W9-CDL-187

# Biological Science
## A Molecular Approach

**BSCS Blue Version**
**Fifth Edition**

**BSCS**

The Colorado College
Colorado Springs, Colorado   80903

**Revision Team:**

Don E. Meyer, Supervisor
Werner G. Heim, The Colorado College
William V. Mayer, President Emeritus, BSCS
Joseph D. McInerney, BSCS
Jean P. Milani, BSCS
Richard R. Tolman, Brigham Young University

With special acknowledgment for contributions:

Phyllis McDowell Popp, St. Charles High School, St. Charles, Illinois
Jack Shouba, Lyons Township High School, Western Springs, Illinois
Pauline Washington, Northwest High School, St. Louis

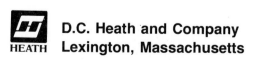

**D.C. Heath and Company**
**Lexington, Massachusetts**      **Toronto**

# Biological Science: A Molecular Approach
BSCS Blue Version, Fifth Edition

**Pupil's Edition**
**Teacher's Guide**
**Study Guide,** Pupil's Edition
**Study Guide,** Teacher's Annotated Edition
**Tests,** Duplicating Masters
**Resource Book of Test Items,** correlated with Fifth Edition text

## Cover Photo:
The surface structure of polyoma virus, which is known to cause cancer in mice. The virus surface is composed of 72 protruding units, each built from 5 protein subunits. This photograph is a computer-generated image of an electron density map of the virus. The structure was determined by X-ray crystallography. Photograph courtesy of Timothy S. Baker, William G. Saunders, Ivan Rayment, and Donald L. D. Caspar.

## Editor:
Toby Klang

## Artists:
William L. Border      Robert F. Wilson
Michael R. Wilson      Holland Victory

## Design Assistance:
Pamela J. Daly

## Administrative BSCS Staff:
Jay Barton II, Chairman, Board of Directors
Jack L. Carter, Director
Joseph D. McInerney, Associate Director

Copyright © 1985, 1980, 1973, 1968, 1963 by BSCS

All rights reserved. Except for fair use as restricted by law, no part of this publication may be reproduced or transmitted in any form or by any means, electronic or mechanical, including photocopy, recording, or any information storage or retrieval system, without permission in writing from the publisher. For permissions and other rights under this copyright, please contact the Permissions Department, D.C. Heath and Company, 125 Spring Street, Lexington, Massachusetts 02173, U.S.A.

Published simultaneously in Canada.

Printed in the United States of America.

International Standard Book Number: 0-669-06769-5

# Foreword

Since its inception in 1958 the BSCS has produced a wide variety of programs. *Biological Science: A Molecular Approach* is designed to present a balanced approach to biology and to serve equally well either as a terminal course in general education or as a college preparatory course in biology. Its central theme is molecular biology, which developed as a field of study around 1920 and has continued to expand as the structure of the cell and the mechanisms of genetic control have been further elucidated.

The chief objective of *Biological Science: A Molecular Approach* is to provide an accurate, modern background to aid students in comprehending the biological issues they will face in the future. Even today, no educated person can afford to be without a knowledge of DNA and its implications. Critical issues of genetic engineering, cellular energy, development, and evolution cannot be understood without a background in molecular biology. The popular media daily report new advances in molecular biology, some destined for major impact, others transient or even erroneous. For the future, knowledge of molecular biology will be essential, as students will be asked to come to grips with such issues whose basis is molecular biology and to vote on directions in which science is likely to be moving.

This new edition represents the cutting edge of current biological research. It is based on 25 years of experience, classroom testing, and continued evaluation. It reflects the thinking of internationally renowned biologists, the pedagogy of thousands of teachers who have used it in the classroom, and the concerns of students with the practical applications of biology for themselves.

An understanding of biology is essential if citizens are to make informed decisions about their current and future life-styles. Biology is the one science that touches on all human activity and that is most relevant to our daily lives. Although no single discipline provides complete comprehension of the human condition, biology affords opportunities for integration with the other natural sciences, the social sciences, and the humanities. *Biological Science: A Molecular Approach* examines aspects of human activity, evolutionary history, structure, function, behavior, relationships to the environment, and the molecular structure on which life is based.

Recent studies have shown the necessity for increased understanding of the process of science, the credibility that can be given its statements, and its successes and limitations. This edition of *Biological Science: A Molecular Approach* is designed to foster scientific thinking, reasoned approaches to problems, and an appreciation of the role science plays in our daily lives. This work is written to engender an understanding of the major concepts that make biology both comprehensible and useful.

For the past quarter of a century the BSCS has looked to students and teachers for critical review and comment. We continue to encourage communication and will acknowledge all questions and commentaries sent us. Those should be forwarded to the director at the address below.

Jack L. Carter
Director
BSCS
The Colorado College
Colorado Springs, Colorado 80903

Jay Barton II
Chairman of the Board
BSCS
University of Alaska
Fairbanks, Alaska 99701

# Contents

# Acknowledgments

Grateful acknowledgment is expressed to the biologists and other scientists who made contributions to this book. Where the contributions are photographs, they are acknowledged separately on page 786. Hundreds of teachers also took part in a Blue Version revision survey or individually submitted suggestions for the revision. Many of those who took part in the Blue Version revision survey did so anonymously and cannot be individually credited. Among the others who contributed to this edition are: Mary E. Acne, Fordham Preparatory School, Bronx, N. Y. Melvin D. Anderson, Ceres High School, Ceres, Calif. Jack D. Arnold, The York School, Monterey, Calif. Tanya Atwater, University of California, Santa Barbara, Calif. James Ausprey, Washington Academy, East Machias, Maine. Albert J. Baraniak, Shannock Valley High School, Rural Valley, Penn. Dorothea Bean, St. Dominic High School, O'Fallon, Mo. Jim Beine, Althoff Catholic High School, Belleville, Ill. Les Bieneman, Monroe High School, Monroe, Wis. Charles E. Biggs, Jr., Susan Wooden Sidwell Friends School, Washington, D.C. Dennis L. Bluge, Trinity Prep School of Florida, Orlando, Florida. Thomas D. Bluni, John F. Kennedy High School, Bellmore, N. Y. Eleanor Budoff, Clarkston High School North, New City, N. Y. Lornie David Bullerwell, Dedham High School, Dedham, Mass. Robert L. Burris, Roosevelt High School, Kent, Ohio. Peggy Brueggemann, Summit Country Day School, Cincinnati, Ohio. Suzanne Ely Byrne, The Bishop's Schools, La Jolla, Calif. Edmund C. Cabot, Milton Academy, Milton, Mass. Alvin S. Caburi, Berkeley High School, Berkeley, Calif. Robert B. Campbell, Incline High School, Incline Village, Nev. Kristina Cannon-Bonventre, Northeastern University, Boston, Mass. Mary Ann Caola, Denver, Colorado. William Carbone, Glen Rock High School, Glen Rock, N. J. Richard Cartner, Modoc High School, Alturas, Calif. Sr. Mary Anne Chase, Convent of Sacred Heart High School, San Francisco, Calif. Melvyn Chopp, Tacoma Public Schools, Tacoma, Wash. Dick Clark, Lancaster High School, Lancaster, Ohio. Robert E. Clark, Virden Community High School, Virden, Ill. Judy Cortese, Hathaway Brown School, Shaker Heights, Ohio. Angelo J. Cortopassi, Palo Alto High School, Palo Alto, Calif. William P. Cote, V. J. Andrew High School, Tinley Park, Ill. Oliver W. Crichton, Tower Hill School, Wilmington, Del. Virginia Curry, Westlake High School, Thornwood, N. Y. Margaret F. Daniel, Collegiate Schools, Richmond, Va. Charles E. Danielski, Deerfield Academy, Deerfield, Mass. Linda M. D'Apolito, Elizabeth Seton High School, Bladensburg, Md. John D. Daulton, Granville High School, Granville, Ohio. Ronald G. Davidson, McMaster University, Hamilton, Ontario. William J. Dooley, Raymore-Peculiar R-II High School, Peculiar, Mo. Gayle Doran, Deerfield-Windsor School, Albany, Ga. Susan K. Duffield, Bush School, Seattle, Wash. Sr. Doris Durant, Marian High School, Omaha, Neb. Cynthia Dunkleberger, St. Josephs High School, Mishawaka, Ind. John Essick, Los Angeles High School, Los Angeles, Calif. Charles F. Farrington, Jr., Roxbury Latin School, West Roxbury, Mass. Mary Ferraro, Franklin High School, Somerset, N. J. Marvin Fietelson, Jefferson Township High School, Oak Ridge, N. J. Frederick J. Fisher, Branham High School, San Jose, Calif. Renee Fishman, Indian Hills High School, Oakland, N. J. Cynthia Fite, Green Mountain High School, Lakewood, Colo. Mary Anne Foerster, Bishop McDevitt School, Harrisburg, Pa. Pam Ford, Rocky Mountain Poison Center, Denver, Colo. Judy Flynn, Bakersfield High School, Bakersfield, Calif. Sr. Sharon Franas, St. Bernard High School, Plaza del Rey, Calif. George H. Freese, Jr., Greenfield Community Schools, Greenfield, Iowa. Vincent A. Frick, Dumont High School, Dumont, N. J. Mrs. I. Gallagher, Sewanhach High School, Floral Park, N. Y. Judith Geller, Dalton Schools, New York, N. Y. Charles Ginsberg, Chicago Vocational School, Chicago, Ill. Vicky Giusti, Mother T. Guerin High School, River Grove, Ill. R. J. Gleason, Bloomfield Jr.-Sr. High School, East Bloomfield, N. Y. Ray Godfrey, Lincoln High School, Cambridge City, Ind. Robert E. Graham, Tilton School, Tilton, N. H. Dody Green, Ursuline Academy, Dallas, Tex. Joyce Greene, Boulder High School, Boulder, Colo. Michael Greminger, Melville Senior High School, St. Louis, Mo. Carolyn Grojean, Sacred Heart of Mary High School, Rolling Meadows, Ill. Barbara Grosz, Pine Crest School, Fort Lauderdale, Fla. Douglas Gruenan, Trinity School, New York, N. Y. Richard A. Harlow, Jr., Tabor Academy, Marion, Mass. Karen Harris, Bishop Kelley High School, Tulsa, Okla. D. Scott Hatcher, Winter Park High School, Winter Park, Fla. Robert D. Higgins, Lyme-Old Lyme High School, Old Lyme, Conn. Phillip Hiller, Evanston Township High School, Evanston, Ill. Joan B. Holmes, Marian High School, Framingham, Mass. Edward W. Hooker, Holland Hall School, Tulsa, Okla. Mark H. Hoskins, Shaker Heights High School, Shaker Heights, Ohio. William V. Houser, West Essex Junior High School, North Caldwell, N. J. Murray Hozinsky, LAB School, Chicago, Ill. John Huddle, Versailles High School, Versailles, Ohio. Larry Hull, Gunn Senior High School, Palo Alto, Calif. James C. Hutten, New Trier Township High School, Winnetka, Ill. Charles J. Ippolito, Marymount School of New York, New York, N. Y. Helen Jacko, Hackensack High School, Hackensack, N. J. Howard S. Janke, Woodward Academy, College Park, Ga. Sr. M. Jeanine, Academy of the Holy Angels, Demarest, N. J. Tom Jinks, Westminster High School, Westminster, Colo. Daniel Lewis Johnson, Wilmington Friends School, Wilmington, Del. Dave Johnson, Francis Parker Jr.-Sr. High School, San Diego, Calif. Steven L. Johnson, Kent Denver Country Day School, Englewood, Colo. Leon E. Jordan, T.B. Browne School, Phoenix, Ariz. Sr. Christine Julie, Chaminade-Julienne High School, Dayton, Ohio. John C. Kay, Iolani School, Honolulu, Hawaii. Rev. David Keener, Bishop Treton High School, Alexandria, Va. Philip T. Kelly, Cedar Crest High School, Lebanon, Pa. Ernest Kenney, Oakmont High School, Roseville, Calif. Johanna O. Killoy, Drehar High School, Columbia, S. C. Richard Kimitsuka, Punahou School, Honolulu, Hawaii. Amy King, Resurrection High School, Chicago, Ill. Gretchen Kingsley, Foote School, New Haven, Conn. Tom Knechtges, Huron High School, Huron, Ohio. Stella Meredith Koch, Edmund Burke School, Washington, D. C. David Koester, Kuemper High School, Carroll, Iowa. Patricia Korn, Herndon High School, Herndon, Va. Julia P. Kron, Rocky Mount Senior

High School, Rocky Mount, N. C. Damon Kross, Thornwood High School, South Holland, Ill. J. Charles Lakinger, Clayton High School, Clayton, Mo. Janet Lasley, Fulton High School, Fulton, Mo. Fran Lauria, Randolph Macon Academy, Front Royal, Va. David G. Less, Holton High School, Holton, Mich. Robert L. Letcavage, Penncrest High School, Media, Pa. George H. Letzner, Solon High School, Solon, Ohio. Diane Liebman, Center High School, Kansas City, Mo. Darlene M. Liem, Greenview High School, Jamestown, Ohio. Daniel R. Lipinski, Bishop Eustace Prep School, Pennsauken, N. J. Betty Little, Center High School, Kansas City, Mo. Michael Logsdon, Bexley High School, Columbus, Ohio. Ralph H. Long, Jr., Mt. Desert Island High School, Mt. Desert, Maine. Barbara Lukomski, St. Josephs High School, Lakewood, Calif. John A. MacDonald, Los Gatos High School, Los Gatos, Calif. William S. Mahalik, Long Branch High School, Long Branch, N. J. Lynn Margulis, Boston University, Boston, Mass. Maurice Maurier, Trinity High School, Manchester, N. H. John Mazzaferro, Rome Free Academy, Rome, N. Y. Terry McGinniss, Edgewood High School, Madison, Wis. Steven A. McKay, Anderson Valley Secondary School, Boonville, Calif. Joseph McNair, Southern Regional High School, Manahawkin, N. J. W. Mealey, Philadelphia High School for Girls, Philadelphia, Pa. Gene Menton, Detroit Country Day School, Birmingham, Mich. Steve Michlovitz, Franklin High School, Somerset, N. J. Robert C. Mills, Putney School, Putney, Vt. Benjamin B. Morgan, Pomfret School, Pomfret, Conn. Frank Morris, Archbishop Ryan High School for Boys, Philadelphia, Pa. Patricia Morris, Wachusett Regional High School, Holden, Mass. Earl S. Morrison, University of New Brunswick, Fredericton, N. B. Beverly D. Mullis, Tampa Catholic High School, Tampa, Fla. Constance T. Noguchi, National Institutes of Health, Bethesda, Md. Steven J. Novek, Maret School, Washington, D. C. Anthony Nusbaumer, Lyons Township High School, Western Springs, Ill. Dean L. Oborn, Roy High School, Roy, Utah. Sr. Helen O'Connell, Marian High School, Birmingham, Mich. G. Owens, Whitfield, St. Louis, Mo. Muriel Paananen, Fostoria High School, Fostoria, Ohio. Douglas N. Packard, New Milford High School, New Milford, Conn. David N. Paulus, Neenah High School, Neenah, Wis. William Peppard, Thornton High School, Harvey, Ill. Cheryl Perkins, Mother T. Guerin High School, River Grove, Ill. Sr. Imogene Perrin, Memphis Catholic High School, Memphis, Tenn. Joann Phillips, Incarnate Word Academy, Corpus Christi, Tex. Robert Phipps, Parkersburg South High School, Parkersburg, W. Va. Cyril Ponnamperuma, University of Maryland, College Park, Md. Phyllis McDowell Popp, St. Charles High School, St. Charles, Ill. Steve Proulx, Robert Louis Stevenson School, Pebble Beach, Calif. Cecilia Quinones, Episcopal Cathedral School, Santurce, P. R. Sharon V. Radford, Paideia School, Atlanta, Ga. Robert L. Ragley, Beachwood High School, Beachwood, Ohio. Evelyn Rees, Caldwell High School, Caldwell, Kans. Mary Riordan, Holy Name High School, Worcester, Mass. Mark E. Rostvold, Niles North High School, Skokie, Ill. Ron Royer, Ben Logan School, Zanesfield, Ohio. Christos T. Sarris, Westwood High School, Westwood, Mass.

Andrew Saunders, Springfield Catholic High School, Springfield, Mo. Alan N. Schechter, National Institutes of Health, Bethesda, Md. William A. Schubert, Girard High School, Girard, Pa. Phyllis Schwartz, New Canaan High School, New Canaan, Conn. Buff Seirup, Mercy High School, Middletown, Conn. Joel Shapino, Clara Barton High School, Brooklyn, N. Y. Esther Shigezawa, Moanalua High School, Honolulu, Hawaii. Jack Shouba, Lyons Township High School, Western Springs, Ill. Larry Sigel, Notre Dame High School, Harper Woods, Mich. Barbara A. Silber, Fieldston School, Bronx, N. Y. John B. Simmons, Washington Community High School, Washington, Ill. Edward Simon, Flintridge Preparatory School, La Canad, Calif. Carl Smith, St. Paul Academy, St. Paul, Minn. Richard S. Smith, Marple Newtown School District, Newtown Square, Pa. Toni Smith, Johnston High School, Johnston, R. I. Frank R. Spica, Roycemore School, Evanston, Ill. Michael R. Spurgeon, Unified District 368 High School, Paola, Kans. Byron Elliott Stout, Marin Academy, San Rafael, Calif. Donald C. Stubbs, Ponagauset High School, North Scituate, R. I. Sr. Mary Sullivan, Ramona Convent High School, Alhambra, Calif. William A. Sumner, Jr., Iolani School, Honolulu, Hawaii. David Swin, West High School, Aurora, Ill. Barbara Tester, Ransom Everglades School, Miami, Fla. Marv Theroff, Blue Springs R-4 High School, Blue Springs, Mo. Martha Thompson, John F. Kennedy High School, Manchester, Mo. Donald Thorn, Irvington High School, Irvington, N. Y. Marilyn Tokoff, Clarkston High School North, New City, N. Y. Anthony J. Toto, Boston College High School, Dorchester, Mass. Robert G. Troutman, East Longmeadow High School, East Longmeadow, Mass. Carolyn Trunca, State University of New York, Stony Brook, N. Y. William Utley, Yuba City High School, Yuba City, Calif. Dennis Urba, Mason City High School, Mason City, Iowa. Victoria Vargo, St. Mary Academy, Monroe, Mich. Phillip D. Vavala, Salesianum School, Wilmington, Del. Thomas M. Vibert, Wheeler School, Providence, R. I. Gerald T. Vlasah, Argo Community High School, Argo, Ill. Gabriel Walker, Jr., Portland High School, Portland, Maine. Caroline Baker Watts, Morgantown High School, Morgantown, W. Va. Ralph Weddington, Isidore Newman School, New Orleans, La. Milo F. Wetzel, Delta High School, Clarksburg, Calif. Arthur Wheeler, Newburyport High School, Newburyport, Mass. Michele Whitehead, Immaculate Heart of Mary High School, Westchester, Ill. Gordon R. Will, St. Patrick High School, Chicago, Ill. Bro. William, St. Francis High School, Athol Springs, N. Y. Marilyn J. Williams, Highland Park High School, Highland Park, N. J. Robert D. Williams, Golden Senior High School, Golden, Colo. Roger W. Wilson, El Morino High School, Forestville, Calif. Marie A. Zupan, St. Joseph Academy, Cleveland, Ohio. JoAnne S. Gray, Corliss High School, Chicago, Illinois.

PART ONE

# Unity Within Variety

An alert observer would be overwhelmed by the numbers and variety of living things in the world. Patterns that can be detected help biologists organize knowledge of the many different kinds of life. The need for water is one pattern. The giraffes share the water hole with many other creatures that have the same need. What features of living things create such similarities in patterns? In what ways are all living things related?

# The Science of Life 1

Being a part of the living world is a wondrous and complicated experience. **Biology** is the science that deals with living things (*bios* = life and *logie* or *ology* = science or study of). If you like to puzzle about the tremendous variety of living things, you will find plenty of unsolved mysteries in biology. If you like to wonder why living things are as they are and how they work, you have much in common with biologists.

Biologists have a tremendous variety of living things and life activities from which to choose as they select their area of study. In doing their work they are like detectives trying to solve a mystery. They try to be observant and alert to new ways of looking at things. In this chapter you can start to experience the methods used by biologists as they investigate the mysteries of life. In later chapters you can use these methods to investigate many of the mysteries yourself.

# Getting Started

## 1–1

## Characteristics of Life

You are alive! You have been growing and changing since before you were born. Other things grow and change as well. In underground caverns, rock formations called stalactites grow larger with the passing of time. In the sky, clouds form and then change in shape and appearance. You know the clouds and the stalactites are not alive. But what about things that are less familiar to you? How is it possible to tell whether something is alive?

To answer a question, it is helpful to gather information which may then provide you with clues. Collecting information by using your senses is called **observation.** By making observations of unfamiliar things, you may be able to tell whether or not they are alive. But what information should you look for? What characteristics do living things have in common?

Movement and growth are two characteristics that come to mind. However, both living and nonliving things may move and grow. What makes living things different?

To help answer this question, biologists consider not only *what* something does but also *how* it does it. Clouds move because they are pushed by the wind. Clouds do not move on their own. As for stalactites, their growth occurs because underground water deposits more material on them. Living things grow by a different process. They take in material from the environment and *change* it to suit their needs. For example, your body changes the food you eat into materials you can use for energy or to make new bones, muscle, and blood. No rock or cloud can do that!

Living things are *organized* according to how they function. Biologists call them **organisms** (OR-gan-iz-ums). You can often see features of this organization when you observe an organism. A mouth, a head, or a leaf and stem are visible examples. Even microscopic organisms have life-supporting structures that you can see under magnification.

---

←Life tackles Earth's harshest environments. Biological questions to investigate are found everywhere. How can you be prepared to recognize them?

**Figure 1–1** Living or nonliving? Look for clues in photographs *a* through *h*. Determine, as best you can, which of the objects are living and which are not. Then turn to page 15 to find out the identity of each object.

Biologists look for common characteristics among living things. But detecting these characteristics is not always easy. Somewhere there is always some unusual living or nonliving thing that is hard to identify (Figure 1–1). However, biologists have developed the following list of characteristics commonly found in living organisms, which serves as a guide.

- Organisms have a specialized structural and chemical organization responsible for their appearance and activities.

- Organisms have coded "information molecules" (MOL-uh-kyoolz) that contain instructions for maintaining the organization and activities of the organisms.

- Organisms take in and use materials and energy from the environment and give off by-products, or wastes.

- Organisms sense and react to many conditions in their surroundings.

- Organisms modify their activities to suit changes in the environment.

- Organisms grow and develop (change as they grow) during some part of their lives.

- Organisms reproduce others of their own kind.

Many organisms show one or more other characteristics:

- They communicate with others of their own kind.

- They move under their own ability.

In this chapter you will begin a closer examination of some familiar kinds of organisms. You must make careful observations! Keen observing is a skill that takes practice as you will find out starting with an ordinary peanut.

**Figure 1–2** Peanuts—how individual are they?

## 1–2
## Becoming a Keen Observer

You wouldn't have any trouble recognizing your own dog or cat but how about a peanut (Figure 1–2)? Observe a peanut and become better acquainted with it. A close look will reveal differences that make each peanut unique. In fact, most living things of the same kind are not as much alike as they appear at first glance.

### MATERIALS
6 bowls of unshelled peanuts
paper and pencil
metric rulers (See **Appendix 1–A,** Measurement in Science, page 686.)
string
balance

### PROCEDURE
You or your group will be assigned a bowl of peanuts. Without looking into the bowl, take one peanut. If its shell is cracked or broken, set the peanut aside and take another. When you have a peanut that is not discolored or broken, take it to your work area. Begin to make some observations. Get to know your peanut well enough so that you can pick it out of a crowd! This is what you will have to do later.

Observe your peanut as carefully as you can and record all your observations in a list on a sheet of paper. Describe the peanut's shape, or better, sketch and label it. Measure the peanut and record the measurements. Do anything else except mark or crack the peanut.

When you have recorded as many observations and measurements as you can, return your peanut to its original bowl. Have a partner mix up the peanuts in the bowl. Then use your notes to find your peanut.

Was your peanut hard to find? If you had any difficulty, start over with another peanut. This time compare your methods with those of some other students. (Biologists frequently ask each other for suggestions.) Work more on your observations and measurements so that you will not have difficulty finding the peanut again.

When you have recorded your observations and measurements as completely and accurately as possible, your teacher will give you instructions for one more part to this exercise. It will be a realistic test of just how keen an observer you were in your work and how carefully you recorded your observations.

### QUESTIONS

1. What were the different ways you found to distinguish one peanut from another?
2. What proved to be the most helpful information in finding a specific peanut?
3. How important were your notes of your observations and measurements in locating the peanut? If your memory was a better guide than your notes, what does this suggest about your notes?

### DISCUSSION

People often confuse *observations* with *inferences*. When you let experience with a lot of peanuts guide what you say, you may not be making an observation of your particular peanut. Instead, you may be drawing an inference. Observations are collected at the scene, using your senses. Inferences are ideas or conclusions based on what you observe or already know.

Based on this distinction, which of the following are observations and which are inferences?

The shell will crack easily.
The shell has a rough surface.
The shell is uniformly colored.
The shell has two lobes and is smaller in diameter between them.
The peanuts have a skin around them.
There are two peanuts in the shell.
The peanuts are roasted.
The surface markings on the shell are in rows, running lengthwise.
The shell has 13 rows of surface markings.

Now look at your notes again and label any inferences that you included.

## 1–3
## Asking Questions

Making observations and asking questions are closely related activities in biology. Observations often lead to questions that should be investigated. Once asked, questions may point to further observations that should be made. In either order, observing and questioning support one another.

Observing and questioning are related in another way. Both depend on skills. Like effective observation, effective questioning develops with practice. Knowing *what* question to ask is sometimes the hardest step.

Initially, a question may be based on only one or a few early observations that are likely to limit the way you ask the question. As a result, you may look for the answer in the wrong place or in the wrong way. In fact, few scientists who have written about their work could report asking their questions right the first time.

A famous example of this situation in biology began in 1665. A scientist named Robert Hooke was first to use a microscope (Figure 1–3) to study parts of plants. Among the things Hooke exam-

**Figure 1–3** Hooke's microscope, as it can be seen today in the Science Museum in London, England. Tiny objects to be viewed were placed on the point of the needle beneath the lowest lens of the microscope.

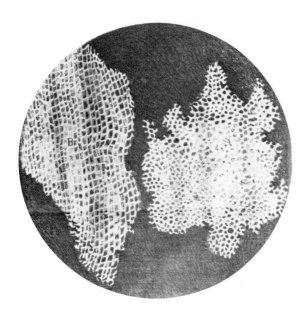

**Figure 1–4** A photograph of Hooke's drawings of cork cells, as seen under the microscope. The drawings appeared in Hooke's book *Micrographia,* published in 1665.

ined were shreds of cork. Under the microscope, these shreds from the bark of the cork oak tree revealed an inner structure.

When magnified many times, little boxlike units could be seen (Figure 1–4). No one had ever noticed them before. They appeared empty; Hooke could see right through them.

Hooke called these structures *cells*. In time, other biologists saw them too in many different plants. Sometimes identification was difficult because parts of live plants were filled with fluid, changing the appearance of the boxlike structures (Figure 1–5, middle and right). However, increasing numbers of plants revealed cells. Botanists began to conclude that all plants were built of cells.

But what about other living things like animals? Were they also composed of the boxlike cells? Now you will see how the nature of a question can mislead investigators. Biologists could

not find the boxlike cells in animals. Could it be that animals were not made of cells?

Fortunately, the matter did not end there. A botanist (plant biologist) named Robert Brown found a structure within the fluid in living plant cells. Brown called this structure the **nucleus** (NOO-klee-us). It was very difficult to see, but it was found repeatedly in different plant cells.

Then, in 1839, a zoologist (animal biologist) named Theodor Schwann (SHVON) re-examined the cell question. Though no boxlike cells could be found in animals, careful study showed that small bits of animal material seemed to be self-contained (Figure 1–6). Often these bits of material from animals looked like fluid-filled sacs. And floating in the fluid was what appeared to be a nucleus! To Schwann's credit, he realized that the cell question was incorrectly based on the boxlike cell structure instead of what was *inside* cells.

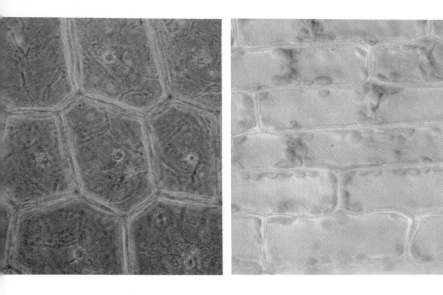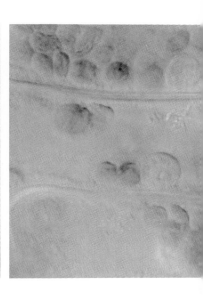

**Figure 1-5** Three photographs of living plant cells. The cells at the left are in a flat layer of cells that cover and protect other cells in a small herblike plant (*Zebrina*). The cells in the middle and at the right are green food-producing cells in a water plant (*Elodea*). The enlarged view at the right shows the nucleus of a cell at the center of the photograph. (Look for the largest body in the cell that is fainter than the other bodies.)

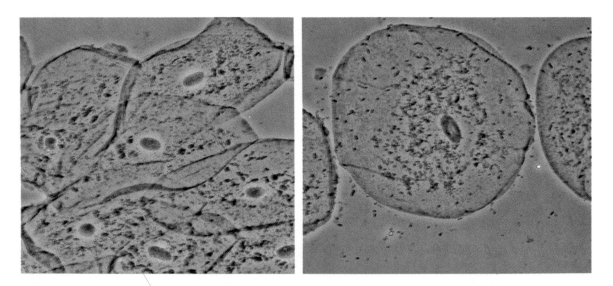

**Figure 1-6** Two photographs of cells recently scraped from the inside of a person's cheek. Notice the nucleus near the center of each cell. Photographs like the ones shown here and in Figure 1–5 require special equipment and lighting effects. Schwann and Schleiden could not see living cells this clearly under their microscopes.

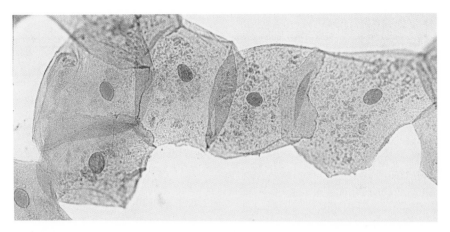

**Figure 1–7** Through the microscope, human cheek cells like these can be seen clearly because the cells have been stained. The color is caused by iodine in the stain. In Figures 1–5, 1–6, and this figure, what cell parts can you see?

The botanist M. J. Schleiden (SHLY-dun) came to the same conclusion Schwann had reached. Schleiden and Schwann advanced the idea that both plants and animals are made of cells that contain nuclei and cell fluid.

All this occurred by the middle of the 1800s. Within a few years, knowledge of cells began to advance rapidly. Methods of staining cells made the nucleus easier to see (Figure 1–7). Other smaller structures within the cell fluid were discovered. Each cell was contained by what is known today as the **plasma membrane.** Outside this membrane in plants, but not in animals, were **cell walls,** which gave cells a boxlike appearance.

You can see that the question about cells in animals was first asked in a way that hindered the search. No amount of careful scientific work would have revealed cells in animals so long as cells were thought of as having boxlike walls. But once the right question was asked, animal cells were quickly recognized.

**Try Investigation 1–A** The Compound Microscope, page 567.

**CAPSULE SUMMARY**

Biologists use numerous different characteristics to distinguish living from nonliving things. Activities such as growth and movement may at first appear similar for both, but how the activities are carried on reveals whether or not something is living.

Developing skills in making observations and asking questions is important in studying characteristics of living things. Observing and questioning usually go together. Learning to ask the right questions is often the key to finding the answer to a problem.

**SELF CHECK**

1. How does growth differ between living and nonliving things?
2. Do all living things have the same characteristics? Explain.
3. What name do biologists give to living things?
4. What observation limited the cell question as it was first asked about animals?

# Skills of Investigation

## 1–4

### Proposing a Hypothesis

With limited information, how can you improve the way a question is asked? Biologists who raise new questions search for clues in related work done by other biologists.

Most work in biology is indexed and summarized in special publications to make searches easier. A library with the indexes in a computer can find all related published work in minutes! Careful study of related work helps an investigator improve the way a question is asked.

Often a great deal of information about the question turns up during the search. A biologist then adds this information to his or her own. The combination of the borrowed information and the investigator's observations are the **initial data** (DAY-tuh) relating to the question.

Using the data, the investigator proposes a **hypothesis** (hy-POTH-uh-sis) for the answer to the question. The hypothesis is a trial solution that should meet two considerations:

1. It should fit the data or help explain them.
2. It should be stated in a form in which it can be tested.

How do you word a hypothesis? How do you even *recognize* a hypothesis? Another famous example of observation and questioning in biology shows how a hypothesis can develop. You may even find the resulting discovery familiar.

In 1928, Alexander Fleming was growing bacteria in laboratory dishes when molds invaded some of the dishes. Fleming intended to discard these dishes but left them sitting while trying for pure growths of the bacteria in other dishes. These particular microscopic organisms (*Staphylococcus*) were bacteria that caused many infections.

Even in the midst of further work Fleming noticed that bacteria were no longer growing near one mold in a contaminated dish. This puzzling observation was to become a lifesaving one. The question it raised kept distracting Fleming: *Why weren't the bacteria growing near that particular mold?*

Abruptly the work on pure growths of bacteria stopped. Fleming searched the work of other biologists for information on the mold. He found it was a common mold (*Penicillium*) known chiefly as a fruit mold (Figure 1–8). Much of the related work was concentrated on how to prevent growth of the mold!

Fleming returned to the observations of the mold and the bacteria. The mold *itself* was not growing on the bacteria. Instead, a clear zone separated the two. The clear zone appeared to be in a ring around the mold. Wherever the ring

**Figure 1–8** The chances are that you have discovered the same mold that Fleming did. It is a common fruit mold. No bacteria have made a visible start near it on this orange. But you would not ordinarily be looking for bacteria. Fleming was studying bacteria, not molds. The bacteria were already in the laboratory dishes when a mold invaded. Why was Fleming prepared to notice something that might happen to the bacteria?

came in contact with the bacteria, the bacteria stopped growing.

From these initial data Fleming suggested a hypothesis:

The mold produces a colorless substance that inhibits growth of the bacteria.

The hypothesis is worded as a direct statement. It could also be worded as a question, or as an "If . . . , then" statement:

Does the mold produce a colorless substance that inhibits growth of the bacteria?

*If* the mold produces a colorless substance that inhibits growth of the bacteria, *then* the substance can be extracted and shown to inhibit bacterial growth in the absence of the mold.

Fleming did extract the substance and successfully tested it against other growths of the bacteria. He had discovered penicillin.

# 1–5
## Testing a Hypothesis

How a hypothesis is stated is up to the investigator. Whether as a question, a direct statement, or an "If . . . , then" statement, it can be tested in the same way. But the advantage of the "If . . . , then" statement is in suggesting the test that may follow. The "then" clause always is a **prediction,** indicating the test and how it will turn out *if the hypothesis is true*.

Prediction is one of the most helpful tools that people use in their thinking (Figure 1–9). In biology, using hypotheses (hy-POTH-us-seez, plural) to make predictions is one of the most important investigative skills. Often different predictions can be made from the same hypothesis. The "If" clause remains the same, but the "then" clause (the prediction) changes, also changing the test. For many hypotheses, a number of different kinds of tests are possible.

The type of test suggested for a hypothesis usually determines the skills that will be needed for the test. The skills used most often in testing hypotheses include the following:

1. *Observation*. Observation, described earlier as "collecting information by using your senses," also includes using instruments that extend the range of your senses. The microscope is such an instrument. Observation is called *qualitative* when no measurement is involved.

2. *Measurement*. Measurement makes many kinds of observations more precise. Observation by measurement is called *quantitative*. Wherever possible, biologists use measurement to achieve greater accuracy. Measurements can also be independent of observations.

3. *Prediction*. Prediction, as described earlier, suggests tests of hypotheses and possible results of the tests. Predictions may also grow out of the tests (for example, see *Modeling*).

4. *Modeling*. Models may be of several kinds. In hobbies, three-dimensional models are usually reduced in size. In science, they are more often enlarged. Investigators may build an oversized model as a hypothesis for a chemical structure they cannot see. Then they can check each part of the model against known chemical data. When the model fits all the known data, it may represent what the chemical structure really looks like. A few key parts of the model may represent data not yet discovered. These parts then become predictions for the unknown data.

   A model may also be a computer program. Your whole community could be represented by a computer model that would be used to study the community's growth. Whatever problems the computer reveals become predictions of what may actually happen in the real community.

*a*    *predicting what will happen*          *b*    *predicting how it happened*

**Figure 1–9** Prediction in biology is a skill that can be applied to both the future and the past. For each scene in column *a*, try to predict what will happen. For column *b*, can you offer any predictions to explain what caused each scene?

5. *Designing Experiments.* Experimenting consists of setting up actual situations, or living models, to test hypotheses. An experiment is usually the best possible test of the observations, questions, research, and predictions that precede it. Conducting experiments is such an important skill that it is discussed separately in Section 1–6.

**Try Investigation 1–B**  How Are Pieces of Potato Affected in Size by Water and by Different Concentrations of Sugar in Water?, page 569.

6. *Organizing and Recording Data.* When experiments and other tests end, only the records of the test data remain. Therefore, skills in orga-

nizing and recording data are essential. You discovered their importance firsthand while working with a peanut. Much of your laboratory time will be devoted to organizing and presenting the data you collect.

Other skills may also be involved in testing hypotheses. In fact, some hypotheses are proposed before ways of testing them are even known. New skills and procedures as they are developed frequently lead to future tests.

## 1–6
## The Experimental Method

When a question has been raised and a hypothesis suggested, a test in the form of an experiment may become possible. For example, earlier in this chapter (page 7) you learned that plant cells, but not animal cells, have cell walls. The discovery of this difference raised the question: *How do cell walls function in plants?* One of the many hypotheses in answer to this question is that cell walls help insulate plant cells from heat and cold. Can an experiment be designed to test this hypothesis?

Many initial data exist concerning this question. For example, young plant cells have thinner walls than older cells. Furthermore, the younger cells occur mainly at the growing tips of plants.

Given these data, a prediction is possible:

*If* cell walls help insulate plant cells from heat and cold, *then* the growing tips of plants are least protected and should be damaged first by heat or cold.

With the necessary facilities, the prediction can be tested by an experiment. The experimental procedure will be the following:

1. Maintain a dozen or more plants of the same kind indoors. Provide equal light, water, and mineral requirements. Inspect the plants daily, removing all that appear unhealthy.

**Figure 1–10** Which group of plants appears sturdiest? Which appears best cared for? If you find differences, then an experiment using these plants may not explain later differences you observe among them. All three groups of plants should be alike until the temperature for two groups is changed. What is the purpose of the third group?

*experimental group to be exposed to heat*

*experimental group to be exposed to cold*

*control (to be kept at moderate temperature)*

2. Divide the remaining plants into three groups (Figure 1–10). Place one group in a chamber in which the temperature will be lowered. Place the second group in a chamber in which the temperature will be raised. Leave a third group unchanged, at moderate temperatures.

3. Continue to provide equally for the requirements of the three groups. Temperature should be the only condition changed.

This procedure describes a **controlled experiment.** The group of plants that will be maintained at moderate temperatures is the normal group or **control group.** Each of the other two groups is an **experimental group.** Temperatures can be raised or lowered for the two experimental groups. In the meantime, the control is a basis for comparison, showing how plants would respond with no change in temperature or other conditions.

Each condition in the experiment that can affect the plants is called a **variable.** Water is a variable, light another, disease (if present) a third. Here, temperature is the **experimental variable.** It will be changed for both of the experimental groups. Only one variable will be tested. If more than one is changed, there is no way to know which variable is responsible for whatever may happen to the experimental plants.

The controlled experiment is one of science's most powerful tools. You will work with it often in the laboratory. However, you should not conclude that one control is all that is necessary in an experiment. Some experiments require several different kinds of controls to provide the proper standards for comparison.

**Try Investigation 1–C** Do Active Living Things Give Off a Common Substance?, page 571.

# 1–7
## Hypotheses, Assumptions, and Theories

How biologists draw conclusions from investigations can be a simple or a complex process. It is simple when the results clearly speak for themselves. You can look at a hypothesis and then at the experimental data obtained and know at once how an investigation turned out. Drawing conclusions can be complex when the results first must be interpreted. Investigators should be careful not to interpret evidence as favorable to a hypothesis *if* any other reasonable explanation could exist.

In biology, as in other sciences, a safeguard exists to help investigators with their interpretations. Investigations are repeated by other biologists for **verification.** If other biologists obtain the same results from the same experiments, the hypothesis becomes more firmly established.

Biology always includes questions and hypotheses. As quickly as some are settled, others are raised. Some hypotheses are tested over many years. Other hypotheses, new and old, are likely to remain untested until a new generation of biologists figures out how to test them.

Many hypotheses will be identified in this book. You will work with qualitative and quantitative data. In addition, two other levels of thinking will be included—**assumption** and **theory.**

A scientific assumption is a provisional acceptance of the truth of something, based on incomplete evidence. For example, biologists assume that Earth's atmosphere has changed over time as you will read in Chapter 5. Generally, assumptions include partly tested hypotheses *if* all tests to date have supported the hypotheses.

Theories begin as hypotheses. However, theories are heavily supported by evidence. They attempt to simplify large masses of biological data. They offer explanations for the data, and they attempt to relate them to one another.

**Figure 1–11** Blue whales are the largest living animals, and yet their bodies are built of cells and other parts made by their cells. Observers rarely see a whole blue whale at once. (Upper left) A blue whale is surfacing and blowing. (Upper right) A young blue whale is swimming at the surface. (Lower left) An adult whale arches its back at the start of a dive. (Lower right) The same whale is diving. Its flukes disappear last.

An example today is the **cell theory.** Until the cell question arose (page 5), many organisms appeared to have little in common. They ranged in size from bacteria to blue whales (Figure 1–11). Organisms were of all shapes and appearances. The discovery of cells gave them a unity. Organisms could be understood as being built of cells. Their different body structures were made of different kinds of cells. The variety among organisms became more understandable.

You will read more about the cell theory in Chapter 2. A modern statement of it is expanded to explain that organisms and their parts are made of cells *or products made by cells.* (Bones, shells, and numerous other structures are thus explained.)

Theories account for data and, like hypotheses, make predictions possible. The predictions lead to new tests, the tests to answers, and the answers to new questions and hypotheses. The process goes on and on (Figure 1–12). The result is an increasingly better understanding of the living world.

*The cell theory predicts the discovery of cells or their products in a newly found tropical plant.*

*Microscopic examination and chemical tests confirm the prediction.*

*One of the cell products has never been encountered before, raising a question. What is its function?*

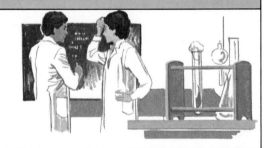

*The question leads to hypotheses and to new predictions.*

*If the substance attacks the growth of competing plants, then...*

*If the substance regulates the plant's use of...*

**Try Investigation 1–D** Microscopic Measurements, page 573.

---

**CAPSULE SUMMARY**

When questions arise, biologists search the work of other biologists to help acquire initial data. Then they suggest hypotheses in answer to their questions. Learning to use hypotheses to make predictions that can be tested builds a very important skill. "If . . . , then" statements of hypotheses are especially helpful in making predictions.

Depending on what predictions are made, hypotheses can be tested in a number of different ways. Skills such as observation, measurement, modeling, organizing and recording data, and experimenting are used.

In a controlled experiment, all variables except the experimental variable are treated alike between an experimental group and a control group. More than one control may be required.

Hypotheses, assumptions, data, and theories interact in biology. The great organizing ideas are the theories. They arise as hypotheses that explain or predict relationships among masses of data.

**SELF CHECK**

1. What is a hypothesis?
2. What two conditions must a hypothesis meet?
3. What is a variable? an experimental variable?
4. If theories originate as hypotheses, what are the differences between the two?

---

**Figure 1–12** Questions lead to answers that lead to more questions. Can you explain why the investigation pictured here will not stop with what is learned from the new hypotheses?

# CHAPTER SUMMARY

## HIGHLIGHTS

Organisms share a number of characteristics. Biologists study not only these characteristics but also others that vary from organism to organism.

Observations in biology often lead to questions. For each new question, initial data are drawn from the observations and from related work by other biologists. Possible answers are explored as hypotheses to be tested. The skills used in testing a hypothesis depend upon the predictions made. Among the skills are observing, measuring, modeling, experimenting, and organizing and recording data.

Drawing conclusions from investigations may involve interpretations. Conclusions are verified by other biologists who repeat the investigations.

Information in biology is usually stated as hypotheses, assumptions, data, and theories. The hypotheses and theories support predictions that lead to new investigations and new discoveries. Theories also organize biological information into understandable patterns or relationships.

## REVIEWING IDEAS

1. What process is described as using your senses, or instruments that extend your senses, to collect information?
2. How are observation and measurement related?
3. What name do biologists give to living things?
4. Where would you expect to find boxlike cells? saclike cells?
5. How did Schleiden and Schwann revise the first question asked about cells in animals?
6. After gathering initial data about a question, what step do investigators take next?
7. What observation led Fleming to the discovery of penicillin?
8. What is a hypothesis? What two conditions must it meet?

9. What is a scientific assumption?
10. What is the role of theories in biology?

## USING CONCEPTS

11. How do observations and inferences differ?
12. What advantage does an "If . . . , then" statement of a hypothesis have over other ways of stating the same hypothesis?
13. Hairs grow—for example, those on your head. Do they grow at the tip, the base, or all along their length? Select a possibility and state an appropriate hypothesis.
14. How could you test your hypothesis about hair growth?
15. Why is a control needed in an experiment?
16. Explain the difference between the way people use *theory* in everyday conversations and the way biologists use the term.
17. What conditions must a hypothesis meet to be accepted as a theory?

## RECOMMENDED READING

Bernstein, J. *Experiencing Science: Profiles in Discovery.* New York, E. P. Dutton, 1980 (paperback). A series of episodes about scientists and their discoveries.

Heath, A. F. *Scientific Explanation.* New York, Oxford University Press, 1982. Many useful perspectives on scientific thinking.

Klemm, W. R., ed. *Discovery Processes in Modern Biology: People and Processes in Biological Discovery.* Huntington, N. Y., Krieger, 1976. Essays by a number of eminent biologists on the *how* of research.

**Answer key for Figure 1–1:**
(a) a living silversword plant in Maui, Hawaii; (b) living "stone plants" in a rock garden in South Africa; (c) frost "ferns" in winter on a window pane, nonliving; (d) a living sea urchin; (e) bubbles on water, nonliving; (f) mud flats, nonliving; (g) living yellow lichens on a rock face; (h) a living "rock plant" in Texas

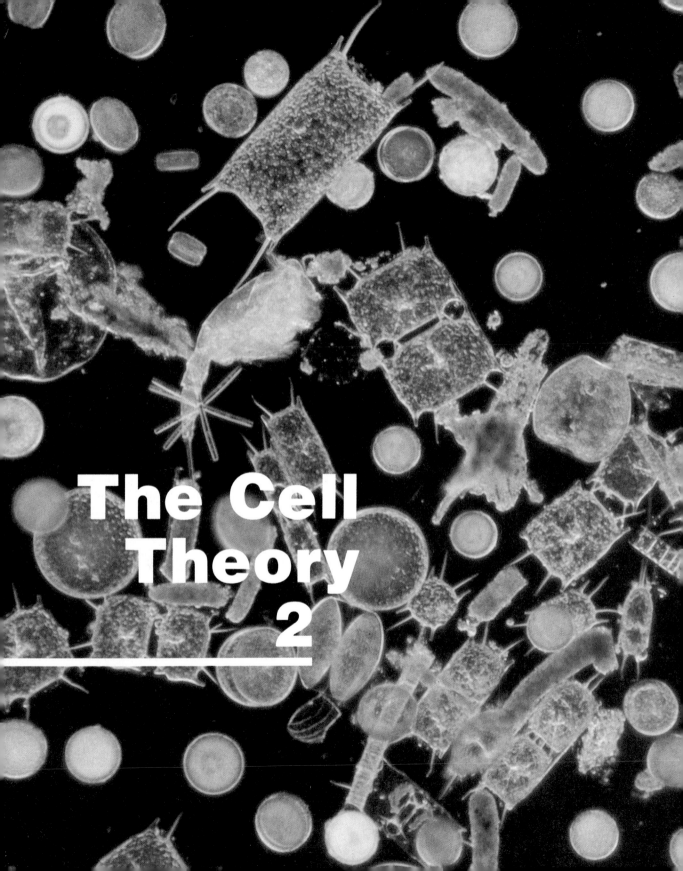

# The Cell
# Theory
# 2

Interested in making millions? Would 100 trillion suit you better? It would if you are talking about cells. You make millions every week. You keep at least 100 trillion in your cell account all the time.

Is your cell account really what you are? For that matter is one cell all there is to life for a tiny microorganism? Both are important questions for you because you began life as one cell. Biologists have puzzled over such questions for more than 100 years. Organisms appear too complicated to be just collections of cells. However, except for cells and their products, no other parts of organisms have been found.

How much life can be packed into a cell? And what happens as cells increase in number and begin to work together?

# One Cell—A World Within a World

## 2–1

## The Cell Is the Basic Unit of Life

Biologists were familiar with a host of microorganisms by the 1830s, when Schwann and Schleiden published their work on plant and animal cells. Anton van Leeuwenhoek ( LAY-van-hook) had discovered microorganisms only 30 years after Hooke discovered cells. Leeuwenhoek was an expert lens-maker who had made a number of microscopes. Though they were made later than Hooke's microscope, they were less advanced. Each of Leeuwenhoek's microscopes had only one lens. (See Figure 5–1, page 88.) Yet one of Leeuwenhoek's lenses helped this part-time biologist discover life in a drop of water. Water from ponds, rain barrels, and the river at Delft, Holland, revealed a wealth of tiny creatures.

Leeuwenhoek published this first news of microscopic life through the Royal Society of London. Soon there were other **microbiologists** (MY-kroh-by-OL-uh-jists) looking for living things through their microscopes. Bits of soil, spoiled food, and almost every other source revealed more microorganisms. The problem of studying these tiny organisms was the same problem botanists and zoologists faced studying animal and plant cells. Improved microscopes and lighting made microscopic images less shadowy but more transparent. It was difficult to observe details in organisms while looking right through them.

As colored stains came into use, part of the problem was solved. Although most stains killed cells and microorganisms, staining made their detailed structures visible. Microbiologists could compare the bodies of microorganisms (Figure 2–1) with the bodies of animals and plants, part for part.

Staining revealed cells in larger microorganisms, but the smaller microorganisms had no correspondingly smaller cells. Instead, individually, they appeared to be about the size of one cell from a larger organism. The idea quickly took hold that

←Microscopic life from the surface waters of the ocean. During daylight hours, these organisms use the energy of sunlight to make the food they require.

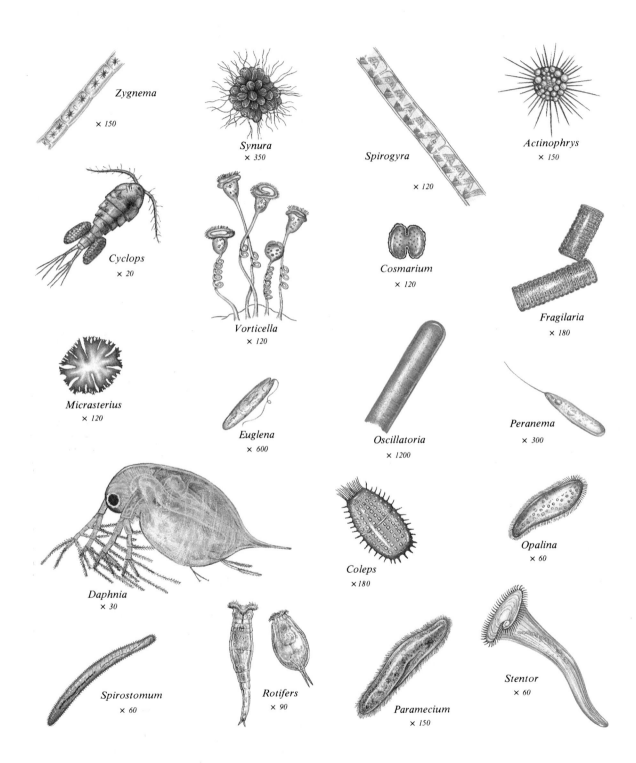

Zygnema
× 150

Synura
× 350

Spirogyra
× 120

Actinophrys
× 150

Cyclops
× 20

Vorticella
× 120

Cosmarium
× 120

Fragilaria
× 180

Micrasterius
× 120

Euglena
× 600

Oscillatoria
× 1200

Peranema
× 300

Daphnia
× 30

Coleps
×180

Opalina
× 60

Spirostomum
× 60

Rotifers
× 90

Paramecium
× 150

Stentor
× 60

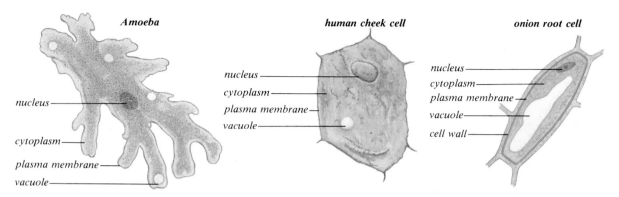

**Figure 2–2** Most microorganisms share a number of features with animal and plant cells. This amoeba is one of a group of the same name (*Amoeba*). Amoebas of other groups may show certain variations, such as having more than one nucleus.

they were **unicellular** (YOO-nih-SEL-yoo-lar), made of only one cell.

Nuclei were discovered in many of these microorganisms. Plasma membranes were also identified. Often however, these outer membranes appeared to contain tough fibers and other specialized materials, or appeared to be surrounded by cell walls or glasslike shells.

Inside these microorganisms, as well as in plant and animal cells, was a fluidlike substance containing additional structures. This substance together with its structures became known as the **cytoplasm** (SYT-uh-plaz-um). All materials outside the nucleus but inside the plasma membrane were part of the cytoplasm.

Bubblelike structures holding fluid or food were found in the cytoplasm. These structures, called **vacuoles** (VAK-yuh-wohls), were identified in both cells and microorganisms. Biologists continued to draw such comparisons. Figure 2–2 summarizes an example, comparing an amoeba (uh-MEE-buh) with an animal and a plant cell.

No one could miss the direction in which these comparisons were leading. A large group of biologists advanced the conclusion that the cell is the basic unit of life. By their reasoning, a cell could be a complete organism. Alternatively it could be part of a **multicellular** (MUL-tih-SEL-yuh-lar), or many-celled, organism.

## 2–2
## The Cell Theory Faces Its Tests

From plants to animals to all life were two great leaps for a proposed cell theory. If the idea was correct, it related every living thing to every other living thing.

As inviting as the idea was, many biologists were unconvinced. They discovered exceptions. For example, the muscles in your arms are not typically cellular. They have many nuclei in long

**Figure 2–1** Some of the many small organisms, usually microscopic, found in pond water.

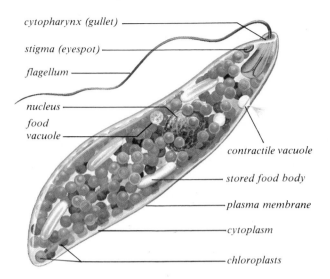

cytopharynx (gullet)
stigma (eyespot)
flagellum
nucleus
food
vacuole
contractile vacuole
stored food body
plasma membrane
cytoplasm
chloroplasts

**Figure 2–3** *Euglena* shares the same features with animal and plant cells that an amoeba does. But numerous other features are also prominent in a *Euglena*.

fibers. Certain whole organisms also have many nuclei but no plasma membranes dividing their bodies into cells. However, in each case other biologists proved that cells caused the development of these exceptions. "Cells or products made by cells" appeared to apply to all life.

One difference still remained between microorganisms and the cells of larger organisms. The cells appeared limited in their abilities, which varied with the roles they played in an organism's body. Microorganisms appeared to be independent, able to carry out all life activities.

To emphasize this contrast, imagine replacing the amoeba in Figure 2–2 with the *Euglena* (yoo-GLEE-nuh) in Figure 2–3. The *Euglena* has a more complicated structure than the amoeba. You can anticipate that this changes the comparison to the animal cell and the plant cell in Figure 2–2.

Both the amoeba and the *Euglena* have a contractile (kun-TRAK-til) vacuole that fills up and expels excess water from the organism. Both can

move about, but the *Euglena* moves more rapidly. It swims expertly, propelled by the movements of its **flagellum** (fluh-JEL-um). It also has a **stigma,** or *eyespot,* that is not an eye but is sensitive to light. In addition, the *Euglena* has two options for getting food. It can take in food from the environment like an animal. It can also make food like a plant. In this case, the food is made by green structures in the cytoplasm called **chloroplasts** (KLOHR-uh-plasts). Can an organism that packs so many structures and functions in one tiny body really be considered a cell?

The answer to this question came from studying cells in multicellular organisms. For example, a muscle cell in an animal has limited functions—it helps the animal move. Yet biologists succeeded in producing a whole animal from an egg whose nucleus was replaced by a muscle cell nucleus. The muscle cell nucleus could do *everything* required to control the building of the complete animal. However, it did not use all these abilities when functioning in a muscle cell. On the other hand, the smallest microorganisms do not have specialized cells to share the building of structures and carrying out of functions. Their tiny bodies must *build* everything and *do* everything in a space no larger than a cell. Thus most biologists consider microorganisms to be very highly developed cells—unicellular organisms.

## 2–3
## The Cell Theory Is Established

Schwann and Schleiden (page 7) did not discover cells. Yet they were the biologists chiefly responsible for the cell theory. Their discovery that cells exist in animals as well as plants affected the work of the microbiologists who extended the cell theory to microorganisms. A physician and biologist, Rudolph Virchow (FIR-koh), added another hypothesis to the growing body of information about cells. One of Virchow's special interests was life in the past and how it was related to present forms of life. Discoveries of cells in more and more organisms suggested to Virchow that their wide occurrence was no coincidence.

Numerous biologists had observed cells dividing, producing more cells. Similarly many microbiologists had observed microorganisms dividing, producing more microorganisms. Virchow saw in these events a principle—cells producing more cells in a procession through time. If this was true, cells must have a long history.

Virchow stated the hypothesis simply—"All cells come from cells." But it meant that investigations of the cell theory were extended into the past to the ancestors of living cells.

Today the cell theory can be expressed in two statements:

1. Cells or products made by cells are the units of structure and function in organisms.
2. All cells come from preexisting cells.

**Try Investigation 2–A** Microorganisms in Pond Water, page 575.

---

**CAPSULE SUMMARY**

When the cellular nature of animals and plants was recognized, microorganisms were not included. Some of the microorganisms have since been found to be multicellular. Others are considered to be unicellular. The structures of unicellular organisms frequently appear more complex than those of cells from multicellular organisms. These structures reflect the complexities of carrying on all functions of life in a single cell.

Today the cell theory applies to organisms of all kinds. It also applies to their ancestors, recognizing that living cells have come from preexisting cells.

**SELF CHECK**

1. Apart from appearance, what was the greatest difference between Hooke's microscope (page 5) and Leeuwenhoek's microscope?
2. What are some similarities between microorganisms and cells of larger organisms?
3. What differences are likely to exist between unicellular organisms and cells of larger organisms?
4. How did Virchow's contribution to the cell theory extend cell investigations into the past?

---

# Cell Structure

## 2–4

## Knowledge of Most Cells Developed Slowly

Cells in multicellular organisms are often referred to as **in vivo** (in VEE-voh). This phrase means "in life" or "in the living body." In larger organisms, cells in vivo cannot be studied under the microscope unless they are in a very thin part of the body. An example is cells in the tail of a fish.

As an alternative, cells can be removed from multicellular organisms and studied **in vitro** (in VEE-troh). This phrase means "in glassware." More broadly it has come to mean "outside the living body in an artificial environment."

Most knowledge about cells of multicellular organisms has been discovered from cells in vitro. Biologists are aware that a living cell may undergo changes in vitro. This is a problem they acknowledge. They assume that a living cell in vitro may not function as it did in the organism.

Another problem is that unstained living cells are difficult to observe. Special lighting techniques can sometimes help deal successfully with this problem.

Stains are often used to bring out detailed structures in cells. However, most stains kill cells. Other materials or processes used to preserve or fix cells for study may change the appearance of the cells.

All such problems explain why, for almost 100 years following Schwann's and Schleiden's work, cell knowledge advanced slowly. One exception was the study of how cells divide to produce more cells. You will study cell division in Chapter 11.

Generally the cell structures that were known early in this century are the same ones you will observe directly under the microscope, such as the following:

- **cell walls** in plant cells (Figure 2–2). They protect cells and make up a network that supports the plants. Some of their many other functions are still being investigated today.
- **plasma membrane** (Figure 2–2). This membrane, looking like a thin sheet around the cell, is partly fluid and very active. Most of its activity is regulating traffic of materials that enter and leave the cell.
- **cytoplasm** (Figure 2–2). Many activities take place in the cytoplasm. It is very complex because it contains so many specialized, smaller structures.
- **vacuoles** in the cytoplasm (Figure 2–2). These vacuoles carry food particles, cell products, or a variety of other materials needed by the cell.
- **plastids** in the cytoplasm of plant cells. The principal plastids are chloroplasts, which are used in making food. They are similar to the chloroplasts in *Euglena* (Figure 2–3).

- **centrioles** (SEN-trih-ohls) in the cytoplasm of animal cells. They function during cell division (Chapter 11).
- **nucleus** (Figure 2–2). The nucleus is the control center of a cell. It contains almost all the cell's information molecules.
- **nucleolus** (noo-KLEE-oh-lus), a structure within the nucleus. The nucleolus helps process special information molecules.
- **chromatin** (KROH-muht-in), a network of material in the nucleus. The chromatin is largely the information molecules, which control the cell.

**Try Investigation 2 –B** Cell Structure, page 576.

## 2–5

## An Information Explosion Is Under Way Today

An important new instrument, the **electron microscope,** was developed in the 1930s. Soon it was used in cell studies. Electron microscopes use electrons rather than light. You do not look through the microscope directly at an object. Instead, a beam of electrons is directed through the object onto a viewing screen something like a TV screen. This particular type of electron microscope is a **transmission microscope** (Figure 2–4). A high-voltage transmission electron microscope can magnify parts of a cell as much as 300,000 times. Just imagine—this is like magnifying your hand so that it is more than 40 kilometers long!

Under a compound microscope, surface cells from a plant root tip would appear similar to those in Figure 1–5 (left), page 6. A thin section of one of these cells would reveal greater detail when examined with a transmission electron microscope (Figure 2–5). Structures in the cell can be enlarged many more times for closer examination.

A second type of electron microscope is a **scanning microscope** (Figure 2–4). In this instrument, the electron beam scans the surfaces of whole objects, instead of passing through thin slices taken from them. You see images of objects from the outside (Figure 2–6). The magnification is not as high as that obtained with a transmission electron microscope.

**Figure 2–4** Two electron microscopes. The larger one (right) is a high-voltage transmission microscope. The smaller one (below) is a scanning microscope. Note that the transmission microscope is almost two stories tall. (The operator of the microscope is on the lower floor.) The scanning microscope sits in a small part of one room.

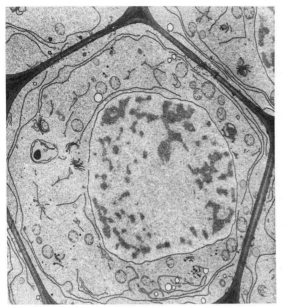

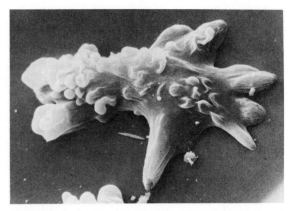

**Figure 2–6** A scanning electron microscope produced this exterior view of an amoeba.

**Figure 2–5** An ultrathin section through a single cell is shown in this photograph made using a transmission electron microscope. Compare this picture with that of *Zebrina* cells shown in Figure 1–5. The cells in both photographs are from layers of cells that cover and protect other cells.

Studies with electron microscopes have revealed many previously unknown cell structures. Complicated chemical tests have helped show how the structures work. As a result, knowledge of cells and their parts has become much more detailed. (See **Appendix 2–A,** Structures of the Generalized Eukaryotic Cell, page 688.) Figure 2–7 shows a cell diagram that includes both animal cell and plant cell features. Among the structures that are first mentioned in this diagram are the following:

- **mitochondria** (my-tuh-KON-dree-uh; singular, mitochondrion, my-tuh-KON-dree-un). Cells that contain these miniature ''powerhouses'' can release much more energy from their food substances than cells without them. Mitochondria sometimes can be detected under a compound microscope as small, oblong particles.

- **lysosomes** (LY-soh-sohmz). Lysosomes are vacuoles containing digestive fluids.
- **ribosomes** (RY-buh-sohmz). Ribosomes are miniature ''factories'' where protein materials are made.
- **endoplasmic reticulum** (EN-doh-plaz-mik reh-TIK-yoo-lum). The ER, as it is abbreviated, is a network of membranes inside a cell. The ER helps give a cell its inner structure and provide sites for different cell functions. The ER is very difficult to detect in the moving cytoplasm of a living cell. Under the electron microscope the ER appears rough where ribosomes occur on it but smooth elsewhere. It may be attached to the inside of a cell's plasma membrane.
- **Golgi** (GOHL-jee) **complex.** The Golgi complex packages materials made along the ER and elsewhere. The packaging material is a mem-

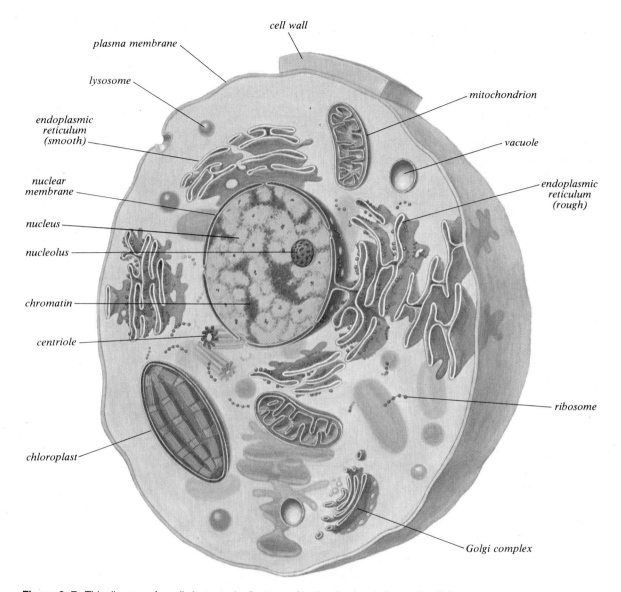

**Figure 2–7** This diagram of a cell shows major features of both animal and plant cells. Only a portion of a cell wall is shown (top). A single cell from either an animal or a plant would not show all of these features.

brane, like the plasma membrane. Packaging is very important when materials could damage the cell or vice versa, and when materials are to be passed through the plasma membrane.

• **nuclear membrane.** The nucleus of a cell is enclosed within its own membrane. The ER attaches to this membrane too. Notice the pores that appear in the nuclear membrane.

After pores were discovered in the nuclear membrane, biologists expected to find pores in a cell's plasma membrane. Instead, they found quick-changing membrane activities that permit the passage of materials. These materials pass through the plasma membrane in a "now you see it, now you don't" fashion. One method of passage is suggested in Figure 2–7. At the upper left, a bit of the plasma membrane is folded inward, making a small pocket. Materials can enter the pocket. The plasma membrane then closes over the materials and releases the pocket inside the cell as a vacuole. In the reverse operation, packaged products for delivery outside the cell come against the inside of the membrane. The membrane opens, and the materials are expelled. The same kind of small pocket is left behind for an instant, but this time the pocket is the emptied package or vacuole.

You will be investigating the work of cells in most organisms that you study in biology. Chemical methods of investigation have advanced so rapidly that you will even read about functions of individual molecules of cell materials.

---

**CAPSULE SUMMARY**
Knowledge of cells developed slowly until well into this century. The invention of electron microscopes was one factor in a new information explosion about cells. The invention of many remarkable chemical methods of investigation was another factor.

Most knowledge of cells has come from studies of fixed cells or of living cells in vitro. The study of cells in vivo still presents great difficulties.

**SELF CHECK**
1. What does it mean to describe cells as *in vivo?* as *in vitro?*
2. What is one disadvantage of using stains on living cells?
3. Give at least one reason why it is important for cells to package some of their products.
4. Explain one way in which the plasma membrane of a cell is unlike an artificial membrane or plastic bag.

---

# Multicellular Organization

## 2–6

## A Group of Cells May Show Cooperation

When one-celled organisms divide, the new cells of some may remain together in a cluster (Figure 2–8). However, a cluster of cells is not necessarily a multicellular organism. Each cell has an individual life and may break away from the cluster at some point.

Among multicellular organisms, the cells are more closely related. One of the least complex examples is *Volvox.* It may be found in many ponds during the spring and early summer. A *Volvox* organism, or colony, is shaped like a hol-

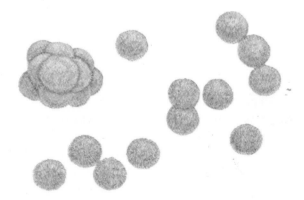

**Figure 2–8** Though bacteria like these exist in clusters, chains, and as isolated cells, every bacterium is still an individual organism.

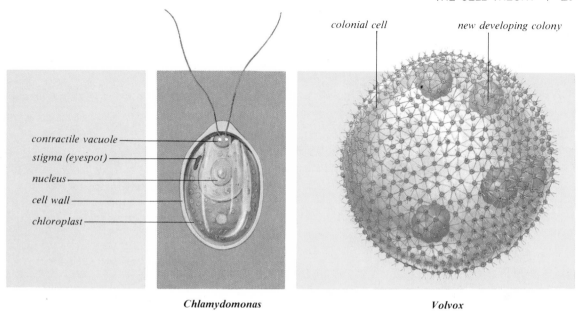

*contractile vacuole*

*stigma (eyespot)*

*nucleus*

*cell wall*

*chloroplast*

*colonial cell*

*new developing colony*

**Chlamydomonas**

**Volvox**

**Figure 2–9** Individual cells of a *Volvox* colony (right) are similar in appearance to a unicellular organism known as *Chlamydomonas* (left).

low ball (Figure 2–9, right). Inside the colony may be other developing colonies. Each colony has several hundred to tens of thousands of cells.

The cells of *Volvox* resemble the one-celled organism *Chlamydomonas* (Figure 2–9, left). Each cell has a nucleus, two flagella, contractile vacuoles, an eyespot (stigma), and a cup-shaped chloroplast. A gelatinlike layer surrounds each cell and separates it from its neighbors. Under the microscope a *Volvox* colony looks like a gelatinous sphere with cells imbedded in it.

If the cell wall and plasma membrane of a *Chlamydomonas* are punctured, the organism dies. If a *Volvox* cell is punctured, the cell dies, but the rest of the colony continues to live.

If you observe *Volvox* under high magnification, you can see delicate strands connecting the cells (Figure 2–9, right). You can also see that certain cells are larger than the rest. The colony appears

to have a front end and a back end. As flagella move the *Volvox* through the water, the larger cells are usually at the back.

*Volvox* moves in a coordinated way. If each cell's flagella were to move at random, only irregular motion of the colony would result. But the colony spins on its front-to-rear axis as it moves through the water. All the cells have to move their flagella in the same pattern to achieve this motion. Thus the cells are organized into a working unit as the colony moves.

Different-sized cells in the colony may have different functions as well. Only a few cells in the colony are capable of producing the offspring colonies. *Volvox* is useful for investigating the functions of cells in simple multicellular organisms. Damage to, or removal of, cells can test whether those cells carried on any essential function for the whole organism.

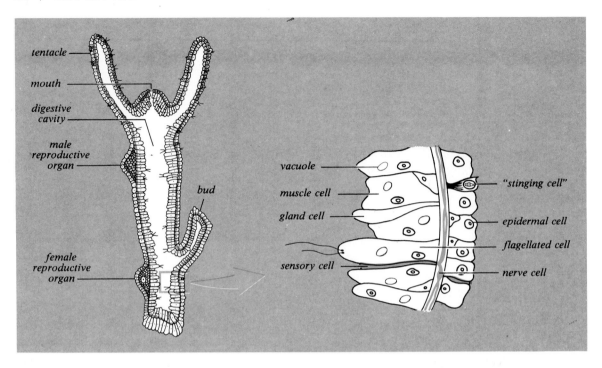

Figure 2–10 A drawing of a section through a *Hydra* (left), and an enlarged view of some of the specialized cells in its body wall (right).

## 2–7

## Division of Labor Begins

In multicellular organisms more complex than *Volvox,* many different kinds of cells exist. All the cells must carry on some basic activities of life. However, each kind of cell often takes on a special job as well. For example, one kind of cell, a gland cell, is efficient at making certain kinds of chemicals. Another, a nerve cell, is efficient in conducting nerve impulses. Still another kind of cell, a muscle cell, is efficient in movement. Even the cells that form an organism's outer covering, **epidermal** (ep-ih-DER-muhl) **cells,** may be specialized. The drawing of a *Hydra* in Figure 2–10 shows cells with such specializations.

A *Hydra* is a very small threadlike organism with a ring of tentacles at one end (Figure 2–11). It is a freshwater animal. Its cells show a beginning

Figure 2–11 A *Hydra* viewed under low magnification. The animal is barely visible without magnification.

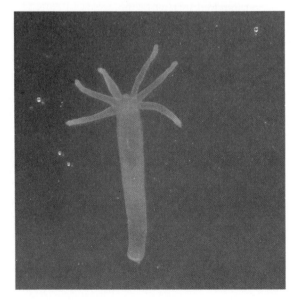

of differences in appearance, along with differences in specialization. In later chapters and in your laboratory work, you will see that cells of larger organisms are much more distinctive in appearance. Nerve and muscle cells are very long and thin, blood cells are almost round, and so on.

In multicellular organisms, a group of cells with the same specialization usually works together. Each specialized group of cells is called a **tissue.** The cell that is labeled *epidermal cell* in Figure 2-10 is part of a tissue. You can see similar cells on either side of it. They form the covering tissue of the *Hydra,* along with stinging cells and sensory cells.

Most kinds of animals and plants have many tissues. Tissues of different kinds may be organized into **organs** (eyes, hearts, and stomachs, for example). Organs may be incorporated into **systems** of organs. For example, a circulatory system usually includes a heart, blood vessels, and blood. No matter how specialized the structures in an organism become, cells or their products are the building blocks.

The division of labor by cells in multicellular organisms accounts for their differences from unicellular organisms. Specialized cells have fewer but more highly developed functions.

**Try Investigation 2–C** What Special Structures Do Some Smaller Organisms Have That Aid in Obtaining Food?, page 577.

## 2–8

## Large Organisms Have Highly Specialized Systems

In multicellular organisms, the inner cells cannot obtain materials directly from the outside environment. In addition they cannot pass their wastes directly to the outside environment. Specialized systems handle deliveries between the environment and the cells (Figure 2–12). In animals a circulatory system is involved. In fact, in most animals more than one system is involved.

**Figure 2–12** Two diagrams of cells in a multicellular organism. Cells that are not in direct contact with the organism's environment are shown in blue on the left. To obtain food and get rid of wastes as efficiently as outer cells, these inner cells require a system for deliveries as shown on the right.

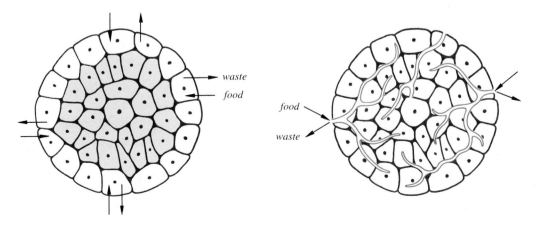

# Biology
# Brief

## Anticell Cells

"Visiting" cells are very common in your body. You are a host to microorganisms from the environment almost all the time. What kind of host are you?

Unlike the way you greet your friends, your attitude toward microorganisms is definitely antisocial. Specialized cells of your own act as your personal body-guards, roaming through your body by way of the bloodstream. They quickly recognize strangers that drop in, and intercept them. In comparison to the size of the visitors, some of the cells you employ in this work are monsters. These friendly monsters (at least they are friendly to you) are not like other body cells that stay together where they work. These large blood cells and their relatives live alone, often work alone, and travel freely. The one restriction they share is that they cannot survive for long outside your body.

A scanning electron microscope produced the photograph you see here of several cells of the roaming type. Getting them together for a family photograph required special laboratory techniques. All the pictured cells are *white blood cells,* though they are of several types that have different names. The monster in the group is a *macrophage* (MAK-ruh-fayj), from *macro-* meaning "large."

White blood cells can work in or out of the bloodstream, destroying microorganisms anywhere in your body. These cells move through your body tissues in a way much like microorganisms themselves. Along with various molecules, the white blood cells are your chief protectors against harm from some of the microscopic life around you.

Most multicellular plants also have some system of transport. A tree's leaves admit air but cannot absorb water from the air. The water and minerals come from the soil. A transport system takes water from where it is absorbed in the roots to where it is needed. Minerals are carried in solution in the water. Another transport system carries food produced in the leaves to other parts of the tree. Both systems extend throughout the tree.

In general, specialized systems account for most of the complexity of multicellular organisms. Most of the systems, in turn, are necessary for these three reasons:

1. a division of labor occurs among cells;
2. many individual cells cannot work together without regulation and coordination;

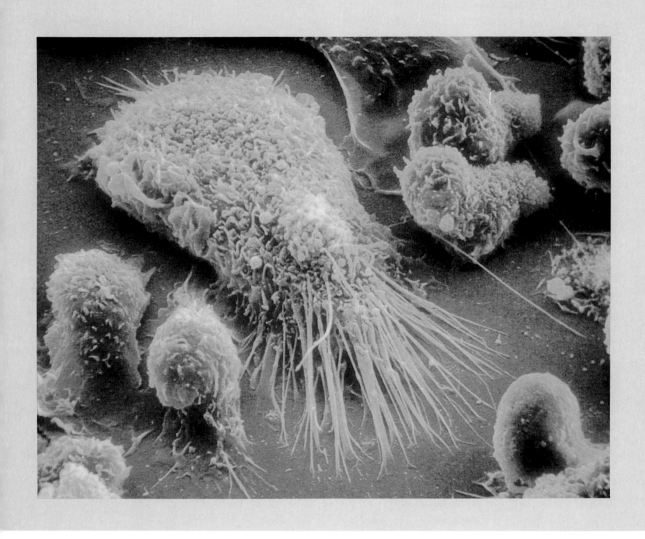

3. the majority of the cells are not in direct contact with the outside environment.

The different systems in an organism unite all its parts into a smoothly functioning whole.

In many organisms, added specializations have developed within their specialized systems. For example, cells whose jobs involve travel occur in your circulatory system. Some of these cells play no part in transport but instead have other specialized tasks (See Biology Brief above). Thus continuing specialization has led to greater and greater numbers of types of cells.

Specialized systems have contributed enormously to the variety, complexity, and sizes of multicellular organisms. In Chapter 3 you will take a look at some of this variety of life.

**CAPSULE SUMMARY**

*Volvox* is one of the least complicated multicellular organisms. Its swimming movements reveal that its cells are coordinated. All the cells look mostly alike, but a few of their functions show differences. In *Hydra* some cells are organized into tissues. Epidermal tissue and nerve tissue are examples.

Tissues, organs, and systems become more complex in larger multicellular organisms. In fact, most of the complexity of such organisms is found in their specialized systems.

**SELF CHECK**

1. How does the death of a cell reveal a difference between unicellular and multicellular organisms?
2. Why are specialized systems necessary in large multicellular organisms?
3. Arrange these terms in increasing order of complexity: cells, organ systems, organs, tissues.
4. Can a single cell form a system or a tissue? Explain.

# CHAPTER SUMMARY

## HIGHLIGHTS

Microorganisms as well as animals and plants show cell structure. The cell theory applies to organisms of all kinds.

Knowledge of cells developed slowly. However, after electron microscopes and modern chemical methods of investigation were developed, a great variety of cell structures were discovered. Their functions continue to be discovered in greater detail. Even functions of many individual molecules in cells have been discovered.

In most multicellular organisms, cells form tissues. Tissues of complementary kinds become organized into organs. Organs become part of organ systems. The complexity of organisms increases accordingly until a great variety of organisms result.

## REVIEWING IDEAS

1. What characteristics of the smaller microorganisms suggest that they are cells?
2. Define *unicellular* and *multicellular*.
3. What was Virchow's contribution to the cell theory?
4. State the cell theory in your own words.
5. Where in a cell are a nucleolus and chromatin found?
6. What difficulties are encountered in studying living cells of multicellular organisms?
7. Where in a cell are mitochondria and ribosomes found?
8. Why is it important for cells to package some of their products?
9. What cell structures release most of the energy from food substances?

10. How does the environment of cells differ for a unicellular and a multicellular organism?

## USING CONCEPTS

11. Some microorganisms, principally bacteria, have no clearly defined cell nuclei. What other evidence would you look for in trying to determine whether they are cells?

12. What cell part specializes in packaging certain materials? Give an example of how the plasma membrane also can package materials.

13. In view of Virchow's addition to the cell theory, what hypothesis would you offer to describe the body structure of ancient organisms on Earth?

14. Describe your understanding of a cell's plasma membrane in contrast to a plastic bag.

15. Explain some of the reasons why knowledge of cells developed so slowly during the century following Schwann's and Schleiden's work.

16. In what way might you expect cells with mitochondria to have different capabilities than cells without mitochondria?

17. Some biologists once wondered whether the ER (endoplasmic reticulum) was formed only after death by the process used to fix cells for study. Why might they have asked such a question?

18. If cells are the units of structure and function in organisms, why would tissues and organs be needed?

## RECOMMENDED READING

Avers, C. J. *Cell Biology,* 2nd ed. New York, D. Van Nostrand, 1981. A clearly written textbook with good diagrams and photographs.

Hillman, H., and P. Sartory. *The Living Cell.* Philadelphia, International Ideas, 1980. A very short but well-illustrated book about cells.

Hoover, R. B. "Those Marvelous, Myriad Diatoms." *National Geographic,* June 1979. Beautiful photographs that may help identify some freshwater microorganisms for Investigation 2–A.

# The Variety of Life 3

You share planet Earth with incredible numbers and kinds of living things. Some are familiar to you; others you have never heard of. Some are microscopic in size, others, like whales and redwood trees, are so large that you have to stand well back to view them whole. Some appear to be always on the move, others always in one spot. Every body of water and every land mass on Earth is inhabited by organisms.

Trying to picture all the varieties of living things at once is a mind-boggling task. No person can store so much information. Biologists solve this problem by grouping and classifying organisms. Then it is possible to think about the groups instead.

What constitutes a group of organisms? Would a group be all the organisms that live in one place? Would it be all the organisms that fly? Do all the organisms of one color make a group? If these categories determined the groups, too many organisms would be members of many different groups. What defines a group must be considered much more carefully. In this chapter you will learn about biologists' ideas on grouping and classifying.

# Bringing Order to Variability

## 3–1

## Species

Variability is a characteristic of life. No two students in your school are exactly alike, not even if they are twins. The trees in your neighborhood, cats, dogs, and other organisms are also individual in their appearance. Yet similarities also exist between organisms.

Those organisms that are similar enough to one another so that they renew their population by reproduction, are recognized as belonging to the same **species.** The species concept was established in the 17th century by the naturalist John Ray. To Ray, a species consisted of similar parents and their offspring. Thus species came to stand for an identifiable group of organisms.

Through time, the definition of *species* has changed. The ability of individuals in a species to reproduce remains a necessary condition. Within that limit, what constitutes a species is determined by the specialists who study the organisms in question.

In general, biologists have identified more than two million species of organisms. Probably another one million species, most of them microorganisms, remain to be identified. No single biologist can know so many species well. Instead, biologists specialize in studying particular groups

---

←Swimming pools can get a bit crowded. These sea lions surface for air. They cannot obtain oxygen underwater as fishes do. Why not?

of organisms. Thus species of birds are determined by **ornithologists** (or-nuh-THOL-uh-jists). Species of fishes are determined by **ichthyologists** (ik-thee-OL-uh-jists). Species of plants that lived long ago and left traces in the rocks are determined by **paleobotanists** (pay-lee-oh-BOT-un-ists). For these special fields of study to exist, all known species of organisms must be grouped by similarities, yet distinguished by differences. To make sense of the vast variety of living things, scientists must classify them.

## 3–2

## Early Classification Systems

The Greek philosopher and biologist Aristotle, who lived about 350 B.C., tried to classify the limited number of plants and animals that were then known. Aristotle's system was not consistent. Plants were classified by whether they were herbs, shrubs, or trees. However, animals were grouped by whether or not they had red blood. Within the resulting two groups, animals were further grouped by body structure and then grouped by how they reproduced.

Every human population seems to have been concerned with classifying the living world. The Indians of southwestern United States developed systems for the classification of cultivated, edible, and medicinal plants. The Aztec people of Central America developed systems for classifying the plants and animals they used in their daily lives. However, these classification systems had little effect on the European work on which modern classification is based.

During the great age of exploration, from the 15th through the 18th centuries, European biologists returned from foreign lands with organisms never before seen in Europe or the Near East. Expeditions were sent out to discover still more organisms. Great collections of plants and animals were assembled over which biologists labored to provide names and identifications.

One of the explorers was the 18th-century botanist Carolus Linnaeus (Karl von Linné). Linnaeus felt that a major aim of science was to find order in nature. As a solution, Linnaeus selected organisms with particular structural characteristics as the ideal types. Other organisms that resembled an ideal type in structure were grouped with it. Those that did not were compared to still other ideal types. This was a *type specimen* approach to species classification.

Linnaeus believed that varieties and species of organisms were fixed and unchanging. The variability that presented itself in the face of this belief went unquestioned.

## 3–3

## Binomial Nomenclature

Many biologists contributed to the development of early classification systems for plants and animals. One of the first attempts to use a two-name system was made more than 100 years before Linnaeus. The Swiss botanist Caspar Bauhin classified plants and named them according to their groups. However, it is mostly to Linnaeus that biologists owe the present species-naming system of **binomial nomenclature** (a two-word naming system). The first word in the species name is the **genus** (JEE-nus; plural: **genera,** JEN-er-uh). This name identifies a larger group to which a species belongs. The second word is the so-called descriptive, or **trivial,** name that applies only to one species in the genus. Together, both words are the

**Figure 3–1** Cats show great variety but have so many features in common that identifying an animal as a cat may not be difficult. Can you match these cats to the names of their species in the text?

species name, but not either word alone. For example, the cat genus is *Felis* (FEE-lis). One species of cat is *Felis leo,* the lion. The species of house cats is *Felis domesticus;* that of the tiger, *Felis tigris;* the leopard, *Felis pardus;* and the American cougar, *Felis concolor.* All are cats, but each is of a different species (Figure 3–1). In addition, there are still other species of cats.

Why a binomial system? Why not just call organisms lions or roses, dogs or gophers? First, a classification system has to be internationally understood, while remaining unaffected by the inevitable changes that occur in spoken languages. For this reason, Latinized names are used rather than names in some particular modern language. The following lines from a textbook used in Yugoslavia refer to a species of organism you may be able to identify, even though you do not know the language in the text:

Te besede se slišijo, kot da bi bile bakterije reagirale po Lamarckovi teoriji. (Poglavje 3–2). Naslednji opis eksperimenta, pri katerem so uporabili bakterijo *Staphylococcus aureus,* vam bo pokazal, ali je ta proces res lamarckovski ali ne.

A second reason for the binomial system is that it is precise. Common names are regional and imprecise. For example, if people from different parts of North America are discussing a gopher, they may not be talking about the same species at all. In California, a gopher is a small burrowing rodent with the scientific name *Thomomys bottae.* Across the Midwest, a gopher is a 13-striped ground squirrel whose scientific name is *Spermophilus tridecemlineatus.* In Florida, a gopher is a kind of turtle or tortoise whose scientific name is *Gopherus polyphemus.* Imagine how difficult it is

for people who use the same common name for different organisms to communicate without confusion. The use of scientific names avoids this problem.

## 3–4

## The Basis for a Scientific Classification System

Think of the ways in which organisms could be classified. You could use color, size, shape, or hundreds of other features as a basis for classification. If you classified organisms by color, earthworms, some roses, and some birds might be grouped together (Figure 3–2). If you used size, mice and mushrooms could be grouped together. If you used shape, fish, mammals such as porpoises, and even some worms would fall into the same group.

Biologists seek more fundamental similarities and differences as a basis for classifying organisms. Similarities of structure that indicate *related ancestry* are the principal criteria. These relationships are called structural **homologies** (ho-MOL-uh-jees). For example, the flipper of a whale, the wing of a bat, and the arm of a human have many homologies in their bone and muscle structure (see Figure 23–5, page 474). Similarly, fish, amphibians, reptiles, and birds share this same limb pattern with mammals. The limbs have the same relationship to the body, and they develop in the same way in the young.

There are also chemical homologies—similarities in blood or other body substances—that are

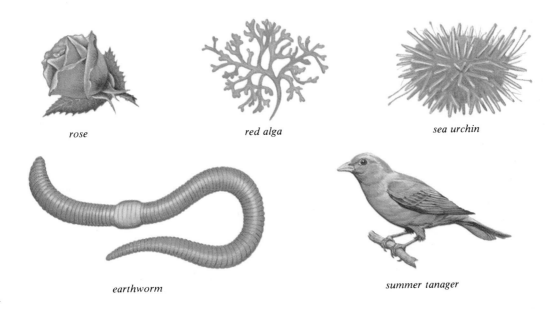

*rose*      *red alga*      *sea urchin*

*earthworm*      *summer tanager*

**Figure 3–2** One similarity among these organisms is obvious—their color. But how else are they alike? Three live on land, but the red alga and the sea urchin live in the ocean. The red alga makes its food, but the sea urchin obtains food from the environment. Are any two of the organisms as much alike as the five species of cats in Figure 3–1? Color is rarely used in classifying organisms, unless it indicates similar chemical substances and similar chemical processes (see algae pictured on page 51).

recognized as important indicators of close relationships. In the previous examples, bones and muscles of the limbs, their cells, and the chemicals in the cells all indicate relationships and common ancestry.

Based on such homologies, organisms of different species are grouped into larger, more general categories (Table 3–1). Closely related species are grouped into genera, as in the cats of the genus *Felis*. Related genera are grouped into the same **family,** related families into the same **order,** and related orders into the same **class.**

At the class level, cats, whales, bats, and people are placed in the class **Mammalia.** All organisms in this class have hair and provide milk for their young. They also share other characteristics.

Related classes are grouped in the same **phylum** or **division.** Zoologists use the term *phylum;* botanists use the term *division.* Phyla or divisions, in turn, are grouped under a number of primary categories called **kingdoms.** Relationships are thus shown in larger and larger groupings from species through kingdom. The discipline of classification has grown complex. It has given rise to a special field of study known as **taxonomy** (tak-son-uh-mee), or **systematics.** The science of classification continues to change as the knowledge about living things expands.

## Table 3-1. CLASSIFICATION OF TWELVE ANIMALS

| Common Name | Species Name |
| --- | --- |
| Man | *Homo sapiens* |
| Lion | *Felis leo* |
| House cat | *Felis domesticus* |
| Tiger | *Felis tigris* |
| Dog | *Canis familiaris* |
| Gopher | *Thomomys bottae* |
| Gopher | *Spermophilus tridecemlineatus* |
| American robin | *Turdus migratorius* |
| European robin | *Erithacus rubecula* |
| Gopher turtle | *Gopherus polyphemus* |
| Green frog | *Rana clamitans* |
| Bullfrog | *Rana catesbeiana* |

### CAPSULE SUMMARY

More than two million species of organisms live on Earth. To study this great variety of life, biologists need some method of classification. Every society and culture on Earth has developed a way of classifying plants and animals. The naturalist Carolus Linnaeus classified organisms by structure. Linnaeus gave each species a scientific name consisting of two parts. This system of binomial nomenclature is in use today. Exactly what constitutes a species is determined by specialists who study the organisms. The definition of the term includes the requirement that a species must be a naturally reproducing group of organisms.

Systematics is concerned not only with naming species, but with indicating relationships among species of organisms. To this end, a seven-layer ranking system is used from species to kingdom.

### SELF CHECK

1. Why is it that a biologist cannot study and know about all the organisms on Earth?
2. How does classification help in understanding the living world?
3. What condition is necessary for organisms to be considered members of the same species?
4. Describe how a species name is constructed. Give an example.

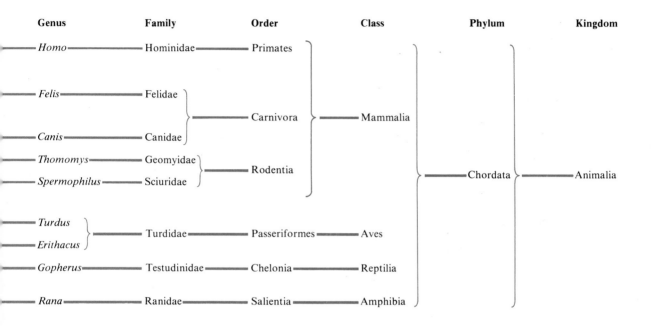

| Genus | Family | Order | Class | Phylum | Kingdom |
|-------|--------|-------|-------|--------|---------|
| *Homo* | Hominidae | Primates | | | |
| *Felis* | Felidae | Carnivora | Mammalia | | |
| *Canis* | Canidae | | | | |
| *Thomomys* | Geomyidae | Rodentia | | | |
| *Spermophilus* | Sciuridae | | | Chordata | Animalia |
| *Turdus* | Turdidae | Passeriformes | Aves | | |
| *Erithacus* | | | | | |
| *Gopherus* | Testudinidae | Chelonia | Reptilia | | |
| *Rana* | Ranidae | Salientia | Amphibia | | |

# The Kingdom Problem

## 3–5

### Prokaryotes and Eukaryotes

From species to kingdom, each successively broader category contains more organisms. The more organisms or species, the more difficult it is to find homologies among them. In addition, it is more difficult to find features that set them apart from other groups at the same systematic level.

In Chapter 2, the cell theory stated that organisms are made up of cells or cell products. Just as the cell is a basic unit of structure and function, it also contains clues about the relationships among

organisms. On the basis of cell structure, biologists can separate organisms into two major groups: the **prokaryotes** (pro-KARE-ee-ohts) and the **eukaryotes** (yoo-KARE-ee-ohts).

The prokaryotes—bacteria and blue-green algae—are cells with cell walls but without a well-defined cell nucleus (no nuclear membrane exists). Movement of the cytoplasm within the cell does not seem to occur. Prokaryotic cells also do not have such structures as mitochondria, lysosomes, a Golgi complex, or plastids (Figure 3–3). Their chromatin often is limited to a single large information molecule, a much-folded, circular

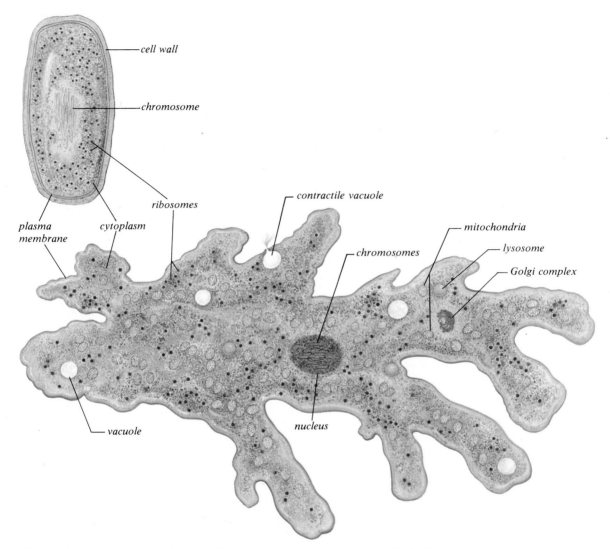

cell wall

chromosome

contractile vacuole

mitochondria

lysosome

Golgi complex

ribosomes

chromosomes

plasma
membrane

cytoplasm

vacuole

nucleus

**Figure 3–3** A prokaryotic cell (upper left) compared with a eukaryotic cell (below). The prokaryotic cell is a bacterium; the eukaryotic cell is an amoeba. Almost all prokaryotic cells are much smaller than eukaryotic cells.

**chromosome** (KROH-muh-sohm). Sometimes there are also smaller, circular information molecules called *plasmids*. When prokaryotes move, they glide (blue-green algae) or use flagella (many bacteria).

Eukaryotic cells are found in your body and, in fact, in most of the organisms with which you are familiar. Eukaryotic cells are distinguished by a definite nucleus bounded by a membrane. Cell walls may be present or absent. The cytoplasm often appears to move or stream within the cell. Among the cell structures of eukaryotes are mitochondria, lysosomes, a Golgi complex, and, in plants, plastids (Figure 3–3).

Between prokaryotic and eukaryotic cells there are greater differences than between plants and animals. Using these basic differences in cell structure, biologists divide all organisms into pro-karyotes and eukaryotes. Within these two categories, further major groups can then be identified.

## 3-6
## How Many Kingdoms of Prokaryotes?

Just because prokaryotic cells have a similar cell structure does not mean that they all function in the same fashion. Bacteria, for example, display more varied chemical and functional patterns than all of the eukaryotes. Like many eukaryotes, some of the bacteria use the energy of sunlight to pro-duce food—a process called **photosynthesis** (foh-toh-SIN-theh-sis). Unlike green plants, however, the bacteria use a wider variety of substances as their raw materials. Other bacteria produce food by using energy obtained from chemicals—a pro-cess called **chemosynthesis** (kee-moh-SIN-theh-sis). Still others do not produce food but are feed-ers in various ways. Organisms that derive their energy and produce food from nonliving sub-stances are called producers, or **autotrophs** (OT-uh-trohfs). Many bacteria and the blue-green algae are autotrophs. Organisms that take their food and energy from other organisms, either liv-ing or dead, are called consumers, or **heterotrophs** (HET-er-oh-trohfs). Many bacteria are hetero-trophs.

The great diversity in chemical makeup and functional patterns among the prokaryotes suggests that there are several kingdoms of bacteria in addi-tion to the blue-green algae. In fact, the blue-green algae may even be considered as another kingdom of photosynthetic bacteria. All these kingdom dif-ferences are not yet clearly resolved. Until they are, it is simpler to consider all the prokaryotes as a single kingdom, the **Monera** (muh-NER-uh). This

kingdom (Figure 3–4) can be divided into some 16 phyla, depending on the criteria used to distinguish one phylum from another.

## 3-7
## How Many Kingdoms of Eukaryotes?

Most eukaryotes can be divided according to whether they are autotrophs or heterotrophs. Some, however, are both. For example, *Euglena* (page 20) sometimes makes its own food and uses ready-made food at other times.

Eukaryotes can be further divided as to whether they are single cells (unicellular) or made up of many cells (multicellular). However, neither this criterion nor a related one, the size of the organ-ism, resolves all the difficulties of placing eukary-otes into kingdoms.

One- or two-parent reproduction (asexual or sexual) is another factor that is considered. How the organisms process their food and convert en-ergy is taken into account too. Structure and func-tion in general are categorized. Still, problems of classification remain.

Currently eukaryotes are placed in four separate kingdoms (Figure 3–4). One of these kingdoms, the **Protista** (pro-TIST-uh), includes organisms that do not fit well into the other three kingdoms. Most protists are alike in being microscopic. In fact, most protists are unicellular. However, some organisms that can be seen without a microscope (such as slime molds) are also included. The kingdom Protista is divided into 27 phyla to which such organisms as amoebas, *Euglena,* and the nucleated algae belong.

Another kingdom of eukaryotes is the **Fungi** (FUN-jye). These organisms reproduce by spores, have cell walls, lack flagella, and have no chloro-phyll. Fungi range in size from microscopic spe-cies to large mushrooms. They reproduce both sexually and asexually. The role of the fungi as

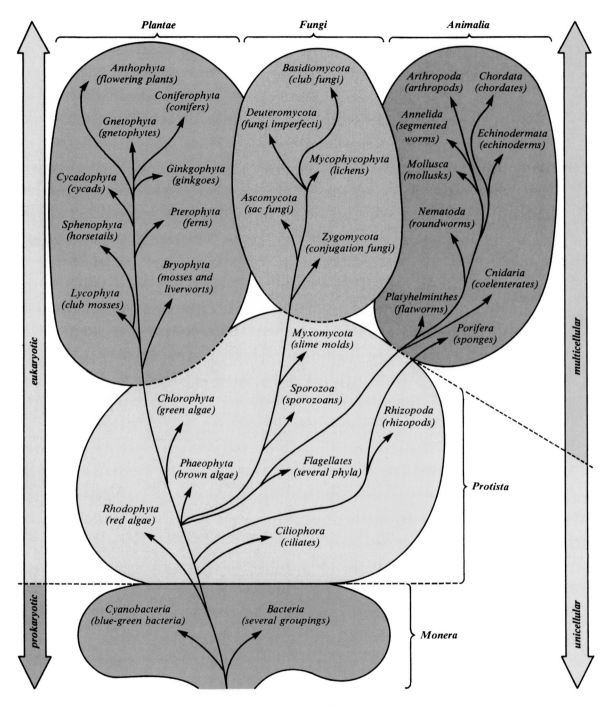

**Figure 3–4** Currently all organisms may be classified in the five kingdoms shown in this diagram. However, future changes may create more kingdoms of prokaryotes (see text).

## Table 3-2. CLASSIFICATION OF AN ORGANISM FROM EACH KINGDOM

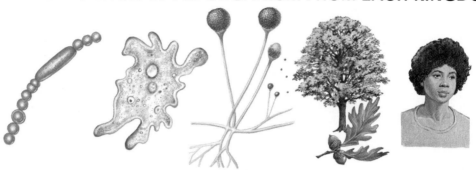

|  | *Anabaena*<br>blue-green algae | *Amoeba* | *Rhizopus*<br>bread mold | *Quercus alba*<br>white oak | *Homo sapiens*<br>human being |
|---|---|---|---|---|---|
| **kingdom** | Monera | Protista | Fungi | Plant | Animal |
| **phylum/division** | Cyanophyta or<br>Cyanobacteria | Sarcodina | Zygomycota | Anthophyta | Chordata |
| **class** | Eubacteria | Lobosa | Phycomycetes | Dicotyledoneae | Mammalia |
| **order** | Oscillatoriales | Amoebina | Mucorales | Fagales | Primates |
| **family** | Nostocaceae | Amoebidae | Mucoraceae | Fagaceae | Hominidae |
| **genus** | *Anabaena* | *Amoeba* | *Rhizopus* | *Quercus* | *Homo* |
| **species** | *Anabaena<br>circinalis* | *Amoeba<br>proteus* | *Rhizopus<br>stolonifer* | *Quercus<br>alba* | *Homo<br>sapiens* |

decomposers is important in the natural world. The fungi include lichens, yeasts, molds, bracket fungi, and mushrooms. There are at least five separate phyla of fungi.

Most of the autotrophic, multicellular eukaryotes that make their own food by photosynthesis belong to the kingdom **Plantae** (PLAN-tee). The exceptions are multicellular algae in the kingdom Protista. Plants have cellulose-containing cell walls, reproduce sexually (for some, also asexually), and contain green plastids in their cells. The bulk of the world's food and much of its oxygen are derived from plants. This kingdom can be separated into nine divisions.

The heterotrophic, multicellular eukaryotes are placed in the kingdom **Animalia** (an-uh-MAYL-yuh). Their size covers an extreme range which includes microscopic organisms and even giant whales. Reproduction is usually sexual, but some asexual reproduction occurs. At least 35 animal phyla have been identified.

Table 3–2 shows the complete classifications of five organisms, one from each of the five kingdoms.

**Try Investigation 3–A** Classifying Flowering Plants, page 579, or **Investigation 3–B** Structural Characteristics of Animals, page 583.

# Biology Brief

## Weekend Botany

Teaching biology is a full-time job, but Dr. Joyce Greene also finds time for her studies as a botanist. Over weekends she identifies and classifies mountain plants and investigates how they survive under harsh conditions at high altitudes.

Aspen trees (*Populus tremuloides*) in the Colorado mountains are one of the hardiest species of trees. People picture them in colorful mid-altitude groves (photo above). Dr. Greene has also found them growing, dwarfed and stunted, where high winds and cold sweep the upper mountain reaches (photo facing page, left). You must look closely to see a few leaves on the misshapen little aspen tree in the photograph. It survives at an altitude of 3350 meters.

*Populus tremuloides* is much more than a classification. It is a way of life.

## 3-8
## Changing Classification Patterns

Classification systems are not static. They change as biological knowledge changes. As more and more knowledge about organisms is acquired, biologists are better able to group them. The understanding of relationships improves with each new discovery about the structure and function of organisms.

Classification occasionally changes for certain organisms at all levels from species to kingdom. What is a species? What is a kingdom? How are organisms related one to another? Biologists are still investigating questions such as these. The goal is a better understanding of the living world and the functions and relationships of the organisms it contains.

Aspens at all altitudes face many hazards. The higher trees cannot flower in spring. On all the trees, frost kills many leaves in spring. Insects attack the trees in summer. Frosts begin again early in autumn. Wind-driven snows imprison some of the trees all winter, bending younger ones over with the force of the advancing snowpack. Each summer these young trees grow back in zigzag correction to their "posture," telling of their seasonal stresses in S-shaped trunks: ⌇. An added winter hazard is bark feeding by hungry elk. Dr. Greene is shown examining an elk-damaged tree (above, right) now exposed to greater future insect damage.

**CAPSULE SUMMARY**

Organisms are classified on the basis of cell structure as prokaryotes or eukaryotes. Prokaryotes do not have all the same cell structures as eukaryotes, although in some ways they are even more diversified. In particular, prokaryotes do not have nuclei bounded by membranes, and they do not have mitochondria, lysosomes, plastids, or a Golgi complex.

Currently all prokaryotes are grouped in one kingdom. The eukaryotes are grouped in four kingdoms.

**SELF CHECK**

1. In what kingdom are bacteria currently grouped?
2. How do the blue-green algae differ from other algae?
3. What are the four kingdoms of eukaryotes?
4. What kingdom is characterized in part by plastids in cells?

# CHAPTER SUMMARY

## HIGHLIGHTS

Classification is necessary if biologists are to study effectively the great variety of organisms that exist or have existed on Earth. A system that names organisms and indicates their relationships has been developed. This system is accepted by biologists throughout the world. It removes language differences so that biologists can understand one another when discussing particular organisms. Originally the classification system was based on structural homologies. Modern classification has introduced chemical homologies as well.

Currently all organisms are classified in five kingdoms–Monera, Protista, Fungi, Plantae, and Animalia. As biologists learn more about the natural world, classification systems become more refined and accurate. Systematics is a dynamic and changing branch of biology, attempting always to do a better job of classifying the world's organisms. Future discoveries can be expected to change classification further.

## REVIEWING IDEAS

1. What is a species? Who determines what constitutes a species?
2. What were the defects in Aristotle's classification system?
3. How did Linnaeus deal with variability?
4. How does binomial nomenclature provide information on classification?
5. Why is binomial nomenclature needed when organisms usually have common names?
6. What are chemical and structural relationships called that indicate related ancestry?
7. What is the difference between autotrophs and heterotrophs?

8. How do prokaryotic and eukaryotic cells differ?
9. Describe the characteristics that distinguish each of the five kingdoms.

## USING CONCEPTS

10. What considerations suggest that division of kingdoms by cell structure—prokaryotes and eukaryotes—may eventually result in approximately the same number of kingdoms of each?
11. What factors cause biologists to change the way they classify organisms?
12. Suppose that one of the two cell types—prokaryote and eukaryote—could have been ancestral to the other. Present arguments for which may have been the ancestral type.
13. Bats, birds, butterflies, and certain extinct reptiles all have or had wings. Why not place them in the same class because of this feature?

## RECOMMENDED READING

The following books are a few of many that may help you identify unfamiliar organisms:

Nowak, R. M., and J. L. Paridaso. *Walker's Mammals of the World.* Baltimore, Johns Hopkins University Press, 1983.

Perry, F., and R. Hay. *Field Guide to Tropical and Subtropical Plants.* Princeton, N.J., Van Nostrand Reinhold, 1982.

Peterson, R. T. *Field Guide to the Birds,* 4th edition. Boston, Houghton Mifflin, 1980.

Stubbendieck, J., et al. *North American Range Plants: Two Hundred Descriptions as a Guide to Identification.* Lincoln, Nebraska, Natural Resources Enterprises, 1981.

*A brief survey of organisms*

The variety of organisms seems almost endless. They vary from those that carry out all of the functions of life within a single cell (unicellular) to highly specialized collections of trillions of cells (multicellular). Some make their own food from energy and materials in the environment (autotrophs). Others require ready-made food (heterotrophs). Some move about in their environment; they are said to be motile. Others are fixed to one spot; they are said to be sessile. The great variety of size, shape, color, and way of life of organisms can be seen from the examples in this survey. All living organisms can be divided into five major kingdoms: Monera, Protista, Fungi, Plantae, and Animalia. Each kingdom may be divided into smaller groups called phyla (singular phylum) or division (for plants). In turn, phyla and divisions can be divided into classes. Where possible, common names are given for the illustrated organisms as well as a size indication. However, many organisms have no specific common names; their scientific names are used. For each group, major characteristics are listed. For more complete and detailed information on a specific group of organisms, specialized reference works should be consulted.

**Kingdom Monera:** *the most numerous and among the smallest organisms on Earth; all are prokaryotic; many are unicellular; some are autotrophs, others heterotrophs; reproduction is generally asexual; about 4,000 described species and many more undescribed; 16 phyla.*

bacteria (several phyla): the smallest living cells; basically unicellular; autotrophs and heterotrophs; motile members move by means of flagella; cell walls with no cellulose; asexual and sexual reproduction.

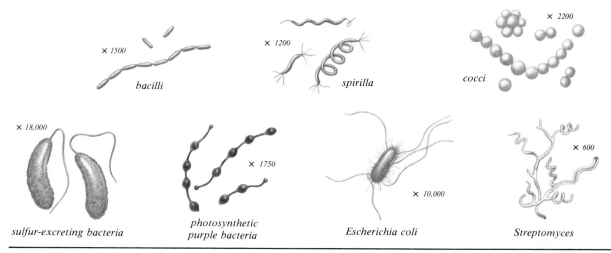

× 1500

bacilli

× 1200

spirilla

× 2200

cocci

× 18,000

sulfur-excreting bacteria

× 1750

photosynthetic purple bacteria

× 10,000

Escherichia coli

× 600

Streptomyces

blue-green algae (Phylum Cyanophyta), also classified as blue-green bacteria (Phylum Cyanobacteria): usually unicellular or in filaments; autotrophs; chlorophyll not in chloroplasts; gelatinous outer sheath; asexual and sexual reproduction.

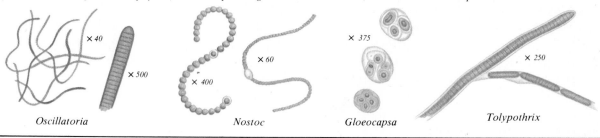

× 40

× 500

Oscillatoria

× 60

× 400

Nostoc

× 375

Gloeocapsa

× 250

Tolypothrix

**Kingdom Protista: eukaryotic; most are unicellular, but some form multicellular colonies; some are autotrophs, others heterotrophs or both; reproduction is asexual and sexual; more than 100,000 known species; 27 phyla.**

*flagellates (several phyla): motile, using flagella; unicellular or colonial; autotrophs, heterotrophs, or both in one.*

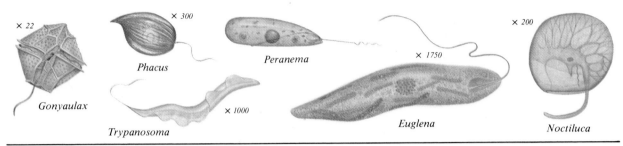

× 22

Gonyaulax

× 300

Phacus

Peranema

× 1000

Trypanosoma

× 1750

Euglena

× 200

Noctiluca

*ciliates (Phylum Ciliophora): usually motile, using cilia; generally unicellular; heterotrophs; macro- and micronuclei.*

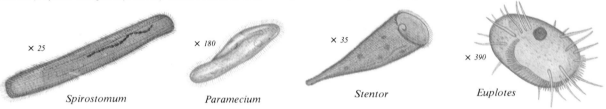

× 25

Spirostomum

× 180

Paramecium

× 35

Stentor

× 390

Euplotes

*rhizopods (several phyla): may form pseudopods; unicellular; heterotrophs; many with pore-studded shells called tests.*

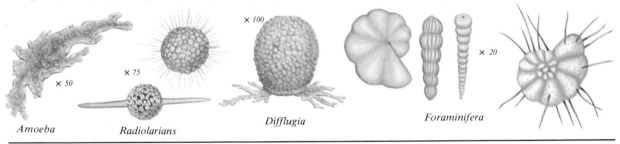

× 50

Amoeba

× 75

Radiolarians

× 100

Difflugia

× 20

Foraminifera

*sporozoans (Phylum Sporozoa): no locomotion; unicellular; heterotrophs; all parasites; complex life cycles.*

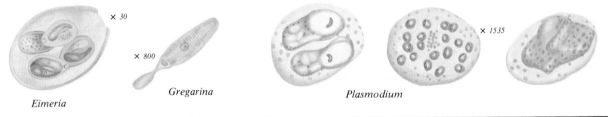

× 30

Eimeria

× 800

Gregarina

× 1535

Plasmodium

*slime molds (Phylum Myxomycota): amoebalike colonies; heterotrophs; sexual reproduction by spores formed on upright stalks.*

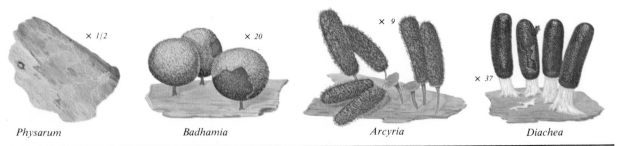

× 1/2

Physarum

× 20

Badhamia

× 9

Arcyria

× 37

Diachea

*yellow-green algae (Phylum Chrysophyta): unicellular or multicellular; autotrophs; largest group is the diatoms, with shells or tests in two parts called valves; tests contain silica.*

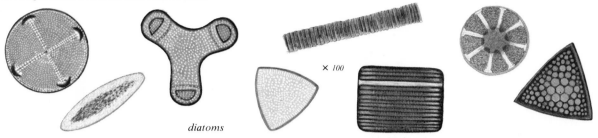

× 100

diatoms

*brown algae (Phylum Phaeophyta): multicellular; autotrophs; up to 100 meters in length; generally sexual reproduction.*

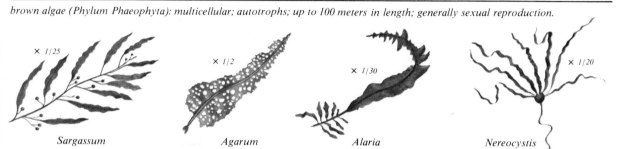

× 1/25          × 1/2          × 1/30          × 1/20

Sargassum          Agarum          Alaria          Nereocystis

*red algae (Phylum Rhodophyta): multicellular; autotrophs; source of agar; sexual reproduction.*

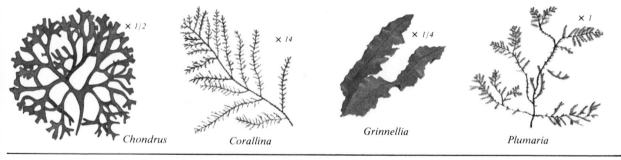

× 1/2          × 14          × 1/4          × 1

Chondrus          Corallina          Grinnellia          Plumaria

*green algae (Phylum Chlorophyta): unicellular or multicellular; autotrophs; plantlike cell walls; ancestors of plants; asexual and sexual reproduction.*

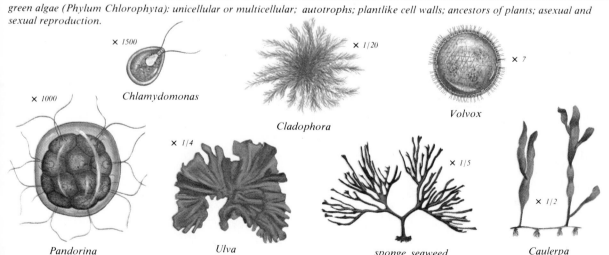

× 1500

Chlamydomonas

× 1/20

Cladophora

× 7

Volvox

× 1000

Pandorina

× 1/4

Ulva

× 1/5

sponge seaweed

× 1/2

Caulerpa

**Kingdom Fungi: eukaryotic; unicellular or multicellular; heterotrophs; reproduction is sexual by spores; more than 100,000 species; 5 phyla.**

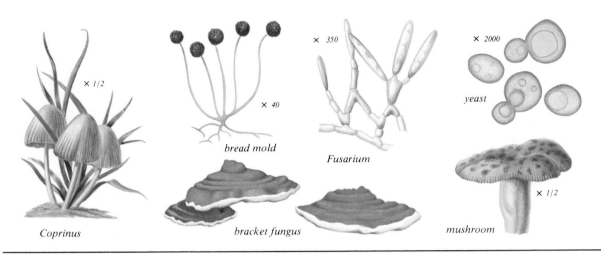

× 1/2

× 40

× 350

× 2000

yeast

bread mold

Fusarium

× 1/2

Coprinus

bracket fungus

mushroom

---

**Kingdom Plantae: eukaryotic; multicellular; autotrophs; cells contain green plastids; reproduction is usually sexual; more than 500,000 species; 9 divisions.**

mosses and liverworts (Division Bryophyta): nonvascular (no conducting tissues); small; live in moist places on land.

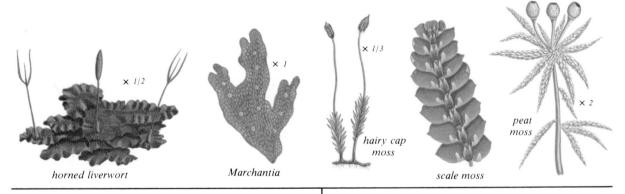

× 1/2

× 1

× 1/3

× 2

horned liverwort

Marchantia

hairy cap moss

scale moss

peat moss

---

horsetails (Division Sphenophyta): vascular; jointed stems; rough texture caused by silica in outer cells.

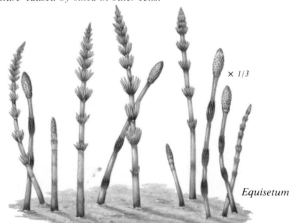

× 1/3

Equisetum

club mosses (Division Lycophyta): vascular (conducting tissue); spores borne on conelike tips (clubs).

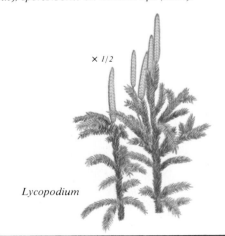

× 1/2

Lycopodium

*ferns (Division Pterophyta): vascular; leaves grow from underground stems; no seeds.*

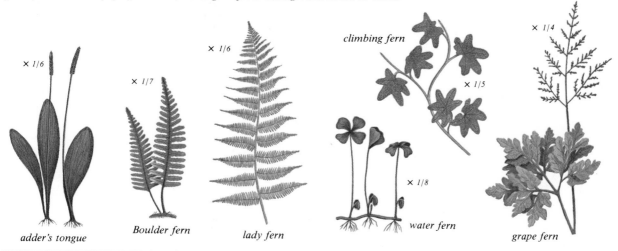

× 1/6

× 1/7

× 1/6

climbing fern

× 1/4

× 1/5

× 1/8

water fern

*adder's tongue*

*Boulder fern*

*lady fern*

*grape fern*

*cycads (Division Cycadophyta): vascular; naked seeds (not in ovaries); unbranched stems.*

× 5

× 1/80

*cycad*

*ginkgoes (Division Ginkgophyta): vascular; naked seeds; fan-shaped leaves close to branches.*

× 1/4

*Ginkgo*

*conifers (Division Coniferophyta): vascular; naked seeds borne in cones; most have needle-shaped leaves; many are evergreens.*

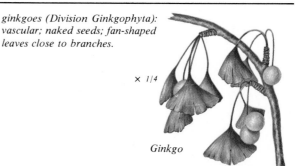

× 1/4

× 1/2

× 1/4

× 1/950

× 1/2

*juniper*

× 1/240

*bald cypress*

× 1/1080

*larch*

× 1/950

*blue spruce*

*gnetophytes (Division Gnetophyta): vascular; naked seeds borne in cones; both small- and large-leaved.*

*Welwitschia*

× 1/60

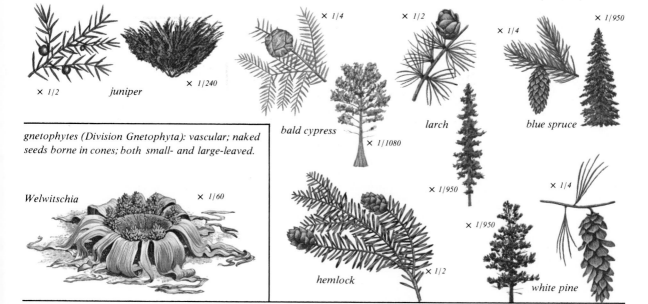

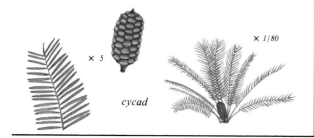

× 1/950

*hemlock*

× 1/2

*white pine*

× 1/4

*flowering plants (Division Anthophyta): vascular; enclosed seeds that develop in flowers rather than cones.*

*monocotyledons (Class Monocotyledonae): flower parts in threes or multiples of threes; leaves mostly parallel-veined; one seed leaf in the embryo within the seed.*

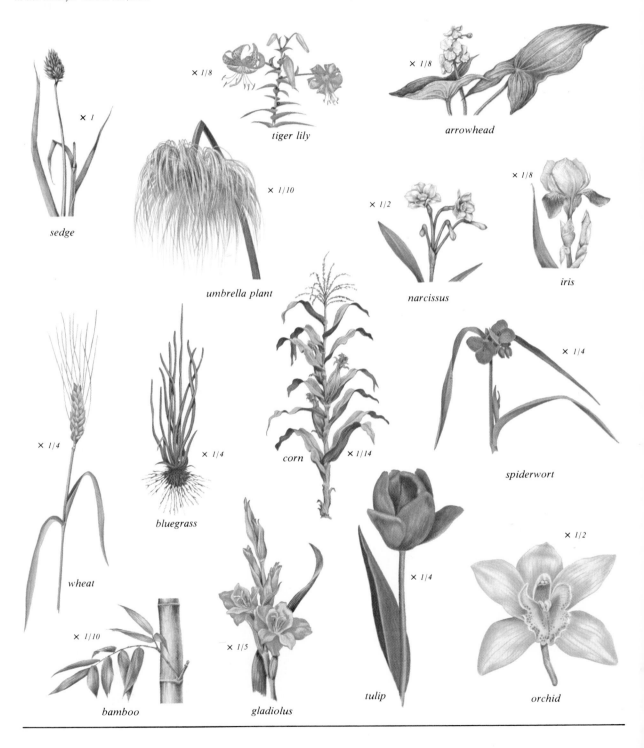

× 1/8

*tiger lily*

× 1/8

*arrowhead*

× 1

*sedge*

× 1/10

*umbrella plant*

× 1/2

*narcissus*

× 1/8

*iris*

× 1/4

*spiderwort*

× 1/4

*wheat*

× 1/4

*bluegrass*

× 1/14

*corn*

× 1/10

*bamboo*

× 1/5

*gladiolus*

× 1/4

*tulip*

× 1/2

*orchid*

*dicotyledons (Class Dicotyledonae): flower parts in fours or fives; net-veined leaves; two seed leaves in the embryo within the seed.*

butter-and-eggs

× 1/3
rose

× 1/6
larkspur

× 1/4
sunflower

× 1/2
columbine

× 1/6
field mustard

× 1/2
wild rose

mint

× 1/720
× 1/4
white oak

× 1/4
snapdragon

× 1/3
water lily

× 1
buttercup

× 1/2
sweet pea

× 1/2
cactus

× 1/2
wild carrot

**Kingdom Animalia:** *eukaryotic; multicellular; heterotrophs; reproduction is usually sexual; over 1 million species; 35 phyla.*

*sponges (Phylum Porifera): no movement (sessile); body has pores; no organs or appendages; asexual and sexual reproduction.*

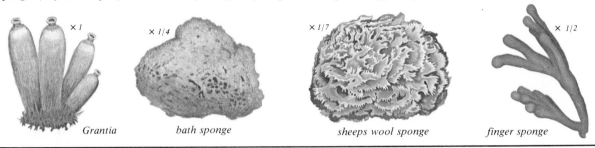

× 1          × 1/4          × 1/7          × 1/2

*Grantia*          *bath sponge*          *sheeps wool sponge*          *finger sponge*

*coelenterates (Phylum Cnidaria): mouth surrounded by tentacles; saclike digestive cavity; nerve network; no circulatory, respiratory, or excretory organs; asexual and sexual reproduction.*

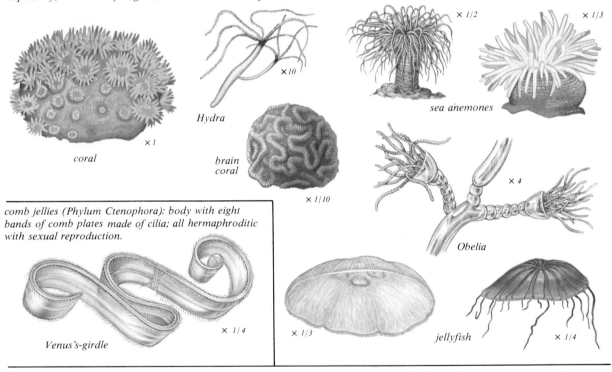

× 1/2          × 1/3

× 10

*Hydra*

*sea anemones*

*coral*          × 1

*brain coral*

× 1/10

× 4

*Obelia*

*comb jellies (Phylum Ctenophora): body with eight bands of comb plates made of cilia; all hermaphroditic with sexual reproduction.*

*Venus's-girdle*          × 1/4

× 1/3

*jellyfish*          × 1/4

*flatworms (Phylum Platyhelminthes): flat, soft body; no circulatory system; excretion by flame cells; asexual and sexual reproduction.*

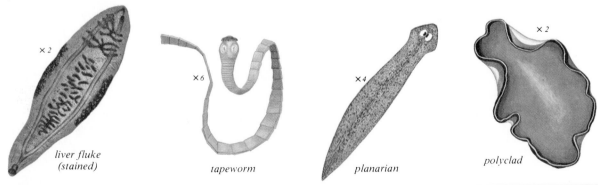

× 2

× 6

× 4

× 2

*liver fluke (stained)*          *tapeworm*          *planarian*          *polyclad roundworms (Phylum Nematoda): slender, cylindrical body; complete, straight digestive tract; longitudinal muscles only; sexual reproduction.*

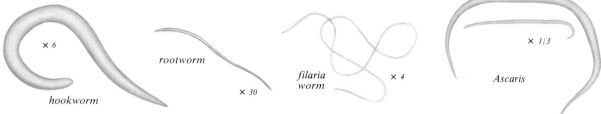

× 6

*rootworm*

× 30

*filaria worm*

× 4

× 1/3

*Ascaris*

*hookworm*

*rotifers (Phylum Rotifera): named for the wheel-like appearance of moving cilia at the "head" end; asexual and sexual reproductive stages.*

*lampshells (Phylum Brachiopoda): covered by dorsal-ventral shells; sexual reproduction.*

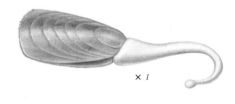

× 28

× 1

*segmented worms (Phylum Annelida): body divided into similar segments; true body cavity; asexual and sexual reproduction.*

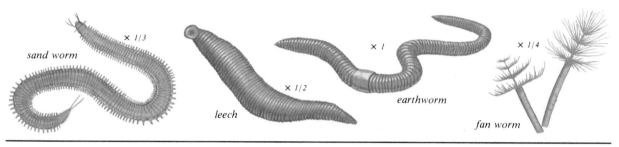

× 1/3

*sand worm*

× 1/2

*leech*

× 1

*earthworm*

× 1/4

*fan worm*

*mollusks (Phylum Mollusca): soft-bodied, usually with shell; radula to bore or scrape for food; sexual reproduction.*

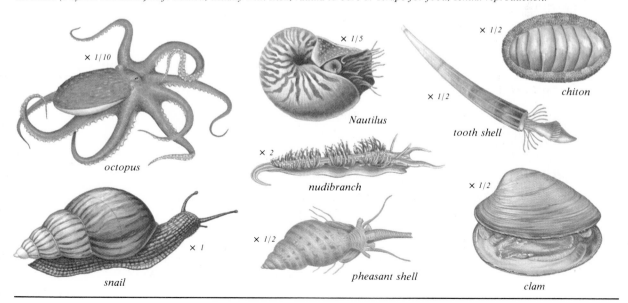

× 1/10

× 1/5

× 1/2

*Nautilus*

× 1/2

*tooth shell*

*chiton*

*octopus*

× 2

*nudibranch*

× 1/2

× 1

*snail*

× 1/2

*pheasant shell*

*clam*

**arthropods** (*Phylum Arthropoda*): segmented body; usually two or three body sections; jointed appendages; exoskeleton; usually sexual reproduction.

**crustaceans** (*Class Crustacea*): two body sections; two pairs of antennae; respiration through gills.

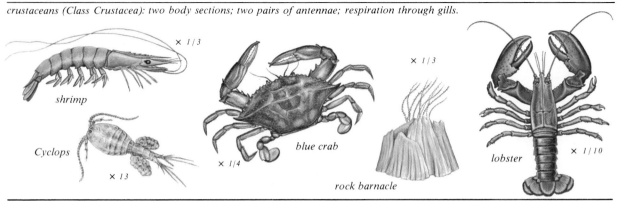

shrimp  × 1/3

Cyclops  × 13

blue crab  × 1/4

rock barnacle  × 1/3

lobster  × 1/10

**insects** (*Class Insecta*): three body sections; generally one or two pairs of wings; one pair of antennae; three pairs of legs; respiration through trachea.

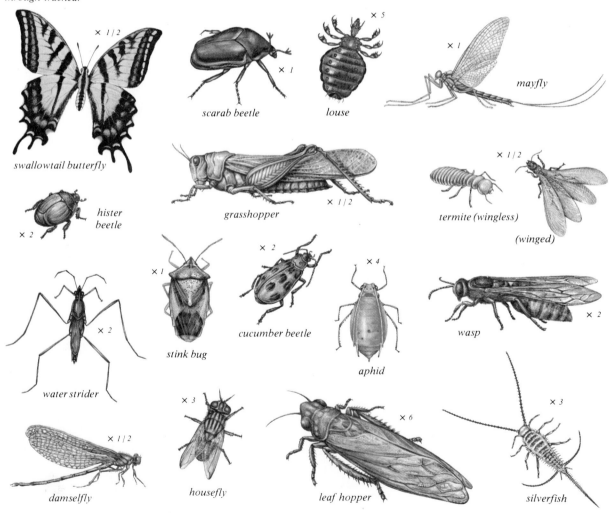

swallowtail butterfly  × 1/2

scarab beetle  × 1

louse  × 5

mayfly  × 1

hister beetle  × 2

grasshopper  × 1/2

termite (wingless)  × 1/2

(winged)

water strider  × 2

stink bug  × 1

cucumber beetle  × 2

aphid  × 4

wasp  × 2

damselfly  × 1/2

housefly  × 3

leaf hopper  × 6

silverfish  × 3

*arachnids (Class Arachnida): usually two body sections; no wings; no antennae; usually four pairs of legs; respiration through trachea, lungs, or gill books.*

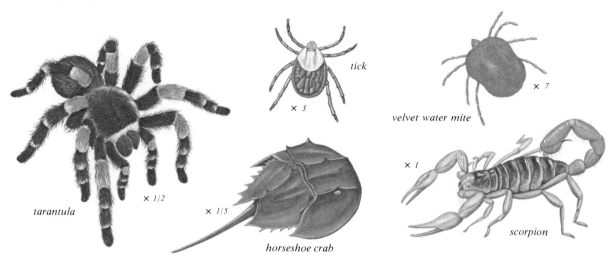

tick
× 3

× 7

velvet water mite

× 1

tarantula
× 1/2

× 1/5

horseshoe crab

scorpion

---

*centipedes (Class Chilopoda): many-segmented, flattened body; one pair of long antennae; respiration through trachea.*

*millipedes (Class Diplopoda): many-segmented, cylindrical body; one pair of short antennae; respiration through trachea.*

*peripatus (Phylum Onychophora): unsegmented; one pair of short antennae; a link between annelids and arthropods.*

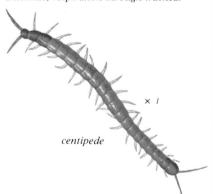

× 1

centipede

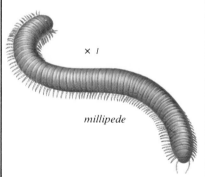

× 1

millipede

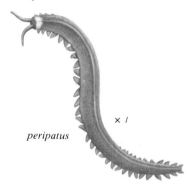

× 1

peripatus

---

*echinoderms (Phylum Echinodermata): no head; no segmentation; water-vascular system; chordatelike larvae.*

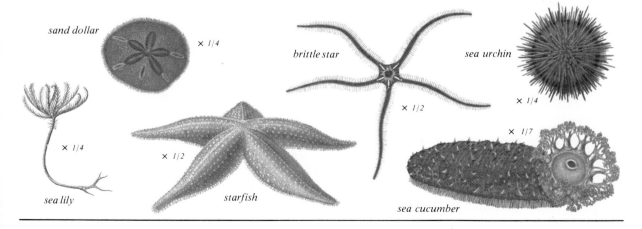

sand dollar
× 1/4

brittle star

sea urchin
× 1/4

× 1/7

× 1/4

× 1/2

× 1/2

sea lily

starfish

sea cucumber

**chordates (Phylum Chordata):** *pharyngeal breathing device; hollow dorsal nerve cord; notocord as dorsal support during part of life.*

*lower chordates (several subphyla): no vertebrae (backbone); no brain; no cranium.*

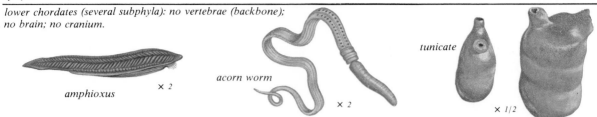

amphioxus × 2

acorn worm × 2

tunicate × 1/2

**jawless fishes (Subphylum Agnatha):** *vertebrates, with skeleton of cartilage; no true jaws or paired appendages; no scales; respiration through gills.*

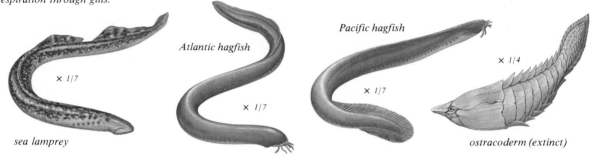

Atlantic hagfish

Pacific hagfish × 1/4

sea lamprey × 1/7

× 1/7

× 1/7

ostracoderm (extinct)

**cartilaginous fishes (Class Chondrichthyes):** *vertebrates, with skeleton of cartilage; jaws; paired fins; respiration through gills.*

× 1/40

× 1/30
shark

× 1/25

Chimaera

× 1/100

hammerhead shark

stingray

× 1/14

Dinichthys (extinct)

**bony fishes (Class Osteichthyes):** *vertebrates, with bony skeleton; jaws; most with paired fins; translucent, overlapping scales; respiration through gills.*

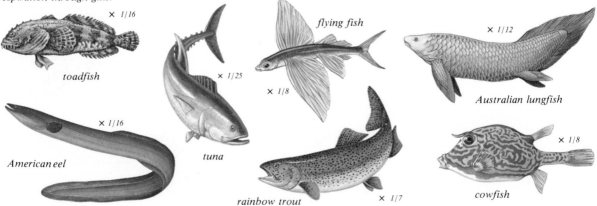

× 1/16
toadfish

flying fish

× 1/12

× 1/25
tuna

× 1/8

Australian lungfish

American eel × 1/16

rainbow trout × 1/7

cowfish × 1/8

*amphibians (Class Amphibia): vertebrates, with bony skeleton; no external scales; moist, glandular skin; most with two pairs of limbs; three-chambered heart; respiration through skin or lungs.*

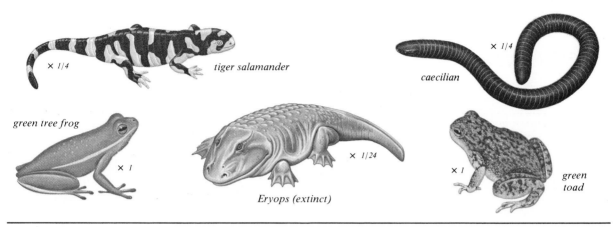

× 1/4    tiger salamander

× 1/4    caecilian

green tree frog    × 1

× 1/24    Eryops (extinct)

× 1    green toad

*reptiles (Class Reptilia): vertebrates, with bony skeleton; dry, usually scaly skin; most with two pairs of limbs; incompletely divided four-chambered heart; respiration through lungs.*

6-lined race runner    × 1/3

× 1/4    box turtle

× 1/40    alligator

× 1/10    rattlesnake

× 1/6    Gila monster

corn snake    × 1/6

× 1/120    Pteranodon (extinct)

chameleon    × 1/4

× 1/115    Triceratops (extinct)

Brontosaurus (extinct)    × 1/120

*birds (Class Aves): vertebrates, with bony skeleton; scaly skin with feathers; no teeth; forelimbs modified as wings; hard-shelled eggs; four-chambered heart; closely regulated body temperature; respiration through lungs.*

× 1/80

ostrich

× 1/8

mourning
dove

× 1/30

brown pelican

× 1/6

robin

broad-tailed
hummingbird

× 1/12

kiwi

× 1/3

× 1/4

tree sparrow

× 1/4

chaffinch

× 1/7

yellow-headed
parrot

× 1/14

turkey vulture

× 1/14

ring-necked
pheasant

× 1/14

heath hen

× 1/8

grebe

× 1/20

albatross

× 1/16

red jungle fowl

× 1/10

barred owl

× 1/9

quetzal

× 1/20

flamingo

× 1/20

Hesperornis
(extinct)

× 1/30

king
penguin

mammals (Class Mammalia): *vertebrates, with bony skeleton; body usually covered with hair; nourish young with milk from mammary glands; four-chambered heart; closely regulated body temperature; respiration through lungs.*

× 1/40
rhinoceros

× 1/30
aardvark

× 1/20
armadillo

× 1/16
horse

× 1/20
koala

× 1/10
duck-billed platypus

× 1/14
cottontail rabbit

× 1/55
great red kangaroo

× 1/120
elephant

× 1/8
long-eared bat

× 1/80
manatee

× 1/30
porcupine

× 1/15
baboon

× 1/36
human

× 1/10
pika

× 1/40
cougar

× 1/30
gorilla

× 1/430
blue whale

× 1/24
seal

# Evolution

## 4

The variety of organisms the world over has raised basic questions. Many kinds of living things appear clearly related to each other. Relationships today suggest common ancestors in the past, when species different from those of today inhabited Earth.

How and why have former species given way to new ones? Some hypotheses about changing forms of life, or **evolution,** will be investigated in this chapter. The first hypothesis was proposed by a biologist named Jean Baptiste Lamarck. A second was proposed by several biologists independently of one another, among them Charles Darwin. Other hypotheses related to Darwin's are still being proposed today, showing the continuing role of inquiry in biology.

# Meaning and Evidence of Evolution

## 4–1

## Evolution Helps to Explain the Variety of Life

When biologists say that living things have *evolved,* they mean that former species have given rise to those of today. The old species may have died off—become extinct—or some of them may have continued to the present day. Buried remains or traces of life forms are major clues that there once were organisms on Earth that no longer exist. These remains or traces of former life are called **fossils** (FOS-uls). The existence and nature of fossils have been recognized by scholars throughout recorded history.

How did so many different kinds of living species come about? A theory of evolution must offer an explanation—and evidence—to answer such a question.

←Fossil bones are uncovered and cleaned at Dinosaur National Monument in Colorado.

A scientific theory is always open to question and testing. It is subject to change if new facts call for a change. People often have different views of how the variety of life came about. Biologists share the view that evolution has taken place but continue to investigate questions of *how* it has done so. The unresolved questions point to a need for more evidence about particular events of the past, and about hereditary change. Yet a great deal of evidence has already thrown light on the history of many species of living things.

Having a theory of evolution gives biologists a more logical way to classify organisms. A new grouping of the yucca plant and the Joshua tree illustrates a change in classification that came from using evidence of evolution. An earlier classification placed the plants in widely different categories because they appeared to be different in structure. The study of their flowers, however, has convinced botanists that the two plants have similar ancestors. Therefore, based on their ancestral re-

**Figure 4–1** A study of their flowers has convinced biologists that the Joshua tree (left) should be classified with the yucca plant (right).

lationships, the modern system places them in the same genus, *Yucca* (YUK-uh). These plants are shown in Figure 4–1.

A second example of change in classification involves the horseshoe crab, *Limulus* (LIM-yoo-lus). (See Figure 4–2.) It was formerly grouped with other crabs in the class *Crustacea* (krus-TAY-shuh), because it looked somewhat like other crabs. Studies of its blood chemistry, however, have shown that the horseshoe crab is unlike other crabs. A review of all the evidence indicates that the horseshoe crab is more closely related to spiders. It is now grouped with spiders in the class *Arachnida* (uh-RAK-nih-duh).

Linnaeus' system of classification, based on structure, is still usable even in the light of modern evolutionary thought. One reason is that evolution usually implies that organisms of similar structure

have similar ancestry and are closely related. Yet exceptions may occur, as between crabs and the horseshoe crab. Evolution also usually implies that organisms which appear different in structure have different immediate ancestors and are not closely related. Again, exceptions may occur, as between the Joshua tree and the yucca plant.

## 4–2
## Fossils Give Evidence of Former Species

Fossils are remains or traces of life that have withstood the passage of time. Fossils can be bones or teeth or even plant or animal imprints preserved in rock since prehistoric time. The appearance of

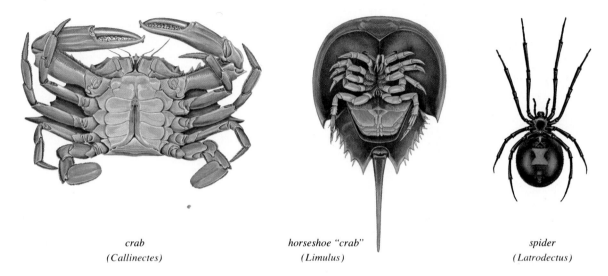

crab
(*Callinectes*)

horseshoe "crab"
(*Limulus*)

spider
(*Latrodectus*)

**Figure 4–2** Although *Limulus,* the horseshoe crab, looks like a crab, its blood is more like the blood of spiders than crabs. Therefore, *Limulus* is now classified with spiders.

fossils in rock has been a source of wonder and fascination to people for centuries. The fossil of an ancient sea animal was even found among the possessions of a prehistoric human being. Many people have tried to explain fossils. Aristotle believed they were the remains of living creatures, but thought the creaures grew in the rocks. Some people believed that fossils were placed in rocks by evil spirits. Other explanations were remarkably modern. For example, Herodotus (hih-ROD-ah-tus), a famous Greek historian, observed fossil seashells in the Libyan desert in 450 B.C. and guessed that the Mediterranean Sea had once spread much farther to the south than it does today.

Fossils were preserved in rocks by a series of lucky accidents. Unless special conditions exist, dead organisms will quickly disappear. A dead plant or animal usually begins to decay immediately. Fortunately, the minerals in organisms are recycled very quickly. Nature in the form of bacteria and other organisms returns the chemical materials of dead organisms back to the land, water, and air. Even bones decay unless they are somehow preserved. In rare cases and places, organisms can be preserved as fossils. In polar regions and high mountain tops, few scavenging or predatory organisms are around to consume the dead tissues. The low temperatures also retard decay. Water burial can lead to the preservation of a dead organism also. (See Figure 4–3.) If an animal or plant dies near a stream, ocean, or sea, it may be quickly buried by sediment and sand that settle out of the water. The water helps prevent predation and decay. Eventually minerals in the water seep into the bones of the animal and preserve them. The floors of oceans and shallow seas have frequently proved to be our richest source of fossils.

**Figure 4-3** Fossil formation. Underwater sediments are oxygen-poor, discouraging the presence of oxygen-requiring microorganisms that consume (decay) plant and animal remains. Dead fish, or their skeletons, may remain intact in these sediments over long periods of time. Eventually minerals circulating in underground water replace the bone substance of the fish's skeletons. The mineralized skeletal replacements are fossils.

**Figure 4-4** Buried fossils may be exposed by any of the forces that uplift segments of Earth's crust and expose these segments to erosion.

The eruption of a volcano can produce fossils by burying all the nearby animals and plants in several feet of ash and cinders. Protected from the air and other animals, these organisms may be preserved as fossils. Still other fossils, such as those dug up at Rancho La Brea in the city of Los Angeles, are the remains of organisms trapped and preserved in tar pits.

Time passes and the layers of mud, sand, ashes, and other sediment containing the fossils become covered by more deposits. The weight of new sediment presses down on the sediments holding the fossils and hardens these layers into rock. The rock layers accumulate and the fossils become buried deep in Earth. Much later they may be exposed again by changes in Earth's surface. Mountain-building movements may cause Earth's crust to rise. Or whole continents may drift, and giant plates in the earth's crust grind together burying surface land here and raising buried rock there. Streams then cut gorges or canyons through the raised rock layers containing fossils. Or wind and rain wear away the surface and expose the fossils, as shown in Figure 4-4.

Scientists can tell approximately how old fossils are by the rock layers in which they are found. The lowest layers of rock are the oldest unless the layers have been disturbed by geologic movements. A variety of laboratory dating methods independently dates samples from the rock layers, based on changes in the materials within them.

# 4-3

## The Fossil Record and the History of Life

The fossils preserved in successive vertical layers indicate the sequence in which animals and plants evolved. The oldest rocks contain fossils of simple forms of life. Most of these forms are now extinct. The rocks of later ages have fossils of more complex kinds of organisms. Fossils form a record in the rocks that supports the idea that life has evolved over very long periods of time from simple to more complex varieties. Some varieties of life may continue to exist, some may become extinct, and some may give rise to still other forms of life. The variety of life, once thought to be fixed and unchanging, turns out to be dynamic, always changing.

The fossil of a small four-toed animal about the size of a fox terrier was found preserved in layers of rock. Modern techniques of dating found that the rock and fossil were about 60 million years old. The discovery and dating of other fossils have enabled scientists to trace a branching line of descent showing gradual changes from the dog-sized animal to the modern horse. Stages in this evolution are shown in Figure 4-5. A painting of this ancient "horse" is shown in Figure 4-6. Modern horses were not the only descendants of the dog-sized ancestor. Other branches of descent produced related animals that persisted for long periods of time, then became extinct. Lines of descent are typically much-branched.

Similar lines of descent have been traced for elephants, giraffes, camels, and certain other animals. The fossil evidence suggests that life has been changing slowly from one form to another over all the time the fossils represent.

---

**CAPSULE SUMMARY**

The fossil record introduced the idea that new species arise from old ones by a process of evolution. Awareness that evolution has occurred added a new perspective to the classification of organisms. Today biologists interpret similarities of structure among organisms as evidence of common ancestry. Exceptions are detected by comparisons of the organisms' chemical makeups.

**SELF CHECK**

1. Why do biologists agree that evolution has occurred if they do not agree on *how* it has occurred?
2. How has the awareness of evolution affected biological classification?
3. Are fossils numerous or scarce? Explain.
4. How are fossils formed? How are they exposed?

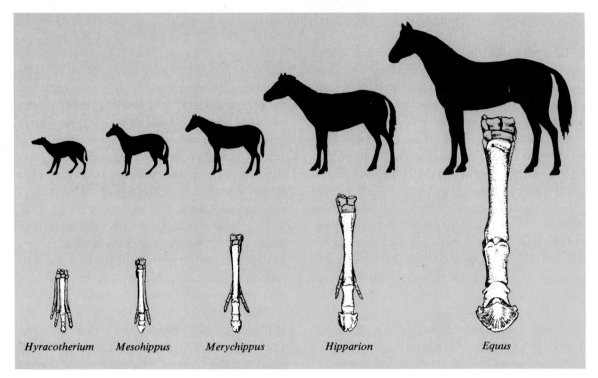

Hyracotherium   Mesohippus   Merychippus   Hipparion   Equus

**Figure 4–5** Stages in the evolution of the horse. Of the four toes found on *Hyracotherium,* only one evolved as the hoof on *Equus*.

**Figure 4–6** A reconstruction of the probable appearance of *Hyracotherium,* no bigger than a dog. It is the earliest known ancestor of the horse.

# The Means of Evolution: Two Views

## 4-4

### Lamarck Explains Evolution

The idea of evolution is very old. It dates at least to the Greek philosopher Empedocles, who lived 25 centuries ago. Empedocles proposed that the development of life on Earth was a gradual process. However, the term *evolution* was not coined until the 19th century.

In the 18th century many biologists had become interested in the idea of evolution. In 1794 Charles Darwin's grandfather, Erasmus Darwin, published a long poem entitled "Zoonomia," containing the belief that evolution probably occurred in plants and animals. The elder Darwin accepted the idea of evolution but did not propose any hypothesis to explain how it happens. One important question therefore remained unanswered: How does evolution occur? This question later concerned both Jean Lamarck and Charles Darwin.

In 1809, the very year Charles Darwin was born, Jean Baptiste Lamarck published a book called *Zoological Philosophy*. This book presented Lamarck's ideas on evolution. Lamarck, a French biologist, was the first biologist to offer a well-developed hypothesis to explain how plants and animals might evolve.

Lamarck reasoned that a great change in the environment of an animal species would result in the need for a corresponding change in that species itself. This need for change, brought on by the animal's inner feelings, would cause the animal to form new habits to adjust to its new environment.

Lamarck made two major assumptions based on a study of nature and on the idea of the need of an organism for change. The first assumption is known as the principle of use and disuse. Lamarck assumed that as any part of the body is used more and more, it develops and enlarges. The parts that are not used weaken slowly, become

**Figure 4-7** Lamarck's theory stated that the giraffe developed its long neck, and made its front legs longer than its hind ones, by stretching for leaves over countless generations. What makes this theory unacceptable?

smaller, or even disappear. Lamarck's second assumption is called the inheritance of acquired characteristics. It stated that an animal could pass on to its offspring the characteristics it had gained, or acquired, during its lifetime. Thus the offspring

# Biology Brief

*The earth then . . .*

*and now*

PANGAEA

—*India*

*Antarctica*— —*Australia*

## Continents Adrift

Like to start a trip around the world? Then just stay where you are—the continent you are on is adrift! Its speed is only a few centimeters a year, but in your lifetime, you may be more than two meters along in the journey. Exciting?

The supercontinent *Pangaea* was once joined together at the continental shelves. Look where India was. When India eventually drifted up and smashed into southern Asia, it pushed up the world's highest mountain chain. Mt. Everest, the highest mountain in the world, was built in this collision between Asia and India.

Actually the continents themselves do not correspond to the movable plates in Earth's crust; they ride along inside of larger plates, which include both continents and oceans. Each plate moves somewhat differently, causing changes in the shapes of the continents and the oceans over many millions of years. The

would inherit those characteristics that had become enlarged from use, or that had grown smaller from disuse. Lamarck based the hypothesis of the process of evolution on these two assumptions. They suggested that new species evolve after many generations from acquiring new traits or losing old traits.

Lamarck thought that birds, like the heron, developed long legs by stretching them to keep their bodies out of the water. Similarly, Lamarck reasoned that the webbed feet of ducks and geese were the result of their use in swimming.

An often-quoted example of Lamarck's reasoning is an explanation of how the giraffe's neck grew so long. (See Figure 4–7.)

The giraffe lives in places where the ground is almost invariably parched and without grass. Obliged to browse upon trees it is continually forced to stretch upwards. This habit maintained over long periods of time by every individual of the race has resulted in the forelimbs becoming longer than the hind ones, and the neck so elongated that a giraffe

study of these surface plates and their movement is called *plate tectonics*. You may have heard about two of the plates that are slipping past one another in California. Earthquakes occur up and down the coast where these plates rub and grind in passing. One plate is mostly under the Pacific Ocean. The other includes most of North America.

Long ago, living things could move more freely between continents. Even today, the ongoing drift and plate movement continue to affect life. Scientists like Dr. Tanya Atwater (above) have studied the plate movements in California and elsewhere, and are even taking underwater expeditions to study the ocean-floor spreading where Earth's surface plates are coming apart.

can raise its head to a height of almost six meters without taking its forelimbs off the ground.[1]

This line of reasoning seems especially convincing because Lamarck's first major assumption is correct: parts of animals do change as a result of use or disuse. You have probably seen many examples. Athletes, for example, develop larger, stronger muscles with use.

Lamarck's second hypothesis proved false. Numerous observations and experiments have failed to show that acquired traits can be inherited by offspring.

Though Lamarck's hypothesis about the means of evolution may have been wrong, its importance as a reasoned approach is not forgotten. Lamarck recorded many careful observations of nature in a series of interesting books. The ideas on evolution failed to stir the imagination of the people of that time. Yet, just fifty years later, Charles Darwin fired the interest of the western world with new evidence for evolution and another explanation of the way it may occur.

**Figure 4–8** The extinct glyptodon was many times larger than the present-day armadillo (shown to scale in the smaller drawing), yet they are similar in many ways.

## 4–5

## Darwin's Voyage on the H.M.S. *Beagle*

In 1831, Darwin sailed from England at 22 years of age as ship's naturalist on the H.M.S. *Beagle*. The crew of the *Beagle* was to chart the distant coasts of South America and the islands of the Pacific for Great Britain. As ship's naturalist Darwin collected animal and plant specimens and kept a record of biological and geographical observations.

Darwin also dug up fossil remains of large mammals, unlike any animals living today. In Argentina Darwin found a giant extinct mammal that resembled a living armadillo. Yet these monsters, four meters long, could hardly be of the same species as present-day armadillos. Figure 4–8 shows some of the differences between the two.

Some 950 kilometers off the west coast of South America the H.M.S. *Beagle* came upon the Galápagos (guh-LAH-puh-guhs) Islands, shown on the map in Figure 4–9. Darwin found different finches and tortoises on each of the islands visited. Darwin wrote:

During the voyage of the *Beagle,* I had been deeply impressed by discovering in the Pampean formation [the plains] great fossil animals covered with armor like that on the existing armadillos; secondly by the manner in which closely allied animals replace one another, in proceeding southwards over the continent; and thirdly, by the South American character of most of the productions of the Galápagos . . . and more especially by the manner in which they differ slightly on each island of the group; none of the islands appearing to be very ancient in the geological sense.

It was evident that such facts as these, as well as many others, could only be explained on the supposition that species gradually become modified; and the subject haunted me. [2]

The variation within species that Darwin observed seemed to demand an explanation. Why shouldn't members of a species be alike, no matter where they are found? During the voyage, Darwin read *The Principles of Geology,* a book written by a close friend, Charles Lyell. One of Darwin's teachers had advised reading the book but "on no account to accept the view advocated therein." Lyell's book set forth the hypothesis that the forces of nature today were also those of the past, acting in the same ways. These forces could account for changes in the landscape of Earth throughout the ages. Darwin began to think about all the different life forms in view of Lyell's ideas.

**Try Investigation 4 – A,** Variation Within a Species, page 586.

## 4–6

## Malthus Gives Darwin Another Clue

Darwin returned to England after five years away on the *Beagle*. The following years provided time to study and think about the variation within spe-

cies. At one point, Darwin read an essay by Thomas Malthus, an English minister writing about the struggle for survival among people. In Darwin's words,

In October, 1838, that is, fifteen months after I had begun my systematic enquiry, I happened to read for amusement Malthus on Population, and being well prepared to appreciate the struggle for existence which everywhere goes on . . . , it at once struck me that under these circumstances favourable variations [in a species] would tend to be preserved, and unfavourable ones to be destroyed. The result of this would be the formation of a new species. Here, then, I had at last got a theory by which to work; but I was so anxious to avoid prejudice, that I determined not for some time to write even the briefest sketch of it. [3]

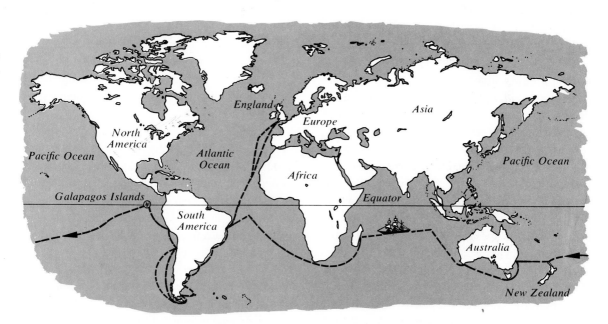

**Figure 4–9** The route of the *Beagle.* Darwin found some of the most important evidence for the theory of natural selection in South America and on the Galápagos Islands.

*pouter*

*jacobin*

*fantail*

*rock pigeon*

**Figure 4–10** If the enormous differences in these domestic pigeons that people have bred from the wild rock pigeon were found in a group of wild animals, a naturalist would place them in different species.

## 4–7

## Darwin Finds Clues from Observation and Experience

Darwin's observations of nature along with the research of other scientists all pointed to one thing—that species do change. Darwin accepted the following as a scientific hypothesis: Species, contrary to almost universal belief, are not fixed and unchanging but actually do change over long periods of time.

Added groundwork for the hypothesis came from a study of variation among organisms of domestic (tame) species. Back in England, Darwin noted the work of animal and plant breeders. Much more variation had been produced in species of domesticated animals and plants than Darwin had observed in species of wild animals and plants. Darwin experimented in raising and breeding domestic varieties of pigeons. Planned matings of pigeons with different traits led after

some generations to completely new varieties of pigeons. These new varieties resembled the wild pigeon, yet differed in many ways. Figure 4–10 shows the wild pigeon and unusual varieties produced from it.

Darwin discovered that breeders were able to bring about such unusual variation of animals and plants by *selection*. They deliberately selected those animals or plants for mating that had the particular traits they wanted.

The question for Darwin became: If people *select* to produce new domestic types of plants and animals, what produces new types in nature? If Galápagos residents were brought a Galápagos tortoise, they could tell which island it came from by slight but clear differences in its shell. Is this variation among island tortoises evidence of a process of change to new types? If so, Darwin thought, it is not selection directed by people, but selection by nature itself. Darwin realized that deliberate selection by people can lead to new types in a fairly short time, but that selection by nature probably proceeds more slowly.

## 4–8
## Darwin Proposes a Hypothesis of Natural Selection

Darwin's observations and experience, Charles Lyell's book, and the population essay of Malthus helped Darwin shape a hypothesis of evolution. Darwin hypothesized that new species came about by a process of **natural selection.** Darwin's first assumption was that all species tend to reproduce in geometric ratio from generation to generation. This is different from an arithmetic ratio of 1, 2, 3, 4 or 1, 3, 5, 7, and so on. When something increases by steps in a geometric ratio it is multiplied in each step by the same number. For example, if 1 amoeba divides to form 2 amoebas, then those 2 will divide to form 4. Following generations will produce 8, 16, 32, 64, 128, and on and on.

In all of Darwin's studies of animal and plant populations such gigantic increases in numbers were not the rule. Many offspring die or are killed and eaten. Darwin's second assumption, therefore, was that although organisms tend to reproduce in greater numbers, the total number in any species usually remains about the same.

Darwin's third assumption was that variation occurs in every species. Certain variations would help members of a species survive in a certain type of environment, while other variations would not.

Darwin reasoned that, as a rule, those organisms with favorable variations would be most likely to survive and reproduce. Many of the organisms with unfavorable variations would die out. The survivors would pass their variations on to their offspring. The favorable variations would accumulate over a period of time. As these favorable variations accumulate, organisms would be-

come so different from members of the original species that a new species would finally evolve.

Darwin's own words show the reasoning behind the concept of natural selection:

> If under changing conditions of life organic beings represent individual differences in almost every part of their structure, and this cannot be disputed; if there be, owing to geometrical rate of increase, a severe struggle for life at some age, season, or year, and this cannot be disputed; . . . But if variations useful to any organic being ever do occur, assuredly individuals thus characterized will have the best chance of being preserved in the struggle for life; and from the strong principle of inheritance, those will tend to produce offspring similarly characterized. This principle of preservation or survival of the fittest, I have called Natural Selection.[4]

Darwin's hypothesis of natural selection attempted to explain how a new species could develop from an old species and how the great variety of life on Earth has come about. A summary of the ideas follows in list form:

1. All organisms tend to increase in number at a geometric rate.
2. Over many generations, however, the number of individuals in a species remains nearly constant.
3. So there must be a struggle to survive.
4. Variations (which may be inherited) are found among individuals in each species.
5. Some variations are favorable to an organism in a particular environment and help it to survive and reproduce abundantly. Surviving organisms pass on their hereditary variations to their offspring.
6. In time great differences arise, until a new species evolves from an old species.

## 4-9

## Darwin Announces the New Hypothesis

Darwin hesitated to publish the new hypothesis until a large body of evidence could be gathered to support it. For more than 20 years Darwin continued to collect facts to help produce a completely convincing work.

In 1858 Darwin received a letter from Alfred Russel Wallace, a fellow naturalist writing from Malaya. Enclosed with the letter was an essay Wallace had written; Wallace asked Darwin to read it and pass it on to Charles Lyell. In this essay Darwin found the hypothesis of natural selection, as independently discovered by Wallace. Darwin was willing to give Wallace the honor of being the first person to announce the hypothesis. However, a friend of Darwin's arranged to present short articles by both scientists simultaneously. Strangely enough, the articles were received without much excitement. And no one was aware that a hypothesis of natural selection had been published earlier in the century, in a book primarily on another subject. (Its author was named Patrick Matthew.)

Darwin went on to complete a book that succeeded in gaining the wide attention the articles had not aroused. The book was entitled *On the Origin of Species by Means of Natural Selection.* It has since become famous, as the hypothesis advanced by Darwin, Wallace, and Matthew was accepted as a theory.

The development of a theory of evolution by means of natural selection was a remarkable achievement in the 19th century. Much knowledge that would have aided its discoverers was not yet known. They were familiar with plant and animal breeding. However, the work of Gregor Mendel in establishing the study of inheritance, now called **genetics** (juh-NET-iks), was unknown to them. The study of cells, **cytology** (sy-TOL-uh-jee), was still in its infancy. Only the

study of fossils, **paleontology** (pay-li-un-TOL-uh-jee), was well under way. However, even it provided very few fossils compared to the number now available.

At the end of *On the Origin of Species by Means of Natural Selection,* Darwin states:

> There is a grandeur in this view of life, with its several powers, having been originally breathed into a few forms or into one; and that, whilst this planet has gone cycling on according to the fixed law of gravity, from so simple a beginning endless forms most beautiful and most wonderful have been, and are being evolved. [5]

---

**CAPSULE SUMMARY**

Lamarck's ideas and Darwin's are related but different. Both acknowledged evolution. Both wondered how it occurred. Lamarck noted that organisms acquired greater development of body parts with constant use. Could this development be inherited, leading to evolution? Lamarck thought that this was how evolution came about.

Unlike Lamarck, Darwin did not speculate about how inheritance occurs in organisms. He observed that an abundance of hereditary characteristics existed in each species studied. Breeders could "evolve" new types of organisms merely by selecting for the traits wanted. In nature, *natural selection* could favor organisms with useful traits.

**SELF CHECK**

1. What were Lamarck's two assumptions?
2. What was Lyell's hypothesis? How did it remove some of the mystery associated with past ages?
3. How did Darwin and Lamarck differ in their assumptions about how evolution occurs?
4. State the basic assumptions in the theory of natural selection.

**Figure 4–11** The Galápagos finches were able to adapt to many different food sources, because few species competed with them. Note the variations in the sizes and shapes of the beaks.

# Adaptation and Natural Selection

## 4–10

## Darwin's Finches

The Galápagos are volcanic islands that erupted out of the ocean about a million years ago. The islands were never connected to the South American mainland. Therefore, only those animals which reached the islands by chance could populate them. Very few land species live there, only two kinds of mammals, five kinds of reptiles, and about a dozen kinds of land birds.

During the *Beagle's* visit to the Galápagos Islands, Darwin collected many specimens of a rather drab, dull-colored bird, the finch. There were 13 different species of finches: six of ground finches, six of tree finches, and one species, the warbler finch, which feeds in bushes. If you look at the drawings (Figure 4–11) of these finches, you can see what Darwin observed. Although the finch bodies are very much alike, the beaks are different in size and shape. Darwin observed dietary differences among the different finches. Darwin believed that these finches, with their different beaks and different diets, all had a common ancestor. The ancestral species may have lived on the South American mainland. Some ancestral finches reached the islands and, with time and evolution, gave rise to the various finch species of the islands.

The mainland finches do not show this variety. It seems that the Galápagos finches, being isolated from the mainland, had to compete for food only among themselves and with a few other birds. Thus the island finches were able to invade different environmental **niches** (NIH-chez). A niche is a way of life in an environment. The finches adapted to different diets through natural selection. Meanwhile the mainland finches remained in competition with other mainland birds.

The different beaks of the island finches are **adaptations.** An adaptation of this kind is an inherited variation in an organism that improves its chance to survive and reproduce in its particular environment. The variation may be in one inherited characteristic or a combination of several.

## 4–11

## Laboratory Experiments on Natural Selection

The biologist who investigates selection in the laboratory must try to reproduce the conditions of nature in order to observe natural selection at work. One example of such an experiment used deer mice. There are two color variations in this species—buff and gray, as shown in Figure 4–12. Under carefully controlled conditions in a University of Michigan laboratory, both varieties of mice were placed in a room with a barn owl. A "jungle" of interlacing sticks gave the mice some place to hide. The room was kept almost dark so that the owl saw its prey "by night." One day the floor would be covered with pale-colored soil that matched the buff-colored mice, and the next day with darker soil matching the gray mice.

Four mice of each color were released each day and exposed to the owl for 15 minutes. According to the color of soil used, one set of mice was more easily seen against its background, and one set was less easily seen. In 44 trials on each soil type, almost twice as many more easily seen than less easily seen mice (107 to 65) were taken by the owl. Other experiments like this one have shown the way variations in a species can be an advantage or a disadvantage.

You have probably heard that certain bacteria have "developed a resistance" to penicillin. This wording sounds as though the bacteria responded according to Lamarck's ideas (Section 4–4). The following discussion of experiments using the bacterium *Staphylococcus aureus* (staf-ih-loh-ĸoĸ-us aw-rih-us) may help you to decide whether or not the process really is Lamarckian.

When about 100 million bacterial cells in a dish were exposed to a weak dose of penicillin, fewer than 10 cells survived. These few cells were able to multiply in the presence of the penicillin. However, nearly all their descendants were killed when the dose of penicillin was doubled. Again, survivors were allowed to multiply. Then again, the penicillin dose was increased. Eventually, a strain of bacteria was obtained that could withstand a dose of penicillin 2500 times stronger than the weak dose first used.

Was the process Lamarckian? In another experiment, cells that had not been exposed to penicillin were isolated from one another. Each isolated cell was allowed to reproduce. Then the first dose of penicillin was applied to each group of off-spring. The drug wiped out group after group. Then a group was observed that appeared to be unaffected, and another group that was little affected. Each of these groups had descended from an individual resistant to a drug it had not encountered. Need had not led to resistance. The hereditary variations for the "resistance" pre-existed.

## 4–12
## Questions Today About Natural Selection

Massive outdoor sprayings of the insecticide DDT once killed off large numbers of mosquitoes. Soon the disease malaria, which is transmitted by mosquitoes, was brought under control. But the effect was temporary. As the few DDT-resistant mosquitoes multiplied, new cases of malaria also multiplied. Today the disease is again uncontrolled in some parts of the world, and DDT is no longer effective.

**Figure 4–12** The coat color of mice must blend with the background if the mice are to have their best chance for survival.

The resistance of bacteria to penicillin and the resistance of mosquitoes to DDT are only two of many known examples of natural selection. They support Darwin's observation that hereditary variations exist among species. They also support Darwin's theory that natural selection acts on organisms with these variations. In the cases of the bacteria and the mosquitoes, humans changed the environment by introducing penicillin and DDT. Natural selection did the rest.

Today the theory of natural selection is widely accepted in explaining adaptation. However, the role of natural selection in the evolution of new species is not as clear. Darwin's view was that as adaptations of different kinds accumulated, descendants would slowly become different from their ancestors. Eventually they would constitute a new species. Most biologists support this view. It is important to note that natural selection as the cause of evolution has been neither proved nor disproved.

Some biologists question whether evolution can be explained as Darwin proposed. They suggest that greater, more sudden changes could occur that would give rise to a new species. Natural selection would have nothing to do with causing such changes. Instead, some event would result in large-scale changes in the material that controls heredity. These changes would cause the appearance of organisms very different from their original species. Natural selection would then act on the changed organisms. One hypothesis about such large-scale changes is called **punctuated equilibrium;** it will be discussed in Chapter 15.

What Darwin viewed as gradual, some biologists view as a leap or jump. The important point to note is that natural selection has its role in adaptation in both views of evolution. In Darwin's view, natural selection *causes* evolution. In the other view, natural selection shapes the results. Thus, in both views, natural selection influences the directions in which evolution is successful.

**Try Investigation 4–B** Natural Selection, page 588.

---

**CAPSULE SUMMARY**

Much evidence supports adaptation by natural selection. This adaptation is the survival and reproduction of individuals that have existing, favorable hereditary characteristics. It is not the adjustment of an individual to its surroundings.

Darwin and Wallace proposed that natural selection gradually leads to changed, then new, species. Some biologists today propose that evolution is more sudden. In their view greater hereditary variations could occur than are usually seen in species. Natural selection would act on the result.

**SELF CHECK**

1. Give an example of a hereditary adaptation.
2. Why do biologists explain adaptation in terms of Darwin's theory rather than Lamarck's ideas?
3. Describe two views held today about hereditary variation and the evolution of species.

---

# CHAPTER SUMMARY

### HIGHLIGHTS

Fossils have long intrigued people. The idea that living things have evolved preceded attempts to discover how the evolution occurred. In the 19th century Lamarck proposed a hypothesis based on use or disuse. Lamarck reasoned that organisms with perceived needs developed their bodies or functions in response to those needs. Characteristics acquired in this way were inherited by the offspring of the organisms. Similarly, disused features eventually were no longer inherited.

The work of Darwin and others on a theory of evolution by natural selection eclipsed consideration of Lamarck's proposal and won scientific support. Darwin argued that natural selection acted on hereditary variations. The immediate result would be adaptations. A long-term, eventual result would be evolution of new species.

Evidence for natural selection in adaptations of organisms has become unquestioned. However, questions are asked about whether such adaptations lead to new species. Some biologists propose that new species arise more suddenly than by the gradual accumulation of adaptations. Both views are being investigated today.

## REVIEWING IDEAS

1. What is a fossil? Name at least two examples.
2. How may fossils be formed?
3. What explanation did Lamarck give for the giraffe's long neck?
4. Why was the horseshoe crab reclassified with the spiders instead of remaining with the crabs?
5. How did Lyell's hypothesis help Darwin think about the past?
6. Who may first have proposed that life on Earth appeared or evolved gradually?
7. How did Darwin explain adaptation using natural selection?
8. What is a niche in an environment?
9. What conclusion did Darwin arrive at for the cause of new species?
10. Give an example of adaptation by natural selection.

## USING CONCEPTS

11. Which of Lamarck's two basic assumptions was true, and which was false?
12. Darwin's observations provided evidence for three assumptions supporting the idea that a process of natural selection must occur among organisms. What were the three assumptions?
13. What was the difference between adaptation as Lamarck described it and adaptation as Darwin described it?
14. What is hereditary adaptation?
15. What part of the theory of natural selection has accumulated the greatest amount of evidence?
16. Describe two views of biologists today about evolution by means of natural selection.

## RECOMMENDED READING

Darwin, C., and A. R. Wallace. "Evolution by Natural Selection." New York, Johnson Reprint Corporation, 1971. The original joint paper.

Hitching, F. *The Neck of the Giraffe*. New Haven and New York, Ticknor and Fields, 1982. A readable review of the evidence about evolution, favoring punctuated equilibrium.

## REFERENCES

1. J. B. Lamarck, as quoted in A. E. E. McKenzie, *The Major Achievements of Science*. Cambridge, England, Cambridge University Press, 1960, p. 116; also New York, Simon & Schuster, 1973.
2. C. Darwin, *The Autobiography of Charles Darwin,* ed. F. Darwin (1892). New York, Dover Publications, Inc., 1958, pp. 41–42.
3. C. Darwin, *op. cit.*, pp. 42–43.
4. C. Darwin, *On the Origin of Species by Means of Natural Selection* (1859). New York, Mentor Books, 1958, p. 128.
5. *Ibid.*, p. 450.

PART TWO

# Evolution of Life Processes

What earth was like when life began has intrigued biologists for centuries. Today we are closer to knowing, although the answers have held some surprises. There was little or no oxygen in the early atmosphere, so that life began without requiring free oxygen. Most biologists agree that a broth of organic compounds in the waters of Earth was the source of materials for the first life, and thereafter was its first food. Some life processes today still reflect the earlier conditions.

# Forerunners
# of
# Life  5

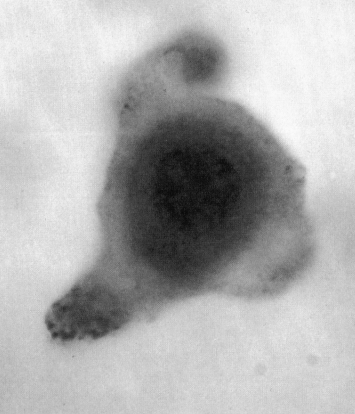

A biologist looking at the photograph you see here would say there is no question it is a cell. The largest plants and animals on Earth are made of cells. This cell, however, probably lived as a one-celled microorganism. Its significance to biology is the fact that it is almost half the age of Earth—a very old fossil. Along with still older fossil evidence, this cell measures life's origin by billions, not millions, of years.

When Darwin proposed evolution by natural selection, fossils this old were unknown. Yet the world was thrown into a turmoil of speculation about life's origin. If the organisms living today evolved from their ancestors, and they, in turn, from their ancestors, how did life first begin? What were the first forms of life like? Today we have evidence that life evolved when Earth was still young, that populations of microorganisms arose first and flourished.

# The Question of Life's Origin

## 5–1

## Life from Nonlife?

Scientists must always be aware that their basic assumptions have an effect on the way they see and interpret facts. Assumptions along with facts once clouded a scientific issue for 22 centuries: Can life arise from nonlife?

Early Greek philosophers fueled the debate. They observed events in nature when science with experimentation was unknown. Assumptions became theories without passing through the stage of hypotheses to be tested (except by observation). Consider the consequences: The Greek philosophers observed, for example, pond life disappearing when ponds dried up, but reappearing when the ponds filled again with rain! All the fishes, eels, and other organisms that started life anew in the ponds were never observed to be in the raindrops.

Therefore, the Greeks assumed that the organisms formed from the mud of the pond bottoms. These and similar events were carefully described and recorded, with the observation that "Life can be renewed by Earth itself."

The eggs of most pond organisms were small and difficult to observe. Microscopes were unknown. Laboratory methods of collecting organisms and observing their reproduction and development were almost unknown too. The Greek observers knew that organisms reproduced but had no reason to believe that this was the only method by which organisms could arise. To them, reproduction explained neither life's origin (as it does not today) nor its reappearance following fire, drought, or other natural disasters. The belief in **spontaneous generation** of life from Earth or from other materials appeared to be a straightforward observation that anyone could make. Many people made this observation and it seemed to be a fact.

---

←A living cell? Yes, once upon an early Earth. Its fossil is two billion years old.

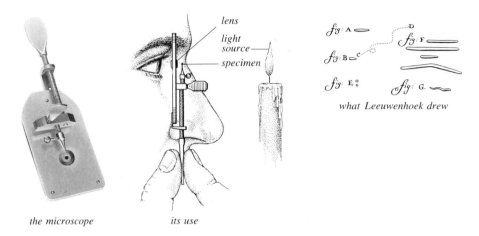

*lens*

*light source*

*specimen*

*what Leeuwenhoek drew*

*the microscope*          *its use*

**Figure 5–1** Leeuwenhoek used a simple microscope with one lens to see many small objects and details. Figures A through G, top right, show bacteria and one pattern of their motion. Leeuwenhoek discovered bacteria and many other microorganisms.

From the 4th century B.C. to the 17th century A.D. spontaneous generation was widely accepted. As experimentation was introduced in biology, however, active doubt arose. Some biologists openly expressed skepticism. Yet even as they designed experiments to test some of the accepted observations, new examples of spontaneous generation were reported. As late as 1652, an experiment by a Belgian physician described the spontaneous generation of mice. Baby mice appeared in 21 days, the report stated, in a pot containing only a sweaty shirt and kernels of wheat. The sweat in the shirt was cited as the important ingredient. (The Greeks, too, had believed that some "active principle" influenced spontaneous generation.) From your vantage point today, what other hypothesis would you suggest to explain the appearance of the mice? Could you design a controlled experiment to test your hypothesis?

Spontaneous generation of maggots on decaying meat was one of the widely observed examples supporting the centuries-old belief. (Maggots develop from the eggs of flies and mature into pupae that produce new adult flies.) An experiment in which meat was kept covered was suc-

cessful in excluding flies; no maggots appeared on the meat. Disproof of spontaneous generation was not this simple, however. Critics of the experiment could have claimed that the cover over the meat kept out a needed "active principle" in the air. The experiment was repeated with a finely meshed cloth that effectively kept all flies away from the meat. Air circulated freely through the cloth mesh, but again no maggots appeared. (See **Appendix 5-A,** Redi's Experiments Yield Evidence Against Spontaneous Generation, page 690.)

Even with this and other careful investigations, spontaneous generation for some organisms was difficult to exclude. One by one the examples yielded—until only microorganisms remained in question. The microscope (invented around 1600) was first used to detect microorganisms by Leeuwenhoek (page 17). He discovered them a few years after the experiment on maggots was performed. From the point of view of the spontaneous generation controversy, microorganisms were discovered just in time to add another century or more to the dispute. Leeuwenhoek's microscope and drawings of bacteria that he observed are shown in Figure 5–1.

Once discovered, microorganisms were found everywhere. Wrapping or sealing foodstuffs was of no use against them; they continued to attack the food. In many experiments, investigators even boiled liquid preparations (hay and water, or sugar and water) to kill any microorganisms present. Table 5–1 shows why this procedure did not always work. Thus, many biologists and others came to accept the idea that microscopic life was spontaneously generated. The dispute about spontaneous generation raged as growths of microorganisms continued to appear in supposedly sterile liquids.

**Table 5–1  Average time that different organisms (or their spores) can survive being boiled**

| Organisms | Survival time (in minutes) |
|---|---|
| Protists | 0 |
| Bacteria | |
| Most species | 0 |
| *Bacillus subtilis* | 14 |
| *Clostridium perfringens* | 20 |
| *Clostridium botulinum* | 360 |

About a century ago the long controversy was brought to an end. A better understanding of sterilization led to improved methods for killing microorganisms. When these methods were used, ''spontaneous generation'' no longer occurred in experiments. Biologists at last united in accepting as a principle, ''All organisms arise only from others of their kind.''

**Try Investigation 5–A**  Where Do Bacteria and Other Microorganisms Come From?, page 591.

## 5–2

## The Question of Life from Nonlife is Reopened

The biologists who discredited spontaneous generation were concerned only with linking organisms with parents of the same species. Evidence that the organisms would not appear unless the parents (or their eggs or spores) were present was sufficient. Darwin's work went further. He accepted the idea that organisms arise only from others of their kind. What concerned him was the hereditary variations that occurred from generation to generation in the same species.

Evolution, in Darwin's view, increased the numbers of species as a result of the variety among individuals in pre-existing species. The Galápagos finches (page 79) were an example; all of them were probably descended from the same ancestors. Even Darwin's pigeon-breeding experiments suggested the potential for variation within one species. More kinds of organisms could always be expected to evolve from fewer before them, if Darwin's view was correct.

Darwin's hypothesis implied fewer and fewer species farther and farther into the past. Thus, all species could have come from the same ancestral species living at the time when life must have originated. As you have read on page 78, Darwin concluded *On the Origin of Species by Means of Natural Selection* with this thought.

The early Greeks also had questioned the origin of life. However, they assumed that each species arose separately by spontaneous generation. In a different way, Darwin reopened the question of how life may have begun.

Fossil studies have not contradicted this hypothesis of one or a few initial forms of life. In fact, the oldest fossil records support the hypothesis; they reveal few species. One possible reason is the erosion, weathering, and recycling of the

*first reptile*
*(over 280 million
years ago)*

*reptiles today*
*(four living orders
and 6000 species)*

*the Golden Age of Reptiles*
*(16 or more orders and tens of thousands of species,
extending through almost 200 million years)*

**Figure 5–2** The Golden Age of Reptiles produced tens of thousands of species from small lizards to flying reptiles and giant dinosaurs. Turtles, alligators and crocodiles, lizards, and snakes are the only surviving orders or major kinds of reptiles today.

oldest fossil-bearing rocks. Yet none of the surviving older rocks suggests a great variety in species. Delicate fossils of microscopic organisms are all that are found.

Spectacular illustrations of Darwin's ''fewer-many'' argument are found in the fossil record at later times. Evolution often branched to produce a ''golden age'' for a particular group of organisms. The ''Golden Age of Reptiles'' included a greater variety of species than among reptiles today. Dinosaurs and flying reptiles are the examples for which the age is best known. Yet they made up only a minority of the many species (Figure 5–2). The ''Golden Age of Mammals'' was a later example. You are a member of this group, whose greatest diversity also appears to be past.

When there were more reptiles, there were fewer mammals and almost no birds. When there were more mammals, reptiles were declining and birds were evolving into more species. This pattern appears in each age in the fossil record. Across all groups, Darwin's ''fewer-many'' view fits. Within each group, the ''fewer-many'' view also fits, up to a point (or golden age). Thus, more different species of organisms have evolved from fewer before them.

The pathway is more complicated than Darwin knew. One group would flourish, then succumb to changes in the environment or to competition from other groups. Another group would then increase to its greatest variety in numbers of species. But, there was a remote time, before any known golden ages of larger organisms, when relatively few species of organisms apparently existed.

Were these organisms ancestral to all later ones? Were they themselves far from life's beginning? How did the very first organisms arise? Difficult as these questions are to comprehend, biologists are aware that they again are facing an investigation of life from nonlife.

# 5-3

## Approaches to Investigating Life's Origin

Professor Elso S. Barghoorn of Harvard University discovered the two-billion-year-old fossil cell shown on page 86. He also discovered the bacteriumlike fossil, more than three billion years old, shown in Figure 5–3. Other investigators have discovered algalike or bacterialike fossils in ancient rock 3.5 billion years old. Fossil traces of the pond scum that the latter organisms formed led to further evidence of the fossil microorganisms themselves.

But the search is not as simple as looking for older and older rocks, with older and older fossils. The oldest rocks formed on Earth have not remained unchanged. If the fossil record once included traces of the first life forms on Earth, it no longer does. Other, less direct methods of investigation must be employed.

The evidence derived about life today, and about fossil life extending 3.5 billion years into the past, is the most reliable evidence biologists have from which to form hypotheses about the origin of life. This evidence indicates a continuing evolutionary relationship between past and present living things. If evolution is the thread that links life through the ages, then there is reason to investigate the origin of the first life as a part of evolution. That is, life itself may have originated by evolution. This hypothesis presupposes that the chemical substances necessary to form a living thing were present on Earth long ago. Biologists have discovered that at least *some* investigation of this view is possible, even today.

Evolution is therefore being studied as the process by which life not only diversified, but first arose. Taking this hypothetical step also makes it possible to predict what the first life was like—it was very small and relatively unstructured. The reason it would not include large organisms with

**Figure 5–3** This ancient fossil bacterium (left) and its imprint were found in rocks more than three billion years old. The line of scale represents one micrometer.

specialized body parts is that evolution cannot build everything at once, but works in stages. You can think of evolution as a remodeler, not an architect. It could only have worked at first with whatever small cluster of particles were present on Earth.

The fossil record supports this reasoning. Fossils of the earliest known life are all microscopic in size. Not a single exception has been found.

As you will be reading in this and the next several chapters, biologists and other scientists are studying the evolution of Earth, the other planets, and the sun for many kinds of clues. Space explorations have helped to gather data in probes of the sun's other planets. Even planets around other stars are important to the search, for if life evolved on Earth, it may have evolved elsewhere as well. However, planets around other stars are very difficult to detect. Only indirect evidence that such planets exist has been obtained so far, as in the multiple objects observed circling the star *Vega* (VAY-guh). Sending out space probes to the areas around such stars is not likely in the near future.

**CAPSULE SUMMARY**

A belief in spontaneous generation satisfied people's questions for 22 centuries about most of the mysteries surrounding living things. Observation alone, without experimentation, could not dislodge this belief. Even experimentation at first failed to do so. A belief in spontaneous generation of microorganisms persisted until experimental procedures could be improved to show otherwise.

Fossil evidence indicates that microorganisms were the first organisms on Earth. Thus the question of their origin is very important in biology. A first-life hypothesis based on evolution is the basis for investigation today.

**SELF CHECK**

1. How does the spontaneous generation of a frog from pond mud differ from the hypothesis of evolution of early cells from nonliving materials?
2. Why is fossil evidence of life's origin not possible?
3. What size are the oldest known fossils?
4. What was Darwin's "fewer-many" argument?

# The Evolving Earth When Life Began

## 5-4

### The Earth and Other Planets

Little about the evolution of Earth or of the other planets is established beyond question. First comes the sun—its origin is the first necessary clue. The sun is a star, and studies of the birth of other stars in space provide all the information known on how the sun may have been formed. A revolving cloud of gas and dust, as seen for other stars, is the suggested answer. Hydrogen is always the major element in the gas. Hydrogen is the sun's major element and nuclear fuel today.

As the solar system's early gas cloud revolved it may have trailed arms or wisps around its edges. (These, too, are seen in giant revolving clouds of gas in space.) When the sun condensed from the gas it would not have recovered all the distant, trailing arms. Four of these arms probably condensed separately and formed the giant planets Jupiter, Saturn, Uranus, and Neptune. Other remnants of the gas remained partly as gas and condensed partly into many smaller bodies. Much later, some of these smaller bodies may have collided and acquired combined sizes to form the smaller planets, including Earth.

All these events began about 15 billion years ago (for the sun) and ended for Earth about 4.7 billion years ago when it was formed.

If Earth encountered some of the remaining hydrogen gas from the cloud, as its first atmosphere, the hydrogen slowly escaped again. Hydrogen is the lightest element and requires a greater force of gravity than Earth's to hold it permanently in an atmosphere. Heavier gases are held more easily.

Early Earth, without (or stripped of) any atmosphere, probably heated and partly melted. The sun's heat on the barren planet is not believed to be the cause, but rather radioactive elements inside Earth. Eventually, as most of these reactions faded, Earth began to cool again.

It is at this point that events became very significant for the origin of life.

Earth's second atmosphere (if there was a first) came from within the planet itself as it cooled over millions of years. Volcanoes and giant ruptures in the cooling surface poured out gases at a rate difficult to imagine today. (Volcanoes, however, still do pour out such gases.) Hydrogen and heavier gases were released from the planet's interior. Some of the hydrogen combined with other gases and was retained in the atmosphere.

Free oxygen was not among all these gases, or else very little of it was present. Because oxygen is necessary to all but a few species of organisms today, this particular assumption about the early atmosphere attracted much attention. A great deal of research has been done; volcanoes and the gases they release today have been studied all over the world. No evidence has been found that free oxygen, or much of it, existed in the early atmosphere. In fact, it is now believed that the green plants and their ancestors later added oxygen to the atmosphere.

## 5–5
## The Early Atmosphere

Today about 78 percent of Earth's atmosphere is nitrogen gas and about 21 percent is oxygen gas. The remaining one percent is made up of small amounts of other gases, of which carbon dioxide is the most important for life. The primitive atmosphere, however, could not have been the same if it formed from gases escaping from the interior of the planet through volcanic activity. It would have contained water vapor, carbon dioxide, carbon monoxide, nitrogen, and hydrogen. Some scientists suggest that this was the atmosphere for the first life. Others suggest that some of the nitrogen and hydrogen reacted to form ammonia (used by microorganisms and plants today), and that hydrogen reacted with carbon gases to form methane (used today as natural gas). If so, ammonia and methane were added to the atmospheric gases.

(Ammonia and methane are also found today at heated vents or fissures in the ocean floor.)

As Earth cooled, water vapor would have condensed, starting massive rains. Rivers, lakes, and oceans would have begun to form.

An atmosphere with little or no oxygen would mean that the first life must have been able to live without oxygen. Many modern bacteria and certain fungi can live without oxygen. Moreover, an oxygen-rich early atmosphere could have *prevented* life from evolving. Oxygen is a chemically reactive gas that would have destroyed naturally occurring organic compounds. Without these compounds, no life could have been possible.

All organisms today carry on certain chemical processes that probably originated in cells living without free oxygen.

## 5–6
## The First-Life Hypothesis

The Russian scientist, A. I. Oparin (oh-PAHR-in), published the first extensive development of the first-life hypothesis. You have already read certain predictions about this first life. An English biologist, J. B. S. Haldane (HAWL-dayn), also helped develop the first assumptions about pre-life (or chemical) evolution.

Not everything today is assumption. You will be reading conclusive evidence that many organic compounds, including some used by organisms today, formed naturally and are found even in meteorites from space (page 104). Oparin and Haldane both argued that chemical evolution, as it occurred throughout the universe, produced organic compounds. The most interesting arguments are about the first life itself, however.

The first life was microscopic (you have read this prediction and why it was made). What did these first living things use for food? Such a question tempts biologists to suggest that the first life made its own food. Green plants and other such organisms today do so; they are the autotrophs, or producers. However, as they use carbon dioxide and water in food manufacture, they give off oxygen. They also require oxygen to make use of their own foodstuffs. Among all living organisms today, only a few kinds of bacteria can make their food by a different process, neither using nor giving off oxygen. When you remember that bacterialike fossils are among the oldest found on Earth, you might wonder whether evolution took this route. Possibly it did, but the food-making apparatus is a complex thing to add to all the other complexities of being alive. If evolution took the fewest possible steps, the first living things would have been heterotrophs. For food *they could have used the supply of naturally occurring organic compounds.*

The **heterotroph hypothesis** is favored by many biologists. They propose that the very first life fed on the same organic compounds from which it evolved. This would have made the first organisms consumers. They could not synthesize (SIN-theh-size) all the organic compounds they needed as food. Yet these heterotrophs would have required fewer evolutionary steps to develop than would the more complex autotrophs. Evolution would have gone on and by small steps resulted in the food-making apparatus and processes somewhat later. (Otherwise life as heterotrophs would have evolved and come to a dead end when the supply of natural organic compounds was exhausted in food use.)

An autotroph could have lived in much simpler surroundings than a heterotroph, but it would have required even more complex surroundings to have evolved first. You can think about this as biologists have. They believe they may be right, unless evolution somehow took a great many complex steps almost simultaneously.

In Figure 5–4, notice that the earliest life had appeared and was well established by the time Earth was only one third as old as it is today.

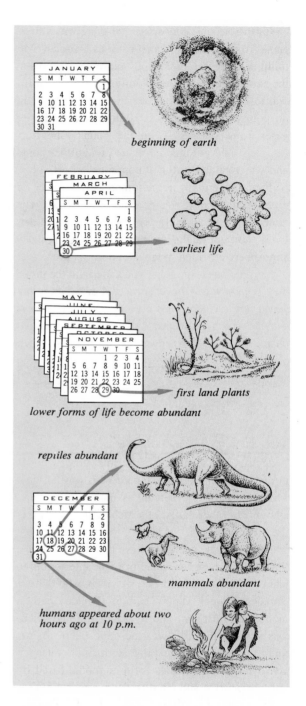

**Figure 5–4** In this calendar, 4.7 billion years of Earth's history are compressed into one year. Each day is equal to almost 13 million years on Earth.

**CAPSULE SUMMARY**

Scientific evidence indicates that Earth is about 4.7 billion years old. If there was a first atmosphere (largely hydrogen), it was lost. The planet provided its own second atmosphere as it cooled and vented gases in widespread volcanic activity. Water vapor, carbon dioxide, carbon monoxide, nitrogen, and hydrogen were probably among these gases. Methane and ammonia were probably formed by reactions in the atmosphere.

Little or no free oxygen was present in the early atmosphere. If it had been, it would have destroyed the naturally occurring organic compounds from which life is believed to have evolved. The first organisms, then, had to be able to live without free oxygen. A number of species of such organisms exist today.

Biologists believe heterotrophs (consumers) evolved first and used the supply of natural organic compounds as food.

**SELF CHECK**

1. How much older may Earth be than the oldest known fossils?
2. What gases did the early (second) atmosphere contain?
3. How might rivers, lakes, and oceans have formed on Earth?
4. Why do biologists believe heterotrophs (consumers) evolved first?
5. Explain why the relative absence of oxygen in the early atmosphere once gave biologists a problem, then provided them with the solution to another problem.

# The Chemistry of the Primitive Atmosphere

## 5-7

## Atoms and Molecules Provide the Key to the Chemistry of Matter

To understand how substances needed for the structure of organisms, and for their food, might have come to exist, you need to know something about the chemical nature of matter. Only a few basic principles can be discussed here, but these will help you understand how living cells function today and the assumptions biologists make about the origin of life.

Of all the gases that were in the early atmosphere, the one most familiar is water vapor. Water is abundant on Earth today—as a gas, as a liquid, and as a solid. The physical state of water depends on its temperature. If the temperature is high enough, water becomes a vapor. If the temperature is low enough, water freezes to ice. Although its form may change, its chemical composition remains the same. Water has some unusual physical and chemical properties that have had a powerful effect on the evolution of life. If you take a closer look at the chemistry of water, some general ideas about the chemical nature of matter will become evident.

Suppose you found a way to subdivide a drop of water into smaller and smaller droplets until finally you could not even see them under a microscope. No matter how small the water droplet, it would still be made of identical units that are called **molecules.** Molecules of water are the smallest units into which water can be subdivided and still have the properties of water.

When an electric current flows through water a remarkable change takes place. Water is changed into two gases. One is the lightest gas, hydrogen. It will burn with a very hot flame in air that contains oxygen. The other gas is oxygen. Any burning object thrust into oxygen will continue to burn with a more brilliant flame.

Thus, when an electric current is passed through water, the water molecules are broken down into two new substances, hydrogen and oxygen. Neither hydrogen nor oxygen looks like or has the same properties as water.

If molecules can be broken down, what are the particles of which molecules are made? This question brings up the most important of all chemical theories: the **atomic theory.** In 1805, the British teacher and chemist John Dalton finished a long series of experiments and measurements that indicated every substance is made of minute particles. Dalton believed these particles could not be broken into smaller particles, so he named them atoms (from the Greek word *atomos* meaning indivisible). He stated several principles to describe their chemical behavior, which helped to clarify many different observations that scientists had made. Other discoveries have changed the atomic theory since Dalton's time, but this theory is still basic to an understanding of chemistry and biology.

Molecules are made of atoms that have been chemically combined. Molecules may be made from more than one kind of atom (as in water), or they may be made from atoms of the same kind. For example, hydrogen gas consists of hydrogen atoms that exist in combination with each other. Two hydrogen atoms form a molecule of hydrogen (see Figure 5–5). The same arrangement is true of oxygen; two oxygen atoms combine to form a molecule of oxygen. (Oxygen also forms molecules of *ozone* that contain three atoms of oxygen.)

A substance made of only one kind of atom is called an **element.** Over 100 different elements are known today. A substance made of two or more different kinds of atoms, such as water, is called a **compound.** Elements can combine chemically in many ways to form the millions of compounds that give Earth its variety of materials.

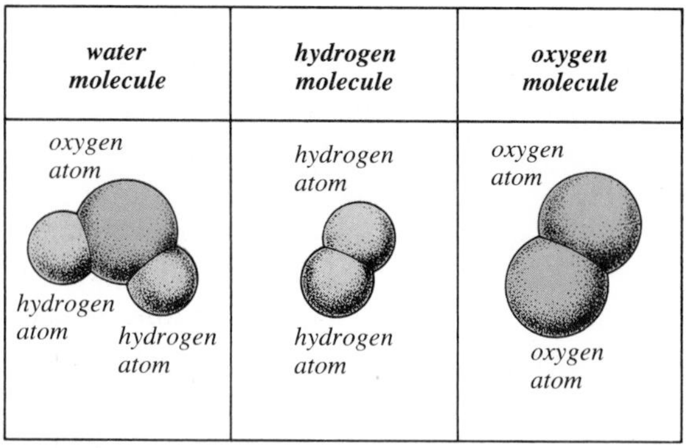

**Figure 5–5** These models of a water molecule, a hydrogen molecule, and an oxygen molecule show that molecules are composed of atoms.

Chemists have given each element a symbol for convenience. The symbol is made of letters taken from the element's name. H stands for hydrogen, O for oxygen, C for carbon, and N for nitrogen. But iron is Fe, derived from the word *ferrum,* reflecting the fact that some symbols come from an element's Latin or Greek name.

Despite all this variety of materials, organisms are made of compounds more than 96 percent of which contain only five elements—carbon, hydrogen, oxygen, nitrogen, and phosphorus. The compound present in organisms in the greatest amount is water. The remaining four percent of the materials in organisms varies but contains small amounts of other elements. The basic five elements are essential to *every* organism. A limited number of others are essential, too, but only in smaller amounts.

Are the elements essential for life the most abundant elements in the environment? Free oxygen is abundant today but was not in the early atmosphere. However, both oxygen and hydrogen were and are abundant in water and other compounds. Carbon, nitrogen, and phosphorus—the other three most common elements in organisms—are not among Earth's most abundant elements. (See **Appendix 5–B,** Elements Essential for Life, page 691.)

The useful chemical properties of elements, rather than their abundance, are what make them essential to living things. Nevertheless, organisms are influenced by the chemical environment in which they live. For example, the chemical composition of the blood of many marine animals is very similar to that of seawater. This hereditary adaptation helps the animals live in the oceans. But these same animals also require materials that are not among the ocean's most abundant materials.

## 5–8
## Compounds Contain Fixed Proportions of Atoms of Elements

The atomic theory, like other theories, organizes and explains facts and predicts others. For example, in a demonstration of the use of an electric current to decompose water molecules, unequal amounts of hydrogen and oxygen are collected. By volume, twice as much hydrogen as oxygen is yielded. This fact is explained to mean that water contains two atoms of hydrogen for every one atom of oxygen. Data on all other compounds tested show that in a certain compound, atoms are always present in the same proportion. Therefore, the prediction is made that in *all* compounds, atoms of different elements are present in fixed or constant proportions.

This idea may be written in a short statement called a chemical equation. The chemical equation for the decomposition of water is as follows:

$$2H_2O \xrightarrow{\text{electricity}} 2H_2 + O_2$$

| 2 molecules of water | 2 molecules of hydrogen | 1 molecule of oxygen |

Why is it necessary to use two molecules of water in the equation? Remember that hydrogen

and oxygen molecules each consist of two atoms (Figure 5–6). A single molecule of water does not yield enough oxygen atoms to make an oxygen molecule, but two molecules of water do. The equation is written to reflect this fact. Notice that the number of molecules is shown by a numeral *preceding* the symbols, or formula, for the molecule. The number of atoms of each element in the molecule is shown by a subscript *following* the symbol for the element (the number "one" is always understood and is not written). For example, the formula for carbon dioxide, $CO_2$, means that a molecule of this gas contains one carbon atom and two oxygen atoms. A molecule of ammonia, written as $NH_3$, contains one nitrogen atom and three hydrogen atoms. Finally, a molecule of methane is written $CH_4$. You can tell what elements are in each molecule, and how many atoms of each element the molecule contains.

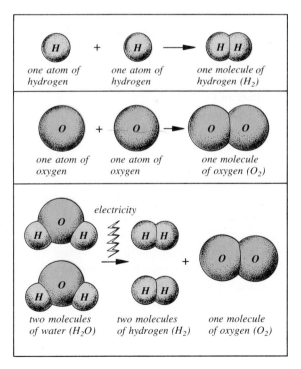

**Figure 5–6** In the decomposition of water, twice as many hydrogen molecules as oxygen molecules are produced.

**Figure 5-7** Two ways of picturing the hydrogen atom. At left, a simplified representation of the electron (*e*) moving about the nucleus, which consists of one proton (*p*). At right, a cloud represents the likelihood of the electron's presence at any position.

## 5-9

## Atoms Are Composed of Smaller Particles

Dalton thought atoms were indivisible. Scientists today know that they are not. Atoms are built of many smaller particles. The particles basic to an understanding of biology are electrons, protons, and neutrons.

The most familiar of these particles is the electron. It carries a negative charge in an atom just as it does when moving in an ordinary electric current. A proton has a positive charge and a neutron has no charge.

Protons and neutrons remain in the center, or nucleus, of the atom. The electrons, however, seem to be everywhere at once *except* in the nucleus. The rapidly moving electrons form a negatively charged cloud around the nucleus.

The simplest of all atoms is hydrogen. A hydrogen nucleus has a single proton, no neutron, and a single electron that moves about the nucleus (Figure 5-7). If the electron is removed, or if it is shared with another atom, a chemical change has occurred. Removal of the electron leaves a nucleus, made of a single positively charged proton that is represented by the symbol $H^+$.

Atoms of elements other than hydrogen are more complex than the hydrogen atom. For example, an atom of carbon (Figure 5-8) has six protons and six neutrons in its nucleus, and six electrons outside the nucleus. The number of neutrons may vary, but six protons and six electrons in an atom always signify carbon. Similarly, nitrogen has seven protons and seven electrons, and oxygen has eight protons and eight electrons (Figure 5-8).

In any atom, the number of protons and electrons is equal. Thus the charges are balanced, and the atom has no overall electric charge. However, the atoms of most elements can undergo chemical change by having one or more electrons added, removed, or shared with other atoms.

Only electrons in the outer energy levels of the atoms pictured in Figure 5-8 interact when the atoms combine during a chemical change. Many elements have atoms with electrons in more than two energy levels, but again, only the outermost electrons normally interact during changes. The outer electrons give chemists a reliable indicator of the chemical activity of an element's atoms. However, it should be remembered that whole atoms also exert profound influence on chemical reactions.

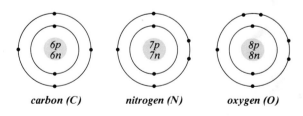

carbon (C)          nitrogen (N)          oxygen (O)

**Figure 5-8** The models shown here of carbon, nitrogen, and oxygen atoms represent the numbers of protons (*p*), neutrons (*n*), and electrons (black dots) in the energy levels (circles) of each atom. The number of electrons in the outer level determines chemical activity.

Atoms of different elements differ in their number of protons, neutrons, and electrons. However, atoms of a single element can differ only in their numbers of neutrons. They always have the same number of protons and electrons, and the same chemical behavior. Atoms of an element that differ in their number of neutrons are called **isotopes** (EYE-suh-tohps). Oxygen provides an example. Ninety-nine percent of oxygen atoms are like the one pictured in Figure 5–8. This atom is called the oxygen-16 isotope—named for the sum of its protons and neutrons. However, oxygen-17 and oxygen-18 also exist, with nine and ten neutrons respectively.

Isotopes are valuable in biology because they can be detected, or traced, in the compounds an organism makes. Most useful as tracers are **radioactive isotopes.** The number of neutrons in their nuclei somehow makes the nuclei unstable. One result is that radiation energy escapes from these atomic nuclei and can be detected. Radiation detectors are very sensitive. If an organism is supplied with just a small amount of a radioactive isotope for some of its needs, any compound made with the isotope can be identified. For example, the common form of the element carbon is carbon-12 (with six protons and six neutrons). However, carbon-14 (with two extra neutrons) is a radioactive isotope. Biologists can trace the path of carbon-14 in many complicated reactions inside living cells.

## 5–10
## Atoms React Chemically with One Another

You have learned already that atoms do not exist singly in many instances. Two or more atoms are often combined to form compounds.

**Chemical bonds** between atoms are formed by the attraction, sharing, or transfer of outer electrons from one atom to the other. Such bonds be-

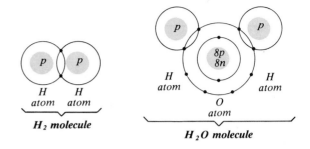

**Figure 5–9** In a molecule of hydrogen (left), two hydrogen atoms form an electron-sharing (covalent) bond. In a molecule of water (right), the oxygen atom forms an electron-sharing or covalent bond with each hydrogen atom.

tween atoms can be broken, the atoms rearranged, and new bonds formed. A **chemical reaction** is actually the making and breaking of chemical bonds. Chemical reactions are always occurring in living organisms. Living organisms are sometimes compared to chemical factories, but the number and the complexity of chemical reactions that occur in living organisms is vastly greater than in any factory.

When atoms interact, they form mainly two types of chemical bonds. In one type of chemical bond, two atoms share a pair of electrons. The diagrams in Figure 5–9 show two examples of electron-sharing or **covalent** (KOH-vay-lent) **bonds.** Two atoms of hydrogen are joined to form a molecule of hydrogen gas ($H_2$) by sharing a pair of electrons. In a molecule of water, each of the two hydrogen atoms shares a pair of electrons with the same oxygen atom.

Chemical formulas are often written to show both the numbers and the arrangement of atoms in molecules. Such formulas are called structural formulas. In writing structural formulas of compounds, an electron-sharing or covalent bond is indicated by a line. For example, the structural formula for water is written H—O—H. Sometimes two atoms will share two pairs of electrons between them, forming a double bond that is

| name | molecular formula | structural formula | models | |
|---|---|---|---|---|
| | | | space-filling | ball-and-stick |
| hydrogen | $H_2$ | H—H | | |
| water | $H_2O$ | H—O—H | | |
| ammonia | $NH_3$ | H—N—H<br>\|<br>H | | |
| methane | $CH_4$ | H<br>\|<br>H—C—H<br>\|<br>H | | |

**Figure 5–10** A variety of symbols and models can be used to represent chemical molecules. Still another model is the electron-dot diagram, in which H:H represents a hydrogen molecule and H:O:H represents a water molecule. Each pair of dots represents a shared pair of electrons in a covalent bond.

shown by a double line (═). When three pairs of electrons are shared by two atoms, they form a triple bond that is represented by three lines (≡). Figure 5–10 shows structural formulas and models of several molecules that existed in the early atmosphere of Earth.

The second major type of chemical bond is formed when electrons are transferred from one atom to another. This type of chemical bond is found in many substances including table salt, also known as sodium chloride (NaCl). As the latter name suggests, table salt is made of two elements, sodium (Na) and chlorine (Cl). When atoms of these two elements react, an electron passes from an atom of sodium to an atom of chlorine. The result is that the sodium atom becomes positively charged, for it has one more proton than electrons. It becomes a sodium **ion** (EYE-on), written as $Na^+$. The chlorine atom becomes negatively

charged, for it has one more electron than protons. It becomes a chloride ion, written as $Cl^-$. Note the change in name from chlorine to chloride.

As these examples suggest, an *ion* can be defined as an atom or a group of atoms that has acquired a positive or negative charge as a result of gaining or losing one or more electrons. By this definition a molecule can also become an ion by gaining or losing an electron.

Table salt is made of positively charged sodium ions and negatively charged chloride ions, each strongly attracted to the other. The result is that each sodium ion is surrounded by chloride ions and vice versa. The ions are arranged in a formation represented by Figure 5–11.

The attraction between oppositely charged ions is called an **ionic** (eye-ON-ik) **bond.** Ions are very active chemically, primarily because of their electric charge. Note that there is no sharing of electrons in an ionic bond.

**Figure 5–11** Small positively charged sodium ions attract larger negatively charged chloride ions to form a sodium chloride crystal like the one shown in this model. The bonds are not electron-sharing, or covalent. What kind of bonds are they?

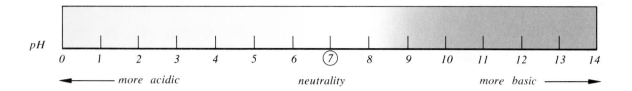

$pH$

0  1  2  3  4  5  6  ⑦  8  9  10  11  12  13  14

◄───── *more acidic*      *neutrality*      *more basic* ─────►

**Figure 5–12** The *pH* scale is used to describe acid and base solutions.

## 5–11

## Ions in Solution Affect Living Cells

When table salt is dissolved in water, the ionic bonds are broken. $Na^+$ and $Cl^-$ ions separate and remain as ions in solution. A reaction in which a substance separates into ions is called **ionization.**

One of the most important ionization reactions for living cells is the ionization of water. A water molecule ($H_2O$) breaks down or ionizes into a hydrogen ion ($H^+$) and a hydroxide ion ($OH^-$). Notice that the hydrogen ion, $H^+$, is a hydrogen atom that has lost its only electron. In other words, a hydrogen ion is the same as a proton. The missing electron is held by the hydroxide ion, $OH^-$, which is made up of an atom of oxygen, an atom of hydrogen, and an extra electron.

Calculations show that only one in every ten million molecules of water breaks down into ions. Yet all life processes depend on this tiny amount of ionization of water. Living cells control their internal levels of $H^+$ and $OH^-$ ions within narrow limits. Small changes in the amounts of these ions can influence important cellular reactions.

Chemists and biologists use a convenient device known as a *p*H scale to describe the level of $H^+$ and $OH^-$ ions in solution. The scale runs from 0 to 14. A solution that has the same number of $H^+$ and $OH^-$ ions is said to be neutral and to have a *p*H of 7. Pure water has a *p*H of 7. A solution having more $H^+$ than $OH^-$ ions is said to be acidic and will have a *p*H less than 7 (low *p*H). Such a solution is sour to the taste. A solution that has more $OH^-$ ions than $H^+$ ions is said to be basic (or alkaline) and will have a *p*H greater than 7 (high *p*H). Thus a solution with a *p*H of 2 is strongly acidic and a solution with a *p*H of 10 is strongly basic. (See Figure 5–12.)

The *p*H scale is important in biology because organisms vary greatly in their response to *p*H changes. Certain fungi and bacteria can grow in solutions that are acidic but not in solutions that are basic. On the other hand, some marine organisms have become so adapted to the slightly basic *p*H (7.8 to 8.6) of seawater that they cannot live in acidic solutions. Human blood remains at a constant *p*H of 7.4. Death results if the blood *p*H falls to 7.0 or rises above 7.8.

**Try Investigation 5–B** What Are the Acid or Base Characteristics of Some Common Biological Materials?, page 592.

| CAPSULE SUMMARY | SELF CHECK |
|---|---|
| Water is a compound which may be decomposed by means of an electric current into molecules of the elements hydrogen and oxygen. These molecules are composed of still smaller particles, called atoms, each of which has a system (protons and electrons) of electrical charges. Various atoms combine to form molecules of millions of different compounds. The electron sharing or attractions which hold atoms together in molecules are called chemical bonds. | 1. What is the difference between atoms and molecules?<br>2. What is a compound?<br>3. What is the evidence for the assumption that a water molecule contains twice as much hydrogen as oxygen?<br>4. What elements may have made up the gases of Earth's ancient atmosphere?<br>5. What is a chemical bond?<br>6. What is an ion? How do ions form? |

# The Formation of Organic Compounds

## 5–12

### Organic Compounds Before Life

Many chemical compounds, aside from water, are needed for life to exist. The most important are the **organic compounds.** You have already run across this term. The name ''organic'' was coined long ago when these compounds were thought to be formed only by living cells. Chemically speaking, organic compounds are carbon compounds in which the carbon atoms are combined with hydrogen, usually oxygen, and with nitrogen, sulfur, or phosphorus. A few carbon compounds were never included with organic compounds: carbon dioxide ($CO_2$), carbon monoxide ($CO$), and carbonic acid ($H_2CO_3$).

The idea that only living cells could form organic compounds was shown to be wrong in 1828 when the German chemist, Friedrich Woehler, was able to synthesize in the laboratory an organic compound, **urea** (yoo-REE-uh). Urea was previously known to be formed only in animals and excreted in urine. Since then millions of different organic compounds have been synthesized by chemists in the laboratory. There is no longer any reason to call these compounds ''organic,'' but the

name was so well established that it still is widely used to describe the carbon compounds essential for life.

You read earlier (page 93) that two scientists, A. I. Oparin and J. B. S. Haldane, independently conceived the idea that organic compounds could have been formed under Earth's primitive conditions before life arose. They reasoned that when Earth was young it had in abundance powerful energy sources such as ultraviolet radiation from the sun, electrical energy from lightning, radiation from radioactive rocks, and heat from volcanoes. (Today very little of the sun's powerful ultraviolet radiation penetrates the oxygen-rich atmosphere and reaches Earth.) The energy from these sources would have broken apart the gas molecules in the early atmosphere and re-formed the released carbon and other elements and ions into organic compounds. (For a discussion of energy see **Appendix 5–C,** Energy, page 692.) Driving rains would have washed the organic compounds into oceans and ponds. Without living organisms to consume them and free oxygen to destroy them, organic compounds needed for life would have accumulated in the waters of Earth. The ancient waters thus became nutrient solutions that could nourish emerging life forms.

## 5–13

## Primitive Earth Conditions in the Laboratory

Specifically, what organic compounds were formed before life emerged? Harold Urey and Stanley Miller worked on this problem at the University of Chicago. They thought of imitating in a laboratory experiment the conditions that might have existed on Earth long ago. Miller, now at the University of California, built and sterilized the airtight apparatus in Figure 5–13. Methane, hydrogen, and ammonia gases were placed in the apparatus and circulated past a high-energy electrical spark.

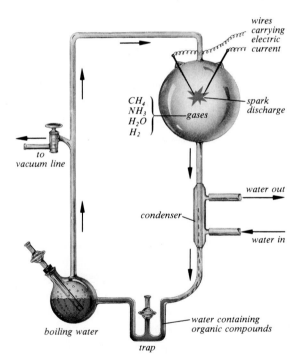

**Figure 5–13** A drawing of Miller's apparatus, in which conditions thought to exist in the primitive atmosphere were reproduced in the laboratory. What was Miller trying to find out?

Heat and water vapor were supplied by a container of boiling water connected to the apparatus. As the water vapor circulated, it cooled and condensed as "rain." Thus Miller created some of the conditions that may have been present in the early atmosphere. Those conditions were the gases, heat, rain, and flashes of lightning.

After circulating the gases for a week, Miller examined the liquid in the apparatus. The only visible difference was that the liquid, colorless at the start of the experiment, was now red. Chemical tests, however, showed that the liquid contained several compounds that were not present when the experiment began. The atoms of some of the gas molecules had recombined to form new and more complex molecules.

When the substances in the liquid were identified, Miller found that organic compounds known as **amino** (uh-MEE-noh) **acids** had been formed. This was an exciting discovery because amino acids are the building units that make up **proteins** (PRO-teenz), the most abundant organic compounds in living cells on Earth. No Earth form of life is possible without proteins. Miller's experiment did not prove that amino acids were formed in this way under early conditions on Earth. But the experiment indicated that a similar process *might* have occurred in the early atmosphere of Earth.

More recently, other scientists have carried out similar experiments using different energy sources, including ultraviolet radiation, and different combinations of the gases likely to have been in the early atmosphere. These experiments were also successful. They showed that other compounds essential for life might have been formed under Earth's primitive conditions. It is now clear that one of the key assumptions of the heterotroph hypothesis, the formation of organic compounds before life emerged, is not pure guesswork.

Exciting evidence has been found that organic compounds are formed even beyond Earth, in space. The conclusive tests were made by Cyril

Ponnamperuma (Po-nam-puh-RU-ma) and others in 1970, at the Ames Research Center in California. They found amino acids and other organic compounds in a meteorite that fell to Earth near Murchison, Australia, in September 1969 (Biology Brief, page 106). Of the seven amino acids found, two do not even occur in organisms on Earth. Such a mixture might be expected from random synthesis of amino acids somewhere in space.

Since 1970, other meteorites have revealed organic compounds that originated somewhere in space. Even before 1970, amino acids had been found in meteorites. However, until the test of the Murchison meteorite, the possibility of contamination by terrestrial protein had never been ruled out. New meteorites and new methods changed that.

Impressive as all this evidence is, you must not jump to the conclusion that all questions about the origin of life are now settled once and for all. The heterotroph hypothesis is the best hypothesis that science can now offer to explain this riddle. Much remains to be learned, particularly about the transition from organic compounds to the first living cell.

## 5–14
## Building Proteins

As already mentioned, without proteins life would be impossible. Every living cell contains a number of different proteins essential to the functioning of the cell. Each cell makes its own proteins by linking about 20 different amino acids together in long chains. Each of the different amino acids may occur in many places in the chain, so that different protein molecules may contain from about 50 to 3000 amino acid units.

Since new proteins are being formed throughout the life span of an organism, each living cell needs a continuous supply of amino acids. Some cells, like those of green plants and certain bacteria, are able to make all of the amino acids as they need them. Other cells, such as those in human beings, can make only some of the 20 amino acids and therefore must obtain the others from the proteins in food. The amino acids people cannot synthesize themselves are called ''essential amino acids.'' Strictly speaking, all the amino acids that make up proteins are essential for life, but the essential amino acids must be in your diet. **Appendix 5–D,** The Amino Acids, page 693, lists the 20 amino acids found in proteins and shows which are the so-called essential amino acids.

Most proteins contain all the 20 different amino acids, and one protein may contain more or less of certain amino acids than another protein. (See **Appendix 5–E,** Amino Acid Sequence of Ferredoxin, page 694.) A most important difference between proteins is the order or sequence in which the amino acids are arranged within the protein molecule. The amino acid sequence of a protein that has a certain function in one species will resemble closely the amino acid sequence of a protein that has the same function in another species. The closer different species are related to each other the fewer will be the differences between their amino acid sequences. The example in **Appendix 5–F,** Similarities in the Amino Acid Sequence of Cytochrome $c$ from Horse, Human, Pig, Rabbit, Chicken, and Tuna, page 694, illustrates the similarities in the amino acid composition of a protein that functions in the respiration of all these six animals.

What are the amino acids made of? All amino acids contain carbon, hydrogen, oxygen, and nitrogen atoms. The basic structure of an amino acid includes a central carbon atom (C) to which are attached a hydrogen atom (H), an amino group ($-NH_2$), an acid group ($-COOH$), and one of a variety of atoms or groups of atoms symbolized by R. Figure 5–14 illustrates the general structural formula of amino acids and gives the structural formulas of two of them. Observe that in the

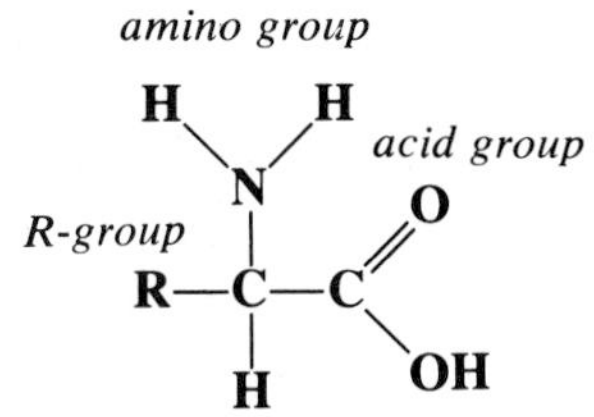

*amino group*

H      H

N

*acid group*

*R-group*        O

R—C—C

H        OH

*general formula*

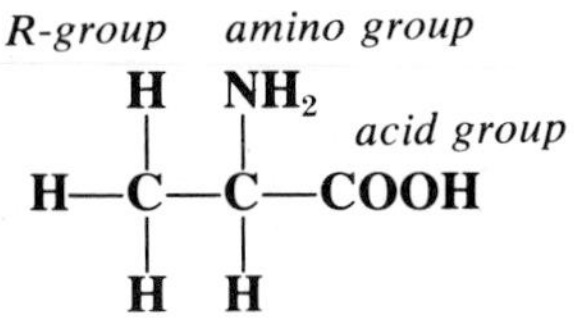

*R-group*     *amino group*

H    NH$_2$

*acid group*

H—C—C—COOH

H    H

*alanine*

*amino group*

NH$_2$

*R-group*         *acid group*

H—C—COOH

H

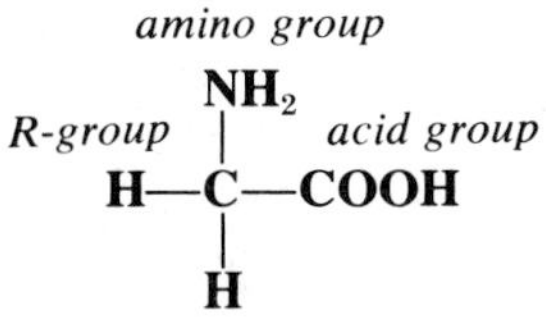

*glycine*

**Figure 5–14** Amino acids (except for proline) have a central carbon atom bonded to a hydrogen atom, an amino group, an acid group, and an R-group.

amino acid alanine (AL-a-neen) R is a CH$_3$ group and in glycine (GLY-seen) R is an H atom.

A protein is an example of a large and complex molecule that is built up from simpler organic compounds, in this case the amino acids. Any two molecules of amino acid may combine by forming a bond between the amino group of one and the acid group of the other. This bond, called a **peptide bond,** forms by a process in which a single molecule of water is removed. The formation

of a peptide bond is described in **Appendix 5–G,** Formation of a Peptide Bond, page 695.

When two amino acid molecules form a peptide bond, the new larger molecule still has an amino group at one end and an acid group at the other. (See **Appendix 5–G.**) Other amino acid molecules may then join the new molecule by forming peptide bonds with it. Such a chain of amino acids is called a **polypeptide.** Additional amino acid molecules may be attached until perhaps thousands are linked into a protein molecule.

A particular protein is distinguished from all other proteins by the number and the order in which its different amino acids are combined. It has been estimated that an animal cell may contain about 2000 different kinds of proteins. Some of these proteins are found only in one species.

How did amino acids combine to form the first proteins? In all living cells amino acids are combined by peptide bonds in several steps. Each step is controlled by a regulator that is itself a protein. This process requires energy. How could proteins have been made before there were living things to produce them?

To solve this puzzle, scientists have tried to invent ways to link amino acids together into proteinlike molecules without using existing proteins. One method was demonstrated by Sidney Fox of Florida State University, who heated a dry mixture of amino acids to temperatures above the boiling point of water. The water given off during the formation of the peptide bond evaporated. When the mass was cool, Fox found many amino acids bonded together into more complex molecules with certain properties of proteins.

The experiments of Fox do not prove that heat joined single amino acids into proteins under Earth's primitive conditions. However, they do provide more support for the heterotroph hypothesis, by showing how complex molecules could be formed from simple organic compounds without the aid of living organisms.

# Biology Brief

## Stones from the Sky

On December 17, 1807, a fireball with a luminous tail suddenly appeared in the sky over Weston, Connecticut. With a loud roar that sounded like cannon fire to those nearby, the fireball rapidly approached Earth. Those who witnessed the event included two professors who saw the fireball suddenly vanish, followed by the fall of a rock that hit Earth.

The event was so unusual that Thomas Jefferson, then President of the United States, is reported to have said, "I could more easily believe that two Yankee professors would lie than that stones would fall from heaven." Even earlier, the French Academy of Sciences in Paris had issued a memorandum stating that the "falling of stones from the sky is physically impossible" and that what witnesses saw were ordinary terrestrial rocks that had been struck by lightning.

Stones from the sky are now called meteorites. The Weston meteorite was probably the last meteorite to be judged so skeptically. Except for rocks from the moon, meteorites are the only fragments from elsewhere in our solar system that have reached Earth. If life or conditions favorable to life exist beyond Earth, meteorites might provide the evidence. The important question was whether meteorites contained organic compounds, without which life could not exist.

Evidence for organic compounds in meteorites has been reported for almost a century by a number of scientists. But doubts remained. Most of the meteorites examined have been on Earth a long time and might have become contaminated by terrestrial substances. For example, amino acids have been found in meteorites but in a pattern that was similar to traces of amino acids in human fingerprints. Had not the amino acids come from handling the samples?

The meteorite that fell near Murchison, Australia, on September 25, 1969, gave at last a positive answer to the question: Are organic compounds formed beyond Earth? The meteorite is shown above about actual size, and also on the desk of Dr. Cyril Ponnamperuma, who headed the successful research team.

**CAPSULE SUMMARY**

It has been assumed that the chemical bonds of molecules of simple gases in the early atmosphere might have been broken and that the atoms might have recombined into carbon-containing molecules such as those of amino acids. In turn, these molecules may have formed peptide bonds with other amino acids to produce proteins as a start toward the long, slow evolution of life itself.

**SELF CHECK**

1. What sources of energy might have brought about the changes in the chemical bonds of gas molecules in Earth's early atmosphere?
2. Name some organic compounds.
3. Describe the structure of an amino acid.
4. How can amino acid molecules become linked together to form proteins?
5. In what way are the results of the experiments carried on by Miller and Fox similar?
6. If these experiments did not prove the heterotroph hypothesis, of what value were they?

# Emergence of Life in Ancient Waters

## 5-15

### From Clusters of Organic Compounds to Primitive Cells

Important as amino acids and proteins are, other complex carbon compounds also must have been formed under Earth's primitive conditions to make life possible. The first structure to resemble a primitive cell must have been even simpler than the most elementary bacterial cell in existence today. These primitive cells must have been able to reproduce and grow. However, if they were to reproduce themselves, they needed special organic compounds to control reproduction. (You will learn about these in Chapter 9.)

The heterotroph hypothesis assumes that the organic compounds needed for reproduction were also formed by nonbiological reactions. They, along with other complex compounds, were probably washed down by rain into lakes, rivers, and oceans. The ancient waters of primitive Earth thus formed a "thin soup" or nutrient broth of all the compounds needed for the first primitive cell. Without living organisms to use them, these organic compounds could have accumulated in the waters. The best place for these compounds to accumulate was not in the vast oceans, but in smaller lakes and ponds and even in mud flats. Particles of mud and clay, and cooler temperatures, might have served to concentrate the various types of molecules. For this reason, some scientists think that life first appeared in tidal flats or mud flats on the edges of oceans, or even in smaller bodies of water than the oceans.

As time went by, some amino acids in the nutrient broth formed polypeptides and proteins. Other simple organic molecules also formed larger, more complex molecules. Eventually, some of the large molecules combined into clusters and the clusters merged to form a primitive cell.

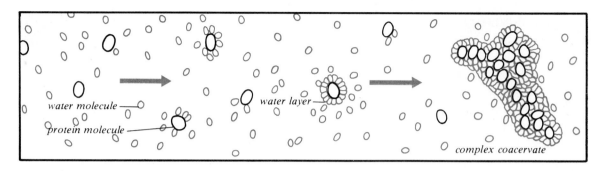

*water molecule* —
*protein molecule* —
*water layer* —
*complex coacervate*

**Figure 5–15** This drawing shows how a complex coacervate is formed when a water layer surrounds a cluster of protein molecules.

This is a far-reaching assumption. The formation of primitive cells from clusters of organic compounds is more difficult to explain than the formation of the organic compounds themselves under Earth's primitive conditions. The assumption is that at first, large organic compounds in the nutrient broth were grouped together at random, forming many types of aggregates. These different types of aggregates may have competed with each other for the organic molecules in the broth that were needed for growth and reproduction. In this competition, some aggregates had a composition and an organization that made them more successful than other aggregates. Eventually, natural selection crowded out the less successful ones.

Oparin proposed a model for a pre-cell—droplets of a type called **coacervates** (koh-AS-er-vayts). The name is derived from a Latin word meaning "heaped," or "clustered." Coacervates are clusters of proteins or of proteinlike substances held together in small droplets within a surrounding liquid. When proteins are dissolved in water, part of the protein molecules gain an electric charge. The electrically charged protein molecules attract molecules of water, so that an organized layer of water molecules forms around a large protein molecule. A *complex coacervate* is produced from a cluster of protein molecules surrounded by a water layer (Figure 5–15).

Fox has suggested another model for a precell—**microspheres.** Microspheres are cooling droplets from a hot water solution of polypeptides. Each microsphere forms its own double-layered boundary as it cools. Certain other cell-like features also develop.

The ancestors of primitive cells could easily have been of several kinds. Different kinds, with different capabilities, may have come together. In this way some of the features may have developed that are seen today in the simplest heterotrophic bacteria. The cell ancestors formed a membrane that separated them from their external world. They began to grow by using compounds in the surrounding environment for spare parts and energy. They evolved a process of reproduction, producing others like themselves.

**Try Investigation 5–C** Coacervate Formation, page 593.

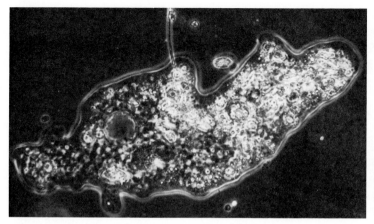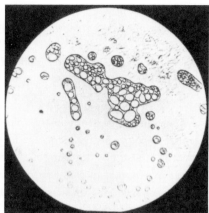

**Figure 5–16** A living *Amoeba* (left) is much more complex than a coacervate droplet (right), which is not alive. Yet the two look very similar.

## 5–16

### What Is Life?

A biologist is embarrassed when asked to give a simple definition of life. Of course, it is easy to say that a cow is living and a stone is nonliving. She or he can also say that an *Amoeba* is living and a coacervate is not. (See Figure 5–16.) However, when the biologist tries to set up an exact classification system for living versus nonliving things, trouble results.

You may recall from Chapter 1 that certain characteristics of organisms are shown by nonliving things. If a salt crystal is added to a concentrated salt solution, it will grow and start the formation of other crystals. There is a difference, however, between this kind of growth and that of organisms. The salt crystal can grow only by taking material of the same composition from the environment. Primitive cells proposed by the heterotroph hypothesis may also have grown by first taking materials like their own from the environment. But the environment eventually became depleted of these materials. Today organisms can

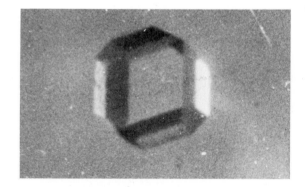

**Figure 5–17** This single crystal of polio virus, magnified 600 times, appears hollow because the crystal is transparent. This crystal contains about 200 million viruses.

take and use materials from the environment that differ significantly from themselves. They show few superficial resemblances to crystal growths.

Viruses provide a biological puzzle in this connection. Like salt, some viruses can be crystallized (Figure 5–17) and even stored. Yet when placed inside a living cell they can take over the cell and cause it to destroy itself, reproducing more viruses. Outside a cell, viruses are inactive—they cannot take in and use materials from the nonliving environment. Are viruses alive? The following is what N. W. Pirie, a British biochemist, has said about the problem:

> . . . systems are being discovered and studied which are neither obviously living nor obviously dead, and it is necessary to define these words or else give up using them and coin others. When one is asked whether a . . . virus is living or dead the only sensible answer is, 'I don't know; we know a number of things it will do and a number of things it won't and if some commission will define the word "living" I will try to see how the virus fits into the definition.' This answer does not as a rule satisfy the questioner, who generally has strong but unformulated opinions about . . . the words 'living' and 'dead'.[1]

This statement probably makes a good description of the situation in which biologists find themselves. There is no commission to decide on a definition of life. At present, there is no way to decide how complex a system must be before one would call it living. The difference between a cow and a stone is obvious. The difference between the simplest living organism and the most complicated nonliving system is not so obvious.

**CAPSULE SUMMARY**

A "nutrient broth" may have resulted from the accumulation of organic compounds in Earth's ancient waters. As time went by, the simpler molecules in the broth formed more complex molecules and then the complex molecules formed a primitive cell. The primitive cell absorbed compounds needed for growth and reproduction from the surrounding soup. Eventually, the primitive cell increased in complexity to resemble a heterotroph cell. Biologists have always found it very difficult to define the term "life." This difficulty is explained by the assumption that only a fine line separates the most complex cluster of molecules from the simplest organism.

**SELF CHECK**
1. Describe how scientists think primitive cells might have formed.
2. Where could primitive cells have found the energy they would need?
3. What is a coacervate? a microsphere?
4. Why is it so difficult to draw a line between life and nonlife?
5. Would you conclude from the heterotroph hypothesis that it is difficult to distinguish between life and nonlife? Why?

## CHAPTER SUMMARY

### HIGHLIGHTS

Spontaneous generation, a common belief for 22 centuries, did not prove to be a plausible explanation for how new life comes about. Darwin's theory of evolution, however, has led to many predictions of what the first life was like. Based on these predictions, scientists turned to studying the evolution of Earth itself.

Scientists now think Earth is about 4.7 billion years old and that its early atmosphere was probably made of gases that escaped from the planet's interior through volcanoes and hot springs. These gases included little or no free oxygen, but did include water vapor, carbon dioxide, carbon monoxide, nitrogen, and hydrogen. The first reactions may have produced methane and ammonia. The heterotroph hypothesis assumes that the bonds between these molecules of gases were broken by ultraviolet light and other less abundant forms of energy in the early atmosphere. The atoms recombined to form simple organic compounds such as amino acids. These compounds were washed down by rains into rivers, lakes, and oceans.

Some of the small carbon molecules in the ancient waters began to form more complex molecules. Later some of the complex molecules combined to form clusters of complex molecules. These clusters then grew in size by taking in other molecules from the surroundings. Dividing clusters "reproduced." A number of such different clusters might have arisen, resulting in competition for useful carbon compounds. Some clusters that had a composition and organization better adapted to the environment grew at the expense of others and became the ancestors of living cells.

## REVIEWING IDEAS

1. What does "spontaneous generation of life" mean?
2. According to fossil evidence, how long ago did life exist on Earth?
3. What do the oldest known fossils reveal about early life on Earth?
4. Distinguish between elements and compounds.
5. What is an isotope? a radioactive isotope?
6. Describe two types of chemical bonds.
7. How does an ion differ from the atom from which it formed?
8. If there was no free oxygen in the early atmosphere of Earth, what is the source of the oxygen in today's atmosphere?
9. Why do many biologists think heterotrophs evolved before autotrophs?
10. Why are biologists interested in structures or droplets such as coacervates and microspheres?

## USING CONCEPTS

11. If more species have evolved from fewer pre-existing ones, as Darwin believed, then why are there fewer species of reptiles today than during their "golden age"?
12. Why would events on Earth of long ago have proceeded differently if the early atmosphere had been rich in oxygen?
13. What is meant by the statement that evolution is a remodeler, not an architect?
14. Distinguish between amino acids and peptides; between peptides and polypeptides.
15. Explain how Miller's experiment supported but did not prove the heterotroph hypothesis.
16. In what ways would an autotroph hypothesis for the first organisms on Earth appear to be more suitable than the heterotroph hypothesis? less suitable?
17. How does the atomic theory explain isotopes? Try to name three ways in which all isotopes of an element are alike.
18. What part, or parts, of an atom are involved in forming chemical bonds? in tracing radioisotopes through organisms?

## RECOMMENDED READING

Deamer, D. W. and P. B. Armstrong. "The Edge of Life." *Natural History,* February 1983. An easy-to-read article on microspheres (page 108).

Dickerson, R. E. "Chemical Evolution and the Origin of Life." *Scientific American,* September 1978. An article on how life may have originated in an atmosphere rich in hydrogen compounds.

## REFERENCE

1. N. W. Pirie, "The Meaninglessness of the Terms Life and Living," in *Perspectives in Biochemistry,* ed. Joseph Needham and David E. Green. New York, Cambridge University Press, 1937, p. 12.

# Chemical
# Energy
# for Life
# 6

According to the heterotroph hypothesis, the early evolving cells gradually began to resemble some of the unicellular heterotrophs that still exist today. A boundary, or membrane, separated them from their watery environment. Some organic molecules from the surrounding nutrient broth could pass through the membrane. These molecules supplied the energy and building materials needed by cells to maintain their structure and to grow. In this chapter you will see how organic molecules supply energy to cells living without oxygen, like the first heterotrophs living under Earth's primitive conditions. A great advance of science in the last 50 years was the discovery that some of the chemical mechanisms by which primitive cells obtained energy from foodstuffs are still used by living cells today, including those of you and other humans.

# Cells and Energy

## 6–1

### Cell Organization Requires Energy

There was one basic way in which the molecules in the primitive one-celled heterotrophs resembled the molecules in living cells today. They were no longer freely floating in the surrounding water but were contained within a restricted space and surrounded by a boundary, a plasma membrane. This arrangement requires organization, and organization requires energy.

If you have a room of your own at home, you already know a great deal about organization and energy. A room has a tendency toward disorderliness, it would seem. When you take off your clothes, they do not put themselves into the right place in the closet. Beds do not make themselves. Dust may accumulate. Games, books, and hobby tools may get scattered around the room, on the floor, under the bed, and so on. When the state of disorderliness reaches a certain level, a firm parental voice may command: ''Clean up your room!'' You know how much energy you can spend just getting your room back in order or in keeping it that way. You have to use energy to organize the unorganized parts of your room.

An orderly system of any kind is attained only by the use of energy. Every living organism is a system of molecules organized in precise patterns. The more organization a system has, the more energy has been put into it. Living cells are organizations of molecules. Energy is required to keep them ''in order,'' to allow them to grow and form new cells.

---

← The first energy-releasing life processes probably arose somewhere in ancient oceans.

**Figure 6−1** The arrangement of crystals in a granite rock (left) shows less organization than the highly ordered structure of skeletal muscle (right) in higher animals. Both views are magnified.

One major property of life is its high degree of organization when compared to inanimate objects. Figure 6−1 compares the relatively unordered structure of a nonliving substance with the highly organized structure of living things. In general, the more advanced a form of life is, the more highly organized it has become. You are an example of an extremely complex, highly organized system of molecules.

A living cell needs a controllable and constant source of energy for (1) making large, complex molecules; (2) organizing these molecules into structural patterns; (3) maintaining their organization; and (4) reproducing the same organization for a new generation. What was the source of energy at the beginning of life? Lightning and the ultraviolet radiation of the sun both carry large amounts of energy. But such large amounts of energy

would have been uncontrolled. They would be more likely to break up and destroy the early cells than to increase their organization. For living cells to exist, a more constant and more gentle source of energy must have been available.

Biologists assume that during the millions of years before life appeared, large numbers of organic molecules collected in the ancient waters. These molecules were probably formed over great periods of time by an input of energy. That energy was mainly from the sun's ultraviolet radiation and also possibly from lightning or heat. What became of this energy? Some of it was changed into chemical energy and stored in the chemical bonds that held together the atoms in the organic molecules. The organic molecules in the ancient waters became a tremendous storehouse of energy in the form of chemical energy.

## 6-2

# Organic Compounds Are Used as Energy Sources

What organic compounds supplied energy to the early cells? No one knows for sure, but very likely they were similar to the organic compounds that supply energy to living cells today. The most important sources of energy for living things are the **carbohydrates** (*carbo,* carbon; *hydrate,* water). They are found in all living cells. In addition to carbon atoms, they contain atoms of hydrogen and oxygen in the same ratio as in water (two to one). The simple carbohydrates are called sugars. The most important sugar, glucose, is readily used by most organisms as a source of energy. Glucose is sometimes known as dextrose, or grape sugar. It is the sugar carried in the human bloodstream to all the cells of the body. Glucose contains six carbon atoms. Figure 6–2 shows two structural formulas representing two forms of glucose in solution. The ring form, in which five carbon atoms and an oxygen atom form a closed ring, is the most abundant. A small amount of glucose in solution exists in the straight, or open chain, form.

Other simple sugars may contain three, four, five, or more carbon atoms. The most familiar sugar is sucrose. It is also known as cane or beet sugar. Sucrose is a double sugar, made up of one molecule of glucose and one molecule of another six-carbon sugar, fructose or fruit sugar, found in ripe fruits and in honey.

Simple sugars bond together to build complex carbohydrates, just as amino acids bond together to build proteins. The complex carbohydrates that are most commonly formed by plants are starch and cellulose. Starch is the main energy-storage reserve for most plants, as in potatoes, wheat, and rice, which are very important energy sources for people. Cellulose is an important part of wood and cotton fibers. It is the most abundant carbo-

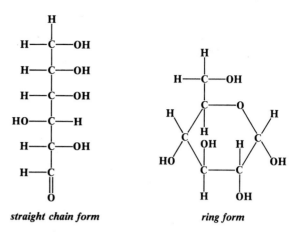

*straight chain form*          *ring form*

**Figure 6–2** Glucose, a six-carbon sugar, can exist in two forms: a straight chain and a ring form.

hydrate in nature. The human liver and muscles store carbohydrates in the form of **glycogen** (GLY-ko-jen). Glycogen is also known as animal starch. Starch, cellulose, and glycogen are each made up of glucose units. These complex carbohydrates have no fixed size. They may contain up to 10,000 glucose units.

Another important source of energy for life is fats. Like carbohydrates and proteins, fats are also made up of simpler units, glycerol (GLIS-uh-rawl) and fatty acids. (See **Appendix 6–A,** Chemical Nature of Fats, page 696.) If there is a shortage of carbohydrates and fats, cells can obtain energy from the amino acids of proteins, but these are used more often for building new cell protein.

Cells have evolved special mechanisms for releasing and using the chemical energy stored in carbohydrates, fats, and other organic molecules. This energy can be used to bring about combinations of other molecules; for example, to bind amino acids together into proteins. Some organic molecules thus provide energy, and others provide the building material for new molecules. By this means, larger and more complicated molecules are continuously being formed by living cells.

# Biology Brief

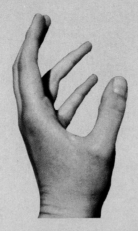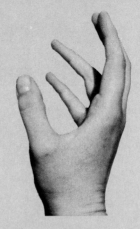

## Right-Handed and Left-Handed Molecules

Do you have polarized sunglasses? They admit only light traveling in a single plane. The light is no longer scattered, causing glare. It is called polarized light, or plane-polarized light.

When this light passes through organic compounds its plane is usually turned or rotated toward the right or toward the left. A century ago the French chemist Louis Pasteur (1822–1895) began studying this strange effect.

Pasteur found that a common acid contributing to the sharp taste of fruits, tartaric acid, rotated polarized light to the right. But another form, paratartaric acid, had no effect on the light. Under the microscope the latter showed a mixture of two different crystal forms.

An exciting thought occurred. Was one of the two crystal forms identical to the tartaric acid of most fruits? If so, it would turn polarized light to the right. Pasteur separated the two forms and tested them in water solutions. One turned the light to the right, the other to the left. In a mixture they had no effect on the polarized light.

## 6–3

### Energy Can Be Released from Chemical Bonds

The energy stored in the chemical bonds of organic molecules cannot be released unless the bonds are changed in some way. In any chemical reaction, substances interact with one another, bonds are broken, and new bonds are formed. The products of the reaction contain the same number and the same kinds of atoms as the original substances, but the atoms are bonded together in new ways.

The new chemical bonds will have either more energy or less energy than the old bonds. If the new bonds have more energy, then energy has been added from the environment. By contrast, if the new bonds have less energy than the old bonds, some energy has been released to the environment

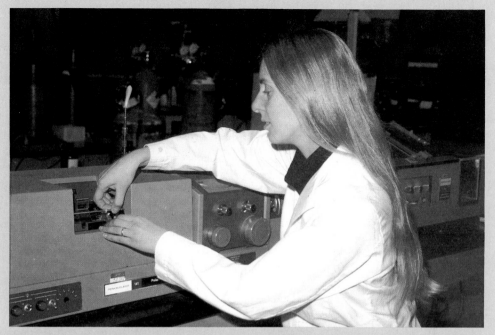

Right- and left-handed molecules and mixtures! Pasteur ran out into the hall and exclaimed to a fellow scientist, "I have just made a great discovery. I am so happy I am shaking all over and cannot keep my eyes on the apparatus."

Why all the fuss? Dr. Mary Ann Caolo, pictured above, can tell you what Pasteur's discovery has meant. Scientists have learned that living things usually make organic compounds of L (left-handed or left-rotating) form, or of D (right-handed) form—but not both. Tartaric acid is D. On the other hand, amino acids made by living things are L. (Glycine, the only exception, is neither right- nor left-handed.) Dr. Caolo can test amino acids and determine their form. The L-amino acids made by living things change only slowly to mixed form.

Do you remember the Murchison meteorite (page 106)? The amino acids found in it were of mixed form, D and L. Two were unknown in *either* form in life on Earth. Why were scientists so excited?

during the reaction. An example of energy release is the explosive reaction of hydrogen and oxygen to form water. In this reaction both heat and light energy are released.

Chemists have worked out a mental picture, or hypothesis, of how chemical reactions take place. This hypothesis, described briefly in the next few paragraphs, attempts to take into account the facts known about chemical reactions.

Chemical reactions happen when molecules collide. The energy needed to produce a collision powerful enough to bring about a chemical reaction is called **activation energy.** An outside source of activation energy is often necessary to get many reactions started. For example, molecules of hydrogen and oxygen gas can exist together without reacting until energy is added by a lighted match or a spark. The added energy will cause the molecules of hydrogen and oxygen to react with each other and form molecules of water. The chemical bonds in the newly formed water molecules have less energy than the old bonds in the hydrogen and oxygen molecules. Therefore, energy will be released. Some of the released energy will serve as activation energy for more molecules of hydrogen and oxygen to react with each other. In this way, the reaction will continue as long as there is a supply of free hydrogen and oxygen molecules. Once the reaction of hydrogen and oxygen is started, it gives off enough activation energy to supply the other molecules and keep the reaction going.

Heating a mixture of substances usually provides activation energy and increases the rate of chemical reaction. But a high temperature would not be a good way for a cell to obtain activation energy. Too much heat would harm a cell. Cooking demonstrates this; it destroys any cells still alive. There is one way to increase the rate of reactions, however, that is not harmful. When certain chemicals, called **catalysts** (CAT-uh-lists), are present, molecules can interact without the need for extra heat. This means that catalysts act to lower the amount of activation energy needed. Think of the energy of activation as a mountain which molecules must climb before they can interact. The catalyst opens a pass around or through the mountain and thereby makes it easier for the reaction to proceed. Catalysts might, for example, attract one or both of the reacting molecules and hold them in place close enough to react. Thus the contact necessary for reaction is more likely. In this way catalysts speed up slow reactions at moderate temperatures. Catalysts affect the rate of a reaction and become involved in it, but they are not permanently changed by it. Because catalysts are not consumed in the reaction, they can be used over and over again.

Many proteins show this activity as catalysts. Their use by early, evolving cells probably was crucial to life. These proteins help living cells carry out a multitude of chemical reactions at mild temperatures favorable to life. Otherwise, these reactions would occur only at high temperatures that are harmful to life.

**Try Investigation 6–A** What Do Cells Contain to Promote the Chemical Activity of Life Processes?, page 594.

---

**CAPSULE SUMMARY**

For the evolving cell, energy was essential to make complex molecules, organize them into patterns, and maintain the patterns. Direct use of the energy from the sun's ultraviolet radiation and from lightning would have harmed the primitive cells. However, when this energy was converted into chemical energy, stored in the bonds of organic molecules, it became available to living cells through chemical reactions.

By lowering the activation energy needed for chemical reactions, catalysts allow the reactions to proceed at moderate temperatures. Catalysts probably became part of living cells very early in their evolution.

**SELF CHECK**

1. Under what conditions does the environment receive energy from a chemical reaction?
2. Under what conditions does the environment give energy to a chemical reaction?
3. What is activation energy?
4. What are catalysts? What are their unusual properties?
5. Discuss two ways in which the rate of a chemical reaction can be increased.
6. Why does the heterotroph hypothesis assume that an evolving cell would need a constant and controllable source of energy?

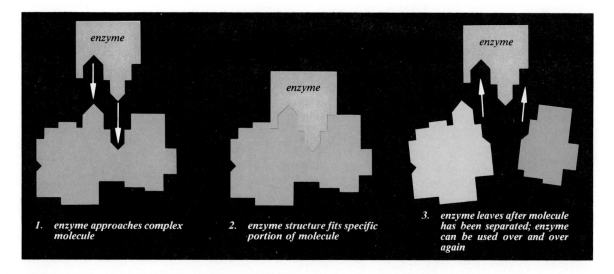

1. *enzyme approaches complex molecule*
2. *enzyme structure fits specific portion of molecule*
3. *enzyme leaves after molecule has been separated; enzyme can be used over and over again*

**Figure 6–3** An enzyme can break a chemical bond and split one complex molecule into two smaller ones. The enzyme takes part in the reaction but is only temporarily changed. It emerges again in its original form.

# Energy Release Without Oxygen

## 6–4

## Catalysts Are Found in Living Organisms

Most chemical reactions in organisms living today take place within a fairly narrow range of temperatures. These temperatures are not high enough to supply the activation energy needed to start most reactions. Biologists have found that nearly all the chemical reactions of living things take place with the help of catalysts.

A number of substances, including water, can act as catalysts to increase the rate of chemical reactions. Recent studies have shown, however, that almost all chemical reactions that take place in living organisms are catalyzed by a wide variety of

protein molecules. Protein molecules that are catalysts are called **enzymes.** Often the protein molecule is joined to a nonprotein part. But the major part of most enzymes is a protein.

Living organisms have many different kinds of enzymes. The nonprotein parts of many enzymes are formed from minerals, such as iron, and from vitamins, especially the B vitamins. Such enzymes that use a vitamin or mineral cannot function without it. This helps explain why minerals and vitamins are so necessary in your diet.

An important biological discovery was made when it was found that enzymes can continue to function outside an organism. It is often difficult to be sure that a specific chemical reaction actually

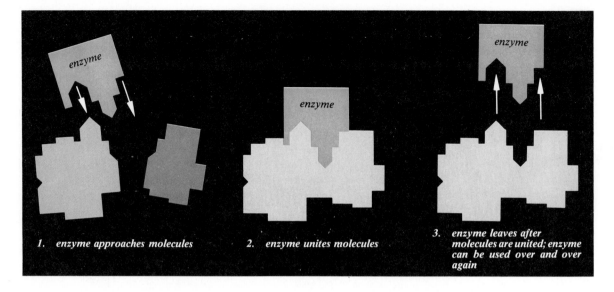

1. *enzyme approaches molecules*

2. *enzyme unites molecules*

3. *enzyme leaves after molecules are united; enzyme can be used over and over again*

**Figure 6–4** The enzyme from Figure 6–3, or possibly a different enzyme, may have an opposite role. It may catalyze a reaction that forms a chemical bond between the two smaller molecules to build the more complex molecule. Again, the enzyme emerges from the reaction in its original form.

takes place within an organism. It is much simpler to study the reaction if an enzyme and the raw materials can be put together in a test tube (in vitro). In this way, the reaction can be studied without all the other chemical reactions that normally go on at the same time in a cell.

For example, hydrogen peroxide is a poisonous by-product of reactions in cells. An enzyme, **catalase** (CAT-uh-lays), must break it down quickly into harmless substances. In the laboratory, you can investigate this reaction in vitro.

The reaction catalyzed by an enzyme depends on the molecular structure and shape of a small area of the enzyme called the **active site.** The active site can attract and hold only specific molecules. An enzyme and the molecules on which it acts—the **substrates** (SUB-strayts)—may fit together like a lock and key. Sometimes the enzyme changes shape slightly when it interacts with the substrate, much as a glove assumes the shape

of a hand. Each enzyme can catalyze only one or a few chemical reactions because only a few molecules are sufficiently alike in structure and shape to fit the active site.

To act as a catalyst, an enzyme must temporarily take part in a chemical reaction. The reacting molecules combine with the active site of an enzyme, forming an **enzyme-substrate complex.** By bringing the reacting molecules together, the enzyme lowers the activation energy so that chemical changes can be completed rapidly. One of the characteristics of enzymes is that they greatly speed up reactions that otherwise would take place very slowly. Once the reactions are complete, the newly formed molecules break away, leaving the enzymes the same as they were before the reactions. (See Figure 6–3.)

A major characteristic of reactions catalyzed by enzymes is that they are often reversible. With the aid of enzymes, two reacting molecules may combine to form a single molecule, or the single molecule may separate into the two smaller molecules. The direction in which the reaction goes is influenced by the concentrations of the smaller and larger molecules in the cell. A different enzyme may catalyze each reaction. Alternatively, the same enzyme assisted by different coenzymes—other active compounds in cell reactions—may catalyze both reactions (Figures 6-3 and 6-4).

Two aspects of enzyme activity are very important to cells. Enzyme reactions are faster at higher temperatures but only within a narrow temperature range. Above certain temperatures, the enzymes themselves break down, as do all proteins. Enzyme activity also varies with the acidity of the solution. Thus the temperature and the degree of acidity (*p*H) must be at the right level for enzymes to act effectively.

## 6–5

## All Cells Can Use the Chemical Energy of ATP

Although enzymes lower the activation energy, many chemical reactions in living cells still need an input of additional energy. How is this energy quickly supplied? Cells build several kinds of molecules that have groups of atoms attached, which hold available energy in their bonds. One of these kinds of molecules is the cell's main standby energy source. It is named **adenosine triphosphate** (uh-DEE-no-seen tri-FOS-fate), **ATP** for short. (See Figure 6–5.)

ATP has been called the energy currency of living cells. To see why ATP has been compared to money in this way, imagine foreign tourists arriving in New York without any American money but with only the different kinds of money used in their own countries. It would be difficult for them to pay for a dinner, a newspaper, or a theater ticket in New York with their different kinds of money.

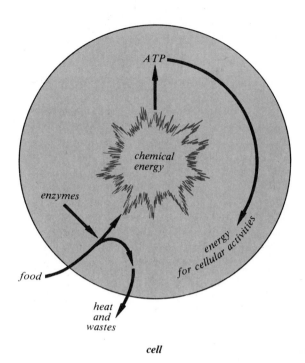

**Figure 6–5** The cell breaks down food and complex molecules to provide energy. The energy is stored in ATP molecules.

Now suppose that the tourists change their foreign money into the local currency of dollars and cents. All these purchases now become simple and easy. In a similar manner a cell changes the chemical energy of different organic compounds to the chemical energy carried by the molecules of ATP. Not all, but most of the energy "bills" inside a cell are then "paid" by ATP.

How do molecules of ATP carry energy in living cells? Note the structure of an ATP molecule in Figure 6–6. **Appendix 6– B,** Structural Formulas for Adenosine Triphosphate (ATP), Adenosine Diphosphate (ADP), and Adenosine Monophosphate (AMP), page 697, gives the chemical formula of ATP.

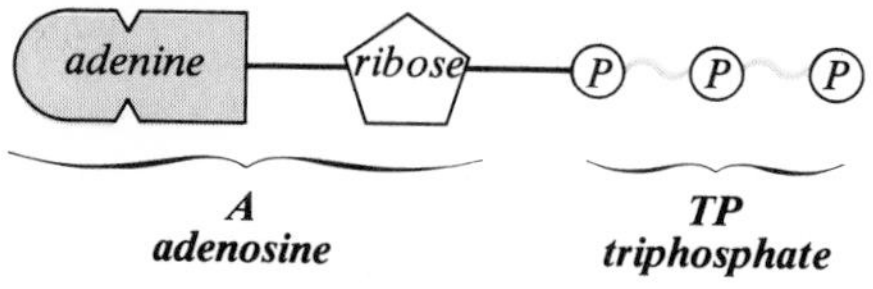

**Figure 6-6** Adenosine triphosphate (ATP) is named for the substances that compose it: adenosine and three phosphate groups.

*adenine*

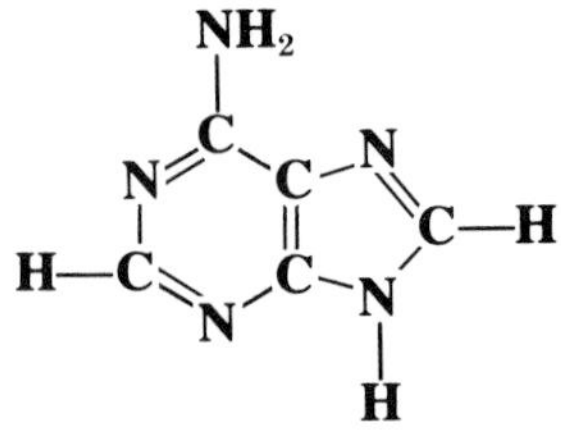

**Figure 6-7** The structure of adenine. Adenine and a five-carbon sugar, ribose, make up adenosine, part of ATP.

ATP consists of two organic compounds joined to a chain of three phosphate groups. Those compounds are the nitrogen-containing adenine (AD-eh-neen) (Figure 6–7) and a five-carbon sugar called ribose (RY-bohs). A phosphate group has one atom of phosphorus, one of hydrogen, and three of oxygen. Most of the energy of the ATP molecules is in the bonds of the two phosphate groups at the end. When an ATP molecule reacts with water, the bond between the second and third phosphate groups is broken. Energy is released that can be measured as heat energy. This bond is called an energy-rich phosphate bond. ATP has one more energy-rich phosphate bond between the first and second phosphate groups. (Notice that the two energy-rich phosphate bonds in ATP are marked by squiggles $\sim$ in Figure 6–6.)

In living cells, only *some* energy in the two energy-rich bonds of ATP is lost as heat. The rest is used to do cellular work. For example, ATP may transfer its end phosphate group to another molecule. With the phosphate group also goes some of the energy that had been held in the high-energy phosphate bond. The molecule that accepts the phosphate group from ATP gains energy and becomes activated. It can now react with other molecules in the cell. In this way the energy of ATP is used to supply activation energy. It is also used to "drive" energy-requiring reactions that bring about growth and reproduction of the cell.

There is usually very little ATP in cells. ATP is continually being used up and remade. When a molecule of ATP gives up one energy-rich phosphate group, it becomes adenosine diphosphate, abbreviated as ADP. When ATP gives up both of its energy-rich phosphate groups, it becomes adenosine monophosphate, abbreviated as AMP. (The formulas of ADP and AMP are also shown in **Appendix 6–B.**) To form a molecule of ATP again, ADP must combine with one phosphate group and AMP must combine with two phosphate groups. The linking of phosphate groups with ADP or AMP uses energy that is supplied by the breakdown of organic compounds within the cell. For example, the energy released by the breakdown of a molecule of glucose is saved by being used at once to form energy-rich phosphate bonds between ADP and phosphate. ATP thus acts as an energy carrier, a go-between for those reactions in the cell that release energy and those reactions that consume energy.

Could ATP or a similar molecule have been available to primitive heterotrophs? Recent laboratory experiments seem to show that energy-rich phosphate bonds could have been formed under Earth's primitive conditions before life emerged. The adenine and ribose that make up ATP, as you saw in Figure 6–6, were produced in laboratory experiments similar to those of Miller (Chapter 5). Phosphates were present in Earth's crust and may have leached from there into the ancient waters.

To sum up, ATP is the principal energy carrier of all living cells today and was probably an energy carrier of the primitive heterotrophs. When a person walks, when a fish swims, when a bud opens into a flower, when a yeast cell divides, ATP is used. The use of ATP as an energy carrier in all living cells—from primitive heterotrophs to cells of humans—is strong evidence for the unity of all life on Earth.

In living things today the formation of new ATP molecules from ADP and phosphate is brought about through a series of energy-releasing reactions catalyzed by enzymes.

## 6–6

## Energy Carried by ATP Has Many Uses

The cell uses the chemical energy carried by ATP in many different ways. It has already been noted that chemical energy is needed to build large molecules from their simple subunits. For the construction of a molecule of protein, hundreds of amino acid molecules must be joined (see **Appendixes 5-F and 5-G**), and each amino acid molecule must first be activated by ATP. Energy is also used to carry substances into the cell and to arrange them inside the cell. Substances that the cell needs for growth are often present in small amounts outside the cell. Work is required to gather them together in the cell.

Energy is needed to move unwanted substances out of the cell. Harmful substances need to be pumped out, or excreted, by the cell. The energy of ATP is also used for mechanical work by living cells. Such mechanical work—for example, muscular activity—is easily observed in higher organisms. Even single cells move from place to place. During cell division they change shape and pull apart the cell contents. All this work is powered by energy carried by ATP.

## 6–7

## Life Without Oxygen: The Process of Fermentation

As you will learn in Chapter 8, the most effective process for ATP formation in living cells uses oxygen gas. But since we have assumed that the primitive atmosphere did not contain free oxygen gas, we must look for a process that forms ATP in cells without the help of oxygen. Such a process is **fermentation,** a series of reactions in which energy is released from the organic molecules of foodstuffs in the absence of oxygen.

Fermentation was used by people before recorded history. Tribes of nomads must have learned that under certain conditions milk would turn sour or would change to a solid or semisolid material—cheese. Part of these changes in milk resulted from fermentation by certain bacteria. For centuries people have also been fermenting fruit juices by means of yeast to produce alcoholic beverages. More recently, knowledge of the chemical details of fermentation has contributed to knowledge of life itself.

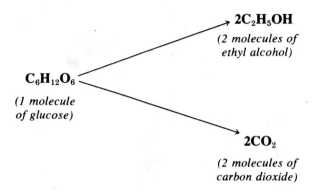

**Figure 6–8** In one of several different fermentation processes, alcohol and carbon dioxide are formed from glucose.

Near the end of the 18th century, knowledge of chemistry was just beginning to develop. At that time the French scientist Antoine Lavoisier (luh-vwah-ZYAY), a founder of modern chemistry, discovered that fermentation of glucose can produce carbon dioxide and alcohol. A little later, in 1810, another French chemist, Joseph Louis Gay-Lussac (GAY-lew-SAK), showed by a chemical equation the amounts of carbon dioxide and alcohol that are produced from glucose (Figure 6–8).

There were many heated debates in the 19th century about the relationship between chemical reactions and living organisms. Some scientists felt that fermentation was an activity of living things and therefore could not take place outside of living cells.

In the 1850s the French wine industry was having serious trouble with wine that had spoiled. The French emperor Napoleon III called in Louis Pasteur to help. Pasteur knew that the fermentation which produced wine was caused by living yeast. (See Figure 6–9.) But certain bacteria in the wine were also carrying on fermentation. Pasteur discovered that fermentation by bacteria spoils wine because it produces vinegar (acetic acid) instead of the alcohol produced by yeast. Pasteur suggested that the winemakers heat the wine for a short time to destroy the bacteria. They were horrified, but it worked. The process, pasteurization, is used today, especially for milk.

For many years there was lively discussion about the nature of fermentation. Pasteur defined fermentation as life without air. This definition held that fermentation was the way of life of microorganisms in **anaerobic** (an-ay-RO-bik) environments (environments where there was little or no oxygen gas). Only living cells, according to Pasteur, could carry on fermentation. In 1897, two years after Pasteur died, Eduard Buchner, a young German chemist, accidentally made a great discovery about fermentation. In order to preserve some juices that had been squeezed from yeast, Buchner added sugar to them. Using sugar as a preservative was well known in the preparation of jams and jellies. The yeast juices contained no living cells, but to Buchner's surprise the sugar began to ferment. Buchner decided that the juices must therefore contain an enzyme which caused fermentation to take place.

In further experiments Buchner found that within an hour after the sugar was added, the mixture started to produce bubbles of carbon dioxide. This activity could continue for days. These experiments showed that a yeast enzyme can catalyze a chemical reaction after the enzyme has been removed from the yeast cells.

Buchner thought that the yeast juice contained one enzyme that fermented sugar, giving alcohol and carbon dioxide. Today it is known that not just one, but many enzymes are involved. Buchner's discovery that enzymes produced by yeast can work after the yeast is killed had far-reaching results. Knowledge that enzymes could work outside of cells led to research that identified many enzymes and explained their function in living cells.

Today we know that yeast cells contain a dozen or more enzymes that are involved in fermentation. Each catalyzes a separate step in the process.

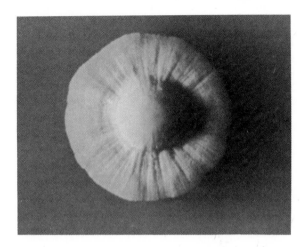

**Figure 6-9** A giant colony of brewer's yeast cells, 15 to 20 mm across, is shown growing on malt-extract gelatin (left). Pasteur's concerns for the quality of fermentation are still concerns of brewers today. Purification and studies of the yeast are part of the work of technologists like Sharon Moore (right) of the Research & Development Microbiology Department of a major brewer.

## 6-8

## Fermentation Is a Source of Energy

The special feature of fermentation is that it releases energy from organic molecules without using oxygen. There are different types of fermentation. The one we will discuss first is the fermentation by yeast cells of glucose into alcohol and carbon dioxide. A much-shortened diagram of the main reactions is shown in Figure 6-10. The process is outlined in detail in **Appendix 6-C,** Fermentation of Glucose to Ethyl Alcohol or Lactic Acid, page 699.

The process of fermentation is divided into two stages. (See Figure 6-10.) No ATP is produced in Stage I. In fact, ATP is consumed to supply the activation energy needed for the reactions in Stage II which produce ATP. When a phosphate group from ATP combines with glucose, the resulting compound gains activation energy that can be used to take part in enzyme-controlled reactions. Each

molecule of glucose eventually reacts with two molecules of ATP to form a six-carbon compound, with two phosphate groups, that splits in half. Each half is a three-carbon compound with one phosphate group.

Stage II of fermentation begins when a second phosphate group is added to each three-carbon compound. This time, however, phosphate comes from an inorganic phosphorus compound, not from ATP. In the reactions so far, the organism has gained no energy at all. In fact it has used two molecules of ATP. Beyond this point, however, reactions occur which provide the cell with energy.

In the next series of reactions each of the two "glucose halves" releases energy which is used to form new molecules of ATP. Two new molecules of ATP are formed from each "glucose half" by combining its two phosphate groups with two molecules of ADP. On giving up their phosphate groups the two "glucose halves" become converted to two molecules of pyruvic (pie-ROO-vik) acid. Pyruvic acid is then broken down to carbon

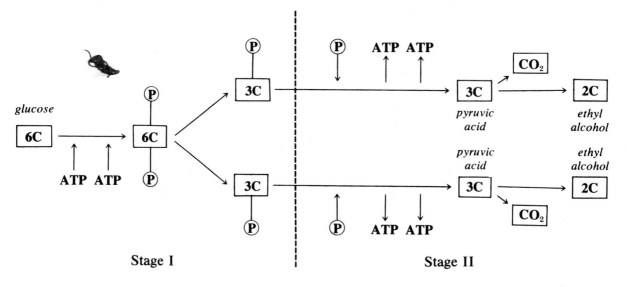

**Figure 6-10** In fermentation, two ATPs are used by the reactions that split glucose into two 3C compounds. Each 3C compound yields energy for two more ATPs. All steps are catalyzed by enzymes.

dioxide and alcohol, completing the process of fermentation.

Notice that each glucose molecule uses up two ATP molecules to start fermentation. Also notice that each glucose molecule produces four ATP molecules during fermentation (two for each "glucose half"). Thus for each glucose molecule there is a net gain of two ATP molecules. This means that in alcohol fermentation, energy is released. This energy is stored in the phosphate bonds of ATP. In addition, two molecules of alcohol and two molecules of carbon dioxide are produced.

The most important advantage of the sequence of changes in fermentation is that some of the chemical energy contained in the glucose molecule is made available to the cell as ATP. The amount of energy released is relatively small, but the energy in the ATP is easily used by the cell. When glucose is fermented by yeast, enough ATP is produced to keep the yeast alive and growing.

Fermentation of glucose or a process similar to it is carried on in all living organisms today, although in most organisms the release of energy does not stop there. Only one difference occurs between yeast cells and your own cells in the breakdown of glucose, at least to the point when pyruvic acid is formed. Yeast enzymes change pyruvic acid to carbon dioxide and alcohol. Certain bacterial enzymes change pyruvic acid to carbon dioxide and acetic acid instead. In other organisms enzymes change pyruvic acid to lactic acid (the acid in sour milk). You may be surprised to learn that during vigorous exercise, fermentation of glucose to lactic acid takes place in your muscle cells. (See **Appendix 6-C-II,** Fermentation of Glucose to Lactic Acid, page 699.)

Organic compounds other than glucose can be used as starting materials for fermentation. However, the basic process of fermentation is always the same. In every case the process is carried on without oxygen. It consists of a series of separate steps, each catalyzed by a different enzyme. The final result is that the organism gains energy for life and growth.

**CAPSULE SUMMARY**

Catalysts act to speed up chemical reactions. Enzymes are protein molecules that act as catalysts within living things. Chemical energy for the cell is available from ATP and certain other molecules. ATP acts as an energy carrier between reactions in the cell that release energy and those that consume energy.

Pasteur defined fermentation as life without oxygen. Starting with Buchner, scientists have analyzed all the reactions that take place during fermentation. Each reaction is catalyzed by a particular enzyme. Two ATP molecules are required to start the process of fermentation of glucose, and four ATP molecules are finally produced.

**SELF CHECK**

1. How was the discovery that enzymes can function outside of organisms important?
2. What did Pasteur contribute to the understanding of fermentation?
3. What are some of the products of different fermentation processes using glucose?
4. How does fermentation carried out by yeast cells differ from the process in other organisms? How is all fermentation similar?
5. How are enzymes like other catalysts?

# Transfer of Materials Across Cell Boundaries

## 6–9
## Cells Have a Membrane

So far you have learned that the primitive heterotroph cells probably obtained their nourishment from the organic compounds that surrounded them in the ancient waters. But before these compounds could be used they had to pass from the water into the cell. These compounds were of no use to the organisms if they remained outside, just as your food is of no use to you until it is taken into the body. How do organic compounds enter living cells? To answer this question you must first understand how molecules move from one place to another.

The molecules in a gas or in a liquid are in constant motion, moving in all directions. As you know, if a drop of perfume evaporates in one corner of a room, the scent will soon permeate the entire room. Similarly, if you place a lump of sugar in the bottom of a glass filled with water, all of the water in the glass will taste sweet after a while. Each of these cases is an example of **diffusion,** that is, a movement of molecules from an area of greater concentration into areas of lesser concentration. The moving molecules continually collide and in the end become uniformly distributed. In the above examples, each corner of the room gained the same fragrance and every drop of water in the glass became equally sweet.

Could diffusion explain the entrance of organic molecules into a cell? Recall that a cell has an outer boundary. This boundary is the plasma membrane. The membrane is made up primarily of fat and protein materials. Under the high magnification of an electron microscope, the width of the plasma membrane (Figure 6–11) can be measured. It is only about 10 nanometers.

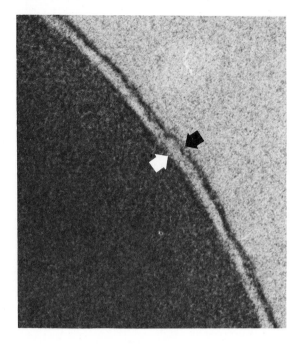

**Figure 6–11** Cross section of the plasma membrane of a human red blood cell, photographed through an electron microscope (× 300,000).

The presence of the plasma membrane limits the diffusion of molecules into and out of the cell. However, the limitation is not like that of the walls of a room limiting the diffusion of the perfume molecules. Recall that the plasma membrane is itself made of large molecules. Smaller molecules, like those of oxygen, carbon dioxide, and water, can diffuse freely between the molecules of the plasma membrane. Glucose, a six-carbon sugar, moves through more readily than sucrose, a larger, twelve-carbon sugar. However, the size of the molecule is not the only factor that determines entry. Compounds that dissolve in fats pass fairly readily through the membrane. Yet electrically charged particles, or ions, do not—even though many of them are very small. (See Section 5–11 for a review of ions.) The plasma membrane has a very high electrical resistance.

Experimental evidence shows that the plasma membrane's structure includes not only fats and proteins, but also carbohydrates. The fatty, or **lipid** (LIP-id), material forms the major portion of the membrane as two layers of lipid molecules. One of these molecules is diagrammed at the upper right in Figure 6–12. Protein molecules are partly or wholly embedded in the lipid layers. Other protein molecules are located on the surface of the lipids. Carbohydrates are attached to some of the lipid and protein molecules.

The membrane is almost fluid. In fact, a two-layered fluid membrane of lipids in water will form by itself under certain conditions.

**Try Investigation 6–B** What Controls the Movement of Materials into and out of Cells?, page 597, and **Investigation 6–C** What is the Relationship Between Diffusion and Cell Size?, page 600.

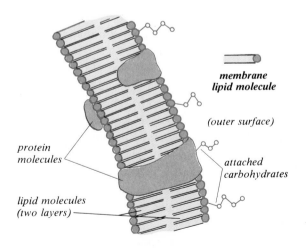

**Figure 6–12** A diagram of a portion of the plasma membrane of a cell. A sandwich appearance is produced, seen also in Figure 6–11.

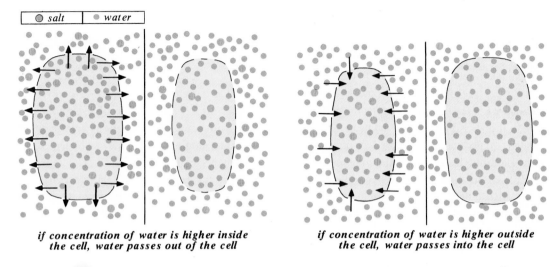

| ◉ salt | • water |
|---|---|

*if concentration of water is higher inside
the cell, water passes out of the cell*

*if concentration of water is higher outside
the cell, water passes into the cell*

**Figure 6–13** A diagram of osmosis. When water concentration is higher inside the cell (left), the cell shrinks. When water concentration is higher outside the cell (right), the cell swells. In the diagram, salt is represented by one kind of particle for simplicity, but in water it ionizes into two kinds of particles, sodium ions and chloride ions.

## 6–10

## Osmosis

Under normal conditions, water constantly passes into and out of cells through their plasma membranes. This uninterrupted diffusion of water through membranes that restrict passage of many other materials is called **osmosis** (os-MOH-sis). Like other substances, water diffuses from a region of higher concentration to a region of lower concentration. For example, suppose a living cell is placed in a solution that has a higher salt concentration than the cell has. The cell membrane repels most of the ions formed by the salt. The concentration of water is therefore lower outside the cell than inside it. Figure 6–13, left, shows what will happen. The cell will lose water and shrink.

On the other hand, if the concentration of water molecules is greater outside a cell, osmosis will cause the cell to swell with water (Figure 6–13, right). In distilled water, a cell may burst.

In the preceding examples of osmosis there were extreme differences between the concentration of materials inside and outside the cells. When these cells are in their normal environment, however, the differences are not as great. Some osmosis occurs, but not to an extent that it destroys the cells.

## 6–11

## Molecules Can also Enter the Cell by Active Transport

Osmosis of water and diffusion of other substances through the plasma membrane save the cell work when needed materials are supplied or kept in balance inside and outside the cell. But for most materials this is not true. If osmosis and other diffusion were the only processes of materials exchange, many of the cell's food and other molecules would soon be evenly distributed throughout the environment! Think what that would do to the cell.

The cell must maintain a high concentration of many needed substances and a low concentration of wastes, in relation to its surroundings. This means the cell must do work and therefore expend energy. The use of energy by the cell to transport materials through the plasma membrane is called **active transport.** Though not completely understood, active transport is known to occur in a variety of ways. Many molecules and ions that are able to diffuse through the membrane may also be *actively* transported through it. Even molecules too large to diffuse through the membrane may be transported. Sometimes they interact with substances in the membrane itself. At other times the membrane may fold inward forming a tiny "pocket" (see the upper left of the cell diagram in Chapter 2, Figure 2–7), which fills with fluid and particles from the cell's surroundings. The membrane then closes over the pocket and releases it into the cell. The bubblelike result is a new vacuole containing fluid and particles that were once outside! If this activity occurs in the reverse, materials can be expelled from the cell. Through active transport, cells can maintain a much greater

concentration of many materials (and much less of others) than in the surrounding environment.

How can it be shown experimentally that a substance is more concentrated inside a cell than outside? It is usually difficult to determine the contents of a single living cell. However, the freshwater alga *Nitella* is one of a number of organisms with some unusually large cells. Because of their size, single *Nitella* cells can be isolated and their contents can be removed. The amount of potassium, for example, in a single cell can be measured. The concentration of potassium in the cell can then be calculated and compared to the concentration in the water where *Nitella* grows. The ratio of potassium in *Nitella* to potassium in the water may be as much as 1000 to 1!

Every living cell constantly exchanges materials with its surroundings. But the exchange is regulated. Diffusion, osmosis, and active transport are combined in such a way that the cell almost always selects what it takes and keeps. That is, the plasma membrane of the cell is **selectively permeable** (PER-mee-uh-bul) to the cell's material needs, and to wastes that the cell ejects.

---

**CAPSULE SUMMARY**

Cells are enclosed by plasma membranes that admit or transport certain materials but not others. Diffusion and osmosis are natural processes that cause water and other materials to enter and leave cells. The cells expend no energy in these processes. However, it is active transport that establishes the selective balance of materials in cells. All forms of active transport require the expenditure of energy.

**SELF CHECK**

1. What does it mean to say that a plasma membrane is selectively permeable?
2. Do osmosis and diffusion stop when substances are evenly distributed?
3. What kind of evidence informs biologists that active transport occurs?
4. Give an example of active transport.

# CHAPTER SUMMARY

## HIGHLIGHTS

Enzymes and ATP are organic molecules found in all cells. Enzymes lower the amount of activation energy needed for reactions to take place. Thus, they not only promote reactions but cause them to take place at temperatures that are not harmful to life.

Fermentation is a process that releases energy in the absence of oxygen. Because Earth's early atmosphere contained little free oxygen, the first heterotrophs may have used a process similar to fermentation. In fermentation, two ATP molecules pass high-energy phosphate groups to glucose, activating the glucose. After several further steps, energy is released and stored in four molecules of ATP. Thus, for each fermented glucose molecule, a net gain of enough energy for two ATP molecules is achieved.

Osmosis and diffusion must have operated in the first heterotrophs. As processes of active transport were developed, cells acquired more control over the materials they exchanged with their environment.

## REVIEWING IDEAS

1. Why do biologists think that early heterotrophs obtained energy from organic compounds rather than from lightning or ultraviolet radiation?
2. Why does a cell exchange materials with its environment?
3. Why was fermentation difficult to understand until Buchner's discovery?
4. What is activation energy? What supplies activation energy in fermentation?
5. How can an enzyme be used more than once, if it takes part in a reaction?
6. How are enzymes and other catalysts alike? How are they different?
7. What is the principal kind of molecule in a cell's plasma membrane?
8. How are diffusion and osmosis related?
9. How does active transport differ from diffusion in terms of
   a. cell energy?
   b. changing the distribution or concentration of materials?
10. How many molecules of ATP are required to ferment a molecule of glucose? How many molecules of ATP are formed from the energy released?

## USING CONCEPTS

11. Predict whether ATP from plants could be used successfully in an animal enzyme experiment. Defend your reasoning.
12. Why do cells use different enzymes to catalyze different reactions?
13. Explain the difference between
    a. providing activation energy, as in fermentation, and
    b. driving energy-requiring reactions that build needed cell materials.
14. A cell uses materials as it needs them. How does this influence the direction in which a reversible reaction goes in the cell?
15. The motion of molecules in diffusion is random. That is, the molecules move in all directions, colliding with other molecules. Based on this information, how can diffusion occur in "one" direction?

## RECOMMENDED READING

Keeton, W. T. *Biological Science*. Third edition. New York, Norton, 1980. A college textbook with a readable account of fermentation.

Sharon, N. "Carbohydrates." *Scientific American*, November 1980. The many important roles (energy, structural, and others) of carbohydrates.

# Light as Energy for Life

## 7

In the last chapter you learned that ancestral heterotrophs could have lived in a world without oxygen by obtaining energy from fermentation. Certain bacteria that live today without oxygen are probably quite similar to those primitive heterotrophs. But the rich variety of forms now living on Earth could not have existed on the primitive Earth. Energy processes in most organisms have changed. What made it possible for Earth later to become the home of so many new and different forms of life?

It all probably started several billion years ago when the primitive environment began changing and some of the heterotrophs began using sunlight as a source of energy. This was a development of enormous importance for life on Earth. It provided a continuing source of energy and assured a dependable supply of food. In time it also changed Earth's atmosphere by supplying it with oxygen gas. You will learn in this chapter about life today in sunlight.

# Photosynthesis in a Changing World

## 7-1

## The Changing Environment Favors a New Form of Life

What fundamental change of environment may have happened during the early history of life? The nutrient broth of organic materials probably became more dilute as the primitive heterotrophs consumed the available amino acids, proteins, fats, and sugars. The materials that had accumulated over millions of years could not support a growing population of heterotrophs forever. More organic compounds probably were being made by ultraviolet radiation and lightning, but not fast enough to feed the increasing numbers of heterotrophs. Thus, as organic compounds in the primitive waters and soil were used up, food probably became scarce.

How could some organisms have adapted to the food shortage and managed to survive while other organisms could not? Organisms that could use a

second source of energy would have had a great advantage. Eventually, changes in some organisms might have made them able to use sunlight as an extra source of energy. Sunlight was probably not an important energy source for the primitive heterotrophs until the ready-made organic molecules became scarce. With less food, ability to use light made an organism and its descendants more fit for survival.

## 7-2

## The Sun Supplies Energy for the Life of Autotrophs

You read earlier that the main source of energy in making organic compounds before life evolved was the sun's ultraviolet radiation. However, the first living things probably could not use the sun's ultraviolet radiation to make other organic compounds. The energy of ultraviolet radiation is so great that it could have destroyed any forms of life not shielded by water. Some primitive heterotrophs, in their watery environment, began to use

---

←Light in lagoons and tidal flats may have fostered the first energy-capturing processes.

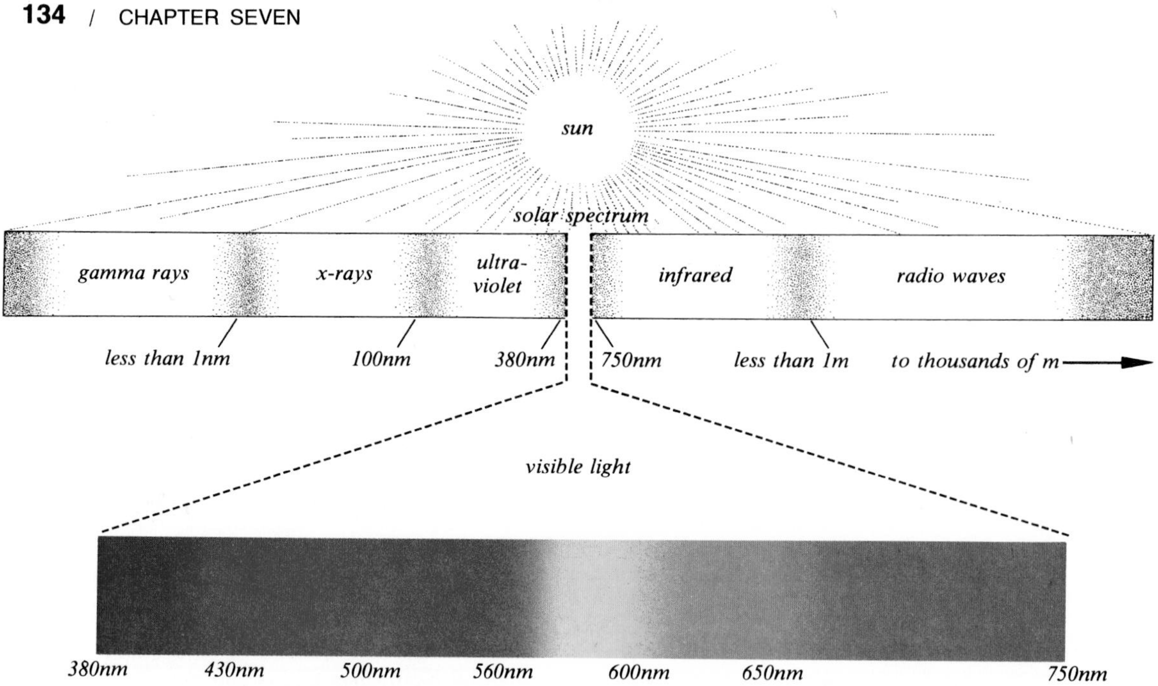

**Figure 7-1** The radiation spectrum is continuous, although in our uses of it we visualize it as divided into bands (light, X rays, and radio waves are examples). Visible light to humans is the portion of the spectrum with wavelengths longer than 380 nanometers and shorter than 750 nanometers. This is a very small portion of the spectrum.

the visible light from the sun as a source of energy. The difference between visible light, ultraviolet radiation, and other radiations from the sun is illustrated in Figure 7–1. A more complete discussion is given in **Appendix 7–A,** The Sun and Its Radiation, page 699.

The first organisms able to use sunlight would probably have acted partly like heterotrophs, taking in existing organic compounds, and partly like autotrophs, making other organic compounds with the energy from sunlight. There are forms of bacteria living today that show exactly these properties. These organisms are certain purple-colored bacteria that were originally thought to be only heterotrophs. It was later discovered that they contain a substance that the usual heterotrophs do not. They contain **chlorophyll** (KLOR-uh-fill), a pigment that absorbs light. They can use the energy of the absorbed sunlight to make new cellular materials from organic compounds taken in from the environment. These bacteria are heterotrophs that can use sunlight as an extra source of energy.

An even more remarkable group of cells exists today. Certain purple and green bacteria also contain chlorophyll, live only in light, and do not require any ready-made organic compounds at all. They are true autotrophs. They use the energy of sunlight to make *all* of their essential organic compounds from carbon dioxide and a few other compounds and elements.

Still another remarkable group of bacteria lives in water with a very high concentration of salt (six or seven times that of the oceans). They have a purple pigment in their cell membranes much like the visual pigment in your eyes. The purple pigment in your eyes absorbs light energy and lets you see. In the "salt-loving" bacteria the purple pigment absorbs light energy that is used to make ATP (page 121). The ATP then is used in making needed organic compounds.

All these groups of bacterial cells that use light energy to form organic compounds are jointly known as photosynthetic bacteria. They are bacteria that carry on the process of **photosynthesis** (foh-toh-SIN-theh-sis). As the name suggests (*photo,* light; *synthesis,* putting together), photosynthesis is the process by which living cells use light energy to make organic compounds.

You will soon learn the enormous importance of photosynthesis to life on Earth. There are actually several different types of photosynthesis. The photosynthetic bacteria in Figure 7–2 are anaerobes; they do not use oxygen. Some are even damaged by the mere presence of oxygen. They carry on the oldest type of photosynthesis— photosynthesis that does not produce oxygen. Such bacteria might have thrived several billion years ago before Earth's atmosphere contained oxygen. Anaerobic photosynthetic bacteria today live in freshwater and saltwater habitats with little oxygen.

Anaerobic photosynthetic bacteria have a great advantage over other anaerobic cells. They obtain energy directly from light and thus do not have to compete, or compete as much, for energy-rich compounds in their environment. Perhaps when life was new on Earth, these photosynthetic bacteria became very abundant in the ancient waters where they were protected from harmful solar radiation. The water would have stopped the harmful ultraviolet wavelengths but would have allowed the useful wavelengths of sunlight to reach the bacteria.

Today, anaerobic photosynthetic bacteria are not a major source of new organic compounds, as they once may have been. The most important type of photosynthesis today is photosynthesis that produces oxygen, the type carried on by green plants and freshwater and ocean algae.

**Try Investigation 7–A**  Photosynthesis, page 601.

**Figure 7–2**  (left) *Rhodospirillum,* a photosynthetic bacterium that can also live as a heterotroph. Note its flagella. (center) Another such bacterium (*Ectothiorhodospira mobilis*) seen with the electron microscope. P is the photosynthetic membrane system; R indicates ribosomes; PM is the plasma membrane; CW is the cell wall; and N is the nuclear material, not membrane-enclosed. (right) Several different species of purple photosynthetic bacteria.

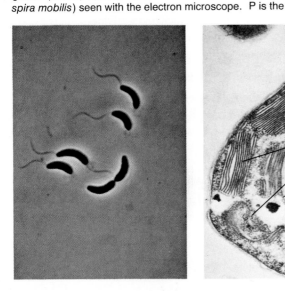
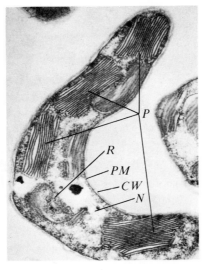
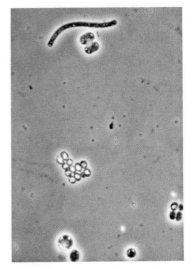

**Figure 7-3** Joseph Priestley discovered that plants restore air that has been "used" by animals or by a burning candle. Soon it was understood that plants carry on activities that release oxygen.

## 7-3

# Photosynthesis with Oxygen Is Discovered

Scientists discovered photosynthesis by plants almost 200 years ago, about 100 years before they discovered photosynthetic bacteria. In 1772 the British scientist Joseph Priestley (Figure 7-3) published a paper in London which read in part:

> I have been so happy as by accident to hit upon a method of restoring air which has been injured by the burning of candles and to have discovered at least one of the restoratives which nature employs for this purpose. It is vegetation.[1]

If Priestley had used an equation to summarize this discovery, it might have been written:

$$\text{bad air} \xrightarrow{\text{plants}} \text{pure air}$$

Priestley's discovery aroused tremendous excitement in the world of science. It was the first good explanation of how the air has remained healthful for millions of years despite the continuous breathing of people and other animals. In 1773, Priestley was presented the Copley Medal of the Royal Society and the citation read in part:

> From these discoveries, we are assured that no vegetable grows in vain, but . . . cleanses and purifies our atmosphere.

Priestley was hailed as the discoverer of the secret of what might be called Earth's ventilation system: how the air was constantly being restored to purity after being spoiled by the breathing of animals and the burning of fires. However, the enthusiasm which greeted Priestley's discovery was soon followed by doubts. Other investigators were unable to confirm the findings. In fact, Priestley, too, on returning to this subject six years later, was unable to repeat the earlier results.

This puzzle was cleared up by the Dutch physician Jan Ingenhousz (INN-ghen-howz), who made a very important discovery in the summer of 1779. Ingenhousz described the new discovery in these words:

> I observed that plants not only have a faculty to correct bad air in six or ten days, by growing in it, as the experiments of Dr. Priestley indicate, but that they perform this important office in a complete manner in a few hours; that this wonderful operation is by no means owing to the vegetation of the plant, but to the influence of the light of the sun upon the plant.[2]

Thus, Ingenhousz discovered the role of light in photosynthesis. Priestley's first experiments must have been carried out in light. Attempts to repeat the experiments later may have been made without enough light—no one knows for sure.

If Ingenhousz had used an equation to summarize the later findings, the equation might have been written:

$$\text{bad air} \xrightarrow[\text{light}]{\text{plants}} \text{pure air}$$

# The Secret of Vegetation

People have long realized that they and all other animals grow and develop by eating plants, or by eating other animals that feed on plants. But what is the "food" that plants eat? The keenest observers of plants could find no sign that plants ever consumed any food. The lack of food intake, the observers reasoned, explains why plants excrete no waste products.

But how then could plants develop and increase in size? In the 17th century a physician named Jean Baptiste van Helmont announced an astonishing conclusion reached not by observing plants in nature but by performing what had never been done before: a quantitative scientific experiment on plant growth. In van Helmont's own words, "I took an earthenware pot, placed in it 200 lb of earth dried in an oven, soaked this with water, and planted in it a willow shoot weighing 5 lb. After five years had passed, the tree grown therefrom weighed 169 lb and about 3 oz. But the earthenware pot was constantly wet only with rain or (when necessary) distilled water . . . and, to prevent dust flying around from mixing with the earth, the rim of the pot was kept covered with an iron plate coated with tin and pierced with many holes . . . Finally, I again dried the earth of the pot, and it was found to be the same 200 lb minus about 2 oz. Therefore, 164 lb of wood, bark, and root *had arisen from the water alone*."

Van Helmont performed a beautifully simple experiment and tried to measure carefully, but did not take account of the air or consider the missing two ounces of soil very important. This small soil loss gave a hint of what we now know is an uptake of soil minerals by plant roots. Secondly, and most important, neither van Helmont nor anyone else for another 100 years had any reason to suspect that the "food" which made plants grow and develop was being silently and efficiently manufactured in the leaves, by a mysterious chemical process that required carbon dioxide from the air and sunlight.

In this chapter you will learn about the nature of this mysterious process that escaped detection for many thousands of years. This light-requiring process accounts for over 90 percent of all plant substance.

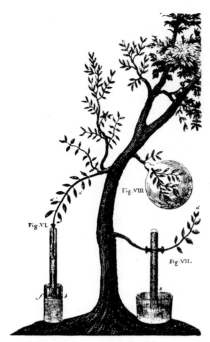

Fig.VIII

Fig.VI

Fig.VII.

**Figure 7–4** One of de Saussure's quantitative experiments with photosynthesis. Differing amounts of carbon dioxide were made available to plants. Then the plants were weighed to see how much weight they had gained. De Saussure showed that carbon dioxide and water were both used to produce carbohydrates.

Another idea came to this rapidly developing subject from the growing science of chemistry. "Bad air" was recognized as carbon dioxide and "pure air" as oxygen. Using the new names, the equation for the new process would become:

$$\text{carbon dioxide} \xrightarrow[\text{light}]{\text{plants}} \text{oxygen}$$

In 1796, Ingenhousz went a step further. If the green plant was not just acting as a gas exchanger, then it had to be deriving important nourishment from this process. Ingenhousz thought about this and wrote that a plant in sunlight absorbs the carbon from carbon dioxide, "throwing out at that time the oxygen alone, and keeping the carbon to itself as nourishment." This was a new idea, and very close to the truth. When carbon dioxide

was split by the light, or so Ingenhousz believed, the carbon was retained by the plant to form organic compounds to use for its own nourishment. The remarkable behavior of plants in light was thus important for two reasons, instead of just one. First, it purified the air of our planet. Second, it resulted in new carbon compounds. In equation form, Ingenhousz's new idea could be written:

$$\begin{matrix} \text{carbon} \\ \text{dioxide} \end{matrix} \xrightarrow[\text{light}]{\text{plants}} \begin{matrix} \text{organic} \\ \text{compounds} \end{matrix} + \text{oxygen}$$

A few years later, in 1804, a Swiss scientist, Nicolas Theodore de Saussure (de-soh-SUR), showed that water also takes part in this process. By means of careful experiments, de Saussure found that plants carrying on photosynthesis increased in weight by more than the amount of carbon dioxide they could take in. Water seemed to account for this difference (see Figure 7–4). The equation for photosynthesis thus underwent another change in understanding:

$$\begin{matrix} \text{carbon} \\ \text{dioxide} \end{matrix} + \text{water} \xrightarrow[\text{plants}]{\text{light}} \begin{matrix} \text{organic} \\ \text{compounds} \end{matrix} + \text{oxygen}$$

In the following years, as chemists began analyzing plants, they found that the main products of photosynthesis were carbohydrates. Since the ratio of carbon, hydrogen, and oxygen in carbohydrates is represented by the formula $CH_2O$, the equation for photosynthesis came to be written in chemical symbols as:

$$CO_2 + H_2O \xrightarrow[\text{light}]{\text{plants}} CH_2O + O_2$$

This equation for plant photosynthesis is widely used today, although the words "plants" and "light" are usually not written. $CH_2O$ is also not an actual plant compound but shows only the *ratio* of carbon to hydrogen to oxygen. If everything in the equation is increased sixfold, however, then the equation shows the formation of $6 \times CH_2O$, or $C_6H_{12}O_6$. This compound is the common plant sugar glucose. The equation thus becomes:

$$6CO_2 + 6H_2O \longrightarrow C_6H_{12}O_6 + 6O_2$$

Plants use the glucose formed by photosynthesis as raw material to make other carbohydrates, amino acids, proteins, fats, vitamins, and all the other materials needed by cells for growth and reproduction. They also form some amino acids directly in photosynthesis. The process of photosynthesis is thus the key to the formation of all organic compounds by plants. Since animals eat plants, they also indirectly depend on photosynthesis for their food. Even those animals that live on land and in the ocean by preying on other animals depend indirectly on photosynthesis for their food. There is always a ''food chain'' in nature that begins with a photosynthetic organism as the food producer and leads through one or more steps to an animal as the food consumer. Keep in mind, however, that photosynthetic algae and plants are also consumers of the food they make; they use it as a source of energy and raw materials for their own growth and reproduction. These algae and plants are both producers and consumers of food, whereas animals are only consumers.

**Try Investigation 7–B** Do Plant Parts Without Chlorophyll Carry on Photosynthesis When in the Light?, page 603.

---

**CAPSULE SUMMARY**

As the population of heterotrophs increased, the organic material they used for energy decreased. Certain organisms that could use sunlight for the synthesis of food evolved over millions of years. This new way of making food, known as photosynthesis today, was a radical change from the process that produced an organic broth by the action of ultraviolet light on chemicals in the atmosphere. Some bacteria living today carry on a primitive type of photosynthesis that produces organic compounds but does not produce oxygen. The most important type of photosynthesis today is photosynthesis by green plants and ocean algae. In this process oxygen and sugar are produced.

**SELF CHECK**

1. What evidence in existing organisms today suggests that part-heterotrophs, part-autotrophs may have evolved early in Earth's history?
2. Name the most important pigment in photosynthesis today.
3. What were the first major discoveries that led to further studies concerning photosynthesis?
4. What two important discoveries concerning photosynthesis were made by Jan Ingenhousz?
5. Photosynthesis requires a living plant and visible light. What other substances are involved?

---

# The Two-Part Sequence of Tasks in Photosynthesis

## 7–4

## Photosynthesis Includes Light and Dark Reactions

The scientists who first discovered what substances went into the process of photosynthesis and what substances were produced left one important question unanswered: What happens to the light energy which plants absorb during this process? Remember that energy cannot be created or destroyed. (See **Appendix 5-C**, Energy, page 692). It can only be converted from one form into another. Years after the discovery of photosynthesis it was recognized that the organic compounds formed by this process contain more chemical energy than the carbon dioxide and water they came from. Thus the extra chemical energy could have come only from light. It became clear then that photosynthesis is a process which converts light energy into chemical energy.

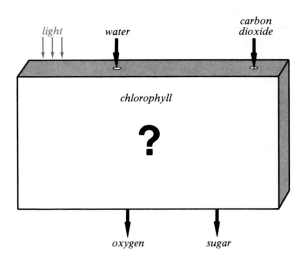

light water carbon dioxide

chlorophyll

**?**

oxygen sugar

**Figure 7–5** Knowledge of photosynthesis was limited at the end of the nineteenth century. The raw materials, the products, and the importance of light were well understood. The big mystery (shown here as a box hiding whatever goes on inside) was how plant cells convert the raw materials into the energy-rich products.

Photosynthesis was thus recognized as the bridge between the sun's energy and the energy needs of life on Earth. Cell processes other than photosynthesis cannot use solar energy directly. They can use it only after it is converted into chemical energy. This energy conversion is carried out by photosynthetic organisms when they absorb solar energy and use it to "reshuffle" the atoms of water and carbon dioxide and to make new energy-rich chemical bonds between them. The products of this "reshuffling" are oxygen gas and organic compounds that supply the energy needs of plants and animals.

Once it was understood what happens in photosynthesis, scientists turned their efforts to answer the big question of how it happens. The inner workings of photosynthesis were a complete mystery, hidden as if they were in a box, as shown in

Figure 7–5. To solve this mystery, to find out what goes on inside the box, became a challenge to scientists in our own century.

The first hint as to the inner workings of photosynthesis came in the early 1900s when it was recognized that photosynthesis may include both a light-requiring reaction and a reaction that may proceed either in light or darkness. The steps that led to this conclusion are described in **Appendix 7–B,** Photosynthesis Includes a "Dark Reaction," page 701.

The existence of a dark reaction in photosynthesis was a new idea. Scientists could now investigate what part of photosynthesis depends on light and what part of photosynthesis is independent of light.

**Try Investigation 7–C** Does the Rate of Photosynthesis Depend on the Intensity of Light?, page 603.

# 7–5
## The "Light Reaction" Involves Water

Photosynthesis uses two different materials, water and carbon dioxide. It is possible then that one material is involved in a light reaction and the other in a dark reaction. But which is which? At one time most scientists favored the idea that light splits carbon dioxide. You may recall from Section 7–3 that this idea was first suggested by Ingenhousz in 1796.

An entirely different hypothesis, however, was developed in the 1930s by C. B. van Niel of Stanford University. Van Niel investigated bacterial photosynthesis like that described in Section 7–2, which does not produce oxygen. Some photosyn-

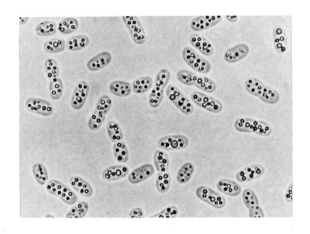

**Figure 7–6** These photosynthetic bacteria use hydrogen sulfide instead of water to make carbohydrates. In this process they give off sulfur instead of oxygen. The round bodies inside the cells are the globules of sulfur being released by photosynthesis.

thetic bacteria use the compound hydrogen sulfide ($H_2S$) instead of water ($H_2O$) in making carbohydrates from carbon dioxide. In this type of bacterial photosynthesis sulfur is the by-product (Figure 7–6). When water is used, oxygen is the by-product. Both kinds of reactions, however, use the same second material, carbon dioxide. If the oxygen is split from the carbon dioxide, why is it not released in both types of photosynthesis?

Van Niel reasoned that the light reaction splits hydrogen sulfide ($H_2S$) or water ($H_2O$), and not carbon dioxide. In other words, the light reaction is probably similar in both plant and bacterial photosynthesis.

This hypothesis suggested the conclusion that photosynthesis in green plants is basically a transfer of hydrogen from water to carbon dioxide. You may recall (from page 97) that splitting water into hydrogen and oxygen takes a great deal of energy.

But what of the dark reaction in photosynthesis? According to the new hypothesis the dark reaction involves carbon dioxide. As shown in Figure 7–7, the mysterious box that held the secrets of photosynthesis can now be thought of as being divided into two smaller "boxes": (a) a "light box" that holds the secret of how light splits water into hydrogen and oxygen, and (b) a "dark box" that holds the secret of how carbon dioxide is converted into sugar or another organic compound.

You learned in Chapter 1 that biology advances whenever hypotheses are tested and supported by experiments. Van Niel's hypothesis was based on similarities between photosynthesis in plants and in bacteria. Because some parts of these processes were alike, other parts might also be alike. But no one was prepared to learn that the dark reaction, or reactions much like it that do not require light, could be carried on by animals as well as by plants and photosynthetic bacteria.

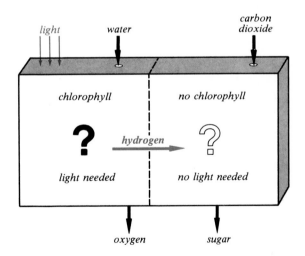

**Figure 7–7** Continuing studies suggested that photosynthesis consists of two distinct types of reactions, a "light" reaction and a "dark" reaction. The light reaction decomposes water into oxygen and hydrogen. The dark reaction uses the hydrogen, and carbon dioxide, to make sugar.

## 7–6

## Heterotrophs, Too, Build Organic Compounds from Carbon Dioxide

Developments in one scientific field often help to advance another. In the late 1940s, biological research received a powerful boost from two developments in other fields. First, physicists discovered how to make radioactive isotopes. (See Section 5–9.) Radioactive carbon dioxide became available for biological research. The carbon atom of radioactive carbon dioxide gives off radiation and can thus be ''traced'' in whatever compound it is present. Second, chemists developed a method, called paper chromatography, for detecting very small amounts of organic compounds. By this technique the individual compounds in a mixture can be separated out on a sheet of filter paper. Once the compounds are separated, they can be analyzed and identified. Paper chromatography soon led to improved methods of chromatography handled automatically by machines of advanced design.

The first biological experiments with radioactive carbon dioxide gave some surprising results. Scientists found that even cells that do not contain chlorophyll and cannot use light energy nevertheless can take in and use carbon dioxide. For example, in one experiment liver cells formed radioactive carbohydrates from radioactive carbon dioxide.

These findings shattered the idea held by scientists for almost 150 years that only autotrophs can form organic compounds from carbon dioxide. It became clear that all cells, heterotrophs as well as autotrophs, can use carbon dioxide in this way. Was there then no difference between the way that autotrophs and heterotrophs formed organic compounds? One important difference remained—the energy. To convert carbon dioxide into organic compounds takes energy. Heterotrophs can obtain this energy only by breaking down other organic compounds. There is, therefore, no gain in the total amount of organic compounds. But when autotrophs form organic compounds during photosynthesis, they use energy that comes from light. Autotrophs, therefore, can increase the total amount of organic compounds.

This new insight into the chemistry of living cells supported some of the ideas of scientists about the dark reaction in photosynthesis. It certainly seemed reasonable to suppose that if heterotrophs could build organic compounds from carbon dioxide in the absence of light, so could autotrophs. In other words, there could indeed be a dark process in photosynthesis.

## 7–7

## The Carbon Cycle Is the Dark Phase of Photosynthesis

Although in green plants it is the light reaction that comes first, the first part of photosynthesis to be experimentally explained was the synthesis of organic compounds from carbon dioxide and hydrogen. Direct evidence that the use of carbon dioxide in building organic compounds is the ''dark reaction'' of photosynthesis came from the work of Melvin Calvin and others at the University of California at Berkeley. Calvin started with the hypothesis that carbon dioxide is changed to carbohydrate in a series of separate chemical reactions. If the reactions could be stopped part way, intermediate compounds might be found. If a green plant was supplied with radioactive carbon dioxide, the intermediate compounds would be ''tagged.'' They would contain radioactive carbon and could be distinguished from all the other carbon compounds in the cell. If these ''tagged'' intermediates were separated and identified by chromatography techniques, the ''path of carbon'' from carbon dioxide to carbohydrate would become known.

This approach gave interesting results. When cells carrying on photosynthesis were exposed to radioactive carbon dioxide for only a few seconds, almost all of the radioactive carbon turned up in one three-carbon (3C) compound, phosphoglyceric acid. This 3C acid is known to be produced when glucose is broken down by fermentation. Calvin's later experiments showed that the formation of the 3C acid is one of a series of reactions by which carbon dioxide is converted into glucose. All the reactions together form a **carbon cycle.** The main features of the carbon cycle are shown in a "dark box" in Figure 7–8. Read the following summary as you study the figure.

1. Carbon dioxide ($CO_2$) enters the reaction and combines with a five-carbon (5C) compound to form an unstable six-carbon (6C) intermediate. The intermediate breaks up into two molecules of the 3C acid.
2. The 3C acid is then converted into simple 3C sugars.
3. Some of the simple sugars are converted into glucose as the product of photosynthesis. The rest of the simple sugars are used toward rebuilding the 5C compound that will again combine with $CO_2$ in another turn of the carbon cycle.

The carbon cycle is explained in more detail in **Appendix 7–C,** The Carbon Cycle in Photosynthesis, page 703. The carbon cycle turned out to be more complicated than a single "dark reaction" for the incorporation of carbon dioxide in photosynthesis. Altogether, 12 different enzyme reactions are needed to convert carbon dioxide into glucose. Nevertheless, the idea of a "dark" process proved basically correct because all these reactions operate independently of light. Biologists therefore call them jointly the **dark phase** of photosynthesis.

It was stated earlier that the formation of organic compounds from carbon dioxide requires

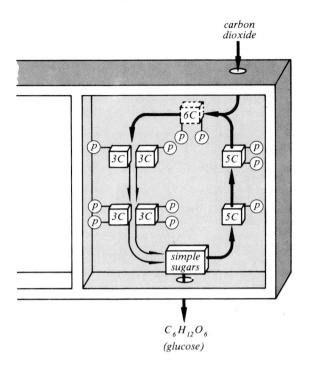

*carbon dioxide*

$C_6H_{12}O_6$
*(glucose)*

**Figure 7–8** The dark phase, or carbon cycle, in photosynthesis. Carbon dioxide enters the cycle and reacts with a 5C compound, forming an unstable 6C compound. The 6C compound breaks down into two 3C acids. The 3C acids go through reactions that change them into simple sugars. Both glucose and more of the 5C compound that starts the cycle are made from the simple sugars. (The P's represent phosphate groups.)

energy. The carbon cycle of photosynthesis needs a constant input of energy. It turns out that the energy is supplied by two substances, ATP and NADPH.

ATP, you will recall (Chapter 6), is the most general form of energy currency in cells. $NADP^+$ is an electron and hydrogen carrier in cells. The initials NADP stand for nicotinamide adenine dinucleotide phosphate (nih-kuh-TEEN-uh-myde AAH-duh-neen dye-NU-klee-oh-tyde FOS-fayt). The formula of $NADP^+$ is given in **Appendix 7–D,** $NADP^+$, page 704. $NADP^+$ combines with a hydrogen ion and two electrons to form NADPH. When living cells form new organic compounds,

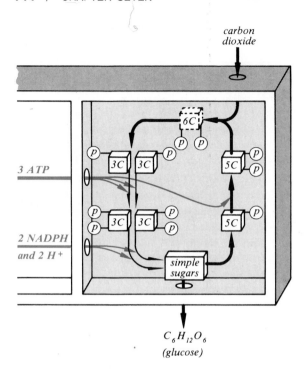

carbon dioxide

3 ATP

2 NADPH and 2 H+

simple sugars

$C_6H_{12}O_6$
(glucose)

**Figure 7–9** Three molecules of ATP and two of NADPH provide the energy needed for one carbon dioxide molecule to go through the carbon cycle.

some of the needed hydrogen is carried by NADPH. Remember that splitting hydrogen from water requires energy. Thus NADPH must be energy-rich. It carries a hydrogen ion and two electrons from water. A second hydrogen ion ($H^+$) from water is in solution within the cell.

Not all the steps in the carbon cycle require an input of energy. The blue arrows in Figure 7–9 show where ATP and NADPH are needed. Three molecules of ATP, two molecules of NADPH, and two hydrogen ions (from solution within the cell) are needed to incorporate one molecule of carbon dioxide into the carbon cycle. Six times these amounts are needed to build one hypothetical molecule of glucose from inputs of carbon dioxide and hydrogen.

## CAPSULE SUMMARY

The hypothesis that photosynthesis involves a light-requiring reaction and another that may proceed either in light or in darkness suggested that water may be involved in one (the light reaction) and carbon dioxide in the other (the dark reaction). Van Niel then proposed that the energy of sunlight splits water molecules, not carbon dioxide molecules; otherwise, photosynthetic bacteria might be expected to give off oxygen as green plants do, since these bacteria also use carbon dioxide in photosynthesis. But the bacteria do not give off oxygen.

Further evidence that carbon dioxide enters the dark reaction intact came with the discovery that heterotrophs as well as autotrophs can use carbon dioxide to build organic compounds. Calvin's work then affirmed that carbon dioxide (with other inputs, too) enters a carbon cycle that results in glucose being manufactured in the dark phase of photosynthesis.

## SELF CHECK

1. How did van Niel come to suspect that water, not carbon dioxide, was split by sunlight in the light reaction of photosynthesis?
2. How did the discovery that animals can use carbon dioxide in building organic compounds support the hypothesis of a dark reaction in photosynthesis?
3. If the hydrogen in NADPH comes from water, is energy required or released by the transfer? How do you know?
4. How did Calvin propose to identify the steps in building a sugar molecule?
5. How did the carbon cycle (for building a sugar molecule) turn out to be different from the equation for photosynthesis (page 139)?

# The Mechanisms of the Light Phase in Photosynthesis

## 7–8

### The Light Phase Produces Oxygen, ATP, and NADPH

Calvin found another pathway in the carbon cycle, which produced an amino acid (page 103) instead of a glucose molecule. But it, too, required carbon dioxide, ATP, and NADPH. In other words, the requirements appeared similar no matter what organic compound the green plant built during the dark phase. This conclusion concentrated attention on how ATP and NADPH are formed using the energy of sunlight.

Since at least two compounds are produced, the "light reaction" (like the "dark reaction") suggested a whole series of reactions and soon came to be called the **light phase** of photosynthesis.

Remember that oxygen is a product of photosynthesis in plants, but that oxygen is not produced by the carbon cycle. You must therefore expect that oxygen is produced along with ATP and NADPH during the light phase of photosynthesis.

The light phase of photosynthesis powers the entire process. In an automobile the power comes from the engine. The engine converts the chemical energy of its fuel into the mechanical energy that moves the wheels. What is the "engine" in photosynthesis that converts light energy into chemical energy?

You might guess that the engine of photosynthesis contains chlorophyll, since, as you read earlier, chlorophyll is the major plant pigment that absorbs light. If you examine a section of a leaf under the microscope (Figure 7–10), you will see chlorophyll located in separate plastids within the cells. These plastids are the chloroplasts (Chapter 2), a name derived from Greek words that mean "green shape."

The number of chloroplasts in photosynthetic cells varies. A leaf cell may have from 20 to 100 chloroplasts. A single-celled alga may have only one or two. Chloroplasts also vary in shape. Those of higher plants are usually shaped like disks about five micrometers ($\mu$m) in diameter and about two $\mu$m thick. (Recall that a micrometer is 0.001 millimeter.) A hundred chloroplasts placed end to end would be no bigger than the period at the end of this sentence. Biologists have recently

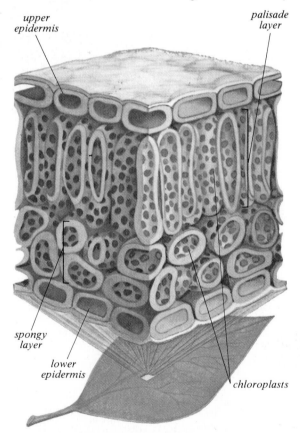

*upper epidermis*

*palisade layer*

*spongy layer*

*lower epidermis*

*chloroplasts*

**Figure 7–10** A small section through a green leaf. The upper and lower layers (epidermis) are the leaf surfaces. They are coated by an almost waterproof substance. The spongy and palisade layers of cells between the upper and lower epidermis contain chloroplasts. Photosynthesis is carried on in the chloroplasts.

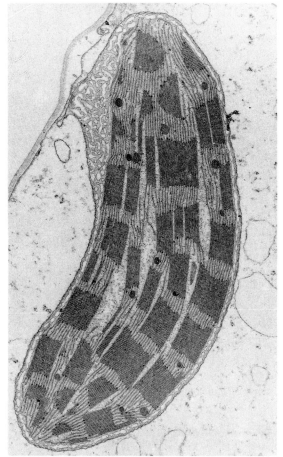

**Figure 7–11** An electron micrograph of a single chloroplast. The darker areas are stacks of thylakoids. Each thylakoid is a disk or flattened sac enclosed by a membrane. Photosynthetic pigments are in the thylakoid membranes.

learned much about the structure of chloroplasts by using the electron microscope. Figure 7–11 illustrates the details of the structure.

Inside a chloroplast, flattened sacs called **thylakoids** (THY-luh-koyds) occur in stacks called **grana** (GRAY-nuh). The darker areas in Figure 7–11 are the grana, each containing numerous thylakoids. Chlorophyll, other photosynthetic pigments, and enzymes of the light phase are embedded in the thylakoid membranes. The lighter

areas of the chloroplast contain the enzymes of the carbon cycle.

Almost a hundred years ago plant scientists thought that the entire process of photosynthesis probably occurred in chloroplasts, but no one was able to demonstrate this until much later. In 1937, Robert Hill of Cambridge University, England, found that when chloroplasts were isolated from living cells and placed in the light, they could produce oxygen. They only needed to be supplied with certain compounds of iron. This reaction became known as the Hill reaction. However, there was still no evidence that isolated chloroplasts could form carbohydrates from carbon dioxide, completing the process of photosynthesis.

The subject was further investigated by Daniel Arnon and others at the University of California at Berkeley. They made two discoveries. First, they found that isolated chloroplasts could indeed convert carbon dioxide into carbohydrates. Second, they found that isolated chloroplasts could form ATP in light even when no carbon dioxide was supplied. (They named this new process of ATP formation photosynthetic phosphorylation, or photophosphorylation for short!) We will refer to this process as ATP formation in the light. The overall reaction can be summarized as:

$$ADP + P \xrightarrow[\text{light}]{\text{chloroplasts}} ATP$$

The discovery of ATP formation in the light seemed at first to explain the origin of all the ATP in photosynthesis. But this proved to be only part of the story. Arnon's research team discovered later a second type of ATP formation in the light, in which ATP formation was linked to the formation of NADPH and oxygen gas. The overall reaction in this type of ATP formation in the light can be summarized as

$$2NADP^+ + 2ADP + 2P + 2H_2O \xrightarrow[\text{light}]{\text{chloroplasts}}$$
$$2NADPH + 2ATP + O_2 + 2H^+$$

The first process of ATP formation in light, the process that makes only ATP, is cyclic. The second process, in which ATP is produced together with oxygen and NADPH, is noncyclic. The nature of the light reactions in these two processes is discussed in **Appendix 7–E,** The Light Reactions in Photosynthesis, page 705.

The noncyclic process yields all the three products that are expected from the light phase of photosynthesis: ATP, NADPH, and oxygen. The cyclic process produces additional ATP. The plant uses some of this additional ATP during the reactions of the dark phase. Turn back to the diagram of the carbon cycle in Figure 7–9. Observe that *three* molecules of ATP and *two* of NADPH are needed for each molecule of carbon dioxide put into the cycle. The noncyclic process provides ATP and NADPH molecules in equal numbers. The cyclic process adds more ATP.

**Try Investigation 7–D** Is the Green Coloring in Leaves a Single Substance or a Mixture of Different Substances?, page 605.

## 7–9
## Light Energy Establishes a Flow of Electrons

So far, only the *results* of the light phase of photosynthesis have been presented. Nothing has been said about *how* sunlight is converted to chemical energy in ATP and NADPH.

Electrons that absorb light energy are said to be "excited." These excited, or high-energy, electrons may escape from their usual energy levels in a molecule (see page 98) to higher energy levels. They may even escape from the molecule completely, carrying the extra energy with them.

Chlorophyll and related pigments absorb light energy this way and lose the resulting high-energy electrons. Other molecules present in the chloroplast accept these electrons. This electron-transfer

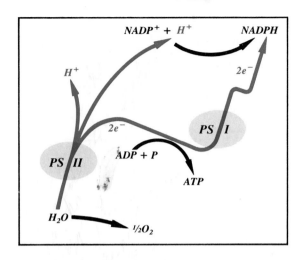

**Figure 7–12** A diagram of the relationship between the two photosystems (PS I and II). Electron flow goes from water to PS II to PS I to NADPH. Thus NADPH has a hydrogen ion and two electrons originally derived from water.

process converts sunlight to energy used in photosynthesis. When the high-energy electrons bind to the other molecules, the energy becomes chemical energy. These carrier molecules can pass electrons on to other carrier molecules, including $NADP^+$. Energy can also be released to form ATP.

Two groups of pigment molecules take part in the noncyclic reactions of the light phase of photosynthesis. These groups are called Photosystems (or PS) I and II. Both photosystems absorb light, but of slightly different wavelengths. Electron-carrier molecules connect the two photosystems. (See Appendix 7–E.) When light energy is absorbed, chlorophyll molecules in both systems lose high-energy electrons to carrier molecules. Water is also separated into hydrogen ions, electrons, and oxygen. A flow of electrons is set up. Those from water replace the ones lost by PS II. Those lost by PS II replace the ones lost by PS I. ATP is formed as electrons are transferred between the two photosystems. At the end of the electron flow, $NADP^+$ accepts electrons and a hydrogen ion to become NADPH. (See Figure 7–12.)

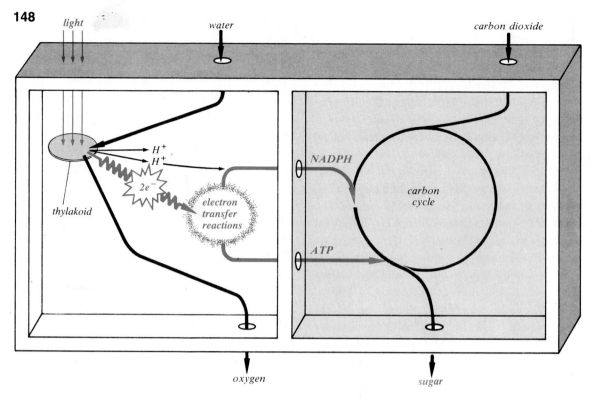

**Figure 7–13** The light and dark phases of photosynthesis. In the light phase (left), light is absorbed by electrons of chlorophyll molecules. Electron transfer reactions produce ATP, transfer a hydrogen ion and electrons to NADP+ to produce NADPH, and release oxygen. The ATP and the NADPH are used in the dark phase (right) that incorporates carbon dioxide in the carbon cycle and produces sugar as its chief end-product.

Figure 7–13 brings together in one diagram the two phases of photosynthesis, the light phase and the dark, and shows how they are connected. In the light phase the absorption of light by chlorophyll molecules leads to electron-transfer reactions that release the oxygen from water and produce ATP and NADPH. This ATP and NADPH are used in the dark phase to operate the carbon cycle that converts carbon dioxide into sugar.

## 7–10

## Chlorophyll Absorbs Certain Wavelengths of Light

Photosynthesis depends on "chemical machinery" that includes pigments, enzymes, and other catalysts. If you did Investigation 7–D, you studied some of the plant pigments. The most important is chlorophyll, the green pigment that absorbs light. Other photosynthetic pigments are also present— among them yellow and orange pigments. They absorb additional wavelengths of light and transfer the energy to chlorophyll.

There are even several kinds of chlorophyll. Chlorophyll *a* and chlorophyll *b* are found in green plants. Chlorophyll *a* is the essential pigment in both Photosystems I and II. Both PS I and PS II may contain chlorophyll *b*, and PS II may contain chlorophyll *c*. Each kind of chlorophyll molecule contains atoms of carbon, hydrogen, oxygen, nitrogen, and a single atom of magnesium. Differences in the structures of the molecules cause slight differences in the wavelengths of light they absorb. It is chlorophyll that is responsible for the familiar green color of leaves. Chlorophyll absorbs most of the violet and the red wavelengths of light but very little of the green. The wavelengths of light that are not absorbed by chlorophyll are reflected toward our eyes and we see leaves as green.

In 1882, Theodore Engelmann devised an ingenious experiment to show which wavelengths of light were most important in photosynthesis. Because oxygen is produced by photosynthesis, Engelmann reasoned that the rate of photosynthesis could be measured by the rate of oxygen production. The more rapid the rate of photosynthesis, the more oxygen produced. Therefore, Engelmann measured the rate at which oxygen was produced at different wavelengths of light. Passing white light through a prism produced light of different colors: red, orange, yellow, green, blue, and violet. You will recall from Figure 7–1 that these

different colors correspond to the different wavelengths of light. Engelmann used long strands of algae to carry on the photosynthesis. As a "measure" of the oxygen, special oxygen-loving bacteria were introduced that would crowd together wherever oxygen was present.

When Engelmann illuminated the long strands of algae with the spectrum of light from the prism, startling results appeared. The greatest cluster of bacteria gathered where red light was shining on the strand of algae. A second cluster, somewhat smaller, gathered in violet light. Between these extremes very few bacteria were seen at all (see Figure 7–14). Since Engelmann's bacteria concentrated where oxygen production by photosynthesis was the greatest, the experiment showed that photosynthesis was most active in red and violet light. From other experiments, Engelmann concluded that photosynthesis depends directly on the

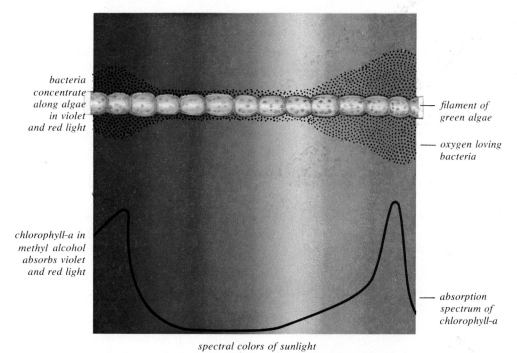

bacteria concentrate along algae in violet and red light

filament of green algae

oxygen loving bacteria

chlorophyll-a in methyl alcohol absorbs violet and red light

absorption spectrum of chlorophyll-a

spectral colors of sunlight

**Figure 7–14** A graphic representation of the results of Engelmann's experiment. Oxygen was produced in the greatest amounts by the algae in violet and red light. The clusters of bacteria indicated the differences in oxygen production.

# Biology Brief

## Light for Profit

When you are a commercial plant grower like Miss Shawn Sullivan (shown harvesting carnations), photosynthesis must be prescribed to fit the particular plants you raise. The number of hours of illumination each day and light intensity (including optimum light at each wavelength) can be matched to each variety of plant for greatest yield and greatest beauty. Miss Sullivan is responsible for the timely growth (chrysanthemums, carnations, lilies, etc., during their season) of over 2000 different varieties of plants. Each has its own best conditions for growth. Light in her greenhouses is controlled by screens that are draped in a varying number of layers from the roof area. (See facing page.) Light meters monitor the intensity of the incoming light, and increases or decreases are made with artificial lighting or selective screening to offset seasonal differences throughout the year. This careful regulation helps time the harvests for peak periods of demand.

light absorbed by chlorophyll. This conclusion was verified by many later investigations, which also revealed other pigments that absorb light at a few other wavelengths.

## 7–11

## Photosynthesis Occurs on Land and in the Water

How long has photosynthesis existed on Earth? Biologists do not know exactly when it started, but only that it is a very old process. The oldest fossils that give evidence of photosynthesis are remains of cells that resemble the blue-green algae (or blue-green bacteria), a group of photosynthetic organisms living today. The fossil evidence was embedded in rocks that are 3.5 billion years old (page 91).

Scientists think that photosynthesis by anaerobic bacteria is even more ancient. Blue-green algae closely resemble anaerobic photosynthetic bacteria in the structure and organization of their

One of Miss Sullivan's largest continuous crops is carnations. (See above right.) Experiments with these carnations in her greenhouses have revealed the different growth factors that effect the highest yields. The most successful beds have the plants growing in gravel instead of soil, with automatic watering devices regulating the amount of water and soil nutrients. The light, the temperature, and any symptoms of diseases are carefully monitored in the best-producing beds. In a highly competitive market, Miss Sullivan is continually looking for a biological edge on her competitors so that she can grow plants more efficiently. But most of the real satisfaction in her work, she feels, is in being surrounded by the plants she has brought to near-perfect quality in the greenhouses.

Photosynthesis is the link between many careers serving human needs and a rich variety of interests. How many other examples can you name, and how would you group them as serving need or interest?

cells, but their photosynthesis differs in one important respect: it produces oxygen. Today most blue-green algae live where oxygen is present. Some, however, live in the same environments as anaerobic photosynthetic bacteria, such as in muddy river bottoms where the oxygen content is very low. Blue-green algae probably evolved from ancient photosynthetic bacteria that were anaerobic. Thus the blue-green algae became the first photosynthetic organisms that produced oxygen.

Most photosynthesis today is carried on by plants that produce oxygen. Anaerobic bacterial photosynthesis may have been the first form of photosynthesis on Earth, but today it is very minor in comparison with photosynthesis of the oxygen-producing type. The amount of oxygen produced by photosynthesis is enormous. Photosynthesis will have replaced all the oxygen that is now in Earth's atmosphere in a little over 2000 years. This is a short period compared with the 4.7 billion years that is the estimated age of Earth. Such calculations convinced scientists that all the oxygen in Earth's atmosphere has come from photosynthesis.

Today, photosynthesis is the largest single chemical process on Earth. It has been estimated that each year about 140 billion metric tons of carbon dioxide and 110 billion metric tons of water are used to produce over 90 billion metric tons of organic matter and about 100 billion metric tons of oxygen gas by the process of photosynthesis. The photosynthesis of ages past is responsible for the fossil fuels—coal, oil, and natural gas—that have made our industrial civilization possible.

The first photosynthetic organisms, photosynthetic bacteria and blue-green algae, lived in water habitats. Most of the photosynthesis in oceans and lakes is still carried on by microscopic algae. But today land plants account for much of the total photosynthetic activity on Earth, too.

Photosynthesis constantly supplies oxygen to Earth's atmosphere. Most organisms require oxygen and give off carbon dioxide. The carbon dioxide is used again in photosynthesis. A useful cycle exists. But the carbon dioxide content of the atmosphere is increasing. Large amounts of this gas are released by the burning of modern fuels. The burning of these fuels also uses oxygen.

Measurements show that the oxygen content of the atmosphere has remained almost constant over the past century despite the increased burning of fuels. However, as the carbon dioxide level continues to increase, many biologists are concerned that its insulating effect in the atmosphere will change Earth's climates.

To preserve a balance in the oxygen and carbon dioxide levels in the atmosphere may be of vital importance to life on Earth. Much study is being given to this problem today.

---

**CAPSULE SUMMARY**

The light phase of photosynthesis produces oxygen, ATP, and NADPH. The energy is supplied by sunlight and stored as chemical energy. The hydrogen ions, electrons, and oxygen come from water molecules split during the light phase.

Two photosystems, PS I and PS II, channel electrons from water and boost them in energy. Different amounts of chlorophyll $a$, $b$, and $c$ allow the differing wavelengths of light to be absorbed by PS I and PS II. Other photosynthetic pigments also contribute to the differences.

Photosynthesis is the largest chemical industry on Earth, and the most significant.

**SELF CHECK**

1. What is a thylakoid? Where is it found?
2. What are grana?
3. Which type of photosynthesis, aerobic or anaerobic, is dominant today?
4. Why are both electron carriers and chlorophyll needed for photosynthesis to occur?
5. How was Engelmann able to show which wavelengths of light were absorbed more than others in photosynthesis?

---

## CHAPTER SUMMARY

### HIGHLIGHTS

As the original supply of dissolved organic materials became scarce, organisms that could use other sources of energy had a great advantage. Organisms developed that could use sunlight for energy. These organisms contained photosynthetic pigments, probably early kinds of chlorophyll.

Today the most widespread kind of photosynthesis uses carbon dioxide and water as raw materials. Oxygen gas is released as a by-product. The key part of photosynthesis is the conversion of light energy into chemical energy, as high-energy electrons are captured by electron-carrier molecules. The reactions involved are the light reactions. They produce ATP and NADPH.

NADPH and ATP carry the chemical energy and hydrogen made available by the light reactions to enzymes that control the dark reactions of photosynthesis. The dark reactions operate the carbon cycle which makes glucose, other sugars, amino acids, and other compounds.

The evolution of photosynthetic organisms had two very important results. First, organisms were no longer dependent on the diminishing supply of naturally-occurring organic compounds. Second, oxygen gas became a part of Earth's atmosphere.

## REVIEWING IDEAS

1. What two contributions by Ingenhousz advanced ideas of plant function from air purification to photosynthesis?
2. Both plants and animals make organic compounds using carbon dioxide. What is the important difference in these reactions?
3. When is light energy converted to chemical energy in photosynthesis?
4. What are the raw materials of photosynthesis in green plants?
5. Name three products of the light reactions of photosynthesis.
6. In which reactions, light or dark, do thylakoids and grana take part?
7. Name at least one product of the dark reactions of photosynthesis.
8. Which reactions in photosynthesis yield chemical energy?
9. How did van Niel discover that the oxygen released in photosynthesis came from water, not carbon dioxide?

## USING CONCEPTS

10. Trace a hydrogen ion and a pair of electrons from water through Photosystems I and II to their destination in the carrier molecule NADPH.
11. Hydrogen and oxygen react explosively to form water, releasing a great deal of energy. Sunlight is used by plants to decompose water. Use this information and the work of Photosystems I and II to explain how you know that NADPH is energy-rich.
12. How does the actual operation of the carbon cycle differ from the notion expressed in the following equation?

$$6CO_2 + 6H_2O \longrightarrow C_6H_{12}O_6 + 6O_2$$

13. From the product produced, how do you know that cyclic photophosphorylation does not split water molecules?

## RECOMMENDED READING

Arms, K., and P. S. Camp. *Biology,* Second Edition. Philadelphia, Saunders College Publishing, 1982. Contains a clearly written chapter on photosynthesis, with many excellent diagrams.

Revelle, R. "Carbon Dioxide and World Climate." *Scientific American,* August 1982. Favorable and unfavorable aspects of change in the amount of carbon dioxide in the atmosphere.

## REFERENCES

1. J. Priestley, "Observations on Different Kinds of Air." *Philosophical Transactions of the Royal Society of London,* Vol. 62, 1772, p. 147.
2. J. Ingenhousz, *Experiments upon Vegetables, Discovering Their Great Power of Purifying the Common Air in Sunshine and Injuring It in the Shade and at Night.* London, Elmsly and Payne, 1779.

# Life with Oxygen

# 8

You have learned that the atmospheric oxygen on which most life today depends is itself a product of life. The oxygen was released to the air by photosynthesis. The change from a primitive atmosphere without oxygen to today's atmosphere with oxygen was gradual. It began over two billion years ago and had an enormous influence on the distribution and development of living organisms on Earth. In this chapter you will learn how the presence of oxygen made it possible for living organisms to invade areas where no life had existed before. At the same time, as the oxygen level of the atmosphere kept rising, living cells developed a very efficient way of obtaining energy from organic compounds, using the oxygen. The organic compounds were now being continuously produced by the process of photosynthesis. Life on Earth became dependent on photosynthesis as a source of oxygen and of organic compounds.

# Oxygen and Energy

## 8–1

## Ozone Becomes the Shield of Life

Oxygen gas has a very interesting property: It absorbs ultraviolet light. On absorbing ultraviolet light, an oxygen molecule ($O_2$) breaks down to two oxygen atoms ($2O$). Oxygen atoms produced in this way combine to give a new kind of gas that has molecules made of three atoms of oxygen ($O_3$). Oxygen in this form is called ozone (from a Greek word which means "to smell"). Ozone is a blue gas with a very sharp odor.

The ozone layer in the atmosphere absorbs almost all the ultraviolet radiation that could destroy life. The small amount of ultraviolet radiation that gets through the ozone layer may still cause a painful sunburn, but it does not destroy life. Today life on Earth is protected by a layer of ozone that surrounds Earth about 48 kilometers above the surface of the planet.

The formation of the ozone layer had a tremendous effect on the spread of living organisms on Earth. Survival no longer depended on protection by water from ultraviolet light. Life became possible on the water's surface. For the first time in the history of Earth, even the surface of the land became safe for living organisms. Organisms could now spread out in all directions and live in previously dangerous places.

When did these enormous changes in the character of life on Earth take place? It is not known for sure, but according to one hypothesis, a turning point might have come about 600 million years ago. Enough ozone would have collected by then to allow many colonies of photosynthetic organisms to live closer to the surface in the waters of oceans, rivers, and lakes. As photosynthetic activity in the waters increased, the amount of oxygen in the atmosphere and the thickness of the ozone layer also increased. Finally, perhaps 400 million years ago, the ozone layer became thick enough to screen out all dangerous ultraviolet radiation. Living organisms could now for the first

---

←Blue sky—what was its appearance before free oxygen was added to the atmosphere?

**155**

time safely "crawl out" from the waters and begin to live and develop on land.

Interestingly enough, the known fossils fit into this timetable of evolution. Only primitive life forms are found in fossils older than 600 million years. Fossils formed between 600 and 400 million years ago show many new and more complex life forms. Some scientists speak of a "biological explosion" that occurred during that period.

The formation of an ozone layer in the atmosphere had another important effect.

In Section 5–13 you learned that the sun's ultraviolet radiation was an important source of energy for the formation of the organic compounds that nourished the heterotrophs. What happened when the ozone layer prevented most ultraviolet radiation from reaching Earth? The solar radiation that penetrated the ozone layer was mainly visible light. Visible light has too little energy to make organic compounds directly. Only through photosynthesis can the energy of visible light be used to make new organic compounds. Photosynthesis became, therefore, the only process that could add to the supply of organic compounds on Earth. Earth's organisms became dependent on photosynthesis for their food supply. The only exceptions are certain bacteria, still living today, that can obtain energy from inorganic compounds without using photosynthesis. All other organisms today depend on the food produced by photosynthesis. Nearly all also depend on the oxygen produced by photosynthesis.

## 8–2

## In Respiration, Oxygen Is Used to Release Energy

In Chapter 6 you learned that the most primitive organisms obtained their energy by the process of fermentation. Production of oxygen by photosynthesis made possible a new, efficient way of obtaining energy from organic compounds. By using

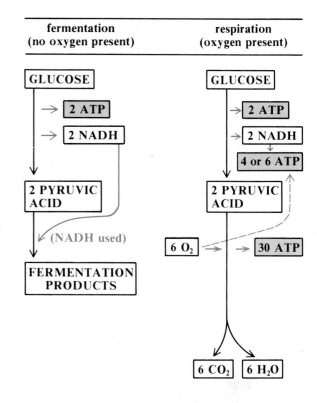

**Figure 8–1** Respiration (right) releases much more energy (36 or 38 ATP) from a glucose molecule than does fermentation (2 ATP).

oxygen, organisms could obtain more energy from the same amount of food (see Figure 8–1).

The great difference that oxygen makes in the release of energy from food was first observed by Louis Pasteur in 1861. Pasteur grew yeast cells both with and without oxygen gas, using glucose as a source of energy. With the same amount of glucose, up to 20 times more yeast grew with oxygen than grew without oxygen.

The results of Pasteur's experiments can now be fully explained. In the absence of oxygen, yeast cells undergoing fermentation released only part of the chemical energy stored in the glucose molecule. In the presence of oxygen, yeast cells could release all of the chemical energy stored in the glucose molecule. **Respiration** is the process in which oxygen is used by living cells to release the chemical energy that is stored in foodstuffs.

Glucose is an important source of energy for many forms of life, including human life. Therefore, this sugar is a good example to use in studying fermentation and respiration.

In fermentation, energy is released when a molecule of glucose is decomposed to two molecules of pyruvic acid. The net energy gain to the cell is two molecules of ATP. In respiration, the same molecule of glucose would yield at least 36 molecules of ATP—in some cells, 38. No wonder Pasteur found yeast growth to be so much greater when oxygen was present.

Why is so little chemical energy released by fermentation? Actually, there is more energy, which is released to a hydrogen and electron carrier called NADH (related to NADPH in Chapter 7). Notice in Figure 8–1 that in respiration, NADH is used to make more ATP. But in fermentation, NADH is used to convert pyruvic acid to the fermentation products. There is no energy gain. You can read more about NADH in fermentation in Appendix 6–C, page 699.

Additional energy exists in the fermentation products, but is not released. By contrast, respiration decomposes glucose to its starting materials, carbon dioxide and water:

$$C_6H_{12}O_6 + 6O_2 \longrightarrow 6CO_2 + 6H_2O$$
glucose

Note that this equation is the reverse of the equation on page 139 for the formation of glucose by photosynthesis. In photosynthesis, energy had to be added to form glucose from its starting materials, carbon dioxide and water. In respiration, the energy stored in the glucose molecule during photosynthesis is released. Much of this released energy is trapped in ATP, that is, in a form that all cells can use.

A comparison of respiration and photosynthesis leads to very important conclusions about the flow of energy and materials in the living world (see Figure 8–2). Energy for life flows in one direction only. It comes from the sun, is absorbed in photosynthesis, is released by respiration, and is used in life processes. By contrast, carbon dioxide, water, and oxygen are being continuously exchanged between respiration and photosynthesis and are used over and over again. In photosynthesis, carbon dioxide and water combine to form organic compounds and oxygen. In respiration, when oxygen reacts with organic compounds, carbon dioxide and water are set free and can be reused in photosynthesis.

**Try Investigation 8–A** Does an Oxygen Supply Affect the Rate of Growth and Reproduction of Cells?, page 607.

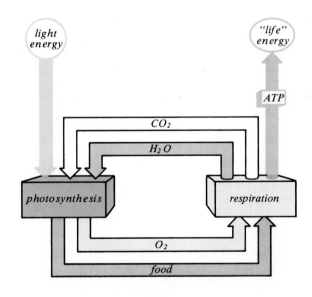

**Figure 8–2** Follow the path of the energy (yellow and orange) in the living world. Energy flow is one way. It begins as light energy from the sun and ends as the energy released by respiration. The materials, however, are reused in a cycle.

**CAPSULE SUMMARY**

The oxygen produced by photosynthesis had very important consequences for life on Earth. Oxygen gas gradually became a permanent part of Earth's atmosphere. The oxygen in the atmosphere formed a layer of ozone. This ozone absorbed the sun's ultraviolet radiation that could destroy life. Under the protection of the ozone layer, organisms could live safely on land and on the surface of waters. The presence of oxygen in the atmosphere has also made possible the development of respiration, a process in which oxygen is used by living cells to release the chemical energy that is stored in foodstuffs. Respiration is much more efficient than fermentation in releasing energy from foodstuffs. For example, the yield of ATP that is obtained from glucose is 18 or 19 times greater in respiration than in fermentation.

**SELF CHECK**

1. Why do scientists think that photosynthesis preceded the formation of atmospheric ozone?
2. What were two important consequences of formation of the atmospheric ozone layer?
3. What interesting effect did Pasteur notice about the relationship of glucose, air, and the growth of yeast cells?
4. Does photosynthesis seem more the opposite of fermentation or of respiration? Why?
5. How do photosynthesis and respiration differ with regard to oxygen?

# The Process of Respiration

## 8-3
## The Carbon Pathway in Respiration

The release of energy in respiration depends on the breakdown of organic compounds to carbon dioxide and water. The discovery of the steps of this process is one of the great achievements of modern biochemistry. Glucose will be used as an example, but the main facts are the same for all foodstuffs. In the last 40 years biochemists have found that the process of respiration includes a large number of chemical reactions, each controlled by a separate enzyme. These chemical reactions can be divided into two main groups. One group of reactions frees the carbon atoms from glucose, releasing them as carbon dioxide. These reactions will be called the **carbon pathway.**

Another group of reactions transfers the hydrogen atoms of glucose to oxygen, forming water. These reactions are called the **hydrogen pathway.** The carbon and the hydrogen pathways are linked together. Consider the carbon pathway first.

The first steps in respiration are the same as in fermentation. Without using oxygen, a living cell breaks down a molecule of glucose to two molecules of pyruvic acid (Figure 8–1). So far no carbon dioxide is given off. The two molecules of pyruvic acid each contain three carbon atoms. Together they contain the same six carbon atoms that were present in the molecule of glucose.

The release of carbon dioxide in respiration begins with the breakdown of pyruvic acid. The three carbon atoms of pyruvic acid will give rise to three molecules of carbon dioxide. Pyruvic acid is first decomposed to one molecule of carbon dioxide and a two-carbon compound (2C). Vitamins take part in making the two-carbon compound, an "active" form of acetic acid. Next, this "active" acetic acid is decomposed to yield two molecules of carbon dioxide by a series of reactions known collectively as the Krebs cycle or the citric acid cycle. Sir Hans Krebs of Oxford University, England, is the biochemist who first tracked down the complete carbon pathway in the breakdown of pyruvic acid.

A detailed picture of the Krebs cycle is given in **Appendix 8–A,** The Krebs Cycle, page 707. The main features of the Krebs cycle are summarized in a simplified manner in Figure 8–3 and as follows:

1. The 2C compound combines with a 4C compound to give a 6C compound.
2. The 6C compound splits off one molecule of carbon dioxide to give a 5C compound.
3. The 5C compound splits off one molecule of carbon dioxide to give a 4C compound. After undergoing several changes, the 4C compound is ready to combine with another molecule of the 2C compound.

Figure 8–3 shows that one turn of the Krebs cycle yields two molecules of carbon dioxide. These two molecules, and the one molecule of carbon dioxide released earlier when the 2C compound was formed, are the three molecules of carbon dioxide produced from one molecule of pyruvic acid. At the same time, the 4C compound is changed back to its original form to "take on" another molecule of the 2C compound and go through the cycle again.

It was originally thought that the Krebs cycle explained only the breakdown of carbohydrates in respiration, since all carbohydrates from foodstuffs are broken down to glucose or to pyruvic acid, the 3C compound. But more recent research has shown that the Krebs cycle also explains the

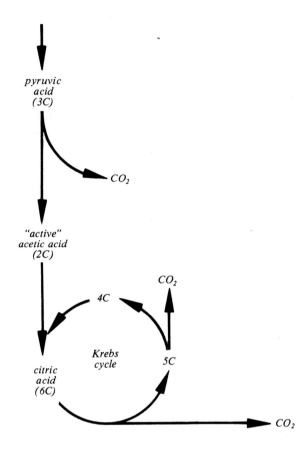

**Figure 8–3** The Krebs cycle. Pyruvic acid gives off a molecule of carbon dioxide and forms a 2C compound, which combines with a 4C compound to form a 6C compound. Following reactions remove two molecules of $CO_2$, and the 4C compound is re-formed to begin the cycle again.

breakdown of fats and proteins. These two classes of foodstuffs are also often used as sources of energy in respiration. When fats are used for energy, they are broken down to the same 2C fragments (active acetic acid) as carbohydrates. The acetic acid is then decomposed by the Krebs cycle to give off two molecules of carbon dioxide.

When proteins are used in respiration, they are first decomposed to amino acids. The carbon "skeletons" of the amino acids are in turn broken up into the same 3C, 2C, 4C, and 5C compounds that are shown in Figure 8–4. These compounds are then decomposed by the Krebs cycle to give off carbon dioxide. As Figure 8–4 shows, the Krebs cycle is the main pathway of carbon for the three classes of foodstuffs that are used in respiration: carbohydrates, fats, and proteins.

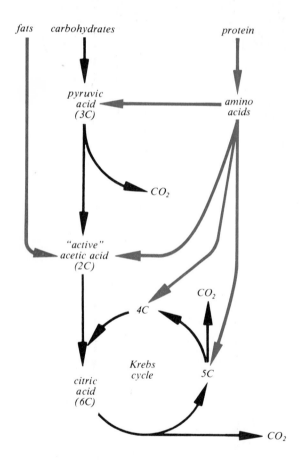

**Figure 8–4** The Krebs cycle (or citric-acid cycle) is the main pathway of carbon in the respiration of carbohydrates, fats, and proteins. Compare this figure with Figure 8–3.

## 8–4
## The Hydrogen Pathway in Respiration Is Linked to the Energy-Releasing Reactions

Since energy release was stressed as the important part of respiration, you may wonder why nothing was said about energy when the carbon pathway was discussed. ATP is not produced by the carbon transfers, but by the simultaneous transfers involving hydrogen. Hydrogen is transferred to oxygen in a series of energy-releasing reactions. Like the carbon transfers, the hydrogen transfers begin before the Krebs cycle and continue during it.

Hydrogen and oxygen readily combine to form water, releasing a large amount of energy. Thus a mixture of hydrogen and oxygen gas is highly explosive. In respiration, the combination of hydrogen and oxygen takes place in a special way that makes the released energy useful for life.

Consider first the explosive reaction between hydrogen and oxygen gas. Obviously an explosion would not be a good way to release energy for life processes. In an explosion, no matter how small, the energy is released all at once in an uncontrolled way. (Look at the waterfall on the left in Figure 8–5. Then look at how it has been controlled through a series of power stations, on the right.) In respiration, energy is released in a controlled way. Hydrogen does not combine with oxygen in one step but approaches oxygen in a series of steps. At some steps, hydrogen-carrier molecules accept the hydrogen. At other steps, electron-carrier molecules accept only electrons from the hydrogen. That is, the hydrogen sometimes exists as hydrogen atoms and at other times it exists as hydrogen ions and electrons ($H^+$ and $e^-$). This situation should remind you of the way electrons move in photosynthesis (Chapter 7) before combining with hydrogen ions in NADPH. As you might expect, at each step along the way in

**Figure 8–5** A waterfall releases all its energy at once. If it is run through several steps turning turbines at each step, its energy is released in controllable amounts.

respiration, the hydrogen or the electrons release a bit of their total energy. Much of this released energy is stored in ATP.

Biologists speak of **electron transport** as the key to energy release in respiration. In the final step of respiration, the electrons are transferred to oxygen. At the same time, hydrogen ions are transferred to the oxygen, so that hydrogen is formed again in reaction with oxygen to make water.

The compounds that accept hydrogen and electrons from food molecules in the cell are usually $NAD^+$ and $NADP^+$. You know $NADP^+$ for its role as a hydrogen and electron carrier in photosynthesis to form NADPH. Similarly, NADH is

formed from $NAD^+$. The only structural difference between $NAD^+$ and $NADP^+$ is that $NADP^+$ has a phosphate group attached to a ribose part of the molecule (Appendix 7–D). Both $NAD^+$ and $NADP^+$ contain nicotinamide (nih-kuh-TEEN-uh-myde), also known as niacin, one of the B vitamins.

You first read about NADH earlier in this chapter. It is formed in fermentation but does not lead to the formation of ATP. NADH is also formed in respiration and leads to the formation of ATP.

The hydrogen and electrons of NADH and NADPH are transferred to a complex series of enzymes known collectively as the **respiratory chain.** Each enzyme in the chain has an "active

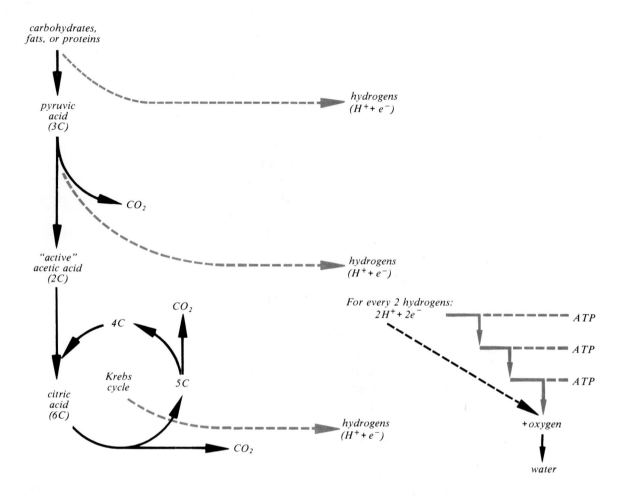

**Figure 8–6** The hydrogen released in respiration is the source of energy for the cell. Eight hydrogens are released by each turn of the Krebs cycle alone. Three molecules of ATP are usually formed for every two hydrogens released, although there are a few exceptions. The hydrogen combines with oxygen to form water.

group'' that accepts hydrogen or electrons. The active groups of some of the enzymes contain riboflavin, another B vitamin, and minerals such as iron and sulfur. Other enzymes contain iron or copper. Now you know at least one very important reason why vitamins and minerals are needed in the diet.

Each enzyme in the respiratory chain accepts hydrogen or electrons from the preceding enzyme. Some energy is released in the transfer. Then the hydrogen or electrons are passed on to the next enzyme. Again some energy is released in the transfer. There are many enzymes in the respiratory chain. During three of the many transfers, enough energy is released from a pair of electrons to make ATP from ADP. (See **Appendix 8–B,** The Respiratory Chain, page 708.) Usually the energy released from each pair of electrons does in fact lead to formation of three molecules of ATP (Figure 8–6). However, the exact manner in which this occurs is still being studied, as you will read in Section 8–6.

# 8–5

## Respiration Releases Energy and Supplies Building Materials for the Cell

Almost 200 years ago scientists recognized that both a flame and respiration yield energy from fuel. The flame changes the chemical energy of the fuel into heat and light in a single step. Respiration, in many controlled step-by-step reactions, changes the chemical energy stored in foodstuffs into a form of chemical energy (ATP) that is readily used by cells. Respiration releases heat, too, but much more slowly than a flame. The heat may be important to many organisms in keeping warm. Heat-regulating mechanisms in humans and many other animals keep the body's internal temperature constant within narrow limits. Your own body temperature, for example, stays the same within one or two degrees. It may go up a few degrees when you are ill but drops back to normal when you are well.

Figures 8–1 and 8–6 summarize the features of respiration that are presently known. The first part, as shown in Figure 8–1, yields two molecules of ATP and two molecules of NADH. With the formation of NADH, the hydrogen pathway has begun even before the steps similar to fermentation have ended.

Unlike all later NADH generated in respiration, the first NADH formed is made during the fermentationlike steps. The NADH is unable to move to places in the cell where the respiratory chains occur, so a series of chemical reactions is required to transfer the energy of NADH. In cells of your heart, liver, and kidneys, the transfer of energy is made to the beginning of a respiratory chain. Six molecules of ATP are generated. But in most of your other body cells, the energy transfer is made to a carrier molecule that functions in a later step of the respiratory chain. Only four ATP molecules are generated.

In the second part of respiration, hydrogen ions and electrons continue to be released. They are released both before and during the Krebs cycle, as indicated in Figure 8–6. Figure 8–1 shows that the ATP yield in this part of respiration is 30 molecules of ATP. Thus, the total yield of ATP from one molecule of glucose in respiration is 36 or 38 molecules.

The pre-existing reactions of fermentation have not been discarded in respiration. You may recall from Chapter 5 that evolution acts as a remodeler, not an architect. This remodeling accounts for the aerobic reactions added after pyruvic acid forms (Figures 8–1 and 8–6). First, a net gain of two molecules of ATP is generated as in fermentation. Then the fate of the NADH generated in fermentation is modified to yield more ATP. Respiration exploits the energy release that is only begun by fermentation.

The tremendous increase in energy yield in respiration is accompanied by a second advantage. The breakdown of large organic molecules, all the way to carbon dioxide and water, completes a cycle. Photosynthesis requires carbon dioxide and water; respiration releases them again. The materials can be used over and over. The supply of building materials for cells of most organisms is renewed each time the photosynthesis portion of the cycle occurs.

**CAPSULE SUMMARY**

The first steps in respiration are the same as in fermentation. No carbon is given off in the breakdown of glucose until after pyruvic acid begins to be decomposed. However, hydrogen and electrons are given to NAD$^+$, forming NADH. In fermentation, the energy of the NADH is used again in making the fermentation products. In respiration, the energy is shuttled to a respiratory chain and used to make ATP. This shuttle step determines whether the ATP yield from one molecule of glucose will reach 36 or 38 molecules.

Most of the ATP from the respiration of glucose is formed from the breakdown of pyruvic acid. All in all, 30 of the 36 or 38 molecules of ATP are formed in these later steps of respiration. The Krebs cycle is involved, and both carbon and hydrogen are given off before as well as during the Krebs cycle. The hydrogen (or electrons), but not the carbon, passes along respiratory chains to oxygen, releasing energy.

**SELF CHECK**

1. What role do NAD$^+$ and NADP$^+$ play in respiration?
2. What role do vitamins and minerals play in respiration?
3. What is a respiratory chain?
4. Why does the yield of ATP from glucose in respiration differ for different cells in your body?

## 8–6

## Respiration Takes Place in Special Parts of a Cell

No process like respiration can proceed in a haphazard way. It involves many enzymes and many chemical reactions. How are all the necessary substances coordinated in the cell? How can the product of one enzyme reaction be handed over to the next enzyme in the chain without getting lost

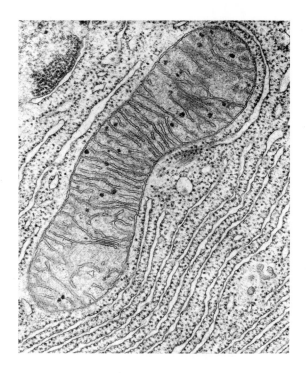

**Figure 8–7** A mitochondrion in the pancreas of a bat, as photographed through an electron microscope (×25,000).

among the many reactions taking place within the cell?

Cells have evolved special compartments that "house" the Krebs cycle and respiratory chains. Each compartment is called a **mitochondrion** (Figure 8–7). You may recall from Chapter 2 that mitochondria are often called the powerhouses of the cell.

Some cells may have only 10 to 20 mitochondria. Others may have several thousand. The number of mitochondria is related to a cell's functions and energy requirements. The size of each mitochondrion is very small, usually only two or three micrometers (μm) in length and about one μm in thickness. When properly stained, larger mitochondria may be seen under a compound microscope. However, their detailed structure is revealed only by the electron microscope.

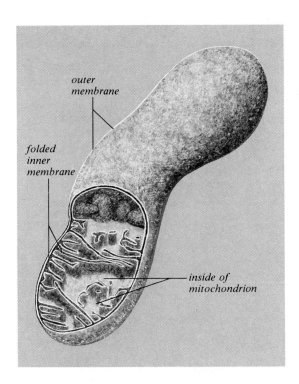

**Figure 8–8** A three-dimensional drawing of the mito-chondrion shown in Figure 8–7. Respiration occurs as food products enter the mitochondrion.

A mitochondrion has two membranes (Figures 8–7 and 8–8). Like a cell's plasma membrane, they are made of lipid and protein molecules. However, they contain so many enzymes that they are more protein than lipid. This is especially true of the inner membrane. It has many folds extending into the inside of the mitochondrion. In and on this inner membrane are

- all enzymes of the respiratory chains;
- enzymes for ATP formation;
- some of the enzymes of the Krebs cycle.

Most of the enzymes of the Krebs cycle are in the open, inside area of the mitochondrion.

The fermentationlike steps in respiration take place in the cell cytoplasm. The remaining steps take place in the mitochondria. The NADH formed during the fermentationlike steps cannot enter a mitochondrion through its two membranes and reach a respiratory chain. That is why a chemical "shuttle" operates to transfer the energy of NADH into the mitochondria. All other NADH or NADPH is actually made in the mitochondria where the respiratory chains occur.

ATP is made on the same inner membrane where electron transport takes place in the respiratory chains. Yet molecules that transfer energy from respiration to the enzymes that make ATP have never been found. (See **Appendix 8–C,** The $H^+$ Pump, page 709.)

All in all, mitochondria are amazingly complex structures for their size. They contain enzyme systems that biologists consider too highly developed to have arisen in one "remodeling" step in evolution. How did they come to be so similar in cells of so many different organisms?

## 8–7
## Did Mitochondria Evolve from Tiny Organisms?

Prokaryotic cells (page 41) do not have mitochondria. Yet many bacteria carry on respiration. The entire cells of some of these small bacteria are much like mitochondria.

Eukaryotic cells generally have mitochondria, but there are exceptions. The giant amoeba *Pelomyxa palustris* does not have mitochondria. It lives in mud at the bottom of ponds, where oxygen is in short supply. You might expect the amoeba to live by fermentation. However, close study reveals that the amoeba carries on respiration. Under an electron microscope it even appears to contain objects somewhat like mitochondria. The objects are bacteria, living inside the amoeba!

If the bacteria in the amoeba are killed with antibiotics, respiration stops. The amoeba then accumulates fermentation products. This accumulation is an indication of the mitochondrionlike role

# Biology Brief

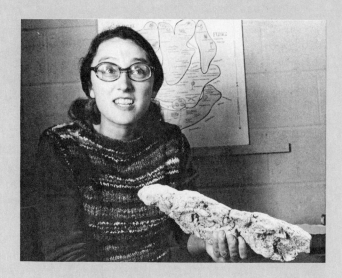

## The Cell Symbiosis Hypothesis

The oldest known fossil cells appear to have been prokaryotic. Traces of Cyanobacteria (page 49) 3.5 billion years old have been found in Australia. Fossil bacteria (Figure 5–3, page 91) more than 3 billion years old have been found in South Africa. The differences between these early cells and eukaryotic cells of larger organisms are very great. How did eukaryotic cells originate?

Professor Lynn Margulis (shown above) of Boston University is one of the foremost proponents of the cell symbiosis hypothesis. This hypothesis proposes that specialized prokaryotic cells of long ago may have come together in symbiotic relationships that led to eukaryotic cells. Some of the early prokaryotic cells carried on fermentationlike processes; others, photosynthesis. Still others evolved that used oxygen given off by photosynthesis to help break down the by-products of fermentation. A host cell carrying on fermentation would be beneficial to a guest cell using oxygen in obtaining energy from the host cell's wastes. The great increase in energy yield could in turn be beneficial to the host cell. The oxygen may have been harmful to the host cell; eventually, defenses against it would have evolved. Symbiotic relationships beginning almost by chance may have become necessary to the partner cells. They would then evolve together as a more complex cell.

the bacteria play in the life processes of the amoeba.

Certain other organisms can carry on photosynthesis because photosynthetic algae or bacteria live inside them. Indeed, a photosynthetic bacterium (Figure 7–2, center, page 135) looks much like a chloroplast (Figure 7–11, page 146).

Such observations have raised the question of

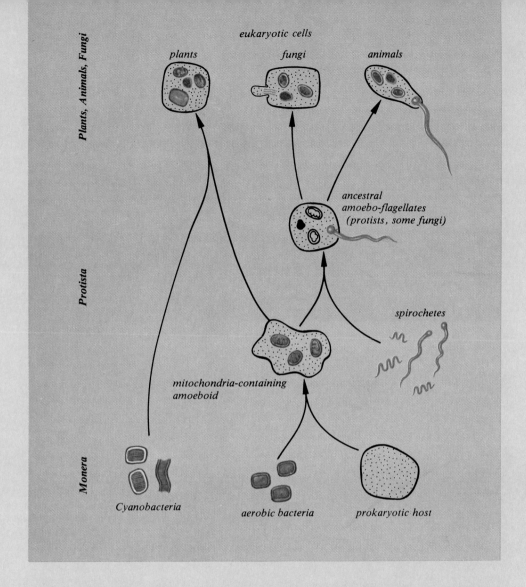

*Plants, Animals, Fungi*

*Protista*

*Monera*

eukaryotic cells

plants    fungi    animals

ancestral
amoebo-flagellates
(protists, some fungi)

spirochetes

mitochondria-containing
amoeboid

Cyanobacteria

aerobic bacteria    prokaryotic host

Bacteria that carried on respiration could have been the ancestors of mitochondria in eukaryotic cells. Cyanobacteria could have been the ancestors of chloroplasts in eukaryotic cells. Motile bacteria, especially spirochetes (see figure above), may even have been the ancestors of mechanisms for motility in eukaryotic cells, according to Professor Margulis. Thus, cilia and flagella in eukaryotes would have derived from bacteria too. As biologists discover more about cell structures, questions about ancestral symbiosis multiply.

whether chloroplasts and mitochondria in eukaryotic cells evolved from smaller cells living within larger ones. If so, then these relationships among several different kinds of prokaryotic cells could help explain the origin of eukaryotic cells. (See Biology Brief above.) **Symbiosis** (sim-bih-OH-sis) is the name given to such close living associations between organisms.

**CAPSULE SUMMARY**

The enzymes of the Krebs cycle, the respiratory chains, and ATP formation occur together in mitochondria. Only the fermentationlike steps of respiration occur outside the mitochondria, in eukaryotic cells. ATP is also formed in the cell cytoplasm during fermentationlike steps.

The cell symbiosis hypothesis suggests that eukaryotic cells evolved from symbiotic relationships among specialized prokaryotic cells. Even today, symbioses that permit photosynthesis in nonphotosynthetic organisms are observed. So are symbioses that permit respiration in eukaryotic cells lacking mitochondria. Most eukaryotic cells have mitochondria, but symbiosis in cells that do not have these structures suggests what the origin of the mitochondria could be.

**SELF CHECK**

1. Where are the enzymes of the respiratory chains located in mitochondria?
2. Why is a shuttle necessary for NADH generated in fermentationlike steps of respiration?
3. What is the probable origin of mitochondria?
4. What new environmental substance is required by cells containing mitochondria?

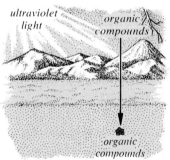

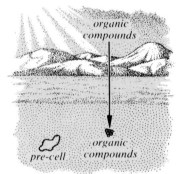

**1. primitive atmosphere**

**2. organic compound formation**

**3. pre-cell formation**

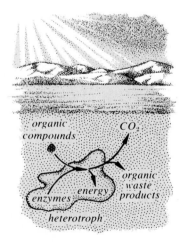

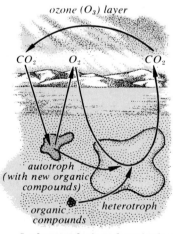

**4. simple fermentation**

**5. photosynthesis and respiration**

**Figure 8–9** The heterotroph hypothesis assumes that life processes developed gradually. It assumes that the first living things existed without oxygen and that photosynthesis and respiration were later developments.

# CHAPTER SUMMARY

## HIGHLIGHTS

As the oxygen produced long ago by photosynthesis escaped to the atmosphere, it formed a layer of ozone that absorbed most of the ultraviolet radiation from the sun. With a protective ozone screen above them, living organisms no longer had to remain in the water. They began to live where no life had existed before. For the first time in the history of Earth, life on land became possible.

Living cells developed a new process—respiration—using oxygen. Respiration is much more efficient than fermentation. The net yield in molecules of ATP from one molecule of glucose is 36 or 38, instead of 2 as in fermentation. In eukaryotic cells, all but the fermentationlike steps of respiration are carried out in the mitochondria. The mitochondria may have evolved from bacteria that carried on respiration.

A review of the general assumptions of the heterotroph hypothesis is shown in Figure 8–9. The fifth scene in the figure shows the developments of life on Earth with oxygen in the atmosphere.

## REVIEWING IDEAS

1. What happens when ultraviolet radiation acts on oxygen gas?
2. About how many times greater is ATP production by respiration than by fermentation?
3. Why would you not expect to find mitochondria in anaerobic organisms?
4. Which part of a hydrogen atom is always transported by a respiratory chain?
5. Explain how respiration completes a materials cycle with photosynthesis.
6. What major requirement of organisms cannot be recycled? How is it renewed?
7. What types of organic compounds can the Krebs cycle break down?
8. To what element are hydrogen ions and electrons transferred at the end of a respiratory chain?
9. How many molecules of carbon dioxide and of water result from the breakdown of one molecule of glucose in respiration?
10. Name one reason why the membranes of mitochondria are rich in proteins compared to lipids.

## USING CONCEPTS

11. How are the Krebs cycle in respiration, and the carbon cycle in photosynthesis, alike? How are they different?
12. Respiratory chains occur only in mitochondria. What effect does this have on NADH produced outside the mitochondria during the fermentationlike steps of respiration?
13. What must happen to the rest of the energy from glucose in eukaryotic cells that generate 36 instead of 38 molecules of ATP from a glucose molecule?
14. How is your breathing related to respiration in your cells? Suggest how the two processes differ.
15. Certain organisms that carry on fermentation cannot live in symbiosis with mitochondrionlike bacteria. Why are these organisms limited to fermentation? How do they resemble the earliest heterotrophs?

## RECOMMENDED READING

de Duve, C. ''Microbodies in the Living Cell.'' *Scientific American,* May 1983. This article discusses several little-known cell structures and their origins.

Margulis, L. *Early Life.* San Francisco, W. H. Freeman, 1981. The cell symbiosis hypothesis is explored in a short, readable, well-illustrated book.

Weisz, P. B., and R. N. Keogh. *The Science of Biology.* Fifth edition. New York, McGraw-Hill, 1982. A college textbook with good coverage of cell respiration.

# PART THREE

# New Life

A young elephant grows and matures as its parents age. Reproduction renews the species. All organisms are eventually replaced by others due to disease, fire, flood, drought, starvation, and other hazards that compete with aging to affect life spans. How can life be transferred from existing individuals to new ones? Why are the new individuals the same species as the old? Both these questions underlie the related processes by which different species maintain their populations.

# Master
## Molecules 9

By now you have learned that in cells all the processes essential for life are catalyzed by enzymes. Enzymes are proteins. Proteins are made of up to 20 different amino acids. The amino acids are arranged in many different combinations like letters in the alphabet that are arranged differently in different words. How are proteins formed? What controls the different orders in which amino acids combine to form different proteins? How are the instructions to form the same proteins transferred from a parent cell to a new cell? These are questions we will now try to answer.

# The Nucleic Acids

## 9–1
## Nucleic Acids Are Found in All Cells

To many biologists the most fascinating molecules found in living organisms today are the **nucleic** (new-KLEE-ik) **acids.** All recent experimental evidence indicates that nucleic acids are the molecules that exert primary control over the synthesis of protein enzymes, which in turn control the basic life processes of all living organisms. Nucleic acids form the chemical link between the generations. To understand how this one type of molecule can play such a dominant role in all living things, scientists have carefully studied the structure of nucleic acids. In the last few years, much has been learned about these molecules. Some of the most exciting discoveries in biology are being made as scientists all over the world study the structure and the action of the nucleic acids.

Nucleic acids were first isolated from white blood corpuscles and fish sperm by a Swiss biochemist, Friedrich Miescher (MEE-sher), in a remarkable series of investigations which began in 1869. The isolated substances belonged to a new

class, different from proteins and other known substances in cells. They were acidic in nature and rich in the element phosphorus. Because they were found in cell nuclei, Miescher called them "nuclein." Today they are called nucleic acids. Miescher speculated that they were the cell's hereditary materials. When more and more organisms were examined, it soon became apparent that they all contained nucleic acids.

As the methods for analyzing nucleic acids were improved, the nucleic acids from many different kinds of organisms were compared. To the astonishment of chemists and biologists, nucleic acids were found to be very similar in all forms of life, from bacteria to green plants to humans. Upon further investigation it became clear that nucleic acids were found not only in the nuclei but also in other parts of the cell. The term *nucleic acids* is still used even though it is not entirely accurate.

## 9–2
## The Nucleic Acid Molecule Has Several Parts

To understand the composition of nucleic acids, scientists analyzed them chemically. By gathering together great numbers of cell nuclei, they could obtain enough of the nucleic acids to determine their composition. When nucleic acids were split

---

← If things go well, a trout dinner for two is developing in the sheltered, shallow water. But what directs the formation of these fishes from beginnings so very small?

apart, they were found to be made of a few relatively simple units repeated over and over again. The resultant molecules of nucleic acids are huge—the largest molecules found in living cells. The secret of the importance of nucleic acids in living systems lies in the smaller units.

The basic unit of a nucleic acid is a **nucleotide** (NEW-klee-oh-tyd). A nucleic acid molecule contains four kinds of nucleotides. These four kinds of nucleotides are arranged in a long chain. Just as one might arrange red, blue, yellow, and green beads on a string in a great many ways, so the four kinds of nucleotides can be arranged in many different ways. Different species of organisms differ in the number and arrangement of the nucleotides in their nucleic acid molecules.

Each nucleotide can be broken down into three parts. One of these parts is always a sugar. One kind of nucleic acid contains a five-carbon sugar, ribose. (See Figure 9–1.) Nucleic acids that contain ribose are called **ribonucleic** (ry-boh-new-KLEE-ic) **acids,** or **RNA** for short. The structural formula for ribose shows that four of its carbon atoms are joined by an oxygen in the form of a

**Figure 9–1** RNA and DNA are named after the sugars ribose and deoxyribose. Every molecule of nucleic acid contains one or the other of these sugars. The only difference between the sugars is one atom, at the point outlined in blue.

ring. Notice in the diagram that one of the hydroxyl groups (—OH) is shown in blue. The reason for this emphasis will become clear in the next paragraph.

Another kind of nucleic acid contains a very similar form of five-carbon sugar, deoxyribose. This form, shown also in Figure 9–1, has a hydrogen (—H) atom instead of the hydroxyl (—OH) group at the same carbon atom. Compared to ribose, one oxygen atom is missing. This sugar is called "de-oxy-ribose"; *deoxy* means "minus one oxygen." The nucleic acids which contain deoxyribose are called **deoxyribonucleic** (dee-OK-sih-ry-boh-new-KLEE-ic) **acids.** This is abbreviated as **DNA.** These two general types of nucleic acids, RNA and DNA, are named after the sugar molecule their nucleotides contain.

The two other parts of nucleotides in addition to sugar are: (1) a phosphate group made from phosphoric acid ($H_3PO_4$); and (2) a ring-like structure of carbon, hydrogen, and nitrogen, known as a nitrogen base. The bases in nucleic acids have either a single-ring or a double-ring structure.

Each of the four different kinds of nucleotides in DNA contains the same sugar and phosphate groups but has a different base. (See Figures 9–2 and 9–3.) For example, adenine nucleotide is made by the bonding together of one molecule each of a base (adenine), a sugar (deoxyribose), and phosphoric acid. The other three nucleotides of DNA contain three other bases: thymine (THY-meen), guanine (GWAH-neen), and cytosine (SY-toh-seen). Thymine and cytosine are single-ringed compounds of a type known as pyrimidines (pih-RIH-mih-deens). Their formulas (see Figure 9–2) contain a single closed ring with other atoms bonded to it. Adenine and guanine are double-ringed compounds (see Figure 9–3) of a type known as purines (PURE-eens). Figure 9–4 is a diagram of the four DNA nucleotides.

Nucleotides, especially adenine nucleotides, are also key substances in other cell processes. ATP,

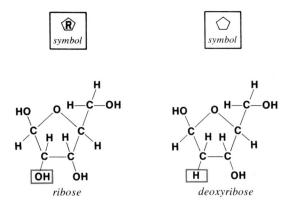

the carrier of chemical energy in all living cells, is an adenine nucleotide. It contains adenine, ribose (instead of deoxyribose), and three molecules of phosphate. (Compare Figure 9–4 with Figure 6–6 on page 122). Adenine nucleotide also makes up about half of $NADP^+$ (see Appendix 7–D), the hydrogen carrier molecule that plays an essential role in photosynthesis and respiration.

Scientists can now experimentally put together a nucleic acid molecule. A research team headed by Arthur Kornberg (now at Stanford University) successfully isolated an enzyme from bacteria which catalyzes the synthesis of DNA from its four nucleotides. This laboratory-made DNA had the same properties as the DNA made by the living cell. For the first time scientists could observe the synthesis of DNA outside the living cell!

How does the structure of RNA (ribonucleic acid) differ from that of DNA? One difference is that the sugar of RNA is ribose instead of deoxyribose. The other difference is that the base thymine is not found in RNA but is replaced by a similar compound, uracil (YUR-uh-sil), also a pyrimidine. The other three bases, adenine, guanine, and cytosine, are the same in RNA and DNA. Figure 9–5 shows the structure of the base uracil and the nucleotide that is formed from it.

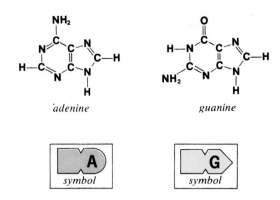

**Figure 9–3** The purines adenine and guanine. Each has a double-ring structure.

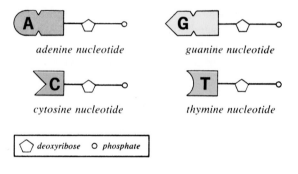

**Figure 9–4** Symbols represent the adenine, guanine, cytosine, and thymine in these diagrams of nucleotides. Each nucleotide contains one of the bases, one sugar, and one phosphate group. The sugar is deoxyribose, making these the four nucleotides of DNA.

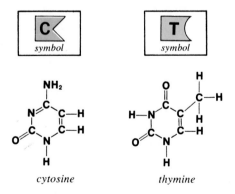

**Figure 9–2** The pyrimidines cytosine and thymine. Each has a single-ring structure.

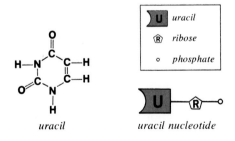

**Figure 9–5** If the sugar in Figure 9–4 were ribose, three of the four nucleotides (but not the thymine nucleotide) would be found in RNA. A uracil nucleotide, diagrammed above, is found as the fourth nucleotide of RNA.

In RNA, just as in DNA, the nucleotides are arranged in long chains. The number and arrangement of the nucleotides vary in RNA as they do in DNA. These different arrangements of nucleotides are of great importance. They provide the key to how these molecules may account for the variety of organisms living on Earth.

nucleus, whereas RNA is found in both the nucleus and the cytoplasm. RNA differs from DNA in that it contains a different sugar and has the base uracil instead of thymine.

**SELF CHECK**

1. What are the two basic chemical differences between RNA and DNA?
2. What are the chemical building blocks of which nucleic acids are constructed?
3. How many kinds of nitrogen-containing bases are found in DNA? in RNA?
4. How does the chemical structure of ribose differ from that of deoxyribose?
5. What are nucleotides? Describe the structure of a typical nucleotide.
6. Compare ATP to the adenine nucleotide in DNA.

**CAPSULE SUMMARY**

Nucleic acids are very large molecules found in all forms of life today. Nucleic acids are made up of chains of smaller units called nucleotides. Each nucleotide is made up of three parts: a phosphate group, a sugar, and a nitrogen base.

The two kinds of nucleic acids are deoxyribonucleic acid (DNA) and ribonucleic acid (RNA). In eukaryotic cells, DNA is found mainly in the

## Nucleic Acids and Cells

### 9-3

### Nucleic Acids in Action

The first real proof that nucleic acids have something to do with inheritance in cells came in 1944. It came from the work of Oswald Avery, Colin McLeod, and Maclyn McCarty (at the Rockefeller University in New York City). They were working with pneumococcus (new-moh-KOK-us) bacteria, which can cause the disease pneumonia. To understand why scientists were surprised by this work we have to know something about the bacteria they studied.

**Try Investigation 9-A** Bacteria, Pneumonia, and DNA, page 608.

Two kinds of pneumococcus bacteria were known to exist. In one kind, each pair of bacterial

cells is surrounded by a capsule of a sugarlike substance. The other kind has no capsule around the cells. Both kinds can reproduce, giving rise to cells like themselves. When cells with capsules divide, they form new cells with capsules. Cells without capsules form new cells without capsules. (See Figure 9-6.)

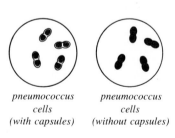

*pneumococcus cells (with capsules)*     *pneumococcus cells (without capsules)*

**Figure 9-6** Diagrams of two different strains of pneumococcus bacteria.

*live cells
(without capsules)*

*live cells
(with capsules)*

**Figure 9–7** Mice react differently to injection of the two strains of pneumococcus.

The most significant fact about these bacteria is that those with capsules can cause pneumonia. Mice injected with these cells sicken and die. Mice injected with cells that have no capsules are unaffected. (See Figure 9–7.)

Avery, McLeod, and McCarty tested many different parts of the pneumococcus cells for the cause of this difference. They knew that hereditary material was involved. They expected to find that a protein was the active hereditary substance. They eventually found, however, that the hereditary characteristics of the bacteria were determined by DNA. They grew the pneumococcus cells with capsules, and after a period of growth they broke open the cells and extracted the DNA. They then added the extracted DNA to a culture of pneumococcus cells without capsules. These cells would normally give rise to new cells without capsules that did not cause pneumonia. But now something unusual happened: among the new cells were some with capsules. When these were injected into healthy mice the mice developed pneumonia. The only explanation that fitted these facts was that the "foreign" DNA from cells with capsules changed some of the harmless cells without capsules. The "foreign" DNA transformed these cells into disease-causing cells with capsules that gave pneumonia to healthy mice.

The importance of these experiments was that for the first time heredity had been traced to the action of a particular chemical substance. Scientists had speculated that some day the carriers of heredity might prove to be proteins. Few since Miescher had suspected that this role belonged to nucleic acids. Could the same role for nucleic acids be demonstrated in other systems? To answer this question, scientists turned to viruses.

## 9–4
## Viruses Contain Nucleic Acids

Section 5–16 discussed the question of whether or not viruses are living. Outside a living organism, they are like a chemical and can remain inert almost indefinitely. Once they enter a living cell, however, they often take over control of that cell. They then direct the cell's "machinery" to produce more viruses.

The first virus crystals were obtained in 1935 by Wendell Stanley at the University of California at Berkeley. Stanley was able to purify and obtain crystals of tobacco mosaic virus, which infects and kills the cells of tobacco leaves.

Tobacco mosaic virus was originally thought to be made entirely of protein. Eventually research showed that the virus crystals are in part made of protein and in part nucleic acid. Since that discovery, the chemical nature of many other viruses has been investigated. All of them, regardless of the cells they infect, appear to be composed primarily of nucleic acid and protein.

RNA is the kind of nucleic acid found in many viruses, such as tobacco mosiac virus, polio virus, and influenza virus. DNA is found in many other viruses including those viruses that attack bacterial cells and reproduce within them.

## 9–5
## Some Viruses Reproduce Within Bacteria

Like other viruses, bacterial viruses are composed primarily of nucleic acid and protein. These viruses are also called **bacteriophages** (bak-TEER-ee-uh-fay-jez), or just "phages" (FAY-jez) for short. (The word "phage" comes from the Greek *phagos,* one that eats.) Phages live at the expense of the bacteria they inhabit. They are reproduced within the bacterial cells and eventually may destroy the very cells that produced them.

The interaction between phages and bacteria has now been studied extensively. In one well-known case, a tadpole-shaped phage called T2 attaches itself to a bacterial cell. (See Figure 9–8.) The phage then injects its long, single fiber of DNA into the cell. The bacterial cell has its own DNA, the substance that governs its normal life activities. But when the viral DNA enters the cell, it takes over the "manufacturing plant" of the bacterium. The viral DNA causes the bacterium to produce more virus substance instead of more bacterial substance. The materials within the bacterium are built into more viral DNA and more viral protein, and eventually the bacterium dies. Figure 9–9 pictures the stages of these events.

The new DNA directs the cell to produce complete viruses. In less than 30 minutes the cell bursts and several hundred newly formed viruses are released to the outside. Each of these virus particles can now infect another bacterial cell, and in time an entire population of bacteria may be destroyed.

**Figure 9–8** An electron photomicrograph of T2-phage viruses. The phages can inject their DNA into bacteria.

## 9–6
## Nucleic Acids Control Cell Activities

The study of bacterial viruses and of the way they reproduce within living cells tells us a great deal about DNA. It is important to note that viral DNA goes further than directing an invaded cell to make more viral DNA. The cell is also directed to make the protein coats of the viruses and to assemble the completed viruses. Together, these steps suggest that DNA is the material that controls cellular events. These experiments with viruses and bacteria also show that there are differences in their DNA. The virus DNA may take over control of the bacterium from the bacterium's own DNA.

Experiments on DNA in viruses and bacteria continue today. Many other experiments with DNA now involve animal eggs and the cells they produce in developing animals. These cells have a great number of functions that have already been extensively studied, as you will learn in Chapter 11. Thus, cells in developing animals make ideal subjects for experiments investigating how DNA affects each of these known functions.

In eukaryotes from protists to human beings, DNA is located chiefly in long nuclear strands called **chromosomes.** Prokaryotes have no nucleus but have a chromosome, as viruses also do.

In some viruses, RNA is the hereditary material. RNA is also found in all organisms (in both the nucleus and the cytoplasm of eukaryotes). Organisms use their DNA to synthesize RNA. However, to a limited extent the reverse also occurs. Enzymes that use nucleotides to make new copies of a cell's DNA require RNA as a starter or primer (as you will read later in this chapter).

---

**CAPSULE SUMMARY**

DNA and RNA are the information molecules of cells. DNA from pneumococcus bacteria has been shown to transform a harmless strain into the disease-causing strain. Moreover, DNA from a bacterial virus can take over a bacterium. The viral DNA causes the bacterium to make more viral DNA, plus protein coats, and assemble new viruses. Continuing experiments with viruses, bacteria, and eggs of many animals have added more evidence that nucleic acids control cell functions.

**SELF CHECK**

1. What is meant by information molecules?
2. When mice were injected with a mixture of living pneumococcus cells without capsules and DNA from dead cells with capsules, why were the mice expected to remain healthy?
3. What evidence is there in the phage experiment that DNA can direct the manufacture of more molecules like itself?
4. In what kinds of molecules would you expect to find the "biological instructions" to the next generation of cells?

---

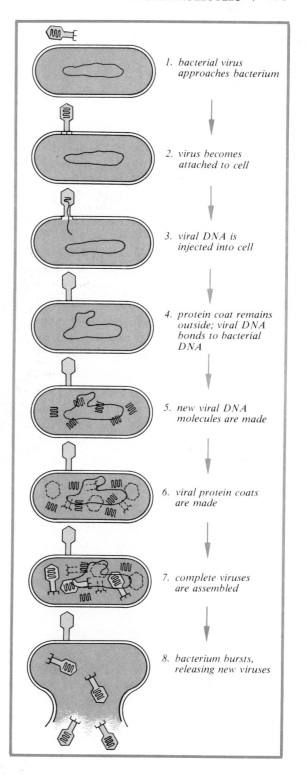

1. *bacterial virus approaches bacterium*

2. *virus becomes attached to cell*

3. *viral DNA is injected into cell*

4. *protein coat remains outside; viral DNA bonds to bacterial DNA*

5. *new viral DNA molecules are made*

6. *viral protein coats are made*

7. *complete viruses are assembled*

8. *bacterium bursts, releasing new viruses*

**Figure 9-9** A single phage becomes attached by its "tail" to a bacterium. The phage DNA passes into the bacterium. It directs the bacterium to produce phage DNA, make protein coats, and assemble the new phages. The bacterium is destroyed.

# A Molecular Model of DNA

## 9–7
## Clues to the Structure of DNA Led to a Model

When scientists realized that DNA is the substance that determines heredity, they became very eager to understand its structure. They thought that if they could learn how the nucleotides are arranged in a DNA molecule, they might be able to learn how the molecule functioned. In other words, they might find in the structure of DNA a clue to its function. Biochemists wanted to know how the nucleotides might be attached to one another.

More information about the DNA molecule became known. Pure samples of DNA were obtained, and its molecular structure was studied by a procedure called X-ray diffraction. X rays are a form of radiant energy, as are ultraviolet and visible light. (See Figure 7–1, page 134.) When a small sample of a pure chemical substance is placed close to a source of X rays, the X rays will pass through the substance. The X rays are diffracted, or bent, in different directions as they pass through the substance.

The pattern of X-ray diffraction makes a "shadow picture" on film. A single molecule can be distinguished using this technique (Figure 9–10). The shadows can tell a great deal about the molecule, but training is required to interpret the different structures the shadows could represent. Measurements can also be made from the X-ray diffraction photograph. Calculations usually follow. They are then compared with available chemical data.

The X-ray diffraction photograph of DNA in Figure 9–10 was obtained and analyzed by Maurice H. F. Wilkins at King's College in London. Wilkins and his colleague Rosalind Franklin made many different X-ray diffraction photographs of DNA molecules such as this one. They interpreted the pictures to mean that the bases, which are flat molecules, were stacked one on top of another.

Another piece of experimental evidence was obtained by comparing the chemical composition of DNA molecules taken from different kinds of organisms. It was found that in any kind of DNA the number of adenine nucleotides was always the same as the number of thymine nucleotides. Also, the number of guanine nucleotides was always the same as the number of cytosine nucleotides. This evidence seemed to indicate that nucleotides occurred in pairs in the DNA molecule.

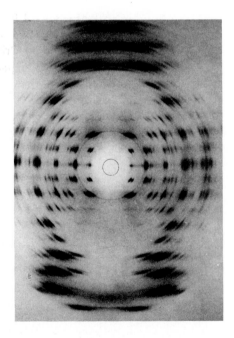

**Figure 9–10** X-ray diffraction photograph of DNA. The top and bottom bands correspond to the recurring bases in the molecule. The circular central pattern of dark spots indicates that the molecule is coiled.

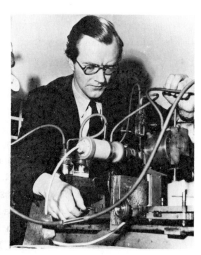

**Figure 9–11** In 1953 James D. Watson (left) and Francis H. C. Crick (center) proposed a model for the DNA molecule based partly on the X-ray diffraction studies of M. H. F. Wilkins (right). The three shared the Nobel prize in 1962.

These clues to the DNA mystery were pieced together by James D. Watson, an American geneticist working with Francis H. C. Crick, a British biophysicist at Cambridge University, England. In 1953, when Watson was only 25 years old and Crick was 37, they proposed a model for the DNA molecule which took into account the facts that were then known about DNA. In 1962 Watson, Crick, and Wilkins were jointly awarded the Nobel Prize for physiology and medicine. (See Figure 9–11.) Their work provides the basis for the chemical part of the study of heredity, the modern science of genetics.

What is a model of a molecule? In a sense, a molecular model has some things in common with models of planes, ships, and automobiles that you can purchase in a hobby shop. A model of a ship, for example, is an approximation of the real object, except that the model is much smaller. The model helps us to understand how a ship is built and how it operates.

In the same way, a model of a molecule gives an idea of how the molecule is built. In this case, since the molecules are too small for their structure

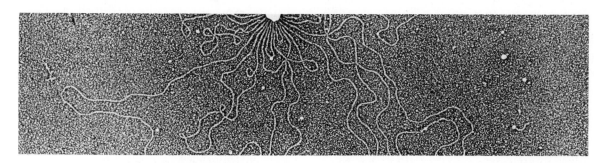

**Figure 9–12** The long thread issuing in loops from the top of the photograph is one continuous strand of DNA, photographed at about the time Watson, Crick, and Wilkins were honored for solving its molecular nature.

to be seen with the eye or with most microscopes, the real thing cannot be observed directly. A molecular model must be constructed from indirect molecular measurements and from what is known about the chemical behavior of the molecule. An electron microscope gives a picture of DNA, shown in Figure 9–12, but the picture does not tell how the atoms are arranged within the molecule. However, it does give some idea of the length and diameter of the molecule. In the same way, the X-ray diffraction pictures do not tell directly the arrangement within DNA but give indirect evidence that the flat bases are stacked together. Using these facts, the scientist can construct a model.

In science, then, a model is a way of picturing a hypothesis, based on the known facts. A model makes it easier to visualize the structure and to understand the relation of different parts. This is what the model of DNA proposed by Watson and Crick did for scientists.

## 9–8

## The Structure of DNA Was Seen as a Type of "Ladder"

Watson and Crick proposed their model of the DNA molecule in a paper published in 1953. Using the data from Wilkins' and Franklin's X-ray diffraction studies, Watson and Crick concluded that the DNA molecule consists of two strands twisted about one another in the form of a **double helix.** They wrote the following about their hypothesis:

> We wish to put forward a radically different structure for . . . deoxyribose nucleic acid. This structure has two helical chains each coiled around the same axis. . . .[1]

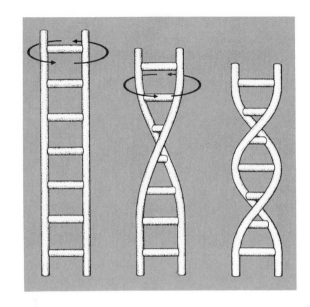

**Figure 9–13** A double helix can be formed by twisting a ladder that has flexible uprights. Watson and Crick used this idea of a double helix to picture a DNA molecule.

A double helix is like a double coil. It can be understood by imagining a ladder, as shown in Figure 9–13. This impractical ladder has flexible uprights. The bottoms of the uprights of the ladder are held in place so that they cannot move. Twist the ladder from the top, and a double helix is formed.

The uprights of this special ladder are made of the phosphate and deoxyribose portions of nucleotides. The rungs are made of nitrogen bases. The Watson-Crick model points out that the bases are paired in the rungs:

> . . . The novel feature of the structure is the manner in which the two chains are held together. . . . They are joined together in pairs, a single base from one chain being hydrogen-bonded to a single base from the other chain, so that the two lie side by side. . . . [These pairs are: thymine (single

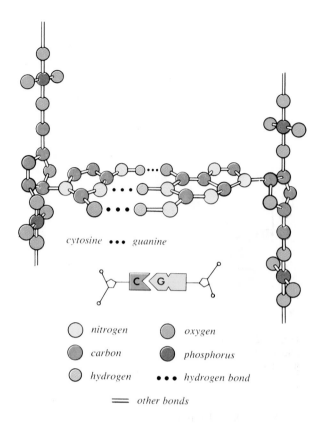

cytosine ••• guanine

C G

○ nitrogen   ○ oxygen

○ carbon     ● phosphorus

○ hydrogen   ••• hydrogen bond

══ other bonds

**Figure 9–14** A diagram of one rung of the DNA "ladder," with a key to its structure. Hydrogen bonds complete the rung, bonding cytosine (on the left) to guanine (on the right).

each case these bases are connected by weak chemical bonds called **hydrogen bonds.** These are chemical bonds established between hydrogen atoms and certain larger atoms, such as oxygen and nitrogen. Figure 9–14 shows how cytosine "fits" with guanine and how they are connected by means of hydrogen bonds.

In Figure 9–15, you can see how the ladder is transformed into a DNA molecule, as hypothesized by Watson and Crick. To summarize the Watson-Crick model of the DNA molecule:

1. The molecule is made of two strands wound about each other in a double helix.
2. Each strand is made up of a chain of nucleotides.

ring) with adenine (double ring), and cytosine (single ring) with guanine (double ring).] . . . In other words, if an adenine forms one member of a pair, on either chain, then on these assumptions the other member must be thymine; similarly for guanine and cytosine.[2]

Here, briefly and completely, was set forth the rest of the model. Each rung consists of a single-ring base matched with a double-ring base. Adenine would always be paired with thymine. Guanine would always be paired with cytosine. In

**Figure 9–15** The double-helix "ladder" has uprights made of phosphate (P) and sugar (S), and rungs made of adenine-thymine pairs and cytosine-guanine pairs.

3. A nucleotide is composed of a phosphate group, a deoxyribose group, and a nitrogen base.
4. The nucleotides in a single strand are linked together by phosphate-to-sugar bonds.
5. The strands are held together by forces that include weak hydrogen bonds between each single-ring base and its double-ring partner.

One other point emerged: the two strands appear to "face" opposite directions. This best explains the spacing of neighboring parts of the molecule.

Even though each hydrogen bond is weak in itself, there may be thousands of hydrogen bonds holding together the bases of the two strands in a single DNA molecule.

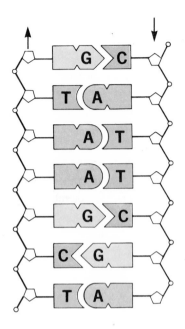

## 9–9

## How Useful Is the Model?

One measure of the value of a scientific model is its usefulness in solving problems. A model should be able to suggest new questions and predict their answers, as well as answer old questions. One problem was how the DNA molecule could be copied. It was known that each new cell receives the same kind of DNA as the original cell. You will recall from Section 9–3 that the transformed pneumococcus cells passed their capsule-forming ability on to their offspring. Each new cell received instructions from the parent cell on how to perform. These instructions were carried in the DNA molecules. Therefore, the DNA molecules must be accurately duplicated by the parent cell.

Here the Watson-Crick model is very useful, for it provides a simple explanation of how DNA undergoes duplication. The duplication process depends on the shape of the base molecules. Since

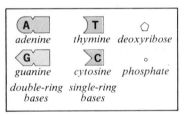

**Figure 9–16** Another diagram of the DNA "ladder," without its helix or spiral form. Sugar-phosphate bonds connect the nucleotides in the uprights. Hydrogen bonds connect the nucleotides in the rungs. Notice that the uprights "face" opposite directions; that is, the two strands have opposite orientations.

hydrogen bonds function only over short distances, the shapes of these molecules require adenine to pair only with thymine, and guanine to pair only with cytosine. According to the model, the number of adenines present in a particular kind of DNA should always be the same as the number of thymines; and the number of guanines should be the same as the number of cytosines. This is what the experimental evidence clearly showed.

Let us return to the symbols for the various kinds of nucleotides, as introduced in Figure 9–4. By uncoiling a small part of the DNA model and using the nucleotide symbols to represent it, then this structure would appear as in Figure 9–16.

Notice in Figure 9–16 that the strand on the left does not appear to have the nucleotides arranged in any particular order other than to pair correctly with those on the right. In a model, the nucleo-

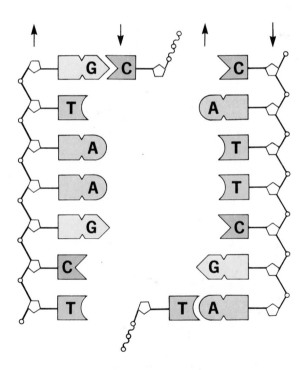

**Figure 9–17** Two strands of DNA are separated by enzyme action. New nucleotides begin to pair with those of the original strands. A feature to notice is that the new nucleotides carry extra energy-rich phosphate groups. Can you suggest how the energy may be needed and used? (See Figure 9–18.)

tides on a single strand can be in any sequence at all. Thus a great number of arrangements is possible. However, once the sequence of nucleotides on one strand is known, the sequence on the other strand is also known. For according to the model, a thymine must pair with an adenine, and a cytosine with a guanine.

A whole team of enzymes is required to duplicate DNA. First, some of the enzymes unwind a portion of a DNA molecule. Other enzymes break the hydrogen bonds between the paired nucleotides. The two strands separate (Figure 9–17). New nucleotides can now be added to each strand.

A cell's storehouse of raw materials contains many nucleotides. Improper ones for any pairing are temporarily rejected. On the left in Figure 9–17, a guanine nucleotide can pair only with a new cytosine nucleotide. On the right, an adenine nucleotide can pair only with a new thymine nucleotide.

As you read in the caption for Figure 9–16, the two strands of DNA are oriented in opposite directions. You can tell by examining the deoxyribose (sugars), then the added arrows. New nucleotides are added to the strands according to the direction in which an original strand is oriented. Because the enzymes that carry out this task can work in only one direction, the new nucleotides must be added from opposite ends of the DNA fragment's two strands (Figure 9–17).

Little by little, new nucleotides of the proper kinds continue to be added, as shown in Figure 9–18. The phosphate of one nucleotide is covalently bonded (page 99) to the sugar of the next. Soon each original strand of DNA has a new partner like the old, as in Figure 9–19.

Notice that neither new fragment of DNA is *all* new or *all* old. Each fragment contains one new and one old strand. Because of this feature, biologists say that the DNA has been **replicated** (REP-lih-kay-tud) rather than duplicated.

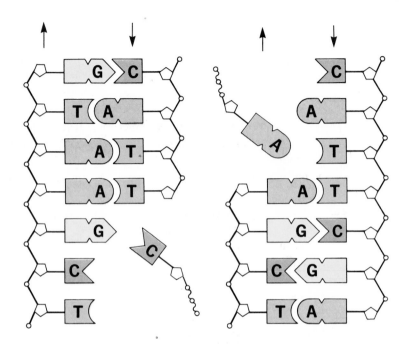

**Figure 9–18** New nucleotides continue to be brought into place. The energy of their extra phosphate groups is used to bond these new arrivals to the preceding nucleotides.

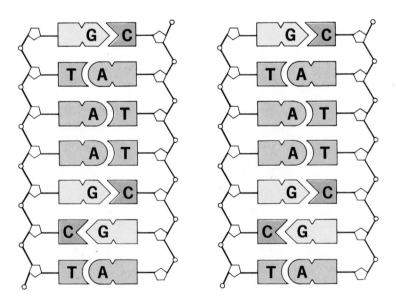

**Figure 9–19** Two new fragments of double-stranded DNA are completed. Compare them to one another and to the original in Figure 9–16. Has the replication been exact?

**9-10**

# The Model Is Tested

Watson and Crick said, "It has not escaped our notice that the specific pairing we have postulated immediately suggests a possible copying mechanism for the genetic material." The copying mechanism in Figures 9–17 and 9–18 illustrates their prediction. Compare the DNA fragments before and after replication (Figures 9–16 and 9–19). Can you see differences?

Observations and experiments with DNA from chromosomes eventually suggested a new problem. Recall that Figures 9–16 through 9–19 show only a short fragment of a DNA molecule. In the very long molecules of DNA from chromosomes, replication begins at many sites and proceeds in both directions on both strands until all replicating portions meet.

It is the "both directions on both strands" phenomenon that is puzzling. Remember that the enzymes work in only one direction. Further investigation revealed that replication takes place in one direction as expected.

$$\longrightarrow$$

However, replication also proceeds elsewhere in many simultaneous short steps that together account for the *opposite* direction.

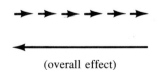

(overall effect)

This short-step operation takes no more time for completing a new DNA strand, toward the left in the diagram, than continuous replication would require if it proceeded in that direction. The result is replication that appears to go in two directions.

Wherever DNA replication starts, the first molecules must be in place. The enzymes for replication can only *add to* molecules already there. However, no new DNA molecules are in place at the beginning of replication. It turns out that the molecules in place are RNA. DNA replication is RNA-primed—that is, begun with RNA molecules. Just before the replicating DNA segments meet and are joined, the RNA is cleaved out and replaced by DNA. This means that DNA and RNA are each involved in the synthesis of the other.

---

**CAPSULE SUMMARY**

Evidence from X-ray diffraction and chemical studies were combined by Watson and Crick as they worked out their model of DNA. Observations and experiments confirmed their model: DNA is normally double-stranded, and the strands are oriented in opposite directions. Replication takes place in one direction, primed by RNA and activated by enzymes. Nucleotide pairing— A with T and C with G—governs the pattern of replication.

**SELF CHECK**

1. In a DNA "ladder," what forms the "uprights"? What forms the "rungs"?
2. What is a helix? Give some examples.
3. Which nucleotides pair with each other in a DNA molecule?
4. How does RNA help enzymes replicate DNA?

# Biology Brief

## The Chicken and the Egg

Which came first, DNA or primitive life? In a way, this is another question like "Which came first, the chicken or the egg?"

Viruses contain only DNA, or RNA, and protein coats. They cannot reproduce themselves. Their DNA must get inside living cells to find the enzyme systems and materials necessary to virus reproduction. Then the virus DNA can take over the cells, reproducing more viruses until the cells are destroyed.

Sometimes virus DNA enters and changes a cell without destroying it. The virus DNA joins the cell's DNA and adds new genes to the cell. When the cell reproduces, both its DNA and the virus's DNA are reproduced. The new cells are of the changed kind that their parent cell became when the virus DNA contributed the new genes. The cells have been *transformed*.

Viruses that infect human beings can produce similar, or even unpredictable, effects. The *Herpes simplex* (HER-peez SIM-pleks) virus can invade human cells and produce symptoms of infection or may simply be added to the cell's DNA. In the latter event, the person may not know he or she has the virus. But sometime later, even years later, the virus DNA may separate from the cell DNA. Then the symptoms of infection appear. Could the adding on of DNA from one source to that from another source have made living things more complex early in Earth's history? Or did different pre-life or early living forms come together and unite as part of evolution? You have already read a hypothesis about the second of these questions—the cell symbiosis hypothesis—on pages 166 and 167. Such questions and their answers help biologists think about which came first, DNA or primitive life.

Meanwhile, research on viruses continues to add new information to the store of biological knowledge. The biologist shown here is injecting viruses into eggs to see whether the viruses will reproduce. Could it be that the egg will not be affected?

# CHAPTER SUMMARY

## HIGHLIGHTS

Primitive heterotrophs had to be able to reproduce. To do so they first required some means to replicate their information molecules. These master molecules controlled cell structure, repair, and all cell activities. Even the enzymes necessary for the information molecules to replicate were made using information from these molecules.

For many years scientists debated whether proteins or nucleic acids were the hereditary materials—the information molecules. Experiments with bacteria settled the question; one kind of bacterium could be transformed into another, disease-causing kind by a transfer of DNA. Later experiments confirmed these findings for other organisms including plants and animals.

The Watson-Crick model of DNA structure solved the major problem that had hindered research on hereditary materials. Knowing the structure of DNA has helped make possible many kinds of studies of DNA-controlled processes.

## REVIEWING IDEAS

1. What kind of nucleic acid contains:
   a. deoxyribose?      c. thymine?
   b. uracil?            d. ribose?
2. Name five bases found in nucleotides.
3. If all DNA is made of the same four nucleotides, how can differences in DNA exist?
4. What evidence exists that a nucleic acid can pass through a bacterium's plasma membrane?
5. Which nucleic acid contains the same kind of sugar found in ATP?
6. How are enzymes and RNA essential to the replication of DNA?
7. Where is DNA found in a cell? RNA?

8. Who first suspected that nucleic acids were the hereditary materials of cells?
9. Where on a chromosome does replication begin?
10. How do extra phosphate groups contribute to adding a nucleotide to DNA?

## USING CONCEPTS

11. Which nucleotides pair with each other in an RNA molecule?
12. What evidence first indicated that adenine and thymine nucleotides are paired in DNA?
13. When continuous, or unbroken, replication is taking place in one direction on a strand of DNA, explain the replication that is taking place in the other direction.
14. Contrast replication of a DNA molecule with duplication of a molecule.
15. How do viruses illustrate the importance of enzymes to replication of DNA?

## REFERENCES

1. J. D. Watson and F. H. C. Crick, "Molecular Structure of Nucleic Acids." *Nature,* Vol. 171, No. 4356, 1953, pp. 737–738. (Reprinted in *Classic Papers in Genetics,* ed. J. A. Peters, Englewood Cliffs, N.J., Prentice-Hall, 1959.)
2. *Ibid.*

## RECOMMENDED READING

Keeton, W. T. *Biological Science.* Third Edition. New York, Norton, 1980. A college textbook that includes excellent coverage of DNA.

Sheeler, P. *Cell Biology: Structure, Biochemistry, and Function.* Second Edition. New York, John Wiley & Sons, 1983. Includes a more advanced coverage of DNA and RNA.

# The Genetic Code 10

Biology takes a great step forward whenever a new discovery helps explain the life of organisms on Earth. The discovery that DNA controls heredity, as in pneumococcus bacteria, was this type of event. No matter how different the millions of species of organisms on Earth are, all of them have DNA in their cells. They also have RNA. Viruses, too, have DNA or RNA.

The concurrent discovery that DNA can be replicated suggested an explanation for how organisms of each species can reproduce others of their kind. In this chapter you will see how the language of life is written in a molecular code in DNA and RNA. The coded messages are most often for proteins, including the enzymes that control life processes. Through these enzymes, the coded messages control every activity of living cells.

# The Language of Life

## 10–1

## How Do Organisms Pass On Their Characteristics?

Whether an organism is unicellular or multicellular, its life processes depend upon its cells. Multicellular organisms also depend upon special cells for reproduction, as you will read in Chapter 11.

How can a cell transmit its particular characteristics, or those of its species, to its descendants? A hypothesis was once suggested that perhaps each kind of molecule in a cell could make an exact copy of itself. Each cell structure could then be duplicated before the cell divided to make two cells.

The trouble with this hypothesis was that no evidence has been discovered that most cell materials have this remarkable ability to make copies of themselves. However, consider another hypothesis. Suppose that one group of molecules is replicated. Suppose further that these particular molecules contain the information necessary to make all the others.

Many kinds of experiments have confirmed that these master molecules exist and that they are nucleic acids. In particular, experiments have established that nucleic acids carry instructions for the manufacture of a cell's proteins. Protein synthesis is basic to life. Each cell constantly and simultaneously makes hundreds of different kinds of proteins.

Some of these proteins are structural, helping to make up the various parts of cells. Other proteins are regulatory, like the hormone insulin and most other hormones. Most proteins, however, are enzymes that catalyze the multitude of cell reactions on which life depends. Some of these enzyme-controlled reactions manufacture other materials within a cell. Many of the reactions also release energy required for life. Thus by controlling protein synthesis, nucleic acids control the cell and its functions.

---

← It isn't easy to stand out in a crowd. DNA in these red crabs produces characteristics similar to those of both crabs and shrimp.

A molecular code raises many questions. Biologists know that the code is transmitted from one generation of cells to another, and from one generation of organisms to another. But how is the code carried by a nucleic acid molecule? In Chapter 9 you learned that DNA and RNA are each made up of four nucleotides. The nucleotides themselves are identical from one species of organism to another. The hypothesis arose that the nucleotides must differ in their *arrangement* from species to species. By examining other kinds of codes you can see the results different arrangements produce.

## 10–2
## Codes Use Symbols

A code is a system of symbols used to store information. Anyone who knows the code can translate the information from one form into another. Written language is one kind of code devised by people. By using just a few symbols, anyone can communicate ideas and experiences to someone else. For instance, English contains 26 symbols, the letters of its alphabet. With these 26 letters, an unlimited number of code words can be formed, and an unlimited number of books can be written with stored information. And yet, to the person who does not know this particular code system, nothing written in English has meaning. This person would have to use a dictionary to translate the code system. Figure 10–1 shows the use of a code.

Codes may contain any number of symbols, and the same symbols may be used in more than one code system. For example, other languages may use fewer or more letters than the English alphabet. The Hawaiian alphabet uses only 12 of the 26 letters used in English.

Perhaps you have seen some of the cards used in modern accounting machines and computers. Many of the bills your parents receive in the mail are cards with some coded information from a computer printed on them. The coded symbols on the bill are used to process the payment. Although

**Figure 10–1** A code uses symbols to translate information from one form into another.

the symbols can be translated by someone who knows the code, they are intended to be decoded by a machine designed for that purpose. Other kinds of codes may be simpler, using only two or three symbols. For example, the Morse code represents the English alphabet by using a varying number of dots (•) and dashes (—). It also uses precisely controlled spaces.

How many symbols might there be in a DNA code? Although molecules of DNA may be very long, they are made of only four nucleotides. The DNA ''alphabet'' can therefore have only four ''letters''—the four nucleotides. The small size of this alphabet poses a new problem. In Chapter 5 you saw that proteins are made of 20 smaller units called amino acids. The difference between one protein and another lies in the frequency and position of individual amino acids in the polypeptides (page 105) that make up the protein molecule. Even if two proteins had exactly the same number of amino acids, but had them arranged in a different sequence, they would have different properties. Recall that the same three letters *a t r* arranged one way mean ''art'' and arranged in two other ways mean ''tar'' and ''rat.''

Now imagine that DNA molecules might send a message to ''Add a certain amino acid to a chain of amino acids to form a particular protein.''

How many DNA nucleotides would be needed to code a message giving directions about a single amino acid? Each message must be distinct, so that the cell will not confuse one amino acid with another. Since there are 20 kinds of amino acids in proteins, at least 20 different messages are needed—one for each amino acid. If a single kind of nucleotide were to code a single amino acid, then only four amino acids in all would be coded with four nucleotides—adenine (A), thymine (T), cytosine (C), and guanine (G).

It is evident that four single letters are not enough to code 20 amino acids. More complicated messages are needed. Perhaps two nucleotides in

a particular order could mean that a particular amino acid should be added. The possible orders would be: AA, AT, AC, AG, TA, TT, TC, TG, CA, CT, CC, CG, GA, GT, GC, and GG. Thus 16 amino acids could be coded by the nucleotides. That still is not enough messages! Thus groups of at least three nucleotides are needed to code enough information to specify each of the 20 amino acids. When three nucleotides are grouped at a time, 64 triplet combinations like CTG, TAC, ACA, etc., are possible. A code using three nucleotides at a time would be more than enough to specify 20 amino acids. In fact, there are enough extra code messages so that more than one message can specify the same amino acid. In English, there are also different words that code the same meaning (for example, *also* and *too*). Recent experiments indicate that this is true of the DNA code as well.

## 10–3
## The Genetic Code Is Carried by a Messenger

One of the most rewarding chapters in the history of biological investigation has been the work of research biologists and chemists who cracked the code of life, now known as the **genetic code.** These scientists were able to attach meaning to ''words'' made from the nucleotide alphabet. They discovered the particular triplet of nucleotides that was the code message for each amino acid. To understand how these discoveries were made you must know something about protein synthesis in cells.

When biochemists investigated protein synthesis they learned that DNA does not control protein synthesis directly. Instead, DNA works through RNA according to this scheme:

DNA ⟶ RNA ⟶ protein
(which means DNA controls RNA synthesis,
and RNA controls protein synthesis).

It had long been suspected that RNA was associated with protein synthesis in the cell because cells that were making large amounts of protein always contained large amounts of RNA. Most of the RNA in the cell is found in the cytoplasm. By using techniques that split cells into their parts, biochemists found that much of the RNA in the cytoplasm was contained in the tiny granules called **ribosomes.** Ribosomes can be seen in the electron photomicrograph in Figure 8–7.

Studies using amino acids marked with radioactive isotopes (page 99) showed that new strands of amino acids are formed on the ribosomes. These strands are used to make up proteins. The RNA particles must have contained the instructions for assembling the amino acids. How did the instructions get there? One thing was certain—they could not come from the DNA directly because the DNA remained in the nucleus.

It turned out that the DNA was indeed a sort of master tape that is kept securely locked up in a safe, that is, in the nucleus. But from this master DNA tape are made working tapes that carry the genetic instructions to the ribosomes. These working tapes are special RNA molecules called **messenger RNA.** The genetic message carried by much of the DNA is transcribed onto messenger RNA molecules, which carry it to the ribosomes.

Messenger RNA strands are synthesized in the nucleus directly alongside the DNA strand whose genetic instructions they copy. This copying must be done very exactly. All messenger RNA molecules copied from one DNA strand must be alike. This ensures that all of the protein molecules

| The DNA alphabet | | The RNA alphabet | |
|---|---|---|---|
| A | adenine nucleotide | A | adenine nucleotide |
| C | cytosine nucleotide | C | cytosine nucleotide |
| G | guanine nucleotide | G | guanine nucleotide |
| T | thymine nucleotide | U | uracil nucleotide |

**Table 10–1** The DNA and RNA "alphabets." A, C, and G occur in both alphabets, although the sugar in them differs (ribose in RNA, deoxyribose in DNA). The T in DNA and the U in RNA are the major differences.

whose synthesis is controlled by one DNA strand will be identical. In code language, this means that the nucleotides in the new strand of messenger RNA must match the nucleotides of DNA. The major difference is that the RNA strand is later shortened by deleting the extra code that is not used. A second difference is that the T in DNA is replaced by U in RNA (Table 10–1).

Recall that in DNA cytosine pairs with guanine, and adenine pairs with thymine. The only difference when a strand of RNA is made from DNA is that uracil replaces thymine. Thus, where a cytosine nucleotide is located on the DNA strand, a guanine nucleotide will be located on the RNA strand. (See Table 10–2.) But where an adenine nucleotide is located on the DNA strand, a uracil nucleotide will be on the RNA strand.

| DNA code message | RNA code message | Amino acid built into protein |
|---|---|---|
| CCA | GGU | glycine |
| AGA | UCU | serine |
| CGA | GCU | alanine |
| CAA | GUU | valine |

**Table 10–2** DNA and RNA codes for four amino acids.

## 10-4

# The Genetic Code Is
# Finally Cracked

It was the messenger RNA that gave the clue to the genetic code. A young American biochemist, Marshall Nirenberg, working at the National Institutes of Health in Bethesda, Maryland, studied protein synthesis in an extract of bacterial cells that contained ribosomes. Nirenberg found that adding messenger RNA isolated from one kind of cells increased protein synthesis by the ribosomes from another kind of cells. In other words, ribosomes started producing more protein molecules even when they received instructions from a "foreign" RNA. This suggested an idea for an experiment. If ribosomes could follow instructions from a strange RNA, would they also follow instructions from a synthetic RNA, an RNA made in the laboratory and never before present in a living cell?

To keep matters simple, Nirenberg prepared RNA molecules which consisted of only one ribonucleotide, uracil, repeated over and over again. A custom-made chain of uracil nucleotides (-U-U-U-U-U-U) was added to each of twenty different test tubes. Each test tube contained ribo-

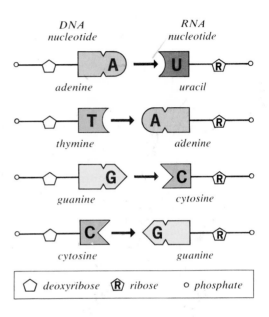

**Figure 10–3** The letters of the DNA alphabet are transcribed into RNA letters.

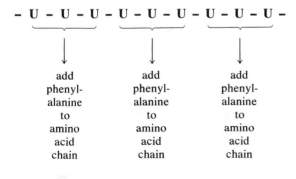

**Figure 10–2** Each group of three uracil (U) molecules specifies the addition of one molecule of phenylalanine to a polypeptide chain of a protein.

somes, enzymes, and other factors needed for protein synthesis. However, each test tube contained a different radioactive amino acid. The results were astonishing. In nineteen of the test tubes nothing happened, but in the twentieth the radioactive amino acid was incorporated into polypeptides. The radioactive amino acid was phenylalanine. When the polypeptides were analyzed, they were found to consist only of phenylalanine units, one joined to another (Figure 10–2).

Biochemists had previously concluded that a triplet of nucleotides may represent a code word that specifies the particular amino acid to be incorporated into protein. Nirenberg discovered the first triplet. It was UUU and it meant: attach one molecule of the amino acid phenylalanine to the polypeptide chain. This was a remarkable discovery for which Nirenberg later received the Nobel Prize.

Nirenberg's work electrified the scientific world. Many biologists followed his lead with other experiments. A second, more complicated technique was discovered. Using either the second technique or Nirenberg's procedure, different investigators discovered the code messages for the rest of the amino acids. Table 10–2 shows only four of the code messages. A much more complete code is shown in **Appendix 10–A,** Messenger RNA Code for Twenty Amino Acids, page 709. Figure 10–3 shows how the DNA code is transcribed into this RNA code.

The genetic code is nearly universal. Almost no differences in it have been detected in organisms studied to date. However, in eukaryotic cells, mitochondria in the cytoplasm have some of their own genetic information molecules. Also, some of the mitochondrial genetic code is different. This puzzling observation raises new questions about the origin of mitochondria (see Chapter 8, pages 165–167).

## 10–5
## Building Protein Molecules

The first step in synthesizing polypeptide chains to build proteins is to get the necessary instructions from the cell nucleus to the ribosomes in the cytoplasm. Messenger RNA carries these instructions. But how is the messenger RNA made?

During DNA replication, all the DNA unwinds and is copied, but when messenger RNA is to be made, only a portion of a DNA molecule unwinds. Unlike replication, where both strands of DNA are copied, only one strand of the DNA is involved in synthesizing messenger RNA.

An enzyme recognizes and binds to a site on a DNA strand to start making RNA. A supply of nucleotides is available in the nucleus. The pairing of new nucleotides of RNA with those of the DNA begins and continues until the enzyme recognizes a sequence of nucleotides in the DNA that is a termination signal.

The resulting RNA strand, with uracil nucleotides instead of thymine nucleotides, is called *messenger RNA precursor*. Both it and the DNA strand on which it was made contain sequences of nucleotides that do not code for the amino acids in proteins (Figure 10–4). In DNA these extra or intervening sequences are called **introns** (IN-trahns). The functions of introns are unclear and are currently being investigated. However, the *intron RNA* produced from them has no function in building proteins.

The intron RNA must be removed from the messenger RNA precursor. Until this is done, the precursor RNA strand remains in the cell nucleus (Figure 10–4).

The amino acid-coding segments of the precursor molecule were made on portions of the DNA molecule called **exons** (EK-sahns). Exons code for RNA that in turn codes for amino acid sequences in polypeptides and proteins. The *exon RNA* usually is much less than half of the length of the strand of messenger RNA precursor.

In the cell nucleus, enzymes and small RNA molecules remove intron RNA from the precursor strand and splice the exon RNA together. Other enzymes add a cap and a tail to the two ends of the strand. The messenger RNA molecule is now completed. It leaves the nucleus through a pore in the nuclear membrane (Figure 10–4).

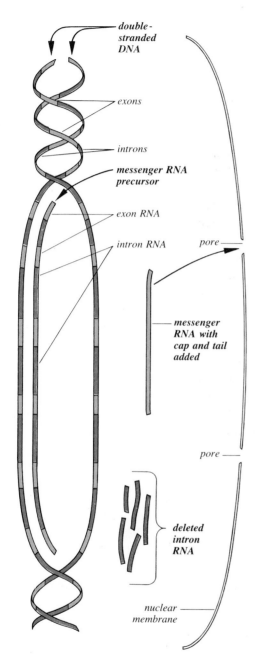

**Figure 10–4** The strands of DNA and a messenger RNA precursor are so long that individual nucleotides cannot be shown in this diagram. The messenger RNA precursor is coded from one strand of DNA. On the right, intron RNA has been removed from a precursor molecule that was made earlier.

Ribosomes in the cell cytoplasm have their own RNA, made like messenger RNA in the nucleus. The nucleolus processes this **ribosomal RNA,** which then becomes a part of the ribosomes. Completed ribosomes are ready to synthesize polypeptides. However, they require messenger RNA to specify *which* polypeptides to synthesize. In other words, a ribosome is like a factory awaiting an order and assembly-line instructions.

An arriving messenger RNA molecule carries the order and instructions for a polypeptide. The raw materials are amino acid molecules in the cell cytoplasm. These amino acids become chemically bonded to special RNA molecules known as **transfer RNA.** A part of each transfer RNA molecule has a single triplet code message. There are numerous different transfer RNA molecules, and each will bond to only one kind of amino acid. For example, a transfer RNA molecule with a CCA triplet picks up and carries the amino acid glycine. A GGU triplet (see Table 10–2) of messenger RNA specifies glycine, and it is the CCA-coded transfer RNA that can provide the glycine. Remember that G pairs with C, and U pairs with A. Therefore, a temporary bond can form between the GGU of messenger RNA and the CCA of the transfer RNA to put the amino acid in place.

Figure 10–5 shows how messenger RNA, transfer RNA, and a ribosome work together to synthesize amino acids into a chain. The signal to start is in two parts—an initiation site of several nucleotides in the cap of messenger RNA *and* the first of the triplet code messages. This first triplet code message is always AUG.

The AUG signal once puzzled biologists because AUG means to add a specific amino acid (the amino acid methionine, as shown in Appendix 10–A). Yet most polypeptides do not have this amino acid in the first position. The mystery was solved when investigators discovered that a ribosome does start a polypeptide with this amino acid, but that enzymes may later cleave it off.

*a. The ribosome begins synthesis of a polypeptide.*

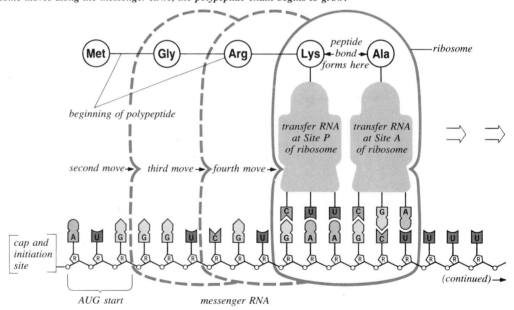

*b. As the ribosome moves along the messenger RNA, the polypeptide chain begins to grow.*

**Figure 10–5** Part **a** of this diagram shows a ribosome (in blue) at the first two triplet-code positions on a messenger RNA molecule. Usually the ribosome begins one position earlier (blue dashes) with AUG alone, then moves to this position. The amino acids are shown by abbreviations of their names in black circles. They are on the opposite side of transfer RNA molecules from the three nucleotides that are complementary to the messenger RNA code. In part **b**, the ribosome has moved along several positions. The beginning of the polypeptide can be seen in the chain of amino acids that is forming.

A ribosome accommodates two triplet code messages at a time on messenger RNA (Figure 10–5). At one of the two ribosome sites an amino acid is added. Then the ribosome moves the length of one code message along the messenger RNA. This shifts the amino acid just added to the other site on the ribosome, where an enzyme forms a peptide bond between this amino acid and the next new one coming in at the first site. In this way a chain is formed between the amino acids as they appear, one at a time.

Some of the enzymes can proofread their work. They expend considerable energy to check the amino acid just added and to check the peptide bond formed between it and the previous amino acid. At first you might think that this is a waste of energy. If the ribosome and transfer RNA molecules work correctly and the messenger RNA is coded correctly, the synthesis of a polypeptide should be almost automatic. But errors do occur. Many are caught and corrected, but a few slip by.

Why do errors occur? One reason is that several different triplet code messages may mean the same thing, as you can see in Appendix 10–A. Reading 20 different code messages for 20 amino acids would be efficient, but messenger RNA has more than 60 different code messages for the 20 amino acids. Only AUG and UGG are unique, and AUG is also part of the starting signal.

There are many other possible causes of errors, some of which can be traced back to DNA in the cell nucleus. There, proofreading also occurs. Some segments of DNA are repeated frequently. Some of the repeated segments become inverted, coding backwards. Some segments mysteriously jump to a new location on the DNA molecule. Yet the correct segments are needed to transcribe coding to messenger RNA. You can now see why energy continues to be expended for proofreading by enzymes as polypeptides are synthesized.

Figure 10–5 shows the beginning of a polypeptide. Amino acids are added until the ribosome encounters one of the three code messages UAA, UAG, or UGA. None of these triplets codes for an amino acid. The ribosome has reached a blank space, and so synthesis stops.

Some proteins consist of a single polypeptide chain. Most proteins have two or more chains that are synthesized separately, then joined. Structural proteins, enzymes, many hormones, and all other proteins a cell makes are produced at the ribosomes, starting with amino acids.

**CAPSULE SUMMARY**

DNA coding may have many functions. The one that has been investigated most is coding for messenger RNA that in turn codes for polypeptides in protein formation. Through proteins, DNA can control cell functions, including the synthesis of all nonprotein materials by enzymes.

Biochemists have made dramatic progress in cracking the genetic code. When the four nucleotides of DNA or RNA are used three at a time, 64 combinations can be formed. This is more than enough code messages to code the 20 amino acids. In messenger RNA, 61 of the combinations code for amino acids and the other three are termination codes. One of the 61 is also part of the start signal that begins the synthesis of a polypeptide at a ribosome. Thus starting, coding for amino acids, and terminating a polypeptide are all accounted for in protein synthesis.

**SELF CHECK**
1. How many symbols are used in DNA coding? RNA coding? How do the two sets differ?
2. Where are the master instructions located for building cell proteins?
3. What are introns? What are exons? How is each involved in messenger RNA production?
4. How does messenger RNA function?

# New Code Messages

## 10-6

## Genes Are DNA Code Messages

A segment of DNA that codes for an RNA molecule is called a **gene.** Other segments of DNA that participate only in turning on, regulating, and turning off the activity of such genes are also considered genes. These segments work without actually coding for more RNA.

This gene definition may not seem to match familiar expressions people use, such as "the gene for blue eyes," or a gene that causes a human hereditary disorder. But the different definitions and descriptions actually agree.

A gene may code for ribosomal RNA that becomes part of the ribosomes. Or it may code for small nuclear RNA that helps process messenger RNA precursor. A gene may also code for a transfer RNA molecule. In such cases the RNA is the end product.

A segment of DNA that codes for messenger RNA is also a gene. Here, however, the RNA is not the end product. In eukaryotes, the messenger RNA precursor contains many segments of intron RNA. When the intron RNA is eliminated (by nuclear RNA and enzymes), the resulting messenger RNA molecule is a much shorter strand than before. It typically codes for a single kind of polypeptide. Two or more genes are necessary to code for a protein, unless the protein is a single polypeptide or is made of identical polypeptides.

In prokaryotes, messenger RNA has no intron RNA. The messenger RNA may be long enough for several different polypeptides, one after the other, that are assembled into a protein. One gene may code for the whole protein.

In both prokaryotes and eukaryotes, genes code (through messenger RNA) for proteins that are enzymes, structural proteins, and other kinds of proteins. When the protein is an enzyme, the end product is not really the enzyme itself but *the process it catalyzes.* Thus genes (through messenger RNA and enzymes) code for the synthesis of sugars, fats, vitamins, and other products. In larger numbers, genes code for all the structures of an organism and all the materials it makes. Eye structure and eye color are examples.

The particular characteristics of every species, including all the hereditary variations, are determined by genes. The problem in investigations is that biologists start with the characteristics, which can usually be observed directly, and work backwards. The investigators must try to determine how many genes affect a given characteristic. They must also work out the complicated pathways by which the genes exert their effects.

## 10-7

## Mutations Are Changes in Code Messages

There is almost no limit to the number of possible DNA messages. Their differences lie chiefly in different numbers and sequences of the same four nucleotides. Yet different code messages do not always produce different effects. In Appendix 10-A, you can see that several different RNA code triplets specify the same amino acid. If these RNA codes are transcribed into DNA codes, you discover that different DNA triplets can also mean the same thing with regard to protein synthesis.

Except for such duplications in genetic meaning, other differences that arise in coding usually change the effects produced by genes. Many chemicals, as well as ultraviolet light and other forms of radiation, can damage DNA and lead to code changes. For example, in human skin cells, ultraviolet light often causes two adjacent thymine nucleotides in DNA to form a new chemical bond between them. The "fused" nucleotides block the interpretation of the code beyond them. Replication of DNA or transcription of DNA to messenger RNA stops abnormally at the blockage. Fortunately, repair mechanisms exist for this ultraviolet damage to DNA. Special enzymes cleave out the two defective thymine nucleotides and replace them with new ones.

All organisms have DNA-repair mechanisms. If DNA strands break during replication, enzymes usually repair them. However, even repair mechanisms are limited. Thus some ultraviolet damage to DNA in human skin cells goes uncorrected, as in ultraviolet-induced skin cancer. Some broken DNA strands may remain broken, or may be reattached incorrectly.

The example of ultraviolet damage to thymine nucleotides also occurs in bacteria. DNA damage by chemicals, ultraviolet light, radioactive sources, and other causes affects all organisms. Often by studying other organisms, biologists learn much about DNA changes in humans too.

A change in the DNA code of a gene is called a **mutation** (myoo-TAY-shun). A change in the DNA code affecting many genes simultaneously is also a mutation. Some biologists call these larger mutations **macromutations.** An example of a macromutation is the deletion of many genes from a DNA strand, caused by some type of damage. Many other kinds of macromutations also exist. All in all, a mutation may involve from one or a few nucleotides in a gene to tens of thousands of nucleotides comprising many genes.

Mutations are often harmful to an organism, and sometimes fatal. However, some mutations may be beneficial, improving the efficiency of gene effects. Still other mutations are neutral, increasing genetic variety without ill effects.

**Try Investigation 10–A** How Can Mutant Strains of Bacteria Be Isolated?, page 611.

## 10–8
## A Mutation May Affect the Life of a Cell or Organism

The effects of mutations are most easily studied in microorganisms that can live on a mixture of simple food substances in test tubes. From these simple substances the microorganisms can manufacture all the rest of the organic molecules they need (Figure 10–6, top view).

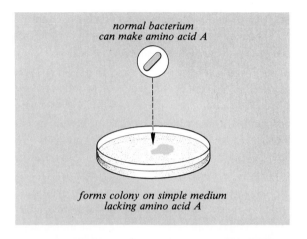

*normal bacterium can make amino acid A*

*forms colony on simple medium lacking amino acid A*

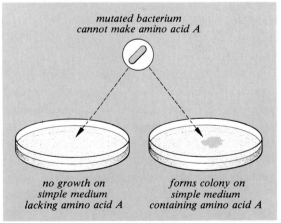

*mutated bacterium cannot make amino acid A*

*no growth on simple medium lacking amino acid A*

*forms colony on simple medium containing amino acid A*

**Figure 10–6** A mutation in the DNA of a bacterium may stop the manufacture of an amino acid necessary for the bacterium to live. Adding the amino acid to a culture medium enables the bacterium to survive and reproduce.

What happens when a mutation occurs? One example of a mutation in some bacteria is the loss of ability to manufacture a particular amino acid. The mutation affects an enzyme needed for the synthesis of the amino acid. A bacterium with the mutation can no longer manufacture proteins that require the missing amino acid. To offset this mutation, biologists can supply the needed amino acid to the bacterium (Figure 10–6, bottom view).

In another microorganism, a particular species of mold, biologists have observed a mutation that stops the mold from manufacturing a vitamin. Without the vitamin, the mutant mold dies. If the vitamin is supplied to the mold, it survives and reproduces.

One of the first molds used for genetic studies was the pink mold *Neurospora* (new-RAH-spoh-ruh). This fungus, which often grows on bread and many other substances, can also be grown in a test tube.

When *Neurospora* is chemically analyzed, it is found to contain many different complex molecules: a wide range of proteins, carbohydrates, fats, vitamins, nucleic acids, pigment molecules, and other substances. Even though *Neurospora* mold is a relatively simple organism, it has a very complex chemical makeup. Its nutritional requirements are very few. *Neurospora* builds its complex molecules from a dilute mixture of salts (containing nitrogen, sulfur, and phosphorus), sugar, and one vitamin, biotin. Compare this with the nutritional requirements of humans. You can see that *Neurospora* can synthesize a great many more chemical compounds than humans can. For example, thiamine is a vitamin necessary for the proper growth and development of both humans and *Neurospora*. Humans acquire thiamine by eating foods that contain it. *Neurospora,* on the other hand, manufactures its own supply of thiamine from the basic substances noted before. Both organisms need thiamine, but humans must rely on other organisms to make their supply.

In its reproductive cycle, *Neurospora* produces spores from which a new growth of mold can develop. Since the new growth of *Neurospora* can also survive on media having only salts, sugar, and biotin, the ability to synthesize complex molecules must be passed along from one generation to the next through the spores. A mutation in the genetic material that controls synthesis of complex molecules could alter the ability of *Neurospora* to survive.

**Try Investigation 10–B** Effects of Radiation on Microorganisms, page 614.

## 10–9
## Genes Direct the Production of Polypeptides

From studies of organisms such as *Neurospora,* biologists have learned much about the kinds of reactions that normal genes control. Each gene is responsible for the synthesis of polypeptides that are combined to form a specific protein or a particular enzyme. When the gene functions normally, the enzyme it controls is produced in the cell. Each enzyme catalyzes a specific reaction. If the gene is damaged or changed, then the enzyme will also be changed. Frequently the change will be harmful and the organism may not be able to survive. In some instances the changed gene may prove beneficial. For example, a mutation may make it possible for the mutant organisms to live in more environments than they could before.

A relationship between genes and enzymes was assumed before the steps from DNA to protein synthesis were known. At that time biologists

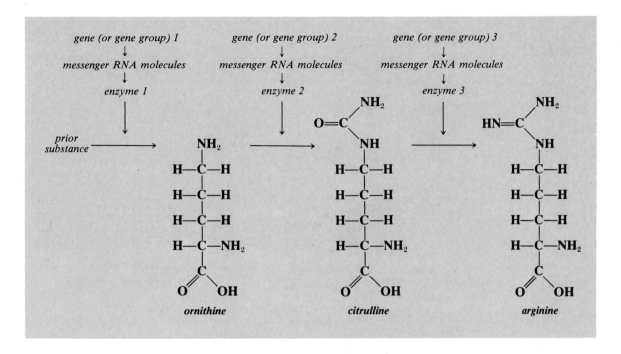

**Figure 10–7** One or a group of genes controls the production of an enzyme. In the diagram above, each enzyme helps change an amino acid into a more complex amino acid. The result of each gene group's message is the addition of more atoms to the amino-acid structure. Many steps may be required to build a complex amino acid.

believed that one gene controlled the production of a complete protein. You have read that in prokaryotes, such as bacteria, this may be true for some proteins. But *Neurospora* is a eukaryote. In this mold, as in human beings, one gene controls the production of messenger RNA for only one polypeptide. Two or more genes are required to control production of most proteins.

In Figure 10–7, an interrelationship in the work of three enzymes is diagrammed. These enzymes are involved in synthesizing one of the 20 amino acids listed in Appendix 10–A—arginine (AR-juh-neen)—from its precursors. George W. Beadle and Edward L. Tatum (Figure 10–8) investigated and identified this process in *Neurospora*.

Genes (or gene groups) 1, 2, and 3 control the production of enzymes 1, 2, and 3. Each of the enzymes is necessary to synthesize arginine from simpler amino acids. If any gene is missing or defective, the next amino acid in line will not be made from the preceding one. This amino acid will have to be supplied in the diet of the *Neurospora*, or the mold will not survive.

In Figure 10–7 you can see that each enzyme changes the molecule slightly by catalyzing the addition or removal of a few atoms. The three enzymes obviously work as a team.

An effective team of enzymes may remain much the same over millions of years, even though life has evolved in many directions. The synthesis of arginine, as shown in Figure 10–7, takes place not only in the pink mold *Neurospora* but also in

**Figure 10–8** Edward L. Tatum (left) and George W. Beadle (right) experimented with various amino-acid requirements in *Neurospora*.

many other organisms including humans. It is now known that arginine is manufactured in humans by the same steps as in *Neurospora*. Biologists have thus been able to gain a greater understanding of the biochemistry of humans by studying the biochemistry of a mold. You can study some of the work with *Neurospora* in Inves-

tigation 10–C. For this work, Beadle and Tatum were awarded shares in a Nobel Prize.

**Try Investigation 10–C** What Controls the Synthesis of Large Molecules in an Organism?, page 616.

---

**CAPSULE SUMMARY**

A segment of DNA that codes for an RNA molecule is called a gene. Other DNA segments involved in the regulation of these genes are also considered to be genes. Genes produce their effects in various ways, usually through RNA or the proteins (including most enzymes) for which messenger RNA codes.

Chemicals, ultraviolet light, radioactive sources, and other agents may cause damage to the DNA in cells. Organisms have repair mechanisms for DNA, but inevitably some damage is not repaired. Mutations, including macromutations, are changes in DNA code messages. When the mutant DNA is replicated, the resulting DNA will also be mutant. Mutations are therefore hereditary.

The effects of mutant genes can be studied most readily in microorganisms. Many microorganisms have simple nutritional requirements and reproduce rapidly. Investigators can therefore study the effects of mutations in millions of descendants of the original mutant organism.

**SELF CHECK**

1. What evidence is there that DNA exists in many different code sequences?
2. Is ultraviolet damage to an RNA molecule in a skin cell a *mutation?* Explain.
3. How do mutations within genes differ from macromutations?
4. How could genes determine whether hair (made of protein) is straight or curly?

# New Genetic Patterns

## 10–10
## Chromosomes Are Sets of DNA Molecules

Chromosomes are found in all organisms. In eukaryotes they are found in the nucleus of each cell. Most of the time they appear to be distributed throughout the nucleus in a network called chromatin. You first encountered chromatin in Chapter 2 (Figure 2–7, page 25).

Chromatin, unless stained, cannot ordinarily be seen under a compound microscope. When analyzed chemically, it yields slightly more than half protein, less than half DNA, and a small amount of RNA. This is the chemical environment in which the genetic code is kept.

The long strands of DNA are held in place by a network of proteins in the chromatin. Proteins called **histones** (HISS-tohnz) form groups of molecules around which DNA winds. These combinations of DNA and histones are called **nucleosomes** (NEW-klee-oh-sohmz). Still other histones are attracted to the DNA strands between the nucleosomes, forming them into packed clusters. As a result, the long strands of DNA are kept in an orderly network in the chromatin. Otherwise, the DNA might easily snarl like string unwound from a large ball.

Interestingly, histones are not found in the chromosomes of prokaryotes. Also, prokaryotes are not made of different types of cells that require different combinations of working genes. In contrast, the body cells of multicellular eukaryotes are of many types. Think of your own body. As you think, you are using brain cells. While you think, muscle cells in your heart are contracting rhythmically, pumping blood cells throughout your body.

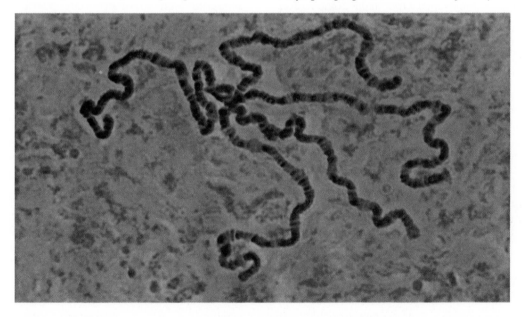

**Figure 10–9** These prominent chromosomes occur naturally from repeated replication of the DNA. They are from a salivary gland cell in the larva of a fruit fly (*Drosophila*). The photograph was taken under a compound microscope.

Nerve cells are carrying messages that coordinate many body activities. Gland cells are producing their chemicals. Skin cells are being made to replace others that you lose.

Each kind of cell requires that different kinds of genes be in control, while others are kept inactive. Otherwise, genes for every function in your body would be at work in each cell.

Many segments of DNA, as well as a number of separate compounds, have been identified as being responsible for turning genes on and off. To be turned on, the genes must be accessible. One hypothesis about gene accessibility is that histones help keep genes locally coiled and packed when they are not in use. In each kind of cell, different genes are kept inactive all the time.

Before a cell divides, its chromosomes become condensed into a short, thick form. At this time they are easy to see under a microscope when stained. However, all the activities you have read about in this and the preceding chapters take place when the chromosomes are in their extended form (except for localized coiling and packing). The chromosomes are hardest to see at this stage.

Exceptional chromosomes exist that can be observed almost any time when stained. These chromosomes are prominent because their DNA has replicated many times, until as many as 1,000 strands lie alongside each other in a chromosome. Figure 10–9 shows some of these chromosomes in the gland cell of a larva from a fruit fly.

## 10–11
## Chromosomes Change Over Time

One of the most perplexing problems of the heterotroph hypothesis is how chromosomes were formed in early heterotrophs. Until recently chromosomes appeared to endure with so few changes that their early evolution was difficult to consider at all. How could collections of genes have gotten started?

Modern discoveries have made the question approachable. Chromosomes show obvious scars of evolution. Their genes contain many introns (page 196). Many genes are present in more than one copy, but not always on the same chromosome. Breaks and reattachments have sometimes turned segments of DNA around, inverting the nucleotide sequences.

There are gene mutations and chromosome mutations (macromutations). Segments of DNA can mysteriously jump to new locations on a chromosome (page 199). These DNA segments, called **jumping genes,** can even jump to different chromosomes. A question being investigated today is whether they may jump from one organism to another. For example, when a bacterium invades another cell, can a gene jump between the two organisms? If so, many more possibilities for evolution may exist.

Even a mutation that adds a single nucleotide to a gene may be a major mutation. The whole code of the gene from that point will be changed because the members of every triplet from that point on will change by one nucleotide.

Somehow many teams of genes have persisted in the face of all the changes that are possible. Repair mechanisms undoubtedly have played a part. You have read that a team of genes and enzymes in *Neurospora,* leading to synthesis of the amino acid arginine (Figure 10–7), is found in humans as well. Yet *Neurospora* and humans are in separate biological kingdoms (Chapter 3).

The change in many genes and the persistence of others has apparently been the pattern of evolution of chromosomes. Neither feature alone—stability or change—characterizes the chromosomes over time.

## 10–12

## Two-Parent Reproduction Leads to New Combinations of Chromosomes

Bacteria (Figure 10–10) and many other microorganisms can produce offspring by undergoing cell division. One-parent, or asexual (AY-sex-yoo-ul), reproduction results in offspring that have the same genetic makeup as the parent. Two-parent, or sexual, reproduction gives the offspring some of the genes of both parents.

Sexual reproduction is common in many eukaryotic microorganisms. However, until recently,

prokaryotes were thought to reproduce only asexually. Then an experiment with bacteria, by Joshua Lederberg and Edward L. Tatum, produced some very puzzling results.

Lederberg and Tatum were studying two nutritional mutants in a species of bacteria. Each mutant was much like the *Neurospora* mutant of page 203. The chief difference was that each bacterial mutant required *three* substances added to its food. None of the three substances was the same for the two mutants.

Lederberg and Tatum supplemented food with three substances for one mutant, and with three different substances for the other mutant. In this way the bacteria were grown in isolation from each other. Then some of each mutant were put together on food to which all six substances had been added. Again the bacteria reproduced successfully and formed colonies.

The investigators transferred some bacteria from the mixed colonies to food that did not contain any of the six substances. It was food that would support normal bacteria, but that had failed to support either mutant. Some of the bacteria survived and formed new colonies!

Lederberg and Tatum pondered this new development. Had the bacteria mutated back to normal again? But if new mutations had occurred, it seemed unlikely that they would be exactly the ones needed to correct the nutritional deficiencies. Mutations may have occurred, but they could affect *any* genes. It probably would have taken millions of generations of bacteria before mutations occurred by chance that were precisely those needed to return either of the two bacterial mutants to normal. Yet normal bacteria had appeared here in a short time.

The investigators recalled an experiment you read about in Chapter 9 (pages 176 and 177). Avery, McLeod, and McCarty had transferred DNA from pneumonia-causing bacteria to other

**Figure 10–10** These two bacteria were photographed through an electron microscope. Can you suggest why the investigator was interested in them?

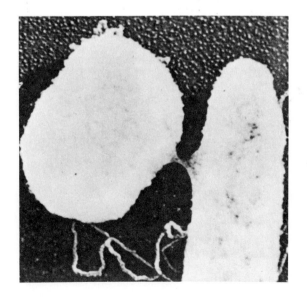

bacteria that were harmless. Some of the harmless bacteria were transformed into the kind that caused pneumonia.

Was it possible that living bacteria had a way of transferring DNA between them? If so, then either mutant could have given the other the DNA needed to return it to normal. Lederberg and Tatum reached this conclusion and published the report of their experiment.

Some years later photographs like the one in Figure 10–10 were obtained through the electron microscope. The photographs showed that bacteria can form tubelike bridges between them through which hereditary material can be transmitted. In the meantime, Lederberg's and Tatum's work had been repeated by others. The two shared a Nobel Prize with George W. Beadle (Figure 10–8), with whom Tatum had also worked.

Bacteria that can transmit chromosome material to other bacteria are designated as (+), and bacteria that receive chromosome material are designated as (−). The *plus* bacteria have been discovered to carry a sex factor that always makes them donors. This characteristic is similar to that of males in most eukaryotic species. Males are donors of sperm that carry chromosomes to the egg of the female. Hence, sexual reproduction occurs in both prokaryotes and eukaryotes.

One advantage of sexual reproduction is shown by the Lederberg-Tatum experiment itself. Without sexual reproduction, the mutant bacteria probably would have perished when they were placed on the simple food that lacked the substances they needed. In other words, without sexual reproduction organisms are limited to changes that occur by mutation. But sexual reproduction provides new combinations of chromosomes from different parents. A damaging mutation inherited from one parent may be offset by genes inherited from the other. Similarly, a beneficial mutation may become established more rapidly. In short, greater genetic variety results among the offspring.

## 10–13
## New Gene Combinations Are Produced by Gene-Splicing Techniques

The deciphering of the genetic code has opened the door for many new genetic techniques. Enzymes used by living cells to cleave DNA, to sequence new DNA, and to splice broken DNA fragments are used by biologists to introduce new genes into bacteria and other organisms. In bacteria, many genes are contained in circular **plasmids** (PLAZ-mids) that are separate from the rest of the chromosomal DNA. (See Figure 10–11.) The plasmids have been observed to pass between bacteria, not only during sexual reproduction but occasionally at other times. Thus, they are natural vehicles for introducing new genes into bacteria.

Figure 10–12 is a diagram of one method by which a new gene can be introduced into a bacterium. Another method is to attach the new gene to the DNA of a phage-type virus, which is then introduced into the bacterium. The virus is especially efficient at inserting its DNA into a bacterial plasmid. Still other methods are being developed and used.

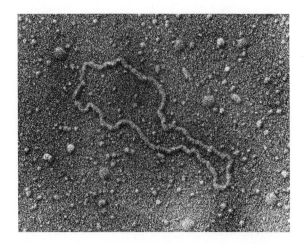

**Figure 10–11** This DNA molecule is a plasmid from a bacterium, photographed through an electron microscope.

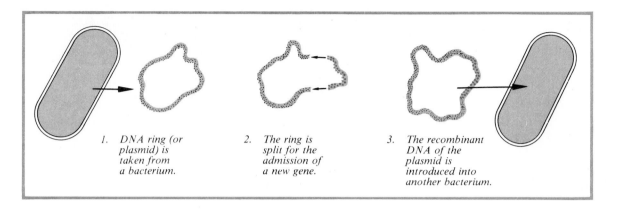

1. *DNA ring (or plasmid) is taken from a bacterium.*

2. *The ring is split for the admission of a new gene.*

3. *The recombinant DNA of the plasmid is introduced into another bacterium.*

**Figure 10–12** One method of gene-splicing in bacteria is suggested by this diagram. The plasmid removed from a bacterium is cleaved by restriction enzymes, and a new gene (shown in blue) is inserted. An enzyme for DNA repair is used to splice the new gene into place. Finally, the plasmid is inserted into another bacterium.

Gene splicing, or **recombinant DNA** techniques, are now used frequently to insert genes into bacteria. One such gene codes for messenger RNA for human insulin. Because the bacteria reproduce rapidly, human insulin is produced in increasing quantities. The bacteria are maintained to produce insulin needed by people who suffer from diabetes (Chapter 21, pages 440 and 441).

This transplanted gene for human insulin was assembled artificially from nucleotides in the laboratory. "Designer genes" like this one will become increasingly numerous as investigators continue their progress with gene synthesis and gene splicing.

Naturally-occurring genes can also be isolated from DNA in organisms and used in gene-splicing. Experiments in gene splicing have even been conducted in animals, where the techniques are more difficult than with bacterial plasmids. Yet successful experiments have been conducted involving cells of mice, rabbits, and monkeys.

Treating human genetic disorders by gene splicing involves many problems. Humans have too many cells for direct treatment in this way. However, if a disorder caused by a known gene can be detected in a human embryo very early in a pregnancy, treatment may become possible. You can see that recombinant DNA research has exciting future possibilities.

Researchers have not overlooked plants in their plans for new gene combinations by gene splicing. For example, one of the great problems in agriculture today is the cost in energy and dollars to produce nitrogen fertilizers for crops. Certain bacteria and algae can take nitrogen from the air and build it into compounds that plants can use as their nitrogen source. Can the sequences of genes responsible for this activity in the bacteria or algae be spliced successfully into the reproductive cells of crop plants?

Much of the biological news you will read in the future is likely to be about gene splicing.

# Biology Brief

## The Golden Mutation

On February 12, 1879, the first California Citrus Fair took place in the new, small settlement of Riverside. Most of the new settlers came to grow oranges—a crop that was just becoming commercially established in California.

The new growers were not sure what orange varieties to plant. They hoped that a citrus fair would put on exhibit all local varieties. Oranges had been grown in California on a small scale from seeds introduced a century earlier by the Franciscan Fathers.

The first prize at the 1879 Citrus Fair was awarded to two plates of unusual oranges. The fruit was large, readily identified by a navel mark. It also had excellent color and flavor and (conveniently for the eater) no seeds.

In 1880 and 1881, Riverside held a second and a third Citrus Fair. In both years the first prize went again to the same strain of navel oranges, now billed "King of Oranges." Where did these splendid new oranges come from? They were all traced to two trees grown in Riverside by Mr. and Mrs. Luther C. Tibbets. Mrs. Tibbets had freely given buds from these trees to neighbors. They inserted these buds underneath the bark of their old "stock" trees. When the union grew, the new buds formed leaves, shoots, and finally the prize-winning oranges. Bud grafting is a vegetative method of propagation widely used for citrus and many other fruit trees. It was necessary for the navel orange, which had no seeds.

SCENE IN THE GROVE

Where did the Tibbets' trees come from? Early in 1873, just prior to starting for her new home in California, Mrs. Tibbets was in Washington, D.C. There she visited the propagation greenhouses of the U.S. Department of Agriculture and saw a new variety of orange trees that had arrived three years before from Bahia, Brazil. The superintendent, Mr. William Saunders, offered Mrs. Tibbets two of these trees for a trial in California. When they arrived in Riverside, they were planted on the Tibbets homestead.

The Bahia orange had originated around 1810 as a mutation in a Brazilian orchard. Grafts were transferred to other trees. An American missionary reported these events to Mr. Saunders, who procured twelve of the trees. Two of these he sent to the Tibbets homestead in Riverside.

The new variety became known as the Washington Navel orange. Why Washington Navel and not Bahia Navel? Mrs. Tibbets, probably forgetting the name "Bahia," always told her friends that the trees came from Washington. One of the original Tibbets trees is still growing in Riverside. Its progeny in California alone now occupy more than 100,000 acres with millions of trees.

**CAPSULE SUMMARY**

Both prokaryotes and eukaryotes have genes grouped in chromosomes. In eukaryotes the chromosomes are distributed throughout the chromatin network of each cell nucleus until just before the cell divides. At that time the chromosomes become condensed as short, thick structures.

Chromosomes can change in many ways. Mutations occur, jumping genes relocate, many gene codes become repeated, and inversions occur, among other events. Yet many genes persist in the face of all the changes. Some teams of genes and enzymes may be hundreds of millions of years old.

Genetic change is usually not limited to a single line of descendants of the organism in which the change first occurred. Both prokaryotes and eukaryotes may reproduce sexually, dispersing changes and increasing genetic variety.

Recombinant DNA research has produced techniques of gene splicing that promise great future benefits in medicine, health, agriculture, and probably other fields.

**SELF CHECK**

1. What three kinds of compounds are found in chromatin?
2. Name some features of chromosomes that biologists interpret as signs of change over time.
3. How did Lederberg and Tatum arrive at the conclusion that bacteria can reproduce sexually?
4. How can new genes be introduced into bacteria using recombinant DNA techniques?

# CHAPTER SUMMARY

### HIGHLIGHTS

Breaking the genetic code was one of the greatest achievements in genetics. The four nucleotides of DNA and the four of RNA are arranged in groups of threes in the code. Once geneticists learned the code, they could analyze sequences of DNA and RNA and read code messages.

Most genes that have been studied code for messenger RNA that in turn codes for polypeptides and proteins. Other genes code for transfer RNA, ribosomal RNA, and nuclear RNAs. Still other genes may not code for RNA at all, but instead have regulatory functions affecting other segments of DNA.

Through protein synthesis, genes control the synthesis of other materials and structures of cells and organisms. Most enzymes are proteins, and teams of enzymes control the chemical reactions that take place in cells.

New code messages arise chiefly by mutations. Mutations may be within a gene or may be macromutations that affect many genes. Chromosomes show many signs of change over time in introns, inversions, gene repetitions, and even different code triplets that mean the same thing in amino-acid sequencing in polypeptides. New mutations today may be produced by chemicals, ultraviolet light, radioactive sources, and perhaps other agents.

In spite of changes in chromosomes, many genes persist. Some DNA-RNA-enzyme teams are so old that they are found in organisms of different biological kingdoms.

Biologists have learned to introduce new changes to chromosomes by gene-splicing techniques. Synthetic genes or genes from other organisms are introduced into bacterial plasmids. New genes have also been introduced to animal cells, using gene splicing. These techniques show promise for practical use in medicine and other fields.

## REVIEWING IDEAS

1. How was the genetic code broken by investigators?
2. How are DNA and RNA codes similar? How are they different?
3. What is a gene?
4. What is a mutation?
5. In what way does a mutation that adds an extra nucleotide to a gene change the gene's code?
6. Distinguish between a gene mutation and a macromutation.
7. Where are proteins synthesized in a cell?
8. What is the function of transfer RNA?
9. What is the chief difference between messenger RNA precursor and messenger RNA?
10. Explain how the Lederberg-Tatum experiment suggested that bacteria reproduce sexually.
11. What is gene splicing?
12. What is the chief difference between messenger RNA in prokaryotes and eukaryotes?

## USING CONCEPTS

13. For what type of RNA would you expect a gene that affects eye color to code? Explain.
14. Occasionally a gene that codes for RNA contains a uracil nucleotide where a thymine nucleotide formerly existed. Would you predict that this mutation is beneficial, harmful, or neutral?
15. In transfer RNA, only the first two nucleotides must always match the messenger RNA code. Sometimes the third may not. Using this information and Appendix 10–A, decide whether the number of different transfer RNA molecules necessary to code for 20 different amino acids is less than, equal to, or greater than

   a. the number of different amino acids;
   b. the number of messenger RNA code triplets that code for amino acids.

16. Suppose a mutation occurred in the code triplet TAC that codes for messenger RNA. Would you predict that this mutation would be beneficial, harmful, or neutral?
17. If a gene does not code for RNA, how do you know that its function is not expressed outside the nucleus?
18. What feature of a chromosome may help minimize the effects of a gene inversion?

## RECOMMENDED READING

Chilton, M. D. "A Vector for Introducing New Genes into Plants." *Scientific American,* May 1983. Gene splicing using bacteria that invade plants.

Eigen, M., W. Gardiner, P. Schuster, and R. Winkler-Oswatitisch. "The Origin of Genetic Information." *Scientific American,* April 1981. An argument that RNA came first, interacting with proteins—with DNA coming later.

Evans, D. A. and W. R. Sharp. "Single Gene Mutations in Tomato Plants Regenerated from Tissue Culture." *Science,* September 2, 1983. Technical, but with a clear message—tissue culture of cells in the laboratory can cause mutations.

Grivell, L. A. "Mitochondrial DNA." *Scientific American,* March 1983. Code differences between mitochondrial DNA and nuclear DNA.

Lake, K. A. "The Ribosome." *Scientific American,* August 1981. An excellent article on the cell's protein factories, and on the RNAs and enzymes that operate them.

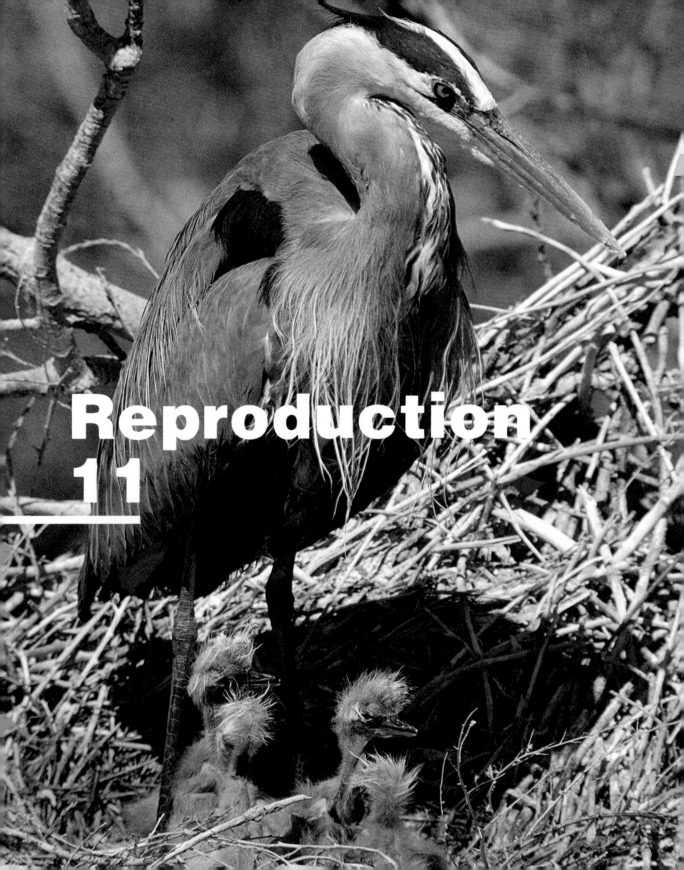

# Reproduction
## 11

Living things face many hazards. Very few live to a ripe old age, for many reasons. One life process, reproduction, provides replacement organisms for the future. Through reproduction, DNA is replicated and distributed to cells that start a new generation.

Reproduction differs from other life processes because it is not essential for the life of the individual. It is significant only for preserving the species. If the reproductive function in all members of a species were to stop, the species would be doomed after the current generation.

In short, reproduction preserves the species rather than the individual. Through billions of years of evolution, a variety of ways have evolved in which organisms reproduce their kind. In this chapter you will study some of these patterns of reproduction.

# Cell Division and Asexual Reproduction

## 11-1

## All Cells Come from Pre-existing Cells

Cell division is a process that produces two cells from one cell. Depending on whether an organism is multicellular or unicellular, cell division serves different purposes. In multicellular organisms, cell division is required for growth, repair, and reproduction. For example, many plants grow by extending their stems upward, their roots downward, and by adding new leaves. All the tissues of the growing plant are made of cells produced through cell division. You grow in much the same way. Many new cells, including bone, muscle, skin, nerve, and blood cells, are produced through cell division. These cells replace worn-out cells and also result in an increase in your overall size.

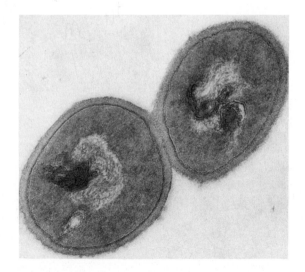

**Figure 11-1** Two bacteria newly reproduced from one, as seen through an electron microscope. The chromosomal material is clustered near the center of each new cell. Cell division in prokaryotes such as these differs in some respects from cell division in eukaryotic cells. (×72,000)

←Color distinguishes the downy appearance of newly-hatched blue herons in their nests. Other characteristics will appear later.

In unicellular organisms, all life activities are limited to one cell. When the cell divides, it produces *two* unicellular organisms (Figure 11–1). The details of the division vary from species to species, but for these organisms cell division is always reproduction.

In these examples, cell division serves different purposes, but one feature does not vary. Whether division is for growth, repair, or reproduction, before the cells divide, their chromosomes are replicated. Each new cell receives a complete set of chromosomes like that of its parent cell. The only exception is in reproduction involving two parents.

Does this mean that replication of chromosomes is part of the process of cell division? Look at the following pieces of evidence drawn from observations of many species of organisms:

1. For most kinds of cells, cell division will not take place unless the chromosomes have first been replicated.
2. However, some cells undergo DNA replication without producing new chromosomes (Figure 10–9, page 205). Some cells produce new

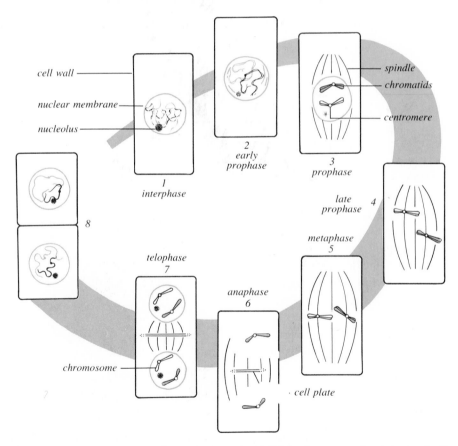

**Figure 11–2** This diagram outlines mitosis and cell division in a generalized plant cell. For simplicity, only one pair of chromosomes is shown, although such a cell would contain many pairs. The process is divided into several stages according to microscopic examination of fixed (dead) plant cell specimens. In a living cell the process is continuous; there are no stops or stages.

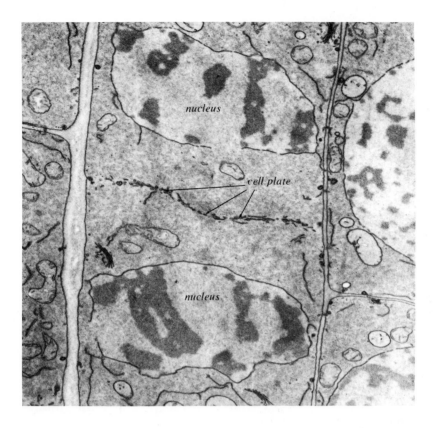

**Figure 11–3** As a plant cell divides, a new cell plate (middle of photograph) begins to form between the two new nuclei (top and bottom). By contrast, in animals (Figure 11–5), a dividing cell usually pinches partly in two before new plasma membrane forms. This photograph, taken through an electron microscope, shows stage 7 of Figure 11–2. (×12,000)

chromosomes and two or more cell nuclei per cell without dividing to become two cells.

3. In cell divisions that produce sperm and eggs, one cell division takes place without replication of the chromosomes.

Because of this varying evidence, replication of chromosomes and the formation of two nuclei from one are distinguished from cell division. However, in most cases these events are interdependent.

## 11–2

## Mitosis and Cell Division Follow a Pattern in Plants

The formation of two cell nuclei from one, each with a complete set of chromosomes as in the parent nucleus, is called **mitosis** (my-TOH-sis). Mitosis begins with the replication of the chromosomes represented by stage 1 in Figure 11–2.

Mitosis ends with the formation of two new nuclei represented by stage 7.

Does the cell divide while mitosis is taking place? The answer for plant cells is usually no. The cell begins to divide when mitosis is ending, as evidenced by the formation of a cell plate during stage 7. Figure 11–3 shows a photograph of cell division under way with the formation of the cell plate.

Because mitosis and cell division usually occur together in a continuous series of events, they are often referred to as a single process, mitotic cell division. The names of the phases in Figure 11–2, beginning with **interphase,** correspond to particular events as they occur in sequence. Cells are often fixed and stained for study of these events (Figure 11–4).

During interphase the chromosomes are replicated. Strung out in their chromatin network (page 25), they are very difficult to see. However, during **prophase** the replicated chromosomes condense. Shortened and thickened, they become easy to see under the compound microscope when stained. Each chromosome is a doubled (replicated) structure joined at the **centromere** (SEN-troh-meer—Figure 11–2). The two replicas of a chromosome are called **chromatids** (KROH-muh-tids) until they later separate. During prophase, however, they remain together.

Also during prophase a fibrous spindle forms in the cell. The chromosomes become attached by the centromeres to the fibers of the spindle.

During the next stage of mitosis, **metaphase,** the chromosomes become arranged on the spindle across the center of the cell, approximately where a cell plate will later form. At this stage it is sometimes possible to count the chromosomes. As **anaphase** begins, the centromeres divide, and the two chromatids separate into individual chromosomes on the spindle fibers. Notice in stage 6 of Figure 11–2 that a set of replicated chromosomes is moving toward either end of the cell.

During **telophase,** a nucleolus appears near each set of chromosomes (the darkened spots in stage 7, Figure 11–2). New nuclear membranes form as mitosis is completed. A cell plate begins to form across the middle of the cell, signaling the start of cell division.

By stage 8, cell division has been completed. Each new cell is only about half the size of the parent cell but will begin to grow. As growth occurs, new material will be made that extends the cell walls around the cells. Added cell wall materials will also thicken the walls as the new cells mature.

## 11–3
## Mitosis and Cell Division Are Similar in Plants and Animals

Only a few differences occur in mitosis and cell division in animals as compared to plants. The processes are so similar that you can easily follow the events in animal cells once you are familiar with them in plant cells. Figure 11–5 illustrates the differences:

1. Animal cells contain a pair of **centrioles** (see Figure 2–7, page 25). As mitosis begins, the centrioles are duplicated. One pair gradually moves toward the opposite side of the nucleus from the other pair. The spindle fibers begin to form between these two poles as the nuclear membrane breaks down.

2. No cell plate forms. Instead the cell constricts, or pinches, across the middle as cell division begins. A new plasma membrane forms across the constricted portion of the cell.

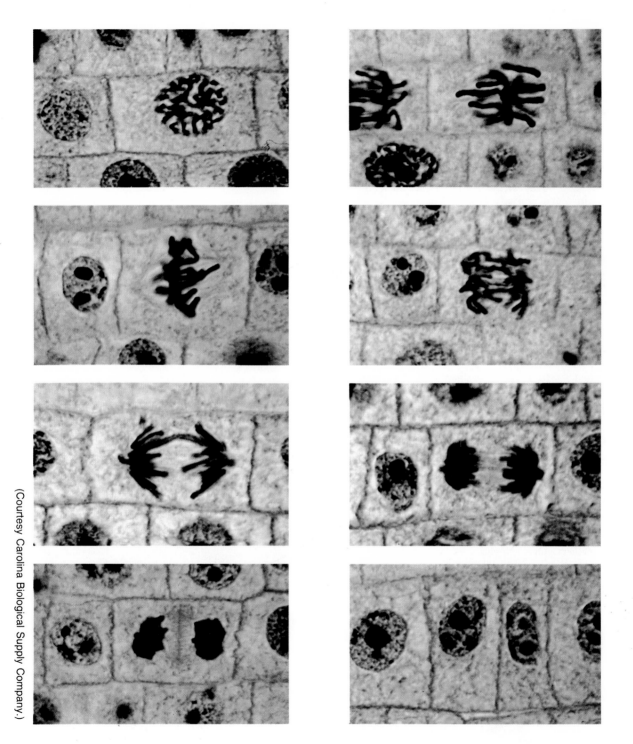

(Courtesy Carolina Biological Supply Company.)

**Figure 11–4** Dividing cells in onion root tip. The stages of mitosis seen here are (left to right, top to bottom) early prophase, prophase, metaphase, anaphase, anaphase, telophase, and telophase. Two newly divided cells are seen in the last view.

3. Cell division is usually evident earlier during mitosis in animal cells (anaphase) than in plant cells (telophase). The cells in Figure 11–5 are shown in anaphase. A constriction is already evident across the cells. Cell division may even be completed before new nuclear membranes are completed around each nucleus.

In some animal cells, the new plasma membrane that forms deepens the pinching effect until the cell appears to pinch in two. In others the new plasma membrane forms across the neck of the constriction before the pinching effect becomes complete. In both cases the new plasma membrane is forming between the dividing cells.

**Try Investigation 11–A** What Are Some of the Cell's Nuclear Activities That Precede the Division of One Cell into Two Cells?, page 619.

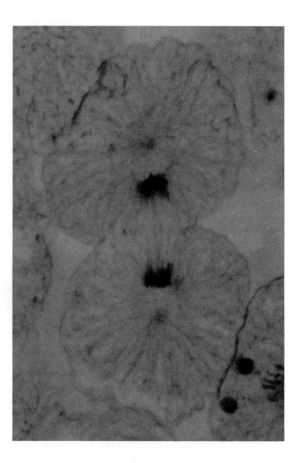

constriction of
plasma membrane

centrioles

**Figure 11–5** Two distinctive characteristics of mitosis and cell division in an animal cell are the presence of centrioles and the absence of a cell plate. A third characteristic is also evident in the drawing and photograph shown here. An indication that the cell is about to divide usually occurs in anaphase, one stage earlier in the mitosis of animal cells than in most plant cells. Here the cells in both the drawing and the photograph show constrictions.

## 11-4

## Asexual Reproduction

**Asexual reproduction** is a method of reproduction that requires only one parent to reproduce an offspring. The type of cell division involved in this form of reproduction is usually mitotic cell division. Prokaryotes also reproduce by cell division, but the process is slightly different; they have no nuclear membrane around their chromosome. The chromosome is replicated and each new cell receives a copy. Chromosome replication and cell division are a single continuous process.

Some organisms reproduce asexually in every biological kingdom. However, examples that are familiar to most people occur among plants, and to a lesser extent among animals.

**Figure 11-6** An example of asexual reproduction. *Bryophyllum,* often called the "air plant," produces little plants on the leaves of the parent plant. Each little plant may fall to the ground and grow as a new plant.

Grasses that spread by means of underground stems are one of many illustrations. These grasses extend their stems horizontally, beneath the soil surface. At points along the stems, cell division starts new roots downward and new blades of grass upward, producing new plants. The aspen trees described in the Biology Brief in Chapter 3 often reproduce from new sprouts on the roots of old trees. The young trees that result are genetically identical to the old. The roots remain connected underground. Red cedar trees are another species of trees that can also reproduce this way.

Another example of asexual reproduction occurs with the potato plant. A new plant may sprout from each eye of a potato. Potatoes are commonly cut into pieces and planted to take advantage of this means of reproduction.

Some plants even produce new plants at positions along their leaf edges, as shown in Figure 11-6. Still other examples of asexual reproduction are shown in Figure 11-7.

Among plants and animals, small outgrowths from the parent's body called *buds* (different from flower buds) may grow in size and take on the shape of a new organism like the parent. Later, these buds become detached as new individuals. Hydras are among the animals that can reproduce this way, as well as sexually (Figure 11-8).

A common characteristic of asexual reproduction in plants and animals is that mitotic cell division is involved. The cells of new organisms will contain chromosomes identical to those of the parent organism. The only exception will be the occasional occurrence of a mutation (page 201). Organisms that are genetically identical to their parent are known as **clones.** In all of the examples you have just read about, new plants and animals grew from one parent — an organism whose cells underwent mitosis. Each new asexually-produced offspring is genetically identical to its parent unless a mutation has occurred. Thus each offspring is a clone of its parent.

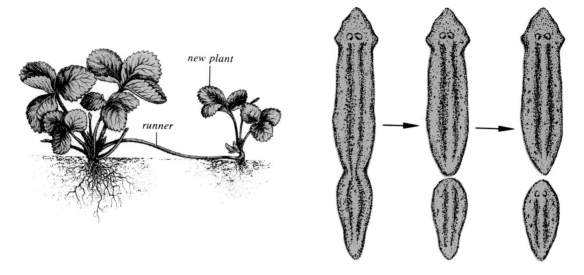

**Figure 11–7** More examples of asexual reproduction. The strawberry plant gives rise to a new plant by sending out runners. Many plants reproduce asexually this way and also reproduce by sexual methods. The planarian reproduces asexually by dividing into two pieces.

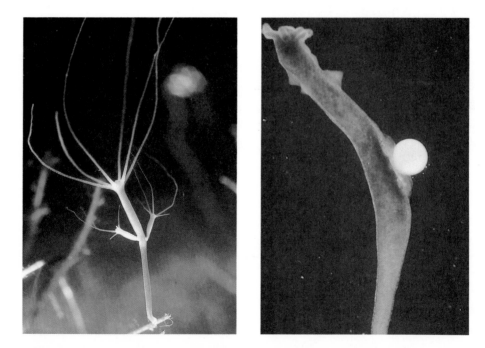

**Figure 11–8** (Left) A *Hydra* producing two offspring asexually by budding. (Right) Another *Hydra* showing sperm-producing organs near its short tentacles, and an ovary at midbody discharging a fully developed egg. In some *Hydra* species, individuals are either male or female but not both; in other species, one individual can produce both sperm and eggs.

**CAPSULE SUMMARY**

The production of two cell nuclei from one, each with a set of chromosomes identical to the chromosomes of the parent nucleus, is called mitosis. Mitosis ordinarily occurs before cells divide. It may also occur without being followed by cell division, producing a cell with more than one nucleus.

A process similar to mitosis occurs in prokaryotic cells before they divide, but prokaryotes have no nuclear membrane around their chromosome. The chromosome is replicated and each new cell receives a copy.

Cell division in conjunction with mitosis takes place in most kinds of eukaryotic cells. In animal cells, evidence that the cell is dividing usually occurs in anaphase. In plant cells, cell division more typically occurs with the formation of a cell plate in telophase. Animal cells form no cell plate. Animal cells have centrioles that are involved in the formation of the spindle. In both animal and plant cells the replicated chromosomes become attached to the spindle.

Asexual reproduction in eukaryotes begins with mitotic cell divisions. The offspring that are produced are clones of the parent organisms.

**SELF CHECK**

1. What two processes are involved in mitotic cell division in eukaryotes?
2. Why do biologists say that a process similar to mitosis, but not mitosis itself, occurs in prokaryotes?
3. What is the difference between a chromatid and a chromosome?
4. During which phase of mitosis are the chromosomes replicated?
5. A centromere is part of what structure in a dividing cell?
6. What are clones?
7. Name three or more examples of asexual reproduction in plants.
8. Name an example of asexual reproduction in animals.

# Cell Division and Sexual Reproduction

## 11–5

## Chromosome Numbers Remain the Same in Each Species

In asexual reproduction the numbers and kinds of chromosomes remain constant from parent to offspring. The chromosomes occur in pairs, except in prokaryotes. The prokaryotes generally are considered to have only one chromosome, but it may be divided between a long central loop and one or more smaller plasmids (page 208).

Each species has a characteristic number of chromosomes. In humans the number is 46. Tropical fish called black mollies also have 46 chromosomes, but they are not the same chromosomes nor do they have the same genes as those in humans. Fruit flies (*Drosophila*) have eight chromosomes. Houseflies have twelve. Corn has twenty.

Because chromosomes occur in pairs in eukaryotes, the number of chromosomes in each species is an even number. The two chromosomes of each pair, except for the one pair called the sex chromosomes, are similar in size, shape, and the genetic characteristics their genes control. For example, a gene on each of two paired chromosomes affects whether your basic blood type is A, B, or O, as you will read in a later chapter. The two chromosomes of a pair are **homologous** (hoh-MOL-uh-gus)—similar in their structure and genetic functions and having the same evolutionary origin.

Mitosis accounts for all chromosomes when it occurs in a cell. Thus offspring from asexual reproduction have the same pairs and the same number of chromosomes as the parent.

When an organism has *two* parents, different events occur. **Sexual reproduction** takes place when the nuclei of two cells, each from a different parent, fuse to start the life of a new organism. If the cells from the parents were produced by mitotic cell division, the chromosome number of the offspring would then be double that of each parent. Yet the chromosome number remains constant from generation to generation. Why? Close examination of reproductive cells from each parent reveals that those cells are different from the parent's other cells. The reproductive cells have only *one* chromosome of each homologous pair!

These male and female reproductive cells are called **gametes** (GAM-eets), from the Greek word meaning "to marry." Most commonly the male gametes are called sperm, or **spermatozoa** (spur-mat-uh-ZOH-uh), and the female gametes are called eggs, or **ova** (OH-vuh). Because gametes contain only one chromosome of each homologous pair in the respective parents, they are described as

**haploid** (HAP-loid) cells. (Haploid is from a Greek word meaning "single.") On the other hand, cells with both the chromosomes of each pair are described as **diploid** (DIHP-loid) cells. (Di means "two.") The union of two haploid cell nuclei—sperm and egg—restores the chromosome number to diploid (see Figure 11–9). Note that in the figure, the diploid number is four—two pairs of chromosomes.

A constant chromosome number is maintained from generation to generation in sexual reproduction. The number is not doubled at fertilization because each of the two gametes has only one chromosome of each homologous pair. How the haploid number is achieved in the gametes involves another kind of cell division.

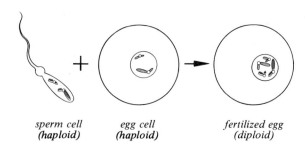

*sperm cell (haploid)*      *egg cell (haploid)*      *fertilized egg (diploid)*

**Figure 11–9** Gametes unite in the process of fertilization. The new individual has a combination of chromosomes from the two gametes.

## 11–6
## Meiotic Cell Divisions

In cells that give rise to gametes, mitosis does not occur. Instead another series of events called **meiosis** (my-OH-sis) takes place. Cell divisions are always associated with meiosis.

First, the chromosomes are replicated just as at the start of mitosis (Figure 11–10, stage 1) so that

## *Meiosis*

1. *Following replication, each chromosome consists of two chromatids.*

2. *Chromatids remain together, and homologous chromosomes come together in pairs (synapsis).*

3. *Homologous chromosomes move to spindle in pairs.*

4. *Chromatids remain together, but paired homologous chromosomes separate.*

5. *Following cell division, each cell has only one chromosome of each pair. However, each chromosome still consists of two replicated chromatids.*

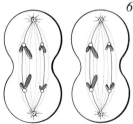

6. *As a second cell division begins, the chromatids separate into individual chromosomes.*

7. *Following the second cell division, each cell has only two chromosomes, each identical to one chromosome of each pair in the original parent cell.*

## *Mitosis*

1. *Following replication, each chromosome consists of two chromatids.*

2. *Chromatids remain together, and homologous chromosomes remain separated.*

3. *Homologous chromosomes move to spindle individually.*

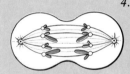

4. *Chromatids separate into individual chromosomes. Identical sets (two pairs) of chromosomes move in opposite directions.*

5. *Following cell division, each cell has two pairs of chromosomes identical to those of the parent cell.*

**Figure 11–10** The differences between meiosis and mitosis, in relation to cell division of a cell with two pairs of chromosomes. The four cells of stage 7 may have different combinations of chromosomes if one pair of chromosomes in stage 3 at the upper left is flipped over, left to right, on the spindle.

each chromosome is made of two chromatids. Then, an event unlike any in mitosis occurs. The replicated chromosomes of each homologous pair come together (Figure 11–10, stage 2). This coming together of the chromosome pairs is called **synapsis** (sin-AP-sis). The chromosomes are attached to the spindle in synapsis (stage 3).

As the cell divides, homologous chromosomes are separated. Each new cell receives only one chromosome of each pair (Figure 11–10, stages 4 and 5) and is therefore haploid. However, each chromosome is still double, made of replicated chromatids. Cell division occurs again, separating the replicated chromatids (stages 6 and 7). The four resulting cells are all haploid, with single (unreplicated) chromosomes.

The division of cytoplasm among cells formed by meiotic cell division is not always equal. Animals often produce four equal-sized sperm in meiotic division. However, when eggs are produced, division is usually unequal. Only one cell receives most of the parent cell's cytoplasm and becomes an egg. The other three cells produced with the egg usually have little cytoplasm. They are called **polar bodies** and usually die, but their fate varies in different species of animals.

Meiotic cell division usually occurs in animals only when gametes are produced. However, in some plants, meiosis produces cells that grow into new, multicellular haploid plants. As these haploid plants mature they produce the male and female gametes.

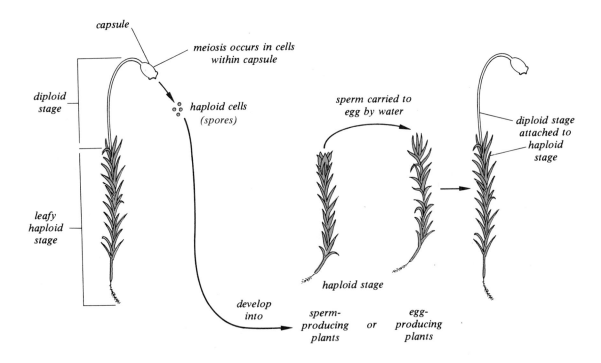

**Figure 11–11** The haploid stage of the moss plant is more prominent than its diploid stage.

# Sexual Reproduction of Flowering Plants

## 11-8

## Flowers Contain Reproductive Organs

Flowering plants produce gametes in specialized structures located in the flowers. The two organs of the flower that are important in the reproductive process are the **stamen** (STAY-men) and the **pistil** (PIHS-til). (See Figure 11-12.)

The **ovary** is at the base of the pistil. The haploid egg cells develop in **ovules** (OH-vewls) within the ovary. There may be from one to a great many ovules in an ovary. Each ovule produces a single egg. Follow the process diagrammed in Figure 11-12. The embryo develops from the fertilized egg. Note that two other nuclei are involved in formation of the endosperm, which serves as food for the embryo. The endosperm tissue forms the bulk of the starchy food grains—wheat, rye, and oats, among others.

The structure at the tip of the stamen is called the **anther** (AN-ther). Hundreds of diploid cells in the anther undergo meiosis. The nucleus in each resulting haploid cell divides, but the cell does not. Each of these cells, with two haploid nuclei, is called a pollen grain. (See Figure 11-12.)

Pollen is shed by the anther and may be carried to the pistil of the same or of different flowers by wind, water, insects, birds, or other animals. The transfer of pollen from anther to pistil, where fertilization takes place, is termed **pollination.** Cross-pollination (pollination between two different plants of the same species) provides more genetic variety because the offspring get a haploid set of chromosomes from each of two different parents. (See **Appendix 11-A,** Pollination by Insects Aids Fertilization, page 710.)

A chemical from the pistil stimulates the pollen to form a tube that grows down through the pistil toward the egg. One nucleus remains in the tube and is involved in the formation of the tube. It is often called the tube nucleus. The other nucleus divides into two **sperm nuclei** that move down to the ovule. One sperm fertilizes the egg cell, and the other fuses with the two endosperm nuclei. The short haploid stage of the flowering plant is now ended. Other nuclei of the ovule generally die. The embryo and endosperm are enclosed in the ovule wall and this entire structure is called the **seed.** Seeds, like those of the milkweed shown in Figure 11-13, may be carried by the wind. Still others are transported over great distances because they stick to the fur of animals. A coconut drifting with an ocean current may be transported many thousands of miles from one island to another.

The size of the seed varies with the species of plant. For example, orchids produce seeds the size of dust particles, whereas the double coconut from islands in the Indian Ocean may produce a seed weighing 18 kilograms (40 pounds). By what means do you think seeds of such different sizes may become distributed?

**Figure 11-13** Milkweed seeds (below), dandelion seeds, and many others have attached, fluffy structures that make them easily airborne.

**Figure 11–14** Flowering plants grow in many different environments. The woodland fire pink (left), a desert cactus (top right), and the mountain dwarf clover (bottom right) provide examples.

Plants that produce flowers are found in widely different environments (Figure 11–14). There are desert-dwelling species and mountain flowers. Some even inhabit shallow coastal waters. As far as biologists know, only the open ocean and polar wastelands are uninhabited by these plants. The following adaptations of flowering plants evidently contribute much to their success: (1) a self-sufficient diploid stage with a very much reduced haploid stage; (2) the evolution of highly efficient and specialized ways of getting sperm cells of one plant to egg cells of another, thus ensuring that chromosomes are reshuffled; (3) the evolution of the seed, providing food and protection for the young plant; and (4) a variety of methods of seed dispersal.

**Try Investigation 11–B** Reproduction in Flowering Plants, page 621.

**Figure 11–15** A variety of edible fruits. How are the seeds dispersed?

## 11–9

## Seeds and Fruits

After fertilization has occurred the ovule develops into a seed. At the same time, the tissues of the ovary usually grow and develop into a **fruit.** Very often the fruit of a plant is specialized to aid in spreading the seeds. The fruits that are most familiar have fleshy, edible tissues. These are favored as food and are often carried for miles by birds and other animals. Because the seeds of these fruits are often not digested, they leave the animal's digestive system intact and can germinate. Some types of fruit have barbs that attach to animal fur. Other fruits, such as maple, have wings that allow them to be carried by the wind. Can you determine how the fruits in Figure 11–15 and other types of fruits become distributed from the plant that produced them? How does this distribution relate to successful propagation of the species of plant that produces the fruits?

---

**CAPSULE SUMMARY**

In flowering plants, the haploid phase is greatly reduced and the diploid phase is more prominent.

Flowering plants have highly specialized reproductive structures and have developed many methods for pollination and for the transportation of sperm nuclei to egg nuclei. The fertilized egg develops into an embryo that is enclosed within the seed and sometimes, also, the fruit. Flowering plants have developed many mechanisms for the distribution of their seeds.

**SELF CHECK**

1. How does the egg cell develop in a flowering plant?
2. What is a pollen grain? How is a pollen grain formed?
3. How does a pollen grain function in reproduction?
4. What purpose does the endosperm serve?
5. What is a seed? What is a fruit?
6. In what ways are flowering plants equipped to survive in a wide range of environments?
7. List some plant adaptations in seed dispersal.

---

# Sexual Reproduction in Animals

## 11–10

### Gametes of Aquatic Organisms Unite Externally

Sexual reproduction is the most common pattern of reproduction in the animal kingdom. Almost all animals that reproduce sexually have separate organs for the production of male and female gametes. These specialized organs are of two types: **ovaries,** which produce eggs, and **testes** (TES-teez) (singular, testis), which produce sperm.

In many species of lower animals the same individual produces both eggs and sperm. This is true of hydras, earthworms, some sponges, and a variety of other organisms. Individuals that produce both eggs and sperm simultaneously are not known in any vertebrate species. Contrast this with the higher plants, in which flowers normally produce both sex cells.

The eggs of higher animals cannot move about by themselves, but the sperm can. The sperm move with a swimming motion that requires a liquid. Most aquatic animals simply release their gametes into the surrounding water. Many are destroyed in one way or another. For example, large numbers of the eggs are eaten by other water-dwelling organisms. However, the release of large numbers of gametes, a process known as spawning, usually ensures that enough eggs will be fertilized to preserve the species. (See Figure 11–16.) Salmon lay up to 17,000 eggs at a time and codfish lay over 6,000,000.

Amphibian eggs are also fertilized externally. Amphibians represent an intermediate stage of

**Figure 11–16** The many eggs of a single brook trout. They are shown about twice their natural size.

evolution, because part of their life cycle takes place in the water and part on land. Frogs, for example, can live on land but must lay their eggs in water. The eggs are small, have no shell, and contain only enough stored food for the embryo to develop to the tadpole stage.

Since an animal sperm contains little nourishment, it cannot live long after being released. If a sperm is to reach an egg, both must be shed at approximately the same time and place. There are many patterns of behavior that bring this about, and they are far from being fully understood.

One behavior pattern is the exact timing shown by the grunion, a saltwater fish, in releasing male and female gametes. The grunion swim ashore on the highest waves of the highest night tides of the month. During the brief intervals between waves, the female deposits her eggs in the sand and the male fertilizes them. The fertilized eggs hatch in time to be carried out to sea by the highest tides of the next month. Very little is known about the factors that control the grunion's spawning activity. Perhaps the movement of the tides is a direct influence. At any rate, elaborate patterns of animal behavior that ensure the union of eggs and sperm have evolved during the course of millions of years.

## 11–11
## Fertilization Is Internal in Land Animals

In all land animals and in some aquatic animals, systems have evolved that further ensure the meeting of egg and sperm for fertilization. Sperm are released into the female reproductive tract, so that fertilization of the egg occurs within the body of the female. Liquid necessary for movement of the sperm is often produced by the male reproductive organs. When eggs are released from the ovary of the female, they are likely to be fertilized if sperm are present.

Internal fertilization protects the gametes from the hazards of the outside environment. What might some of these hazards be?

Relatively small numbers of gametes are needed by animals having internal fertilization but there is still a problem of timing. In most cases, the tiny sperm can live only a short time because they contain little stored food. The fertilizing capacity of a human sperm, for example, does not extend beyond a few days. Furthermore, the egg is able to receive a sperm for only a brief time. In most mammals the egg is fertile for only a few hours. The human egg usually remains fertile for about a day and usually only one egg cell is produced per month. If fertilization is to take place, egg and sperm must be released at about the same time. If a sperm makes contact with an egg during the time that fertilization can take place, the sperm releases enzymes that break down the outer layers of the egg, making it possible for the nuclei of the egg and sperm to unite. (See Figure 11–17.)

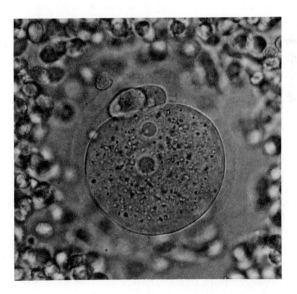

**Figure 11–17** Fertilization of human and other mammalian eggs is internal, and similar from species to species. This photograph shows a living fertilized egg of a mouse. Two polar bodies and two pronuclei are visible.

In many insects the problem of timing and release of the gametes is solved by the storage of sperm within a special pouch of the female. Sperm are released from the pouch as the eggs are laid. Bees may store sperm for an entire life span. Just how this is accomplished is not fully understood.

In many higher animals the timing of gamete release is controlled by complex systems of organic compounds called **hormones.** Hormones are produced and secreted by specialized cells in both plants and animals. Each hormone affects only specific areas of the organism. You will learn later in this chapter about some of the hormones that control reproduction.

## 11–12
## Development of Animals

Fertilization is only one part of reproduction. After fertilization takes place, the newly developing organism must be nourished and protected from danger. Maintaining the developing embryo is far more complex for animals than for plants. You can probably guess some of the reasons. A developing green plant can begin to make its own food supply quite early in life. An animal, however, must compete with other animals for food, and so it must reach a relatively advanced stage of development before starting out on its own.

Most reptiles and birds can spend their whole life on land and lay their eggs there. This is true partly because they have a pattern of internal fertilization and partly because of a special egg structure. The egg has a firm outer shell, which helps to keep it from drying out. In addition, within its membranes it contains a lot of stored water. A large part of the egg serves as a food supply for the developing embryo. The yolk performs the same functions in animals as the endosperm does in plants.

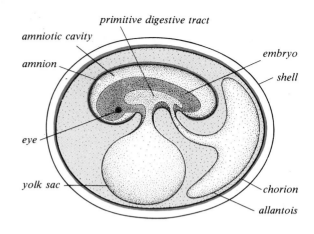

**Figure 11–18** A drawing of a developing reptile egg, showing the four embryonic membranes (yolk sac, amnion, allantois, and, surrounding all three of these, the chorion).

Early in the development of the reptilian or bird embryo, four specialized membranes are formed. (See Figure 11–18.) The **yolk sac,** which surrounds the yolk, is an extension of the embryo's digestive system. The **amnion** (AM-nee-on) is a fluid-filled sac that develops around the embryo. The embryo thus develops under water even though the egg is on land. What do you think are the advantages of the fluid environment?

The **allantois** (ah-LAN-toh-is) grows out of the digestive tract of the developing organism and becomes another large, saclike structure. It collects wastes from the digestive tract. The **chorion** (KOHR-ee-on) completely surrounds all the other membranes enclosing the embryo and lies very close to the shell of the egg. The chorion and allantois together serve as a respiratory organ, allowing ample diffusion of oxygen and carbon dioxide into and out of the egg. The shell is porous enough to allow diffusion of gases; at the same time, it prevents most bacteria from entering.

## 11–13

## Development Inside the Mother's Body Provides Additional Protection and Nourishment

One of the major trends in the evolution of animals has been toward increased care for young organisms, both in the embryonic stage and following it. Internal development of the young occurs in some sharks, in certain other fish, in some reptiles, and in almost all animals with reproductive patterns similar to humans'—the mammals.

As you probably know, most mammals are born rather than being hatched from eggs. An exceptional mammal, whose young are hatched from eggs, is the duckbilled platypus (PLAT-ih-pus).

Though it is an egg-laying animal, the duckbilled platypus is definitely a mammal. It has hair and the female has **mammary** (MAM-uh-ree) **glands** that produce milk. The newly hatched offspring lick the milk from their mother's fur, and thus are nourished until they can get their own food.

The American opossum and the pouched mammals of Australia, such as the kangaroo, the wombat, and the koala, belong to another group of primitive mammals called marsupials. The developing young remain within the mother's body for only a short period of time. Then they are born very immature. (See Figure 11–19 below.) A tiny immature opossum displays a remarkable agility.

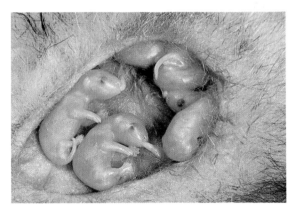

**Figure 11–19** Newborn opossums (above) are incompletely developed but manage to crawl into the mother's pouch and attach to a nipple. The enlarged view of one of the offspring (top right) shows that the eyes are still developing and are covered by a membrane, the ears remain undeveloped, the front and hind feet are still developing, and the entire animal is still naked, or hairless. Twelve to fourteen weeks later (right), the litter of baby opossums has begun to explore the immediate environment, but still never far from their mother. (Left and top right: Courtesy Carolina Biological Supply Company. Right: ANIMALS, ANIMALS/© Lloyd Beesley.)

Though born while it is still less than a centimeter in length and only partially developed, it crawls into the mother's belly pouch. In the pouch, opossums complete their development and are sheltered and nourished by milk from the mammary glands located in the pouch.

The most highly evolved mammals not only have internal fertilization and development and a supply of milk for the newborn young, but they also have a **placenta** (pluh-SEN-tuh). The placenta is a membrane of double origin, formed partly from the embryo and partly from the mother. Although present in marsupials, too, it reaches its highest development in placental mammals. The placenta, rich in blood supply, becomes a pathway for food, oxygen, and other materials needed for the developing new organism. Waste materials also pass through the placenta and are disposed of by the systems of the mother. In the next section you will learn more about the placenta.

## CAPSULE SUMMARY

In most species of animals there are specialized organs for the production of male and female gametes. Eggs are produced by the ovaries. Sperm are produced by the testes. Usually, one individual has either ovaries or testes. Sexual reproduction requires that an egg and a sperm from two different parents be brought together. The result is a mixing of their genetic material as the nuclei fuse.

Most aquatic animals release thousands of gametes at approximately the same time and place. The young are usually left to fend for themselves.

The embryos of egg-laying animals are protected by surrounding membranes and a hard shell. The embryos are nourished by yolk contained within the shell.

In most higher animals, fertilization occurs within the body of the female. When fertilization is internal, few gametes need be produced.

Organisms with the most highly evolved pattern of reproduction, the placental mammals, provide nourishment and internal protection for the developing young and continued care after birth.

## SELF CHECK

1. How is the number of eggs produced related to the method of fertilization and development?
2. What are some of the functions of the membranes and the shells of the eggs of reptiles and birds?
3. Name two characteristics of mammals.
4. What is the source of the placenta in marsupials and in placental mammals?

# Reproduction in Placental Mammals

## 11–14

## The Male Reproductive System Produces Sperm Cells

The human reproductive system will be used as an example of reproduction in placental animals. In general, the reproductive systems of other placental mammals function in a similar way.

In human males, the testes, the organs that produce sperm, are located in the **scrotum** (SCROH-tum), an outpocketing of the male's body wall. Different groups of mammals show wide variation in the location of the testes. Experiments have shown that human sperm do not develop if the temperature is above a certain point. The location of the human testes in the scrotum, outside the body wall, is an advantage because the temperature is lower than it is within the body. Sperm cells develop by meiosis in the highly coiled tubes of the testes, shown in Figure 11–20. The sperm are stored in the testes for only a short time. Additional structures, the **prostate** (PROS-tayt) **gland** and **seminal vesicles,** produce a fluid, the **semen** (SEE-men), which serves for the transport of sperm. When sperm are ejaculated, they travel through the sperm duct and out of the body through the urethra, carried along by the liquid semen. If not ejaculated, sperm eventually die and are absorbed by tissues of the testes. The average male produces many millions of sperm compared to the number of eggs produced by the female.

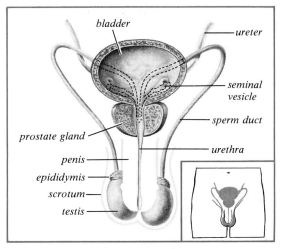

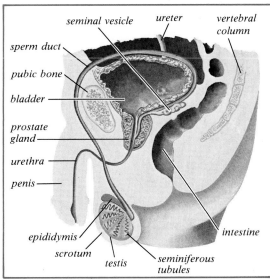

**Figure 11–20** The human male reproductive system. Sperm are produced in each testis within the scrotum. Follow their path to the outside of the body.

## 11–15

## The Female Reproductive System Produces Eggs

In human females, the ovaries, the organs that produce eggs, are located inside the body wall

(Figure 11–21). Eggs (which are smaller than a pinhead) are normally discharged one at a time from the ovaries. The egg then enters one of the two tubular structures called the **oviducts.** Sperm from the male are ejaculated through the penis into the **vagina** (vuh-JY-nuh) of the female. The sperm swim from the vagina into the **uterus** (YEW-ter-us) and then into the oviduct. There they are transported in oviductal fluid. If the egg is fertilized, it enters the uterus from the oviduct, becomes attached to the wall of the uterus, and starts to develop into a new human organism. If the egg is not fertilized, it disintegrates within the uterus and a new cycle begins.

In the human female, the reproductive cycle usually begins and ends within a month's time and is therefore called the **menstrual cycle.** (*Mensis* is the Latin word for "month.") The cycle is often referred to as the reproductive cycle even though reproduction occurs only occasionally if at all. Reproduction cannot occur, however, without certain specific functions of the cycle.

In some mammals the reproductive cycle can occur only once a year. In other mammals it occurs twice a year and, in some, more often.

Events in the human menstrual cycle may be summarized, in order, as follows. (Also see Figure 11–24 on page 241.)

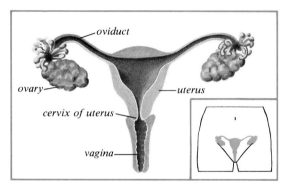

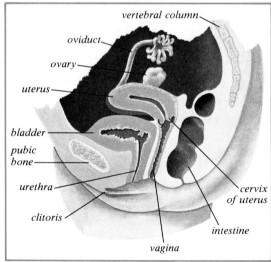

**Figure 11–21** The human female reproductive system. Eggs develop in the ovaries and enter the oviducts, where fertilization takes place. Usually one egg matures and is released at a time; if it is fertilized, it implants in the wall of the uterus and the embryo develops there.

1. **Menstruation** (men-stroo-AY-shun)—The soft tissues in the uterus break down and are discharged. The first day of the menstrual flow is usually taken as the beginning of the menstrual cycle. This stage averages about five days in length.

2. **The follicle stage**—A new follicle (FOL-ih-kul) and egg mature in an ovary. The follicle is a saclike structure which becomes larger and filled with fluid as the egg matures. The follicle stage lasts until the time of ovulation, about 14 days. During this stage the inner lining of the uterus is building up in preparation for an embryo.

3. **Ovulation**—The follicle ruptures and the mature egg that is released from it normally enters an oviduct. Ovulation occurs about midway in the cycle. The inner wall of the uterus is now thick, soft, and rich in blood supply.

4. **The corpus luteum stage**—After ovulation, the ruptured follicle develops into a new structure called the **corpus luteum** (COR-pus LEW-

tee-um). (*Luteus* is the Latin word for "yellow.") In some animals the corpus luteum is yellow. As you will see, the corpus luteum plays a very important role in the control of the reproductive processes. For about 10 days, the corpus luteum grows and secretes progesterone which brings about the final preparation of the uterus. The egg arrives in the uterus in the middle of this period. If the egg has been fertilized, it continues to develop within the uterus. If it has not been fertilized, menstruation takes place and a new cycle begins. (Figure 11–22 shows some of the detail of the corpus luteum.)

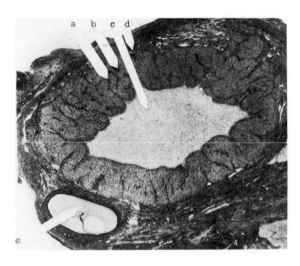

**Figure 11–22** An enlarged view of a corpus luteum from a human ovary. The labels a, b, c, and d are to structures in the corpus luteum; the label e at the lower left points to a nearby developing follicle.

## 11–16

## How Does the Ovary Bring About Changes in the Uterus?

A frequently used procedure in attempting to determine the function of an organ in an animal is to remove the organ. Then a study is made of the effects of the absence of the organ. After the ovaries are removed from a placental mammal, the uterine tissue does not grow in preparation for a fertilized egg. The results suggest that the ovary or some substance from the follicle of the ovary affects the growth of the uterus. Many experiments of this kind have been performed. Biologists now know that each ovarian follicle, as it matures, secretes a chemical substance, a hormone called **estrogen** (ES-troh-jen). This hormone causes the soft tissues of the lining of the uterus to increase. Estrogen does this by a threefold action on the inner uterine cells:

1. Estrogen speeds up mitosis.
2. Estrogen increases the blood supply to the cells.
3. Estrogen increases the amount of tissue fluid.

The corpus luteum, formed from the ruptured follicle, secretes small amounts of estrogen and another hormone, **progesterone** (proh-JES-tuh-rohn). Progesterone causes further buildup of the uterine wall by stimulating gland and blood vessel development. Under the influence of estrogen and progesterone the uterus is prepared for implantation of a fertilized egg. The corpus luteum degenerates if a fertilized egg has not implanted itself. If sperm have been released into the opening of the female reproductive tract, the vagina, they swim at random through the uterus and into the oviduct. If an egg has been released from the ovary and has entered the oviduct, a sperm and the egg may unite (fertilization). Normally the fertilized egg will become implanted when it reaches the uterus. In this case, the corpus luteum does not break down but remains through the time of embryonic development and continues to secrete estrogen and progesterone. It secretes particularly high levels of progesterone, without which the uterine wall and the implanted fertilized egg could not be maintained.

**Try Investigation 11–C** What Regulates the Schedule of Egg-Laying by Female Frogs?, page 622.

*Hi Matt !!!*

## 11–17

## If Hormones of the Ovary Regulate the Uterus, What Regulates the Ovary?

A tiny gland at the base of the brain, the **pituitary** (pit-TEW-ih-ter-ee) gland, controls the reproductive cycle. The pituitary merges into a region of the brain, the **hypothalamus** (hy-po-THAL-a-mus). (See Figure 11–23.) Hormones called releasing factors (**RF**) are produced by the hypothalamus and travel by way of the bloodstream to the pituitary. Releasing factors of the hypothalamus stimulate the pituitary to secrete hormones that bring about changes in the ovary and uterus. Releasing factors (RF) of the hypothalamus change in concentration in response to changing levels of the hormones produced by the ovary.

Some of the hormonal interactions of human reproduction are summarized in Figure 11–24. Notice that hormones can have a negative influence and cause an inhibition as well as a stimulation. The inhibiting influence is often referred to as negative feedback, the stimulating influence as positive feedback.

Under hypothalamic influence, the follicle-stimulating hormone (**FSH**) of the pituitary increases in concentration. The FSH stimulates the growth of the ovarian follicle in which the egg is maturing. The follicle cells are secreting estrogen, and the estrogen reaches the uterine wall causing growth of the lining of the uterus.

Under the influence of the hypothalamus the luteinizing (LOOT-e-un-i-zing) hormone (**LH**) of the pituitary also increases in concentration. LH causes further development of the follicle and egg, and increased output of estrogen by the follicle.

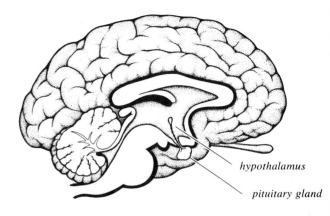

**Figure 11–23** A drawing of a section through the human brain, showing the locations of the hypothalamus and the pituitary gland.

Just after LH and FSH reach their peak, the follicle ruptures, releasing the egg (ovulation).

After ovulation, the follicle transforms into the corpus luteum. A rapid decrease in FSH and LH concentration results in part from the production of another hormone in the corpus luteum, progesterone. Progesterone and estrogen remain in relatively high concentration during the next 14 days. If an egg has not been implanted in the uterus during this time, the corpus luteum then breaks down, estrogen and progesterone concentrations decrease, and menstruation occurs. The decreasing concentrations of estrogen and progesterone in the blood free hypothalamic-releasing factors to stimulate increased production of FSH and LH again. The cycle starts over.

If a fertilized egg has become implanted in the uterus, LH remains high. The corpus luteum is maintained and goes on producing estrogen and high levels of progesterone.

Among mammals there is great variety in how often sufficient hormones are produced to cause ovulation. Recent experiments indicate that perhaps the hypothalamus or some other nearby portion of the brain may possess a built-in biological

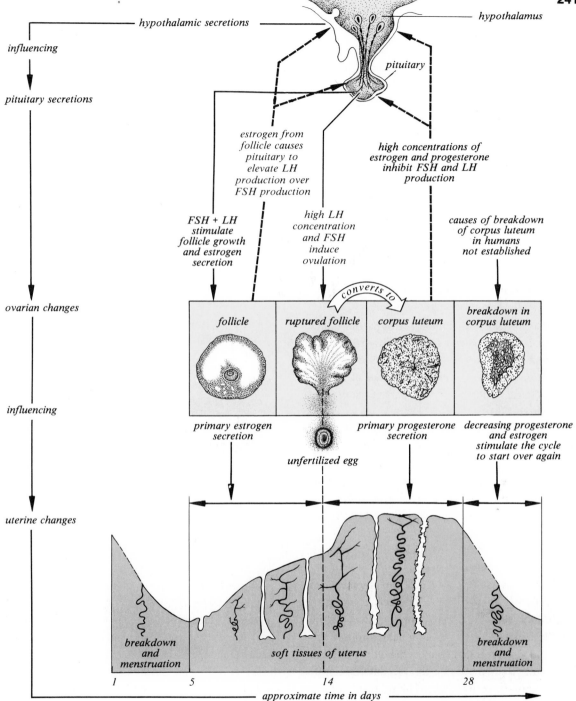

**Figure 11–24** The coordination of the events that take place in the human female reproductive system is shown here for one cycle (i.e., an egg matures and is released but is not fertilized).

clock. Though not completely understood, this information is significant. When biologists speak of biological clocks in a living organism, they are referring to the causes (often unknown) of regularly timed changes that result in certain predictable, physiological events.

The pituitary hormone **prolactin** (pro-LAK-tun), also controlled by the hypothalamus, induces milk production for the young. Prolactin contributes as well to maintaining a functional corpus luteum when a fertilized egg has been implanted.

## 11–18
## The Placenta and Embryonic Membranes Maintain and Nourish the Embryo

The chorion and the amnion surround the human embryo, as in bird and reptile embryos. During development of the human embryo, however, tiny projections grow from the outer surface of the chorion to make up the embryonic part of the placenta (Figure 11–25).

It is known that in some mammals the placenta secretes hormones that function like those of the pituitary gland and the corpus luteum of the ovary. During the last six months of human pregnancy the placenta produces particularly large quantities of progesterone, along with some estrogen. These hormones help maintain a very rich supply of blood to the uterine wall and help the embryo to remain implanted.

After the first few weeks of development, the edges of the amnion come together, forming the **umbilical** (um-BIL-ih-kul) **cord.** (See Figures 11–26 and 11–27.) The umbilical cord is a tube with blood vessels that connect the embryo and the placenta. Remember that the placenta is a structure composed of intertwined tissue from both the mother and the fetus. It is through the placenta that the fetus receives nourishment and rids its own bloodstream of waste products. The blood of the fetus and that of the mother do not normally mix. The blood vessels of each come in close contact in the placenta, and exchanges are made by diffusion through the maze of membranes making up the placenta.

The yolk sac is present in the human embryo for only a short time. It is a good example of a vestigial organ, or remnant.

## 11–19
## Milk Production Is Coordinated with the Birth Process

By the ninth month of human pregnancy, the head of the fetus is usually turned down toward the opening of the uterus (Figure 11–27). Sometimes, however, the feet are turned toward the

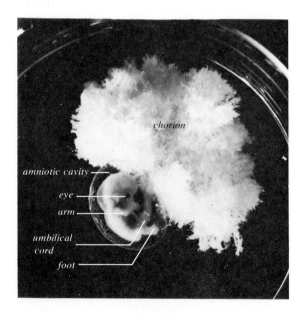

**Figure 11–25** A human fetus at about seven weeks of development. The embryo is within its amnion. The chorion that ordinarily surrounds the embryo has been peeled back to expose the amniotic sac.

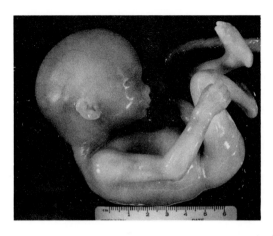

**Figure 11–26** A human embryo at about three months showing the umbilical cord.

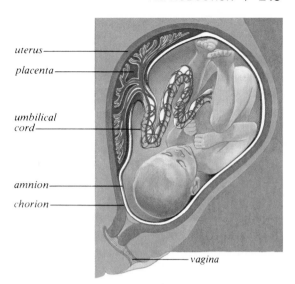

uterus

placenta

umbilical cord

amnion

chorion

vagina

**Figure 11–27** A drawing of a full-term human fetus, with its head downward toward the opening in the uterus. The umbilical cord with its blood vessels is still the lifeline of the fetus for food, oxygen, and waste disposal.

opening. This makes the delivery more difficult.

Childbirth begins when the muscle layers of the uterus start to contract and relax. These actions are known as labor. They cause the labor pains felt by the mother. Exactly how the childbirth mechanism is started is a complex event that biologists do not understand completely. At first, the contractions are just strong enough to move the baby slowly toward the vagina. Generally, at this stage, the fluid sac (the amnion) surrounding the baby breaks and releases its fluid content. This is a sign that labor is in progress. Stronger and more frequent contractions push the baby through the vagina, out of the mother's body. The umbilical cord is then tied or clamped off. The small piece of cord that remains attached to the baby eventually dries up and drops off. After the birth of the baby, muscular contractions of the uterus continue until the placenta, commonly called the afterbirth, is expelled.

During late pregnancy the mammary glands of the mother undergo changes that prepare the breasts for production of milk after the offspring is born. Estrogen and progesterone contribute to these changes. During pregnancy, and also in the nonpregnant cycle, progesterone inhibits the hypothalamus so that it, in turn, inhibits secretion of prolactin by the pituitary. At delivery, the inhibition to the hypothalamus ceases and the hypothalamus stimulates the pituitary to secrete prolactin. Prolactin is necessary for milk production. If the newborn baby does not feed from the mother's breast, milk secretion soon ceases and the reproductive cycle begins again. Sometimes ovulation, fertilization, and a new pregnancy may start even during the period of milk secretion.

The average duration of internal development or pregnancy varies among mammals. Some approximate times are as follows: mouse, 21 days; rabbit, 32 days; dog and cat, 60 days; horse, 350 days; and whale, 360 days. Pregnancy in the human normally lasts about 280 days.

## 11–20

## Hormones Also Control the Male Reproductive System

Whereas in the female, the pituitary hormones FSH and LH regulate the ovarian and uterine activities, in the male these same hormones regulate the activities of the testes. Releasing factors from the hypothalamus stimulate the pituitary as in the female. FSH and LH from the pituitary then stimulate the testes to secrete **androgens** (AN-droh-jenz) and produce sperm. Because it is the female of the species who has the potential of growing a new individual inside her body, her hormonal system is more complex, especially during pregnancy and birth.

Although both males and females produce estrogen and androgens, the concentrations vary with the sex of the individual. The amount of estrogen is high in females and low in males. Androgen concentration is high in males and low in females. Androgens, including **testosterone** (tes-TOS-ter-ohn), are secreted by the testes in the male and control the development of secondary sex characteristics. In humans the androgens cause changes in the voice and body hair distribution from the beginning of puberty until maturity. Throughout the animal kingdom there are often prominent differences in the appearance of males and females of the species. (See Figure 11–28.) Often the differences can be traced to hormonal differences in the sexes.

**Figure 11–28** An example of secondary sex differences. The more brightly colored duck is the male. At nesting time each year the male's coloration confers an advantage in distracting intruders from detection of the female. Her color blends in with the grass and reeds of the nesting area.

# Biology Brief

## The Open Odds in Orchid Breeding

Suppose that meiosis were to fail—altogether—when gametes were formed. What would happen? Taking into account the gametes of both parents, you can see that the offspring's chromosome number would be doubled! Such events are rare, but *polyploidy,* or multiple chromosome numbers, is known to have contributed to the evolution of new species in the past. One of the largest families of flowering plants, the orchid family, includes many examples.

Polyploidy is not without problems. The fertilized egg often dies. Or the offspring may be infertile. Orchids have proved amazingly adaptable to polyploidy, and orchid-breeders take advantage of this fact to increase the variety in orchids. In their cross-breeding experiments they try crosses between plants with known different chromosome numbers.

The lady in her greenhouse, (left) is Mrs. Pat Trumble of Boulder, Colorado. The orchid plant she is holding has grandparents of three different genera! First, orchids from two genera were crossed. A fertile plant from this mating was then crossed with a plant from a third genus. This cross produced the orchid you see—it won a prize, although no one knew whether it was fertile.

If the plant is infertile, asexual reproduction may come to the rescue. The plant may reproduce by sending out a new growth. Or *meristem* tissue, which you will read about in the next chapter, can be removed from the plant's growing tips and cultured in laboratory culture dishes. Orchids that produce flowers exactly like those of the parent plant can be cloned from the culture. Mrs. Trumble's new orchid will then be copied more perfectly than by further breeding. Can you explain why?

**CAPSULE SUMMARY**

In humans, sperm are produced in the testes. Eggs develop in the ovaries, and the embryo develops within the uterus. Two ovarian hormones, estrogen and progesterone, cause the buildup of the uterine lining to receive the fertilized egg.

Follicle-stimulating hormone (FSH) and luteinizing hormone (LH) stimulate the growth of the ovarian follicle. After ovulation the uterine lining deteriorates in 14 days unless a fertilized egg is implanted. The placenta also secretes hormones and nourishes the developing embryo. Prolactin stimulates milk production.

The male, like the female, has estrogen. Both also have the male hormones, the androgens. But the concentrations of these and other hormones are quite different in the two sexes.

**SELF CHECK**

1. Where is the egg of a placental mammal usually fertilized?
2. What is the uterus?
3. What usually happens to a fertilized egg when it enters the uterus?
4. How does the hypothalamus of the brain affect the female reproductive cycle?
5. What two pituitary hormones affect both the female and the male reproductive processes?
6. What two hormones in the female promote the development of the uterine wall?
7. What are the functions of the placenta?
8. Of what advantage is the amnion?
9. What hormones affecting the male reproductive system are secreted by the testes?
10. How do the hypothalamus of the brain and the pituitary gland affect the male reproductive system?

# CHAPTER SUMMARY

## HIGHLIGHTS

Many different forms of reproduction have evolved. All of them function to preserve the species. Offspring may be produced asexually or sexually. In asexual reproduction, mitosis or a process similar to it leads to replication of the chromosomes and their distribution to new cells that are produced. New cells receive a full complement of chromosomes identical to those of the parent cell. New individuals are clones of their parent.

Meiosis is involved in sexual reproduction. The chromosomes are replicated, then paired in synapsis. Homologous chromosomes are separated in a first cell division, and the chromatids of each chromosome are separated in a second cell division. The gametes that are produced are haploid; they have only one of each pair of chromosomes characteristic of their parent cell. When an egg and sperm unite in fertilization, the diploid number of chromosomes is reestablished. Sexual reproduction increases genetic variety in a species because offspring receive chromosomes from two parents.

Most plants and animals have a prominent diploid stage of life, but some—moss plants, for example—have a more prominent haploid stage of life. Complex life cycles and reproductive cycles are associated with sexual reproduction in flowering plants and vertebrate animals. In humans, the reproductive cycle is so complex that parts of it are still being investigated.

## REVIEWING IDEAS

1. Which of these processes—mitosis or meiosis—is involved in the growth of a multicellular organism?
2. How is the chromosome number of a species maintained in asexual reproduction?
3. How is the chromosome number of a species maintained in sexual reproduction?
4. How are mitosis and cell division related? How are they different?
5. What are clones? Give an example.
6. If you look through a microscope and observe chromosomes in synapsis, what process are you likely to be observing?
7. What is the evidence that haploid moss plants are part of a sexual life cycle?
8. What are the male and female organs of a flower?
9. In what part of the female reproductive system does fertilization usually occur in humans?
10. What ovarian hormones promote growth of the inner lining of the uterus in humans?
11. What are secondary sex characteristics? Give examples.
12. How does a human fetus obtain nourishment?

## USING CONCEPTS

13. Explain the interrelationship of the hypothalamus, the pituitary gland, and the ovaries in controlling hormones in the female reproductive cycle.
14. Can haploid cells be maintained and multiplied by mitotic cell division? Explain.
15. Why are the chromosomes of a pair said to be homologous?

16. In what respect is mitosis different from the chromosome replication that must take place in prokaryotes before cell division?
17. Which cell division associated with meiosis is similar to one associated with mitosis?
18. Name one method by which 18-kilogram coconuts on an island in the Indian Ocean might be dispersed.
19. Fertilization is internal in land animals and in most land plants. Among what types of land plants would you look for exceptions?
20. Compare and contrast the development of the young in marsupials and placental mammals.

## RECOMMENDED READING

Avers, C. J. *Cell Biology*. Second edition. New York, D. Van Nostrand, 1981. A college textbook with further discussions of mitosis and meiosis.

Beaconsfield, B., B. Birdwood, and R. Beaconsfield. "The Placenta." *Scientific American*, August 1980. A well-illustrated article on this essential structure in mammals.

Fawcett, D. *The Cell*. Second Edition. Philadelphia, Saunders College Publishing, 1981. Includes many photographs taken through the electron microscope, showing structures involved in cell division, among others.

Parish, J. H. (ed.) *Developmental Biology of Prokaryotes*. Berkeley, University of California Press, 1980. An advanced book about these lesser-known organisms.

Prescott, D. M. *Reproduction of Eukaryotic Cells*. Burlington, NC, Carolina Biological Supply Company, 1978. A readable, well-illustrated book.

# Development
# 12

In the last chapter you learned how a number of different kinds of organisms reproduce others of their kind. In this chapter you will consider some of the interrelated processes by which organisms develop from their beginnings in fertilized eggs. Increased knowledge of some of the environmental influences on development is just one of the factors that make this a field of widening importance.

Offspring of the simpler organisms resemble their parents almost immediately. When an amoeba, a bacterium, or a one-celled alga divides, its living substance is divided between the two new cells, and the parent cell loses its identity.

In higher plants and animals, however, the process of sexual reproduction does not immediately result in the formation of individuals that resemble their parents. The fertilized egg undergoes striking changes as it divides, grows, and finally develops into a fully formed organism with characteristics of its parents.

# Patterns of Development in Plants

## 12–1

### How Does a Single Cell Develop into a Multicellular Organism?

All methods of reproduction are similar in the sense that each parent contributes a part of itself to the new individual. The process by which the cells contributed by the parent, or parents, grow into complete new individuals is called **development.** In sexual reproduction the chromosomes of both egg and sperm are active in the development of new individuals. This fact was not established until late in the 19th century.

What kinds of processes take place while an organism develops from a tiny fertilized egg into

an adult? Think of yourself, for example. It is not difficult to list the main ways in which you differ from the fertilized egg that was the starting point of your development: First of all, you now consist of trillions of cells, whereas the fertilized egg was a single cell. Second, you are much larger than the fertilized egg. And third, you are made of many different kinds of cells, organized into different tissues and organs and systems, whereas the egg was only one kind of cell.

Growth is usually thought of as an increase in the amount of living substance present. At different periods in development certain parts of the organism are in rapid and critical periods of growth. The growth rate usually slows down when the organism approaches a certain size. Some parts of an organism, however, may continue to grow throughout life. Growth is really the net result of three closely interrelated cell processes:

---

←Care for the developing young. Look in the cells for the wasp larvae.

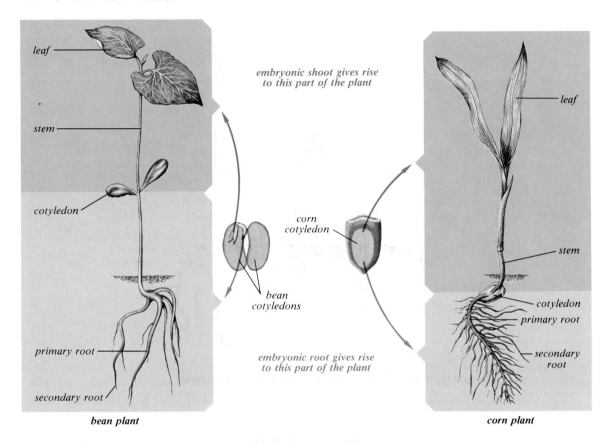

leaf

stem

cotyledon

primary root

secondary root

*bean plant*

*embryonic shoot gives rise to this part of the plant*

*corn cotyledon*

*bean cotyledons*

*embryonic root gives rise to this part of the plant*

leaf

stem

cotyledon
primary root

secondary root

*corn plant*

**Figure 12–1** Compare the young bean and corn plants. The bean plant has two cotyledons, the corn plant one. How else are the plants different? How are they similar?

1. **Cell division.** The egg begins to divide quite soon after fertilization, and cell division continues throughout life. Many cells of your body are being constantly renewed by cell division.

2. **Cell enlargement.** Following cell division the two resultant cells usually enlarge. Materials are utilized and energy expended to synthesize more cytoplasm and enlarge the cells.

3. **Cell differentiation.** As cells divide, and as the organism grows, the cells become more and more different from one another. Various types of cells specialize and perform particular functions.

## 12–2

## Development in Higher Plants Begins in the Seed

Although plants have evolved reproductive mechanisms that are quite different from those in animals, the same basic steps are present. The development of the plant begins almost immediately after fertilization. (See Section 11–8.) In most cases the small embryo begins to develop while it is still attached to the parent plant. The seed protects and nourishes the young embryo until it can begin a life of its own. The seeds of higher plants

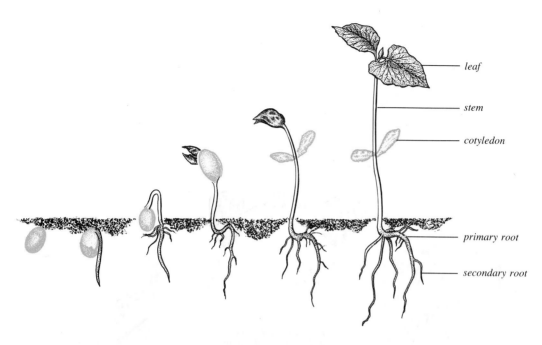

*leaf*

*stem*

*cotyledon*

*primary root*

*secondary root*

**Figure 12–2**  As a bean seedling develops from a seed, it grows both above and below the cotyledons.

contain **cotyledons** (kot-ih-LEE-dunz). Cotyledons are the first, or seed, leaves which, along with the endosperm, provide food for the growing embryo.

Some plants have only one cotyledon in the seed. These plants are called **monocotyledonous** (MON-oh-kot-ih-LEED-un-us) plants, or just monocots for short. Corn is a common monocot. Grasses, lilies, and orchids are other examples of monocots. The **dicotyledonous** (DYE-kot-ih-LEED-un-us) plants, or dicots, those whose seeds have two cotyledons, include all the legumes (beans, peas, clover), the common trees and shrubs (except evergreens), and most flower and vegetable garden plants.

The three regions of the plant embryo can easily be identified: the embryonic shoot, the embryonic root, and the cotyledons. (See Figure 12–1.) The cotyledons contain enough food to give the young plant nourishment until it can grow leaves and begin to manufacture its own food by photosynthesis. Cotyledons of some plants carry on photosynthesis for a short time. The embryonic shoot is the beginning of much of the stem, the leaves, and eventually, the flowers and fruit. The embryonic root develops into the roots of the plant and into the lower part of the stem.

If a seed is planted and provided with the proper conditions of moisture, oxygen, and temperature, it will usually sprout (germinate). Figure 12–2 shows stages of bean development.

**Try Investigation 12–A**  What Is There in a Seed That Can Grow into a Complete Plant?, page 627.

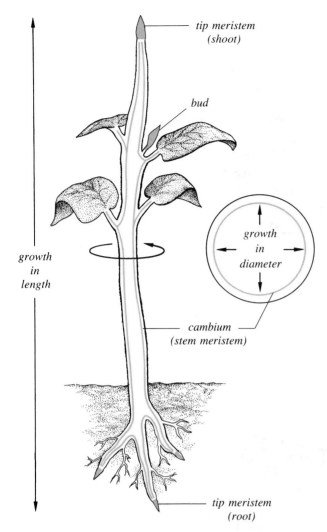

**Figure 12-3** The primary growth tissues of this dicot plant are called meristems. They include the cambium, the tip meristem, and the meristem of other buds.

remain throughout the lifetime of most plants. All permanent tissues of a plant are derived from one or another of these meristems. (See Figure 12–3.) **Cambium** (KAM-bih-um), which allows growth in the diameter of a stem, is rarely present for long in monocot plants. Thus, most monocots can grow taller, but not much thicker.

The dicots usually retain their cambium layer which produces both **xylem** (ZYE-lem) and **phloem** (FLO-em) cells. Xylem is the woody tissue in the plant that is involved in supporting the plant and in transporting water throughout the plant. Phloem is the food-conducting tissue. The addition of new cells, especially during the growing seasons, causes an increase in width. The seasonal layers are seen as annual rings. (Figure 12–4.)

The center of a large tree is nonliving; but the thick and tough walls of its once-living cells usually remain, making up the wood of the tree. Even if these inner cell walls are destroyed, the tree can continue its normal growth because the living tissue of a tree trunk is part of the bark. The cambium which is the innermost layer of the bark is continually producing new layers of cells. The well-known "Chimney Tree" is a giant redwood whose interior was burned out, so that only the outer shell remains. You can walk inside the base of the trunk and look straight up through the center of the tree and see the blue sky above. From the outside the tree looks normal and it continues to grow like other redwood trees.

## 12–3

## Plant Embryos Develop Primary Growth Tissues

By rapid mitosis, new cells push out from the primary growth layers, causing the plant to increase in height or diameter and to develop such structures as stems, leaves, and flowers. The primary growth tissues are called **meristems** and

**Figure 12–4** The pattern of rings in the wood of the tree trunk marks its growth each year. The annual rings are added by the cambium, the meristem tissue under the bark. Water- and mineral-carrying xylem cells continue to form from the cambium during the entire growing season. Cells made later in the season are smaller than those made earlier, accounting for the rings (1, 2, 3, 4 in the drawing). Food-conducting phloem cells also originate from the cambium.

**CAPSULE SUMMARY**

Parents contribute some part of themselves to the next generation. The development of the new individual is achieved by the growth processes of cell division, cell enlargement, and differentiation. In plants the embryos produce cotyledons, special structures that nourish and protect the developing organisms. Meristems are specialized regions of growth from which all permanent tissues of a plant are formed.

**SELF CHECK**

1. What are three cell processes involved in the development of a multicellular organism?
2. What is the meristem tissue of plants? What is its function?
3. What are cotyledons? What is their function?
4. What are monocots? dicots?
5. What is the cambium tissue? Where is it in most trees?
6. What conditions seem to be necessary for the proper growth and development of plant embryos?

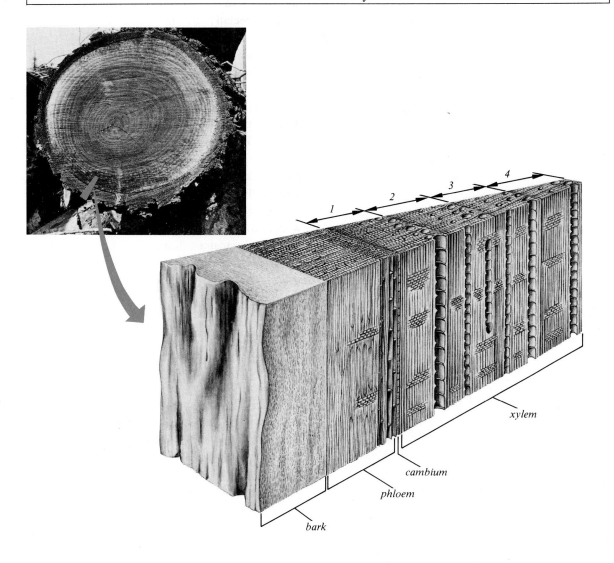

xylem

cambium

phloem

bark

# Patterns of Development in Animals

## 12–4

### Earlier Ideas About Development

Before Aristotle's time no one knew how a chick developed from a hen's egg, or a tadpole from a frog's egg, or a plant from a seed. Aristotle observed the development of the chick, and came to the conclusion that the chick developed gradually from unorganized substances in the egg. Aristotle thought that the raw material from which the organism developed was the "female principle" and that the semen, or "male principle," provided the "creative spark" for development. The idea that a new individual develops gradually from unorganized raw materials is called **epigenesis.**

Other people believed that a tiny, completely formed individual existed in either the egg or the sperm. This idea is called **preformation** (Figure 12–5). It was not until better microscopes were developed and more emphasis was placed on both actual observation and experiments that arguments were settled between those who believed in either preformation or epigenesis. A set of careful observations of incubated chicken eggs revealed that there was continuous growth and gradual development of the organs of the chick.

Modern biologists now know, however, that the egg is not unorganized. There seems to be some preformation and a great deal of epigenesis in the development of any organism. Some of the experiments that provided the evidence are described later in this chapter.

Chicken eggs proved easier to observe than mammalian eggs, which are very small. Karl von Baer, in the 19th century, was probably the first person to find and see a mammalian egg. Von Baer studied both rabbit and dog development, observing the egg of a dog with a microscope.

The egg cells of other mammals were later discovered, and eventually human eggs were also

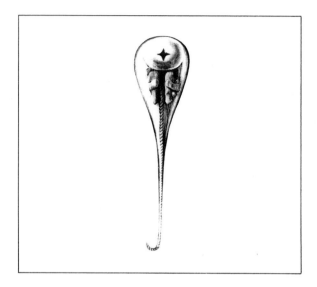

**Figure 12–5** Like an embryo plant that can be seen in an opened seed, this little human being in a sperm was perceived from dim outlines "seen" by early scientists with very crude microscopes. Other scientists contested this interpretation. Some saw the little being in the egg, not the sperm. Others flatly denied that it was in either of the two.

observed. Under the microscope the human egg looks no different from the eggs of other mammals. In fact, all mammalian eggs are about the same size. The egg of a whale is just a little larger than the egg of a mouse. Figure 12–6 compares the egg and sperm cells of several vertebrates.

## 12–5

### The Early Developmental Processes of Cleavage

One group of animals whose eggs have long been used in the study of early developmental stages is the **echinoderms** (eh-KY-noh-derms). Starfish and sea urchins belong to this group. These animals produce large numbers of eggs which can be easily

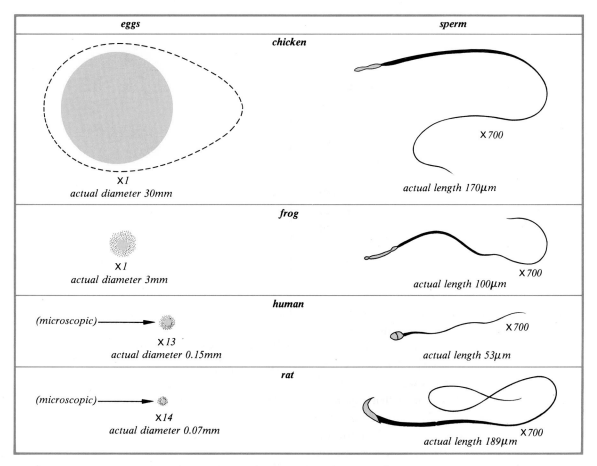

**Figure 12–6** Compare the sizes of these vertebrate egg cells and sperm cells. How would you account for the great difference in size between the chicken egg and a human egg?

fertilized in the laboratory. Then it is possible to study in detail key steps from the fertilized egg to the fully developed animals. As biologists came to learn, these embryos resemble the early stages of development of most other animals that develop from fertilized eggs (Figure 12–7).

In the process of **cleavage,** the fertilized egg undergoes many mitotic divisions and finally it becomes a tight ball of a great many cells. (See Figure 12–8, on page 257.) What do you think is the energy source for all these divisions?

Figure 12–9, also on page 257, shows the two-cell stage of a fertilized human egg. Cleavage continues until hundreds of smaller cells are produced. From some of these cells the embryo itself develops. From other cells, membranes develop which protect and nourish the embryo within the body of the mother. Echinoderm embryos do not have these membranes.

**Try Investigation 12–B** Chicken Embryo Development, page 629.

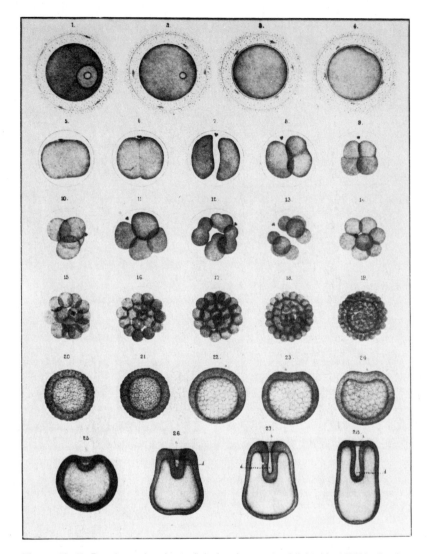

**Figure 12–7** Drawings of early starfish development published in 1877 by Louis Agassiz. Stage 28 occurs 22 hours after fertilization.

## 12–6

## Embryos Develop Internal Cavities After Cleavage

A fluid-filled cavity forms within the mass of cells formed by cleavage. At this stage the embryo is known as a **blastula** (BLAS-choo-luh). (See Figures 12–8 and 12–10.) The blastula cavity is only temporary, but it makes room for the first series of foldings that occur as the embryo develops.

In the next stage of development, the cells on the surface of the embryo push to the inside of the embryo. This infolding of the cells causes the blastula cavity to get smaller. The embryo that

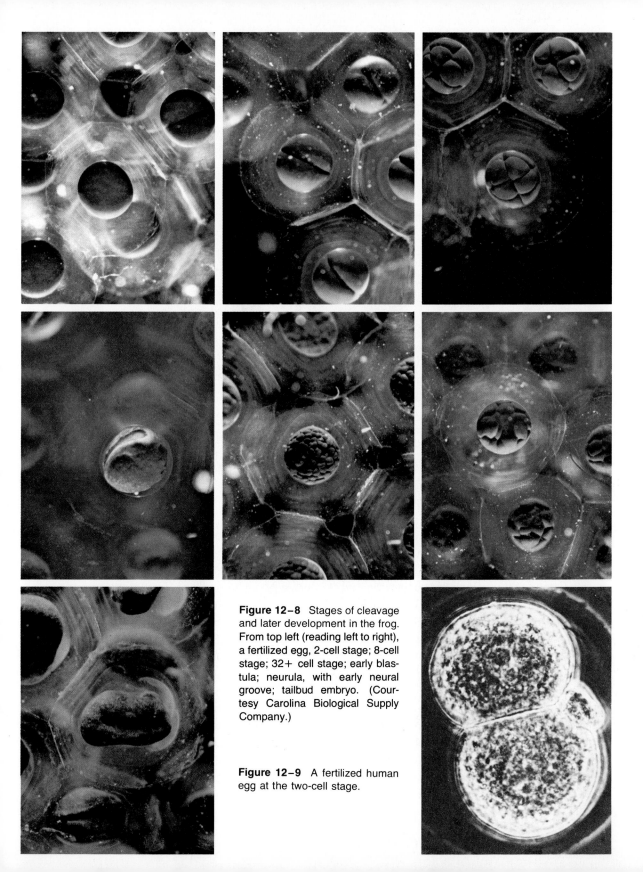

**Figure 12–8** Stages of cleavage and later development in the frog. From top left (reading left to right), a fertilized egg, 2-cell stage; 8-cell stage; 32+ cell stage; early blastula; neurula, with early neural groove; tailbud embryo. (Courtesy Carolina Biological Supply Company.)

**Figure 12–9** A fertilized human egg at the two-cell stage.

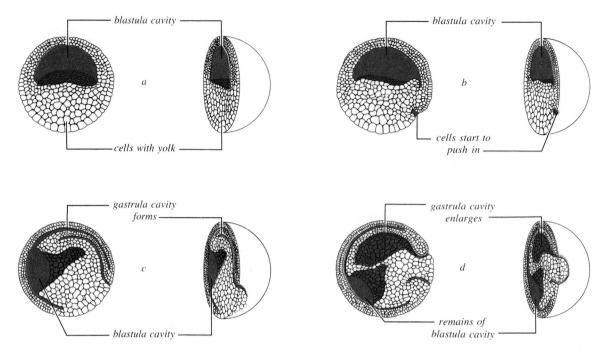

**Figure 12-10** Blastula and gastrula stages in a frog embryo. The blastula cavity (a) grows smaller (b, c, d) and eventually disappears as the infolding of the surface cells forms a gastrula cavity.

results from this cell movement is called a **gastrula** (GAS-troo-luh). (Study drawings b, c, and d in Figure 12–10.)

The gastrula cavity eventually becomes the cavity of the digestive system. It joins cells that have pushed in from the front end of the embryo to form the mouth of the animal. A similar breakthrough occurs at the tail end, forming the anus. The cavity of the digestive system is a tube which runs through a second tube, the body cavity. (See Figure 12–11.)

Three layers of the embryo are formed by the movement of cells to the inside of the embryo. Harmless bits of red and blue dye have been placed on the surface of developing amphibian eggs. When the embryos were later sectioned, the vari-

ous spots of color could be found in a variety of internal organs. This same kind of experiment can be done in chick embryos by placing particles of charcoal on the embryo, and tracing the movements of the charcoal as the chick develops.

The three layers, or cell layers, that are formed are **endoderm** (EN-doh-derm), on the inside; **ectoderm** (EK-toh-derm), on the outside; and **mesoderm** (MEH-soh-derm), in the middle. These three cell layers contain the "germ" or beginning of all the tissues of the adult body. In humans, for instance, the mesoderm gives rise to the reproductive, skeletal, and circulatory systems, among others. The ectoderm gives rise to such different systems as the nervous system and the skin and its derivatives. Refer again to Figure 12–11.

## CAPSULE SUMMARY

A fertilized egg develops according to a pattern of cell division, enlargement, and differentiation. In many animal embryos development begins with a series of rapid cell divisions. This is called the cleavage stage. This stage ends with the formation of a blastula. The blastula consists of an embryo in the shape of a ball with an internal cavity filled with fluid. Then an infolding of cells begins, known as the gastrula stage. Three cell layers form by movement of cells: the ectoderm, the mesoderm, and the endoderm. Out of these, all the tissues and organs of the body develop.

## SELF CHECK

1. What is cleavage?
2. What kind of cell divisions occur in cleavage?
3. Describe the blastula stage of an embryo.
4. What happens in an embryo's gastrula stage?
5. In general, what tissues and organs develop from each of the three early cell layers?

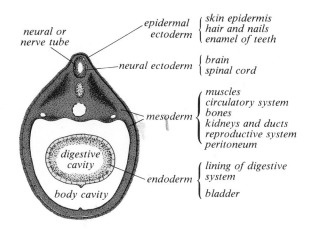

**Figure 12–11** The three primary cell layers in a vertebrate embryo (shown in cross section). Some of the adult structures each layer produces in development are listed on the right. The ectoderm is divided into epidermal and neural ectoderm.

# Explanation of Development

## 12–7

### Early Experiments Suggested Two Types of Developmental Patterns

Being able to describe what actually happens in development is quite different from being able to explain how it takes place. How can a frog egg develop into a tadpole, and then into a frog, and how can a bean seed develop into a bean plant? Biologists began to realize that the way to understand more about normal development was to study what happens when normal development is interfered with. Sometimes in nature, normal development is disturbed and unusual organisms may develop from apparently normal eggs or normal seeds.

One of the most important early experiments was done in 1888 by the German scientist Wilhelm Roux. Frog eggs were fertilized and allowed to divide once. Then Roux poked a hot needle into one of the two cells produced by each egg to kill that cell. The other cell was not injured. Roux then found that the healthy cell developed into a *half* embryo—sometimes a head end, sometimes a tail end, sometimes a left half, and sometimes a right half, but always a half embryo, never whole (Figure 12–12).

Let us think about Roux's experiment. It *seems* to be evidence for some sort of preformation—not preformation of a body, but preformation of a pattern that controls development. If one of the first two cells develops into a left half of an embryo, that cell must have had only the pattern for this one side. The one surviving cell is not able to alter its organization and form a whole embryo.

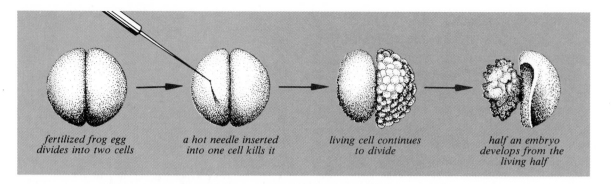

*fertilized frog egg
divides into two cells*     *a hot needle inserted
into one cell kills it*     *living cell continues
to divide*     *half an embryo
develops from the
living half*

**Figure 12–12** Roux's experiment to investigate how embryos develop. At the two-cell stage, one cell was killed. The surviving cell usually formed half an embryo—only the head or the tail half, or only the right or the left half.

Roux's experiment was so interesting that many people began doing similar experiments, poking eggs with needles or separating the first two cells in some way. One of these investigators was Hans Driesch, who did an experiment similar to Roux's but with a different animal. Driesch used sea urchin eggs that were at the two-cell stage, and separated the two cells instead of killing one. The result was very different from that of Roux: each cell gave rise to an *entire* embryo. This result led Driesch to believe that an explanation similar to epigenesis is nearer the truth than preformation. Each half egg, which preformationists thought would normally contribute to only half an embryo, could actually produce a whole embryo.

Roux and Driesch began a long argument. They wrote articles in scientific magazines, each saying the other was wrong. We now know they were both partly right. Modern biologists have repeated Roux's experiment and have discovered that half frog eggs do sometimes develop into whole embryos. Whether one gets a half embryo or a whole embryo depends on how the experiment is done. Thus if one actually removes one of the first two cells instead of killing it, the remaining cell usually gives rise to an entire embryo. In Roux's original experiment, apparently the mere presence of the dead cell prevented the formation of a whole embryo.

Driesch's experiments with the sea urchin have also been repeated and the same results obtained. However, sometimes a half sea urchin egg forms only a half embryo rather than a whole embryo. If the two cells formed *at the first division* are separated, either one can give rise to an entire embryo (Figure 12–13). But, if the egg cell is cut through in a plane perpendicular to the normal cell division, neither half gives rise to a whole embryo.

A whole series of experiments shows that most eggs behave this way. The results depend upon the way the experiments are done. Development is largely epigenetic. There is no preformed tadpole in a frog egg or sperm, no tiny human being in a human gamete. New structures do continuously make their appearance in development.

But there is an element of truth in preformation, too—though not in the way it was first conceived. In a sense one can say that the embryo is preformed because it receives genes from the parents. Its development will depend on the action of these genes. Thus, an embryo inherits a preformed genetic makeup. But this is very different from the theory of preformation that was believed for so long.

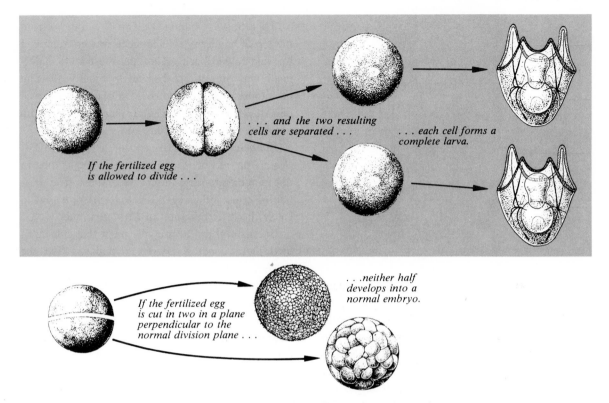

*. . . and the two resulting cells are separated . . .*

*. . . each cell forms a complete larva.*

*If the fertilized egg is allowed to divide . . .*

*. . .neither half develops into a normal embryo.*

*If the fertilized egg is cut in two in a plane perpendicular to the normal division plane . . .*

**Figure 12–13** Driesch separated the living cells at the two-cell stage (top sequence). Each cell developed to form a complete larva. Dividing or cutting the egg in any way different from the normal division plane, however, produced abnormal results (bottom sequence).

## 12–8

## Are the Cells in the Early Embryo All Alike?

Some of the most fundamental experiments to throw light on the nature of the embryonic cells were done by Hans Spemann (SHPAY-mahn). The most famous of these experiments dealt with the differentiation of the embryonic nervous system. From embryos, Spemann cut out the ectoderm that normally becomes the nerve tube (refer back to Figure 12–11) and put these pieces of ectoderm in a separate dish. Each embryo from which this piece was taken healed and lived, but it had either a defective nervous system or none at all. Moreover, the isolated pieces of ectoderm did not form nervous systems, though they remained alive and healthy. Why did each piece form a nervous system if left in the embryo, but not by itself?

Possibly something in the relation of neural ectoderm to the rest of the embryo was necessary to start development of a nervous system. Spemann concluded that the piece of ectoderm needed to be attached to the embryo in order to develop properly. If you think back to the early structure of the embryo, you will remember that there is a layer of mesoderm underneath the ectoderm. Spemann thought that perhaps the mesoderm stimulates the ectoderm to develop into the nervous system. So a second experiment was begun.

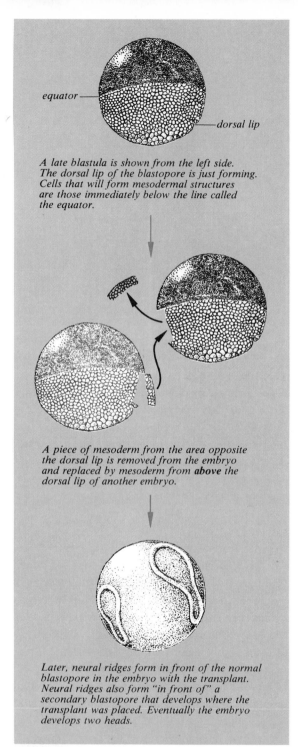

*equator*

*dorsal lip*

*A late blastula is shown from the left side. The dorsal lip of the blastopore is just forming. Cells that will form mesodermal structures are those immediately below the line called the equator.*

*A piece of mesoderm from the area opposite the dorsal lip is removed from the embryo and replaced by mesoderm from **above** the dorsal lip of another embryo.*

*Later, neural ridges form in front of the normal blastopore in the embryo with the transplant. Neural ridges also form "in front of" a secondary blastopore that develops where the transplant was placed. Eventually the embryo develops two heads.*

**Figure 12–14** Spemann's experiment. The mesoderm moves inside the embryo, where it stimulates the ectoderm to develop neural ridges, and later, a nervous system.

This time Spemann cut a flap of ectoderm from the top of an embryo. The piece was not removed but just folded back. Then the mesoderm underneath was cut out and discarded. Finally, the flap of ectoderm was folded back in place. The ectoderm healed and looked quite healthy, but it did not develop into a nervous system.

Spemann's hypothesis appeared to be proved. When the mesoderm is removed, the ectoderm does not differentiate into nerve tissues. The mesoderm must influence the ectoderm somehow to cause the differentiation of nervous tissue.

Spemann did a third experiment that substantiated more conclusively the hypothesis that the mesoderm stimulates the ectoderm to form a neural tube. To understand this experiment, you must know that the mesoderm of a late blastula or early gastrula forms a band extending around the **equator** (Figure 12–14) of the embryo. Two embryos were used in the experiment. From one Spemann removed a piece of mesoderm from immediately in front of the dorsal lip of the blastopore (see Figure 12–14), the area where the neural ridges normally form. From the second embryo Spemann then removed a similar-sized piece from the mesodermal area on the side of the embryo exactly opposite the dorsal lip. In its place the piece of mesoderm from the first embryo was placed. Neural ridges, and later a brain and spinal cord, formed normally in front of the dorsal lip of the embryo's *original* blastopore. Of much greater interest was *the same occurrence in the area where the transplant was made.*

A sort of Siamese-twin embryo was produced. From the belly of an otherwise normal tadpole protruded part of another with a brain and spinal cord.

Obviously there is something very interesting about the mesoderm of the dorsal lip region. If it is removed, the animal produces no nervous system in the normal place. If it is put in a strange place, the animal develops an extra nervous sys-

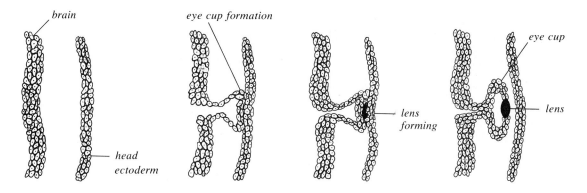

**Figure 12-15** Neural ectoderm (an outpocketing of the brain) induces formation of the lens of the eye.

tem. This area of mesoderm seems to control the differentiation of nerve tissue.

For these experiments and many other important contributions to the experimental study of development, Spemann was awarded a Nobel prize in 1935.

Why are these experiments so important? Biologists try to understand how the cells of a developing embryo become different from one another. They still do not understand fully how these initial differences come about, but once a tissue has been made to differentiate, it may acquire the capacity to cause specific development in some other tissue. The complex structure seen in a fully developed embryo seems to be brought about by a series of interrelated changes, each one dependent on a previous change.

In these experiments the mesoderm is said to have an inductive (in-DUK-tiv) influence on the ectoderm. That is, the mesoderm induces, or causes, the differentiation of ectoderm into nerve cells. Spemann called this process **embryonic induction.** Embryonic induction, the influence of one tissue on another in development, is one of the basic processes of differentiation.

## 12-9

## The Development of the Eye Is an Example of Embryonic Induction

The eye is a very complex structure. When biologists study the development of an eye, they see that it originates partly from ectoderm from the outside of the body, partly from mesoderm, and partly from the neural ectoderm of the nervous system. The eye functions to receive impulses of light from the outside. It converts these light impulses into nerve impulses and sends them through the optic nerve to the brain.

The eye begins its development as an outpocketing of the brain, as shown in Figure 12–15. On each side of the head an extension of the brain grows toward the ectoderm at the front of the head. Each of these extensions forms a cup. The cup inverts, forming a double layer of cells. The double cup closes at the top again, around the forming lens. The cup is connected to the main body of the brain by a narrow stalk. The lining of this double cup of neural ectoderm eventually becomes the retina of the eye, the part of the eye that is sensitive to light energy.

The lens of the eye, the part that focuses light waves upon the retina, is derived from the ectoderm of the head, on the outside of the body. The head ectoderm does not develop into a lens until the neural ectoderm grows out and meets it. In other words, the eye cup touches the outer ectoderm and induces the development of the lens.

In later development other tissues of the eye form, the lens sinks in, and a cornea forms over the front of the eye. The organ is able to function soon after birth. But if the neural ectoderm fails to contact the overlying ectoderm, no lens is formed. This fact can be demonstrated experimentally by placing a layer of cellophane between the optic cup and the overlying ectoderm. The optic cup thus cannot contact the ectoderm, and no lens is formed. But what causes the induction? If a layer of agar is placed between the optic cup and the overlying ectoderm, then the lens does develop. Chemicals that cannot diffuse through cellophane can diffuse through agar. These chemicals were isolated and were shown to cause induction.

Many other cases of embryonic induction in the development and differentiation of tissues and organs have been discovered. The modes of induction have not all been the same and some still remain unsolved.

## 12–10

## Plant and Animal Tissues Can Be Grown Outside the Body

The technique of culturing tissues outside the body of the organism has developed rapidly in recent years, and holds great promise for unraveling more of the mysteries of development.

Tissue culture techniques have proved to be of great value in medical research. They were used, for example, in the procedures which led to the development of polio vaccine. Cancer cells can be grown and studied in tissue culture. Normal cells can be grown in tissue culture and inoculated with viruses in much the same way as bacteria have been inoculated with bacterial viruses. These are a few applications of tissue culture techniques.

Embryonic induction has taken place in tissue culture. When a select square of ectoderm from a frog embryo is put in a dish with a square of inducing mesoderm, nervous tissue forms in the piece of ectoderm.

Important recent work has also been done in the culture of plant tissues. The tip of a plant can be removed and placed in tissue culture containing the nutrients necessary for the plant. Growth and differentiation occur and, eventually, an entire plant develops. The new plant is a clone (page 221). It can be transplanted to soil and will continue to grow normally.

Still more recent work has demonstrated that even certain multicellular animals can be cloned from specially treated cells. Transplant of cell parts is often involved, in addition to tissue culture.

---

**CAPSULE SUMMARY**

Biologists sought explanations for differentiation by interfering with normal development. One technique was to observe the development of a part of an early embryo. When only one cell of the two-cell stage was allowed to develop, conflicting results were obtained, depending on the organism and the experimental method used. It was eventually learned that half of an early embryo could become a complete individual under certain conditions. Much of development depends on physical contact, materials interchange, and tissue interaction during development. Some cells and tissues can be grown away from the body in tissue culture.

**SELF CHECK**

1. How did Roux and Driesch each interfere with normal development, and with what results?
2. How were the conflicting results obtained by Roux and Driesch explained and reconciled?
3. Describe other evidence which has been added to Spemann's studies indicating the importance of embryonic induction to normal development.

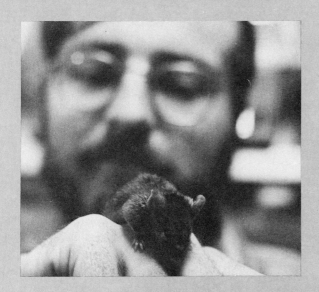

# Mammals with Multiple Parents

During development, a mammal acquires the ability to chemically recognize foreign protein, meaning any protein that is not its own. In humans, this ability causes a problem in organ and tissue transplants. When someone needs to have an organ replaced and a healthy organ is available, a transplant may be performed. However, the recipient's body usually recognizes the organ's protein as foreign and rejects the transplant. This occurs because the tissues of the replacement organ are attacked and destroyed by cells and cell-produced substances that are specialized for this function in the recipient's body. Only transplants of one organ—the liver—have progressed beyond the experimental stage to the point where liver recipients can enjoy long-term transplant benefits.

What are the factors involved in an animal's immune responses? Researchers are continually conducting experiments to understand and answer this question. One experiment that was performed involved the use of eight-cell embryos from two different inbred strains of mice. The embryos were merged to permit scientists to study whether or not the two different types of cells could live together. In this procedure, the two very early-stage embryos are placed together in a drop of culture medium and gently brought in contact with each other until they fuse. The fused "double" embryo is then implanted into the body of a female mouse that acts as a foster mother and eventually gives birth to the young mouse. The mouse you see in the picture above was produced this way—it has four genetic parents! Some of the cells of the newborn mouse are derived from one pair of parents, and some are derived from the other pair. Yet the tissue fluid of the mouse contains substances that block rejection of either type of cell from the original four parents. Learning more about these substances and how they act could make organ transplant surgery more promising.

# Variations in Development

## 12–11

### Plants and Animals Can Replace Lost Parts

Growth and development continue to differentiate the specialized body parts in an embryo until a completely formed individual is produced. In some ways, however, development continues as the individual matures to an adult. Even then, injury may renew developmental processes. Many plants and animals, for example, can replace lost body parts. The process is called **regeneration.**

In regeneration, the same pattern found in the embryo appears again—cell division, cell enlargement, and differentiation. This time only the missing body part is usually the target, although many plants retain an amazing ability to reproduce an entire plant. (You have read about this as asexual reproduction in Section 11–4.)

When a tree trunk is damaged, the tree repairs it, even producing new bark. Only when the damage extends completely around the trunk (cutting off all water and food circulation) will the trunk and branches die. The tree still may not die; new shoots may be produced from the trunk *below* the encircling damage. People prune their trees and shrubs to shapes and sizes desired, counting on the plants' amazing regenerative capacity.

Many animals can replace lost parts in varying degrees. If one of the rays of a starfish is removed, a new ray will begin to regenerate very shortly. The new ray will continue to increase in size until it has the same form and functions as the ray it replaces. Even more amazing, the ray that has been removed from the starfish, provided it retains a portion of the center of the body, may develop into a whole new starfish! And so, depending upon the organism, regeneration and reproduction overlap.

Even some vertebrate animals have a remarkable capacity for regeneration. If a leg is removed from a salamander, the salamander will form a new leg. Most surprising, the leg will be a near duplicate of the one that was amputated. The bones, muscles, nerves, and blood vessels will be replaced accurately, and the leg will function perfectly.

The capacity to replace lost parts varies greatly among vertebrates. Most groups of vertebrates have less regenerative power than their evolutionary ancestors. In general, the more complex an animal, the less regenerative power it has. Human beings have some regenerative powers, though they cannot regenerate a limb or even a finger. Skin wounds heal by regeneration of the cell types found in skin. When there is a greater loss of tissue, the wound heals somewhat imperfectly, leaving a scar.

Some internal organs of humans can also regenerate to a certain extent. The tongue, when injured, has a good capacity for regeneration. Likewise, when portions of the liver have been removed surgically, the liver tissue can regenerate a large part of its normal mass. Bone and muscle tissues can be regenerated when the injury has not been too great.

There is still much to be learned about regeneration, but it seems clear that regeneration of lost parts involves the same kinds of processes that take place in the original development of an organism.

**Try Investigation 12–C**  What Happens to the Pieces of Cut-Up Planarians?, page 632.

## 12–12

### Heredity and Environment May Produce Variations in Development

Although the processes of development are remarkably accurate generation after generation, abnormalities do occur. These abnormalities may have their origins in gene mutations (Chapter 10). Or some occurrence during the developmental period may affect the organism permanently.

If the genes that control developmental processes are not functioning properly, abnormal development may result. For instance, the mice of one genetic strain are very fat and weigh several times as much as normal mice. In humans, there are individual cases of unusual development, resulting in dwarfism or giantism. There are also entire populations known for their large or small stature. Members of the Watusi tribe of Africa often exceed two meters in height, while not far away live the dwarf Pygmy tribes. The individuals of these tribes are abnormal only when compared with the majority of humans.

A dramatic instance of the effect of an external agent on normal development was seen in 1962. It was discovered in Europe that some mothers who had taken a particular kind of drug for nausea, thalidomide (tha-LID-oh-myd), gave birth to abnormal babies. Some of the babies had shortened or deformed arms and legs, and also various kinds of internal disorders. When the unsuspected effect of the drug was discovered, it was removed from the market. Unfortunately, hundreds of women had taken the drug during the early stages of pregnancy, when the arms and legs of the embryo were forming. Early experimental tests on laboratory animals did not show that this drug caused abnormal development. Later tests did reveal the same results as in the affected human infants.

It is known that embryonic tissue is highly susceptible to environmental factors that would have less or no harmful effect on the fully developed organism. In general, the younger the organism, the higher the risk.

## 12–13

### Uncontrolled Cell Division May Produce Cancer

As an organism approaches maturity, the rate of development gradually diminishes. Differentiation slows or stops when all the organs have reached their adult form and function. Cell division continues in most tissues, but at a slower rate. Just enough cells are produced to replace those that are lost. Overall growth stops when an organism reaches its mature size. Humans characteristically do not grow any taller than two meters. Trees may reach a height of more than 30 meters. Among dogs, the very large Great Danes and the very small Chihuahuas (chi-WAH-wahs) each reach a definite size.

Even though the rate of cell division generally drops to a low level, some kinds of cells must still be manufactured at a high rate. Red blood cells, for instance, wear out relatively quickly: They live approximately 120 days. Every second the body must replace about 10,000 red blood cells just to keep a constant number in the circulating blood. Plants continue to put forth new stems, leaves, and flowers throughout life, although their overall size may change very little.

If the rate of cell division in an organ suddenly increases again, the chances are that somewhat different cells are produced than are needed by the body. Some abnormal cells can cause cancerous growth. The word 'cancer' refers not to a single disease, but to a variety of different types of abnormal growth and development. Leukemia, a particular form of cancer, for instance, is a condition in which large numbers of immature white blood cells are produced and released into the bloodstream. (See Figure 12–16.) There are even different kinds of leukemia.

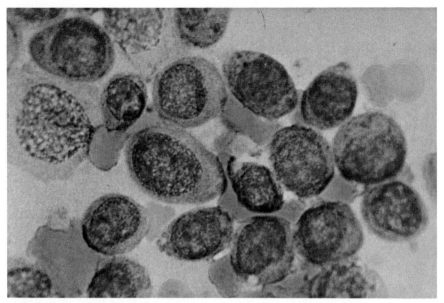

**Figure 12–16** Abnormal numbers of these white blood cells with prominent nuclei help to identify a type of leukemia. The normal balance of the blood cannot be maintained.

Much progress has been made in cancer research, but the problem is still a long way from solution. A new direction in chromosome research has provided promising new clues. You learned in Chapter 10 that chromosomes may break and segments become transferred to other locations on the same or different chromosomes. Researchers reason that genes associated with cancerous growth may exist in inactive segments of chromosomes. Breakage and relocation may put them in active segments and expose them to the right combination of activating genes and enzymes. A cell in which these events occur may thus become cancerous and produce other cells like itself.

**Try Investigation 12–D** Growth Patterns, page 633.

**CAPSULE SUMMARY**

Throughout their lifetime many plants and animals retain the ability to replace lost parts. This property of regeneration is greater in some groups than in others, but even advanced organisms, such as humans, retain some regenerative powers. Development may be influenced by both internal and external factors, which may cause abnormalities of various kinds. While the rate of development slows as an organism approaches maturity, sometimes isolated cells or tissues begin to grow again in uncontrolled numbers and type, resulting in cancerous growth.

**SELF CHECK**
1. What is regeneration?
2. How is regeneration related to differentiation?
3. What are some regenerative powers in humans?
4. What is an example of variation in development due to genetic variation?
5. What are some examples of variation in development due to the use of external agents?

# CHAPTER SUMMARY

## HIGHLIGHTS

Three cell processes are involved in growth and development: (1) cell division, (2) cell enlargement, and (3) cell differentiation. The primary cell layers in animal embryos give rise to definite structures in adults, as demonstrated by experiments that interfere with or change the cell environment of selected regions of cells in embryos. In plants, new cells and tissues arise only from the regions of growth called meristems.

Biologists can experimentally change the circumstances of embryonic development. However, even with experiments they have not discovered how embryonic induction occurs in every part of an embryo. Experiments and chemical analyses continue. Research is also conducted on regeneration, cancer development, and other normal or abnormal processes that may be related to embryonic development. Cancer research has also focused on changes in chromosomes.

## REVIEWING IDEAS

1. What cell processes are involved in growth?
2. How does reproduction differ from development?
3. How have experiments on development helped explain the differentiation of cells into tissues?
4. What does cell differentiation mean?
5. How is regeneration in plants and animals related to development?
6. How does a fertilized egg differ from a blastula? from a gastrula?
7. From what primary cell layer in an animal embryo does each of the following tissues arise?
   a. brain          d. lining of the stomach
   b. heart          e. reproductive system
   c. skeleton       f. skin and hair
8. What are meristems, where are they found, and what purpose do they serve?
9. In what ways were both preformation and epigenesis wrong as explanations for development?
10. Of what value are studies of development to an understanding of abnormal processes such as cancer?

## USING CONCEPTS

11. A human developmental disorder called phocomelia (foh-coh-MEE-lee-uh) results in arrested development of arms and legs. How does understanding the way thalidomide affects embryos add to an understanding of developmental disorders?
12. What evidence that genes and environment interact in the development of an organism did Spemann's work provide?
13. Babies have been born as thalidomide victims, as drug addicts, and as victims of alcoholism. In what way are all these findings related?
14. Why are drugs that have been tested only with laboratory animals used with humans?
15. If embryonic induction is strongly environmental, what care should be exercised in experiments with embryos in culture fluids?

## RECOMMENDED READING

Bishop, J. M. "Oncogenes." *Scientific American,* March 1982. The origin and activation of genes that may cause cancer.

Orr, R. T. *Vertebrate Biology.* Fifth Edition. Philadelphia, Saunders College Publishing, 1982. Includes selective coverage of development in vertebrates.

Saunders, J. W. *Developmental Biology: Patterns, Problems, and Principles.* New York, Macmillan, 1982. The many areas of research in studies of development.

# PART FOUR

# Genetic Continuity

To the three giraffes, the trees may all look alike. How difficult would it be to identify the giraffes individually? Likenesses are an expression of genetic makeup. Genes preserve remarkable similarities among individuals of a species without making these individuals identical. The giraffes and the trees show the same degree of variability in appearance that you and your friends do. For more than a century biologists have investigated these characteristics of species.

# Patterns of Heredity
# 13

In sexual reproduction the link between one generation and the next is a very small egg cell that has been fertilized by an even smaller sperm cell. Amazingly, each fertilized egg can develop into a complex organism by the chemical instructions coded in the DNA molecules of the cell's nucleus.

After a period of development the new individual comes to resemble its parents in most respects. In many ways, however, it may differ from one or both of its parents. You probably resemble your parents in many ways and differ from them in many other ways. In this chapter you can learn about how your genes and your environment interact to make you the unique person that you are.

# Heredity and Environment

## 13–1

## What Is Genetics?

A basic plan seems to be passed on from each generation to the next. And yet, by observing humans and other organisms it becomes obvious that there are also differences between parents and their offspring.

Charles Darwin was aware of these differences and called them **variations.** Darwin's theory of the mechanism of evolution was based on the idea that favorable variations survived through the process of natural selection. What factors contribute to the similarities and differences in organisms?

One factor is **heredity.** An individual's heredity consists of the chemical instructions coded in DNA and received from the reproductive cells of the parents.

A second important factor that influences development and later life of an individual is its **environment.** The environment of any individual is very complex. It includes all the substances and forces and organisms that affect an individual during the time it develops, and indeed during its entire life.

Genetics is the branch of biology that attempts to detect and explain the factors that contribute to hereditary similarities and differences. The word *genetics* contains the word *gene,* which is the unit of heredity. You may recall from Chapter 10 that a gene is a segment of DNA that codes for an RNA molecule or acts as a regulator.

## 13–2

## Selective Breeding Was Begun by Early Humans

Early in history people domesticated, or tamed, animals and plants that were especially useful. Animals were selected that were good to eat, that provided milk, or that could be used for transportation or hunting. Plants were selected that produced more fruits, more vegetables, or more grains than other similar plants. The next generation was bred from these selected plants. In this manner,

←Look-alikes and do-alikes. The little prairie dog copies its mother's sitting behavior.

by selective breeding over thousands of years, people developed a variety of plants and animals. (See Figure 13–1.)

A record of heredity over a number of generations is called a **pedigree.** A pedigreed animal, one whose ancestry for many generations is known, is often prized above all others. Farmers want pedigreed cattle from which to breed their milk cows. Hunters want pedigreed dogs. The farmers purchase their seed corn from those who know the pedigrees of their breeding strains in great detail.

**Figure 13–1** The ears of corn pictured here are several times the size of the first domesticated corn in Mexico or the Southwestern United States. Early Indians raised corn which produced ears only about 7 to 8 cm long. The developing bananas are a tropical fruit. The sheep and pigs are modern breeds but are derived from lineages domesticated more than 2500 years ago in Europe and Asia.

Pedigreed animals and plants are selected for particular traits that have characterized their ancestors for many generations. Thus they are more likely to have these characteristics than individuals with unknown ancestors. Also, undesirable traits have been bred out.

Selective breeding, by a trial-and-error procedure, was not always successful. Breeders of Dalmatian dogs (coach hounds), for instance, wanted their animals to have many small and distinct black spots. They selected dogs that had the coat pattern they wanted. But, generation after generation, no matter what the coat patterns of the parents, the pups were born with coats of every kind. Some had nearly white coats. Others had big black patches instead of neat round spots.

In short, people knew that selective breeding worked sometimes but not always. They knew that heredity affected the results, but they did not know how. They also knew from careful observations that heredity affected the health of humans. As early as the sixth century people realized the connection between heredity and hemophilia (bleeders' disease). This was the state of affairs for thousands of years. Then, about a hundred years ago, the science of genetics rapidly developed and with it an explanation for heredity.

**Try Investigation 13–A** Why Do Plants Develop Chlorophyll?, page 635.

## 13–3
## Environment Plays a Key Role in Development

When biologists became interested in problems of heredity, they began to make a list of characteristics, or traits, that appeared to be inherited. They saw that most aspects of life have a hereditary basis and that many traits can appear in more than one form. For instance, humans may have blond, red, brown, or black hair. They may have one of

several different eye colors, one of several different types of blood, one of several colors of skin. Their ear lobes may be attached or free (Figure 13–2). They may or may not be able to manufacture certain enzymes. Some of these traits are much more important to the life of the individual than others, but all of them are hereditary.

Geneticists cannot possibly analyze all the traits of an organism at once. Instead, they study only a few traits at a time. Many other traits are present. This background of other traits is always present and may affect the outcome of experiments and observations. As they work out the solution to each hereditary mystery, geneticists must not forget that all organisms live in a complex environment, both internal and external. The environment may affect the degree to which hereditary traits develop. Geneticists must try to find out which of the many parts of the environment may affect their results. They must try to keep these factors as constant as possible by using controlled experiments. Only then can they tell whether the differences they observe are more likely due to heredity than to environment.

**Figure 13–2** Free ear lobes (left) and attached ear lobes (right). Many variations of free or semi-attached ear lobes exist, but usually a person can be classified as nearer one of these two types than the other.

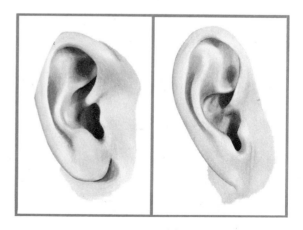

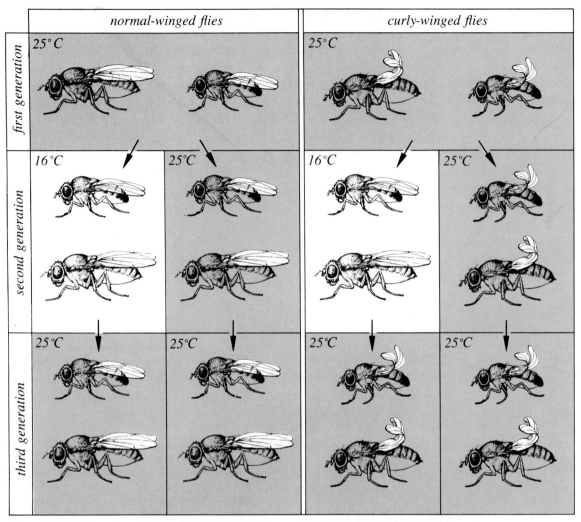

**Figure 13-3** Curly wings in *Drosophila* result from a temperature-influenced trait. If the third generation of curly-winged flies had been raised in a 16°C environment, what would their wings look like?

Heredity determines what an organism *may* become, not what it *will* become. What an organism becomes depends on both its heredity and its environment. These two forces working together determine the final outcome. Some relationships between heredity and environment provide a few examples:

1. Some hereditary traits are expressed only under certain environmental conditions. The small fruit fly, *Drosophila,* may have a hereditary trait of curly wings. The expression of this trait is affected by the temperature at which the organism has grown. At 25° C, the wings are curled. The same flies exhibit the normal wing pattern if they are raised at 16° C. (Study Figure 13-3.)

2. Some traits do not appear to be affected much by the external environment. One of the first hereditary traits studied in humans was poly-

dactyly (pol-lih-DAK-tih-lee). An individual with polydactyly has more than ten fingers or toes, as shown in Figure 13–4. This trait does not seem to be affected by the external environment to any noticeable extent. Other human traits such as color-blindness, blood type, eye color, and free or attached ear lobes do not as a general rule seem to be greatly influenced by the environment either.

3. Many environmental factors permanently change the characteristics of an organism. Those that affect a developing fetus are especially serious. For example, low birth weight has been shown to result from maternal smoking. Other fetal effects, which may even include mental retardation, are associated with alcohol use during pregnancy. The tranquilizer thalidomide caused the birth of many infants with short, malformed limbs. Maternal infection with a viral illness such as *rubella* (German measles) may cause severe defects in the fetus.

4. Heredity and environment interact in the expression of many traits. The nutritional status of the mother during pregnancy, as well as eating patterns established after birth, are as important as genes in determining a person's body build. Many behavioral traits such as IQ depend on environmental as well as genetic influences.

## 13–4
## Identical Twins and Nature and Nurture Studies

Many animals have more than one offspring at a time. In humans, however, only one embryo usually develops during one pregnancy. About once in 85 births, two embryos develop in the uterus and are born at the same time. Rarely, three, four, or even five or more embryos may develop together.

Most twins are **fraternal twins.** Fraternal twins develop from two separate eggs. If two eggs are present at the time of fertilization, each may receive a sperm and develop into a separate individual. Fraternal twins are no more closely related genetically than are any other brothers and sisters. They may look very much alike, or quite different from each other. They may be the same sex or different sexes.

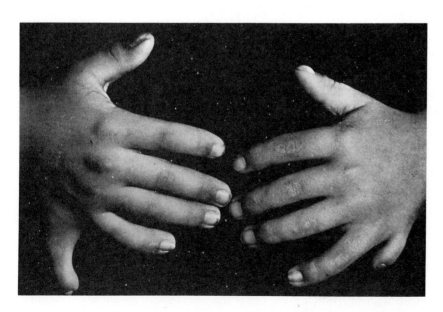

**Figure 13–4** Polydactyly. Extra fingers or toes are rare. Whenever they occur, they are almost always abnormal in position or structure and are usually surgically removed.

**Figure 13–5** Identical twins. Temporarily you can tell the two apart because one twin is wearing braces on her teeth. Yet X rays of their jaws and teeth coincide almost exactly. As a science fair project, one of the twins conducted a study of how the two see themselves, how they compare on physical and psychological tests, and how their friends see them. The outcome was that only strangers could not tell them apart.

Occasionally, the cells developing from a single fertilized egg may separate into two groups. Two complete embryos may then be formed. This is similar to what Driesch observed in sea urchin eggs (Section 12–7), except that in humans, the separation usually takes place at a later stage of development. Excluding the possibility of genetic accidents, the two embryos have exactly the same genetic makeup and thus are called **identical twins.** Identical twins are always the same sex. They always resemble each other very closely physically and have the same basic hereditary traits, such as eye color and blood type. If they dress alike, it may be quite difficult to distinguish one twin from the other. Figure 13–5 shows a pair of identical twins.

Because identical twins have the same genetic makeup, they provide geneticists with the only reasonably controlled human situations for the study of the influences of heredity (nature) versus environment (nurture). If a trait seems to be very different in many identical twins, this lends support to the idea that the trait is heavily environmentally influenced. If, however, the trait seems to be the same in many identical twins (especially if raised in different environments, as may occur through separation and adoption), then it supports the belief that the trait is genetically controlled.

**CAPSULE SUMMARY**

Genetics is the branch of biology that studies and attempts to explain the similarities and differences between parents and offspring. Early humans began to select for breeding those plants and animals that were particularly useful or attractive. Over the years many distinct genetic types were developed in this way. In time, particular patterns of heredity came to be understood. It was realized, also, that the environment of an organism affects the way its heredity is expressed.

**SELF CHECK**

1. How is selective breeding carried out for plants and animals?
2. Give some examples of traits that are influenced by the environment.
3. List several human hereditary traits that do not seem to be affected by the external environment.
4. How are identical twins produced? How can they be used to study the effects of environment versus heredity?

# The Work of Mendel

## 13–5

### Gregor Mendel and the Science of Genetics

Gregor Mendel (Figure 13–6) grew up in the 19th century in what is now Czechoslovakia and was ordained a priest. University studies in mathematics and science influenced Mendel in his experimenting with garden peas in a monastery garden plot. These experiments led to the first in-depth understanding of heredity and the beginning of the science of genetics.

Mendel's first reports record more than eight years of experimental work. The remarkable success of the studies stemmed in large part from mathematical as well as biological principles. The experiments differed in three important respects from earlier ones.

First, instead of including only the few offspring from a single mating, the studies dealt with all offspring of many pairs of genetically similar parents.

Second, since there were large numbers of offspring, mathematics could be used to analyze the data and reveal any statistical trends.

**Figure 13–6** Gregor Mendel's studies of heredity laid the foundation of modern genetics.

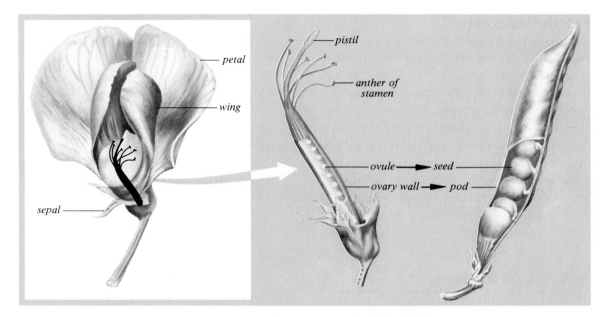

**Figure 13–7** The petals of the pea flower (left) completely enclose the reproductive organs. As a result the pollen from the anthers (center) falls on the stigma, or top, of the pistil of the same flower. The pollen tubes grow down through the pistil until they reach the ovules in the ovary. There self-fertilization occurs. The ovules develop into seeds (right), and the ovary wall develops into the pod. Usually all the seeds in the pod are fully formed.

Third, the studies were directed toward particular traits, not everything about all the offspring at once. A selected few hereditary traits of pea plants were studied in detail. Further, these traits were clearly contrasting, such as stem length (short or tall) and seed shape (round or wrinkled).

There is one additional point to keep in mind. At the time when Mendel worked, nothing was known about genes or chromosomes or the processes of cell division. Any principles to be discovered were based only on the results of the plant-breeding experiments. Nothing was known about changes taking place in the cell. It was not until many years later that knowledge about the cell was successfully related to Mendel's principles, as you will see in the next chapter. To understand this early work you will examine some of the original data.

Mendel selected garden peas for these experiments because they had many desirable features. The plants were easy to cultivate and produced many generations in a short time. Numerous varieties could be purchased. The offspring of matings between different varieties could reproduce readily. The final reason was that it is easy to control fertilization (matings) in garden peas.

Look at the structure of the pea flower in Figure 13–7 to see how fertilization usually occurs. Fertilization in the pea is similar to that in most flowering plants. Remember that the ovules are in the center of a flower. The pollen grains, carriers of the male gametes, are formed in the anthers. Pollen, either from a flower's own anthers or from some other flower, usually falls on the top of the pistil above the ovules and fertilizes the egg within each ovule.

Since the pistil and anthers in a pea flower are completely enclosed by special, fused petals, the ovules are normally fertilized by pollen from the same flower. This is self-pollination. It was important in developing purebred lines of pea plants with which to start the experiments. In some of the actual experiments, Mendel then wanted to pollinate pea flowers with pollen from another flower. To *prevent* self-pollination in these flowers, Mendel removed the anthers from them before the pollen was mature. Each flower's stigma could then be dusted with pollen from the other flower. By cross-pollination, an experimenter can cross plants with known hereditary characteristics. Thus Mendel was able to control the pea-plant experiments.

## 13–6
## Dominant and Recessive Traits

After selecting pea plants for the experiments, Mendel chose characteristics to study. To ensure that the plants were purebreeding, they were left to fertilize themselves for a number of generations. This required several years. The offspring in each generation were studied to make sure that in the selected traits they were like each other and like the parent plant. Mendel then made hundreds of crosses by dusting the pollen from pea plants with a selected characteristic onto the stigmas of pea plants with an opposing characteristic. This kind of cross is called a **parental cross** (P). After making the crosses, Mendel covered the flowers with a paper sack to prevent the chance of accidental cross-pollination.

Mendel found that all the offspring resembled one of the parents and showed no sign of the trait of the other parent. When plants that produced round seeds were crossed with plants that produced wrinkled seeds, all the offspring produced round seeds. Moreover, it seemed to make no difference which of the parent plants provided the pollen. These offspring of the parental cross are the **first filial generation,** or $F_1$ generation.

In the $F_1$ generation, one trait seemed to rule or dominate over the other trait. Therefore, Mendel called these traits **dominant,** for they always appeared in the offspring of parents with contrasting traits. For example, round seed shape dominated wrinkled, and green pod color dominated yellow. Altogether, Mendel described results for seven different pairs of contrasting traits. In each pair, one trait was always dominant to the other. The dominant traits are recorded in Table 13–A–1 in **Appendix 13–A,** Samples of Mendel's Records, page 711.

Mendel considered other traits as well but selected these for their clear pattern of dominance. Then, in the second major step of the experiments, the $F_1$ plants were left to pollinate themselves. The plants resulting from this second cross became the $F_2$ generation. Three quarters of the $F_2$ generation had round seeds, but one quarter of the offspring had wrinkled seeds. Since the characteristic of wrinkled seeds apparently receded and was not visible during the $F_1$ generation, Mendel called that trait **recessive.** In Mendel's work, a trait was called dominant or recessive according to the way it behaved in actual breeding experiments.

Table 13–A–2, in Appendix 13–A, shows the results Mendel obtained when the members of the $F_1$ generation produced an $F_2$ generation by self-fertilization. In each case, the dominant trait appeared in approximately three fourths of the $F_2$ generation, while the recessive trait appeared in one fourth of these offspring. You can now see the importance of mathematics in the experiments. In each case the ratio of plants with the dominant trait to plants with the recessive trait was close to 3:1. Mendel recognized that these ratios were the same, whether the trait studied was seed shape, length of stem, or another. Mendel recognized in these mathematical ratios a principle that would help to explain the inheritance of many different traits. This principle became basic to many later studies of genetics.

**Try Investigation 13–B** How Are Traits in Fruit Flies Inherited?, page 636.

## 13–7

## At Least Two Genes Determine Each Trait

To explain the results of the experiments, Mendel used simple letter symbols for each trait. With these and mathematical ratios, the patterns of heredity could be expressed much more easily than if written descriptions had been used. Mendel used a capital letter ($R$, for example) to represent the factor for the dominant trait and the same letter, though small ($r$), to represent the factor for the recessive trait. This convenient system of symbols is still used. Today these factors are called genes and are known to be specific portions of DNA molecules. Many of these genes code for the production of polypeptides.

Mendel had noticed that some $F_1$ plants with the dominant trait produced some offspring with the recessive trait. How could this happen? First, it was obvious that the $F_1$ plants with the dominant trait must have had a gene for this dominant trait. But since they produced offspring with the recessive trait they must also have had a gene for the recessive trait. In other words, Mendel concluded that each plant must have had at least two genes for each trait. Alternate forms of a gene that affect a specific trait ($R$ and $r$, for example) are called **alleles** (uh-LEELZ). Mendel reasoned that only one allele for each trait is passed on to the offspring from each parent.

A plant from parents that always produced round seeds could therefore be symbolized by $RR$. This meant that the offspring received two alleles for round seeds, one from each parent. Similarly,

a plant that bred true for wrinkled seeds could be symbolized by $rr$, showing that it had received an $r$ allele from each parent. This description of the alleles for a trait, indicated by paired symbols, is called the **genotype** of an organism. How the genotype is expressed in the appearance or function of the organism is known as the **phenotype.**

Mendel was now able to test these assumptions about alleles. Knowing the genes present in each parent made it possible to predict the kinds of genes that would be present in their eggs and sperm. Even the proportions in which these genes would be distributed could be predicted. Mendel could then predict the kinds and proportions of offspring the gametes would produce.

Suppose, for example, a plant's genotype was $RR$. What kinds of gametes could it produce? Mendel's rule was simple: Only one allele of each pair goes to a gamete. So, in the case of an $RR$ plant, where the members of the pair of alleles are the same, all the gametes, whether sperm or eggs, will contain the same allele. According to the rule above, each gamete will contain one $R$ allele.

Consider a second plant whose gentoype is $rr$. All its gametes, whether sperm or eggs, will contain an $r$ allele, since $r$ alleles are the only kind this parent can provide.

A third case is possible; the plant could have a genotype of $Rr$. According to the rule, a single gamete may have one allele or the other, but not both. It would be expected that one half of the gametes would have $R$, while the other half would have $r$.

The rule that the members of a gene pair separate and end up in different gametes is called the **principle of segregation.** According to Mendel's rule, chance played an important role in heredity. It was a matter of chance which of the two alleles a particular gamete received. The combinations in which these gametes came together during fertilization could also be explained as the result of chance events.

## CAPSULE SUMMARY

The data from a well-planned series of experiments with garden peas enabled Gregor Mendel to work out the first principles of heredity. Mendel used many pairs of similar parents to get large numbers of offspring, which could then be studied mathematically. One form of a trait appeared to be dominant to a second form of that trait when the two varieties of the plant were crossed. The second, recessive trait could reappear in a later generation. Mendel assigned symbols to various traits and concluded that each trait was represented by a pair of alleles in each plant. When gametes are formed, only one allele of each pair goes to a gamete. Which allele goes to a particular gamete appeared to be a matter of chance.

## SELF CHECK

1. How did Mendel make certain of having pure-breeding strains of garden peas?
2. What is a dominant trait? a recessive trait?
3. What is an allele?
4. What is meant by the term genotype? phenotype? Give at least one example of each.

# Probability and Genetics

## 13–8

### Principles of Probability

Genetic reasoning involves probability, the mathematical science that tries to predict the chances that a certain event may happen. Probability is a tool for dealing with chance, or random, events.

The most obvious examples of chance events are found in games of chance. When a coin is tossed, how often will it fall heads? (See Figure 13–8.) What is the chance of its falling tails?

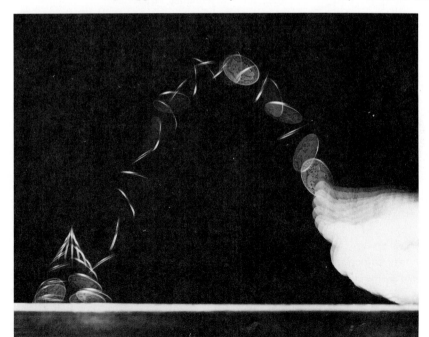

**Figure 13–8** Heads or tails? This stroboscopic photograph shows the tumbling of a tossed coin. What is the chance for the result to be heads?

Many games of chance use a deck of playing cards. In such a deck there are four types of cards: hearts, diamonds, clubs, and spades. In a normal deck there are thirteen cards of each type. When drawing a card from this kind of deck, you can ask such questions as: What is the chance that the card will be a heart? or an ace? or an ace of hearts?

These are all typical chance events and the question "How often?" is a quick way of asking a question which the science of mathematical probability tries to answer. A more accurate way to put the question is: How often should this event be expected to happen in a given number of trials? Notice that the question is "How often should it be expected to happen?", not "How often will it happen?" Why is this distinction important?

An easy way to express a probability is by a simple fraction. If, for example, an event is expected to happen five times in a thousand trials, the probability is expressed simply as $^5/_{1000}$.

Now express the probabilities of some simple and familiar events. For practice, explain to yourself why the probability of each of the following situations is correct:

1. The chance of drawing a spade in a single draw from a full deck of cards: $^1/_4$

2. The chance of an $A$ gamete from an $AA$ parent: $^1/_1$

3. The probability of an $a$ gamete from an $AA$ parent: $^0/_1$

4. The probability of an $A$ gamete from an $Aa$ parent: $^1/_2$

5. The chance of an $a$ gamete from an $Aa$ parent: $^1/_2$

Two principles of probability are important to genetics. The first contradicts a commonly accepted superstition but is true nevertheless:

The result of one trial of a chance event does not affect the results of later trials of the same event.

Consider the following example: Suppose you toss a coin five times and every toss comes up heads. At this point, just before the sixth toss, what is the chance that you will toss tails? The coin does not know what happened in earlier tosses. It is just as likely to fall heads or tails on the sixth toss as on the first. In other words, chance events have no memory.

Suppose that the first three children in a certain family are all girls. What is the probability that the fourth child will be a boy? The egg and sperm involved in the origin of this new embryo were not involved in any previous births in the family. They unite in complete independence of the prior events. So the chance, assuming that male and female births are equally frequent, is simply $^1/_2$, as it was in every previous birth in the family. A run of luck does not alter the probabilities of events if they are truly chance situations.

The second principle of probability is equally simple:

The chance that two independent events will occur together is the multiplication product of their chances of occurring separately.

To illustrate this principle, suppose you roll one of two dice. What is the chance of it showing a three face up? The answer is $^1/_6$. Now you roll the other die. What is the chance of it showing a three face up? The same, $^1/_6$. Now for the new question: What is the chance of both of them, rolled together, showing threes face up? The answer is $^1/_6 \times ^1/_6$, which is $^1/_{36}$, the product of their independent chances. Read more about such applications of probability in the following section.

## 13–9

## How Are Principles of Probability Applied?

Suppose in a certain city one girl in every two has brown hair. Also suppose that one girl in three is slim. What is the chance that the next girl passing by will have brown hair and be slim? The answer is $1/2 \times 1/3$, or $1/6$.

Now suppose that in that city one girl in two has brown hair, one girl in three is slim, and one girl in ten is witty. What is the chance that the next girl passing by will have brown hair, be slim, and be witty? The answer is $1/2 \times 1/3 \times 1/10$, which is $1/60$. The chance that the first girl one meets in that city is slim, has brown hair, and is witty is itself very slim!

Now consider one more example before turning to genetics again. If you toss two coins at a time, what is the probability they will both come up heads? As you learned in the preceding section, the answer is $1/2 \times 1/2$, or $1/4$. What is the chance that they will both come up tails? The answer is again $1/2 \times 1/2$, or $1/4$. Now for the tricky part of the problem: What is the chance that one will fall heads and the other tails? The answer is not $1/4$. It is $1/2$. Why?

This answer does not go against the rule that the probability of a combination of events is a product of their independent probabilities. This result comes about because there are two ways of getting a head and a tail. The first coin could fall heads (chance, $1/2$), and the second could fall tails (chance, $1/2$). The chance of getting a head and a tail together that way would have a probability of $1/4$. But the first coin could have fallen tails (chance, $1/2$), and the second coin could have fallen heads (chance, $1/2$). So there are two ways of getting a head-tail combination, each with a probability of $1/4$. Twice $1/4$ is $1/2$, the answer to the problem.

To calculate the probabilities of all possible combinations of two coins (or two alleles), you always proceed in the same way. Let $H$ stand for heads and $T$ stand for tails. For each coin, there is a probability of $1/2$ for heads ($1/2\ H$) and $1/2$ for tails ($1/2\ T$), so the total chances for that coin are $1/2\ H + 1/2\ T$. To figure the odds for each combination the two coins can have, you multiply the probabilities for the coins. The total adds up to 1.

probabilities for one coin: $\qquad 1/2\ H + 1/2\ T$
probabilities for other coin: $\underline{\times\ \ 1/2\ H + 1/2\ T}$
$\qquad\qquad\qquad\qquad\qquad \underline{1/4\ HT + 1/4\ TT}$
$\underline{1/4\ HH + 1/4\ HT \qquad\qquad}$
$1/4\ HH + 1/2\ HT + 1/4\ TT$

## 13–10

## Probability Applied to Gametes and Offspring

The simpler problems in genetics are exactly like the problem of tossing two coins. Nothing new is added except that genes or gametes are used instead of coins, and the kinds of offspring are predicted instead of combinations of heads and tails.

Suppose one parent has a genotype of $AA$. What kinds of gametes will it produce, and in what proportions? Remember that when parents produce gametes, a pair of alleles separates into different gametes. One and only one allele of each pair goes to a gamete. This is like the toss of a coin that has heads on both sides. Half of the gametes formed will get $A$, and the other half will get the other $A$.

probable gametes from $AA$ parent:
$1/2\ A + 1/2\ A$ (all $A$)

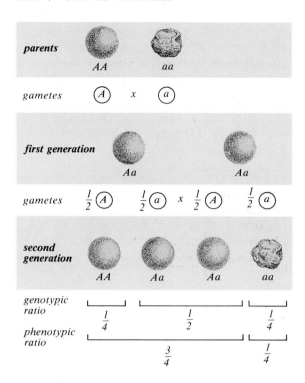

| | |
|---|---|
| *parents* | AA    aa |
| *gametes* | (A) x (a) |
| *first generation* | Aa    Aa |
| *gametes* | ½(A)  ½(a) x ½(A)  ½(a) |
| *second generation* | AA   Aa   Aa   aa |
| *genotypic ratio* | ¼    ½    ¼ |
| *phenotypic ratio* | ¾    ¼ |

**Figure 13-9** When Mendel crossed plants producing round peas with plants producing wrinkled peas, these results were obtained. Which characteristic is dominant?

There are only two other possibilities, and they can be listed in the same way:

probable gametes from *aa* parent:
$\frac{1}{2} a + \frac{1}{2} a$ (all *a*)

probable gametes from *Aa* parent:
$\frac{1}{2} A + \frac{1}{2} a$

If an organism has the genotype *AA* or *aa*, both alleles are alike and the individual is called **homozygous.** (*Zygo-* means a pair, and *homo-* means the same or alike.) If an organism has the genotype *Aa*, each allele is different and the individual is called **heterozygous.** (The prefix *hetero-* means different or other.) In a heterozygous indi-

vidual, the dominant trait will be expressed in the phenotype; the recessive trait will not. At least, this is true if the inheritance of the traits follows a pattern in which the dominant trait completely masks expression of the recessive one. The peas Mendel chose happened to follow this simple pattern. (See Figure 13-9.)

Now solve a simple genetic problem: If an individual with different genes (*Aa*) is mated with an individual with similar genes (*aa*), what kinds of offspring might be expected? The genotypes of the zygotes (fertilized eggs) can be determined by multiplying the probabilities for the gametes produced by one parent by those for the gametes produced by the other:

gametes from *Aa* parent:      $\frac{1}{2}A + \frac{1}{2} a$
gametes from *aa* parent:      $\times \quad \frac{1}{1} a$
$$\overline{\frac{1}{2} Aa + \frac{1}{2} aa}$$

Another way to picture the solution of this problem is to use a type of checkerboard called a Punnett square. It works much like a multiplication table. The probable gametes from one parent are placed along one side of the table, and the gametes from the other parent along the top, as shown below. Then the numbers in the boxes are multiplied in order to arrive at all possible combinations of gametes.

| | probable gametes from *Aa* parent | |
|---|---|---|
| | ½ *A* | ½ *a* |
| probable gametes from *aa* parent    $\frac{1}{1} a$ | ½ *Aa* | ½ *aa* |

Now solve a problem in which both parents are heterozygous. This is exactly the same as the problem involved in the self-fertilization of the $F_1$ plants in Mendel's experiments. Again, separate the alleles into gametes with their probable frequencies, and multiply:

probable gametes from one
*Aa* parent:                          $\frac{1}{2}A + \frac{1}{2}a$

probable gametes from other
*Aa* parent:                      $\times \frac{1}{2}A + \frac{1}{2}a$

$$\overline{\quad \frac{1}{4}Aa + \frac{1}{4}aa \quad}$$

$$\frac{1}{4}AA + \frac{1}{4}Aa$$

probable offspring:     $\overline{\frac{1}{4}AA + \frac{1}{2}Aa + \frac{1}{4}aa}$

Refer again to Figure 13–9. You will get the same results as shown there if you apply the Punnett square. Try it.

So, in the cross of two heterozygotes, the probabilities are that $\frac{1}{4}$ of the offspring will be homozygous for the dominant trait, $\frac{1}{2}$ will be heterozygous, and $\frac{1}{4}$ will be homozygous for the recessive trait.

# 13–11
# How Are Mendel's Results Interpreted?

Now turn to Mendel's experimental results and work out an explanation. If *A* stands for the allele for round seeds, and *a* stands for the allele for wrinkled seeds, then Mendel's original pure-breeding lines were evidently *AA* and *aa* in the genotype. Table 13–1 shows this parental cross.

| P phenotypes | round | $\times$ | wrinkled |
|---|---|---|---|
| P genotypes | *AA* | $\times$ | *aa* |
| P gametes | $\frac{1}{1}A$ | $\times$ | $\frac{1}{1}a$ |
| $F_1$ genotype | | $\frac{1}{1}Aa$ | |
| $F_1$ phenotype | | all round | |

**Table 13–1**

In obtaining the next generation ($F_2$), Mendel permitted the $F_1$ plants to self-fertilize, so the problem is like one that you solved in Section 13–10. It is the heterozygote $\times$ heterozygote cross, as in Table 13–2. Another way to express the proportion of $\frac{3}{4}$ round to $\frac{1}{4}$ wrinkled is by using the ratio $3:1$ or $\frac{3}{1}$.

| $F_1$ phenotypes | round | $\times$ | round |
|---|---|---|---|
| $F_1$ genotypes | *Aa* | $\times$ | *Aa* |
| $F_1$ gametes | $(\frac{1}{2}A + \frac{1}{2}a)$ | $\times$ | $(\frac{1}{2}A + \frac{1}{2}a)$ |
| $F_2$ genotypes | $\frac{1}{4}AA + \frac{1}{2}Aa$ | $+$ | $\frac{1}{4}aa$ |
| $F_2$ phenotypes | round      round | | wrinkled |
| | $\frac{3}{4}$ | $+$ | $\frac{1}{4}$ |

**Table 13–2**

In one large-group experiment using parents with round peas, Mendel obtained 7324 offspring. Of these, 5474 had peas that were round, and 1850 had peas that were wrinkled. This is a ratio of $2.96/1$. Notice that the actual results are very close to the expected ratio of $3/1$. These results are shown in Table 13–A–2 of the Appendix.

Looking at the data with the rules of probability in mind, Mendel was able to draw some conclusions. Although he used the word *element* or *factor* instead of *gene*, the meaning was the same. The conclusions can be summarized in the following statements:

1. There are different factors (genes) that determine the inheritance of traits.
2. For a single trait, a plant possesses two alleles, which may be alike or different.
3. When the two alleles are different, the dominant trait will be expressed, while the recessive trait will remain hidden.
4. Both alleles are distributed unchanged into the gametes with an equal probability.

**Figure 13–10** The strain of Ancon sheep (center and right) was developed from a mutation causing short legs. The strain was popular with sheep herders since the sheep could not jump fences easily. The short-legged sheep carry two alleles for this recessive trait.

5. At fertilization there is a chance union of gametes, which results in a predictable ratio of traits among the offspring.

Figure 13–10 shows the dominant-recessive principles derived from the garden pea in a trait of another domestic organism—one of many confirmations of Mendel's work.

**CAPSULE SUMMARY**

Mendel applied a knowledge of mathematics and biology to the results obtained by crossing garden peas of distinctive purebreeding lines. In this way a hypothesis to explain the distribution of traits in the offspring of garden peas was tested.

Mendel's explanation was based on probability. He stated that the distribution of genes into the gametes and their union in fertilization were subject to the laws of chance. Biologists use these techniques today to solve many types of genetic problems.

**SELF CHECK**

1. What two principles of probability are used in genetics?
2. How does the use of probability help in experiments with large numbers of organisms?
3. Give an example of a homozygous pair and a heterozygous pair of alleles.
4. How is a phenotype related to a genotype?
5. Why were symbols useful to Mendel?
6. If the probability of maleness in a human birth is $1/2$, and the probability of being red-haired in the same family is $1/4$, what is the probability that the next child in the family will be a red-haired boy?

# Hereditary Patterns

## 13–12

## Dominance Occurs in Many Traits But Not in Every Trait

Most traits are not as simple as those Mendel selected for study in the garden pea. It took some time to find these traits in which only two "characters" or "factors" seemed to be at work, with one or the other clearly expressed. Further, Mendel's conclusions were based on experiments with a limited number of kinds of plants—with the garden peas foremost. Without performing similar experiments on many different organisms— animals, plants, and protists—Mendel could not be sure that these principles applied in general to the inheritance of traits in all living organisms. It is now known that a variety of relationships exists, ranging from complete dominance-recessiveness at one extreme to complete lack of dominance at the other.

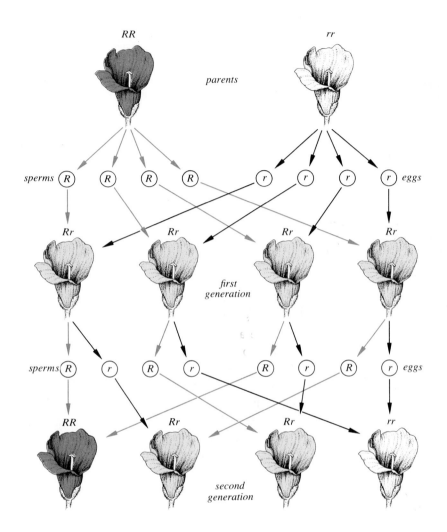

**Figure 13–11** In a cross between purebred red and white snapdragons, the phenotype of the first generation is visually different from that of either parent. This is an example of codominance.

For example, a snapdragon genetically pure for red color (*RR*) crossed with one pure for white (*rr*) yields only pink offspring. If numbers are large, the ratio in the F$_2$ will approach $^1/_4$ red, $^1/_4$ white, and $^1/_2$ pink. This is an example of complete lack of dominance, or **codominance.** In such cases, the phenotype completely reveals the genotype. (See Figure 13–11.)

In shorthorn cattle, certain color traits also show codominance. Crosses between red and white cattle usually result in roan, an intermediate color (Figure 13–12). Close examination shows that roan is due to a mixture of red and white hairs. In the heterozygous state, the effects of both alleles for hair color are seen. What color offspring would result from a cross between two roan cattle?

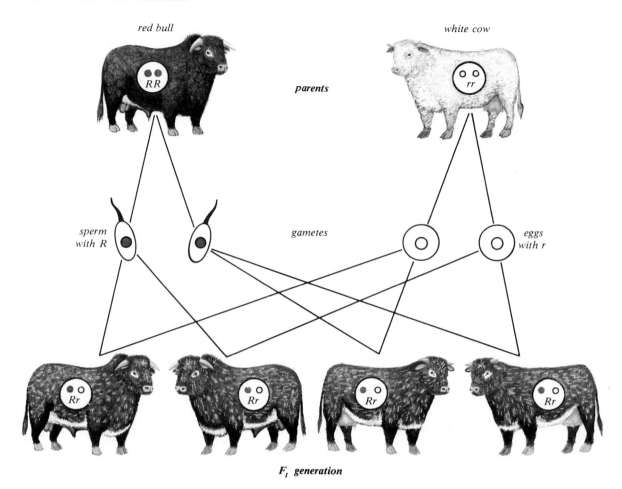

**Figure 13–12** A cross between shorthorn cattle, one red and one white, produces all roan offspring in the F₁ generation.

## 13–13

## Making a Test Cross

In snapdragons and shorthorn cattle, the genotype for color is revealed in the phenotype. This is not true in the peas discussed earlier, however. Since roundness is dominant, a round pea may be either homozygous or heterozygous for roundness. When it is important to know whether or not such an individual is heterozygous, a **test cross** can be made.

To make a test cross, the organism whose genotype is being tested is crossed with an organism showing the recessive trait. (Why can it be assumed that such an organism is homozygous for the recessive trait?) Every offspring from such a mating would receive one allele for the recessive trait from the homozygous parent. If any offspring shows the recessive phenotype, then it also must have received an allele for the recessive trait from the parent being tested. Thus the genotype of the test parent is revealed. In the case of the plant with the unknown round pea, it would be crossed with a plant producing wrinkled (homozygous recessive, *rr*) peas. If any one of the offspring

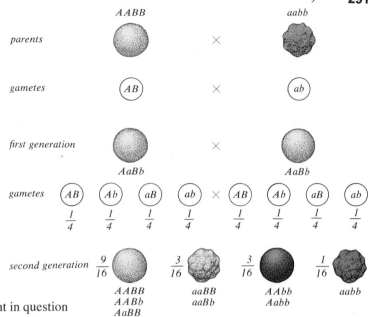

**Figure 13–13** Probabilities of combinations when two traits are traced together.

plants has wrinkled peas, then the plant in question must have been a carrier of the recessive allele and therefore heterozygous ($Rr$).

Refer back to Figure 13–9. What would be your expectations if you crossed a plant producing wrinkled peas ($rr$) with one that is homozygous for round peas ($RR$)? What if the genotype of the plant producing round peas was $Rr$?

## 13–14
## Following the Inheritance of Two Traits at Once

In several of his experiments on peas, Mendel followed two pairs of alleles simultaneously. For example, the alleles for shape and the alleles for color can be followed together. The same methods are used. Since each pair of alleles in this example behaves independently, you can first deal with them separately and then combine them by using the second principle of probability.

Mendel followed the traits of seed shape (round or wrinkled) and seed color, as determined by the cotyledons in the seed (yellow or green), in the same experiment. An earlier cross with seed color had revealed that yellow color is dominant to green

color. Mendel then crossed a plant that produced round, yellow seeds with a plant that produced wrinkled, green seeds.

From earlier work you know that the cross of a plant homozygous for round seeds with a plant homozygous for wrinkled seeds will yield plants with all round seeds in the $F_1$, and will produce $3/4$ plants with round seeds, $1/4$ plants with wrinkled seeds in the $F_2$. Mendel also found that a plant homozygous for yellow seeds, when crossed with a plant producing green seeds, yielded all plants with yellow seeds in the $F_1$, and $3/4$ plants with yellow seeds, $1/4$ plants with green seeds in the $F_2$. Trace the results of combining both sets of traits in Figure 13–13.

In order to get the expected proportions of seeds with the various traits, multiply the $F_2$ results from these two independently acting pairs of alleles:

| $3/4$ round | + | $1/4$ wrinkled | | |
|---|---|---|---|---|
| $\times$ $3/4$ yellow | + | $1/4$ green | | |
| $9/16$ | $3/16$ | $3/16$ | $1/16$ |
| round | + wrinkled | + round | + wrinkled |
| yellow | yellow | green | green |

# Biology Brief

# Mendel in Medicine

Finding out about human genotypes is a special problem: humans are not used in breeding experiments. Most of what is learned is discovered when things go wrong. Disorders that run in families provide most of the data.

Tay-Sachs disease is a genetic disorder whose inheritance fits Mendel's principles. A pair of alleles controls it. The dominant trait is due to a normal allele that controls production of an enzyme known as Hex A (hexosaminidase A). A defective allele causes the recessive trait when Hex A is no longer produced as it should be. In the absence of Hex A, lipids (fats) accumulate in body cells and especially in nerve cells.

A child must receive two alleles for the recessive trait to develop Tay-Sachs disease. At first the baby appears healthy, but as lipids accumulate, brain cells and other nervous tissues are destroyed. The child usually dies by age four.

Prospective parents who are heterozygous for Tay-Sachs may not know it. They feel no ill effects. A genetic counselor, such as Dr. Marie-Louise Lubs, can have tests made and advise the parents when they are carriers of the allele for the recessive trait. Here is how Dr. Lubs or another counselor might proceed after a positive test.

A Punnett square can be used to solve this same problem, but the procedure is much longer and more complicated. Such a table is shown in the Appendix, Table 13–A–3. The summing of results from the nine different genotypes is shown in Table 13–A–4.

Mendel discovered that genes for different traits appear to behave independently as they are as-

sorted in the gametes. This conclusion is called the **principle of independent assortment.**

## 13–15

## What Are Multiple Alleles?

You have now seen how to solve genetic problems in which there are two unlike alleles such as *A* and

Use $t$ for the Tay-Sachs allele and $T$ for the normal allele. If the genetic counselor learns that only one prospective parent is a carrier, the counselor can explain these probabilities:

$Tt$ (one parent)                $TT$ (other parent)
1/2 $T$ and 1/2 $t$ gametes       $T$ gametes only

Probabilities for children:
1/2 $T \times 1T = 1/2$ $TT$ noncarriers      1/2 $t \times 1T = 1/2$ $Tt$ carriers

No children will have the disease, but some, all, or none may be carriers.

Now suppose the genetic counselor finds out that both prospective parents are carriers:

$Tt$ (one parent)              $Tt$ (other parent)
1/2 $T$ and 1/2 $t$ gametes      1/2 $T$ and 1/2 $t$ gametes

Probabilities for children:
1/2 $T \times$ 1/2 $T =$ 1/4 $TT$ noncarriers ⎫
1/2 $T \times$ 1/2 $t =$ 1/4 $Tt$ carriers      ⎬ no Tay-Sachs disease
1/2 $t \times$ 1/2 $T =$ 1/4 $Tt$ carriers      ⎭
1/2 $t \times$ 1/2 $t =$ 1/4 $tt$ with Tay-Sachs disease

Notice that the odds are like those of Mendel's $F_2$ generation: 3 to 1, or by actual genotypes, 1 to 2 to 1. The genetic counselor will be careful to point out to the prospective parents that each fertilization of an egg is an independent event. Therefore, the same probabilities exist for every pregnancy. There is a clear risk.

Fortunately, even tests of unborn babies are possible for Tay-Sachs. The counselor will tell the prospective parents this as well. You will read more about this testing process in Chapter 14.

$a$. In many cases, however, there are more than two different alleles affecting a particular trait. These are called **multiple alleles.** Inheritance of the human ABO blood types is an example of multiple alleles.

There are four blood types (or phenotypes) in the ABO system (Table 13–3). Three major alleles are involved, although only two of them can occur in any one individual. The two may be present in any combination of the three possible alleles.

The ABO blood types are determined by the presence or absence on the red blood cells of two protein substances. These two types of protein are identified by the letters $A$ and $B$. In blood type A, only the A protein is present on the red blood cells. In blood type B, only the B protein is present. Type AB blood results from the presence of both A and B proteins on the red blood cells. If neither is present, the blood type is O. The symbols $I^A$, $I^B$, and $i$ are used to show that codominance as well as complete dominance operates in this multiple-allele system.

**Table 13–3** Genetics of ABO blood types.

| phenotype | genotype | protein on red blood cells |
|---|---|---|
| type A | $I^A I^A$ or $I^A i$ | A |
| type B | $I^B I^B$ or $I^B i$ | B |
| type AB | $I^A I^B$ | A and B |
| type O | $ii$ | neither A nor B |

**Try Investigation 13–C** How Are A, B, AB, and O Blood Groups Inherited?, page 637.

The alleles for blood groups and for thousands of other traits studied in different organisms appear to assort independently in the gametes. This supports Mendel's conclusions based on the hereditary factors in garden peas. But even with independent assortment, occasionally certain gene combinations in a number of organisms occur more frequently than chance can explain. Earlier in the chapter you read that three girls in a row, in one family, do not affect whether the fourth child will be a boy or girl, *if the situation is truly chance.* However, some gametes in certain families turn out to be less likely to survive than others, because of some unknown genetic trait. The gametes that survive to take part in fertilization may be mostly female-determining. Then the events are no longer chance. However, the great majority of all genes and their alleles appear to be subject to fair play, or chance, as Mendel first determined with the garden pea studies.

---

**CAPSULE SUMMARY**

Observed traits are the outcome of a variety of interactions among the alleles affecting those traits. A dominant trait is one in which homozygous and heterozygous individuals have the same appearance or phenotype. In the case of a trait involving codominance, the heterozygote is easily distinguished from either homozygote. In many cases multiple alleles exist for the same trait; for example, in human blood types. However, only two of the multiple alleles can be present in one individual. Dominance may be present or lacking in traits with multiple alleles, depending on the particular pair of alleles present in the individual.

**SELF CHECK**

1. Give an example of an inherited trait where no dominance is present. Is there a difference between the genotype and phenotype?
2. What are multiple alleles?
3. If parents have type O and type AB blood, what blood types can their children have? Explain.
4. How is the second probability rule applied to a problem of inheritance involving two traits?
5. Are Mendel's principles as worked out with garden peas applicable to other types of organisms? Explain.

# CHAPTER SUMMARY

## HIGHLIGHTS

Two important forces control the development and life of an individual: heredity and environment. What an organism becomes depends upon a complex interaction of both heredity and environment.

Heredity was poorly understood before Gregor Mendel began experimental studies of garden peas. Mendel's results suggested that heredity was controlled by a number of independent factors, later called genes. Each inherited trait, such as seed shape, or flower position, or height of plant, appeared to be controlled by a pair of alleles.

One of Mendel's important contributions was to recognize that the individual alleles of a pair are segregated into gametes (the principle of segregation). These alleles are then assorted, by chance, among the offspring (principle of independent assortment).

Mendel further assumed that different alleles of a gene pair were not modified by being together in the cells of an organism. This appeared to be true because although alleles for recessive traits did not have any apparent effect in the heterozygote, the recessive traits reappeared unchanged in the offspring of some plants. The gene for white seed coat, for instance, remained the same determiner of whiteness, in spite of being associated with a gene for colored seed coat.

Most genes and their alleles investigated since Mendel's time fit the assumptions made for the hereditary factors in garden peas, although a few exceptions are now known. Few traits, however, are controlled by only two alleles. The ABO blood types are an example of multiple alleles. Complete dominance is also not as common as Mendel's studies first indicated.

The principles of probability help scientists understand experimental results and predict the kinds and proportions of offspring expected from certain matings.

## REVIEWING IDEAS

1. What is the relationship of purebred animals and plants to homozygous or heterozygous genotypes?
2. What characteristic of the flowers of pea plants made these plants more reliable than many other kinds of plants for breeding experiments?
3. What experimental procedures contributed to Mendel's success as a geneticist?
4. Distinguish between $P$, $F_1$, and $F_2$ as terms applied to different generations in breeding experiments.
5. If $A$ is dominant to $a$, what does the expression $1/4\ AA + 1/2\ Aa + 1/4\ aa$ mean?
6. Explain *dominance, codominance,* and *multiple alleles.*
7. Under what conditions do phenotypes reveal genotypes? Under what conditions must phenotypes be tested to determine genotypes? How can this testing be done?

## USING CONCEPTS

8. Could a hospital's maternity ward depend entirely on blood typing as a way to keep babies identified? Explain.
9. Describe the procedure you would use to determine the genotype of a round, yellow-seed pea plant.
10. What colors and proportions of calves could be expected from a roan bull and white cows? Could a true-breeding roan herd eventually be established? Explain.

## RECOMMENDED READING

Curtis, H. *Biology,* 4th edition. New York, Worth Publishers, Inc., 1983. A beautiful book with eight good chapters on genetics.

Goodenough, U. *Genetics,* 3rd edition. New York, Saunders College / Holt, Rinehart and Winston, 1983. A general introductory text with emphasis on molecular genetics.

# Genes
# and
# Chromosomes
# 14

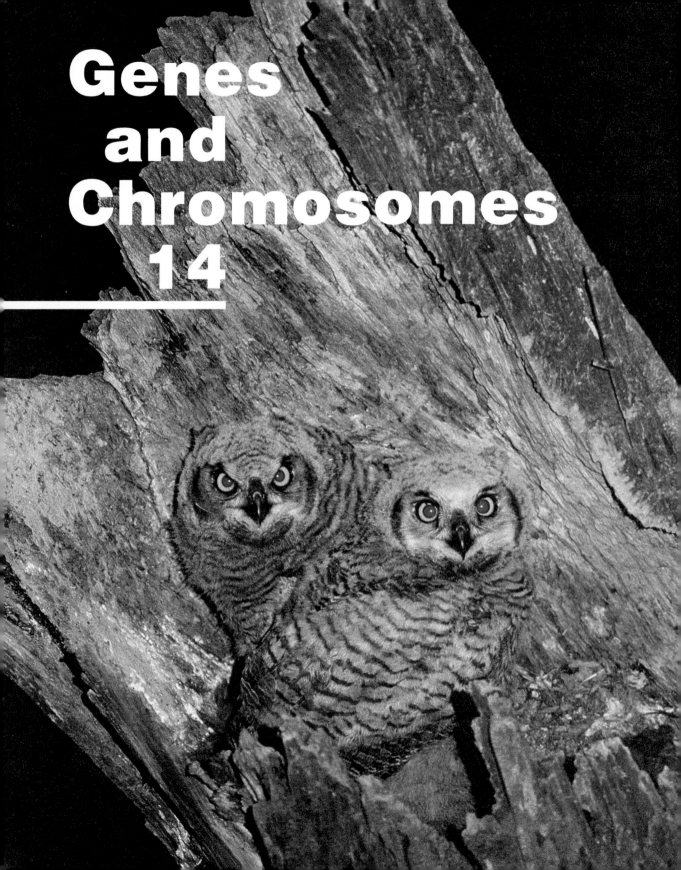

Without a microscope or a knowledge of chromosomes, Mendel uncovered evidence of genes. What were these hereditary "factors"? Genes appeared in pairs in garden peas, but the pairs were split up and reassorted from one generation to the next. Some genes, when present, always affected a plant's appearance. Others could exist in the plant unnoticed, only to affect a trait in the next generation.

Mendel assumed that chance determined the pairing of genes in each new generation. Chance accounted beautifully for the results in each trait studied in pea plants. With the passing of time, however, the heredity of other organisms came into question. How could chance explain that some traits appeared in males, others in females, of many species? Did the principle of independent assortment perhaps not always apply? Was new information still to be obtained, and would it add to Mendel's data or conflict with it? Principles that could explain more about genetics were eagerly sought.

# Seeking an Explanation for Mendel's Principles

## 14–1

### Mendel's Work Comes to Light After 35 Years

Mendel's garden pea studies were published in 1865. During the years that followed, many different plants and animals were used in breeding experiments. Although biologists tried to make sense of their results, they were not always successful. Most plant and animal breeders did not know that Mendel's paper existed. Those who did know of the paper apparently did not realize its significance. They did not know that answers to many of their questions were already available.

The long neglect of Mendel's paper is an interesting chapter in the history of science. A few biologists did know about Mendel's paper but they would not admit that mathematics could explain a biological process such as plant breeding. Mendel showed a great deal of foresight in stating that the findings were important to the study of evolution. However, biologists were not prepared to understand or appreciate the mathematical analysis.

It was not until 1900, thirty-five years after Mendel presented the results and sixteen years after his death, that the value of the paper was realized. Three biologists were working independently on the same kind of breeding problem that Mendel had investigated. Each was working with a different organism in a different country in Europe and each obtained results that agreed with those of Mendel. Each of these three biologists, Correns in Germany, De Vries in the Netherlands, and Tschermak in Austria, came across Mendel's paper when they were writing their own experimental results. Apparently the time was ripe for the development of the science of genetics.

←Which of them is which? Two young great horned owls show their genetic likenesses. Are they identical twins? Match their characteristics one at a time to find out.

**Try Investigation 14–A** Why Are Some Pea Seeds Wrinkled and Some Not?, page 639.

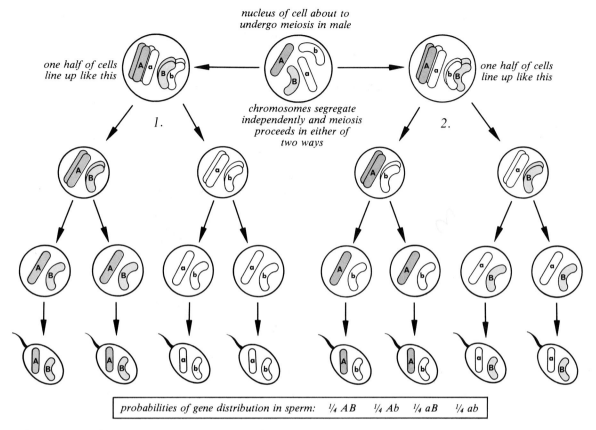

*nucleus of cell about to undergo meiosis in male*

*one half of cells line up like this*

*one half of cells line up like this*

*chromosomes segregate independently and meiosis proceeds in either of two ways*

*1.*

*2.*

*probabilities of gene distribution in sperm:* ¼ *AB* ¼ *Ab* ¼ *aB* ¼ *ab*

**Figure 14–1** Two pairs of genes—A, a and B, b—on chromosomes in a cell nucleus about to undergo meiosis. Follow how the Boveri-Sutton theory of where the genes are located supports the probabilities Mendel worked out.

## 14–2

## The Chromosome Theory Fits Mendel's Predictions

By 1900 biologists knew that each species has a constant number of chromosomes. Theodor Boveri of Germany established that each chromosome is an individual structure that retains its identity from generation to generation. Biologists generally thought that chromosomes carry the hereditary material. Boveri's experiments with the eggs of sea urchins showed conclusively that each chromosome carries different hereditary material.

The connection between chromosomes and Mendel's factors was made independently in 1902 by Boveri and an American, W. S. Sutton. The following year Sutton elaborated on this idea in what later became known as the chromosome theory of heredity. The hypothesis may be summarized to include the following three points:

1. Genes are actual physical units located on the chromosomes.
2. Two alleles of any given gene are present, one on each chromosome of a homologous pair.
3. One chromosome of each homologous pair is from the female parent and the other is from the male parent.

Given these assumptions, the behavior of chromosomes during meiosis and fertilization accounts for the results Mendel obtained from his breeding experiments.

Different genes on separate pairs of homologous chromosomes are diagrammed in Figure 14–1. Follow the different alleles through meiosis and see how their movements could explain the Mendelian ratios.

The hypothesis that genes are located on chromosomes seemed to be a good one. However, more evidence was needed before biologists would be completely convinced. (See **Appendix 14–A,** The Boveri-Sutton Theory, page 712.)

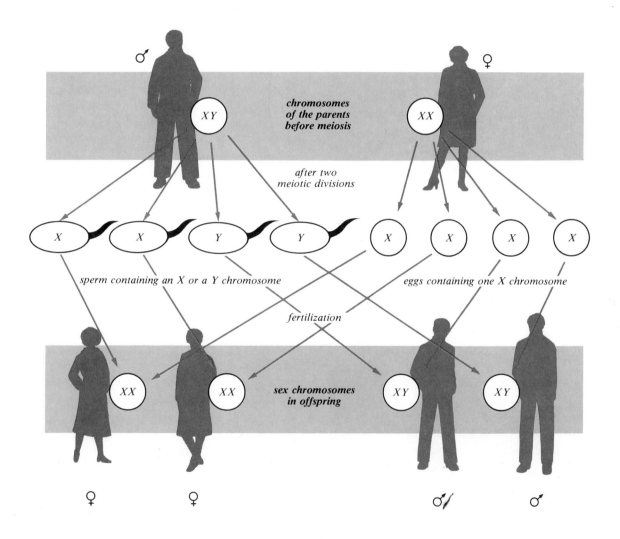

**Figure 14–2** Sex in humans is determined at the moment of fertilization by the sex chromosomes of the egg and the sperm. XX produces a female; XY produces a male. The symbol ♀ represents female; ♂ represents male.

## 14–3

## Chromosomes Determine the Sex of Offspring

The first evidence supporting the chromosome theory came from studies of insects. Some insects have one fewer chromosome in the males than in the females. In other insects the numbers in both sexes are the same but one sex has a chromosome pair made of unlike chromosomes.

Biologists came to recognize the existence of specific chromosomes that determine the sex of the individual. These **sex chromosomes** are usually designated X and Y to distinguish them from the other chromosomes, known as **autosomes** (AWT-uh-sohms). In humans, the female has two large X chromosomes and the male has one X and one much smaller Y chromosome. Under normal conditions, females pass one of their two X chromosomes to each offspring and males pass either an X or a Y chromosome to each offspring (Figure 14–2). Many organisms have this XX-XY pattern of sex inheritance, though the mechanisms of sex determination may still differ. For example, *Drosophila* will be female so long as there are two X chromosomes present (Figure 14–3). In rare cases where two X chromosomes and a Y are present, the *Drosophila* is still female. In humans, however, if a Y chromosome is present with two X chromosomes, the person will be male.

## 14–4

## X-Linked Inheritance Is Discovered

Further evidence supporting the chromosome theory came from Columbia University. There a group of biologists led by Thomas Hunt Morgan was working with fruit flies. Wild fruit flies usually have dark red eyes. While examining *Drosophila* cultures, Morgan found a male fly that had white eyes. He isolated it with a red-eyed female and the two flies mated. All the $F_1$ generation had red eyes, supporting Morgan's assumption that the white-eye trait is recessive.

Flies of the $F_1$ generation were then mated to each other. In the $F_2$ generation, a ratio of $^3/_4$ red-eyed flies to $^1/_4$ white-eyed flies was obtained. This ratio of eye colors also was expected. Strangely, however, all the white-eyed flies were males. Although not all males were white-eyed, this trait seemed nevertheless to be linked to a fly's sex. Further experiments confirmed this finding.

Morgan's knowledge of meiosis led him to predict that female fruit flies produce one kind of egg, carrying one of their two X chromosomes, plus one chromosome from each pair of autosomes (Figure 14–4). Males, on the other hand, produce two kinds of sperm. Half of the sperm carry an X chromosome and half carry a Y chromosome. Each sperm also carries one chromosome from each pair of autosomes. The Y chromosome, though responsible for producing a male, apparently was inactive in the inheritance of eye color. Therefore, a single allele for the recessive trait, *if on the X chromosome*, could result in a white-eyed male (Figure 14–4). Thus Morgan discovered that

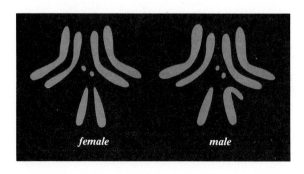

*female*          *male*

**Figure 14–3** Chromosome pairs in male and female *Drosophila*. Which pair of chromosomes shows a difference between the two sexes?

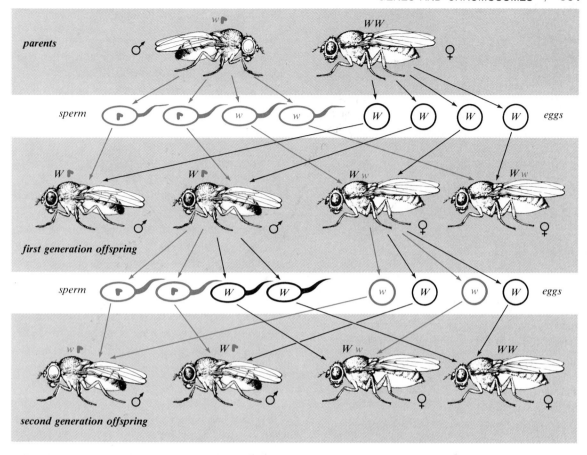

*parents*

*sperm*                                                                                    *eggs*

*first generation offspring*

*sperm*                                                                                    *eggs*

*second generation offspring*

**Figure 14–4** Morgan's work on X-linked inheritance in *Drosophila* helps explain inheritance of white eyes. The gene that determines white eyes is located on the X chromosome. What kind of eyes would result if a white-eyed female were mated with a red-eyed male?

the gene for eye color in fruit flies is on the X chromosome. Any trait whose gene is carried on the X chromosome is called an **X-linked trait.** Eye color in fruit flies was the first X-linked trait to be identified.

## 14–5

## Nondisjunction—An Exception That Establishes the Chromosome Theory

In time, a large number of genes in *Drosophila* was found to be X-linked. These genes were all

inherited in the same way as white eyes, and therefore were apparently all located on the X chromosome.

One of Morgan's graduate students, Calvin B. Bridges, worked with another allele for eye color on the X chromosome of *Drosophila*. This recessive trait, known as vermilion (bright red) eye color, results when two of these alleles are present. Normal or wild-type *Drosophila* have darker red eyes. From your knowledge of X-linked characteristics, what color eyes would you expect to find in the offspring of a vermilion-eyed female and a normal-eyed male?

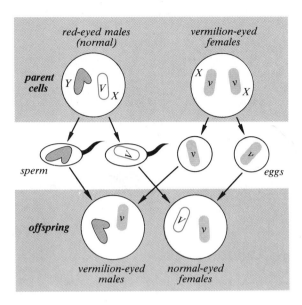

**Figure 14−5** The normal inheritance in *Drosophila* of vermilion eyes, an X-linked trait. *V* represents the gene for the dominant trait of normal, dark red eyes; *v* represents the gene for the recessive trait of vermilion eyes. Which sex chromosome does not carry either allele? (How does this affect the expression of the recessive, vermilion-eyed trait?)

This cross of eye color traits is diagrammed in Figure 14−5. Only the X and Y chromosomes are shown, since only they are involved in the inheritance of this trait.

Figure 14−5 shows that the normal separation of the X and Y chromosomes in meiosis results not only in the determination of the sexes, but also in the distribution of the gene for vermilion eyes. This observation agrees with the experimental evidence that the gene for vermilion eyes is located on the X chromosome. Moreover, the Y chromosome has no gene for eye color. Although the vermilion eye trait is recessive, it appears in males because there is no allele on the Y chromosome to counteract it. Thus, in this type of cross all the females are normal-eyed, but all the males are vermilion-eyed.

In making the cross shown in Figure 14−5 hundreds of times and observing thousands of offspring, Bridges noticed that occasionally (about once in every 2,000 flies) a female with vermilion eyes was produced. Occasionally a male with normal eyes was also produced. These flies were clearly exceptions to the rule and raised some doubts about the validity of the chromosome theory of heredity. Could these exceptions be explained without giving up the theory?

According to the chromosome theory of heredity, for a vermilion-eyed female to be produced two genes for vermilion eyes would be required, one on each X chromosome. A gene for normal eye color on either X chromosome would result in a female with normal eye color, because vermilion eye color is a recessive trait. One of the two genes required was definitely contributed by the mother in the egg cell. But where did the other gene come from?

By studying Figure 14−5 again, you can see that there was no gene for vermilion eyes on the X chromosome of the father. Therefore, both X chromosomes of the vermilion-eyed female must have come from the mother. For this exceptional event to occur, the mother's two X chromosomes, each carrying a gene for vermilion eyes, must have failed to separate in meiosis. They could then pass into the same egg. Bridges gave the name **nondisjunction** to this apparent failure of homologous chromosomes to separate in meiosis.

Figure 14−6 shows the possibilities if nondisjunction of the X chromosomes occurs. When the two chromosomes do not separate, two kinds of eggs are produced: those with unseparated X chromosomes (and therefore two genes for the vermilion trait) and those with no X chromosome at all. When the abnormal eggs are fertilized by normal sperm, the zygotes (fertilized eggs) will also contain an abnormal chromosome number. Remember there are two kinds of normal sperm, those

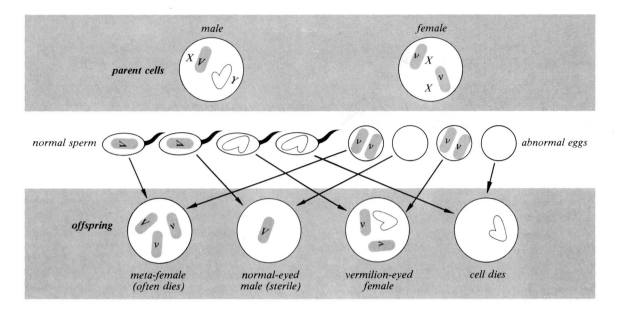

**Figure 14–6** Bridges explained the existence of rare, vermilion-eyed females by suggesting that sometimes the X chromosomes fail to separate during meiosis. This diagram shows the offspring that would result from the abnormal eggs.

containing an X chromosome and those containing a Y chromosome. When the eggs with two X chromosomes are fertilized by normal sperm, half the zygotes will be XXY, and half will be XXX, as shown in the diagram. When the eggs have no X chromosome, the zygotes will have only the sex chromosome contributed by the sperm—X or Y. The zygotes with XXX may survive, but those with no X chromosomes do not because their genetic disturbance is evidently too great. A fly with only one X chromosome and no Y looks male but is sterile.

Bridges examined the cells of flies used in the suspected crosses and found that the hypothesis of nondisjunction was supported by a perfect agreement between (1) the inheritance of vermilion eyes, (2) the sex of the fly, and (3) the chromosomes of the fly. The exceptional vermilion-eyed females, for instance, which were thought to have the genotype of *vvo,* did in fact have two X chromosomes and one Y chromosome. (The *o* is used here to show that the Y chromosome has no allele for vermilion eyes.) Each *v* is located on an X chromosome.

Bridges' experiments and examinations of the chromosomes were a dramatic and convincing demonstration that the genes are, indeed, located on chromosomes. Bridges published a paper titled "Nondisjunction as Proof of the Chromosome Theory of Heredity" in 1916. The chromosome theory of heredity was firmly established. Studies of heredity and observations of cells had come from two different directions to establish the basis of the modern science of genetics.

**CAPSULE SUMMARY**

Mendel's work on heredity lay neglected for 35 years. After its rediscovery, biologists sought a physical explanation for the behavior of Mendel's hypothetical genes. Boveri and Sutton independently noted striking similarities between the assumed behavior of genes in heredity and the observed behavior of chromosomes. Sutton proposed the hypothesis that the genes are physical units located on the chromosomes.

Differences between one pair of chromosomes in the male and female of many organisms helped establish the chromosome theory of heredity. Chromosomes comprising this pair are called the sex chromosomes. Morgan found genetic characteristics that are X-linked in fruit flies. The study of X-linked characteristics was easier because there are no alleles for these genes on the Y chromosome.

Further work by Bridges on an X-linked gene led to the discovery of flies with characteristics that did not seem to fit the chromosome theory. However, examination of the chromosomes of these flies revealed that the X chromosomes had failed to separate in meiosis. An unusual event in heredity was therefore correlated with an unusual chromosome event. The chromosome theory of heredity became established.

**SELF CHECK**

1. Why was the importance of Mendel's work not recognized when it appeared?
2. What conclusion did Boveri and Sutton draw from the parallels between chromosome activity and gene behavior?
3. What are linked genes?
4. What is the result of nondisjunction?

# Linked Genes Are Responsible for Many Traits

## 14–6

## Humans Also Have X-Linked Traits

The sex chromosomes of humans show similarities to those of *Drosophila*. Thus it is reasonable to expect that some human hereditary traits would turn out to be X-linked. More than 200 X-linked traits are now known in humans. Most of these traits are recessive.

The distinctive patterns of inheritance associated with X-linked recessive traits are apparent in pedigree charts such as those in Figure 14–7 for red-green color blindness. Red-green color blindness is the inability to distinguish red, green, or both of these colors from others. It is a rather common trait.

There are many more color-blind males than females. A male whose X chromosome carries

the gene for color blindness will be color-blind. No allele exists on the Y chromosome to offset the gene for color blindness on the X chromosome. In order for a female to be color-blind, both of her X chromosomes must carry the gene for color blindness. That means her father, who contributed one of her X chromosomes, must be color-blind. Her other X chromosome was contributed by her mother, who could either be color-blind or a **carrier** for color blindness. A female with one X chromosome carrying a gene for a recessive X-linked trait is a carrier for that trait, but does not show the trait herself.

The frequency of color blindness in males ranges from 5 to 9 percent in different populations. That means that approximately five X chromosomes in 100 carry the gene for color blindness. To find out how often females would be color-blind, apply the second rule of probability. Remember from Section 13–8 that this principle states that the chance of two independent events occurring together is the product of their chances of occurring separately. The chance of a female getting two X chromosomes, each carrying the gene for color blindness, is the product of the two separate probabilities: $0.05 \times 0.05$, or 0.0025 (25 in 10,000). Thus, females who are color-blind would be only about one twentieth as prevalent as color-blind males.

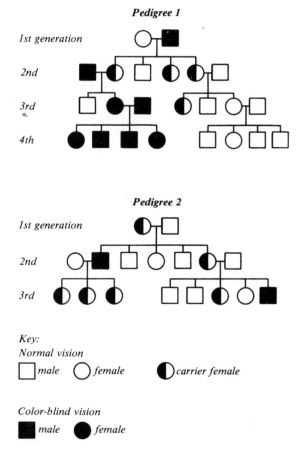

**Pedigree 1**

*1st generation*

*2nd*

*3rd*

*4th*

**Pedigree 2**

*1st generation*

*2nd*

*3rd*

*Key:*
*Normal vision*
□ *male*  ○ *female*  ◐ *carrier female*

*Color-blind vision*
■ *male*  ● *female*

**Figure 14–7** Two pedigrees for red-green color blindness. A marriage is shown by a horizontal line joining a circle and a square. Note the characteristic pattern of inheritance of this X-linked trait.

A quite rare, but much more serious, X-linked recessive trait in humans is hemophilia. In this condition the blood fails to clot or clots very slowly. Normal blood clotting requires the interaction of several specific clotting factors. Hemophilia is caused by a mutant allele of the gene that controls the synthesis of one of those factors. In hemophilia, that factor is produced in a form that does not function correctly. As a result, such individuals may have increased bruising and prolonged bleeding if they are injured or have a tooth extracted. In more serious cases, there may be frequent and painful bleeding in the joints, often leading to crippling deformities. Severe bleeding can be controlled with transfusions and administration of the specific clotting factor. Female carriers of hemophilia do not usually have any symptoms of the disease.

Color blindness and hemophilia have been used as examples of X-linked recessive inheritance for many years. Today many other X-linked conditions are known, including several that are dominant. One of these is a type of rickets (see **Appendix 23–A,** Hormones That Control Bone Formation, page 735). Can you work out the pattern of inheritance of such an X-linked dominant trait?

At least one important gene is located on the Y chromosome. It controls production of a substance essential to the embryonic development of the male sex organs. Assignments of other genes to the Y chromosome are still tentative.

## 14–7

## The Lyon Hypothesis Explains an Observation

A female who is homozygous for mutant genes carried on her two X chromosomes is usually no more seriously affected than a male who has only one such gene on his single X chromosome. For many years geneticists did not understand why. A hypothesis that seems to explain this observation was first proposed by Mary F. Lyon, a British geneticist.

The Lyon hypothesis, also called the X inactivation hypothesis, maintains that in the early embryonic development of a normal female, one X chromosome becomes inactivated in each body (nonreproductive) cell. Chance is believed to govern which of the two X chromosomes is inactivated in any given cell, but the mechanism of inactivation is not yet completely understood. Research indicates that a portion of the inactivated X chromosome remains active.

Several kinds of evidence are offered in support of the hypothesis. One kind of evidence relates to a darkly staining mass that appears in the nucleus of certain cells. This structure, called a Barr body, is named after one of the discoverers who showed that it is normally present only in female cells (Figure 14–8). Lyon hypothesized that the Barr body is an inactivated X chromosome.

Further evidence came from studies of a red blood cell enzyme called G6PD. A deficiency of G6PD results in destruction of red blood cells, which causes anemia. In humans, the gene that controls production of this enzyme is X-linked. Investigators have shown that the activity of the enzyme in normal males and females is the same. Furthermore, there are no differences among individuals with three or more X chromosomes.

One may conclude that the genes on only one X chromosome remain active. It is believed that X inactivation occurs only when there is more than one X chromosome present. Thus, because males normally have only one X chromosome to begin with, inactivation does not occur in their cells. Moreover, because of X inactivation, males or females who have an extra X chromosome may have few medical problems.

The Lyon hypothesis also helps to explain why X-linked conditions tend to have a variable expression in female carriers. For example, although carriers of hemophilia do not usually have symptoms of the disease, tests show great variation in the amount of the clotting factor present. To date, this can best be explained by random X inactivation. The coloring pattern in tortoise-shell cats (see Biology Brief) is also a result of X inactivation.

## 14–8

## Genes Are Linked on Autosomes as Well as on Sex Chromosomes

Biologists have tried to identify as many genetic traits as possible. In humans alone, hundreds of genes are known by the traits they control. Because there are far more genes than chromosomes, many genes must be located on a single chromosome. Sutton suggested this same idea years ago. All genes located on the same chromosome are said to be linked. This observation implies that all the genes on a chromosome are inherited together. Luckily most of the traits Mendel studied were not determined by linked genes. Otherwise the principle of independent assortment could not have been developed from the pea experiments.

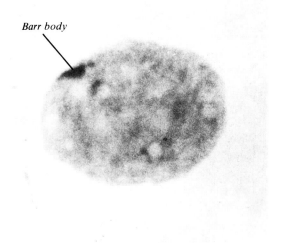

*Barr body*

**Figure 14–8** A cell with one Barr body.

Further investigation showed that linked genes do not always remain together. Chromosomes may break almost anywhere along their length. When homologous chromosomes pair in meiosis, they often exchange fragments, resulting in an exchange of alleles (Figure 14–9). This exchange of alleles between homologous chromosomes is called **crossing-over,** and it greatly increases the genetic variability that results from sexual reproduction. The farther apart two genes are on a chromosome, the more likely a break will occur between them. If two genes are far enough apart on a chromosome, breaks between them may be so frequent that the principle of independent assortment will apply to their inheritance. Some of the

genes in Mendel's experiments assorted independently for this reason.

The frequency with which two linked traits become separated gives a measure of the relative distance on the chromosome between the genes for those traits. With this information, geneticists can construct accurate maps showing the sequence of genes on chromosomes. This can be done without ever seeing the genes themselves or the detailed structure of the chromosomes. Genetic maps now exist for chromosomes of humans and many other organisms.

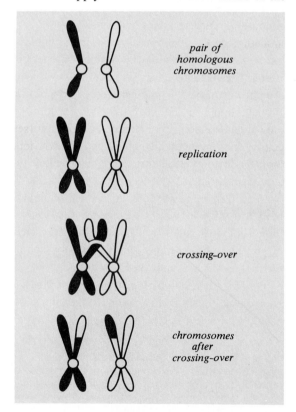

**Figure 14–9** Crossing-over frequently occurs between homologous chromosomes during the early stages of meiosis. Only one chromatid in each of the homologous chromosomes is involved.

pair of homologous chromosomes

replication

crossing-over

chromosomes after crossing-over

**CAPSULE SUMMARY**

Since the work of Morgan and others established the existence of X-linked traits, many such traits have been identified in humans. They are generally more prevalent in males than in females, and their pattern of inheritance is distinctive.

The Lyon hypothesis of X inactivation explains the varying degrees of expression in female carriers of X-linked traits. It also explains the observation that individuals with an extra X chromosome may not have severe medical problems.

Linked genes on any chromosome do not always remain together. Crossing-over during meiosis results in an exchange of genes between homologous chromosomes. By measuring the frequency of crossover, biologists have constructed gene maps for a number of organisms.

**SELF CHECK**

1. What are some X-linked traits in humans?
2. In what ways is the inheritance of X-linked traits distinctive?
3. How does the Lyon hypothesis help explain varying degrees of expression of X-linked traits in carrier females?
4. How does crossing-over affect linkage?
5. How is crossing-over used to construct gene maps?

# Advancing Techniques Uncover More About Genes and Chromosomes

## 14–9

## Techniques Reveal More About Human Chromosomes

The study of human chromosomes advanced slowly at first. Chromosomes are very small. They were studied in tissues difficult to obtain and often in poor condition. The tissue was specially prepared, stained, and thinly sliced. Despite careful study, even the total number of human chromosomes was in dispute for many years.

In 1956, human chromosome study improved with the development of a technique introduced by J. H. Tjio and A. Levan. They used smears of cells grown in tissue culture. They treated cells that were undergoing mitosis to make the chromosomes separate and swell. Their preparations showed all the chromosomes beautifully spread out, not bunched and tangled inside a tiny nucleus (Figure 14–10).

The first benefit to be derived from these new techniques was an accurate count of human chromosomes. Biologists found that there are only 46 chromosomes in a normal individual instead of 48 as had been thought earlier. Biologists also found that they could distinguish each chromosome from the others by carefully measuring its length and noting the location of the centromere (see page 218). The autosomal pairs were numbered from 1 to 22. The two sex chromosomes, X and Y, became the twenty-third pair (Figure 14–10).

Unusual chromosome numbers may cause abnormal conditions. Lejeune and his co-workers showed in 1959 that persons suffering from Down syndrome have 47 chromosomes. A syndrome is a group of symptoms that occurs together in a particular condition. Individuals who have Down syndrome have limited mental abilities, short stat-

ure caused by retarded physical development, and abnormalities of the face, hands, and feet. These individuals have an extra chromosome 21. For the first time in humans, a severe condition was associated with the presence of a particular extra chromosome. Bridges' discovery of nondisjunction in *Drosophila* now helped to explain a new discovery in human biology. The extra chromosome could be accounted for by assuming that nondisjunction had occurred in a gamete of one of the parents. In this way, three instead of two of these chromosomes would be in a fertilized egg, a condition known as **trisomy** (TRY-sohm-ee).

Today several abnormal syndromes in humans can be associated with nondisjunction of some particular chromosomes. Trisomy 21 (Down syndrome) occurs about once in every 1,000 births. Women of age 35 and older, although constituting only about five percent of all mothers, give birth to nearly one-fourth of all babies with Down syndrome. Trisomy 18 and trisomy 13 are more severe than trisomy 21 and occur once in every 5,000 or more births. Fewer than 20 percent of infants born with these trisomies survive the first year of life. Biologists still do not know how the presence of an extra chromosome brings about the abnormalities associated with these syndromes.

Of great interest to biologists and physicians has been the discovery that variations in the number of

**Figure 14–10** (Above) The 46 chromosomes of a human male. Each appears double because of duplication prior to cell division. The chromosomes have been separated from the rest of the cell. The *karyotype* (below) is a display of the chromosomes arranged in their homologous pairs. It was prepared by cutting the individual chromosomes out of the photograph and arranging them in their 23 pairs. Note the X and Y chromosomes.

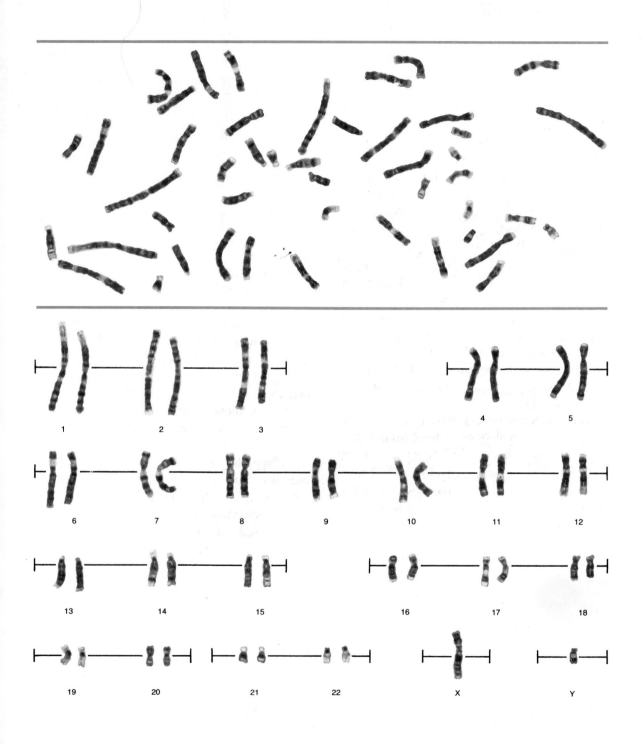

# Biology Brief

## Too Many Chromosomes

Male tortoise-shell cats (mixed black and orange coats) are as rare as 1 in 3000. The gene for black coat color is located on an X chromosome. An allele of this gene, for orange coat color, is also located on an X chromosome. Tortoise-shell females (XX) are to be expected—but tortoise-shell males? Males (XY) are normally black or orange, but not both.

Even before chromosomal analysis, the male tortoise-shell cat can be predicted to have an abnormal chromosome pattern. This proves true. At least one extra X chromosome (XXY), sometimes more than one, is found. Scientists study these cats to try to understand the causes of nondisjunction, not only in cats but in humans as well. The *effects* of the nondisjunction are also studied. The XXY cats rarely father litters. They are either not fertile, or fertile for only a short time.

Tortoise-shell males show a remarkable similarity to a human male condition. On analysis, the human chromosome pattern in this condition turns out to be XXY—the same nondisjunction! XXY human males, unlike the cats, do not have hair of mixed color. But they may have problems that they do not know are partly caused by their chromosomes. Their particular sex-chromosome condition is called the Klinefelter syndrome. Men with this condition frequently are fairly tall,

sex chromosomes may interfere with the normal development of sex characteristics and mental abilities. Some individuals have only one sex chromosome, an X chromosome. Biologists call this a 45,XO condition. Medically it is known as Turner syndrome. These persons are females who are usually short, underdeveloped, and sterile. They frequently have various abnormalities of

the skin and skeleton. Another kind of chromosome arrangement in humans is an XXY condition that results in Klinefelter syndrome. It is similar to the condition discovered by Bridges in *Drosophila*. However, in humans these persons are males. They are often tall and sexually underdeveloped, and may have some intellectual impairment.

sometimes have problems adjusting socially, may or may not have some degree of mental impairment, and may or may not be fully developed and fully fertile.

Biologists like Dr. Carolyn Trunca, pictured above, specialize in studying and counseling people with abnormal chromosome patterns. Dr. Trunca is director of a clinical cytogenetics laboratory which provides diagnostic services for such people. She also is carrying on research in meiosis to help establish risk estimates for people who carry unbalanced chromosome rearrangements. Many people may not realize they have chromosomal irregularities. They are more fortunate than those whose symptoms of chromosomal disorders are severe. Dr. Trunca and many others are at work in research and counseling in order to help.

Scientists studying human chromosomes have found other unusual chromosomal conditions such as XYY, XXX, XXXY, XXXX, and even XXXXY. These conditions are apparently all due to nondisjunctions. Nondisjunctions in formation of *both* sperm and egg would be necessary to account for some of these conditions. In general, the greater the number of X chromosomes, the greater the degree of disorder or disability. Recall that if even one Y chromosome is present, the individual is a male. Research to date indicates that an extra Y chromosome causes few, if any, problems.

In addition to variations in chromosome number, biologists have detected many changes in chromosome structure in humans. A **deletion** occurs when a piece of a chromosome is missing.

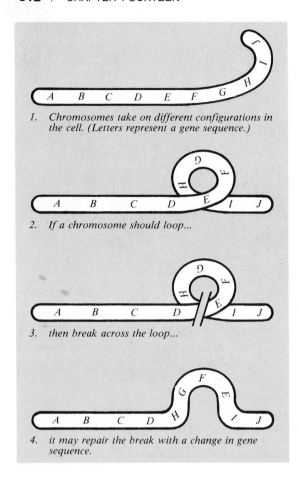

1. *Chromosomes take on different configurations in the cell. (Letters represent a gene sequence.)*

2. *If a chromosome should loop...*

3. *then break across the loop...*

4. *it may repair the break with a change in gene sequence.*

**Figure 14–11** Inversion in part of the gene sequence of a chromosome. A sequence of four genes—E, F, G, and H—has been inverted in order, following looping, breakage, and repair.

Sometimes a portion may be broken off and attached to some other chromosome—an event known as **translocation.** A breakage and its later repair somewhere along the length of a chromosome also can occur. This may result in reversal of a gene sequence, known as an **inversion,** on part of that chromosome (Figure 14–11). Most of these changes cause severe physical and mental disorders. Many cause death during development

of the fetus or soon after birth. More than half of the miscarriages that occur may be due to abnormalities in chromosome structure or number. Chromosomal rearrangements appear to play a central role in human cancers. Specific translocations, deletions, or trisomies have been found to be consistently associated with specific types of tumors.

In general, the effects suggest that changes in autosomes are not tolerated to the same degree that changes in the sex chromosomes are. Individuals missing a sex chromosome, such as those with Turner syndrome (45, XO) often survive into adulthood. There are no known instances where a human fetus missing an autosome survived until birth.

## 14–10
## Newer Techniques Continue to Be Discovered

One of the most important laboratory procedures for studying human chromosomes employs special staining techniques that produce patterns of banding on the chromosomes (Figure 14–12). Since the banding pattern is distinct for each chromosome, the process of identifying and distinguishing different chromosomes has become very accurate. Earlier techniques stained the chromosomes uniformly all along their length. With the specific banding patterns it is possible to correctly match homologous chromosomes and to distinguish between two nonhomologous chromosomes that are the same size, such as number 7 and X (Figure 14–13). Missing or extra chromosome portions and rearrangements can now be detected.

New techniques have made it possible to match more than 650 genes, each to a particular chromosome. Furthermore, many of the specific regions

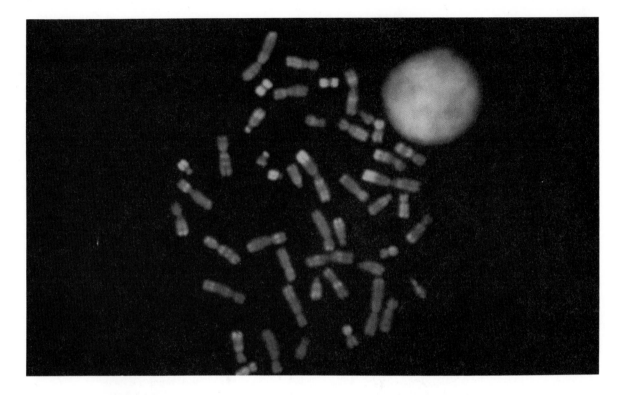

**Figure 14–12** Human chromosome spread. The banding patterns are the result of differences in absorption of stains by different regions of the chromosomes. Examining banded chromosomes has enabled biologists to detect missing or extra chromosome parts more easily than by examining chromosomes that have been uniformly stained. The banding patterns have also made the mapping of genes on the chromosomes more accurate.

where these genes are located on a chromosome have been identified. Some of these are shown in Figure 14–14. At the present time the number of genes that are mapped doubles every two years.

A very important medical advance has been the

**Figure 14–13** Human chromosomes 7 and X. The banding patterns seen in the photographs are represented in the diagrams. These two chromosomes are almost the same length, and their centromeres are located in the same relative positions. They can be distinguished by their different banding patterns.

*(drawing) (photo)*
***No. 7 showing chromatids***

*(drawing) (photo)*
***X showing chromatids***

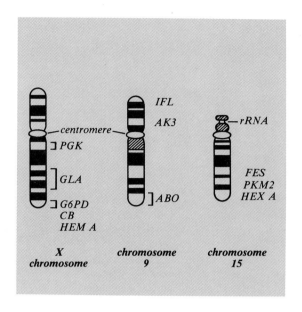

**Figure 14-14** A few of the genes that have been mapped on the X chromosome and on autosome numbers 9 and 15 are shown. The numbering system is that used in human karyotypes (see Figure 14-10). On these particular chromosomes are located the genes for color blindness (CB), hemophilia (HEM), the enzyme G6PD, ABO blood groups, and Hex A (Biology Brief, page 292). IFL is an interferon gene family. Interferons are naturally occurring substances that help cells resist viral infections. FES is a gene that is related to a type of human cancer. The other symbols stand for various enzymes.

diagnosis of genetic disorders in a fetus while it is still developing within the mother's uterus. Several diagnostic tests have been developed. One such test is **amniocentesis** (am-nee-oh-sen-TEE-sus), which involves withdrawing from the uterus a small amount of the fluid that surrounds the fetus (Figure 14-15). This procedure is usually done between the fourteenth and sixteenth weeks of pregnancy and does not require hospitalization. While the woman is under local anaesthetic, a needle is inserted through her abdomen and uterine wall into the amniotic sac. The small amount of fluid that is withdrawn during the procedure is replaced naturally in about four hours. The fluid

withdrawn from the amniotic sac contains living cells from the fetus. These cells can be grown in tissue culture. The culturing and subsequent tests can take up to four or five weeks. The cultured fetal cells are used to determine the genetic characteristics of the fetus or to look for certain biochemical abnormalities.

The amniotic fluid itself also can be used for diagnosing fetal disorders. For example, high levels of a substance called **alphafetoprotein** (AFP) in the fluid can indicate the presence of defects of the neural tube. When the neural tube of the fetus—which becomes the central nervous system—fails to close properly, increased amounts of

AFP are released into the amniotic fluid. This condition is known as spina bifida.

Before the procedure for amniocentesis begins, the patient's abdomen is scanned with **ultrasound**. High-frequency vibrations are translated into an image of the fetus and the surrounding structures in much the same way as sonar equipment is used on ships to identify submerged objects. The ultrasound image appears on a television screen and the viewers, including the parents, can actually see the fetus in the amniotic fluid. The image allows the physician to obtain an accurate estimate of the fetal age by determining its size. The picture also shows the location of the placenta and the fetus so that injury can be avoided during amniocentesis. Twins can be identified

**Figure 14–15** Prenatal diagnosis of genetic disorders by amniocentesis. Fetal cells from the amniotic fluid are cultured for later chromosomal and biochemical analyses. Biochemical analysis of the fluid can also reveal certain problems.

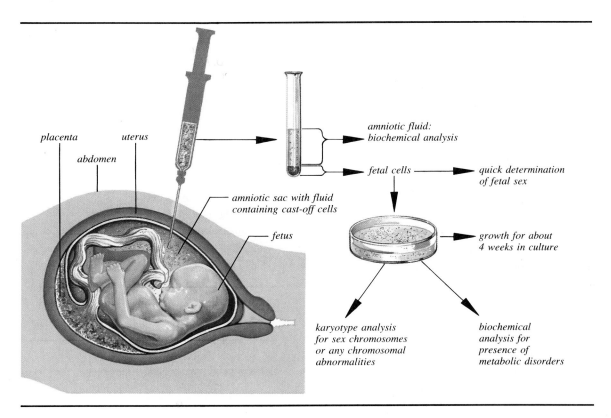

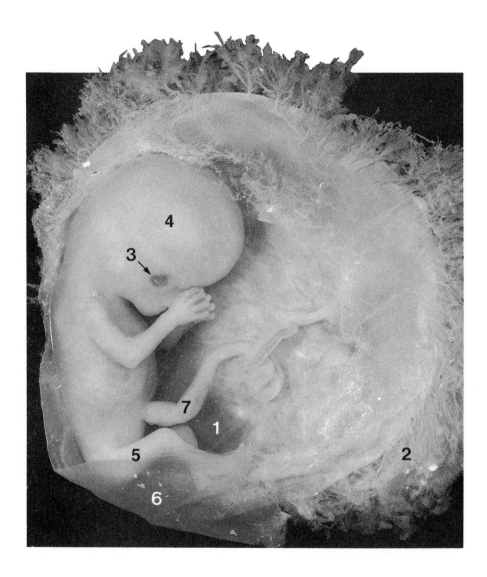

**Figure 14–16** A nine-week fetus with the chorionic sac opened. The fetus is still enclosed in the transparent amnion (1). The chorionic villi (2 and at the top of the figure) develop from the fertilized egg and therefore contain the same chromosomes as the embryo. The technique of chorionic villus biopsy provides a larger sample of fetal tissues than amniocentesis, and test results can be known more quickly. It is hoped that this technique will eventually make possible the early detection of more than 3,000 genetic disorders. (1—amnion, 2—chorionic villi, 3—eye, 4—head, 5—leg, 6—smooth chorion, 7—umbilical cord)

easily. Also, fetal sex can be detected with a high degree of certainty in the second trimester (four to six months).

Several fetal abnormalities can now be detected with ultrasound technology. These include enlarged or absent kidneys, hydrocephalus (water on the brain), certain forms of dwarfism, neural tube disorders, and even some cases of congenital heart disease (defects in the structure of the heart that are present at birth). When done by well-trained professionals the risks of amniocentesis and ultrasound have been low. Studies continue to assess any possible long-term effects.

In 1982, medical geneticists developed a new technique for sampling fetal cells in the eighth week of pregnancy—even earlier than amniocentesis. The obstetrician inserts an instrument into the woman's vagina and through the cervix. A small piece of chorionic villi is then snipped off. The chorionic villi are hairlike projections of the chorion, a membrane that surrounds the fetus. (See Section 11–12.) The chorion is derived from fetal cells which therefore contain fetal chromosomes. Chorionic cells can be analyzed for chromosomal and biochemical disorders, and the results known within days or even hours. Research is continuing on the safety of this new technique, known as **chorionic villus biopsy.** (See Figure 14–16.)

The procedures described above have made it possible for couples who are at risk of having children with severe genetic disorders to make informed decisions through genetic counseling. Consider, for example, a couple whose first child is diagnosed at one year of age as having Tay-Sachs disease (see Biology Brief on page 292). Before the availability of prenatal diagnosis of Tay-Sachs, few if any parents chose to take the chance of having additional children with such a tragic and as yet untreatable disease. Today, with the knowledge that a fetus with Tay-Sachs can be detected prenatally, many parents make the opposite choice.

Almost always, the chance of having a perfectly normal child is far higher than the risk of any problem. Thus in most cases, test results are normal, and the parents are reassured. When a positive test indicates that a fetal abnormality is likely, a genetic counselor will usually discuss with the couple all possible medical options.

Research in human genetics has allowed rapid progress in the detection, prevention and treatment of genetic disorders. It has also shed new light on other areas such as the control of gene action and the genetic relationships between species.

---

**CAPSULE SUMMARY**

The study of human chromosomes has advanced rapidly in recent years with the development of techniques for culturing human tissues, observing their chromosomes, banding them with stains, and analyzing them. The chromosomes can be measured and identified, and certain abnormal physical conditions can be related to abnormal chromosome patterns. Techniques for prenatal diagnosis have made it possible to detect genetic disorders before birth.

**SELF CHECK**

1. Name some of the techniques developed for the study of human chromosomes.
2. What is a translocation? What is a deletion?
3. Describe some problems associated with abnormal numbers of human chromosomes.

# CHAPTER SUMMARY

## HIGHLIGHTS

The concept of the gene was based upon breeding experiments involving organisms that differed in one or more traits. In order to explain his data, Mendel hypothesized that there must be genetic units which are not only distinct, but which also behave independently of other units. He had no knowledge of the physical structure of these units. Once chromosomes had been discovered and their behavior in mitosis and meiosis worked out, the hypothesis followed that the genes are located on the chromosomes.

The chromosome theory of heredity was further strengthened with Bridges' demonstration that unusual genetic events could be fully explained by unusual chromosomal activity. Nondisjunction of chromosomes has now been found to occur in many organisms, including humans. Certain abnormal conditions in humans, such as Down syndrome, are related to abnormal chromosome distribution in meiosis.

Genes located on the sex chromosomes control traits that show an unusual pattern of inheritance. X-linked inheritance is known in many kinds of organisms, including humans. Genes located on the X chromosome are expressed in males, because there are almost no alleles on the Y chromosome to offset their effects. X inactivation provides an explanation of the varying degrees of expression seen in female carriers of X-linked traits.

Much has been learned about the structure of chromosomes. New staining techniques produce banding patterns in human chromosomes, making more accurate study possible. Genetic maps of chromosomes continue to be constructed for many organisms. Techniques for prenatal diagnosis enable physicians to detect genetic disorders early in fetal development.

## REVIEWING IDEAS

1. In what way did Boveri's work lay a foundation for development of the chromosome theory?
2. What basic assumption did Sutton make in relating genetics and cell structure?
3. In what way did experiments with *Drosophila* provide evidence for the chromosome theory of heredity?
4. What are autosomes? What are sex chromosomes?
5. What new aspect was added to the gene-chromosome theory as a result of Morgan's experiments with *Drosophila?*
6. How is sex determined in fruit flies? How is sex determined in humans?
7. What is nondisjunction? What assumptions did Bridges make to explain the exceptional inheritance of vermilion eye color in *Drosophila?*
8. How is hemophilia in humans related to Morgan's experiments with *Drosophila?*
9. Describe experiments that led to the conclusion that there are X-linked traits.
10. What evidence can you describe that supports the chromosome theory of heredity?

## USING CONCEPTS

11. How must Mendel's principle of independent assortment be modified in the light of present-day knowledge?
12. What are Barr bodies? How many Barr bodies would be found in cells of a person with the XXY condition? XXXY? XXXX? XYY?

13. Nondisjunction can occur during the first or second meiotic division, during formation of sperm or eggs. Describe where nondisjunction might have taken place in each of the four conditions listed in question 12.

14. Under what two conditions would you expect genes to assort independently?

15. In a breeding experiment with *Drosophila,* consistently more females than males were produced. Suggest one or more reasons why.

## RECOMMENDED READING

Allen, G. E. *Thomas Hunt Morgan—The Man and His Science.* New Jersey, Princeton University Press, 1978. An interesting biography of Morgan and the team that worked with him.

BSCS *Basic Genetics: A Human Approach.* Dubuque, Iowa, Kendall/Hunt Publishing Company, 1983. An excellent source for further information on some of the topics covered in the chapter.

Fuchs, F. "Genetic Amniocentesis." *Scientific American,* June, 1980. An understandable explanation of this technique and its uses.

Mange, A. P., and E. J. Mange. *Genetics: Human Aspects.* Philadelphia, Saunders College, 1980. A clearly written genetics textbook.

Sturtevant, A. H. *A History of Genetics.* New York, Harper & Row, 1965. A readable account by a scientist involved in much of the history.

# Origin
of New
Species
15

Genes exist in most species in an astonishing variety of forms or alleles. Many alleles are neutral in natural selection; others are not. Chance differences of alleles occur from group to group within a species. If the groups have no contact, new mutations may increase these differences. Natural selection adds to chance events, helping to make each group distinct.

Natural selection also connects or relates the isolated groups within a species. It preserves in each group the essential characteristics of the species, by eliminating harmful mutations. It also acts through mating preferences against individuals that vary too greatly from others. How, then, does a new species arise? In this chapter you will examine some of the knowledge of genetics in populations, then investigate two views of the origin of new species.

# Genes in Populations

## 15-1

## A Population Has a Gene Pool

A **population** consists of individuals of a species that live at the same time in the same area. The area makes up the breeding range of all, or most, members of the population.

The population's **gene pool** includes all of the genes of its individuals. Many of these genes are alleles that reflect the genetic variation among individuals. The term *pool* suggests that new combinations of alleles may be drawn from anywhere within the population, from two individuals of opposite sex.

For detailed studies, the gene pool is divided into several subpools. Often the subpools represent parts of the population that live in different localities within the population's total area. A **gene flow** exists between these subpools; that is, individuals from different localities may interbreed when they come into contact with one another.

At times, different subpools may be used for males and females within a population. Genetic differences between males and females are greater for some species than for others.

The number and diversity of alleles in a gene pool is almost impossible to estimate. You probably have at least 40,000 genes, all or almost all of them in pairs. Alleles of these genes become recognized chiefly when they cause genetic disorders or differences in appearance. Neutral alleles that cause no change are likely to go undetected until they turn up during laboratory analysis of human DNA.

Alleles account for most of the genetic differences between populations within a species, although other chromosome changes may also be involved. The biological diversity of the alleles in a gene pool makes it possible for a population to adapt to change in the environment.

The study of gene pools and gene flow of populations is called **population genetics.** Identifying alleles, mating patterns, and changes in the percentages of individuals carrying certain alleles all are part of a population geneticist's work.

---

←Going fishing? The long parts of a heron's body look exaggerated on land but play coordinated roles in food-seeking. Long legs, long neck, long beak—how closely related are they in their genetic origins?

## 15–2

## Gene Pools Are Frequently Stable in Stable Environments

Both chance and natural selection always act on a population in some ways. However, when a species is highly adapted to an environment, natural selection rarely promotes change. Instead it preserves the essential characteristics of the species by acting against most changes.

The boojum (BOO-jum) tree and the cardon cactus plants in Figure 15–1 grow in certain deserts of North and South America. As you study the adaptations of these plants, you may find it difficult to list genetic changes that could be beneficial to them. Boojum trees have miniature branches and leaves. The small leaves, with their almost waterproof coating, lose a minimum of water to the dry desert air. The trees grow upward but often arch over and take root again at their tips. Thus these trees are adapted both to obtain water through their multiple root systems and to conserve the water they obtain.

The tall cardon cactus plants have only spiny remnants of ancestral leaves. The green trunks of the plants store water and carry on photosynthesis. Except for openings for air exchange, and other openings made by birds and insects, the trunks are waterproof.

Increased tropical storm activity in the Pacific Ocean increases the rainfall on North American populations of these plants. If rainfall is above desert levels (40 cm) for several years in a row, the desert floor becomes dotted with more than the usual number of new plants. Some of these plants are new genetic varieties of boojum trees and cardon cactuses. As rainfall decreases again, only varieties much like their parents continue to grow. The others die.

In environments that are less restrictive than a desert, a greater variety of adaptations persists in the populations of many species. Nevertheless, remarkably stable populations are found. Often an environmental change introduced by human activities provides the most obvious clues that natural selection is operating. For example, the use of insecticides on flies and mosquitoes promotes the selection of individuals for alleles that were formerly neutral. At first the populations of flies and mosquitoes are depleted by use of the insecticides. Then resistant individuals multiply and replenish the populations. The gene pools of the new populations contain the same alleles as the old populations. The stability of the new populations results from the presence of more individuals with resistance-producing alleles.

**Try Investigation 15–A** A Model Gene Pool, page 641.

## 15–3

## Gene Frequencies Can Be Studied from Generation to Generation

Population geneticists often study how frequently certain genetic characteristics appear in individuals of a population. If the inheritance patterns for the characteristics are known, the geneticists can determine how widespread the alleles are in the population's gene pool. Dominant, recessive, and codominant characteristics can be studied in this way. Characteristics determined by more than one pair of genes are more difficult to study.

In a simple case, two alleles of one gene may determine a characteristic. For example, in humans, A and B blood proteins are not the only blood proteins found on red blood cells. Another set is determined by two alleles designated as $B^M$ and $B^N$. Allele $B^M$ causes production of a protein called M. Allele $B^N$ causes production of a slightly different protein called N. Because $B^M$ and $B^N$ are codominant, an individual who is heterozygous ($B^M B^N$) produces both proteins on the

**Figure 15-1** Natural selection starkly advertises its effects on desert plants. No large leaves susceptible to great water losses are found on any of these plants. The boojum tree has arched over and taken root again at its tips. Water is the desert's limiting factor. Temperature extremes are usually second.

red blood cells. Thus three blood phenotypes are associated with $B^M$ and $B^N$—M, MN, and N. Proteins M and N both appear to be neutral in natural selection, and they are not associated with human sexual differences. Because these proteins also cause no difficulties in blood transfusions, they are not often included in determining human blood types.

A study of the human population of Sweden was undertaken to determine the distribution of these neutral red blood cell factors. An estimated sixteen percent of Swedish individuals have type N blood. These individuals are known to be homozygous ($B^N B^N$). From this information, calculations can be made to estimate the percentages of individuals with type M and type MN blood.

Using a table as you did in Section 13–10, you can fill in the beginning information:

| | allele frequencies in male gametes | |
|---|---|---|
| | ? $B^M$ | ? $B^N$ |
| allele frequencies in female gametes   ? $B^M$ | | |
| ? $B^N$ | | 0.16 $B^N B^N$ |

If the gene frequencies are the same in both sexes, then the frequency of $B^N$ in either sex, multiplied by itself for the other sex, must equal 16 percent (0.16). To calculate this frequency, find the square root of 0.16:

$$\sqrt{0.16} = 0.4 \text{ or } 40 \text{ percent}$$

The frequency of the $B^M$ allele must therefore be 60 percent in each sex, for there are only the two alleles.

All the missing values in the table are now known or can be determined:

| | allele frequencies in male gametes | |
|---|---|---|
| | 0.6 $B^M$ | 0.4 $B^N$ |
| allele frequencies in female gametes   0.6 $B^M$ | 0.36 $B^M B^M$ | 0.24 $B^M B^N$ |
| 0.4 $B^N$ | 0.24 $B^M B^N$ | 0.16 $B^N B^N$ |

According to the calculations, approximately 36 percent of the Swedish population has type M blood. (An actual sample of 1200 people in Sweden revealed that 36.1 percent of the sample has type M blood.) Approximately 48 percent (0.24 plus 0.24), according to calculations, has type MN blood. (The sample revealed 47 percent.) The remaining 16 percent (16.9 percent in the sample) has type N blood.

Are the differences between the calculations and the sample important? They may only indicate an error in the beginning estimate. Or the sample itself may not have reflected the exact gene frequencies for the entire population.

The most interesting feature of the calculations is that they also predict gene frequencies for future generations of the Swedish population. For each generation, the calculations will be identical. The completed table already contains the predicted allele frequencies in male and female gametes. Sixty percent (0.36 + 0.24) of the alleles will be $B^M$ and forty percent (0.16 + 0.24) will be $B^N$, provided that the two alleles remain neutral in natural selection. Samples can be tested in future generations to confirm the population's stability for these alleles.

The stability of populations for neutral alleles was discovered by two investigators for whom the mathematical principle was named. (See **Appendix 15–A,** The Hardy-Weinberg Principle, page 713.) Their principle is based on a number of assumptions about population size, chance, natural selection, new mutations, and breeding. Populations do not match every assumption, but the principle nevertheless fits many observed data for population stability.

---

**CAPSULE SUMMARY**

A population has far more alleles in its gene pool than any few individuals can have. A gene flow exists between subpools in the population. A great capacity to adapt to change in the environment also exists because of the variety of alleles in the gene pool. The population can remain stable or establish a new stability in response to change, simply by changes in the frequencies of some alleles.

**SELF CHECK**

1. Define a population.
2. What is a gene pool?
3. What is population genetics?
4. Describe gene flow in gene pools.
5. What are some factors in population stability over many generations?

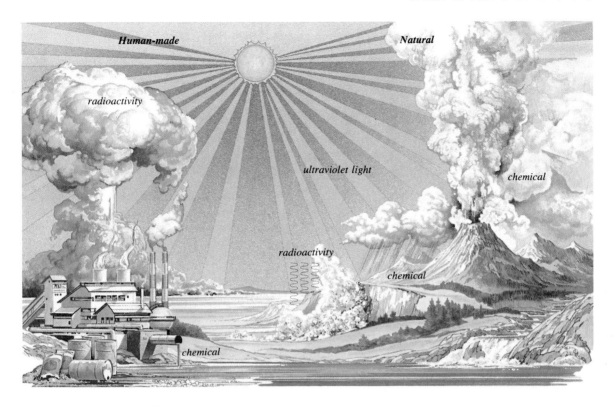

**Figure 15–2** Known mutagens include several forms of radiation and a variety of chemicals. The mutagens occur both naturally and as a result of human activities.

# Change in Populations

## 15–4

### Mutations Have Many Causes

A substance or source of energy that can change the chemical composition of a gene is called a **mutagen** (MYOOT-uh-jin). Mutagens give rise to the alleles in a population. Some kinds of mutagens are well known today (Figure 15–2), but until the late 1920s none had been proved to cause mutations. Then H. J. Muller and L. J. Stadler conceived similar experiments with X rays. Muller bombarded fruit flies with X rays. Stadler did the same to barley. The offspring produced by the irradiated flies and plants astonished even the inves-

tigators. In Muller's words, mutations "ugly and beautiful" produced "a motley throng." In the flies, varieties never seen before appeared in eye color, eye shape, different wing structures, body size and color, and tolerance to light and heat. Offspring followed through the $F_2$ generation also revealed too few males, suggesting harmful recessive mutations on the X chromosome.

Some of the X-chromosome mutations in flies were **lethal,** killing the developing males. Others were lethal in a second way—making some flies sterile.

# How Can We Recognize Mutagens in The Environment?

Relatively few forms of radiation are mutagens. Chemicals are a different problem. More than 70 thousand synthetic chemicals are used by business and industry. Many of these chemicals are known mutagens. Thousands of others are suspected mutagens and must be tested, along with new chemicals that come into use each year.

The National Center for Toxicological Research in Jefferson, Arkansas, develops tests to determine whether such substances are mutagens. The problem increases all the time, because new chemical products are constantly being introduced by industries across the nation. Other toxicological research is also carried out by the center in its role as one of the bureaus of the Food and Drug Administration of the Department of Health and Human Services.

Typically, a substance being tested as a possible mutagen undergoes all the following procedures:

It is tested for its impurities, or for its ingredients if it is a mixture of substances.

Each ingredient or impurity, as well as the major compound or product itself, is reviewed for its chemical relationship to any known mutagen.

Tests are made using microorganisms as indicators of mutagenic substances. The biologist pictured on the facing page is setting up such a test, called the Ames test.

A number of different kinds of radiation subsequently have been shown to cause mutations. Heat is also a mutagen, as are many chemicals (see Biology Brief). One way a chemical can produce a mutation is by being a look-alike for a large, flat nucleotide in a DNA strand (Chapter 9). If the chemical is wedged somewhere in the strand when the strand is replicated, the new DNA that is produced may contain an extra nucleotide. Because gene messages are read three nucleotides at a time, the message will be different beginning where the new nucleotide has been inserted.

Such a mutation is limited to one gene. The next gene on the chromosome is protected by its starter sequence of nucleotides. However, not all chemical effects are limited to one gene.

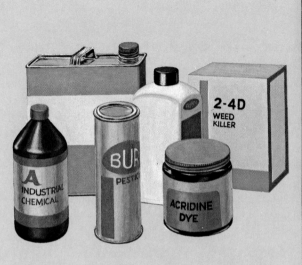

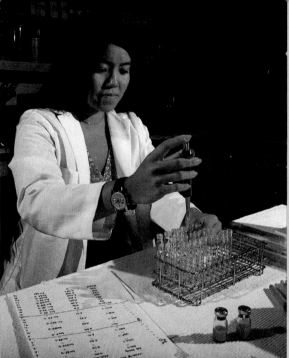

Other tests are made on cell cultures of mammalian tissues.

If indicated, further tests are made on living laboratory mammals, usually rodents.

By-products of any substances changed by an animal's metabolism are identified and studied.

Plants, especially plant roots and growing tips where mitosis and cell division are frequent, are susceptible to mutagens too, but most tests are made on microorganisms and laboratory animals. The microorganisms are *rapid* indicators of many mutagens. Laboratory mammals, on the other hand, are more likely to indicate whether a potential mutagen may affect humans.

Keeping an eye on suspected mutagens is a formidable task. The National Center for Toxicological Research is one of the principal safeguards of human health.

Both chemicals and radiation may produce macromutations (Section 10–7). The greater the number of genes affected, the less the probability that the macromutation will be neutral in natural selection. An individual with such a mutation may not be greatly affected, because the mutation may be in only one or a few cells. However, if a cell that produces gametes is affected, descendants may be produced with the mutant genes in every cell of their bodies. The individuals may or may not survive.

How often do new mutations usually occur in gametes? The rate varies. For some species, one mutation in some gene may be expected in every 2,000 gametes, for others one in only every million or more gametes.

## 15–5

# Other Chromosome Changes May Occur

No clear distinction exists between isolated mutations and other chromosomal changes that may occur. Chromosomes, once thought to be unchanging structures, are now known to undergo many kinds of modification (Sections 10–12 and 14–9). If a segment of a DNA molecule becomes inverted, the inversion is a mutation only if that segment would have been read for its instructions. Sometimes the inverted sequence may merely separate other gene sequences on the chromosome. In that event, another readable copy of the original sequence may still exist elsewhere.

Extra or inverted copies of genes that separate other genes make it easier for other chromosomal changes to occur. "Jumping genes" (see page 206) can jump without damage if protected at both ends by inverted DNA sequences. Crossing-over can also occur without damage.

A great many chromosome changes have occurred during evolution. Studies of chromosomes of living species from different families, orders, and classes have revealed evidence of past

1. increase in chromosome number by nondisjunction;
2. production of larger chromosomes by the splicing of two chromosomes end to end;
3. production of certain small chromosomes by breakage of ancestral chromosomes;
4. addition of genes to chromosomes by viruses or bacteria that invade cells;
5. exchange of segments between chromosomes.

Some of these phenomena occur today, usually producing individuals acted upon unfavorably by natural selection. In some varieties of plants, however, nondisjunction has doubled the chromosome number without ill effects—and without

producing new species. Macintosh apples are an example.

Biologists suggest that chromosomal changes are most likely to contribute to the origin of new species when regulatory sequences of DNA are among those that are affected, not merely genes that lead to structures. A Macintosh apple is simply larger. No change has occurred in how the regulatory genes help to produce the apple on the tree. A change in how the regulatory genes work would produce a very small effect in the fertilized egg nuclei of an apple blossom. However, the effect would be multiplied many times over as the embryo plants were produced in the seeds. The fruit would appear different, and the trees that grow from the seeds would multiply the effects again.

In Chapter 16 you will read about some remarkable similarities between proteins produced by chimpanzees and humans. The relationship is so close that biologists suspect regulatory genes, rather than structural genes, are involved in most differences between the two species. Regulatory genes are a leading clue to genetic change.

## 15–6

# Many Factors Contribute to Population Change

The factors that can play a part in population change are not all genetic. At least five factors are usually involved.

**1. Migration.** A population's gene pool is changed when individuals enter or leave that population. When individuals from another place join a population, they may bring with them alleles that the population did not have. When individuals leave and start a new population elsewhere, the gene pool of the parent population will change very little. However, chance affects the gene pool of

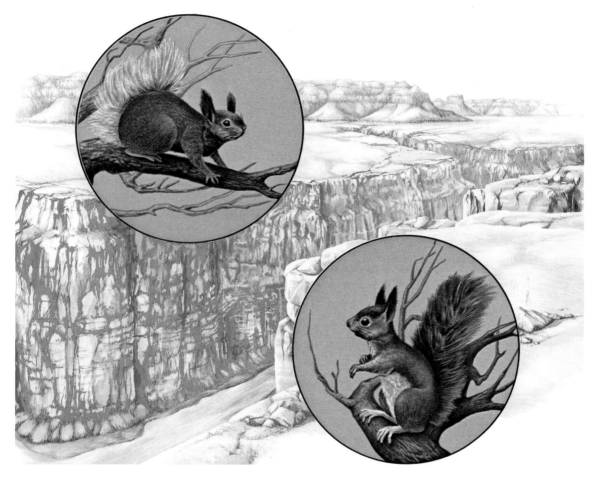

**Figure 15–3** The Kaibab (left) and the Abert (right) squirrels are related. When they became geographically isolated on different rims of the Grand Canyon, they began to develop differences. How many differences can you see?

the departing population to the extent that many alleles of the larger population will not be represented. Thus population differences will begin with the migration.

**2. Isolation.** No gene flow exists between populations that are completely isolated from one another (Figure 15–3). More often, isolation is incomplete. *Geographical isolation* may be a matter of distance instead of impassable barriers. Gene flow can then occur but is reduced.

Another form of isolation, *behavioral isolation,* may follow geographical isolation. For example, gene flow would be prevented if mutations and other chromosome changes affect the time of flowering in plants or of breeding in animals. Mating preferences in animals may also be affected. Thus only limited gene flow may occur between populations that come in contact after lengthy separation.

*Genetic isolation* and *isolation in time* are the two biologically complete forms of isolation.

Genetic isolation exists when crosses produce only sterile offspring, or none at all. Isolation in time occurs because organisms living at different times can have no contact. Genes passed from ancestors to their descendants provide the only link between these organisms.

### 3. Mutations and other chromosome changes.

Mutations or chromosome rearrangements occur whether a species is found in one or many populations. Mutation rates for different populations within a species will be similar unless one population is in contact with more mutagens.

Some mutations and other chromosome changes occur more than once. They can occur independently in two isolated populations. Other mutations occur and are often restricted to the populations in which the mutant individuals live.

### 4. Natural selection.

How do biologists recognize natural selection? Look at the leopard frogs in Figure 15–4. Are the alleles that affect their spots and color neutral? If so, how did the differences come to exist?

Chance can account for many differences in populations, but a hypothesis of natural selection can be offered for the frogs. Consider those from Massachusetts and Arizona. Their spots and color may help protect them from predators. That is, both may be camouflaged in their respective environments. In Massachusetts, vegetation is more dense and varied than in Arizona. The angle of the sunlight is also lower, increasing the interplay of light and shadows. The darker, more distinctly spotted frog may be hard to see. In Arizona, however, the light is brighter and the contrasts fewer. The lighter, more evenly colored frog may be better protected.

How would you test this hypothesis, using owls or snakes as the predators?

Such differences between populations, when caused by natural selection, arise very slowly. A

**Figure 15–4** Leopard frogs formerly were considered all of one species, *Rana pipiens*. However, today biologists consider some of the populations separate species. The three frogs pictured are from Massachusetts (top), Oklahoma (middle), and Arizona (bottom).

hundred generations or more may be required for a single beneficial mutation to spread through a population. Charles Darwin remarked on the slowness of natural selection when he contrasted it to the rapid effects of artificial selection by plant and animal breeders (Chapter 4).

**5. Chance.** Chance may sometimes act more quickly than natural selection on populations. An example is a new gene pool started by individuals that migrate from a population. Their gene pool has fewer alleles than the parent population's gene pool. Moreover, some of the alleles of the smaller population may spread or disappear by chance. If a single new generation includes no offspring with a particular allele, that allele disappears from the gene pool.

A change in alleles or their frequencies as a result of chance is called **genetic drift.** Genetic drift may begin with migration and continue as chance acts on the new gene pool. Another kind of genetic drift also affects populations, regardless of their size. Neutral alleles will be selected when carried by individuals favored for other reasons by natural selection. As a result, certain neutral alleles may increase or decrease in frequency. Linked genes (Section 14–8) may contribute to the outcome.

## 15–7

## Isolation and Selection Are Demonstrated in Breeding

The cattle in Figure 15–5 are a result of selective breeding. None of them closely resembles the wild park cattle from which modern breeds have descended. Their observable differences from one another are greater than those of the leopard frogs in Figure 15–4. Not only do the cattle differ in color, but the shapes of their heads, ears, and bod-

**Figure 15–5** The Santa Gertrudis breed of beef cattle (bottom) resulted from crossing Brahman cattle (top) with Shorthorn cattle (center).

ies differ. The Shorthorn and the Santa Gertrudis also have more meat in proportion to their bones. The three breeds differ in their resistance to drought and their tolerance for high and low temperatures. The frogs in Figure 15–4 may also differ in the latter ways, but their differences took much longer to evolve.

Selective breeding speeds up the appearance of differences between populations within a species. Many of the differences do not coincide with those that chance and natural selection would produce. However, selective breeding demonstrates the potential that exists for differences in a large gene pool. With new mutations and other chromosome changes, the potential increases.

Almost every type of plant and animal raised for food is a product of selective breeding. Decorative plants and pet animals are also selectively bred. Some of the varieties are bred almost wholly for appearance. Easily observable differences therefore occur, as in pigeons (Figure 4–10) and dogs. Dogs such as Pekingese and Great Danes cannot even interbreed.

An evolutionary problem produced by selective breeding is the disappearance of many wild-type alleles of genes. New strains of disease-producing organisms often appear and attack crop plants or animals bred for meat. To search for a gene resistant to the disease-producing organisms, backcrosses to wild, ancestral types of these plants and animals could be made. However, no one raises the wild, ancestral types because the yields are too poor. To date a few remaining small populations of wild plants and animals have been found to serve this particular need. However, the wild-type gene pools are disappearing.

The problem of disease points to a difference between natural and artificial selection. Natural selection, together with chance, maintains a greater diversity of alleles in gene pools. Artificial selection reduces the variety of alleles in the gene pools to a minimum.

**CAPSULE SUMMARY**

Mutations may have numerous causes, not all of them known. The principal mutagens appear to be a few types of radiation, heat, and many chemicals. The mutations themselves may be in a single gene or may be macromutations affecting more than one gene. The greater the number of genes changed by a mutation, the less the chance that the mutation may be neutral.

Not all chromosome changes are mutations. Evolution includes evidence of increases in chromosome number by nondisjunction, new chromosomes formed by breakage or by end-to-end splicing of two chromosomes, and numerous other chromosome changes.

Factors that contribute to population change and evolution, by causing changes in gene pools, include migration, isolation, mutations and other chromosome changes, natural selection, and chance. The opportunities for change often are vividly illustrated by artificial selection in plant and animal breeding. However, artificial selection proceeds at such a rapid pace that variety in the gene pools is reduced to a minimum. The risks of genetic disorders and susceptibility to new diseases are increased. Natural selection and chance, working together, maintain greater variety in gene pools, thereby reducing such risks.

**SELF CHECK**

1. What type of mutagen was first demonstrated by biologists?
2. Give an example of genetic drift.
3. How do geographical isolation and behavioral isolation differ?
4. Explain why natural selection requires so many generations to change a characteristic of a population.
5. What is genetic isolation?
6. Describe ways in which natural and artificial selection differ.

# How New Species May Originate

## 15–8

### Natural Selection Explains Many Closely Related Species

Darwin used the evolution of different species of finches on the Galápagos Islands to illustrate the theory of evolution by means of natural selection. The finches differ from one another in size, body proportions, color, and adaptations for obtaining food, including characteristics of their beaks. According to Darwin, adaptations for obtaining food played a principal role in natural selection. The finches that arrived on the islands from South America multiplied until they became their own chief competitors for food. Natural selection thereafter favored birds with characteristics that enabled them to explore other environmental niches (Chapter 4) for their food.

Geographic isolation from mainland South America provided the opportunity for a new species to evolve. In all, 13 species evolved. Notice in Figure 15–6 that not all the species are found on a single island. This fact suggests that geographical isolation on different islands interacted with adaptations for obtaining food, contributing to

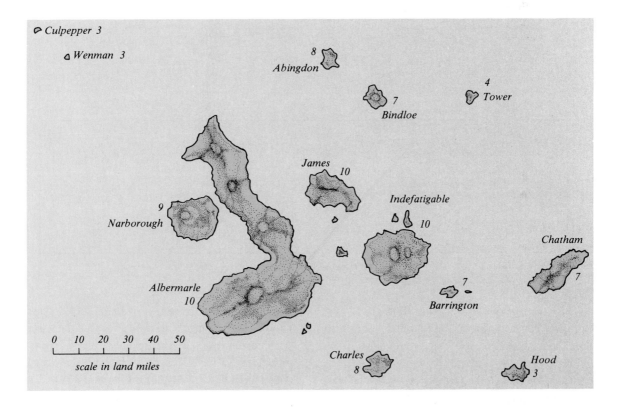

**Figure 15–6** This map of the Galápagos Islands shows where many of the 13 species of Darwin's finches are found on each island. The 13 species are pictured in Figure 4–11. None of the islands has all 13 species in permanent residence. Three outlying islands—Culpepper, Wenman, and Hood—have only three species each.

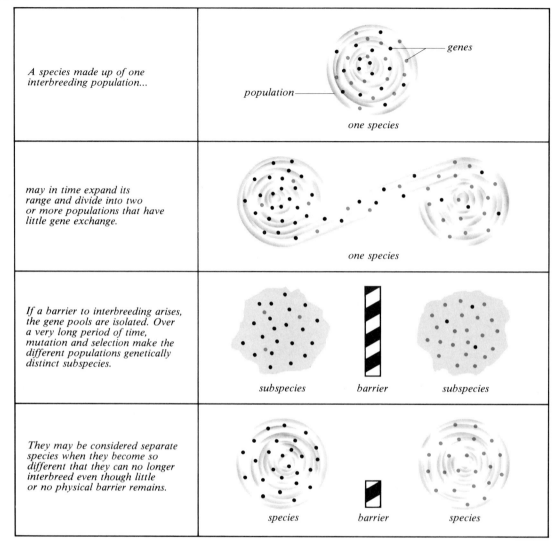

| | |
|---|---|
| *A species made up of one interbreeding population...* | *genes* *population* one species |
| *may in time expand its range and divide into two or more populations that have little gene exchange.* | one species |
| *If a barrier to interbreeding arises, the gene pools are isolated. Over a very long period of time, mutation and selection make the different populations genetically distinct subspecies.* | subspecies    barrier    subspecies |
| *They may be considered separate species when they become so different that they can no longer interbreed even though little or no physical barrier remains.* | species    barrier    species |

**Figure 15–7**  A simple model of how two populations within a species may become isolated and evolve to produce two species.

some of the species of finches. Biologists today study organic deposits on the islands to determine how the finches were distributed in the past. Why might this task be difficult?

The evolution of the Galápagos finches appears to fit both views of natural selection that you read about in this chapter's introduction. One is that natural selection and chance contribute to differences between isolated populations from the same

species. The other is that even in such isolated populations, natural selection preserves the essential characteristics of the species against harmful mutations. The Galápagos finches still share many characteristics with finches on the mainland. The characteristics that are no longer shared have diverged, showing numerous genetic variations for an essential activity—obtaining food. Natural selection does not preserve a species against *bene-*

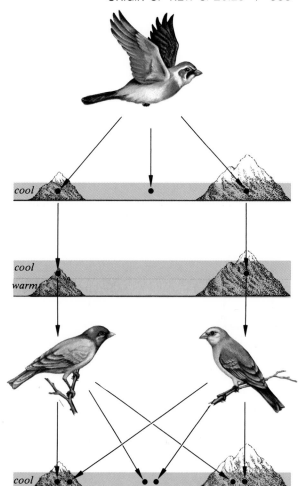

1. *A single species of bird restricted to cool zones is found on two mountains 200 kilometers apart and on the wide connecting plain.*

2. *In time the climate changes, and the lower elevations become warm. The birds can no longer live in constant contact and the two populations become mostly isolated. (Individuals flying between mountains are exceptions.)*

3. *Over thousands of years mutations and selection make the two populations genetically distinct.*

4. *Still later, the cool zone moves again and once more includes the valley. The two populations, although they are now in the same area, cannot interbreed. They have become two separate species.*

**Figure 15–8** A model similar to the one in Figure 15–7, applied to the origin of two closely related species of birds.

*ficial* mutations. In the island environment, with increasing competition for food, a variety of new genetic characteristics proved beneficial. The finches, while still diverging from mainland finches, began diverging from one another.

The Galápagos finches are a more complex example of evolution than the Kaibab and Abert squirrels (Figure 15–3). The differences between the squirrels may be explained according to the model in Figure 15–7. Leopard frogs (Figure 15–4) also fit this model, but in their case, gene flow has not completely stopped. It exists through other populations that live between the more widely separated ones. However, this limited gene flow is insufficient to maintain all the leopard frogs as a single species.

A variation on the model in Figure 15–7 appears in Figure 15–8. The set of circumstances illustrated could explain the origin of two species of birds from two incompletely isolated populations. Distance and climate combine to reduce gene flow between the populations.

Only examples of the evolution of closely related living species have been presented. Evolution over longer spans of time must be studied in the fossil record and in DNA and protein differences between different groups of living organisms. DNA and proteins are not preserved in the rock strata of Earth. Thus fossils are studied on the one hand, and chromosomes and proteins of living species on the other. Chromosome and protein differences are the only remaining genetic evidence of the evolution of divergent living groups from common ancestors.

For many examples of evolution, both the beginning and the end are buried in the past. In the case of the dinosaurs, no living representatives of the group exist, so no chromosomes are available to help determine how dinosaurs evolved from small ancestral reptiles. Only an incomplete fossil record is left. Thus there are important differences between studying the evolution of taxonomic groups that have living representatives and studying those that do not. Closely related living species provide the best established examples of evolution by natural selection. Few biologists doubt that the Galápagos finches evolved this way. The Kaibab and Abert squirrels, the leopard frogs, and many other examples of closely related species are accepted as examples of isolation and natural selection. However, questions are raised about the fossil record. The principal question is why fossil species do not show the same continuous relationships that living species do.

Many gaps appear in the fossil record, but they do not seem to be as great for some groups as for others. Partial reconstructions have been made of the evolution of horses (Chapter 4), elephants, many other animals, and some plants.

The incomplete fossil record may, in time, reveal more. Previously unknown fossils are discovered almost every year. Moreover, fossils of certain extinct species, whose existence was predicted from living species, have been found.

Every species of today has ancestors, whether or not the fossils of the recent ancestors are eventually discovered.

The conditions necessary to preserve fossils are not the usual circumstances that existed at the time and place where many organisms died. This observation is especially true of organisms that lived on land. The fossil record contains many more remains of marine organisms than of terrestrial ones. A Biology Brief in Chapter 16 discusses some of the reasons for fewer and poorly preserved fossils of land animals.

Are missing fossils the explanation for the gaps in the fossil record? Or is there another explanation? A number of biologists have suggested that rapid evolutionary changes, rather than missing fossils, may explain many of these gaps.

## 15–9
## Another Hypothesis Is Offered to Explain Gaps in the Fossil Record

The hypothesis of *punctuated equilibrium* (Chapter 4) is based on two characteristics of the fossil record. One characteristic is the apparent stability of different species over millions of years. Often, more species appeared *unchanged* than changed during long periods of time. The second characteristic is the disappearance of many of these long-surviving species during a shorter period of time. Then fossils of new species suddenly increased in frequency and another long period of little change began. Thus long periods of relatively few changes were *punctuated* by short periods of greater change. Because of this repeating pattern, *equilibrium* has characterized more of Earth's past than change has. Figure 15–9 summarizes this idea.

**Figure 15–9** A diagram that represents the fossil record as long periods of relatively little change punctuated by shorter periods of greater change. The letters represent species; A through D and F are the oldest species represented in the diagram.

During the periods of greater change, the relatively rapid shift from old to new species left gaps in the fossil record. Is the record incomplete at these points, or did evolution jump many of the apparent gaps?

You have already read (page 328) that recent studies of chromosomes from organisms of different taxonomic groups have revealed major chromosomal changes during evolution. The hypothesis of punctuated equilibrium cites these studies for supporting evidence.

Briefly stated, the hypothesis says that major chromosomal rearrangements may have caused new species to evolve in relatively few steps. Although mutations and macromutations may not have increased in rate, the rearrangement of genes on chromosomes would have caused major changes in the effects of many genes. The regulatory genes that control the development of organisms would have operated differently. New types of organisms, instead of the old, would have resulted.

New genera and families of organisms would have been represented by some of the new species that appeared. All the chromosome changes may have been completed within a few thousand to tens of thousands of years, so that natural selection may not have had a full opportunity to act.

Many features of the hypothesis of punctuated equilibrium are attractive. The time periods described in the hypothesis fit the shorter periods of change found in the fossil record. Major chromosomal changes could have occurred at these times. However, some biologists point out that organisms would have little chance of surviving a *series* of such changes if natural selection had such limited time to act. Indeed, natural selection could not have been excluded. Although slow, it would still have produced its own effects on each change over the period of years involved. Thus the hypothesis of punctuated equilibrium cannot be separated completely from natural selection. The two views of evolution are closely interrelated.

Scientists are cautious in accepting revisions of theories. The burden of supplying evidence rests with those who propose the changes. The theory of natural selection has been modified before by additions. In fact, the concept of macromutations and major chromosomal changes constitutes one of those additions. However, the idea that evolution could occur by *successive* major changes in a brief geologic time has not yet been established.

The prevailing view is that organisms surviving *one* such major change would almost certainly be out of step in some ways with their new genetic and environmental relationships. A long period of natural selection would be required to obtain the best combinations of alleles for successful adaptation.

Did major chromosome changes really occur so close together in geologic time? If so, some biologists predict that punctuated equilibrium and natural selection will eventually become two mechanisms of an expanded theory of evolution.

---

**CAPSULE SUMMARY**

Evolution by natural selection can be studied most successfully using examples that lead to species living today. Genetic evidence and observations of how each species lives can be added to the evidence of fossil ancestors.

The fossil record is immense but incomplete. The conditions necessary for fossil formation did not always exist at the right time and place to aid biologists who are today searching for fossils to fill gaps in the record.

A somewhat different explanation for these gaps from that offered by the theory of natural selection is the hypothesis of punctuated equilibrium. Evolution may have bridged these gaps with relatively few steps. Thus more than one mechanism of evolution may exist.

**SELF CHECK**

1. How may evolution occur by natural selection?
2. In what ways are living species, rather than fossils, necessary to obtain direct information about natural selection?
3. What is meant by a gap in the fossil record?
4. What is the hypothesis of punctuated equilibrium?

# CHAPTER SUMMARY

## HIGHLIGHTS

A gene flow exists between populations that are not completely isolated. All the genes of individuals in each population make up a gene pool. The gene pool contains far more alleles than any small number of individuals may have.

When the gene flow between populations is reduced or stopped, genetic differences may accumulate. Chance (genetic drift) and natural selection may cause the evolution of two or more related species from one.

Several forms of radiation, heat, and many chemicals are known mutagens. Not all mutations are limited to single genes. Macromutation and other chromosome changes also occur. Evidence for these major chromosomal changes is revealed by comparisons of chromosomes from living organisms of different taxonomic groups.

Both the theory of natural selection and the hypothesis of punctuated equilibrium offer explanations of evolution whenever major chromosomal changes occur. The theory of natural selection suggests a long adaptation period following any such major genetic change. The hypothesis of punctuated equilibrium suggests that the major changes can occur in succession with little intervention by natural selection. New species of different genera and families could result in only thousands of years. If gaps in the fossil record remain as they are today, evaluating the two views of evolution across these gaps will be a continuing problem for biologists.

## REVIEWING IDEAS

1. What factors contribute to stability in gene pools?
2. What factors contribute to change in gene pools?
3. Explain how natural selection and genetic drift differ. How may they occur together?
4. How does isolation of populations contribute to evolution of two species from one?
5. How are behavioral isolation and genetic isolation related? Which usually occurs first?
6. What problem does selective breeding create in the gene pools of many plants and animals?
7. What does punctuated equilibrium mean?
8. What reasons can you give for gaps in the fossil record?
9. How are the theory of natural selection and the hypothesis of punctuated equilibrium interrelated?
10. How do the theory of natural selection and the hypothesis of punctuated equilibrium differ?

## USING CONCEPTS

11. Natural disasters are often cited as a factor in the disappearance of species. What natural disasters that occur today may have been more widespread in the past?
12. What kinds of natural disasters on Earth might be caused by events originating in space?
13. The theory of natural selection is based upon evidence observed in living species, as well as upon the fossil record. Why is it more difficult to establish a hypothesis based largely on the fossil record, instead of events occurring today?
14. Why are regulatory genes more influential in evolution than many other genes?

## RECOMMENDED READING

Grant, P. R. and N. Grant. ''The Origin of a Species.'' *Natural History,* September 1983. The origin of two finch species from one, involving geographical isolation but a later contact.

Myers, Norman. *A Wealth of Wild Species.* Boulder, Colorado, Westview Press, 1983. The problem of saving alleles in wild-type populations of the plants and animals that people breed (Chapters 1 and 2).

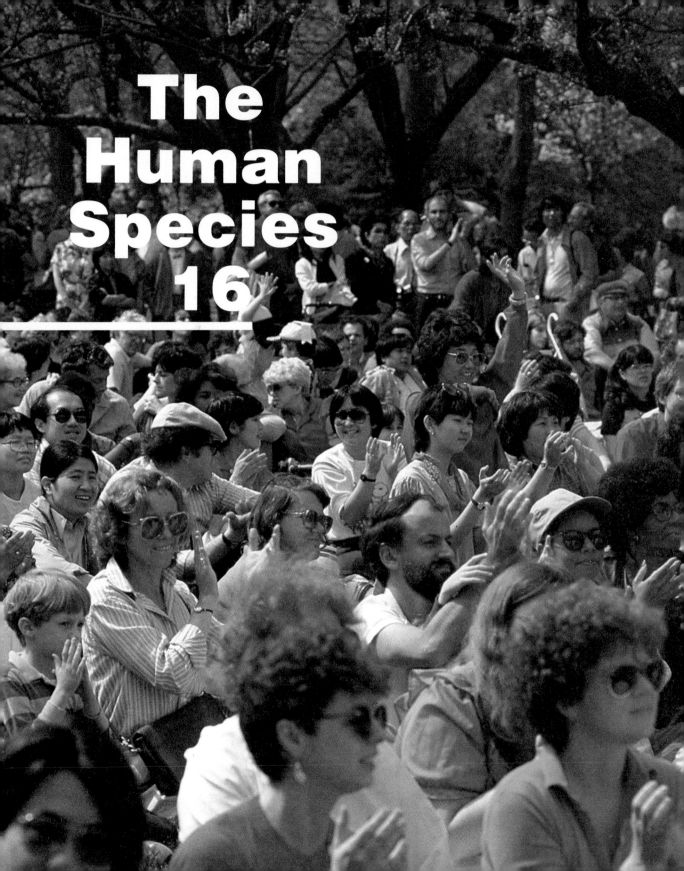

# The Human Species

# 16

If new species evolve from old, from what species did modern human beings evolve? Biologists agree that it was another human species. The history of humans is known to have included several different species, although only one exists today.

No genetic barriers to interbreeding exist among the living members of the species *Homo sapiens*. The only genetic differences between human groups are those of long separations racially, socially, and geographically. Yet we are separated by time from other species of the genus *Homo* in the past. Genetic differences accumulate with time. Did different species of humans once compete in their contacts with one another? Or were these species in the past also separated by time? Anthropologists—biologists who study human culture and evolution—are not sure of the answers. They are still seeking more data.

In this chapter you will learn some of what is known about the complex genetics and the history of evolution of humans.

# The Evolution of Humans

## 16-1

### How Are Human Traits Inherited?

Most discoveries in human genetics have been made from things that go wrong. When things go right, humans are excluded from many procedures used to investigate genetics.

Even our ABO blood groups were discovered as a result of things that went wrong. In early attempts to save lives by blood transfusions, the donor's blood cells frequently clumped or clotted in the patient's body. In time it was learned that this reaction was caused by blood of a different genetic type from the blood of the patient. The patient's body defenses responded by clumping and isolating the donated cells.

Gradually, enough has been discovered about human genetics to indicate that most human characteristics that have been investigated have definite

---

← Even a small crowd such as this one testifies to the great variety contained in the human gene pool.

genetic roots. Genes for more than 650 traits have now been mapped on the human chromosomes. But over 40,000 genes in all may be on these chromosomes. Their action is far more difficult to analyze than once thought. Even traits believed to be determined by a single pair of genes have usually been found to be controlled by several alleles, or by two or more pairs of genes. Eye and hair color and the shapes of ear lobes are examples; they are not single gene pair traits. Biologists continue to grow more and more aware of the complex evolutionary history of the 46 human chromosomes. Mutations and other genetic accidents over billions of years have produced these chromosomes. The result is a human genetic machinery so complicated that it apparently has few traits that are as simply determined as those Mendel studied in garden peas. Even Mendel had to search for several years before identifying the handful of garden pea traits that appeared possible to study. Garden peas, too, are the product of long ages of evolution of interacting genes.

**Figure 16–1** Sarah the chimpanzee has two plastic "words" that she associates with the meanings "same" (light color) and "different" (dark color). She has watched a full container of liquid like the one at the left poured into the wide-mouthed jar at the right. This intelligence task is known as *conservation of liquid quantity.* One jar now appears to have more liquid than the other, doesn't it? But Sarah, left alone, thinks it over and places the plastic word "same" in the circle between the two jars. Not all human beings Sarah's age (14 years) or younger do as well.

Human facial features, body size, and body shape are among the physical characteristics whose genetic patterns have proved very difficult to investigate. Not one of these characteristics is simply determined by one or two pairs of genes, and environmental influences play a role, too. Human intelligence is an even more puzzling characteristic genetically. Intelligence tests, for example, recognize many different qualities in human intelligence. That is why every standard intelligence test is divided into many different kinds of tasks and subtests. Can you remember what some of these subtests were?

Biologists are keenly aware that some of the characteristics called "intelligence" are not even uniquely human. Other higher animals display them, too, in varying degrees (Figure 16–1). If you stop to think, you would expect evolution to work this way instead of producing, all at once, all the traits that determine intelligence in only one kind of organism. Human beings undoubtedly inherited from their ancestors many traits affecting intelligence. Other traits continued to evolve.

Environmental factors further complicate the study of characteristics like body size and shape or intelligence. Improved human diets over much of the world have led to increased body size. Similarly, regular physical activity increases muscle development and changes the body shape. As for intelligence, many factors like home, neighborhood, and cultural surroundings affect it (or the ways in which it is measured), especially in young children. Environment may even act on the development of intelligence before birth. A deficient diet for a pregnant mother, especially in the early weeks of a human embryo's development, may negatively affect the rapid differentiation and growth of the embryo's brain.

Genetics is one key to understanding evolution. Yet you can begin to see that human genetics itself is not yet well understood. There are good reasons for this lack of understanding. Human beings are not ideal organisms for the study of heredity. The many years of a human generation, the difficulty of accurately measuring many characteristics, the improbability of using planned matings, and the small number of offspring per family represent difficulties for the geneticist. In spite of these difficulties, our understanding of human heredity has increased rapidly. Eventually it may help complete a picture of how people evolved.

**Figure 16–2** During the last glacial period early humans inhabited the caves of Europe. Often they painted the cave walls with scenes of animals and objects that were part of their lives.

In the meantime, geneticists and biochemists have found a shortcut around the problem of unobtainable genetics data in the study of human evolution. The structure of the DNA of genes, and of proteins made under the control of genes, can be analyzed chemically. Such structures in humans can then be compared to DNA and protein structures of other organisms. Enzymes, hormones, and other proteins (structural parts of the body) are the major substances manufactured under the direction of the genes. Clues to human evolution may be found by biochemical comparisons of DNA and proteins of humans and other higher animals. You will read the results of a few of these biochemical studies later in the chapter. Most of the evidence for human evolution, however, has been discovered from fossil studies.

## 16–2
## Who Are the Ancestors of Humans?

Fossil remains of humanlike skulls and bones have been found and studied for more than a century. At first, no one realized their age or their significance. Ancient cave sites in France and other parts of Europe and the Near East helped lead people to some understanding of how long their ancestors had occupied the land before them. Remains of fires, charred bones of animals, and even beautiful paintings (Figure 16–2) could be found in these caves. While these finds were known to be old, early investigators had no real idea of how long ago human life on Earth began.

Until this century, the oldest known humanlike fossils were a skull, teeth, jawbones, and an upper leg bone found in Java, an island of the Indonesian chain off the coast of southeast Asia. The skull

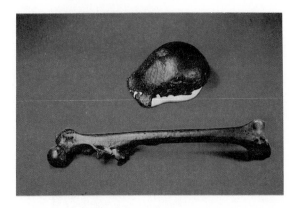

**Figure 16–3** A cast of the skullcap and femur (upper leg bone) from the first humanlike fossils found in Java. The originals, which also include a jawbone and teeth, are in a museum in the Netherlands.

was incomplete (Figure 16–3). The jaw protruded forward, however, and the brain cavity was small (around 1100 cubic centimeters, as compared with 1400 for living peoples). The structure of the upper leg bone indicated a creature that walked upright. At first the fossils were not assigned to the human genus, *Homo*. Today they are. Additional discoveries of such fossils with chipped and flaked stone tools, charcoal from fires, and collected bones of animals that were probably used for food suggest that the upright beings were humans. The fact that they collected their food and brought it to a home site where they may have shared it is considered very important in their identification as human. This kind of food-collecting and food-sharing behavior is inborn among certain insects. (For example, ants in an ant colony collect food and bring it back to the nest.) But the same kind of behavior is not inborn among the higher mammals; it is voluntary or learned. As voluntary behavior, it fits a social pattern best known among human beings. People share food as one consequence of their division of labor between obtaining food and other tasks.

The fact that these earlier upright beings had brains smaller than those of humans today is not considered necessarily significant in their identification as human. Within broad limits brain size and intelligence are not well correlated, even among living peoples. The *structure* of the brain, within a relative range of brain size, is more significant than a measurement of the actual size.

Fossil finds supporting the earliest ones in Java have since been made in Asia, the Near East, Europe, and Africa. These fossils are assigned to the species *Homo erectus* (meaning erect or upright humans). Yet even these people, dating back as far as 1.5 million years ago, may not have been the first humans.

As long as 20 to 35 million years ago, advanced creatures larger than those that gave rise to monkeys lived. They are known from many jaw, tooth, and bone fragments. These early creatures are assigned to the genus *Dryopithecus* (dry-oh-PITH-eh-kus). Somewhat later fossils show that five other genera of such creatures appeared 10 to 15 million years ago. One of them, *Ramapithecus* (rom-eh-PITH-eh-kus), had a small face, as also indicated by jaw and tooth fossils. No complete or even nearly complete fossils of any of these early creatures have been found. From this you can understand that a great deal of uncertainty surrounds the suggestion that *Ramapithecus,* with the small face and less apelike jaws and teeth, may have been ancestral to human beings.

A gap in the fossil record exists from the time of *Ramapithecus* to about 3 to 4 million years ago. Beginning then, and extending to less than a million years ago, several species of interest to anthropologists lived and left fossils. These later fossils represent hundreds of individuals. For most only teeth, jaws, skullcaps, and sometimes part of a leg bone have been found. Some almost complete skulls have also been found, and for one individual, parts from most of the skeleton. The story of humans held a surprise.

## 16-3

## The Link to Humans

More than a million years ago, *Homo erectus* shared Africa with at least one other tool-using species that walked upright. This other species was one of two, or possibly three, such species that stood and walked erect.

There is no conclusive evidence that these species used tools regularly, or that they made the tools they used. Tools of opportunity—conveniently shaped stones battered at both ends—have been found with the fossils. Long trails of fossil footprints have also been found.

The fossil skulls in Figure 16-4 are of individuals assigned to the genus *Australopithecus* (ostray-loh-PITH-uh-kus). The older of the two, *Australopithecus africanus,* preexisted humans but may have survived until the first individuals of the genus *Homo* appeared. The younger of the two, *Australopithecus robustus,* shared its environment with *Homo erectus.*

Fossils of *Homo erectus* found in Africa are frequently closely associated with stone tools that are chipped to a particular shape. These tools are not the same as tools of opportunity. They imply that the toolmakers used tools regularly since they went to the trouble of making the tools. Other objects found with fossils of all three species include smashed skulls and broken bones of other animals, presumably used as food.

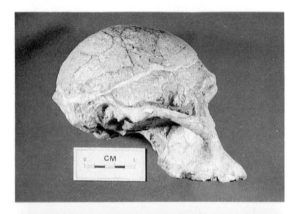

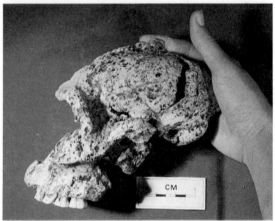

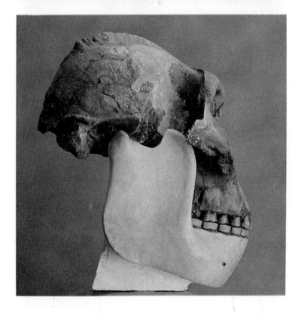

**Figure 16-4** (Top) An australopithecine skull of the → species named *Australopithecus africanus.* Its features are finer than those of the other skulls shown in this figure. (Middle) A skull of the species named *Australopithecus robustus.* Notice the bony ridge on top of the skull. (Bottom) Another skull of *Australopithecus robustus,* with its bony ridge on top of the skull and with a reconstruction of what its massive lower jaw was like. All three skulls were missing their lower jaws. However, representative lower jawbones have been found separately, indicating smaller lower jawbones for *A. africanus* than for *A. robustus.*

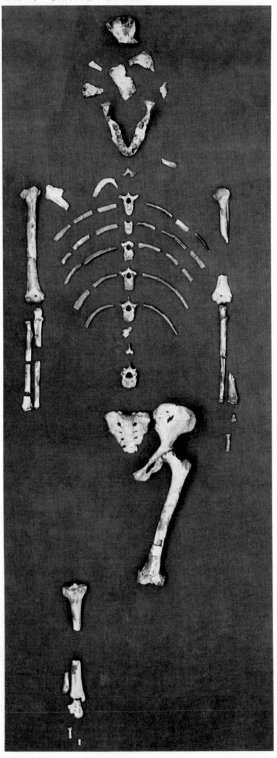

Most of the questions that remain unanswered concern the older fossils among the finds in Africa. Neither of the two *Australopithecus* species in Figure 16–4 is considered ancestral to humans unless the skeleton in Figure 16–5 is considered to be a member of *Australopithecus africanus.* If so, then *A. africanus* existed at least 1.3 million years before *Homo erectus* and may have become extinct as humans arrived on the scene. However, this ancestral relationship is only a possibility, not an established link. The same reasoning would eventually have to include the possibility that *A. africanus* gave rise to both *A. robustus* and to humans, and possibly survived to coexist with one or both of them.

Another possibility is that the oldest members of *Australopithecus,* like the one in Figure 16–5, were a separate species. The name *Australopithecus afarensis* has been proposed for this group. This species might have been ancestral to humans and to one or both other species of *Australopithecus.* Only as additional fossil deposits are found will more conclusive information be obtained. Even the date when humans first appeared is uncertain.

Was *Homo erectus* the first human species? The answer to this question is not known. Fossils ranging in age from several hundred thousand to 1.5 million years of age establish that *Homo erectus* (Figure 16–6) lived in Africa, Europe, the Middle East, and Asia over a time period of more than a million years. Chipped and flaked stone tools, fire, and bones of hunted animals have all been associated with this species.

Two kinds of evidence suggest that another human species may have existed earlier than *Homo*

**Figure 16–5** Lucy, the most complete skeleton known for any member of the genus *Australopithecus.* She stood only slightly more than a meter tall and lived from 2.8 to 3.2 million years ago. Lucy and more than 12 other individuals of her species, whose fossils were found with her, were overtaken simultaneously by an unexplained disaster.

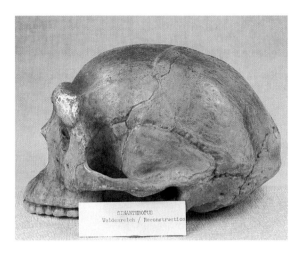

**Figure 16–6** Two views of a reconstruction of one of the most famous *Homo erectus* skulls. The original fossil skull fragments were part of the largest assemblage ever found, including twelve skullcaps and other remains (teeth, jawbones, leg bones) of some 40 individuals. The fossils were unearthed near Peking, China. They were much studied and photographed, then lost or destroyed during World War II. Further quantities of *Homo erectus* fossils have since been discovered in China, Java, East Africa, Europe, and the Middle East.

*erectus*. Crudely made stone tools have been found in deposits almost a million years older than the oldest *H. erectus* fossils. And the fossil skull shown in Figure 16–7 has been found, along with fragments of others like it. In some ways this skull is more like a human skull of today than it is like *Homo erectus*. For example, the bony ridges above the eyes are not as prominent as in *H. erectus*.

A new species name is not quickly assigned to one fossil skull and fragments of others. Even so, the name *Homo habilis* has been proposed. The skull may be related to tools that predate known *Homo erectus* fossils. However, it was not found with any of these tools.

An intriguing mystery thus surrounds the oldest *Homo* and *Australopithecus* fossils and the oldest stone tools. The question of ancestry is very complex. Was *A. afarensis* ancestral to *A. africanus*? Was it also ancestral to *H. habilis*? Somewhat later, was *A. africanus* ancestral to *A. robustus*, and was *H. habilis* ancestral to *H. erectus*? Some

**Figure 16–7** Skull 1470, named for its index number at the National Museums of Kenya, in East Africa. The skull is at least 1.8 million years old, based on the younger of two major datings. From its relation to the deposits in which it was found, it is probably not older than 2 million years. Skull fragments of other individuals have been found, but skull 1470 is the most nearly complete. Thus, it is the oldest known fossil skull of the genus *Homo*.

anthropologists once thought that if more fossil finds as rich as those known today could be discovered, the basic questions about human ancestry would be answered. They were only partly right. The pattern of evidence for evolution of species that walked upright is even richer than anthropologists imagined. But it has raised new questions.

One of the most interesting questions is whether early humans were responsible for the extinction of the genus *Australopithecus*. Future fossil evidence may not answer this question. Furthermore, the pressures put on both *Australopithecus* and *Homo* by predatory animals and disease-causing organisms are also not likely to become fully known.

## 16–4

## The Human Story

How old is the oldest human species? This question cannot be definitely answered today. Perhaps it can never be. You have read about some of the problems. It is difficult to even agree on a definition of what being *human* means. *Australopithecus* used crude tools; chimpanzees also use crude tools today (Figure 16–8). Yet at one time, the ability to use tools was thought to be uniquely human. Upright posture was once also thought to be limited to humans but is now known to have been a characteristic of *Australopithecus* too.

What the fossil record shows is that upright-walking species, both *Homo* and *Australopithecus*, evolved along with apes over a period of millions of years. *Homo, Australopithecus,* and apes alike could probably all use crude tools. To this extent all were "intelligent."

Chimpanzees today have proved intelligent in a wide variety of tasks. They perform very well on many intelligence tests (Figure 16–1). They can even be taught to carry on conversations with humans in sign language. Biochemical tests of DNA and protein similarities have been made between chimpanzees and humans, and between humans

and other animals. These tests indicate that the closest living relatives to human beings are the chimpanzees (Table 16–1). Certain other tests of gene similarities, chromosome by chromosome, appear to indicate the same closeness of relationship between gorillas and humans. The evolutionary distance between chimpanzees and humans, and between gorillas and humans, may be less than the distance between foxes and dogs, and about the same as that between horses and zebras.

**Table 16–1**  Examples of Protein Similarity Between Chimpanzees and Humans

| Protein | Amino Acid Differences | Number of Amino Acids |
|---|---|---|
| Hemoglobin | 1 | 579 |
| Myoglobin | 1 | 153 |
| Cytochrome c | 0 | 104 |
| Serum albumin | 6(?)* | 580 |
| Carbonic anhydrase | 3(?)* | 264 |
| Transferrin | 8(?)* | 647 |

*Data approximated by comparative methods. Exact amino acid sequences not yet determined.

Most of these biochemical data are expressed as percentages of agreement in amino acid sequences in proteins, and in nucleotide sequences in DNA. Some of the data are also based on chromosome banding techniques (Chapter 14) and comparisons

**Figure 16–8**  Jane van Lawick-Goodall first publicized → the toolmaking behavior of chimpanzees. In her field studies in Africa in the early 1960s, she observed the chimpanzees breaking blades of grass and stripping twigs to obtain sticklike tools. The chimpanzees used the tools to obtain one of their favorite "snacks"—termites from termite mounds.

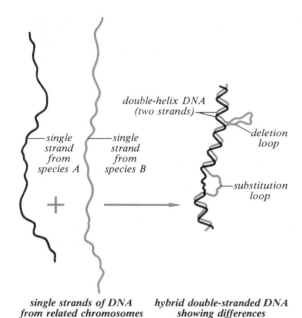

*double-helix DNA
(two strands)*

*single
strand
from
species A*

*single
strand
from
species B*

*deletion
loop*

*substitution
loop*

**single strands of DNA
from related chromosomes
of two different species**

**hybrid double-stranded DNA
showing differences
between species**

**Figure 16–9** When double-stranded DNA is separated into its single strands, a test of relationship between the DNA of two different species of organisms can be made. One DNA strand from one species, and one from the same portion of a related chromosome of the other, can be brought together. Wherever the two strands are alike they form the typical double helix of a DNA molecule. The more closely they fit together, the more closely they are related. In this figure, species B has one segment that species A lacks. The two species also differ in another segment.

and *Australopithecus* about 3 to 4 million years ago, with *Australopithecus* then becoming extinct.

Changes in human populations became continuous. Many fossils seem to reflect this continuous evolution; they are difficult to assign to one species or another. Even recent examples can be puzzling. One is the case of the Neanderthal people (Figure 16–10) of Europe, Asia, and Africa, who disappeared only 40 to 50 thousand years ago. Were Neanderthals the end of the species *Homo erectus?* Were they the beginning of the species *Homo sapiens?* Or were they neither, but a separate species as earlier anthropologists once proposed—*Homo neanderthalus?* Many anthropologists try to look at different peoples of the past as they would look at different racial stocks of people living now. They accept that the Neanderthals could have been *Homo sapiens*. They also ques-

**Figure 16–10** A fossil Neanderthal skull. The disappearance of these widely distributed people has never been satisfactorily explained. They survived as recently as 40,000 to 50,000 years ago.

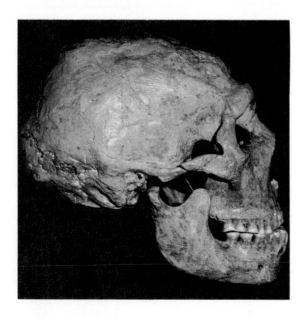

of the bandings for different species. A still simpler test of DNA relationships is illustrated in Figure 16–9.

Unfortunately, proteins and DNA do not survive in fossils. Otherwise, biochemical tests of kinship between extinct species and the one living species of *Homo* could be made.

Probably the evolution of humans, *Australopithecus,* and apes branched for the apes between 5 million and 15 million years ago, and for humans

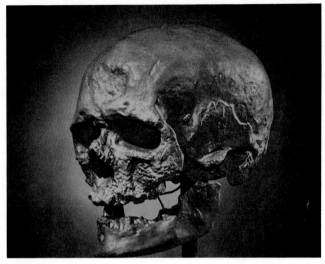

**Figure 16–11** Two Cro-Magnon skulls, possibly representing two somewhat genetically different populations. Cro-Magnon peoples, like all people today, have been classified as *Homo sapiens*.

tion whether the Neanderthals really became extinct. An argument can be made instead that *Homo sapiens* saved many Neanderthal genes in some of the variations of facial features and body proportions found among modern human beings.

Certainly Cro-Magnon people (Figure 16–11) of 30,000–35,000 years ago were *Homo sapiens*. They were cave dwellers of taller stature than their ancestors. Many were even of taller stature than most people today. They made beautiful stone tools, and other fine tools from the ivory tusks of wooly mammoths. They also drew superb pictures in caves (Figure 16–2) and in general confirmed that *Homo sapiens* had arrived. They were chiefly European and today are recognized as only one of several different *Homo sapiens* stocks living at the same time on different continents. This early diversity adds to the mystery of the disappearing Neanderthals. Anthropologists continue to wonder why Neanderthal fossils do not appear related definitely to one of the surviving *Homo sapiens* stocks.

If a people who lived as recently as 40 to 50 thousand years ago can leave behind questions that anthropologists cannot answer, you can see that other questions about still older peoples may always exist. The origins of human speech, for example, have not been mentioned because fossil evidence has not helped directly in discovering them. Yet the development of meaningful speech must have had a dramatic effect on the evolution of human beings from that point onward.

# Biology Brief

## "Kristie and Lucas at Site DK, Olduvai"

This snapshot turned up with the photos you have seen of human and *Australopithecus* fossils. How did it get in the group? Who are Kristie and Lucas? The legend on the snapshot was only seven words, handwritten (see title).

Efforts were soon started to find out about Kristie and Lucas. Olduvai is a name associated with rich fossil finds in East Africa. The late Dr. L. S. B. Leakey, his wife Mary Leakey, and his son Richard Leakey discovered many of the fossils at Olduvai and other sites not far from it that you have read about. Dr. Donald Johanson discovered Lucy (Figure 16–5) far to the north of Olduvai.

In time Lucas was found, but he proved out of reach by telephone. He was at the fossil sites, on the resident staff. Contacting Kristie, however, proved more successful. She is now in the United States, as a professor at Northeastern University in Boston. Her full name is Dr. Kristina Cannon-Bonventre.

How did Kristie and Lucas come to be photographed at Olduvai? Was it on a day of discovery? No, Kristie replied in a telephone interview, it wasn't that. She explained the underlying need of fossil-hunting expeditions to discover how to ask the right questions and seek the right answers in interpreting fossil finds.

When they were photographed, Kristie and Lucas were engaged in *taphonomy,* the painstaking excavation of sites in efforts to understand the geological and environmental conditions that affect preservation and distribution of animal remains. Both ancient and contemporary sites are studied. Taphonomy and a related field, *ethnoarchaeology,* accumulate data about what happens when animals die and their remains are left to be scattered by scavengers, or to decay, or to be

---

**CAPSULE SUMMARY**

Human genetics is very complex and cannot yet answer certain questions about human evolution. However, the structure of human proteins and human DNA can be analyzed and compared to the structures of these substances in other organisms. In this way the evolutionary "distance" between species of living animals can be estimated.

Most of the direct evidence for human evolution is obtained from fossil studies. The fossil evidence indicates that species of humans, of *Australo-* *pithecus,* and of apes all evolved separately and that the species of *Australopithecus* eventually became extinct. For humans, *Homo erectus* fossils date back at least 1.5 million years in time. Almost a million years earlier, sites of toolmaking, tool use, and food-collecting at a "home" area existed. A human skull almost two million years old also has been discovered, but not in association with either tools or game-food animals. Thus the earliest human beings remain little known.

Mysteries surround even more recent human

buried.  Human campsites are of special interest in these studies.

When campsites are along the shores of lakes, changes in the water level are important.  The sites, and any bones, may be covered by water and buried under sediments.  They will be protected from scavengers and oxygen-requiring micro-organisms of decay.  Another kind of burial that affords similar protection of animal remains is burial by volcanic ash.  East Africa still has active volcanoes.  Without burial, however—and this exposure is most common—anything can happen.  Scavengers chew and scatter the bones, the sun bleaches them, other animals trample and crush them, and within a year only bone fragments may be left.  Eventual geological burial will preserve only meager evidence of the original skeleton.  This is exactly what most two-million-year-old fossil sites reveal.

Finding fossils?  Apparently this constitutes only the first giant step.  How you interpret them in their surrounding deposits is the test.  And this is what Kristie and Lucas were investigating.

groups, notably the Neanderthal people.  Their disappearance from the fossil record shortly before Cro-Magnon fossils appeared in the fossil record is still a subject of study by anthropologists.

## SELF CHECK

1. How do most human characteristics differ in their inheritance from the traits Mendel studied in garden peas?
2. If traits affecting intelligence have evolved in the manner other traits have, what organisms might you want to test for their intelligence?
3. What evidence other than fossils themselves do anthropologists consider in determining whether the fossils may be of humans?
4. How long ago may humans have lived, based on earliest fossil evidence and excavated home sites?  On what later date do most anthropologists agree for *Homo erectus?*
5. What possible explanations would you investigate for the disappearance of Neanderthal people?

*percent*

- 0–5
- 5–10
- 10–15
- 15–20
- 20–25
- 25–30

**Figure 16–12** The distribution of the human blood group allele $I^B$ for type B blood in Europe, western Asia, and northern Africa. The frequencies are expressed as percentages of the population in which the allele is found.

# Changes in Human Populations

## 16–5

### Differences in Gene Pools Reflect Partial Isolation

Neanderthal and Cro-Magnon peoples were quite different. Even Cro-Magnon peoples were not all alike. Three distinct cultures, all Cro-Magnon, coexisted in Europe. Other cultures of people inhabited probably every continent except Antarctica. The age of modern human beings began with all the genetic variation, or more, found in human populations today. Thus, earlier populations of humans, like later ones, reflected their geographic isolation from one another.

Occasional small bands of adventurers did not keep the gene pools of different populations mixed. Among very large human populations today, not even frequent immigrations—made easier by world travel—produce much effect on the larger native population's gene pool. Among smaller human populations, however, gene pools have changed significantly with increased travel and colonization by groups from other cultures.

The ABO blood groups once provided a clear-cut example of population differences. Blood typing for these ABO groups was discovered around 1900. Around 1920, samples of blood from populations all over the world were analyzed for blood type. Imagine the surprise of geneticists to discover that most American Indians, Basques of northern Spain, and aborigines of southern Australia had no $I^B$ genes! The geneticists now believe this gene was absent from these populations until interbreeding introduced it.

The search for more data on blood-group gene frequencies has continued. Scientists now have enough data so that they can draw maps showing the frequencies of blood-group genes in various parts of the world. Study the gene-frequency map of Europe in Figure 16–12. You will see that the frequency of the gene for type B blood is more than 25 percent in extreme eastern Europe and western Asia. It gradually decreases in all directions westward until it falls below 5 percent in small areas of France, Spain, Portugal, and Scandinavia. On a similar map that includes all of Asia, you would see that the high frequency of the type B gene extends all the way across Asia to the Pacific and southward to the Indian Ocean. It seems that the genes have spread from a center of high concentration. Can you explain the spreading and the different zones of frequency it produced?

Determining the distribution of blood-group genes is only one way to study human populations. Other genes have also been studied, and the same kinds of differences in distribution have been found. Perhaps you could even identify a particular population if you knew enough about the frequencies of the various genes in that population and were shown the gene data. Such information has led to new insights into the development of human populations.

Another blood characteristic found in human populations is sickle-cell anemia. Studies have shown that when the oxygen supply is low in the red blood cells of affected persons, the hemoglobin—the substance that carries oxygen—becomes aggregated, or clumped. The aggregated hemoglobin molecules decrease the flexibility of the red blood cells and can cause them to assume a sickle shape (Figure 16–13). These inflexible

**Figure 16–13** In sickle-cell anemia, the DNA triplet that codes for the sixth amino acid of one of the protein chains of hemoglobin is altered so that an abnormal chain is formed. Unlike normal hemoglobin, the hemoglobin formed from this abnormal chain aggregates (clumps) when the oxygen content is low. This aggregation inside the red cells reduces their flexibility and can cause sickling. The figure is adapted from a diagram courtesy of Drs. Alan N. Schechter and Constance T. Noguchi, National Institutes of Health.

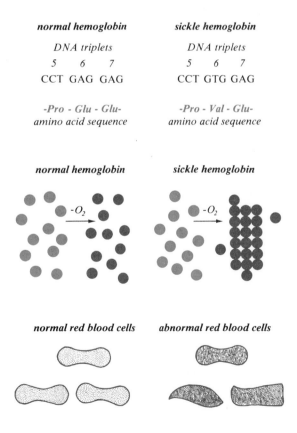

*normal hemoglobin*

*DNA triplets*

| 5 | 6 | 7 |
|---|---|---|
| CCT | GAG | GAG |

*-Pro - Glu - Glu-*
*amino acid sequence*

*sickle hemoglobin*

*DNA triplets*

| 5 | 6 | 7 |
|---|---|---|
| CCT | GTG | GAG |

*-Pro - Val - Glu-*
*amino acid sequence*

*normal hemoglobin*

*sickle hemoglobin*

*normal red blood cells*

*abnormal red blood cells*

cells clog the smaller blood vessels and block the flow of blood to nearby tissues. The resulting loss of nutrients and oxygen damages the tissues and causes swelling and pain. This condition is called a sickle-cell crisis. Persons with sickle-cell anemia suffer many of these painful crises and may die at a young age.

Tests have shown sickle-cell anemia to be a common inherited disorder. It occurs primarily in black populations but is also found in some Mediterranean areas and as far east as India. The allele probably originated as a random mutation and then spread with migration. This is an example of gene flow, discussed in Section 15–1.

Carriers who inherit the allele from one parent are said to have sickle-cell trait. Few carriers have been reported to show symptoms even under extreme stress, such as while suffering from an infectious illness or climbing at high altitudes. Those individuals who inherit the allele from both parents usually suffer severe symptoms and are said to have sickle-cell anemia.

Numerous genetic disorders are mostly restricted to specific populations of people. Eye and hair color, hair texture, skin color, and many other traits are also different for different populations. The differences in these traits reflect differences in the gene pools of the populations. These variations are evidence of long periods of geographic and genetic isolation of each population from others.

**Try Investigation 16–A** A Blood Abnormality in the Human Population, page 644.

## 16–6
## The Human Species Shows Great Variety

Differences in gene pools of human populations give geneticists new insights into what formerly were called races. Easily visible characteristics like facial structure, skin color, hair texture, presence or absence of facial hair, eye color, and others (Figure 16–14) once led to the racial classifications. Research into other genetic traits, however, has not preserved these divisions. In fact, classification by gene pools produces many times the number of human groups represented by races. Nevertheless, certain general groupings have proved useful to distinguish a few major varieties of people. These groupings include the Caucasoid (wavy hair, narrow nose, "white" skin), the Negroid or Black (wooly hair, broad nose, "black" skin), the Mongoloid (straight hair, moderately broad nose, "yellow-brown" skin), and the Australoid (curly hair, moderately broad nose, "brown" skin).

The members of different human populations are not as physically isolated today as they once were. Travel has broken down barriers. Yet population growth has kept pace with the rate of migration and intermarriage for many populations. Exceptions are groups like American Indians. They have been genetically swamped by the immigration and growth of other populations. In the eastern United States, most Indian descendants are now also immigrant descendants.

In other parts of the world, rapidly growing populations native to those areas are not so greatly affected by immigration and intermarriage. Only a minority of people, even today, travel more than a few hundred kilometers from their place of birth. Huge gene pools are relatively little changed by contributions from limited numbers of immigrants. And so isolation, even with world travel, continues genetically. It is true, however, that the boundaries between the gene pools of various populations are slowly becoming less distinct.

**Try Investigation 16–B** Variation in the Human Species, page 646.

**Figure 16-14** Traveling around the world to observe people of different facial features and different skin, hair, and eye color is not necessary today. All these photos were taken in a single western city in the United States.

## 16-7

## The Future of the Human Species

If genus *Homo* is 2 million years old or older— even 3 million—this span of time is less than one percent of life's 3.5 billion years or more of age on Earth. Humans are thus very young in life's evolution. What clues do biologists have to human life in the future?

1. Some geneticists speculate that the separate populations of people will someday merge into one. Other geneticists take the opposing view. Can you supply some of the evidence for both sides of the argument, from what you have read?

2. Average life spans may continue to increase dramatically. Better nutrition and better health and medical care are major contributors to the longer life spans. Human populations of the future may routinely include four generations at the same time. In the past only two generations, then three, overlapped in life spans.

3. Agents of natural selection will be changed, and are changing even today. The treatment of many hereditary disorders is making possible more offspring with these disorders. Successful treatment of heart, circulatory, and other disorders that may also have a genetic component makes possible more offspring with these genetic tendencies, too. On the opposite side,

new selective agents are now operating in the form of environmental stress from pollution and other technological causes.

4. The world population will continue to grow. Increased life spans, and a birthrate above the replacement level, together mean continued population growth. More people will mean more crowding, more expenditures of energy resources, and new problems of food supply. Environmental pollution will also increase even though pollution-control will be exercised, because industries must multiply to make products for the increasing numbers of people. Today the world's human population exceeds 4 billion. When you are an adult, the population may be 5 billion.

5. People may become their own competitors. Human societies are growing and evolving too rapidly for most of their members to plan ahead. Future planning may be the most important human need today. The capacity to invent and to produce more and more competes with the growing need to plan. Interestingly, producing more and more new types of products includes more and more new human-made mutagens—mutation-causing products and wastes. Apart from damaging mutations, will other mutations also occur that might speed up human evolution? Could there ever be another species of *Homo?*

6. People may even modify themselves. Recombinant DNA (Section 10–14) could mean new genes on human chromosomes in the future. Artificially synthesized genes, or natural genes from other organisms, are already being introduced experimentally into microorganisms. Thus, a bacterium that can produce needed human insulin has been developed. The insulin-coded genes were added to the bacterium's own genes. Even more recently, a gene from a rabbit has been recombined with genes in monkey cells grown in tissue culture. The monkey cells promptly began producing one of the rabbit's chains of hemoglobin (the oxygen-carrying protein of red blood cells). If recombinant DNA techniques are applied to humans in the future, they would open a new field of **genetic engineering.** You can quickly guess that the gene pools of people would be affected. At the present time, genetic engineering is being considered only to replace faulty genes associated with genetic diseases.

**CAPSULE SUMMARY**

The gene pools of many different populations make up *Homo sapiens*. Probably this was true even at the time of Cro-Magnon peoples. Variation, including racial stocks, has persisted. Some geneticists predict that the different human populations will eventually merge into one. Others believe that only small populations are genetically swamped, and that larger ones will persist separately because their gene pools are huge and immigration is limited even today. Most geneticists agree, however, that the boundaries of gene pools will become less distinct. In time, this will affect the larger gene pools, at least to an extent.

The future of *Homo sapiens* holds many questions. Populations continue to grow, and societies continue to become more complex. The agents of natural selection are changing; even genetic engineering has become a foreseeable possibility.

**SELF CHECK**

1. What are the arguments in favor of the prediction that world populations will someday merge into one? What are the arguments against it?
2. What are some of the new agents of natural selection in a technological society?
3. What is recombinant DNA? On what groups of organisms has it been demonstrated?
4. If you were proposing laws to regulate genetic engineering, what activities would you promote? What activities would you forbid?

# CHAPTER SUMMARY

## HIGHLIGHTS

Human origins are apparently closely related to those of another, now extinct genus, *Australopithecus*. At one time, members of this genus coexisted on Earth with humans. The existence of humans has been traced back at least 1.8 million years. *Australopithecus* has been traced back to as much as 2.8 to 3.2 million years. Members of both *Homo* and *Australopithecus* stood and walked erect, used tools, and probably reflected a common ancestry long after the ancestors of today's apes branched off in their own lines of descent.

By the time of the disappearance of Neanderthals and the rising prominence of Cro-Magnon peoples, the modern species *Homo sapiens* was becoming established. Then and now, a variety of different groups or racial stocks existed.

Geneticists who study human populations today find that the gene pool of each population is far more revealing than superficial characteristics of racial stocks. Gene pools also reveal a far greater number of distinctive human groups.

The future holds many questions for the human species. At a time when planning is important, rising population makes planning more difficult to undertake. How humans deal with this problem will become significant in the future.

## REVIEWING IDEAS

1. Where are the gaps in the fossil record of human ancestry?
2. Why is it important that scientists continue to look for evidence of the ancestors of modern humans?
3. What higher animals use, or are known to have used in the past, crude tools?
4. Why do anthropologists suspect that the genus *Homo* may be more than 2 million years old?

5. What do protein and DNA analyses reveal about the genetic relationship between humans and chimpanzees?
6. What does fossil evidence reveal about the close genetic relationships between humans and other species of animals in the past?
7. Why do genetic differences exist among different populations of people today?
8. What is genetic engineering? How might it be employed in medicine?

## USING CONCEPTS

9. What characteristics would you consider in suggesting whether fossils found in a layer of deposits are human?
10. What are some of the reasons why more animals do not leave fossils?
11. Explain how a genetic disorder could arise and be associated with one group of people but not others.
12. The ancestors of American Indians are believed to have crossed the Bering Strait to Alaska from Asia. Why did they not bring the $I^B$ blood allele to America? Suggest two different possible reasons.

## RECOMMENDED READING

Harland, W. B. et al. *A Geologic Time Scale.* New York, Cambridge University Press, 1983. A brief, readable account of the problems and processes of establishing dates in the past.

Johanson, D. and M. Edey. *Lucy: the Beginnings of Humankind.* New York, Simon and Schuster, 1981. Lucy's story by her discoverer.

Leroi-Gourhan, A. ''The Archaeology of Lascaux Cave,'' *Scientific American*, June 1982. Research on Cro-Magnon cave paintings in France.

PART FIVE

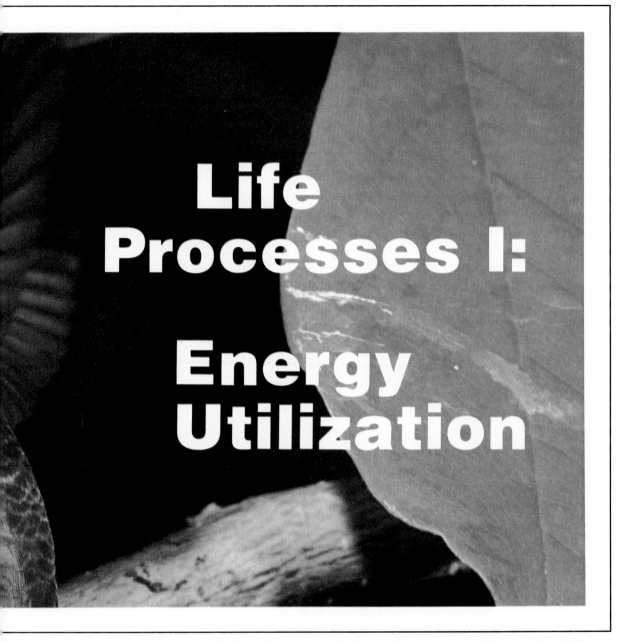

# Life Processes I:

# Energy Utilization

A broad-tailed female hummingbird reveals the pattern of her day's activities—feeding herself and her young. A camera, but not the eye, can "see" her wings in motion. You would see only a blur, and hear the humming sound the wings make as they propel the air. Up to 80 wingbeats a second! A tremendous amount of energy must be supplied constantly to her cells. And so she hovers near flowers, always feeding. Energy is essential for all life activity.

# Transport
# Systems 17

Every living cell requires materials and energy. Cells must also get rid of certain wastes. A multicellular organism must constantly transport materials from one part of its body to another.

The basic source of energy on Earth is the sun. Some of its radiant energy passes to living things during photosynthesis. Complex plants have special transport structures that supply cells with materials for photosynthesis. These special transport structures also distribute the products of photosynthesis for the plants' use.

Complex animals take in energy in the form of food. They too require transport systems to distribute essential substances great distances to huge numbers of cells. In this chapter you will explore how complex plants solve the problems of transporting the raw materials for photosynthesis, and distributing its products to all parts of the plants. You will be able to compare these methods with the patterns developed by complex animals for the transport of food and oxygen to all their cells and the transport of wastes away from the cells.

# Evolution of Transport Systems in Plants

## 17–1

### The Multicellular Plant Is Adapted to Life on Land

About 440 million years ago in the course of evolution, plants began to live on land as well as in water. Most botanists agree that photosynthetic protists somewhat similar to the green algae were the most likely forerunners of today's land plants. The types of pigment found in the cells of present-day green algae are similar to the pigments of land plants, and both groups produce starch from photosynthesis.

The process of photosynthesis is much the same in a single-celled green alga as it is in a cell of a maple leaf. But large multicellular land plants face many problems that algae do not. For example, the raw materials for photosynthesis simply diffuse into a single-celled alga living in water. Many of these raw materials are not directly available to a cell in a maple leaf. In the multicellular green plant, special structures have evolved that allow the plant to obtain materials from the environment, transport them to individual cells, use them, and store new materials made from them. Some of these activities carried on by plants are summarized in Figure 17–1 on the next page.

← A plant leaf shows its branching network of veins. What do the veins do besides provide support?

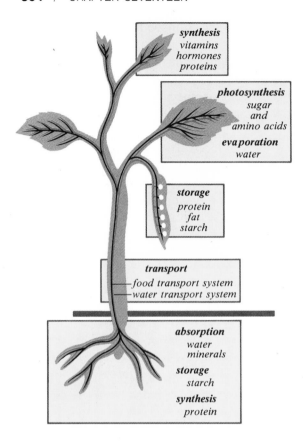

**Figure 17–1** Different parts of a plant have different activities. All these activities involve materials that must be transported where needed. Water is the material needed in greatest amounts. It also serves as the transport fluid, carrying minerals in one kind of plant tissue and plantmade foods in another.

## 17–2

## The Leaf Is an Efficient Structure for Photosynthesis

Some fossil plants show structures similar to present-day plant leaves, but smaller. (See Figure 17–2.) The presence of leaves increases the surface area exposed to light, an adaptation favorable to photosynthesis. In addition, complex plants have leaves with bundles of conducting cells called veins, which carry water to the leaf cells and the products of photosynthesis (chiefly glucose) to other parts of the plant.

Exposure to the air would have quickly evaporated all the water from a primitive aquatic plant. Thus, to live on land, plants had to develop a waterproof outer surface. The waxy coating, or **cuticle** (KEW-ti-kul), found on modern land plants appears in very ancient fossil plants as well. The cuticle is not a layer of cells, but simply a thin film covering the outer surfaces of the plants. Examine the structure of a typical leaf in Figure 17–3, page 366. Notice that the upper and lower surfaces are covered by the waxy cuticle that prevents water loss.

The major function of a leaf is photosynthesis. Carbon dioxide and water must be available as raw materials for photosynthesis. At the same time, the leaf must conserve water in periods of dryness. The underside of the leaf has openings or pores in the cuticle, through which water vapor and carbon dioxide pass. These pores are called **stomata** (STOH-muh-tuh). (See Figure 17–3.) The term "stomata" is the plural of the Greek word **stoma,** meaning mouth or opening. The fossil record shows that stomata were present in the outer coverings of plants even before leaves had developed.

Each stoma is bounded by two **guard cells,** specialized cells that change shape to open or close the stoma. Figure 17–4 on page 367 shows that the edge of the guard cell next to the stoma is thicker than the edge away from the stoma. When the guard cells take in water and become swollen, the pressure exerted on the cell walls causes the thinner walls to bulge outward. This outward bulging forces the thicker inner walls apart, thus opening the stoma. When water pressure in the guard cells decreases, the opposite action occurs. The thicker inner walls come together and close the stoma. (See **Appendix 17–A,** Opening and Closing of Stomata, page 716.)

The cells inside the leaf (Figure 17–3) just

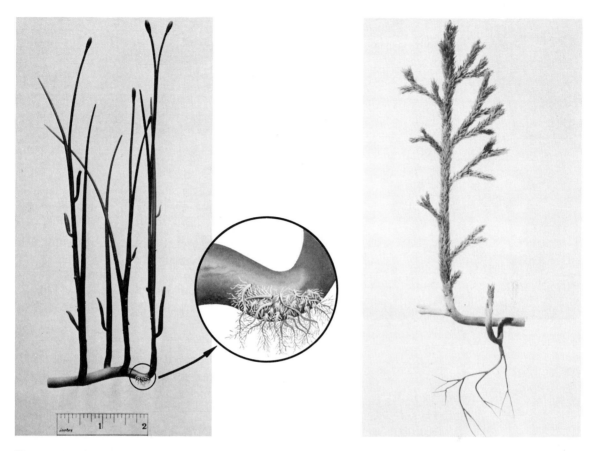

**Figure 17-2** The fine root hairs on the horizontal stem of the fossil plant at the left are shown in an enlarged view next to the plant. Compare these root hairs with the rootlike structures of the more advanced fossil plant at the right. The stem of the more advanced plant also had leaflike extensions.

above the stomata have spaces between them. This open, spongy arrangement of cells permits carbon dioxide to diffuse directly and rapidly into each cell in the leaf that is carrying on photosynthesis. Would you consider this arrangement an example of evolutionary adaptation?

Plants use carbon dioxide and release oxygen when photosynthesis occurs. Yet all the plant cells use oxygen for respiration and release carbon dioxide, just like animal cells. Part of the oxygen released in photosynthesis is used immediately by the cells for respiration. During the daylight hours, photosynthesis produces much more oxygen than is needed immediately for respiration. The excess oxygen diffuses out of the plant through the stomata to the air. However, at night when only the dark reactions of photosynthesis (Section 7-7) are occurring, oxygen for cells carrying on respiration must diffuse from the air through the stomata into the interior of the leaf. Carbon dioxide released by the respiration at night diffuses out of the leaf.

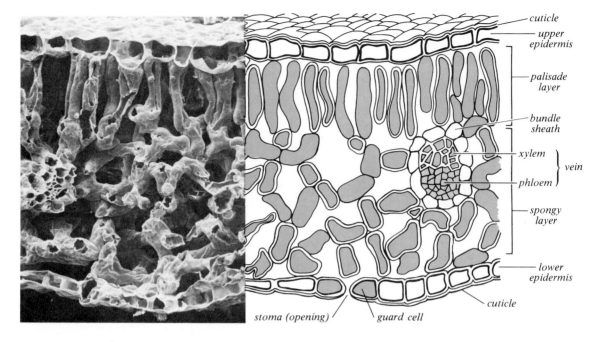

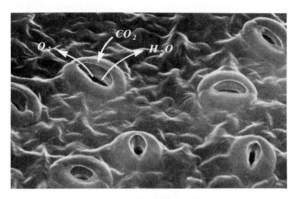

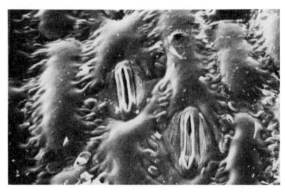

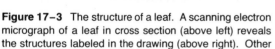

**Figure 17–3** The structure of a leaf. A scanning electron micrograph of a leaf in cross section (above left) reveals the structures labeled in the drawing (above right). Other scanning electron micrographs show the leaf stomata opened (lower left) and closed (lower right). How is the leaf adapted on the inside to air circulation?

Water, in the form of water vapor, can move through the stomata. The rate of movement is influenced by the relative humidity of the air. (The humidity in the leaf is always higher than in the air.) When the humidity of the air drops, water will evaporate from the leaf through the stomata at a greater rate. How would the rate of water evaporation be changed when there is a rise in temperature? How would the rate be changed by a drop in temperature?

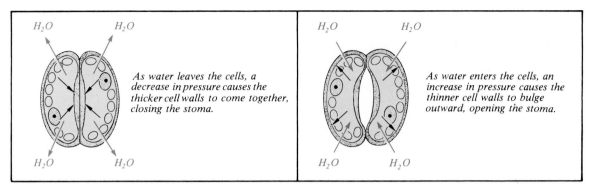

**Figure 17-4** The guard cell walls surrounding a stoma move according to the water pressure inside the cells, thus closing or opening the stoma.

## 17-3

## Water and Minerals Are Absorbed by the Roots of Plants

One of the striking differences between water plants and land plants is the root system. As land plants evolved into larger and more complex organisms, a far-reaching, branching system of true roots developed. (See **Appendix 17-B,** Fossil Record of Root Development, page 717.) True roots differ from the simple rootlike structures of primitive plants in that they are connected to the transporting tubes that go through all parts of the plant. Figure 17-5, on page 368, shows the main water-conducting structures in a tree. Some root cells have long, thin projections, the **root hairs.** Water and minerals in solution enter the cells through the root hairs. The water and minerals then diffuse from the root hairs into other root cells, and finally enter water-transport channels.

The root cells require energy to transport these materials. Where do they obtain the energy to perform their functions? If water can be transported upward from the roots into the rest of the plant, could glucose, produced in the leaves by photosynthesis, be transported downward to provide energy to the roots? Experiments have shown that this is actually what happens.

## 17-4

## Channels Transport Materials Through the Plant

Transport systems that could move water, minerals, and organic compounds around in the plant body appeared early as an adaptation of land plants. Fossil plants had bundles of cells running up and down their stems as well as in their leaves. Botanists believe that these were the forerunners of the complex systems of conducting tubes seen in present-day plants. The primitive bundles of cells evolved into two types of channels. One channel type, called the **xylem** (ZY-lem), transports water and minerals. The other channel type, called the **phloem** (FLOH-em), transports food. The phloem is located nearer the outer part of the stem, and the xylem is located closer to the center of the stem. Figure 17-6, on page 369, illustrates these two kinds of conducting tubes in a woody plant. Notice the relationship of the xylem and phloem to the cambium. **Cambium** is a layer of cells that produces new tissues in every growing season.

The cells that make up the xylem tubes are dead. Some xylem cells, the tracheids (TRAY-kee-uds), have pointed ends and thick walls with pits that connect them to nearby cells. Other xylem cells, the vessels, are short tubes with no

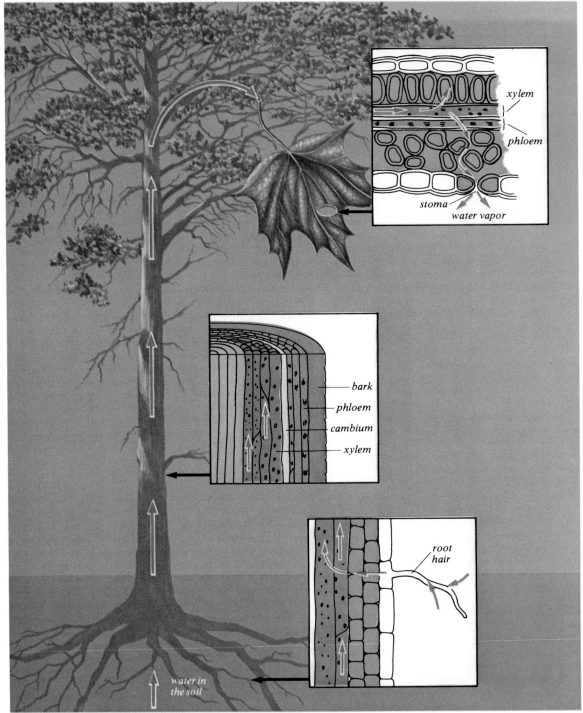

xylem

phloem

stoma

water vapor

bark

phloem

cambium

xylem

root
hair

water in
the soil

**Figure 17–5** The red arrows identify the principal water-conducting structures of this tree. Trace the path of the water from the root hairs through xylem tissues to the leaves.

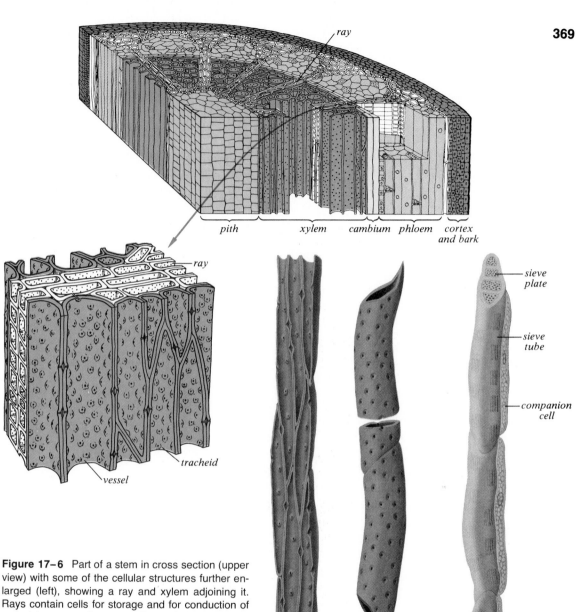

**Figure 17-6** Part of a stem in cross section (upper view) with some of the cellular structures further enlarged (left), showing a ray and xylem adjoining it. Rays contain cells for storage and for conduction of materials across the stem. Two principal kinds of xylem cells and a sieve tube of phloem cells are shown separately, at the right.

*ray*

*pith    xylem    cambium    phloem    cortex and bark*

*ray*

*tracheid*

*vessel*

*tracheid cells    vessel cells    phloem cells*

**xylem cells**

*sieve plate*

*sieve tube*

*companion cell*

end walls. End-to-end, these cells form a continuous channel. The phloem through which food travels is made of living cells joined end to end. The ends of the phloem cells have tiny pores through which the contents of the cells can mix. Because the porous areas at the ends of these cells resemble tiny sieves, the phloem channels are often called **sieve tubes.**

---

**CAPSULE SUMMARY**

Leaves, roots, and conducting vessels evolved very early. Leaves provide a maximum surface for photosynthesis. Openings on the leaf surfaces, called stomata, regulate the passage of carbon dioxide, oxygen, and water vapor into and out of leaves. Water and minerals absorbed from the soil are transported to other parts of the plant by the tracheids and vessels in the xylem channels. The products of photosynthesis are transported from the leaf to all parts of the plant through the sieve tubes in the phloem channels.

**SELF CHECK**

1. From what type of primitive autotroph living in the water did the first land plants probably evolve?
2. How do leaves enhance photosynthesis in a multicellular land plant?
3. What structures of roots absorb water and minerals from the soil?
4. What is the principal difference between the cells of the xylem and the cells of the phloem?

---

**Try Investigation 17–A** What Controls the Movement of Water in Plants? page 649.

# Operation of Transport Systems in Higher Plants

## 17–5

### An Engineering Problem: How Is Water Transported in Plants?

Water enters the plant through the root-hair cells and is transported through the xylem to all parts of the plant. Water evaporates from the leaf surfaces through the stomata. Tremendous amounts of water evaporate from large land plants every day. For example, a typical red maple tree growing in a humid climate may lose as much as 200 liters of water a day. This water must be replaced if the plant is to survive. The water entering through the roots must often be transported upward for great distances. Yet plants do not have built-in pumps like the hearts of animals.

Any hypothesis developed to explain the rise of water in plants must account for all the observations made by botanists over a long period of time. They have noted that:

1. Some trees are over 100 meters tall.
2. Work must be done to move water upward. Therefore, some form of energy is needed.
3. Water loss can be rapid. For this reason, the movement of water must also be rapid.
4. Water loss is greatest on a hot sunny day and least at night.
5. Branches removed from plants can take up water even though no roots are present.
6. Stems in which the phloem cells have been killed can still conduct water. (Remember that the channels of the xylem are composed of dead cells.)

Three explanations have been suggested for water transport in plants:

1. Capillary action can raise water to a limited height in tubes.
2. Root pressure, at least at certain times, can raise water to a height of 30 meters.
3. Cohesion-tension forces could raise water to a height of more than 100 meters.

**Capillary action** can be demonstrated by placing one end of a narrow glass tube into a container of colored water or India ink. The liquid in the tube will rise to a higher level than the liquid in the container. The smaller the diameter of the tube, the higher the liquid will rise in it. The liquid rises in the tube because the molecules on the surface of the liquid are attracted to the molecules on the sides of the tube. The capillary rise of fluid in small tubes is not very rapid and not very high. Therefore, capillary action would not explain water transport in very tall plants.

**Root pressure** has also been used to explain the upward rise of water in plants. When the stem of a plant is cut off, water and other materials ooze out of the cut surface. The pressure that causes this oozing is exerted by the root system. However, root pressure has been measured and would not by itself account for the rise of water in trees taller than 30 meters.

The **cohesion-tension** hypothesis explains how water is lifted to great heights in a tree. According to this idea, water exists in a continuous column in xylem cells from the bottom to the top of a tree. The leaf cells lose water by evaporation through the stomata. Cohesion, the force holding the water molecules together, causes more water to move into the leaf cells from the xylem. The remaining water in the xylem is placed under tension and pulled upward in an unbroken column. More water is furnished by the root cells to the xylem. The root cells extract water from the soil by osmosis. Osmosis occurs because the concentration of inorganic compounds within the root cells is greater than the concentration of the compounds in the soil. Thus an unbroken column of water under tension extends in the tree from the root cells to the leaf cells. The forces of cohesion and tension in this column account for the upward rise of the water.

This pulling force can be measured. It is large enough to account for the movement of water to a height of more than 100 meters. (See **Appendix 17–C,** Böhm's Cohesion-Tension Experiment, page 717.) The cohesion-tension hypothesis is favored by most biologists today as the best explanation of the rise of water in plants.

If the water column is cut at a point around the tree, water continues to rise around one or both sides of the cut. Is the water column broken by cutting the xylem in this way (introducing air where the cut is made)? Or is the water column in the tree a continuous network all around the inside of the trunk, interrupted only at a spot where a cut is made? (See **Appendix 17–D,** Postlethwait's and Rogers' Radioisotope Experiments, page 718.)

## 17–6

## Food Is Transported in Plants Through the Phloem

How is food transported in the phloem? A number of facts are known about this problem, but a full explanation has not yet been found. Remember that phloem cells are living, and any explanation must take into account that the food must pass through the cytoplasm of these cells.

At one time it was thought that slow, simple diffusion or protoplasmic streaming moved the food molecules along the phloem tubes. However, the speed at which materials flow through the phloem has been measured. At certain times the rate of flow is as high as 100 centimeters per hour, indicating that diffusion or protoplasmic streaming is not the major mechanism of food transport in the phloem.

A more recent hypothesis is based on differences in fluid pressure in different parts of the plant. According to this hypothesis, water and dissolved carbohydrate food flow through the sieve tubes from an area of higher pressure to an area of lower pressure. As carbohydrate food is produced by photosynthesis in the cells of green leaves, water moves into these leaf cells through the process of osmosis. This movement of water raises the fluid pressure inside the leaf cells. High pressure

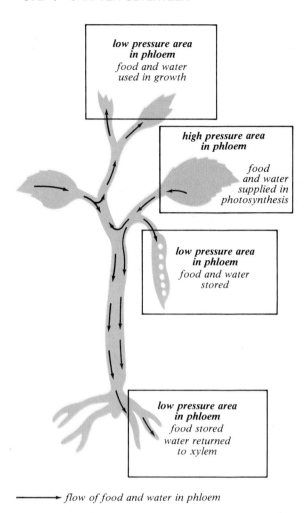

low pressure area
in phloem
*food and water
used in growth*

high pressure area
in phloem

*food
and water
supplied in
photosynthesis*

low pressure area
in phloem
*food and water
stored*

low pressure area
in phloem
*food stored
water returned
to xylem*

→ *flow of food and water in phloem*

**Figure 17–7** A hypothesis based on fluid pressure, for the transport of food and water in phloem.

in one cell tends to force substances into adjoining cells. The phloem cells in the leafy parts of plants are considered to be under higher pressure than the other parts. Consequently, water and dissolved carbohydrate food are forced into the sieve tube cells from the leaves to the other portions of plants. In storage organs and actively growing parts of plants, sugars and carbohydrate food are being stored or used. As carbohydrate food is

removed from the sieve tubes in the storage organs or growing areas, these sieve tube cells tend to lose water. The loss of water results in a drop in fluid pressure. Within the sieve tube system, then, there are areas in the plant under higher fluid pressure and other areas under lower fluid pressure. Water and dissolved carbohydrate food move from the areas of higher pressure (usually the leaves) to areas of lower pressure (usually storage areas or rapidly growing plant parts). The entire process is dependent on an uptake of water by cells in the leaves and a loss of water by cells in the storage areas or areas of rapid growth. (See Figure 17–7 and **Appendix 17–E,** A Practical Application, page 719.)

The fluid carried in the phloem tubes can be collected and analyzed chemically. This fluid contains a number of complex sugars, some amino acids, phosphorus compounds, and inorganic ions. These chemicals are products of photosynthesis and metabolism in the leaves' cells.

An ingenious method of obtaining very pure samples of the fluid in the phloem is illustrated in Figure 17–8. This method makes use of insects called aphids. The aphids insert their very fine mouth parts into a single cell of the phloem. The pressure of the flow of material in the phloem cell forces material through the aphid's digestive tract, forming droplets of "honeydew" at the hind end of the aphid. Pure samples of the material can be collected by first detaching the body of the aphid from the mouth parts. The material can be collected as it flows through the mouth parts. Thus, it does not come into contact with the aphid's internal organs.

Different materials in solution move up and down the stems of plants through the xylem and the phloem. Water, salts, and other soluble materials also move sideways from the xylem to the phloem, or from the phloem to the xylem, through the **ray cells.** Figure 17–6 shows how these ray cells are arranged in relation to the xylem and the phloem.

**Figure 17–8** An aphid's proboscis is buried in a phloem cell of a tree as the insect sucks juice from the phloem. Note the drop of "honey-dew" at the end of the aphid's abdomen.

Pits in the walls of the ray cells open channels to pits in both the xylem and the phloem. Water and minerals are supplied to the phloem. Food material is supplied to dividing cambium cells as they are enlarging to form plant tissue. Substances can also pass sideways in the plant through rays, so that all the cells are provided with the necessary materials.

**CAPSULE SUMMARY**

Transport systems provide all plant cells with the organic products of photosynthesis and with water and minerals from the soil. The cohesion-tension hypothesis is the most commonly accepted explanation of how water is transported in xylem. This hypothesis states that the evaporation of water from leaves creates a pulling force. Cohesion holds the water molecules together, and the water is drawn upward in an unbroken column. Organic materials move through sieve tubes in the phloem.

**SELF CHECK**

1. How do water and minerals from the soil get to the transport system of the roots?
2. What structures in the stem of a plant would conduct water between the veins of the leaf and the water-conducting vessels of the roots?
3. If you were able to inject some air bubbles into the xylem vessels of a tree, what would happen to the transport of water in these vessels? Why?
4. Would loss of water from the surfaces of leaves have any effect on the transport of materials in the sieve tubes of the phloem?
5. What are ray cells?

# Transport Systems in Animals

## 17–7

### Circulatory Systems Have Evolved in Multicellular Animals

Although plant and animal transport systems differ in structure and operation, they serve the same basic functions. They carry essential substances to the cells, carry away the products of the cells' activities, and thereby help maintain a constant internal environment for the cells of the body.

Even single-celled organisms seem to have a simple kind of transport system. You may have watched a *Paramecium* take in food and form a vacuole. The food vacuoles are carried around the cell in a definite direction by the movement of the *Paramecium's* cytoplasm, as diagrammed in Figure 17–9. The *Hydra,* a simple multicellular animal, also seems to have a "circulation." The fluid in the *Hydra's* body cavity contains food, oxygen, and carbon dioxide. The fluid moves as the body of the *Hydra* moves. Flatworms and roundworms also have no special structures for fluid transport. The structures in echinoderms are very limited. Mollusks, annelids, and arthropods have the most highly developed transport structures among invertebrates.

As larger animals evolved, pumps that could push fluids, and tubes that would contain them, developed. The pumps are usually called **hearts,** and the tubes are called **blood vessels.** These transport systems in multicellular animals are "closed" or "open." The earthworm, shown in Figure 17–9, has a closed system, with a series of connecting vessels including a number of contractile hearts. Blood from these hearts is pumped under pressure into a main vessel under the digestive tract. From this large vessel the blood flows into many smaller vessels, the **capillaries,** which

extend into all the organs of the earthworm. Food, water, and waste products are exchanged through the walls of the capillaries. The blood then passes back to a larger vessel running above the digestive tract, and returns to the hearts to be pumped around the body again.

The grasshopper has an open system, shown also in Figure 17–9. The grasshopper's transport fluid, its "blood," is pumped by a muscular seven-chambered heart into large, open spaces among the body tissues. These spaces, called **sinuses** (SY-nuh-sez), are distributed around the body. The blood flows through the sinuses and back to the heart. This kind of transport system is described as open because the blood is not always enclosed within vessels. Note the difference between the earthworm's transport system and the grasshopper's.

The transport systems in both vertebrates and invertebrates bring food and oxygen to the cells of the body and remove waste products and carbon dioxide. The human heart pumps blood under pressure into arteries, where it then flows into capillaries, and finally into veins before it returns to the heart. (See **Appendix 17–F,** William Harvey Discovers That Blood Circulates, page 719.)

**Try Investigation Figure 17–B** Variations in the Heartbeat of *Daphnia,* page 652.

**Figure 17–9** Transport in a protist and some inverte- → brate animals. Compare the simple transport systems of the *Paramecium* and *Hydra* with the more complex systems of the earthworm and insect. Both the insect and earthworm have contractile hearts, but which one has a continuous system of blood vessels?

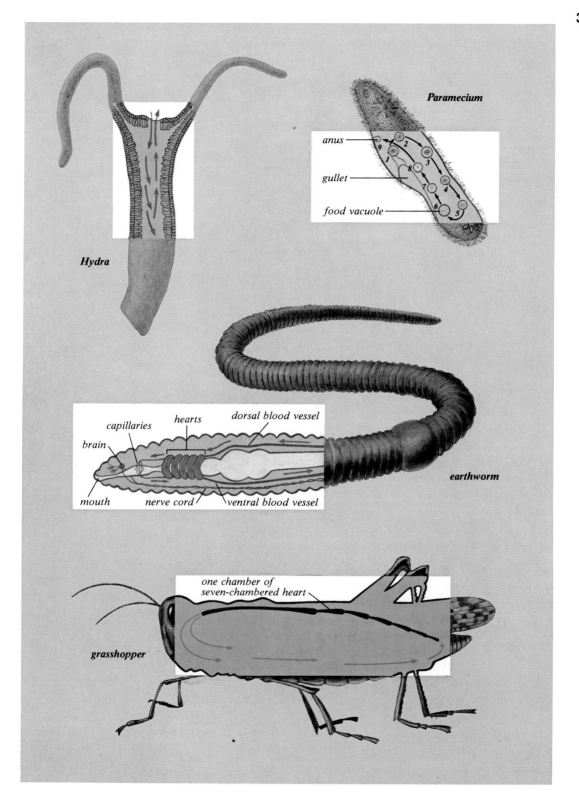

Hydra

Paramecium

anus

gullet

food vacuole

capillaries   hearts   dorsal blood vessel

brain

mouth   nerve cord   ventral blood vessel

earthworm

one chamber of
seven-chambered heart

grasshopper

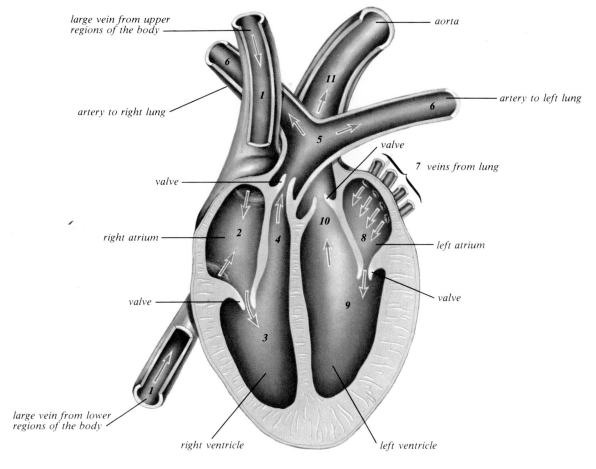

large vein from upper regions of the body

aorta

6

1

11

artery to right lung

artery to left lung

6

5

valve

valve

7 veins from lung

right atrium

2

4

10

8

left atrium

valve

9

valve

3

1

large vein from lower regions of the body

right ventricle

left ventricle

**Figure 17–10** A drawing of a section through a human heart and the blood vessels leading to and from it. How can you account for the wall of the left ventricle being thicker than the wall of the right ventricle? Trace the flow of blood into and out of the heart by following the numbers and arrows.

## 17–8

## The Human Heart Pumps Blood to the Body

The human heart is a two-part pump (Figure 17–10). Each side of the heart has two chambers. The upper chamber, called the **atrium** (AY-tree-um), has a thinner wall than the lower chamber, the **ventricle** (VEN-trih-kul). The wall of the ventricle is very thick and muscular. The heart beats in two steps. First, the muscles of the wall of the atrium contract, acting as a kind of priming pump to force the blood into the ventricle. Then muscles in the thick-walled ventricle squeeze the blood with great force into the arteries.

William Harvey, an English physician and scientist, studied the beating of the heart in many kinds of animals. Harvey observed that the contractions of the heart seem to start in the heart muscle itself. Later experiments have shown that under proper conditions the hearts of some animals

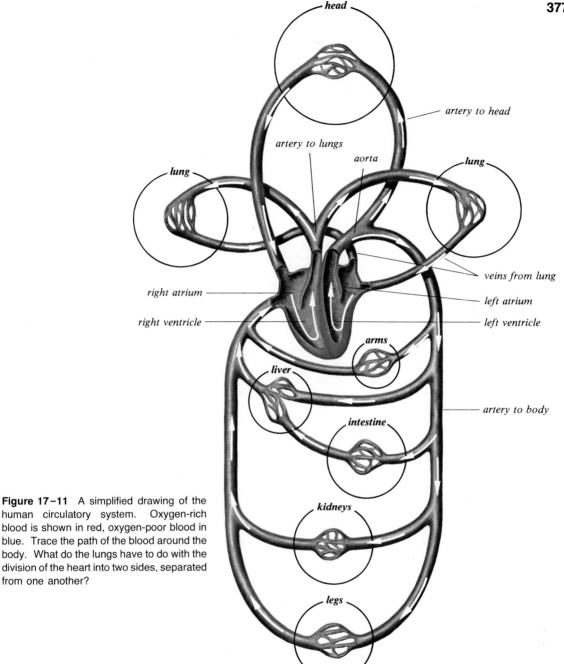

**Figure 17–11** A simplified drawing of the human circulatory system. Oxygen-rich blood is shown in red, oxygen-poor blood in blue. Trace the path of the blood around the body. What do the lungs have to do with the division of the heart into two sides, separated from one another?

will continue to beat even when they are removed from the body. The heartbeat results from a rhythmic impulse that comes from cells in the heart itself. This impulse arises in the cells of specialized muscle tissue called the **pacemaker.** The pacemaker of humans and some other animals is

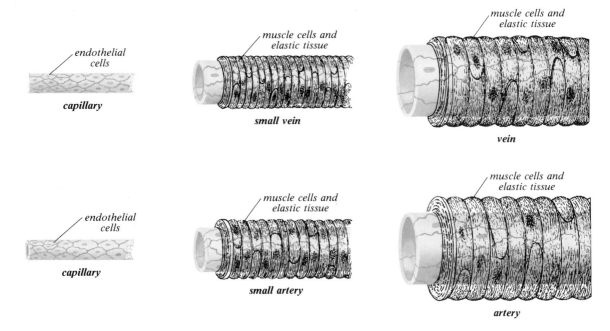

**Figure 17–12** The structure of arteries, veins, and capillaries corresponds with their functions in the circulatory system. Arteries are thicker walled with their combination of muscular and elastic tissue than veins. Capillaries have the thinnest walls.

located in the wall of the right atrium. The heartbeat impulse spreads from there throughout the heart muscle. Although the heartbeat starts in the heart itself, the rate of the heartbeat is controlled by nerves outside the heart.

You will notice in Figure 17–10 that the openings between the atria and ventricles have the flaplike folds of tissue that Harvey called valves. The valves operate like one-way gates, so that the blood in the ventricles cannot back up into the atria.

The path of the blood through the two sides of the heart is shown in Figure 17–11. Blood enters the right atrium from the veins. At this point the blood is low in oxygen and high in carbon dioxide, having just returned from the organs and tissues of the body. From the right atrium the blood enters the right ventricle. Then it is forced into the pulmonary artery where it goes to the lungs. In the lungs carbon dioxide is given off from the blood and oxygen is taken in.

The blood enters the left atrium from the lungs, where it has gained oxygen. The blood from the left atrium goes to the left ventricle. From there it is forced into a large artery called the **aorta** (ay-OHR-ta). The aorta branches into arteries that carry the blood to all parts of the body. In this way, the oxygen-rich blood coming from the left side of the heart is pumped to all the tissues and organs of the body.

Although the heart's double pump sends blood through two separate pathways, the right and left sides of the heart act in rhythm with each other. As a certain amount of blood is pumped out of the left side of the heart, an equal amount enters the right side. (See **Appendix 17–G,** How Much Blood Does Your Heart Pump?, page 721.)

## 17-9

## The Structure of Blood Vessels Is Related to Their Function

The whole circulatory system provides a good example of the interrelationship of structure and function. Blood vessels differ in the amounts of muscle and elastic tissue in their walls. For example, the largest arteries have walls made up largely of elastic tissue. (See Figure 17–12.) When the heart contracts, forcing blood into these arteries under great pressure, the walls of the large arteries, because of their elasticity, stretch and expand. This expansion allows more space for the blood to enter and prevents the pressure from increasing greatly. During the relaxed phase of the heartbeat the stretched elastic walls of the arteries continue to exert pressure on the blood, helping to push it along and maintain blood pressure. In a disease called arteriosclerosis, the arterial walls become rigid and are unable to expand with each surge of

blood. As a result, the blood pressure rises and the heart is put under a great strain.

The smaller arteries have walls made up of muscle and elastic tissue. Under control of the nervous system these arteries can contract and expand. They control the direction and amount of blood that flows into different parts of the body. The resistance to blood flow by the very small arteries and capillaries also aids in maintaining pressure.

The capillaries supply individual cells with the materials necessary for life. To provide the billions of cells within an animal with these materials, the circulatory system depends on a network of tiny capillaries that extends into every tissue of every organ of the body. Figure 17–13 shows how the arteries and veins connect with capillaries by way of smaller vessels. Materials are exchanged between the blood and the fluids surrounding the tissue cells through the thin capillary walls. In spite of the size of an average human

**Figure 17–13** Arteries and veins connect with capillaries by way of smaller vessels or connecting channels. Blood can pass from arteries to connecting channels to capillaries or directly through the connecting channels to veins.

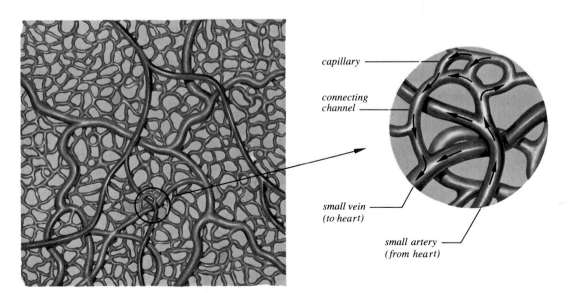

capillary

connecting channel

small vein (to heart)

small artery (from heart)

being, no cell is very far from a capillary. An example will give you some idea of the enormous extent of the network of capillaries in the body and their extremely small size. It has been estimated that the capillaries of a single person, if put together in a sheet almost 30 cm wide, would extend for 20 kilometers! This sheet would be so thin that if you rolled up all 20 kilometers, the roll would be no thicker than a lead pencil.

The blood returning to the heart through the veins is under much lower pressure than blood flowing in the arteries. Veins have thinner walls with less muscle and elastic tissues than arteries.

(See Figure 17–12.) Blood flow through the veins is aided by several factors. Valves in the veins prevent the blood from flowing backward. In some parts of the body, contraction of the skeletal muscles around the veins helps to push the blood along. Gravity also helps to return the blood to the heart, especially from the head regions. Part of the reason astronauts lie flat during blastoff and reentry of their space vehicles is to keep increased gravity from returning too much blood to the heart.

**Try Investigation 17−C** Capillary Circulation, page 653.

---

**CAPSULE SUMMARY**

Transport systems in animals carry essential life substances to the cells of the body, and carry away the waste products of cell activity. Transport vessel systems may be of two types: open systems in which the fluids are not entirely enclosed in vessels, and closed systems in which the circulating fluid is always within vessels. Larger animals have pumping organs, or hearts, that drive the transport fluids around the body.

The heart of higher vertebrates is a double pump. Blood goes to the body from the left side of the heart, and to the lungs from the right side. The arteries carry blood to all parts of the body. Blood is returned to the heart through the veins. Arteries are muscular and elastic and aid in controlling blood pressure. The blood in arteries moves toward capillaries under rather high pressure. The flow of blood into the capillaries is controlled by the small arteries leading to them. Capillaries are very small and abundant. No cell of the body is very far from a capillary. The total surface area of the capillaries is tremendous. Blood reaches all

the tissue spaces of the body by way of the capillaries. Blood pressure decreases as the distance from the heart becomes greater. Blood in the veins is therefore under less pressure than in the arteries. Veins have thinner walls with less elastic and muscular tissue than arteries. The return of blood to the heart through the veins is aided by several factors including valves, skeletal muscle contractions, and gravity.

**SELF CHECK**

1. Why is it necessary for many animals to have transport systems?
2. Distinguish between open and closed transport systems in animals.
3. In humans, where is blood pumped after it leaves the right ventricle of the heart? After it leaves the left ventricle?
4. Why is the blood pressure in the veins less than the blood pressure in the arteries?
5. Name one factor which aids the return of blood in the veins to the heart.

# Regulation of the Internal Environment

## 17–10

### Blood Is the Transport Fluid

The transport system in large and complex animals performs two basic functions: It brings essential substances to the cells, and it carries away waste products of cellular activity. Blood performs other functions as well.

Blood consists of cells of different kinds suspended in a fluid. In humans, blood transports oxygen in specialized cells called **red cells.** Red cells contain a red pigment called **hemoglobin** (HEE-muh-gloh-bin). In other animals, pigments of different chemical structure and colors combine with oxygen and transport it to cells. (See **Appendix 17–H,** Oxygen–Transport Pigments in Animals, page 721.) Any decrease in the ability of the red cells to carry oxygen can be detected and often treated. Blood also carries carbon dioxide.

Red cells are constantly being renewed. A red cell lives only about three months. In humans a young red cell contains a nucleus, but as the cell matures the nucleus is lost. Therefore, red cells cannot reproduce themselves. They are specialized for one function, the carrying of oxygen. New red cells are manufactured in the bone marrow of the long bones of the body.

The specialized **white cells** form the first line of defense against invading organisms such as bacteria. A white cell surrounds bacteria and absorbs them in much the same way as an amoeba takes in food. When there is an infection in the body, the number of white cells increases greatly. The white cells help to combat the disease by destroying the bacteria. The pus that forms in an infected wound consists largely of white cells that have died after engulfing bacteria. Other substances in blood, called **antibodies,** also help fight disease. Figure

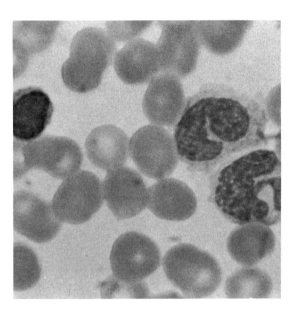

**Figure 17–14** Human blood from a healthy individual. Some red blood cells (erythrocytes) appear to have holes because they are thinner in the middle. Two large white cells (monocytes) are seen to the right and a smaller white cell (lymphocyte) to the left.

17–14 shows some of the types of cells found in human blood.

The fluid portion of the blood, called **plasma,** is water containing dissolved proteins, salts, amino acids, sugars, and other substances. Blood absorbs digested food from the intestine and carries it in the plasma to all the cells of the body. Unusual variations in the amounts of amino acids, sugars, or fats may sometimes indicate that the organs or glands of the digestive system are not functioning properly.

Glands secrete hormones such as the reproductive hormones you read about in Chapter 11.

These hormones are carried in the plasma through-out the body. Upsets in the hormonal system can sometimes be detected by a blood analysis.

Blood also can clot, or *coagulate,* acting like a sealing glue to close a wound. If you cut yourself, small structures called blood platelets disintegrate and start the interaction of certain substances in the blood. The enzyme **thrombin** (THROM-bin) acts upon a soluble plasma protein, **fibrinogen** (fy-BRIN-uh-jin), to produce insoluble **fibrin** (FY-brin). The fibrin is the essential part of the covering. Red blood cells become trapped on the fibrin to form a temporary patch over the cut. It is possible for a clot, or *thrombus,* to form within a blood vessel, blocking circulation. In this in-stance, the clot may be harmful but can sometimes be dissolved.

## 17–11

## Fluid Is Exchanged Between Blood and Body Cells

Blood reaches the cells of the body through the capillaries. Oxygen and food are exchanged for waste molecules through the capillary walls. The exchange is a fluid exchange between the blood in the capillaries and the spaces between body cells.

In the late 1890s Ernest Starling, an English biologist, suggested a hypothesis to explain fluid exchange. Starling hypothesized that **blood pres-sure** forced fluid through the capillary walls where it moved into the tissue spaces to supply the cells with food and oxygen. Starling suggested that the forces of osmosis moved the fluids back into the capillaries (you learned about osmosis in Section 6–10). At that time it was thought that the protein molecules suspended in the blood plasma were too large to move through capillary walls. Thus, the only fluid passing out of the capillaries into the spaces between the cells would be a watery sus-pension of smaller molecules like sugars, amino

acids, salts, and other substances. The fluid out-side the capillaries between the body cells contains more water molecules than the blood plasma in the capillaries. Water would therefore move into the capillaries by osmotic pressure because water mol-ecules are more concentrated in the tissue fluid than in the capillaries.

Starling also pointed out that the blood pressure at the arterial end of the capillary is higher than the osmotic pressure. Thus, at the arterial end, more fluid would leave the capillary than would enter. At the venous end, the blood pressure would be less than the osmotic pressure and more fluid would pass into the capillary from the tissue spaces. Starling's hypothesis is diagrammed in Figure 17–15.

Starling knew that another system of vessels, the **lymphatic** (lihm-FAT-ik) system, also carried some of the tissue fluid from the spaces between the cells back into the bloodstream. The fluid in the lymphatic system, which contains certain kinds of cells, water, large protein molecules, salts, and other substances, is called **lymph** (LIMF). Lymph passes through the walls of small lymph capillaries into larger lymph vessels. Finally, all of the lymph fluid empties into the bloodstream from the two largest lymph vessels which are attached to veins in the chest.

Recent experiments show that Starling's as-sumption that large protein molecules do not pass through the capillary wall is not true. Various blood proteins were tagged with radioactive atoms in experimental animals. These tagged protein molecules leaked out of the capillaries along with the fluid. In the course of a day about half of the total proteins circulating in the blood were passed out of the capillaries. Since the body does not lose half of its blood proteins every day, they must return to the bloodstream in some way. The radioactive proteins were traced. It was found that these proteins returned to the blood through the lymph vessels.

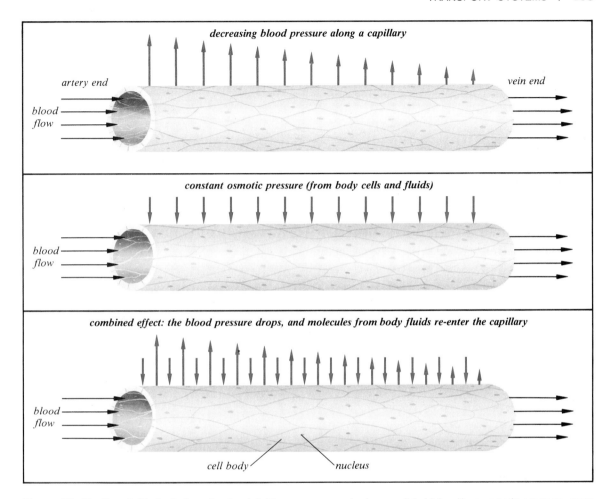

**decreasing blood pressure along a capillary**

artery end

vein end

blood flow

**constant osmotic pressure (from body cells and fluids)**

blood flow

**combined effect: the blood pressure drops, and molecules from body fluids re-enter the capillary**

blood flow

cell body          nucleus

**Figure 17–15** Ernest Starling's hypothesis of fluid exchange. Osmotic pressure of body fluids against the capillary walls (blue arrows) is constant. Where blood pressure (red arrows) is higher than osmotic pressure, more fluid leaves the capillaries. Where blood pressure is lower than osmotic pressure, more fluid re-enters the capillaries.

## 17–12

## The Transport System Helps to Maintain a Stable Internal Environment

Most organisms live in an external environment that is constantly changing. Yet the internal environment of living things, the fluids that are transported to the body cells and tissues, must be kept rather constant, with balanced amounts of oxygen and food molecules. Waste materials must be continuously removed from the cells.

The balance maintained in the internal environment by various body processes is called **homeostasis** (HOH-mee-oh-STAY-sis). Claude Bernard (bair-NAHRD), a great French scientist of the 19th century, pointed out the importance of an organism's ability to maintain a constant internal environment.

Bernard emphasized the importance of the transport system in the maintenance of homeostasis. For instance, people may change their diets greatly at different times of the day. One meal may include a large amount of sugar, with very little in the next meal. Yet the amount of sugar in the blood is almost the same throughout the day. During heavy exercise large amounts of oxygen molecules are needed by the muscles, and they release much carbon dioxide. But oxygen and carbon dioxide levels of the blood do not vary greatly. The temperature outside a person's body may change greatly in a very short time, but the temperature of the body's blood remains remarkably constant, about 37° C (98.6° F).

In order to maintain the internal fluid environment at constant levels, many control mechanisms have evolved. These controls must be able to detect changes in the external environment. They must also be able to make necessary adjustments to keep the internal fluid environment constant. The nervous system and the endocrine system are the two systems most directly responsible for this control. You will learn about many of these regulatory activities in coming chapters.

---

**CAPSULE SUMMARY**

Blood is the fluid in the transport vessels of animals. Essential substances are carried by the blood to cells of the body, and waste products are carried away. The internal environment that surrounds and bathes cells is the fluid that diffuses from the capillaries into the tissue spaces. Movement of this fluid through the capillary walls is caused by a combination of blood pressure and osmotic pressure. Most of the fluid between cells is returned to the blood through the capillary walls, but some of it is returned through the lymphatic system. The regulation of the internal environment is carried on by body processes which maintain the blood in a balanced condition. The maintenance of the balance of the internal environment is called homeostasis.

**SELF CHECK**

1. What is the function of the red cells of the blood?
2. According to Starling's hypothesis, in which direction would more fluid move between the venous end of a capillary and the adjacent body tissue spaces?
3. In very cold weather, capillaries of the skin constrict, so that less blood flows to the exposed surface of the body. Relate this occurrence to homeostasis.

---

# CHAPTER SUMMARY

## HIGHLIGHTS

The major function of transport systems is to carry essential substances from one place in the organism to another. The cells of smaller organisms are in close contact with the external environment. Therefore, the essential substances can diffuse in and out of the body surface and reach each cell.

Larger organisms consist of large numbers of cells, most of which are isolated from the external environment. A special transport system is necessary to carry nutrients, wastes, water, and gases to and from the cells and the external environment.

In higher plants, materials move through the xylem tracheids and vessels and phloem sieve tubes by means of complex mechanisms. In large complex animals a muscular pump, the heart, moves the blood from place to place in a system of vessels. Specialized cells are carried in the fluid part of the blood of higher animals. The blood acts as a common carrier of materials between different parts of the body.

The constancy of the internal environment is called homeostasis. The maintenance of homeostasis depends on many systems of the body. The transport system is the connecting link.

## REVIEWING IDEAS

1. Why is a specialized transport system more necessary to a large organism than a small one?
2. Compare and contrast the transport system of a grasshopper and an earthworm.
3. What is the function of the valves in the veins of humans?
4. How do cells of the xylem differ from cells of the phloem?
5. Through what vessels does blood pass from arteries to veins?
6. Describe how guard cells operate to open and close the stomata.
7. Give two reasons why botanists believe land plants arose from protists similar to today's green algae.
8. What explanation best accounts for water transport in plants?
9. What is the chief function of red blood cells?
10. In what part of the blood is food carried to the body cells?

## USING CONCEPTS

11. How do land plants prevent dehydration?
12. Relate the structure of a capillary to its function.

13. Describe how both osmotic pressure and blood pressure are thought to operate in Starling's hypothesis.
14. What is the role of blood cells in fighting infections?
15. Explain how the structure of a leaf is related to the process of photosynthesis.
16. How does the circulatory system maintain homeostasis in humans?
17. Trace a drop of blood from the left ventricle to your thumb and back to the left ventricle. Through what types of vessels and what chambers of the heart does it pass en route?
18. Explain the hypothesis that best accounts for the transportation of food in the phloem.
19. Where do root cells obtain the energy necessary to transport water and minerals?
20. What would happen if the lymphatic system were blocked and its fluid did not return to the bloodstream?

## RECOMMENDED READING

Doolittle, R. F. "Fibrinogen and Fibrin." *Scientific American,* December, 1981. How blood clots are formed and broken down.

Jones, C. *The Circulatory System of Insects.* New York, C. C. Thomas, 1977. Typical arthropod circulatory structure and function.

Moorby, J. *Transport Systems in Plants.* New York, Longman, Inc., 1981. A comparative view of transport in plants.

Rose, N. R. "Autoimmune Diseases." *Scientific American,* February, 1981. Lymphocytes and their role in the immune defense system.

Zucker, M. B. "The Functioning of Blood Platelets." *Scientific American,* June, 1980. The role of platelets in the blood in health and disease.

# Respiratory
# Systems
# 18

The breath of life. We all know that breathing air is absolutely necessary if we are to continue living. Yet breathing is only the beginning of a long series of events that carry oxygen from the air to all the cells of our bodies. Many organisms do not breathe as we do, but they have some mechanism for exchanging respiratory gases with their environment. In this chapter you will compare the evolution, structure, and function of some of these systems of gas exchange in different animals.

# The Exchange of Gases in Multicellular Organisms

## 18–1

## Respiration Is Life with Oxygen

Nearly all cells use oxygen to release energy from organic molecules. Carbon dioxide is the by-product of this release of energy. The whole process of oxygen use, energy release, and carbon dioxide production by the cells is called **cell respiration.** You first studied cell respiration—and compared it to fermentation—in Chapter 8. In order for cell respiration to proceed, oxygen must be continuously supplied to the cells. Carbon dioxide must also be removed. The necessary oxygen is present in the environment surrounding the organism. Oxygen is taken in through the surface of the body, or openings in it, and then transported to the cells. Excess carbon dioxide also leaves the body through its surface or through surface openings. This process of taking in oxygen and releasing carbon dioxide is called **general respiration.** In higher land organisms air is moved in and out of the body by breathing.

Organisms have varying requirements for oxygen. In Chapter 6 you learned how primitive organisms, and many modern ones, release energy

through fermentation, a process that requires no oxygen. However, most organisms require large amounts of oxygen to live and function successfully. (See **Appendix 18–A,** Understanding of Respiration Developed Slowly, page 722.)

**Try Investigation 18–A** Comparing Oxygen Consumption in Small Vertebrates, page 655.

## 18–2

## The Amount of Respiratory Surface Varies in Animals

Respiration takes place in the cells, and the necessary materials must be transported there. Several kinds of respiratory organs have evolved in animals. They all function to exchange gas molecules between the surface of the body and the internal fluids of the transport system. The gases are then transported to and from the cells and tissues where cell respiration occurs.

Almost all cells, whether individual (free-living) microorganisms or part of the tissues of an animal or plant, obtain oxygen and give off carbon dioxide by gaseous diffusion through the plasma membrane. Even the largest multicellular plants

---

← Sunning, swimming, and—most importantly—breathing. River otters are lung-breathers.

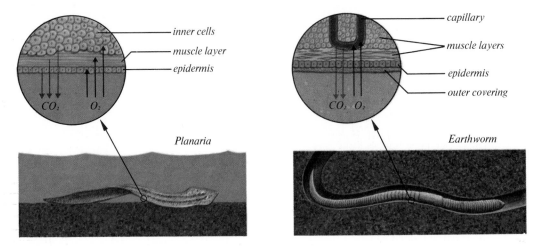

**Figure 18–1** Planarians and earthworms have no special respiratory organs. Gases are exchanged directly between these organisms and the environment through the skin.

exchange oxygen and carbon dioxide with the environment by diffusion.

Smaller multicellular animals, such as planarians (flatworms), obtain oxygen and give off carbon dioxide directly through the surfaces of their flat bodies (Figure 18–1). These animals do not need a specialized respiratory system because all their cells are fairly near the external environment.

The earthworm also obtains oxygen and gives off carbon dioxide by diffusion through the skin (Figure 18–1). The outer surface of the earthworm is covered with a film of a moist, mucuslike material. Gas molecules dissolve in this moist material and diffuse through it. Notice that the earthworm has a transport system, consisting of capillaries and larger vessels. The blood supplies the body with oxygen that diffuses through the skin.

Larger and more complex animals need specialized surfaces for the exchange of gases. Different kinds of respiratory surfaces have developed in organisms that live in different habitats. In general, these surfaces are made up of folds or pockets of tissue that greatly increase the surface area and therefore the amount of diffusion of gases.

The respiratory organs found in many animals that live in water are called **gills.** Gills provide these water dwellers with a large respiratory surface. Since there is no problem of drying out, gills are usually folds of tissue on the outer surface of the animal. Some aquatic worms, crustaceans, and mollusks breathe through gills. A gill of a fish, as shown in Figure 18–2, is made up of many fine threadlike filaments. Each filament consists of a thin layer of cells surrounding a network of capillaries. Oxygen and carbon dioxide are exchanged between the blood circulating through these capillaries and the water surrounding the filaments. Water contains dissolved oxygen, but only in small amounts. To supply enough oxygen to the blood, water must constantly pass over the gill surfaces. The water is taken in through the mouth of a fish, forced over the gills, and passed out of the body through an opening in the cavity that surrounds the delicate gill filaments.

The respiratory organs found in many animals that live on land, and some that live in water, are called **lungs.** Lungs are internal sacs used for taking oxygen from the air.

Some fishes have lunglike swim bladders. The fish can survive periods of drought by using these swim bladders for exchange of gases in respiration. The rest of the vertebrates—amphibians, reptiles, birds, and mammals—have complex lungs and associated breathing structures.

Although land-dwelling vertebrates do not use gills for breathing, some of their water-dwelling ancestors did. Structures that are part of lung-breathing systems seem to have been modified from structures used for gill breathing. For example, the artery that goes to the lungs of higher land-dwelling vertebrates seems to have been modified from a pair of arteries that carried blood to a pair of gills in water-dwelling vertebrates.

## 18–3

## Specialized Structures Are Used for Breathing Air

At most, water can hold only about 0.5 percent of oxygen by volume. In atmospheric air, 20 percent of the total volume is oxygen. Thus, the air passing across the respiratory surfaces of a land-dwelling animal is far richer in oxygen than the water passing over the gills of a water animal. It is not surprising, then, that warm-blooded animals with a high rate of metabolism and a great need for oxygen have evolved only from air-breathers. (See **Appendix 18–B,** Oxygen Consumption Is Related to Temperature Regulation in Animals, page 722.)

The greatest disadvantage of air-breathing is the danger of the respiratory gas-exchange structures' drying out. Just as the multicellular land plants developed a waxy cuticle that protects them from drying out, land animals have various waterproof coverings. For example, you may have handled a frog and noticed that the skin has a somewhat

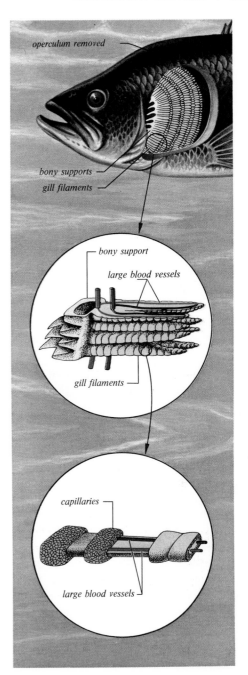

**Figure 18–2** In fishes, gills are thin filaments supported by bony structures and richly supplied with blood vessels. Each filament is made of delicate plates containing many capillaries. A covering over the gills called the operculum protects the delicate filaments.

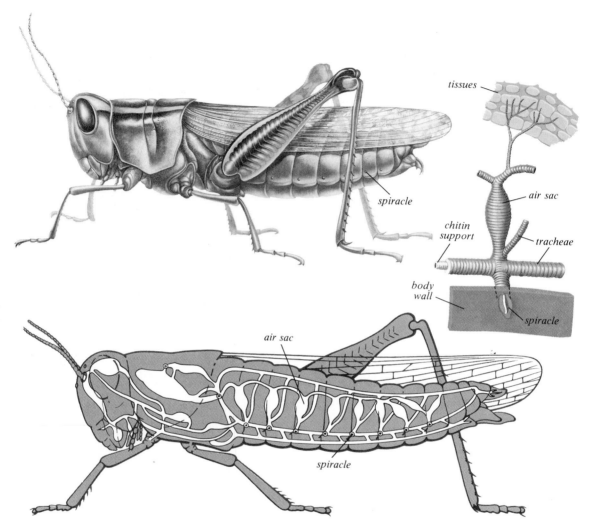

**Figure 18–3** In insects, oxygen and carbon dioxide are exchanged through branching air tubes called tracheae.

slippery film covering it. This film is made of a mucuslike substance that prevents water from evaporating. The same kind of film covers smaller land-dwelling animals, such as earthworms and snails, that live in moist habitats.

In some air-breathing spiders and scorpions, structures for the exchange of oxygen and carbon dioxide are found to be very much like gills of fish. However, these structures are well protected from the drying effect of air by membranes that cover them.

Land-dwelling insects have developed a system of air tubes called **tracheae** (TRAY-kee-ee). Air enters the insect through openings, called **spiracles** (SPY-rih-kuhls), along the side of the body and passes into air-filled cavities or sacs. From these sacs, the tracheae branch into smaller and smaller tubes, as shown in Figure 18–3. The smallest tubes are in direct contact with muscle and other body cells. Thus the body cells can easily receive oxygen and give off carbon dioxide by diffusion, both through their membranes and through the walls of the air tubes. The tracheae are held rigid by an inner lining of **chitin** (KY-tin). Chitin is a hard substance that also makes up the hard outer skeleton covering the insects. Movements of the insect's body can inflate and deflate the air sacs, but the flow of air within the tracheal tubes is under relatively little pressure.

There is no connection between the insect's tracheal system and its circulation. How do you think this fact relates to the "open" type of circulatory system described in Section 17–7?

Among mammals, including humans, the breathing movements are produced by the actions of two groups of muscles, the **diaphragm** (DY-uh-fram—see Figure 18–4) and the rib muscles. These muscles act together to change the size of the chest cavity. (See **Appendix 18–C,** The Mechanics of Lung Breathing, page 724.)

**Figure 18–4** The human respiratory system. Two enlargements show clusters of alveoli and their blood supply. Figure 18–5 shows the appearance of alveolar walls and blood capillaries under the microscope.

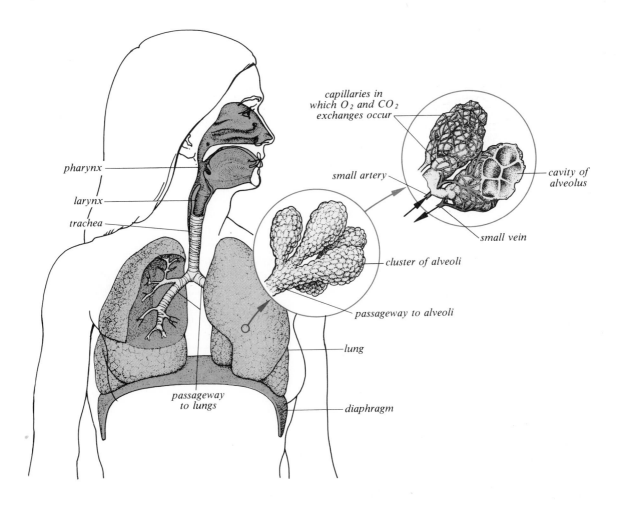

# Warning: Breathing May Be Hazardous to Your Health!

Smog in cities is unpleasant and irritating. It spreads to cover much of the surrounding countryside. Under certain weather conditions, called inversions, a blanket of still, warm air will form over cooler air close to the ground. The cooler, more dense air acts like a blanket and traps air pollutants that normally would be carried away. When such conditions persist for more than a few days, dangerous and even deadly concentrations of pollutants may build up. Some people become ill. The death rate rises above its normal level.

What is the source of the pollutants? The burning of sulfur-containing fuels in heating and electrical generating plants is one source. It produces sulfur dioxide, which is extremely irritating to breathe. Mixed with rain, the sulfur dioxide forms an acid that is damaging to plant life.

Automobile exhaust is the main source of air pollutants. One of these pollutants is carbon monoxide. Breathing exhaust fumes containing carbon monoxide is very dangerous, because the carbon monoxide combines with hemoglobin in the red blood cells. The hemoglobin then cannot carry oxygen. Automobile exhaust gases mixed with air are also acted on by sunlight, causing reactions that create an ozone layer close to the ground. Ozone is another molecular form of oxygen, $O_3$, not the $O_2$ you normally breathe. Ozone is another irritant.

Changes in the size of the chest cavity affect the gas pressure in the lungs. When the chest cavity expands, the pressure within the chest falls. Because of this reduced air pressure, air is forced in from the outside, where it is under greater atmospheric pressure. When the volume of the chest cavity is reduced, the internal pressure becomes greater than atmospheric pressure and gas is forced out. The rhythmic increase and decrease in the chest cavity's volume is the mechanical pump which drives air in and out of the lungs.

Atmospheric air is dry, sometimes cold, and

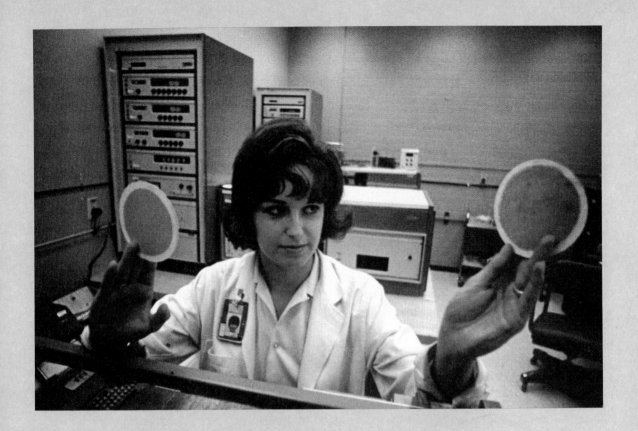

Soot and ashes from the incomplete burning of fuels add the dirty particles seen in polluted air. The pollution technician pictured above is holding up two white filters clogged with pollutant particles. Monitoring of air pollution by city, state, and federal agencies does not present a hopeful picture for cleaner air. Yet this monitoring is very important. It provides the data necessary to convince governments at each level that transportation and fuel-based industries in our society need to be reexamined.

What can you do about all this? Join car pools. Ride your bicycle (but safely). Support well-developed laws designed for effective use of fuels, and promote use of more fuel-efficient vehicles, heating processes, and industrial plants.

often dirty. The air you breathe passes through your nose and down the trachea, or windpipe. The air is moistened, warmed, and cleaned by cells lining the air passageways. These passageways enter the lungs and end in the **alveoli** (al-VEE-uh-ly). The alveoli are cavities formed by folded sheets of cells. Each lung has millions of these cavities, with their walls richly supplied with capillaries. The human respiratory system and details of the alveoli are illustrated in Figure 18–4. The photomicrograph in Figure 18–5 shows the closely associated, often fused, alveolar walls and blood

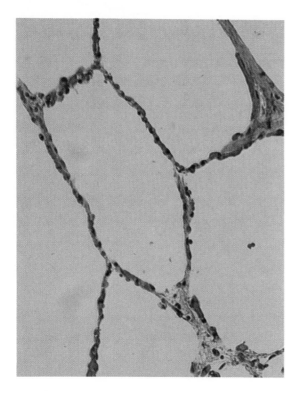

**Figure 18-5** Alveolar walls and blood capillaries in the human lung. Note the large air spaces inside the alveoli. The alveoli are in such close association with capillaries that the walls of the two sometimes merge. The round darker and lighter objects are red blood cells.

capillaries. It is in the alveolar walls that oxygen diffuses into the bloodstream. The lung can exchange a large volume of gases in a very short time because the numerous alveoli of the lung provide an enormous amount of surface area. If the surface of the human alveoli were spread out flat, it would cover an area of about 60 square meters (about the size of 2 large parking spaces).

## 18-4

## Some Animals Use More Than One Respiratory System

Many animals use more than one respiratory system for exchange of oxygen and carbon dioxide.

Even though frogs have well-developed lungs, they can take in oxygen and pass out carbon dioxide through their moist skins. This skin breathing is similar to the diffusion of molecules in and out of the body surface of the earthworm, which was described earlier.

Some animals use different respiratory systems at different times in their life. The frog, for example, changes from gill breathing to lung breathing during its transition from tadpole to adult frog. You may have watched the development of the frog as an optional investigation after doing Investigation 11-C. At one stage gills are very evident. Respiration in the gills of a tadpole is essentially the same as in the gills of a fish. When the water-dwelling tadpole begins to change to the land-dwelling frog, the gills disappear and lungs develop. Because of this change from water- to land-dwelling in its development, the frog is classified in the group called Amphibia, meaning "double life." Some other amphibians are toads and salamanders.

The embryos of reptiles, birds, and mammals also have respiratory structures that differ from the lungs of the adults. You read about the embryonic membranes of the chick. Remember that the chorion and the allantois together serve as the respiratory surface for the developing chick. These membranes are pressed close to the shell, where oxygen and carbon dioxide diffuse easily between the shell and the membranes. The many capillaries in the membranes bring oxygen to and remove carbon dioxide from the body tissues of the developing chick. In most mammals, the placenta serves as a respiratory surface. It supplies the embryo with oxygen by bringing the oxygen-containing blood from the mother's circulation into close contact with the blood of the developing embryo. Diffusion of oxygen then occurs. As soon as a chick hatches or a mammal is born, however, its own lungs begin bringing in oxygen from the environment and giving off carbon dioxide.

**CAPSULE SUMMARY**

Nearly every animal and plant needs oxygen to live. Cells obtain oxygen and give off carbon dioxide by diffusion. Diffusion of gases at the surface of the organism also provides plants with oxygen and carbon dioxide. Many small animals are provided with oxygen in the same way. Large animals have developed specialized respiratory surfaces. Gills, tracheae, and lungs have developed in many of these animals for respiration. Breathing air presents special problems that have been solved in different ways. The embryos of some animals may respire by means of different structures from those used by the adult. Movements of the chest force air into and out of the lungs, in mammals. The alveoli of the lungs provide a great increase in the respiratory surface of higher animals. Thus, the capacity for absorbing oxygen is greatly increased in larger animals.

**SELF CHECK**

1. What is the main difference in the ways oxygen and carbon dioxide enter and leave the cells in the flatworm and the earthworm?
2. Name two ways in which the respiratory surfaces of air-breathing animals are protected.
3. Describe the differences between the respiratory structures of land and water animals.
4. What kind of respiratory structures do whales, porpoises, and seals have?
5. What kind of respiratory structures do amphibians have?

# Transport of Oxygen and Carbon Dioxide

## 18–5

## What Causes the Blood to Take Up and Release Oxygen?

Blood has a great capacity to carry both oxygen and carbon dioxide. Yet oxygen is not very soluble in water (or plasma) under normal atmospheric conditions. One hundred milliliters of water will hold only about 0.5 milliliters of oxygen in solution. Under the same conditions, however, 100 milliliters of blood can hold about 20 milliliters of oxygen. You have learned that blood consists of cells suspended in a watery plasma. If you measured the dissolved oxygen in just the plasma part of the blood you would find only about 0.3 milliliters of oxygen in 100 milliliters of fluid. Therefore, practically all of the oxygen in the blood must be carried by the cells. How do the cells carry oxygen?

Richard Lower observed in the 1660s that blood changed color when exposed to air. He wrote:

> . . . it is evident that this red colour is entirely due to the particles of the air which enter the blood, since it only becomes red in the lungs because of the direct and intimate intermingling which takes place between its corpuscles with the particles of the air. In the same way the surface of venous blood which is put onto a plate only takes a red colour because it is exposed to the air. This is further proved by the certainty that if this surface were skimmed with a knife, that which is immediately underneath would be changed in a short time to the same colour by a similar contact with the air.[1]

Why does air change the color of blood? Red blood cells contain large quantities of a red-colored protein called hemoglobin. Hemoglobin is one of a group of substances known as transport pig-

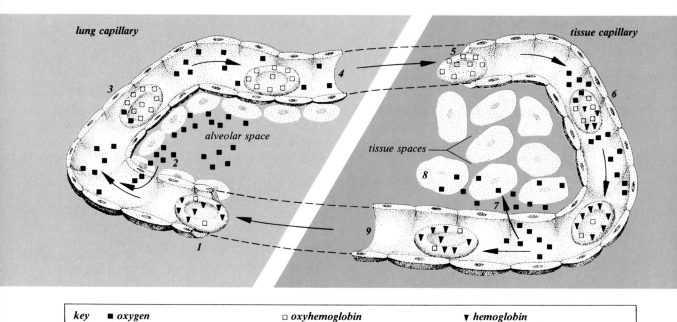

| key ■ oxygen | □ oxyhemoglobin | ▼ hemoglobin |

1. *Blood cell enters lung capillary.*

2. *Oxygen from alveolar space enters lung capillary plasma.*

3. *Oxygen enters blood cells from plasma; combines with hemoglobin to form oxyhemoglobin.*

4. *Blood cells carry oxyhemoglobin out of the lungs to the body tissues.*

5. *Oxygen-laden cells enter tissue capillary.*

6. *Oxyhemoglobin breaks down, releasing oxygen into the plasma.*

7. *Oxygen leaves plasma and enters tissue space.*

8. *Oxygen enters tissue cells from tissue space.*

9. *Blood cell moves through the tissue capillary and through the circulatory system to return to the lungs.*

**Figure 18–6** The steps in the transfer of oxygen from the lungs to other body tissues by way of the bloodstream.

ments. Transport pigments are complex organic molecules that each contain one atom of a metal. The metal atom in the hemoglobin molecule is iron. The transport pigment in the blood of some animals contains an atom of copper. (See Appendix 17–H, Oxygen-Transport Pigments in Animals, page 721.)

Transport pigments increase the oxygen-carrying capacity of blood in both invertebrate and vertebrate animals. In vertebrates the hemoglobin is always carried in cells, but in invertebrates it is dissolved in the fluid portion of the blood. This difference is important because the red cells can hold much more hemoglobin than the fluid part of the blood. For example, if all the hemoglobin in human blood were dissolved instead of being held in red cells, the total protein concentration of the blood would be about 20 percent. The rate of flow would be that of syrup and would require the heart to do a tremendous amount of work to pump the blood. Cells as particles in a thinner blood fluid can be moved more efficiently. With the hemoglobin in red cells a very large amount of oxygen can be carried in a unit of blood. In part, this makes it possible for vertebrates to have a higher rate of metabolism than some invertebrates.

How does hemoglobin release oxygen to the tissues? You will recall from Section 6–9 that water molecules diffuse from a region of higher concentration to a region of lower concentration. Oxygen molecules also diffuse from higher to lower concentrations. The air coming from the outside into the alveolar spaces of the lung has a high concentration of oxygen. The blood coming from the body through the capillaries of the alveoli has a low concentration of oxygen. Thus, oxygen will diffuse from the alveoli into the blood. The iron atoms in the hemoglobin molecules of the red cells combine with the oxygen. The hemoglobin then becomes bright red and is called **oxyhemoglobin** (ok-see-HEE-muh-glo-bin). Oxyhemoglobin is transported in the red cells to the tissues. The concentration of oxygen in the intercellular spaces is low. Oxygen can be easily released from the weak chemical combination with hemoglobin. Oxygen will therefore leave the red cells and diffuse into the tissues. The hemoglobin becomes darker red in color when this happens.

The ease with which oxygen passes into and out of red cells makes the oxygen-exchange system in the body quick and efficient. Figure 18–6 summarizes the reactions of hemoglobin and oxygen in the lungs and in body tissues.

## 18–6

## Carbon Dioxide Is Also Carried by the Blood

Blood coming from the tissues to the lungs contains more carbon dioxide than does the air in the alveolar spaces. Carbon dioxide diffuses from the capillaries (higher concentration) to the alveolar spaces (lower concentration). Figure 18–7 illustrates the diffusion of carbon dioxide from the tissue spaces into the capillaries, and then into the air spaces of the lungs. Only a small amount of carbon dioxide dissolves in the water of the plasma. Most of the carbon dioxide enters the red blood cells where it reacts with water to form carbonic acid ($H_2CO_3$). You may know this acid because it is the source of the gas that bubbles from many soft drinks. The production of carbonic acid and the formation of the bicarbonate ion are reversible reactions.

$$CO_2 + H_2O \rightleftharpoons H_2CO_3 \rightleftharpoons H^+ + HCO_3^-$$

carbon water carbonic hydrogen bicarbonate
dioxide  acid  ion  ion

Almost all the carbonic acid quickly breaks down to form hydrogen ions and bicarbonate ions. (See Figure 18–7.) This reaction takes place in the red cells. Most of the carbon dioxide in the blood, then, is carried as bicarbonate ion ($HCO_3^-$). (See **Appendix 18–D,** Carbon Dioxide Transport in the Red Blood Cells, page 724.)

Once bicarbonate is formed, it diffuses out of the red corpuscles into the plasma. It is carried to the lungs where, once again, the bicarbonate enters the red blood cells. Here the bicarbonate combines with hydrogen ions to form carbonic acid. The carbonic acid then breaks down into carbon dioxide and water. The carbon dioxide diffuses into the lung cavities and is exhaled to the external environment. Some of the water passes off in the form of water vapor. This mechanism again illustrates the complex, well-regulated functions of the body. (See **Appendix 18–E,** Carbon Dioxide and the Nervous System's Control of Breathing, page 724.)

**Try Investigation 18–B** Measuring Carbon Dioxide Concentration of Human Breath, page 657.

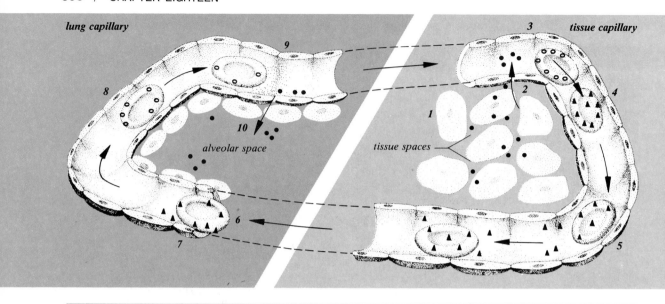

*lung capillary*

*tissue capillary*

*alveolar space*

*tissue spaces*

**Figure 18–7** The steps in the transfer of carbon dioxide from body tissues to the bloodstream and lungs. Red blood cells play a central role in both oxygen and carbon dioxide transport.

**key** ● *carbon dioxide* ○ *carbonic acid* ▲ *hydrogen + bicarbonate ions*

1. Carbon dioxide leaves cells and enters tissue spaces.

2. Carbon dioxide enters capillaries.

3. Carbon dioxide reacts with water in the red blood cells to form carbonic acid.

4. Carbonic acid splits into hydrogen ions and bicarbonate ions.

5. Bicarbonate ions leave red blood cells and enter plasma.

6. Blood travels to lungs through transport system and enters lung capillary.

7. Bicarbonate ions leave plasma and enter red blood cells.

8. Bicarbonate ions combine with hydrogen ions to form carbonic acid.

9. Carbonic acid breaks down to water and carbon dioxide. Carbon dioxide enters the plasma.

10. Carbon dioxide leaves lung capillary and enters alveolar space.

**CAPSULE SUMMARY**

Hemoglobin in the red blood cells of vertebrates is a transport pigment. In the lungs, it binds to oxygen and in the capillaries of the tissues, it releases oxygen. Carbon dioxide is transported in the blood in the form of the bicarbonate ion. Oxygen and carbon dioxide diffuse from regions of higher concentrations of gas to regions of lower concentrations. In the body tissues oxygen moves from the capillaries into the intercellular spaces. In the lungs, oxygen moves from the alveoli to the capillaries. The movement of carbon dioxide is just the opposite.

**SELF CHECK**

1. Describe how oxygen is carried in your blood.
2. How is carbon dioxide carried in your blood?
3. Why was the evolution of specialized ways to transport oxygen and carbon dioxide of value?

# CHAPTER SUMMARY

## HIGHLIGHTS

Oxygen is required by most forms of life to release energy. This enzyme-controlled process in the cells is called cellular respiration. Respiratory systems make gas exchange possible between the body cells and the external environment. Gills, tracheae, and lungs have relatively large surface areas where oxygen and carbon dioxide are exchanged with the external environment. Several types of transport pigments have evolved. These pigments increase the blood's capacity to carry oxygen. Hemoglobin, one type of transport pigment, carries a large amount of oxygen and releases it readily to the cells. Respiratory and transport systems are the lifelines carrying oxygen and food to every cell of a large, complex organism.

## REVIEWING IDEAS

1. Why is oxygen required by most living organisms?
2. What is the process by which cells take in oxygen and give off carbon dioxide?
3. What are the common features of gills and lungs? How do they differ?
4. What role does the placenta play in respiration in mammals?
5. How is respiration affected by surface area?
6. Plants have no respiratory system. How do they respire?
7. What is the function of transport pigments such as hemoglobin?
8. In what form is most of the carbon dioxide carried in the blood?
9. What is the function of the diaphragm in breathing? What other muscles play an important role in breathing movements?
10. What is the function of a respiratory organ?

## USING CONCEPTS

11. Compare and contrast cell respiration, general respiration, and breathing.
12. What is the evolutionary relationship between gills and lungs?
13. What effects can pollution have on respiration?
14. Trace the path of a molecule of oxygen from the air to a human red blood cell.
15. What would happen if your hemoglobin were not in your red blood cells but in the fluid part of your blood?
16. How does the transport system relate to the respiratory system in humans?
17. What roles do carbon dioxide, carbonic acid, and the bicarbonate ion play in respiration?
18. How is the danger of drying of the respiratory surfaces reduced in land organisms?
19. How does the respiratory system of insects differ from that of mammals?
20. What structures besides lungs are used by vertebrates for respiration?

## RECOMMENDED READING

Dickerson, R. E. "Cytochrome C and the Evolution of Energy Metabolism." *Scientific American,* March, 1980. The evolution of chemical respiratory mechanisms from bacterial ancestry.

Mill, J. P. *Respiration in Invertebrates.* New York, St. Martins Press, 1973. Pigments, structures, and mechanisms of invertebrate respiration.

Randall, D. J. et al. *The Evolution of Air Breathing in Vertebrates.* New York, Cambridge University Press, 1981. Variation in respiratory systems of terrestrial vertebrates.

## REFERENCE

1. M. L. Gabriel and S. Fogel, eds. *Great Experiments in Biology.* Englewood Cliffs, New Jersey, Prentice-Hall, 1955, pp. 88 and 93.

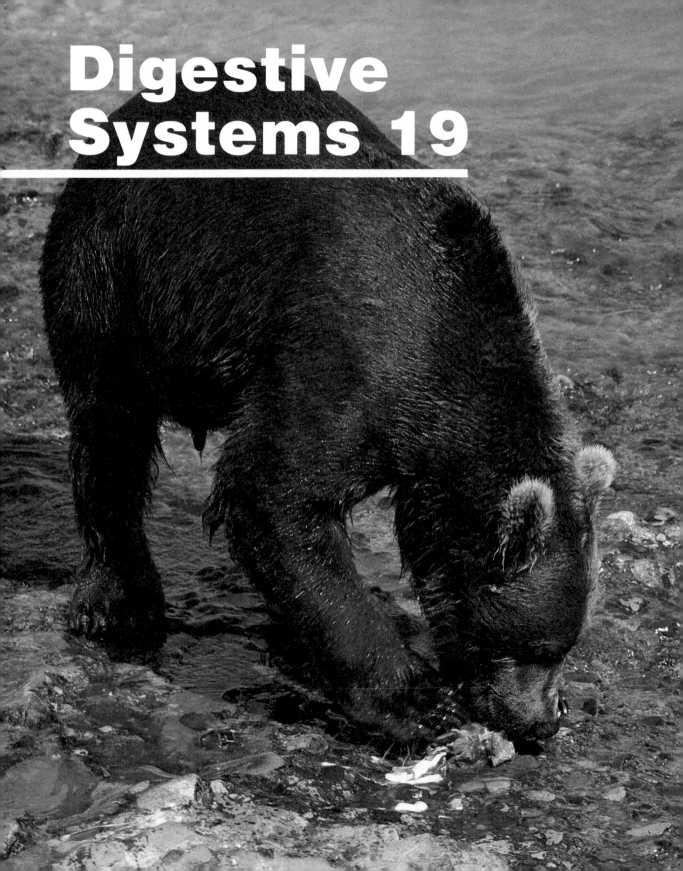

# Digestive
# Systems 19

According to the heterotroph hypothesis, the most primitive cells were not able to make their own food. They supplied their needs with small organic molecules from the environment. Among these molecules were sugars, amino acids, and other simpler compounds used for energy and as building materials. Like certain sugars you eat today, most of these molecules required no digestion.

Once organisms had built more complex molecules from these simpler ones, the situation changed. The naturally occurring nutrients were no longer as plentiful. In their place were the larger molecules built up by different organisms. These larger molecules no longer fit every organism's needs. Instead they fit only the structure and functioning of the kind of organism that had built them. Digestion and photosynthesis renewed the food supply. Digestion made possible breaking down the larger molecules and recycling their nutrients. Photosynthesis made the sun's light a continuing source of food energy.

# Patterns of Digestion

## 19–1

### Digestion Is a Chemical Process

The simpler molecules used by almost all organisms for energy and building materials are commonly called **nutrients.** Simple sugars, vitamins. and amino acids are examples. In addition, even simpler molecules such as the minerals plants take in and use in foodmaking are often called nutrients. So are the minerals in animal diets.

Nutrients may be interchangeable from one organism to another, but the larger compounds, and the cells and tissues of which different organisms are made, are not interchangeable. This is true even though many of them may contain the same nutrients. **Digestion** is the chemical process of breaking down these larger parts of organisms for the nutrients they contain.

**Foods** are compounds or tissues that can be digested. An organism is food for another organism if the second has the enzymes necessary to digest parts of the first. Wood, grass, and other plant parts whose food energy is stored in cellulose are not useful foods for you because human beings do not have enzymes that digest cellulose. You eat plant parts that are rich in proteins, sugars, starch, vitamins, and minerals. The materials that can be used as foods are always determined by an organism's digestive enzymes.

Digestion involves the chemical process of **hydrolysis** (hy-DROL-uh-sis), splitting a food molecule by adding water. During hydrolysis, large food molecules are split into smaller molecules. Most of the food of an organism consists of carbohydrates, fats, and proteins. Each of these large

---

← Salmon for lunch for a large Alaskan heterotroph, a brown bear.

**Figure 19–1** A Venus flytrap in action. As soon as an insect lands on a leaf, the spiked blades start to close. Once trapped, the insect (in this case, an ant) is digested by plant enzymes secreted into special leaf cavities. But why a carnivorous plant at all? Biologists hypothesize that such plants could have evolved in nitrogen-deficient soils. Carnivorous plants obtain some of their nitrogen compounds from their insect prey.

different molecules is acted upon by special kinds of digestive enzymes that speed up hydrolysis.

Some of the smaller molecules produced by the digestion of food may not be needed immediately by the cells of the organism. These molecules are stored in the tissues for future use. In animals, stored food is built into larger molecules as fat or as a carbohydrate called glycogen. Plants usually store reserve food in the form of starch, another kind of large carbohydrate molecule. Starch is usually found in roots, seeds, or fruits. Some plants, such as peanuts, coconuts, and castor beans, store fat molecules in their seeds. The reserve food supply, however, must be digested again, or broken down into a simpler substance once more, in order to be used by the cells.

**Try Investigation 19–A** Starch Digestion, page 660.

## 19–2

## Digestion May Take Place Outside or Inside of Cells

Plants do not usually have specialized digestive organs. Certain plants, however, have the ability to capture insects and digest them in special cavities in the leaves. Figure 19–1 shows a Venus flytrap plant capturing an insect. After the insect is trapped, the plant cells secrete enzymes into special leaf cavities to digest it. This process is called **extracellular digestion** because it takes place outside the cells.

Most plant digestion takes place inside the cells. The foods digested are those the plant has made itself. This is **intracellular digestion.** The exceptions, as with the Venus flytrap, may involve a way to obtain nitrogen in foods (such as insects) when the plant has evolved in soils that are nitrogen-poor.

Many heterotrophs produce enzymes that digest food outside of the cells. The bread mold and its relatives digest materials from dead plants and animals. Bread molds secrete enzymes that diffuse out of the cells to digest foods. The molds then absorb the products of digestion into their cells. Figure 19–2 shows how bread is digested by a mold. You may also have seen rotting wood covered with molds. These molds obtain their food from the wood and in the process help to decay organic material. Soil is enriched by the digestive action of such molds. Other molds cause fruits and vegetables to decay and spoil.

The external environment contains different substances necessary for cell life. The substances outside the cell may be in the form of small molecules, large molecules, or larger groups of many molecules. How does the cell, either as a separate organism or as one unit in a multicellular form, take in and use materials of different sizes?

Small molecules in the surrounding environment can enter the cell by diffusion. For example, amino acids, sugars, minerals, water, and oxygen can diffuse into the cell. However, large molecules cannot enter the cell by diffusion. How do large molecules get into cells?

Sometimes the surface of a cell folds inward to form a small pocket. Some of the fluid surrounding the cell will flow into the pocket. The fluid may hold large molecules in solution. The edges of the pocket then close to form a fluid-filled bubble inside the cell (Figure 19–3). The fluid containing the large molecules is now within the cell as part of the cytoplasm, but is isolated in a spherical membrane. The membrane and its contents are now called a **vacuole** (VAK-yuh-wohl). Many kinds of cells, including some in the stomach and small intestine of humans, are able to take in large molecules by this process, called **pinocytosis** (pin-oh-sy-TOH-sis).

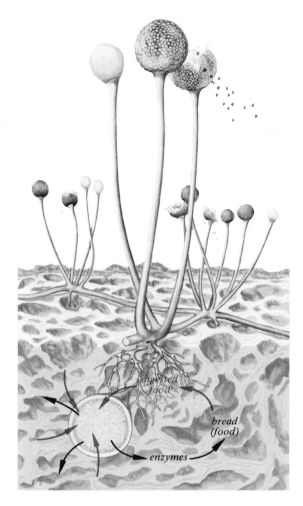

**Figure 19–2** (Right) Enzymes from bread mold diffuse into the bread, digesting complex carbohydrates to their component sugars. The sugars are then absorbed by the mold.

**Figure 19–3** (Below) Pinocytosis. How many infoldings or "pockets" can you count in this electron micrograph of a capillary cell? What functions of blood capillaries account for such heavy traffic in materials passing through?

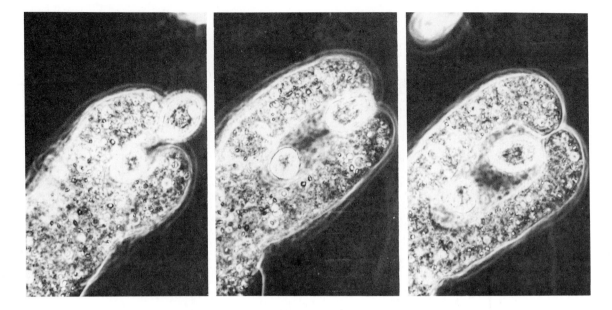

**Figure 19–4** Phagocytosis. The protist *Amoeba* contacts food (left), surrounds it (center), and forms a food vacuole (right).

Some cells can take in solid pieces of food as well as fluid simply by surrounding the particles with extensions of the cell body. This process is called **phagocytosis** (fayg-oh-sy-TOH-sis). You may have observed an *Amoeba* in the laboratory "eating" food this way. Figure 19–4 shows an *Amoeba* taking in food and surrounding it with a membrane. In the human bloodstream white blood cells may surround and consume bacteria in much the same way as the *Amoeba* engulfs and digests food. (See Section 17–10.)

Protists like *Paramecium* have permanent structures for taking in food. Figure 17–9 shows the formation of food vacuoles in *Paramecium*. The cells lining the internal cavities of simpler multicellular animals such as sponges or *Hydra* also take in solid bits of food. Figure 19–5 (upper right) shows some cells of *Hydra*.

The large molecules and the solid particles taken in by cells are digested by enzymes. This is an example, in protists and animals, of intracellular digestion. Enzymes produced in the cell are secreted into the food vacuoles where digestion takes place. The smaller molecules produced by digestion then move across the membrane of the vacuole and into the cytoplasm of the cell.

Why don't cells digest themselves? The way digestive enzymes are secreted suggests an answer. Specialized parts of many cells secrete the enzymes into protective vacuoles called **lysosomes** (LY-soh-sohms). The lysosomes then merge with new food vacuoles. In still other cells the enzymes may be secreted directly into the food vacuoles. Biologists are still studying these processes, but it appears that cells have evolved ways to isolate their digestive enzymes from cell parts these enzymes might digest.

**Try Investigation 19–B** Do Plants Contain Enzymes That Digest Starch?, page 662.

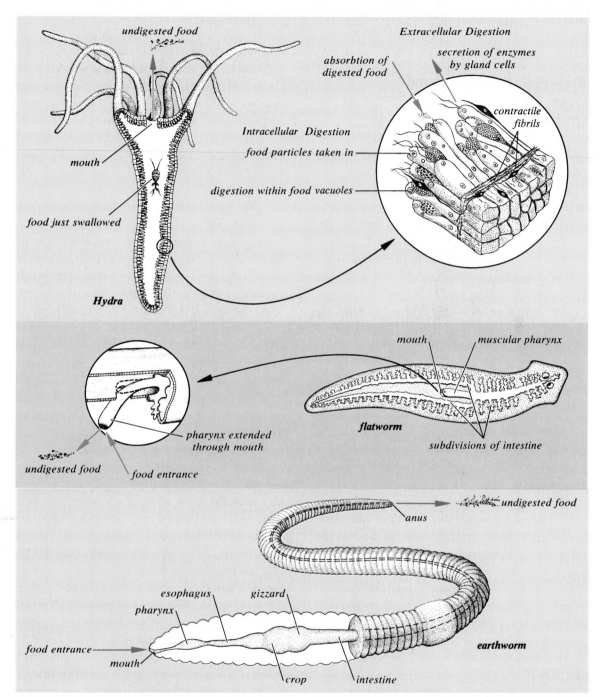

**Figure 19-5** Digestive systems of three increasingly complex animals: *Hydra*, flatworm, and earthworm. *Hydra*, the simplest of the organisms shown here, uses the same opening for both taking in food and eliminating wastes. Its intracellular and extracellular digestive processes are detailed in the insert. The flatworm's digestive cavity is more specialized than that of *Hydra*, but it too has only one opening. The earthworm's system is an example of the complete digestive tube with two openings—the mouth at one end, through which food is taken in, and the anus at the other end, through which wastes are eliminated. Digestion occurs extracellularly, within the tube.

## 19–3

## Multicellular Organisms Have Specialized Digestive Systems

In multicellular animals food is digested in specialized cavities or tubes. For example, special cells of the *Hydra* secrete enzymes into the central or digestive cavity, where they digest food. (See Figure 19–5.) The products of this extracellular digestion are absorbed by the body cells of the *Hydra*. As you learned in Section 19–2, some of the cells lining the central cavity in the *Hydra* can also take in undigested food and digest it within the cell.

The central cavity of the *Hydra* has only one opening. Materials that cannot be digested—for example, cellulose—pass out the same way that food enters.

The flatworm's digestive cavity is more complex than that of the *Hydra,* but it also has only one opening (Figure 19–5). A muscular organ in the flatworm called the **pharynx** (FAR-inks) takes in bits of solid food. The food is digested in a branched digestive cavity, then absorbed by the body cells.

Digestion in larger, more complex animals is carried on in digestive tubes that have two openings. Food enters the mouth at one end of the tube, and material that cannot be digested is passed out of the **anus** (AY-nus) at the other end of the tube. The earthworm's digestive system, shown in Figure 19–5, is an example of a digestive tube with two openings. The movement of food and undigested wastes becomes one-way traffic in complex animals with an opening at each end of the digestive tube.

The digestive tube of most complex animals also is divided into different regions with specialized functions. The specialization may depend on the diet of the animal. For instance, snails and

their relatives have rasping, filelike structures near the front of the digestive tube that tear food into pieces. Many of the higher vertebrates have jaws and teeth to chew their food. What effect does tearing pieces of food into smaller pieces have on the rate of digestion? Think of the greater surface area exposed to digestive enzymes by many smaller particles of food as opposed to one or two larger pieces.

In the earthworm, as in the flatworm, the pharynx is a muscular organ that mixes the food with a moistening secretion and pushes it farther along the tube. As you can see in Figure 19–5, the earthworm's digestive tube has an enlargement called the **crop** where food is stored. Birds (Figure 19–6) also store food in a crop region. Food is moved from the crop into the **gizzard** in both earthworms and birds. The gizzard is a muscular organ which grinds food particles into smaller pieces. Birds swallow gravel or small stones that help in the grinding process. Earthworms take in sand and other rough particles along with their food, in the soil they eat.

In the earthworm, the intestine is a region where digestive enzymes are secreted by cells of the intestinal lining. This is true of larger, more complex animals, too. Many of the latter, however, also have specialized organs called digestive glands that secrete more digestive enzymes into the digestive tube. The crayfish has an organ that not only secretes digestive enzymes, but also stores digested nutrients. Spiders have a similar gland surrounding the intestine. In vertebrates, the pancreas performs this function of secreting enzymes, and the liver secretes chemicals which break fat globules into smaller particles. You may have heard of this secretion of the liver called **bile.**

The intestine is the major organ of absorption of small food molecules after digestion. The surface of the intestine is usually folded, sometimes in a very complex manner, increasing the surface area for absorption. In animals with a circulatory system, the intestine has many capillaries and lymph vessels where food molecules are picked up and transported to the cells of the body. (See **Appendix 19–A,** Other Organisms with Highly Specialized Digestive Systems, page 725.)

The stomach is an organ not found in the *Hydra* or in flatworms and earthworms. It is found in birds (Figure 19–6) and many other animals, especially other vertebrates. The stomach may secrete digestive enzymes and absorb nutrients, too. In cows it is a complex organ with several compartments and a related series of functions.

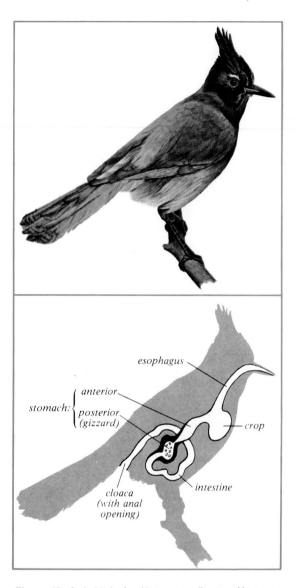

**Figure 19–6** In birds, food is temporarily stored in a crop. Farther along the digestive tract, a specialized part of the stomach—the gizzard—grinds up food to aid digestion. The walls of the gizzard are thick and muscular (see drawing). Within the gizzard is gravel, eaten by the bird. Can you complete a description of the grinding action?

---

**CAPSULE SUMMARY**

Animals obtain food in many ways according to their complexity and environment. Most plants make their own nutrients and foods. Digestion in different organisms may be extracellular or intracellular or both. Although differences exist, the final result of digestion is the same in all organisms: small essential molecules are made available for cellular use. The process of breaking down food into these essential molecules is called digestion. Food must be digested because cells cannot absorb or use large molecules made to fit the structure and functioning of some other organism.

Digestive systems are of many kinds. The more highly specialized ones are found in larger, more complex animals.

**SELF CHECK**

1. What is digestion?
2. Why is digestion necessary?
3. What substances carry on digestive processes?
4. What is intracellular digestion? What is extracellular digestion?
5. How do plants carry on digestion without digestive organs?

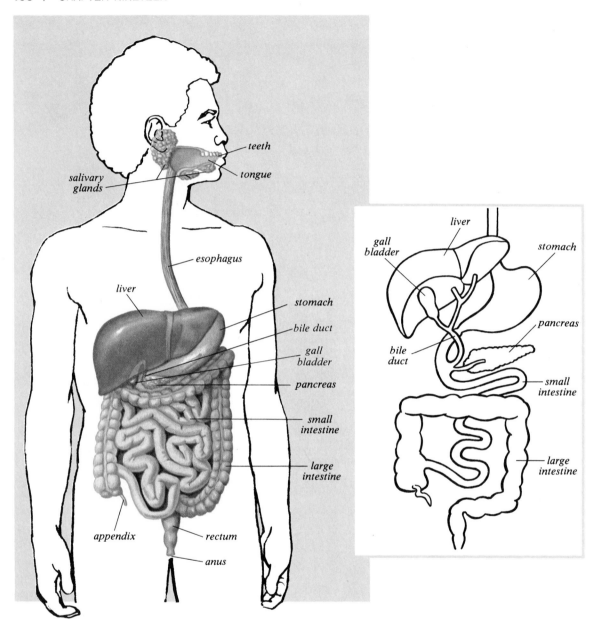

**Figure 19-7** The human digestive system. It is a continuous tube with highly specialized organs and tissues along its length. It produces some of its own enzymes and is supplied with other enzymes by nearby glands.

# The Human Digestive System

## 19–4

## Different Regions of the Human Digestive System Have Special Functions

The human digestive system is basically a tube with a series of specialized regions. Different phases of digestion occur in each region. Figure 19–7 shows the parts of the human digestive system.

Food is chewed and broken into smaller pieces in the mouth by the action of the jaws, teeth, and tongue. The food is also mixed with **saliva** (suh-LY-vuh), which moistens and lubricates the food particles and adds the first digestive enzyme. The tongue aids in the mixing process and then pushes the food to the rear of the mouth cavity. Then the food is swallowed and passed down the throat into the **esophagus** (ih-SOF-uh-gus). The respiratory tube, or **trachea** (TRAY-kee-ah), is very close to the esophagus. Food is prevented from entering the trachea and the **larynx** (LAR-inks), or voice box, by the **epiglottis** (ep-ih-GLOT-is). (See Figure 19–8.)

From the esophagus, food passes into the stomach. Strong contractions of muscles lining the

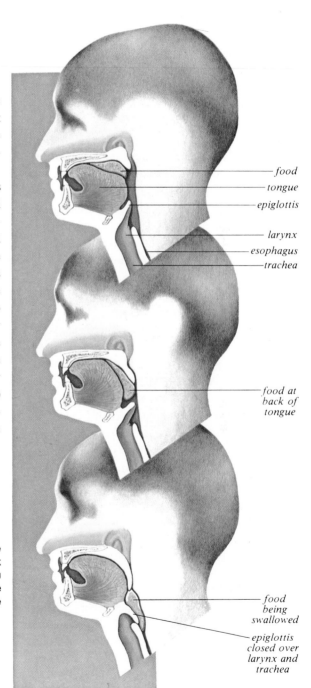

food
tongue
epiglottis

larynx
esophagus
trachea

food at back of tongue

food being swallowed

epiglottis closed over larynx and trachea

**Figure 19–8** The process of swallowing. Follow the diagrams to see how the epiglottis keeps food and drink out of the trachea (windpipe). Occasionally, when you involuntarily choke and cough while taking a drink, the epiglottis has not completely closed the opening over the larynx and trachea.

stomach wall thoroughly break up and mix the food with secretions of the stomach. These secretions, called gastric juice, have an acidic $pH$ and include more enzymes. After this mixing, the food is in the form of a semiliquid mass, called **chyme** (kime). Still more digestive enzymes are added after the food leaves the stomach and enters the small intestine. The $pH$ is changed (to basic, or alkaline), and the breakdown of larger molecules into smaller molecules is completed here in the small intestine. Nutrient absorption, which began in the stomach, takes place mostly in the intestine. Nutrient molecules are absorbed through the walls of the small intestine into capillaries and lymph vessels. After digestion is completed, undigested material passes into the large intestine. Most of this material is eliminated through the anus.

The digestive enzymes functioning in each region of the digestive tube are produced by gland cells. Some enzymes are secreted by cells of the stomach lining, and others by cells of the small intestine. Enzymes and other substances necessary in digestion are also secreted by digestive glands that are connected to different parts of the digestive tract by small tubes called ducts. For instance, the **salivary** (SAL-uh-vehr-ee) **glands** secrete saliva that mixes with food in the mouth. Also, the **pancreas** (PAN-kree-us) and the liver secrete substances that are carried to the small intestine by way of the **pancreatic** and **bile ducts,** which often join (see Figure 19–7).

Food is moved through the digestive tube by means of alternate contractions and relaxations of muscles in the wall of the tube. This wavelike series of movements of the digestive tube is called **peristalsis** (pehr-ih-STAWL-sis). The passage of food from the esophagus to the stomach, and from the stomach to the small intestine, is controlled by rings of muscle that act like valves. When the rings are opened, portions of food move from one region to the next. Another ringlike muscle controls the passage of material from the anus.

## 19–5

## Digestion of Carbohydrates Provides the Body's Primary Energy Source

Most carbohydrates enter the body in the form of starch, glycogen, or complex sugars. Starch and glycogen are very large molecules formed by joining many glucose molecules. Sucrose, ordinary table sugar, is an example of a complex sugar. The sucrose molecule is composed of two six-carbon sugars bonded together.

Carbohydrates are the primary energy source coming into the animal's body in food. However, the energy in the carbohydrates cannot be used by cells until the starch and complex sugars are broken down into glucose and other simple sugars. The digestion of carbohydrates takes place in two regions of the digestive tract, the mouth and the small intestine.

Carbohydrate digestion begins in the mouth with the action of an enzyme in saliva. This enzyme is called salivary **amylase** (AM-uh-lays). Amylase acts on starch. The enzymes of the group to which amylase belongs act on different carbohydrates and therefore are called **carbohydrases** (kar-boh-HY-drays-ez). Enzymes are often named after the substances they act upon.

Like all digestive enzymes, salivary amylase acts by breaking chemical bonds. In the laboratory you may have investigated the breakdown of starch. Amylase breaks some of the bonds in starch molecules and adds parts of the water molecules of saliva to the products of the breakdown. The equation below represents the breakdown of starch molecules by amylase.

$$\text{starch} + \text{water} \xrightarrow{\substack{\text{salivary} \\ \text{amylase}}} \underset{\text{(maltose)}}{\text{sugar}}$$

In the mouth or elsewhere, enzyme action depends on the concentration of acids or bases (*p*H) in the surroundings. Salivary amylase functions only in basic (alkaline) solutions. Saliva is alkaline. The contents of the stomach, however, are very acid. Therefore, starch digestion by salivary amylase stops in the stomach because the enzyme is inactivated. No carbohydrate digestion takes place in the stomach.

Carbohydrate digestion is completed in the small intestine, where pancreatic juices convert the acid food mixture to a basic *p*H again. The maltose produced by the salivary amylase is further broken down to glucose by added amylases in the intestine. Starch that was not broken down in the mouth is also digested in the small intestine. Amylases from the pancreas and other carbohydrases from the intestine itself work together in breaking down starch into sugars.

The final result of most carbohydrate digestion is glucose, a carbohydrate that cells can use in respiration. Glucose is a sugar molecule with six carbon atoms.

When certain complex carbohydrates are digested, other sugars are produced that have five-carbon atoms. Ribose is an example of a five-carbon sugar. Why is ribose important in the functioning of cells?

## 19–6

# Protein Digestion Begins in the Stomach

An early series of experiments by an army physician, Dr. William Beaumont, showed that secretions of the stomach help to digest food. (See **Appendix 19–B,** Beaumont's Experiments on Digestion, page 726.) Many other observations and experiments have shown that the stomach acts particularly on the proteins in food. Protein digestion is actually a two-part process. The first takes place in the stomach. The second part takes place in the small intestine.

When food enters the stomach, the *p*H of the food is basic (alkaline) because of the secretions of the salivary glands of the mouth. However, the breakdown of large protein molecules in the stomach requires an acid condition. Hydrochloric acid secreted by some of the gland cells of the stomach lining starts the protein-digesting action in the stomach. Protein-digesting enzymes are called **proteinases** (PRO-teen-ays-ez). The active proteinase in the stomach is **pepsin** (PEP-sin).

The hydrochloric acid secreted by the gland cells is so concentrated that it could destroy living tissue. The cells of the stomach lining are not harmed, however, because the acid is immediately diluted by the food mixture in the stomach. Some of the cells lining the stomach also continuously secrete a thick coat of mucus which protects the cells from acid. Only when these protective functions fail can stomach cells be attacked by the acid and partly digested by the enzymes. Wounds in the stomach wall called stomach ulcers may result.

Studies on experimental animals have shown that acid secretion by stomach cells is governed by the presence of food in the stomach. As food enters the stomach, certain cells are stimulated to release a hormone called **gastrin** (GAS-trin). Acting as a chemical messenger, gastrin enters the bloodstream and comes in contact with other stomach cells that secrete hydrochloric acid. The gastrin then signals these stomach cells to secrete hydrochloric acid. Secretion of stomach acid is also controlled, in part, by the nervous system. Stress and tension can influence the formation of ulcers.

The enzyme that breaks some of the peptide bonds of protein molecules is pepsin. But pepsin is produced by the cells and secreted in an inactive form called **pepsinogen** (pep-SIN-uh-jen). Hydrochloric acid changes pepsinogen to active pepsin.

The secretion of pepsinogen by stomach gland cells is also controlled by the action of gastrin. Gastrin is the same hormone that controls secretion of hydrochloric acid. Further, the conversion of pepsinogen into pepsin is speeded up by a few molecules of active pepsin. Thus, the presence of food in the stomach, the secretion of gastrin, the production of hydrochloric acid, and the conversion of pepsinogen into pepsin are all related. You can see that the entrance of food into the stomach starts a complex sequence of digestive steps.

Pepsin breaks some of the peptide bonds of the large protein molecules. This results in smaller molecules called polypeptides. Each of the polypeptide molecules, however, has a large number of amino acids still bound together. Further digestion is necessary to break all the peptide bonds. This next step in protein digestion takes place in the small intestine.

## 19–7

## Protein Digestion Is Completed in the Intestine

Food from the stomach enters the upper part of the small intestine in an acid condition. You have already read that the pancreas secretes a substance that mixes with the food and changes it from acidic to basic. The food must be basic for the enzymes in the intestine to act. But almost no secretion takes place from the pancreas unless there is food in the small intestine. What controls this mechanism?

Two English physiologists, W. M. Bayliss and E. H. Starling, found in 1902 that food entering the small intestine causes a hormone to be secreted by the cells of the small intestine. This hormone, called **secretin** (sih-KREET-in), enters the bloodstream and circulates to the pancreas, where it stimulates the gland to produce and secrete pancreatic juice.

Figure 19–9 shows the relationship of the pancreas to the small intestine. The pancreatic juices enter the intestine through the pancreatic duct, or its juncture with the bile duct.

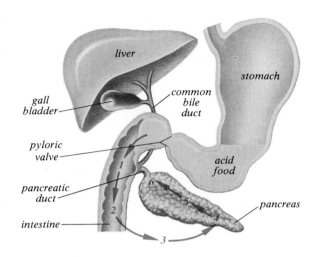

**Figure 19–9** Acid food enters the small intestine (1 above) through the pyloric valve and stimulates secretion of the intestinal hormone secretin (2). The secretin enters the bloodstream (3) and circulates to the pancreas (4). In the pancreas secretin stimulates production of pancreatic juices (5) that flow through a duct to the intestine. The pancreatic juices change the $p$H of the food mixture from acid to basic. They also supply trypsin, an enzyme that breaks peptide bonds in proteins in the food.

In addition to the substance that changes the food mixture from an acidic to a basic condition, pancreatic juice also contains a powerful enzyme called **trypsin** (TRIP-sin). Trypsin comes into the small intestine in an inactive form called **trypsinogen** (trip-SIN-uh-jen). Trypsinogen is changed into active trypsin in the intestine by the action of another enzyme secreted only when food is present in the intestine, and therefore active trypsin is formed only when food is present. Trypsin also triggers still more conversion of trypsinogen into trypsin.

Ordinarily the cells lining the intestine are not attacked by trypsin. Some of these cells produce protective mucus. You can compare the intestine's protective mechanism—that is, in forming trypsin from trypsinogen only when food is present—with the way in which gastric juice is prevented from

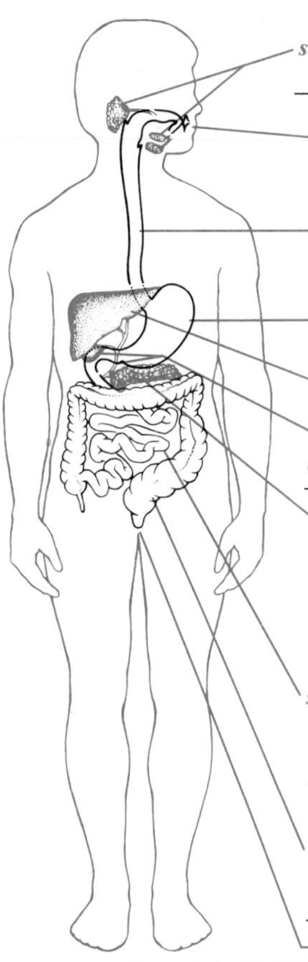

| parts of the digestive system | major function | major secretion | source of secretions | substances acted on | products of action |
|---|---|---|---|---|---|
| salivary glands | secretion of saliva | salivary amylase | salivary glands | starch | complex sugar (maltose) |
| mouth and teeth | food entrance; chewing; some starch digestion | | | | |
| esophagus | carries food to stomach | | | | |
| stomach | protein digestion | hydrochloric acid pepsinogen (pepsin) | gland cells of stomach | proteins | polypeptides |
| liver gall bladder and bile ducts | secretion, storage, and transport of bile | bile salts | liver cells | large fat droplets | small fat droplets |
| pancreas | secretion of pancreatic juice | trypsinogen (trypsin) lipase amylase | pancreas | polypeptides fats carbohydrates | amino acids fatty acids and glycerol maltose |
| small intestine | digestion and absorption | proteinases lipases carbohydrases | gland cells of small intestine pancreas | peptides fats complex sugars | amino acids fatty acids and glycerol glucose |
| large intestine | resorption of water; collection of undigested wastes | | | | |
| anus | waste exit | | | | |

**Figure 19–10** A summary of the parts and functions of the human digestive system. Imagine a plain hamburger on a bun. Start at the top of the chart, with the salivary glands, and describe the digestive system's action on the meat (including fat) and bread. Where is the hamburger sandwich, after digestion, absorbed into the bloodstream?

harming the stomach. Gastric juice may also harm the intestine if not inactivated. For example, ulcers of the upper part of the intestine may form when the food mixture entering the intestine from the stomach is not neutralized. The acidic food mixture and the protein-digesting enzymes may digest part of the intestinal wall. The pancreatic juices prevent this in most people.

Trypsin breaks the peptide bonds of the polypeptides coming from the stomach. Trypsin can also act on any larger protein molecules that were not broken down in the stomach by pepsin. The gland cells lining the small intestine also secrete enzymes that can split peptide bonds. (See Appendix 4–F to learn about the peptide bond.) The end products of all of the processes of protein digestion are amino acids.

**Try Investigation 19–C** Fat Digestion, page 663.

# Biology Brief

## Danger!  Poison.

Not everything that reaches people's stomachs is food.  Absent-mindedly reaching for the wrong glass to take a drink can result in poisoning.  Or forgetting that you have taken your medicine and taking it again may cause poisoning.  Sometimes food itself is poisonous.  Toxins from harmful microorganisms occasionally contaminate the food.  Botulism, one example of food poisoning, leaves no telltale appearance or odor, yet it can be fatal.

Does your community have a poison-control center?  One of the largest in the nation is the Rocky Mountain Poison Center in Denver.  It is staffed by 6 physicians, 2 doctors of pharmacology, 2 registered pharmacists, a chemist, 11 public health nurses, and more than 20 other staff members.  In an emergency, any hour of the day or night you can telephone the Center:

From Denver, telephone 629-1123
From out-of-state, telephone 1-800-332-3073

Emergency service is often faster than calling your doctor, because your doctor may be out of the office or involved in another emergency.  Lines are always open to the Rocky Mountain Poison Center.  Only long-distance lines, on holidays, may be tied up.

The Center's head nurse, Pam Ford, is shown responding to a call.  Emergency-treatment information is flashed on her TV screen by POISINDEX®, which covers more than 250,000 products, their ingredients, and the recommended emergency treatment procedures.  A second system, DRUGDEX®, is also in use.

## 19–8

### Fats Are Digested in the Small Intestine with the Help of the Liver

Fats are digested in the small intestine.  Unlike carbohydrates and proteins, fats do not mix with water.  Enzymes can act on fat molecules only on the surface of the fat droplets.  Large droplets of fats are broken down into smaller ones, increasing the surface area of the droplets available to the fat-digesting enzymes.  The breakdown is accomplished by bile salts secreted by the liver.  Bile reaches the small intestine through the bile duct, as shown in Figure 19–9.

Liver bile does not contain any enzymes for digesting fat molecules, however.  The fat-digesting enzyme, **lipase** (LY-pays), is present in pancreatic juice.  It splits fats into fatty acids and glycerol.  Fatty acids and glycerol are sources of

414

The telephone number of your nearest poison-control center is one of the emergency numbers you should keep posted on your telephone. Use this number (or the number of The Rocky Mountain Poison Center) when you have questions about any of these:

1. Poisonous mushrooms, plants, snakes, or spiders
2. Food poisoning
3. Household products such as cleaning supplies and cosmetics
4. Disposal of hazardous products and chemicals
5. Drug overdoses, drug interaction (two or more drugs), and drug effects and side-effects
6. Drugs that affect an unborn child or may be secreted with breast milk
7. Inhalation of poisonous fumes and gases
8. Pesticides (insecticides and herbicides)
9. Massive poisonings and public health hazards (truck spills, radiation, and so on)

energy used by the body when carbohydrates are not available. Food may be stored in the form of fat in animals and in plant seeds.

## 19–9

## The Products of Digestion Are Absorbed into the Transport System

Figure 19–10 summarizes the human digestive processes. The end products of digestion of pro-

teins, starch, and fats are amino acids, simple sugars, fatty acids, and glycerol. Which of these nutrients is in each type of food?

These end products of digestion have three features in common: (1) They are small molecules that can pass through the cell membranes. (2) They are molecules that cells can use for energy. (3) They are the kinds of molecules that cells can use to rebuild their own structure.

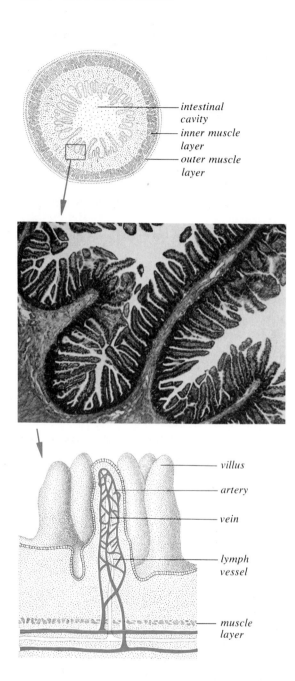

These small molecules pass through the cells lining the small intestine. The surface area inside the intestine is increased tremendously by millions of small outgrowths called **villi** (VIL-ee; singular, villus). Each villus contains capillaries and a lymph vessel (Figure 19–11). Simple sugars, amino acids, some glycerol, minerals, and vitamins pass through the cells of the villi and enter the capillaries. The products of fat digestion also pass through the cells of the villi, but enter the lymph vessel instead of the capillaries. Bile salts aid in the absorption of fatty acids by the lymph vessels. Eventually the lymph vessels bring the fatty acids into the bloodstream also. (See Section 17–11.)

The blood carries the products of digestion to the cells. Inside the cells the molecules are either broken down further to yield energy or put together again to synthesize the substances needed for growth and repair of the organism.

**Figure 19–11** A cross section of the small intestine (top), with a photomicrograph (center) and drawing (bottom) of intestinal villi. Digested foodstuffs enter the bloodstream through the villi.

## 19–10

## The Large Intestine Reabsorbs Most of the Water

Undigested food passes along the small and the large intestines by the muscular movements of peristalsis. Numerous bacteria, present in the large intestine, play a part in producing several vitamins, gases, and other compounds. The vitamins are absorbed and used by the body. As the undigested food moves onward, much of the water is absorbed by the walls of the large intestine. This absorption partly dries out the wastes, called **feces** (FEE-seez). The feces are eventually eliminated through the anus.

**CAPSULE SUMMARY**

The human digestive system is a highly specialized tube in which different kinds of food molecules are broken down to smaller molecules by the action of digestive enzymes. The enzymes are produced either by special glands connected to the digestive tube, or by some of the cells lining the tube itself. These enzymes are activated in different parts of the digestive system by complex mechanisms. Amylase is an enzyme that breaks down starch and glycogen, pepsin and trypsin break down proteins, and lipase breaks down fats. Starch and glycogen are broken into glucose molecules, proteins into amino acids, and fats into fatty acids and glycerol.

These molecules are the building blocks for growth and repair of the cells. They are also the sources for the energy that supports the life of the organism.

**SELF CHECK**

1. What are the major parts of the human digestive tract?
2. What digestive action is caused by the presence of the enzyme in saliva?
3. What is the role of the small intestine in digestion?
4. What effect does acid have on pepsinogen?
5. How are fats broken down in digestion?

## CHAPTER SUMMARY

### HIGHLIGHTS

Digestion is the process of breaking food down into molecules small enough to be absorbed and used by individual cells. Digestive enzymes, which act chemically, cause the food to be broken down. The different enzymes are manufactured in plants, protists, and animals. In intracellular digestion, used by some plants and many animals, digestion takes place within the individual cells that will use the food. More advanced animals accomplish most of their digestion by extracellular digestion, which takes place within a tube specialized for digestion. The small molecules that are the end products of digestion can be used by living cells as a source of energy or as materials for growth or repair of the cell.

### REVIEWING IDEAS

1. What are nutrients? What are foods? In what way do the two usually differ?
2. Why is it necessary for proteins, fats, and most carbohydrates to be digested?
3. What is the final result of the digestion of carbohydrates? of fats? of proteins?

4. How is the stomach lining protected against being digested by pepsin?
5. What sort of controls act to stimulate or inhibit secretion of juices by the stomach?
6. What is the special role of the pancreas in the digestive process?

### USING CONCEPTS

7. What advantages with regard to types of food does extracellular digestion give an animal?
8. In all animals, how is the actual breaking down of large molecules to small molecules accomplished?
9. Birds have no teeth. How do they grind food into smaller particles?
10. What steps in digestion are started by the entrance of food into the stomach?
11. Compare and contrast pinocytosis and phagocytosis.
12. How is digestion affected by chewing food well, in contrast to swallowing large bites?

### RECOMMENDED READING

Moog, F. "The Lining of the Small Intestine." *Scientific American*, November, 1981. The role of cells lining the intestine in processing food.

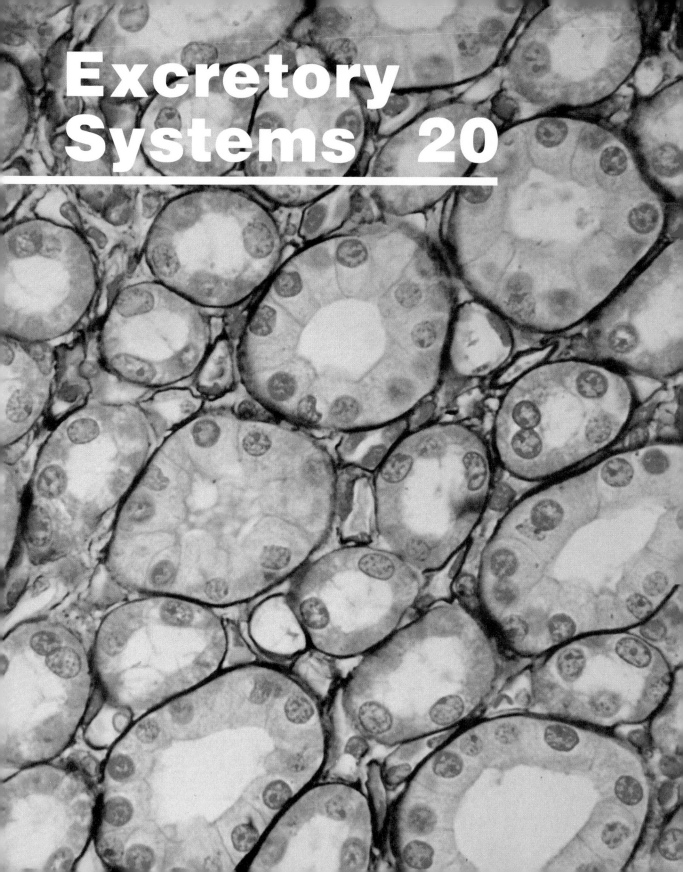

# Excretory
# Systems   20

The life of an organism depends upon the life of its cells. Supplying these cells with food and oxygen is one necessity of life. Removing the cells' wastes is another. But both are only part of maintaining the cells' balance of materials in the organism's physical environment. In this chapter you will explore some of the adaptations for maintaining homeostasis and for removing wastes, in a variety of different organisms from protists to plants to people.

# Homeostasis and Materials Exchange

## 20-1

### Excretion Helps Maintain a Balance with the External Environment

All organisms' surroundings differ from the organisms themselves in many materials and in their relative abundances. The organisms use osmosis, diffusion, active transport, breathing, and eating to obtain the particular environmental materials they need. Each cell of very small organisms is near the external environment and the materials required from it. The circulating blood in more complex organisms is the key link between body cells and the external environment.

Because all organisms must exchange materials with the environment to live, unneeded as well as needed materials may pass between the organism and its surroundings. The organism will take in materials it does not need along with those it does. In turn, it will lose some needed materials to the environment. Selective mechanisms in cell membranes help keep such unproductive transfers to a minimum, but different materials of similar molecular size and shape easily "fool" these mechanisms. Homeostasis (see Section 17–12) will be disrupted unless some way of restoring the balance exists.

Needed materials can be a problem, too, when available in amounts insufficient or surplus to an organism's life and well-being. Fresh water organisms, for example, require water in their bodies, as all other organisms do. Water constantly enters these organisms beyond their needs. The problem in homeostasis is to eliminate the excess water without losing significant quantities of soluble body salts.

Organisms that live in salt water have a problem almost opposite that of freshwater organisms. In saltwater fishes and some invertebrates, the body salt concentration is usually lower inside the organisms than the salt concentration of the surrounding ocean water or salty lake water. Therefore, water from the organisms tends to be lost by osmosis to the surrounding salt water. Replac-

← Collecting tubes in a human kidney show their cellular walls in cross section.

**419**

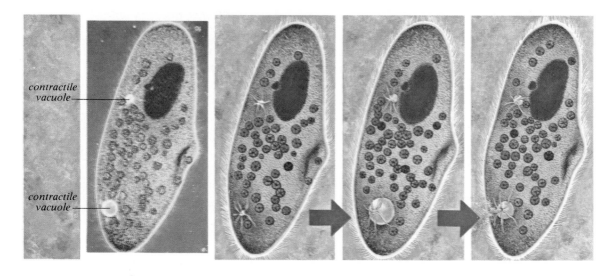

**Figure 20–1** Contractile vacuoles in *Paramecium* rid it of excess water. The vacuoles expand as water fills them through their radiating canals. Then the vacuoles contract and eject the water from the organism.

ing the lost water with salt water requires elimination of excess salts from the replacement water. The problem in homeostasis for these organisms is retaining their body water and excreting salts from water taken in to offset body water losses.

Land-dwelling organisms are somewhat similar in water and salt problems to saltwater organisms. Water must be retained and salt excreted by land-dwelling animals, including humans.

Keeping both water and salt in balance in an organism are just two examples of how body mechanisms work to conserve needed materials and eliminate others. There are many other instances when either the type or the chemical balance of the materials must be maintained.

A more special problem is created by the wastes organisms produce as they use materials and energy. Nitrogen-containing wastes are a by-product of food use. So is carbon dioxide. Acid wastes or excesses are still other by-products. In body fluids these acid excesses are an accumulation of hydrogen ions ($H^+$), lowering the internal $p$H (Section 5–11). Organisms must have a means of excreting these wastes.

The exchange of materials with the environment thus involves at least two general problems for all organisms. One is maintaining homeostasis as materials are gained and lost. The other is a particular part of this problem, but still a general one—removing wastes. These wastes obviously include the by-products of food use and cell respiration. The not-so-obvious wastes include damaged and worn-out cell parts, enzymes, hormones, and other components of organisms that are being replaced or recycled. (Remember, from Section 17–10, how often just the red blood cells alone must be replaced?)

## 20–2

### Protists Have Mechanisms for Water Balance and for Excretion

Osmosis and diffusion are not the only mechanisms for materials exchange in protists. Many protists living in fresh water have structures called **contractile vacuoles** that remove excess water which constantly enters the organisms. Water collects in the vacuoles, and contractions of the vacuoles squeeze the water out of the cell. Figure 20–1 shows how the contractile vacuoles in *Paramecium* operate. *Amoeba* and *Euglena* have similar contractile vacuoles, as do many other freshwater protists.

Some protists have specialized parts used for food intake, but wastes are usually excreted through the plasma membrane. Carbon dioxide and nitrogenous food wastes are excreted in this way. Only incidentally are nitrogenous wastes occasionally included with the water eliminated by the contractile vacuoles.

## 20–3

### Plants Have Mechanisms for Water Balance and for Excretion

Land plants more often are involved in conserving water than in eliminating excess water. The waxy cutin coating the leaves and stems retards water loss, as does the closing of leaf stomata (Section 17–2). Most water loss that occurs takes place through the stomata by diffusion, but occasionally plants do have a water excess in terms of environmental moisture, temperature, and their own digestion of their food. In some plants water can be removed by special structures located at the edges of leaves. Drops of water from these structures are part of the "dew" that you may have seen on grass

**Figure 20–2** These strawberry leaves have droplets of water forming on their edges. If the water is a product of a cell activity, what cell activity do you think it is?

and other plants early in the morning. Figure 20–2 shows this kind of water removal from leaves.

Carbon dioxide is not a waste in green plants. As it is produced by cell respiration, it is usually used in photosynthesis. However, it is produced by cell respiration even at times when it is not needed for photosynthesis. At these times the carbon dioxide is lost by diffusion, chiefly through the stomata. Other substances may be excreted by root cells into the soil. Still others may be changed into insoluble materials that remain in the plants. Why would insoluble waste products not be harmful to the plants?

Certain plants that grow in soils with a high calcium content must rid themselves of the excess calcium they absorb. They eliminate the excess calcium by depositing it in the leaves, which are eventually shed.

Leaf-edge structures that eliminate excess water may at times eliminate excess soluble salts, too. You may have seen light-colored deposits appear at the edges of leaves on house plants that are growing in soil which has been too richly fertilized.

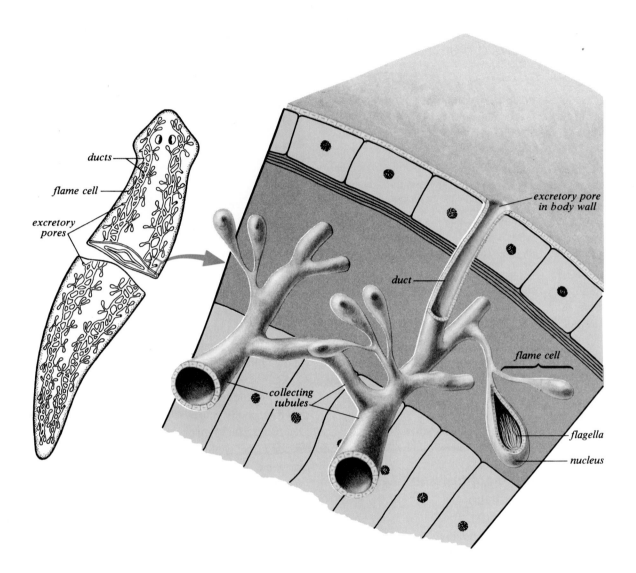

*ducts*

*flame cell*

*excretory pores*

*excretory pore in body wall*

*duct*

*flame cell*

*collecting tubules*

*flagella*

*nucleus*

**Figure 20–3** The flame cells of the flatworm, and the duct system of which they are a part, have the same function as the contractile vacuoles in *Paramecium*. Both organisms live in fresh water and have more water entering their bodies than they need.

## 20–4

## Animals Have Evolved Systems for Materials Balance and for Excretion

Like protists, sponges and *Hydra* excrete wastes from each cell directly through the external surface. In animals larger and more complex than these, however, not enough of the body cells are in contact with the external environment for each cell to dispose of its own wastes. Thus, larger species of animals have evolved special organs for excretion, and sometimes other organs for maintaining their water balance.

Planarians are freshwater organisms. Like other freshwater organisms, they have an overabundance of water entering their bodies. Water is removed constantly from tissue fluids by a system of ducts (Figure 20–3). Some wastes and other soluble materials are in the water. **Flame cells,** so named because the beating of their flagella resembles the flickering of a flame, create a current in the tubular system. The water is moved through ducts and eliminated through pores. The pores are openings of the ducts in the body wall.

Carbon dioxide in planarians is excreted by diffusion through the body wall. Nitrogenous wastes, like soluble ammonia ($NH_3$), and any additional wastes are also excreted through the body wall and through the mouth (Figure 19–5).

The grasshopper, as a land dweller, has a different problem of water balance from that of planarians. The grasshopper must avoid large losses of water. Its excretory organs are adapted to removing nitrogenous wastes from the blood and body fluids and excreting these wastes in an almost insoluble form, as **uric acid.** Very little water is needed to excrete uric acid crystals from the body.

The grasshopper has specialized excretory tubes called **Malpighian tubules** (Figure 20–4). They extend into the body cavity where the blood circulates. (You will recall that the grasshopper has an open type of circulatory system, with the blood not

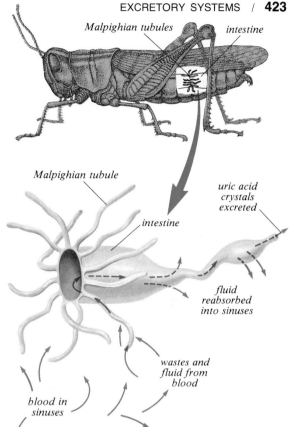

**Figure 20–4** Wastes and fluid from the blood of the grasshopper enter the Malpighian tubules. The tubules empty into the digestive tract, from which the fluids are reabsorbed. The wastes are excreted as uric acid crystals, along with undigested food remnants from the digestive system.

always in blood vessels. In the body cavity the blood circulates freely in the space, or sinuses.) The Malpighian tubules float freely in the circulating blood of the sinuses. Wastes and fluid from the blood are passed into the tubules. Nitrogenous wastes are changed into uric acid crystals. The tubules empty into the digestive tract, from which fluids are reabsorbed into the sinuses. The uric acid crystals are excreted through the anus along with undigested food remnants.

Carbon dioxide is excreted by the grasshopper through its air tubes, or tracheae (Figure 18–3).

## 20–5

## Forms of Nitrogenous Wastes Differ Among Different Animals

The three major forms of nitrogenous wastes excreted by animals are ammonia, uric acid, and urea. Ammonia is very toxic. The dilution of ammonia in large quantities of water makes the ammonia a safer excretory product in freshwater and saltwater protists and animals. *Amoeba, Paramecium, Euglena,* and planarians all excrete ammonia through their cell membranes or body coverings, as you have read. Later you will read that ammonia is also the chief nitrogenous waste of some vertebrates, the ocean fishes.

Uric acid is not toxic because it is almost insoluble. Uric acid excretion has evolved as an adaptation of many land animals. Little loss of water is involved. Not only grasshoppers (and other insects) but reptiles, birds, and many mammals excrete nitrogenous wastes as uric acid crystals.

Urea is toxic, but less so than ammonia. It is safe as an excretory product when diluted in sufficient water. Certain mammals, including humans, and many fishes and amphibians excrete nitrogenous wastes either partly or chiefly as urea. Humans, like many other mammals, also excrete uric acid, although normally in very small amounts as compared with urea. You will read later how uric acid crystals in the human kidneys can cause problems.

The chief fact that emerges from a review of different kinds of nitrogenous wastes is that they show important evolutionary patterns. That is, animals which have evolved in water and land environments show differences in nitrogenous wastes related to the abundance or scarcity of water. Look back over the discussion of ammonia and uric acid to see that this is true. Urea is not as toxic as ammonia, but it requires more water than uric acid for its excretion. Hence, urea fits into the evolutionary patterns when you think of it as somewhere between uric acid and ammonia in its requirement for dilution in water.

**Try Investigation 20–A** Earthworm Excretory Structures, page 664.

---

**CAPSULE SUMMARY**

Living cells are continuously building up and breaking down chemical compounds, producing wastes as a by-product. In addition, these cells must maintain the differences of materials that exist between them and their environment. One-celled and multicellular organisms have evolved a variety of ways to conserve needed materials, eliminate excess materials, and excrete the waste by-products of their living activities.

Water and salt balance is maintained in different ways by organisms that live in different environments. Nitrogenous waste excretion is related to the water balance problem. Carbon dioxide excretion is accomplished in a variety of ways ranging from diffusion to removal by respiratory systems.

In general, saltwater and land animals have developed water-conserving methods of nitrogenous waste excretion and salt excretion. Freshwater organisms have developed other ways that also involve the removal of large quantities of water.

**SELF CHECK**

1. What is the difference in function between contractile vacuoles and Malpighian tubules?
2. How are contractile vacuoles and flame cells related in function?
3. How do protists excrete nitrogenous wastes? How do planarians and grasshoppers excrete these wastes?
4. What kind of nitrogenous waste would you expect a small freshwater organism to produce?
5. In what kinds of animals is uric acid the nitrogenous waste that is produced and excreted?

# Vertebrate Excretory Systems

## 20–6

## Different Kinds of Mechanisms for Water Balance and Excretion Have Evolved in Vertebrates

In vertebrates a closed circulatory system is closely related to both maintaining a water-salt balance and to excreting wastes. The blood, instead of body fluids in general, is regulated for replenishment or excretion of materials. Why would keeping the blood in balance keep the whole body in balance?

Ocean fishes, like all other vertebrates, take oxygen into their blood and excrete carbon dioxide from it. In these fishes the excretion of carbon dioxide takes place in the gills (Figure 18–2), the same organs through which the supply of oxygen is obtained. Excreting salt to help maintain the body's water balance takes place in special cells that are also in the gills. Nitrogenous wastes are excreted chiefly as ammonia—once again as the blood circulates through the gills. Hence the gills are the chief excretory organs of ocean fishes. These fishes have kidneys, too, that excrete urea in a watery **urine.** But little urea needs to be excreted in addition to the ammonia excreted through the gills. So little water is lost in urine.

Sea turtles and birds that feed on ocean organisms excrete salt through special glands in their heads. Like other air-breathing animals with lungs, they excrete carbon dioxide from the blood as it passes through the lungs. Their kidneys function more in excretion of nitrogenous wastes than the kidneys of ocean fishes.

In mammals and especially humans, the kidneys have become the chief excretory organs. They not only remove nitrogenous wastes from the blood but also regulate the water-salt balance. The urea they excrete is formed in the liver, where most of the body's wastes are processed and some are even

recycled. Many toxic substances are changed in chemical form and rendered harmless in the liver. The small amount of uric acid excreted along with urea in urine is also formed in the liver. In many respects, then, the liver is also an excretory organ, and a very important one. It passes substances along in the blood to the kidneys.

As in other mammals, carbon dioxide is excreted by humans from their blood as it passes through the lungs. Some salt and water are excreted through the skin. Undigested food remnants are eliminated through the digestive tract, as in all other animals with a complex digestive tract. In a strict sense the undigested food remnants have never entered the bloodstream or body cells and so are eliminated by the same continuous food tube through which the food entered. This is not the same as excretion of the body's cell wastes from the blood in the liver, kidneys, and lungs.

The oxygen-carbon dioxide exchange in the lungs was discussed in Chapter 18. In this chapter, you will read about what happens to blood when it reaches the kidneys after it has passed through the liver and other organs.

## 20–7

## The Human Kidneys Contain Many Excretory Units

Each human kidney is a bean-shaped organ about 16–18 cm long. There are two kidneys, one on each side of the body just above waist height, against the back wall of the body cavity (Figure 20–5). The working units of a kidney are the **nephrons** (NEF-rons), seen in the sectioned kidney as a closely packed system of tubules in the kidney's **cortex** (Figure 20–6). Each kidney contains about a million nephrons.

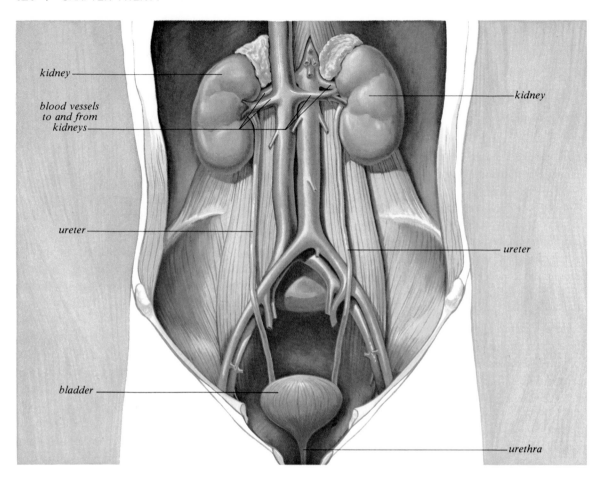

**Figure 20–5** Though the lungs, intestine, and skin may also serve excretory functions in humans, the major part of the excretory system is shown here. The kidneys are against the back of the body wall. The ureters lead from the kidneys to the bladder. The bladder empties through the urethra to the outside of the body. Note the relationship of the kidneys to the two major blood vessels between them.

A nephron is long and coiled (Figure 20–6). One end opens into a duct that collects urine. The other end is a cup fitted over a mass of blood capillaries. Still other blood capillaries form a network around the tube of the nephron all along its length. This intimate relationship between the blood and the kidneys is an important linkup. As Figure 20–6 shows, the intertwined capillaries and

nephrons show clear visual evidence of their close relationship.

The cup of a nephron is called a **Bowman's capsule.** The ball of capillaries in the cup is called a **glomerulus** (glaw-MER-yoo-lus). The wall of the tubule is never more than a single cell thick and often in direct contact with a blood capillary wall, also a single cell thick. In fact, in places along the

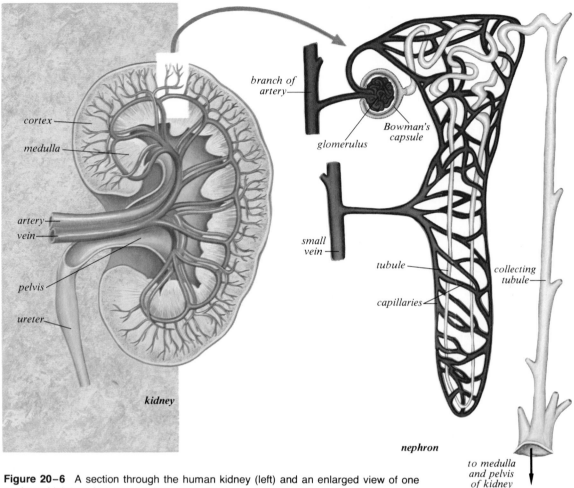

cortex

medulla

artery

vein

pelvis

ureter

**kidney**

branch of
artery

glomerulus

Bowman's
capsule

small
vein

tubule

capillaries

collecting
tubule

**nephron**

to medulla
and pelvis
of kidney

**Figure 20–6** A section through the human kidney (left) and an enlarged view of one nephron (right) and its surrounding capillaries.

tubule the capillary and tubule walls appear merged into one undivided structure. (This also occurs sometimes in the alveoli of the lungs, where capillary and lung tissue appear to merge.)

The tubule of a nephron leads out into a collecting tube. This tube in turn leads to a larger one, until all the urine in a kidney flows into one large tube, a **ureter,** that leads from the kidney to the urinary bladder (Figure 20–5).

The kidneys treat all of the blood in the body at a rate that amounts to about 30 times or more, for the entire blood supply, each day. This accounts for the rich supply of blood vessels you see in Figures 20–5 and 20–6.

The question is, How do the kidneys do all that they do, with their two million or so nephrons?

## 20–8

## The Blood Is Filtered by the Nephrons

Important data about the kidneys have been collected for about 40 years. A very delicate technique is used to gain the data. Tiny glass tubes are stuck into different parts of individual nephrons in anesthetized laboratory animals (Figure 20–7). Through these glass tubes, fluid is withdrawn from the different places in a nephron and analyzed chemically. The fluid differs from place to place.

Human patients with kidney problems have also been studied closely for many years. As a result of all the studies, probably more is known of human kidney functions than of many of the excretory organs of other animals that you have read about earlier in this chapter.

The glass tube experiments have revealed that as blood flows through the glomerulus, all parts of the blood except most of its proteins and red and white cells may cross the membranes and enter the collecting tissue as filtrate in the Bowman's capsule. Nitrogenous wastes are in this almost whole blood plasma. So are excess hydrogen ions. So is much of the blood's water content.

As the filtered liquid from the blood flows along the tubule, more wastes are removed from the surrounding blood capillaries. In turn, the blood reabsorbs useful substances that passed into the Bowman's capsule from the blood there. This exchange of materials is not passive; it requires specialized cell functions and active transport. Glucose, amino acids, and many other substances are reabsorbed by the blood. The concentration of wastes in the collecting tubules increases.

Through glucose reabsorption the nephrons help conserve blood sugar. Regulation of blood-sugar level is very complex, and the kidneys play only one role. If the sugar level is too high, as in patients with diabetes, some glucose will be excreted in the urine. If the blood-sugar level is low, al-

most no glucose will be in the urine.

The increasingly concentrated wastes and liquid continue to flow through the collecting tubes. In the larger portions of the tubes in the kidney's **medulla** (Figure 20–6), the water-salt balance is regulated. Here, about 99 percent of the water that has left the blood capillaries and has entered the nephrons is reabsorbed by the blood. The kidney manages this by maintaining a high salt concentration in the tissues of the medulla, causing water to leave the collecting tubes by osmosis and re-enter the tissues and the bloodstream.

As water is reabsorbed and the urine becomes more concentrated, most of the nitrogenous wastes are in the form of urea. Some are uric acid crystals produced by the liver's breakdown of damaged nucleic acid molecules. The uric acid crystals, if they grow, can form kidney stones and block the passage of urine through a ureter. "Passing a kidney stone" through a ureter is very painful. Normally, however, the almost insoluble uric acid crystals are very small and are flushed out of the kidney by the urine.

As a net result of the kidney's activities, blood sugar is conserved; nitrogenous wastes are removed from the blood; water-salt balance is regulated (and water reabsorbed by the blood); and excess salt, within limits, is excreted. However, the kidneys cannot excrete high concentrations of salt—nor can the skin glands, in perspiration. Normally humans do not eat or drink substances with high salt concentrations. When they do, as in drinking ocean water, they are in trouble. For instead of replenishing their body water they will lose still more water than before in trying to excrete the salt. This is why shipwrecked people can so easily perish from dehydration on rafts or in lifeboats before they are found.

Still another function of the kidneys' nephrons is regulating the $pH$ of the blood, as you read earlier. Normally blood in the arteries is very slightly alkaline ($pH = 7.4$). If the $pH$ goes

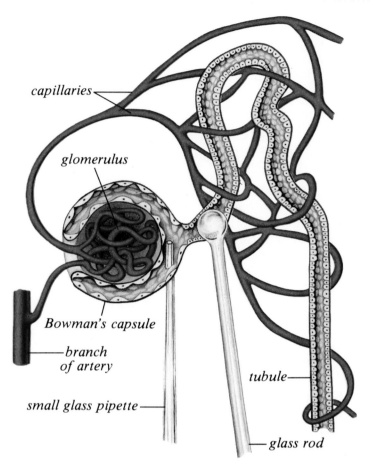

**Figure 20–7** With a glass rod blocking the nephron, fluid is withdrawn from the Bowman's capsule through a small glass pipette. The fluid is analyzed. The block-and-tap procedure can be repeated all up and down the nephron. The fluid withdrawn at each point is analyzed. By this series of samplings biologists have learned what materials from the blood pass into the Bowman's capsule and where along the nephron's length each material needed by the body is reabsorbed from the nephron into the blood.

higher, the nephrons in the kidneys excrete from the blood some bicarbonate and other ions that otherwise could combine with hydrogen ions and continue to keep the hydrogen ion supply too low. More hydrogen ions will then be left in the blood, and the $p$H will drop slightly. If, on the other hand, too many hydrogen ions are in the blood, the $p$H may drop to 7.3 or 7.2. Then the nephrons in the kidneys will remove hydrogen ions from the blood until the $p$H is raised slightly again.

The kidneys have other functions such as participation in the regulation of blood pressure, but blood sugar reabsorption, water-salt balance, nitrogenous waste excretion, and $p$H regulation set the human kidneys apart from the kidneys of, for example, ocean fishes. Look back at the limited function of kidneys in the ocean fishes (page 425) to see how much more the kidneys have evolved in their functions in humans. In the next chapter you will see how hormones control such functions.

# The Artificial Kidney, a Life-Saving Machine

This patient is undergoing hemodialysis, or blood cleansing, under the supervision of Kathy Johnson, Registered Nurse. The patient's kidneys are not functioning normally. Without help from the artificial kidney machine she would be very ill. Waste products collecting in her blood would begin to poison her body. Hemodialysis by means of the kidney machine removes these wastes much as the real kidneys normally would.

Notice the two tubes to the patient's arm. One, connected to an artery, carries blood from the patient to the kidney machine. The other, connected to a vein, carries "cleansed" blood from the machine back to the patient. The kidney machine itself consists of pumps and mixing chambers to pump the blood and mix the dialysate bath properly. The dialyzer or artificial kidney consists of a semipermeable membrane that permits diffusion of some substances across it (urea and creatinine) but not others (proteins, blood cells). The dialysate bath bathes the *outside* of the semipermeable membrane while the blood circulates through the *inside* of the membrane. Electronic controls monitor all the machine's functions. Kathy Johnson, RN, monitors the machine and the patient throughout the treatment. Because the machine's functions and the patient's condition could mean life or death, nurses working in dialysis receive intensive, indepth training and become specialists in hemodialysis and renal nursing.

You used a dialysis tube in Investigation 19-A. The dialysis membrane on the machine is essentially similar; it is a semipermeable membrane made of refined cellophane or a plastic substance. Materials that pass through the walls of blood capillaries and kidney nephrons can also pass through the walls of the dialysis membrane.

**CAPSULE SUMMARY**

Although ocean fishes have kidneys, their major excretory and water-salt balance functions are carried out by the gills. Sea turtles and birds that feed on ocean organisms have salt-secreting glands in their heads; their kidneys are more advanced than those of ocean fishes.

Human kidneys are very highly advanced in their functions. Along with the liver they excrete nitrogenous wastes, chiefly urea but also some uric acid, in urine. The kidneys are also the human organs of water-salt balance, contributing in this way, as well as in waste removal, to homeostasis. And the kidneys are the human organs that directly affect

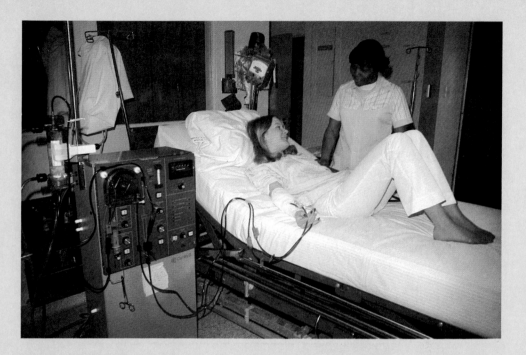

The dialysate bath in the machine contains a solution of substances or chemicals normally found in the body—salts, calcium and magnesium, as examples. The chemicals in the solution are in lower amounts than in the body. As the patient's blood circulates through the membrane bathed by the dialysate, chemicals move from the patient (high) through the pores in the membrane and into the dialysate (low) and are then disposed of. This process continues throughout the treatment (4 to 6 hours, 2 or 3 times weekly). The machine is very efficient and can remove urea and creatinine faster than normally-functioning kidneys can.

A kidney machine does not duplicate *all* of a normal kidney's functions. However, patients can live indefinitely using the machine. Even patients with normally-functioning kidneys who are poison victims may have overdoses of aspirin, barbiturates, and bromides dialyzed rapidly out of their blood by the machine. Removal of chemicals by dialysis depends on the molecular weights and structures of the chemicals—that is, whether they can pass through the pores of the dialysis membrane.

the conservation of blood sugar and the regulation of $p$H, contributing still again to the maintenance of homeostasis.

**SELF CHECK**

1. What is a nephron?
2. What is the major nitrogenous waste in ocean fishes? What other nitrogenous waste in fishes is the major nitrogenous waste excreted by humans?
3. What are kidney stones?
4. How is water-salt balance maintained in ocean fishes? Sea turtles? Humans?
5. How is $p$H regulated in humans?

# CHAPTER SUMMARY

## HIGHLIGHTS

Maintaining water-salt balance is one of the problems of homeostasis in organisms. Freshwater organisms solve it by eliminating water that constantly enters the body, while conserving body salts. Contractile vacuoles in protists and flame cells in planarians function chiefly in eliminating water. Saltwater and land organisms may have the opposite problem, in that they must conserve water and excrete salt. Water-salt balance is only one of many problems in maintaining a materials balance in homeostasis, but it is a major problem.

Excreting wastes is a special problem in homeostasis. Every living cell of an organism constantly produces waste by-products of its cell activities. In addition, cell parts, enzymes, hormones, and nucleic acids become damaged or worn out and must be replaced and removed as wastes. The nitrogenous wastes are excreted chiefly in three forms—ammonia, urea, and uric acid. Carbon dioxide is excreted as a gas, by diffusion through body coverings or by diffusion from the blood to the trachea (in insects), gills (in fish), or lungs (in ocean mammals and land vertebrates, including humans).

Nitrogenous wastes are related in form to the water-salt balance and the environment of an organism. Ammonia is toxic but can be diluted in large quantities of water. It is the principal waste product of freshwater and ocean organisms. Urea is less toxic than ammonia but also requires water, though less than for ammonia, for its excretion. Uric acid is nontoxic because it is almost insoluble; this form of nitrogenous waste has evolved in animals that must conserve water (as examples, insects, reptiles, birds, and some mammals).

Mammalian kidneys have evolved beyond the kidneys of many other organisms in regulating homeostasis. They remove nitrogenous wastes, conserve blood-sugar, and maintain water-salt balance and blood $p$H. They also regulate other materials in order to maintain homeostasis. The chief form of nitrogenous waste in humans is urea, diluted in water (containing other wastes) as urine. A secondary form of nitrogenous waste in humans is uric acid, which may form kidney stones if not flushed regularly in the urine. Uric acid in humans seems to be formed chiefly from nucleic acid breakdown by the liver.

## REVIEWING IDEAS

1. How do plants normally lose or eliminate water? How may some plants also eliminate excess water?
2. How may plants excrete salts? (Name two plant organs involved.)
3. In what way is depositing wastes in leaves a form of excretion for plants that lose and replace their leaves?
4. Which of the following structures have one or more of the same functions as human kidneys?

    a. kidneys in fishes
    b. gills in fishes
    c. salt glands in sea turtles
    d. plasma membranes in protists
    e. lungs in birds
    f. Malpighian tubules in grasshoppers
    g. contractile vacuoles in protists
    h. tracheae in insects

5. Which one of the structures in question 4 has exactly the same function as flame cells in planarians?
6. What is a nephron? Describe its interaction with the blood in the capillaries that fill its Bowman's capsule and the capillary network that surrounds its tubule.
7. Under what conditions will sugar be excreted in the urine of humans?

8. Which of these functions is not carried on by human kidneys?

   a. regulation of water-salt balance
   b. regulation of blood $pH$
   c. regulation of oxygen-carbon dioxide balance
   d. conservation of blood sugar
   e. excretion of nitrogenous wastes

9. How do planarians remove excess fresh water from their bodies?

10. What is the chief excretory organ of an ocean fish?

## USING CONCEPTS

11. How is the way in which an organism excretes its nitrogenous wastes usually related to the amount of water available to the organism?

12. Describe at least three adaptations in different organisms for eliminating carbon dioxide from the body.

13. What are the problems of homeostasis in ocean fishes? What other organisms share these problems?

14. What problem in water balance does a freshwater fish have that an ocean fish does not?

15. Describe how the human kidney controls water-salt balance. How does it control blood $pH$?

16. What salt level, relative to the environment, would you predict that an ocean microorganism has in its cell fluid, if it has an active contractile vacuole?

17. In what structure of the kidney does diffusion play the principal role? active transport? Explain these roles.

18. If you knew an organism excreted nitrogenous wastes only as uric acid, what hypothesis would you make regarding the organism or its environment?

19. As a tadpole, a frog lives completely in water. As an adult, it spends part of its time on land. How does this change in life-style affect its excretory system?

20. In what ways is a dialysis machine more effective than a human kidney? In what ways is it less effective?

## RECOMMENDED READING

Marsh, D. J. *Renal Physiology*. New York, Raven Press Publishing, 1981. A review of kidney function.

Silverstein, A., and V. B. Silverstein. *Excretory Systems: How Living Creatures Get Rid of Waste*. New York, Prentice-Hall, 1972. An introduction to a wide variety of excretory patterns.

PART SIX

# Life Processes II: Regulation and Coordination

This is how a ptarmigan looks in its summer plumage. And yet in winter this bird will be pure white. Seasonal differences account for the ptarmigan's summer and winter colors. (What factors do you think are at work?) Both sex and seasonal differences are internally regulated in multicellular organisms. So are all other life processes. Hormones and the nervous system are the controls.

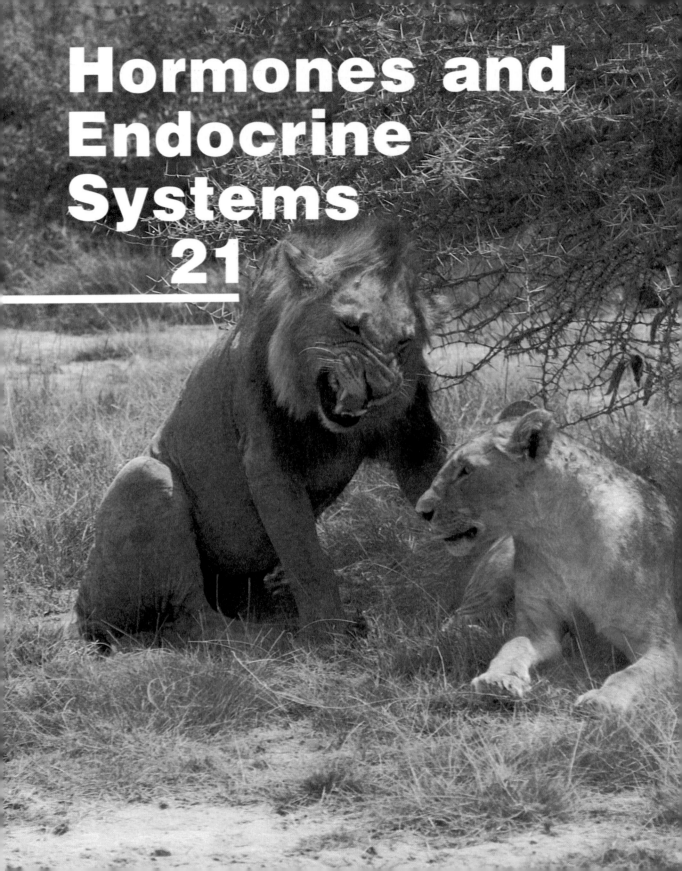

# Hormones and Endocrine Systems

## 21

Investigation of the functions of hormones has been going on for over 100 years. Tiny amounts of these substances have profound effects on the regulation of body processes. You have already read about hormonal regulation in the digestive and reproductive systems. Many other activities of animals and plants are regulated by hormones. In this chapter you will see how our knowledge of hormones has grown. You may also gain some insight into this fascinating subject by your own investigation. Because of the complicated nature of hormone balance, you will study only a few examples. Many of the functions of hormones are known, but other functions are still being detected and investigated by scientists today.

# Chemical Regulation in Plants and Animals

## 21-1

### Plant Hormones Control a Variety of Plant Activities

**Plant hormones** are substances that regulate internal plant functions such as growth. Hormones are produced in small amounts. They act on parts of the plant other than the part that produces them. The **auxins** (AWK-sins) are the specific hormones that control plant growth. The action of these hormones has been studied in experiments similar to the ones you will read about in Investigation 21–A. Other plant hormones regulate such activities as the start of flowering and fruiting, or the loss of leaves in autumn.

Plant hormones are produced by individual cells distributed throughout the plant body. These cells are not grouped together in specific locations as are the glands in animals.

Plant tissues may also produce hormones which slow down or prevent growth. These are called **plant inhibitors.** Several inhibitors have been isolated and found to control such activities as germination of seeds and budding in plants. (See **Appendix 21–A,** Inhibitors in Desert Plants, page 728.)

Biochemists have been able to make synthetic plant-growth regulators. A well-known weed killer, called 2,4-D, is a synthetic auxin that destroys weeds by chemical means. Weeds sprayed with 2,4-D grow very rapidly, then shrivel up and die. The way in which 2,4-D kills the weed is not clearly understood.

The continued study of natural plant hormones will bring more insight into the chemical regulation of plants. Testing of different kinds of organic molecules will help produce synthetic regulators that will either promote or inhibit plant growth. The results of these studies will help humans supply their increasing need for food.

**Try Investigation 21–A** What Causes a Plant to Grow Toward Light?, page 666.

**Try Investigation 21–B** How Does Light, or Its Absence, Affect the Growth of Plant Stems?, page 669.

---

← Related hormones in different mammals, influencing male and female behavior, can almost make you think these are "people" you know.

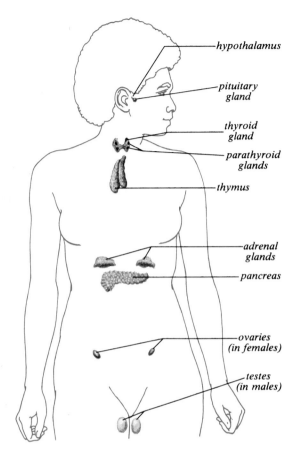

*hypothalamus*

*pituitary gland*

*thyroid gland*

*parathyroid glands*

*thymus*

*adrenal glands*

*pancreas*

*ovaries (in females)*

*testes (in males)*

**Figure 21–1** Some of the major endocrine glands in the human body. The hypothalamus is part of the brain, connecting the nervous and endocrine systems. It also secretes its own hormones. Many other cells and organs of the body also produce hormones.

## 21–2

## Chemicals Help Animals Maintain Homeostasis

About 100 years ago, the physiologist Claude Bernard pointed out how the many parts of a multicellular animal work together. Bernard concluded that the many body processes must be "directed by some invisible guide," regulating them in relationship to one another (Section 17–12). The idea of **homeostasis,** maintaining a constant internal environment, appeared to Bernard as the most striking feature of all living things.

Scientists have since discovered that Bernard's invisible guides are actually chemical substances dissolved in body fluids. Cells in one part of the body may influence cells in other parts of the body by chemical means. Some body-regulating chemicals such as oxygen, vitamins, and minerals come from outside the body. The body makes other chemicals, such as enzymes and hormones, that help to maintain the internal environment.

Hormones have been discovered in most organisms that biologists have investigated for these substances. One hypothesis to explain the presence of hormones is that they are cell messengers that promote the ability of individual cells to work together. Possibly cells in all animals and plants produce hormones. Only in more complex animals, however, do specialized glands occur that produce greater quantities of certain hormones.

The most well-known human hormones are the chemical substances secreted into the bloodstream by specialized tissues called **endocrine** (EN-duh-krin) **glands** (Figure 21–1) These hormones cannot be delivered directly to the organs they will regulate because no ducts or tubes connect the endocrine glands to those organs.

Many other glands in the body do have delivery tubes or ducts. Sweat glands, salivary glands, and digestive glands deliver their secretions through tubes directly to places where they are used. Hormones cannot be delivered in this way. Instead, the hormones are carried in the bloodstream and in this way are delivered to their target organs.

Not all hormones secreted into the blood come from the endocrine glands. Some hormones are secreted by individual body cells and they may enter body tissues as well as the bloodstream. Hormones also are secreted by cells of body organs that are not primarily endocrine glands. For example, you have already studied the stomach, which secretes the hormone gastrin (Section 19–6), and the intestine, which secretes secretin (Section 19–7).

Some hormones are proteins, but others are different chemical compounds. It is sometimes difficult to draw a sharp line between the action of hormones and the action of other chemical regulators such as vitamins and certain minerals. A very small amount of hormone may produce a great effect on the organ it regulates, or on the entire body. You have read how hormones produce a dramatic effect on the tissues of the uterus during the female reproductive cycle (Sections 11–16 and 11–17). Hormones from the hypothalamus, the pituitary (Figure 21–1), and the ovaries interact to regulate this reproductive cycle.

Hormones and nerves act together in many ways to regulate organ activity. Some nerve cells even secrete hormones. The nervous and endocrine systems are interconnected through the hypothalamus. Nerves stimulate many hormone secretions, and a number of hormones, in turn, affect nervous responses. You can see that the processes of regulating systems of the body are complex.

---

**CAPSULE SUMMARY**

Organisms including animals and plants produce chemical regulators called hormones. Plants have no specialized glands that produce hormones, but plant cells produce auxins and other hormones that regulate the plants and plant growth. A variety of synthetic chemicals related to plant hormones is used to promote crop growth or kill unwanted plants.

In animals as well as plants, hormones are produced by body cells, including some cells of organs that have other functions. Some of the higher vertebrates, including humans, have endocrine glands that produce still greater quantities of certain hormones. The most well-known human hormones are those produced by the endocrine glands.

**SELF CHECK**

1. What is an auxin? Where is it produced?
2. What is an endocrine gland?
3. How are hormones from endocrine glands delivered to organs they affect?
4. Name some substances other than hormones that have regulatory effects in the body.

---

# Interaction of Hormones

## 21–3

### Several Hormones Interact to Regulate the Blood's Glucose Level

In some cases a number of hormones work together to regulate the increase and decrease of a specific activity. An example of this control is the regulation of how much glucose is in the blood. Glucose is an important energy source for cells. Glucose molecules continually leave the bloodstream to enter cells all over the body. At the same time, great numbers of glucose molecules enter the blood from the intestines and liver. Yet the concentration of glucose in the blood remains remarkably constant.

**Insulin** (IN-suh-lin) and **glucagon** (GLOOK-uh-gon), two hormones formed in the pancreas, and **adrenaline** (uh-DREN-uh-lin), formed in the **adrenal** (uh-DREEN-ul) **glands,** work together to regulate the blood glucose level. (See Biology Brief: The Discovery of Insulin.) Insulin speeds the removal of glucose molecules from the blood by stimulating their entry into body and liver cells. In the body cells, glucose molecules may be used

# The Discovery of Insulin

A disease called **diabetes mellitus** has been known by different names since the time of the Roman Empire. It has caused many deaths. *Diabetes* means "to pass through" and *mellitus* means "honey-sweet." Sugar (glucose) is passed through the kidneys into the urine in this disease. Normally this key sugar in the bloodstream is not excreted. Its presence in the urine may be caused by a number of different conditions. In diabetes the cause is too high a blood-sugar level.

Homeostasis is difficult to maintain by people who are diabetic. Their body chemistry is unbalanced. When the symptoms of diabetes become extreme, the patient's life is in danger. Although this disease has been known for many centuries, its cause and treatment remained undiscovered until this century.

One of the first steps in discovering the cause of diabetes occurred when the pancreas was removed from several experimental animals. Scientists noticed flies swarming to the spots where the animals urinated, following recovery from surgery. A test of the urine revealed sugar. Other tests showed that the animals were suffering from a condition similar to diabetes in humans. The scientists treated the animals with extracts from the pancreas, but no improvement occurred.

The pancreas was found to consist of two kinds of gland tissue. One kind secretes some of the enzymes of digestion through a tube leading to the intestine. The other kind, scattered in small islands, was named the **Islets of Langerhans** after the scientist who discovered them. (See smaller photo, page 441.) Suspicion centered on the Islets as somehow being involved in diabetes.

At the University of Toronto, in 1920, F. G. Banting, a Canadian surgeon, and C. H. Best, a medical student, began a new series of experiments on dogs. Banting and Best hypothesized that grinding the pancreas to obtain extracts would cause digestive enzymes to mix with and digest whatever substance the Islets might produce. They tied off the pancreatic duct in each of the pancreases of their experimental dogs. The cells that produced digestive enzymes shriveled and became

for energy or may be stored for future use. Glucagon, on the other hand, tends to increase the passage of glucose into the blood from the intestines and liver. Adrenaline speeds up glycogen breakdown to glucose in the liver and causes still more glucose to be released into the blood. The way in which the glucose level of the blood is regulated is shown in Figure 21–2 on page 442.

How do these regulators work together to keep the concentration of blood glucose nearly constant? When the glucose concentration in blood is low, adrenaline and glucagon may be secreted.

Eli Lilly and Company

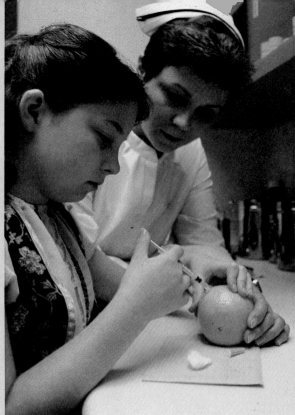

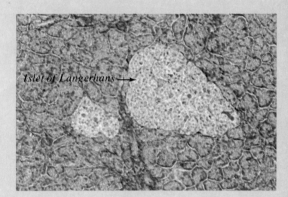

*Islet of Langerhans* →

inactive. The Islets, however, survived this treatment. Extracts from the Islets were then injected into diabetic dogs. The level of sugar in the dogs' blood was promptly reduced!

The substance the Islets produced was identified as a hormone and named insulin. Banting and Best were correct in believing that the Islets produced a substance necessary to the control of blood-sugar level.

Treatment with insulin has saved millions of lives. Most diabetics can lead almost normal lives given modified diets and regular injections of insulin. (The child you see above is learning the procedure, under a nurse's supervision, by practicing on an orange.) Still better means of controlling diabetes are constantly sought, because some disabilities can eventually occur even with treatment. Will recombinant DNA play a role in the control of *diabetes mellitus* in the future?

These substances cause the concentration of glucose in the blood to increase. Higher levels of glucose present in the bloodstream bring about a greater secretion of insulin by the pancreas. The insulin, in turn, causes the glucose molecules to leave the blood and enter the cells.

How the blood glucose level can affect the formation and the release of insulin and glucagon is still unknown. However, this kind of active balance is constantly maintained in your body. The kidneys also function in maintaining blood glucose level (page 428).

**441**

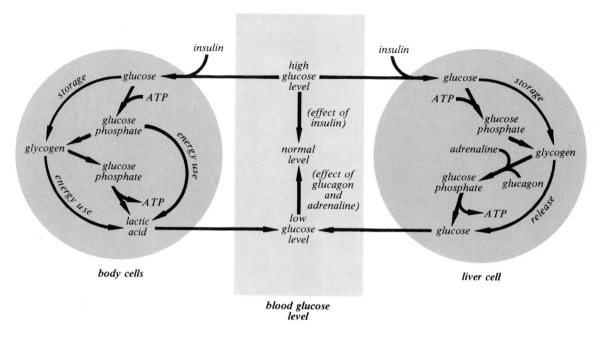

**Figure 21–2** The mechanism for the regulation of glucose level in the blood.

## 21–4

### The Thyroid Gland Secretes a Hormone That Controls Cell Activity

The thyroid gland secretes a hormone, called **thyroxine,** that regulates the speed of many basic cellular processes of the body. (See **Appendix 21–B,** The Function of the Thyroid Gland Is Discovered, page 728.) The activity of cells is called **metabolism.** One measure of metabolic activity is the amount of oxygen that the cells use. (See Investigation 18–A, Comparing Oxygen Consumption in Small Vertebrates.) Oxygen consumption by cells increases greatly when more thyroxine is secreted. As with other hormones, thyroxine is distributed by the bloodstream. If the thyroid gland secretes large amounts of hormone, body processes are speeded up. If the thyroid

gland secretes only small amounts of hormone, body processes are slowed down. In spite of a great deal of research we still do not know exactly how thyroxine acts on cells to regulate metabolism. We do know that this hormone causes an increased production of certain enzymes in cells, especially some that are involved in cellular respiration. Thyroxine also affects growth and development, especially in immature animals.

The human thyroid gland consists of two lobes connected to each other by a thin strip of tissue. The lobes are located on each side of the trachea, or windpipe, just below the voice box (Figure 21–3). Blood vessels and nerves penetrate each lobe. The lobes consist of small roundish sacs. These sacs, called follicles, are made of cells surrounding a cavity filled with colloid, a gel-like material. The colloid and the thyroxine are produced by the secretory cells (Figure 21–4). The hormone is stored in the colloid until needed. The amount of colloid within the follicles varies according to the health of the animal.

When the thyroid gland secretes either too much or too little hormone, the size of the gland generally increases, a condition known as goiter (see Figure 21–5).

An important discovery about the thyroid gland was made about 1900. It was observed that there was a very high concentration of iodine in the thyroid gland, hundreds of times more iodine than in other body tissues. It was also found that the thyroid glands of people living near the seacoast contained more iodine than those of people living farther inland.

About that time David Marine, a young American doctor living near Cleveland, Ohio, began experiments on the assumption that a lack of iodine might possibly produce goiter. It had been noticed that goiter was a rare disease along the seacoast. It

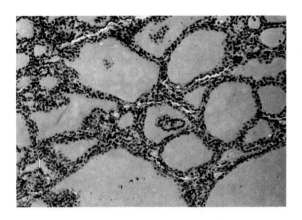

**Figure 21–4** A photograph of normal thyroid gland tissue. The spaces are filled with a colloid, an iodine-containing protein produced by the rings of surrounding tissue. The colloid contains several hormones produced by the thyroid, including thyroxine. (Courtesy Carolina Biological Supply Company)

was also known that iodine is present in seawater and all seafoods. Regions away from the sea, such as the Middle West or the Great Lakes, do not have much natural iodine.

Dr. Marine gave healthy experimental animals a diet with no iodine and they soon developed goiter. The next step in Marine's experiment was to add low concentrations of iodine to the diets of animals with goiter. After they were given iodine,

**Figure 21–5** An enlarged thyroid gland produces the condition called goiter.

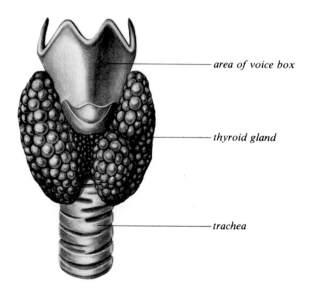

*area of voice box*

*thyroid gland*

*trachea*

**Figure 21–3** The human thyroid gland is in the throat. It has two lobes, one on each side of the windpipe, or trachea, just below the voice box.

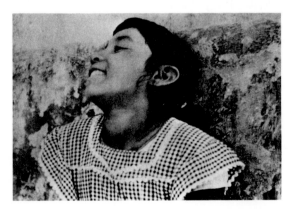

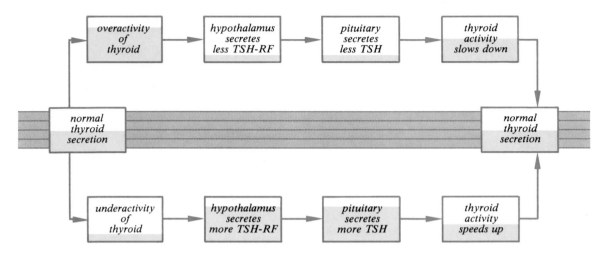

**Figure 21-6** The feedback system controlling the thyroid gland. The hypothalamus and pituitary are part of similar feedback systems controlling other endocrine glands.

the animals returned to normal health, and their goiters disappeared. This led Marine to propose that iodine be added to all drinking water and to table salt. It was fully 10 years before Marine's proposal was accepted. The use of iodine reduced the occurrence of goiter among the school children of Detroit from 36 percent in 1924 to 2 percent in 1931. Today, most table salt has iodine added.

## 21-5

## What Regulates the Thyroid Gland?

Experiments have shown that if the pituitary gland is removed from an experimental animal, the animal eventually becomes deficient in thyroxine. This indicates that normal thyroid function depends on the pituitary gland. But the story is more complex than this. The hypothalamus, where nervous system control and hormone regulation work together in many functions, is also involved. You first read about the hypothalamus in the regulation of the female reproductive cycle in Chapter 11.

In normal thyroid secretion of thyroxine (Figure 21-6, left), the hypothalamus, the pituitary, and the thyroid gland all work together with balanced hormone secretions. If an imbalance occurs, the hypothalamus releases more or less of a hormone called **TSH-releasing factor,** or **TSH-RF.** This hormone acts on the pituitary and causes it to release more or less **TSH** (thyroid-stimulating hormone). TSH then acts on the thyroid gland to secrete corresponding amounts of thyroxine. An increase or decrease in the thyroxine that is secreted affects the hypothalamus; its secretion of TSH-RF is adjusted accordingly. This is a good example of a feedback system, with constant interaction between the hypothalamus, the pituitary, and the thyroid.

Thyroid gland secretion is also influenced by changes in the external environment. For example, when rats are exposed to a very cold environment, the cells of their thyroid gland are enlarged and secretion is increased. Evidence indicates that the environment affects thyroid activity in humans, as well. Thyroid structure seems to vary widely according to many individual and geographic factors. Among the reasons for this variability are diet, climate, general health, exposure to radiation, and physiological makeup. (See **Appendix 21–C,** Thyroid Disorders Represent Abnormal Regulation, page 729.)

## 21–6

## How Could the Thyroid Gland Have Evolved?

When biologists searched for evidence of thyroid glands in animals, they made some interesting discoveries. Although the evidence is certainly not conclusive, a pattern of possible evolution of the thyroid gland can now be pictured.

Thyroxine-like compounds were discovered in the ''skeletons'' of sponges and corals. Mollusks, worms, and insects have been found to contain thyroxine-like compounds and even traces of thyroxine. But these invertebrates do not have glands to produce these compounds. The iodine-bound molecules are found in the hard parts of the body, such as the hard covering of insects. Some invertebrates have hard, toothlike parts in the pharynx that contain thyroxine. The location of thyroxine in different kinds of invertebrates is shown in Figure 21–7, *a* and *b*. How invertebrates use these compounds has not been determined.

The lancelet, a fishlike animal slightly more primitive than the vertebrates, lives on the ocean floor. In the lancelet, thyroxine is concentrated in a gland on the floor of the pharynx (Figure 21–7*c*). This is not an endocrine gland but releases its chemicals into the digestive system.

Thyroid glands have been found in all classes of vertebrates. The lamprey, an eel-like fish and a primitive vertebrate, shows an intermediate stage in the evolution of the thyroid gland. While young, the lamprey feeds on microorganisms in the mud and debris of lakes. The thyroid gland of the young lamprey, like that of the lancelet, lies at the

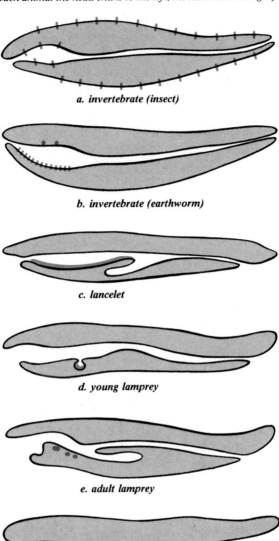

*location of thyroxine-like compounds in different animals (in each animal the head end is to the left, the tail end to the right)*

*a. invertebrate (insect)*

*b. invertebrate (earthworm)*

*c. lancelet*

*d. young lamprey*

*e. adult lamprey*

*f. complex vertebrate*

**Figure 21–7** The evolution of the thyroid gland is studied in terms of thyroxinelike compounds found in other animals. In the diagrams here, evidence of these compounds is shown in color. However, a true endocrine gland that produces thyroxine is not found in insects, earthworms, lancelets, or young lampreys. It is found in adult lampreys, and thyroid glands are common in the more complex vertebrates.

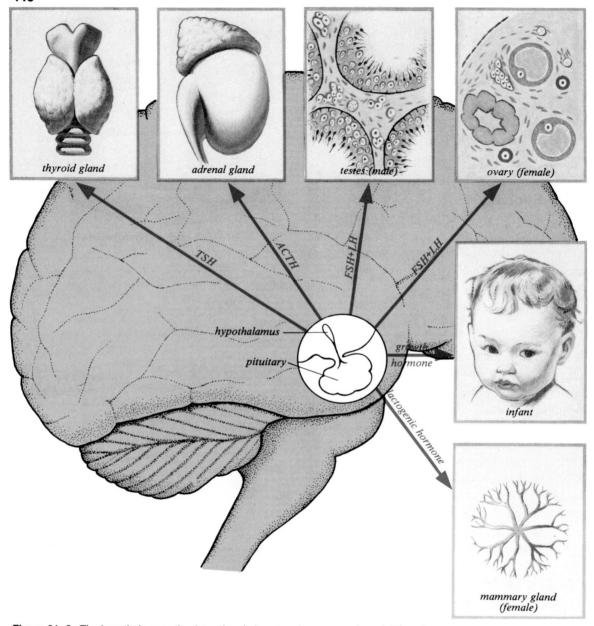

**Figure 21–8** The hypothalamus stimulates the pituitary to release a number of different major hormones. Most of these hormones stimulate other endocrine glands to secrete and release their hormones.

floor of the pharynx. But the gland of the young lamprey has evolved as a cuplike cavity with an opening or short tube leading into the pharynx. This is shown in Figure 21–7d.

The adult lamprey develops a funnel-like mouth lined with teeth. This permits the lamprey to attach itself to a living fish and suck blood for food. In the adult lamprey (Figure 21–7e), the tube from the thyroid gland is buried in tissue under the pharynx. At this stage, the thyroid is a true endocrine gland, for the hormone is released directly into the blood of the organism. The adult lamprey's thyroid gland is similar to the type found in more complex vertebrates, as shown in Figure 21–7f.

Using this kind of evidence, biologists are able to piece together evolutionary patterns. Because glands are made of soft tissues, they do not leave fossil evidence. Other means of detection are necessary. In this case, the chemical similarity between thyroxine-like substances in present-day invertebrates and vertebrates provides much of the evidence. It seems reasonable that the thyroid glands in vertebrates may have developed through the evolutionary path shown in Figure 21–7.

## 21–7

## Hormones from the Hypothalamus and the Pituitary Control Many Other Endocrine Glands

The hypothalamus, in the mid-region of the brain, and the pituitary gland, at the base of the brain, regulate many endocrine glands. The pituitary gland has sometimes been called the master gland because its hormones (Figure 21–8) control the secretions of other endocrine glands. But the hypothalamus controls the secretion of these regulatory pituitary hormones, as you saw with TSH-RF and TSH in affecting secretion of thyroxine by the thyroid gland.

In the discussion of the female reproductive system in Chapter 11, you read (Section 11–17) how the hypothalamus and pituitary interact with the ovaries. FSH-RF and LH-RF from the hypothalamus, and the corresponding two hormones, FSH (follicle-stimulating hormone) and LH (luteinizing hormone) from the pituitary, stimulate development of the ovarian follicles. The follicles produce more estrogen, which inhibits any further

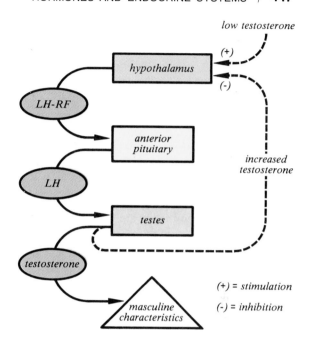

**Figure 21–9** The feedback system controlling the level of testosterone in males. The hypothalamus and the pituitary are part of each feedback system for the endocrine glands. (See Figures 11–24, 21–6, and 21–11.)

secretion by the hypothalamus and pituitary. This negative feedback, however, promotes release of a different ovarian hormone, progesterone. Progesterone and estrogen concentrations build up. The process continues through alternative hormone interactions that take place depending on whether or not an egg is fertilized and pregnancy occurs.

Similar interactions take place in human males. The hormone from the testes, testosterone, is produced under the influence of releasing hormones from the hypothalamus and the pituitary. The testosterone levels then inhibit further secretion by the hypothalamus and pituitary (Figure 21–9).

For another example, the adrenal glands are endocrine glands located just above the kidneys (See Figures 21–1 and 21–8). The outer part of each adrenal, the cortex, secretes a variety of hormones. There is a feedback control system operating between the adrenal cortex, the hypothalamus, and the pituitary, the latter of which secretes adrenocorticotrophic hormone (ACTH).

A summary of major human endocrine glands and hormones would require several pages because of the complex interactions between the hypothalamus, pituitary, and the other glands. Excluding all the releasing hormones or factors from the hypothalamus, a reasonable summary of other glands, some of their major hormones, and the functions of these hormones are given in Figure 21–10.

Hormones produced by body cells are not included in Figure 21–10. For example, for many years biologists wondered why fatty acids, obtained from digestion of fats, were essential to the body. Then some compounds built from fatty acids were discovered in human cells and cells of many other animals. These compounds acted to lower blood pressure and cause smooth muscle to contract. In addition, some compounds worked oppositely to known hormones. In every way they appeared to function as a large group of hormones themselves, regulating many processes in cells and tissues. All these fatty acid-derived, hormonelike substances are called **prostaglandins** (prah-stuh-GLAND-ins). There are a great many of them, perhaps as many as all other known hormones taken together. The prostaglandins appear to be synthesized all over the body in cells and tissues. At least 14 are known in the human male reproductive tract alone. As their functions are better understood they will be more fully included in discussions of hormone regulation in the body. How, for example, are they affected by the hypothalamus and pituitary, which exercise control over so many other hormone functions?

**Try Investigation 21–C** Regulation of Secondary Sex Characteristics in Chickens, page 670.

## 21–8

## The Hypothalamus and the Pituitary Are Both Very Complex in Their Structure and Function

Whether to call the hypothalamus an endocrine gland (Figures 21–1 and 21–8) or a part of the brain has been a question for many years. In recent years research has established that the hypothalamus fills both functions.

Direct nerve links exist between the hypothalamus and the pituitary. Some of the nerve cells, or **neurons** (NYOO-rons), from the hypothalamus are connected to a blood vessel that leads to the front part, or **anterior lobe,** of the pituitary gland. Other neurons from the hypothalamus lead directly to the back part, or **posterior lobe,** of the pituitary. No blood vessel is involved here.

How does the hypothalamus act on the pituitary with these two different kinds of connections? Scientists now believe that hormones are synthesized in the neurons of the hypothalamus. A number of these hormones have actually been detected in close association with the neurons. Some are secreted by the neurons into the blood vessel that leads to the anterior pituitary. These hormones are the releasing factors (RFs) that you have read about. They stimulate the anterior pituitary to produce its own hormones that act, in turn, to stimulate other endocrine glands to produce their hormones. The male and female reproductive functions, the thyroid function, and other functions you have studied are examples of this type.

The nerves leading from the hypothalamus to the posterior pituitary are also believed to secrete hormones. But they secrete these hormones directly into the posterior pituitary, where they are stored until their release. The posterior pituitary therefore releases hypothalamic hormones in at least some cases, instead of making its own hormones in response to those secreted by the hypothalamus.

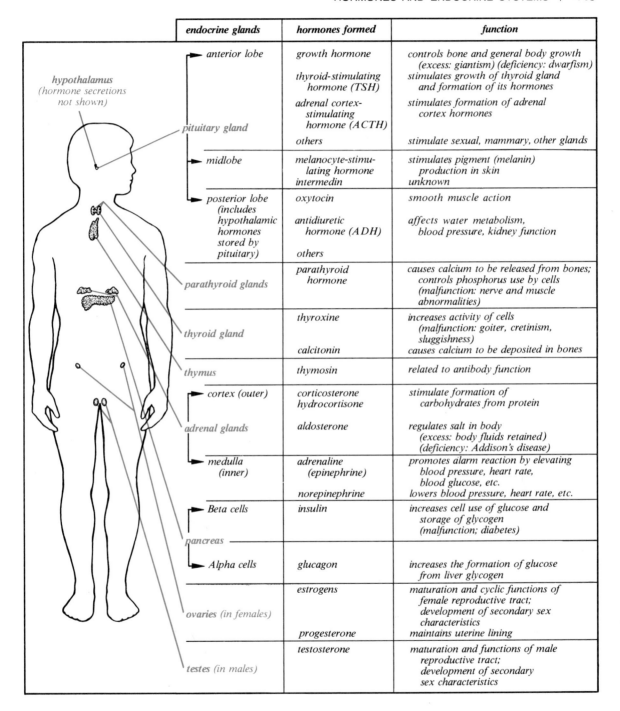

| endocrine glands | hormones formed | function |
|---|---|---|
| *anterior lobe* | *growth hormone* | *controls bone and general body growth (excess: giantism) (deficiency: dwarfism)* |
| | *thyroid-stimulating hormone (TSH)* | *stimulates growth of thyroid gland and formation of its hormones* |
| | *adrenal cortex-stimulating hormone (ACTH)* | *stimulates formation of adrenal cortex hormones* |
| *pituitary gland* | *others* | *stimulate sexual, mammary, other glands* |
| *midlobe* | *melanocyte-stimulating hormone* | *stimulates pigment (melanin) production in skin* |
| | *intermedin* | *unknown* |
| *posterior lobe (includes hypothalamic hormones stored by pituitary)* | *oxytocin* | *smooth muscle action* |
| | *antidiuretic hormone (ADH)* | *affects water metabolism, blood pressure, kidney function* |
| | *others* | |
| *parathyroid glands* | *parathyroid hormone* | *causes calcium to be released from bones; controls phosphorus use by cells (malfunction: nerve and muscle abnormalities)* |
| *thyroid gland* | *thyroxine* | *increases activity of cells (malfunction: goiter, cretinism, sluggishness)* |
| | *calcitonin* | *causes calcium to be deposited in bones* |
| *thymus* | *thymosin* | *related to antibody function* |
| *cortex (outer)* | *corticosterone hydrocortisone* | *stimulate formation of carbohydrates from protein* |
| *adrenal glands* | *aldosterone* | *regulates salt in body (excess: body fluids retained) (deficiency: Addison's disease)* |
| *medulla (inner)* | *adrenaline (epinephrine)* | *promotes alarm reaction by elevating blood pressure, heart rate, blood glucose, etc.* |
| | *norepinephrine* | *lowers blood pressure, heart rate, etc.* |
| *Beta cells* | *insulin* | *increases cell use of glucose and storage of glycogen (malfunction; diabetes)* |
| *pancreas* | | |
| *Alpha cells* | *glucagon* | *increases the formation of glucose from liver glycogen* |
| *ovaries (in females)* | *estrogens* | *maturation and cyclic functions of female reproductive tract; development of secondary sex characteristics* |
| | *progesterone* | *maintains uterine lining* |
| *testes (in males)* | *testosterone* | *maturation and functions of male reproductive tract; development of secondary sex characteristics* |

*hypothalamus (hormone secretions not shown)*

**Figure 21–10** Some of the hormones secreted by human endocrine glands, together with a summary of the hormones' functions.

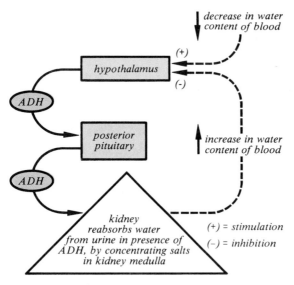

**Figure 21–11** The feedback system controlling the level of water in the blood. What is different about the contributions of the hypothalamus and the pituitary in this particular system?

An example of the work of the hypothalamus and the posterior pituitary is the maintenance of the body's water-salt balance, which you read about in the last chapter. One of the hormones synthesized in neurons of the hypothalamus and secreted directly into the posterior pituitary is **antidiuretic hormone** (ADH). A decrease in the water content of the blood stimulates release of stored ADH from the posterior pituitary (Figure 21–11). The ADH travels through the bloodstream and reaches the kidneys, where it concentrates salt in the medulla of each kidney. The high salt concentration "pulls" water, by osmosis, from the dilute urine passing through the tubules in the medulla of each kidney. The water is returned to the bloodstream, raising its water content again. The return of the water content of the blood to normal acts as negative feedback on the hypothalamus and pituitary. Less ADH is released until the water content of the blood falls below normal again.

Does nerve stimulation from the hypothalamus take two different forms in acting on the posterior pituitary? If some neurons of the hypothalamus secrete hormones that the posterior pituitary stores, do other neurons stimulate the posterior pituitary to secrete hormones of its own? This seems possible based on present research, although much remains to be clarified about the hormones that are released, if not made, in the posterior pituitary. In fact, much remains to be learned about both the hypothalamus and the pituitary. (For example, the pituitary has a mid-lobe, too; see Figure 21–10.) New answers will continue to be obtained for many years into the future.

---

**CAPSULE SUMMARY**

A specific body function may be regulated by more than one hormone. For example, the level of glucose in the blood is kept constant by the interaction of glucagon, insulin, and adrenaline.

Another example of the interaction of body regulators is the relationship between the thyroid, the hypothalamus, and the pituitary gland. Thyroxine from the thyroid gland regulates the speed of basic cellular processes throughout the body. The thyroid is in turn affected by a pituitary gland hormone. The pituitary is affected by a releasing hormone from the hypothalamus.

The hypothalamus and the pituitary have proved to be very complex. Some hypothalamic hormones stimulate the pituitary to make its own hormones. Other hypothalamic hormones are stored in the pituitary and released by it; in these cases the pituitary is not making its own hormones.

**SELF CHECK**

1. How does iodine affect the thyroid gland?
2. How does hormone interaction contribute to homeostasis?
3. How would the lack of insulin affect glucagon and adrenaline production?
4. How does the hypothalamus interact with the anterior and posterior lobes of the pituitary?

# CHAPTER SUMMARY

## HIGHLIGHTS

Hormones appear to have developed early in evolution. In all multicellular organisms, hormone production occurs in different individual cells. In the more complex vertebrates, a system of endocrine glands produces greater quantities of certain hormones.

Most plant hormones that have been investigated regulate growth. Animal hormones have been identified that regulate many of the major functions in the bodies of animals. Sometimes several hormones may interact, as in the regulation of blood-sugar level.

The hypothalamus, the pituitary, and various endocrine glands interact in producing hormones that regulate many body functions. Hormones produced in different body cells are also involved in these interactions, but in ways that are still largely unknown. Much remains to be learned about hormones, especially the many hormones produced by body cells.

The hypothalamus is part of both the brain and the endocrine system. It is a link in the close coordination of endocrine gland and nervous system functions.

## REVIEWING IDEAS

1. The pancreas includes both digestive and endocrine glands (Islets of Langerhans). How do the two kinds of glands differ in the way they deliver their secretions?
2. Which two glands in the endocrine system are always involved in interactions with other endocrine glands?
3. How was iodine discovered to be necessary for thyroid gland function?
4. A deficiency in which endocrine gland produces the disorder called diabetes?

5. What are releasing factors or releasing hormones? Where are they produced?
6. Name a hormone that speeds up cell processes and increases the amount of oxygen the cells use.
7. What three hormones interact in regulating blood-sugar level?

## USING CONCEPTS

8. Explain how a feedback system works in the regulation of a body process by hormones.
9. Without investigation, should biologists assume that thyroxine found in invertebrates has the same functions it has in complex vertebrates? Explain.
10. Research indicates that organs as different as the brain and the testes may produce their own insulin. How does this finding relate to the way in which biologists think hormone production evolved in animals?
11. How do positive (+) and negative (−) feedback differ in a feedback system of hormones?
12. How do endocrine glands and the kidneys work together in maintaining water-salt balance?

## RECOMMENDED READING

Keeton, W. T. *Biological Science*. Third edition. New York, Norton, 1980. A college textbook with an excellent chapter on chemical control.

Mysteries, "Why Do Women Live Longer than Men?" *Science 83*, October issue. A brief article that includes the role of sex hormones.

Research News, "New Theory of Hormones Proposed." *Science*, 12 March 1982. More about the hypothesis that hormones are made by many cells in all organisms, and that endocrine glands developed later.

# The Nervous System and Sensory Mechanisms

## 22

A variety of mechanisms control and regulate the internal environment of multicellular animals. Among these mechanisms the nervous system is the chief coordinating system. Almost every body function is controlled, monitored, and continuously regulated by the nervous system. Sensitivity to the organism's external environment as well as its internal environment is part of this regulation and control.

The endocrine system, another control system, is largely regulated by the nervous system and so is operationally a part of it. In Chapter 21 you learned that some of the pituitary hormones are secreted by the nerve cells in the hypothalamus. In this chapter you will learn more about how the nervous and endocrine systems work together to bring order to the many body activities of animals.

# Structure and Function of the Nervous System

## 22–1

### Organisms Respond to Changes in the Environment

An environmental change that may cause an organism to respond is known as a **stimulus** (STIM-yoo-lus)—plural, stimuli. The response can be a change in the organism internally or in its outward behavior. You receive stimuli through **sensory receptors.** These receptors are specialized tissues and nerve cell endings that react to events both in your body and in your surrounding environment (see Figure 22–1).

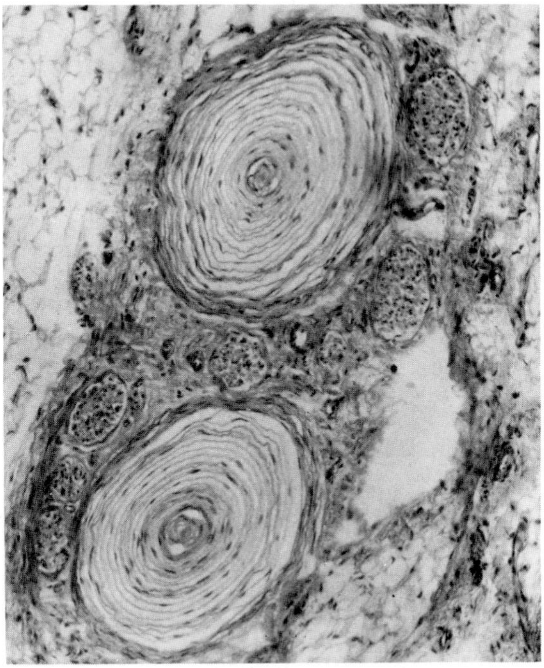

**Figure 22–1** (Right) These touch receptors, shown → in cross section, are located in the finger.

←Keeping a sharp lookout—an eagle eye—on things is the activity for which this bird of prey is noted.

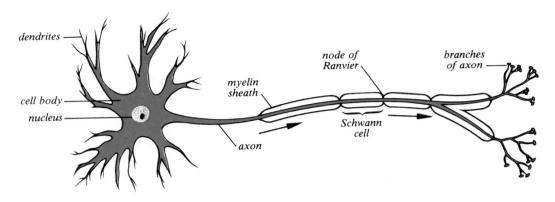

**Figure 22-2** A diagram of a motor neuron of a vertebrate. The axon carries impulses away from the cell body, as the arrows indicate.

Receptors may be grouped together in **receptor organs.** Each receptor or group of receptors is specialized to receive a specific kind of stimulus. Receptors in the eye, for instance, are stimulated by light waves. Some of the receptors in the ear react to sound waves. The organs of smell and taste react to a variety of chemical substances. To how many different kinds of stimuli are you sensitive? Imagine that you go into a closet and shut the door, excluding all visible light. You hear nothing and see nothing. However, if you took a radio into the closet, you would find that the air is full of stimuli. Your ears alone cannot pick up the stimuli, but the radio can. A television set would pick up other stimuli. Obviously people's eyes and ears reveal very few of the many events going on around them. The eyes and ears provide only glimpses into the physical world.

Any one type of receptor receives only a small portion of the stimuli present in the environment. The receptors of the eye are stimulated only by light waves that vary from the short violet waves to the long red waves. These waves, called visible light, represent only some of the many waves actually present (see Figure 7-1). For instance, the waves shorter than violet, called ultraviolet, cannot be picked up by the human eye. Waves longer than red, the infrared and radio waves, are also invisible to humans. Some of these waves can be detected by other organisms. They can also be detected by special instruments.

In Investigation 22-A you will begin to study some of your own responses to stimuli. You probably will notice that certain parts of your skin are more sensitive than others. The more sensitive areas contain more sensory receptors or receptor organs than the less sensitive areas do.

**Try Investigation 22-A** What Does Your Touch Tell You?, page 672.

**Try Investigation 22-B** The Mammalian Eye: Its Parts and How They Work, page 673.

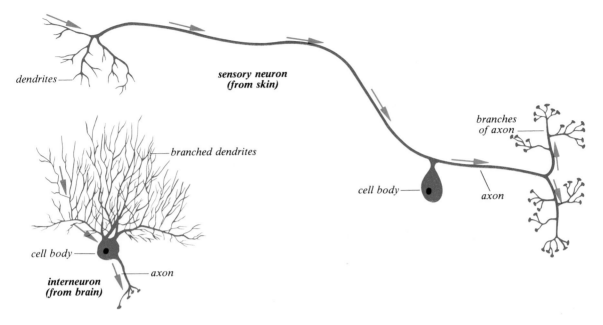

dendrites

*sensory neuron*
*(from skin)*

*branches*
*of axon*

*cell body*

*axon*

*branched dendrites*

*cell body*

*axon*

*interneuron*
*(from brain)*

**Figure 22–3** Different neurons from different parts of the vertebrate nervous system may have different shapes, but you can recognize them by their structure. The arrows indicate the direction in which nerve impulses normally travel.

## 22–2

## The Nervous System Is Made Up of Nerve Cells

A **nervous system** is an organized network of **neurons** (NYOO-ronz), or nerve cells. A typical nerve cell is shown in Figure 22–2. The nerve cell has three main parts: the **dendrites** (DEN-dryts), the **cell body,** and the **axon** (AK-son). The dendrites and axon are extensions of the cell body. The dendrites carry nerve signals, or impulses, toward the cell body. The axon carries signals away from the cell body. The nucleus is located in the nerve cell body. Although the general structure is similar, the shape of neurons varies in different animals, and even within different parts of the nervous system of one animal (see Figure 22–

3). Neurons vary greatly in length and thickness. The axons of some cells of vertebrate animals have a special covering called the **myelin** (MY-uh-lin) **sheath.** The myelin sheath is formed from coils of the membrane of **Schwann cells.** The Schwann cells are highly specialized and almost completely enclose the axon. The areas between Schwann cells are called **nodes of Ranvier.** Figure 22–4 on page 456 shows how the Schwann cell's membrane has been coiled to form the myelin sheath.

Axons covered with myelin sheaths transmit their signals at fast rates, up to about 120 meters per second. Axons without myelin sheaths carry signals more slowly, often at less than one tenth of the rate for myelinated axons.

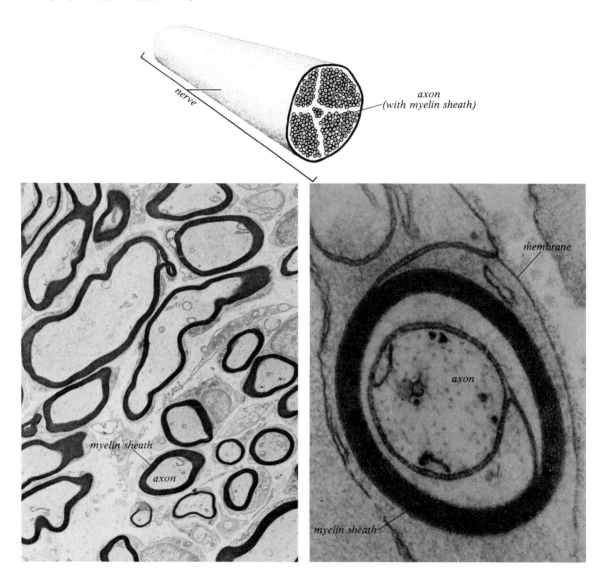

**Figure 22–4** A nerve cross section (top) shows bundles of axons. The drawing is magnified about 100 times over actual size. At a magnification of 2500 (photo at left) and 100,000 (photo at right), you can see a single axon in increasing detail. Each axon is surrounded by a myelin sheath made up of coils of the membrane of a Schwann cell.

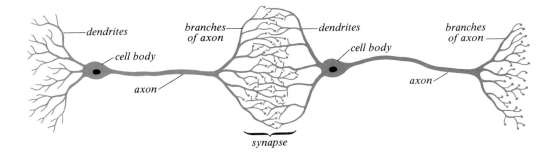

**Figure 22-5** Trace the path of an impulse across the synapse. In which direction does the impulse travel from neuron to neuron?

The dendrites and the axons of a neuron are sometimes called **nerve fibers.** In some cases they are long nerve fibers and may be a meter in length. A **nerve** is a bundle of these long fibers. When a nerve is cut and observed under a microscope, the end view looks like a cable. Each axon or dendrite in a cross section is like a wire in the cable, as shown in Figure 22–4.

If you could trace a nerve signal from your foot to your brain, you would find that several neurons would be involved. Nerve cells can receive and pass on signals. The dendrites of one neuron lie close to the axons of another (see Figure 22–5). The place where two neurons meet is called a **synapse** (SIH-naps). Figure 22–6 shows a highly magnified picture of the ends of an axon at the synapse. The two neurons are not connected. In fact, a small gap between the two cells is found at the synapse. However, the neurons are close enough for chemical signals to pass from one to the other. These signals pass over the gap in only one direction, from the axon of one neuron to the dendrite of the other neuron.

**Figure 22-6** An electron micrograph of part of a synapse, showing terminal knobs on the ends of the branches of the axon. An impulse coming to the ends of the axon stimulates the synaptic knobs to secrete a chemical messenger, or neurotransmitter. The chemical crosses the gap and stimulates the dendrites of neighboring neurons, re-initiating the impulse in them.

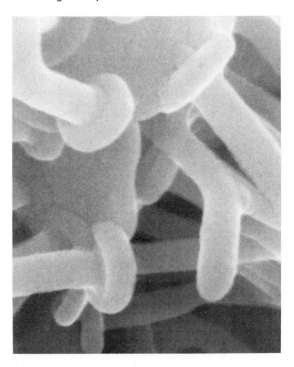

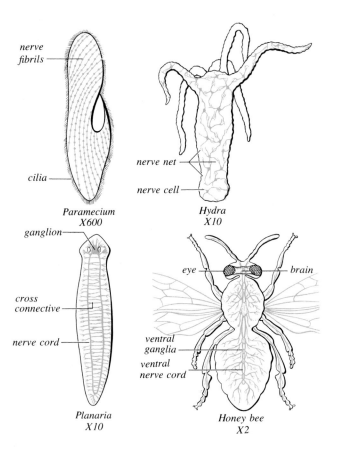

*nerve fibrils*

*cilia*

*Paramecium X600*

*ganglion*

*cross connective*

*nerve cord*

*Planaria X10*

*nerve net*

*nerve cell*

*Hydra X10*

*eye*

*brain*

*ventral ganglia*

*ventral nerve cord*

*Honey bee X2*

**Figure 22–7** *Paramecium* does not have a nervous system but does have fibrils that cause its cilia to beat rhythmically. *Hydra* has a nerve net made up of nerve cells that are all alike. A planarian has a nervous system with two nerve cords, many nerve cells, and a ganglion in the head region. A honeybee has an even more advanced nervous system, in which the two nerve cords and ganglia along them form a single cord. The honeybee also has a brain.

## 22–3

### Nerve Structures Vary in Different Organisms

Plants and unicellular protists do not have specialized nerve cells. However, these organisms are able to respond to certain stimuli. For example, as you learned in Section 21–1, plants respond to light by chemical means. Many unicellular organisms also react to stimuli by chemical means. The sensitivity of these cells to stimuli indicates that response to a stimulus is a general characteristic of living tissue.

Paramecia can respond to stimuli such as changes in light, temperature, and acidity. They also have a series of fibrils interconnecting the bases of their cilia. These fibrils can be seen with an electron microscope (see Figure 22–7). If the fibrils are cut, the cilia no longer beat.

All major groups of multicellular animals except the sponges have definite nerve cells. However, even without nerve cells, sponges are able to respond to external stimuli. One sponge cell can transmit the effect of a stimulus to a neighboring cell by chemical means.

A *Hydra* has a nervous system made up only of nerve cells evenly distributed throughout the animal and connected to each other by synapses (see

Figure 22–7). Such a system is called a **nerve net.** When a stimulus is applied to any point on a *Hydra,* the resulting impulse eventually spreads along the nerve net in all directions through the whole organism. For an effect to spread very far, however, the stimulus must be strong and last a long time. The nerve net carries signals more slowly than do the nerves of higher organisms.

Higher animals have both nerve nets and more organized nervous systems. In this type of system most of the cells are more centrally located into clusters and cords. The planarian, for example, has a centralized nervous system in addition to a nerve net. Although vertebrates have complex and highly organized nervous systems, nerve nets are found in the walls of both their blood vessels and their intestines.

The simple nervous system of the planarian contains the basic structures found in more complex systems. In the head region, the planarian has two clusters of nerve cells called **ganglia** (GANG-glee-uh)—singular, ganglion. A ganglion is a collection of nerve cell bodies enclosed by sheaths of connective tissue. When many ganglia are located in the head region, the cluster is usually called a **brain.** A separate **nerve cord** consisting of chains of ganglia runs along each side of the planarian's body. These nerve cords are joined by connecting links (see Figure 22–7). Many variations of this basic type are found in the animal kingdom.

Basically, the honeybee's nervous system is similar to the planarian's (see Figure 22–7). In the insect there is a pair of nerve cords very close together under the digestive system. They are usually referred to as a single cord. The head ganglia, the brain of the insect, are made up of thousands of nerve cells that extend into the nerve cords. From the nerve cords, more nerves lead to the segments of the insect's body.

In vertebrates, the nerve cord is a single tube lying above the digestive tract. The brain, an

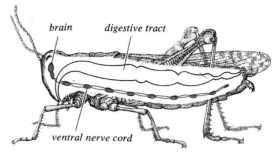

*arthropod*

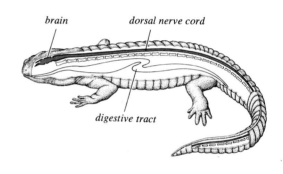

*vertebrate*

**Figure 22–8** In insects the nerve cord is ventral, beneath the digestive tract. In vertebrates it is dorsal, above the digestive tract.

anterior extension of the nerve cord, is also above the digestive tract. In Figure 22–8, the location of the nerve cord in an insect is compared with that of a vertebrate. Note that in the insect, the brain lies above the digestive tract while the nerve cord lies below the digestive tract. A complex web of nerves transmits stimuli from receptor organs to the nerve cord and all parts of the organism.

The most important factor in the evolution of the vertebrate nervous system is the development of the brain. You will find out more about the evolution and functions of the brain later in this chapter.

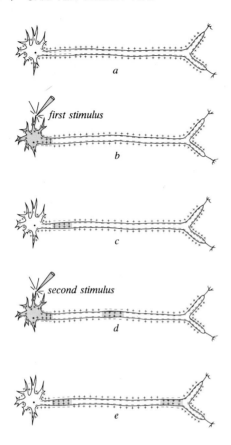

**Figure 22–9** (a) A neuron in a ready state, not yet stimulated. Plus and minus signs indicate a relative difference in electrical charge. The plasma membrane is more positive on the outside than on the inside. (b) A stimulus is applied. The electrical state reverses as the impulse is initiated. (c) The impulse moves as a wave of changes in electrical charges. (d) A second stimulus is applied after recovery. (e) Both impulses, spaced apart, move along the axon.

## 22–4

## How Does a Nerve Signal Travel Along a Neuron?

A stimulus at the end of a nerve fiber or neuron starts a process of chemical and electrical changes that travels like a wave over the length of a neuron. This wave of change is called a nerve impulse. The chemical reactions that occur in the nerve impulse at any given segment of a neuron consume oxygen and require energy. In addition, the reactions produce carbon dioxide and a rise in temperature.

Electrical changes accompany the chemical changes. Experiments have shown that the outside of a nonstimulated fiber of a neuron is electrically more positive than the inside (see Figure 22–9a). The difference in electrical charge arises from the neuron plasma membrane's difference in permeability to charged ions, principally sodium (Na$^+$) and potassium (K$^+$).

When the dendrites of a neuron are stimulated, electrical changes indicate the start of a nerve impulse (see Figure 22–9b). The inside of the neuron at the stimulated point becomes more positive and the outside becomes relatively more negative. This sudden change in electrical charge is caused primarily by the admittance of sodium ions (Na$^+$) from the outside to the inside of the neuron's plasma membrane. The nerve impulse then starts a similar change in the next small segment. Each segment along a neuron's length is then stimulated by an impulse traveling from the segment before it. The impulse moves from one end of the neuron to the other as a wave of local chemical and electrical changes. Neurons need time to recover before they receive a new stimulus. Sodium ions must be pumped back outside the plasma membrane, using active transport. A smaller number of potassium ions must be moved inside the membrane. Thus charges are redistributed (see Figure 22–9c). A second stimulus too soon after the first may elicit no response. However, in some neurons the recovery time may be as brief as a thousandth of a second. After recovery the neuron can carry another impulse (see Figure 22–9d, e). (See **Appendix 22–A,** How Does a Nerve Respond to Various Stimulus Strengths?, page 730).

**Try Investigation 22–C** Chemical Receptors of Taste and Smell, page 675.

# Biology Brief

# Biofeedback Training

A youth sits in a darkened room, wired to an oscillograph. The machine detects very small amounts of electricity produced by the brain cells. The experiment is on learning—an unusual kind of learning. Do you think you could learn to increase your brain's output of a selected pattern of brain waves?

That is what the subject of the experiment is doing. Normally the brain waves called *alpha waves* are produced for short periods at a rate of about 8 to 14 per second. The oscillograph and a computer have been connected to a speaker, so that each time alpha waves are produced, a beeping tone is heard. The waves are also recorded on an EEG (electroencephalogram). With this positive feedback the youth is learning how to control brain activity and increase the length of time alpha waves are produced. Why would this be useful? The only fact known for sure is that alpha waves are associated with a state of full, yet relaxed, alertness during periods of peak mental performance.

Experiments like this are called biofeedback training. Some of the results indicate better mental performance. Others show learned control over body functions that are normally involuntary, relating to the heart, circulation, digestive system, and various glands. Conscious control like this has long been practiced by mystics, meditators, and even hypnotists.

Applications of biofeedback training, if viewed with some caution, offer some interesting possibilities. A person with high blood pressure might learn to maintain a blood pressure low enough to prevent headaches and dizziness, as well as help prevent coronary attacks and strokes. Individuals suffering from much tension or fatigue might benefit by being trained to induce muscle relaxation. Good athletes are aware that great mental concentration is required to accomplish complicated physical feats. They might benefit by practicing the necessary concentration, using feedback signals of brain waves to indicate the moment of optimum preparation. Biofeedback training could be used in teaching machines to signal when the attention of the student is lost. Alternative teaching procedures could be built into the teaching program to recapture the attention.

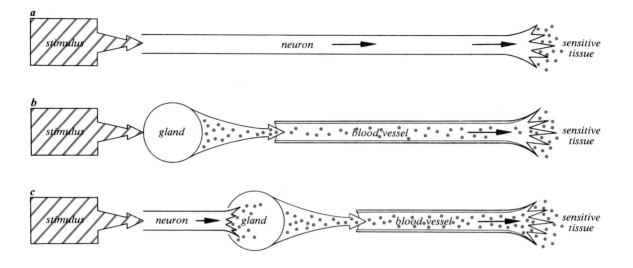

**Figure 22–10** Nerve impulses and endocrine functions both involve secretion of chemicals that affect sensitive organs or tissues. Which method brings about a response more quickly?

## 22–5

### How Do Nerve Impulses Travel Between Neurons?

More and more evidence has accumulated to show that the transmission of impulses between neurons is different from conduction of impulses *along* neurons. The small gap between the cells at the synapse prevents a direct continuation of the impulse. Experiments have shown that specific chemical substances produced at the ends of the nerve fiber bridge the gap.

When impulses come to the ends of an axon they cause the release of the chemical substance. The chemical diffuses across the synapse and causes a new nerve impulse to be initiated in the dendrites of the next neuron. The chemicals are produced only at the ends of the axons (see Figures 22–5 and 22–6) and not in dendrites. Therefore, the nerve impulses can travel only in one direction along a series of neurons.

The substance released by some neurons is a relatively simple compound, **acetylcholine** (uh-seet-il-KOH-leen). It transmits impulses across many types of nerve endings. Acetylcholine is called a **neurotransmitter** (nyur-oh-trans-MIT-er). A neurotransmitter is any substance released by nerve endings that transmits an impulse from one neuron to another neuron, or to a muscle, or to a gland. In each case the neurotransmitter causes a different reaction. In another neuron it causes a new nerve impulse to start. In muscle cells contraction occurs. In gland cells secretions are released.

## 22–6

## Nerves and Hormones Work Together to Regulate Various Activities

Nervous regulation and hormonal regulation of various organs and cells are similar in many ways (see Figure 22–10). Receptors receive stimuli and impulses are transmitted along neurons to sensitive structures—cells, tissues, or organs (Figure 22–10a). But, at the ends of neurons, neurotransmitters are released. It is these chemicals, not the nerve impulse, that actually cause the responses.

Interestingly, a neurotransmitter may be identical to a hormone. The neurotransmitter **norepinephrine** (nor-ep-eh-NEH-freen), released in muscle tissue, is identical to a hormone of the same name produced by the adrenal glands.

Endocrine glands receive stimuli and secrete hormones (Figure 22–10b). These hormones circulate in the bloodstream to a sensitive structure where they regulate its activity. Nerve impulses travel very rapidly. Blood circulation is much slower. Therefore, nervous regulation is much more rapid than hormonal regulation.

In many cases both nerves and hormones control the activity of a single organ. For example, neurons from the brain running to the heart control its rate of beating. A hormone from the adrenal gland (see Figure 21–10), adrenaline, also helps to control heart rate. (See **Appendixes 22–B,** the Autonomic Nervous System, page 730, and **22–C,** Neurotransmitters and Hormones Control the Rate of the Heartbeat, page 732.)

Neurons and endocrine glands also operate in sequence to regulate activities (Figure 22–10c). Stimuli received by neurons cause a nerve impulse. The impulse travels over the neuron to an endocrine gland. The gland, in response to the impulse, secretes a hormone. The hormone circulates in the blood to a sensitive tissue or organ.

Thus the nervous system and the endocrine system work together to regulate the activities of the body that are important in maintaining a homeostatic balance.

---

**CAPSULE SUMMARY**

Receptors permit organisms to receive stimuli from their surroundings. In human beings these receptors are widely distributed inside and on the surface of the body, including the skin and tongue. Receptors are also grouped into complex organs like the ear and the eye. Response to stimuli is a general characteristic of living tissues. Most animals have specialized nerve cells and tissues.

The basic structural unit of the nervous system is the nerve cell, or neuron. The nerve impulse travels along a neuron by a series of chemical and electrical changes. Impulses may cross the synapse between neurons by means of neurotransmitters.

Neurotransmitters from nerves and hormones from endocrine glands work together to control many activities of animals.

**SELF CHECK**
1. What are stimuli?
2. Describe a nerve cell and nerve net.
3. In what direction do nerve impulses normally travel over a neuron?
4. Describe a synapse.
5. Describe various ways neurons and endocrine glands can regulate sensitive tissue.

# The Central Nervous System—Control and Homeostasis

## 22–7

### The Brain and Spinal Cord Are the Center of a Human's Nervous System

In humans the nervous system consists of several interdependent systems:

1. The **central nervous system** is made up of the **brain** and **spinal cord.**
2. The **peripheral** (peh-RIF-er-ul) **nervous system** is made up of the nerves that connect directly to the central nervous system.
3. The **autonomic** (ot-oh-NOM-ik) **nervous system** (Appendix 22–B, page 730) is made up of ganglia and neurons in pathways leaving the central nervous system, and regulating functions that are not under conscious control.

The spinal cord (Figure 22–11) extends from the base of the brain to the lower back and is protected within the backbone. The brain is a large extended part of the spinal cord and is protected inside the skull. Both the brain and the spinal cord contain neurons and fluid and are covered by membranes.

Twelve pairs of cranial nerves connect directly to the brain. Thirty-one pairs of spinal nerves connect to the spinal cord. Some of the cranial and spinal nerves contribute neurons that lead into the autonomic nervous system. However, the majority of neurons issuing from, or leading to, these nerves are part of the peripheral nervous system, and as such involve conscious sensations and functions.

**Sensory neurons** carry impulses from the body's sensory receptors to the spinal cord and the brain. All the impulses are chemically and electrically the same. Any of these neurons can be stimulated experimentally to carry impulses with a mild

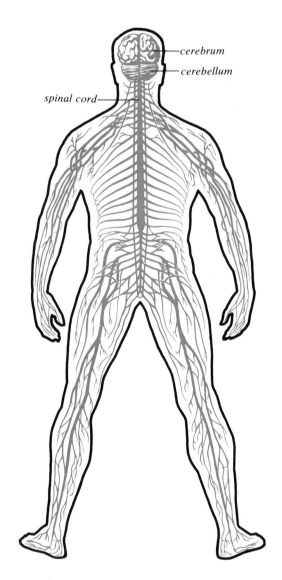

*cerebrum*
*cerebellum*
*spinal cord*

**Figure 22–11** In humans, a network of nerves is connected to the brain and spinal cord.

electrical shock. If a neuron in your eye is stimulated, an impulse is then sent to the brain and you have the sensation of seeing. If a neuron in your ear is stimulated, the impulse arriving in your brain produces the sensation of hearing. The many different sensations that arise from identical impulses in different neurons are made possible by the brain's own billions of specialized neurons. Different areas of the brain control different sensory and other body functions.

The sensations of seeing, hearing, tasting, smelling, and feeling are experienced in the part of the brain called the **cerebrum** (SEHR-e-brum). The sensory neurons from each type of receptor organ end in specialized areas of the cerebrum. Some of these locations are shown in Figure 22–12.

The functions of the cerebrum are continually being studied in brain-injured humans as well as in controlled experiments on laboratory animals. From such studies scientists know that conscious sensations like hearing and sight, voluntary control of muscles, speech, understanding, and memory are centered in parts of the cerebrum. Yet not all the functions of the cerebrum are known. How does one think, learn, and feel emotions? A person's cerebrum is probably involved in each of these activities. (See **Appendix 22–D,** The Cerebrum Became Larger as the Brain Evolved, page 733.)

The brain not only translates messages from sensory neurons; it also directs impulses to neurons that cause a response. These neurons, called **motor neurons,** conduct impulses from the brain and spinal cord to muscles and glands. When stimulated by motor neurons, the muscles and glands act. The muscles contract and the glands secrete their substances.

The brain is far more complex than a computer. The computer excels in memory, but the brain responds to totally unexpected situations. It both directs and controls the responses of organisms. In addition to the brain-controlled activities of which one is aware, the brain controls a whole range of physical activities without con-

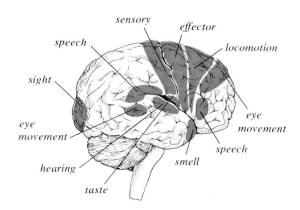

**Figure 22–12** Different areas of the outer portion of the cerebrum, or cerebral cortex, are associated with different functions. Most of these areas have been identified as a result of diagnosing patients with accidental brain injuries.

scious knowledge. For example, during exercise, the cells increase their use of glucose and oxygen and their production of carbon dioxide. These changes are under hormonal control. In response to these changes caused by hormones, the rate of breathing is increased and the heart rate increases to speed the movement of the blood. The brain causes these changes by sending more frequent nerve impulses to the rib muscles, the diaphragm, and the heart. The rate of breathing is controlled by the rate of contraction of the rib muscles and diaphragm. (See **Appendix 22–E,** How Does the Brain Control the Breathing Rate?, page 734.)

Impulses carried by neurons coming from the brain allow muscles to control the flow of air over the vocal cords during speech. Speech is one of many conscious actions. The movements of the body in swimming, dancing, and running are also conscious actions. They are dependent on the controlled contraction of many muscles that are coordinated by impulses from the nervous system. With training, even these actions can occur with less conscious thought and effort.

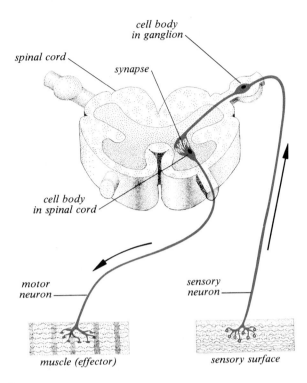

*cell body*
*in ganglion*

*spinal cord*

*synapse*

*cell body*
*in spinal cord*

*motor*
*neuron*

*sensory*
*neuron*

*muscle (effector)*

*sensory surface*

**Figure 22–13** Trace the path of a simple two-neuron reflex arc from the sensory neuron to the motor neuron.

## 22–8

## Some Nerve Actions Take Place Through the Spinal Cord

How can a snake or a chicken move after its head has been cut off? Why does your knee jerk when struck in a certain way? The answers to these questions require an understanding of **reflex activity,** involuntary responses for which the stimuli are usually channeled through the spinal cord.

Knowledge of the reflexes of the spinal cord is based on the pioneering work of the English physiologist C. S. Sherrington and other biologists who worked in the earlier years of this century. Very simple reflex activity is brought about by two neurons connected in what is called a **reflex arc.** A simple reflex arc is illustrated in Figure 22–13.

The pathway of such a reflex arc starts at a sensory surface. It then continues along the sensory neuron to the spinal cord and then along the motor neuron to the effector, usually a muscle. Such an arc is involved in the human knee-jerk reflex.

The knee-jerk reflex action takes place if the tendon just below the kneecap is struck. Stretch receptors in the tendon give rise to impulses that travel by way of a sensory neuron up the leg to the neuron's cell body in a ganglion just outside the spinal cord. A short axon continues from the cell body in the ganglion to the spinal cord. In the spinal cord the ends of the axon come into close association with the dendrites of the motor neurons at a synapse. Impulses travel back along a motor neuron from the spinal cord to the muscles or effectors of the thigh. These impulses cause the muscles at the front of the thigh to contract, while those at the back of the thigh are relaxed. As a result, the leg jerks forward, partly straightening at the knee.

A person who has been struck below the kneecap is aware of the fact that a blow has been struck. This is because the sensory impulses also travel along paths other than the ones just described. Some sensory impulses can pass from the sensory neurons up the spinal cord to the brain. However, the spinal reflex of the knee jerk does not depend on awareness. Reflexes can occur in deep sleep. They can occur even if the spinal cord's connection to the brain is cut and the sensory impulses cannot reach the brain at all.

Most reflex arcs are much more complicated than the knee-jerk reflex path and usually involve more than two neurons. What happens when you receive a pain-causing stimulus by stepping on a nail? You know from your own experience that you pull your foot up, bend the knee, and often contract other muscles of the leg as well. This reflex is largely accomplished by a three-neuron reflex arc: a sensory neuron, a connector neuron in the spinal cord, and a motor neuron (see Figure

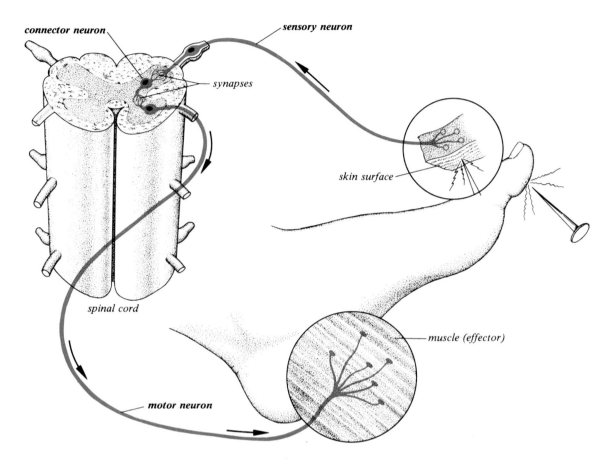

**Figure 22-14** Stepping on a nail initiates a three-neuron reflex. Most reflexes involve three neurons, sometimes more. Compare this diagram with Figure 22-13.

22–14). Exactly the same response to a pain-causing stimulus is seen in other vertebrate animals. It is thought that this is one of the basic evolutionary patterns of reflex response to a pain-causing stimulus and possible injury. It is a protective response. This kind of reflex will occur if the spinal cord is intact, even if the brain is destroyed.

Reflex pathways may go up or down the spinal cord. More than one reflex arc may be involved in a spinal reflex activity. One stimulus may cause one muscle to act. The contraction of that muscle may stimulate another nerve which stimulates another muscle, and so on. This complex reflex activity partly explains how a headless snake is able to wriggle, or a headless chicken is able to run. Such reflex responses are extremely complex, but the movement is partly caused by a chain of reflexes. (See **Appendix 22–F,** The Brain Performs Reflex and Unifying Activities, page 734.)

**CAPSULE SUMMARY**

Stimuli received by specialized receptor cells are carried to the brain and spinal cord by sensory neurons. The most highly specialized regulation in the nervous system is performed by the brain. Motor neurons conduct impulses from the brain and spinal cord to the muscles and glands that respond. Many different pairs of nerves leading to and from the brain and spinal cord work similarly in the nervous system's control over internal organs such as the stomach, intestine, and kidneys. The autonomic nervous system is also involved, as is the endocrine system.

Simple reflex activity is brought about by two or three neurons grouped in a reflex arc that passes through the spinal cord. In humans, spinal reflexes are also influenced by controls from the brain. The wink reflex of the eyelids is a brain reflex.

**SELF CHECK**

1. What is a receptor?
2. Describe a neuron.
3. What is the function of a motor neuron?
4. How is the brain related to the spinal cord?
5. Describe a reflex arc.
6. What is a spinal reflex action?

# CHAPTER SUMMARY

### HIGHLIGHTS

The nervous system integrates the activities of all parts of the body. The central nervous system, composed of the brain and spinal cord, is a coordinating center. The cranial and spinal nerves are the peripheral nervous system. Impulses are transmitted along neurons from receptors to effectors, linked by the selective coordinating responses of the brain. When a given receptor is stimulated, the right effector usually responds. This kind of unifying activity is a major function of the nervous system.

The basic unit of the nervous system is the neuron. All neurons are fundamentally alike, consisting of an axon, dendrites, and a cell body. Messages are carried over the neurons in the form of chemical and electrical changes called nerve impulses.

Neurons bring about unifying activity. Their simplest pattern is a two-neuron reflex arc. Many other more complex reflex activities are known to play an important part in an organism's interaction with the environment.

### REVIEWING IDEAS

1. What is a sensory receptor? What is a receptor organ? How do they put you in touch with the environment?
2. Describe the parts of a neuron.
3. In what way is sending a message by a nerve impulse more efficient for a large multicellular animal than sending the message using a hormone?
4. How is the nervous system of a planarian more advanced than the nerve-net organization in a *Hydra?*

5. Describe the pathway of a nerve impulse in a reflex arc.
6. What part of the brain is more developed in humans than in other animals?
7. How do sensory neurons and motor neurons differ in their functions?
8. How are neurons whose axons are covered by myelin sheaths more efficient than neurons whose axons are not?
9. What is a neurotransmitter?
10. How does the brain control the function of such activities as circulation and respiration?
11. What is a ganglion?
12. When a great many ganglia are located in the head region of an animal, what are they collectively called?

## USING CONCEPTS

13. Name as many kinds of sensory receptors and receptor organs in humans as you can. Where is each located?
14. It is possible for impulses to travel in either direction in a neuron. What may stop a wrong-way impulse from being transmitted to the next neuron?
15. Describe the chemical and electrical events that indicate a neuron has been stimulated.
16. When a particular area of the cerebrum is stimulated by mild electrical shock, a person may experience a nonexisting event. How is this evidence useful in determining the nature of impulses in neurons of the brain?
17. Why may certain reflexes found in some animal species have evolutionary significance? Use a pain-causing stimulus and the resulting reflex as an example.
18. As you read in Chapter 21, many cells of the body produce hormones. How may this be related to the fact that motor neurons in muscle tissue produce norepinephrine?

## RECOMMENDED READING

Jensen, D. *The Human Nervous System.* Englewood Cliffs, NJ, Appleton-Century-Crofts, 1980 (paperback). A detailed coverage of the human nervous system and how it works.

Mann, M. D. *The Nervous System and Behavior.* Philadelphia, Lippincott, 1981 (hardback and paperback). An advanced book that includes summaries of medical and experimental case histories.

Nathan, P. *The Nervous System.* Second edition. New York, Oxford University Press, 1982. A textbook on the nervous systems of different animals, but emphasizing the human nervous system.

Orr, R. T. *Vertebrate Biology.* Philadelphia, Saunders College Publishing, 1982. A textbook that includes more information on the nervous systems of vertebrates.

# Skeletal and Muscular Systems 23

As multicellular organisms evolved, cell specialization was accompanied by larger body size. Among the cell specializations that became important were those that provided body support and made coordinated movement possible. Can you suggest why larger organisms required these added features?

Body-supporting cells and tissues are of many kinds, including muscles used in movement as well as cartilage, bone, and the chitin in the body coverings of insects and many other animals. Protection, support, and movement are the functions of the skeletal and muscular systems.

# Supporting Structures

## 23-1

### Two Kinds of Skeletal Systems Are Found in Organisms

A multicellular organism has not only the problem of supplying its cells with their needs and removing their wastes, but of protecting and supporting its entire body. In many animals, support is provided by both muscles and a skeleton. The skeleton may be protective as well as supporting. For example, a skull protects the brain of a vertebrate animal.

Skeletons are of two general types: **exoskeletons** (ek-so-SKEL-uh-tunz), those formed outside the animal's body; and **endoskeletons** (en-doh-SKEL-uh-tunz), those formed inside the body. Some examples of animals with these two skeletal types are shown in Figure 23-1 on page 472.

Exoskeletons are made of different materials. For example, the single-celled diatoms, found in the oceans and fresh waters of the world, live in glass houses. Their exoskeletons consist largely of silicon, from which glass is made. The common garden snail has an exoskeleton made largely of lime. And yet other living forms such as the grasshopper and crayfish have exoskeletons made of chitin, a complex organic material which is secreted by a layer of living cells just under the exoskeleton. Regardless of how or from what material exoskeletons are made, they protect, support, and often aid in the movement of the organism they enclose.

Endoskeletons are found in many animals. Sponges have microscopic internal rods, or fibers. Since these supporting structures are inside the body, they are considered to be internal skeletons. The starfish skeleton is internal because it is covered with a thin layer of tissue. The skeletons of all vertebrates are internal, jointed, and movable at many of the joints. Many vertebrate skeletons are also flexible where cartilage instead of bone forms part of the supporting framework.

---

←Awkward on land but graceful at sea—the green sea turtle's coordinated movement is best shown in swimming.

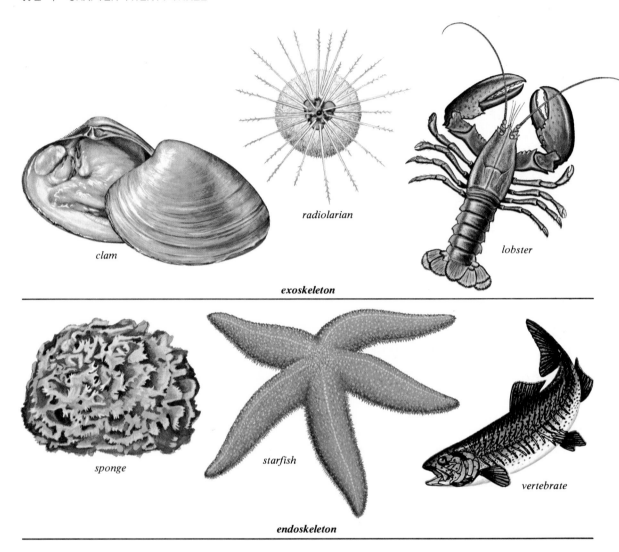

**Figure 23–1** Two groups of animals, one group with endoskeletons, the other with exoskeletons. Only a single layer of living cells may be outside the spicules or skeletal parts over much of the sponge's or starfish's body. By contrast, several to many cell or tissue layers usually cover a vertebrate's skeleton. (However, biologists are always alert to exceptions. Is a turtle's shell an exception? Is the shell part of the turtle's skeleton? Are teeth part of your skeleton?)

An external skeleton can grow with added secretion of material, as in a clam's or snail's shell. Or it can be shed as an animal grows. A new, larger exoskeleton is then secreted, as by a lobster or a grasshopper.

An internal skeleton, however, better fits the growth pattern of larger animals. It grows as the animal does. Internal skeletons are characteristic of animals such as elephants and whales, which have attained great size.

## 23–2

## Vertebrates Have Highly Developed Internal Skeletons

The vertebrates are named after the small, jointed sections of the backbone that protect the nerve cords of these animals. These sections of the backbone are called the **vertebrae** (VERT-uh-bree); see Figure 23–2. If you touch the lower part of the back of your neck, you can feel the ends of your own vertebrae. Feeling bones like this through your skin and other tissues is direct evidence of an internal or endoskeleton. Try to feel the bones in your arms and in your shoulders.

As you can see in Figure 23–2, the vertebrae of your backbone interlock to provide flexible support. The back of a vertebrate can be bent because of these joints in the backbone (see Figure 23–3). What would your own movements be like if, instead of vertebrae, you had a single, rodlike backbone?

The earliest vertebrates were ancestral to fishes and lived in the oceans. Yet little is known of them because no fossil vertebrates older than fishes have been found. However, the evolution of vertebrates after this earliest stage has been traced in the fossil

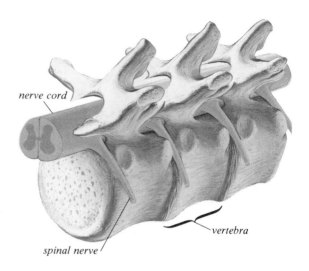

*nerve cord*

*spinal nerve*

*vertebra*

**Figure 23–2** Part of the vertebral column of a human. Notice how the three sections fit together, providing flexible support for the body and protecting the spinal cord.

**Figure 23–3** These two views of a running dog demonstrate the flexibility of the vertebral column. The vertebrae arch (left) to provide a bowlike spring to the action of running (right). Notice the positions of the legs and feet in each case.

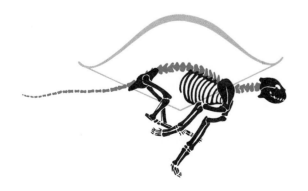
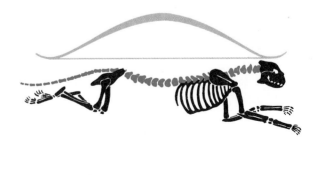

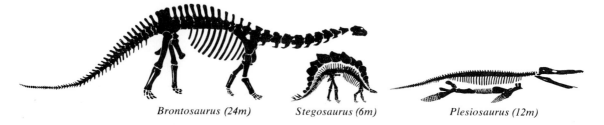

*Brontosaurus (24m)*      *Stegosaurus (6m)*      *Plesiosaurus (12m)*

**Figure 23–4** Drawings to scale of the skeletons of three fossil reptiles. *Brontosaurus* and *Stegosaurus* were land-dwellers. *Plesiosaurus* lived in the sea. How do the skeletons reflect these facts?

remains of their skeletons. The history of dinosaurs (Figure 23–4) and the evolution of the modern horse (Figure 4–5) are just two stories that were pieced together using fossil bones as clues. Biologists are continuing to uncover skeletal remains of ancient organisms all over the world.

You can begin to understand why biologists believe vertebrates are closely related if you compare similar bony parts of their bodies. The bones of the forelimbs of various vertebrates are compared in Figure 23–5. At first glance, you might think that the left forelimbs of the salamander, crocodile, bird, bat, whale, mole, and a human are very different. You know that these limbs are used for different activities: walking, flying, swimming, digging, and handling. Yet if you look closely, you will see that the bones of these limbs are remarkably similar. Each limb has a bone like

**Figure 23–5** Bones of the forelimbs of seven vertebrates. Follow the color key to similarities; they indicate to biologists that these animals once had a common ancestor. Also check the structure of each forelimb for its adaptations to the animal's way of life.

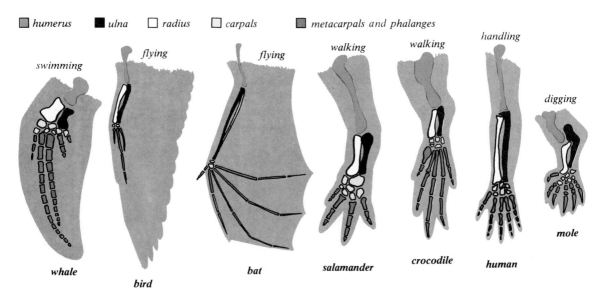

■ *humerus*   ■ *ulna*   □ *radius*   □ *carpals*   ■ *metacarpals and phalanges*

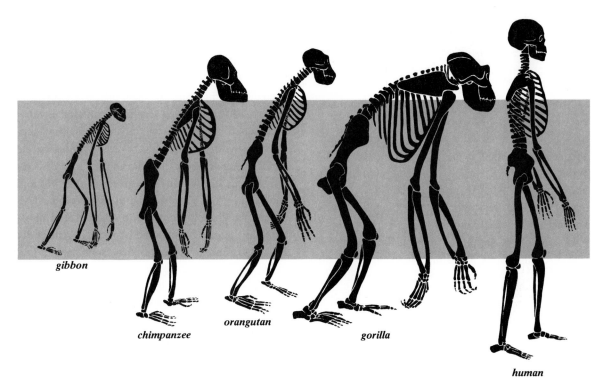

*gibbon*

*chimpanzee*

*orangutan*

*gorilla*

*human*

**Figure 23–6** Skeletons of the great apes and of a human being. Compare their bone structures as you did the structures of the vertebrate forelimbs in Figure 23–5.

your upper-arm bone, although the bones vary in length and shape. Bones like the two from your elbow to your wrist can be found in each of the other limbs shown. Most of the bones of your hand resemble those in each of the other limbs shown. The arrangement of muscles, blood vessels, and nerves is also somewhat alike. The way these limbs develop in the embryo has also been found to be similar. Biologists believe these similarities exist because these vertebrates share a common ancestry.

The more closely related vertebrates are, the more similar their skeletons are. Skeletons of some upright or almost upright walking vertebrates are shown in Figure 23–6. Compare each to the others.

## 23–3

## Bone and Cartilage Are the Building Materials of Vertebrate Skeletons

The supporting skeleton of vertebrates is composed of bone and cartilage. **Bone** consists of living bone cells surrounded by organic fibers and by a hard, nonliving substance. This dense material is secreted by the bone cells themselves. The cells are linked to each other by a series of canals that run between them. These canals connect the bone cells to each other and to blood vessels.

The chemical composition of bone differs greatly from that of the soft body tissues. Only 25 percent of the bone tissue of a young adult is water, while the other tissues may be 60 to 90 percent water. About 45 percent of bone consists of calcium combined with either phosphate or carbonate. These minerals give bone its rigidity and hardness.

The minerals in the bones are not fixed in place like the minerals of a rock. They are withdrawn from bone when needed by other parts of the body and are redeposited in bone when needed there. When radioactive ions of calcium, sodium, or phosphate are injected into the bloodstream, they appear in bone very quickly. Calcium ions, for instance, move back and forth between the blood plasma and bone so quickly that the entire population of calcium ions in the plasma exchanges with the bone calcium within one minute. Similarly, phosphate and other ions are rapidly exchanged between the body fluids and bone tissue.

The other major tissue of vertebrate skeletons is **cartilage.** It is composed of living cells surrounded by some of the same organic fibers found in bone, and by a protein called *chondrin*. It does not contain the hard material of bones. In humans, much of the skeleton in infancy is cartilage, which is later replaced by bony tissue. Cartilage continues to bind and connect the bones at joints in adults. In certain other vertebrates, cartilage may form a major part of the skeleton, as in sharks.

The cells of body tissues other than those of the skeleton require calcium and phosphate ions much as bone does. In humans, if there are not enough minerals in the diet, these ions will be removed from the skeleton. In starvation, the bones may give up as much as a third of their natural content to the blood and other body tissues. This loss leaves the bones soft and spongy and easily broken. During pregnancy, an expectant mother's body supplies the infant's body with materials to build its skeleton. Minerals may be withdrawn from the mother's skeleton to meet these increased demands. Thus, expectant mothers frequently add minerals to their diet.

## 23–4

## Bone Formation Is Controlled by Hormones, Vitamins, and Minerals

Normal bone structure is the result of a balanced exchange of materials between the bone tissue and the rest of the body. A balanced mineral level is maintained in bone by minerals and vitamins supplied by the diet and by hormones. Three separate endocrine glands produce hormones that directly affect bone formation and growth. The thyroid and parathyroid glands in particular produce hormones which help control the calcium and phosphate levels in the blood and bone. See **Appendix 23–A,** Hormones That Control Bone Formation, page 735.

The growth of the skeleton is governed by a hormone produced in the pituitary gland. When the hypothalamus in the brain, and the pituitary gland, are not functioning together normally, too little or too much of the growth hormone may be secreted by the pituitary. The effects are easily recognized. If the disorder occurs in youth, the effect may be a midget or a giant. If it occurs later, the effect may be overgrowth of jaws, hands, and feet.

## 23–5

## Organisms Have Different Kinds of Body Coverings

Endoskeletons provide support for animals, but except for the skull, rib cage, backbone, and hip-bones they do not protect soft parts of the body from injury or drying out. These functions are carried out by a softer, more flexible layer of cells called the **epidermis** (ep-ih-DUR-mis). The epidermis protects all soft-bodied creatures, whether they have an internal skeleton or not. Sometimes the epidermis secretes protective substances, such as mucus, horn, and nail. The epidermis of soft-bodied invertebrates is only a single layer of cells.

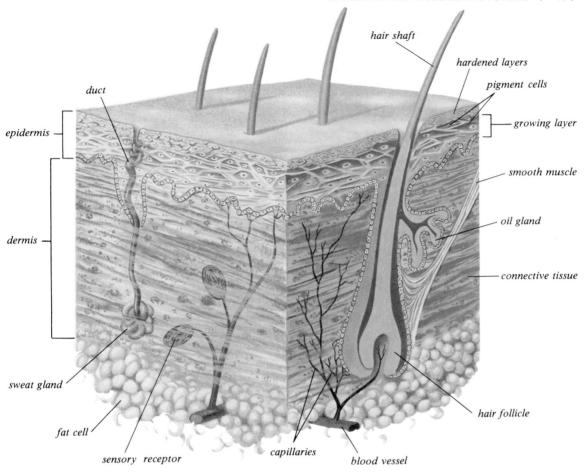

**Figure 23-7** A drawing of a section through the skin of a human being. The skin of other mammals is similar but with many more hair follicles and hairs.

Examples of this can be found among the sponges, flatworms, and slugs. The epidermis of earthworms, tapeworms, and roundworms secretes a thin covering that provides some protection against drying out. However, these organisms must still live in an environment that is moist. The epidermis of organisms with exoskeletons secretes the materials of these exoskeletons.

Vertebrates with their endoskeletons have evolved more complex body coverings. The body

of a vertebrate is covered by a skin made up of two layers, an outer **epidermis** and an inner **dermis.** The epidermis of fish covers a nonliving sheath of scales and contains mucus-producing glands. The frog's epidermis also secretes a substance that keeps it moist. In land vertebrates, the epidermis is several cell layers thick. The outer layer of the epidermis contains hardened dead cells. Thus the skin of reptiles, birds, and mammals is hardened, dry, and tough. As these outer cells rub off, they are replaced by cells from the growing epidermal layer beneath. This kind of skin helps conserve body fluids. It also helps to minimize the seriousness of many surface injuries, such as bruises and scrapes.

Nonliving growths of the epidermis include the scales of reptiles, the feathers of birds, and the hair of mammals. All these provide physical protection and insulation against temperature changes. All of them can be lost and replaced from time to time.

Human skin is similar to the skin of other mammals. A cross section through the epidermis and dermis is shown in Figure 23–7. The epidermis is only 0.07 millimeter thick, and dermis is from two and a half to five millimeters thick. The cells of the dermis contain blood vessels, nerves, pigment, and fibrous connective tissue. Humans have less body hair for insulation than most other mammals. Sweat glands in the dermis of human skin provide a means for cooling the surface body temperature. As the moisture given off by the sweat glands evaporates, heat energy is given off and the skin is cooled. Evaporation of moisture from the skin is one of the means by which the body temperature is regulated.

---

**CAPSULE SUMMARY**

Many multicellular organisms are supported and protected by both muscles and skeletons. Exoskeletons are found outside the body; endoskeletons are inside the body, or at least inside the epidermis. Vertebrate skeletons are internal, jointed, and movable at many of the joints. They are made of bone and cartilage. Bone consists of living cells in hard nonliving material. The formation and maintenance of bone is regulated by hormones and diet. Endoskeletons do not protect organisms from drying out as exoskeletons do, but the hardened cells of the epidermis prevent loss of moisture in organisms with endoskeletons.

**SELF CHECK**

1. How do exoskeletons differ from endoskeletons? Give an example of an animal having each kind of skeleton.
2. What are the functions of a skeletal system?
3. Describe several factors that influence bone growth.
4. What kinds of ions are continually interchanged between body fluids and bone tissue?
5. What is the major function of the dry skin of reptiles, birds, and mammals?

---

# Muscle–Its Structure and Function

## 23–6

## Muscle Provides Movement and Support to Organisms

Muscles as well as skeletons provide support for animal bodies. Muscles also act to bring about movement. Since the earthworm has no skeleton, its muscles perform both of these functions—body support and movement. The same muscles that sheathe the earthworm and maintain its shape are used by it for movement. The earthworm is held together, literally, by muscles. Even in animals with skeletons, muscles function in both movement and support. What would happen to a human being's abdominal organs, for example, if the abdominal muscles were removed?

It is easy to see the body movement of a person walking or an earthworm crawling, but muscles also control movements that cannot be seen. The movement of blood, for example, is the result of muscular activity of the heart and blood vessels, as you learned in Sections 17–8 and 17–9. In all higher animals, the movement of food through the digestive tract is the result of muscular activity of digestive organs.

A secondary, but important, function of muscles is producing body heat. You are certainly aware of the large amounts of body heat produced by dancing, playing tennis, or any form of muscular activity.

## 23–7

## Vertebrates Have Evolved Several Kinds of Muscle Tissue

The cytoplasm of all cells has at least some ability to move. Tiny fibers called **fibrils** in the cytoplasm of cells of many lower animals increase this ability to move. The fibrils can contract (grow shorter) and resume their "relaxed" length again. In some cells the fibrils are in long extensions branching from the main cell body. In other cells they are central to the cell body, which may be elongated in the direction of the fibrils' length. Muscle cells may have evolved from such simple beginnings. In a muscle cell the fibrils have come to be so many that even the cell's nucleus may be off to one side (Figure 23–8). Cytoplasm and the cell's energy "powerhouses," the mitochondria (Section 8–6), are squeezed in between the fibrils and around the cell's edges.

Contractile fibrils in extensions from body wall or epidermis cells show the beginning of muscle-like structure in the simpler multicellular animals. (See Figure 19–5, upper right, the enlarged view of cells of *Hydra*.) Specialized muscle cells, singly or in a loose network among other cells, show the next step. The one feature these cells share, apart from their muscle fibrils, is their general shape. Muscle cells tend to be long and narrow instead of round or oblong or rectangular. (Why?) By the stage at which worms and many

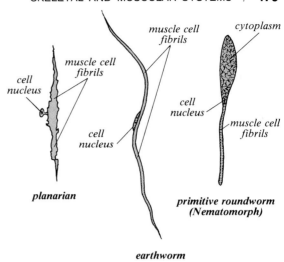

**Figure 23–8** In these muscle cells from several invertebrates, the nucleus is at one side or at one end away from the muscle cell fibrils. Muscle cells may have evolved from cells with extensions of contractile fibrils, or increasing numbers of fibrils in the main cell body.

other organisms had evolved, the muscle cells no longer are isolated or loosely clustered. They are continuous, fitted side by side and overlapping at the ends in muscle tissues. These tissues form sheets of muscle. Different types of muscle tissue in the body wall and the digestive tract show still further specialization even in the same organism.

Among the vertebrates, different types of muscle cells are often named for their appearance. The cells that form the walls of the digestive tract and of arteries in the circulatory system appear very smooth or even in texture all along their length. They are called **smooth muscle** cells. Other muscle cells, including those of the muscles that are attached to the skeleton, show cross-stripes under the microscope. They make up **striated muscle.** The muscle cells of the heart are also striated but are not identical in appearance to other striated muscle. These heart muscle cells form **cardiac muscle.**

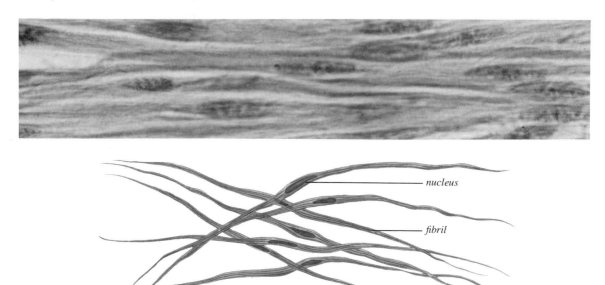

nucleus

fibril

×220

**Figure 23–9** (Top) Smooth muscle cells in the intestinal wall, magnified 850 times. (Bottom) A drawing of several cells under lesser magnification. This type of muscle has clearly defined cells, each with a single, centrally located nucleus. Smooth muscle tissue contracts in wavelike motion, regulated but involuntary. Contractions are abrupt only during spasms. Can you name an example?

Smooth muscle in vertebrates contracts and recovers more rhythmically and more slowly than striated muscle. Smooth muscle contractions usually are involuntary—that is, not controlled by the conscious part of the brain. Such muscles move your food along your digestive tract with no thought or planning from you involved.

As you see in Figure 23–9, the smooth muscle cells are shaped like slender rods tapered at each end. Compare them with the muscle cell of the earthworm illustrated in Figure 23–8. A smooth muscle cell is a few tenths of a millimeter in length and contains a single nucleus located within the center portion of the cell. Under a microscope the smooth muscle cell appears to be almost uniform in composition except for its nucleus. When such a cell is given special chemical treatment, however, tiny fibrils can be seen running along its length.

The muscle fibrils are the part of the smooth muscle cell that produces muscular contraction.

Striated muscle in vertebrates differs from smooth muscle in many ways. First, the striated muscle contracts much more rapidly than smooth muscle. Second, nervous control of striated muscle is generally voluntary. Conscious messages from the animal brain can bring about an increase or decrease in the rate and degree of muscular contraction. Thus, when you hear the signal for the start of a race you respond by running. How rapidly you run depends on the messages sent by your brain to your leg muscles. If the race is close, your leg muscles respond to brain messages by contracting strongly, at a maximum rate and to a maximum degree. You run at top speed. When the race is over, your leg muscles again obey orders from your brain. You slow down and stop.

Cardiac muscle is striated but is involuntary. It constantly contracts and relaxes in a continuing rhythmic pattern. During the entire life span of an individual, the only rest that the cardiac muscle gets is a momentary pause before each contraction of the heart.

Besides differing in function, striated and smooth muscles also differ in structure. Compare Figure 23–9 with Figure 23–10. Clearly defined individual cells cannot be seen in the structure of striated muscle. When this muscle is formed, repeated division of a single cell produces a long, continuous fiber in which there do not seem to be separations between the cells. The fiber therefore contains many nuclei. The tiny fibrils of striated muscle fiber are crossed with alternate light and dark bands called **striations.** The cross striations result from the arrangement of even smaller threads or filaments within the fibrils.

## 23–8

## How Are Muscles Organized in Vertebrates?

Except for cardiac muscle, the muscles in the walls of internal organs of vertebrates are smooth muscles. The faster-reacting striated muscles are located in the arms, legs, face, the chest wall, the abdominal wall, and the back.

How fast can striated muscle contract? A few examples include a hummingbird hovering in the air at 80 wing-beats per second, a human eye muscle contracting in 0.01 second, and a bird's heart beating several hundred times per minute.

**Figure 23–10** Striated muscle fibers ($\times$ 3000). The alternating thick (dark) and thin (light) bands are the striations. (See Figures 23–13, 23–14, and 23–15.)

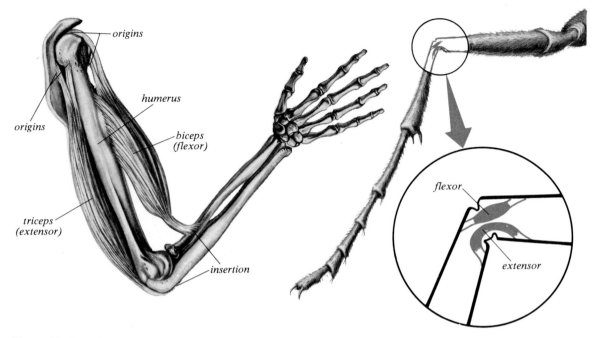

**Figure 23–11** A flexor-extensor muscle pair in the human arm (left) and in an insect leg (right). Flexors bend a limb at a skeletal joint; extensors straighten the limb again. Note the similarities in the muscle arrangements in the two animal limbs. What is the principal difference?

Most striated muscles move bones. Those that do are often called **skeletal muscles.** For a muscle to move a bone it must be attached to that bone, and attached at its opposite end to some "anchoring" bone or bones. Skeletal muscles are attached to bones by tough, cordlike bundles of tissue called **tendons.** The attachment to the "anchoring" bone or bones is called the **origin** of the muscle. The attachment to the bone that the muscle moves is called the **insertion** of the muscle. Without such attachment points the muscle could produce only a fraction of its effect in moving a part of the body.

Skeletal muscles usually act in pairs. The action of one muscle of a pair is opposite the action of the other. When a skeletal muscle contracts, it may cause a body part to move. Then its companion muscle contracts to return the moved part to its original location. Most of the skeletal muscles are arranged in such opposing, or "doing-undoing," pairs. A good example of an opposing pair is the combination of a flexor muscle and an extensor muscle. A flexor muscle bends a joint, and an extensor muscle straightens it out again (see Figure 23–11). A flexor-extensor pair is used to bend the elbow. Even in an invertebrate a similar arrangement of muscles inside an exoskeleton moves the limbs, as in an insect or a lobster. You should be able to think of many other examples of flexor-extensor pairs.

A joint can be held in a rigid position when both muscles of an opposing pair contract at the same time. This rigidity is necessary, for example, when standing still. In order to support the body the knees must be held straight. For ordinary movement, however, one of the two muscles must relax.

## CAPSULE SUMMARY

From lower to higher animals, muscle cells and muscles reflect their probable evolution. In invertebrates with exoskeletons, and in vertebrates with their endoskeletons, both muscles and skeletons protect and support the animal and are involved in its movement.

In vertebrates there are two general kinds of muscle: smooth and striated. They differ from each other in form, speed of contraction and recovery from contraction, and nervous control. Smooth muscle is made up of individual cells. It contracts more slowly and is usually under involuntary control. Striated muscle in vertebrates has dark and light bands. It does not have clearly defined individual cells. It contracts rapidly and, except for cardiac muscle, is usually under voluntary nervous control. Striated muscle includes skeletal muscle, which along with the skeleton itself is responsible for the body movements of vertebrates.

## SELF CHECK

1. How did muscle cells probably evolve?
2. How do muscles bring about movement in an organism?
3. Where is smooth muscle found in higher animals?
4. Why must skeletal muscles be fastened or anchored?
5. How do skeletal muscles work in opposing pairs?

# Muscular Contraction

## 23-9

## What Stimulates Muscle to Contract?

Muscles contract in response to nerve impulses. Microscopic examinations such as the one in Figure 23-12 show that each muscle fiber in a striated muscle has a motor nerve ending. The branches of a single motor nerve may be in close contact with as many as 200 muscle fibers.

If a motor nerve is destroyed, the muscle fibers it activated are said to be "paralyzed." They no longer respond. Diseases like polio that damage nerves to muscles lead to partial paralysis. The muscle fibers that cannot be used waste away; the muscle grows smaller. Careful programs of physical activity may encourage further growth of other

**Figure 23-12** Nerve endings on striated muscle fibers. Nerve impulses stimulate the nerve endings to secrete their chemical messengers, leading to contraction of the muscle fibers.

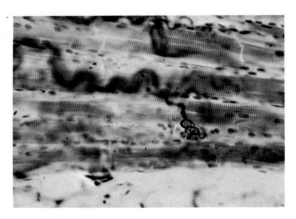

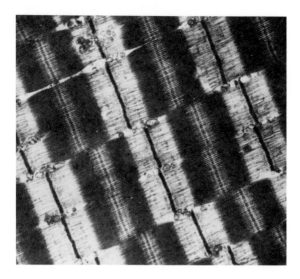

**Figure 23–13** Under higher magnification ($\times$ 24,000) than the muscle fibers in Figure 23–10, this rabbit muscle tissue shows individual fibrils within a fiber and filaments within the fibrils. Compare this photo with the drawings in Figure 23–14.

muscle fibers that retain their nerve connections. If the damage has not been too great the development of new muscle fibers can partly repair the muscle as a whole.

All this knowledge has been acquired through experience with illnesses that affect nerves and muscles. It does not tell biologists how muscle cells work. What is contraction, for example? What makes striated muscle fast to react, and fast to recover for repeated reaction? What makes just enough muscle fibers in a striated muscle contract to do a given job?

If all the fibers in the biceps muscle (Figure 23–11) contracted when you picked up a pencil, you would throw the pencil over your shoulder. Instead, you pick up the pencil gently. Individual fibers in a muscle cannot adjust to tasks like this. Each fiber contracts all the way, or not at all; it has only an "on-off" nerve switch. Only the muscle

as a whole can adjust, through the number of fibers that contract to do a given job. Such observations make the mystery of how muscles work all the more fascinating.

**Try Investigation 23–A** Making Muscles Move, page 677.

## 23–10

## Hypotheses Attempt to Explain the Contraction of Striated Muscle

The way muscle becomes shorter during contraction has been investigated for many years. The structure of striated muscle fibers, as seen through an electron microscope, has provided many clues (Figure 23–13). As you can see, there are light and dark bands that produce the striations. The bands run *across* the muscle fibrils. But the individual filaments in the fibrils (look at the figure closely) run lengthwise through the bands.

Figure 23–14 starts with a muscle and shows a succession of closer-in views. In *a* a complete muscle is shown. In *b*, a small section has been magnified to show that the muscle is composed of individual fibers with definite cross striations. In *c*, a section of an individual fiber has been magnified. Notice the many nuclei of the fiber and the difficulty of finding distinct cellular structure. (See also Figure 23–10.) Notice also that the fiber itself is composed of many individual fibrils. These fibrils are the parts of striated muscle tissue that contract. A section of one of these fibrils has been enlarged in *d* to show more clearly the nature of the alternate light and dark bands. These are the bands, in several fibrils, that you see in Figure 23–13. In *e*, you can see that the fibrils are composed of even smaller parts called filaments.

Starting in the center of *e,* and working back to *d,* note how the light band in the middle of *d* corresponds to the parallel arrangement of the two kinds of filaments. The darker bands on either side of this light band result from areas where both thick and thin filaments appear, and overlap. The very light areas beyond the dark areas result from the parallel arrangements of thin filaments. Finally, the very narrow, dark lines that run *across* the filaments at the ends of the view shown in *e* indicate where the thin filaments pass through a zone of very dense protein material. The structural details of the protein are not yet completely understood. In muscle tissue the individual fibrils are lined up so that the dark band of one fibril is exactly parallel to the dark band of another fibril. The light bands are also lined up with each other. Thus, when striated muscle tissue is observed under the light microscope (Figure 23–10), this ordered arrangement produces the alternating light and dark bands that we call the striations.

The thick filaments are composed of a protein called **myosin** (MY-oh-sin). The thin filaments are composed of another protein called **actin** (AK-tin). On the thin actin filaments are also two other proteins (called troponin and tropomyosin). These two added proteins are involved in the thick and thin filaments' reactions with each other.

Calcium ions trigger muscle contraction. This has been known for years. When the calcium is absorbed or taken up again, the muscle relaxes.

**Figure 23–14** Successive magnifications from muscle to fiber to fibril to filaments. This figure should help you interpret what you see in Figures 23–10 and 23–13. The mechanism for the contraction of striated muscle is in the overlapping filaments.

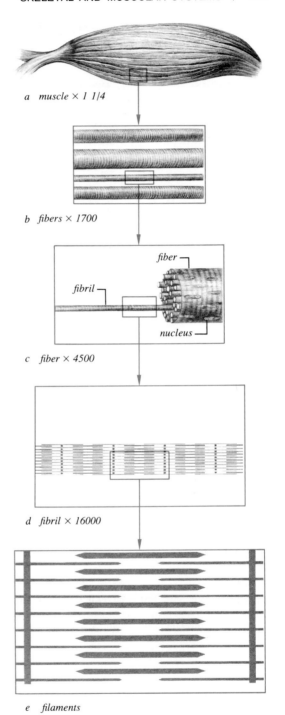

*a   muscle × 1 1/4*

*b   fibers × 1700*

*fiber*

*fibril*

*nucleus*

*c   fiber × 4500*

*d   fibril × 16000*

*e   filaments*

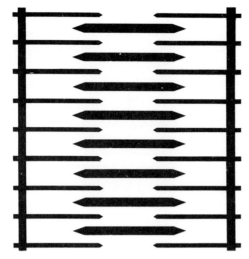

*relaxed position*

*contracted position*

**Figure 23–15** The positions of the filaments in these two drawings indicate how striated muscle contracts. The contraction is triggered by calcium ions. It involves the thick filaments (myosin) attracting and attaching temporarily to the thin filaments (actin).

1. Motor nerves carry impulses from the brain and spinal cord to the muscles.
2. Each motor neuron releases a chemical messenger into the muscle fibers.
3. The chemical messenger works by triggering the release of calcium ions.
4. The calcium ions react with the two proteins (troponin and tropomyosin) that cover parts of the thin actin filaments. The tropomyosin moves slightly and *un*covers active sites on the actin.
5. The thick myosin filaments attach to the active sites on the actin and pull on the actin filaments.
6. The result is that the thick and thin filaments, now attached, slide past each other. The muscle fibrils contract.
7. When calcium ions are absorbed or taken up again, the tropomyosin interrupts the myosin's (thick filaments') attachment to the actin (thin filaments).
8. The now unattached filaments slide past one another again to their relaxed or former position.

Figure 23–15 illustrates the relaxed and contracted positions of the filaments in a short section of a striated muscle fibril.

The "sliding filament" hypothesis was first proposed by the English scientist H. E. Huxley. Today this idea is well established, based on the work of many other scientists in discovering and suggesting the roles of the two proteins covering parts of the thin filaments. How active sites are covered and uncovered, governing the attachment of thick to thin filaments, is one of the newest hypotheses in the continuing investigations into muscle contraction.

The combination of known experimental evidence and several hypotheses produces the current understanding of how striated muscles contract:

**Try Investigation 23–B** What Causes Fatigue in Skeletal Muscles?, page 678.

## 23–11

## The Right Amount of Effort Is Exerted for the Task

Muscle fibers have not only motor neuron endings, but sensory ones too. The sensory receptors originate in certain specialized sections of the striated muscle fibers. The hypotheses you have read explained contraction and recovery and how rapidly they can occur as calcium ions are freed and reabsorbed. But these hypotheses do not explain why the calcium ions are freed in some fibers and not others. What determines how many muscle fibers are involved as a muscle begins to contract?

Apparently you put judgment into the task and govern the degree of muscle involvement, but sometimes you miss your guess. At other times you don't have the opportunity to guess at all. Something, or someone, may land upon you or bump into you from behind. What brings more muscle fibers into action to help you regain your balance?

Correcting your estimates and responding to surprise demands on your muscles appears to begin with the sensory receptors in the striated muscle fibers. These sensory receptors are *stretch receptors*. They are activated as the specialized sections of muscle fiber are pulled on by contraction at their ends. The receptors start impulses along the sensory neurons. The impulses go to your brain. Although the impulses end up in your cerebral cortex, you are not aware of them. They result in motor impulses that travel down your spinal cord and to more of the motor neuron endings in your muscles. More muscle fibers respond by contracting, to fit the increased demand.

If someone hands you an object that is much heavier than you expected, your arm drops under the load, but recovers almost instantaneously with a greater second effort of your muscles. Only if you continue to hold the object out in front of you will the muscles grow fatigued and let your arm fall. Regulation of muscle effort by the sensory neurons that originate in the muscles, and by the brain, will work only as long as the muscle fibers can respond without fatigue.

After a time even standing still tires some of your muscles. If you think about this, you will realize that standing in one spot and keeping a steady balance requires uninterrupted contractions of opposing muscles. The sensory neurons that originate in the muscles keep the opposing contractions occurring. Organs of balance in your head are involved, too. All the impulses are coordinated in your brain.

Instant responses to greater (or continuing) demands on the muscles are not limited to human beings. They are characteristic of vertebrates generally and of many other animals. Thus the star of a western movie can leap from a high balcony onto the back of a horse and ride away, in a successful film take. But you can make calculations to show that the force of a 75-kilogram body falling three meters or more makes the horse the true star of the show!

## 23–12

## Physiologists Explain the Chemistry of Muscle Contraction

Any activity requires energy. Striated muscle fibers require more energy than many other kinds of cells. In 1949, before the compound that supplies the energy was known, a remarkable experiment was performed. Albert Szent-Gyorgi (sent-JUHR-jee), a physiologist at the Institute for Muscle Research in Woods Hole, Massachusetts, dissected muscle fibers from rabbits and attached these fibers to frames to keep them from changing their length. The fibers were then killed in a chemical bath, rinsed, and placed in a dilute solution of salts. Calcium ions were supplied in the solution.

**Figure 23–16** Albert Szent-Gyorgi, who discovered that ATP supplies energy that enables muscle fibers to contract. From Szent-Gyorgi's work came the suggestion that ATP could be the major energy source for all cells.

The fibers remained inactive until Szent-Gyorgi (Figure 23–16) applied some ATP. The fibers contracted! Even after the fibers had been dead for months they would contract when ATP was added. This experiment was very important in first suggesting that ATP is the major energy source in living cells.

Other energy-rich compounds in muscle cells include glucose, glycogen, and creatine phosphate. None of these causes muscle cells to contract, however, if they are applied experimentally, as in Szent-Gyorgi's experiment.

Other physiologists soon reasoned that if ATP is a muscle fiber's energy source, then a recently exercised fiber should contain less ATP than a fiber which has been at rest. However, experimental measurements failed to show a difference in the amount of ATP in such fibers. Only less creatine phosphate is found in recently exercised fibers, as compared with resting fibers.

Much related data has been discovered. As a result, the sequence of energy-dependent events in muscle cells has gradually been established. Muscle cells, like other cells, take in glucose from the bloodstream. They convert some of the glucose to glycogen, as the liver also does. When energy is needed, the glycogen is broken down to glucose again. The glucose is split as in fermentation (Chapter 6). Pyruvic acid molecules are the product, along with a small supply of energy. In the presence of oxygen the pyruvic acid is broken down by cell respiration, yielding far more energy than in the fermentation step. The energy is stored in ATP and in creatine phosphate.

As a muscle fiber uses energy it depletes its supply of ATP. But this supply is immediately replenished by the transfer of energy-rich phosphate groups from creatine phosphate to ADP, producing ATP again. This explains why the creatine phosphate level drops in active or recently exercised muscle fibers.

The cause of muscle fatigue has been explained, too. Glucose can be broken down to pyruvic acid in the absence of oxygen, but the pyruvic acid can be broken down only in the presence of oxygen. When you exercise vigorously, you soon run short of oxygen. Yet you can go on exercising.

When a muscle fiber runs short of oxygen, it continues to change glycogen to glucose to pyruvic acid, and to store the energy in creatine phosphate and ATP. But the pyruvic acid cannot be broken down in the absence of oxygen and is only converted to lactic acid. Accumulations of lactic acid begin to affect the muscle fiber. For example, lactic acid changes the $p$H, until the muscle fiber can no longer respond. Other effects of the lactic

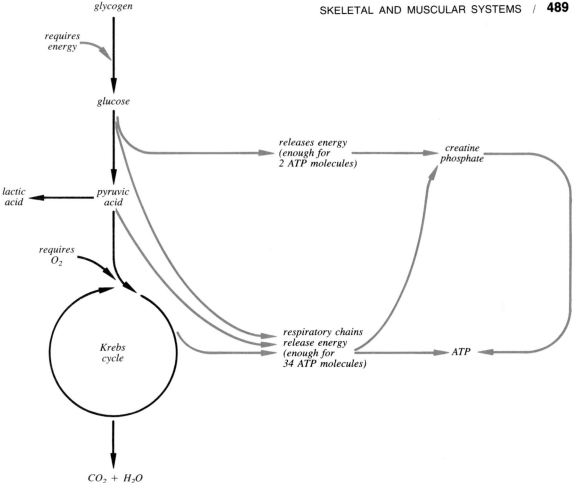

**Figure 23–17** Energy for movement. The same cell respiration processes take place in muscle cells that take place in other cells. (Refer back to Figures 8–3, 8–4, and 8–6.) Muscle fatigue starts when oxygen runs low; the reactions on the left in the diagram then stop short of the Krebs cycle, which requires oxygen. The pyruvic acid is converted only to lactic acid, which piles up, changing the muscle fiber's $p$H. Little energy gets through to the right, to replenish the creatine phosphate supply. If the muscle fiber goes on working, more creatine phosphate will be used than is replenished, and its supply will be lowered. Only after the oxygen debt is paid and the Krebs cycle is in full operation again will the energy flow to the right shown at the bottom of the diagram be resumed.

acid also contribute to blocking the fiber's further activity. You experience this as muscle fatigue.

Figure 23–17 illustrates the energy process in muscle cells. When enough oxygen is present, the whole process is carried through. When oxygen is low, only the step similar to fermentation occurs. An "oxygen debt" is the result. The lactic acid accumulates and begins diffusing out of the muscle

fibers into the bloodstream. When oxygen is available again, the liver takes the lactic acid from the bloodstream and converts it back to glycogen. A small portion of the lactic acid that has not yet diffused out of the muscle fibers is broken down there and its energy used to replenish the creatine phosphate and ATP supply. Most of the lactic acid, however, eventually diffuses from the muscle

# Biology Brief

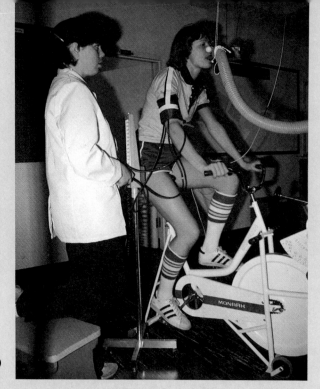

# Feeling Fit?
# How Fit Are You?

You don't have to be in shape to visit a Human Performance Laboratory, but you will discover the shape you are in. The college student pedaling the "bicycle" in the photo is engaged in one of many tests in the Human Performance Laboratory at the University of Denver. With her, taking her blood pressure during exercise, is Margaret Cooney, a graduate student and member of the laboratory staff. The air hose in the student's mouth, above and on the facing page, is being used by Dr. Clarence L. H. Baer, the laboratory director, to measure the student's pulmonary ventilation during exercise.

Human Performance Laboratories exist in many cities, often on college or university campuses. Athletes, physical education students, members of the campus community, and various business and governmental groups are frequently served by such laboratories.

fibers and is converted by the liver back to glycogen. The "oxygen debt" is then paid. The muscle cells are ready for use or exercise again.

Energy is required in the muscle contraction process from its beginning. Without energy, calcium ions cannot affect the proteins covering part of the thin (actin) filaments. Tropomyosin uses energy from ATP in being moved off the active sites that it covers on the actin filaments. Each subsequent step in binding the thick filaments (myosin) to the active sites on the thin filaments (actin) continues to use energy from ATP. As the ATP supply is used, some of the creatine phosphate supply is used to replenish it. Usually four to six times as much creatine phosphate as ATP can be found in striated muscle fibers. The energy of the creatine phosphate increases the quick-energy supply in the muscle fibers, even as the glycogen → glucose → pyruvic acid breakdown continues.

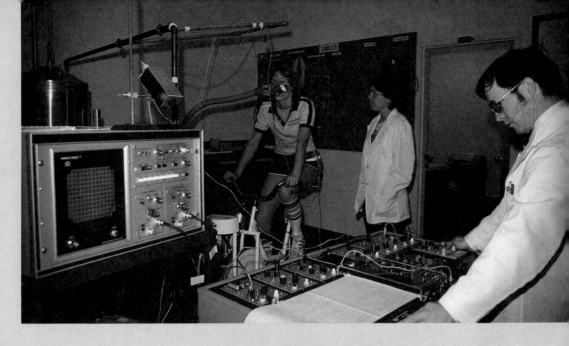

Most human activity each day is muscular activity. You are so used to standing, sitting, bending, walking, and climbing stairs that you don't think much about these activities. Yet most people exercise too little in all these daily tasks. Finding that you are out of shape involves more than a comparison with your own best periods of fitness; it involves comparisons with others too. For these comparisons, only laboratory tests can provide the information you seek.

Many of the laboratories are equipped to take electrocardiograms and make blood tests. As you bicycle, or run on the treadmill, your heart rate and its peaks and rhythms can be monitored. At rest, tests of glucose, cholesterol, and triglycerides in the blood can be made. Exercise programs possibly may lower the cholesterol and triglyceride levels. Proper exercise may also help to reduce the amount of body fat (also measured at the laboratory.)

A personal fitness program can be designed on the basis of your fitness and performance tests. Later the program can be modified to meet your changing needs. It could usefully be followed for a lifetime.

## 23–13

### Exercise Builds Muscle Fibers

Earlier you read that some diseases, such as polio, may destroy nerve connections to muscles. By working vigorously with muscle tissue that is still responsive, polio victims can sometimes regain much of their muscle activity. They do it by exercising healthy muscle fibers until these build up to offset the loss of others. Growing new motor neuron endings to new muscle fibers appears to be possible from healthy neurons. But muscle fibers formerly served by neurons that have been destroyed cannot be reactivated. These muscle fibers degenerate.

Everyone loses a certain number of muscle fibers. Active programs of exercise are not for victims of diseases alone. Physical fitness programs are widely encouraged for all people of all ages, provided that these persons do not have other disabilities which could make vigorous physical activity dangerous for them. The biology brief discusses some topics associated with regular physical exercise and fitness activities.

What is true of skeletal and other striated muscles does not necessarily apply wholly to smooth muscles, too. However, the filaments of some smooth muscles are identical to the thin (actin) filaments of striated muscles. Much more remains to be learned about the contraction of both striated and smooth muscles, and about the nature and arrangements of fibrils in smooth muscles.

---

**CAPSULE SUMMARY**

Nerve impulses that release chemical messengers in the muscle fibers start the events leading to contraction of the muscle fibers by freeing calcium ions. The calcium ions, in the presence of ATP, interact with two proteins covering active sites on actin filaments. One of these proteins moves off the active sites, making it possible for the myosin filaments to engage the actin filaments and pull on them. The actin filaments are pulled alongside the myosin filaments. This is the process of contraction. Reabsorption of the calcium ions ends contraction.

This quick release and reabsorption of calcium ions, and the quick interaction of the ions with the proteins on the muscle filaments, help make striated muscle fast to react and recover. The organization of the striated muscle fibers as compared to smooth muscle fibers is also a factor. Still another factor is motor neurons with myelin sheaths, which carry impulses faster than neurons without these sheaths, as you learned in Chapter 22. The motor neurons leading to your skeletal muscles have myelin sheaths. Many of those leading to smooth muscles do not (see Appendix 22–B, The Autonomic Nervous System).

Contraction and recovery involve energy and oxygen. Energy is supplied by ATP, backed by creatine phosphate, in turn backed by glycogen and glucose. When oxygen runs low, glucose breakdown stops with pyruvic acid and its conversion to lactic acid. The lactic acid piles up, changes the $p$H, and causes muscle fatigue. Much of the lactic acid enters the bloodstream. As the oxygen supply returns to normal, the lactic acid is removed from the bloodstream by the liver and reconverted to glycogen.

**SELF CHECK**

1. How are striated muscles stimulated?
2. How is the number of muscle fibers engaged in a muscle's contraction kept regulated?
3. Describe the energy source for muscle contraction.
4. How is lactic acid both an energy source and a fatigue factor?
5. What is the function of creatine phosphate in muscle fibers?

---

## CHAPTER SUMMARY

### HIGHLIGHTS

Muscles and skeletons provide animals with body support and methods of locomotion. Some animals have no skeleton at all; the earthworm, for example, has sheathlike muscles that both support and are used for locomotion. Other animals have exoskeletons; the grasshopper's skeletal muscles are attached to the inside of an exoskeleton. Vertebrates have endoskeletons; the striated muscles are outside the bones and cartilage of the skeleton.

Many kinds of muscle cells have evolved in animals. In vertebrates, striated and smooth muscles are both found. Heart or cardiac muscle is a kind of striated muscle.

An individual muscle cell or fiber contracts all the way or not at all; it has only an "on-off" switch. The strength of a muscle's contraction is determined by how many of its fibers contract. Research has established the structure and the sliding-filament method of contraction of striated muscle. Motor nerves secrete a chemical messenger that frees calcium ions, which trigger muscle contraction if ATP is present to provide energy.

A working muscle fiber can keep up its energy supply because it has creatine phosphate to replenish its ATP. It can also split glycogen to glucose (requiring energy) and glucose to lactic acid (releasing energy) to keep up its energy supply even in the absence of oxygen, until the lactic acid accumulates and brings on fatigue.

Regular physical exercise enlarges skeletal muscle fibers. New fibers may also be formed. Everyone loses some muscle fibers at times but can more than replace the loss through regular vigorous exercise.

## REVIEWING IDEAS

1. Explain the difference between exoskeletons and endoskeletons.
2. How do animals with exoskeletons grow? Give several examples.
3. What relationship exists between the size of an animal and the presence or absence of a skeleton?
4. How do muscle cells appear to have evolved?
5. What kinds of filaments in striated muscle give it the striations?
6. What sources of energy do striated muscle fibers use?
7. How is "oxygen debt" related to lactic acid accumulation in striated muscles?

8. What allows muscles to continue to work in the face of an "oxygen debt"?
9. How does smooth muscle differ in its microscopic structure from striated muscle?
10. What is the difference between a skeletal muscle and any other striated muscle?
11. Explain how a flexor-extensor pair of muscles works in bending a joint, straightening a joint, and standing still.
12. What are actin and myosin? How do they function in muscles?

## USING CONCEPTS

13. How do tropomyosin and troponin contribute to the functioning of muscle cells?
14. Most invertebrates have arginine phosphate instead of creatine phosphate in their muscle cells. Vertebrates have creatine phosphate. How could investigation of this and other chemical differences in muscle functioning add to biologists' knowledge of the evolution of muscle cells?
15. If a muscle fiber contracts all the way, or not at all, how can muscular effort be adjusted for different tasks? What role do stretch receptors play in adjusting muscle effort?
16. If fairly large animals exist that have no skeleton, in what type of environment would you expect to find them? Try to name an example.

## RECOMMENDED READING

Alexander, R. M. *Locomotion of Animals*. New York, Methuen, 1982. An advanced book, but excellent on details of how animals move.

Bulbring, E. et al. (eds.) *Smooth Muscle: An Assessment of Current Knowledge*. Austin, TX, University of Texas Press, 1981. How smooth muscle functions in the walls of internal organs.

Litt, J. Z. *Your Skin and How to Live in It*. Shaker Heights, OH, Corinthian Press, 1982 (paperback). The use and abuse of your skin.

PART SEVEN

# Higher Levels of Organization

Nerves, hormones, and gland and muscular coordination control the working of an animal's body. But what describes it as an individual, interacting with a population of its kind? For animals like these baboons, different behaviors organize the whole troop socially. But behavioral studies start with far smaller and simpler animals than baboons. Some surprises are in store for you, in studies ranging from individuals to populations to ecosystems with *over* populations.

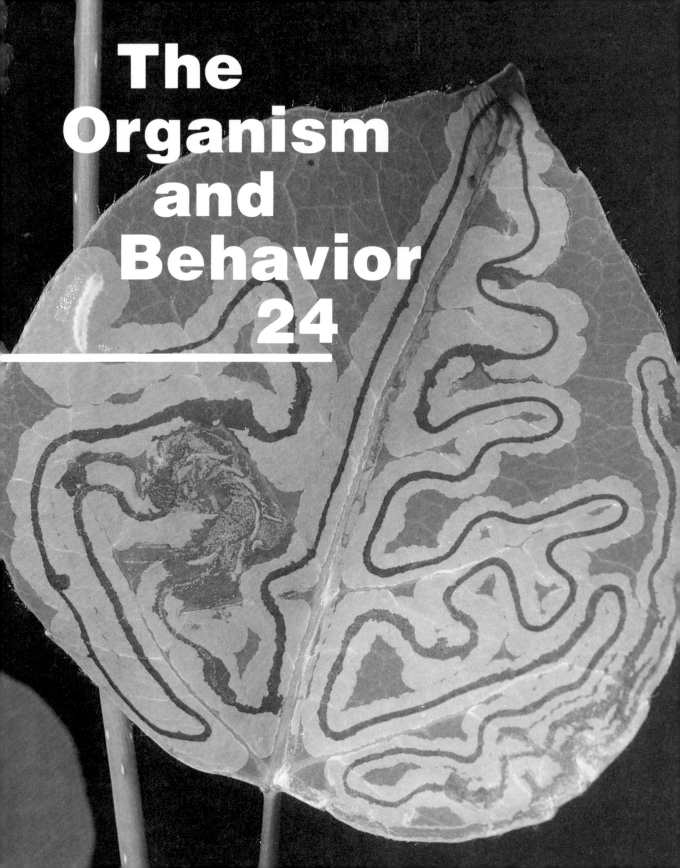

# The Organism and Behavior

# 24

Complex organisms made of millions of cells have many different parts carrying on different functions. All of these parts and functions must work together if the organism is to thrive. As you have seen in earlier chapters, the many parts of multicellular organisms are regulated by complex systems including genetic molecules, hormones, enzymes, and nerves. This regulation allows the living plant or animal to function as a single organism, rather than as millions of independent cells. In this chapter you will start to explore the behavior of whole organisms, including humans, and the factors that influence and control such behavior.

# A Relatively New Science

## 24-1

### Why Study Behavior?

How do you explain why a species of insect may devote more care to its young than many higher animals such as fishes do? Or why a plant such as the Venus flytrap (page 402) may "turn the tables on" insects and eat *them?* Or why lions and wolves, usually thought of as killers, apparently inflict less death on their own numbers than people do on theirs?

Naturalists have long studied the behavior of other organisms, understandably fascinated by all its variety. But the study of behavior proved difficult to approach as a science because it appeared so variable and complicated in many organisms. Scientists reacted here as they react to all other natural phenomena. They have felt compelled to understand why things are as they are. This drive is at the very root of scientific inquiry.

Another and potentially more important reason than scientific curiosity also exists for biologists to study the behavior of other living things, especially other animals. If evolution is a clue to behavior, we need many clues to understanding our own behavior. Some of our characteristics and the resulting strife they create have become increasingly difficult to live with in our crowded world. Intolerance and aggressiveness are two examples. Thus the study of how other social animals solve the problems of living together can be of great potential value to us.

How does an organism behave when its environment changes? How does a plant react when the amount of light it receives per day is suddenly reduced? Or when it receives only red light, instead of the mixture of wavelengths that make up sunlight? How does an animal react when it meets another animal of its own species? Is its reaction, when the other animal is a male, different from its

---

← Do you like mazes? Follow this one. The moth larva is chewing its way through the leaf.

reaction when the other animal is a female? Is the reaction influenced by the time of the year, or by the surroundings? Do animals and plants in groups react differently than they do when they are alone? Do animals "learn" by past experience? Are animals born with patterns of activity already established, or are these patterns developed during their lives? Do protists learn and do they show patterns of behavior?

These are the kinds of questions that are asked by biologists who study behavior. Physiologists, behavioral biologists, zoologists, ecologists, anthropologists, and geneticists are today jointly engaged in scientific behavior studies. The most recent and perhaps the most important addition to this group has been the geneticists, since more and more evidence suggests that behavioral differences in plants and animals are due in large part to genetic differences.

Getting started in behavior studies is often quite simple. To study many animals, just binoculars and a place to hide are enough to begin. But from this simple beginning lead many complexities. If the animals see or hear or smell the observer, their behavior will be changed. The activities the animals carry on must be reported many times, in as great detail as possible. (Eventually motion picture film helps; it can be stopped and started and replayed at slow speed.) Interpreting behavior is especially complex because it is comparative. The behavior of many different individuals of the same species must be observed and recorded. Then the behavior patterns of this species can be compared and contrasted to those of other species. However, it is important to avoid interpreting one species' behavior in terms of another's. Evolution suggests differences as well as similarities.

When changes are introduced into the natural environment, they should be planned carefully. To what extent is an artificial, as opposed to a natural environment, affecting an animal's behavior? Tests made in laboratory situations have a different purpose. Laboratory intelligence tests are an example. They tell observers much about the evolution of intelligent behavior. They also make the observers more knowledgeable about possibilities to watch for in further studies of the animals in their natural environment. Physiological experiments in the laboratory inform biologists about an animal's potential behavior based on the physical and biochemical working of its body systems.

## 24–2

## What Is Behavior?

**Behavior** is the way an organism acts. You have probably inferred this meaning in the many uses already made of the word *behavior*. More broadly, behavior is the sum of all the activities of an organism. It includes the influences of other organisms of the same kind, of organisms used as food, and of organisms that try to use *this* organism as food. Behavior also includes all the responses of an organism to such things as the changes in light, temperature, day or night, time of year, and each other characteristic of the ecosystem in which the organism lives. In brief, behavior includes, or must try to account for, everything in an organism's life.

You have already studied the separate internal organ systems that help bring about unified, outward expressions of organized behavior in multicellular organisms. The nerves and hormones of an animal's regulatory systems help control behavior from within, while the skeletal and muscular systems bring about most of the outward responses of behavior. For example, the sense organs of animals receive stimuli from the environment and send messages to the central nervous system. The central nervous system, in turn, sends messages to the muscles and causes hormones to be released into the bloodstream. Muscles and other organs receive these messages from nerves and hormones and react in some unified way. This unified act of the animal, whatever it is, is part of that animal's total behavior.

Behavior is a reaction to environment, both internal and external. Organisms react to many environmental factors—to heat and cold, to the pull of gravity, to light, sound, and chemicals. An organism also reacts to the objects around it, both living and nonliving. If an animal reacts to its particular environment in a way that helps it to survive, the behavior of that organism can be called successful.

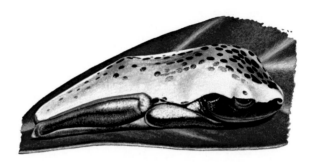

**Figure 24–1** An example of how camouflage and behavior can help a species to survive. Motionless during daylight hours, the tiny frog appears from above as a bird dropping.

## 24–3

## Behavior Is an Aspect of Evolution

Not only does behavior affect individual survival, but it also plays a part in preserving the species. If the behavior of individuals is successful, they may live to produce many offspring. The number of descendants affects the survival of a species as a whole. Therefore, the behavior of each member of a species helps to determine whether the species continues to reproduce and thrive.

For one example, the tiny tropical frog pictured in Figure 24–1 must remain totally motionless during the daylight hours if predators are to see it as a bird dropping. Its innate behavior pattern provides for night activity and long, motionless hours during the day. Thus it survives. Species that exist today are adapted to the conditions in which they live. Indeed, they may eventually give rise to new species. Thus, because behavior helps an organism survive, it is closely related to the evolution of the species.

Behavior is only one aspect of adaptation. Adaptation (Section 4–10) is a combination of inherited characteristics which improve an organism's chances to survive and reproduce. Poorly adapted organisms do not usually survive. Their species may eventually become extinct. Those adaptations that help an organism live successfully in its environment are an important part of the study of both evolution and behavior. Figure 24–2 on page 500 shows four interesting examples of adaptations.

---

**CAPSULE SUMMARY**

Biologists are increasingly concerned with the study of behavior. It is related to every other aspect of functioning and survival for an organism and its species. Behavior is the way an organism acts, the sum of its activities. Knowledge about behavior in one species helps lead to study and understanding of behavior in other species. Behavior expresses the coordination of all the body systems and their interdependence in the life of an organism.

**SELF CHECK**

1. Why are people interested in the behavior of other living things?
2. What is behavior?
3. What are the pros and cons of comparing behavior patterns in different species?
4. How does behavior reflect adaptations?
5. What is the relationship of an organism's behavior and its evolution?

**Figure 24–2** Animal adaptations are clues to their ways of life. Powerful muscles, padded feet, a keen sense of smell, retractable claws, and flesh-tearing teeth characterize the stalking leopard (top photo). The spotted coat is an adaptation, too, although not to new growths of savannah grass. Where would the coat camouflage the leopard? Below and to the right of the leopard is an animal whose appearance is a perfect adaptation for camouflage. Can you find the walking stick in the picture? The pelican (lower left) is another kettle of fish, or its bill usually is. Its webbed feet are an adaptation, too, but not to the post on which it is sitting. The bat (lower right) has small eyes and large ears, flesh-piercing teeth, and wings. (The eyes do not show in this photograph.) The bat flies at night. Does it see in the dark? Consider again the large ears. Do you know the unusual adaptation that gives the bat an electronic-age guidance system? (Look up the meaning of the word *sonar*.)

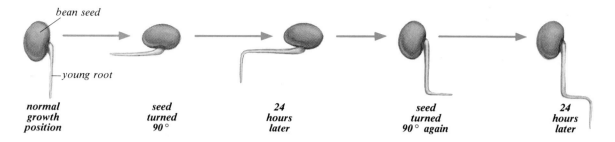

bean seed

young root

| normal | seed | 24 | seed | 24 |
|--------|------|----|------|-----|
| growth | turned | hours | turned | hours |
| position | 90° | later | 90° again | later |

**Figure 24-3** This behavior in a growing root is called a tropism. Follow the steps in the experiment. They indicate that gravity is influencing the bean seedling's root. The adaptation is a geotropism.

# Plant and Animal Behavior

## 24-4

### Some Plant Movements Are Called Tropisms

Plants show responses to their environment. The response of turning toward or away from a stimulus is called a **tropism.** In Chapter 21 you learned about auxins, including the hormones that cause plants to bend by growing toward the light. In addition to light, other factors such as gravity, chemicals in the environment, humidity, and temperature also affect plant growth and behavior.

The response to gravity is called **geotropism.** (*Geo* is a prefix meaning "earth.") Different parts of a plant may respond to gravity in different ways. As you observed in a seedling, for example, the young root usually grows toward the center of the earth (see Figure 24-3). The root is **positively geotropic.** The young stem, however, usually grows in the opposite direction, away from the attraction of gravity. The stem is **negatively geotropic.** For additional details on geotropism and other types of plant movements see **Appendix**

**24-A,** An Explanation of Tropisms and Other Plant Movements, page 737.

Try Investigation 24-A How Does Gravity Affect Plants?, page 681.

## 24-5

### What Are the Different Types of Animal Behavior?

In the broadest sense behavior is considered to be either **instinctive** or **learned.** Instinctive behavior is considered to be inherited or genetically determined. It is most commonly referred to as **innate** behavior, which means inborn. It is a behavioral pattern ready to function when the organism is hatched or born. Environmental influences may trigger innate behavior but do not explain it. Nor does learning explain it when no previous experience is involved. For example, the kitten pictured

**Figure 24–4** This Siamese kitten has never fallen or been dropped. It has had no experience with high places. The drop you see here is only visual; a plate of glass gives the kitten firm underfooting. Yet the kitten hesitates. Such experiments are used to help determine when behavior is innate and when it is learned.

in Figure 24–4 is standing on a checkerboard surface while looking down a visual cliff or drop. The drop is visual, not actual, because a plate of glass covers it. Yet the kitten will not venture out onto the glass. This particular kitten has had no experience with heights or falling. The reaction can be classified as innate in response to the visual stimulus.

Learned behavior consists of all those responses that an organism develops as a result of environmental experiences. Animals with well-developed nervous systems can learn to behave in new ways. Learned behavior may range from simple changes that modify innate behavior in lower animals to the kind of complex learned behavior used to operate a microscope or drive a car.

Oftentimes, even in the higher animals, it is difficult to know whether observed behavior is innate or learned. For instance, does a salamander learn to swim naturally when it reaches a certain stage of development? Questions of this sort can only be answered by the use of well-designed experiments.

In one experiment on this question, a group of salamanders was anesthetized at an age before swimming movements normally begin. A control group was allowed to develop normally. At first the control group made feeble efforts to swim, as if they were learning, and then swam normally. When the experimental salamanders were allowed to recover from the anesthetic, they immediately swam normally. This experiment showed that mature swimming movements in this kind of salamander occur naturally, at a certain stage of development. Thus the ability to swim in these animals is innate. They do not have to learn.

Innate behavior can be changed by learning, however. A series of experiments with the southern toad indicates how experience may change the behavior of a vertebrate. The toad is a natural predator of the robber fly and flips this insect down its throat with a quick motion of the tongue. However, the bumblebee resembles the robber fly in size, shape, and color. When a bumblebee is first presented to the toad, its tongue reaches out to flip the insect into its mouth just as it did with the robber fly. The bumblebee, however, stings the toad's tongue and then escapes. The toad meanwhile ducks its head, blinks its eyes, and holds its tongue out. After recovering from this experience the toad does not attempt to catch robber flies. It does, however, continue to flip out its tongue to capture other kinds of insects. The toad has changed its innate tongue-flipping behavior: It no longer flips its tongue at insects that look like bumblebees.

For many years scientists have argued the question of whether many kinds of behavior are innate or learned. However, most scientists agree today that the answer is not entirely one or the other. There are probably elements of both heredity and learning in many behavior patterns once thought to be only learned or only innate.

**Try Investigation 24–B** Do Paramecia Behave Sensibly?, page 682.

## 24–6
## Reasoning Is the Most Complex Process in Behavior

Human beings are able to develop concepts, deal with abstract matters, and solve problems involving new situations. These abilities are recognized as part of people's reasoning power. Do animals other than humans have this reasoning ability? The reasoning ability of animals can be studied experimentally with "detour problems." In such a problem, an animal must follow an indirect path to get to a desired object. The animal must first move away from the desired object in order to reach it (Figure 24–5).

In experiments with the detour problem the important question is, Did the animal use reason or simply trial and error in solving the problem? Of

**Figure 24–5** A detour is necessary if the raccoon is to reach the food. This experiment provides data on trial-and-error and reasoning.

**Figure 24–6** Three "stills" from a motion picture film of a chimpanzee, a bunch of bananas too high to reach, and some empty boxes. The chimp sized up the situation (left), stacked the boxes (center), and obtained the bananas (right).

the many animals tested in this type of experiment, only monkeys and chimpanzees were able to solve the problem quickly without much trial and error. Rats, dogs, and raccoons learned how to make the detour, but they seemed to use trial-and-error methods, not reasoning. For more of trial-and-error learning see **Appendix 24–B,** Innate Behavior, page 738.

Chimpanzees and monkeys also show the ability to solve even more difficult problems. In a classic demonstration of reasoning ability, some bananas were hung out of reach of a chimpanzee. Several boxes on the floor, if stacked, would provide possible access to the bananas. Figure 24–6 shows the chimpanzee's response. In other, more recent experiments, chimpanzees have used plastic tags (Figure 16–1) and computer keys to respond to tests.

In any learning experiment it is not always easy to decide how the problem was solved. Was it by reasoning or by application of some previous experience? Reasoning actually goes beyond the effect of stored experiences. How are reasoning, experience, and trial and error to be distinguished in each experiment?

The answers to these questions are at the heart of exciting work in the field of behavior. How humans and other animals learn is an important phase of scientific research. The chimpanzee experiment in Figure 24–6, for example, and many other such studies have consistently indicated that chimps are intelligent animals. Yet all attempts to teach them to speak failed. At length it developed that the human experimenters, not the chimps, were failing! Chimpanzees do not have human organs of speech. When sign language was used, not only chimps but gorillas began to communicate with their human trainers.

Communications skills, it develops, are not uniquely human. Continuing research will help develop more knowledge of complex reasoning processes. Apparently we share these processes in varying degrees with many other animals. This is consistent with the idea that nervous systems and mental processes evolved, too, just as other organ systems have.

## 24–7
## Imprinting, Habituation, and Conditioning

One limited kind of learning is known as **imprinting.** An example is the process in which newly hatched birds learn to follow their mother. It was first thought that baby birds instinctively follow their mother. Experiments to test this idea were carried out by Konrad Lorenz, an Austrian zoologist. When Lorenz acted like a mother goose, waddling along and honking in front of newly hatched goslings that had never seen their mother, the goslings followed along behind. When the goslings were later given the opportunity to follow their own mother or other birds, they still followed Lorenz (Figure 24–7). They did not "recognize" their own mother. The goslings apparently learned to follow the first object they saw that moved and made honking sounds.

**Figure 24–7** Konrad Lorenz, "mother" to the goslings following along behind. Greylag geese are so easily imprinted to the first moving object they see that special care must be taken in moving them from an incubator to a foster home with other geese. The person who moves them must be careful not to be seen.

In fact, further investigation showed that a gosling would follow a large colored box containing a ticking clock—if the box was the first moving object it observed! When the colored box was pulled along by a wire, the gosling followed. Even later, when its own mother was present, the gosling still followed the box, not its mother.

Imprinting is an unusual form of learning. It can take place only during a very limited period of time. These experiments showed that a gosling's early attraction to its mother is not instinctive. The gosling learns to follow its mother because the mother bird is usually the first moving object that the gosling sees.

Another kind of simple learning might be called tuning-out behavior or **habituation.** If an animal is exposed to a stimulus over and over again it may slowly lose its degree of response to such a stimulus. For example, a dog responds to the sound of an airplane passing overhead and turns its head. If airplanes continue to fly overhead, the dog may learn to disregard the sound. Such a reaction can be thought of as learning not to respond to stimuli which are of little importance to the animal.

A more complex kind of learning is known as **conditioning.** Conditioning occurs when the patterns of an innate reflex are changed. In the early 1900's the Russian physiologist Ivan Pavlov (PAV-lof) did pioneer work on the subject of conditioned reflexes. Pavlov's most famous experiments involved the innate reflex of the flow of saliva in a dog when food is placed in its mouth. This reflex can be explained as follows: An impulse from the taste receptors on the tongue travels along the neurons to the brain and back to the salivary glands, causing saliva to be secreted. Thus, very soon after the dog is given a piece of meat, it salivates.

Pavlov first showed that when a bell was rung the dog did not produce a flow of saliva. Then the bell was rung as meat was presented to the dog.

The dog secreted saliva. The acts of ringing the bell and presenting the meat were repeated together many times. After many trials there was a change in the dog's reflex behavior. Eventually the dog secreted saliva upon hearing the bell, even when no food was present. Pavlov reasoned that a new reflex had been set up. Some kind of change had come about in the neuron pathway between receptors of the ears, the brain, and the salivary glands of the dog.

Pavlov performed many other experiments with conditioned reflexes. Dogs were conditioned to light, electric shock, the ticking of a metronome, and many other stimuli. Pavlov's work became so famous that much of behavior was at one time explained only in terms of reflexes and conditioning. But today it is realized that behavior is much more complicated. Remember that in a conditioned response one stimulus is substituted for another. An animal learns to respond to a new stimulus in the same way that it had responded to a first stimulus.

Experimenters have tried to develop conditioned responses in many types of animals. One of the most interesting experiments was performed on planarians. In the early 1950's two biologists developed a conditioned response in planarians. First, they shined a strong light on a planarian. Several seconds later, they administered a mild electric shock. The planarian's normal response to the light was to stretch. Its normal response to the shock was to contract or turn its head. This sequence, in which the light was followed by the shock, was repeated about 100 times. Soon the response to the light alone was about the same as though the electric shock had been given also. This sequence is outlined in Figure 24–8. A "trained" planarian would show a shock response when the light was turned on 23 out of 25 times. However, it soon forgot its lesson unless it was retrained periodically.

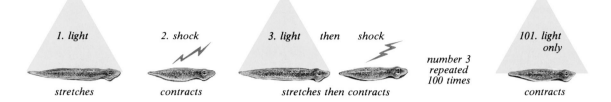

1. light
stretches

2. shock
contracts

3. light    then    shock
stretches then contracts

number 3
repeated
100 times

101. light
only
contracts

**Figure 24-8** A conditioned-reflex experiment with a planarian. As a result of the conditioning, the planarian eventually responds to light as it would to an electric shock.

In later experiments, planarians conditioned to the light-shock response were cut in half. Each half was allowed to grow. The tail half grew a head and the head half grew a tail. The regenerated planarians were then subjected to the light-shock experiment. It was found that both types of planarians, those regenerated from the head half and those regenerated from the tail half, responded to conditioning more quickly than planarians being conditioned for the first time. Apparently something had occurred in planarians regenerated from tail pieces as well as in those regenerated from head pieces that permitted faster conditioning.

A somewhat higher level of learning is trial-and-error learning. Some biologists prefer to call this trial-and-success learning. An animal faced with two or more responses may eventually be taught the preferred one when a reward is given for this response. Other responses may result in punishment. Many organisms learn, after many trials, to make the "correct" response.

**CAPSULE SUMMARY**

It is difficult to determine whether observed behavior is innate or learned. Well-designed experiments are required to obtain more data on such questions. The behavior of most organisms consists of both innate and learned behavior. Innate behavior can often be changed by learning. The most complex process in behavior is reasoning. The capacity to reason is innate. Its development and use involve learning.

Learning may be by imprinting, habituation, conditioning, or more complex processes. Some of these forms of learning occur not only in humans, but also in much simpler, invertebrate organisms.

**SELF CHECK**

1. What is a tropism?
2. What is the difference between innate and learned behavior?
3. Can the conclusions from the salamander swimming experiment be applied to other animals?
4. What does the experiment with toads, robber flies, and bumblebees suggest to you about the toad's capacity to learn or to alter innate behavior?
5. How can we determine whether animals other than human beings can reason?

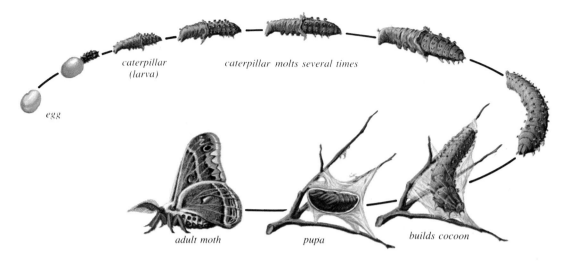

*caterpillar (larva)*

*caterpillar molts several times*

*egg*

*adult moth*

*pupa*

*builds cocoon*

**Figure 24-9** The life cycle of the Cecropia moth, or American silkworm. An egg develops into a small caterpillar in 10 days. The caterpillar, or larva, eats leaves, molts four times and grows up to 10 centimeters in length in several weeks. It then spins a cocoon around itself, and the pupa develops within the cocoon. The adult moth emerges in the spring.

# The Biological Roots of Behavior

## 24-8

### Behavior Is Affected by Both External and Internal Stimuli

Today the study of animal behavior includes subjects ranging from how an animal functions as an individual to how it communicates with others of its kind. The latter, or social behavior, is the subject of the next chapter. But the environment plays a role in determining even behavior as an individual. Both internal and external stimuli are almost always at work.

The study of how the American silkworm, the Cecropia moth, constructs its cocoon reveals how both external and internal stimuli interact to determine an organism's behavior. Scientists observed that during the larval stage of its life, this silkworm spins almost two kilometers of silken thread into a cocoon. The cocoon is a record of the animal's spinning behavior. Figure 24-9 shows the life cycle of the silkworm.

The larva or caterpillar form of the moth spins the cocoon at the end of summer. The adult moth comes out of the cocoon the following spring. The Cecropia cocoon has two thick layers. They are baglike structures, one inside the other, with a small opening on the upper end of each bag. These openings serve as an escape hatch for the adult moth. Between the two bags of the cocoon is a loose network of silk thread. Such a cocoon insulates the animal from its external environment and allows it to survive through a cold winter.

Since the silkworm larvae do not have any opportunity to learn how to spin a cocoon, cocoon-spinning behavior must be inherited. What, therefore, starts and controls the silkworm's spinning behavior?

Scientists have studied and compared the American silkworm with another species of silkworm, the kind raised commercially to produce silk. The commercial silkworm usually spins a cocoon with only a single bag. However, biologists found a mutant of the commercial silkworm, one that spins a cocoon with the double bag like that of the Cecropia. Breeding experiments with this mutant silkworm showed that double-bag spinning was controlled by a single dominant gene.

Is cocoon-spinning behavior therefore determined solely by genes? The difficulty with such a conclusion is that the ability to learn and carry out new behavior patterns is also determined by genes. In fact, all kinds of behavior patterns have some genetic factors.

Biologists wondered why the silkworm spins its cocoon at the particular time that it does. It was found that during the larval stage, the organism loses its skin, or molts, a number of times. Before each molt the larva secretes a small pad of silk. When it molts, the larva pulls away from its old skin, leaving it attached to the small pad of silk. This process is repeated each time the animal molts. However, before the last molt, the caterpillar builds the double-bag cocoon.

In further investigations, biologists found that a pair of glands in the insect's head controls cocoon-spinning. If these glands are surgically removed early in the life of the caterpillar, it will spin a tiny cocoon instead of a silk anchor-pad the next time it molts. From experiments like this, a hypothesis is suggested: Hormones from these glands prevent cocoon-spinning until later in the development of the caterpillar. This hypothesis predicts that these glands will stop secreting hormones at the last molt and that the cocoon will then be spun. Further experiments have supported this hypothesis. Thus you can see that hormones are important in insect behavior.

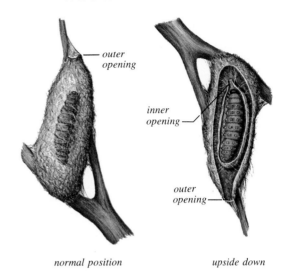

*normal position*          *upside down*

**Figure 24–10** The normal cocoon of the Cecropia moth (left) has an inner and outer bag with the entrances to both facing upward. These openings provide an exit for the adult moth. In an experiment, the cocoon was turned upside down after only the outer bag was spun. Although the entrance to the outer bag was on the bottom, the caterpillar built the inner bag with its opening on the top (right). What do you think happened to the moth?

Scientists have also studied external influences on this caterpillar's behavior. What will happen if the organism is turned upside down after it has spun its outer envelope with an opening at the top but before it has started to spin the inner envelope? If, in the new position, the animal spins the inner bag with the opening upward, the adult moth will be trapped. On the other hand, if the silkworm receives the message that it is now upside down, it will make the opening of the bag on the downward side. In actual experiments the animals are observed to build the inner bag of the cocoon with the opening upward. As a result, the bags have openings in opposite directions, as shown in Figure 24–10. The experiments suggest that these animals may use gravity as an environmental clue. Such experiments point out the importance of considering external stimuli in the study of behavior.

In another set of experiments, caterpillars just ready to spin were placed inside inflated balloons. In this environment the caterpillars spread their silk in flat sheets on the inside surface of the balloon. They apparently are unable to spin cocoons. If the caterpillars are taken out of the balloons after spinning about half their silk, they spin only the tight inner-cocoon bags. It appears that the inner envelope is started only after a certain amount of silk thread is secreted. The caterpillar must have a method for measuring the amount of silk secreted. The animal seems to change behavior from spinning the outer envelope to spinning the inner envelope according to the internal stimulus of how much silk is secreted.

In a continuing series of experiments, it has been found that cocoon-building behavior remains unchanged even when large parts of the brain are removed. The removal of certain other tiny parts of the brain, however, results in strange cocoons. In one experiment, for example, the brain-injured animal spread a flat sheet of silk completely covering the floor of its cage instead of spinning a cocoon.

Many studies such as these with different animals have shown the importance of internal stimuli in animal behavior. All in all, the experiments show that behavior is not only a reaction to stimuli from the external environment, but it is also controlled by internal stimuli. Perhaps you can now see why the study of animal behavior is difficult, but fascinating. It will take work in the fields of evolution, genetics, and physiology to gather data for better understanding of animal behavior.

## 24–9

## External and Internal Stimuli Interact in Vertebrates

Complex instinctive behavior frequently depends on the animal's physiology. For example, the distinctive courting and reproductive behavior of

birds and fishes depends on the amounts of certain hormones in the organisms. The amounts of hormones, in turn, may be due to external factors such as the length of day.

The courting and reproductive behavior of the three-spined stickleback fish has been widely studied as one example of the interaction of internal and external stimuli. In early spring reproductive hormones cause changes in both the appearance and the behavior of the stickleback. The hormones trigger a whole sequence of mating behavior in the fish. The male moves to the warm, shallow edge of the pond to select a breeding area, or territory. Physical change, such as the red color of the male's belly, becomes an external stimulus for the behavior of the females. The whole sequence of mating behavior is shown in Figure 24–11.

Experiments have shown that a certain kind of behavior by the stickleback occurs in response to specific stimuli. For example, the male stickleback defends its territory against other males of the same species. The male will defend its nest against even a dummy fish of any shape in the same territory as long as the dummy has a red belly. On the other hand, if a model of a male stickleback without a red underside is presented, the male stickleback does not show fighting behavior. The specific external stimulus of the red underside seems to start the male's defense behavior.

Another example of how a specific stimulus evokes instinctive behavior is shown by the herring gull. Young gulls in the nest will beg for food when they are shown dummy gull heads. The strength of the young gulls' responses depends partly on the shape of the dummy's beak and partly on the presence of a spot of color on the beak. If there is no spot at all, responses are weak.

The study of internal and external stimuli in the instinctive behavior of some vertebrates has been of tremendous interest to biologists. Instinctive behavior, although unlearned and characteristic of

**Figure 24–11** At breeding time a male stickleback has a red belly. The male attracts a female with dancelike swimming motions and leads her to the nest he has built. The female lays eggs, then leaves. The male enters the nest, fertilizes the eggs, and thereafter guards the nest from intruders.

a particular species, is not as rigid and unchanging as was once thought. Changes are sometimes observed. These differences in the nature and strength of responses depend on both the external stimuli and the internal condition of the animal. When a certain pattern of response is often repeated, biologists assume that it has great survival value to the species.

# Biorhythms

Are you a morning person or a night person? Does your body chemistry function best if you go to bed early and get up early? Or are you wide awake at midnight and slow to wake in the morning?

Scientists are now exploring these and other questions related to biological rhythms. Flowers bloom, birds migrate, leaves change color at times related to relative lengths of day and night (time of year) and other factors. Body temperature, blood pressure, respiration, pulse rate, enzyme activity, hormone secretions, and even cell division vary in daily rhythms. These are called circadian rhythms, from the Latin *circa diem,* which means "about a day."

Many scientists are convinced that the evidence indicates internal biological "clocks" in different organisms. None of these clocks is well understood. Many rhythms are affected by such changes in living as late-shift work and airplane travel to different time zones. Other rhythms go right on even in changed circumstances. Some have been maintained during experiments in which people lived for months in artificial lighting, not knowing whether it was night or day.

Results of biorhythm studies are being tested in many applications. For example, there appear to be times of day at which medicinal drugs work best. A profile of a patient's pulse, blood pressure, and other body activities can help pinpoint the times at which the smallest dose of a drug may have the greatest effect.

Several years ago a Japanese railroad company determined a number of biorhythm patterns of 500 train engineers and entered these patterns in a computer.

## 24–10

### What Guidelines Are Suggested in Studying Human Behavior?

Behavior becomes more and more complicated to study the higher up the evolutionary scale the investigator is working. Patterns of behavior that are instinctive or innate make up less of the total behavior observed. In terms of genes and the environment, the environmental influences upon learning grow greater. By the time human beings are reached, the highest level of conscious behavior is being studied. The human subjects often

"Ups" and "downs" in alertness and behavior were predicted by the computer for each engineer. The railroad claimed that the accident rate dropped 50 percent the first year when engineers were cautioned about predicted "bad days."

Other studies have contradicted the Japanese railroad experience. A number of controlled experiments have suggested that biorhythm predictions, at least as presently made, are nonsense. These experiments show that when people are not told which days are computed to be "bad days," the computer predictions are not supported by actual patterns of mishaps or accidents. The value of the Japanese railroad experience was simply that the company took an individual interest in each of its engineers and stressed safety continually with each of them.

It seems that biological rhythms are not yet well enough understood to suggest conclusions. However, you may find biorhythm studies in your future.

express an opinion that they determine their own behavior. Does this mean that human beings are freed of their evolutionary and genetic heritage?

You should already know that this cannot be true. Much of the human body is controlled and coordinated involuntarily. People blink, blush, breathe, digest a meal, and get goose bumps involuntarily—there are hundreds more of such examples. Although learning plays a greater role among human beings than among other animals, there is no reason to believe that human behavior is free of evolutionary and genetic influences.

Survival value is easy to identify as a hypothesis explaining some examples of human behavior. But people, as the most complicated species behaviorally, are also the most puzzling. Their behavior is full of inconsistencies. Much of the time survival is not at stake. Even when it is, people may adapt on one occasion and rebel or fight on another. Adaptation, for humans as for other animals, is related to survival. Sometimes, however, adaptation is more clearly for acceptance of an individual by a group than for the group's (including the individual's) survival. Revolutionary political or social movements provide examples. Unrest and conflicting values and intolerance mark the human species as the only animal species in which different groups or populations engage in organized wars. How is survival then at stake for the species? For individuals?

Human beings also are the only organisms able to contemplate their species' past and future. Yet people's behavior may be deeply rooted in the evolutionary past. Awareness that their activities are producing negative effects for their descendants in the future creates more and more unrest. But the pre-existing behavior and activities continue. Populations, their energy use, industrialization, and environmental impact continue to grow. How is survival involved for the species in these circumstances? How is it involved for presently living individuals and populations?

All species are constantly faced with the problem of adapting to a changing environment or becoming extinct. Biologists review the overall effects of behavior and of evolution using such statements. A species does not behave or adapt as an organized whole, however. The human examples help illustrate this. Species consist of individuals past, present, and future. Only living individuals are involved with survival and with behavior influencing survival. Innate reproductive behavior strongly affects these individuals, as with the stickleback—or, again, human beings. It promotes survival of the species, as opposed to survival of individuals.

In many animal populations and societies, innate behavior plays a much greater role than it plays in human societies in determining individuals' roles. You will look into some of these other animal societies in the next chapter.

---

**CAPSULE SUMMARY**

Behavior is innate or learned, or a combination of both. The levels of behavior are related to the complexity of the organism. Internal and external stimuli are both nearly always at work. Both genes and the environment affect behavior.

Studies of cocoon-spinning by silkworms and of courting behavior by stickleback fish provide good examples of how behavioral studies are pursued by biologists. Innate behavior, as in these examples, contrasts vividly with the diversity of behavior observed in human beings. Humans have innate behavior, too. However, much of their behavior is learned, showing inconsistencies as compared with innate patterns of behavior.

**SELF CHECK**

1. In what way is spinning a cocoon a record of Cecropia behavior? How do biologists determine whether learning, or reasoning, is involved in spinning the cocoon?
2. If genes determine innate behavior, what determines learning?
3. How would you classify the courting and reproductive behavior of the male stickleback fish?
4. How does behavior appear to be related to evolution?
5. Why is the study of human behavior of increasing importance?

# CHAPTER SUMMARY

## HIGHLIGHTS

The behavior of an organism is defined as its total activity in interacting with its living and nonliving environment.

Plant tropisms illustrate a limited part of the behavior of plants. Overall, plant behavior may be chemically complex, but it is more limited in physical activity than animal behavior.

A multicellular organism's behavior is affected by hormones, other body chemicals, and, in animals, the nervous system. The behavior may be innate, learned, or both. Innate behavior is not as unvarying for some organisms as once thought. For both innate and learned behavior, reasoning is the highest level of behavioral activity.

Behavior is an important aspect of evolution and is heavily influenced by genes. Among more complex animals, including humans, behavior becomes less consistent and more difficult to classify biologically as learning increases. Some of the inconsistencies of learned behavior affect species survival.

## REVIEWING IDEAS

1. What is behavior?
2. What are some environmental changes that might bring about responses by organisms?
3. How is behavior related to survival of an individual organism?
4. How is behavior related to survival of a species?
5. How do tropisms in plants represent reactions having survival value?
6. What is innate behavior? What advantages does it have for organisms? Give examples.
7. How is learning demonstrated by a conditioned reflex?

8. How did investigators verify that cocoon-spinning by Cecropia moth larvae is innate?
9. How is the study of animal behavior useful in approaching a study of human behavior?
10. How does reproductive behavior differ in survival value from other behavior?

## USING CONCEPTS

11. Explain how individual survival and species survival in humans may correspond in some behavioral situations, but conflict in others.
12. Suggest how behavior can be a factor in evolution.
13. Some plants produce chemicals that interfere with normal hormone functioning in animals that feed on the plants. Is this an example of plant behavior? Explain.
14. How would you plan an experiment to test imprinting in baby chicks? What useful background information might be obtained from a commercial hatchery?
15. People may respond to a human behavioral study with improved performance that is unrelated to the study itself. The human subjects try harder. How could you design a control for this unwanted effect on the study?

## RECOMMENDED READING

Barnett, S. A. *Modern Ethology: The Science of Animal Behavior*. New York, Oxford University Press, 1981. A modern textbook on the study of animal behavior.

Cloudsley-Thomas, J. L. *Tooth and Claw: Defensive Strategies in the Animal World*. London, J. M. Dent, 1980. Defense behavior as a major example of survival-oriented behavior.

Tuthill, J. E. ''The Bugs of Winter.'' *Science 83*, January/February issue. The effect of temperature and insect-made antifreeze on the behavior of insects that are active in winter.

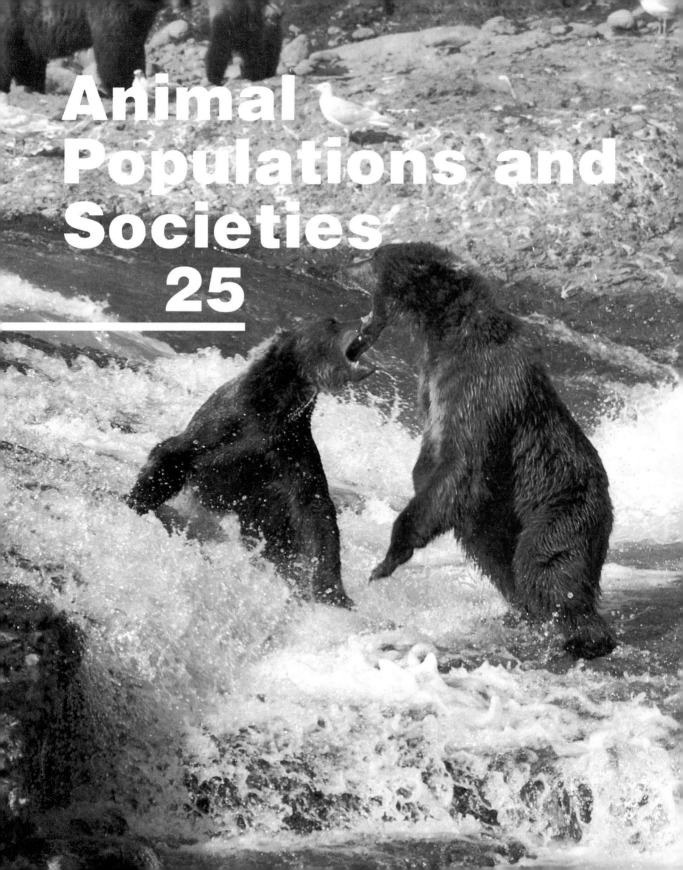

# Animal Populations and Societies
# 25

Animals live with or near others of their kind. Is a group in one area just so many individuals? Or is it, instead, organized in ways biologists can detect in behavioral studies?

Animals depend on other organisms for their food. Do the members of a group cooperate, or merely compete, in seeking food? Do animals cooperate in any other ways? Reproduction obviously involves cooperation. The male and female stickleback fish you read about in the last chapter are interdependent for reproduction. Are other life activities organized in any way? In this chapter you will find that the answers differ for different animal species.

# Populations and Their Organization

## 25-1

### Populations Are Made Up of Like Organisms

A biologist may underline the interdependence of all living things by pointing out that the world population is not merely four billion-plus people. It includes other living organisms, making the total number astronomical. Experimentally, however, populations are not studied for all species together. By agreement, the term **population** is defined as all the organisms of a single species that live at the same time in the same area. You have seen it used this way in earlier chapters. The group that makes up the population can be further broken down into the adult and juvenile populations. Or it can be divided into the male and female populations. But unless such a division is specified, the population is considered to be all the individuals of one species living in the place named. Other populations of the same species may exist in other places.

Many animal populations are a group only in the sense of their common habitat. They are not knit together or organized in any way. At least biologists have not been able to determine specific interactions except in reproduction and in competition for food. For these animals, the gene pool and gene flow provide almost the only population characteristics. Populations of this kind occur among many of the animals that produce and fertilize eggs in great numbers and then abandon them.

---

←Who was there first matters less than the threat display. Bears have evolved societal behavior in which threats are usually sufficient to protect territories or fishing rights.

**Figure 25–1** Organized activities suggesting cooperation are clues to an animal society. Pictured here are two groups of animals—beetles and ants. One of the photographs has recorded behavior suggestive of social cooperation. Which is it? Which of these groups of animals would you choose to investigate?

Sponges, many insects, frogs (Investigation 11–C), and most fishes appear to fit this description, but it is too general to be a guide. Each species must be investigated. What can you see in Figure 25–1, for example, that suggests some kind of organization or cooperation in one of the species of animals pictured?

Usually what is easiest to overlook in considering possible organization in populations is innate or instinctive behavior. Animals do not necessarily have to be thinking animals to organize their activities. Complicated behavioral patterns may be genetically transmitted. Some kinds of ants, for example, not only have job specialization in the colony but also maintain herds of aphids. The ants place the aphids on succulent plant leaves and ''milk'' the aphids to obtain some of the colony's food supply.

How much do you know of the populations of insects, birds, and other creatures whose representatives you frequently see on your way to and from school? Are these individuals' activities haphazard? Or are their activities a part of an organized whole?

**Figure 25-2** King penguins come together to form a breeding colony. Each pair of penguins, male and female, broods a single egg, taking turns at the task.

## 25-2
## Societies Are Organized Populations

Leaders, followers, individuals doing different jobs, and others settling who goes first—or feeds first—are evidence of organized and usually cooperative behavior in a population. If the evidence can be confirmed on investigation, it is said to identify an **animal society.**

Societies may be loose-knit or very highly organized. The dogs in your neighborhood probably do not constantly fight but instead have established relationships beginning with the "top dog." That is, one dog may be dominant over all the others. A new dog in the neighborhood quickly adapts or becomes engaged in many fights. The dogs—as well as wolves, their wild relatives—have many characteristics of behavior that reveal **hierarchies,** levels in the society where individuals fit. You can watch the behavior of dogs that meet without fighting and observe the behavioral acts that concede, for one dog, a higher place in the hierarchy to the other.

Many animal societies are so highly organized that the survival of the population depends on each kind of individual doing its job. You will read about some of these societies, which have **caste systems.** A caste of soldier ants differs even in physical characteristics from the caste of worker ants of the same species.

**Figure 25–3** Musk oxen, shown in this drawing, and caribou will stand shoulder to shoulder and sometimes form a ring around a large herd to face the threat of wolves. Unprotected young, and old or isolated adults, are easy targets. But a defensive line prevents cooperative attacks by the wolves on one individual. The outcome is that cooperation by the musk oxen or caribou overcomes cooperation among the wolves.

Cooperation, achieved by different means, is part of all animal societies. A hierarchy replaces constant competition with dominance relationships, within which individuals in the society cooperate. A caste system divides the work or functions of the society among the different castes. What similarities to human society do you see in such methods of organization?

You can very easily determine one necessity for a society. There must be some method of communication. Otherwise cooperation could not be maintained. A hierarchy could not be established at all without communication. Nor could castes cooperate efficiently.

Time may be an important element in the observations made of an animal society. A pattern of behavior you observe at one time may not be present at another. King penguins, for example, nest only on the shores of remote islands near Antarctica, and only at a certain time of the year. Each year during the breeding season the penguins gather on these shores and form large breeding colonies. Here the males and females take turns protecting and warming their eggs (Figure 25–2) and rearing their young. Far away, in the northern hemisphere, an observer of musk oxen and caribou would observe a loosely knit organization of herds most of the time. A hierarchy could be identified for at least some of the animals. But at a time of danger from intruders the organization of the herd becomes very specialized. Males may form a line (Figure 25–3) or even a ring around the herd, standing shoulder-to-shoulder facing the threat. Females and young will be protected behind the line or ring. Or, females may be in the line, too, depending on the numbers of individuals present, the ''surprise'' element in the timing of the threat or attack, and the time of year relative to breeding.

When studying populations you will see many kinds of societies. Some of these societies with strong social instincts have been studied extensively, as you will see in reading about insects first, then birds and mammals.

## 25–3

## Honeybee and Other Insect Societies

Many of the social insects, such as ants, termites, wasps, and bees, have a division of labor that is accompanied or determined by bodies that are adapted to special jobs. These insects have working caste systems. Biologists have discovered many features of these societies in hundreds of separate behavioral studies.

Among termites, the females that reproduce the members of the society have enlarged abdomens. The workers are sterile males and females of different sizes. Workers perform tasks according to their size. They may gather the food, build and repair the shelter, or care for the young. The soldiers that defend the society are equipped with a variety of protective and attacking devices. Their skeletons are sometimes heavily armored, and their jaws are large and strong, adapted for deadly biting. Some of the soldiers can release chemical substances that act much like a poison gas. Such a society shows clearly different castes.

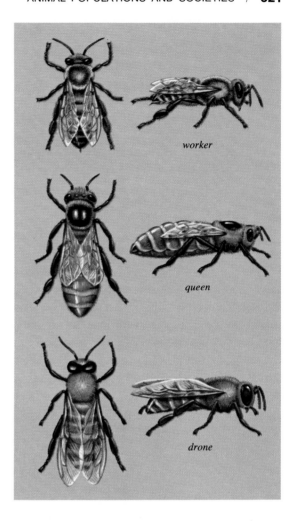

**Figure 25–4** Individuals of three castes of honeybees. What differences among the castes do you see in the body structures of the bees?

The honeybee society has three castes: the queen, the drones, and the workers. The drones are responsible for the production of offspring by the society. A drone supplies the sperm, and the queen supplies the eggs. The workers carry out all other activities of the hive. Compare the bodies of the queen, drone, and worker honeybees in Figure 25–4. The differences between the specialized body structures of the queen and the workers are determined by diet, not heredity. The workers and the queen all develop from female larvae, the drones from male larvae. During development the workers and queen bee are all fed "royal jelly" for the first three days. After that only one larva is usually fed royal jelly. More than one queen can be produced, however. A fight to the death follows. The lone survivor becomes the hive's queen.

The workers, after the first three days of their development, receive only "bee bread" made of pollen and honey during the rest of their development.

Both the queen and the drones have reproductive organs that occupy a large portion of their bodies. The reproductive organs of the drone are arranged so that all the sperm can be instantly deposited into the reproductive tract of the queen. The reproductive tract of the queen is adapted in a special way. The tract is large enough to accept and store for her entire lifetime the sperm received from one or more matings. What advantage to the hive's survival can you find in such an adaptation?

Neither the queen nor the drone is concerned with food-gathering or food-processing. Organs associated with these activities are reduced or absent. The digestive system is reduced in size. The jaws, legs, and hairs of the body are not specialized for food-gathering as they are in the workers. Also, the sense organs, particularly the antennae of the queen, are small. However, the sense organs of the drones are highly developed. A drone must catch a flying queen in order to mate. Therefore, the drones with well-developed sense organs, long antennae, and long wings are most successful in mating.

The workers gather the food, produce wax, rear and protect the brood, and carry on all the work of the hive. Such special body adaptations increase the work efficiency of the hive and thereby the chance of the society's survival.

## 25–4
# Baboon Society

The division of labor in many vertebrates, including humans, is not based on castes as distinct as the bee's. A recurring social structure of vertebrate groups is divided into adult males, adult females, infants, and juveniles. Usually these group members do not differ in physical structure except for size and sexual differences. Social behavior and ability, rather than body types, determine the division of labor. Leaders, pathfinders, sentinels, and guardians of the group may look the same but behave differently. These roles in the group are not necessarily static. Individuals change roles from time to time, or assume new roles. Age and experience play a part. John Phillip's description of a troop of baboons can give you an idea of the organization of one vertebrate society as in the observations quoted below:

The sentinel is exceedingly sharp and detects the least noise, scent, or appearance of man or leopard. . . . The sentinels are often the largest, strongest males, that is, with the exception of the real leader of the group; they will remain faithfully at the post 'waughing' (the typical note of danger is "waugh, waugh," very guttural and somewhat alarming) despite the proximity of danger. Upon these notes of warning reaching the ear of the leader, he will immediately assemble the members of the group, marshalling the males at the rear and along the sides, the females and the young at the forefront, or within the cordon of the males; he himself will alternately lead or bring up the rear, according to the plan of flight or degree of danger. When things get too hot for the sentinels, they scamper off a short distance, mount some high position, and give a further warning to the leader.[1]

**Figure 25–5** A mother baboon and her offspring. When the mother is sitting or resting, the young baboon crawls around to her breast and nestles in her arms.

Evolutionary influences on behavior are an obvious hypothesis for societal similarities among baboons and many other higher animals. Oral communication, although not necessarily complex speech, is more versatile than it might appear at first. Family and group influences and the care and affection given offspring (Figure 25–5) are very noticeable. Many of the features of family or group living are common from species to species, from baboons to humans.

---

**CAPSULE SUMMARY**

Populations of different species show many differences in composition and in the behavior of the members. Many populations are organized into animal societies. In each society, some degree of cooperative behavior can be found ranging from a hierarchy to definite castes. A hierarchy may place the largest, strongest members of a population in higher positions, but otherwise it may not reflect permanence in individual assignments. Leaders and dominant members can change. Body structure and appearance is usually very similar among members of a population. The caste system of social insects, however, reflect body differences as well as different assignments within the society. Each caste is fixed in its existence and job specialization within the society.

**SELF CHECK**

1. Define a population.
2. What is an animal society?
3. Contrast a social hierarchy with a caste system.
4. Using animals you know, give an example of a behavioral adaptation to life in a society. Also give a human example.
5. How might behavioral changes in tasks or roles be brought about in non-caste societies?

# Structure of Societies

## 25–5

### Group Structure May Be Influenced by Sexual Differences

How does a society divide its work among specialists? Sometimes labor of a group may be divided according to sex. In your family, for example, your mother may be largely responsible for raising children and managing the home. Your father may be largely responsible for providing income for food, shelter, medical care, and education. Yet in some human families, these responsibilities are reversed. In still others, both parents may work at outside jobs and share in home responsibilities. Human society, in other words, is adaptable, and it is changing. Some people now prefer to live in larger or extended families. Other people prefer a more traditional family, but with the roles of the family members no longer determined by sex.

A division of labor exists at the level of society as well as at the family level. Some divisions of labor in human society include farmers, cattle ranchers, merchants and salespeople, artists, physicians, mechanics, teachers, soldiers, secretaries, scientists, musicians, athletes, and government leaders.

In past times these jobs were sometimes thought of partly in terms of sexual differences. But the technological age, moving away from the primarily agricultural age, has changed the needs of human societies. Most specializations in society are now based on education, ability, and preference rather than on an individual's sex or other factors. The structure of human society is therefore determined by differences in behavior.

Often changes in human society begin with the reactions of its younger, rather than older, members to the changing world.

## 25–6

### Societies with Hierarchies Are Numerous

Social hierarchies among animal societies have been studied since the 1880s. A Norwegian biologist, Thorlief Schjelderup-Ebbe, discovered the "peck order" in chickens in the early 1900s. Later Warder Allee and others studied flocks of chickens and of other birds in greater detail. Their work prompted others to look for similar relations in different animal societies. Social hierarchies were found to exist in societies of insects, fish, lizards, rodents, carnivores, hoofed animals, and humans. In Allee's own words:

> The social order (in chickens) is indicated by giving and receiving of pecks, or by the reaction to threats of pecking; and hence the social hierarchy among birds is frequently referred to as the peck order.

> When two chickens meet for the first time there is either a fight or one gives way without fighting. If one of the two is immature while the other is fully developed, the older bird usually dominates. Thereafter, when these two meet, the one which has acquired the peck-right, that is, the right to peck another without being pecked in return, exercises it except in the event of a successful revolt which, with chickens, rarely occurs.[2]

Allee's results with 13 brown leghorn hens are summarized in Figure 25–6. The plus sign ( + ) in

| bird | birds | | | | | | | | | | | | |
|---|---|---|---|---|---|---|---|---|---|---|---|---|---|
| | M | L | K | J | I | H | G | F | E | D | C | B | A |
| A pecks | + | + | + | + | + | + | + | + | + | + | + | + | |
| B pecks | + | + | + | + | + | + | + | + | + | + | + | | |
| C pecks | + | + | + | + | + | + | + | + | + | + | | | |
| D pecks | + | + | + | + | + | + | + | + | + | | | | |
| E pecks | + | + | + | + | + | + | + | + | | | | | |
| F pecks | + | + | + | + | + | + | + | | | | | | |
| G pecks | + | + | + | + | + | + | | | | | | | |
| H pecks | + | + | + | | + | | | | | | | | |
| I pecks | + | + | + | + | | | | | | | | | |
| J pecks | + | + | + | | | + | | | | | | | |
| K pecks | + | + | | | | | | | | | | | |
| L pecks | + | | | | | | | | | | | | |
| M pecks | | | | | | | | | | | | | |

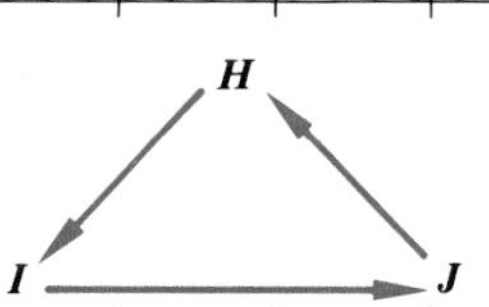

**Figure 25–6** The peck order in a flock of brown leghorn hens.

this illustration indicates that the chicken listed in the left-hand column pecks the chicken listed in the upper row. For example, you can see that chicken A in the left-hand column pecks all the other chickens in the flock. Chicken B pecks all the other chickens in the flock except chicken A. Chicken C pecks all the other chickens in the flock except chickens A and B, and so on.

Following chicken G, a triangle appears. This triangular arrangement shows that H pecks I, I pecks J, and J pecks H. Although chickens H, I, and J have a triangular peck-order among themselves, each of these maintains its peck-right over the remaining birds: K, L, and M.

Not all birds have as rigid a peck order as these leghorns, or as the white leghorns illustrated in Figure 25–7. Flocks of pigeons, ring doves, canaries, and parakeets have a more flexible social organization. This point can be illustrated by one of Allee's experiments with a flock of 14 white king pigeons. Allee found that in pair contacts (threats or fights between a pair of birds), one bird did not always dominate another. In a series of pair contacts a bird would win some conflicts and lose some. Thus a looser peck order was established. It has also been found that the peck order becomes looser or less rigidly established as the flock grows larger, beyond 10 or so.

**Figure 25–7** Dominance relationships in white leghorn hens. The hen in the upper left in her first contact has been dominated by another hen. In the foreground, the lowest hen in the flock is pecked by the top hen. Three other hens, intermediate in the peck order, rushed to the food when the top hen left.

In general, the larger, stronger, and more mature animal wins a pair contact. There may be sex differences: in some societies males may dominate females, in others females dominate males. Animals with young tend to win over animals without young. Animals who are ill tend to lose. Animals in a winning streak continue to win. Can you suggest other factors that might have an influence on the outcome of a pair contact?

A social hierarchy seems to have survival value for any society. In the case of Allee's birds, an established pecking order reduces energy loss by bringing the activities of the group into harmony. The peck order establishes a means by which mates and food are found with less strife and competition. Aggression among members of the flock is reduced. The social hierarchy also influences the way animals share or divide their living space.

## 25–7

## What Is the Function of a Leader in a Society?

Leadership and social dominance are not one and the same. There are leaders in colonies of ants, but no peck order is known. The leaders in flocks of hens are often found in the middle of the peck order. In some groups of mammals the leader is the dominant member in the peck order. In other groups the leader is not necessarily the strongest animal of the group, or the fastest, or the one out front when the group is moving. Leadership may depend on other qualities.

A leader is an animal that can furnish guidance to the group. Those animals that are most alert to danger, most concerned with the welfare of the group, and cleverest in devising escapes may become the leaders. In some herds of mammals, like those of the red deer of Scotland, the leaders are older, experienced females. In groups of other animals, such as rhesus monkeys, an experienced and aggressive male is the leader. The howler monkeys of the Panama Canal Zone have a group of male leaders. Leadership is based on more than force. It involves protection and concern for others and an interdependence between the leader and the followers. Both the leader and the followers have roles involving obligations.

There can be no leader if others are not willing to follow. The young must learn to follow a leader. They are prepared for their later roles in the group by their play activities. Perhaps you have seen young lambs playing "follow the leader." Some deer play a game of "tag" much like the one you played when you were younger. They chase and touch each other with their front legs. Such play is the beginning of dominance relations and the roles of leader and follower. An example of such play by juvenile baboons in the presence of a dominant male is illustrated in Figure 25–8.

**Figure 25–8** Among baboons, dominance relationships begin as the young play in the presence of an older, dominant member of the group.

The social life of animals is clearly based on cooperative behavior. For what kinds of animals do you think such behavior is innate (inherited)? For what others do you think it combines inheritance with learning?

## 25–8

## Territorial Behavior

Every living organism requires a certain amount of space in which to live, find food, and reproduce. The living space that an animal may defend is called a **territory,** and the behavior of an animal defending its living area is known as **territoriality.**

This sense of property is well developed in many animals, including humans. Animals may defend the territory until the brood has been reared.

Much has been learned about territoriality in many species. Probably more is known about territorial behavior in birds than in any other animal except humans. The male bird occupies a suitable area before the mating season begins. He warns other male birds with his song that this territory is his. When a female finds a male and his area attractive, the two birds mate and nest. The male continues to defend the territory until the brood has been reared.

Howler monkeys provide another example. These monkeys travel in groups that vary in size from 4 to 35 individuals. The average group has about 17 members. Each group has a territory that it defends for its own use. However, the territorial boundaries are not clearly defined and often overlap those of neighboring groups. Early each morning the groups perform a ritual of howling to estimate the distance to their neighbors. The distance helps to define their territory. If two groups come together, a loud vocal battle begins with roaring and bluffing but with little or no physical contact. Most animal behavior, like this example, stops short of physical violence. Fighting is the exception, not the rule. Usually noise and threats effectively keep neighboring groups apart.

In some ways the behavior of "staking out" territory is similar to social dominance and the leader-follower relationship. These three forms of behavior all arise from contacts and competition with others of the same species. All three forms of behavior have survival value for the group.

**Try Investigation 25–A**  Observing Crayfish in a Small Habitat, page 683.

## 25–9

## Humans Show Territorial Behavior

An examination of human society raises some interesting questions. For example, why do people live in walled houses, fence their back yards, and put up "No Trespassing" signs? Territoriality provides much of the answer.

Does human territoriality have survival value? Consider the following example. The Bill of Rights of the Constitution of the United States says:

> The right of the people to be secure in their persons, houses, papers and effects against unreasonable searches and seizures shall not be violated. . .
> No person may be deprived of life, liberty or property without due process of law; nor shall private property be taken for public use without just compensation.

Besides territoriality, do humans show additional forms of behavior demonstrated by other animals? For example, are there peck orders in human society? Is there, for example, a peck order in your school, in your social group? Do there seem to be peck orders in military organizations, in political parties, in your local government? Is striving for dominance a part of human life?

Is human society concerned about leadership? How often have you heard of educational leadership, military leadership, athletic leadership, civic

# How to Slug-a-bug or Croakaroach

To kill an insect is almost instinctive to humans. This is the result of the age-old competition between insects and people for food. It is added to by recent knowledge of the role insects play in causing certain diseases. Actually not all insects are harmful to people. Some are harmless and others are very helpful. In fact, only $1/10$ of one percent are classified as being harmful. This $1/10$ of one percent consists of insects that eat or destroy humans' food or cause disease. By far the largest percentage of these harmful insects directly compete with people for food.

In recent years the food supply has become increasingly critical to support an expanding human population. As a result, the age-old war against insects has been escalated. Killing insects by methods based on their behavior is a new approach. Behavior is more specific to certain insects than their absorption of widespread poisons like DDT. DDT is blind. Instead of killing only the target insect, it kills many harmless and helpful insects. In addition, it is extremely persistent, lasting for many, many years and becoming widely distributed in the environment where it poisons still other animals. The experience with DDT has produced an urgent and worldwide search for the so-called "ideal" insecticide.

The "ideal" insecticide has a number of specific characteristics. For example, it should kill only the target insects, be a substance to which they cannot become resistant or immune, quickly break down in the environment into harmless substances, and be cheap and easily applied. Not a single product has yet been produced with all these characteristics. But the search goes on. The behavior of each species of harmful insect is studied to provide clues.

At present, two classes of chemicals seem to hold particular promise as possible "ideal" insecticides. One, the so-called "juvenile hormone," prevents further development of the insect larvae or pupae if applied at the correct time. The other chemical is secreted by insects as a sexual attractant. Chemical sex attractants secreted by females can be detected by males at incredible distances, up to 10 kilometers. Sexual attractant chemicals are called **sex pheromones** (FER-o-mohns). As insecticides they are used to attract target insects to traps.

One insecticide company held a national contest to name one of its products, a hormone-type insecticide. Some of the entries are shown above.

leadership? Will you, one day, be a leader or a follower? Might you one day be dominated by a person or persons, but still be a leader?

Territoriality, dominance, and the leader-follower relationship appear in so many species that they are probably the product of an evolutionary trail almost as old as multicellular life.

---

**CAPSULE SUMMARY**

Species and their populations have evolved many behavioral adaptations with survival value. These adaptations provide advantages and offset the disadvantages of living together. Populations that have evolved such cooperative adaptations in behavior are called societies. In societies, order is kept and jobs are done by means of (1) the caste system, (2) the peck order, and (3) leader-follower adaptations. Territorial behavior enables a society

to protect living space for its members. Although many species seem to share these forms of behavior, there are always differences. Every animal society is unique. Each must be treated as its own case study and over a long period of time.

**SELF CHECK**
1. What is the evidence for social hierarchies within animal groups?
2. What factors seem to be associated with achieving high status in the peck order?
3. What is the value of territoriality?
4. What are some of the factors that determine leadership in animal groups?
5. What evidence can you give for and against the claim that peck orders exist in human society?
6. What advantages do noise displays, threats, and bluffing have over fighting?

---

# Animal Communication

## 25–10

### How Do Animals Communicate?

For a society to evolve and work cooperatively, some method of communication among its members is necessary.

Many animals can communicate by sound. For example, the soldier termites vibrate their heads against a tunnel wall when they are disturbed. Fellow soldiers and other termites are warned. The hunting wolf gives a characteristic combination of a short bark and howl when closing in for the kill. A human may scream with alarm and pain when attacked by surprise. All these sounds tell something specific to the listener. And the listener reacts by fleeing or hurrying to help, depending on the sound.

Different animals can also communicate by sight, smell, touch, and possibly taste. The

**Figure 25–9** The alarm signal from a pronghorn antelope. The white rump patch of hairs usually lies flat. When muscles cause these hairs to stand erect, other nearby antelope are warned of an intruder or other danger.

**Figure 25-10** The pathway of a bee doing the round dance.

**Figure 25-11** In the waggle dance the bee moves its abdomen from side to side as it follows the indicated pathway.

pronghorn antelopes of the western United States signal sudden danger to other members of the group by flashing the white hair of their rump patch (Figure 25–9). When termites are dipped in scented liquids from a different colony, they are treated as invaders in their own colony. And they are treated as fellows in the colony that provided the scent! In humans and other higher animals a touch can communicate alarm, safety, or love. Insects commonly touch antennae to communicate. Information can be passed on from one individual to another in many ways. Without such communication the division of labor in a society would be impossible.

## 25–11
## Honeybees Communicate by Dancing

Karl von Frisch, of the University of Munich, found that when a dish of sugar-water is placed some distance from a beehive, many hours may pass before a bee finds the dish. However, when one scout bee finds the sugar-water, several more bees will find it in a short time. This simple observation made von Frisch suspect that the scout bee somehow passes along information on the location of the food supply to the other bees. Von

Frisch was curious to learn how bees could communicate the presence of food at a new location. Von Frisch found after years of study that the scout bees do a dance on the vertical surface of the honeycomb when they return to the hive. The dance communicates both the direction and distance to the source of the food.

Von Frisch described two types of dances. The round dance shown in Figure 25–10 is used when the food is close to the hive, from 10 to 80 meters. The waggle dance shown in Figure 25–11 is used when the food is 80 to 100 meters or more from the hive. Von Frisch discovered that the bees convert the angle between the sun and the food to an angle between straight up and down in the direction of their dance on the vertical surface of the hive. Thus, straight up and down on the vertical surface of the hive honeycomb is always the direction of the sun. Therefore, as shown in Figure 25–12,

A tail wagging run pointed upward means the source of food lies in the direction of the sun; the same part of the dance directed downward announces the food is opposite to the sun. If the tail wagging run points 60° left of straight up, the food source is 60° to the left of the sun. . . .[3]

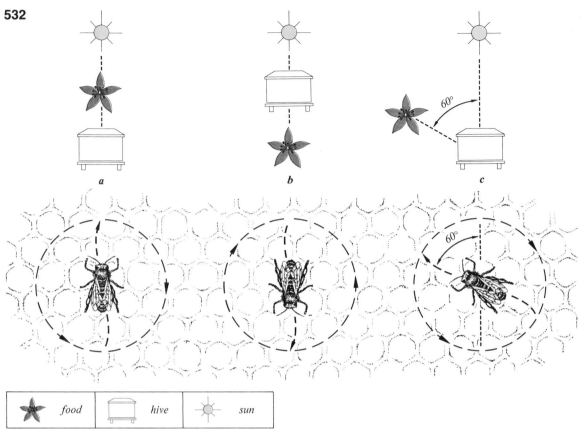

| ✿ | food | ⌂ | hive | ✸ | sun |

**Figure 25-12** The returning bee does a waggle dance. The direction of the dance apparently tells observing bees where the food is in relation to the sun. For instance, in view *a*, the food is in a straight line from the hive to the sun; in *b*, the food is on the opposite side of the hive from the sun; and in *c*, the food is 60 degrees to the left of the sun.

Many other researchers have experimented to test this theory of communication. The previous experience of the bees, food scent carried by the scout bee, and hive scent left at the feeding station by the scout have all been investigated. While these variables have not been ruled out, von Frisch appears to be right. Bees apparently use the most abstract method of communication known for any animal other than humans. Recently, researchers at the California Institute of Technology and the University of Oregon conducted carefully controlled experiments that were variations of von Frisch's original experiments. The researchers have concluded that the honeybee dance does indeed communicate direction to the food source.

## 25-12
## Higher Animals Communicate in Many Ways

Communications and behavior have also been studied in wild chimpanzee societies. Jane van Lawick-Goodall and her colleagues conducted field studies in east-central Africa from 1960 to 1965. These studies reveal that chimpanzees communicate in many different ways. When chimpanzees play, they use a panting laughter. When young chimpanzees are frightened or lonely, they whimper. When they meet after separation, the chimpanzees often greet each other much like humans. They also have a sound to show rage or anger, the savage "wraa" bark.

**Figure 25–13**  The female chimpanzee (left), unsure of the intentions of the male, hides her baby behind a tree and reaches out her hand toward the male. He reassures the female by touching her hand. Such physical contact is common in wild chimpanzee communication.

Chimpanzees communicate by physical contacts also, like the touch of reassurance shown in Figure 25–13, or the embrace of two old friends.  They pat each other on the back, embrace, and even hold hands.  Physical contact, then, seems to extend their vocal communication system.  Do chimpanzees have feelings of acceptance, rejection, love, anger, and friendship?  Apparently they do, and they can also learn to communicate facts and feelings (or judgments) to human beings.  You have already read about the experiments in which chimpanzees (and gorillas) have been taught sign language to communicate with human beings.

Humans have the most highly organized societies of all.  These societies are made possible by the most abstract system of communications in the animal kingdom.  In human societies all sorts of information, general and specific, are passed among individuals and from generation to generation. Human communication, as you know, uses a wide variety of written and vocal symbols and other signals (Figure 25–14).  It also involves much physical contact such as that described for chimpanzees.  It commonly uses the other senses and instruments that are extensions of the senses. These elaborate systems of communication make possible our highly organized human society.

**CAPSULE SUMMARY**

Information can be passed from one individual to another in many ways.  Without this communication, social organization could hardly be maintained.  Communication by sight, sound, smell, touch, and perhaps taste is common in animal societies.  Some animals communicate primarily by one of these senses.  Many animals, however, including some of those that rely most heavily on one of the senses, actually use many senses for communication.

**SELF CHECK**

1. Why is communication necessary in societies?
2. What senses are used in animal communication?
3. In what ways is communication similar in chimpanzees and humans?
4. In what ways are field studies of chimpanzee and gorilla populations of value in understanding human communication?
5. How does a returning scout honeybee communicate the direction of its food find to the other bees in the hive?

**Figure 25-14** Gestures and body language play a large part in human communication. Which of these photos states, "Who knows?" What does the other photo communicate?

## CHAPTER SUMMARY

### HIGHLIGHTS

A society is a special kind of animal population that has an internal organization and communication among its members. A division of labor may produce distinct castes as in social insects, or be based on behavioral differences of otherwise similar individuals. Cooperation among the members of a society is based on different behavioral patterns. Hierarchies in higher animals probably arise from pair contacts and the competition between individuals. At the group level the social adaptations of dominance, leadership, and territoriality develop. Group adaptations, however, can work well only if animals have sense organs and can use them to exchange information. In this way the activities of the group members may be directed toward a common goal.

Human societies are a product of the most complex of all communication systems. Some authorities believe that humans, just like other animals, show territoriality, dominance, and leader-follower adaptations. If such adaptations are partly instinctive in other animals, they are probably partly instinctive in humans. Thus our social behavior may be deeply rooted in the evolutionary past.

In the next chapter you will examine some of the biological problems that people have created with their complex societies and rapidly growing populations.

### REVIEWING IDEAS

1. Explain how a society differs from other populations.
2. How may dominance and leader-follower relations be similar? different?

3. How does the formation of a group affect the life of its members? How do castes solve problems of conflict vs. cooperation?

4. What kinds of social roles have humans developed?

5. How does innate or instinctive behavior affect formation of societies? How may learning be related to social behavior?

6. Could a society exist without communication? Explain.

7. Have human societies evolved castes like the bees and the ants? Would you enjoy living in this sort of social structure?

8. How would you determine whether a peck order exists in one of the following groups? What evidence would you seek?
   a. a group of your friends
   b. a group of children on a playground
   c. one of your classes at school
   d. your family

## USING CONCEPTS

9. Ants spread scent trails from the anthill to food. How would you find out whether the ants require the scent trails to find their way back to the anthill?

10. Compare the scent trails of ants with the dancing of honeybees. Are the two functions similar? Are *both* forms of communication? Explain.

11. Which is more efficient, a society organized by conscious cooperation or by instinctive (innate) behavior? Defend your reasoning with examples.

12. Communication implies information. Name a species in which communication is used to obscure information, or to convey misinformation. What is the effect of this practice on individuals? on the species?

13. It was suggested early in this chapter that societies are a product of evolution. What kind of evidence supports this idea?

14. For communication to exist among plants, what form would it be likely to take? How would your answer shape the direction of an investigation?

15. What type of group or social behavior is associated with each of the following?
   a. a telephone call    c. a school election
   b. a wedding ring    d. a school sports contest

## RECOMMENDED READING

Fossy, D. "Close Encounters with Great Apes." *Science Digest,* August 1983, and *Gorillas in the Mist,* Boston, Houghton Mifflin, 1983. An article and a book on the social behavior of gorillas.

Raeburn, P. "An Uncommon Chimp." *Science 83,* June issue. Examples of humanlike behavior in pigmy chimpanzees.

Topoff, H. (ed.) *Animal Societies and Evolution: Readings from Scientific American.* San Francisco, W. H. Freeman, 1981. A collection of articles on many different animal societies.

## REFERENCES

1. W. C. Allee and others. *Animal Aggregations: A Study in General Sociology.* Chicago, University of Chicago Press, 1931, p. 349.

2. W. C. Allee. *The Social Life of Animals.* Boston, Beacon Press, 1958, p. 130.

3. M. Lindauer. *Communication Among Social Bees.* Cambridge, Harvard University Press, 1961, p. 32.

# Interrelationships
## 26

No organism lives alone. It is part of a population of its kind. The population also does not live apart from other kinds of organisms. Not even human beings in cities succeed in doing this. Every population depends on others. Plants depend on animals for carbon dioxide. Animals depend on plants for food and oxygen. Animals depend on one another in other food relationships. Plants depend on the animals for mineral wastes that are returned to the soil and the oceans.

Interdependent populations in the same environment form a community. If the community supports itself for almost all the materials its populations need, it and its physical environment together are called an **ecosystem.** Materials are used and reused within the ecosystem. Only energy is spent. The energy supply is constantly renewed by plants as they carry on photosynthesis in sunlight.

People, and the growth or decline of populations of every kind of organism, affect every ecosystem. People take food from all lands and oceans. They seek and modify other of Earth's materials, too. Human-fashioned products and altered environments have become expected features of the world. All ecosystems are being changed. Because some of the changes have led to problems, biology today includes looking into our own behavior as we exploit the world's ecosystems.

# Materials and Energy for Life

## 26–1

### Populations and Food Supply

A great blue whale dies. One hundred metric tons of flesh, bones, fats, and oils sink slowly into the depths of the ocean. A feast for the creatures below! The giant carcass descends past fishes at many levels, which tear at its flesh. It is so large that it arrives at the bottom little more than skinned and prepared for creatures there to feed upon. They strip it. The skeleton comes to rest like an old Spanish galleon, open ribwork without its hull of skin and muscle and its cargo of internal organs.

The living whale was a mammal—it lived near the ocean's surface where it could obtain its air. Life far below did not concern it. But it was part of the ecosystem of the life below, because no sunlight reaches the depths to support plant life and photosynthesis. Food for the bottom-dwelling creatures must drift down from above. The materials are slowly recycled from the bottom, sometimes taking hundreds of years to be carried by currents to the surface again. Once at the surface, the materials that were part of the whale provide minerals for photosynthetic microorganisms that inhabit the sunlit surface waters. These organisms

---

←A deserted mine in mountain wilderness. Human beings have reached into the remotest parts of their world.

**Figure 26–1** A blue whale feeding. This largest of the world's living animals feeds exclusively on some of the world's smallest animals, little shrimplike organisms commonly called krill.

use the minerals and the energy of sunlight to make new food. Small shrimplike animals feed on the photosynthetic microorganisms. Then another great blue whale scoops up the small shrimplike animals, huge mouthfuls at a time (Figure 26–1). These tiny animals are the whale's food. And when this whale, too, finally dies, its corpse provides food for the animals far below. The cycle goes round again.

The photosynthetic microorganisms, the shrimplike animals, the great blue whales, and the flesh-eating creatures below form a **food chain** (Figure 26–2). There are many other food chains in the ocean. But all of them start with the photosynthetic microorganisms. Shrimps and related small creatures, jellyfish, squid, cuttlefish, many kinds of fishes, and other ocean organisms enter the food chains. All the food relationships taken together make up the ocean's entire **food web.**

How many great blue whales will the ocean's populations of shrimplike animals support? How many of these little animals will the ocean's populations of photosynthetic organisms support? What other ocean organisms compete for the same food sources? Is a population's size regulated simply by the food available to it? In the oceans, the supply of suitable space and other life requirements appears to be so great that only food is the limiting factor in determining each population's size. Is this true in all ecosystems?

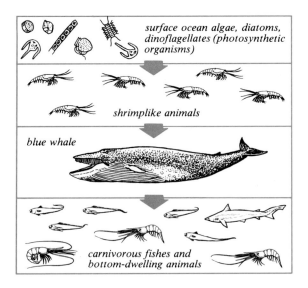

**Figure 26-2** The simple food chain of which the blue whale is a part. Like all food chains it begins with producers (top), photosynthetic organisms.

*surface ocean algae, diatoms, dinoflagellates (photosynthetic organisms)*

*shrimplike animals*

*blue whale*

*carnivorous fishes and bottom-dwelling animals*

## 26-2

## Many Studies Have Been Made of Factors Affecting Population Growth

Biologists have studied many populations to determine what regulates population size. Records like those shown for two land-inhabiting animals in Figure 26-3 have been collected. Much like populations of blue whales and shrimplike animals, populations of lynxes and hares are related. Lynxes eat hares as a normal part of their food supply. Fluctuations in the lynx population closely follow fluctuations in the hare population. This suggests that the number of hares partly determines the number of lynxes. But is it possible to put a third line on the graph which might explain the fluctuations of both populations as more than just food supply? (Some completely different data such as snowfall and temperatures might also be

**Figure 26-3** Fluctuations in the populations of the Canadian lynx and the snowshoe hare over a period of almost 100 years. The hare is part of the lynx's diet.

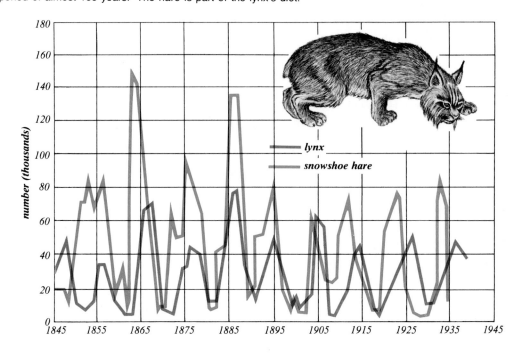

*number (thousands)*

lynx
snowshoe hare

useful.) Data like those in the graph are helpful, but conclusions must be reached cautiously. Collecting data on animal populations in the wild is very difficult and inexact.

Biologists have tried to learn more by studying animal populations in well-defined areas. At the University of Wisconsin, a team of research biologists headed by John Emlen studied the population of house mice in some old buildings. The mouse colony was provided with 250 grams of food daily. The mouse population grew rapidly.

Soon the number of mice became greater than the 250 grams of food per day could support. The researchers were interested in what would happen next. They found that mice began leaving the colony. The rate of emigration was about the same as the birthrate. The population living on the 250 grams of food supplied each day leveled off because of the emigration.

The same investigators then performed another experiment. This time they prevented the mice from emigrating. The population grew until a food shortage developed. Soon after, the birthrate declined and the population stopped increasing. This event, too, limited the size of the population.

A third experiment was performed. This time food was provided in abundance. As in the second experiment, emigration was prevented. Again the population increased rapidly. A new factor became important—space. The colonies became very crowded. Fighting increased dramatically. So did cannibalism, the practice of eating the newborn in the crowded nesting spaces. Most of the female mice stopped taking care of their nests and their young. The death rate among the young increased to almost 100 percent, even though the birthrate remained high. In this experiment, an increased death rate from fighting and cannibalism offset the increased birthrate. The result was a limiting of the population.

Experiments similar to this last experiment were tried in England. The English researchers had

different results. They found that fighting and cannibalism did not develop. The population increased with unlimited food until, in very crowded conditions, reproduction almost stopped.

In both the Wisconsin and English experiments the populations of mice reacted in ways that limited further population growth. At the University of Wisconsin limits were established by emigration, low birthrate, or high death rate. The conditions of each of the three experiments differed. In England, under conditions like those of the third Wisconsin experiment, a limit came about through a lowered birthrate. Can you suggest some reasons why these populations of mice reacted in different ways? For the last two experiments especially, what variables might not have been carefully controlled from Wisconsin to England?

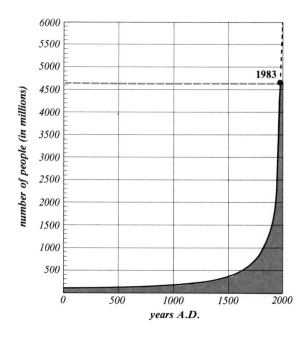

**Figure 26–4** Human population growth. Fluctuations, as in the lynx–snowshoe hare graph, have been evened out by compressing almost 2000 years of data into one graph. But these fluctuations, caused in the past by such diseases as the plague, no longer occur.

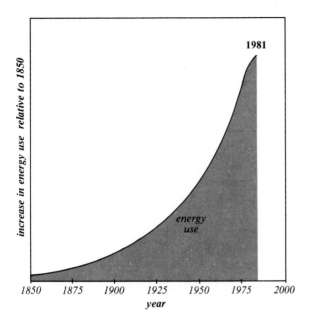

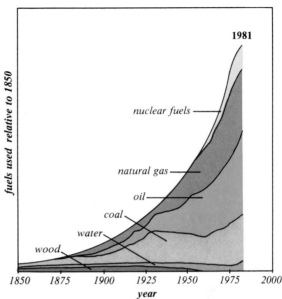

**Figure 26–5** Since 1850, U.S. energy use has increased 37 times over that year's total (graph at left). The population has increased 11 times over the 1850 population. The sources of all the energy used have become increasingly varied (graph at right). Developed nations still account for most of the increases in the use of energy. Other nations view this unequal demand as wasteful of limited world resources.

Many data on populations have been collected by biologists for a long period of time. Some species of animals seem to have built-in patterns for maintaining their population numbers within a range their food supply or living space can support. What about the human species? We cannot run controlled experiments with humans or place them in stress situations as with the mice. Thus, it is difficult to know exactly what might influence the human population as numbers of people continue to multiply.

## 26–3
## We Modify Our Ecosystem

You have undoubtedly heard of the human population explosion. Figure 26–4 shows the data. Notice the rate of population growth each century. Where does the term explosion begin to apply? When you look at the growth rate now, you see a line going almost straight up.

The world's human population is increasing by about two percent each year. This doesn't seem like much. However, the two percent has a compounding effect just like the bank's interest on a savings account. At this rate of increase the population will double in less than 40 years. This period is called the **doubling time** (DT) of the world population.

The rate of population growth varies from zero to a DT of 17 years for different nations. Five European nations have stopped growing in population, at least temporarily. They are Denmark, Sweden, Hungary, East Germany, and West Germany. No other countries in the world have achieved stable population numbers. Most nations have a DT of 30 years or less. Even the United States has a DT of less than a century.

Should the world be concerned about the size of its population? People modify their environments to fit their needs. The food supply can be in-

# Biology Brief

## Energy and Agriculture

A century ago, no one knew that the yields of food crops could be as large as they are today. People struggled to obtain a sixth of the 200 to 300 bushels of corn per hectare that are now the annual yield in the midwestern Corn Belt. Not even biologists were able to forecast the future correctly.

creased. The human population has always solved at least some of its own problems of growth.

However, if the population of the world doubles in 40 years or less, twice as much food, other materials, and energy will be required. These amounts would only maintain today's standard of living. On a worldwide basis this standard is not

very high. To improve it, even more food, other materials, and energy would be required. Break-throughs in agriculture in even the most advanced agricultural nations would be necessary. The greatest initial responsibility would fall on countries like the United States, which already use more energy than they can produce (Figure 26–5).

Such facts have led many people to discount current forecasts that the world is in population trouble. They point out that increases similar to that of the corn yield have taken place in other crops and in improved breeds of animals for meat. Not counting farmland, many regions of Earth are still relatively uninhabited. New discoveries of natural resources will be made, even if not on a scale with former discoveries. The world can go on supporting human population growth indefinitely, in this view.

Is this optimistic outlook realistic? To find out, the cost of progress can be analyzed. Although any example could be used, the one taken here is the corn crop, the leading agricultural crop of the United States.

One hundred years ago, the energy used in raising corn was the food energy of farmers and their draft animals. Other, nonrenewable energy was used only in the manufacture of horse- or mule-drawn farm equipment. Even fifty years ago, trucks and tractors required a small fraction of the nonrenewable fuels devoted to agriculture today. Chemical fertilizers were used on less than 30 percent of the land on which corn was raised.

Today, chemical fertilizers are used on more than 95 percent of the nation's cornfields. The cost in natural gas to manufacture the fertilizers is more than 2.5 billion cubic meters of natural gas each year. The cost in gasoline and diesel fuel for mining certain ingredients and for transporting the fertilizers is more than 15 billion liters of fuel each year. These costs are met merely to make the fertilizers and get them to the farms. Fuel used in making and transporting farm machinery, pesticides, operating the machinery, force-drying the grain, and transporting the corn to market quadruple these energy costs.

Crops that can help fertilize themselves by using nitrogen from the air are being investigated in genetics experiments. Gene-splicing (Section 10–13) may make this advance possible. Otherwise, greater crop yields require greater fuel expenditures, in a race against human reproduction.

Whether humans can obtain so much food, building materials, consumer products, and fuels and energy is an often-debated topic. Some people are very optimistic about the prospects, others are pessimistic (see Biology Brief). The decisions to be made will be decisions of priorities. For example, if the quality of life becomes the priority, then space, pollution control, and more resources per person will become important. The growing population will then be of increasing concern. However, if population growth continues to be encouraged for industrial and economic reasons, then the quality of individual life cannot remain indefinitely high.

When you are looking back on these views later, you will have your own experience to add. The same human values will still be questioned when you are twice your present age. There will be more people then. Biologists will have reported more studies on what regulates population growth in other animals. People will continue to invent new ways to design living space, improve their own food-raising, find alternative energy sources, and be confident about the future. Yet you will notice that places you visited as outdoor recreation areas have become suburbs, with houses, families, schools, and shopping centers.

Then, if not now, you will see why biologists are studying populations. In nature, reproduction matches risks. Natural selection has proceeded in a way that insures replacement. Reproductive processes yield more offspring than the numbers of their parents. In some animals, a single reproductive act yields from several to thousands of possible offspring. In humans, the pattern is one at a time, with exceptions. Natural selection has offset this slow human generation rate by providing a long number of years of possible childbearing. In the meantime, the risks to human offspring have been reduced. Because of science and medicine, only a small percentage of children is lost today to starvation, disease, or accident. As a result, each generation is replaced by a larger new one.

The human population seems to have an unlimited ability to expand. Yet the world does not expand with it. Space, water, land suitable for food-raising, all needed materials, and most energy sources are limited. Someday in the future a growing population must run into one of these limits. It is a simple question of arithmetic that science cannot solve with new processes. Improvements will run out against the limits of living space and the supply of raw materials. What will people decide then?

It is safe to assume that the world population will go on increasing in the near future. Questions of continued future growth will be more frequent. Difficult political questions will be asked. Biologists' animal studies cannot provide all the information needed to address these questions adequately in terms of human beings.

## 26–4

## Food Pyramids Exist in Ecosystems

In any ecosystem there is a greater supply of food organisms than of those that eat them. Generally it takes about ten times an organism's body mass in food organisms to support it. This relationship goes on as long as an organism lives. Part of the reason for this 10-to-1 ratio is that when one thing eats another, the consumer is not very efficient at utilizing the materials and energy. One organism usually does not eat all the parts of another. A cow eats only the tips of blades of grass; the main part of each plant, and its roots, go untouched and produce more growth of grass blades. A mountain lion eats its fill of a fresh kill and leaves the rest behind. Also, for most organisms, even those food parts eaten are not all digestible. Of the parts that are digested much is used for energy to run the organism's body. Only a relatively small part of the eaten organism is actually incorporated into another organism's body. Biologists show these relationships in the form of a **food pyramid.**

Look at Figure 26–6. As you study the figure you can see that no level can be the same size as the one beneath it. An upper level cannot even approach closely the **biomass** (total mass of organisms) in a lower level. Whenever a population grows so large that its members eat all of the immediately available food, widespread starvation sweeps through its ranks. The population size is thus cut back to the number of individuals that can be supported in the pyramid.

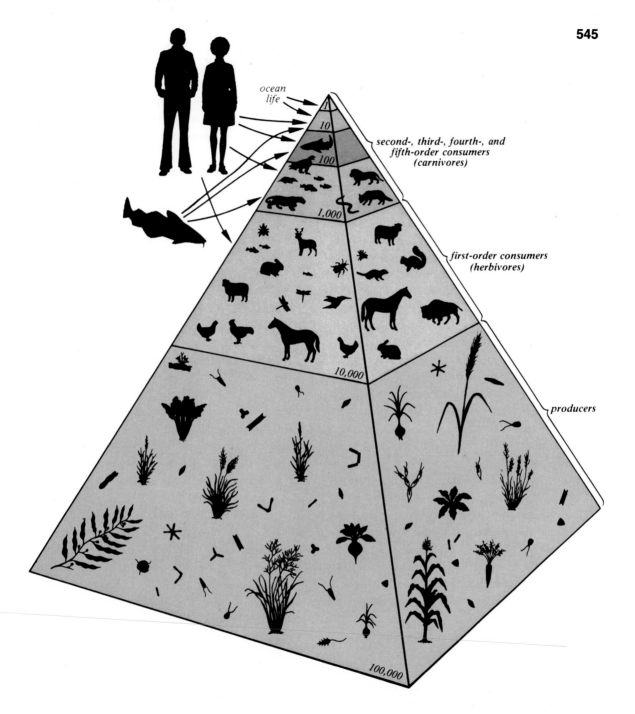

*ocean life*

*second-, third-, fourth-, and fifth-order consumers (carnivores)*

*first-order consumers (herbivores)*

*producers*

1
10
100
1,000
10,000
100,000

**Figure 26–6** A food pyramid. Each level is one tenth the biomass of the one beneath it. The other nine tenths of the biomass one level lower is (a) eaten, used for energy, and the materials excreted; (b) eaten but not digested; and (c) left uneaten. Notice that some organisms are difficult to place on only one level. Humans are an example; the cod shown at the left is another. Even the eagle shown near the top of the pyramid (next to the number 100) occupies both the levels that its body overlaps. These animals and many others feed at several different levels below them.

Notice that the food pyramid is shown with the ratio of 10-to-1 for each change in level. At the bottom of the pyramid are photosynthetic organisms, the basic **food producers** or autotrophs. Only $\frac{1}{10}$ of their biomass can be supported in first-order consumers (**herbivores,** or plant-eaters). These first-order consumers are on the second level of the pyramid. Moving up to the third level, you find second-order consumers. A second-order consumer is a **carnivore,** or flesh-eater, that eats herbivores. Only $\frac{1}{10}$ of the biomass of the herbivores can be supported in second-order consumers. This general biomass relationship continues up the pyramid as each higher level of consumers is reached. Only the bottom level of the pyramid is made up of autotrophs. All the other levels are occupied by heterotrophs.

Many other examples of this 10-to-1 ratio of food biomass to consumers are known. Beef cattle will gain a kilogram in weight for each 6 kg of feed (mixed grains and grasses) they eat. Chickens and turkeys will gain a kilogram in weight for each two kilograms of feed they eat. These apparently much better than average figures (less than 10-to-1) are really deceptive. The figures do not show that the feed itself is very select. Cattle that are fed grain, for example, eat no more than 50 percent of the biomass of the plants from which the grain is taken. So the cattle ratio, instead of being 6 to 1, is more nearly 12 to 1. Similarly, chicken feed is about 25 percent of the biomass of the plants it is taken from. The chicken-feed ratio must be multiplied by 4; it is 8 to 1.

In the wild, ratios of 20-to-1 and 30-to-1 are not uncommon for active carnivores that use a great deal of energy searching for food. And in the oceans particularly, where third-, fourth-, and fifth-order consumers are very common, food relationships that extend over many levels produce surprisingly high ratios. From partial calculations it has been estimated, for example, that 100,000 kg of algae are necessary to produce 1 to

5 kg of cod! The exact food ratio is difficult to determine because the cod is a mixed second-, third-, and fourth-order consumer. Young cod are second- and third-order; they feed on tiny animals that feed on one another and on the ocean's photosynthetic algae. Older cod feed both this way and on other fishes that feed as young cod do. What the cod illustrates is that it is very difficult to place some organisms accurately on the food pyramid. Food relationships can be very complex.

Humans also have a mixed diet. As you eat a pizza you may be a first-, second-, and third-order consumer all at the same time. (Anchovies on the pizza could account for the third order.) People are multiple consumers ranging from first-order (for fruits and vegetables) to second-order (for beef, lamb, chicken, cheese, and so on) to third-, fourth-, and fifth-order for cod and other ocean fishes and still other seafoods.

More and more organisms of all kinds are being investigated by biologists each year to obtain more data on food relationships. The 10-to-1 biomass ratio shown for the food pyramid has not changed during these studies. As an average, this ratio is often more useful to know than isolated data about one organism and the food it eats. But what implications does this pattern hold for the human population?

For one thing, we can be more energy-efficient as herbivores (first-order consumers) than as carnivores (second- or higher-order consumers). When we eat plants, we can support several times the number of people we can by feeding the plants to a steer and then eating the steer. We can't digest the cellulose in grass and many other plants. However, we can digest the starch and proteins of grains. Some people argue (vegetarians especially) that we should eat the grains that we feed to cattle and stop raising and killing cattle. Like the question of a growing population, this related food issue is difficult to consider for clear-cut right or wrong answers. For example, we have learned to like meat, and to give food and our meals more significance than their survival value alone. The problem of population growth and food problems can only be debated. For your part, what do you believe should be the important points?

---

**CAPSULE SUMMARY**

Food relationships are the major factor regulating population size for each kind of organism in an ecosystem. A simple food chain with photosynthetic microorganisms, the shrimplike animals that feed on them, the great blue whales that eat these small creatures, and flesh-eating animals that feed on the whales' carcasses illustrates these food relationships.

Food is not the only factor that influences population size. Any other requirement of living organisms can also be a limiting factor if it is in short supply. Biologists have carried out many experiments with groups of animals to find out what kinds of environmental stresses affect growing populations, and how the populations react. The results are informative but not directly applicable to world human population growth.

The human population can be studied in terms of its food pyramid. If food should become a limiting factor in human population growth, a change to a vegetarian diet could support many more people than meat-centered diets now do. But many important questions about the quality of life would have to be considered. Biologists can only provide the data for these considerations.

**SELF CHECK**

1. Describe two or more food chains that lead to you. Begin with photosynthetic plants for each.
2. If the food chains in question 1 do not overlap, describe still others that do overlap with them. Put these food chains all together in the beginning of a food web. Can you go on adding to the web?
3. What are the reasons for the 10-to-1 food ratio in a food pyramid?
4. Is a first-order consumer a herbivore or a carnivore?
5. Considering all the foods you eat, on how many levels of the food pyramid can you place yourself?

---

# Materials Flow and Cycles

## 26–5

### Unwanted Materials Enter the Food Pyramid

The environment always contains many more materials than the life-nourishing ones. Think of all the things you consider inedible that are around you right now. Others are buried beneath Earth's crust and would not normally concern us if we did not mine them for our own uses. Once brought to the surface, these materials enter the living environment.

A whole new source of environmental materials has resulted from human activity, not only in mining but also in industry (Figure 26–7). Far more than 100,000 mined or manufactured materials are produced and processed each year. Waste gases and other lightweight materials are vented into the atmosphere through chimneys, smokestacks, and jet plane and automobile exhausts. The heavier materials tend to accumulate on land, in streams, coastal waters, and the oceans. Because people are inventive, this kind of material

**Figure 26–7** The life-nourishing materials that enter the food pyramid are only a small fraction of all the materials in the environment. Others have always existed in nature, and human activities have added to the supply. Bringing concentrations of buried materials to the surface has been one form of adding to the supply. Creating new materials in manufacturing, and producing wastes in processing them, has multiplied environmental materials many times over. High-voltage electricity and the major fossil fuels (coal, oil, natural gas) have put energy at the service of everyone. All these activities have not only changed the landscape, but have led to unexpected intrusions of materials into the food pyramid.

addition to the environment will probably continue.

Many of Earth's naturally occurring materials as well as a great many of the manufactured ones are harmful to organisms. You might like to think that plants and animals—including you—could just select the materials they need from the environment and screen the rest out. To an extent your body defenses do this: How do your nose and trachea, for example, screen and reject materials from the air you breathe? Yet this screening is not possible at the molecular level for many materials. Both in the air we breathe and the food we eat, we often get high levels of other, unanticipated materials.

The food pyramid tells a different story for these nonfood materials than for foods and nutrients. Consider first the nonfoods absorbed by plants, on the bottom level of the pyramid. Once the plants absorb any materials that they cannot use or get rid of, these materials are "trapped" in their living system. As the plants are eaten, the materials move up the food pyramid. Absorbed nonfoods are not like plant nutrients. They are not broken down and used. If they also cannot be excreted, they can only remain in the cells of each organism that eats them. Because herbivores feed on so many plants (remember the 10-to-1 biomass ratio), they end up with *many times as much absorbed nonfood materials* as the individual plants had. A carnivore that is a second-order consumer then eats the herbivores. If you again use the 10-to-1 ratio, the carnivore may end up with *100 times the concentration of the nonfood materials* that was in the original biomass of plant material. Going on up the pyramid, each food chain continues to higher-level consumers. The concentrating effect at each added level is usually another factor of about 10 (Figure 26–8). Thus a fourth- or fifth-order consumer can get a real "knockout drop" of certain toxic, nonfood substances that found their way into the original plant population.

This is the biological explanation for why there are no "low" levels or "safe" levels for the use of toxic substances in industry or anywhere else in the environment. Once these substances are absorbed by plants, they are concentrated tenfold at each step up the food pyramid until they may "knock out" some high-order consumers.

The insecticide DDT provides an example. It and its toxic breakdown products remain in the environment for a long time. DDT was widely used not too many years ago. In studying its effects the concentration phenomenon became very obvious. The concentration of DDT in the tissues of organisms increased nearly 200 times in moving up the food chain from algae to clams and minnows to ospreys, in one study. Some humans were found to contain DDT concentrations similar to those of the ospreys in the same areas. Ospreys, pelicans, and even penguins in the Antarctic were eventually affected by the concentrated DDT. So were many other organisms. At one point, some bird populations were nearly killed off because the DDT interfered with formation of sturdy shells around eggs.

Today so many nonfood materials are produced that the Department of Agriculture (which has to test all the materials) has a serious problem that is not easily solved. Pesticides are sprayed or dusted directly on food plants and therefore present a high risk of absorption into the food pyramid. A simple solution to this problem would be to stop their use. But if this were done a new problem would emerge. Insects and fungus would claim up to 40 or 50 percent of the food crops, and we would not have enough food to feed our population.

Biologists who advise industries and government agencies on the manufacture and use of nonfood materials are aware of the many problems. They advance several guidelines about *all* materials, to try to avert accidental poisoning of the environment. In question form, these guidelines are:

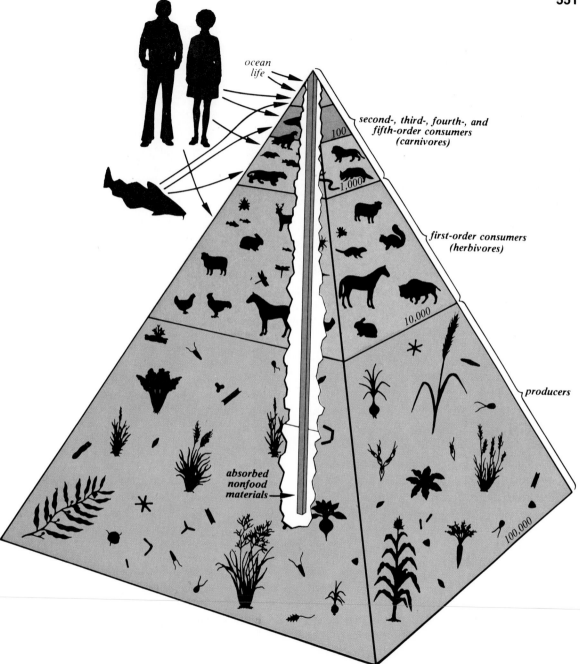

*ocean life*

*second-, third-, fourth-, and fifth-order consumers (carnivores)*

100

1,000

*first-order consumers (herbivores)*

10,000

*producers*

*absorbed nonfood materials*

100,000

**Figure 26–8** As foods are used the residue of absorbed nonfood materials in the food pyramid becomes proportionately greater and greater. Why are these nonfood materials often harmless at the bottom of the pyramid but harmful at the top?

**Figure 26–9** This scientist is studying corneal tissue from eyes to determine how different chemicals might damage it. The test she is running for evidence of damage is called a protein molecular weight distribution.

1. Have the materials been long in use and been demonstrated harmless, from experience?
2. If not, can they be demonstrated not to harm laboratory animals when fed to the animals in concentrations equal to or greater than those that could occur in the food pyramid?
3. If the materials cannot be demonstrated to be harmless by tests or experience (Figure 26–9), can they be made **degradable?**

Degradable materials are designed to break down or decompose before they can work their way up the food pyramid. **Naturally degradable** materials are decomposed by the action of sunlight or by other nonliving processes. **Biodegradable** materials are decomposed by some of the same kinds of organisms that feed on the dead remains of plants and animals from the food pyramid.

Naturally degradable and biodegradable materials are especially attractive, but they pose another problem of their own. Whatever they degrade into must be studied for harmful effects, too. DDT and another widely used pesticide had harmful breakdown products.

Toxic materials are not new. Naturally occurring ones have existed all through life's history. Humans, however, seem to be increasing the frequency at which new substances or pollutants enter the environment. Many people are studying these suspected hazards. Almost always, the potential hazard must be studied in the context of the concentrating effect that occurs in the food pyramid. We are already aware of the continued use of potentially dangerous pesticides on food crops—with the reluctant permission of the Department of Agriculture until safe, effective pesticides are known.

Each day, new nonfood products are being discovered that create new industries with new jobs for new people, in a still-growing population. And more people will need still more food. Can reasonable solutions to more new environmental materials problems be found? Obviously the solutions are not simple. There are economic, personal, political, environmental, biological, and other considerations that must be weighed as each new approach is considered.

# 26–6

# Recycling Renews the Supply of Materials for Life

It takes grain or grass to produce beef. In fact, as you recall, it probably takes about 12 kg of plants to produce 1 kg of beef. Not all the plant material is eaten. What is eaten provides basically two important things for the steer—materials and energy.

Every time a carbon-hydrogen bond in the food is broken, some energy is released. Some of the energy may be retained in chemical form to build new compounds. Energy used in motion or lost as heat, however, escapes from the living system. It cannot be recaptured and used again. A great deal of energy escapes in these ways in any energy change. Thus, energy flow in the food chains and food webs of life is one-way—from the producers up through all the various levels of consumers and eventually to the surroundings in used forms, mostly heat. Once changed from its chemical form in foods, energy can be used only immediately, then lost to an organism's surroundings. It cannot be recycled.

Materials, however, are recycled in nature. Fragments of the organic compounds in food are either used to build other needed organic compounds or are broken down further until all or nearly all of their available chemical energy is obtained, and their carbon and hydrogen is combined with oxygen. The $CO_2$ and $H_2O$ are then given off—to air, or soil, or water. Nitrogen, phosphorus, and other materials may also be given off, depending on what organic compounds have been broken down for energy.

The $H_2O$ enters the water cycle (Figure 26–10) and is available to organisms again in rain or soil water, ponds, streams, or the oceans. The nitrogen enters the nitrogen cycle (Figure 26–11). The $CO_2$ enters a carbon cycle, the phosphorus enters a phosphorus cycle, and so on. The result is that minerals, $CO_2$, and $H_2O$ are made available to plants again for new foodmaking activities.

Important parts of the cycles depend on organisms that consume previously uneaten or undigested parts of plants and animals. At each level in the food pyramid some of the food biomass is not eaten by the consumers; plant parts, animal bones, skin, fur, and a few internal organs remain. And at the top of the pyramid, even the most successful carnivores eventually die. When they do, they give up their materials and energy to add to the biomass of uneaten remains of other organisms. All these plant and animal remains, along with some of the nitrogen wastes and undigested food given off by other animals, are attacked by **decomposers.** The decomposers are organisms, too—mostly soil and water microorganisms that live on decaying organic remains. But they include mushrooms, toadstools, and a related bracket fungus that grows on dead or dying tree trunks. When considerable quantities of decaying animal remains are available, vultures, jackals, and maggots (the young of houseflies and other flies) often precede the decomposers in feeding on the remains.

Tree trunks are broken down and their materials made available again by the bracket fungus and other organisms. The leaves of trees, along with other plant parts, are broken down by soil microorganisms. Animal remains are broken down by larger, and then smaller, organisms. The materials freed from the decaying plant and animal biomass go back by different routes to the air, land, and water. They are again where they were before they were taken up by plants and used in making the organic compounds that have been broken down. They can be reused in the same way. The only new requirement is energy. The constant input of

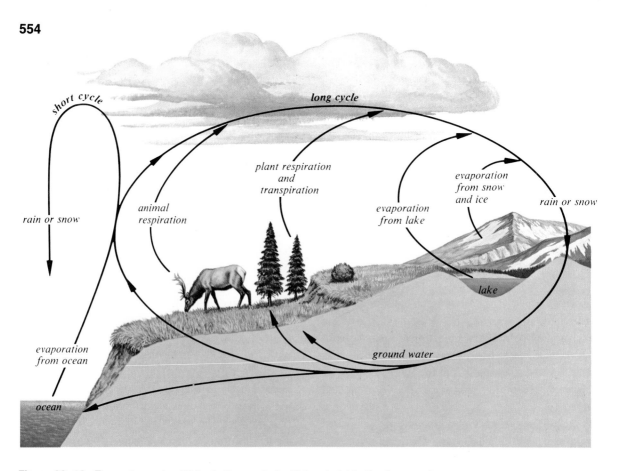

short cycle

long cycle

plant respiration
and
transpiration

evaporation
from snow
and ice

rain or snow

rain or snow

animal
respiration

evaporation
from lake

evaporation
from ocean

lake

ground water

ocean

**Figure 26–10** The water cycle. Water is the most plentiful material in the tissues of organisms. Its decomposition in photosynthesis is offset by its reappearance as a by-product of cell respiration. The water is cycled over and over.

new energy from the sun renews the energy supply for all life but that of a few bacteria.

If the materials necessary for life are naturally recycled, then why do industries turn out millions of metric tons of fertilizers each year? The fact is that food and materials for life are not a problem at nature's own rate. But recycling in nature often takes long periods of time. People are impatient. We do not want to wait for things to decay and replenish needed elements for our farmland. We want to grow more food *this* year, not just later. As you will consider in the next section of this chapter, our human concerns are for more than just living—they are for a better life-style.

---

**CAPSULE SUMMARY**

Both needed and unneeded materials in food, water, and air enter organisms. The food materials are used in the food pyramid. Nonfood substances cannot be digested; if they also cannot be excreted, they accumulate in the food pyramid. That is, foods decrease in biomass going up the food pyramid while nonexcretable substances remain. A higher-order consumer may get a harmful amount of toxic materials that were not concentrated, or were at the ''safe'' level, when first absorbed by plants. In general, foods decline in biomass 10-to-1; other materials, if not excreted, thus accumulate 1-to-10 at each level in the food pyramid.

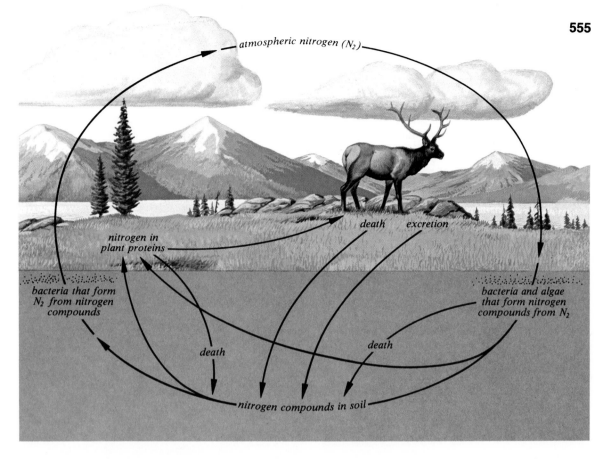

**Figure 26–11** The nitrogen cycle. Not only water and nitrogen, but calcium, phosphorus, oxygen and carbon dioxide, and the other materials necessary for life are recycled.

Materials from the food pyramid are recycled. Eventually they are made available to plants again as the minerals and $CO_2$ needed in new food-making activities. The energy from the food pyramid is not recycled, however. Food energy that has been used by an organism is changed mostly to heat and lost to the atmosphere. Only what is passed on as chemical energy can be used by another organism. New energy input from the sun to green plants and algae is constantly necessary.

Humans add to the materials cycle by artificial fertilization. More food crops and food animals can then be produced. Human activities also add more toxic nonfood materials to the environment.

**SELF CHECK**

1. The biomass of food decreases at each level in the food pyramid. Where do the "lost" materials and energy at every level go?
2. How do materials that cannot be digested or excreted become more concentrated at each level in the food pyramid?
3. Why is a "low" level or "safe" level for the use of toxic substances in the environment not biologically possible?
4. What are biologists' three recommended tests for the use of nonfood materials?
5. What are decomposers? How are they related to degradable materials?

# Materials, Energy, and Human Life-styles

## 26–7

### The Ecosystem and the Economy

Two words with the same word root have become central ideas in our lives. The words *economy* (*oikos* = house + *nomos* = manager) and *eco-* *system* (*oikos* = house + *system* = to bring together, combine) are closely related. The human ecosystem (Figure 26–12) includes our food relationships with other organisms throughout the entire world. The economy includes the ecosystem

**Figure 26–12** Today most human beings live in cities (center). Their ecosystem reaches over the rest of the world, from which food and other products are transported to them.

wholesale beef distributor

harvest of apples

vegetables

cattle feedlot

fish farm

plowing the fields

cotton

ocean fishing boat

New York City

high-yield rice field

grains

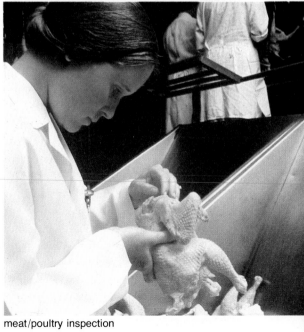

meat/poultry inspection

and all nonbiological processes and products as well— mining, manufacturing, marketing, and investing for the exploitation of nonliving resources for fuels and for industrial, military, and home products.

You are a part of a human economy and a human-influenced ecosystem neither of which you can avoid. The economy includes everything around you—the streets, the sewers, the buildings, the cars, the plants, the grocery store, the gas station, the broken windows, the people, the animals, the crops in the fields, and on and on. Because both the economy and the ecosystem are made up of so many interconnected and interacting components, it is often difficult to determine what part you play or what your contribution is. If you take time to reflect on everything you purchase, use, discard, eat, destroy, consume, recycle, protect, cherish, and dislike you will start to appreciate the many interconnections in everything affecting human life.

When the economy and the ecosystem can be made more productive, more money is earned and more new jobs are created. This prosperity encourages population growth. Yet we are beginning to realize that both systems have built-in limits. Our population increases in size, but our world does not. If our economy or our ecosystem is pushed beyond its limits, either system can be upset or even destroyed. There are limits, for example, to most of our natural resources. If we suddenly push our use of fossil fuels beyond reasonable limits it would have great consequences upon our economy and our ecosystem. We already know that our current use of oil, natural gas, and other fuels is affecting our economy.

There are other kinds of limits besides those of supplying needed foods, fuels, and other materials. There are limits to the rate at which giant systems can change. Because of their size and complexity, and their division among many nations

of the world, these systems are difficult to manage, and they tend to change only slowly. There are limits to the rate at which the systems can adapt to new materials or get rid of unwanted old ones. Today the costs and the problems of getting solid and gaseous wastes out of the air, getting the wastes out of water, and even disposing of our garbage, are good examples of the heavy expense of modern human activities.

Another problem of the complicated world economy and ecosystem is that events can have very unexpected effects. Since there are so many interacting and interdependent components, almost any event can produce more than the planned result. An unexpected effect may appear in a far-removed part of either system. Thus, predicting the consequences of actions is very difficult. This problem has often been stated as ''You can't do just one thing.'' One action always seems to have more than one result (Figures 26–13 and 26–14). You have seen examples of this earlier in this course. No one predicted DDT-resistant flies when DDT was first used, or penicillin-resistant bacteria when penicillin was first used. In Egypt, the construction of the Aswan Dam and a vast system of irrigation canals brought thousands of acres of desert under cultivation. But in addition it also allowed the spread of snails that carry a dreaded human parasite. One result has been an increase in a particularly disabling disease. Now, ten farmers along the Nile who have these parasites can do the work of only three or four. There have been many other such examples of unpredicted consequences. Our pollution problems are in this category. A ''little'' pollution never seemed a problem, but the price we pay now and in the future to clean up the world's air and water will be much greater than the sum of the little prices we might have paid along the way.

Almost everything in the current world ecosystem and economy seems to be part of a trade-off

**Figure 26–13** Pollution associated with use of horses was once a major problem in cities. Odors and particles of dried dung polluted the air. Fresh dung, remnants of horse feed, feed buckets, and broken harnesses littered the streets. The automobile (left in drawing) seemed to be a clean solution. But one action always seems to have more than one result. From a few hundred automobiles to a few hundred thousand to hundreds of millions of automobiles later, the pollution problem has grown anew. An energy problem has grown with it: how can energy continue to be supplied for all the world's vehicles?

situation. You can do this . . . but if you do, then this . . . will result. For example, people in industrialized nations can have more automobiles and industries discharging wastes into the air, or they can have cleaner air, but they cannot have both. Or, you can have continued great variety in foods or continued world population growth, but not both—not indefinitely. We can dig more coal and ores or keep more land protected from mining activities and surface changes, but not both. What trade-offs are the best choices?

## 26–8

## Change Has Always Been Part of Life

All these consequences of human activities have added to the complexity of the living world you have studied in your biology course. Not only millions of years of natural selection, but also, very recently, human intervention have brought the world to its current state.

Many people spend a great deal of time writing and predicting future trends. Such activities are extremely valuable in forcing us to consider all the

**Figure 26–14** The "solution" to the horse pollution problem. Most of the smog over American cities is produced by automobile exhaust fumes. The next solution presents a greater challenge than the last.

possible alternatives. Biologists' discoveries have proved especially valuable, as in learning about the concentration effects of toxic substances in the food pyramid.

The one thing that can be said about the future was also true of all times past—the world is in a state of change. The world has *always* been in a state of change. Living things are not static and never will be. An organism described as human hundreds of thousands of years ago (Chapter 16) is not the same as a human today. The humans who are here today are not the same as those who will be here many thousands of years from now. All living things are part of a long continuum of living history.

The forces of natural selection have left a very understandable pattern of past history. Our biological hindsight is good and getting better. Our ability to look ahead and see what is coming in our evolution may be no better than it has ever been. Yet humans do have a unique ability. We are the only organisms able to understand and contemplate our own evolution. Our understanding is advanced to the level that we know our future evolution is largely in our own hands. Decisions made now are shaping the human world of the future. Yet amazingly we still have little ability to look forward and determine what direction we should take. What an exciting, confusing, and challenging point in time to be alive and a part of human history!

One thing is certain: biology reflects nature's balances. When thinking about a problem, it is useful to consider its biological relationships. They provide a model or comparison for changes in society. For a change to be beneficial very far into the future, it should bear a resemblance to balances in the relationships among organisms in nature.

Otherwise better life-styles now may be future mistakes, taking some biological toll from people who will be living later. The major importance of your biology course is in helping you become able to look at all life situations in a partly biological way.

---

## CAPSULE SUMMARY

People have built their economy and modified their ecosystem to work together. Both have grown very complex, making it difficult to foresee what results an action can have in addition to the planned result. The unforeseen results have helped show that both systems have limits. There are limits in supply, limits in rate of change, and limits in costs of controlling pollution. Many decisions about the economy and the ecosystem have become trade-offs. People can have one thing or another but not both, as in cars and industries vs. cleaner air.

Biological patterns of thinking about problems are a most valuable kind of input. A biology course allows you to consider aspects of the human ecosystem and economy that would be difficult, if not impossible, to consider without a biological background.

## SELF CHECK

1. Which system, the economy or the ecosystem, is included in the other?
2. The human ecosystem has sometimes been called the "city-world ecosystem." Can you explain this meaning?
3. What kinds of limits do the human economy and ecosystem have?
4. What does "You can't do just one thing" mean, in terms of the economy and the ecosystem?
5. Why are biological relationships a good model for predicting further changes in the human economy?

---

## CHAPTER SUMMARY

### HIGHLIGHTS

Every organism is a part of a food chain, and because most organisms have varied diets, usually part of a more complex food web. An ecosystem is a physical environment with a community of microorganisms, plants, and animals that are reasonably self-supporting in their food and other requirements. The ecosystem's food web may be very complex.

Populations grow in relation to the abundance of food, water, living space, and other factors in the environment. Biologists' studies of animal population growth have revealed both food supply and crowding as limiting factors. Studies of human population growth cannot be made experimentally. The effects must be analyzed as the growth actually occurs.

Health and starvation risks to humans have been reduced so much that the prediction of continued human population growth is certain. But space, water, land available for food-raising, and all needed materials and most energy sources are limited because the world does not grow, too. Limits to population growth must be foreseen for some time in the future.

Not only foods but other materials get into food chains and the food pyramid. Biologists have proposed guidelines for the use of nonfood materials, based on studies of damaging effects of some of those materials to animal populations. Pollution extends beyond food relationships to the air, water, and land in other respects, too. Most questions about environmental quality have become trade-offs.

Change has been a part of every species' existence. People have accelerated the changes in their own lives. The changes affect both the people and all or most other species of organisms. With a biological background, you can be ready to participate in decisions affecting changes in the future.

## REVIEWING IDEAS

1. What is an ecosystem?
2. What is the difference between a food chain and a food web?
3. Name two factors that limit the population growth of some animals.
4. Where are the autotrophs found in the food pyramid? the heterotrophs?
5. What are decomposers? How do they affect the recycling of materials in an ecosystem?
6. What does *degradable* mean? *biodegradable?*
7. Why are there no "safe" levels for the use of toxic substances that can enter the food pyramid?
8. What is the difference between the human economy and the human ecosystem?

## USING CONCEPTS

9. What is the importance to a nation of the distinction between food energy and the energy used to help produce food crops?

10. Contrast the passage of 10,000 metric tons of food and 10,000 metric tons of nonexcretable pesticides through a food pyramid.
11. Describe the relationships among populations, communities, and ecosystems.
12. The population doubling time for Canada is 85 years, for the United States 95 years, and for Mexico 27 years. How do these data help explain where immigration problems exist in North America? How do they help explain where food problems are greatest?
13. Explain the effect that population growth may have on agricultural land in the farming areas of the United States.
14. Many bacteria and some algae can take nitrogen from the air and make ammonia and nitrates. Crop plants require ammonia or nitrates for their nitrogen source. Describe the gene-splicing experiment that these data suggest.

## RECOMMENDED READING

Bernard, H. *The Greenhouse Effect*. New York, Harper-Row, 1981 (paperback). Will the increased carbon dioxide in the atmosphere caused by greater fuel use change Earth's climate?

Boserup, E. *Population and Technological Change: A Study of Long-Term Trends*. Chicago, University of Chicago Press, 1981. A reference book on all the problems described in this chapter.

Gwatkin, D. R. and S. K. Brandel. "Life Expectancy and Population Growth in the Third World." *Scientific American*, May 1982. Concentrations of humans where food is scarce.

National Geographic. *Saving Energy*. Washington, D.C., National Geographic Society, 1981. Guidelines for saving some of the energy that people use needlessly.

Uhl, C. "You *Can* Keep a Good Forest Down." *Natural History,* April 1983. The ruin of many portions of the Amazonian rain forests.

# Investigations

# Introduction to Laboratory Work

The laboratory is a scientist's workshop. Only in the laboratory can ideas be tested and proved. In the laboratory portion of this course, you will have the opportunity to see evidence that supports major biological concepts. To pursue your investigations effectively, you will need to learn certain basic techniques, including safe laboratory practices. Careful observation of the following rules and procedures should help you acquire these skills and techniques.

## Laboratory Safety

1. Do not perform any experiments that have not been assigned by your teacher.
2. A laboratory apron should be worn at all times in the lab.
3. Eye protection should be worn at all times when chemicals are being used in the lab.
4. Know the locations of safety equipment such as the eye-wash fountain, fire extinguisher, and first-aid kit.
5. In case of any accident or injury, notify your teacher immediately.
6. Clean up all spills immediately. If your skin comes in contact with a corrosive substance (acid or base), wash the affected area immediately with large amounts of water. Check the information under **First-Aid Procedures** for how to neutralize the acid or base.
7. Never taste any chemical substance in the laboratory unless directed by your teacher. Food should never be consumed in the lab area. Never use your mouth to draw liquid into a pipette.
8. Never use a scalpel or other cutting device with more than one cutting edge.
9. Specimens should be properly supported during dissection. Never dissect a hand-held specimen.
10. Seal petri dish cultures with tape to prevent the spread of microorganisms.
11. Bacterial cultures should be killed before petri dishes are cleaned. Your teacher will explain how to do this. Clean all culture media by sterilizing with a strong disinfectant and washing with a strong cleaning agent. Wear rubber gloves.
12. Use proper illuminations with microscopes. Reflected sunlight can cause eye damage.
13. Handle all chemicals with care. Read the labels of all bottles before using the chemical. First-aid procedures should be listed on all bottles purchased from a chemical supply house.
14. Tie back long hair and avoid wearing clothing with loose sleeves when working in the presence of open flames. Keep combustible materials such as alcohol away from open flames.
15. Do not use chipped or broken glassware. Be sure heat-resistant glass containers are used when a procedure requires heating. Place broken glass and solid substances in the proper waste containers. Keep insoluble materials out of the sink.
16. When heating a substance in a test tube, never point the mouth of the test tube at another person or at yourself.

17. In case of fire, extinguish all flames (from burners). Use a fire extinguisher to douse the fire.

## First-Aid Procedures

Burns–flush with cool water

Cuts–apply pressure to stop the bleeding, clean the affected area and bandage with materials from the first-aid kit. For severe bleeding, apply pressure and call for medical help immediately.

Matter in the eyes–flush with plenty of water from the sink, eye-wash fountain, or eye-wash bottle

Poisoning–note the poisoning agent, call the poison control center in your area

Acid burns–wash with plenty of water, neutralize with sodium hydrogen carbonate, $NaHCO_3$ (baking soda)

Base burns–wash with plenty of water, neutralize with boric acid, $H_3BO_3$

## Use of Living Things in the Lab

1. Obtain background information on the care of the organisms kept in the classroom. Appropriate living quarters should be provided. Animals should not be subjected to disturbances caused by varying classroom activities.
2. Proper food and drinking water should be available in suitable containers.
3. Any experiments done with living organisms should be strictly supervised by your teacher.
4. No experimental procedure should be attempted on a vertebrate animal that would cause pain or discomfort to the animal.
5. Pathogenic organisms should not be used in the classroom.

## Performing Experiments

1. Read the assigned investigation before coming to the laboratory. You will need the entire period for experimental work.
2. Wait for instructions before handling materials or equipment.
3. Arrange and label materials before beginning an experiment.
4. Follow directions precisely. For example, ''one minute'' means exactly one minute by the second hand.
5. Record all experimental activities in a data book.

## Recording Experimental Data

1. Organize your record of each experiment in a logical form. Use your own plan or one suggested by your teacher. You may use the following outline:
   a. title and number of experiment
   b. purpose
   c. materials and equipment
   d. procedure
   e. observations and measurements
   f. interpretation of data
   g. conclusions or generalizations
2. Write in simple, clear language.
3. Wherever possible, express data quantitatively, using the metric system. Make the precision of your data consistent with the precision of your equipment or measurements. For example, do not record a value of 1.002 grams when the precision of your balance is 0.1 gram. Similarly, do not record beyond the first decimal place the average of measurements made to one decimal place.
4. Express your data in graphs, tables, and drawings wherever possible. Label graphs and tables with appropriately descriptive titles. Make simple outline drawings, also properly labeled.

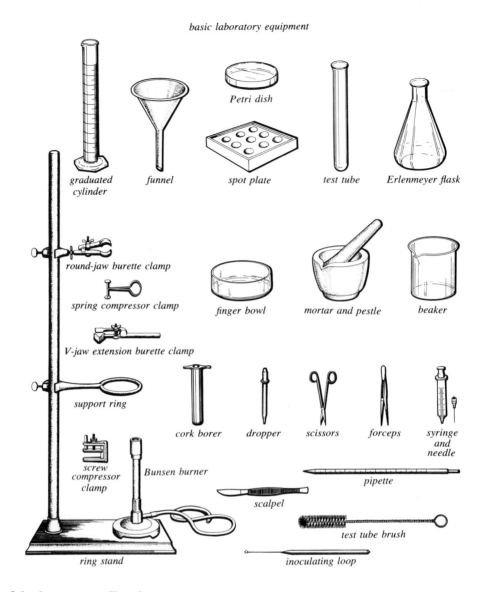

*basic laboratory equipment*

graduated cylinder · funnel · Petri dish · spot plate · test tube · Erlenmeyer flask

round-jaw burette clamp · spring compressor clamp · finger bowl · mortar and pestle · beaker

V-jaw extension burette clamp · support ring · cork borer · dropper · scissors · forceps · syringe and needle

screw compressor clamp · Bunsen burner · scalpel · pipette

test tube brush

ring stand · inoculating loop

## Care of Laboratory Equipment

1. Handle equipment carefully.
2. Avoid contamination, especially in experiments requiring sterile methods.
3. Wrap refuse in paper towels and put it in the appropriate waste container. Do not leave refuse in the sink.
4. After use, wash glassware and instruments with cleaning powder and rinse in clear water. Hard-to-clean items, such as pipettes or stained slides, should be soaked in water, slightly acidified with dilute hydrochloric acid.
5. At the end of the working period, wipe the sink and work surfaces with a sponge or damp paper towels.
6. Follow your teacher's instructions for putting away materials and equipment.

# The Science of Life

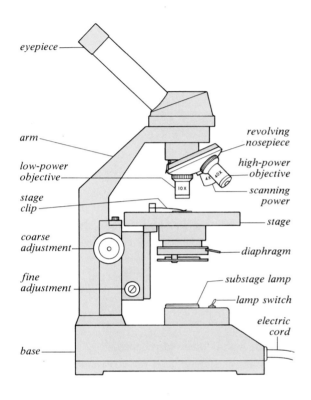

**Figure 1–A–1** Parts of a compound microscope.

## 1–A

### The Compound Microscope

The human eye cannot distinguish objects much smaller than 0.1 mm in size. The microscope is designed to extend vision to much smaller objects. The most commonly used compound microscope (Figure 1–A–1) is monocular (one eyepiece). Objects are viewed with one eye. Light usually reaches the eye after being passed through the object to be examined. Rarely, light is reflected off the object to the eye.

A pair of knobs called the coarse and fine adjustments is used to focus the view of an object. To determine how greatly magnified the view is, multiply the number inscribed on the eyepiece by the number on the objective being used. If the eyepiece is inscribed 10× and the objective 10×, the magnification is 100 times.

In this investigation you will learn how to use and care for a microscope.

### MATERIALS

Compound microscope, 3 slides, cover slips, scissors, water, dropper, newspaper.

### PROCEDURE

**a. Care of the Microscope** The microscope is a precision instrument that requires proper care.

1. Always carry the microscope with both hands, one hand under its base, the other on its arm.
2. When setting the microscope on a table, keep it away from the edge. If a lamp is attached to the microscope, be careful of the wires. Keep everything not needed for microscope studies off your lab table.
3. Avoid tilting the microscope when using temporary slides made with water.
4. The lenses of the microscope cost almost as much as all the other parts put together. Never clean lenses with anything other than the lens paper designed for this task.
5. Before putting the microscope away, *always* return it to the low-power setting. The high-power objective reaches too near the stage to be left in place safely when a slide is next mounted on the stage. Locating an object to be viewed is also easier under low power.

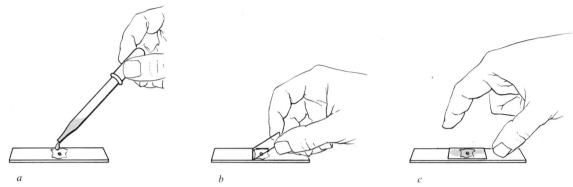

*a*        *b*        *c*

**Figure 1–A–2** Preparing a wet mount with a microscope slide and cover slip.

## b. Setting Up the Microscope

1. Rotate the low-power objective into place if it is not already there. When you change from one objective to another you will hear a click as the objective sets into position.
2. Move the mirror so that light is reflected upward through the opening in the stage, or turn on the substage lamp. Most microscopes are equipped with a diaphragm for regulating light. Some materials are best viewed in dim light, others in bright light.
3. Make sure that the lenses are clean. Wipe lenses with lens paper only.

## c. Practice in the Use of the Microscope

1. Cut out a lower-case *o* from a piece of newspaper. Place it right side up on a clean slide. With a dropper place one drop of water on the letter. This type of slide is called a **wet mount.**
2. Wait until the paper is soaked before covering it with a cover slip. Hold the cover slip at about a 45° angle to the slide and then slowly lower it. Figure 1–A–2 shows these first steps.
3. Place the slide on the stage and clamp it down. Move the slide so that the letter is in the middle of the hole in the stage. Watch the stage from one side of the microscope as you use the coarse adjustment knob to lower the low-power objective. Lower the objective until it is about 1 mm from the cover slip.
4. Now look through the eyepiece and use the coarse adjustment knob to raise the objective slowly, until the letter *o* is in view. Use the fine adjustment knob to sharpen the focus. Position the diaphragm for the best light. Compare the way the letter looks through the microscope with the way it looks to the naked eye.
5. Cut out a lower-case letter *c*. Make a wet mount and examine it under low power. Describe how the letter appears when viewed through the microscope.
6. Make a wet mount of the letter *e* or the letter *r*. Describe how the letter appears when viewed through the microscope. What new information (not revealed by the letter *c*) is revealed by the *e* or *r*?
7. Look through the eyepiece at the letter as you use your thumbs and forefingers to move the slide slowly away from you. Which way does your view of the letter move? Move the slide to the right. Which way does the image move?
8. Make a pencil sketch of the letter as you see it under the microscope. Label the changes in image and movement that occur under the microscope.

9. Make a wet mount of two different-colored hairs, one light and one dark. Cross one hair over the other. Position the slide so that the hairs cross in the center of the field. Sketch the hairs under low power, then go to part **d**.

#### d. Using the High-Power Objective

1. With the crossed hairs centered under low power, adjust the diaphragm for the best light.
2. Turn the high-power objective into viewing position. Do not change the focus.
3. Sharpen the focus with the fine adjustment knob only. Do not focus under high power with the coarse adjustment knob.
4. Readjust the diaphragm to get the best light. If you are not successful in finding the object under high power the first time, return to step 1 and repeat the whole procedure carefully.
5. Using the fine adjustment knob, focus on the hairs at the point where they cross. Can you see both hairs sharply at the same focus level? How can you use the fine adjustment knob to determine which hair is crossed over the other? Sketch the hairs under high power.

If time permits, use low and high power to examine cork cells and other materials provided by your teacher.

## 1–B

## How Are Pieces of Potato Affected in Size by Water and by Different Concentrations of Sugar in Water?

What will happen to the sizes of potato cores placed in water, or in sugar solutions of water, for 24 hours? An experiment to answer this question requires two sets of data. First, the initial sizes of the potato cores must be determined. Then their sizes after 24 hours in water or in sugar solutions must be determined.

This investigation will give you a chance to use some scientific measuring instruments and the metric system of measurement. (See **Appendix 1–A**, page 686.) The following materials and procedures will help you collect information. In certain later investigations you can decide on materials and procedures yourself.

### MATERIALS

White potato, razor blade, metric ruler, balance, labels, cork borer (5- to 10-mm diameter), graduated cylinder, dissecting needle, aluminum foil or plastic wrap, large test tubes or small beakers, 10% sugar solution (90% water), 20% sugar solution (80% water), distilled water (100% water).

### PROCEDURE

1. Using a cork borer, cut three cores from a potato. Trim each core so that its length will be at least 30 mm. Figure 1–B–1 shows the relationship of millimeters to centimeters. Make all cores as nearly the same length as possible. Keep these cores separated and identify them as core A, core B, and core C.

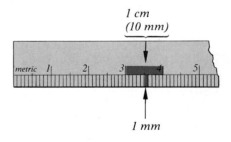

**Figure 1–B–1** Metric rule divided into centimeters and millimeters.

| measurements | core A (100% water) | | | core B (90% water) | | | core C (80% water) | | |
|---|---|---|---|---|---|---|---|---|---|
| | 1st day | 2nd day | gain or loss (+ or –) | 1st day | 2nd day | difference (+ or –) | 1st day | 2nd day | difference (+ or –) |
| length (mm) | | | | | | | | | |
| diameter (mm) | | | | | | | | | |
| volume (ml) | | | | | | | | | |
| weight (g) | | | | | | | | | |

**Table 1–B–1**  Potato core data chart.

2. Measure the length and diameter of each core to the nearest millimeter and record the measurement in your data book. See Table 1–B–1 for data recording.

3. Measure the volume of each core by the following method. Pour water into the graduated cylinder until it is about half full. Hold the cylinder at eye level and read the line on the level with the lower part of the curved surface of the water, as in Figure 1–B–2. This curved liquid surface is called the **meniscus** (men-IS-kus). Record this exact amount of water.

   Holding the core by a needle, sink it under the water and record the new water level. The difference between the two water levels represents the volume of the core in milliliters. Record the volume of each core in a table like Table 1–B–1.

4. Your teacher can show you how to weigh a core, using the balance scale. After proper instruction, weigh each core to the nearest tenth or hundredth of a gram. Again, record your results in a form like Table 1–B–1.

5. Place each core in a different test tube and label each tube A, B, or C according to the core identification. Pour distilled water (100% water) into tube A until core A is covered.

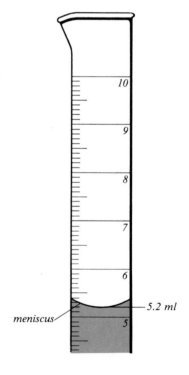

**Figure 1–B–2**  Read water volume from the bottom of the meniscus.

Add a 10 percent sugar solution in water (90% water) to tube B until core B is covered; then add a 20 percent sugar solution in water (80%

water) to tube C in the same way. Cover each tube with foil or plastic wrap and store it away until your next class period.

6. At the following class period, remove the cores from the tubes and repeat procedures 2, 3, and 4. Record your results in the table you set up.

## DISCUSSION

1. In addition to the changes shown by your data, what other changes occurred in each core?
2. How does the change in volume of core A compare with the change in its weight?
3. What is the relationship between the concentration of water and the change in potato core weights?
4. Plot on a graph form like the one in Figure 1–B–3 the changes in weight of the three cores.
5. Predict the water concentration at which a potato core would not change in weight.
6. Describe an experiment that would test your prediction.
7. Several students measuring the same potato core got the following data for length: 30 mm, 31 mm, 29 mm, 28 mm. How do you account for the variation in data?
8. Has this investigation answered the question stated in the title? Explain.

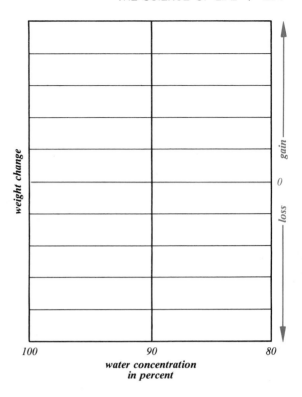

**Figure 1–B–3** Units of measure for weight changes can be entered on the left and a graph plotted for changes in weight of potato cores at different water concentrations.

## 1–C

## Do Active Living Things Give Off a Common Substance?

In Investigation 1–B you made observations and measurements of the size of potato cores and recorded changes that occurred. These observations were *quantitative*. Quantitative observations require careful measurements.

Observations that are *qualitative* also require great care. For example, chemical tests with carefully planned controls can reveal that you modify the composition of the air that you breathe. You probably know that you take oxygen from the air and add carbon dioxide to it.

To identify unknown substances, scientists often use special materials to test the substances. Litmus paper is an example of a material used to test liquids. It yields the qualitative observation of whether the liquid is an acid or a base. This information depends on the color of the litmus paper after it is immersed in a liquid. The litmus paper is an **indicator.**

Your teacher can demonstrate the use of litmus paper or other chemical indicators. In this investigation you will use indicators in liquid form to make qualitative observations.

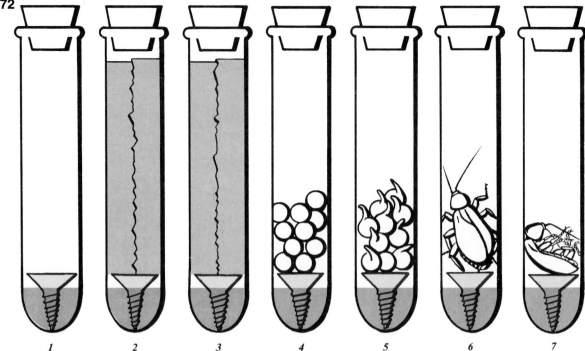

**Figure 1–C–1**  How to set up test tubes for the investigation.

## MATERIALS

Phenol red, limewater, carbonated water, dilute acid, droppers, straws, paper towels, 2 test tube racks, 7 small test tubes with stoppers, 7 small brass screws to fit into the test tubes, 6 standard-sized test tubes, yeast-sugar solution, boiled yeast-sugar solution, 5–10 dry seeds (melon, radish, sunflower, for example), 5–10 sprouted seeds of the same kind, 1 small live insect, 1 small dead insect.

## BRIEF PROCEDURE

**a.** Add different items to each of 7 test tubes containing an indicator (phenol red). Observe and record any color change that takes place in the phenol red of any of the tubes.

**b.** Perform some tests with known substances to determine what the color change of phenol red indicates. Also conduct some tests with limewater to see how it can be used as an indicator.

## DETAILED PROCEDURE

**a. Testing Materials with Phenol Red**  Set up 7 small test tubes in a rack and add 5 drops of phenol red solution to each tube. Tilt each tube slightly and gently slide a screw to the bottom, point first. Now, add the following materials to the tubes as indicated in Figure 1–C–1:

Tube 1: Nothing

Tube 2: A small, rolled piece of paper towel moistened with yeast-sugar solution

Tube 3: A similar piece of paper towel moistened with boiled yeast-sugar solution

Tube 4: 5–10 small dry seeds of one kind

Tube 5: Like number and kind of sprouted seeds

Tube 6: A live insect

Tube 7: A dead insect

Stopper the tubes only after all seven have been prepared. Watch for changes in the phenol red solution and record the approximate time required for the change to take place. Record your observations in a table like Table 1–C–1.

| tube number | material added | indicator change | time for change |
|---|---|---|---|
| *1* | | | |
| *2* | | | |
| *3* | | | |
| *etc.* | | | |

**Table 1–C–1** Record of observations.

## b. Determine Meaning of Phenol Red Change

The following series of tests will help you interpret the results of part **a**.

Set up 6 standard-sized test tubes in a rack and label them 8, 9, 10, 11, 12, and 13. In tubes 8, 9, and 10 place 10–12 drops of phenol red. Fill tubes 11, 12, and 13 about one-quarter full of limewater. Record on your table the indicator changes as the following substances are added:

Tube 8: 1–5 drops of a dilute acid (hydrochloric, acetic, or sulfuric)

Tube 9: 5–10 drops of carbonated water (water with carbon dioxide added)

Tube 10: Your breath blown through a straw for 30 seconds into the phenol red solution

Tube 11: 15–20 drops of an acid

Tube 12: 5–10 drops of carbonated water

Tube 13: Your breath blown through a straw into the limewater for about 30 seconds

### DISCUSSION

1. According to the results of the tests in tubes 8 and 9, what kind of substance does carbon dioxide form when it is dissolved in water?

2. If a certain substance causes a color change in phenol red like that in tube 9, can you be sure the substance contains an acid? Can you be sure it contains carbon dioxide?

3. How can you know that your breath contains a substance that forms an acid when mixed with the water of the phenol red solution?

4. Judging from the results of the tests in tubes 10 and 13, does your breath contain carbon dioxide? Explain.

5. How do the materials that caused a change in tubes 2–7 differ from those that did not?

6. For which tubes is tube 1 a control?

7. How does each of the following pairs of tubes form a controlled pair?
   a. tubes 2 and 3     c. tubes 6 and 7
   b. tubes 4 and 5

8. What hypothesis can you give to account for the color change in some of the first 7 tubes?

9. What indicator could be used to give support to your hypothesis?

10. Why were materials that caused no change in the indicator included in this investigation?

## 1–D
## Microscopic Measurements

How can the microscope be used to measure very small objects (Figure 1–D–1)? In this investigation you will learn several techniques.

### MATERIALS

Compound microscope, plain slide, measuring slide, cover slips, scissors, plastic metric ruler, dropper, water, section of a magazine photograph.

### BRIEF PROCEDURE

Use a measuring slide under the microscope, then a plastic metric ruler, for measurement. Also determine the diameter of the low-power field in terms of a small hand-drawn circle. Count magazine newsprint dots and spaces to compare the diameters of two, or all three fields, of the microscope.

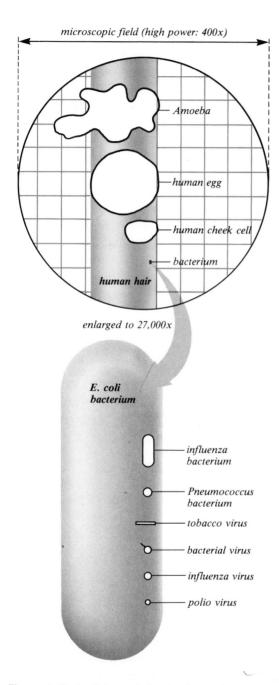

*microscopic field (high power: 400x)*

—Amoeba

—human egg

—human cheek cell

—bacterium

**human hair**

*enlarged to 27,000x*

**E. coli bacterium**

—influenza bacterium

—Pneumococcus bacterium

—tobacco virus

—bacterial virus

—influenza virus

—polio virus

**Figure 1–D–1** Objects similar in size to those in the high-power field of view (circle at top) can all be studied and measured under the compound microscope. Viruses and some bacteria (bottom) cannot be seen.

## DETAILED PROCEDURE

1. Set up the microscope using the procedure you learned in Investigation 1–A.

2. If your school laboratory has metric measuring slides, mount one on the stage of your microscope. Bring the scale on the slide into focus under low power and determine the diameter of the low-power field of view. Record this measurement, then switch to high power and repeat the measurement. Which field has the larger diameter? Depending on the magnifying power of a third objective on the microscope, your teacher may ask you to determine its width of field, too.

3. For most of your work you will not be using measuring slides. Lay a thin, plastic, metric ruler over a plain glass slide and bring the ruler into focus under low power. Again determine the diameter of the low-power field. *Do not switch to the high-power objective; it may collide with the ruler and be damaged.*

4. With a freshly sharpened pencil draw a very small circle of the diameter determined with the plastic ruler for the low-power field. Cut out the circle and make a wet mount of it. Bring the edge of the circle into focus under low power. Adjust the position of the slide to determine whether the circle fills the low-power field. If not, lay the plastic ruler on top of the slide and recheck your measurements. Continue until you have a circle that represents the low-power field. Reproduce this circle in your laboratory notebook and label it for the size of the low-power field.

5. Cut out a small section of a photograph from a magazine. Make a wet mount of the slip of paper and examine it under low power. Count a single line of dots across the center of the field. Record the count, then switch to high power using proper procedure. Center a line of dots and count them across the high-power field. Record the count. Express the two

counts as a fraction, with the high-power count as the numerator and the low-power count (the larger number) as the denominator. Multiply this fraction times the diameter you have already determined for the low-power field. The result should be the diameter of the high-power field. Check the result against that obtained with a measuring slide, if you used one (step 2).

6. Calculate the diameter of the high-power field indirectly, using the diameter of the low-power field and the magnification numbers on the low- and high-power objectives. Fill in these values in the following formula:

$$\frac{\text{high-power magnification}}{\text{low-power magnification}} =$$

$$\frac{\text{low-power field diameter}}{\text{high-power field diameter}}$$

7. Recheck your various measurements of the field diameters for your microscope. Make sure the results by different methods agree. If not, repeat the preceding steps. Include calculations for the third objective on your microscope if your teacher has given you directions for the use of that objective.

8. The unit of microscopic measurement is the **micrometer** ($\mu$m). One $\mu$m equals 0.001 mm, or 1 mm equals 1,000 $\mu$m. Express the field diameters for your microscope in micrometers. Record this data in your laboratory notebook. Which field of view is greatest in diameter? Which field is greatest in magnification?

9. Write a paragraph describing how you could use the microscope to determine the dimensions of a cell or those of a microorganism (provided that the microorganism is not moving too fast).

# Investigations for 2:

# The Cell Theory

## 2–A

## Microorganisms in Pond Water

Many organisms are familiar to you, but almost all of these organisms are large enough to be seen without a microscope. The hidden world of microorganisms includes distinctive kinds of living things just as diversified as larger organisms.

### MATERIALS

Beaker or jar, pond water, finger bowls, bits of dried grass and leaves with a pinch of soil, stereoscopic and monocular microscopes, slides, cover slips, dropper.

### PROCEDURE

1. Add to the jar or beaker bits of grass, leaves, and a pinch of soil to a depth of about 1 cm. Finish filling the container with pond water. Mark the jar with your name and the date.

2. Store the container in a warm, lighted place. Avoid too much heat and direct sunlight.

3. Examine the container from day to day for the next several days. Note any change in clarity, color, odor, or other characteristics.

4. Once a scum has formed on the surface of the water, make a microscopic examination. If your school laboratory has some stereoscopic microscopes, you can begin by using both eyes at low magnification, using one of these microscopes. Draw off a little water in a finger bowl and examine it through the stereoscopic microscope. Some of the smallest microorganisms may not be visible at this low magnification, but if your pond culture includes small multicellular organisms, you should be able to see them clearly. Roundworms, *Daphnia, Cyclops,* rotifers, and the immature young (larvae) of insects are among the multicellular creatures that could be in your pond water. Some of the one-celled organisms may also be visible under the stereoscopic microscope. To see these and other smaller creatures more clearly, put one or two drops of the water on a slide and examine under low power with your monocular microscope. Under low power the slide will not require a cover slip. However, add a cover slip before switching to high power.

5. Try making some high-power observations, keeping in mind that most of the organisms are transparent, or almost transparent. This makes them harder to see at higher magnification with brighter light. Your teacher may want you to try dark-field illumination. Also, some of the organisms move about and are hard to find under high power. However, the cover slip will slow some of them down, or actually pin some of them in place.

6. Measure some of the organisms.

7. Make observations on future dates for several weeks and compare the types of organisms, and their frequencies, with those observed earlier.

## DISCUSSION

1. What kind of microorganism seemed to be most abundant first? (Hint: What caused the culture to become cloudy and produce a bad odor?)

2. Do you think all the types of organisms that you observed on later dates were in the pond water on the day the culture was set up? Explain.

3. What do you think caused a change in the frequency of the various types of microorganisms as the culture got older?

# 2–B
# Cell Structure

In this investigation you will see what some cells from multicellular organisms look like under your microscope. You will also have an opportunity to compare the structure and organization of cells from different organisms.

## MATERIALS

Onion, *Elodea* leaf, toothpick, microscope, slide, cover slip, iodine, forceps, salt solution (5%) in dropper bottle, paper towel.

## PROCEDURE

1. Hold a piece of an onion scale leaf so that the concave surface faces you, then snap it backwards. (See Figure 2–B–1.) A transparent paper-thin layer of cells can be seen along the outer curve of the scale.

2. Using forceps or your fingernails, peel off a small section of this thin layer and place it in one or two drops of iodine on a slide. Add a cover slip.

3. Examine the slide first with low power and then with high power.

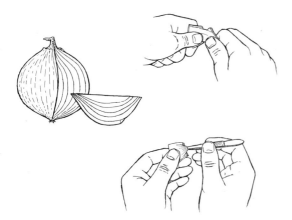

**Figure 2–B–1** Removing the thin layers of cells of an onion scale leaf.

4. Sketch a few cells as they appear under high power. How many dimensions do the cells appear to have when viewed through the microscope? Sketch a cell as it would appear if you could see three dimensions. Measure a cell and record the measurements. Identify the *cell wall, plasma membrane, nucleus,* and *cytoplasm.* You may be able to see a *nucleolus* within a nucleus. (If you cannot see the plasma membrane, add a drop of salt solution at one edge of the cover slip. Then touch a piece of paper towel to the opposite edge of the cover slip, to pull the salt solution into contact with the cells. Continue observing the cells until the plasma membranes separate from the cell walls.)

5. Mount an *Elodea* leaf on a slide and observe it with low and then with high power. Sketch a few cells as they appear under high power. Lift the cover slip and add a drop or two of iodine to the leaf. Observe it again under high power. Are there structures visible now that could not be seen without the iodine? Add these structures to your sketch. Measure a cell and record the measurements.

6. With the broad end of a toothpick, *gently* scrape the inside of your cheek. (Scratching or digging into the cheek tissue is not necessary.) Lay the broad end of the toothpick on a slide. Roll the toothpick gently to dislodge the cheek cells. Discard the toothpick. Add one or two drops of iodine and a cover slip. Examine the cheek cells with the low and then the high power of the microscope. Find a field where the cells are separate and distinct and sketch a few under high power. Measure a cell and record the measurements.

7. Examine slides your teacher can provide and compare their cells with those of your slides.

**DISCUSSION**

1. What cell part did you find around plant cells that you did not find around your cheek cells?
2. Why is it difficult to see the plasma membranes of plant cells?
3. How did the iodine help? Why do biologists use stains to study cells?

## 2–C

## What Special Structures Do Some Smaller Organisms Have That Aid in Obtaining Food?

One-celled organisms take in food directly, but it is difficult for cells of multicellular organisms to do so. By examining several organisms, you can discover how food activities are coordinated, so that all cells can be supplied.

### MATERIALS

Microscopes (monocular and stereoscopic), hand lens, methyl cellulose, slides, cover slips, toothpicks, watch glasses or finger bowls, *Paramecium,* yeast-Congo red preparation, *Hydra, Daphnia,* planarians, dropper.

## PROCEDURE
### Paramecium

1. Place a ring, about 1 cm in diameter, of methyl cellulose on a slide. Into this ring place a drop of *Paramecium* culture. Add a small drop of yeast-Congo red preparation and gently mix with a toothpick. Cover with a cover slip, and observe under low, then high power.
2. Under high power, locate one *Paramecium*. Continue to watch it for some time. Try to see how it takes in its food, what structure it uses for this, and where the food is contained in the cell after ingestion. Look for any movements of food in the cell and any color changes that might occur.
3. Make a sketch of the *Paramecium* indicating the general shape, structure, and location of food-getting parts. Show by arrows any pattern of movement within the cell.
4. Answer Discussion questions 1, 2, 3, and 4.

### Hydra

1. Place two or three *hydras* in a watch glass or finger bowl half full of water. Observe them through a hand lens or stereoscopic microscope until they become extended and relaxed.
2. From a dropper add several living *Daphnia* to the water around the *hydras*. Observe any food-getting activities for several minutes.
3. Make sketches of the *hydras* before, during, and after the food-getting process.
4. Store the containers with the *hydras* and observe them again the following day.
5. Answer Discussion questions 5, 6, and 7.

### Planarian

1. Place a planarian in a watch glass or finger bowl half full of water. Observe with a hand lens or stereoscopic microscope, but do not use strong light. With a toothpick, gently turn the planarian over and observe its underside. Sketch both body surfaces.

2. Obtain another planarian recently fed cooked egg yolk. Again observe both body surfaces. Add any new observations to your sketch.
3. Answer Discussion questions 8 and 9.

## DISCUSSION

1. Does the *Paramecium* have a special place for food to enter?
2. Describe the specific structures of the *Paramecium* for food-getting.
3. What process appears to be indicated by the color change of ingested yeast cells?
4. Describe the general pattern of food movement while digestion is taking place.
5. How does a *Hydra* take in food?
6. Describe the specific structures of *Hydra* that are involved in food-getting.
7. What happens to items taken in by a *Hydra* that cannot be digested?
8. How does a planarian take in food?
9. Which appears to have a more advanced digestive apparatus—*Hydra* or planarian?
10. Match *Paramecium, Hydra,* and a planarian to the digestive pathways in Figure 2–C–1.

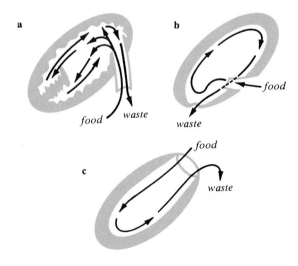

**Figure 2–C–1** Three diagrams of digestive pathways.

# The Variety of Life

## 3–A

### Classifying Flowering Plants

Flowering plants are divided into two classes: monocotyledons and dicotyledons (pages 54–55). To classify these plants you need to become familiar with the structure of flowers and the use of a classification key. Both are included in this investigation. You will be able to identify selected flowering plants to the family level.

### MATERIALS

Representatives of common families of flowering plants, hand lens or stereoscopic microscope, scissors, scalpel, forceps, dissecting needle.

### BRIEF PROCEDURE

Use dissecting instruments and the microscope or hand lens to reveal characteristics of flowers of selected plants. Identify each plant as a monocotyledon or dicotyledon and classify the plant to the family level.

### DETAILED PROCEDURE

1. Select a flowering plant and determine whether it is a monocotyledon or a dicotyledon, using the definitions that follow the Discussion questions.
2. Use forceps, scissors, scalpel, dissecting needle, and hand lens or microscope to reveal key characteristics of the plant's flowers.
3. Match the flower characteristics to the definitions that follow the Discussion questions, and to the illustrations of these definitions in Figure 3–A–1.
4. Use this information and Table 3–A–1 or 3–A–2 to classify the plant.

5. Repeat steps 1–4 for other selected plants.

### DISCUSSION

1. Look up the term *dichotomous* and describe how it applies to the key you have used.
2. Which characteristics seem most important in identifying families of flowering plants?
3. Why were size and color of little help?

### DEFINITIONS

*Monocotyledon:* flower parts in threes or multiples of threes; leaf veins usually parallel.

*Dicotyledon:* flower parts in fours, fives, or multiples of fours and fives; leaf-vein network.

*Superior ovary:* ovary above the bases of petals and sepals (Figure 3–A–1a).

*Inferior ovary:* ovary below the bases of petals and sepals (Figure 3–A–1b).

*Regular flower:* flower parts of each kind (sepals, petals, stamens, etc.) all alike (Figure 3–A–1d).

*Irregular flower:* one or more sepals, petals, stamens, etc., unlike others (not shown).

*United petals:* petals continuous or attached to each other, at least at base (Figure 3–A–1e).

*Separate petals:* petals distinct from one another beginning at their bases (Figure 3–A–1f).

*Receptacle:* stem enlargement at flower base.

*Calyx:* entire group of sepals and their bases.

*Head:* many small flowers, with no stalks, tightly clustered in a group (Figure 3–A–1c,g).

*Umbel:* many small flowers, with stalks, loosely clustered in a group (Figure 3–A–1h).

*Stipules:* small paired structures sometimes present at base of a leaf stalk (Figure 3–A–1i).

*Sheath:* specialized portion of a leaf that encloses the stem (Figure 3–A–1j).

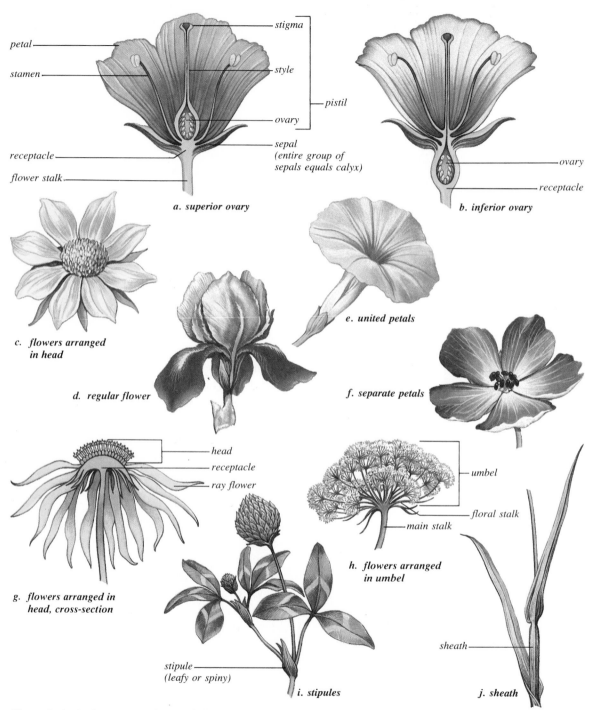

a. superior ovary

petal
stamen
stigma
style
pistil
ovary
sepal
(entire group of
sepals equals calyx)
receptacle
flower stalk

b. inferior ovary

ovary
receptacle

c. flowers arranged
in head

d. regular flower

e. united petals

f. separate petals

g. flowers arranged in
head, cross-section

head
receptacle
ray flower

h. flowers arranged
in umbel

umbel
floral stalk
main stalk

i. stipules

stipule
(leafy or spiny)

j. sheath

sheath

**Figure 3–A–1** Some flower characteristics used in classifying flowering plants.

**Table 3-A-1** Classification key for families of monocotyledons.

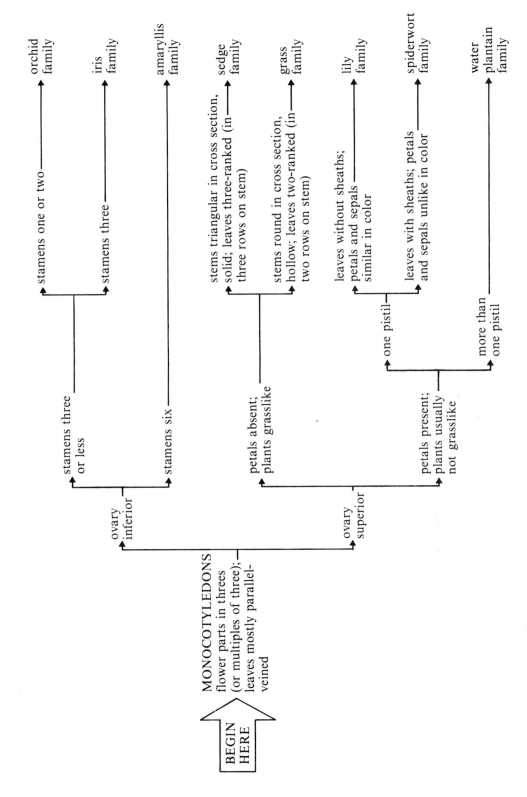

**Table 3-A-2** Classification key for families of dicotyledons

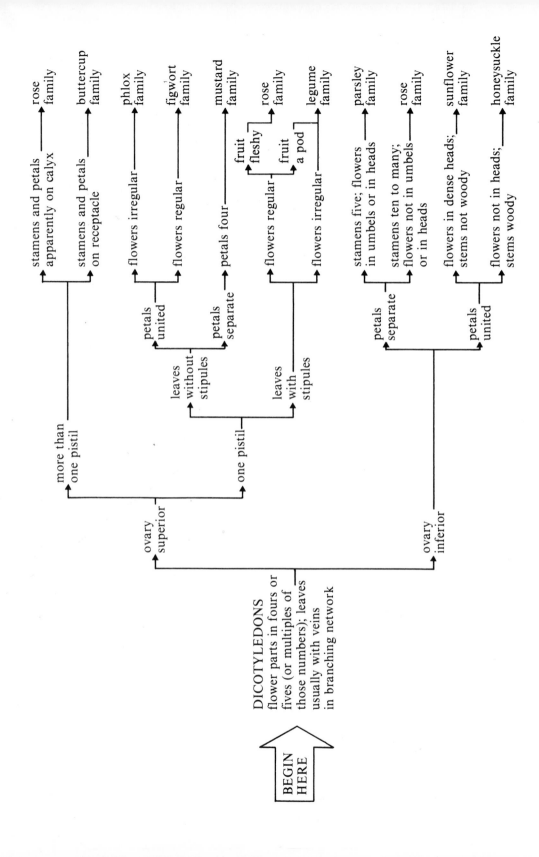

# 3–B

## Structural Characteristics of Animals

On this field trip you will observe selected external characteristics of animals and use these characteristics to classify the animals. Careful observation and note-taking will be required. Two questions that may help guide your observations are "How are these animals similar?" and "How are they different?"

### MATERIALS

Charts of animal characteristics to be observed and recorded, textbook, pen or pencil, notebook or clipboard.

### BRIEF PROCEDURE

This investigation will be a field trip. Your teacher will describe the objectives, schedule, and place or places to be visited. Make careful observations of the animals you see and attempt to work out a classification scheme based on your observations.

### DETAILED PROCEDURE

1. You will be briefed on this field experience. The briefing will include where, when, what to do, and materials and references you will need to carry out your observations.
2. Before the field trip, study the animal classification charts in Chapter 2 and practice making observations and taking notes. Look at animal pictures in other books and magazines and determine where you would place these animals in the classification charts in Chapter 2. Sharpen your skills in observation and in organizing and recording data.
3. On the field trip, observe an animal carefully before you record any data. Note those features that can be used to distinguish its species. Also note the more general characteristics that can be used to group the animal with others that appear related to it.
4. Record your observations on charts similar to those shown in Tables 3–B–1 and 3–B–2 or in charts your teacher will ask you to use.
5. Make additional notes beyond the observations you record on the charts. Save these notes for discussion after the field trip.
6. Repeat steps 3, 4, and 5 for each animal to be observed. If you have questions, try to ask them *before* making entries in the charts.

### DISCUSSION

1. What types of features did you find of greatest value in categorizing the animals you observed?
2. What features were of greatest value in grouping animals together?
3. What features were of greatest value in distinguishing one species from another?
4. Which of the animals you observed seemed most closely related to one another?
5. Which of the animals you observed seemed least closely related to one another?
6. On the basis of your observations, write a short paragraph that distinguishes animals from other organisms.
7. Based on the animals you observed, what changes, if any, would you make in the classification charts you used?
8. What advantages and disadvantages did you find in studying living animals rather than preserved specimens or illustrations in magazines and books?
9. What kinds of characteristics that you were unable to observe would have proved helpful in distinguishing between species of some of the animals you saw?
10. What roles did type of food and characteristics of feeding play in your classification of similar and different groups of animals?

**Table 3-B-1** Classification chart for vertebrates.

| | | NAME OF ANIMAL | | | | | | | |
|---|---|---|---|---|---|---|---|---|---|
| **SKIN STRUCTURES** | Hair present | | | | | | | | |
| | Feathers present | | | | | | | | |
| | Scales present | | | | | | | | |
| | None of above present | | | | | | | | |
| **APPENDAGES** | Wings present | | | | | | | | |
| | Legs present | | | | | | | | |
| | Fins present | | | | | | | | |
| | None of above present | | | | | | | | |
| **SKELETON** | Bony[1] | | | | | | | | |
| | Cartilaginous[2] | | | | | | | | |
| **TEETH** | Present | | | | | | | | |
| | Absent | | | | | | | | |
| | | Class | Class | Class | Class | Class | Class | Class | |

[1]Bony skeleton: a skeleton in which most of the parts are hard and relatively rigid, because of the hard mineral matter they contain.

[2]Cartilaginous skeleton: a skeleton in which all the parts are tough but flexible because they are composed of cartilage—a substance that does not contain significant deposits of hard minerals.

**Table 3-B-2** Classification chart for invertebrates.

| | | NAME OF ANIMAL | | | | | | |
|---|---|---|---|---|---|---|---|---|
| **EXOSKELETON**[1] | Present | | | | | | | |
| | Absent | | | | | | | |
| **BODY SYMMETRY** | Radial[2] | | | | | | | |
| | Bilateral[3] | | | | | | | |
| | Part bilateral, part spiral | | | | | | | |
| **JOINTED WALKING LEGS** | 3 pairs present | | | | | | | |
| | 4 pairs present | | | | | | | |
| | More than 4 pairs present | | | | | | | |
| | Absent | | | | | | | |
| **BODY SEGMENTATION**[4] | Present | | | | | | | |
| | Absent | | | | | | | |
| **TENTACLES**[5] | More than 4 present | | | | | | | |
| | 4 or fewer present | | | | | | | |
| | Absent | | | | | | | |
| **ANTENNAE**[6] | 2 or more pairs present | | | | | | | |
| | 1 pair present | | | | | | | |
| | Absent | | | | | | | |
| | | Phylum | Phylum | Phylum | Phylum | Phylum | Phylum | Phylum |

[1]Exoskeleton: a skeleton on the outer surface of an animal, enclosing the animal.

[2]Radial symmetry: body parts arranged in a circular manner around a central point or region, as in a bicycle wheel.

[3]Bilateral symmetry: matching body parts along the right and left sides of a line running from one end of the animal to the other, as in the body of a bus.

[4]Body segmentation: a structural pattern in which the body is divided into a series of more or less similar sections, the boundaries of which are usually indicated by grooves encircling the body.

[5]Tentacles: slender, flexible structures that can be lengthened or shortened; usually attached near the mouth.

[6]Antennae: slender structures that can be waved about but cannot be changed in length; usually attached to the head.

# Investigations for 4:

# Evolution

## 4–A

### Variation Within a Species

You have probably heard the expression "as much alike as two peas in a pod." Well, just how much alike are two peas in a pod, or two beans in a pod, or leg-lengths of grasshoppers, or heights of people? In a flock of sheep all the individuals would look very much alike, and we would not be able to tell one from another. The baby lambs, however, seem to have no difficulty in finding their own mothers when feeding time comes. There are differences in the mother sheep that the lambs use to identify them. We do not notice these differences by simply looking at them.

The differences by which individuals within a species are identified are known as **variations.** It is possible to describe these differences in pictures, words, or measurements. Probably the best description is made in terms of measurements.

In this investigation you are going to look for differences in a number of living things, to see if there is any pattern to these variations. You will also be asked to think about the survival advantages of some of the variations that you measure.

### MATERIALS

Soaked pea or bean seeds or peas in pods if available, grasshoppers of the same species, millimeter ruler, petri dish or similar container, graph paper, string.

### PROCEDURE
#### a. Collecting Data

1. Peel the outer covering (seed coat) from the seed so it may be easily divided in half. Lay one of the halves of the seed on the millimeter ruler and determine to the nearest half or whole millimeter the longest dimension of the seed. Discard both halves. Repeat with other seeds until you have measurements from about 25 seeds. Record all measurements in a table or chart in your data book, showing the number of seeds with the same length. Pool your data with other students so that you have a record of at least 100 different seed measurements.

2. Measure the length of the femur of the jumping leg of several grasshoppers. It is not necessary to remove the leg. Figure 4–A–1 will help you to locate the femur. Record your measurements in your data book. Pool your data with the entire class so that you have the measurements of all the grasshoppers.

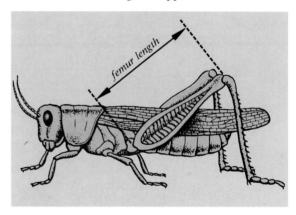

**Figure 4–A–1** The measurement to be made of the femur of a grasshopper.

3. Tie a knot about five centimeters from the end of a piece of string to mark a point of reference. While holding the string across the bridge of your partner's nose, position the knot in the string at the exact outer corner of one

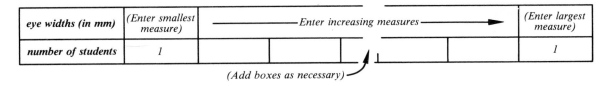

| eye widths (in mm) | *(Enter smallest measure)* | ←————————Enter increasing measures————————→ | | | | | *(Enter largest measure)* |
|---|---|---|---|---|---|---|---|
| number of students | *1* | | | | | | *1* |

*(Add boxes as necessary)*

**Table 4–A–1** Sample data table for student eye widths.

eye. Stretch the string tightly and mark with your thumbnail the point of the outer corner of the other eye. Measure to the nearest millimeter the distance between the knot and your thumbnail. This measurement represents the distance from the corner of one eye to the corner of the other eye. Now have your partner measure this distance on you. Record these measurements in your data book. Pool your data with the other class members.

## b. Organizing Data

1. Arrange your three sets of measurements (bean size, leg length, and eye width) in a manner that will show the number of like measurements. (See Table 4–A–1.)
2. Prepare a graph of each set of data to show the distribution of the variations. To do this, put the range of measurements on the horizontal axis of the graph and the number of individuals having this measurement on the vertical axis. Draw a smooth line (one without angles) connecting or passing near the dots plotted on each graph. (See Figure 4–A–2.) Each set of measurements must be put on a separate graph.
3. Calculate the average length in each set of measurements. Mark this length on each graph by finding the average value on the horizontal axis and making a vertical line to indicate the position of the average length.

## DISCUSSION

1. In what ways are the three graphs alike? How do they differ?
2. The two large halves of the seed are modified leaves containing stored food which will be used by the young plant as it grows. Which of the seeds that you measured would have the most stored food?

**Figure 4–A–2** Hypothetical graph of student eye widths, showing straight lines connecting plotted data.

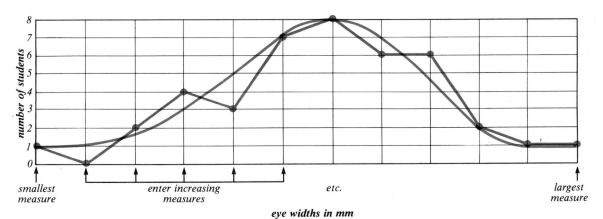

3. What kind of measurement other than length would give you a better answer to question 2?

4. How does large seed size help the young plant to survive?

5. Assuming that a grasshopper with a longer femur can jump farther, how might leg length be a survival factor in the life of a grasshopper? List as many advantages as you can think of, remembering, of course, that these are based on an assumption. Can you think of any disadvantages?

6. An optometrist (a doctor who examines eyes and fits glasses) measures the width of the eyes of all people that he or she fits glasses to. If all the thousands of measurements of eye width that any optometrist has made were plotted on a graph, how would the general shape of that graph compare with the one you made?

## 4–B

## Natural Selection

Charles Darwin collected many facts to support the theory of evolution by natural selection. Darwin had not observed evolution taking place in nature over a short period of time, however. Yet some remarkable examples of natural selection were going on around him in the English countryside. One example is the selection process involving the peppered moth, *Biston betularia* (BIS-ton bet-choo-LAR-ee-a).

The Industrial Revolution began in the middle of the eighteenth century. Since that time tons of soot have been deposited on the countryside around industrial areas. The soot has discolored and generally darkened the surfaces of trees, rocks, and other features of the landscape. It has also destroyed the lichens that once grew in these areas. Lichens are small, flowerless plants which frequently encrust the bark of trees. Many lichens are light in color. Before the Industrial Revolution the peppered moths were also light-colored.

In 1848, the first dark-colored peppered moth was observed and recorded. A century later, in some areas, 90 percent or more of the peppered moths were dark in color. More than 70 species of moths in England changed from light to dark coloration. Similar observations have been made in other industrial nations, including the United States. How did this striking change in coloration come about? Is the change related to the way in which one species is thought to evolve normally from another?

To answer these questions and to interpret the results of the following experiments, it will be helpful to keep the following information in mind:

1. Hereditary characteristics of parent organisms are passed on to their offspring.

2. Changes can occur in the hereditary material of the parents to produce offspring with characteristics different from those of the parents. These changes are known as **mutations.**

3. If the different form, called a **mutant,** survives and reproduces, it may pass on the new trait, or mutation, to future generations.

**a. An Experiment with Chemicals from Soot** The peppered moth has a one-year life cycle. The egg hatches into a larva (caterpillar), which feeds on leaves. The animal then goes through a dormant stage and is finally transformed into an adult moth. In 1926, a British scientist fed leaves treated with certain chemicals found in soot to the larvae of light-colored moths. The larvae were then permitted to go through the normal life cycle. Eventually the larvae changed into light-colored adult moths. These moths were allowed to mate and produce offspring. When the scientist counted these offspring, 8 percent of the new moths were found to be dark-colored. Since this was much higher than the normal rate of mutation, the scientist claimed that the chemicals found in soot caused changes to the hereditary material that determines body color. When the experiment was

**Figure 4-B-1** *Biston betularia,* the peppered moth, and its black form (*carbonaria*) on a lichen-covered tree trunk in unpolluted English countryside (left) and on a soot-covered oak trunk (right) near the industrial city of Birmingham, England.

repeated by other scientists, their results showed much less than 8 percent dark-colored offspring. Moreover, it was found that light-colored moth larvae that were fed on unpolluted leaves produced about as many dark-colored moths as those fed on polluted leaves.

## DISCUSSION

1. What is the value of an experiment that other scientists repeat with different results?
2. What errors could have been made by the scientist who performed the feeding experiment in 1926?
3. What was the ''control'' in the second experiment? Why was it necessary?

## b. An Experiment in an Unpolluted Forest

More recently another experiment was performed with *Biston betularia*. A large number of the moths were captured. The underside of each moth was marked with a small spot of paint for identification. Known numbers of these marked moths were then released in an unpolluted forest. After a while, moths were collected from this forest and

the marked ones were counted. Of 488 dark moths and 496 light moths released in an unpolluted forest, 34 dark moths and 62 light moths were recaptured.

## DISCUSSION

4. Why was the spot of paint placed on the underside of the moth rather than on top?
5. What may have happened to the moths not recaptured?
6. How do the results of this experiment give evidence of natural selection? How might this experiment be performed to give even better evidence of natural selection?

## c. An Experiment on a Light-Colored Tree

In still another experiment, equal numbers of light and dark moths were placed on a light-colored tree in an unpolluted forest. These moths were kept under careful observation. Birds were seen to seize moths from the tree and rapidly carry them away. At the end of a day, approximately twice as many light moths as dark moths were left on the trees. Then the reverse experiment was performed. Equal numbers of light and dark moths were placed on a dark-colored tree in a polluted forest. At the end of the day, approximately twice as many dark-colored moths were left. Motion pictures were taken showing the birds feeding on the moths. Figure 4–B–1 shows the moths on both light and dark trees.

## DISCUSSION

7. What is the chief predator of the peppered moth?
8. Assuming that equally large numbers of both types of moth are present on trees like those shown in Figure 4–B–1, which type of moth would most likely be preyed upon in each case? Why?
9. Does the experiment just described help support the conclusions you have drawn thus far? Explain.
10. Which type of moth is more apt to survive in a polluted forest? In an unpolluted forest?
11. Is it likely that any dark-colored moths existed before the Industrial Revolution?
12. If any dark-colored moths did exist before the Industrial Revolution darkened the forests, what probably happened to them?

## d. An Observation in an Unpolluted Forest

In an old forest in Scotland, far removed from industrial cities, there is a species of moth called *Cleora repandata*. Of about 500 moths observed, approximately 50, 10 percent of the total population, were dark-colored while 90 percent were light-colored. When these moths rest on the bark of pine trees during the daytime, the dark form is more conspicuous. Observation has shown that many moths move from one tree trunk to another during the day if they are disturbed by ants or the heat of the sun. In flight, the dark moth is visible for a distance of about 18 meters, but the light moth is visible for a distance of more than 90

meters. Observers have reported seeing light moths captured in flight by birds.

## DISCUSSION

13. Which body coloration is protective when the moths are resting during the daytime?
14. Which body coloration is protective when the moths are in daytime flight?
15. Explain your answers to questions 13 and 14.
16. Studies have shown that light-colored moths produce 1 dark moth in approximately 200,000 offspring. This is the mutation rate from light to dark, only 0.0005 percent. From these data, how can you explain the fact that 10 percent of the total population of moths in the unpolluted forest are dark?

## e. Interpretation of the Observations

On the basis of your interpretation of the preceding experiments, write a short paragraph using these questions as a guide: How has the striking change in coloration of the moth population come about? (Use Darwin's theory of natural selection and apply it to what you have learned in this investigation.) Is the change related to the mechanisms by which one species is thought to evolve normally from another? (Apply Darwin's ideas on the origin of new species.) Include an explanation of how the dark moth appeared and how the proportion of dark moths changed from 0.0005 percent to more than 90 percent in the polluted forests.

## f. Prediction of the Future

Soot and factory pollution are subsiding as pollution-control measures are practiced in many industrial areas. Non-pollutant fuels may, in the future, replace the coal-burning furnaces of the present factories. Write a short paragraph predicting changes you might expect in the environment and the effect these changes will have on the survival and reproduction of the two colors of peppered moth.

# Forerunners of Life

## 5–A

### Where Do Bacteria and Other Microorganisms Come from?

Cats give birth to kittens. Robins lay eggs which hatch into baby robins. Oak trees produce acorns which will grow into oak trees. It is obvious that living things like these produce more of their own kind, and reproduction is the only way that more of these kinds of living things come into existence. But what about bacteria and other microorganisms? Even today, some people are uncertain about whether these microorganisms come about only by reproduction. Are other hypotheses feasible? In this investigation, modeled after an experiment by Louis Pasteur, you will explore this question.

### MATERIALS

Eight 250-ml flasks, 600 ml of nutrient broth, straight glass tube (8–10 cm long), S-shaped glass tube (18–20 cm long), sealing wax or paraffin, cotton plugs for 5 flasks, cork stopper for 1 flask, aluminum foil, string, boiling waterbath (1000-ml beaker or pan of water on a solid-top hot plate), pressure cooker or autoclave.

### PROCEDURE

1. Put 75 ml of the nutrient broth into each flask. Number the flasks 1–8 and treat them according to the following directions. (See Figure 5–A–1.)

Flask 1: Plug with cotton. Do not heat.

Flask 2: Plug with cotton. Heat gently in a boiling water bath for 10 minutes.

Flask 3: Heat gently in a boiling water bath for 10 minutes. Leave open.

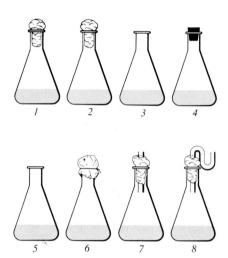

**Figure 5–A–1** Set-up for flasks 1 through 8.

Flask 4: Heat gently in a boiling water bath for 10 minutes. After heating, stopper with a cork. Seal the cork to the glass with wax or paraffin.

Flask 5: Heat in the pressure cooker for 15 minutes at 15 lb pressure. Leave the flask unplugged.

Flask 6: Plug with cotton. Cover the cotton plug and neck of the flask with one or two layers of aluminum foil. Tie securely. Heat in pressure cooker or autoclave, as for flask 5.

Flask 7: Plug with cotton through which the open straight glass tube has been inserted. Heat in the pressure cooker or autoclave.

**591**

Flask 8: Plug with cotton through which the open S-shaped glass tube has been inserted. Heat in the pressure cooker or autoclave.

2. After the proper treatment, store the flasks in the laboratory but not in a closed cabinet or in direct sunlight. Look for changes in the broth, at first from day to day, later from week to week.

3. Along the left column of a page in your data book, make a simple sketch of each flask. In a column next to the sketches indicate briefly the kind of heat treatment, if any, the broth in the flask was subjected to. In another column, indicate your prediction about the possibility of having bacteria form or occur in the broth, either now or later. In the last column, record your observations about changes that occur in the broth. Where could the bacteria have come from to produce these changes? Use your sense of smell as well as sight to describe these changes.

4. When changes in the appearance of the broth have occurred, make a slide with a drop of the broth and observe it under the high power of the microscope. Prepare a slide of fresh broth and compare the two. Save the spoiled broth for Investigation 5–B.

**DISCUSSION**

1. From the observations you have made on the flasks, what are your conclusions about the origin and source of the microorganisms?

2. Judging from your results with flask 6 and flask 8, can bacteria be excluded from broth that has been heated in an autoclave or pressure cooker?

3. Why do bacteria appear in flasks 5 and 7 but not in flask 8?

4. Louis Pasteur was one of the scientists who believed that bacteria cannot originate spontaneously but require other live bacteria before them. Pasteur used "swan-necked" flasks

(similar to your number 8) to trap bacteria in the necks of the flasks, without excluding air. How does your number 8 prove Pasteur's point (and not exclude any "active principle" in the air)?

5. What practical applications are suggested by this experiment?

## 5–B

## What Are the Acid or Base Characteristics of Some Common Biological Materials?

The $pH$ value of a solution can be measured precisely by means of complex electrical instruments, or somewhat less precisely by means of certain dyes. Each of these dyes, like the phenol red you used in Investigation 1–C, changes color at a different point in the $pH$ scale. With a careful selection of dyes you can detect any level of $pH$. In this exercise you will use strips of paper that have been treated with a mixture of several of these dye indicators. When dipped in a solution, the paper will change color, depending on the $pH$ of the solution. By comparing the color to a reference color chart, you can determine the $pH$ level.

During the rest of the year it will be necessary for you to measure $pH$ values quite frequently. The tests you perform in this exercise will introduce you to the $pH$ scale and will show the broad range of $pH$ values found in biological substances.

**MATERIALS**

Dilute hydrochloric acid, distilled water, tap water, lemon juice, tomato juice, spoiled broth from 5–A, unspoiled broth, dilute sodium hydroxide (a base), white vinegar, red vinegar, saliva, urine, blood, fresh milk, sour milk, egg yolk, egg white, $pH$ paper with color chart, drinking straw.

## PROCEDURE

1. Take a small sample of the various materials provided and determine the $p$H of each by dipping a small piece of $p$H paper into the liquid. Compare the color of the wet $p$H paper with the standard color chart.
2. Make a table in your data book and record the substances tested and the $p$H of each. Compare your $p$H numbers with those of others.
3. Mix a substance that has a low $p$H number with a substance that has a high $p$H number. Determine the $p$H of the mixture.
4. Take the $p$H of some tap water. Then, bubble your breath through the water by exhaling through a drinking straw for 30 seconds. Take the $p$H of the water again.

## DISCUSSION

1. Distilled water is neutral—that is, it is neither an acid nor a base. What is the $p$H of distilled water? What other substances did you find to be neutral?
2. Is the $p$H of the hydrochloric acid solution greater than or less than that of the distilled water?
3. In procedure 3 you mixed an acid and a base. What was the $p$H of the substances before they were mixed? What was the $p$H of the mixture? Explain.
4. What substance tested was the most basic? What was the most acidic?
5. What effect did bubbling your breath through water have on the $p$H of the water? What substance in your exhaled breath could have made the change?
6. Arrange all the substances tested from the most acidic to the most basic. Give the $p$H of each.
7. What effect does souring have on the $p$H of milk? Account for the difference on the basis that milk sours because of bacteria that live in it.

## 5–C

# Coacervate Formation

Under certain conditions, the proteins, carbohydrates, and other materials in a solution may group together into the organized droplets called coacervates. Because coacervates have some of the properties of living things, droplets like them might have been an important step in the origin of life. In this investigation, you can produce coacervates and study the conditions under which they form.

## MATERIALS

Gelatin dissolved in distilled water, gum arabic dissolved in distilled water, hydrochloric acid (0.1 M), pipette, dropper, $p$H test paper, test tubes with corks, living amoebas (optional), microscope slides and cover slips, microscope.

## PROCEDURE

1. Mix together 5 ml of the gelatin solution and 3 ml of the gum arabic solution in a test tube. Gelatin is a protein. Gum arabic is a carbohydrate, a carbon compound related to sugars and starches. Measure the $p$H of this mixture.
2. Place a drop of the liquid on a slide and observe it under the low power of the microscope.
3. Carefully add acid, drop by drop, to the test tube. After the addition of each drop of acid, mix well and then wait a few seconds to see if the mixture becomes cloudy. If the liquid in the tube remains clear, add another drop of acid. Continue adding acid a drop at a time until the mixture becomes cloudy.
4. When the material turns cloudy, take another $p$H reading. At this point, carefully observe a drop of the liquid under the microscope. Look for coacervates, structures resembling those in Figure 5–16. If you cannot see them, try adjusting the light and using high power. If you still do not observe coacervates, repeat the

procedure from the beginning, for you may have added acid too rapidly. When you are successful, record your observations and make sketches of the coacervate droplets.

5. Examine a slide of living amoebas and compare their structure and organization with the larger coacervates.

6. When you have finished your observation of the coacervates, add more acid to the test tube, a drop at a time. Mix after adding each drop and measure the $pH$ after every third drop. Continue until the solution becomes clear again. When the liquid becomes clear again, examine a drop under the microscope and measure the new $pH$.

**DISCUSSION**

1. How do the materials that you used to make coacervates compare with those that might have been present in the ancient ocean?

2. In what $pH$ range did the coacervate droplets form?

3. Did the $pH$ change as expected as a result of adding more acid to the solution between coacervate formation and clearing?

4. When hydrochloric acid was added beyond a certain point, the coacervates disappeared. What might you add to the test tube to make the coacervates reappear?

5. How might the coacervate droplets be made more visible under the microscope?

# Investigations for 6:

# Chemical Energy for Life

## 6–A

### What Do Cells Contain to Promote the Chemical Activity of Life Processes?

Almost any chemical activity in a cell could be tested to find out how cells promote their chemical reactions at moderate temperatures. What enables them to do this? The reaction you will investigate involves the compound hydrogen peroxide.

Hydrogen peroxide is a poisonous chemical that is continually formed as a byproduct of reactions in living cells. Since it is poisonous, the cells must either get rid of it or change it to something non-poisonous. If they cannot do this they will die.

In this investigation you will use some plant and animal tissues and determine what happens when hydrogen peroxide is added to them. You will also investigate some conditions that might affect the rate of the activity.

**MATERIALS**

Manganese dioxide powder, fresh 3% hydrogen peroxide solution, pieces of raw liver and potato; small test tubes, graduated cylinder or syringe, forceps, test tube holder, boiling water bath, ice bath, stirring rod, fine sand; $pH$ paper, sodium hydroxide solution (0.1M), hydrochloric acid solution (0.1M), mortar and pestle, wood splints, matches. (Optional for demonstration: gas-collecting apparatus.)

## PROCEDURE

1. Will just anything, when added to hydrogen peroxide, cause a reaction? To determine this, add a pinch of sand to about 2 ml of hydrogen peroxide in a test tube. Describe the reaction as: none, slow, moderate, or fast.

2. Will a reaction occur when a small piece of liver is added to hydrogen peroxide? Use about 2 ml of hydrogen peroxide and a piece of liver about the size of a small pea. Rate the reaction.

3. Will a reaction occur when plant tissue is added to hydrogen peroxide? Use a piece of potato about the size of a small pea and about 2 ml of hydrogen peroxide. Rate the reaction.

4. Will a reaction occur when chemicals other than those from living things are added to hydrogen peroxide? Add a pinch of manganese dioxide to about 2 ml of hydrogen peroxide to determine this. Rate the reaction.

5. The reaction in procedure 2 occurs for a time and finally stops. Why? Was it completed? (Is all the hydrogen peroxide changed?) Or was something in the liver "used up" before all the hydrogen peroxide could be changed? To find out, add a fresh piece of liver to some fresh hydrogen peroxide and wait until the reaction stops. (Use a wood splint to hold the liver in the bottom of the tube if it has a tendency to rise.) When the reaction stops, remove the piece of liver and put it in a clean test tube. Add some fresh hydrogen peroxide to the used liver. What happens? As a control, add some fresh liver to the used hydrogen peroxide in the other tube. From the new reactions, determine which had originally changed—the liver, the hydrogen peroxide, or both.

6. Will grinding the tissue have any effect on the rate of the reaction? Use the mortar and pestle to grind a piece of liver mixed with a pinch of sand. Empty the ground liver and sand into a test tube. Wash the mortar and pestle, and grind a piece of potato in sand. Empty this into

a second test tube. Add about 2 ml of hydrogen peroxide to each test tube and compare the reactions with those of procedures 2 and 3.

7. Does temperature have any effect on the rate of the reaction? Use a stirring rod to **gently** crush some liver in a test tube and stand the tube in a boiling water bath for about 3 minutes. Then add about 2 ml of hydrogen peroxide to the boiled liver. Rate the reaction.

   Put two test tubes, with about 2 ml of hydrogen peroxide in each, into separate water baths. One bath should be warm and one ice cold. After the tubes of hydrogen peroxide have been in the water baths for about 3 minutes, add a small piece of liver to each. Rate the reactions.

8. Does $p$H affect the rate of the reaction? Grind some liver with sand in the mortar and divide it into equal portions in three clean test tubes. Add 2 ml of distilled water to one tube, 2 ml of sodium hydroxide to another, and 2 ml of dilute hydrochloric acid to the third. Check the $p$H of each tube with small pieces of $p$H paper. Pour 2 ml of hydrogen peroxide into each tube and record the rates of reaction.

9. What are the products of the reaction? In other words, what is the gas that is given off during the foaming action, and what is the liquid that remains when the reaction stops? To collect some of the gas, you can prepare a gas-collecting apparatus like that shown in Figure 6–A–1. (Your teacher may ask only one group of students to do this, as a demonstration.)

Using a mortar and pestle grind a chunk of liver, about 1 cm on each side, with sand, and place the mixture in a 250-ml flask. Add about 100 ml of hydrogen peroxide to the flask. After about 5 seconds place the stopper and tubing in the mouth of the flask. Collect two tubes of the gas by transferring the tubing to the second water-filled test tube as soon as the first is filled with the gas.

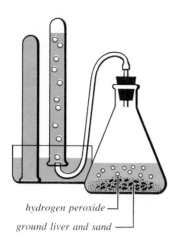

*hydrogen peroxide*

*ground liver and sand*

**Figure 6–A–1**  Set-up for a gas-collecting apparatus.

   Remove one of the tubes of gas, holding it in the inverted position.  Bring a burning match near the open end of the tube.  Record what happens. Remove the other tube and immediately turn it to the upright position.  Insert a glowing splint (not flaming) into the gas of this tube.  (See Figure 6–A–2.)  Record what happens.

**Figure 6–A–2**  Testing for hydrogen (above), and for oxygen (below).  Which test gives positive results?

## DISCUSSION

1. Make a list of the reaction rates.  Organize the list so the materials that produced the fastest reaction are listed first and the others are in descending order, with the materials that produced the slowest reaction last.  Compare your list with those of other groups.
2. Look up the word *catalyst* in a dictionary. Describe what happened in procedure step 5 in relation to this definition.  Does liver tissue contain a catalyst?  Explain.
3. Read about enzymes in Section 6–4.  What is the relationship between a catalyst and an enzyme?  Does liver tissue contain an enzyme? Does potato tissue contain an enzyme?  Explain.

4. Manganese dioxide does not come from a living thing.  Is manganese dioxide a catalyst?  Is it an enzyme?  Explain.
5. Answer the questions in each procedure step 1 through 9.
6. Complete the following chemical equation:

$$2H_2O_2 + \underset{\text{(catalase)}}{\text{enzyme}} \longrightarrow ? + ? + \underset{\text{(catalase)}}{\text{enzyme}}$$

7. Does catalase, an enzyme in living tissue, change hydrogen peroxide into nonpoisonous materials?  Explain.

## 6–B

## What Controls the Movement of Materials into and out of Cells?

The cell's contents are surrounded by a thin membrane. Anything entering or leaving the cell must pass through this plasma membrane. If materials can pass into the cell, what keeps the contents of the cell from leaking out? (If they did, the cell would lose vital substances and die.) In some way the plasma membrane must regulate the passage of substances through it.

In this investigation the movement of substances through membranes will be explored. Some of the membranes will be living plasma membranes, others will be from nonliving material but similar to the membranes of cells.

### a. Will Different Materials Move Through a Dialysis Membrane Equally?

#### MATERIALS

Scissors, about 30 cm of dialysis tubing, two 250-ml beakers, distilled water, one egg, string, balance, dropper, paper towel or other absorbent paper, sugar solution.

#### PROCEDURE

1. Cut the dialysis tubing into two equal lengths (about 15 cm). Twist one end as in Figure 6–B–1, fold the twisted end over and tie it tightly with a piece of string. Prepare both tubes the same way.
2. Carefully break the egg into one of the beakers and separate the yolk from the white. Add the white of the egg to the open end of one of the dialysis bags until it is about three-fourths full. Twist the end, fold it over, and tie tightly with string. Rinse the outside of the bag and dry it with absorbent paper. Discard the egg yolk.

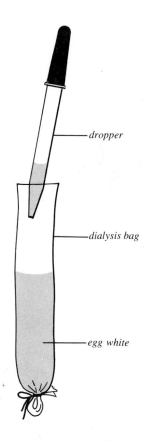

**Figure 6–B–1**  Set-up for dialysis bag.

3. Add sugar solution to the other dialysis bag and tie the open end securely. Rinse and dry as in step 2.
4. Weigh each bag to the nearest tenth of a gram and record each weight.
5. Place each bag in a separate beaker of distilled water for 10 minutes. Have only enough water in the beaker to cover the bag.
6. After 10 minutes remove each bag and dry with absorbent paper. Weigh the bags again. Record the weights.

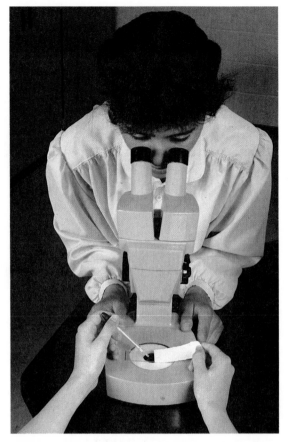

**Figure 6–B–2** Adding sugar or salt solution under a cover slip.

## DISCUSSION

1. What part of the setup was similar to the cell membrane?
2. Account for the change in weight of the two bags.
3. Egg white is a protein whose molecules are composed of several hundred atoms. Water molecules have 3 atoms ($H_2O$). What characteristic of the dialysis membrane would permit water to go in but not permit egg white to come out?
4. Sugar molecules are made of two dozen or so atoms, depending on the type of sugar used. Does this help explain the difference in the

change of weight between the two bags? Explain.
5. Recall the potato-core experiment in Investigation 1–B. Use the evidence from this Investigation (6–B) to explain why the core in distilled water gained weight while the core in 80% water lost weight.

## b. What is the Effect of Different Water Concentrations on the Live Cells of an *Elodea* Leaf?

### MATERIALS
*Elodea* leaf, sugar solution (20%) in dropper bottle, salt solution (5%) in dropper bottle, distilled water, slides and cover slips, microscope, absorbent paper.

### PROCEDURE
1. Place a leaf from the growing tip of *Elodea* in a drop of water on a clean slide. Cover with a cover slip and study under low power. Position the slide so that when you switch to high power you will be looking at the cells along one edge of the leaf.
2. Switch to high power and focus sharply on a few cells near the edge of the leaf. While you watch through the microscope, have your lab partner place a small piece of absorbent paper at the edge of the cover slip opposite the side of the leaf you are observing, as shown in Figure 6–B–2. (Remember, directions are reversed when you look through the microscope.) Then have your lab partner place several drops of sugar-water at the cover slip edge nearest the part of the leaf being observed. The absorbent paper will cause the sugar-water to flow under the cover slip and surround the cells you are observing. It may be necessary to adjust the

focus with the fine adjustment while the water is being replaced with sugar solution. Continue to observe until you see changes in the contents of the cells.

3. Make simple sketches showing the cells both before and after the sugar solution was added.

4. Remove the sugar solution and replace it with distilled water. Use a new piece of absorbent paper and allow two or three drops of distilled water to flow across the slide into the paper to make sure that most of the sugar solution is washed away. Make observations while this is being done by your lab partner.

5. Exchange places with your lab partner. Repeat steps 1, 2, 3, and 4.

6. Repeat steps 1, 2, 3, 4, with a salt solution in place of the sugar solution.

## DISCUSSION

1. Did water move into the cells or out of the cells while the leaf was surrounded by the sugar solution? By the salt solution? What evidence do you have to support your answer?

2. In which direction did the water move through the plasma membrane when the cell was surrounded by distilled water?

3. What do you think would happen to *Elodea* cells if they were left in a sugar solution for several hours? Could *Elodea* from a fresh-water lake be expected to survive if transplanted into the ocean? (Assume that the salt concentration of the ocean is about the same as the salt solution used in this experiment.)

4. An effective way to kill plants is to pour salt water on the ground around them. Explain why the plants die, using principles discovered in this investigation.

5. Bacteria cause food to spoil and meat to rot. Explain why salted pork, strawberry preserves, and sweet pickles do not spoil even though they are exposed to bacteria. Name other foods preserved by the same principle.

## c. Can Membranes of Living Cells Do More Than Membranes of Dead Cells?

### MATERIALS

Suspension of yeast cells in water, Congo Red solution in dropper bottles, 2 small test tubes, Bunsen burner or other source of heat, slides and cover slips, microscope, droppers, test-tube racks and holders.

### PROCEDURE

1. Place one drop of yeast suspension on a slide, cover with a cover slip, and observe the yeast cells under low power and then high power. Describe what you see and make sketches of two or three cells to show their general appearance.

2. Place about 1 ml of yeast suspension in each of two small test tubes. Heat one of the tubes until the contents have boiled for at least 30 seconds. This will kill the yeast cells. Allow the tube and its contents to cool for a few minutes.

3. Add 5 drops of Congo Red solution to the boiled yeast suspension and 5 drops to the unheated yeast suspension.

4. Prepare a slide from each tube and examine under high power. Record any differences between the yeast cells in the two suspensions.

### DISCUSSION

1. In a preparation of unheated yeast solution and Congo Red, a few red yeast cells are usually noticed. What assumption can you make concerning these cells?

2. What effect does heat seem to have on the yeast plasma membrane?

3. Which passes more easily through the membranes of living cells, Congo Red molecules or water molecules? Give a hypothesis that would account for your observation and answer.

## 6–C

## What is the Relationship Between Diffusion and Cell Size?

Does diffusion proceed rapidly enough to supply a cell efficiently with some of its materials? The same question can be asked about removing cell wastes. In this investigation you will discover how the rate of diffusion and the size of a cell are related.

### MATERIALS

3 cubes of 3% agar-phenolphthalein (1 cm, 2 cm, and 3 cm on a side), millimeter ruler, 100 ml of 4% hydrochloric acid solution (HCl), 250-ml beaker, plastic spoon, plastic table knife, paper towel.

### PROCEDURE

1. Measure the agar blocks and trim them to make cubes 3 cm, 2 cm, and 1 cm on a side.
2. Place the agar cubes in the beaker and pour in the hydrochloric acid until the blocks are submerged. Record the time. Turn the blocks frequently for the next 10 minutes.
3. Prepare a table like Table 6–A–1 and do the calculations necessary to complete it.

Surface area of a cube
= length × width × number of surfaces.

Volume of a cube
= length × width × height.

| Cube dimension | Surface area | Volume | Simplest ratio |
|---|---|---|---|
| 3 cm | | | |
| 2 cm | | | |
| 1 cm | | | |
| 0.01 cm | | | |

**Table 6–A–1**   Data table for agar blocks.

Ratio of surface area to volume

$$= \frac{\text{surface area}}{\text{volume}}$$

This ratio may also be written "surface area: volume." The ratio should be expressed in its simplest form (example: 3:1 rather than 24:8).

4. After 10 minutes remove the agar blocks from the hydrochloric acid and blot them dry. Avoid handling the blocks until they are blotted dry. If you wish, use the plastic knife to slice each block in half. Record your observations of the sliced surface. Measure the depth of diffusion of the hydrochloric acid in each of the three blocks.

### DISCUSSION

1. List the agar cubes in order of size, from largest to smallest. List them in the order of the ratios of surface area to volume, from the largest to the smallest ratio. How do the lists compare?
2. Calculate the surface area-to-volume ratio for a cube 0.01 cm on a side.
3. Which has the greater surface area, a cube 3 cm on a side or a microscopic cube the size of an onion skin cell? (Assume the cell to be 0.01 cm on a side.) Which has the greater surface area *in proportion to* its volume?
4. What evidence is there that hydrochloric acid diffuses into an agar block? What evidence is there that the rate of diffusion is about the same for each block? Explain.
5. What happens to the surface area-to-volume ratio of cubes as they increase in size?
6. Most cells and microorganisms measure less than 0.01 cm on a side. What is the relationship between rate of diffusion and cell size?
7. Propose a hypothesis to explain one reason why larger organisms have developed from *more* cells rather than *larger* cells.

# Light as Energy for Life

## 7–A

### Photosynthesis

It took many years to understand the process of photosynthesis. The materials and the products of photosynthesis are shown in the equation developed in Section 7–3:

carbon
dioxide + water

carbo-
hydrate + oxygen

$$CO_2 + H_2O \xrightarrow[\text{light}]{\text{plants}} CH_2O + O_2$$

Look at this equation for a short time. It can be used to raise several questions. These questions can serve as a basis for experiments that should help you to understand the process of photosynthesis.

a. Does a green plant use carbon dioxide in the light?
b. Is light necessary for this reaction to go on?
c. Are the materials shown in the equation involved in any plant processes other than photosynthesis?
d. Do plants release the excess oxygen that is produced by photosynthesis?

How would you design experiments to answer the questions above? You will have to make several decisions. These should be discussed before you set up the experiments.

a. What kind of plant could best serve your purpose, a water plant or a land plant?
b. What factor affecting photosynthesis could best be used to start and stop the process of photosynthesis?

c. What kind of detector can be used to show that photosynthesis has or has not occurred?
d. How can you identify the substances that are produced or given off during photosynthesis?

### a. Does a Green Plant Use CO$_2$ When Exposed to Light for a Period of Time?

**MATERIALS**
Bromthymol blue, *Elodea*, test tubes, stoppers, drinking straw, carbonated water.

**PROCEDURE**
1. Add some bromthymol blue to a test tube, and, with a straw, bubble your breath through it until you see a color change.
2. Add a few drops of carbonated water to a small amount of bromthymol blue in a test tube and observe any color change. Describe the change. What do the carbonated water and your breath have in common that might be responsible for the color change? What action would be necessary to restore the original color of the bromthymol blue after adding one of the above materials?
3. Using *Elodea*, bromthymol blue, and test tubes, set up an experiment of your own design to answer the question asked in the title of part **a**. Hint: Bromthymol blue is not poisonous to *Elodea*.

| Tube | Material Added (procedure) | Expected Indicator Change (hypothesis) | Actual Indicator Change (data) | What the Change Shows (interpretation) |
|------|---------------------------|----------------------------------------|--------------------------------|----------------------------------------|
| 1 | Bromthymol blue, *Elodea,* $CO_2$, and light | Yellow bromthymol blue will turn blue | | |

**Table 7–A–1**  Form for data table for chemical indicators, with sample entry.

## b. Is Light Necessary for a Green Plant to Carry On Photosynthesis?

### PROCEDURE

Using the same kinds of materials as in part **a**, set up an experiment to answer the question asked in part **b**. Use as many plants and tubes as necessary to be sure of your answer.

## c. Is $CO_2$ Taken In, Given Off, or Involved in Any Way While the Plant Is Not Carrying On Photosynthesis?

### PROCEDURE

Using the same kinds of materials, set up an experiment to answer the question of part **c**.

### DISCUSSION

1. Prepare a table listing the tubes you used. Show what you added to each tube, what change you expected in the bromthymol blue, and what change actually occurred. Give an explanation for the change. Table 7–A–1 is given as a sample. The first three columns of the table should be filled in on the day the experiments are set up. The last two columns are to be filled in the next day.

2. Do you have evidence from your experiment that light alone does not change the color of bromthymol blue? What tube or combination of tubes listed in your table shows this?

3. What tube or combination of tubes shows that light is necessary for a plant to carry on photosynthesis?

4. How is $CO_2$ involved in a plant that is not carrying on photosynthesis? What tubes or combination of tubes shows this? What biological process accounts for this?

5. Check your table and determine where your expected changes disagree with the actual changes. Are the differences, if any, due to experimental error or a wrong hypothesis on your part? Explain.

## d. Is Excess Oxygen Produced by a Green Plant That Is Carrying On Photosynthesis?

Your teacher or a selected group of students will set up a demonstration experiment to answer this question. Did you make any observations in the tubes of parts **a**, **b**, or **c** that indicate that the *Elodea* in light was giving off a gas of some kind? How might some of this gas be collected and tested to determine its identity?

# 7–B

## Do Plant Parts Without Chlorophyll Carry On Photosynthesis When in the Light?

Carbohydrates are an important product of photosynthesis. In fact, the total food supply of the earth is directly or indirectly dependent on the carbohydrates produced by plants. The primary food produced by photosynthesis is sugar, but many plants have enzymes in their cells that convert the sugar to starch. Starch is not readily soluble in water and will not diffuse out of the cells where it is made. Thus, plant cells that make sugar and then convert the sugar to starch can be easily detected with a starch indicator, iodine.

In this activity you will investigate the production of starch by a plant whose leaves are partly green and partly white.

### MATERIALS

2 *Coleus* plants (one that has been in the dark for 72 hours), ethyl or isopropyl alcohol (50–70%), forceps, two 250-ml beakers, 1000-ml beaker or pan, iodine solution, solid-top hot plate.

### PROCEDURE

1. Pick one of the healthy leaves from the plant that has been in the light and make a sketch of it showing the distribution of the chlorophyll.
2. Place the leaf in a beaker of boiling water and let it cook for 2 to 3 minutes.
3. Remove the leaf from the boiling water and submerge it in hot or boiling alcohol for about 3 minutes.

**CAUTION:** Do not heat alcohol over an open flame. Immerse a Pyrex beaker of alcohol in a larger beaker or pan of water being heated on a solid-top hot plate (not over a flame).

4. Remove the leaf from the alcohol and let it dry. After drying, submerge the leaf in a beaker of iodine solution for a minute or two. Sketch the leaf again, showing the distribution of starch as revealed by the iodine test.
5. Repeat steps 1, 2, 3, and 4 with a leaf from the plant that has been in the dark for 72 hours.

### DISCUSSION

1. What was the apparent effect of the hot alcohol on the cooked leaf?
2. What cells of the leaves apparently had sugar that was converted into starch?
3. Do all the green parts of a leaf necessarily have starch? Explain.
4. Suppose a fresh *Coleus* leaf, like the ones you experimented with, was placed in a weak solution of glucose for 12 hours. Assume that glucose will diffuse into the cells. Explain the situation that would result in the entire leaf turning black when tested with iodine.
5. Converting sugar into starch is a molecular activity in which many small molecules are linked together to make fewer large molecules. What kind of special substance must be present in the cell to activate this chemical action?
6. This experiment has shown that a plant must have two things in order to produce food. Name them.
7. What are the controls for this experiment?

# 7–C

## Does the Rate of Photosynthesis Depend on the Intensity of Light?

In other investigations it was determined that plants must have light to carry on photosynthesis. In this investigation you will explore the relationship between the photosynthesis rate and light intensity. Use the following background information and hints to design your own procedures to collect data that will determine the relationship between light intensity and photosynthesis rate.

## BACKGROUND

*Elodea* sprigs will carry on photosynthesis while in a test tube exposed to light and filled with water containing a pinch of sodium bicarbonate. The sodium bicarbonate goes through a chemical change and replaces the $CO_2$ that the plant takes from the water by photosynthesis. Thus, no change occurs in the $CO_2$ concentration that might affect the *Elodea's* photosynthesis rate.

Oxygen given off by the *Elodea* comes to the surface of the liquid in small uniform bubbles. Hint: Refer ahead to Investigation 18–A and determine how the volumetric apparatus used with the frog could be used to measure the photosynthetic rate of an *Elodea* sprig. You would need to set the jar upright instead of on its side. What would you put in the jar? How would you use another volumetric apparatus for a control?

Light intensity can be varied by using different-size bulbs in a reflector or by using one size of bulb and changing the distance between the bulb and the plant. Be sure to avoid the effect of temperature changes in the volumeter tubing due to closer light or larger bulbs.

## DISCUSSION

1. What control did you use to show that any changes that occurred were due to the activity of the *Elodea?*
2. Plot a graph showing the rates of photosynthesis in relation to different light intensities. Compare your graph with those of other groups.
3. From the results of this investigation would you hypothesize that a field of wheat does or does not produce more food on a bright sunny day than on a hazy or cloudy day?

## ADDITIONAL INVESTIGATIONS

1. Design an experiment to test the effect of light duration on the rate of photosynthesis. For example, test this rate of photosynthesis by *Elodea* under different periods of light and dark, giving the plant an equal total amount of light by varying the time between the light and dark periods.
2. From what you know about the color of chlorophyll and the absorption and reflection of light by colored materials, form a hypothesis about the effect of different colors of light on the rate of photosynthesis. For example, "Some colors are absorbed most strongly and should give the greatest photosynthesis. These colors are . . ." Then try to test your hypothesis.

You can control the color of light reaching the test plant by adding different dyes to the water surrounding the plant. Start with red, green, and blue. If time is available, try other colors as well. Use your ingenuity to make sure that the light intensity is about the same for each different color of light. A photographic light meter can be very helpful in determining light intensity. Prepare the red solution and measure the amount of light it transmits. Then prepare the green solution by adding green dye slowly to a fresh beaker of water until the light-meter reading is the same.

Prepare a table relating the rate of photosynthesis to the color of light. Then make a graph, plotting colors of light along the horizontal axis according to their order in the spectrum.

3. It is possible to use the same apparatus that you used in this investigation to obtain evidence concerning many other factors that influence photosynthesis. Temperature, $CO_2$ concentration, chlorophyll concentration in the green cells, or variations in the kinds of pigments in the green cells are a few additional factors whose role in photosynthesis you may wish to investigate.

# 7–D

## Is the Green Coloring in Leaves a Single Substance or a Mixture of Different Substances?

You noticed in Investigation 7–B that hot alcohol will remove the green color from leaves. As the leaves become pale in color the alcohol becomes green. Since this green substance is of such great importance in photosynthesis, and since photosynthesis is so important to the world's food supply, it is understandable that biologists and biochemists want to know all they can about the green substance in leaves.

In this investigation you will use a technique called paper chromatography to determine whether the green substance is a single substance or a mixture of substances. Paper chromatography is a technique that separates mixtures of substances into their separate components. Chemical tests can then be made on the separate components to help identify them.

### MATERIALS

Green leaves, two 250-ml beakers, 1000-ml beaker or pan, scissors, solvent mixture, wire hooks (made from paper clips), test tubes, hot plate, toothpicks, large test tube and stopper, filter paper strips, alcohol.

### PROCEDURE

1. Place several green leaves in a beaker of boiling water and let them cook for 2 or 3 minutes.
2. Remove the leaves from the water and place them in a beaker of boiling alcohol. Use only enough alcohol to cover the leaves in the bottom of the beaker. Boil for 2 to 3 minutes.

---

> **CAUTION:** Boil alcohol only in a double boiler. Put the beaker of alcohol in a larger beaker or pan of water on a solid-top hot plate. Do not use a Bunsen burner or an open-coil hot plate.

---

3. Remove the bleached leaves from the alcohol and discard them. Continue boiling the alcohol until the extract is dark green, almost black.
4. Make a J-shaped hook and push it into the bottom of the stopper. Attach the paper strip to the hook and lower it into the empty test tube. Trim the paper so that it hangs straight and nearly reaches the bottom of the tube.
5. Once the paper is fitted to the tube, remove it and apply the green leaf extract. Do this by dipping a toothpick into the extract and drawing a fine line with it across the filter paper about 2 cm from the bottom. Go over and over the line many times, letting the extract dry after each application. The finer and darker the line of extract, the better.
6. When the extract line is dry, pour some solvent into the tube. Add enough solvent so that the end of the paper strip when placed in the tube will be submerged, as in Figure 7–D–1. But be sure the extract line is not submerged.
7. Leave the tube still and in an upright position for 10 to 15 minutes or until the solvent mixture has risen to a point near the top of the paper strip.
8. Remove the paper strip (chromatogram) from the solvent mixture. Let it dry and then make notes and sketches of your observations.

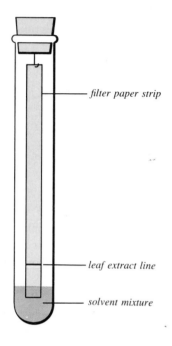

— filter paper strip

— leaf extract line

— solvent mixture

**Figure 7–D–1** Set-up for paper chromatography.

## DISCUSSION

1. Is the green pigment in leaves a single compound or a mixture of several compounds? Explain.

2. Chlorophyll is green. Is all of the pigment in the leaves you tested chlorophyll? Explain.

3. In the fall of the year most leaves on broad-leafed trees die and drop off. How do the observations of this investigation help to explain the various color changes that the leaves go through as they die?

4. How many color bands can you see on your chromatogram? How does this compare with what other groups found, using the same kind of leaves? How does the order of the bands compare with that found by other groups using different leaves?

5. If by special tests and instruments a certain band on your chromatogram was identified as chlorophyll $a$, how could you identify chlorophyll $a$ on someone else's chromatogram?

6. Carrots contain a pigment that gives them their distinct color. Is there any indication that the leaves you tested may have some of this same pigment? Explain.

# Life with Oxygen

## 8–A

## Does an Oxygen Supply Affect the Rate of Growth and Reproduction of Cells?

Oxygen is very important in the release of energy from food. Most organisms, including humans, cannot live without a constant supply of oxygen. Some organisms, however, can get energy from food without oxygen. There are a few kinds of microorganisms that will use oxygen if it is available, but if it is not available they can still get energy from food. In other words, some types of microorganisms are both aerobic and anaerobic. *Aerobacter aerogenes* (AIR-oh-back-ter air-AHJ-ih-neez) is the scientific name of a bacterium that can be either aerobic or anaerobic.

In this investigation you will be given data from an experiment with *Aerobacter aerogenes*. The bacteria were allowed to grow in test tubes containing distilled water to which only a few salts and various concentrations of glucose were added. Some of the tubes were sealed so that no air was available to the cells. Other tubes had a stream of air bubbling through the growth solution.

### PROCEDURES

Using the data shown in Table 8–A–1, construct two graph lines on the same graph. First plot "concentration of glucose" against the "number of bacteria" in series A (tubes without air). Label the vertical axis "millions of cells per ml" and the horizontal axis as "glucose (mg/100 ml)."

For the second graph line, plot the "concentration of glucose" against the "number of bacteria" in series B (tubes with air). Label the first graph line "Growth without air." Label the second line "Growth with air."

| Concentration of Glucose (milligrams per 100 ml of $H_2O$) | Number of Bacteria at Maximum Growth (millions per ml) | | | |
|---|---|---|---|---|
| | Tube no. | Tubes without air | Tube no. | Tubes with air |
| 18 | 1A | 50 | 1B | 200 |
| 36 | 2A | 90 | 2B | 500 |
| 54 | 3A | 170 | 3B | 800 |
| 72 | 4A | 220 | 4B | 1100 |
| 162 | 5A | 450 | 5B | 2100 |
| 288 | 6A | 650 | 6B | |
| 360 | 7A | 675 | 7B | |
| 432 | 8A | 675 | 8B | |
| 540 | 9A | 670 | 9B | |

Table 8–A–1 Effects of different glucose concentrations on growth of bacteria.

## DISCUSSION

1. What are the two most obvious differences between the two graph curves?

2. Look at Table 8–A–1 and compare tubes 4A and 4B. How many times greater was the growth when air was present?

3. Compare the other tubes in the A and B series at the various glucose concentrations. How much greater is the growth in air for each pair of tubes from 1A and B through 5A and B?

4. Notice that the number of bacteria are not given for tubes 6B, 7B, 8B, and 9B. How many bacteria would you predict in tube 6B? In 7B? These numbers were omitted from the table because they are so large.

5. After each tube reached maximum growth, the solution was tested for the presence of glucose. In all the tubes from 1A to 6A and from 1B to 9B there was no glucose. In contrast, tubes 7A, 8A, and 9A contained some glucose even

after maximum growth had been reached. Now compare tubes 4A and 4B. How many bacteria were produced per milligram of glucose in each case?

6. Now offer a hypothesis that can explain the numbers you calculated for question 5. Why are there so many cells per milligram of glucose in the B tubes?

7. Each milligram of glucose has an equal amount of energy available to do work. The B tubes produced more cells per milligram of glucose than did the A tubes. Assuming that each cell produced requires a certain amount of energy, which tubes should contain some products of glucose that still contain some "unused" energy?

8. In additional tests it was also determined that alcohol accumulates in the A tubes. How does this information relate to your answer concerning "unused" energy in question 7?

# Investigations for 9:

# Master Molecules

## 9–A

### Bacteria, Pneumonia, and DNA

Nucleic acids were known for 75 years before their importance in living cells was fully realized. The mystery of how DNA acts was first explored in bacteria. Research biologists first focused their attention on the role of DNA in a particular species of bacterium, *Diplococcus pneumoniae* (dih-plo-KOK-us new-MOH-nih-ee). As you might guess from its name, this is the type of bacterium that

causes the disease pneumonia. The name of the genus *Diplococcus* refers to the fact that the bacterial cells are in pairs and are round in shape (*diplo*, double, *coccus*, berry). A shorter, common name of the species, pneumococcus, is often used.

There are two main kinds of pneumococcus bacteria. In one kind, each pair of bacterial cells is surrounded by a capsule of a sugarlike substance. The other kind has no capsule around the cells. Figure 9–A–1 shows the two kinds. Both kinds can reproduce, giving rise to cells like themselves.

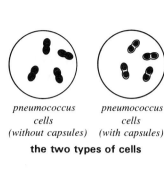

pneumococcus cells (without capsules)   pneumococcus cells (with capsules)

**the two types of cells**

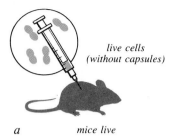

*a*   mice live

live cells (without capsules)

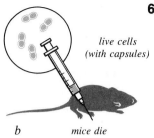

live cells (with capsules)

*b*   mice die

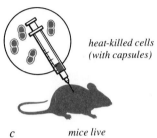

heat-killed cells (with capsules)

*c*   mice live

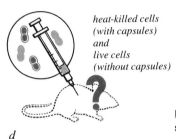

heat-killed cells (with capsules) and live cells (without capsules)

*d*

**Figure 9–A–1** Experiments with two strains of pneumococcus on mice.

When cells with capsules divide, they form new cells with capsules. Cells without capsules form new cells without capsules.

The capsule around the pneumococcus cells is related to another characteristic of these cells. The cells with capsules cause pneumonia and subsequent death when they are injected into mice. Pneumococcus cells without capsules do not cause pneumonia in the mice that are injected.

Because of the dangers involved in handling pneumococcus, it will not be possible for you to carry out any experiments using these disease-bearing bacteria. Below is a description of some experiments that have been performed. Your task is to analyze the results and propose hypotheses concerning the results of these experiments.

## Experiment 1

Healthy mice were injected with a few pneumococcus cells *without* capsules, as in part *a* of the figure. The mice remained healthy.

## Experiment 2

Healthy mice were injected with a few pneumococcus cells *with* capsules. The mice died. Autopsies showed that death was caused by pneumonia. (See part *b* of the figure.)

## Experiment 3

Pneumococcus cells with capsules were killed by heat. These dead cells with capsules were injected into healthy mice. The mice remained healthy. (See part *c* of the figure.)

## Experiment 4

In part *d* of Figure 9–A–1, healthy mice were injected with a mixture of living pneumococcus cells *without* capsules and a few heat-killed pneumococcus cells *with* capsules.

## DISCUSSION

1. Based on the results of Experiments 1, 2, and 3, what do you think happened to the mice in Experiment 4? Explain.
2. Assume that the mice died of pneumonia. Give a number of hypotheses that could account for their having pneumonia.

## Experiment 5

In the actual experiment like the one described in Experiment 4 the mice did get pneumonia and die. The scientists proposed a hypothesis to explain this. Perhaps somehow the pneumococcus cells without capsules gained the ability to produce capsules and could pass this ability along to their offspring. Remember that the capsule must be present for the cells to cause pneumonia. To test this hypothesis, the scientists prepared a mixture of nutrients in which the pneumococcus cells could grow outside the body of a living thing. Such a mixture of nutrients is called a **culture medium.** The experimenters could grow the pneumococcus cells in a culture medium in petri dishes and observe them with microscopes to see whether capsules were formed or not.

The experimenters first grew large numbers of pneumococcus cells with capsules. They then killed these cells, ground them up, and dissolved them in a solution. Such a solution, called an **extract,** contained the materials ordinarily within the cell membranes.

The extract from heat-killed cells with capsules was mixed with living cells without capsules. This mixture was added to a culture medium and allowed to grow, as in Figure 9–A–2, part *a*.

## DISCUSSION

1. According to the results of Experiment 4, what is the most logical hypothesis as to the type or types of bacteria found growing on the culture medium of Experiment 5?

## Experiment 6

Some of the cells from Experiment 5 were injected into healthy mice, as in part *b* of Figure 9–A–2.

## DISCUSSION

1. Assume that the mice died of pneumonia in Experiment 6. What conclusion could be made about the cells growing on the culture medium of Experiment 5?
2. Could these cells have produced pneumonia in mice before they were grown on the special culture medium of Experiment 5? Why?
3. In the actual experiment like the one in Experiments 5 and 6, microscopic examination showed the presence of live cells with capsules. These cells could reproduce to form more bacteria with capsules. When these were

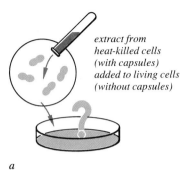

*extract from heat-killed cells (with capsules) added to living cells (without capsules)*

*a*

**Figure 9–A–2**

*b*

injected into mice, they caused pneumonia. How did the bacteria differ after they were grown on the special culture medium? Was this difference only in their structure? Explain.

Hint: Not only were the original cells that were placed on the special medium changed, but their offspring also showed the same new characteristic.

## Experiment 7

At the Rockefeller University in New York City, Oswald Avery, Colin McLeod, and Maclyn McCarty worked to find the part of the extract from the dead cells that caused the change in hereditary material. They wanted to find what it was that made it possible for cells without capsules to produce cells with capsules. They performed very careful experiments in which each part of the extract was tested. They hypothesized that some particular molecule in the extract was being taken up by the living cell and that this molecule was responsible for the new hereditary information. The molecule was finally identified as DNA. Pneumococcus characteristics had been changed as a result of the incorporation of DNA molecules from the extract.

**DISCUSSION**

1. What apparently happens to the DNA of the pneumococcus cells when they divide to form new cells?

2. With what you now know about DNA molecules, give an explanation of what happened in Experiment 4 to cause the mice to die from a pneumonia infection.

# Investigations for 10:

# The Genetic Code

## 10-A

### How Can Mutant Strains of Bacteria Be Isolated?

Because of their small size, rapid rate of reproduction, and relatively simple structure, bacteria are excellent subjects for laboratory studies. This investigation will introduce you to techniques of microbiology that will be of use to you throughout your biological work.

**a. How to Handle Bacteria** Bacteria are everywhere. They can contaminate anything if the necessary precautions are not taken. Even some of the "tamest" bacteria can cause infections if enough are present. You must exercise particular care in all your laboratory procedures in this investigation. Read and remember the following rules. Then practice the suggested techniques. If you have difficulty in mastering any part of this work, be sure to consult your instructor.

**GENERAL RULES**

1. Do not eat in the laboratory.
2. Do not put anything in your mouth in the laboratory. Learn to keep hands and all objects away from your face and mouth.
3. Do not drink from laboratory glassware or utensils.
4. Be as careful and as clean as possible in the use of all laboratory equipment, including microscopes, desks, and so on.
5. In case a live culture is spilled, notify the instructor immediately and disinfect your hands.
6. Always sterilize all cultures before disposing of them. Your instructor will direct how this is to be done.
7. Dispose of liquid waste and agar only in the containers provided for this purpose.
8. At the conclusion of the laboratory, return all equipment to its place and wash the desk tops with disinfectant.
9. Never open petri dishes containing cultures until the dishes are ready to be cleaned. They may contain harmful organisms.

**HOW TO TRANSFER SAMPLES**

All work with bacterial cultures depends on the technique of transferring samples without contaminating them. Carefully observe the demonstration that your instructor will conduct. Then practice the technique without bacteria until you can perform the transfer quickly and smoothly.

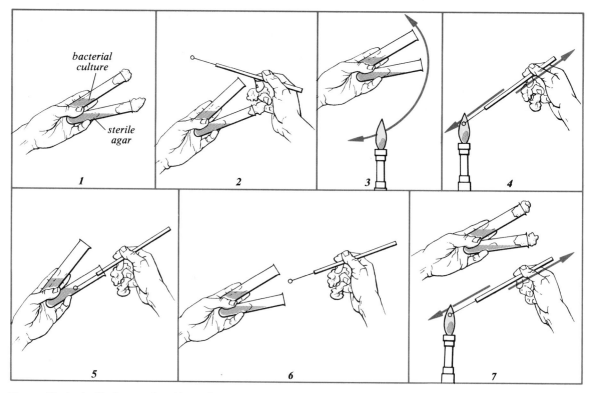

**Figure 10–A–1** Sterile transfer of bacteria.

1. Hold both the test tube containing the bacterial culture and a test tube of sterile agar in your left hand at the angle shown in Figure 10–A–1. Hold the loop or needle in your right hand. (If you are left-handed, you will find it easier to reverse this procedure.)

2. With your right hand, remove the plugs from both test tubes.

3. Flame the mouth of each test tube by passing it through the flame twice.

4. Heat the transfer loop until it glows orange.

5. Cool the loop by laying it along the surface of the agar in the sterile test tube.

6. With the loop remove a small amount of bacterial culture from the surface of the agar and immediately transfer it to the surface of the sterile medium. Do not dig into the agar. The

pressure of the weight of the loop is enough to apply a sample of living bacteria to the culture medium.

7. Flame the loop and pass the mouth of each test tube through the flame as before. Replace the cotton plugs, each in the tube from which it came. Set the test tubes in the test tube rack.

---

**CAUTION:** Throughout the transfer remember that both the glass and the wire will be hot enough to burn your fingers for some time after being passed through the flame.

---

These techniques are not difficult. When you can perform the transfer correctly, proceed with the experiment.

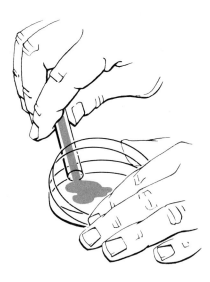

**Figure 10–A–2** Pouring heated agar from test tube to petri dish.

## b. Bacterial Resistance to Antibiotics

### MATERIALS

Pure cultures of *Bacillus cereus,* test tubes of sterile nutrient agar, antibiotic disks (penicillin and aureomycin); forceps soaking in 70% alcohol, sterilized petri dishes, Bunsen burner, transfer loops, water bath at 100 °C.

### PROCEDURE

1. Heat the test tubes of sterile agar medium in the water bath until the agar melts.
2. Remove the test tubes from the water bath. Let them cool enough to hold in your hand, but not so much that the agar becomes solid again. Perform the following transfer as quickly as possible. You must work rapidly so that the liquid agar will not cool and solidify before the transfer is completed.
3. Hold both a test tube of warm agar medium and the test tube containing the culture of bacteria in your left hand. Remove the cotton plugs and pass the mouth of each test tube through the burner flame twice. Flame the loop and cool it. Pick up a loopful of the bacterial culture and transfer it to the warm agar in the second test tube. Shake the loop in the liquid a few times and then remove the transfer loop. Flame the loop and the mouth of each test tube and replace the cotton plugs.
4. Roll the test tube of warm agar between the palms of your hands to mix the bacteria with the agar. Remove the cotton plug and flame the mouth of the test tube. Lift the cover of the sterile petri dish at an angle of slightly more than 45°. Keep the lifted cover directly over the bottom half of the petri dish to avoid contamination as much as possible, as in Figure 10–A–2. Pour the agar into the bottom half of the dish. Be certain that the mouth of the test tube does not touch either half of the petri dish. Remove the test tube and lower the cover. Move the covered petri dish gently along the table top in a figure-eight pattern to distribute the agar evenly. Allow the agar to cool until it becomes firm.
5. Remove the forceps from the 70% alcohol and pass the tips very quickly through the burner flame. Use the forceps to remove the penicillin disks from the container. Try to avoid contaminating the remaining disks with the forceps. Place the penicillin disks on one side of the agar medium by barely raising the top of the petri dish. Then rapidly pass the forceps through the flame again and pick up one of the aureomycin disks. Place this disk on the other side of the agar surface, as in Figure 10–A–3. Flame the forceps and replace them in the alcohol.
6. After a few minutes turn the dish upside down. Let it stand at room temperature, or in an incubator, to allow the bacteria to grow. Observe the dish the next day and on several following days. Describe the color and shape of any bacterial colonies and other features you observe.

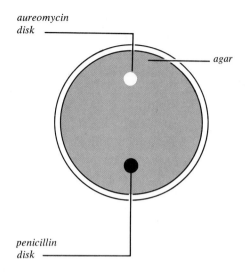

aureomycin disk

agar

penicillin disk

**Figure 10–A–3** Set-up for petri dish with agar and two antibiotic disks.

## DISCUSSION

1. Different bacteria usually produce colonies with different appearances. Do you think that more than one species of bacteria is present in your petri dish? Why do you think so?
2. What areas, if any, are free of bacterial colonies? Why?
3. Which clear area is larger, the one around the penicillin disk or the one around the aureomycin disk?
4. Why might one area be larger than the other?
5. For what purpose might these disks be useful in medical research?
6. Examine the clear area around each disk. You may find one or more small colonies in this area. If you find a colony in this area, how can you account for it?
7. Mutant bacteria that were resistant to the antibiotics probably were present in the original *Bacillus* culture. Why were they not noticed before the experiment? Why do they appear in the clear area?

8. How can you determine whether this colony may have developed because the antibiotic had lost its potency?
9. Assume that there is a penicillin-resistant strain and an aureomycin-resistant strain isolated in the respective clear areas of the culture medium. What kind of experiment could be done to determine whether the strain resistant to one antibiotic is also resistant to the other antibiotic?
10. How would you explain the results of an experiment that showed that penicillin-resistant bacteria are not resistant to aureomycin and that the aureomycin-resistant strain is not resistant to penicillin?
11. Describe an experiment that would be a logical attempt at producing a strain of bacteria resistant to both antibiotics.

## 10–B

# Effects of Radiation on Microorganisms

Exposure to radiation can be fatal to an organism. Within a species, individual organisms vary considerably in the amount of radiation they can tolerate. The most convenient way to describe the effect of radiation on a particular species, therefore, is to speak of some average fatal dose. Such a dose has been defined as the amount of radiation that will kill just 50% of the individuals in a species. (The other half of the population would be killed only if the radiation dose were greater than the average fatal dose.) The term LD–50 means "lethal dose for 50% of the population." In this experiment you will determine the LD–50 for a population of yeast cells.

## MATERIALS

Dry yeast, potato-dextrose or grape-juice agar, sterile petri dishes, germicidal ultraviolet lamp, stopwatch (or clock with a second hand), 1-liter

Erlenmeyer flask with cotton plug, graduated cylinder (or 1-liter volumetric flask), metric ruler, sterile distilled water, sterile pipettes, incubator.

## PROCEDURE

1. If the petri dishes of agar have not already been prepared for you, melt the agar and pour it into 10 sterile petri dishes, using careful, sterile techniques. Label these dishes 1 to 10.
2. Weigh out 0.75 g of dry yeast and suspend it in a 1-liter Erlenmeyer flask of sterile distilled water. Plug with cotton and swirl to mix thoroughly. Pipette 5 ml of the yeast suspension into an empty, sterile petri dish. Using a sterile pipette, transfer 0.1 ml of the yeast suspension to the agar in the petri dishes labeled 1 and 2. Spread the suspension evenly over the surface of the agar by rotating the dish gently in a figure-eight motion. These two dishes will have no exposure to ultraviolet radiation.
3. Set the ultraviolet lamp 10 cm above the table top and turn it on. Place the petri dish containing the 5 ml of yeast suspension under the lamp for exactly 5 seconds.

---

**CAUTION:** Do not look directly into the lamp. It is harmful to the eyes.

---

4. Remove the yeast suspension from under the lamp. Using a sterile pipette as you did in step 2, transfer 0.1 ml of the irradiated yeast suspension to the agar in petri dish number 3. Spread as directed in step 2. Mark the cover of the petri dish to indicate the length of exposure (5 seconds).
5. In the same manner, irradiate the 5-ml yeast suspension 10 seconds more. The yeast cells have now been exposed to the ultraviolet light for a total of 15 seconds. Add 0.1 ml of the irradiated yeast suspension to petri dish number 4. Repeat the irradiation of yeast samples for exposures of 30 and 60 seconds, and 2, 5, 10, and 20 minutes. Add 0.1 ml of the irradiated sample to a different one of the numbered petri dishes after each exposure. Mix each as directed above and mark the dish with its exposure time.
6. Then incubate all 10 inoculated agar plates in the dark at about 25°C for 48 hours. During this incubation period, any surviving cells will multiply sufficiently to form visible colonies.
7. Count the number of colonies formed in each of the nonirradiated cultures of cells. Let the average number of colonies present in these control cultures represent 100% survival. Then compare the number of colonies in each irradiated culture with the average number of colonies in the two untreated cultures to find the percent of survivors. One hundred percent minus the percent of survivors is the percent of cells killed by the radiation treatment.
8. Prepare a graph with "time exposed to irradiation" on the horizontal axis and "percent of original population killed" on the vertical axis. Be especially careful in plotting the time on the horizontal axis. Remember that each square on the graph paper is supposed to represent a certain number of seconds or minutes; the points representing 10 minutes and 20 minutes, therefore, will be much farther apart than the points representing 15 seconds and 30 seconds. Draw a smooth curve through the points.

## DISCUSSION

1. Approximately what length of exposure kills one half the cells? To answer this question draw a straight horizontal line from the point on the vertical axis representing 50% fatalities. Where this line intersects the curve, drop a vertical line to the time scale and read the time.
2. How can you explain the shape of the curve?
3. If you were planning a similar experiment, using the same techniques and exposure times

but a different species of microorganism, would you be able to use information from this experiment to predict the LD–50 for the new species? Explain.

4. Would the shape of the curve obtained for this new species be about the same? Explain.

## 10–C

## What Controls the Synthesis of Large Molecules in an Organism?

George W. Beadle and Edward L. Tatum of Stanford University in the early 1940's directed their scientific research to the question asked in this investigation title. They used a common pink mold called *Neurospora* to determine if the mold spores that start a new generation carry the instructions for building the large specialized molecules that characterize the organisms. It was known that *Neurospora* spores can be cultured on a medium containing only small and simple types of molecules, although the mold makes large complex molecules during growth.

In this investigation you will analyze the results of some experiments similar to those conducted by Beadle and Tatum. For the sake of simplicity, the problems will be restricted to *Neurospora's* ability to synthesize amino acids and vitamins.

### Experiment 1

*Neurospora* spores were placed on agar containing only salts, sugar, and biotin (a vitamin). From now on this will be referred to as the **simple medium.** At the spore stage of the life cycle, the spores were exposed to X-ray irradiation. Single irradiated spores were then placed upon agar that had many vitamins and all 20 amino acids in addition to the substances in the simple medium. This medium will be referred to as the **complete medium.** These spores developed and grew into new mold that produced spores. Some of these spores were then placed on simple medium, and some on complete medium, as in Figure 10–C–1.

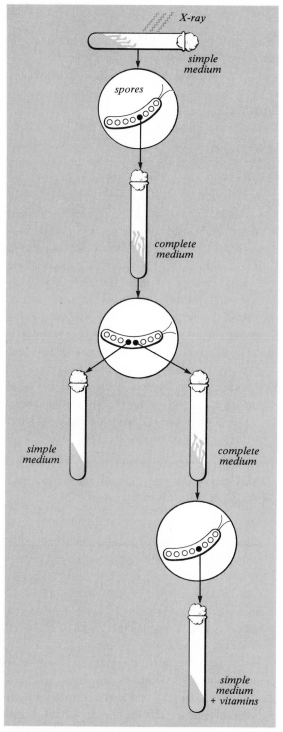

**Figure 10–C–1** Survival requirements for *Neurospora* following irradiation of spores.

All the spores grew on the complete medium, but some did not grow on the simple medium.

## DISCUSSION

1. Which statement best describes the results of this first experiment with *Neurospora?*

    a. X rays kill *Neurospora* spores.

    b. X rays changed something in the spores that interfered with the synthesis of vitamins.

    c. X rays changed something in the spores that interfered with the synthesis of amino acids.

    d. X rays changed something in the spores that interfered with the synthesis of vitamins or amino acids or both.

2. What experiment would now be necessary to determine the change that the X rays produced?

## Experiment 2

Spores from *Neurospora* that would not grow on the simple medium but did grow on the complete medium were then placed on agar in which all the vitamins were added but no amino acids. This is represented in the lower part of Figure 10–C–1. The spores did not grow.

## DISCUSSION

1. Which of the choices in Discussion question 1 of Experiment 1 now most completely describes the effect that X rays had on *Neurospora?*

2. Propose the next step in the experiment now that you know that the irradiated spores will grow on simple medium plus amino acids and vitamins but will not grow on simple medium plus vitamins alone.

## Experiment 3

Beadle and Tatum decided that the X rays had changed or mutated the *Neurospora* so that the spores no longer grew without an outside supply of amino acids. Further experiments showed that the irradiated spores would grow on a simple medium to which all 20 amino acids were added.

## DISCUSSION

1. Is there any way of knowing from these experiments if all amino acids are required?

2. Describe the kind of experiment that would determine if a certain amino acid is sufficient for the irradiated spores to grow.

## Experiment 4

Twenty separate tubes were prepared, each with a simple medium and a different amino acid. Nineteen tubes showed no growth. In one of the tubes the amino acid called arginine had been added to the simple medium. In this tube growth occurred.

## DISCUSSION

1. Describe now the effect that the X rays had on the *Neurospora* spores. Be more specific than you have been in previous descriptions.

## Experiment 5

Beadle and Tatum discovered that some of the irradiated spores requiring arginine would grow if substances similar to arginine were added. In fact they discovered three ways to get some of the mutated spores to grow (add ornithine, citrulline, or arginine) and two ways to get others to grow (add citrulline or arginine). But some would grow only if arginine was added to the medium. The first of these types, which would grow with any of the three substances, they called type 1. The second, needing either citrulline or arginine, was type 2, and the mutants that would grow only with arginine were type 3. (See Figure 10–C–2.) The molecular structure of these three substances is quite similar, as you can see by examining Figure 10–7.

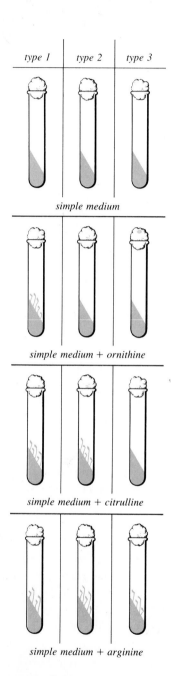

*simple medium*

*simple medium + ornithine*

*simple medium + citrulline*

*simple medium + arginine*

**Figure 10–C–2** Isolation of three types of mutant *Neurospora* spores by growth on simple media supplemented with different amino acids.

## DISCUSSION

1. If ornithine were added to the simple medium and spores from mutant type 3 were placed on the medium, what results would you expect?
2. What would you expect if you used mutant type 2? type 1?
3. What substance would mutant type 2 need to synthesize its own arginine?
4. What substance would mutant type 1 need to make its own citrulline and arginine?
5. In Figure 10–7, which molecule is the most complex? Which is the simplest?
6. What modifications would be necessary to change ornithine into citrulline? citrulline into arginine?
7. The chemical changes discussed in question 6 could go on naturally but they would take a long time. What substances in living cells bring about these changes at a more rapid rate?
8. Which of the following hypotheses would be more reasonable?

   a. DNA coding is directly responsible for the formation of arginine.
   b. DNA coding directs the formation of enzymes which in turn direct the formation of arginine.

9. It seems that some substance in the medium is converted into ornithine by a particular enzyme. Ornithine is converted into citrulline and then arginine by still other enzymes. These different enzymes are present because of the particular coding of the DNA. Form some hypotheses concerning the effects of the X rays that produced the different mutant strains of *Neurospora*. Hint: Ask yourself, where, in the sequence of molecular buildup, has the mutation occurred? What has been affected by the X rays?

# Investigations for 11:

# Reproduction

## 11–A

## What Are Some of the Cell's Nuclear Activities That Precede the Division of One Cell into Two Cells?

To study cell division you will examine groups of cells that have been preserved and then stained. Their nuclear structures will be visible with the ordinary compound microscope. Some of the cells you will see are at very early stages of cell division, some are at later stages, and others may be between cell divisions. Only through painstaking study over a period of many years have biologists been able to trace, from such slides as these, the steps a dividing cell goes through. It is very difficult to tell from slides just which stages come first and which come later. Keep this in mind as you try to reconstruct the process for yourself.

### MATERIALS
Compound microscope, prepared slide of root tip cells, prepared slide of animal embryo cells (*Ascaris* or whitefish), modeling clay (two colors).

### PROCEDURE
1. Place the slide of root tip cells on the microscope stage and examine it under low power. Scan the entire section. Observe that cells far from the tip and cells right at the tip are not actively dividing. Locate the region of active cell division between these two regions.
2. Change to the high-power objective. As you observe the cells, focus up and down slowly with the fine adjustment knob to bring different structures into sharp focus. Find cells at various stages of division. When the slide was prepared, each cell was killed at a different stage of a continuous process. The cells can be compared to scrambled, single frames of a motion picture. Figure out how you would piece the frames of the motion picture together. Refer to Figure 11–2. Make sketches from your slide of *interphase, prophase, metaphase, anaphase,* and *telophase* as described in Section 11–2. Identify each by name.
3. Examine a slide of developing *Ascaris* or of whitefish embryos. Find a cell in which the chromosomes are long and threadlike. Try to count the number of individual chromosomes. (In *Ascaris* eggs this is easy, but in the whitefish embryos it is almost impossible.)
4. Find a cell in which the chromosomes are at the equator of the spindle. Compare the poles of this spindle with those of the spindles in the dividing plant cells you have studied.
5. Find a cell in which the chromosomes are separating and the cell has begun to pinch together in the middle. Compare this method of separation of the new cells with the method you observed in plant cells. What structures do you see in the dividing animal cell that were also present in the dividing plant cell? What structures were not in the dividing plant cell?
6. Refer to Figure 11–A–1 and place cells numbered 2, 7, 9, 11, 12, 13, 16, and 33 in the order in which these stages would occur if you were watching one cell go through mitosis.
7. With two colors of clay and four large sketches of a plant cell, model each stage of mitosis, from prophase to telophase, for a plant cell with two pairs of chromosomes.

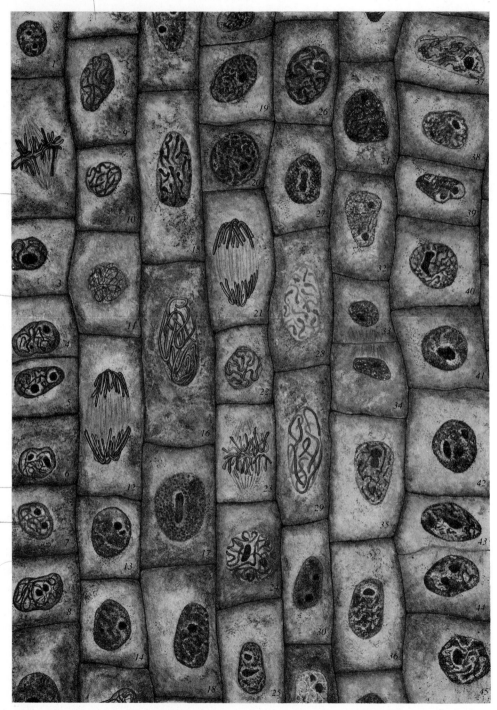

**Figure 11–A–1** Drawing of dividing cells in an onion root as seen through a compound microscope. Arrange cells 2, 7, 9, 11, 12, 13, 16, and 33 in the correct order, demonstrating stages in mitosis.

## DISCUSSION

1. How is mitosis in plant and animal cells similar? List the similarities.
2. How does mitosis in plant and animal cells differ? List the differences.
3. Compare the number and types of chromosomes in the two new nuclei of the clay model with the number and types from the original parent nucleus.
4. If mitosis occurs in a cell but cell division does not occur, what is the result?

# 11–B

## Reproduction in Flowering Plants

If you have ever noticed the flowers of grasses, oak or maple trees, or the various common weeds, you know that flowers are not always beautiful and showy. In fact, the flowers of different kinds of plants vary considerably in structure. Their general function, however, is always the same—to carry on the sexual reproduction of the plant. In this exercise you will study the structure of a flower to observe how it is adapted for its function.

## MATERIALS

Flowers, scalpel or razor blade, forceps, slides and cover slips, hand lens or stereoscopic microscope, monocular microscope.

## PROCEDURE

1. Examine the flower carefully. Compare it to the diagram in Figure 11–B–1 and identify the parts. In what ways is the flower you are examining similar to the diagram, and in what ways different? Compare your flower with the flowers in Figure 3-A-1, page 580.
2. Remove the **sepals** first and then the **petals.** Of what importance are these structures to the function of the flower?
3. The **stamens** are the pollen-producing parts of the flower. If the **anthers** are mature, shake

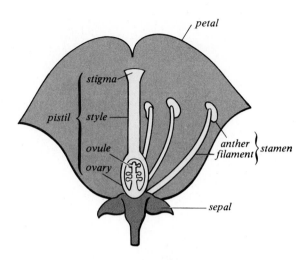

**Figure 11–B–1** Diagram of parts of a flower.

some of the pollen into a drop of water on a slide. Add a cover slip and examine the pollen under the high power of the microscope. Compare the shapes and sizes of pollen from different kinds of flowers. Sketch some of the pollen as it appears under high power.

4. Remove the **pistil** or pistils. Examine one pistil with a hand lens or stereoscopic microscope to see if there is any pollen on it. What is the stigma's special adaptation for holding the pollen that lands on it?
5. Locate the **ovary,** the thickened portion of the pistil. Carefully cut across the ovary so that you can examine the parts inside it. The **ovules** in the ovary are immature seeds. Determine whether this flower would have produced a single seed (like a peach), several seeds (like an apple), or many seeds.
6. If time and materials are available, examine other kinds of flowers. Compare the number of various parts and the way the parts are arranged with respect to each other. These features are important in classifying flowering plants, as you learned in Investigation 3–A.

**Figure 11–C–1** The thousands of eggs in the background were laid by one female frog.

## DISCUSSION

1. Prepare a brief description of the flower. Make sketches to clarify your description.
2. Describe how the flower parts are involved in sexual reproduction and seed formation.

## 11–C

## What Regulates the Schedule of Egg-Laying by Female Frogs?

Female frogs produce eggs during the early spring months, but these eggs are kept in the ovaries until the following spring. Then the eggs are laid. What is there about the frog's internal or external environment that influences her behavior and causes the eggs to be released from the ovaries at a specific time of year? This question, and others, will be explored during this investigation.

## MATERIALS

2 living, mature female frogs, 1 living, mature male frog, 5-cc hypodermic syringe with small needle (No. 18 or No. 19), 80 ml of 10% Holtfreter's solution, distilled water, dissecting kit, dissecting pan, 2 large gallon jars (containers for frogs), 2 pieces of cheesecloth and strong rubber bands, 4 culture dishes (about 10 cm in diameter), glass stirring rod, 2 cc of pituitary preparation, clear plastic wrap.

## a. What Brings About Egg-Laying by the Female Frog at a Specific Time of Year?

Two observations are evident as the time of year approaches for frogs to lay eggs. One, the male and female frogs occupy the same general area; two, the concentration of pituitary hormone increases in the female's blood. As far as the female frog is concerned, the warming of the air and water in spring and the presence of the male frog are a part of the external environment, while the pituitary increase in the blood is an internal environmental change. Which of these has the greatest impact on the reproductive process in the female frog?

**PROCEDURE**

1. Inject 2 cc of distilled water under the skin of the lower abdomen of one of the female frogs. Be very careful not to puncture the internal organs. Put her with the male frog in a large jar. Put cheesecloth over the jar and secure it tightly with a rubber band. Place this jar in a controlled environment, with the temperature and light as much like early spring as possible.

2. Inject 2 cc of the pituitary preparation under the skin of the lower abdomen of the other female frog. Put her in a gallon jar, cover with cheesecloth, and store it under the same conditions as for the other frogs. Label the jars.

3. After 24 to 48 hours remove the female frogs from their containers and check for their readiness to lay eggs. To do this, hold the frog in one hand with her back against your palm. Flex the frog's legs with the other hand while you gently squeeze her abdomen. Start the squeezing action with the first finger just below her front legs and progress downward with the other fingers. This "milking" action will force eggs from the frog if she is in an egg-laying condition. If the experimental treatment has not promoted her readiness to lay, you will not be able to get any eggs by this technique. (Do not injure the frog by squeezing too hard.) If eggs appear, stop the milking action until you are ready to collect the eggs in large numbers. If no eggs appear from either frog, return them to the proper place and try again 24 hours later.

## b. Is Immediate Fertilization Necessary for Normal Frog Embryonic Development?

The natural reproductive process involves immediate fertilization of eggs by the male frog as soon as they are laid by the female. Will fertilization occur and development follow if eggs and sperm are put together 5 or 10 minutes after egg-laying?

**PROCEDURE**

Start only when frog eggs are available.

1. Double-pith the male frog (a technique your teacher will either do for you or give you instructions for, so that you can do it yourself). Open the body cavity of the male frog by inserting the scissors through the skin and muscle wall of the lower abdomen and continuing the cut forward to a point between the front legs. Make lateral cuts at both ends of this first incision so that flaps of skin and muscle can be opened to expose the organs of the abdominal cavity. Pin the flaps of skin and muscle to the bottom of the dissecting pan so that the internal organs are visible.

2. Locate the testes by pushing the stomach and intestines aside. The testes are small, yellow bean-shaped organs lying near the back wall of the abdominal cavity (Figure 11–C–2).

3. With the point of the scissors, detach the testes and remove them from the frog's body. Place both testes in a thin film of 10% Holtfreter's solution in the bottom of one of the culture dishes. Label this dish T. With the scalpel or scissors, cut the testes into small pieces and then crush the pieces with the flat end of the glass stirring rod. Add 20 ml of 10% Holtfreter's solution to the crushed testes. Mark the time you add the Holtfreter's solution.

4. Look at drops of the sperm suspension under the high-power lens of your microscope. Watch for any movement in the sperm. Observe a drop of the sperm suspension at the time it is prepared and about 10 minutes later.

5. Add 20 ml of 10% Holtfreter's solution to three other dishes. Label them A, B, and C.

6. About 10 minutes after the testes were crushed, add about one third of dish T to dish

A. Milk part of the eggs from the female frog directly into dish A. Move the frog around while squeezing the eggs out so that they will not all pile up in one place. Move the female over dish B, which contains only Holtfreter's solution, and continue to strip out more eggs. Mark the time. Continue to dish C, depositing eggs in it. Mark the time. You should now have 3 dishes, each containing about 20 ml of Holtfreter's solution and numerous frog eggs. The first dish also contains frog sperm. With scissors cut the masses of eggs in each dish into small bunches of about 6–12 eggs per bunch.

7. With a dropper take up some sperm suspension from around the eggs in dish A and with it bathe the eggs in dish A several times for the next 5 minutes.

8. Five minutes from the time you added eggs to dish B, take about one third of the sperm suspension from dish T and with it bathe the eggs of dish B. Bathe the eggs several times with this amount of sperm suspension.

9. Ten minutes after depositing eggs in dish C, add about one third of the sperm suspension to them, using the same technique.

10. Observe the eggs and record any changes and any differences among the three masses of eggs that occur in the next 10 minutes.

11. Flood the eggs in each dish with Holtfreter's solution, allow to stand for 5 minutes, and pour off. Cover the eggs with pond water or Holtfreter's solution.

12. If possible observe the eggs carefully during the next hour. Then store the eggs in the place designated by your teacher. Put the female frogs back in their proper place and save for tomorrow's study. Wrap the remains of the male frog in plastic wrap, label, and put in refrigerator.

13. After 24 hours, examine the eggs in the three dishes with a good hand lens or dissecting

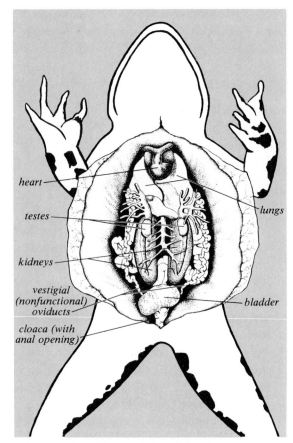

**Figure 11–C–2** Dissected male frog, with some internal organs and tissues moved or removed to expose the reproductive system.

microscope. Which dish contains eggs that seem to be developing? What evidence is there that the eggs are developing?

**c. How Do the Eggs Get from the Ovary to the Outside of the Frog's Body?** The only opening from the organs of the frog's abdomen is the anal opening. This is where the eggs emerge when they are laid. Dissection of the frog to expose the abdominal organs will show that the ovaries are not in direct contact with a passageway leading to the anus. How then, do the eggs get from the ovaries to the outside of the body?

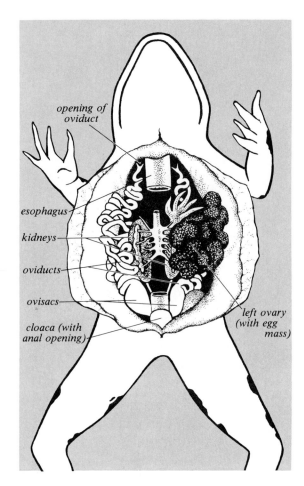

with labels: opening of oviduct, esophagus, kidneys, oviducts, ovisacs, cloaca (with anal opening), left ovary (with egg mass)

**Figure 11–C–3** Dissected female frog, with respiratory, circulatory, and digestive organs removed to expose the reproductive system and egg mass.

## PROCEDURE

1. Double-pith the two female frogs and open their body cavities in the way described for the male frog in part **b**, step 1.
2. Locate the ovaries of the female that did not produce eggs in part **a**. (See Figure 11–C–3.) Describe the appearance of the ovaries.
3. In the frog that produced eggs, see if you can find the pathway that the eggs took in getting from the ovaries to the outside. Cut open organs or tubes that you think might serve as a pathway to see if some eggs might still be present. A comparison of the internal organs of the male with the female will help in locating organs involved in egg-laying.

## DISCUSSION

1. What brings about egg-laying in the female frog? Give experimental evidence to support your answer.
2. From part **a**, do you know what conditions of temperature and day length are necessary? If not, how could this be tested?
3. Why was distilled water injected into the first female frog?
4. Is immediate fertilization necessary for normal embryonic development? Give experimental evidence to support your answer.
5. How do the eggs get from the ovary to the outside of the body? How does this compare with the path of the mammalian egg discussed in Section 11–15?
6. Describe differences in the ovaries and oviducts in the two female frogs you examined.

## ADDITIONAL INVESTIGATIONS

1. Referring to the chart in Figure 11–C–4, continue to observe the eggs for the next several days and keep a record of changes observed.
2. With the aid of Figures 11–C–2 and 11–C–3, locate and identify other organs of the internal anatomy of a frog.
3. You may wish to experiment with the developing frog eggs. Some problems to investigate are these:
   a. What effect do temperature differences have on the developing embryo?
   b. What effect do chemicals such as alcohol or caffeine have on the developing embryo?
   c. Does aeration of the water affect development?
   d. Is rate of tadpole development affected by treatment with thyroid hormones?

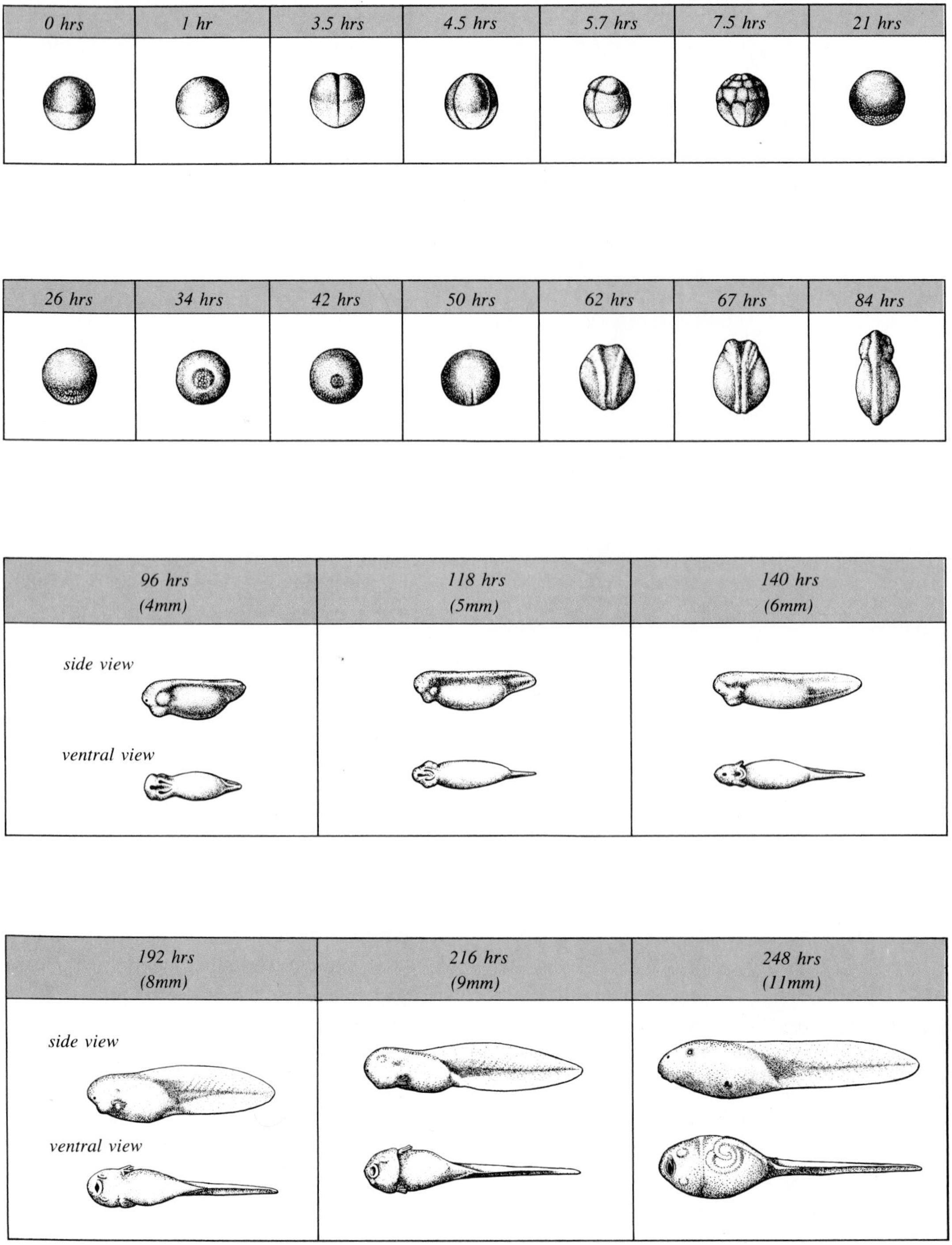

| 0 hrs | 1 hr | 3.5 hrs | 4.5 hrs | 5.7 hrs | 7.5 hrs | 21 hrs |
|---|---|---|---|---|---|---|

| 26 hrs | 34 hrs | 42 hrs | 50 hrs | 62 hrs | 67 hrs | 84 hrs |
|---|---|---|---|---|---|---|

| 96 hrs (4mm) | 118 hrs (5mm) | 140 hrs (6mm) |
|---|---|---|
| side view | | |
| ventral view | | |

| 192 hrs (8mm) | 216 hrs (9mm) | 248 hrs (11mm) |
|---|---|---|
| side view | | |
| ventral view | | |

**Figure 11–C–4** Stages in development of frogs from eggs kept at 18°C.

# Development

## 12–A

### What Is There in a Seed That Can Grow into a Complete Plant?

Plants go through basic stages of development. In many plants, development begins immediately after fertilization. In the bean plant, for example, the embryo reaches a complex stage of development within the seed. When the seed is mature, the embryo stops developing until conditions become favorable for further development.

In this investigation, you will study the plant embryos of some mature seeds. You will determine the conditions necessary to bring about development and the changes that take place in the embryo and seed during development.

### MATERIALS

Pea and bean seeds and corn kernels soaked in water overnight, stereoscopic microscope or hand lens, razor blade or scalpel, iodine, plant marker with waterproof ink, metric ruler, paper towels, beaker or jar, young growing plant, compound microscope, string or rubber band, slide, cover slip.

### PROCEDURE

#### a. Study of Seed Structure

1. Carefully remove the **seed coat** of both a soaked bean seed and a pea seed. Separate the structures called **cotyledons** and find the embryo plant in each seed (see Figure 12–1). Remove the embryo from the cotyledons and put it on a moist paper towel in a petri dish.
2. Examine the embryos under the stereoscopic microscope or hand lens and sketch the general

**Figure 12–A–1** How to section a kernel of corn.

shape and structure. Label any parts of the embryos that you can identify.
3. Lay a corn kernel on a paper towel. Place it so that the small, oval, light-colored area showing through the coat of the kernel is on the top. Position a razor edge along the length of the small oval structure and press down on the razor, cutting the entire kernel in half. (See Figure 12–A–1.) Place a drop of iodine on the cut surfaces. The part that does not turn black is the embryo. Study and record the identifiable parts of the embryo.

#### b. Study of Plant Growth and Development

1. Plant 5 soaked pea seeds and 5 soaked corn kernels in separate paper rolls, (as in Figure 12–A–2). Fasten the roll with string or a rubber band. Stand the rolls in a container of water. Be sure the seeds and kernels are at the top ends of the rolls, not in the water.

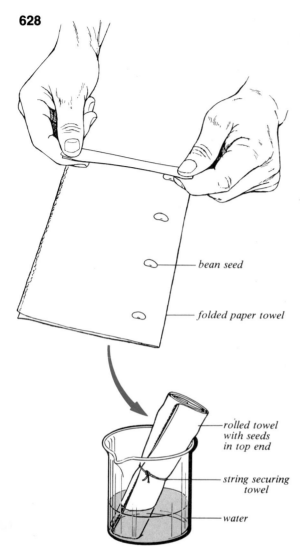

bean seed

folded paper towel

rolled towel with seeds in top end

string securing towel

water

**Figure 12–A–2** Preparing an environment for seed germination.

2. After 3 days of growth unroll the paper planters and examine the seeds and kernels. With water-proof ink in a marking pen and with a metric ruler as a guide, mark the root and stem of a few pea seedlings and a few corn seedlings at regular intervals. Figure 12–A–3 shows you how. Show by a sketch how you marked the seedlings. Return the seedlings to the paper roll for further development.

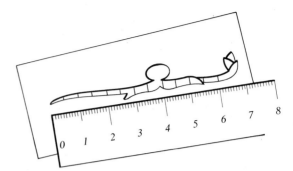

**Figure 12–A–3** Marking developing plants at regular intervals with waterproof ink.

3. After two more days of growth unroll the paper planter and examine the seedlings again. Record your observations with another sketch showing the spacing between the marks.
4. Carefully remove about 2 cm of the growing root tip. Examine this section of root by placing it in a few drops of water on a slide and looking at it through the low power of a compound microscope. Sketch the field that shows the root hairs.

## DISCUSSION

1. What general plant parts did you identify on the plant embryos examined in Procedure step 2 on the first day?
2. How does the pattern of growth and development differ in the pea and corn embryos? Include details about the stem, roots, and leaves.
3. Did growth occur uniformly in each stem? In each root? Explain.
4. What are three possible sources of materials for the increase in the size of the plant as it grew?
5. What is the source of nutrients to the corn seedlings? (Recall the iodine test in step 3, part **a**.)
6. In what general region of the root are the plant cells most actively carrying on mitosis? Explain.
7. What could be the function of the root hairs observed in step 4, part **b** of the procedure?

## 12–B

## Chicken Embryo Development

The development of a fertilized hen's egg may be used to illustrate the many complex changes that take place before a chicken hatches from the shell. Like all eggs, the hen's egg is a single cell. It is quite large, because it has enough yolk to feed the developing chick until the chick hatches.

Actually the egg cell is made up only of the yellow yolk and the small area of clear cytoplasm containing the egg nucleus on top of the yolk. The "white" of the hen's egg, the shell, and some membranes lining the shell are not parts of the egg cell but are secreted by the hen as the egg passes through the oviduct.

It is the clear cytoplasm on top of the yolk which divides into many cells after the egg is fertilized. When many cells have formed, the chick embryo begins to take shape until finally a complete chick develops within the shell. The embryo is enclosed by the membranes you read about in Section 11–12.

All of the complex structures that form a chicken appear in the embryo in a definite order at a definite time. Behavioral patterns also appear while the chick is still within its shell, patterns such as the pecking action which allows the chick to break out of its shell at the proper time. The problem the biologist faces is to discover an explanation for the remarkable series of events that all begin with one fertilized cell on the top of the yolk.

How does this complex process take place? What structures act as organs of respiration, nutrition, and excretion for the developing embryo? In what order do these structures appear in the embryo? From your study of embryonic membranes in Section 11–12, you probably already know some answers to these questions. In this investigation you can further explore these problems of development by examining fertilized chicken eggs at different stages.

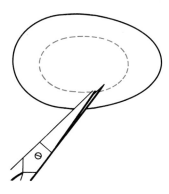

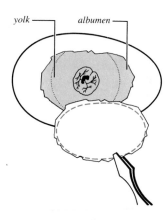

*yolk* — *albumen* —

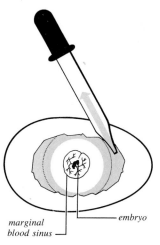

*marginal blood sinus* — — *embryo*

**Figure 12–B–1** Removing a piece of eggshell to expose a chick embryo.

## MATERIALS

Fertilized, unincubated egg, egg incubated for about 3 days, egg incubated for about 5 days, 3 culture dishes, stereoscopic microscope or hand lens, fine-pointed scissors, forceps, dropper, paper towels, watch glass, small plastic spoon, saline solution, filter paper.

## PROCEDURE

1. Place crumpled paper towels in the bottom of each culture dish to keep the eggs from rolling. Mark the upper side of the egg as it is positioned in the incubator. Keep the egg in that same position throughout your investigation. Place the egg in the culture dish.

2. Without removing the egg from the dish, cut away the top part of the shell as shown in Figure 12–B–1. Cut only with the scissors tips so you will not damage the materials beneath the shell.

3. Remove the cut-away part of the eggshell and observe the embryo and the surrounding materials of each egg: unincubated, 3-day stage, and 5-day stage.

4. With the dropper, remove as much of the albumen (egg white) as possible.

5. Cut a paper ring from filter paper and place it over the 3-day embryo as shown in Figure 12–B–2. Carefully cut through the yolk membrane at the outer edge of the paper ring and continue the cut around the paper ring until the embryo is free of the yolk. Hold onto the paper ring with forceps while you are making this cut.

6. Gently lift the paper ring with the attached embryo from the eggshell and place it in a watch glass of saline solution. Observe the embryo under low-power magnification with a stereoscopic microscope or hand lens and compare it with the drawing in Figure 12–B–3.

7. Remove the 5-day embryo in a similar manner. A small spoon under the embryo will help lift it since it is larger and heavier than the 3-day embryo.

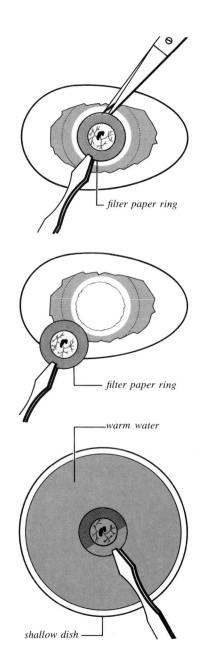

*filter paper ring*

*filter paper ring*

*warm water*

*shallow dish*

**Figure 12–B–2** Preparing the chick embryo for study.

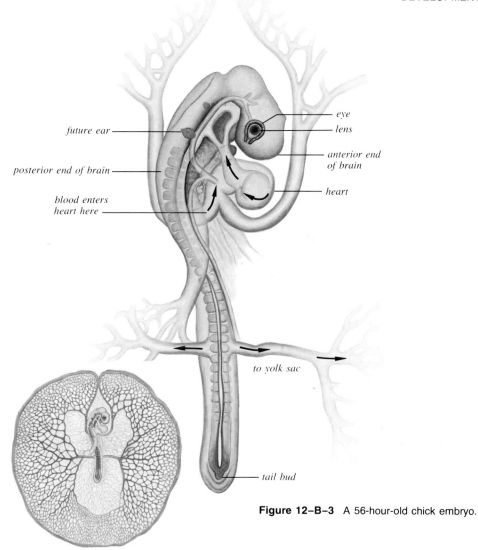

*future ear*

*posterior end of brain*

*blood enters heart here*

*eye*

*lens*

*anterior end of brain*

*heart*

*to yolk sac*

*tail bud*

**Figure 12–B–3** A 56-hour-old chick embryo.

## DISCUSSION

1. What are the functions of the membranes that develop around the chick embryo?

2. The chick embryo has a large supply of food in the form of a yolk. How do the embryos of higher mammals, which do not have a yolk supply, get their nourishment?

3. How does the chick embryo obtain oxygen? How is carbon dioxide given off?

4. Name the main functions of the chorion and the allantois.

5. What effect would coating the eggshell with petroleum jelly have on the developing embryo?

6. From your observation, what system begins to work very early in development? Explain the importance of this system.

7. Write a paragraph describing the changes in the embryo from the third to the fifth day. Use sketches to show the progress of the embryo's development.

## 12–C

# What Happens to the Pieces of Cut-Up Planarians?

Many living things are able to replace or regenerate parts of their bodies that have been lost. Certain flatworms (planarians) have been favorite objects for the study of regeneration since the 18th century. These animals sometimes reproduce by constricting into two pieces; the front piece then grows a new tail, and the rear piece grows a new head.

You may observe in this investigation how the process of regenerating varies in different segments of planarians.

## MATERIALS

Planarians, razor blade or fine scalpel, microscope slide, spring water or chlorine-free tap water, cotton swabs, petri dishes, labels or wax pencils, ice cubes.

## PROCEDURE
### Crosswise Cuts

1. Pour some spring water or chlorine-free tap water into a petri dish. Place a drop of water on a glass slide and place a planarian in the drop of water. The animal may be transferred from the supply dish with a cotton swab.
2. Chill the slide on an ice cube to slow down the movement of the planarian.
3. After the animal has relaxed, cut the body into two equal halves crosswise. (See Figure 12–C–1, part *a*.) Place the two halves in the petri dish of water.
4. Using separate petri dishes, repeat the same operation on one or two other planarians. Cover the dishes, and keep them in a dark, cool place.
5. Examine the pieces every two days. Remove any dead pieces. Observe when the wounds heal and when the regeneration buds appear. How does a bud differ in appearance from the rest of a piece? Make sketches of your observations.

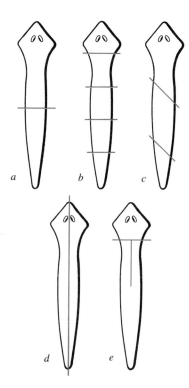

**Figure 12–C–1** Ways to cut planarians for study of regeneration.

**Other Cuts** The preceding experiment really duplicates what happens in normal asexual reproduction in planarians. Can smaller pieces also regenerate into whole worms? What would happen if the cut were made obliquely? What would be the result if a worm were cut lengthwise from head to tail?

To investigate these possibilities, assemble the same equipment as before. Parts *b, c,* and *d* of Figure 12–C–1 suggest some patterns of cutting that you might try. Because smaller pieces cannot be identified easily, you will need separate labeled petri dishes for each kind of planarian section. Keep the animals in a cool, dark place. Examine them every day or two to see if regeneration occurs.

**Partial Separation**   Another interesting possibility is to cut lengthwise partway down the length of the body.  To perform this experiment, first cut off and discard the head, then make the cut indicated in Figure 12–C–1, part *e*.  The difficulty with this experiment is that the partially separated halves will simply tend to fuse together.  Therefore, you have to make the same cut 2 or 3 times during the next 24 hours.  Eventually, the cut parts will remain separated.  Examine the cut planarian every other day and observe what happens.

**DISCUSSION**

1.  How does the new growth differ in appearance from the original piece of planarian?
2.  How large a piece of planarian must be present to produce a new head, a new tail, or both?
3.  Where does regeneration begin?
4.  Do the planarians resulting from the regeneration process appear to be normal animals? Explain.
5.  In what way are generation experiments helpful in understanding embryonic development?

## 12–D

# Growth Patterns

All living things begin life as a single cell.  Mitosis and cell division produce more cells and these also enlarge, differentiate, and divide until finally the organism may consist of billions of cells.  This process is called **growth.**  The pattern of growth in a living thing can be determined by keeping a regular record of some quantitative measurement of the organism.  Your mother probably kept a weekly record of your weight when you were a baby or made a record of your height on each of your birthdays.  A laboratory study of an organism's growth rate would be time-consuming since records must be kept over long periods of time, maybe even years.  Therefore, in this investigation you will work with data collected and recorded by other researchers.  On page 634 are the growth records of three different organisms.  From these data you should be able to determine some general characteristics of growth common to all organisms.

**PROCEDURE**

1.  For each set of data prepare a graph with age on the horizontal axis and size on the vertical axis.
2.  From one of the three sets of data, prepare another graph with *age* or *time* on the horizontal axis, but on the vertical axis plot the amount of growth since the previous measurement.  The bamboo, for example, grew 0.7 m in the first week,  $1.5 - 0.7 = 0.8$ m  in  the  second week, $2.5 - 1.5 = 1.0$ m in the third week, and so on.

**DISCUSSION**

1.  Describe the general shape of the three growth curves you prepared first.  In what ways are the curves similar to each other?  In what ways are they different?
2.  When did the most rapid growth occur?
3.  How do you think these curves would compare with curves describing your own growth in height and in weight, respectively?
4.  What is the relationship between the second type of curve you drew and the first set of curves?
5.  Do you think that in one meal your family could eat the nine-month-old turkey described in Record B?

## Data for 12–D

**Record A.** The height of a stem of bamboo, one of the most rapidly growing of all plants, measured from the time the sprout came up.

| Age in Weeks | 1 | 2 | 3 | 4 | 5 | 6 | 7 | 8 | 9 | 10 | 11 | 12 |
|---|---|---|---|---|---|---|---|---|---|---|---|---|
| Height in Meters | 0.7 | 1.5 | 2.5 | 4.0 | 6.2 | 8.3 | 10.2 | 12.0 | 13.2 | 13.8 | 14.1 | 14.2 |

**Record B.** A turkey weighed every month from the time of hatching to almost full size.

| Age in Months | 0* | 1 | 2 | 3 | 4 | 5 | 6 | 7 | 8 | 9 |
|---|---|---|---|---|---|---|---|---|---|---|
| Weight in Kilograms | 0.05 | 0.60 | 2.06 | 3.95 | 6.22 | 8.37 | 10.64 | 12.65 | 14.58 | 14.82 |

\* just hatched

**Record C.** The average weights of a large number of corn seedlings, recorded every two weeks.

| Age in Weeks | 2 | 4 | 6 | 8 | 10 | 12 | 14 | 16 | 18 | 20 |
|---|---|---|---|---|---|---|---|---|---|---|
| Average Weight in Grams | 21 | 28 | 58 | 76 | 170 | 422 | 706 | 853 | 924 | 966 |

# Patterns of Heredity

## 13-A

### Why Do Plants Develop Chlorophyll?

Albinism is a rare condition found in both plants and animals. The cells of albino animals or plants do not contain certain pigments (chemical coloring matter). Albino plants, for example, have no chlorophyll, the chemical that causes plants to be green. In this section you will investigate the influence of both heredity and environment on the plant's ability to produce chlorophyll.

### MATERIALS

Petri dish, filter or blotting paper cut to fit petri dish, lightproof box or aluminum foil to fit over petri dish, about 100 tobacco seeds.

### PROCEDURE

1. Evenly sprinkle the tobacco seeds over moistened paper in the bottom of the petri dish. The seeds should be separated by at least twice their length.
2. Put the glass cover over the dish. Put the dish in a lighted area for about 4 days. After 4 or 5 days either wrap it in foil or cover with the lightproof box. Put the set-up in a safe place (not in direct sunlight) for 3 or 4 more days. Be sure the paper is moist at all times. Do not expose the seeds to bright light when checking the need for moisture.
3. After the seeds have germinated, usually in about a week to 10 days, remove the lightproof cover, or foil, and examine the seedlings. Observe especially the color of the tiny leaves.
4. Place the petri dish with seedlings in a well-lighted place for a few days. Be sure the glass cover is on the dish and the paper is moist at all times. Observe the seedlings from day to day as they are exposed to the light.
5. After the leaves have shown a color change, count the number of plants that show a color variation. Record observations and numbers in your data book.

### DISCUSSION

1. What was the color of the tobacco plants while they were growing in the dark?
2. Did light have the same effect on all of the plants? Explain.
3. The seeds used in this investigation came from a specially bred tobacco plant. Do you suppose the parent plants were both green, one green, one albino, or both albino? Hint: Consider the role of chlorophyll in the life of a plant.
4. Does light have any effect on the plant's ability to produce chlorophyll? Explain.
5. Is light the only factor necessary for a plant to produce chlorophyll? Explain.
6. This investigation has explored the role of hereditary and environmental influences on the development of chlorophyll in tobacco plants. Which seedlings showed the influence of heredity on chlorophyll development?
7. What was the approximate ratio of green to albino plants that appeared when seedlings were grown in the light for several days? How does this ratio compare with some of Mendel's data in Appendix 13-A?

## 13–B

# How Are Traits in Fruit Flies Inherited?

Among the many experiments conducted by Mendel were crosses between plants having sharply contrasting traits. For example, Mendel wondered what would be the results of crossing a tall garden pea plant and a short garden pea plant. Would the offspring be short like one parent, or tall like the other? Or would they be of medium height, showing a blend of the traits of both parents?

The same kinds of questions can be asked about other organisms. By crossing fruit flies with very different traits, you can observe how those traits appear in the offspring.

### a. The First Generation

#### MATERIALS

Cultures of two different types of *Drosophila*, equipment for handling and examining *Drosophila*, wax pencils, fresh culture vials.

#### PROCEDURE

1. Using the techniques your teacher will show you, examine the two cultures of *Drosophila* provided. One of these cultures is the normal, or "wild," type of fly; the other is a mutant strain. Describe or make a sketch of the observable differences between the two types. By convention in genetics, the symbol + stands for the wild type. Give the mutant strain an appropriate symbol to distinguish it from the wild type.

2. Remove all the adult flies of one type from the culture vial and place them in a fresh bottle or vial. Repeat for the other type. Label the bottles with the date of transfer and the type of fly. These flies will not be used in this experiment, but you may want to develop a fruit fly population for a later experiment. It requires several weeks to develop a fruit fly population.

3. Keep the original containers so that newly emerging flies can be collected. Within 10 hours, examine the containers from which you removed the adults. Remove and anesthetize all adults that have emerged during this time. Your teacher will help you plan a schedule for collecting the flies.

4. Pick out three to five females from one type of fly. They will not yet have mated since the females do not mate until about 10 hours after emergence from the pupae. Do not pick flies with a very pale color and incompletely expanded wings, for they have just emerged.

5. Put the three to five females you have selected in a fresh culture bottle or vial with an equal number of males of the other type. (If the females are of the wild type, the males should be of the mutant type, and vice versa.) Label the bottle according to the male and female types added.

6. After 7 or 8 days, when larvae and pupae are visible, remove the parent flies from the mating bottle and discard them. Be sure to keep the culture bottles or vials at average room temperature (about 25°C). Keep them out of direct sunlight and away from radiators.

7. About 10 to 12 days after the mating, new flies should begin to emerge. Examine 100 to 200 flies of this new generation and record their appearance in a table. Do not record observations past the tenth day after the emergence of the first few flies or the data may be confused by the presence of $F_2$ individuals.

#### DISCUSSION

1. How many of the $F_1$ generation are of the wild type? How many are of the mutant type?
2. How can you account for this?
3. What Mendelian principle is illustrated by the results of this cross?
4. How would you go about determining the gene makeup of flies in the $F_1$ generation?

**b. The Second Generation** In the following experiment, you will allow some of the $F_1$ generation flies you have obtained to mate. The offspring of this mating will be the $F_2$ generation.

**PROCEDURE**

1. Place 5 or 6 pairs of the $F_1$ flies in each of 3 fresh culture bottles or vials. For this mating it does not matter whether the females have mated before the controlled mating. (Why?) Label the containers with the date and the types of flies mated in the cross.

2. As soon as pupae appear (in about 7 or 8 days), remove and discard parent flies.

3. When the second generation ($F_2$) flies emerge, determine how many are of the wild type and how many are of the mutant type. Record the data in a table. Continue observing and counting the flies until you have a total of at least 200 flies. Observations of the $F_2$ generation can only be made for 9 or 10 days because the $F_3$ generation will begin to emerge from their pupae after this time. After you record their appearance, you may dispose of the flies.

**DISCUSSION**

1. What proportion of the flies in the $F_2$ generation are of the mutant type and what proportion are of the wild type?

2. Using the chi-square method (Appendix 15–B), compare the observed $F_2$ results with what you would have expected according to Mendelian principles.

3. Why did the mutant characteristic remain concealed in the $F_1$ generation but reappear in the $F_2$ generation?

4. What Mendelian principles are demonstrated by this investigation?

# 13–C

## How Are A, B, AB, and O Blood Groups Inherited?

The blood types O, A, B, and AB are determined by the presence or absence of the proteins A and B on red blood cells. These human blood types are controlled by multiple alleles—$I^A$, $I^B$, and $i$. Table 13–C–1 summarizes the allele combinations and blood types. Note that more than one genotype may determine two of the four phenotypes. (The paired alleles are the genotype, the resulting blood type the phenotype.)

| Phenotype | Genotype | Protein on Red Blood Cells |
|---|---|---|
| type A | $I^A I^A$ or $I^A i$ | A |
| type B | $I^B I^B$ or $I^B i$ | B |
| type AB | $I^A I^B$ | A and B |
| type O | $ii$ | none |

**Table 13–C–1** The ABO blood types.

In this section you will determine your own blood type. First answer these questions:

1. From the evidence given in the table, is the allele that determines type A blood dominant or recessive to the allele that determines type O blood? Is the allele that determines type B blood dominant or recessive to the allele that determines type O blood?

2. What type of blood is produced when a person inherits allele $I^A$ from one parent and allele $I^B$ from the other parent? Is one allele dominant over the other?

3. In which blood types, A, B, AB, or O, can the genotypes be determined without any knowledge of the parents' blood types? Explain.

## MATERIALS

70% alcohol, cotton, blood lancets (disposable), blood typing serum A and serum B, microscope slides, toothpicks, sterile cotton.

## PROCEDURE

1. Scrub your ring finger clean with cotton and alcohol. Let the finger dry but do not touch it to anything that would contaminate the skin.

2. Let your lab partner or your teacher puncture the finger with the sterile disposable lancet and collect a drop of blood on each of two slides. It may be necessary to squeeze the finger slightly to get a drop of blood from the puncture. Press sterile cotton against the puncture to stop the bleeding.

3. Before the blood has time to clot or dry, mix a small drop of serum A into one blood drop and serum B into the other drop. Use different toothpicks to mix the serum and blood in each drop. Mark the slides according to the type of serum used. Do not get blood on the serum droppers.

4. After mixing, watch for any clumping of the blood cells within the drops. There may be clumping in both drops. There may be clumping in one and not the other. Or there may be no clumping in either. The type of clumping will depend on the type of blood you have. Serum A will clump blood with protein A. Serum B will clump blood with protein B. Both serums will clump AB blood, but neither will affect type O blood.

5. Prepare a table showing the percentage of each blood type for the members of the class.

## DISCUSSION

1. The blood types in the American population are about 44% O, 37% A, 13% B, and 6% AB. Does your class conform to this distribution? Explain any deviations.

2. What is your blood type? What gene combinations could you have to produce your blood type?

3. If you were to marry a person with type O blood, what types of blood could your children have? If you married a person with AB blood, what blood types might your children have?

4. Prepare a pedigree chart of the members of your family to show the known phenotype and genotype of their blood types. If members of your family have not had their blood typed, fill in their pedigree with the different possibilities according to the known types of the other members. Use parents, grandparents, aunts, uncles, brothers, and sisters if data can be obtained.

5. Suppose two newborn babies were accidentally mixed up in the hospital (something that rarely happens). In an effort to determine the parents of each baby, the blood types of the babies and the parents were determined.

| | |
|---|---|
| Baby 1 | Type O |
| Baby 2 | Type A |
| Mrs. Brown | Type B |
| Mr. Brown | Type AB |
| Mrs. Smith | Type B |
| Mr. Smith | Type B |

Show by a pedigree chart which baby belongs to which parents and the genotype of each person.

6. Can the parent-child identification always be determined by blood types? Give examples to support your answer.

# Genes and Chromosomes

## 14–A

### Why Are Some Pea Seeds Wrinkled and Some Not?

Mendel discovered that the shape of pea seeds is under genetic control. Plants with factors (genes) for wrinkled seeds always produced offspring with wrinkled seeds, and plants with factors for smooth seeds always produced offspring with smooth seeds.

The question this investigation is concerned with is how the gene affects the seed coat to cause it to be either wrinkled or smooth. What can a coded message in the nuclei of the seed cells do that would cause the seed to either shrink and wrinkle upon drying, or *not* to wrinkle upon drying?

### a. What Is the Direct Cause of Smooth or Wrinkled Seed Coats in Peas?

#### MATERIALS

10 smooth peas and 10 wrinkled peas, 4 small beakers or other glass containers, balance, paper towels, labels.

#### PROCEDURE

1. Examine the two kinds of peas. What is the obvious difference between them? Is this striking difference between the two seed coats the result of different genes or the result of different methods of drying the peas? In the next two steps you will begin to answer this question by measuring the amount of water each kind of pea can absorb.

2. Determine the dry weight of the 10 smooth peas and then the dry weight of the 10 wrinkled peas. Record these weights in a table. Place the smooth and wrinkled peas in separate beakers or jars and add about 4 times their volume of water. Label your jars for the 2 kinds of peas and put the jars aside for 24 hours.

3. After soaking the peas overnight, pour off the excess water from each bottle and empty each jar of peas into a separate pile on a piece of paper towel. Blot off all the surface water from the peas and again determine their weight. Record the weights of the soaked peas in your table along with the earlier weights of the dry peas. Determine the percent of increase in weight for each kind of pea.

$$\frac{\text{weight difference}}{\text{dry weight}} \times 100 = \% \text{ increase}$$

Record this in your table.

#### DISCUSSION

1. Which seed type, wrinkled or smooth, had the greater ability to absorb water?
2. Is there any conclusive way to find out whether this is a genetic or an environmental difference? Explain.
3. If both kinds of soaked peas were placed in a drying oven and left for 24 hours, do you think they would again show the differences in seed coat?

### b. What Causes a Difference in the Amount of Water Absorbed by Smooth and Wrinkled Seeds?

## MATERIALS

Soaked peas (1 smooth and 1 wrinkled), scalpel or razor blade, microscope slide, 2 droppers, microscope, wax pencil.

## PROCEDURE

1. On one end of a microscope slide mark **W** for wrinkled and on the other end **S** for smooth. Place a drop of water at each end.
2. Cut through a soaked wrinkled seed with a sharp instrument and gently scrape a small amount of the material from the cut surface into the appropriate drop of water, mixing the scrapings well into the drop. Wipe the blade of the instrument clean and repeat the process with the smooth seed.
3. Carefully observe both drops of water with their scrapings under low power of the microscope. Make simple outline sketches showing the shapes of the individual starch grains in each drop. Look at a few slides prepared by other class members and compare them with yours.

## DISCUSSION

1. Which combination of three words from the following list best describes the appearance of the starch grains of the wrinkled seeds? Of the smooth seeds? Compound, simple, whole, divided, oval, round, irregular.
2. Are the starch grains always similar for the one particular type of pea?
3. Is this difference in pea seeds more likely due to genes or environment? Explain how you might do an experiment to make sure.

## c. Is There a Difference in the Rate of Starch Production by Enzymes in Smooth and Wrinkled Seeds? The large starch granules observed in experiment **b** are made up of many starch molecules. The starch molecules are formed in the plant by combining many smaller and simpler sugar molecules.

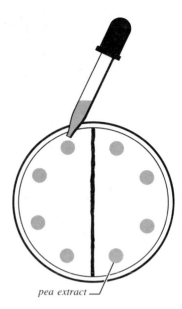

**Figure 14–A–1** Spacing drops of pea extract on a petri dish.

## MATERIALS

10 dry wrinkled pea seeds, 10 dry smooth pea seeds, 2 droppers, petri dish with glucose-1-phosphate agar, centrifuge, cheesecloth, mortar and pestle, graduated cylinder, iodine solution, pliers, funnel, beaker, balance, cotton swabs or paper towels, iodine solution.

## PROCEDURE

1. Weigh out 5 grams of dry wrinkled peas and 5 grams of dry smooth peas.
2. Crush the peas with the pliers and grind each kind separately with a mortar and pestle until no big pieces remain. (This takes much effort.) Add 20 ml of water to each mass of ground-up peas. Mix well and gently continue grinding with the pestle.
3. Remove the larger particles by filtering the mixture through a layer of cheesecloth into an appropriately marked beaker. Squeeze the cheesecloth to get the maximum amount of liquid. Centrifuge the liquid mixture to obtain

a clear solution free of sediment. Be careful not to mix or confuse the extracts from the two kinds of peas.

4. You need about 40 more minutes for the remaining procedures. If you do not have enough time, mark your containers and store the extracts in the refrigerator until the next day.

5. Mark the outside bottom of the petri dish halves. Mark a **W** on one half and an **S** on the other as in Figure 14–A–1. On the **W** side of the dish place 4 drops of the extract from the wrinkled seeds directly onto the agar-glucose surface. Space the drops so they do not run together. Do the same with the smooth-pea extract on the **S** side of the dish. Record the time that the extract meets the agar.

6. After 10 minutes soak up one drop of the extract on the **W** side and one on the **S** side. Immediately apply a drop of iodine solution to both spots where the extract was. Place a drop of the iodine solution on the agar surface at a spot where there was no extract. Record your observations.

7. At 10-minute intervals repeat step 6 with the remaining extract drops. Test only one drop of each extract at each 10-minute interval.

**DISCUSSION**

1. Was there any difference in the amount of starch formed by the wrinkled and smooth peas? How could you tell?

2. Breeding experiments have shown that all the variations in the peas seen in this investigation are controlled by one gene pair. Which condition—the texture of the seed coat, the shape of the starch grain, or the action of the starch enzyme—is closest to being under the direct influence of the gene?

3. Why do some pea seeds have a wrinkled coat? Is it due to environmental influence, direct gene action, or the secondary effects of some other factor controlled by genes? Explain.

# Investigations for 15:

# Origin of New Species

## 15–A

### A Model Gene Pool

If there are two kinds of alleles (*A* and *a*) affecting a certain trait in the gene pool of a population, there are three possible combinations of alleles after fertilization: (*AA*, *Aa*, *aa*). The probability that a particular combination will occur depends on the comparative numbers of each kind of allele in the gene pool.

To understand how certain laws of probability function in a real population of living things, you will set up a model of a gene pool and make allele combinations by picking the model alleles from the gene pool. The random choice of pairs of alleles represents what happens in fertilization, and the resulting pairs will represent individuals of the new generation.

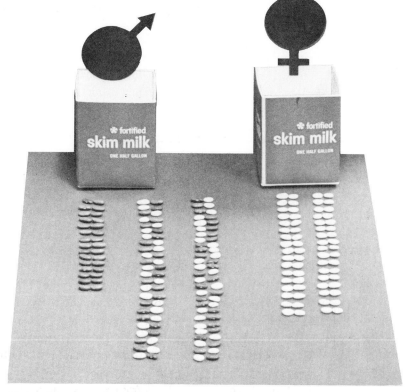

**Figure 15–A–1** Cartons labeled with male and female symbols, and the "gene pairs" selected from the cartons. One member of each pair was taken from the male carton and the other from the female carton.

## MATERIALS

Red and white beans, 2 boxes (bottom of half-gallon milk cartons), one marked ♂ (male) and one marked ♀ (female).

## PROCEDURE

1. Count out two groups of 40 beans of one color (red) and two groups of 60 beans of the other color (white). Place one of the groups of 40 in the box marked male and the other group of 40 in the box marked female. Place one group of 60 beans in the box marked male and the other group of 60 in the box marked female. Each box should have 40 red beans and 60 white beans. Mix the beans by shaking each box gently.

2. One possible combination of alleles of a first-generation offspring can be obtained by randomly picking a bean from each box (male and female). Record the color combination of the pair. Continue picking combinations until the boxes are empty. Provide a separate place for each of the three kinds of pairs (both red, both white, and red and white) on the laboratory table, in three rows or three groups. Save these bean pairs. Figure 15–A–1 shows how the array might look. Record the number of pairs in each group. When you have emptied the boxes, you will have formed all the possible combinations of alleles that random fertilization would produce in this generation of offspring. These combinations represent members of the population that will contribute alleles to the next generation.

| Combinations | Mathematically Expected in % | Individual Results in % | Group Results in % |
|---|---|---|---|
| WW | | | |
| RW and WR | | | |
| RR | | | |

**Table 15–A–1**  Data table for comparison of predicted and actual combinations of alleles.

3. Each pair of beans represents an individual of the population. Half of the pairs of bean combinations represent the males of the population and the other half represent the females. For example, if you have 18 pairs of red-red combinations, nine pairs are males and are to be put back in the "male" box, and nine pairs represent females and are to be put in the "female" box. Divide the other combinations in the same way, putting half of the pairs in the "male" box and the other half in the "female" box. Once you have all three types separated into males and females and have returned them to the gene pool, you are ready to pick new combinations to represent the second-generation offspring. Mix the beans well before picking the new combinations.

4. Again pick pairs that will represent the individuals of the second generation. Count and record these combinations.

5. Combine your results with all other groups by placing your totals on the chalkboard in the proper column. List the first and second generation totals separately.

**DISCUSSION**

1. What was the percentage of each kind of bean in the original male gene pool? In the original female gene pool?

2. At the very beginning of your bean-picking procedure, what chance did you have of picking a white bean when reaching into one box? What were your chances of picking a white bean when reaching into the other box? What were your chances, then, of picking a white bean from each box at once? (Remember that the chance of two events occurring together is the product of their chances of occurring separately.) Make a table like Table 15–A–1. Determine the probability of each combination and record it in the "mathematically expected" column of your table. Remember, your mixed combination can occur two different ways (red-white or white-red).

3. Find the percentages of the combinations that were actually produced when you picked the beans from the boxes the first time. Record them in the column for individual results. Determine the percentages from the data of the whole class and record them in the column for group results.

$$\frac{\text{Number of pairs of one combination}}{\text{Number of pairs of all combinations}} \times 100 = \% \text{ of this combination}$$

4. How do the mathematically derived results (question 2) compare with the actual experimental results (question 3)?

5. How do the actual chance-combination percentages of the first generation compare with those of the second? Determine from your data the number of red and white beans that were put in each box for the second picking. How do these numbers compare with the original num-

bers placed in the boxes? In other words, how does the gene pool of the second generation compare with the gene pool of the first? Is this difference, if any, likely to occur in the same way if the experiment is repeated?

6. From your findings in this study, can you form a hypothesis concerning the gene frequency and gene combinations that occur from generation to generation in an actual population?

# Investigations for 16:

# The Human Species

## 16–A

### A Blood Abnormality in the Human Population

What is the significance of the variations in blood types? Does each variation provide some special advantage to its carrier? These questions are of particular interest to biologists. The modern human species has developed over 40 to 60 thousand years or more, and biologists assume that most variations within the species have some survival value. But could this include even variations that cause diseases? Could a blood disease like *sickle-cell anemia* have survival value? If so, under what circumstances could the disease be an advantage to people?

Sickle-cell anemia is a disorder in which the hemoglobin inside the red blood cells aggregates when the oxygen supply is low, causing the cells to lose their flexibility and assume an abnormal shape. If enough of these cells block small blood

vessels and stop the flow of nutrients and oxygen, vital organs will be damaged and the patient may die. Figure 16–A–1 shows sickle-shaped and normally-shaped red blood cells.

**Figure 16–A–1** Red blood cells of a person with sickle-cell anemia. Sickling of the cells is the most extreme effect of the disorder. Even cells that are not sickled may be too inflexible to pass through small blood vessels.

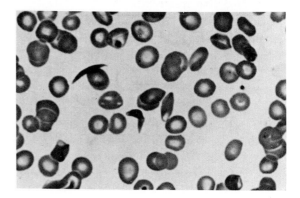

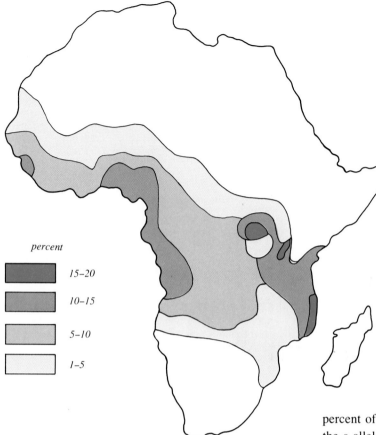

*percent*

| | |
|---|---|
| | 15–20 |
| | 10–15 |
| | 5–10 |
| | 1–5 |

**Figure 16–A–2** Frequency of the gene causing sickle-cell anemia, plotted as percentages of the population gene pool in parts of Africa.

## PROCEDURE

1. Sickle-cell anemia is due to a certain gene (symbol: *s*) when it is present in the homozygous condition. What are the three possible genotypes involving this gene and its normal allele? (Use *S* to represent the normal allele.)

2. What phenotypes would be associated with each genotype you mentioned in answer to question 1?

3. About one-quarter of one percent (0.25%) of American blacks are homozygous (*ss*) for this gene. On this basis what percent of the black population is heterozygous for the *s* allele? Review the Hardy-Weinberg principle in Section 15–3.

4. In Africa about 4 percent of the members of certain tribes have sickle-cell anemia. What percent of this population is heterozygous for the *s* allele?

5. The Hardy-Weinberg principle enables us to predict when the gene frequencies in a population will remain constant. Would you expect the frequency of the *s* gene to remain constant? Because people with sickle-cell anemia usually die in childhood, the frequency of the gene causing this disease might not remain constant. Each death removes a pair of the sickle-cell-causing genes from the population. Nevertheless, your answer to question 4 showed that a high percentage of certain populations is heterozygous for the gene that causes sickle cells. Why does the frequency of this gene remain so high?

6. Figure 16–A–2 shows the locations in Africa where the gene frequency of the *s* gene is highest. These locations are also the areas where a fatal form of malaria is found. Study

of the evidence reveals that the gene causing sickle cells offers some protection against malaria. Refer to the genotypes you gave in answer to question 1. What are the advantages and disadvantages of having each of these three genotypes? Which genotype would you select as having survival value?

7. Consider that in Africa both of the homozygous genotypes could be fatal conditions, one because of malaria and the other because of sickle-cell anemia. Which genotype would tend to survive? What would be the gene frequencies of $s$ and $S$ in a population made up of this surviving genotype?

8. The gene frequencies in the African populations under discussion are not 0.5 for each gene, as you calculated in Procedure step 7. Considering that fact, do you think the assumption in step 7 is reasonable? Which genotype do you think is less likely to be fatal?

9. How can you explain the lower frequency of the gene causing sickle cells among American blacks? (See your answer to question 3.)

10. The sickle-shaped red blood cell is caused by a mutation that affects the hemoglobin in the sickle cells. Hemoglobin is a protein substance and, therefore, made of amino acids. Scientists have been able to compare the chemical structure of normal hemoglobin, **hemoglobin A,** with the kind of hemoglobin found in sickle cells, **hemoglobin S.** They found that both types of hemoglobin molecules contain 560 amino acids of 19 different kinds. Figure 16–A–3 shows that the two molecules are identical except at one point where there is a different sequence of amino acids. What is the significant molecular difference between hemoglobin A and hemoglobin S?

11. Notice that the substitution of a single amino acid within this molecule causes a significant difference in the behavior of the molecule.

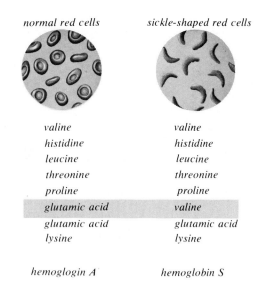

*normal red cells*          *sickle-shaped red cells*

| | |
|---|---|
| *valine* | *valine* |
| *histidine* | *histidine* |
| *leucine* | *leucine* |
| *threonine* | *threonine* |
| *proline* | *proline* |
| *glutamic acid* | *valine* |
| *glutamic acid* | *glutamic acid* |
| *lysine* | *lysine* |

*hemoglogin A*          *hemoglobin S*

**Figure 16–A–3** Amino acid sequences compared for normal and sickle hemoglobin in the portion of the one polypeptide affected.

What are the nucleotide codes for the two amino acids that make the difference between hemoglobin A and hemoglobin S? Consult the genetic code table in Appendix 10–A. What is the simplest mistake in coding that could have occurred to cause the mutation?

**DISCUSSION**

Write a few paragraphs to summarize sickle-cell anemia. Emphasize the ideas of mutation, selection, survival value, and evolution.

## 16–B

## Variation in the Human Species

Variability is a basic characteristic of living things. Reserves of genetic variability are what natural selection acts on as a species meets changes in its environment.

Human beings show variation in many traits that can often be detected easily by phenotype or appearance. Some of these traits may persist partly

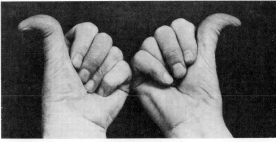

hitchhiker's thumb

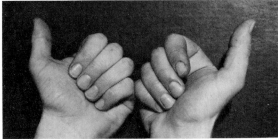

straight thumb

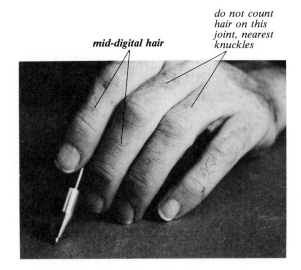

mid-digital hair

do not count
hair on this
joint, nearest
knuckles

**Figure 16-B-1** Hitchhiker's thumb and mid-digital hair on the fingers.

because natural selection is not even involved. That is, some of the traits have no effect on survival today, at least not in any way geneticists can determine.

The following exercise will let you examine variability among members of your class on the basis of as few as six traits. Five of these traits can be determined by inspection (although hitchhiker's thumb shows so many variations you may have some trouble with it—but do your best). The sixth trait is your ABO blood type, which you determined in Investigation 13–C. These six traits may let you arrive at some idea of how different each individual in your class is from all others.

The six traits are:

1. Free vs. attached ear lobes (see Figure 13–2).

2. Nonblue eyes (pigmented) vs. blue eyes (nonpigmented).

3. Hitchhiker's thumb vs. straight thumb (see Figure 16–B–1).

4. Nonstraight hair vs. straight hair.

5. Mid-digital hair on second joint of fingers vs. none (see Figure 16–B–1).

6. Four blood types: A, B, AB, and O.

**PROCEDURE**

1. Determine your own characteristics for the six traits. Use your blood-typing results from Investigation 13–C.

2. Use the genetic wheel (Figure 16–B–2). Start in the middle with the first trait and determine whether it places you on the right or the left side of the vertical line.

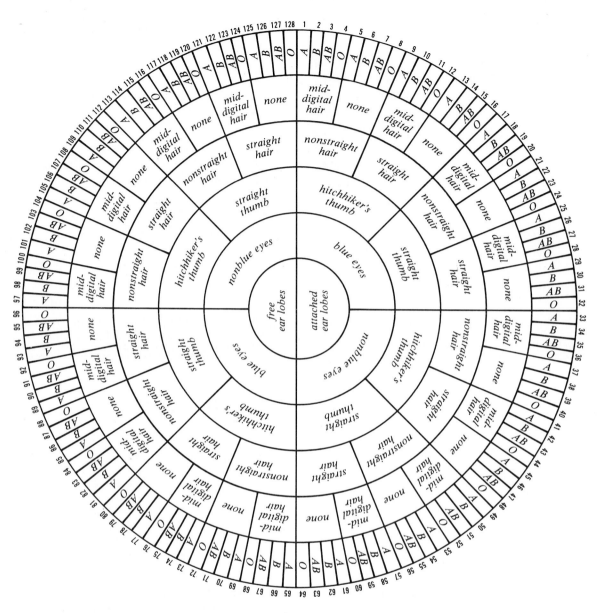

**Figure 16–B–2** The genetic wheel for five pairs of traits (phenotypes) and a sixth trait (blood group) with four phenotypes.

3. Move to the next circle on the wheel and decide which compartment you should select. Continue moving outward, trait by trait, until you come to the outer edge of the wheel. The last trait, blood type, is one of four instead of one of two. Now read the number assigned to your particular combination of traits.

4. Record this number.

5. Obtain the list of numbers your classmates have determined for themselves.

## DISCUSSION

1. Is anyone in the class like you with respect to all six traits? That is, does anyone have the same assigned number you have? (If so, can you name a seventh trait that will distinguish between you?)

2. In what ways would a person with the number 73 be different in these traits from one with the number 56?

3. In what ways would a person with the number 46 be different in these traits from one with the number 80?

4. Try to account for any clusters of the individuals in your class around particular sets of numbers.

5. Assume that in a plane crash, two male individuals and two female individuals having the four numbers 36, 40, 44, and 48 survive on an uninhabited island and start a new, isolated population. What characteristics would you not find in this island population that are present in your class?

# Investigations for 17:

# Transport Systems

## 17–A

## What Controls the Movement of Water in Plants?

The normal pathway of moving water in a living plant is first into the roots, then through the stem, and finally into the leaves. Forces and structures in the plant are involved in moving water. This investigation deals with these questions:

1. What plant structures—roots, stems, or leaves—are most important in the movement of water?

2. What kinds of cells are there in a plant that will allow water to move through them?

3. Is all the water that is delivered to the leaves used or is some lost?

4. From what direction do the forces come to move the water upward against the force of gravity?

## a. Measuring Water Uptake

### MATERIALS

6 test tubes, test tube rack, water, aluminum foil, razor blade, 6 bean (or sunflower) seedlings, petroleum jelly, cotton, glass marker.

### PROCEDURE

Fill 6 test tubes with water to within 2 cm of the top and cover them with aluminum foil. Treat each tube as follows, using Figure 17–A–1 as a guide. Mark the water line only after the plant is in the water.

Tube 1. Mark the water line only.

Tube 2. With a razor blade remove the roots at about 6 cm below the cotyledons. Pierce the aluminum foil with a pencil point and ease the plant through the hole into the water.

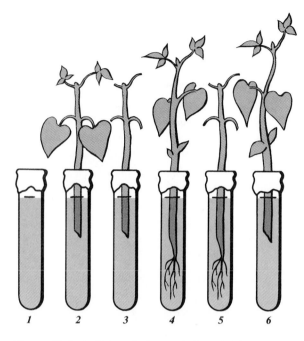

**Figure 17–A–1** Setup of tubes and plants for the water-uptake experiment.

Tube 3. Repeat the procedure outlined for tube 2. Then remove the leaf blades from the plant, leaving only the leaf stems.

Tube 4. Remove the aluminum foil from the mouth of the tube and sink the roots of an intact plant into the water. Mold the aluminum foil to the rim of the test tube so that it seals the tube and supports the plant stem.

Tube 5. Repeat the procedure described for tube 4. In addition, remove the leaf blades from the plant. Only the leaf stems should remain.

Tube 6. Repeat the procedure described for tube 2. In addition, brush petroleum jelly on the upper and lower surfaces of the leaf with a small wad of cotton.

Allow the rack of treated plants to stand in indirect light overnight. After 24 hours mark the new water line on each tube.

Find the difference in millimeters between the original and final water levels for each tube.

**DISCUSSION**

1. What is the purpose of the first tube?
2. Account for the different water levels in each tube.
3. What part of the plant contributes most to the uptake of water?
4. What difference would you have expected in the water level of tube 2 if the plant had had twice the number of leaves?
5. What difference would you have expected in the water level of tube 5 if the plant had had twice the number of roots?
6. What difference would you have expected if the cut end of the plant in tube 6 had been covered with petroleum jelly?
7. Based on your observations of this experiment, which of the following statements is most nearly correct?
   a. Water is pushed upward in a plant by forces created in the lower parts of the plant.
   b. Water is pulled upward in a plant by a force created in the upper parts of the plant.
8. If the water molecules in the test tubes had been tagged so that they could be traced, where do you think most of those that entered the plants could now be found? Describe an experiment that would test your hypothesis.
9. Make a hypothesis that could account for the force that moves the water upward in a plant. (Hint: Water molecules tend to stick together.)
10. How can the results of this experiment help to explain the adaptation of a desert cactus for the conservation of water?

**b. Observing Transport Structures in Plants** You observed in part **a** that water level changed even when leaves or roots were absent. Now you will examine the plant parts under the microscope and determine what structures make the movement of water possible in a plant.

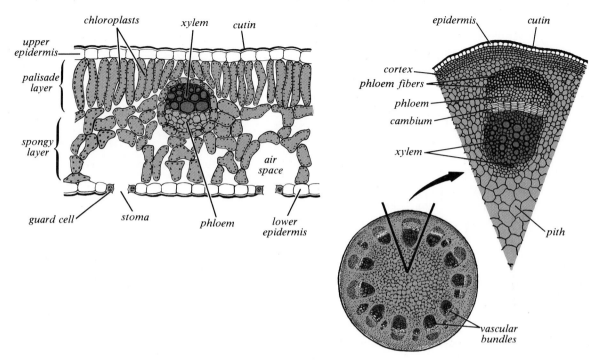

**Figure 17–A–2** Cross section of a leaf (left) and cross section of a young woody stem (right).

## MATERIALS

Prepared slides showing the following: cross section of woody stem, cross section of leaf, leaf epidermis; compound microscope, radish or grass seedlings in a petri dish.

## PROCEDURE

1. Study the cross section of a leaf with first the low power and then the high power of the compound microscope. Identify the following structures using Figure 17–A–2 as a reference.
   **Upper epidermis,** covered with a waxy layer. The cells are thick-walled and flat.
   **Palisade cells,** tightly packed and column-shaped, containing many chloroplasts.
   **Spongy cells,** round, with air spaces between them, containing chloroplasts.

   **Veins,** composed of thick-walled *xylem* cells and *phloem* cells.
   **Lower epidermis,** without chloroplasts but with openings at intervals.
   **Stomata.** These are the openings in the lower epidermis.
   **Guard cells,** two small cells surrounding each stoma and containing chloroplasts.

2. Observe a slide showing the lower epidermis of a leaf under high power. Locate the guard cells enclosing a small slit, the stoma.

3. Study a cross section of a woody stem under the low power of the microscope. Identify the general regions of **pith, vascular bundles, cambium,** and **bark.** Turn to the high power and observe a vascular bundle in more detail. Identify the **xylem,** heavy walled cells toward

the center area of the stem and the **phloem,** small thin-walled cells toward the outside area of the stem. The xylem and phloem cells are separated by a layer of living cells called **cambium.**

4. Carefully place a seedling in a drop of water on a microscope slide and observe with low power. Notice the extent of absorptive area provided by the growth of root hairs. The darker, more dense center region of the young root represents the development of the root's vascular bundles, also composed of xylem, phloem, and cambium cells.

## DISCUSSION

1. What are some of the adaptations of the leaf for the prevention of water loss?
2. In what ways may water loss by leaves help the plant? In what ways might it harm the plant?
3. How is the root adapted to absorb water from the soil?
4. How does water enter the root hairs and epidermal cells?
5. What structure in the stem serves as a connecting link between the water-conducting vessels of the roots and the veins of the leaf?
6. What is the pathway of the water molecules? Refer to part **a** of this investigation.
7. Name the general and specific structures of the root, stem, and leaf that are involved in the transport of water.

## 17–B

# Variations in the Heartbeat of *Daphnia*

*Daphnia* is a small aquatic animal. Although it is commonly called a "water flea," it is actually a crustacean related to crayfish and shrimp. *Daphnia* is a very useful laboratory subject because it is transparent. Its internal organs can be seen at work. In this exercise you will observe the heart

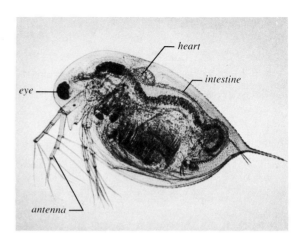

**Figure 17–B–1** *Daphnia.*

of *Daphnia* to determine whether there is a correlation between the rate of its heartbeat and variations that you will introduce into its environment.

## MATERIALS

Microscope, *Daphnia* (live specimens), microscope slides, 0.5% alcohol, droppers, cotton fibers, chlorpromazine, stopwatch or watch with second hand, D-amphetamine sulfate, tea, coffee, cocoa, carbonated beverages, other stimulants and depressants, cover slip.

---

**CAUTION:** Chlorpromazine and other drugs may be harmful if taken internally.

---

## PROCEDURE

1. With the dropper, remove one or two *Daphnia* specimens from the culture and place them on a slide. Withdraw as much water as possible from the slide, leaving just enough to keep the organisms alive. The movement of the animals can be reduced by placing a few cotton fibers under the cover slip. Place the slide under the low-power objective of the microscope. Refer to Figure 17–B–1 to locate body parts.

2. You should be able to observe the heart beating very rapidly in the transparent animal. (Reducing the amount of light may help you to see better. It will also prevent a temperature rise that can be fatal to the animal.) With another student as timekeeper, determine the rate of heartbeat under normal conditions by counting the number of beats per minute for three successive minutes. (Later you will average these counts, but merely record all three rates now.)

3. Place a drop of chlorpromazine on the slide. Note the reaction of *Daphnia*. Determine three one-minute counts of the heartbeat as before. Record the rates. Rinse the dropper well and use it to transfer *Daphnia* back to the culture jar.

4. Place another *Daphnia* on a clean slide, withdrawing as much water as possible. Determine the normal heartbeat rate. Put a drop of D-amphetamine sulfate over the *Daphnia* and observe the results. Determine the heartbeat rates again.

5. On a third specimen of *Daphnia,* determine the normal rate of heartbeat and the rate after treatment with alcohol. If time permits, you might test the effect of other materials, commonly known as stimulants or depressants. Record all the data in tabular form.

6. Determine the average of each set of three figures you obtained, the class average for the controls, and the class average for each experimental treatment.

**DISCUSSION**

1. What serves as a control in these experiments?
2. What is the effect of each of the added chemicals?
3. How great is the variation in the normal heartbeat rate of *Daphnia?* In other words, do all the animals have about the same heartbeat rates or do some individuals vary a great deal from the average?

4. From the class averages of the three experiments, prepare a bar graph. Plot heartbeat rate (in suitable intervals) on the horizontal axis and number of individuals on the vertical axis. Show the normal heartbeat rate in one color and the rates under the effect of each of the chemicals in other colors.

5. What is the likelihood that differences noted in the heartbeat rate actually resulted from chance variations rather than from chemical treatment? Explain your answer in terms of the graph you prepared.

## 17–C

## Capillary Circulation

In the capillaries the blood cells rush, tumble, and squeeze their way along. By observing capillary circulation you will be able to see the important relationship that exists between the bloodstream and the body tissue.

The diameter of the capillaries varies considerably depending upon the amount of blood flow. The thin walls of the capillaries are more elastic than muscular and can stretch and shrink. The flow of blood is largely controlled by the small arteries that lead into the capillaries. These arteries have muscular walls that respond directly to nervous and chemical stimuli. The flushed appearance of a person who has been vigorously exercising is due to increased blood flow and to capillary expansion. Artificial stimuli such as alcohol, nicotine, lactic acid, and sodium nitrite can bring about expansion or contraction in the small arteries.

In this investigation you will first observe normal capillary circulation in living tissue. You will then determine whether various stimuli cause an expansion or a contraction of the small arteries.

## a. Observing the Capillaries

### MATERIALS

Live frog or goldfish, softwood board or petri dish, cloth or paper towels, dropper, pins, string, compound microscope.

### PROCEDURE

Wrap the frog in wet cloth or wet paper towels and fasten it on a board so it cannot move. Stretch one of the frog's hind legs out on the board and hold it down by crossed pins as shown in Figure 17–C–1. The thin web of the foot can then be spread over a hole in the board and held in place with two or three pins as shown. You may place the frog either on its back or on its belly.

**Figure 17–C–1** Living frog in position for observation of blood circulation through capillaries in the web of a foot. Note the hole under the foot, and the crossed pins that hold the leg in position without injury to the frog.

CAUTION: You have a responsibility to treat the frog humanely. The frog should be carefully fastened down to the board, so that it cannot pull away from the pins through the web of the foot; this would cause tearing of tissue and bleeding. Because there are almost no nerve endings in this part of the foot, the frog will feel no pain if the leg is properly immobilized. If the foot is held still, the pinholes, which will be small, will heal almost immediately.

When the setup is complete, wet the web of the foot with water from a dropper. Wet it again every 2 to 3 minutes. Do not allow the web to dry out, for this would harm the circulation.

If you use a fish, wrap the fish (except the tail) in wet cloth or paper and lay it in a petri dish. Wet the bottom of the petri dish and spread the tail out on the wet glass. Add a few drops of water every few minutes to keep the tail moist. Place the petri dish on the stage of the microscope.

Now adjust the frog or the fish on the microscope stage so that a strong light comes through the thin tissue of the web or tail. Examine the tissue under the low power of the microscope. Try to locate small arteries, small veins, and capillaries. You should be able to distinguish vessels of different sizes. Is the speed of flow the same in all vessels? If not, is it faster in the larger or in the smaller blood vessels? Estimate the diameter of the capillaries by comparing them in size to the red blood cells. In the frog, these cells are oval in shape and on the average are 22 $\mu$m long, 15 $\mu$m wide, and 4 $\mu$m thick. (1 $\mu$m = $^1/_{1000}$ mm)

## b. Chemical Control of Capillary Diameter

In this section you will observe the effect of various chemicals on the diameter of the small arteries. Some chemicals cause the blood vessels to dilate, and others cause the vessels to constrict. If you use a frog, use one dilator and one constrictor on the membrane of each foot. If you work with a fish, you can use two dilators and constrictors on the one tail. The chemicals are in two groups to separate the dilators from the constrictors. As you do the experiment, you should be able to tell which group contains the dilators and which group contains the constrictors.

## MATERIALS

Dissecting needle, droppers, toothpicks, Group A chemicals (adrenaline, nicotine), Group B chemicals (lactic acid, histamine acid phosphate, acetylcholine, alcohol, sodium nitrite).

---

> **CAUTION:** Drugs in this list may be harmful if taken internally.

---

## PROCEDURE

Your lab partner should apply one or two drops of a solution directly onto the membrane with a dropper. Observe the capillaries continuously, before, during, and after treatment. Allow 2 to 5 minutes for the chemical to diffuse into the tissues.

It is difficult to see the contraction and expansion. To tell whether the capillaries are expanding or contracting, compare the capillary diameter with the diameter of the red blood cells and watch the rate of blood flow.

After you test the effect of one chemical, thoroughly flush the membrane with water. Then choose a chemical from the other group and test its effect. The effect of nicotine should be tested last.

## DISCUSSION

1. On the basis of this experiment, do you think that a person under the influence of alcohol would be more or less likely to suffer from exposure to extreme cold? Explain.
2. Will a muscle with an accumulation of lactic acid be served more or less effectively by the circulatory system?
3. Why does nicotine (found in cigarettes) affect a person's athletic ability?
4. The treatments applied here are artificial, of course. Under what *natural* conditions might capillary diameter change?

# Investigations for 18:

# Respiratory Systems

## 18–A

## Comparing Oxygen Consumption in Small Vertebrates

**Metabolism** (meh-TAB-uh-liz-um) can be defined as the sum total of all the life processes of an organism. In aerobic organisms the life processes are dependent upon energy derived from cell respiration, using oxygen. Thus, the amount of oxygen that an organism uses is directly related to its rate of metabolism. The metabolic rate of an organism can be determined by measuring the amount of oxygen used per unit of body weight in a given period of time.

In this investigation the rates of oxygen consumption of several small animals will be determined and comparisons can then be made.

## MATERIALS

Volumetric apparatus, mouse, frog, and other small animals, soda lime, thermometer, colored water and dropper, balance, watch with second hand, ice, plastic bag.

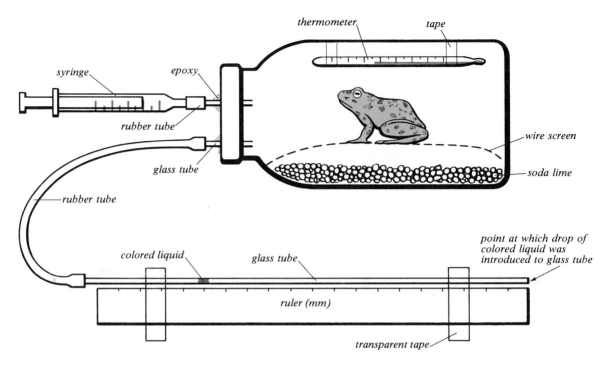

**Figure 18–A–1** Volumetric apparatus for measuring oxygen consumption of a frog (or other small animal).

---

CAUTION: You have a responsibility to treat the animals humanely.

**PROCEDURE**

1. Construct the volumetric apparatus as shown in Figure 18–A–1. Be sure the lid is sealed tightly. Block both sides of the bottle so it cannot roll. The carbon dioxide given off by the animal will be absorbed by the soda lime. As the animal uses oxygen the air pressure within the jar will be reduced. The higher pressure on the outside will force the colored liquid in the tube toward the container. By measuring the distance the colored liquid moves in a given period of time, you can determine the animal's rate of oxygen consumption.

2. Weigh the animal to be used. Place it in the jar.

3. Pull the syringe plunger out to about the $\frac{3}{4}$ mark. Then add a drop of colored liquid to the open end of the glass tube, at the end of the ruler.

4. Start the test and record the distance the liquid moves in a given period of time. The time you use to conduct each test will depend on the rate at which the animal uses oxygen. Between tests remove the syringe from the tubing and open the jar to supply the animal with fresh air. If you have time, make three trials with each animal. Determine the average distance the liquid moves per time period for each animal.

5. After each animal has been tested, determine in milliliters the average volume of oxygen each animal used up. Use the syringe to measure the volume of air that will move the liquid as far as

it was moved by the animal's breathing during the test. This volume will be equal to the volume of oxygen the animal used.

6. If time allows, compare the oxygen consumption of the animals under different temperature conditions. Cool the air in the jar by placing a plastic bag of ice over the outside of the jar. Warm the air by using warm water in the plastic bag. Remove the bag after the air has reached the desired temperature.

## DISCUSSION

1. Plot your data on a graph to compare the oxygen consumed by the animals tested.
2. Determine the average number of milliliters of oxygen that each animal consumes in an hour for every 100 grams of its body mass.
   Example:

   Animal mass: 250 grams
   Oxygen consumed in 3 minutes: 6 ml
   6 ml/3 min = 2 ml per minute for 250 grams
   2 ml/2.5 = 0.8 ml of oxygen used per 100 grams of body mass per minute
   0.8 ml × 60 = 48 ml of oxygen used per 100 grams of body mass per hour

3. Which figure most nearly represents the rate of metabolism for an animal—the total amount of oxygen used in a given period of time, or the amount of oxygen used in a given period of time relative to body mass? Explain.
4. Table 18–A–1 gives some figures for oxygen consumption of various animals. Compare your results with the figures given in the table. Be sure that the units are the same. One milliliter equals 1000 cubic millimeters. (1 ml = 1000 mm³.)
5. Study the results of this laboratory investigation and the figures given in Table 18–A–1. Make some deductions about the various factors that affect the metabolic rates of the different organisms.

| Animal | Oxygen Consumed in mm³ per g Body Mass per Hour |
|---|---|
| Sea anemone | 13 |
| Sandworm | 30 |
| Octopus | 80 |
| Squid | 320 |
| Eel | 128 |
| Human | 200 |
| Hummingbird (at rest) | 3500 |
| Hummingbird (in flight) | 40,000 |

**Table 18–A–1** The oxygen consumption of six animals at rest and of a seventh, a hummingbird, at rest and in flight.

## 18–B

## Measuring Carbon Dioxide Concentration of Human Breath

You know that when you exercise, you breathe in and out faster than when you are at rest. If carbon dioxide is eliminated from your lungs when you exhale, then the faster you breathe the more carbon dioxide you eliminate. On the other hand, the faster you breathe the less time the air is in your lungs and therefore the less time for the transfer of carbon dioxide from the blood into your lungs. This would produce less carbon dioxide per breath. So, can we be sure that breathing faster eliminates more carbon dioxide?

In this investigation you will explore the above conflict of hypotheses and answer the question, How does exercise affect the concentration of carbon dioxide in exhaled air?

## MATERIALS

2 rubber bands, short piece of plastic tubing (6 mm inside diameter), 2 plastic bags (2-liter size), two

250-ml flasks, 30 cm plastic tubing (6 mm outside diameter), 100-ml graduated cylinder, 10-ml graduated cylinder, dropping bottle with 0.04% sodium hydroxide (NaOH), 4-liter jar, deep tray or container (to hold water from 4-liter jar), wax marking pencil, bromthymol blue.

## BRIEF PROCEDURE

Air from your breath will be collected in a plastic bag and then bubbled through a flask of water. The $CO_2$ is soluble in water and reacts chemically to form carbonic acid ($H_2CO_3$). The more $CO_2$ added to the water, the more acid the water becomes. The amount of $CO_2$ in the water can be determined by measuring the amount of a base (of known concentration) that is needed to neutralize the acid. Air from your breath will be tested before and after exercise. The following detailed procedures should be followed carefully so you will have an accurate and reliable measure of the $CO_2$ concentration in your breath.

## DETAILED PROCEDURE

1. Insert the larger plastic tube in the open end of the plastic bag. Secure it tightly with a rubber band. Check for air leaks.
2. Place 100 ml of water in each of the 250-ml flasks. Add 6 to 8 drops of bromthymol blue to each. Mix well by swirling the flasks. If the water is not blue, add drops of sodium hydroxide (NaOH) to each flask until the water is definitely blue. If the NaOH is necessary, be sure to add the same number of drops to both flasks. Label the flasks A and B. Place one end of the smaller plastic tube in the solution of flask A.
3. While you are rested and breathing normally, place the open end of the larger plastic tube in your mouth. Exhale air into the plastic bag. Breathe normally but instead of exhaling into the room exhale into the plastic bag. Do not inhale air from the bag. Do not hold your

**Figure 18–B–1** The experimental procedure for bubbling carbon dioxide through the solution in flask A.

breath before exhaling and do not force your exhalation. Take as many breaths as necessary to fill the bag completely.

4. As soon as the bag is filled with your exhaled breath, quickly insert the end of the small plastic tube in the flask into the larger tube in the plastic bag. Try not to lose any air while connecting the tubes. Lay the air-filled plastic bag on the table. Place your biology text on the bag as shown in Figure 18–B–1. Allow the weight of the book to force all the air through the liquid at a uniform rate.
5. Holding the dropper in a vertical position, add NaOH a drop at a time to the water in flask A. Count the number of drops needed to change the color back to the original blue. Swirl the flask between drops and compare the color of the liquid in flask A with flask B. Record the exact number of drops required to neutralize the acid formed by the $CO_2$.
6. Add the same number of NaOH drops (of a uniform size) to an empty 10-ml graduated cylinder. Record how many ml of NaOH solution they represent.
7. Multiply by 10 the number of ml of 0.04% NaOH required to neutralize the acid produced by the $CO_2$ you exhaled. This product is equal

to the number of **micromoles** of $CO_2$ contained in one bag full of your breath. The micromole is a convenient unit to measure small amounts of substances in solution. Record this figure.

8. Exercise strenuously for three minutes and repeat steps 1 through 7. Have the materials ready so you can exhale into the bag immediately after exercising.

9. To determine the volume of the plastic bag you used, measure the amount of water that is displaced by a bag full of air. To do this, first fill a 4-liter jar or other large container with water. Then, holding your hand over the opening, turn the container upside down in a large tray partly filled with water. Fill the plastic bag with air as you did before. Quickly place the tube under the mouth of the inverted jar of water. Squeeze the bag and notice that as the air enters the jar, the water leaves. Force all the air into the jar. Mark the level of air in the jar with a wax pencil.

10. Remove the jar and empty all water from it. With a large graduated cylinder measure the amount of water required to fill the jar to the line you marked on the side. This volume represents the volume of the plastic bag. Record this volume in liters. (One liter = 1000 ml)

11. Determine the number of micromoles of $CO_2$ you exhaled per liter of air. Do this by dividing the total number of micromoles that you calculated in step 7 by the number of liters of air that you added to the bag (step 9).

12. Record in a table on the chalkboard the following data:

    a. micromoles of $CO_2$/liter of your breath at rest

    b. micromoles of $CO_2$/liter of your breath after exercise

    c. your sex

13. If time allows, perform the following test. Hold your breath for 30 seconds and then exhale into the plastic bag. Measure the micromoles of $CO_2$ contained in this air. How do the results compare with the tests you performed before? Explain your results.

## DISCUSSION

1. Organize the data from the different members of the class. Determine whether the concentration of $CO_2$ is significantly different under any of the recorded circumstances. Compare the data for before and after exercise; compare boys with girls. Use the chi-square test in Appendix 15–B if the differences are not obvious.

2. Illustrate the data on a graph.

3. Are the procedures of this experiment controlled well enough to enable you to reach definite conclusions about the concentration of $CO_2$ in your breath? Explain.

4. What other data would be necessary in order to determine the total amount of $CO_2$ you exhale per minute while at rest and after exercise?

# Investigations for 19:

# Digestive Systems

## 19–A

### Starch Digestion

Starch makes up a large part of the food of living things. It is manufactured by plants and is one of the main sources of energy for the activities of all types of cells in both plants and animals. The digestion of starch for its component sugars is probably the chief source of food energy for people.

In this investigation you will see why starch must be digested before it can be used by cells.

### MATERIALS

5 pieces of dialysis tubing about 10 cm long and 1.5-to-2 cm in diameter, 5 test tubes and stoppers with a diameter larger than the dialysis tubing, 100 ml of Lugol's iodine solution, 100 ml of soluble starch solution, 2 ml saliva mixed with 2 ml water, string (1 meter long), 5 droppers, 6 small test tubes, 20 ml Benedict's solution, 15 ml glucose or dextrose solution, 20 ml diastase solution, scissors.

### BRIEF PROCEDURE

Place different solutions and mixtures in dialysis membrane bags and surround them with other solutions and mixtures. Allow these to stand for a period of time, and then perform some observations or tests to determine whether the solutions or mixtures have been changed and whether they have diffused into or out of the dialysis bag.

### DETAILED PROCEDURE

**a. Pretesting the Indicators** Lugol's iodine solution and Benedict's solution are chemical indicators. To become familiar with the reactions of indicators, perform the following tests and record the changes observed so that you will know what each of the two solutions indicates.

1. Add a few drops of Lugol's iodine solution to a starch solution in a test tube.
2. Add a few drops of Lugol's iodine solution to some water in a test tube.
3. Add a few drops of Lugol's iodine solution to some glucose or dextrose solution in a test tube.
4. Add about 2 ml of Benedict's solution to an equal amount of glucose or dextrose solution in a test tube. Stand the tube in a boiling water bath and observe after about 5 minutes.
5. Add about 2 ml of Benedict's solution to an equal amount of water. Stand the tube in a boiling water bath for about 5 minutes.
6. Add about 2 ml of Benedict's solution to an equal amount of starch solution in a test tube. Stand the tube in a boiling water bath for 5 minutes.
7. Dilute a small amount of glucose or dextrose solution with about 10 parts water. Add 2 ml of this diluted sugar solution to an equal amount of Benedict's solution, and heat in a boiling water bath.
8. Add some Benedict's solution to some of your saliva in a test tube, and heat in a boiling water bath.
9. Add some Benedict's solution to an equal amount of diastase solution, and heat in a boiling water bath.

### DISCUSSION

1. Does Lugol's iodine solution change color when added to a sugar solution? Water? Starch solution?

2. Describe how you could use Lugol's iodine solution to see whether a certain food contained starch. For example, how would you test a raw potato for starch?

3. What color is Benedict's solution when mixed with water and heated?

4. What color is Benedict's solution when mixed with a rich sugar solution and heated? What color is the Benedict's solution when mixed with a weak sugar solution and heated?

5. What substance does hot Benedict's solution indicate?

6. Does saliva contain sugar? Explain.

7. Does diastase contain sugar? Explain.

## b. Diffusion and Digestion Experiments

### PROCEDURE

1. Examine Figure 19–A–1. It shows the setup for experiment A in Table 19–A–1. Each other experiment in the table is similar. Prepare a table like Table 19–A–1 and complete the hypothesis column according to what changes you think will occur. Indicate changes you think will take place in colors of indicators, and why. (Blue-black or purplish-black Lugol's

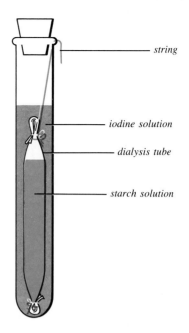

**Figure 19–A–1** Setup for dialysis experiment.

solution indicates starch. Orange Benedict's solution indicates sugar.)

2. Now assemble the materials for experiments A through E as listed in Table 19–A–1. Mark the test tubes A, B, C, D, and E. Add materials to

| Experiment | Materials Added to Dialysis Bag | Materials Added to Test Tube | Hypothesis (expected changes) | Observation (actual changes) | Explanation (what caused changes) |
|---|---|---|---|---|---|
| A | Starch solution | Lugol's iodine solution | | | |
| B | Lugol's iodine solution | Starch solution | | | |
| C | Glucose or dextrose | Water | | | |
| D | $^1/_2$ starch $^1/_2$ diastase | Water | | | |
| E | $^1/_2$ starch $^1/_2$ saliva | Water | | | |

**Table 19–A–1** Data table for digestion experiments.

the dialysis bags and test tubes according to directions in the table. Experiment A, when set up, should look like Figure 19–A–1. Rinse the outside of the dialysis bag for each experiment, A through E, before submerging the bag in the test tube solution.

3. After 5–10 minutes, make observations of tubes A and B and record your observations in the table.

4. Store tubes C, D, and E in a cool dark place for 24 hours.

5. After 24 hours carefully empty some of the contents of test tube C into a clean test tube. Label this tube W for water. Empty the contents of the dialysis bag into another test tube. Label the tube S. Add some Benedict's solution to each test tube and heat. Record observations.

6. Carefully empty the contents of test tube D into two separate new test tubes, and label these tubes W. Also empty the contents of the dialysis bag into two other test tubes, and label them S. Test one of the W tubes for starch and the other for sugar. Test one S tube for starch and the other for sugar. Record the results of these tests in your data table.

7. Repeat procedure 6 with test tube E.

## DISCUSSION

1. What conclusions can be drawn about the comparative sizes of starch particles and the particles of Lugol's iodine solution? Cite evidence from experiments A and B to support your answer.

2. What conclusions can be drawn about the comparative sizes of glucose particles and starch particles? Cite evidence from experiments A and C to support your answer.

3. As far as diffusion is concerned, the dialysis bag is similar to a cell's plasma membrane. What would be a limiting factor in the survival of ''dialysis cell'' C?

4. What two activities of digestion are illustrated by the results of the tests on the materials in experiment D?

5. How did the results of experiments D and E compare? Diastase is an enzyme found in some plants. What enzyme is it similar to that is found in your own body?

6. The acid content of the stomach destroys the action of the starch-digesting enzyme when food is swallowed. Will the starch that is not completely digested by enzymes in saliva go through the remainder of the digestive system unchanged and be of no value to the body? Explain. (See Figure 19–10.)

7. Why do doctors give glucose rather than starch as intravenous injections to patients whose digestive systems are not functioning properly?

## 19–B

## Do Plants Contain Enzymes That Digest Starch?

As you have seen in 19–A, your own saliva can change the starch stored in plants to a form that your body cells can absorb. How do plants use the starch they store? Do plants also have enzymes to change starch into a usable form? Is the finished product of starch digestion the same in plants as in humans? In this section you will have a chance to investigate these questions.

### MATERIALS

Pea or bean plant, sand (about 5 grams), mortar and pestle, cheesecloth (several layers), hot water bath, 10 ml starch solution A, scissors, 3 test tubes, Benedict's solution, funnel, 5 ml starch solution B, Lugol's iodine solution in dropping bottle, sand.

## PROCEDURE

1. Cut the entire plant into small pieces. Put the pieces into a mortar with 10 ml of water and a pinch of sand. Grind them thoroughly with a pestle.
2. Line the funnel with several layers of cheesecloth and set it in a test tube. Filter the crushed plant material through the funnel. Save the resulting filtrate (plant juice).
3. Put 3 ml of the filtrate in a test tube, and add 3 ml of starch solution A. Place 3 ml of distilled water in another test tube and add 3 ml of starch solution A.
4. After about 5 minutes add a few drops of the iodine solution to each of these tubes. Record the results.
5. Pour the remaining plant filtrate into two separate test tubes. Add 3 ml of starch solution B to one and 3 ml of water to the other. After 12–15 minutes, test both tubes for the presence of sugar by adding equal amounts of Benedict's solution to each tube and heating the two tubes in a boiling water bath.

## DISCUSSION

1. From the results of this experiment, what would you conclude about a plant's ability to digest starch?
2. Of what value to the plant is the ability to digest starch? Of what value to an animal is the ability to digest starch?
3. Where do you think digestion takes place in plants?
4. Animals have special glands for the production of enzymes that break large food molecules into smaller ones. What, if any, evidence from the results of this experiment indicates that plant cells possess similar enzymes?
5. Is the product of starch digestion similar in plants and animals? Explain.

## 19–C

## Fat Digestion

In this investigation you will observe the process of fat digestion by testing for the presence of fatty acids. **Pancreatin,** a mixture of substances obtained from the pancreas, is the source of the digestive enzymes for the reaction.

## MATERIALS

3 test tubes, test tube rack, fresh cream or milk, bile salts, fresh pancreatin solution, watch or clock, wax pencil, phenol red solution, water bath, NaOH solution (0.01 M, or 0.04%), droppers and pipettes, thermometer, distilled water.

## PROCEDURE

1. Set up three test tubes in a rack. Label the tubes 1, 2, and 3. Pour 5 ml of fresh cream or milk into each of the tubes. Add 8 to 10 drops of phenol red solution and shake the tubes until the contents are well mixed. What color is the liquid? If it is not pink, add NaOH solution a drop at a time until the liquid turns pink.
2. To the first test tube add 5 ml of distilled water and a pinch of bile salts (about the quantity held on the broad end of a flat toothpick). Bile salts break fat drops into tiny droplets, providing more surface areas on which enzymes can act.
3. To the second tube add 5 ml of the pancreatin solution and a pinch of bile salts.
4. Add 5 ml of the solution of pancreatin juice to the third tube.
5. Shake each tube until well mixed. Place the test tubes in a water bath maintained at about 35° C to 40° C. Watch for color changes; some of them may be rapid. Record the time required for a change from pink to yellow in any of the tubes. A change in color indicates that an acid has been produced.

**DISCUSSION**

1. Which test tube or tubes might be classified as controls?
2. The milk or cream is a complex substance that could contain more than one acid. How does this make tube 1 important to the experiment?
3. Does the presence of bile salts speed up the enzyme reaction? Why?
4. Does fat digestion take place if bile salts are not present? Explain.

5. What kind of acid is produced by the enzyme action on the fat? What kind of molecule other than the acid would you expect to find at this point? (See Figure 19–10.)
6. Describe an experiment to investigate the digestibility of different plant fats such as corn oil, safflower oil, and olive oil, or animal fats such as bacon fat, chicken fat, and beef tallow.

# Investigations for 20:

# Excretory Systems

## 20–A

### Earthworm Excretory Structures

The earthworm has the same problems of homeostasis and excretion as other living things. Water–salt balance must be maintained, and nitrogen-containing waste products must be eliminated. Although the earthworm is a land animal, it lives in moist soil and has a mucus-like covering over its body that reduces water loss. The earthworm's body is completely divided into segments. As you study the excretory system of the earthworm, remember these facts about the animal's structure and habitat.

### MATERIALS

Dissecting pan, dissecting set, dissecting pins, earthworm injected with methylene blue, magnifier, water, paper towels, anesthetic and applicator, colored pencils, slide, cover slip.

### PROCEDURE

1. Line the dissecting pan with paper towels and lay an anesthetized earthworm on it with the darker, more rounded side up.
2. Pin down both ends of the worm. If the anesthesia starts to wear off and the worm becomes active, ask your teacher for directions in applying more anesthetic.
3. Insert the point of a sharp pair of scissors just under the skin at the mouth end. Snip the skin all the way down the length. Be careful not to puncture the organs below or the blood vessels lying nearby.
4. Pin the body wall to the wax in the pan every few segments, securing first one side, then the other. To help expose the organs, cut through the fine tissue found along the digestive tract. (See Figure 20–A–1.)

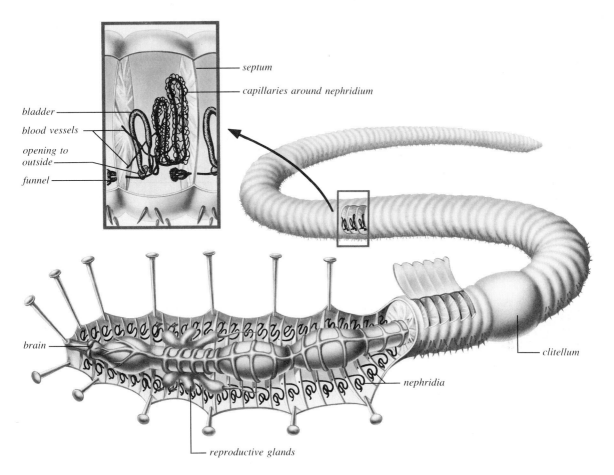

**Figure 20–A–1** Dissection of an earthworm revealing close association of blood vessels and nephridia. Trace the pathway of wastes through the nephridia.

5. Drop some water on the exposed organs and observe them carefully with a magnifier.

6. Locate the **nephridia** (nih-FRID-ee-uh). These are fine tubules coiled up and imbedded in each segment. Each nephridium has a funnel-like opening from a body segment into the next segment to the rear. There the nephridium has many coils and eventually opens to the outside of the body. These tubules remove wastes from the body fluid and carry them outside. Study the enlarged view in Figure 20–A–1 and note the relationship of the blood vessels to a nephridium. Recall that your specimen had a fluid called methylene blue injected into the body cavity to make the nephridia and blood vessels show up better. If a stereoscopic microscope is available, make observations at 15 to 20× magnification.

7. Using a fine forceps, carefully lift out a nephridium and prepare a wet mount. Focus it in the low-power field of your compound microscope. Make a sketch of your observation, coloring it as you see it. Check with your teacher to make sure that what you are observing is a nephridium. Examine the nephridium carefully for any signs of movement of the cilia around the funnel-like opening. Consider what function the cilia may have.

## DISCUSSION

1. In what general area is the blue color concentrated?
2. Recall the way materials diffuse through a membrane. How do you account for the differences of concentration of methylene blue along the length of the nephridium?
3. If a batch of earthworms were injected with methylene blue and one worm was opened every half hour after injection, predict the way the tubules would appear under low power.

Give reasons to support your prediction.

4. Predict the location of methylene blue in an earthworm three days after injection.
5. Compare the excretory systems of the grasshopper (Section 20–4) and the earthworm. How do they differ? What is the relationship of the transport system to the excretory tubules in each animal? Explain how each organism's method for dealing with the problem of water-salt balance is an adjustment to the organism's environment.

# Investigations for 21:

# Hormones and Endocrine Systems

## 21–A

### What Causes a Plant to Grow Toward Light?

You probably have seen evidence that plants adjust to their environment. A common example is the growth of plants toward light. It is often said that this happens because the plant needs the light in order to live and grow. Do you think plants grow toward the light because they "need" to do so? If not, why do plants turn toward light?

Experiments to study growth responses in plants require carefully controlled conditions of temperature, humidity, and light. The plant specimens must be alike and the experimenter must be experienced. For these reasons it will not be practical to do these growth studies yourself. Instead you will examine the data from some experiments that have already been carried out. Suppose that you are a scientist who has performed the experiments and has obtained the results described. Then do what the scientist would do: Analyze the data and draw the logical conclusions.

Five experiments will be described. In each of the experiments, groups of oat seedlings have been used as the experimental material. All plants in the five experiments were grown under the same conditions of temperature and humidity.

The following information will help you to understand the data that will be presented: the shoot of an oat seedling has an outer sheath called the **coleoptile** (koh-lee-OP-til), which covers the developing embryo leaves. The visible growth of the shoot results from the lengthening of cells in the coleoptile. When the shoot reaches a length of 4 to 6 centimeters, the coleoptile stops growing. The enclosed leaves and stem then split through the coleoptile and continue their growth upward. The following series of experiments is concerned with the coleoptiles only during the time when they lengthen rapidly.

## a. Removing and Replacing Coleoptile Tips

Three groups of oat seedlings of the same size were used for this experiment. The plants in the first group were left intact to serve as controls. The tip was cut from each coleoptile of the second group and then replaced on the cut surface. In the third group, the tip was cut off each coleoptile and discarded. All plants were grown in the dark for four hours.

The control plants grew normally, as shown in Figure 21–A–1. Those plants in which the cut tip was put back were only slightly shorter than the controls. Those plants from which the tip was removed completely were the same height as at the beginning of the experiment.

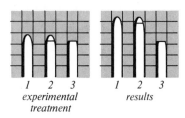

*1    2    3*
experimental
treatment

*1    2    3*
results

**Figure 21–A–1**  Oat coleoptile experiment **a**.

## DISCUSSION

1. In the second group of plants, did the coleoptile grow above or below the cut? (See Figure 21–A–1.)
2. How did the experimental treatments differ for the second and third groups of plants?
3. What evidence is there that some stimulation from the tip was necessary for growth of the coleoptile?
4. What conclusion can you draw from the results of this experiment?

## b. Inserting Agar and Mica Under Coleoptile Tips

Three more groups of oat seedlings were used in this experiment. The first group was untreated. In the second group the tip of each plant was cut off and a block of plain agar 1 mm thick was placed on top of the cut coleoptile. The tip was then put back on top of the agar. The tips were also removed from plants of the third group, but a thin sheet of mica, a substance that prevents diffusion, was placed between the coleoptile and the tip. All plants were grown in the dark.

As shown in Figure 21–A–2, the control plants grew longer. The plants of the second group grew about the same amount as the controls. Plants in the third group did not grow at all.

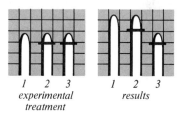

*1    2    3*
experimental
treatment

*1    2    3*
results

**Figure 21–A–2**  Oat coleoptile experiment **b**.

## DISCUSSION

1. How did the treatment of the two groups of experimental plants vary in this experiment?
2. What information is gained as a result of this experiment?

## c. Placing Treated Agar on Cut Tips

Juice was extracted from tips of oat seedlings. The extract was then mixed with agar from which small agar blocks were made. Blocks were also made of plain agar. Again three groups of oat plants were used. The first group was untreated. The tip was removed from each plant of the second group. The tip was then replaced with a block of agar containing juice from growing tips. The tip was also removed from each plant of the third group. The tip was then replaced with a block of agar without the juice. All plants were grown in the dark.

The results are shown in Figure 21–A–3. The control plants grew. Those with the agar blocks containing the juice from oat tips grew about the same as the controls. The group with plain agar blocks did not grow.

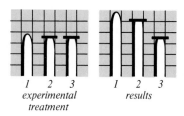

**Figure 21–A–3**  Oat coleoptile experiment **c.**

### DISCUSSION

1. How did the treatment of the two groups of experimental plants vary?
2. Why were plain agar blocks used on one of the groups of plants?
3. Is the coleoptile tip itself required for growth of the coleoptile? Explain.

### d. Placing Treated Agar on the Sides of Cut Tips

Four groups of plants were used in this experiment. The first group was allowed to grow normally, as a control. The tips were removed from the plants of the other three groups. In the second group, a block of agar mixed with juice from growing plant tips was placed on the right side of each cut coleoptile. A piece of agar treated in the same way was placed on the left side of each of the tips of plants in the third group. A block of plain agar was placed on each of the plants in the fourth group. All plants were grown in the dark.

As shown in Figure 21–A–4, the control plants in part **d** grew normally. The plants with the plain agar blocks did not change in length. Plants in the second and third groups each curved away from the side on which the agar block was placed.

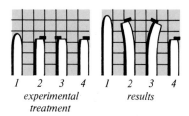

**Figure 21–A–4**  Oat coleoptile experiment **d.**

### DISCUSSION

1. In the plants that curved, where did most of the growth take place?
2. How do you account for the different rates of growth on the left and right sides of the plants in the second and third groups?
3. Recall that these plants were grown in the dark. Try to form a hypothesis to explain the fact that in the presence of light growing plants turn *toward* the light.

### e. Blocking the Growing Tips with Respect to the Direction of Light

The first group of plants was left untreated. In the second group, a small piece of mica was inserted between the growing tip and the rest of each coleoptile on the left side of each plant. A similar piece of mica was inserted into the right side of each plant in the third group. The three groups of plants were illuminated from the right side only.

The control plants curved toward the light. The behavior observed in the plants in the other two groups can be seen in Figure 21–A–5.

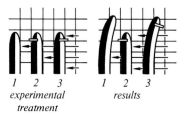

**Figure 21–A–5**  Oat coleoptile experiment **e.**

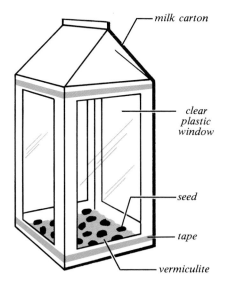

**Figure 21–B–1**  Seed germination containers.

## DISCUSSION

1. Under what lighting conditions were the first four experiments performed?
2. What seems to be the effect of light in experiment **e**?
3. Explain why plants in the second group in experiment **e** failed to grow.

4. Explain how a growing plant turns toward the light.

## 21–B

## How Does Light, or Its Absence, Affect the Growth of Plant Stems?

It is a well-known fact that light is necessary for the life of a green plant. It is the source of energy for the process of photosynthesis. However, the growth of the plant in height depends on the lengthening of its parts, especially the stem. Does light have any effect upon this growth of a plant's height? Which will be longer, a seedling grown in the light or one grown in the dark? Before you experiment to find the answers, form your own hypothesis concerning the effect of light upon the growth of a plant stem. Explain your hypothesis.

### MATERIALS

2 germination boxes (1 with opaque cover, 1 with transparent cover), 20 beans or peas, absorbent material, water, metric ruler.

### PROCEDURE

1. Place absorbent material in each germination box to a depth of about 2 cm. Add water until the material is moist throughout.
2. Place 10 beans (or peas) on the surface of the moist material in each box. (See Figure 21–B–1.) Place the foil on one box and the transparent plastic around the other. Put both boxes in a well-lighted place where the temperature range will be between 15°C and 35°C.
3. Check the boxes daily for moisture content. Add water if necessary, but avoid exposing the plants in the dark box to the light.
4. After one week remove the plants from each box and measure the lengths of the stems. Determine the average length of stems in each box.

## DISCUSSION

1. Do the results of the experiment support or contradict the hypothesis you proposed earlier? Explain.
2. What is the relationship between this experiment and the experiment with the oat coleoptiles in Investigation 21–A?
3. Explain the effect of light on stem growth, using the principles you learned in Section 21–1.
4. A 15-year-old maple tree growing in dense woods among older trees is 10 meters tall. The trunk diameter is 10 cm at one meter in height. The branches start 8 meters above the ground. Another maple of the same species and the same age is growing in a nearby field. It is not surrounded by older trees. It is 6 meters tall with a trunk diameter of 20 cm at one meter in height. The branches start less than 2 meters from the ground.

    If you did not know about auxins, you might explain this difference by saying that the tall, thin tree in the woods needs light for growth. Therefore it has grown tall and thin in order to reach some of the sunlight among the top branches of the older and taller trees. You might say that the second tree is short and bushy because there are no other trees around it to block the light from the sun. Therefore it does not need to grow tall.

    Give a better, more scientific explanation for the difference in growth patterns.

## 21–C

# Regulation of Secondary Sex Characteristics in Chickens

Many hormones regulate the activities necessary for the day-to-day life of an animal. Some of these function continuously. Others act only for a certain length of time, bringing about changes in body processes. The hormones that bring about the development of secondary sex characteristics in animals are of this second type. Secondary sex characteristics are features other than the actual reproductive organs that identify the sex of an individual. For example, as a boy changes to a man, his voice deepens and his beard grows.

In this investigation you will learn what influence testosterone, a male hormone, has on the development of secondary sex characteristics in young male chicks. Biologists use several different techniques to determine the influence of hormones in animals. One way is to remove the gland thought to produce the hormone. By studying what changes occur in the animal without this gland, scientists learn whether it produces the hormone and what effect the hormone has.

Another method of hormone study is to inject hormones into the animal to see what effect higher hormone concentrations than normal have on the animal. This is the technique that you will use in this investigation.

## MATERIALS

Six two-day-old cockerels, felt markers of 2 different colors, testosterone in oil (25 mg per ml), untreated oil, 70% alcohol solution, housing for chicks, 2 hypodermic needles, 2 syringes, cotton.

## PROCEDURE

1. Divide six cockerels into three pairs. Leave one pair unmarked. Mark the second and third pairs on top of the head with different colors. Pair 1 will be untreated; pair 2 will be injected with oil; and pair 3 will be injected with testosterone in oil.
2. Work with another student in the following injection procedure. Thoroughly clean with alcohol-soaked cotton, both a hypodermic needle and the skin in the wing pit (armpit) of one marked chick.
3. Under sterile conditions fill the syringe with the testosterone-oil mixture to the 1-cc mark and

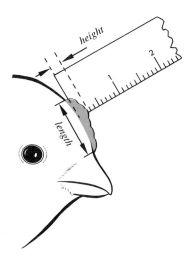

**Figure 21–C–1** Measuring a chick comb with a metric ruler.

expel all the air. Grasp the chick gently in the palm of your hand and turn the chick's lower side up. Raise its wing to expose the wing pit and with your fingers lift up a bit of skin in the wing pit. Holding the needle parallel to the chick's body, insert the needle under its skin and inject the fluid.

4. Rub the skin around the injected area with cotton to distribute the liquid. Replace the chick in its box. Repeat the procedure for the other similarly marked chick. Use the same procedure also to inject untreated oil into the two chicks marked with the second color.

5. Repeat the injection procedure daily for five days.

6. Measure to the nearest millimeter the length and height of the comb of each chick. Repeat this measurement each day for the next seven days, as in Figure 21–C–1. Use the equation to determine a comb factor for each chick each day, so that comparisons of this structure can be made.

$$\text{comb factor} = \frac{\text{comb length} \times \text{comb height}}{2}$$

7. For a few minutes each day during a week observe the behavior patterns of the three pairs. Record any differences between the experimental and the control pairs.

## DISCUSSION

1. What differences that appear to be related to male maturity were noted among the three pairs?

2. What was the purpose of each of the three pairs of chickens involved in the experiment?

3. The testosterone was injected beneath the skin under the wing but its effects were seen elsewhere. How was testosterone distributed throughout the body under these experimental conditions?

4. Under natural conditions the testosterone is produced by special cells in the testes of the maturing male chicken. What evidence do you have to show that the testosterone affects parts of the body other than the testes? How is testosterone distributed throughout the body under natural conditions?

5. Capons are roosters that have their testes removed very early in life. What probable effects would this have upon their appearance when they are mature?

6. What behavior in the experimental group indicates that testosterone affects more than structural characteristics? Do you think capons would show this behavior? Explain.

7. What prediction can you make concerning the production of testosterone by the male chicken as it grows and changes from a cockerel to an adult rooster under natural conditions?

# Investigations for 22:

# Nervous Systems

## 22–A

### What Does Your Touch Tell You?

The skin is sensitive to conditions and changes in the environment in many ways. You can tell whether the air is cold or warm, a point is sharp or dull, or a surface is rough or smooth. In this investigation you will do some exercises that will help you to understand the nature of some of the sensitive areas of your skin.

### a. How Accurate Is Your Skin's Sense of Temperature?

#### MATERIALS

Large container of hot water, large container of ice water, large container of lukewarm water.

#### PROCEDURE

1. Check the hot water to make sure it is somewhat more than comfortably warm, but not hot enough to burn your hand.
2. Put one of your hands in the hot water and the other in the ice water. Leave them there for one minute.
3. After one minute remove your hands from the hot water and ice water. Immediately sink both hands in the lukewarm water.
4. Record in your data book in general terms how the lukewarm water felt to each hand.

### b. How Far Apart Are the Touch-sensitive Areas on Your Fingertip and Back of the Hand?

#### MATERIALS

2 straight pins.

#### PROCEDURE

1. While your eyes are closed and your head is turned away, have your partner gently touch the end of your index finger with the points of both pins. Your partner will place the pins relatively far apart at first. After each contact with the two pins, tell your partner if you feel two points or only one. If two points are felt, your lab partner will lift the pins from your skin and touch your finger tip again with both points a little closer together. Again, tell your partner whether you feel both points or only one. Your partner will keep touching your fingertip with the pins, a little closer each time, until you find that even though both pins are touching your skin, you feel only one point. Don't peek.
2. Draw the outline of your finger in your data book. Put two pencil dots on the outline to represent the closest points where you could feel both pins.
3. Measure the distance in millimeters between the dots on your diagram. Measure in millimeters the width of your fingertip. Express these two measurements as a ratio.
4. Repeat steps 1, 2, and 3 using the back of the hand instead of the fingertip. Start the pin-touching technique with the points at least six centimeters apart.
5. List your ratios in a table on the chalkboard. Compare the ratios of people with large hands and fingers to people with smaller hands and fingers.

## c. Are Cold and Heat Detected at the Same Sensitive Spots on the Skin?

### MATERIALS

Hot-water bath, ice-water bath, 2 large nails.

### PROCEDURE

1. With washable ink, mark a 2.5-cm square on the back of your hand. Make an outline of your hand on a piece of paper. Make a similar square on the drawing.
2. Place one nail in the ice water and the other in the hot water for at least two minutes.
3. After two minutes remove the nail from the hot water. Dry it off, and check to make sure it is uncomfortably warm when touched to the skin but not hot enough to burn.
4. Close your eyes while your lab partner slowly moves the nail along the line around the square on the back of your hand. The head of the nail should maintain steady pressure on the skin. Movement should be slow and continuous.
5. At the times you feel the heat of the nail most sharply say "Mark." At this same point on the square of the drawing a third person will make a small *x*. Keep your eyes closed at all times. Make several trials, reheating the nail between trials.
6. Repeat the procedure using the cold nail. Mark the cold-sensitive areas on the drawing with a small *c*.
7. While your eyes are still closed, your lab partner will touch the back of your hand for only a second with either a hot or cold nail. Relying only on your sense of touch, can you easily tell the difference between hot and cold? Make several trials with the different nails. Determine whether you have difficulty in identifying temperature by touch.

### DISCUSSION

1. Feeling the forehead is a common way to find out whether body temperature is above normal. On the basis of discoveries in this investigation explain how a person with a temperature of 40°C (104°F) might feel cool to the touch.
2. Are the sensitive areas that are stimulated by cold the same sensitive areas that are stimulated by heat? Explain.
3. If a person heard a crackling fire and people talking about heat, and then suddenly was touched with a piece of ice on the back of the neck, what would the first reaction and interpretation probably be? Explain.
4. Is there any correlation between finger and hand size and the distance between touch-sensitive areas?
5. Give a hypothesis that could account for the fact that even though two pins are touching your skin you feel only one.

## 22–B

## The Mammalian Eye: Its Parts and How They Work

The eye is a very complex receptor. In this investigation, you will examine the structure of a mammalian eye. As you perform the dissection, try to understand the role played by each part of the eye in receiving light stimuli. Refer to Figure 22–B–1

**Figure 22–B–1** Diagram of a mammalian eye in cross section.

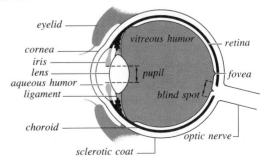

throughout the investigation to help clarify your understanding of the structure and function of the eye.

## MATERIALS

Cow or sheep eye, scalpel, small piece of newspaper, scissors, cover slip, forceps, dissecting pan.

## PROCEDURE

1. If eyelids are present on the eye specimen, cut them off. With sharp dissecting scissors or a scalpel, remove the white, fatty tissue from the rear half of the eyeball. Be careful not to cut off the white stub protruding from the rear of the eye. Look at Figure 22–B–1 to find what this structure is. Use the diagram as a reference to rotate the eyeball to its correct body position. Does the optic nerve enter the eyeball directly behind the lens?

2. Insert the point of the scissors or a sharp scalpel in the back of the eyeball just above the optic nerve. Pierce the tough, white outer coat of the eye. What is the name of this coat? Notice that it is a continuous layer extending over the entire surface of the eye. Observe, however, that in the front part of the eye the coat is transparent. In a preserved specimen this area may appear blue and opaque, but in life it is actually colorless and transparent. Note also that this transparent portion of the **sclerotic coat,** called the **cornea,** may be more sharply curved than the rest of the coat.

3. Cut out the optic nerve, leaving a small opening in the back of the eyeball. Cover the hole with a cover slip to keep the jelly-like liquid that fills the eyeball from escaping. Now hold the eyeball near your own eye so that you can look at the front of the eye through the opening that you have cut. By shifting the position of the eyeball slightly in various directions you may be able to look through it and see the images of objects in front of it. Are these images right side up or upside down?

4. Place the eyeball in the dissecting pan with the cornea downward. Cut the eyeball into two halves, front and rear, by piercing the wall of the eyeball with the point of the scissors and cutting all the way around the eyeball. Lift off the rear half. A jelly-like substance may stick to the front half, particularly to the lens. Remove this jelly-like material with forceps and dissecting needle. Describe the substance. What is it called? What function do you think it serves?

5. Without cutting beyond the cornea, insert the point of the scissors at the outer edge of the cornea and cut all the way around it. Lift off the cornea. A muscular partition called the **iris** is now exposed. Through the opening in the iris, called the pupil, observe the **lens.** The lens is colorless and transparent in life but usually is opaque in preserved specimens. In life the space between the cornea and the lens is filled with a colorless, transparent, watery fluid. What is the name of this fluid? What function do you think it serves?

6. Examine the lens from both the front and the rear. Notice how it is attached to the eyeball by a circular band of delicate fibers. See if you can discover how the shape of the lens changes. The lens is thickest when it is adjusted to bring images of near objects into focus. The lens becomes thinner to bring more distant objects into focus.

7. Carefully cut around the edge of the lens with a scalpel. Remove the lens from its attachments and lay it on a piece of newspaper. What is the shape of the lens? Can you see through it? With your scalpel cut or peel the lens tissue. Is the lens of the eye rigid like a glass lens?

8. Examine the rear half of the eyeball and notice the grayish inside layer. What is the name of this inner coat of the eyeball? Notice the blood vessels that line this layer. This layer also contains the specialized nerve cells, known as **rods** and **cones,** that function as light receptors.

9. Where the optic nerve leaves the eyeball there is a blind spot because no light-sensitive rods or cones are present at this point. You can demonstrate the existence of the blind spot in your own eyes by closing your right eye and focusing your left eye on the cross in Figure 22–B–2. Start with the page about 12 cm from the eye and gradually move the page farther away until the circle disappears. At that position the image of the circle falls on your blind spot.

**Figure 22–B–2** Visual aid for locating the blind spot on the retina. Follow the directions in step 9 of the Procedure.

10. Note the size of the irises and pupils of a classmate's eyes. Now have your classmate cover his or her eyes completely for a period of at least 2 minutes. When they are uncovered again, immediately note the size of the pupils and irises. Continue to observe for at least 15 seconds. Compare the size of the pupils and the irises of your classmate's eyes before covering them and immediately after uncovering them. What happened during the next few seconds after the eyes were uncovered? Does the iris have anything to do with this? Explain.

## DISCUSSION

1. Why can you see better after being in a darkened room for a few minutes than when you first enter?

2. Many people, as they get older, find that they need glasses to improve their vision. List some of the structures in the eye that you think might lose their efficiency with age.

3. Many animals are active at night and apparently see better in the dark than humans do. How are their eyes adapted for night vision?

4. Write a paragraph summarizing how light is received by the eye.

## 22–C

# Chemical Receptors of Taste and Smell

The sensation of taste is produced by changes in the chemical environment of the mouth. Specialized nerve endings located in the taste buds of the tongue are sensitive to the changes. When these nerve endings are stimulated by the chemical changes, nerve impulses are carried to the brain. When the impulses reach the brain, taste is experienced. Smelling, like tasting, is due to a chemical stimulus. The specialized organs for the sense of smell are similar in structure to those for taste. They are located in the upper areas of the nose. When the vapors of a substance reach the moist lining of the nose, they dissolve. The solutions stimulate receptors, cells specialized to receive stimuli. You will investigate how these receptors work.

### MATERIALS

Toothpicks; watch glass; sterile cotton; 1% acetic acid solution; 5 sugar solutions: 0.1%, 0.5%, 5%, 10%, 20%; 5 salt solutions: 0.3%, 1.5%, 2.5%, 4%, 6%; 0.1% quinine sulfate solution; squares of sterile gauze; oil of peppermint; sugar crystals; oil of cloves.

## PROCEDURE

1. **Taste of undissolved substances.** Wipe your tongue dry with a piece of gauze and then place some sugar crystals on the tongue. Do you taste anything? Why do you think it is necessary for a substance to be in solution before it can be tasted?

2. **Temporary change in a sense receptor.** Sniff oil of cloves through one nostril by holding the other nostril closed and breathing the air out through the mouth.

---

> **CAUTION:** Do not hold the bottle of oil too close to the nose, for it may produce a burning sensation.

---

Record the time required before you can no longer detect the odor of cloves. Then try oil of peppermint. Can you smell it?

3. **Location of various types of taste receptors.** To find out the locations of the different taste receptors, place approximately 1 ml or less of 10% salt solution in a watch glass. Dip a small quantity of sterile cotton wrapped around a toothpick into the solution. Apply the solution to a small area on the surface of the tongue. Then apply the solution to other areas until the whole tongue surface has been tested. Avoid applying excess solution. Note the areas where salt can be tasted. Particularly observe those areas where the taste is sharpest. Repeat this test for each of the following solutions: 20% sugar, 1% acetic acid, and 0.1% quinine sulfate. Between applications, rinse your mouth with a small amount of water. Diagram the tongue showing where sensations of salt, sweet, sour, and bitter are most strongly tasted.

4. **Threshold of taste.** Place one drop of 0.1% sugar solution on the area of the tongue most sensitive to sweet. Note whether or not a sweet taste can be detected. Repeat the testing using 0.5%, 5%, 10%, 20% solutions. Rinse your mouth with water between tests. Record the most dilute solution that you can taste. This is your threshold stimulus. Repeat the above procedure with various concentrations of salt solutions: 0.3%, 1.5%, 2.5%, 4%, 6%. Determine your threshold for salt in the area of the tongue most sensitive to salt. Compare your threshold values for salt and sugar with those of the class. Compare these values for salt and sugar for males and for females in your class. Do you notice any other patterns?

# Investigations for 23:

# Skeletal and Muscular Systems

## 23–A

### Making Muscles Move

In Chapter 23 you have seen that vertebrates have two kinds of muscle, smooth and striated. Smooth muscle contracts slowly in involuntary movement; striated muscle is fast-acting and is involved in voluntary movement. Cardiac muscle, a special kind of striated muscle, is involuntary.

Section 23–10 mentions a chemical messenger released by motor neurons into striated muscle fibers. Chemical messengers are of more than one type and affect both striated and smooth muscle. Adrenaline and acetylcholine, as well as norepinephrine, are secreted by nerves. They affect the rate of muscular contraction. Do different kinds of muscles react in different ways to these chemicals?

In this investigation you will determine the effects of adrenaline and acetylcholine upon the activity of cardiac and smooth muscle tissue from the heart and stomach of the frog.

### MATERIALS

Frog, 500 ml Ringer's solution, 2 petri dishes, 2 droppers or syringes, 10 ml adrenaline solution, 10 ml acetylcholine solution, watch with second hand, scissors, forceps.

### PROCEDURE

1. Obtain a frog from your instructor. An operation called "double pithing" has been performed on the frog so that its brain and spinal cord no longer function and it cannot feel pain. Open the abdomen and slit the membrane around the heart. Carefully remove the heart by lifting it gently with forceps and cutting the blood vessels leading to it. Take care not to cut or injure the chamber where the principal veins join before entering the heart.

2. Wash the heart in Ringer's solution to remove any remaining blood. Then put the heart in a petri dish of Ringer's solution. (Ringer's solution is a solution of salts comparable in composition to the body fluid.)

3. Remove the stomach from the abdomen of the frog and place it in the same petri dish with the heart.

4. Observe the activity of each tissue. In a table record the rate of contraction or beats and relative strength of each. Use these figures as the control rate of activity before the drugs are added.

5. Add two drops of acetylcholine solution to the Ringer's solution. Observe the changes in activity, and note any changes in relative strength of contraction of the two tissues. If two drops do not change the strength of contraction, add some more, one drop at a time. Wait about a minute between drops so you can observe any differences in activity. Record the total number of drops you applied.

6. Put the organs in a fresh dish of Ringer's solution. Wait 3 to 5 minutes until the activity of the tissues returns to the original control levels. If the tissues do not return to the original levels, use the new rate as a new control rate. Now add two drops of acetylcholine and record the changes. Then add one drop more. Repeat this at least four times, ending with a dose large enough to stop activity in both tissues. Record the results.

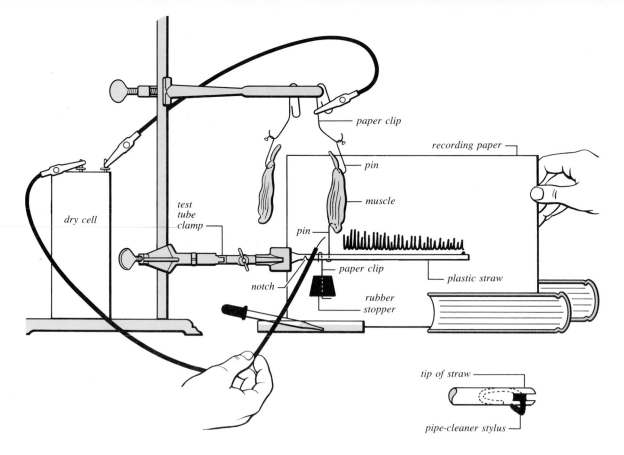

**Figure 23–B–1** Setup for muscle-contraction experiment. The details of fitting the pipe-cleaner stylus in the end of the straw are shown enlarged at the lower right.

7. Put the tissues in a fresh bath of Ringer's solution and repeat the previous steps, using adrenaline instead of acetylcholine. Record the results as before.

**DISCUSSION**

1. What is the effect of adrenaline on cardiac muscle? On smooth muscle?
2. What is the effect of acetylcholine on cardiac muscle? On smooth muscle?
3. How can the activity of cardiac and smooth muscle be changed?
4. Was the response to each drug the same in both tissues?
5. What kind of muscle control is indicated by the fact that the muscles continue to contract even when the nerve connection has been severed?

## 23–B

## What Causes Fatigue in Skeletal Muscles?

The continued contraction of a particular muscle of your body will soon tire you. If the contractions are continued, the muscle will begin to hurt and will finally stop contracting. During a short period of rest, changes occur in the muscle that will enable it to contract again.

Why do muscles stop contracting after a period of continuous stimulation? Do they use up all their energy? What happens during rest to enable a muscle to contract again? The primary energy source of muscle is the food delivered by the blood. Waste produced by the working muscles is removed by the circulatory system. Can a muscle contract and continue contracting without blood circulating through it? Once a muscle is fatigued, or tired, can it be stimulated to contract again without the services of the circulatory system?

In this investigation you will explore some of these questions and determine some of the characteristics of fatigue in a frog leg muscle.

## MATERIALS

Double-pithed frog, dissecting kit, dissecting pan, $1^{1}/_{2}$-volt dry cell or flashlight battery, wire leads for battery, ring stand with clamp and ring, plastic drinking straw, pipe cleaner, straight pins and tool for bending, 2 petri dishes, 100 ml Ringer's solution, watch with second hand, ink and dropper.

## PROCEDURE

### a. Muscle Contraction

1. Assemble the materials as shown in Figure 23–B–1. The recording paper should be taped to a stiff card to give it support. Place two books on the table to make a track through which the card with the recording paper can be moved. Arrange the track so the pipe cleaner stylus makes very light contact with the paper. (Note the enlarged view of the pipe cleaner stylus under the drawing of the overall setup in Figure 23–B–1.) Apply ink to the stylus only after the muscle is attached and everything is ready to start recording.

2. Remove the skin from both hind legs of the frog by cutting the skin around the entire body behind the front legs and pulling it off the lower body and legs like removing a rubber glove.

3. Locate the frog leg muscle (shown in blue in Figure 23–B–2) that corresponds to the calf muscle in humans. Notice where the ends of the muscle are attached. What leg action would be produced by the contraction of this muscle?

4. Remove this muscle from both legs by inserting one point of the scissors under the material that attaches the muscle to the bone. What is this

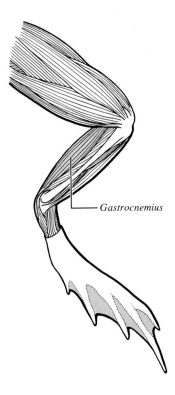

**Figure 23–B–2** The gastrocnemius muscle in a frog's leg.

cordlike attachment material called? Cut each muscle free at both ends and place the muscles in a petri dish of Ringer's solution.

5. Remove the muscles from the solution and attach them to the ring as shown in Figure 23–B–1. Attach only one muscle to the recording device. Add Ringer's solution to the muscles with a dropper. Both muscles must be kept wet with Ringer's throughout the entire experiment.

6. Work in teams of three or four to record the contractions. Stimulate the muscle attached to the straw recorder at one-second intervals until it stops responding to the stimulus. While one student stimulates the muscle by touching the free lead wire to the pin that holds the muscle to the straw, another student will move the recording paper slowly through the book track.

Add ink to the stylus before starting and as needed thereafter. It may be necessary to miss a few contractions while you re-ink the stylus.

One member of the team will serve as the pacemaker by using a watch with a second hand and counting at one-second intervals. Move the paper at a rate that will record one minute of contractions per length of paper. (The marks will be about 0.3 cm apart.) As the recording reaches the end of the paper, invert the paper quickly and continue recording on the other half of the same page, or insert new paper.

Number the records according to the minute intervals so that a continuous series can be made by cutting the papers across the middle and taping the record together in order. Have 4 or 5 recording papers prepared so you can make a continuous record of the muscle contraction without allowing rest periods. Continue stimulating and recording the responses of the muscle until it no longer contracts when stimulated.

7. Allow the muscle to rest for one minute. Then stimulate it again at one-second intervals until it is again exhausted.

8. After five minutes' rest, repeat the procedure.

**b. Sources of Fatigue** The following steps include two experiments. One or two groups in the class should follow steps 1 and 2. Others should follow steps 3 and 4.

1. To investigate whether time alone might be the cause of fatigue, one or two groups should remove the exhausted muscle from the recording apparatus and attach the other muscle. Steps 6, 7, and 8 of part **a** can then be repeated for comparison of the two muscles.

2. Cut the paper in half and tape the strips together for a continuous record of contractions for the second muscle. Compare the two records.

3. To investigate whether muscle becomes exhausted because it has no chance to rest, remove the exhausted muscle and attach the muscle from the other leg to the recording straw. Record the contractions as before but give this muscle a one-minute rest after each minute of contraction. Continue stimulating at one-second intervals for one minute, then resting for one minute, until the muscle is exhausted.

4. To determine the total work done by each muscle, count the contractions and measure the height of each in centimeters. Then weigh the straw and the weight lifted to the nearest gram. The total height in centimeters times the total weight in grams lifted equals work done in gram-centimeters. Compare the work of the two muscles.

**DISCUSSION**

1. For one muscle, how does the strength of contraction in the first minute compare with the strength in the second minute?

2. Why were the experiments done with two muscles from the same frog? Would muscles from different frogs have served as well? Explain.

3. In steps 1 and 2 of part **b,** if the second muscle had been left attached to the frog until it was used in the experiment, would it have served its purpose as well? Explain.

4. Based on your experiment, select the most logical explanation for muscle fatigue:
   a. Muscle fatigue is the failure of a muscle to contract when stimulated, due to lack of available energy.
   b. Muscle fatigue is the failure of a muscle to contract when stimulated, due to accumulation of some by-product that cannot be removed quickly enough by the circulatory system.
   c. Muscle fatigue is the failure of a muscle to contract when stimulated, due to accumulation of some by-product that enzymes in the muscle cell then change in form.

Explain your choice by using data from the experiment as evidence.

# The Organism and Behavior

## 24–A

### How Does Gravity Affect Plants?

You may find it difficult to think of plants as exhibiting behavior. However, behavior is a characteristic of all life, not of animals alone. Plants do not have nerves. Their behavior is controlled by hormones and other chemicals.

In this investigation you will observe plant behavior in response to gravity.

### MATERIALS

4 soaked corn kernels, petri dish, paper towels, masking tape, glass marker, colored pens or pencils, India ink.

### PROCEDURE

1. Space the four corn kernels in the bottom of a petri dish with the cotyledon side down, as shown in Figure 24–A–1.
2. Cushion the kernels on top with moist strips of paper towel. Use enough to make sure that the pointed ends face the center and that the kernels remain in that position when the dish is turned on its side.
3. Cover the dish and secure the lid with strips of masking tape.
4. On the bottom of the dish, label the locations of the kernels A, B, C, and D.
5. Stand the petri dish on edge in a dark place and fasten it in that position with tape.
6. Make a sketch of the setup in your notebook. Each day, sketch the growth of the seedlings. Use different colors for the roots and shoots. Be sure to record the *directions* of growth.

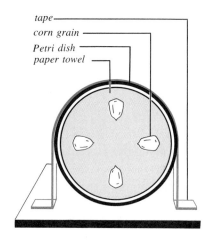

*tape*
*corn grain*
*Petri dish*
*paper towel*

**Figure 24–A–1** Corn kernels wedged in position in vertical petri dish.

7. After two days, remove the lid of the petri dish and use India ink to mark the tips of the roots and shoots of all seedlings. Replace the lid and secure it with tape. Stand the dish on edge as before, then rotate it one-quarter turn so that a seedling that was previously to one side is now on top.
8. Allow the seedlings to grow for two more days. Continue recording data and sketches.

### DISCUSSION

1. In what direction does root growth take place? shoot growth?
2. How does this response of corn seedlings help the plants to survive?
3. How would you design an experiment to show that light or darkness does not cause the growth response of the roots and shoots of seedlings?

## 24–B

# Do Paramecia Behave Sensibly?

Can one-celled organisms like the *Paramecium* detect differences in their environmental conditions? Can they respond in an organized way to the environment? Data collected from the following exercises will help answer these questions.

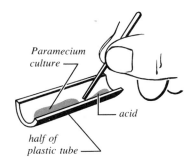

**Figure 24–B–1** Technique for adding acid to a *Paramecium* culture.

### MATERIALS

Grains of sand, 2 inches of $^1/_4$-inch clear plastic tubing cut lengthwise to form a trough, 1 large salt crystal, $1^1/_2$-volt dry cell with wire leads, 1 tube of *Paramecium* culture, 3 droppers, 1 dropping bottle with weak acetic acid, 4 toothpicks, stereoscopic microscope or hand lens, tape.

### PROCEDURE

As you start each numbered experiment, use a clean trough (rinsed in fresh water) and a fresh drop of *Paramecium* culture.

1. **Observing paramecia** Set the clean trough on the stage of the stereoscopic microscope. Place a large drop of the *Paramecium* culture near one end of the trough. Observe the movements of the paramecia for a few minutes and record your observations.
2. **Reaction of paramecia to foreign matter** Place a few grains of sand in the drop of water with the paramecia and observe their reactions. Sketch your observations. Mark the position of the sand grains in your sketch.
3. **Reaction of paramecia to salt** Place a salt crystal in the trough, touching one edge of the water. Sketch the reactions of the paramecia in the area of the dissolving salt.
4. **Reaction of paramecia to acetic acid** Place a small drop of vinegar or weak acetic acid close to (but not touching) a drop of *Paramecium* culture in the trough. Use the end of a toothpick to drag a little acid to the edge of the water drop (Figure 24–B–1). Do not stir or mix the

acid and water. Let the acid diffuse gradually from the point of contact. How do the paramecia react? Use the toothpick to add more acid. Sketch your observations.

5. **Reaction of paramecia to an electric current** Put a large drop of *Paramecium* culture in the plastic trough. Position the trough on the microscope stage so you can observe the entire drop. Place one lead from the dry cell at one edge of the water drop so the wire is just touching the water. Place the other wire at the opposite edge of the water drop. Tape the leads in place. Connect the leads to the dry cell and observe the reactions of the paramecia. Then reverse the leads on the dry cell and observe the reaction. Sketch your observations.

### DISCUSSION

1. Do paramecia react in an organized manner to environmental changes? Give examples.
2. From your sketches make a table of the reactions of paramecia to each condition tested.
3. What effect did reversing the direction of the electric current have on the paramecia? Were the paramecia attracted to a particular pole?
4. How might some of the responses of paramecia help them to survive?

# Animal Populations and Societies

## 25–A

### Observing Crayfish in a Small Habitat

What kinds of behavior described in this chapter do crayfish exhibit? Do they have behavior patterns unique to crayfish? This observation activity will provide some firsthand answers to these questions.

### MATERIALS

Aquarium tank or large plastic tub, broken flower pots, washed gravel, dechlorinated water, 4 or 5 crayfish.

### PROCEDURE

1. Set up an aquatic habitat for a group of crayfish. To do this, place 3 to 5 cm of washed gravel in the bottom of an aquarium tank or large plastic tub. Next, put dechlorinated water into the tank or tub to a depth of about 3 to 5 cm above the gravel. Add the pieces of up to a half-dozen broken flower pots to the new habitat, spreading the pieces out so that the habitat looks something like the drawing in Figure 25–A–1. Compare your group's habitat with that of other groups.

**Figure 25–A–1** Aquatic habitat for crayfish.

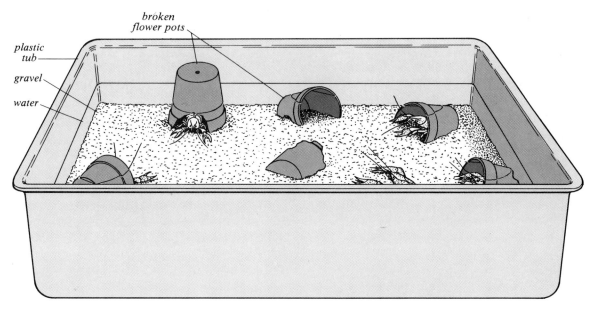

2. Place the habitat on a sturdy table so that your entire working group can observe the crayfish.

3. Use pencil and paper for recording your observations.

4. Place four or five crayfish in their "new" habitat. (Your teacher will instruct you on the correct procedure for handling crayfish.)

5. Observe and record all of the behaviors that result when the crayfish are placed together. (Remember that this is not the crayfish's natural habitat.) If a great deal of interaction results, you may have to designate a different person to watch each crayfish and record its behavior.

6. Observe the crayfish for the remainder of the class period. Locate a unique feature or marking on each crayfish so that you can keep track of each individual.

7. At the end of the class period note where each crayfish is located in the habitat. Observe the crayfish during the next several days and notice any behavior changes or changes in the location or distribution of different crayfish.

## DISCUSSION

1. List and describe the behaviors you noticed with your crayfish.

2. Do crayfish in your artificial habitat exhibit territorial behavior? If so, how quickly can a territory be established? *How* is it established? How can it be changed?

3. How could you further test your answers to question 2?

4. What would you predict would happen if you introduced a new crayfish into the habitat?

5. Based on your classroom observations, what guidelines and questions would you list to help you observe crayfish behavior in a natural habitat? (An example of such a habitat is a shallow stream with a gravel bottom and with rocks protruding above the surface.)

# Appendixes

# Appendixes

## 1–A

## Measurement in Science

The metric system is the standard system of measurement in all nations of the world except one—the United States. Scientists, engineers, and other groups in the United States also use the metric system.

The official name of the internationally standardized metric system is the International System of Units, abbreviated SI (for Système Internationale). Its units of measurement are easily manipulated by doing calculations with ten or powers of ten. Among its basic units of measurement are the **meter** (length), the **kilogram** (mass), the **kelvin** (temperature), and the **second** (time). All lengths are based on that of the meter, and all volumes on a *cubic meter*. All units of mass are based on the kilogram. The intervals, or units, of the temperature scale that you will use, *degrees Celsius,* are equal to kelvins.

The major exception you will take to SI measurement is in the measure of volume. You will use *liters* and decimals of liters, rather than cubic meters and their decimals. Liter measure is widely used for liquids, and most of your volume measurements in biology will be of liquids. Liter measure is accepted by SI, although not officially as a part of it. Like the cubic meter, the liter is also metric (1 liter = 0.001 cubic meter).

Some of the SI units derived from the basic units for length and mass follow:

### 1. Length

| | | |
|---|---|---|
| 1 kilometer | = | 1000 meters |
| 1 hectometer | = | 100 meters |
| 1 dekameter | = | 10 meters |
| 1 meter | = | defined basic unit |

| | | |
|---|---|---|
| 1 decimeter | = | 0.1 meter |
| 1 centimeter | = | 0.01 meter |
| 1 millimeter | = | 0.001 meter |
| 1 micrometer | = | 0.000001 meter |
| 1 nanometer | = | 0.000000001 meter |

Measurements under microscopes are often made in micrometers. Still smaller measurements, as for wavelengths of light used by plants in photosynthesis, are made in nanometers.

Abbreviations of some units of length that you will use in your work are:

kilometer (km)
meter (m)
centimeter (cm)
millimeter (mm)
micrometer ($\mu$m)
nanometer (nm)

Units of area are derived from units of length by multiplication. For example, 1 square meter is written 1 $m^2$; it is also called a *centare*. One square hectometer is a measure often used for biological field studies; it is commonly called a *hectare* and equals 10,000 square meters. Other measures for area include much smaller ones, such as $cm^2$ and $mm^2$, both of which you will use in your laboratory studies.

### 2. Mass

| | | |
|---|---|---|
| 1 kilogram | = | 1000 grams |
| 1 hectogram | = | 100 grams |
| 1 dekagram | = | 10 grams |
| 1 gram (derived from basic unit, kilogram) | | |
| 1 decigram | = | 0.1 gram |
| 1 centigram | = | 0.01 gram |
| 1 milligram | = | 0.001 gram |
| 1 microgram | = | 0.000001 gram |
| 1 nanogram | = | 0.000000001 gram |

Measurements of mass in your biology laboratory will usually be made in kilograms, grams, centigrams, and milligrams. Abbreviations of some of the listed units of mass are as follows:

kilogram (kg)    milligram (mg)
gram (g)         microgram (μg)
centigram (cg)   nanogram (ng)

The units you will use for volume and for temperature follow:

## 3. Volume

1 kiloliter   = 1000 liters (1 cubic meter)
1 hectoliter  =  100 liters
1 dekaliter   =   10 liters
1 liter (derived from the cubic meter)
1 deciliter   =    0.1 liter
1 centiliter  =    0.01 liter
1 milliliter  =    0.001 liter

Your volume measurements in the laboratory will usually be made in glassware marked for milliliters and liters. Abbreviations for these units are as follows: liter (1) and milliliter (ml).

## 4. Temperature

Your laboratory thermometers may read from 0° to 100° Celsius (abbreviated C). Or, since you may be reading temperatures below 0°C, some thermometers may read 30° or 40° below zero.

On the Celsius scale, the freezing point of pure water is 0° and the boiling point is 100°. Atmospheric pressure affects both the freezing point and the boiling point.

Figure 1–A–1 shows the Celsius scale alongside the Fahrenheit scale that is still used in the United States. On the Fahrenheit scale, 32°F and 212°F correspond to 0°C and 100°C.

SI measurement includes still other basic units that you will not use in your biology studies (units of electric current, of force, and of amount of sub-

**Figure 1–A–1**  Temperature-conversion scale.

stance, for example. The basic unit for amount of substance is the **mole.** In the laboratory, molarity (labeled with the letter "M") measures the concentration of a dissolved substance in a solution. You should be aware that a high molarity indicates a high concentration. If you wish to learn still more about SI measurement, write to the U.S. Department of Commerce, National Bureau of Standards, Washington, D.C. 20234, and request their informational booklet entitled *The International System of Units (SI)*.

## 2–A–1 Structures of the Generalized Eukaryotic Cell

| name and approximate dimension of structure | general description of structure | functions and activities of structure |
|---|---|---|
| plasma membrane 6 to 9 nm thick | two lipid layers; surface and embedded proteins; carbohydrates; attached carbohydrates; 2 layers of lipids; proteins | semifluid (fluid mosaic) cell boundary; may or may not be enclosed by cell walls; mostly lipid, permeable to diffusion of many materials; contains enzymes among its proteins; actively transports some materials |
| nucleus 5–10 μm | nuclear envelope contains two unit membranes; chromatin fibers; pores (annul) 50–100 nm; nucleolus | contains most of cell's genetic information; DNA of chromatin carries code for direction of mRNA synthesis; chromatin condenses as individually distinguishable chromosomes during mitosis (or meiosis in gamete-producing cells); nucleolus is described below |
| chloroplasts 2–5 μm long and 0.5–1 μm thick | double unit membrane; thylakoids; stroma (clear); grana | complete cycles (both light and dark reactions) of photosynthesis occur here; contain small amounts of DNA and RNA; chlorophyll and carotenoid pigments are located in the thylakoids of grana where the light reactions produce ATP, NADPH, and $O_2$; $CO_2$ fixation and dark reactions occur in stroma |
| mitochondria 2–10 μm long and 0.5–1 μm thick | inner membrane; space between membranes; outer membrane | Krebs cycle (aerobic respiration) occurs partly inside mitochondria and partly on and in the inner membrane; respiratory chains and ATP-synthesizing enzymes occur on and in the inner membrane; contain small amounts of DNA and RNA (including part of own hereditary material); several hundred or more mitochondria per cell |
| nucleolus 2–5 μm diameter | fibrillar area; dense area | no membrane around nucleolus; site of synthesis and assembly of ribosome RNA and tRNA; mostly protein with about 5% RNA; nucleoli are produced by certain chromosomes; none to 20 nucleoli per cell |

| Organelle | Diagram | Description |
|---|---|---|
| ribosomes 20-22 nm diameter | 60S unit (polypeptide chain grows here); 40S unit (mRNA and tRNA attach here) | contain about 40% RNA and 60% protein; produced by nucleolus; consist of two parts that participate in protein synthesis; ribosomes are also present in prokaryotic cells, nuclei, chloroplasts, and mitochondria; exist in groups called polysomes |
| lysosomes 250-500 nm | unit membrane; enzymes; food vacuole; food particles | contain enzymes that act on RNA, DNA, polypeptides (cathespin), galactosides, and several other compounds; lysosomes fuse with vacuoles containing food particles ingested by the cell, and the enzymes digest the particles; most common in liver, spleen, leucocytes; not present in plant cells |
| endoplasmic reticulum (ER) 5-6 nm diameter | membrane of smooth ER; rough ER (with ribosomes) | a tubular (round or flat) membrane system found in cytoplasm; rough ER is found where active protein synthesis occurs; ER probably functions partly to compartmentalize different activities in the cytoplasm; also channels some enzymes and other secretions; other enzymes are in ER membrane |
| golgi complex 20-40 nm diameter | golgi complex; centrioles; lysosomes | lies near nuclear envelope with centrioles in cuplike proximity; complex is most prominent in synthesizing cells; cell may contain one or more complexes; probable source of lysosomes by placing membrane around enzymes produced on ribosomes; may produce nonprotein secretions |
| cilia and flagella 200 nm diameter by 10-150 μm long | cilium with 9-2 microfibril pattern (cross section); basal body (centriole); plasma membrane | flagella are long cilia; each contains 9 pairs of microfibrils around perimeter with two fibrils in the center—same pattern in plant sperm, protista, and lower animals |
| centrioles 150 nm diameter by 500 nm long | fibrils arranged as 9 triplets; centriole pairs (centrosome) | centrioles and basal bodies of cilia are identical; centrioles occur in pairs during interphase; they exist at each pole of the spindle during mitosis in protista and in animal cells |

## 5–A

## Redi's Experiments Yield Evidence Against Spontaneous Generation

Francesco Redi (1626–1697) was an Italian physician who performed some of the first controlled experiments. People of his time believed that maggots—the immature young of flies—were spontaneously generated in spoiling meat and fish. Redi designed an experiment to test this belief (Figure 5–A–1).

Redi's control was a set of flasks of meat, fish, and eels left open to flies. Maggots developed as these foods spoiled. A similar set of flasks with meat, fish, and eels was sealed. No maggots developed as the foods spoiled.

Critics of Redi's experiment complained that air was excluded from the sealed flasks, preventing spontaneous generation of maggots. The air, they claimed, contains an active ingredient required for spontaneous generation.

Redi designed a new experiment. Again the open control was used. The experimental flasks, however, were not sealed. Instead Redi covered them with a cloth netting to keep flies out. As insurance, he built a frame of cloth netting around the flasks. Air could enter the flasks freely, but flies could not. As Redi predicted, no maggots appeared in the experimental group of flasks.

*meat in open flasks* + *flies* ⟶ *larvae*

*meat in sealed flasks* + *flies* ⟶ *no larvae*

**Figure 5–A–1** No "worms" (maggots or larvae) appeared in flasks of spoiling meat, fish, and eels that Redi sealed against flies.

## 5–B

## Elements Essential for Life

a. Major constituents of all living matter are the elements oxygen, carbon, hydrogen, nitrogen, phosphorus, and sulfur.

b. Other essential elements (including trace elements) are aluminum, boron, bromine, calcium, chlorine, chromium, cobalt, copper, fluorine, gallium, iodine, iron, magnesium, manganese, molybdenum, potassium, selenium, silicon, sodium, vanadium, and zinc.

| Element | Earth's Crust (weight, percent) | Sea Water (percent of total salts) | Air (percent by volume) |
|---|---|---|---|
| Aluminum | 7.90 | trace | |
| Boron | trace | 0.02 | |
| Bromine | trace | 0.19 | |
| Calcium | 3.44 | 1.16 | |
| Carbon | 0.20 | 0.08 | 0.03 (as $CO_2$) |
| Chlorine | 0.07 | 55.2 | |
| Chromium | 0.04 | — | |
| Cobalt | trace | — | |
| Copper | 0.01 | trace | |
| Fluorine | 0.08 | trace | |
| Gallium | trace | — | |
| Hydrogen | 0.22 | — | 0.01 |
| Iodine | — | trace | |
| Iron | 4.45 | trace | |
| Magnesium | 2.40 | 3.7 | |
| Manganese | 0.09 | trace | |
| Molybdenum | trace | trace | |
| Nitrogen | trace | trace | 78.08 |
| Oxygen | 47.07 | — | 20.99 |
| Phosphorus | 0.11 | trace | |
| Potassium | 2.46 | 1.1 | |
| Selenium | trace | trace | |
| Silicon | 28.06 | 0.01 | |
| Sodium | 2.43 | 30.4 | |
| Sulfur | 0.11 | 2.54 | varying (as $SO_2$ in pollution) |
| Vanadium | 0.02 | trace | |
| Zinc | trace | trace | |

**Table 5–B–1**   Relative abundance of elements essential for life.

## 5–C

## Energy

Energy is not as easy to describe as objects. It is present both in and out of objects, and it has no measurable mass. It is defined mathematically, and it is recognized in everyday life by the changes it causes. Change is brought about only by energy; nothing else can do work or effect any other change.

Energy occurs in different forms: chemical, electrical, mechanical, radiant (light and other radiations), heat, and nuclear energy. It can be converted from one form to another, but a large part is always converted to heat. For example, electrical energy is converted to light energy in a lamp, but the bulb heats and continues to give off heat as well as light. Machinery also heats when it is operated—a car, or an electric drill, or a vacuum cleaner. Even your cells give off heat as a byproduct of chemical changes in energy. Heat is therefore the ''downhill'' or ''spent'' form of energy, and it always keeps any energy conversion from being wholly efficient.

Yet energy is never lost in a change or a reaction. Energy can be changed from one form to others (always including heat), but is not destroyed. This is known as the law of conservation of energy.

The source of energy for life on Earth is the radiant energy of the sun. The sun was also the major source of energy on Earth before life began. The sunlight reaching the planet's surface contained rays of ultraviolet that would kill organisms living today. However, early in Earth's history the destructive rays might have promoted the evolution of life by building up a supply of organic compounds. The powerful ultraviolet rays had enough energy to break up the existing bonds between atoms of gas molecules in the atmosphere. Some of the released atoms might have recombined to form the more complex organic compounds that made the beginning of life possible. You will learn in Section 8–1 why very little of the sun's powerful ultraviolet radiation reaches Earth today.

Table 5–C–1 shows that under early conditions on Earth, ultraviolet radiation from the sun was the main form of energy available to form organic compounds.

| Source of Energy | Percent of Total Energy Available |
|---|---|
| ultraviolet radiation from the sun | 99.2 |
| electrical energy from lightning | 0.6 |
| radiation from radioactive elements | 0.12 |
| heat from volcanoes | 0.02 |

**Table 5–C–1** Energy sources available to form organic compounds under early conditions on Earth.

Under these assumed conditions, chemical bonds in the molecules were probably broken mainly by the energy of ultraviolet radiation. The atoms released combined to form organic compounds. Other less plentiful sources of energy that might have been powerful enough to form compounds from the gas molecules of the atmosphere were electrical energy from lightning, radiation from radioactive elements in Earth's crust, and intense heat from erupting volcanoes.

# 5-D
# The Amino Acids

## I. Twenty Amino Acids Found in Proteins

**1  glycine (Gly)**

$NH_2$—$CH_2$—$COOH$

**2  alanine (Ala)**

$CH_3$—$\overset{\overset{\displaystyle NH_2}{|}}{\underset{\underset{\displaystyle H}{|}}{C}}$—$COOH$

**3  valine (Val)**

$\overset{\displaystyle CH_3}{\underset{\displaystyle CH_3}{C}}$—$\overset{\overset{\displaystyle NH_2}{|}}{\underset{\underset{\displaystyle H}{|}}{C}}$—$COOH$

**4  leucine  (Leu)**

$\overset{\displaystyle CH_3}{\underset{\displaystyle CH_3}{C}}$—$CH_2$—$\overset{\overset{\displaystyle NH_2}{|}}{\underset{\underset{\displaystyle H}{|}}{C}}$—$COOH$

**5  isoleucine (Ileu)**

$CH_3$—$CH_2$—$\overset{\displaystyle }{\underset{\underset{\displaystyle CH_3}{|}}{C}}$—$\overset{\overset{\displaystyle NH_2}{|}}{\underset{\underset{\displaystyle H}{|}}{C}}$—$COOH$

**6  serine (Ser)**

$HO$—$CH_2$—$\overset{\overset{\displaystyle NH_2}{|}}{\underset{\underset{\displaystyle H}{|}}{C}}$—$COOH$

**7  threonine (Thr)**

$CH_3$—$\overset{\overset{\displaystyle H}{|}}{\underset{\underset{\displaystyle \overset{O}{\underset{H}{|}}}{}}{C}}$—$\overset{\overset{\displaystyle NH_2}{|}}{\underset{\underset{\displaystyle H}{|}}{C}}$—$COOH$

**8  arginine (Arg)**

$\overset{\overset{\displaystyle NH_2}{|}}{\underset{\underset{\displaystyle HN}{||}}{C}}$—$\overset{\overset{\displaystyle H}{|}}{N}$—$CH_2$—$CH_2$—$CH_2$—$\overset{\overset{\displaystyle NH_2}{|}}{\underset{\underset{\displaystyle H}{|}}{C}}$—$COOH$

**9  methionine (Met)**

$CH_3$—$S$—$CH_2$—$CH_2$—$\overset{\overset{\displaystyle NH_2}{|}}{\underset{\underset{\displaystyle H}{|}}{C}}$—$COOH$

**10  glutamic acid (Glu)**

$HOOC$—$CH_2$—$CH_2$—$\overset{\overset{\displaystyle NH_2}{|}}{\underset{\underset{\displaystyle H}{|}}{C}}$—$COOH$

**11  glutamine (Gln)**

$\overset{\overset{\displaystyle NH_2}{|}}{\underset{\underset{\displaystyle O}{||}}{C}}$—$CH_2$—$CH_2$—$\overset{\overset{\displaystyle NH_2}{|}}{\underset{\underset{\displaystyle H}{|}}{C}}$—$COOH$

**12  asparagine (Asn)**

$\overset{\overset{\displaystyle NH_2}{|}}{\underset{\underset{\displaystyle O}{||}}{C}}$—$CH_2$—$\overset{\overset{\displaystyle NH_2}{|}}{\underset{\underset{\displaystyle H}{|}}{C}}$—$COOH$

**13  aspartic acid (Asp)**

$HOOC$—$CH_2$—$\overset{\overset{\displaystyle NH_2}{|}}{\underset{\underset{\displaystyle H}{|}}{C}}$—$COOH$

**14  lysine (Lys)**

$NH_2$—$CH_2$—$CH_2$—$CH_2$—$CH_2$—$\overset{\overset{\displaystyle NH_2}{|}}{\underset{\underset{\displaystyle H}{|}}{C}}$—$COOH$

**15  cysteine (Cys)**

$HS$—$CH_2$—$\overset{\overset{\displaystyle NH_2}{|}}{\underset{\underset{\displaystyle H}{|}}{C}}$—$COOH$

**16  histidine (His)**

**17  phenylalanine (Phe)**

**18  tyrosine (Tyr)**

**19  tryptophan (Try)**

**20  proline (Pro)**

## II. Amino Acids Essential in the Diet

Nutritional requirements of humans have been discovered partly from experiments with animals. For each nutrient, animals are selected that have similar requirements to humans. Knowledge of the following essential amino acids for humans, i.e., those amino acids that you cannot synthesize but must obtain in your diet, came partly from experiments with white rats.

| | | |
|---|---|---|
| arginine | lysine | threonine |
| histidine | methionine | tryptophan |
| isoleucine | phenylalanine | valine |
| leucine | | |

## 5–E

## Amino Acid Sequence of Ferredoxin

The sequence of 97 amino acids in a molecule of ferredoxin from spinach leaves is shown below:

```
            1
NH₂.Ala-Ala-Tyr-Lys-Val-Thr-Leu-Val-Thr-
        10
     Pro-Thr-Gly-Asn-Val-Glu-Phe-Gln-Cys-
        20
     Pro-Asp-Asp-Val-Tyr-Ileu-Leu-Asp-Ala-
        30
     Ala-Glu-Glu-Glu-Gly-Ileu-Asp-Leu-Pro-
        40
     Tyr-Ser-Cys-Arg-Ala-Gly-Ser-Cys-Ser-
        50
     Ser-Cys-Ala-Gly-Lys-Leu-Lys-Thr-Gly-
        60
     Ser-Leu-Asn-Gln-Asp-Asp-Gln-Ser-Phe-
        70
     Leu-Asp-Asp-Asp-Gln-Ileu-Asp-Glu-Gly-
        80
     Try-Val-Leu-Thr-Cys-Ala-Ala-Tyr-Pro-
        90
     Val-Ser-Asp-Val-Thr-Ileu-Glu-Thr-His-
        97
     Lys-Glu-Glu-Glu-Leu-Thr-Ala.COOH
```

The function of ferredoxin is discussed in Appendix 7–E. The name of each amino acid in the ferredoxin sequence has been abbreviated with a symbol of three or four letters. The symbols and the names in full are given in Appendix 5–D.

The same compound in different organisms may vary slightly in its composition. Often however, it is identical from organism to organism. Biologists are always careful to identify the species for which an analysis of a compound is made, unless the compound is known to be identical in all species tested. (Hence, the ferredoxin sequence was attributed to spinach.)

## 5–F

## Similarities in the Amino Acid Sequence of Cytochrome c from Horse, Human, Pig, Rabbit, Chicken, and Tuna

Cytochrome $c$ is a protein that plays an important role in respiration of animal and plant cells (see Chapter 8). The difference in cytochrome $c$ between different species involves changes in the sequence of some of its amino acids. The closer two species are related in their evolutionary history, the fewer amino acid differences there will be between their comparable proteins. Thus, by comparing the amino acid sequences of cytochrome $c$ from different species, one can determine how closely these species are related.

On the next page is the amino acid sequence for cytochrome $c$ from the horse. (Each amino acid is represented by a symbol; its full name and formula are given in Appendix 5–D. Heme is an iron-containing group that is attached to the protein.) Symbols in capital letters represent identical amino acids in the cytochrome $c$ from horses, humans, pigs, rabbits, chickens, and tuna. Symbols in small letters stand for amino acids that may differ in at least one of these species. The total number of amino acids in the molecule of cytochrome *c* is the same for each species. At one end of the molecule is the free amino group ($NH_2$) of one terminal amino acid, and at the other end of the molecule is the free carboxyl group (COOH) of the other terminal amino acid.

$$NH_2 . GLY-ASP-val-glu-LYS-GLY-LYS-LYS-ileu-\overset{10}{PHE-}$$

$$val-gln-LYS-CYS-ala-GLN-CYS-HIS-THR-\overset{20}{VAL-}$$

$$HEME$$

$$GLU-lys-GLY-GLY-LYS-HIS-LYS-thr-GLY-\overset{30}{PRO-}$$

$$ASN-LEU-his-GLY-LEU-PHE-GLY-ARG-LYS-\overset{40}{THR-}$$

$$GLY-GLN-ALA-pro-GLY-phe-thr-TYR-THR-\overset{50}{asp-}$$

$$ALA-ASN-LYS-asn-LYS-GLY-ILEU-thr-TRY-\overset{60}{lys-}$$

$$glu-glu-THR-LEU-MET-glu-tyr-LEU-GLU-\overset{70}{ASN-}$$

$$PRO-LYS-LYS-TYR-ILEU-PRO-GLY-THR-LYS-\overset{80}{MET-}$$

$$ILEU-PHE-ala-GLY-ILEU-LYS-LYS-LYS-thr-\overset{90}{GLU-}$$

$$ARG-glu-ASP-LEU-ileu-ALA-TYR-LEU-LYS-\overset{100}{LYS-}$$

$$\overset{104}{ala-thr-asn-glu.COOH}$$

## 5–G

## Formation of a Peptide Bond

In the formation of a peptide bond, the acid group (-COOH) of one amino acid joins with the amino group (-$NH_2$) of the second amino acid. The acid group loses an atom of hydrogen and an atom of oxygen. The amino group loses an atom of hydrogen. The two hydrogen atoms combine with the oxygen atom to form a water molecule ($H_2O$). When the water splits off, the two amino acids are connected by a peptide bond. (See Figure 5–G–1.)

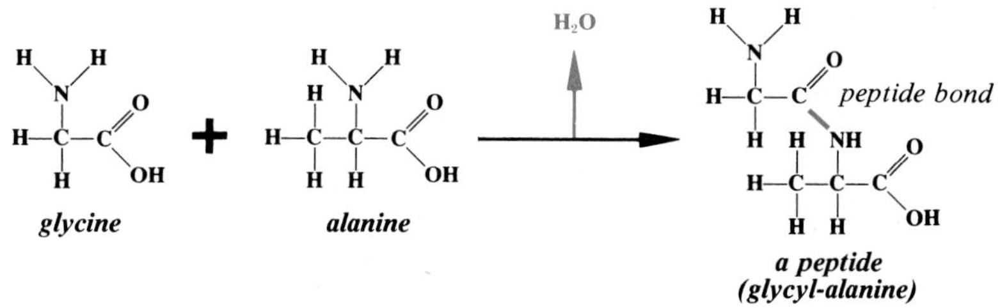

glycine          alanine

*a peptide*
*(glycyl-alanine)*

**Figure 5–G–1** When a peptide bond forms, it joins the acid group of one amino acid to the amino group of another. A water molecule is given off in the process. More peptide bonds can form in the same way, joining together a large chain of amino acids.

## 6–A

## Chemical Nature of Fats

A fat molecule consists of fatty acids joined to a glycerol molecule. Glycerol is an alcohol with a formula $C_3H_5(OH)_3$. To form a fat, one molecule of glycerol combines with three molecules of fatty acids. Each fatty acid consists of a long chain of carbon atoms with attached hydrogen atoms and an acid group (-COOH) at one end. The properties of the different fats depend on their fatty acids. The fatty acids in one fat may all be alike or all different.

The joining together of three fatty acids to one glycerol, forming one molecule of fat (as shown in Figure 6–A–1), releases three molecules of water.

The properties of fatty acids depend on the length of their carbon chains and the bonds between the carbon atoms. The most common fatty acids are those that have a total of 16 or 18 carbon atoms. (Observe that this would mean values of 15 and 17 for n in Figure 6–A–1.) When the carbon atoms of fatty acids are joined only by single bonds, the fatty acids are known as saturated. When some carbon atoms are joined by single bonds and other carbon atoms by double bonds, the fatty acids are known as unsaturated. Stearic acid is an example of a saturated 18-carbon fatty acid. Linoleic acid is an example of an unsaturated 18-carbon fatty acid. Unsaturated fats (that is, fats containing unsaturated fatty acids) tend to be oily liquids at body temperature (example, olive oil). Butter and lard are saturated fats.

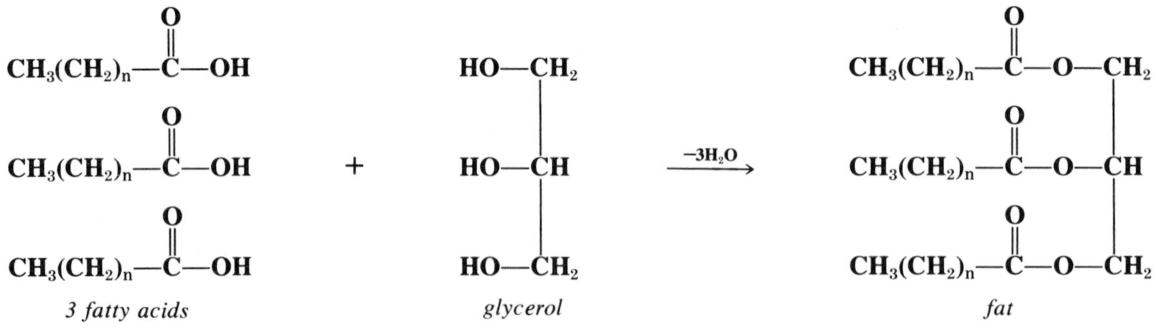

**Figure 6–A–1** The formation of a fat molecule.

**6–B**

**Structural Formulas for Adenosine Triphosphate (ATP), Adenosine Diphosphate (ADP), and Adenosine Monophosphate (AMP)**

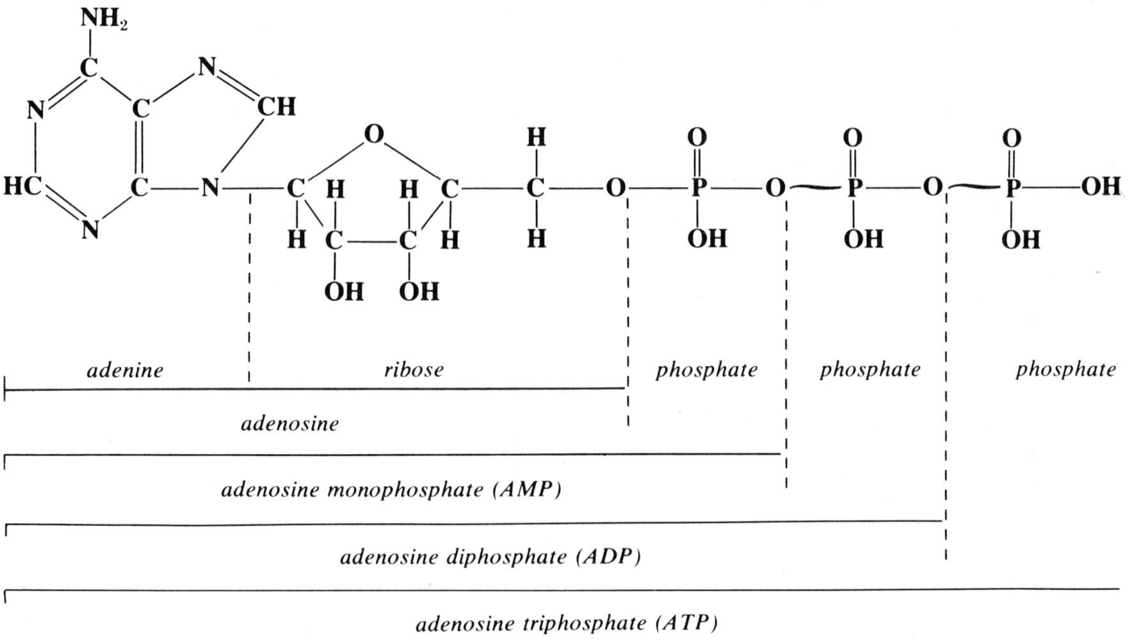

Figure 6–B–1

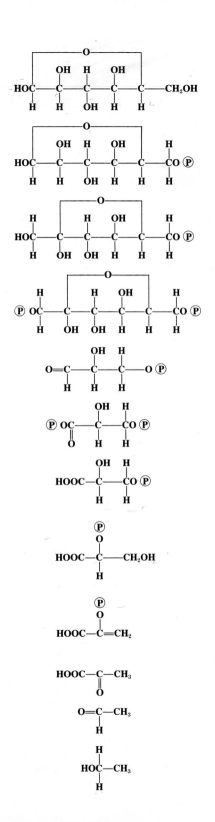

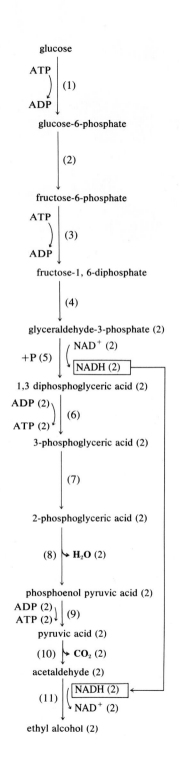

## 6-C

## Fermentation of Glucose to Ethyl Alcohol or Lactic Acid

### I. Fermentation of Glucose to Alcohol

Figure 6–C–1 gives the sequence of reactions in the fermentation of glucose to ethyl alcohol when no oxygen is present. Each numbered reaction step is catalyzed by a different enzyme: (1) hexokinase; (2) phosphohexoisomerase; (3) phosphofructokinase; (4) aldolase; (5) glyceraldehyde-3-phosphate dehydrogenase; (6) phosphoglycerate kinase; (7) phosphoglyceromutase; (8) enolase; (9) pyruvate kinase; (10) pyruvate decarboxylase; (11) alcohol dehydrogenase. Each of these enzymes has been isolated in pure form, and practically every one has been crystallized.

The number two (2) after glyceraldehyde-3-phosphate and all of the compounds that follow it is a reminder that two molecules of these compounds are produced from each molecule of glucose. Although 4 ATPs are produced in these reactions, the net gain to the living system is 2 ATPs, since two other ATPs are required to start the series of reactions.

The sequence for respiration is exactly the same up to the formation of pyruvic acid. The reactions in the respiration process are outlined in Appendixes 8–A and 8–B.

The two reduced $NAD^+$ (NADH) formed when glyceraldehyde-3-phosphate is converted into 1,3-diphosphoglyceric acid are capable of forming four or six ATPs if oxygen is present. The energy released when electrons from NADH pass through

the respiratory chain to oxygen is trapped as ATP. (See Appendix 8–B.) If oxygen is not present, the electrons (and $H^+$) from NADH are used to convert acetaldehyde into alcohol, and no ATP is formed.

### II. Fermentation of Glucose to Lactic Acid

Certain anaerobic bacteria and also muscle cells, when short of oxygen, ferment glucose to lactic acid. The reaction steps (1) through (7), from glucose to pyruvic acid, are the same as in alcohol fermentation. However, in lactic acid fermentation, pyruvic acid is not converted to alcohol but to lactic acid, in a reaction catalyzed by the enzyme lactate dehydrogenase (see Figure 6–C–2).

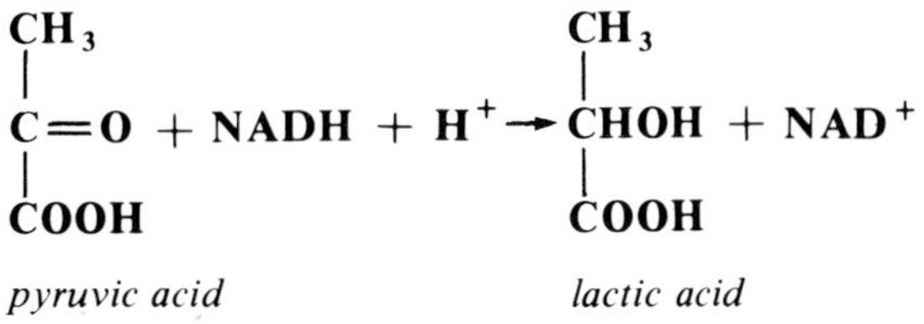

$$
\begin{array}{l}
CH_3 \\
| \\
C{=}O \; + \; NADH \; + \; H^+ \\
| \\
COOH
\end{array}
\rightarrow
\begin{array}{l}
CH_3 \\
| \\
CHOH \; + \; NAD^+ \\
| \\
COOH
\end{array}
$$

*pyruvic acid*          *lactic acid*

**Figure 6–C–2** Formation of lactic acid from pyruvic acid.

## 7-A

## The Sun and Its Radiation

Primitive humans thought of the sun as a ball of fire. According to a Greek legend, Prometheus flew all the way to the sun in order to bring back to mortals some of the sun's heavenly fire. But scientists determined long ago that the sun was not merely burning like a huge bonfire of wood or coal. If the sun's fire were like that of coal, it would have burned for only a few thousand years and would have turned to cinders millions of years ago.

The sun is a medium-sized star that, like all stars, is made mainly of two elements, hydrogen

**Figure 6–C–1** Chemical reactions in the fermentation of glucose to ethyl alcohol. Formulas of reactants are shown at the left, steps in the reactions at the right. Each formula matches the compound named opposite it. The circled Ps in the formulas represent phosphate groups. The numbers next to the arrows (1–11) represent steps.

and helium. The temperature of the surface of the sun is about 6000°C. The temperature increases toward the center of the sun where, 800,000 kilometers deep, it reaches 16,000,000°C. How hot is this? A pinhead of material at this temperature would give off enough heat to kill a person 160 kilometers away. The sun, however, is about 150 million kilometers (93 million miles) away from Earth.

At the enormously high temperatures inside the sun, electrons are stripped away from atoms' nuclei. There are no molecules and no atoms, just a mixture of free electrons and bare atomic nuclei, called plasma. In this special state of matter, an unusual type of reaction called nuclear fusion takes place, in which the atomic nuclei of lighter elements combine to make heavier elements. The net result of nuclear fusion is that four hydrogen nuclei combine to form one helium nucleus. Since hydrogen nuclei, being positively charged, repel each other, very high temperatures of millions of degrees, such as exist in the interior of the sun, are needed for fusion to occur. For this reason nuclear fusion is called a thermonuclear reaction.

The sun's interior may be compared, therefore, to a huge nuclear furnace in which hydrogen is the fuel and helium is the product. What will happen when all of the hydrogen in the sun is converted to helium? The sun will turn cold and "die" and all life on Earth will cease. Fortunately, there is enough hydrogen in the sun to last for 5 to 15 billion years.

The helium nucleus formed by the thermonuclear reaction in the sun has a mass slightly less than that of the four hydrogen nuclei from which it is made. It is this small difference of "extra" matter that accounts for the enormous energy radiating from the sun. At the beginning of this century, Albert Einstein proposed that matter can be changed into energy, according to his famous equation

$$E = mc^2$$

where E stands for energy, m for mass (matter), and c for speed of light (equal to 300,000 kilometers or 186,000 miles per second). Physicists investigating nuclear reactions found that Einstein's formula is correct. The small amount of matter "left over" in nuclear reactions is indeed converted into enormous amounts of energy. In the sun's fusion reaction the mass of the helium nucleus is about 0.6% less than the mass of the four hydrogen nuclei from which it was formed. For the entire sun, this difference comes to almost 4 million metric tons of mass, which, when changed into energy, would supply in one second enough electricity to light a million homes for 160 million years!

However, the energy released in the interior of the sun (and other stars) is not converted into electricity but escapes as radiation. We usually think of the sun's radiation as sunlight or daylight or simply as "light." But light is only that portion of the sun's radiation that is visible to the human eye. The invisible radiation emitted by the sun includes gamma rays, X rays, ultraviolet radiation, infrared radiation, and radio waves. Together with visible light, all these kinds of radiation form a continuous spectrum, known as the electromagnetic spectrum.

Every part of the electromagnetic spectrum travels with the same speed, the speed of light, which, as already mentioned, is 300,000 kilometers a second. At this speed it takes only slightly more than eight minutes for light to travel from the sun to Earth. The daylight that strikes your eyes at this moment left the sun eight minutes ago.

What distinguishes one kind of radiation from another? Radiation travels in waves, and the different kinds of radiation have different wavelengths. A wavelength is the distance between the crest of one wave and the crest of the next. The shorter the distance, the more intense the energy. Shortwave radiations ranging from less than 1 to almost 300 nanometers in wavelength can be damaging to life.

Each kind of radiation includes its own characteristic range of wavelengths. These overlap to a certain extent. Especially important to biology is the range of wavelengths included in visible light. One of the great discoveries in physics was made by Isaac Newton almost 300 years ago when he discovered that visible or "white" light is a mixture of different colors of light. One color of light is distinguished from another color by its different wavelength. Table 7–A–1 gives the range of wavelengths for each color of light and also the wavelengths for the invisible kinds of radiation.

| Kinds of Radiations | Wavelengths of Different Radiations (nanometers) |
|---|---|
| gamma rays | less than 1 |
| X rays | 0.1 to 100 |
| ultraviolet radiation | 100 to 380 |
| visible light | 380 to 750 |
| violet | 380 to 424 |
| blue | 424 to 491 |
| green | 491 to 575 |
| yellow | 575 to 585 |
| orange | 585 to 647 |
| red | 647 to 750 |
| infrared radiation | 750 to $10^5$ |
| radio waves | $10^6$ to $10^{12}$ |

**Table 7–A–1** Radiations and their wavelengths in the electromagnetic spectrum.

Only a small part of the sun's total radiation reaches Earth. Today, the shorter ultraviolet rays (shorter than 290 nm), X rays, and gamma rays cannot get through the atmosphere. This fact is fortunate because these radiations would destroy the present forms of plant and animal life.

It was the infrared and visible parts of the sun's radiation that the emerging photosynthetic organisms began to use as a source of energy. Bacteriochlorophyll, the light-absorbing pigment in photosynthetic bacteria, absorbs light most strongly at wavelengths of 800, 850, and 890 nm. In green plants, chlorophyll *a* has peak absorption for light at 435 and 675 nm and chlorophyll *b*, at 480 and 650 nm. Aside from these absorption peaks, the various other pigments in green plants absorb light, though less efficiently, at other wavelengths in the visible range.

Note that the main type of photosynthesis on Earth, photosynthesis by green plants, uses only the wavelengths of visible light. It does not require either ultraviolet or infrared radiation.

# 7–B

# Photosynthesis Includes a "Dark Reaction"

The first indication that photosynthesis may include both dark and light reactions came in 1905 from the experiments of F. F. Blackman in England. Blackman began by investigating the effects of brightness or light intensity. Since light energy drives photosynthesis, the expectation was that the process would go faster in more intense light. When Blackman measured and plotted the rates of photosynthesis at various light intensities, the curve as shown in Figure 7–B–1 was obtained. At relatively low intensities, increasing the brightness of the light did increase the rate. At higher intensities, however, the rate of photosynthesis did not increase beyond a certain level. A further increase in light intensity made almost no difference.

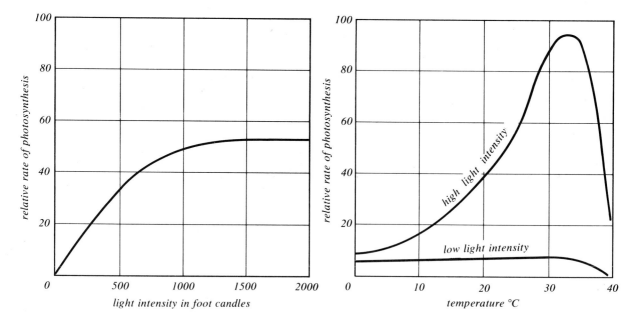

**Figure 7–B–1** Graph showing the relation between photosynthesis and the intensity of light. Notice that beyond about 1200 foot-candles, an increase in the intensity of light does not increase the rate of photosynthesis.

**Figure 7–B–2** Effect of temperature on rate of photosynthesis at different light intensities. At a low intensity of light, an increase in temperature does not affect the rate of photosynthesis. At a strong intensity, the change in temperature has a great effect.

Next, Blackman investigated the effects on photosynthesis of temperature and light together. (See Figure 7–B–2.) Between about 30°C and 40°C it was found that increasing the temperature lowered the rate of photosynthesis, no matter how bright the light. But between 0°C and 30°C, increasing the temperature produced very different effects, depending on how bright the light was. At a low light intensity the increase in temperature had almost no effect on photosynthesis. In contrast, at high light intensity the increase in temperature greatly speeded up the rate of photosynthesis.

To understand Blackman's results, consider the effects of light and temperature on two different kinds of reactions: first, chemical reactions that are independent of light energy and, second, light reactions that are driven only by light energy.

Chemical reactions, including those controlled by enzymes, proceed faster as the temperature increases from 0°C to 30°C. Their rate doubles for each 10-degree rise in temperature. On the other hand, light reactions are not affected by temperature.

Using these principles, Blackman concluded that photosynthesis includes both a light reaction and a dark reaction. A dark reaction may or may not occur in darkness. It is called "dark" to indicate that it can happen without light. Blackman reasoned that when there was little light available, the amount of light was the factor that determined the rate of the entire photosynthetic process. When there is little light available, an increase in temperature will not speed up photosynthesis. But when there is plenty of light available for the light

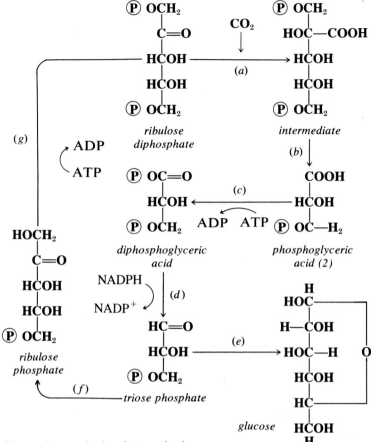

**Figure 7–C–1** The carbon cycle in photosynthesis. Phosphate groups are represented by Ps.

reaction, it is the rate of the dark enzyme reaction that determines the rate of photosynthesis. An increase in temperature speeds up the dark reaction and therefore the overall rate.

The experiments of Blackman made a great impression on scientists who investigated photosynthesis. They had previously thought of photosynthesis as including only light-dependent reactions. Now they began thinking also about the "Blackman reaction," a name they gave to the dark reaction of photosynthesis.

You will learn in Section 7–7 how scientists in recent years extended Blackman's idea and discovered that photosynthesis includes not one but many dark reactions.

## 7–C

## The Carbon Cycle in Photosynthesis

Figure 7–C–1 is a simplified version of the carbon cycle.

(a) Carbon dioxide combines with a five-carbon compound, ribulose diphosphate, having a phosphate group at each end, to give a six-carbon intermediate.

(b) This intermediate compound is unstable and breaks up into two molecules of phosphoglyceric acid (3C–P).

(c) Phosphoglyceric acid accepts another phosphate group and becomes a diphosphate compound, diphosphoglyceric acid (P–3C–P).

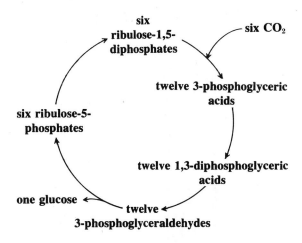

**Figure 7–C–2** The formation of glucose from carbon dioxide (above right) and hydrogen (from NADPH, not shown).

(d) Diphosphoglyceric acid is converted to a three-carbon sugar, triose phosphate (3-phosphoglyceraldehyde, 3C–P sugar).

(e) Part of the triose phosphate is converted to glucose, the product of photosynthesis.

(f) Another part is used to form a five-carbon compound, ribulose phosphate, by a complicated series of reactions (5C–P).

(g) Ribulose phosphate accepts a second phosphate group and is converted to ribulose diphosphate (P–5C–P), which is then ready to combine with another molecule of carbon dioxide, and the carbon cycle starts over again.

Figure 7–C–2 shows how one molecule of $CO_2$ goes through the reactions of the carbon cycle. But one $CO_2$ can contribute only one new carbon atom to the six carbon atoms that make up a glucose molecule. The remaining five carbon atoms would have to be already present in the cell.

To form a glucose molecule entirely from newly absorbed $CO_2$, six molecules of $CO_2$ would need to go through the carbon cycle, as summarized in the diagram at the left.

## 7–D
## NADP⁺

**Figure 7–D–1** Structural formula of NADP⁺ (nicotinamide adenine dinucleotide phosphate).

**Figure 7−D−2** The reaction NADP$^+$ → NADPH involves only the nicotinamide portion of the NADP$^+$ molecule. The rest of the molecule (see Figure 7−D−1) is represented here by R.

# 7−E

## The Light Reactions in Photosynthesis

Many investigations of photosynthesis in intact cells have shown that the process includes two kinds of light reactions. One, known as the "long-wavelength system" or Photosystem I, includes a light reaction that proceeds best in light of wavelengths longer than 690 nm (for a discussion of wavelengths of light, see Appendix 7−A). The second, known as the "short-wavelength system" or Photosystem II, includes a light reaction that proceeds best in light of wavelengths shorter than 690 nm.

When experiments with different wavelengths of light were performed on isolated chloroplasts, it was discovered that cyclic photophosphorylation (page 147) included the long-wavelength Photosystem I light reaction. Noncyclic photophosphorylation (page 147) turned out to be more complicated. All scientists now agree that it includes a collaboration of two light reactions. Most scientists believe that one of these light reactions is of the Photosystem II type, but that the second one is of the Photosystem I type.

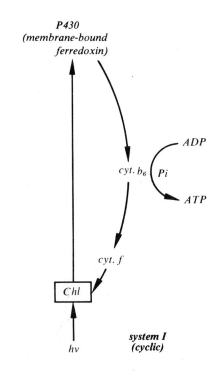

**Figure 7−E−1** Diagram of the cyclic photophosphorylation process as hypothesized.

Figure 7−E−1 illustrates diagrammatically the current hypothesis which explains how Photosystem I liberates energy that is used for ATP formation in cyclic photophosphorylation. Chlorophyll

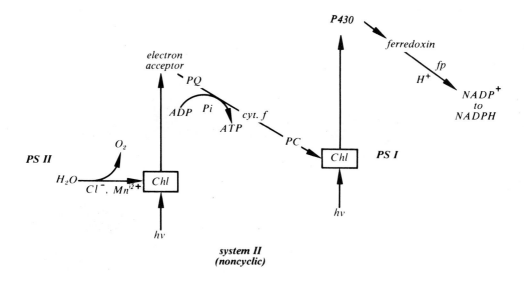

*system II*
*(noncyclic)*

**Figure 7–E–2** Diagram of the noncyclic photophosphorylation process as hypothesized.

energized (excited) by light passes a high-energy electron to P430, an electron acceptor on the thylakoid membrane. Next, the electron is transferred from P430 to an electron-carrier protein known as cytochrome $b_6$, then to a second electron-carrier protein known as cytochrome $f$, and finally back to chlorophyll. Energy is released in these electron-transfer steps and used to form ATP.

Figure 7–E–2 illustrates the current hypothesis which explains how two light reactions collaborate in noncyclic photophosphorylation. In each light reaction (PS I and PS II), chlorophyll (Chl) excited by light (h$\nu$) transfers a high-energy electron to an electron acceptor.

The electron lost by chlorophyll in light reaction PS II is replaced by an electron from water—a reaction which produces oxygen and which is catalyzed by chloride and manganese ions (Cl⁻, Mn⁺⁺). The electron lost by chlorophyll in light

reaction PS I is replaced by the electron supplied by the electron acceptor in light reaction PS II. (See Figure 7–E–2.)

Note that light reactions PS I and II are joined by an electron transport chain which is made up of several components of chloroplasts: plastoquinone (PQ), cytochrome $f$, and the copper protein, plastocyanin (PC). The high-energy electron received by the electron acceptor in light reaction PS II is transferred "downhill" through this electron transport chain. Sufficient energy is released in this downhill electron transfer to form the ATP that is produced by noncyclic photophosphorylation. Finally, the electron reaches the chlorophyll in light reaction PS I.

The electrons transferred by light reaction PS I to P430 go to ferredoxin, then to enzyme $fp$. The enzyme combines the electrons with H⁺ to convert NADP⁺ to NADPH.

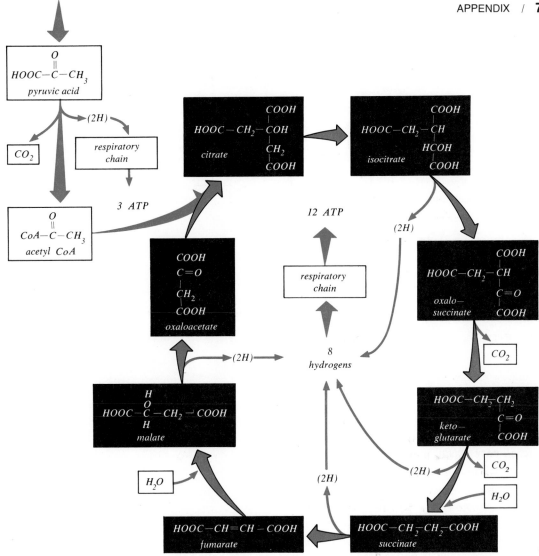

**Figure 8–A–1** The Krebs cycle.

## 8–A

## The Krebs Cycle

In the diagram on this page, the arrows outlined in black connect the compounds that make up the Krebs cycle. One turn of the cycle releases 8 hydrogen atoms. By way of the respiratory chain, these hydrogen atoms give rise to 12 ATP molecules. The role of the respiratory chain in the production of ATP is shown in Appendix 8–B. Since two "active" acetic acid molecules (acetyl-CoA) come from each molecule of glucose, a total of 24 ATP molecules is generated from products of the Krebs cycle.

A complete accounting for the 36 or 38 ATP molecules formed when one molecule of glucose is broken down by cell respiration follows:

|  | ATP |
|---|---|
| Fermentation: 1 glucose molecule to 2 pyruvic acid molecules | $1 \times 2 = 2$ |
| Two NADH generated in aerobic fermentation-like steps | $\left. \begin{array}{r} 2 \times 2 = 4 \\ \text{or} \\ 2 \times 3 = 6 \end{array} \right\}$ |
| Two pyruvic acid molecules converted to acetyl-CoA | $2 \times 3 = 6$ |
| Products of the Krebs cycle: two acetyl-CoA broken down to $CO_2$ and $H_2O$ | $2 \times 12 = 24$ |
|  | Total $= 36$ |
|  | or 38 |

## 8–B

## The Respiratory Chain

The respiratory chain is the chemical pathway through which electrons move from foodstuffs to oxygen. In some steps the electrons are accompanied by protons (hydrogen ions or $H^+$).

Three ATP molecules are formed for most pairs of electrons passed through the respiratory chain. Important places in the chain are held by electron acceptors and carriers such as $NAD^+$ and ubiquinone, and the iron-containing proteins known as cytochromes (Figure 8–B–1). As a pair of electrons is transported through this chain of compounds, the electrons lose energy. The energy is used to make ATP from ADP and an added phosphate group.

Refer to Figure 8–B–1 as you read the following steps. NADH is formed from $NAD^+$, using hydrogen released in the Krebs cycle. The hydrogen is passed to NADH dehydrogenase. The next

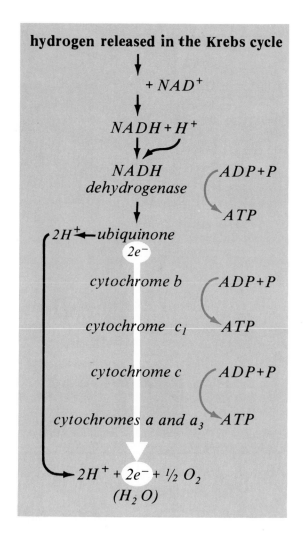

**Figure 8–B–1** Respiratory chain.

electron acceptor, ubiquinone, releases the hydrogen ions and enough energy from the pair of electrons to form a molecule of ATP. Thereafter, the two electrons are passed to a number of cytochromes, where enough additional energy is released for two more molecules of ATP. At the end of the chain, the hydrogen ions and the electrons combine with oxygen to form water.

## 8-C

### The H⁺ Pump

No compound has been found that transfers energy from the respiratory chain to the enzymes that make ATP. Yet ATP is formed during cell respiration.

Evidence has been found of a phenomenon known as a proton pump that is operated in mitochondria by electron transport in each respiratory chain. A proton is a hydrogen ion ($H^+$). The energy released during electron transport is used to actively transport, or pump, $H^+$ from inside the mitochondria to the fluid space between the two mitochondrial membranes. As a result, energy is built up as a *membrane potential*—electrical or electrochemical in nature.

The inner mitochondrial membrane is impermeable to the diffusion of $H^+$ back into the inside of mitochondria, once the $H^+$ is pumped to the outside of the membrane. However, the enzymes in the membrane that make ATP can provide holes through which the $H^+$ can pass. The energy of the membrane potential is believed to be released by $H^+$ reentry through these holes. The enzymes use the energy to make ATP. Thus, hydrogen ions, or protons, as well as electrons become involved in ATP synthesis.

## 10-A

### Messenger RNA Code for Twenty Amino Acids

| Amino acid | Abbreviation | Code Triplets |
|---|---|---|
| Alanine | Ala | GCU, GCC, GCA, GCG |
| Arginine | Arg | AGA, AGG, CGU, CGC, CGA, CGG |
| Asparagine | Asn | AAU, AAC |
| Aspartic Acid | Asp | GAU, GAC |
| Cysteine | Cys | UGU, UGC |
| Glutamic Acid | Glu | GAA, GAG |
| Glutamine | Gln | CAA, CAG |
| Glycine | Gly | GGU, GGC, GGA, GGG |
| Histidine | His | CAU, CAC |
| Isoleucine | Ileu | AUU, AUC, AUA |
| Leucine | Leu | UUA, UUG, CUU, CUC, CUA, CUG |
| Lysine | Lys | AAA, AAG |
| Methionine | Met | AUG |
| Phenylalanine | Phe | UUU, UUC |
| Proline | Pro | CCU, CCC, CCA, CCG |
| Serine | Ser | UCU, UCC, UCA, UCG, AGU, AGC |
| Threonine | Thr | ACU, ACC, ACA, ACG |
| Tryptophane | Tryp | UGG |
| Tyrosine | Tyr | UAU, UAC |
| Valine | Val | GUU, GUC, GUA, GUG |

**Figure 11–A–1** The yucca plant (left) and the Pronuba moth depend on one another for survival. The female moth (right) deposits her eggs in the flower's ovary, where they develop. She also carries a ball of pollen grains to the flower, from another yucca flower in which she mated.

She presses part of the pollen into the stigma of the flower in which she has laid her eggs. This behavioral pattern ensures the development of both the plant seeds and the moth larvae.

## 11–A

## Pollination by Insects Aids Fertilization

Although the flowers of many plants have both male and female organs, most species have some means of cross pollination. Cross pollination provides for more genetic variety and is one of the features in the evolution of sexual reproduction.

Insects are often the agents that carry the pollen from one plant to another. Fossils indicate, in fact, that many flowering plants and insects probably evolved together. The most striking characteristics of flowers—their colors, their scent, and their unusual shapes—may be evolutionary adaptations that attract insects. Pollination by insects seems to make fertilization more likely to

occur. In some cases, the adaptation of plant and insect to each other is very specific. A single species of insect may be responsible or mainly responsible for the pollination of a single species of plant. One of the most extraordinary examples of such a relationship is that of the yucca plant and the Pronuba moth (Figure 11–A–1).

When the yucca flowers open up, the small Pronuba moths, apparently attracted by the fragrance of the flowers, fly to the flowers and mate within them. The female moth then collects pollen from the anthers of the flower and rolls it into a ball. She flies to another yucca, bores into the ovary of a flower, and deposits a fertilized moth egg within it. She then goes to the pistil of the same flower and presses part of the ball of pollen into the pistil. This behavior is repeated until several eggs have been laid and the pistil is well stocked with pollen. Somewhat later, inside the ovary of the yucca, the eggs of the moth hatch into larvae of the moth. In this case, the full life cycle of neither the yucca nor the Pronuba moth is possible without the other. In an area where Pronuba moths were accidentally destroyed by a chemical, the yucca plants examined had not been fertilized and seeds were not produced. This circumstance is indicative of the interdependence of the two types of organisms. This particular relationship does not exclude the possibility, however, that other insects may be attracted to the yucca plants. It would be reasonable to assume that this is fairly likely.

## 13–A

## Samples of Mendel's Records

| Trait Studied | Dominant | Recessive |
|---|---|---|
| seed shape | ROUND | wrinkled |
| seed (cotyledon) color | YELLOW | green |
| seed coat color | COLORED | white |
| pod shape | INFLATED | wrinkled |
| pod color | GREEN | yellow |
| flower position | AXIAL | terminal |
| stem length | LONG | short |

**Table 13–A–1** In early experiments Mendel found that one of each pair of contrasting traits is dominant to the other.

| P₁ cross | F₁ plants | F₁ plants (self-pollinated) | F₂ plants | Actual ratio |
|---|---|---|---|---|
| round × wrinkled seeds | all round | round × round | 5474 round<br>1850 wrinkled<br>7324 total | 2.96 : 1 |
| yellow × green seeds (cotyledons) | all yellow | yellow × yellow | 6022 yellow<br>2001 green<br>8023 total | 3.01 : 1 |
| colored × white seed coats | all colored | colored × colored | 705 colored<br>224 white<br>929 total | 3.15 : 1 |
| inflated × wrinkled pods | all inflated | inflated × inflated | 882 inflated<br>299 wrinkled<br>1181 total | 2.95 : 1 |
| green × yellow pods | all green | green × green | 428 green<br>152 yellow<br>580 total | 2.82 : 1 |
| axial × terminal flowers | all axial | axial × axial | 651 axial<br>207 terminal<br>858 total | 3.14 : 1 |
| long × short stems | all long | long × long | 787 long<br>277 short<br>1064 total | 2.84 : 1 |

**Table 13–A–2** Mendel's breeding results from crossing plants with single contrasting traits.

|  | | Probabilities of Gametes from One AaBb Parent | | | |
| --- | --- | --- | --- | --- | --- |
|  | | $^1/_4$ **AB** | $^1/_4$ **Ab** | $^1/_4$ **aB** | $^1/_4$ **ab** |
| **Probabilities of** | $^1/_4$ **AB** | 1/16 AABB | 1/16 AABb | 1/16 AaBB | 1/16 AaBb |
| **Gametes from** | $^1/_4$ **Ab** | 1/16 AABb | 1/16 AAbb | 1/16 AaBb | 1/16 Aabb |
| **Other AaBb** | $^1/_4$ **aB** | 1/16 AaBB | 1/16 AaBb | 1/16 aaBB | 1/16 aaBb |
| **Parent** | $^1/_4$ **ab** | 1/16 AaBb | 1/16 Aabb | 1/16 aaBb | 1/16 aabb |

**Table 13–A–3**  Probabilities of $F_2$ genotypes when both $F_1$ parents are heterozygous for each of two traits.

| Genotypes | Corresponding Phenotypes | Total of Phenotypes |
| --- | --- | --- |
| 1/16 AABB | 1/16 round, yellow | |
| 2/16 AABb | 2/16 round, yellow | |
| 2/16 AaBB | 2/16 round, yellow | 9/16 round, yellow |
| 4/16 AaBb | 4/16 round, yellow | |
| 2/16 aaBb | 2/16 wrinkled, yellow | |
| 1/16 aaBB | 1/16 wrinkled, yellow | 3/16 wrinkled, yellow |
| 2/16 Aabb | 2/16 round, green | |
| 1/16 AAbb | 1/16 round, green | 3/16 round, green |
| 1/16 aabb | 1/16 wrinkled, green | 1/16 wrinkled, green |

**Table 13–A–4**  A summary of $F_2$ genotypes and phenotypes when $F_1$ parents are heterozygous for each of two traits.

## 14–A

# The Boveri-Sutton Theory

The biological link between generations of multicellular organisms is physically very small. It consists typically of two tiny cells—a microscopic sperm cell from the male and a somewhat larger egg cell from the female. Yet somehow the genes are passed from one generation to the next, indicating that they must be located somewhere within the sperm and egg cells.

Boveri and Sutton started with these observations. Boveri showed experimentally that although the egg and the sperm cells are different, they make equal genetic contributions to the organism they have formed. Mendel had already given evidence for this conclusion. Pollen from peas with round seeds was used to fertilize peas with wrinkled seeds, and pollen from peas with wrinkled seeds was used to fertilize peas with round seeds. Remember from Table 13–A–1 that round seeds are dominant. Mendel found that in the resulting offspring the ratio of round seeds to wrinkled seeds was always the same, regardless of which parent carried the factor for the dominant trait. Mendel concluded that the genes contributed by sperm and egg cells were equally important.

| Hypothesis of Gene Behavior | Observations of Chromosome Behavior |
|---|---|
| 1. Gametes have half the number of **genes** that body cells have. | 1. Gametes have half the number of **chromosomes** that body cells have. |
| 2. The **gene** pairs separate during gamete formation. | 2. **Chromosome** pairs separate during gamete formation. |
| 3. In fertilization gametes unite, restoring the original number of **genes.** | 3. In fertilization gametes unite, restoring the original number of **chromosomes.** |
| 4. The individual **genes** remain unchanged from one generation to the next. | 4. Individual **chromosomes** retain their structure from one generation to the next. |
| 5. The number of possible **gene** combinations can be calculated. | 5. The number of possible **chromosome** combinations can be calculated. |

**Table 14–A–1** A summary of the Boveri-Sutton theory, showing similarities between the hypothesis of gene behavior and actual observations of chromosomes. These similarities led Sutton to propose that genes are located on chromosomes.

Boveri and Sutton reasoned that if the genetic contributions of sperm and eggs are the same, the genes ought to be located in the same place in the two kinds of gametes. Where could this be? Sperm cells are composed mostly of a nucleus, with just a small amount of cytoplasm. The nucleus of the egg is very similar to the nucleus of the sperm. However, the cytoplasm of the egg is very different from the cytoplasm of the sperm. Because of the similarities of nuclei but differences in cytoplasm of egg and sperm, Boveri and Sutton concluded that the nucleus contains the genes.

The chromosomes are inside the nucleus. Careful observations have shown that they seem to behave much as genes were thought to behave. In Table 14–A–1, the activity of chromosomes is compared with the behavior of Mendel's hypothetical factors.

## 15–A

## The Hardy-Weinberg Principle

Early in the 20th century the mathematician G. H. Hardy and the physician W. Weinberg recognized a mathematical relationship in the frequencies of alleles in a population. According to this relationship, the frequencies would stay the same from generation to generation, unless acted upon by natural selection, mating preferences, chance, or other factors.

The actual number of conditions affecting the principle is considerable:

1. The population size must be large enough to offset the effects of chance on the frequencies of different alleles.
2. Natural selection must already have produced stability in the population and not be acting in such a way as to change the existing allele frequencies.

| | allele frequencies in male gametes | |
|---|---|---|
| | 0.6 $B^M$ | 0.4 $B^N$ |
| allele frequencies in female gametes    0.6 $B^M$ | 0.36 $B^M B^M$ | 0.24 $B^M B^N$ |
|    0.4 $B^N$ | 0.24 $B^M B^N$ | 0.16 $B^N B^N$ |

| | allele frequencies in male gametes | |
|---|---|---|
| | $p$ | $q$ |
| allele frequencies in female gametes    $p$ | $pp$ | $pq$ |
|    $q$ | $pq$ | $qq$ |

**Table 15–A–1** Population gene analysis with data (left) and generalized algebraic numbers (right).

3. New mutations must not be occurring. (Today biologists modify this condition to state that new *beneficial* or *neutral* mutations must not be occurring.)
4. Mating effects should be random. If mating preferences are acting selectively, the pattern should be one that produces the same effect overall as random mating.
5. New individuals (with different alleles) should not be migrating into the population.
6. Individuals should not be migrating out of the population.

No population meets all these conditions, or even most of them. However, many populations have stable gene frequencies for the alleles that are studied. In fact, many large populations are found to maintain the same gene frequencies when studied over a number of generations.

Table 15–A–1 reproduces information from the chapter about the frequencies of two alleles in the Swedish population. At the right, the same information is represented mathematically. In the Hardy-Weinberg principle, the frequencies of two alleles are represented by $p$ and $q$. If one allele is dominant, it is represented by $p$. Just as $0.6B^M$ plus $0.4B^N$ add up to 1, or 100 percent of the Swedish population, so do $p$ and $q$ always add up to 1, no matter how the two frequencies differ individually. Hence, $p + q = 1$ is one of two statements in the Hardy-Weinberg principle.

The other statement is: $p^2 + 2pq + q^2 = 1$. Using Table 15–A–1, you can see that for the Swedish population this mathematical statement becomes:

$$(0.6)^2 + 2(0.6)(0.4) + (0.4)^2 = 1$$

You can work this equation out to see that the proportions of the Swedish population having each blood type are those found in the data table.

The Hardy-Weinberg principle is very useful for many population genetics problems. For example, about 0.04 percent of the U.S. population has cystic fibrosis. Cystic fibrosis is a recessive disorder. Only people with a *pair* of alleles associated with the recessive condition are affected. How can the proportion of people who do not carry even one such allele be determined?

In this case, $q^2 = 0.0004$ (0.04 percent of the population). Thus $q$, the square root of $q^2$, is 0.02. This figure is the proportion of gametes with the defective allele. Since $p + q = 1$, $p = 0.98$. The proportion of people who are free of the allele is $p^2$, or $(0.98)^2$:

| $p^2$ | + | $2pq$ | $q^2$ |
|---|---|---|---|
| 0.9604 | | 0.0392 | 0.0004 |
| | | | (cystic fibrosis) |

Roughly 96 percent of the U.S. population is free of the allele. Almost 4 percent (0.0392) have the carrier condition (one defective allele).

It can be expected that about 0.04 percent of the population in the next generation will again have cystic fibrosis. This assumes, of course, that no related mutations occur and that people do not move in or out of the population. This expected percentage also does not reflect any natural selection against cystic fibrosis victims, which would affect their contribution to the gene pool.

## 15–B

## The Chi-Square Test

Suppose that in studying a test-cross between two kinds of tomato plants, a scientist expects half the offspring to have green leaves and half to have yellow. This expectation is based on Mendel's laws and certain assumptions about the genes responsible for the formation of green or yellow leaves. In the actual experiment, however, 671 out of 1240 seedlings turn out to have green leaves and 569 of the 1240 have yellow leaves. Is this a minor difference due merely to chance, or is it a relatively large and significant deviation from the expected numbers?

Scientists have devised a method of determining whether a deviation from expected experimental results is large enough to be significant. This method is called the chi-square test. This test consists of two steps: (1) calculating the chi-square value for the experiment in question and (2) determining how often a chi-square value of that size is likely to be produced by chance alone.

The chi-square value is a measure of the deviation between observed and expected experimental results. In mathematical shorthand, this value can be expressed as follows:

$$\chi^2 = \Sigma \frac{(Ob - Ex)^2}{Ex}$$

where $\chi$ is the Greek letter "chi," $\Sigma$ is the Greek letter "sigma" (our S), standing for "sum" and

meaning here "the sum of all," Ob stands for the observed number, and Ex stands for the expected number. Let us see how this formula is used to find the chi-square value for the experiment described above. In that experiment 620 green-leaved and 620 yellow-leaved plants were expected, but 671 green and 569 yellow were observed. Therefore,

$$\chi^2 = \frac{(671 - 620)^2}{620} + \frac{(569 - 620)^2}{620}$$

$$= \frac{(51)^2}{620} + \frac{(-51)^2}{620} = \frac{2601 + 2601}{620}$$

$$= \frac{5202}{620} = 8.4$$

Thus, the value of chi-square for this experiment is 8.4. Is this a significant value?

Mathematicians have derived tables to provide the basis for judging whether any chi-square value is greater than can be expected by chance alone. From these tables the degrees of probability of some possible chi-square values have been computed. By consulting Table 15–B–1 for the value in the calculations above, you will see that a chi-square of 8.4 for just two classes (green-leaved plants and yellow-leaved plants) is larger than any of the values listed. This means that the probability is less than 1 in 100 that chance alone would produce this big a deviation from the expected results. By custom, when the probability that a deviation is due to chance alone is as little as (or less than) 5 in 100, it is generally agreed that the difference is significant. If a deviation is large enough to be considered significant, then some factors are probably operating other than those on which the expected results were based. In the case of the green- and yellow-leaved tomato plants, for example, it was found that fewer of the yellow-leaved plants germinated and survived because they were less hardy than the green plants.

How is the chi-square test applied to experimental results involving more than two classes of

| Number of Classes | $\chi^2$ Values (Experimental Deviation) | | | | | | | |
|---|---|---|---|---|---|---|---|---|
| 2 | 0.0002 | 0.004 | 0.455 | 1.074 | 1.642 | 2.706 | 3.841 | 6.635 |
| 3 | 0.020 | 0.103 | 1.386 | 2.408 | 3.219 | 4.605 | 5.991 | 9.210 |
| 4 | 0.115 | 0.352 | 2.366 | 3.665 | 4.642 | 6.251 | 7.815 | 11.345 |
| Number of times per hundred that chance alone would produce the deviation | 99 | 95 | 50 | 30 | 20 | 10 | 5 | 1 |

**Table 15–B–1** Significance of some chi-square values.

objects or events? Suppose, for example, that a scientist has crossed pink-flowered four-o'clocks and obtained 236 offspring. From Mendel's laws, the offspring are expected to be red-, pink-, and white-flowered in the ratio of 1:2:1. For the 236 offspring, this would mean 59 red, 118 pink, and 59 white. But the actual results are 66 red, 115 pink, and 55 white. The chi-square test is applied as follows:

$$\chi^2 = \frac{(66 - 59)^2}{59} + \frac{(115 - 118)^2}{118} + \frac{(55 - 59)^2}{59}$$

$$= \frac{49}{59} + \frac{9}{118} + \frac{16}{59} = \frac{98 + 9 + 32}{118}$$

$$= \frac{139}{118} = 1.18$$

By consulting the table, you will see that a chi-square value of 1.18 for three classes is really quite small. Between 50 and 95 times in 100 this value might be produced by chance alone. The experimenter therefore concludes that the observed results actually do agree with the predicted values.

## 17–A
## Opening and Closing of Stomata

Many years ago it was observed that stomata usually close at night and open soon after sunrise. Under certain conditions the stomata also close during the day, particularly during the late afternoon. It has also been found that the opening and closing of the stomata depend on the formation of carbonic acid from carbon dioxide and water vapor. As light strikes the leaves in the morning, photosynthesis begins; more carbon dioxide is used by the leaf in photosynthesis. This results in less carbon dioxide being available to form carbonic acid, and thus a decrease in the concentration of carbonic acid and a subsequent increase in $p$H. This increase in $p$H favors the conversion of starch to sugar in the guard cells of the stomata. With the conversion of each insoluble starch molecule into many soluble molecules of sugar, the number of particles in solution increases greatly. This decreases the concentration of water in the guard cells, and water moves into the guard cells by osmosis from neighboring cells. With this increase in pressure, the stomata are forced open.

As the intensity of light decreases later in the day the reverse occurs. Less carbon dioxide is used in photosynthesis; there is an increase in carbonic acid concentration, which subsequently lowers the $p$H. The lower $p$H favors the conversion of many soluble sugar molecules into fewer insoluble starch molecules. This results in an increased concentration of water in the guard cells. The water moves by osmosis from the guard cells into neighboring cells, reducing the pressure in the guard cells. The reduced pressure lets the guard cells straighten, closing the stomata.

## 17–B

### Fossil Record of Root Development

At the beginning of the 20th century, a French botanist proposed the hypothesis that one of the side branches of an early green alga may have bent over and entered the soil. The fossil record was searched for evidence of primitive land plants with such an anchoring and absorbing system. Fossils of several kinds of plants with these systems were found. Figure 17–2, left, is a reconstruction of one of these simple plants. Another fossil plant with a more advanced rootlike system is shown in Figure 17–2, right. Probably neither of these fossil plants was the actual ancestor of present-day green plants. They can serve, however, as examples of possible forerunners of the land plants of today.

## 17–C

### Böhm's Cohesion-Tension Experiment

Josef Böhm, a 19th century Austrian botanist, performed an experiment using mechanical equipment to imitate the xylem transport system in a tree. Figure 17–C–1 shows the essential points in

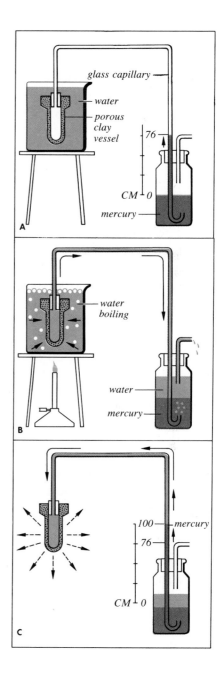

**Figure 17–C–1** Böhm's experiment showing how the forces of cohesion and tension can move water in the xylem of a tree.
a. Porous clay vessel is immersed in water and connected to a bottle of mercury. Note mercury in tube.
b. The boiling water is forced through the walls of the vessel and up the glass tube into the bottle of mercury. The water bubbles through the mercury and out an exhaust tube. Thus, an unbroken column of water is formed, driving all the air out of the system.
c. When the beaker of water is removed, the water in the clay vessel evaporates through the pores, causing the water in the glass tube to move in the opposite direction. As it moves, it pulls the mercury behind it, up to a height of 100 centimeters. Should an air bubble appear anywhere in the system, however, the mercury would fall back to the normal height of 76 centimeters.

Böhm's experiment. Notice particularly that if an air bubble appears anywhere in the system, breaking the continuous column of water, the mercury column will fall back to 76 centimeters, its height under normal atmospheric pressure.

The forces that hold the water molecules together (forces of cohesion) are at least four to five times greater than the force required to move the water upward in the xylem.

## 17–D

### Postlethwait's and Rogers' Radioisotope Experiments

Böhm's experiment suggested that if an air bubble appeared in the xylem transport system, the cohesion-tension force would be lost. S. N. Postlethwait and B. J. Rogers of Purdue University injected radioactive phosphorus ($P^{32}$) into different trees and traced the movement of the phosphorus as it was carried upward with the water through the xylem tracheids and vessels. Figure 17–D–1 illustrates the results of several of their experiments:

In Tree 1, the isotope moved directly up the tree.

In Tree 2, with the xylem purposely damaged by two opposite cuts (A and B) 30 centimeters apart, the isotope moved around both edges of the first cut and with slight spiralling moved up the tree.

In Tree 3, with two pairs of opposite cuts into the xylem (cuts C and D at 90° orientation to A and B), the phosphorus moved around cut A on the left. It then proceeded upward, curving around the edges of the cuts.

In Tree 4, with two pairs of opposite cuts similar to Tree 3's but only 15 centimeters apart, the phosphorus again moved around cut A on the left. It then spiralled upward around the edges of cuts B, C, and D.

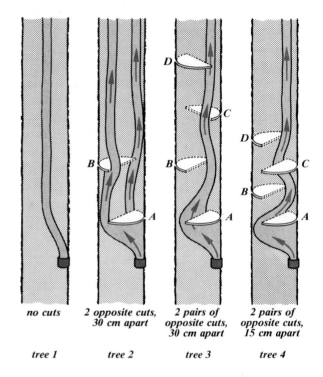

| *no cuts* | *2 opposite cuts, 30 cm apart* | *2 pairs of opposite cuts, 30 cm apart* | *2 pairs of opposite cuts, 15 cm apart* |
| --- | --- | --- | --- |
| *tree 1* | *tree 2* | *tree 3* | *tree 4* |

**Figure 17–D–1** Diagram of the experiments of Postlethwait and Rogers, showing the movement of water upward in the experimentally injured trees.

From the results of Postlethwait's and Rogers' experiments, it appears that the upward movement of water may be more complex than the simple column up each xylem tube suggested by the results of Böhm's experiment. How does water move laterally around cuts in the xylem tracheids and vessels?

## 17-E

### A Practical Application

An interesting application of the knowledge that phloem transports food materials in plants is the practice of "girdling." In one type of girdling, the bark and phloem vessels of a tree are removed back to the cambium in one branch of a plant. Since the food materials produced in the leaves cannot move past the point of girdling, they pass to the fruits growing above the girdle. Such fruits will be exceptionally large. This method is commonly used to produce fruits of extra size and quality. Can you think of other ways in which this procedure of girdling might be used?

## 17-F

### William Harvey Discovers That Blood Circulates

It was not always known that the blood streams around the body in constant circulation. William Harvey was trained as a physician and scientist in England in the 17th century. Harvey was taught that the blood flowed both to and from the head over the same route and through the same vessels, much like the ebb and flow of the tides along the seashore.

One day Harvey's anatomy teacher showed a group of students some tiny flaplike structures discovered in the heart and in certain blood vessels of humans and some lower animals. William Harvey wondered about the function of these structures. It was Harvey's curiosity about these flaps that led to the investigation of the transport system.

During the years after graduation from medical school, Harvey operated on many live animals to observe their heartbeat and the flow of their blood. After many years of patient observation and experimentation, Harvey presented the idea that the blood circulates around the body like a "river with no end." One of the arguments used to support

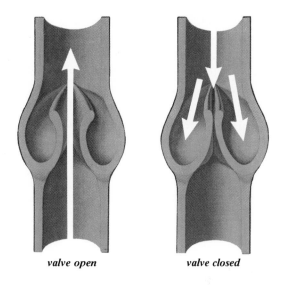

*valve open*          *valve closed*

**Figure 17-F-1** The valves in veins operate something like the locks in a canal, opening and closing to regulate the flow of blood toward the heart. Note that the back pressure of blood tends to keep the valve closed until added pressure of blood on the other side of the valve opens it.

this idea was an explanation of the flaplike structures Harvey had seen as a student. Were these tiny structures valves? A small probing instrument inserted into a blood vessel would go in one direction but not in the other. Harvey reasoned that the structures were valves and that if they prevented a probe from moving in both directions, they would also prevent the blood from flowing backward. Therefore, the blood could not "ebb" back to the heart by the same vessels through which it had come from the heart. Rather, Harvey concluded, the blood must circulate from the heart through one set of vessels, called arteries, and back to the heart through another set, called veins. It was in the veins that the tiny valves had been observed. See Figure 17-F-1.

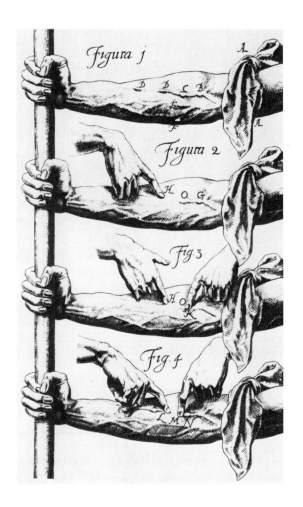

**Figure 17–F–2** Harvey's explanation of the function of valves: "Let an arm be tied above the elbow as (A,A, Fig. 1). In the course of the veins certain large knots or elevations (B,C,D,E,F) will be perceived, and this not only at the places where a branch is received (E,F), but also where none enters (C,D): These are all formed by valves. If you press the blood from the space above one of the valves, from H to O (Fig. 2), you will see no influx of blood from above; yet will the vessel continue sufficiently distended above that valve (O,G). If you now apply a finger of the other hand upon the distended part of the vein above the valve O (Fig. 3), and press downwards, you will find that you cannot force the blood through or beyond the valve. If you press at one part in the course of a vein with the point of a finger (L, Fig. 4), and then with another finger streak the blood upwards beyond the next valve (N), you will perceive that this portion of the vein continues empty (L,N). That the blood in the veins therefore proceeds from inferior to superior parts of the heart appears most obviously."

Figure 17–F–2 shows Harvey's demonstration of the effect produced by valves in the veins of the arm. Harvey's own words are used in the caption so that you may follow the reasoning.

One piece of evidence was lacking in Harvey's demonstration of the circulation of the blood. Harvey could not describe how the blood moved from the arteries to the veins. Several years later, Marcello Malpighi (mal-PEE-gee), an Italian scientist, used a crude microscope to examine the lung of a frog. Malpighi observed that blood flowed from the arteries into fine connecting vessels called capillaries, and then flowed into veins from the other end. With the discovery of these connecting vessels, the circulation of the blood was established beyond reasonable doubt.

## 17–G

### How Much Blood Does Your Heart Pump?

Sitting at rest, take your pulse rate, or have someone else take it for you, using a watch with a second hand. The artery in the wrist is best for feeling the pulse of the heartbeat. Use the average of three readings for your pulse rate. Assume that 60 milliliters of blood (the average amount for an adult) are forced from the heart at each beat. Calculate the volume of blood that is forced from your heart in a minute; in a day.

Now do some moderate exercise such as jumping up and down, running, or walking up and down steps. Quickly take your pulse again and record the rate. Calculate the volume of blood being pumped from the heart in a minute, using the figure given above for milliliters of blood pumped per beat.

Record your results. Compare them with the heartbeat and rate of blood flow when you were at rest. Compare your results with those of a classmate. Is there any difference in the figures obtained for the two sexes? Is there any difference between individuals who are noticeably below or above average body weight?

## 17–H

### Oxygen-Transport Pigments in Animals

A number of different kinds of pigments in various animals are able to combine with oxygen for transport of the oxygen to the cells. Sometimes these pigments are contained in cells; in other cases they are dissolved in the plasma, the fluid portion of the blood. These pigments also differ in their ability to carry oxygen. Table 17–H–1 lists these pigments and some of their characteristics.

| Pigment | Color | Metal Element | Location | Animal | Holding Capacity $O_2$/100 ml Blood |
|---|---|---|---|---|---|
| Hemoglobin | red | iron | red corpuscles | mammals | 25 |
| | | | | birds | 18.5 |
| | | | | reptiles | 9 |
| | | | | amphibians | 12 |
| | | | | fishes | 9 |
| | | | plasma | annelids | 6.5 |
| | | | | mollusks | 1.5 |
| Hemocyanin | blue | copper | plasma | mollusks | 2–8 |
| Chlorocruorin | green | iron | plasma | annelids | 9 |
| Hemoerythrin | red | iron | corpuscles | annelids | 2 |

**Table 17–H–1** Some characteristics of various oxygen-transport pigments.

## 18–A

## Understanding of Respiration Developed Slowly

Even the most primitive humans probably knew that there was a connection between life and the movements of breathing air in and out of the chest. However, the connection between breathing movements and the exchange of oxygen and carbon dioxide in the cells was not understood until the 1700's.

Robert Boyle, one of the founders of modern chemistry, observed during the 1600's that air is essential to life. Boyle compared the death of a mouse in a closed jar with the snuffing out of a burning candle and decided that air was as necessary for the life of the mouse as it was for the burning of the candle. It seems obvious to us now that air is essential for a mammal's life. But suppose someone argued that Boyle's theory that air was essential to life was all wrong. Instead, it was the movement of the chest that was essential to life. How would you prove such an argument incorrect?

Robert Hooke, in 1667, devised an experiment to answer just this argument. Hooke showed that an experimental animal would die soon after the movements of its chest muscles and ribs were stopped. However, if air were immediately blown into the animal's lungs with a bellows, the animal could be kept alive.

Why is air essential to life? Most scientists of Boyle's time believed that the only function of air was to cool the blood as it passed through the lungs. Other scientists suggested that a specific substance in the air was essential to life.

It was Antoine Lavoisier (luh-vwah-ZYAY), a famous French scientist, who showed the importance of oxygen in respiration. On the basis of many experiments, Lavoisier stated, "Air does not simply act as a mechanical force, but as an agency of new combinations." (This quotation is from M. L. Gabriel and S. Fogel, eds. *Great Experiments in Biology.* Englewood Cliffs, New Jersey, Prentice-Hall, Inc. 1955.) It is the oxygen in the air that reacts chemically with other substances in the body during respiration. Lavoisier concluded that oxygen is absorbed by animals from the air and passed from the lungs into the bloodstream. Carbon dioxide is released from the lungs as oxygen is taken in.

In a paper called "A Memoir on Heat," published in 1780, Lavoisier and Pierre Laplace (pee-AIR luh-PLAHS), another great French scientist and mathematician, showed that the respiration of living things was similar to burning. Both processes use up oxygen and produce heat, a form of energy. This explains Boyle's observation that air was needed for a candle flame and for the life of a mouse.

## 18–B

## Oxygen Consumption Is Related to Temperature Regulation in Animals

Oxygen is used by cells in the series of chemical reactions called cell respiration. Like all chemical reactions, the rate of cell respiration depends on the temperature of the organism. If an animal's body temperature is low, cell respiration is slower and less oxygen is used.

In many animals the body temperature is not constant, but varies with the temperature of the surrounding air or water. Animals whose body temperature varies in this way are called **poikilothermic** (poy-KIL-uh-THERM-ik). Fishes, amphibians, and reptiles are poikilothermic vertebrates. Many poikilothermic animals have temperature-regulating processes, but these processes can compensate only for moderate change in environmental temperature. In extreme cold, the animals become sluggish or almost totally inactive. When their surroundings are warmer, their body temperature increases and they become more active. The oxygen consumption also changes with temperature. More oxygen is needed by those animals in warm air or water.

No animal can live if its temperature goes beyond certain limits. To keep alive, a poikilothermic animal must avoid extremes of temperature. For example, on chilly days snakes and lizards often bask on a sunny rock and in this way can become quite warm. In the desert, during the hot days, poikilothermic animals must stay in shaded spots or underground. Thus, they must seek a change in their environment to maintain a suitable metabolic rate.

Birds and mammals are called warm-blooded (homoiothermic) animals, for they can maintain a constant internal temperature even when the temperature of the environment changes. Whether they are in a warm or a cold place, their body temperature remains the same. When some animals that are warm-blooded are too warm, they sweat. The surface of their bodies is cooled as the water evaporates. Other warm-blooded animals have different means of cooling their bodies. Some salivate (camels), and others pant (dogs, birds). Some desert mammals appear not to use evaporative cooling at all.

When the air is very cold, shivering increases body activity, increasing the metabolic rate and warming the body. The increased metabolic rate requires more oxygen. Therefore, a warm-blooded animal actually uses more oxygen when the surroundings get colder. These temperature-regulating mechanisms make it possible for a warm-blooded animal to remain active even in extremely cold temperatures. A poikilothermic animal tends to become inactive in the cold. The difference in oxygen consumption between poikilothermic and warm-blooded animals is thus most apparent in cold temperatures.

Many warm-blooded and poikilothermic animals have a special reaction to extreme cold. They go into a period of dormancy called **hibernation** (hy-ber-NA-shun). Their metabolism slows to a point ordinarily considered near death. The heart beats slowly, the blood circulates very sluggishly, the body temperature drops, and they may breathe as slowly as once every five minutes. By slowing their metabolic rate, they are able to exist for a long period of time on stored body fat. Animals that hibernate, such as frogs, chipmunks, and some kinds of bats, cannot wake up from this dormant period as quickly as they would from normal sleep. They must warm up slowly and gradually increase the rate of their body processes. Some animals, like bears, sleep through the winter, but their body processes merely slow down. This is not considered hibernation, for their metabolic rate is only a little less than their normal rate. On warm winter days they may even awaken and leave their dens in search of food.

**Figure 18–B–1** The arctic ground squirrel (bottom) spends its summer on the Arctic tundra. In the winter it hibernates in its nest (top). Winter temperatures in its burrow range from 0° C to −7° C. Outside, the temperature may drop to −40° C.

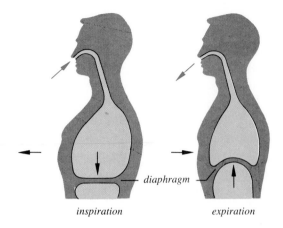

*inspiration*                    *expiration*

**Figure 18–C–1** The movements of the chest wall and diaphragm during inhalation and exhalation change the volume, and therefore the air pressure, in the lungs.

Hibernation causes a massive change in the respiration, metabolism, and whole functioning of the animal. What initiates this great change? How and why do certain tropical animals go into a summer hibernation? These tropical animals seem to be reacting to changes in the environment, particularly changes in the length of day. Scientists are studying the process of hibernation, hoping to discover why and how an animal can change its whole metabolism so drastically.

## 18–C

## The Mechanics of Lung Breathing

Place your hands on each side of your body just above the point where you can feel your ribs end. Take a deep breath and press lightly with your hands. Can you feel the ribs move upward and out? When the sets of muscles between the ribs contract, the chest cavity expands and gets larger. When these muscles relax, the chest cavity gets smaller. When you breathe in, the area just below the ribs pushes downward. This is the diaphragm, a thick sheet of muscles between the chest cavity and the abdominal cavity. When the diaphragm muscles contract, the chest cavity becomes larger.

When they relax, the diaphragm moves upward and the volume of the chest cavity is reduced. The movements of the ribs and diaphragm are coordinated. Such movements cause the air pressure in the lungs to differ from that on the outside, resulting in an air flow. Compare the respiratory movements shown in Figure 18–C–1 with your own.

## 18–D

## Carbon Dioxide Transport in the Red Blood Cells

The reaction of carbon dioxide with water occurs quite slowly in the plasma of the blood. However, inside the red blood cells an enzyme, carbonic anhydrase (an-HY-drayz), speeds up or catalyzes this reaction about 200 to 300 times faster.

$$CO_2 + H_2O \rightleftharpoons H_2CO_3$$

carbon   water   carbonic   carbonic
dioxide           anhydrase   acid

Most of the reaction between carbon dioxide and water takes place within the red blood cells because of the activity of this important enzyme. The carbonic acid ionizes to $H^+$ and $HCO_3^-$ ions.

Carbon dioxide also reacts directly with hemoglobin. As with oxygen, this reaction is a very weak chemical bond. The carbon dioxide is easily released when the blood gets to the capillaries of the lungs. Carbon dioxide combines with hemoglobin at a different point than oxygen does. Therefore, hemoglobin can combine with oxygen and carbon dioxide at the same time.

## 18–E

## Carbon Dioxide and the Nervous System's Control of Breathing

Carbon dioxide is not just a waste by-product of respiration. Carbon dioxide plays a much more important role than oxygen in determining the rate of breathing. The nerves that control breathing are affected by the concentration of dissolved carbon dioxide in the blood. For example, when the carbon dioxide concentration of the blood is high, the rate of breathing is also high. When the carbon dioxide concentration is low, the rate of breathing is low. This mechanism is controlled by a small part of the brain, the respiratory center.

The blood helps to maintain a stable environment around the cells and must be regulated to keep it from becoming too acid or too basic. The rate of breathing is important in regulating the blood's $p$H. Whenever carbon dioxide builds up in the bloodstream, more carbonic acid is formed. More carbon dioxide is removed by the lungs as the rate and depth of breathing are increased. Thus, when carbon dioxide is exhaled, the $p$H of the blood is controlled.

The rate of breathing is increased when very slight changes in the blood $p$H act upon a nervous control center. It is, therefore, an excess of carbon dioxide and not a shortage of oxygen that increases the breathing rate. This mechanism also works the other way. When the blood $p$H rises slightly, carbon dioxide tends to remain in the form of carbonic acid, and the rate and depth of breathing is decreased. Thus, a change in blood $p$H causes a change in the pattern of breathing that tends to restore homeostasis.

## 19–A

## Other Organisms with Highly Specialized Digestive Systems

Many kinds of animals live entirely on plant material. Most of these animals do not have enzymes that digest cellulose, the material of which wood and plant fibers are made. How then can these animals use cellulose? What digestive-system modifications do these animals have? Certain microorganisms that do have enzymes which digest cellulose live in the digestive tracts of larger, plant-eating animals. These microorganisms are

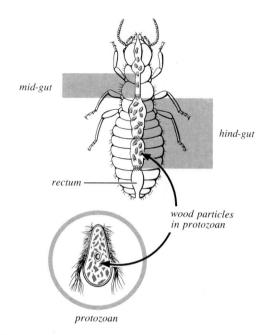

mid-gut

hind-gut

rectum

wood particles in protozoan

protozoan

**Figure 19–A–1** Microorganisms living in the intestine of the termite produce enzymes that digest the cellulose in wood. Termites without these microorganisms would starve on a diet of wood.

able to produce the enzymes that digest the cellulose. For example, bacteria and protozoa digest the cellulose eaten by termites and cows. (See Figure 19–A–1.) If these microorganisms are killed, the host animal will starve to death.

Some organisms have no digestive systems at all. They can absorb food that other organisms have already digested, and therefore they do not need to digest their own food. Plants or animals that obtain food in this way are called **parasites** (PAR-uh-sytes). For example, the mistletoe plant has rootlike suckers that penetrate the phloem of another plant and absorb digested food from it. The tapeworm is another parasite and lives in the intestines of humans and other animals. Tapeworms also do not have any digestive organs; they absorb already-digested food from the host animal's intestines.

**Figure 19–B–1** A painting of Dr. William Beaumont with a frontier nurse and the trapper Alexis St. Martin.

## 19–B

## Beaumont's Experiments on Digestion

Before the days of abdominal surgery, it was rare to directly observe the internal organs of the body as they functioned. Only as a result of the strangest of circumstances could one see inside a living human body. William Beaumont (1785–1853), a physician in the United States Army, observed one of these strange cases.

In 1822 a badly wounded trapper, Alexis St. Martin, was treated by Dr. Beaumont. The accidental discharge of a shotgun had blown a large hole in the left side of the patient. Part of the ribs, muscles, and wall of the stomach had been torn away. Beaumont treated St. Martin (Figure 19–B–1), but the wound did not close properly. For almost two years Beaumont treated infections in the wound and gradually nursed St. Martin back to health. The walls of the stomach grew together with the skin and muscles of the body wall. As a result, a hole leading to the interior of the stomach remained in St. Martin's side. A flap of the stomach wall eventually covered the hole and prevented food from falling out. The flap of tissue could easily be depressed by the finger to permit observation of the inner contents of the stomach.

Beaumont realized that St. Martin could provide an unusual opportunity to an experimenter to study the functioning of the stomach. For eleven years St. Martin remained with the doctor for the purpose of these experiments. The following descriptions, in Beaumont's own words, are two of the experiments as reported in *Experiments and Observations on the Gastric Juice and the Physiology of Digestion,* by William Beaumont, published in 1833.

### Experiment 1

Aug. 7. at 11 o'clock, A.M., after having kept the lad fasting for seventeen hours, I introduced the glass tube of a Thermometer (Fahrenheit's) through the perforation, into the stomach, nearly the whole length of the stem, to ascertain the natural warmth of the stomach. In fifteen minutes, or less, the mercury rose to 100°, and there remained stationary. This I determined by marking the height of the mercury on the glass, with ink, as it stood in the stomach, and then withdrawing it, and placing it on the graduated scale again.

I now introduced a gum-elastic (caoutchouc) tube [a soft rubber tube], and drew off one ounce of pure gastric liquor, unmixed with any other matter, except a small proportion of mucus, into a three-ounce vial. I then took a solid piece of boiled, recently salted beef, weighing three drachms [a drachm is $\frac{1}{8}$ of an ounce], and put it into the liquor in the vial; corked the vial tight, and placed it in a saucepan, filled with water, raised to the temperature of 100°, and kept at that point, on a nicely regulated sand bath. In forty minutes digestion had distinctly commenced over the surface of the meat. In fifty minutes the fluid had become quite opaque and cloudy; the external texture began to separate and become loose. In sixty minutes, a chyme [a souplike mass of food digested in the stomach] began to form.

At 1 o'clock, P.M., (digestion having progressed with the same regularity as in the last half hour,) the cellular texture seemed to be entirely destroyed, leaving the muscular fibres loose and unconnected, floating about in fine small shreds, very tender and soft.

At 3 o'clock, the muscular fibres had diminished one half, since last examination, at 1 o'clock.

At 5 o'clock they were nearly all digested; a few fibres only remaining.

At 7 o'clock, the muscular texture was completely broken down; and only a few of the small fibres floating in the fluid.

At 9 o'clock, every part of the meat was completely digested.

The gastric juice, when taken from the stomach, was as clear and transparent as water. The mixture in the vial was now about the colour of whey [pale yellow]. After standing at rest a few minutes, a fine sediment, of the colour of the meat, subsided to the bottom of the vial.

Figure 19–B–2 illustrates Beaumont's experiment. On the basis of the results of this experiment, would you predict that what happened to the piece of beef in the flask of gastric juice would also happen in St. Martin's stomach? How would you have tested the hypothesis that the piece of beef would undergo the same changes in the stomach as it did in the flask? Beaumont devised the following experiment to test this hypothesis.

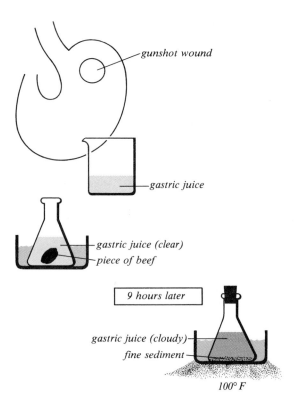

**Figure 19–B–2** A diagram of Beaumont's experiment on the digestion of a piece of beef by gastric juice from a human stomach.

## Experiment 2

At the same time that I commenced the foregoing experiment, I suspended a piece of beef, exactly similar to that in the vial, into the stomach, through the aperture.

At 12 o'clock, M. withdrew it, and found it about as much affected by digestion as that in the vial; there was little or no difference in their appearance, returned it again.

At 1 o'clock, P.M., I drew out the string; but the meat was all completely digested, and gone.

The effect of the gastric juice on the piece of meat, suspended in the stomach, was exactly similar to that in the vial, only more rapid after the first half hour, and sooner completed. Digestion commenced on, and was confined to the surface entirely, in both situations. Agitation accelerated the solution in the vial, by removing the coat that was digested on the surface; enveloping the remainder of the meat in the gastric fluid; and giving this fluid access to the undigested portions.

Do you think Beaumont's second experiment was a good test of his hypothesis–that the gastric juice acted in the same way on the meat in the vial and in St. Martin's stomach? Can you think of any other experiments that could have been performed on St. Martin to find out further facts about the digestion of food in the stomach?

## 21–A

### Inhibitors in Desert Plants

Plant hormones that inhibit growth may have survival value for the plant. For example, consider the following experiment. Seeds from some desert plants did not germinate easily when placed on moist paper in a petri dish. However, after they were placed in running tap water for a number of hours, these seeds readily germinated on the moist paper. How would you explain this?

Further work on these seeds showed that there were inhibitors in the seed coat. Because of these inhibitors many seeds on the desert do not germinate unless there are prolonged rains. The water dilutes and washes out these inhibitors. Under these circumstances the ground would be thoroughly moistened and the germinating seed could survive.

## 21–B

### The Function of the Thyroid Gland Is Discovered

How did we learn about the thyroid and its hormones? The function of the thyroid was under dispute for a long time. Many investigators struggled for hundreds of years to solve the mystery of the thyroid's structure and function. Galen, a Greek physician of the 2nd century, believed that the thyroid secretion contained a lubricating fluid that helped speech. Many learned people accepted this idea for years.

About 400 years ago, however, Vesalius, an Italian anatomist, described the gland and noted that it did not have ducts through which a lubricating fluid could flow to reach the throat. Even with this evidence, investigators of that time held rigidly to the idea that the thyroid was responsible for lubricating the throat.

About 200 years later Albrecht von Haller once more pointed out that there were no ducts connecting the thyroid gland with the throat. The role of the thyroid remained unknown. Indeed, some investigators even believed that the organ had no essential function. Others argued that its large blood supply showed that the gland acted as an overflow to prevent a sudden rush of blood to the head. The name thyroid, from the Greek word meaning "shield-shaped" (Figure 21–3), had been suggested for the gland in 1656 by an English physician, who thought the thyroid served simply to round out and beautify the neck.

Modern experimental work began in 1883 with the observations of Emil Kocher, a Swiss surgeon. Kocher had originally believed that the thyroid had no necessary function, and so had removed the thyroid from 24 patients to help relieve the distress caused by goiters. Sixteen of these patients showed a loss of physical energy, great muscular weakness, and puffy swelling, first of the face, hands, and feet, and finally of the whole body.

The skin of these patients became dry and hard, and their mental abilities slowed down. This condition resembled a disease long known as cretinism (KREE-tin-is-um). Total removal of human thyroid glands was therefore soon stopped. Experiments performed on other mammals showed that removal of the thyroid in early life also caused the symptoms of cretinism to develop. These observations suggested that the thyroid must contain some substance essential for health and normal growth.

In later years another English physician showed that a preparation of dried sheep thyroid helped control certain types of thyroid diseases. Finally it was observed that when dried animal thyroid was given to normal persons, the rate of their total body processes was speeded up. By the turn of the century, physicians were successfully using sheep thyroid to treat patients who did not secrete enough thyroid hormone. It had become obvious that the thyroid contained a powerful chemical substance that was able to influence many other organs.

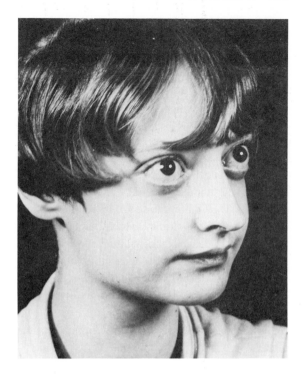

**Figure 21–C–1** A girl with hyperthyroidism, a condition in which the thyroid gland is overactive, secreting too much thyroxine.

## 21–C

## Thyroid Disorders Represent Abnormal Regulation

Sometimes, a child may be born with only part or none of the thyroid. This kind of defect can occur from abnormal development of the embryo. The result is both physical and mental sluggishness. An underactive thyroid has its worst effects in infancy or early childhood. The normal changes in body and facial proportions fail to occur, and bones do not develop properly.

Probably the most common and most serious of all thyroid disorders is the overactivity of the thyroid gland. Characteristics of such a condition are enlarged thyroid and bulging eyes (Figure 21–C–1). When too much thyroxine is secreted, tissues use more oxygen and produce more heat;

blood pressure rises; and circulation and respiration rates increase.

It has been found that the pituitary also plays a role in certain conditions of an overactive thyroid. If a pituitary extract containing TSH is injected into an experimental animal, the same symptoms of overactivity of thyroid occur, including the characteristic bulging eyes. What causes an overactive thyroid in nature is not completely understood. Fortunately, many treatments can help this condition. Some of the treatments used are antithyroid drugs, surgical removal of part of the gland, and high doses of radioactive iodine to destroy some thyroid tissue.

## 22-A

## How Does a Nerve Respond to Various Stimulus Strengths?

A nerve fiber will not transmit an impulse unless the stimulus applied to it is of at least a certain minimum strength, called the **threshold.** A threshold stimulus starts one impulse traveling along the fiber. A stimulus stronger than the threshold also causes an impulse to travel along the fiber, but the impulse will not be any faster or any stronger. Under normal conditions all impulses, no matter what the stimulus, travel along the neuron at the same speed and with the same strength. This kind of response is known as the "all-or-none response." Thus, for any one stimulus, the fiber either transmits a full impulse or it does not transmit an impulse at all. All stimuli above the threshold level trigger the same kind of impulse in the nerve fiber. This is because the energy for carrying the impulse does not come from the stimulus, but from the neuron.

If all impulses travel at the same speed and are of the same strength, how does the body distinguish between stimuli of varying strengths? Surely, you can tell the difference between a pat and a punch. Nerve fibers react to stronger stimuli by transmitting more impulses rather than by transmitting stronger impulses. Usually, once one impulse passes a synapse, other impulses following close behind can pass with greater ease.

It is the number of impulses that cross a synapse then, rather than the strength of the impulses, that varies with the strength of the stimulus. The number of impulses transmitted over a nerve fiber is affected by several factors: (1) how often a stimulus is repeated, (2) the strength of the stimulus, and (3) how long any one stimulus lasts. The difference between the pat and the punch is also affected by the number of neurons stimulated, and by the arrangement and connections between neurons. A single neuron may transmit its impulses to one other neuron or to many other neurons. This would depend on how many other neurons are connected with it.

## 22-B

## The Autonomic Nervous System

In Chapter 22 you studied parts of the nervous system that are voluntary, or under a person's conscious control. You also studied a little about other functions of the nervous system that are involuntary, or not under conscious control. Many of these functions are under the control of the autonomic nervous system. The autonomic nervous system exerts control over the heart, many glands, and over the smooth muscle in the digestive tract, respiratory system, excretory system, reproductive system, and blood vessels.

The reflex arcs explained in Section 22–8 contain one sensory and one motor neuron, often along with a third neuron. The axons of neurons in most reflex arcs have myelin sheaths and conduct reflexes rapidly. In contrast, there are no sensory neurons in autonomic arcs; there are two motor neurons. Usually the second motor neuron of an autonomic arc does not have a myelin sheath. These unmyelinated neurons conduct impulses much more slowly than the myelinated neurons of the reflex arcs.

There are two divisions of the autonomic nervous system. The two divisions are the **sympathetic** and **parasympathetic** systems. The sympathetic and parasympathetic systems differ both in structure and in function (see Figure 22–B–1).

The first motor neurons of the sympathetic system are usually very short. Their cell bodies are in the thoracic region of the spinal cord (see Figure 22–B–1). The synapses between the first and second motor neurons are located in ganglia near the spinal cord. The longer second motor neurons extend from synapses in the ganglia to the target organs.

The cell bodies of the first motor neurons in the parasympathetic system are located in the brain and in the sacral region of the spinal cord (see Figure 22–B–1). In contrast to the short axons of the first motor neurons of the sympathetic system, the axons of the first motor neurons of the parasympathetic system are very long. The synapses between the first and second motor neurons occur near or within the target organs. The axons of the second motor neurons are relatively short.

Most internal organs are connected to both the sympathetic and the parasympathetic systems. The two systems have opposing functions. If the sympathetic system stimulates a particular organ, the parasympathetic system would inhibit that organ. Where the parasympathetic system stimulates an organ, the sympathetic system would inhibit the organ. Usually, however, the sympathetic system serves as a stimulator. It has the same effect as the hormone adrenaline from the adrenal gland. It has an important function in preparing an organism to ''fight or flee'' in emergency situations. Appendix 22–C gives a specific example of how the autonomic nervous system functions in controlling heartbeat rate.

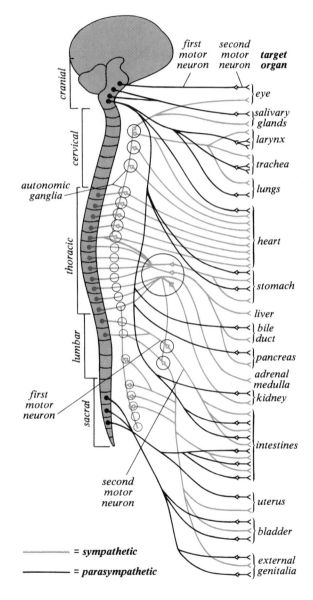

**Figure 22–B–1** Diagram of the autonomic nervous system in human beings. All these neurons are motor neurons; traffic is one-way. Control of the target organs is achieved by contrasting effects of sympathetic and parasympathetic stimuli.

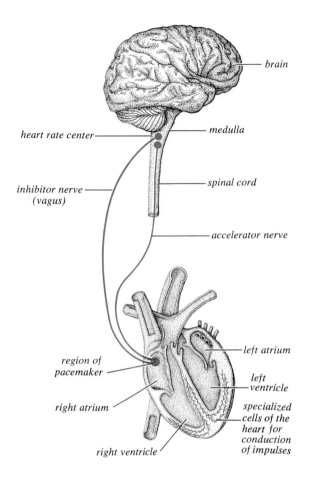

*brain*

*medulla*

heart rate center

*spinal cord*

inhibitor nerve
(vagus)

*accelerator nerve*

region of
pacemaker

*left atrium*

left
ventricle

right atrium

specialized
cells of the
heart for
conduction
of impulses

right ventricle

**Figure 22–C–1** The heartbeat is controlled by two sets of nerves, the accelerator nerves and the vagus nerves. One accelerator nerve carries impulses from stretch receptors in the heart to the medulla of the brain. The stretch receptors are activated by an overload of blood in a heart chamber. The other accelerator nerve carries impulses from the medulla back to the heart. These impulses increase the rate of heartbeat, relieving the blood overload or the sluggish flow in the heart. The vagus nerves, like the accelerator nerves, work as a pair between the heart and the medulla of the brain. However, their effect is to decrease the rate of heartbeat. Only one nerve of each pair is shown in this diagram.

## 22–C

## Neurotransmitters and Hormones Control the Rate of the Heartbeat

You learned in Section 17–8 about Harvey's investigations of the heart. Many observers since Harvey's day have studied the action of the heart. Harvey noted that an animal's heart will continue to beat after its head is cut off. In fact, the hearts of animals like frogs and turtles can beat for days outside the body if they are kept in a suitable solution. These observations suggest that the heartbeat originates in the heart itself. It has been found that the contraction of the heart muscle starts in a special area in the right atrium, the pacemaker (see Section 17–8), and then spreads to other parts of the heart.

The rate and strength of the heartbeat are controlled by factors outside the heart itself. Some of these factors are nerves that run into the heart muscle and chemical substances in the blood, such as carbon dioxide, oxgyen, and hormones.

How do nerves control the rate of heartbeat? Two pairs of nerves go to the heart. One pair, called the **vagus** (VAY-gus) **nerves,** slows down the heartbeat. The vagus nerves are part of the parasympathetic system. The other nerves, called the **accelerator nerves,** carry impulses that increase the rate of heartbeat (see Figure 22–C–1). The accelerator nerves are part of the sympathetic system. The activity of an internal organ is frequently controlled by sets of nerves with opposite effects. These nerves are discussed in more detail in Appendix 22–B, The Autonomic Nervous System.

How was the nature of the control of the heartbeat by nerves discovered? The experiments of Otto Loewi, a physiologist, in 1921, led to an understanding of the control of the heartbeat. Like many experiments performed by truly creative scientists, Loewi's experiment seems very simple. Having found out that stimulation of the vagus nerves would slow down the heartbeat, Loewi

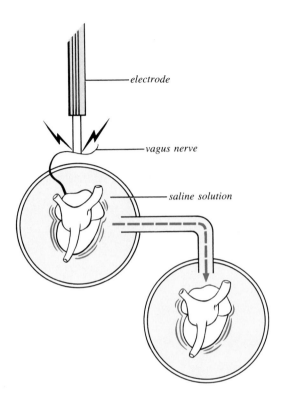

electrode

vagus nerve

saline solution

**Figure 22–C–2** Two hearts affected by a vagus nerve attached to only one of them. What is the evidence, from this experiment performed by Loewi, for the secretion of a chemical messenger?

arranged an experiment like the one shown in Figure 22–C–2. Loewi placed the heart of a frog in a dish and stimulated the vagus nerve electrically. The heartbeat slowed down. Loewi then connected the fluid from this dish to another dish containing a heart without a vagus nerve. The fluid from the first dish caused the unstimulated frog heart, in the second dish, to slow down also. Loewi reasoned that when the vagus nerve to the heart in the first dish was stimulated, a substance was released into the fluid. This substance made the unstimulated heart in the second dish slow down as if its own vagus had been stimulated.

Somewhat later, Loewi identified the substance released by the stimulated vagus nerve as acetylcholine.

The neurotransmitter produced by the accelerator nerves has been identified as adrenaline. Adrenaline is a hormone produced mainly by the adrenal glands, located above the kidney (see Section 21–3 and Figure 21–10). Adrenaline released by the accelerator nerves and from the adrenal glands increases the heartbeat. You may have observed the effects of various substances on the dilation or contraction of blood vessels while doing Investigation 17–C, Capillary Circulation. You will also study the effect of various chemicals on heartbeat rate in Investigation 23–A, Making Muscles Move.

## 22–D

## The Cerebrum Became Larger as the Brain Evolved

Five different vertebrate brains are compared in Figure 22–D–1. Notice that the part called the cerebrum is more prominent in the brain of humans than in the brains of the other animals. Compare the size of the cerebrum with the size of other parts of the brain of each animal. Studies like these are called comparative anatomy. This evidence may suggest a hypothesis about the evolution of the brain in vertebrates: As vertebrates evolved, the size and complexity of function of the cerebrum increased.

The brain is a clue to the biological success of humans, along with the vocal cords, which made complicated communication possible. Chimpanzees and apes have advanced brains, too, and can be taught to communicate by sign language. (They do not have vocal cords permitting humanlike speech.) However, only humans show the degree of specialization that has made their world civilization possible.

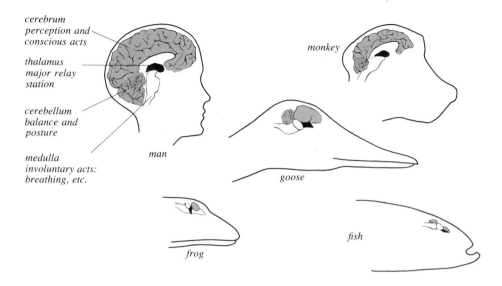

*cerebrum
perception and
conscious acts*

*thalamus
major relay
station*

*cerebellum
balance and
posture*

*medulla
involuntary acts:
breathing, etc.*

*man*

*monkey*

*goose*

*frog*

*fish*

**Figure 22–D–1** Compare these brains of five vertebrates.

## 22–E

## How Does the Brain Control the Breathing Rate?

How does the brain know that the cells do not have enough oxygen and that carbon dioxide is being removed too slowly? A small area of the brain is sensitive to the concentration of carbon dioxide in the blood. If this concentration increases, the part of the brain that is sensitive to carbon dioxide is stimulated. This sensitive part of the brain sends nerve impulses to the part of the brain that controls the rate of breathing. As a result, more nerve impulses pass along the motor neurons to the rib muscles and the diaphragm. Air is inhaled and exhaled more rapidly. The concentration of carbon dioxide in the blood is decreased. With a decrease of carbon dioxide, the part of the brain sensitive to carbon dioxide is no longer stimulated and breathing is restored to normal.

## 22–F

## The Brain Performs Reflex and Unifying Activities

In general, reflexes are thought to go along a path from the place of stimulation to the spinal cord and then out from the cord to the muscle or gland that is activated. Most reflexes do not go through the brain at all. However, even though the brain is not needed for the reflex connection, a person's brain can exert a powerful control over the spinal cord and even over the reflex action.

A person's spinal reflexes seem to stop for a time after the spinal cord has been damaged. For as long as six months, the body seems to be completely paralyzed below the region where the spinal cord is damaged. Only very gradually do reflex movements begin to reappear. Eventually the leg-bending reflex becomes very strong again. The long period before the reflex reappears suggests that normal function of the spinal cord depends on the constant controlling messages of the brain. The spinal cord seems to need a long time to adjust to the loss of brain impulses. A similar situation exists in other animals. However, dependence of the spinal cord on the brain is greater in humans than in other animals.

Other evidence shows that some reflexes can be controlled by the brain. For example, a tightrope walker might step on some sharp object. The reflex response to this stimulus would certainly throw the tightrope walker off balance, but the brain takes over voluntary control of the situation. Training overcomes reflexes so that the tightrope walker can keep the posture needed for proper balance. This ability to exercise voluntary control over reflexes enables humans to adjust to changing situations. It allows us to react to stimuli in many different ways.

Some reflex arcs pass through the brain instead of through the spinal cord. Brain reflex activity is similar to that in the spinal cord. An example of reflex activity that depends on the brain is the wink reflex of the eyelids. Any stimulation of the surface of the eye or the eyelids causes impulses to travel along specific neurons to the brain. In reflex centers in the brain, impulses are relayed to motor neurons that carry them to the muscles of the eyelids. These eyelid muscles then contract, closing the eye in the typical wink of this reflex response. Many spinal and brain reflexes are innate; that is, people are born with them.

In addition to its reflex activity, the brain coordinates the actions in many different parts of the body. This coordination depends in part on sensory impulses coming in from various receptors. The brain interprets these impulses and sends out more impulses to many effectors, muscles, and glands, making it possible for them to act as an efficient unit. These coordinating functions are far more complicated than reflex responses.

A more or less rhythmic increase and decrease of electrical activity goes on in the brain. These measurable electrical changes, or ''brain waves,'' give evidence of brain activity. Brain waves vary, depending on the activity of the brain. During deep sleep in humans, for example, the brain waves are relatively large and slow. They become much smaller, more rapid, and irregular when a person is awake and alert, or if the person is dreaming. What is the meaning of these electrical patterns? Exactly where and how in the brain do they arise? Scientists do not know the answers to these questions, although continued research has provided a partial understanding. So far, the human brain has had only a limited success in attempting to understand itself.

## 23–A

## Hormones That Control Bone Formation

Hormones from the thyroid and parathyroid glands work with another hormone produced in the kidneys to control the amounts of calcium and phosphate in the blood and bones. A compound produced by the action of the ultraviolet part of sunlight on the skin is necessary for the production of the hormone in the kidneys. Without sunlight, the skin is unable to make the compound needed by the kidneys. Without the hormone made in the kidneys, the small intestine cannot properly absorb calcium from food, and bone tissue cannot properly absorb calcium from the blood. As a result, the bones do not become hard.

In the 18th and 19th centuries, rickets was a common bone disease in northern Europe. In fact, rickets is said to be the first air-pollution disease because it spread through northern Europe as the pall of coal smoke from the Industrial Revolution blotted out the sun. In addition, more and more people of that period began to live in the gloomy, narrow, and sunless alleys of industrial city

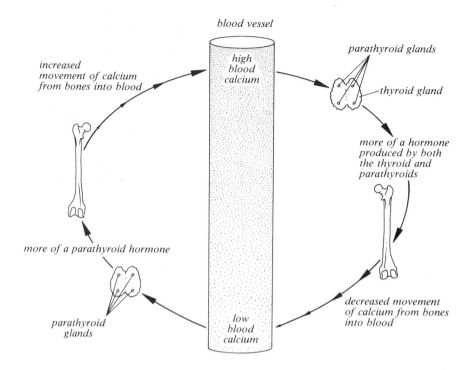

**Figure 23–A–1** A diagram of the action of hormones on calcium in blood and bone.

slums. The lack of sunlight, particularly during the winter months in northern Europe, made rickets the scourge of the rich and poor alike who lived in those cities.

It was stated earlier that hormones of the parathyroid glands in the neck (see Figure 21–10) work to control the level of calcium and phosphate in the blood and bone. There are two of these hormones. One of them is produced by the thyroid gland as well. How these two hormones work is reasonably well understood. When the calcium level of the blood is high, one of the hormones, the one secreted by both glands, is produced in greater amounts. Its action then decreases the movement of calcium from the bones into the blood. As a result, the calcium level of the blood drops. When the calcium level of the blood gets too low, the second parathyroid hormone is produced in greater amounts. Its action increases the movement of calcium from the bone to the blood. As a result, the calcium level of the blood rises. The actions of these two hormones oppose each other. One, a parathyroid and thyroid hormone, protects the bone. The other, a parathyroid hormone, protects the blood. Figure 23–A–1 shows how the actions of these two hormones balance the amount of calcium in the blood and bone. Homeostasis in another body process is the result.

## 24–A

## An Explanation of Tropisms and Other Plant Movements

How can geotropism be explained? Recall the experiments on coleoptiles and light in Investigation 21–A. You saw that the bending of young stems toward light depends on auxins. Can you also assume that the bending of young stems away from gravity depends on auxins?

If you placed a potted plant with the stem in a horizontal position, as shown in Figure 24–A–1, what would happen to the stem? Can you explain the growth of the stem upward in terms of auxins? You might say that more auxin on one side of the stem causes the cells on that side to lengthen and that gravity probably pulls some auxins to the underside of the stems. Lengthening of cells would then be greater on the underside of the stem than on the topside of the stem. This could cause the tip of the stem to bend upward.

The same kind of reasoning would not account for the downward growth of roots. How then can you account for the positive geotropism of the roots of a plant? Several hypotheses may be made. Perhaps root cells react differently to auxins than stem cells do. Or perhaps the roots have more auxin. Experiments have shown that a very high concentration of auxins can sometimes inhibit growth rather than stimulate it. At present, the method by which plant roots react to gravity is not known.

Another kind of plant movement has been observed where the water supply is low. Plant roots grow toward sources of water. It would not be accurate to say that the plants are "seeking" water. It is easy to explain plant and animal behavior in terms of what they are "trying to do in order to survive," but these explanations are misleading. Explanations that assume plants and animals have conscious motives or show human thought and action are called **anthropomorphic**

**Figure 24–A–1** When a potted plant is placed on its side and kept in the dark, the stem turns upward in a few days. How can this be explained?

(an-thruh-puh-MAWR-fik). The word "anthropomorphic" means "having the form of a human." Human attitudes and understandings should be credited only to humans and not to plants and other animals.

What is a reasonable explanation, then, for the observation of roots growing toward water? Very likely, the roots of a plant grow more rapidly and branch more widely in soil that has more moisture. Water from an underground source will tend to diffuse out through very dry soil. The roots of plants that happen to be in this moistened area will grow more rapidly and thus appear to be "purposely" growing toward the source of the water.

Another interesting behavioral response is the tendency of some plants to react to touch. For example, when the tendrils of climbing vines touch solid objects, they react by curling around them. Thus they can wind about the framework of a railing or trellis.

**Figure 24–A–2** Leaflets of the *Mimosa* plant (left). In response to a stimulus, such as touch, heat, or electric shock, the leaflets fold together (right). After a suitable recovery period, the leaflets open again.

The touch reaction in plants is most dramatic in the sensitive plant *Mimosa pudica*. As shown in Figure 24–A–2, the leaves or stem of this plant will close rapidly if they are touched. A sudden change of temperature will also bring about this response. Experiments with *Mimosa* suggest that chemical and electrical activity are involved in these reactions. The reason for this reaction is not known. Perhaps this leaf-closing reaction benefits the plant in some way that helps it to survive.

Another plant with rapid touch reactions is the Venus flytrap (Figure 19–1). This plant traps insects by closing its large leaves around any small object that touches the sensory hair on its leaves.

## 24–B

### Innate Behavior

There are many different kinds of behavior. The *Paramecium* behavior you may have observed in Investigation 24–B is a primitive kind of behavior called a taxis (plural, taxes). A taxis is a change in the direction of movement of protists and animals caused by some stimulus in the environment. Random movements are not taxes, but the *Paramecium's* change in direction in response to a drop of water containing dissolved salt is a taxis. It is a response to a definite stimulus. Because such behavior is usually fixed and unchanging, it is called **innate behavior.** In innate forms of behavior, organisms always react in the same way to the same stimulus.

A more complex kind of innate behavior is **reflex behavior.** In Section 22–8 you learned how the nervous system brings about reflex behavior. One of the simplest reflex actions is the human knee-jerk reflex. When the tendon below the knee is struck, the leg responds with a jerking movement. Reflex behavior is innate behavior because the organism responds to a particular stimulus in a characteristic way. In general, reflexes protect an organism from harm or help it maintain normal conditions.

**Figure 24–B–1** This web spinning spider shows a complex behavior pattern. Different species of spiders spin different kinds of webs.

Many automatic behavioral responses of humans are reflexes. For instance, normal posture is maintained by constant muscle adjustment. This adjustment is stimulated by slight changes in the environment. In any normal movement, such as taking a step, coordination of muscles also depends on a series of reflex acts. These acts involve many muscles, nerves, and sensory receptors located at different parts of the body.

The most complex patterns of innate behavior are those called **instincts.** Instinct is an inherited form of behavior that usually involves a whole series of actions. For example, the nest-building instinct of birds includes all the activities of searching for building materials, bringing them to a good nesting site, and making a particular kind of nest from them. The homing behavior of pigeons and the migratory behavior of certain fish are also examples of instinctive behavior. Such behavior is usually distinctive for a given species. Sometimes the species of an animal can be recognized just by observing the animal's pattern of behavior.

The spider shown spinning a web in Figure 24–B–1 demonstrates another example of instinctive behavior. An expert can tell the species of spider by examining its web. Clues to the evolution of certain spiders may be gathered by analyzing the behavior patterns recorded in their webs. Similarities in webs may show genetic relationships between groups of spiders.

For many years, mazes have been popular for trial-and-error learning in animals. A **maze** is a series of passages in which an animal must choose between alternate paths. If an animal makes the right series of turns, it is rewarded with food. If it makes the wrong series of turns, it may be punished, perhaps with a mild electric shock. By being put through the maze again and again, an animal may learn to make the turns that result in reward rather than punishment.

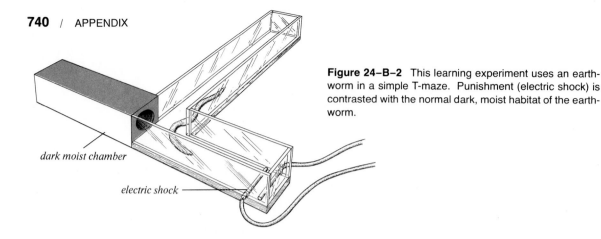

**Figure 24–B–2** This learning experiment uses an earthworm in a simple T-maze. Punishment (electric shock) is contrasted with the normal dark, moist habitat of the earthworm.

*dark moist chamber*

*electric shock*

**Figure 24–B–3** An example of a maze used in trial-and-error learning by ants. The ant has a choice of taking several different paths. Food is usually given as the reward for a successful run.

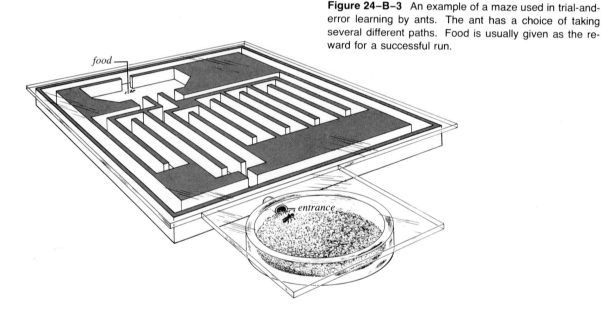

*food*

*entrance*

The simplest kind of maze is the T-maze, where only one choice is involved. Flatworms and earthworms can learn to make the "correct" choice of turns in this maze. Earthworms, for instance, are given the choice either of entering a dark, moist chamber or of receiving an electric shock. (See Figure 24–B–2.) The earthworms in an experiment took about 220 trials in the maze to learn to make the correct turn. After an earthworm had learned, it could make the correct turn 90 percent of the time. If it had not learned, it would have continued to be just as likely to turn left as to turn right.

Some insects show fairly rapid trial-and-error learning in mazes. Even among insects, however, learning ability differs. Ants, for example, are better learners than cockroaches. A maze for testing ants is shown in Figure 24–B–3. Higher animals, like the rat, are able to solve and remember the path through complicated mazes.

# A Dictionary of Biological Terms Used in This Book

# A Dictionary of Biological Terms Used in This Book

Genus and species names are too numerous to be fully represented in this list of terms, although the ones most frequently used in the book have been included. Biographical names are not listed, nor are elements and many of their compounds, except for compounds significant in cell structure or genetics, or otherwise significant as enzymes, hormones, or nutrients. Some of the terms in the book's optional appendixes are included in this listing.

## A

**ABO blood groups:** in humans, an example of multiple alleles for a trait; three alleles influence blood type, but an individual can have only two of the alleles.

**accelerator nerves:** nerves connecting the autonomic nervous system with the heart and carrying impulses that speed up the heartbeat.

**acetylcholine** (uh-seet-il-KOH-leen): a neurotransmitter secreted across synapses by some neurons.

**acid** (or *acidic,* aa-SID-ik): having a $pH$ less than 7, caused by an excess of hydrogen ($H^+$) ions over negatively charged ions.

**ACTH:** the abbreviation for *adrenocorticotrophic hormone* (uh-DREE-noh-kort-ih-koh-TROH-fik HOR-mone), secreted by the pituitary. ACTH stimulates the adrenal cortex.

**actin** (AK-tin): a protein found in muscle fibrils; acted on by myosin, it is pulled toward the myosin to produce contraction of muscle.

**activation energy:** the energy necessary to start a chemical reaction.

**active site:** the part of an enzyme molecule that attracts and holds substrate molecules.

**active transport:** the organized transport of molecules and ions across a cell's plasma membrane, requiring energy expenditure; also observed in mitochondrial and chloroplast membranes.

**adaptation** (uh-dap-TAY-shun): an inherited characteristic, or a combination of inherited characteristics, that increases an organism's chance for survival and reproduction in a particular environment.

**adenine** (AD-eh-neen): one of the four nitrogen bases in DNA or RNA; adenine pairs with thymine in DNA, and with uracil in RNA. It is also found in ATP, $NAD^+$, and $NADP^+$.

**adenosine triphosphate** (uh-DEE-no-seen tri-FOS-fate): *see* ATP.

**ADP:** the abbreviation for *adenosine diphosphate* (uh-DEE-no-seen dy-FOS-fate), the organic compound produced when one of the high-energy phosphate bonds (and phosphate groups) of ATP has been transferred to another compound where the energy will be used in a reaction.

**adrenal cortex** (uh-DREEN-ul KOR-teks): the outer part of the adrenal gland that secretes a variety of hormones.

**adrenal** (uh-DREEN-ul) **gland:** an endocrine gland located just above the kidney.

**adrenaline** (uh-DREN-uh-lin): the hormone secreted by the medulla of the adrenal glands. Adrenaline is also called *epinephrine* (ep-ih-NEF-rin).

**adrenal medulla** (uh-DREEN-ul meh-DUL-uh): the central part of the adrenal gland that secretes adrenaline.

**aerobic** (ay-ROH-bik): air-using; in particular, oxygen-using.

**aggression** (uh-GRESH-un): forceful, attacking behavior usually limited to specific circumstances among animals, such as defending a territory or seeking a mate.

**Agnatha** (AG-nuh-thuh): a subphylum of animals, the jawless fishes.

**air pollutants:** principally automobile exhaust fumes and chimney gases of industries and utilities; soot and other particles are included with the gases. Sulfur dioxide, one of the gases, reacts with water vapor in the air to form acid rain, or with the moisture of the eyes to form acid tears. Many other irritating pollutants are known.

**algae** (AL-jee): aquatic and soil autotrophs less complex in structure than green plants but containing chlorophyll and often several other photosynthetic pigments; most algae are microscopic, although very large seaweeds such as kelps are also algae.

**alkaline** (AL-kuh-lin): having a $pH$ greater than 7, caused by an excess of negatively charged ions over hydrogen ($H^+$) ions; also called *basic*.

**allantois** (ah-LAN-toh-is): one of the embryonic membranes of reptiles, birds, and mammals; in birds and reptiles it may serve a respiratory and waste-collecting function.

**allele** (uh-LEEL): any of two or more forms of a gene for a given trait; alleles occur a pair at a time, one on each chromosome of a homologous pair.

**alphafetoprotein** (al-fuh-fee-toh-PROH-teen): a human fetal protein sometimes present in high levels in amniotic fluid, indicating an abnormality.

**alpha** (AL-fuh) **waves:** brain waves occurring for short periods at a rate of about 8 to 14 waves per second.

**alveolus:** (al-VEE-uh-lus; plural, *alveoli*—al-VEE-uh-ly): a small saclike pouch in the lung; exchange of gases with the blood takes place in the walls of alveoli.

**amino** (uh-MEE-noh) **acid:** an organic compound composed of a central carbon atom to which are bonded a hydrogen atom, an amino group (—NH₂), an acid group (—COOH), and one of a variety of other atoms or groups of atoms. Amino acids are the building blocks of polypeptides and proteins.

**ammonia** (uh-MO-nyuh): a toxic nitrogenous waste excreted primarily by aquatic organisms; also, a gas in Earth's early atmosphere.

**amniocentesis** (am-nee-oh-sen-TEE-sus): withdrawal of a sample of amniotic fluid through a pregnant woman's abdomen, using a surgical hypodermic needle; cast-off cells of the fetus are cultured and studied, along with the amniotic fluid itself, for evidence of genetic health or disorder.

**amnion** (AM-nee-on): a sac or membrane, filled with fluid, that encloses the embryo of a reptile, bird, or mammal.

**amniotic** (am-nee-OT-ik) **fluid:** the fluid surrounding an embryo or fetus in its amniotic sac.

*Amoeba* (uh-MEE-buh): a genus of protists containing one-celled organisms that move and capture food by extending temporary pseudopods.

**AMP:** the abbreviation for *adenosine monophosphate* (uh-DEE-no-seen mon-oh-FOS-fate), the organic compound produced when two high-energy phosphate bonds (and phosphate groups) of ATP have been transferred to other compounds.

**Amphibia** (am-FIB-ih-uh): a class of chordates containing animals that spend part of their life cycle in water and part on land; toads, frogs, and salamanders are amphibians.

**amphibian** (am-FIB-ih-un): *see* Amphibia.

**amylase** (AM-uh-lays): a digestive enzyme that acts on starch, changing it to maltose.

**anaerobic** (an-ay-RO-bik): living in the absence of air. Some but not all anaerobic organisms, or *anaerobes,* are poisoned by oxygen.

**anaphase** (AN-uh-fayz): a stage in mitosis following metaphase; the chromatids of each pair separate and move toward opposite ends of the cell.

**androgens** (AN-droh-jenz): hormones secreted by the testes in male mammals and active in the reproductive functions.

**angiosperm** (AN-jee-oh-sperm): *see* Angiospermophyta.

**Angiospermophyta** (AN-jee-oh-sperm-OFF-ih-tuh): the plant division that contains flowering plants.

**Animalia** (an-uh-MAYL-yuh): the animal kingdom.

**animal society:** an organized population showing cooperative behavior.

**annelid** (AN-uh-lid): *see* Annelida.

**Annelida** (uh-NEL-ih-duh): a phylum of animals, the worms with segmented bodies; also called annelids.

**annual ring:** a ring or layer of xylem cells produced during a growing season by the cambium of a tree trunk or woody plant stem.

**anterior** (an-TIR-ee-er) **lobe:** the front part of the pituitary, producing hormones that stimulate other endocrine glands.

**anther** (AN-ther): the pollen-producing tip of the stamen in a flower.

**anthropologist** (an-throh-POL-oh-jist): a biologist who studies human cultures and human evolution.

**anthropomorphic** (an-thruh-puh-MAWR-fik): interpreting behavior of organisms other than humans in a way that suggests, without evidence, humanlike motives.

**antibiotic** (an-tih-by-OT-ik): a substance produced by a microorganism that inhibits or kills other kinds of microorganisms. Today many antibiotics for medical use are produced synthetically.

**antibody** (ANT-ih-bod-ee): a blood component that combines with a specific foreign particle, or a disease-producing microorganism or its toxin, and neutralizes it.

**antidiuretic hormone** (ant-ih-dye-yoo-RET-ik HOR-mone), or **ADH:** a hormone of the hypothalamus, released by the posterior pituitary, which concentrates salt in the medulla of the kidneys and causes water to be reabsorbed into the bloodstream.

**anus** (AY-nus): the posterior opening of an animal's digestive tract.

**aorta** (ay-OHR-ta): the main blood vessel that in mammals carries blood from the heart to all of the body except the lungs.

**aquatic:** describing a water environment or organisms that live in water.

**arachnid** (uh-RAK-nid): *see* Arachnida.

**Arachnida** (uh-RAK-nih-duh): the class of arthropods containing spiders and scorpions; horseshoe crabs also are arachnids.

**arthropod** (AR-thruh-pod): *see* Arthropoda.

**Arthropoda** (ar-THROP-uh-duh): the largest phylum of animals, with jointed appendages and usually exoskeletons; insects, spiders, lobsters, crabs, shrimp, centipedes, and millipedes are all arthropods.

**asexual** (AY-sex-yoo-ul) **reproduction:** any method of reproduction that requires only one parent or one parent cell.

**assumption:** provisional acceptance of information based on partial evidence.

**atomic theory:** the theory that all matter is made of particles called atoms, different for each element, with the differences accounting for their chemical and physical properties.

**ATP:** the abbreviation for *adenosine triphosphate* (uh-DEE-no-seen tri-FOS-fate), the organic compound that supplies a cell's immediate energy needs; ATP has two high-energy phosphate bonds.

**atrium** (AY-tree-um): a chamber of the heart that receives blood from the body or the lungs and passes it on to a ventricle.

*Australopithecus* (os-tray-lo-PITH-eh-kus): an extinct genus of upright-walking, tool-making individuals closely related to humans.

**autonomic** (ot-oh-NOM-ik) **nervous system:** a part of the nervous system that regulates activities normally independent of conscious control, such as heartbeat, digestion, and breathing.

**autosome** (AWT-uh-sohm): any chromosome other than a sex chromosome.

**autotroph** (OT-uh-trohf): an organism able to make and store food, using sunlight or another nonliving energy source.

**auxin** (AWK-sin): any of a group of plant hormones affecting growth and development.

**Aves** (AY-veez): a class of chordates, the birds.

**axon** (AK-son): the nerve fiber that normally carries impulses away from the cell body of a neuron.

### B

**Bacillariophyta** (bas-uh-lair-ee-OFF-ih-tuh): a phylum of diatoms.

**bacillus** (buh-SIL-us; plural, *bacilli*—buh-SIL-eye): a rod-shaped bacterium.

**bacterial strain:** bacteria bred with a genetic characteristic unlike that of other bacteria of the same species.

**bacteriophage** (bak-TEER-ee-uh-fayj): a virus that infects bacteria.

**bacterium** (bak-TIR-ee-um; plural, *bacteria*—bak-TIR-ee-uh): a prokaryotic microorganism of the kingdom Monera; bacterial cells have no clearly defined nuclei and are among the smallest of all cells.

**bark:** the tough outer covering of woody plant stems; mainly dead phloem cells.

**base** (or *basic*): *see* alkaline.

**behavior:** the sum total of an organism's activity; or, the actions and interactions of organisms with each other and with their environment.

**behavioral adaptation:** a way of reacting to the environment or other organisms that has survival value.

**bicarbonate** (by-CAR-bun-ate) **ion:** the form ($HCO_3^-$) in which most carbon dioxide is carried in the blood.

**bile:** a secretion of the liver that aids in the digestion of fats by breaking large fat droplets into smaller ones more accessible to enzymes.

**bile duct:** a tube from the liver to the gall bladder to the small intestine; from the gall bladder to the small intestine it is usually referred to as the common bile duct.

**binomial nomenclature** (by-NOH-mee-ul NOH-men-klay-chur): the two-word naming system used in systematics or taxonomy.

**biochemical** (by-oh-KEM-ih-kul): denoting chemical events of life processes, or the chemical structure of organic compounds necessary for life.

**biodegradable** (by-oh-dee-GRAYD-uh-bul): made of materials that can be decomposed by the actions of organisms.

**biofeedback** (by-oh-FEED-bak) **training:** the process of making involuntary body activities such as heartbeat and brain waves perceptible to the senses and, if possible, accessible to conscious control.

**biological clocks:** mechanisms in organisms that time events such as reproductive cycles, annual migrations, and even sleeping and waking in relation to day and night.

**biologist** (by-OL-oh-jist): a scientist who specializes in one or more of the biological sciences such as botany, zoology, genetics, paleontology, microbiology, and so on.

**biology** (by-OL-oh-jee): the study of living things in terms of the *methods* of biological investigation, the *knowledge* derived, and the *theories* that organize the knowledge.

**biomass** (BY-oh-mas): the total quantity of living material in a given segment of an environment or ecosystem, or in the ecosystem as a whole.

**biotin** (BY-uh-tin): a vitamin of the B complex.

**birth rate:** the total number of births in a population per unit of time.

**bladder** (BLAD-er): in the excretory system of mammals, a sac that stores urine until it is released from the body; in many other organisms, a sac that contains a liquid or gases.

**blastopore** (BLAS-toh-por): the opening in a blastula through which an infolding of cells takes place to form the gastrula.

**blastula** (BLAS-choo-luh): an early embryo after the cleavage stage, when a fluid-filled cavity develops within the mass of cells formed by cleavage.

**blood:** the transport fluid of multicellular animals.

**blood pressure:** the pressure of the blood against the walls of blood vessels. Blood pressure varies with the contraction and relaxation of the heart muscles.

**blood vessel:** an artery, vein, or capillary in which the blood circulates.

**bone:** the skeletal material of vertebrates, consisting basically of deposits of calcium and phosphorus around living bone cells.

**botanist** (BOT-un-ist): a plant biologist.

**botulism** (BOT-yoo-liz-um): acute food poisoning caused by a toxin of a particular spore-forming bacterium. The spores are resistant to heat-killing.

**Bowman's capsule:** a double-walled cuplike structure surrounding a glomerulus in the kidney.

**Brachiopoda** (bray-kee-OP-uh-duh): a phylum of marine animals, the lampshells.

**brain:** an anterior enlargement of the central nervous system that coordinates higher body functions; in vertebrates it is the site of conscious reaction and memory.

**brain waves:** rhythmic, electric impulses given off by the brain.

**breathing:** the process by which an organism exchanges gas molecules with its external environment. Animals with lungs or gills breathe. Occasionally, even microorganisms are said to "breathe" through their plasma membranes.

**Bryophyta** (bry-OFF-ih-tuh): a plant division of mosses and liverworts.

**budding:** a method of asexual reproduction in yeasts, hydras, and many other small organisms; also, the seasonal start of new growth in higher plants.

### C

**cambium** (KAM-bih-um): a layer of meristem tissue in the stems and roots of plants that produces all growth in diameter, including new xylem and phloem cells.

**camouflage** (KAM-uh-flahzh): concealment or distortion of the natural outlines of an organism by its colors and their patterns.

**cancer:** uncontrolled cell division and growth in which the cells appear to differ functionally from those needed and to crowd out other cells.

**capillary** (KAP-ih-lair-ee): a microscopic blood vessel from which exchanges between the blood and the tissues take place; capillaries connect arteries with veins.

**capillary action:** a way in which liquid can be raised to a limited height in tubes of very small diameter by the attraction of the liquid molecules to the inside walls of the tube.

**carbohydrases** (kar-boh-HY-drays-ez): a group of enzymes that act on carbohydrates.

**carbohydrate** (kar-boh-HY-drayt): an organic compound composed of carbon, hydrogen, and oxygen, with the hydrogen and oxygen atoms in a 2-to-1 ratio such as in water. Examples are sugars, starches, glycogen, and cellulose.

**carbon cycle:** the dark phase of photosynthesis in which carbon dioxide, ATP, and NADPH are used in building organic compounds; also, the carbon cycle in nature in which carbon is used and recycled by organisms.

**carbonic** (kar-BON-ik) **acid:** an acid ($H_2CO_3$) formed when carbon dioxide is mixed with water.

**carbon pathway:** the reactions that release carbon from organic compounds and form carbon dioxide in cell respiration.

**cardiac** (KAR-dee-ak) **muscle:** the striated muscle of a vertebrate's heart.

**carnivore** (KAR-nih-vohr): a meat-eating animal; a second- or higher-order consumer.

**carrier:** an individual who has a gene for a recessive genetic disorder but is not afflicted; also, an individual who has and transmits microorganisms of disease without showing any symptoms of the disease.

**cartilage** (KAR-tih-lij): an elastic connective tissue usually found as part of a vertebrate's skeleton.

**caste system:** a highly organized society in which each member has a specific task that is fixed or unchanging.

**catalase** (CAT-uh-lays): an enzyme that decomposes hydrogen peroxide, a poisonous waste product of plants and animals.

**catalyst** (CAT-uh-list): a chemical that promotes a reaction between other chemicals. The catalyst may take part in the reaction but emerges in its original form.

**cell:** the microscopic organization of a primitive organism, and the structural living unit of which both microscopic and larger organisms are composed. Most cells have a nucleus, and all have cytoplasm and a plasma membrane; some of the structures in the cytoplasm vary in different kinds of cells.

**cell body:** a central portion of a neuron containing the cell nucleus.

**cell division:** the formation of two cells from one, preceded in cells with nuclei by mitosis or meiosis.

**cell plate:** a structure appearing in plant cells after the nucleus has undergone mitosis; the cell plate marks where a new cell wall will be deposited between the two nuclei, completing the division of the cell into two cells.

**cell respiration:** *see* respiration.

**cell symbiosis** (sim-bee-OH-sis) **hypothesis:** the hypothesis that eukaryotic cells arose by associations between prokaryotic cells of different types.

**cell theory:** the theory that organisms are composed of cells and their products, and that these cells are all derived from preexisting cells.

**cellulose** (SEL-yoo-lohs): a plant-made carbohydrate and the most abundant carbohydrate in nature.

**cell wall:** a nonliving covering around the plasma membrane of certain cells, as in plants, many algae, and some bacteria; in plants the cell wall is constructed chiefly of cellulose.

**central nervous system:** the brain and spinal cord of vertebrates.

**centriole** (SEN-trih-ohl): one of a pair of small structures in an animal cell that are associated with mitosis and meiosis; the centrioles duplicate and migrate as two pairs to opposite ends of the cell, where each pair anchors one end of the spindle.

**centromere** (SEN-troh-meer): the region of a chormosome that attaches to the spindle during mitosis and meiosis, and that holds replicated chromatids together.

**cerebrum** (SEHR-e-brum): the largest portion of the human brain; it controls voluntary movements and coordinates mental activity.

**cervix** (SER-viks): in the mammalian uterus, the narrow or constricted portion around the opening of the uterus into the vagina.

**chance:** occurring at random; or, a random event. In single occurrences, chance events are unpredictable.

**chemical bond:** *see* covalent bond *and* ionic bond.

**chemical reaction:** a process of change in chemical bonds.

**chemosynthesis** (kee-moh-SIN-theh-sis): a process of making organic compounds using chemical energy from inorganic materials.

**Chilopoda** (kih-LOP-uh-duh): the class of arthropods containing centipedes.

**Chi-square test:** a mathematical method for determining whether a deviation from predicted experimental results is due to chance or is significant.

**chitin** (KY-tin): a hard organic substance secreted by insects and certain other invertebrates as the supporting material in their exoskeletons.

**chlorophyll** (KLOR-uh-fill): any of several green photosynthetic pigments, or the pigments collectively.

**Chlorophyta** (kloh-ROF-uh-tuh): a phylum of protists containing the bright green algae.

**chloroplast** (KLOHR-uh-plast): a cell structure or plastid that contains chlorophyll and the enzymes of electron transfer and the carbon cycle of photosynthesis. Chloroplasts occur in autotrophs with eukaryotic cells.

**Chondrichthyes** (kon-DRIK-thee-eez): a class of cartilaginous fishes.

**Chordata** (kor-DAY-tuh): a phylum of animals with gill slits at some time during development, dorsal nerve cords, and usually cartilage or bone support along the back near the nerve cord. All vertebrates—fish, amphibians, reptiles, birds, and mammals—are chordates, along with certain other animals.

**chordate** (KOR-dayt): *see* Chordata.

**chorion** (KOHR-ee-on): an embryonic membrane that surrounds all the other embryonic membranes in reptiles, birds, and mammals.

**chorionic villus biopsy** (kohr-ee-ON-ic VIL-us BY-op-see): removal of villi from the human chorion to obtain chromosomes and cell products for diagnosis of disorders in a human embryo.

**chromatid** (KROH-muh-tid): during mitosis and meiosis, either member of a double chromosome; the chromatids are still joined at their centromeres. Upon separation each is an individual chromosome.

**chromatin** (KROH-muht-un): the chromosomal material as it ordinarily appears in a cell's nucleus, with individual chromosomes indistinct.

**chromatogram** (kroh-MAT-uh-gram): the filter-paper record of a test using paper chromatography, showing the pattern formed and the number and identities of components; also, a record produced by automatic methods of chromatography.

**chromosome** (KROH-muh-sohm): a centrally located threadlike structure in the cell containing DNA (genes); for a few viruses the hereditary material is RNA.

**chromosome banding:** use of special dyes to produce cross bands on chromosomes. Study of the banding patterns helps reveal missing, inverted, and repeated chromosome segments, and evidence of crossing-over.

**chyme** (KIME): the semiliquid mass of food formed in the stomach.

**cilia** (SIL-ee-uh): small hairlike appendages on many protists and on planarians. Cilia may also be present on many cells of higher organisms, as on the cells lining the human windpipe. The beating action of cilia propels a protist along in the water—or propels particles out of respiratory passages in humans.

**Ciliophora** (sil-ee-OF-oh-ruh): a phylum of protists that have cilia used for locomotion and food-gathering.

**circadian** (ser-KAYD-ee-un) **rhythms:** regular recurrence of life activities that proceed in cycles of about 24 hours, or that have other repeating regularities in a pattern spaced about a day apart.

**class:** the third-largest grouping, after kingdom and phylum or division, in the biological classification system.

**classification:** placing objects into groups that reflect certain similarities within each group. Classification in biology arranges organisms in groups believed to reflect their related ancestry, or evolution.

**cleavage:** early mitotic cell divisions in a fertilized egg.

**clitellum** (kly-TEL-um): the thickened glandular band around the body of an earthworm or certain other annelids.

**clone:** an offspring that is genetically identical to its parent; or, a group of such offspring.

**cloning:** asexual reproduction of offspring genetically identical to their parents. Many examples occur in nature: strawberries produce runners, potato eyes sprout, yeasts and hydras bud, and aspen trees sprout from the extended roots of other aspen trees. In the laboratory, an egg nucleus may be replaced by a cell nucleus from a body cell, to produce a clone in tissue-culture experiments.

**closed circulatory system:** a transport system in which the liquid always flows in vessels as it goes to and from the heart and all other parts of the body.

**clot:** a thickened lump formed in the blood; blood clots seal wounds when they occur.

**Cnidaria** (ny-DAIR-ee-uh): a phylum of animals, the coelenterates.

**coacervate** (koh-AS-er-vayt): a cluster of proteins or protein-like compounds held together in small droplets within a surrounding liquid.

**coccus** (KOK-us; plural, *cocci*—KOK-sy): a spherical bacterium.

**cockerel** (KOK-er-ul): a male chick.

**codominance:** in genetics, the mixed trait or phenotype produced by two unlike alleles when neither trait is dominant or recessive to the other.

**codon** (KOH-don): the basic unit of a genetic message—a sequence of three nucleotides.

**coelenterate** (suh-LENT-er-ut): any of a group of animals that have tentacles, stinging cells, and a single body opening for food and wastes. Jellyfish, hydras, corals, sea anemones, and similar organisms are coelenterates.

**coenzyme** (coh-EN-zym): a nonprotein, often vitamin or mineral, component of an active enzyme; the coenzyme combines with the protein, or enzyme, activating the enzyme and helping determine the specific reaction it will catalyze.

**cohesion-tension** (koh-HEE-zhun TEN-shun) **hypothesis:** the hypothesis that water is raised upward in an unbroken column in the xylem of plants by the force holding the water molecules together and by the continuing evaporation of water from the top of the column, in the leaves.

**coleoptile** (koh-lee-OP-til): the sheath covering the shoot of an oat seedling and the seedlings of certain other plants.

**colloid** (KOL-oid): a finely divided substance suspended in a medium; or, organic molecules bearing electrical charges and dispersed in a liquid.

**competition:** the struggle among organisms for food, water, space, or any other necessity for the survival of the individual or the continuation of the species.

**compound:** a substance formed by chemical bonds between atoms of two or more different elements.

**compound microscope:** a microscope with two (or more) lenses, one in an eyepiece at one end of the microscope's tube and the other in an objective at the opposite end of the tube. A *monocular* microscope has an eyepiece for only one eye. A *stereo,* or *dissecting,* microscope has eyepieces for both eyes.

**conditioning:** training that associates a response with a stimulus different from the stimulus that causes the response by innate behavior.

**cones** (of eye): sensory receptors in the retina of the eye that function in color vision.

**Coniferophyta** (koh-NIF-er-OFF-ih-tuh): a plant division of cone-bearing trees and shrubs.

**consumer:** a heterotroph; an organism that feeds on other organisms or on their organic wastes.

**contractile fibril** (kun-TRAK-til FY-bril): any of the tiny fibers in the cytoplasm of cells of lower organisms that increase their ability to move.

**contractile vacuole** (kun-TRAK-til VAK-yuh-wohl): a cell structure primarily for the elimination of excess water, in single-celled and certain other lower organisms.

**control group:** subjects that are maintained under normal conditions in an experiment, for comparison with an experimental group.

**controlled experiment:** an experiment in which two or more like subjects or groups (the *experimental* and the *control groups*) are investigated under identical conditions except for one condition (or rarely more than one) that is changed for the experimental group.

**cornea** (KOR-nee-uh): the transparent frontal part of the coat of the eyeball.

**corpus luteum** (COR-pus LEW-tee-um): in a mammalian ovary, a hormone-secreting structure that develops from the ruptured follicle from which an egg has been released.

**cortex** (KOR-teks): the outer layer of an organ such as a kidney, an adrenal gland, or the brain; also, a plant-tissue layer in the outer part of a root or stem.

**cotyledon** (kot-ih-LEE-dun): a seed structure that along with endosperm provides food for the plant embryo. In some plants the cotyledons break the surface of the ground and carry on photosynthesis until true leaves develop.

**covalent** (KOH-vay-lent) **bond:** a chemical bond formed by electron sharing; usually each of two atoms shares an electron with the other, giving both atoms the mutually-held electron pair. Double or triple covalent bonds also occur (the sharing of two or three electron pairs).

**creatine phosphate** (KREE-uh-tin FOS-fate): a secondary source of stored energy in vertebrate muscle cells. As ATP is used, it is replenished by energy from the phosphate bonds of creatine phosphate.

**Cro-Magnon** (kroh-MAG-nun): any of several related populations and cultures of *Homo sapiens* who lived chiefly in Europe, 30,000 to 35,000 years ago.

**crop:** a temporary food storage area in the digestive tract of animals such as earthworms and birds.

**crossing-over:** exchange of genes by homologous chromosomes that overlap, break, and become repaired with exchanged segments.

**cross-pollination:** pollination between flowers of different plants, in which pollen from one flower is deposited on a stigma of the other.

**Crustacea** (krus-TAY-shuh): the class of arthropods containing crabs, lobsters, shrimp, crayfish, and related animals; collectively they are often called crustaceans.

**crustacean** (krus-TAY-shen): *see* Crustacea.

**Ctenophora** (teh-NOF-er-uh): a phylum of animals, the comb jellies.

**culture:** in the laboratory, a planned growth of cells, microorganisms, or small laboratory animals such as *Drosophila* on a nutrient medium in a covered culture dish or tube; in human society, the intellectual, occupational, educational, religious, familial, and leisure values and customs on which the society bases its nature and its standards.

**culture medium:** a preparation of nutrients for the culture of microorganisms or small multicellular organisms.

**cuticle** (KYOO-tih-kul): in plants, a noncellular, waxy outer layer covering certain leaves and fruits.

**Cyanobacteria** (SY-un-noh-bak-TIR-ee-uh): blue-green bacteria, formerly called blue-green algae.

**Cycadophyta** (sy-kad-OFF-ih-tuh): a plant division of cycads.

**cyclic photophosphorylation** (SY-klik foh-toh-fos-for-ih-LAY-shun): a process in which ATP is made in the light phase of photosynthesis.

**cytochromes** (SYE-tuh-krohms): a class of respiratory pigments in cell respiratory chains; cytochrome *c* is the most abundant in different organisms.

**cytology** (sy-TOL-uh-jee): the study of cells and of life processes at the cellular level.

**cytoplasm** (SYT-uh-plaz-um): the area of a cell outside the nucleus, but not including the plasma membrane.

**cytosine** (SY-toh-seen): one of the four nitrogen bases in DNA or RNA; it is present in equal amounts with guanine, with which it pairs in both DNA and RNA.

## D

*Daphnia* (DAF-nee-uh): a genus of small aquatic animals often maintained in the laboratory and useful for study because they are transparent. *Daphnia* are crustaceans.

**dark phase:** in photosynthesis, the carbon cycle of synthesis of carbohydrates or amino acids. A similar synthesis occurs in the metabolism of certain animals, using energy obtained from other organic compounds instead of sunlight.

**data** (DAY-tuh): all the facts related to a particular problem under investigation.

**death rate:** the number of deaths in a given population per unit number of individuals per unit of time.

**decomposer** (de-kum-POHZ-er): an organism, usually a microorganism, that lives on decaying organic material.

**degradable** (de-GRAYD-uh-bul): made of materials that break down or decompose before they can work their way up the food pyramid or accumulate in the physical environment.

**deletion:** loss of a piece of a broken chromosome.

**dendrite** (DEN-dryt): a nerve fiber that normally carries impulses toward the cell body of a neuron.

**deoxyribonucleic** (dee-OK-sih-ry-boh-new-KLEE-ik) **acid:** *see* DNA.

**deoxyribose** (dee-ok-sih-RY-bohs): the five-carbon sugar in DNA.

**dermis** (DER-mis): the deep layer of the skin, supplied with nerves and blood vessels.

**development:** the process by which a fertilized egg becomes a fully formed new individual.

**diabetes mellitus** (dy-uh-BEET-eez MEL-it-us): a disease resulting from the failure of the body to utilize glucose in a normal manner, primarily due to an insulin deficiency.

**dialysis** (dy-AL-eh-sus): separation of substances in solution by means of their unequal diffusion through a semipermeable membrane. The membrane is called the *dialysis membrane* or *dialysis tube*.

**diaphragm** (DY-uh-fram): the sheet of muscle that separates the chest and abdominal cavities in mammals; along with rib muscles it is important in breathing.

**diastase** (DY-uh-stays): a mixture of carbohydrate-digesting plant enzymes.

**dicot** (DYE-kot): *see* dicotyledon.

**dicotyledon** (DYE-kot-ih-LEED-un): a plant having two cotyledons in the seed. Most vegetable plants other than corn, most trees other than evergreens, and many other flowering plants are dicots.

**Dicotyledonae** (DYE-kot-ih-LEED-un-ee): a division of flowering plants that have two cotyledons in their seeds.

**dicotyledonous** (DYE-kot-ih-LEED-un-us): having two cotyledons in the seed.

**differentiation** (dif-er-en-chee-AY-shun): the process by which cells in an organism become different in structure and function although descended from the same egg cell.

**diffusion** (dih-FYOO-zhun): movement of particles through a medium—air, liquid, or solid, including through a plasma membrane—from areas of high concentration to areas of low concentration.

**digestion** (dih-JES-tyun): the process of breaking down large food molecules into smaller ones, by both heterotrophs and autotrophs.

**diploid** (DIH-ploid): having a full chromosome number or both members of every chromosome pair characteristic of the species.

**Diplopoda** (dih-PLOP-uh-duh): the class of arthropods containing millipedes.

**division:** the second-largest grouping, after kingdom, in the biological classification system for plants.

**division of labor:** the existing distribution of tasks within an organism to its cells, tissues, and organs; or, the distribution of tasks within a society to its members based on either instinctive behavior, as in ants, or voluntary behavior, as in humans.

**DNA:** the abbreviation for *deoxyribonucleic* (dee-OK-sih-ry-boh-new-KLEE-ik) *acid,* the hereditary material of most organisms; DNA makes up the genes.

**dominance:** in behavior, the ability to exercise control or authority over others; in genetics, the expression of a gene effect that masks the effect of another allele of that gene.

**dominant:** *see* dominance.

**dominant member:** generally the larger, stronger, and more mature animal within a social hierarchy.

**dorsal** (DOR-sul) **lip:** a lip above the blastopore of an early embryo.

**double helix** (HEE-liks): the shape of a DNA molecule, similar to a pair of spiral, intertwined staircases proceeding upward.

**doubling time:** the period of time during which a given population will increase by 100 percent.

**Down syndrome** (SIN-drohm): in humans, a congenital condition characterized by 47 chromosomes, the extra one being a number 21 chromosome present because of nondisjunction.

**drone:** a male bee.

***Drosophila*** (druh-SOF-il-uh): the genus of the fruit fly, *Drosophila melanogaster* (mel-uh-no-GAS-ter), widely used in genetics experiments.

***Dryopithecus*** (dry-oh-PITH-eh-kus): a genus of fossils believed related to the later evolution of apes, australopithecines, and humans.

## E

**echinoderm** (eh-KY-noh-derm): *see* Echinodermata.

**Echinodermata** (eh-ky-noh-DER-muh-tuh): a phylum of spiny-skinned, ocean-dwelling animals; starfish, sea stars, brittle stars, sea urchins, and sand dollars are all echinoderms.

**ecosystem** (EEK-oh-sis-tem): an almost self-sufficient community of populations of different organisms, together with the physical environment in which they live. Food materials are recycled; few are lost by the environment. However, a constant input of energy from the sun is required.

**ectoderm** (EK-toh-derm): an outer layer of cells, as in an embryo.

**egg:** a female gamete, haploid in chromosome number.

**electrocardiogram** (ih-lek-troh-KARD-ee-oh-gram): a record or tracing of electrical changes occurring during the heartbeat, used in medical diagnosis.

**electroencephalogram** (ih-LEK-troh-en-SEF-uh-loh-gram): the recording of brain waves by special instruments.

**electron** (ee-LEK-tron): the fundamental unit of electricity, and the particle that occurs in varying numbers in the electron clouds surrounding the nuclei of atoms. An electron carries a negative electrical charge.

**electron micrograph** (MY-kroh-graf): a photograph of the image of a specimen that is examined by use of an electron microscope.

**electron microscope:** a microscope that examines specimens with electron beams instead of visible light, hence is capable of much greater magnification than a compound microscope. The image is cast on a screen by the electrons.

**electron transport:** the process by which electrons are transferred from one acceptor or carrier molecule to another in the light phase of photosynthesis and in the respiratory chains of both plants and animals.

**element:** a substance composed of atoms that are all chemically identical—alike in their proton and electron numbers.

**embryo** (EM-bree-oh): an early stage in the development of a new individual from a fertilized egg.

**embryonic induction** (em-bree-ON-ik in-DUK-shun): the influence of one tissue in an embryo on another, in development and differentiation.

**endocrine** (EN-duh-krin) **gland:** a ductless gland that secretes one or more hormones into the circulatory system.

**endoderm** (EN-doh-derm): an inner layer of cells, as in an embryo.

**endoplasmic reticulum** (en-doh-PLAZ-mik reh-TIK-yoo-lum): a system of internal membranes in a cell; the membranes are studded with ribosomes in some places, but are smooth in others.

**endoskeleton** (en-doh-SKEL-uh-tun): the internal skeleton of higher organisms, usually consisting of bone and cartilage.

**environment** (en-VYR-un-ment): an organism's living and nonliving surroundings; also, its internal environment as the environment of each of its cells. In genetics, the external and internal environments are considered as nongenetic influences on the development of the organism, in contrast to genetic influences.

**environmental niche** (nitch): a way of life in a specific environment; or, generally, conditions in an environment that are suitable to a kind of organism with particular adaptations, as in food-getting. As an example, eagles and hawks occupy niches as birds of prey; they hunt chiefly by day, while owls fill a similar niche by night.

**enzyme** (EN-zym): a protein or part-protein molecule made by an organism and used as a catalyst in a specific chemical reaction, or used in electron transfer in respiration and photosynthesis.

**enzyme-substrate complex:** the temporary bonding of an enzyme with the molecules on which it acts.

**epidermal ectoderm** (ep-ih-DER-mul EK-toh-derm): the portion of the ectoderm of an embryo that in mammals will develop into skin, hair, nails, and the enamel of teeth.

**epidermis** (ep-ih-DER-mis) or **epidermal cells:** the outer cell layer, as in the skin or in a green leaf.

**epididymis** (ep-ih-DID-ih-mis): in male mammals, a mass of tubules at the back of a testis.

**epigenesis** (ep-ih-JEN-eh-sis): the belief that a new individual develops from unorganized raw materials in a fertilized egg; epigenesis does not take into account the genetic code.

**epiglottis** (ep-ih-GLOT-is): the flap of tissue that covers the trachea during swallowing.

**equator:** the division between hemispheres of a late blastula.

**erosion** (ee-ROH-zhun): the wearing away of land surfaces by action of wind, water, alternate freezing and thawing, and other causes.

**esophagus** (ih-SOF-uh-gus): the tube through which food passes when swallowed, leading to the stomach.

**essential amino** (uh-MEE-noh) **acids:** the amino acids in the human diet which the human body itself cannot synthesize; these amino acids must be in the proteins of foods.

**estrogen** (ES-troh-jen): a hormone or group of hormones (estrogens) active in the reproductive cycle of female mammals; primarily they promote growth of the soft tissues of the inner lining of the uterus.

**ethnoarchaeology** (eth-noh-ar-kee-OL-oh-jee): the study of the material remains of human habitation, including those of present human cultures, as an approach to studying evidence from older sites.

*Euglena* (yoo-GLEE-nuh): a genus of one-celled green protists that carry on photosynthesis and move about freely, using a whiplike flagellum in their locomotion.

**eukaryote** (yoo-KARE-ee-oht): a cell or organism that has cell nuclei and other specialized cell structures such as mitochondria and plastids.

**evaporation** (ee-vap-uh-RAY-shun): a change in state from liquid to gas, as when water molecules escape into the air through stomata in a leaf.

**evolution** (eh-vuh-LOO-shun): the process of change with time; in biology, the descent of more recent species from former ones.

**excretion** (ek-SKREE-shun): the elimination by a cell of waste by-products of its metabolism, and the elimination of these waste by-products by an organism of which the cell may be a part.

**exon** (EK-sahn): a segment of DNA that codes for messenger RNA and amino acids.

**exoskeleton** (ek-so-SKEL-uh-tun): the external covering of an organism, such as an insect or crustacean, that supports and protects the organism in a fashion similar to a suit of armor.

**experimental group:** the subjects that are manipulated in an experiment, for comparison with a control, or unmanipulated, group.

**experimental variable:** a condition that is changed for an experimental group, for comparison of the results with a normal or control group.

**extensor** (ek-STEN-ser): a muscle that extends a limb or skeletal part.

**external stimulus** (STIM-yoo-lus): an environmental change that reaches an organism from outside and causes it to respond.

**extinct** (ek-STINKT): no longer surviving as a species.

**extracellular digestion** (eks-truh-SEL-yoo-ler dih-JES-tyun): the breakdown of complex food molecules to simpler ones outside an organism's individual body cells, as in the body cavity of a hydra or the digestive tract of humans.

**extract** (EK-strakt): a selected portion, fraction, or solution taken from a culture or other laboratory preparation of whole organisms or some of their body tissues. Often the preparation is centrifuged before the extract is withdrawn.

**F**

**$F_1$:** the first filial generation, or immediate offspring of a parental cross (P).

**$F_2$:** the second filial generation, produced by a cross between members of the $F_1$ generation.

**family:** the fifth-largest grouping, after kingdom, phylum or division, class, and order, in the biological classification system; a group of related genera.

**fat:** a foodstuff made up of fatty acids and glycerol. Fats are a principal form in which many organisms store their reserve food.

**fatty acid:** a chainlike organic molecule composed entirely of carbon and hydrogen except for an acid group (—COOH) at one end; fatty acids combine with glycerol to form fat molecules.

**feces** (FEE-seez): undigested parts of food eliminated from the digestive tract.

**feedback system:** a relationship in which one activity of an organism affects another, which in turn affects the first, yielding a regulatory balance.

**femur** (FEE-mur): the upper leg bone of the hind leg in vertebrates; also, the segment of exoskeleton on the upper hind leg of insects and many other arthropods.

**fermentation** (fer-men-TAY-shun): a series of reactions in which energy is released from the organic molecules of foodstuffs in the absence of oxygen, yielding incompletely digested products such as alcohol, lactic acid, and acetic acid, along with carbon dioxide.

**ferredoxin** (fe-re-DOX-in): an iron-containing compound that acts as an electron acceptor in a cell's respiratory chain; ferredoxin is also an electron acceptor during photosynthesis.

**fertilization:** in sexual reproduction, the union of male and female gametes.

**fetus** (FEE-tus): a developing mammalian offspring when basic body appearance and internal organs are all recognizably developed; in humans, from approximately 90 days onward.

**fibril** (FY-bril): any of the contractile structures that coordinate the action of cilia in an organism such as *Paramecium;* in vertebrates, a contractile unit that makes up the fibers of muscle cells.

**fibrin** (FY-brin): an insoluble protein formed as part of the blood-clotting reactions in mammals.

**fibrinogen** (fy-BRIN-uh-jin): a soluble protein converted to fibrin by enzyme action during the blood-clotting reactions in mammals.

**filament** (FIL-uh-ment): a descriptive term for slender parts of many organisms; in flowers, the filament is the stalk of the stamen; in a fish's gills, a filament is a thin layer of cells; in a muscle, a filament is an element that makes up muscle fibrils.

**Filicinophyta** (fil-ih-sin-OFF-ih-tuh): a plant division of ferns.

**first filial generation:** the offspring (abbreviated $F_1$) of a parental cross.

**first-order consumer:** a herbivore; an organism that eats food producers, such as a cow eating grass.

**flagellum** (fluh-JEL-um): a long, whiplike appendage used in locomotion by many one-celled organisms, or used in creating a current of water by some cells in multicellular organisms.

**flame cell:** a structure used to eliminate excess water in organisms such as flatworms.

**flexor** (FLEK-ser): a muscle that bends a joint; its action is opposite that of an extensor.

**fluid pressure:** the force exerted by a liquid against its container, such as blood pressure in an artery, or water pressure inside a leaf cell.

**follicle** (FOL-ih-kul): in an ovary of a mammal, a saclike structure in which the egg matures; also in mammals, a cavity in the skin from which a hair grows; and, in the thyroid gland, a functional unit in the production and storage of thyroxine.

**food:** an energy and materials source for which an organism has the enzymes necessary to digest principal parts and obtain the materials and energy.

**food chain:** a relationship linking an autotroph (as food producer) to an organism (a herbivore) that eats the autotroph, to another organism (a carnivore) that eats the herbivore, and so on.

**food pyramid:** a representation of food energy passing through an ecosystem, where, in each level, organisms require about ten times their collective body mass (biomass) in food organisms.

**food web:** food chains in an ecosystem taken collectively, showing partial overlapping and competition for many food organisms.

**fossil** (FOS-ul): evidence of an organism preserved in Earth's crust; frozen tissues, mineralized bone or shell forms, and body outlines or casts of body parts in sedimentary rock are all fossils.

**fraternal** (fruh-TER-nul) **twins:** two offspring born at the same time to the same mother, but as products of two different fertilized eggs.

**fructose** (FROOK-tohs): fruit sugar; a six-carbon sugar.

**fruit:** fleshy, usually edible tissues developed by the ovary of a flowering plant around the seed or seeds.

**FSH:** *follicle-stimulating hormone,* produced by the pituitary gland in mammals; in females it stimulates development of the follicle in which the egg is maturing; in males it is also involved in regulation of reproductive functions.

**FSH-RF:** *follicle-stimulating-hormone releasing factor,* a hormone secreted by the hypothalamus; the FSH-RF stimulates the pituitary to secrete and release FSH.

**function** (FUNK-shun): the work or activity of a biological structure or a biochemical compound.

**Fungi** (FUN-jy): a kingdom of organisms that live on decaying remains of other organisms or are parasites of other organisms; examples are mushrooms, toadstools, mildews, rusts, smuts, yeasts, and molds. Fungi have no photosynthetic pigments, nor do they have mouth parts with which to ingest food; they usually secrete enzymes into their surroundings and absorb the nutrients that the enzymes digest.

## G

**gamete** (GAM-eet): a sexual reproductive cell; an egg or a sperm.

**ganglion** (GANG-glee-un; plural, *ganglia*—GANG-glee-uh): a group of nerve cell bodies.

**gastrin** (GAS-trin): a hormone released by stomach cells that starts the secretion of hydrochloric acid.

**gastrula** (GAS-troo-luh): an early embryo at the stage when an infolding of cells from the outside occurs; the gastrula stage follows the blastula stage.

**gene** (JEEN): a unit of DNA or RNA that determines a hereditary characteristic; a segment of DNA that codes for RNA or that has a regulatory function.

**gene flow:** interbreeding between individuals from different populations or subpopulations.

**gene pool:** all the genes of a population of a species considered as being present together, or pooled.

**general respiration:** *see* respiration.

**gene splicing:** insertion of a new gene into the DNA of a cell.

**genetic code:** the triplet code of nucleotides in DNA and RNA; it specifies amino acids for polypeptides that make up enzymes and other proteins.

**genetic counselor:** a professionally trained geneticist who works with persons who believe they may have a genetic disorder, or who may be carriers of genes causing a genetic disorder that would put their children at risk.

**genetic drift:** a change in alleles or their frequencies in a population's gene pool as a result of chance.

**genetic engineering:** the application of recombinant-DNA techniques in producing one or more changes in the genetic makeup of an organism.

**genetics** (juh-NET-iks): the science of heredity, involving the study of the inheritance of characteristics and the hereditary code in the genes of organisms.

**genetic strain:** a population of laboratory animals, plants, or microorganisms reproduced from individuals having a genetic trait unlike that of other populations of the same species.

**genetic "swamping":** the effects on a small population caused by interbreeding with a genetically different and very large population of the same species; the small population's gene pool is quickly modified.

**genotype** (JEEN-oh-type): the genetic makeup (combination of alleles) of an individual for each of its hereditary traits.

**genus** (JEE-nus; plural, *genera*—JEN-er-uh): a group of related species whose biological names all begin with their common genus name (examples: *Felis leo,* the lion; *Felis*

*domestica,* the house cat, and *Felis tigris,* the tiger—all members of the cat genus, *Felis*).

**geotropism** (jee-oh-TROH-piz-um): the influence of gravity upon the direction of growth of plant stems and roots.

**germination** (jer-min-AY-shun): the sprouting of a seed.

**gill:** a respiratory organ chiefly of aquatic organisms, such as fish; in many ocean fish the gills are also the chief excretory organs.

**Ginkgophyta** (gink-GOFF-ih-tuh): a division of ginkgo trees and related plants.

**gizzard:** in animals such as earthworms and birds, a muscular section of the digestive tract in which food is crushed and partially digested.

**gland:** an organ or a single cell that secretes one or more compounds such as mucus or hormones.

**glomerulus** (glaw-MER-yoo-lus): the cluster of capillaries within the Bowman's capsule of a nephron in the kidney.

**glucagon** (GLOOK-uh-gon): a hormone formed in the pancreas that helps regulate the blood's glucose level.

**glucose** (GLOO-kohs): an abundant six-carbon sugar.

**glycerol** (GLIS-uh-rawl): an organic molecule that is the anchoring, or base molecule, in fats; fatty acid chains are bonded to it.

**glycogen** (GLY-ko-jen): animal starch; a carbohydrate made by animals as a food-storage compound.

**Gnetophyta** (nee-TOF-ih-tuh): a division of cone-bearing plants including *Welwitschia.*

**Golgi** (GOHL-jee) **complex:** membranelike structures in a cell's cytoplasm that play a role in secreting cell products.

**grafting:** asexual reproduction by splicing a bud or branch from one plant to a related one, as in the propagation of seedless orange trees.

**granum** (GRAY-num; plural, *grana*—GRAY-nuh): a stack of saucerlike structures or thylakoids containing chlorophyll, within a chloroplast.

**growth:** an enlargement and developmental process involving cell division, cell enlargement, and often cell differentiation.

**guanine** (GWAH-neen): one of the four nitrogen bases in DNA or RNA; it is present in equal amounts with cytosine, with which it pairs.

**guard cell:** one of the two cells regulating the size of an opening, or stoma, in a leaf.

## H

**habitat** (HAB-uh-tat): the home environment of an organism.

**habituation** (huh-bich-yoo-AY-shun): a simple form of learning in which the response decreases as the organism grows accustomed to the stimulus.

**haploid** (HAP-loid): having only one member of each pair of chromosomes characteristic of a species; examples are eggs and sperm.

**Hardy-Weinberg Principle:** a mathematically derived principle providing a method of calculation for predicting frequencies of different genes in a population's gene pool from generation to generation.

**heart:** the pumping organ of the circulatory system in animals.

**heme** (HEEM): an iron-containing compound that combines with one protein to form the respiratory pigment hemoglobin, with another protein to form the enzyme catalase, and with still other proteins to form other respiratory pigments and enzymes.

**hemocyanin** (HEE-moh-SY-uh-nin): an oxygen-carrying blue pigment in the blood plasma of arthropods and mollusks. Hemoglobin also occurs in mollusks.

**hemodialysis** (HEE-moh-dy-AL-eh-sus): separation of wastes from needed substances in blood by means of their unequal diffusion through a semipermeable membrane. The separation is made with a *dialysis tube* in an artificial kidney machine; the solution in the machine is called the *dialysate* (dy-AL-eh-zayt).

**hemoerythrin** (HEE-moh-ee-RITH-rin): an oxygen-carrying red pigment in the blood plasma of many annelids and other worms. Hemoglobin also occurs in annelids, and an oxygen-carrying green pigment, *chlorocruorin* (klor-oh-KROO-oh-rin), is found in certain annelids that inhabit the ocean floor.

**hemoglobin** (HEE-muh-gloh-bin): the oxygen-carrying pigment of red blood cells in vertebrates.

**hemophilia** (hee-moh-FIL-ee-uh): an X-linked recessive hereditary condition in humans, in which blood fails to clot, making death possible from slight wounds such as bruises and cuts. The responsible allele is carried on the X chromosome; the Y chromosome of males has no allele for the gene, so that a single allele causes the disorder in males.

**herbivore** (HER-bih-vor): a first-order consumer; an animal that feeds on plants or algae.

**hereditary variations:** variations in hereditary characteristics in a population or species, mainly as a result of mutations.

**heredity:** the overall DNA code of an individual.

**heterotroph** (HET-er-oh-trohf): an organism that obtains its food by feeding on other organisms or on their remains, or by living as a parasite on another organism.

**heterotroph hypothesis:** the hypothesis that the first life evolved from nonliving clusters of organic compounds and would have been the simplest microscopic life form possible. A microscopic heterotroph that could feed on the naturally-occurring organic compounds is the type of organism specified.

**heterozygous** (het-er-oh-ZY-gus): carrying unlike alleles for a particular characteristic.

**Hex A:** the abbreviation for *hexosaminidase A* (HEKS-ohs-uh-MIN-ih-days), the "A" form of an enzyme not produced in Tay-Sachs disease.

**hibernation** (hy-ber-NAY-shun): a dormant state of certain warm-blooded animals in which metabolism and temperature drop so much below normal that a period of gradual warming and waking is required, in place of rousing as from sleep.

**hierarchy** (HY-er-ark-ee): the arrangement of a group of organisms in order of dominance, task, or other factors.

**histone** (HIS-tone): a type of protein that forms part of the network on which DNA is clustered in a cell nucleus.

**homeostasis** (HOH-mee-oh-STAY-sis): the maintenance of a stable and constant metabolic condition, or a steady-state relationship between an organism and its environment.

**homoiothermic** (HOH-moi-uh-THERM-ik): capable of maintaining body temperature within a narrow range, using internal regulatory mechanisms; warm-blooded, as in birds and mammals.

*Homo* (HOH-moh): the human genus. *Homo sapiens* (SAY-pee-enz) is the surviving species.

**homologous** (ho-MOL-uh-gus): similar or alike in form and origin—often in function as well.

**homology** (ho-MOL-uh-jee): likeness in form, as a result of evolution from the same ancestors.

**homozygous** (hoh-moh-ZY-gus): carrying identical alleles for a particular characteristic.

**hormone** (HOR-mohn): a cell or glandular secretion that has a regulatory effect on the activity of a specific organ, or on a specific biochemical function (for example, regulation of glucose level in the blood).

**humane** (hyoo-MAYN) **guidelines:** in biological investigations, the treatment of living species with a responsible regard for their day-to-day needs and well-being.

**hybrid** (HY-brid): heterozygous for one or more genetic characteristics. Hybrids between different purebred lines will be heterozygous for many characteristics.

*Hydra* (HY-druh): a genus of small freshwater coelenterates with tentacles and stinging cells, popular in laboratory studies of lower animals.

**hydrochloric** (HY-droh-klor-ik) **acid:** the acid found in the stomachs of vertebrate animals.

**hydrogen bond:** a weak attraction between particles, in which hydrogen (bonded to oxygen, nitrogen, or fluorine) exhibits a slightly positive charge that attracts oxygen, nitrogen, or fluorine on an adjacent particle. In great numbers, hydrogen bonds are effective in holding organic molecules together in their configuration. Hydrogen bonds hold the two helical strands of DNA together in their double helix.

**hydrogen pathway:** in cell respiration, the reactions that transfer hydrogen or its electrons from organic compounds through a respiratory chain to oxygen, forming water; energy is yielded and stored in ATP during this process.

**hydrolysis** (hy-DROL-uh-sis): the splitting of a compound by enzyme action, adding a hydrogen atom to one fragment and hydrogen and oxygen to the other—in effect, the chemical addition of water.

**hypothalamus** (hy-po-THAL-a-mus): a cluster of neurons at the base of the brain that regulate pituitary secretion; some of the neurons act directly on the pituitary, but others secrete hormones that act on the pituitary.

**hypothesis** (hy-POTH-uh-sis): a trial solution suggested for a scientific problem, subject to experimental evidence; a hypothesis explains existing data and predicts new data.

## I

**ichthyologist** (ik-thee-OL-uh-jist): a biologist who specializes in the study of fish.

**identical twins:** two offspring with the same genetic makeup, produced from the same fertilized egg whose cells separated during cleavage.

**immune** (ih-MYOON) **system:** all of an organism's biochemical defenses (such as antibodies) and cellular defenses (such as white blood cells) against disease-producing microorganisms, their toxins, and other foreign substances and particles.

**implantation** (im-plan-TAY-shun): the attachment and embedding of the fertilized egg of a mammal in the soft tissues of the lining of the uterus.

**imprinting:** behavior as a fixed response to a particular stimulus, determined by the first response to the same stimulus very early in life.

**indicator:** a chemical useful in laboratory analysis because it undergoes a change, usually in color, in the presence of a certain *p*H or a certain compound, or some other characteristic not directly visible.

**induction** (in-DUK-shun): *see* embryonic induction.

**inference:** a statement based on belief or assumption, related to but not necessarily implied by the facts.

**infrared** (IN-fruh-RED): that portion of the spectrum with wavelengths longer than visible red light but shorter than radio waves.

**initial data:** the first observations and research about a problem to be investigated.

**innate** (in-AYT) **behavior:** behavior that is genetically determined, as in the organization of an ant society. Innate behavior is also called instinctive behavior.

**Insecta** (in-SEK-tuh): the class of arthropods that contains bees, wasps, flies, moths and butterflies, grasshoppers, beetles, and all other such animals with six jointed legs; the largest class of organisms in the animal kingdom.

**insecticide** (in-SEK-tih-syd): a chemical or mixture of chemicals prepared to kill insects.

**insertion:** the attachment of one end of a muscle to the part of the skeleton it moves.

**instinct:** a complex pattern of innate behavior.

**instinctive behavior:** *see* innate behavior.

**insulin** (IN-suh-lin): a hormone produced in mammals by the Islets of Langerhans in the pancreas, and important in the body's use of sugar.

**internal stimuli** (STIM-yoo-ly): causes of behavior that come from within an organism.

**interphase:** the normal condition of a eukaryotic cell when it is not undergoing mitosis and cell division.

**intestine** (in-TES-tin): the portion of the digestive tract leading from the stomach to the anus, important in digestion and absorption of foodstuffs.

**intracellular digestion** (IN-truh-SEL-yoo-lar dih-JES-tyun): digestion that takes place within a cell, as in one-celled organisms and certain cells of many multicellular organisms.

**intron** (IN-trahn): a segment of DNA that intervenes between other segments that code for messenger RNA. Introns code for intron RNA that is removed from the RNA in forming a completed messenger-RNA molecule.

**inversion:** a sequence of genes reversed from their normal order in a segment of a chromosome, often as a result of looping, breakage, and repair; in weather, a warmer layer of air over a cooler layer, trapping the cooler air for an extended period of time.

**in vitro** (in VEE-troh): outside the organism in an artificial environment or laboratory preparation.

**in vivo** (in VEE-voh): inside the organism; in the living body.

**ion** (EYE-on): an atom or molecule that has either gained or lost one or more electrons, giving it a negative or positive charge.

**ionic** (eye-ON-ik) **bond:** a chemical bond formed by attraction between oppositely charged ions.

**ionization** (eye-un-ih-ZAY-shun): conversion of a substance into ions, as by radiation damage, the heat of a nuclear reaction, or, for substances whose bonds are normally ionic, solution in water.

**irradiation** (ir-ray-dee-AY-shun): exposure to a source of high-energy radiation.

**islets of Langerhans** (LAHN-ger-hahns): the islandlike clusters of tissue in the pancreas that secrete the hormone insulin.

**isolation:** the separation of organisms or populations as a result of some barrier between them; the barrier may be behavioral, genetic, or physical or geographic.

**isotope** (EYE-so-tohp): atoms of an element showing variation in their number of neutrons; the proton and electron numbers are always the same.

## J

**jaws:** the biting structures that frame the mouth.

**jumping genes:** genes that move relatively freely in location, on the same or to different chromosomes.

**juvenile hormone:** a chemical that prevents the maturation of insects if applied at the correct time to larvae or pupae.

## K

**karyograph** (KAR-ee-uh-graf): a photographic record of chromosomes arranged and labeled by pairs.

**karyotyping** (KAR-ee-uh-typ-ing): the procedures of preparing a chromosome smear, photographing it, cutting the chromosomes out of the photo with scissors, and matching them in pairs to determine whether the chromosome complement is normal and has no extra or missing chromosome segments.

**kelvin:** the basic unit of temperature in the metric system, equal to a degree Celsius.

**kidney:** an animal organ that removes nitrogenous wastes from the blood.

**kidney stone:** an aggregation of uric acid, calcium, or other crystals that blocks the passage of urine through a ureter.

**kilogram:** the basic unit of mass in the metric system.

**kingdom:** the largest grouping in the biological classification system.

**Klinefelter syndrome** (KLYN-fel-ter SIN-drohm): in humans, a congenital condition characterized by an XXY combination of chromosomes in a male; produced by nondisjunction or a related failure of chromosomes to separate in meiosis.

**Krebs cycle:** the cycle in cell respiration that completes the breakdown of organic molecules from an intermediate stage, releasing hydrogen to the respiratory chain and yielding carbon dioxide and water; also called the citric acid cycle.

## L

**lactic** (LAK-tik) **acid:** a by-product of fermentation of sugar by certain types of microorganisms; also, the by-product of glycogen breakdown in working muscle cells that have run up an oxygen debt and cannot complete the cell respiratory processes.

**lamprey** (LAM-pree): an eellike, parasitic, aquatic vertebrate.

**lancelet** (LANS-let): a small, nonvertebrate aquatic chordate.

**large intestine:** that portion of the digestive tract extending from the small intestine to the anus; in mammals it is shorter in length but larger in diameter than the small intestine, and is a site of water reabsorption.

**larva** (LAR-vuh; plural, *larvae*—LAR-vee): a preadult stage in the life cycle of many animals; usually it is a wormlike stage. Larvae are often significant in living and feeding in ways unlike those of the later adults.

**larynx** (LAR-inks): in humans, the voice box at the entrance to the respiratory tube. The larynx of many other vertebrates is a similar structure but with different vocal adaptations.

**law of conservation of energy:** a natural law expressing that energy cannot be created or destroyed but can be changed from one form to others. Since matter can be converted to energy, as in the sun, the law is often restated more broadly as the law of conservation of matter and energy.

**law of conservation of matter and energy:** a natural law expressing that matter and energy cannot be created or destroyed but can be changed in form; matter can also be changed to energy.

**learned behavior:** behavior developed as a result of experience.

**lens** (convex lens): a transparent disk with smooth curved surfaces, thicker at its center than at the edges. The lens admits light rays and causes them to converge a short distance beyond or behind the lens. Examples are the lenses of the eyes and of a microscope.

**lethal** (LEE-thul): resulting in death or, in genetics, death or sterility.

**lethal mutation** (LEE-thul mew-TAY-shun): a mutation causing the death or sterility of the mutant organisms.

**leukemia:** any of many conditions, all cancerous, in which certain white blood cells multiply out of control, often being released into the bloodstream in an arrested or immature stage of development.

**LH:** *luteinizing* (LOOT-e-un-i-zing) *hormone,* produced by the pituitary gland in mammals. In both males and females it helps to regulate reproductive functions.

**LH-RF:** *luteinizing-hormone releasing factor,* a hormone secreted by the hypothalamus that stimulates the pituitary to secrete and release LH.

**lichen** (LY-ken): an alga and a fungus living in symbiosis on a solid surface such as rock.

**light phase:** the light-requiring reactions of photosynthesis that incorporate sunlight energy as chemical energy in ATP and NADPH.

**linkage group:** a group of genes that are transmitted together because they are on the same chromosome; or, either of two groups of genes exchanged in crossing-over.

**lipase** (LY-pays): a fat-digesting enzyme in pancreatic juice.

**lipids** (LIP-ids): fat-related compounds, including those that make up the major portion of a cell's plasma membrane.

**liver:** a gland of many animals, and the largest gland in the human body; in humans it filters the blood, secretes bile, stores food as glycogen, and disposes of wastes.

**lung:** an internal respiratory structure of most land vertebrates, a few fishes, and aquatic mammals.

**Lycopodophyta** (ly-kuh-poh-DOF-ih-tuh): a plant division of club mosses.

**lymph** (LIMF): the fluid in the lymphatic system.

**lymphatic** (lihm-FAT-ik) **system:** a system of vessels that carries much of the tissue fluid from the spaces between cells back into the bloodstream.

**lymphocyte** (LIM-fo-syt): a type of small white blood cell.

**lymph vessel:** any of the tubes of the lymphatic system, including those of the villi in the small intestine.

**lysosome** (LY-soh-sohm): a cell vacuole containing digestive enzymes.

## M

**macromutation** (MAK-roh-myoo-TAY-shun): a simultaneous heritable change in the DNA of a number of genes.

**macrophage** (MAK-ruh-fayj): a type of large white blood cell.

**maggots:** the wormlike larvae of houseflies and certain other flies.

**Malpighian** (mal-PIG-ee-un) **tubule:** a specialized excretory structure in arthropods such as the grasshopper.

**maltose** (MAWL-tohs): a compound sugar formed by the partial digestion of starch.

**Mammalia** (muh-MAY-lee-uh): a class of chordates containing vertebrates that have hair and that produce milk for their young. Horses, cats, mice, elephants, whales, and seals are some examples of the mammals.

**mammary** (MAM-uh-ree) **glands:** milk-producing glands in mammals.

**mass:** the property of a body that is taken as a measure of the amount of material it contains; *inertial mass* is the measure usually sought, but *gravitational mass* (using a balance in a gravitational field) and *weight* (using a scale in a gravitational field) are the measures most easily obtained.

**maze:** a device constructed with a network of passages, for use in behavioral experiments.

**medulla** (meh-DUL-uh): the central area of an organ such as the kidney or adrenal gland; also, a part of the vertebrate brain.

**meiosis** (my-OH-sis): the replication of chromosomes and the two cell divisions in eukaryotic cells necessary to form sperm and eggs; the chromosomes are replicated once, but the cells divide twice, resulting in gametes with only one member of each chromosome pair.

**meniscus** (men-IS-kus): the curved surface of a liquid in a narrow column in a glass tube, graduated cylinder, or similar container.

**menstrual** (MEN-stroo-ul) **cycle:** in human females, the reproductive cycle, which occurs throughout the year. Other mammals have such a cycle (called the *estrous cycle*) only at certain times of the year.

**menstruation** (men-stroo-AY-shun): the discharge of soft tissues of the lining of the uterus, including blood and blood vessels, when no fertilized egg has implanted in the uterus during the reproductive cycle.

**meristem** (MER-ih-stem): any of the tissues that give rise to plant growth; such tissues are found in stem tips, lateral buds, root tips, and as cambium.

**mesoderm** (MEH-soh-derm): a layer of cells between ectoderm and endoderm in an embryo.

**messenger RNA:** DNA-coded RNA that migrates from the cell nucleus to the cytoplasm with instructions to a ribosome for the synthesis of a particular polypeptide.

**metabolism** (meh-TAB-uh-liz-um): the sum of all the chemical changes taking place in a living organism.

**metamorphosis** (met-uh-MOR-fuh-sis): changes in form, and often in life-style, of an organism at different stages in its life cycle, as in a tadpole and a frog, or a caterpillar and a butterfly.

**metaphase** (MET-uh-fayz): a stage in mitosis following prophase; the chromatids on the spindle form a line across the center of the cell.

**meter:** the basic unit of length in the metric system.

**microbiologist:** a biologist who specializes in the study of microscopic life.

**micrometer** (MY-kroh-mee-ter): a metric unit of microscopic measurement, abbreviated as $\mu$m.

**microorganism** (my-kroh-OR-gan-iz-um): an organism that is microscopic in size.

**microsphere:** a cooling droplet from a hot-water solution of polypeptides; the droplet forms a two-layered boundary or membrane.

**migration:** the movement of a population to a different environment during certain seasons of the year; or, in population genetics, the arrival or departure of individuals who thereby cause a change in the population's gene pool.

**minerals:** water, salts, iron (in compounds), and similar nutrients not used as sources of food energy but necessary to an organism's nutrition.

**mitochondrion** (my-tuh-KON-dree-un; plural, *mitochondria* — (my-tuh-KON-dree-uh): a structure within eukaryotic cells that carries on cell respiration and contains the enzymes of the Krebs cycle and respiratory chains.

**mitosis** (my-TOH-sis): the replication of the chromosomes and the production of two nuclei in one cell. Usually mitosis is followed by cell division.

**MN blood groups:** genetic variation in a protein found on red blood cells, similar to the variation in ABO blood groups but determined by only two alleles, which are codominant (producing M, MN, and N individuals).

**mole:** the basic unit for amount of substance in the metric system.

**molecule** (MOL-uh-kyool): the smallest naturally-occurring particle for elements or compounds whose atoms are covalently bonded to one another.

**Mollusca** (mah-LUS-kuh): a phylum of soft-bodied animals that usually secrete shells around themselves; clams, oysters, and whelks are examples of mollusks, but so are the octopus and the squid, which are without shells.

**mollusk** (MAH-lusk): *see* Mollusca.

**Monera** (muh-NER-uh): a kingdom of bacteria and related microscopic organisms whose one-celled or acellular bodies have no clearly defined cell nuclei or many of the other structures found in cells of higher organisms; that is, the cells are prokaryotic.

**moneran** (muh-NER-un): *see* Monera.

**monocot** (MON-oh-cot): *see* monocotyledon.

**monocotyledon** (MON-oh-kot-ih-LEED-un): a plant having one cotyledon in the seed. Corn, grasses, and orchids are all monocots.

**Monocotyledonae** (MON-oh-kot-ih-LEED-un-ee): a division of flowering plants that have one cotyledon in their seeds.

**monocotyledonous** (MON-oh-kot-ih-LEED-un-us): having one cotyledon in the seed.

**monocyte** (MON-oh-syt): a type of large white blood cell.

**motor neuron** (NYOO-ron): a neuron that carries impulses from the brain or spinal cord to muscles or glands.

**mucus** (MYOO-kus): a slippery secretion that moistens and protects many tissues; it is secreted by special gland cells in the tissues themselves.

**multicellular** (mul-tih-SEL-yuh-lar): composed of many cells, as contrasted to a single-celled organism.

**multiple alleles** (uh-LEELS): a group of alleles, all related to the same hereditary characteristic, of which only two appear in any single individual.

**muscle:** the contractile tissue of most multicellular animals.

**muscle fatigue:** the condition caused by accumulation of lactic acid and the change in $pH$ it brings about in a muscle working without adequate oxygen.

**muscular dystrophy** (DIS-troh-fee): a genetic condition of humans in which the muscles deteriorate and waste away.

**mutagen** (MYOO-tuh-jen): anything that can cause a mutation—radiation, high temperature, or a drug, insecticide, or other chemical.

**mutant** (MYOOT-unt): an organism showing a mutation for a given hereditary characteristic.

**mutation** (myoo-TAY-shun): a heritable change in the DNA of a gene.

**myelin** (MY-uh-lin) **sheath:** the fatty membrane surrounding the axon of some neurons.

**myosin** (MY-oh-sin): a muscle protein responsible for contraction by attaching to and pulling on another muscle protein, actin.

**Myxomycota** (mik-soh-MY-koh-tuh): a phylum of slime molds that during one stage in their life cycle form moving, amoebalike colonies, and in another stage form attached, funguslike stalks with reproductive organs.

## N

**NAD⁺:** the abbreviation for *nicotinamide adenine dinucleotide* (nih-kuh-TEEN-uh-myde AD-eh-neen di-NU-klee-oh-tyde), an electron and hydrogen carrier in cell respiration, related to NADP⁺.

**NADP⁺:** the abbreviation for *nicotinamide adenine dinucleotide phosphate* (nih-kuh-TEEN-uh-myde AD-eh-neen di-NU-klee-oh-tyde FOS-fayt), an electron and hydrogen carrier in cell respiration and in photosynthesis.

**natural selection:** the process in nature that favors survival of organisms with adaptations best suited to a given environment. These organisms become the parents of the next generation and so pass along their hereditary characteristics.

**Neanderthal** (nee-AN-der-thal): a culture of people who lived 40,000 to 50,000 years ago in Europe, Asia, and Africa.

**negative feedback:** feedback from one body process to another that inhibits the latter's rate, or inhibits production or secretion of its product.

**Nematoda** (nem-uh-TOH-duh): a phylum of animals, the unsegmented roundworms.

**nephridia** (nih-FRID-ee-uh): coiled excretory tubules that remove wastes from body fluids in earthworms and other annelids and eliminate these wastes through individual openings of the tubules in the body wall.

**nephron** (NEF-ron): a functional unit in the vertebrate kidney.

**nerve:** a bundle of nerve fibers.

**nerve cord:** a bundle of nerves and ganglia extending from the head region of an animal toward the posterior end of the body.

**nerve fiber:** the axon or dendrite of a neuron.

**nerve impulse:** the electrical and chemical change passing along the length of a neuron as a stimulus is transmitted.

**nerve net:** an interconnected group of neurons that carry impulses in such organisms as hydras and in some organs of animals with more complex nervous systems.

**neural ectoderm** (NYOO-rul EK-toh-derm): the portion of the ectoderm in an embryo that will develop into the brain and spinal cord.

**neuron** (NYOO-ron): a cell of the nervous system, consisting of a cell body and threadlike extensions called the axon and dendrite (or dendrites).

**Neurospora** (new-RAH-spoh-ruh): a mold widely used in genetics studies. Many of its enzyme systems are common to other heterotrophs, including humans.

**neurotransmitter** (nyur-oh-trans-MIT-er): a substance released by nerve endings of an axon that transmits an impulse across a synapse or to an effector such as a muscle or gland.

**neurula** (NYOO-rool-uh): a stage in development of the embryo following the gastrula, in which the embryo becomes elongated and shows evidence of the development of nervous tissue.

**neutron** (NOO-tron): a particle carrying no electrical charge, found in the nuclei of all atoms except those of hydrogen.

**niche** (NITCH): a way of life in a given environment, in relation to other organisms.

**nitrates** (NY-trayts): minerals or ions containing nitrogen chemically bound to oxygen, such as $NO_3^-$. Only certain microorganisms are able to use free nitrogen, while most can use it in the form of nitrates.

**nitrogen base:** any of a certain group of nitrogen-containing organic compounds with ringlike structures, including five found in the nucleotides of nucleic acids: adenine, thymine, cytosine, guanine, and uracil.

**nitrogenous** (ny-TROJ-eh-nus) **waste:** a by-product of protein metabolism that is excreted by an organism.

**node of Ranvier** (NOHD of RON-vyay): a constriction in the myelin sheath of a neuron, between Schwann cells.

**noncyclic photophosphorylation** (NON-sy-klik foh-toh-fos-for-ih-LAY-shun): in the light phase of photosynthesis, a process in which ATP and NADPH are formed, using energy from sunlight; water is also used and its oxygen given off.

**nondisjunction** (non-dis-JUNK-shun): failure of the chromosomes of a pair to separate during meiosis, leading to both chromosomes going to the same egg or sperm cell.

**norepinephrine** (nor-ep-eh-NEH-freen) (also called noradrenaline): a neurotransmitter released in muscle tissue and identical to a hormone of the adrenal gland.

**nuclear membrane:** the membrane surrounding a cell nucleus.

**nucleic** (new-KLEE-ik) **acids:** organic acids characteristically found in a cell's nucleus; in particular, DNA and RNA.

**nucleolus** (noo-KLEE-oh-lus): a structure in the nucleus of a eukaryotic cell; it is associated with the production of ribosomes.

**nucleosome** (NEW-klee-oh-sohm): a bead in a DNA molecule formed by coiling of the DNA around a histone.

**nucleotide** (NEW-klee-oh-tyd): the basic unit of a nucleic acid, made up of a nitrogen base, a five-carbon sugar, and a phosphate group.

**nucleus** (NOO-klee-us): the structure in eukaryotic cells that contains the chromosomes and certain other materials important in control of the cell; also, the central structure in an atom, containing one or more protons and, except for hydrogen, one or more neutrons.

**nutrient:** a food substance in a form, usually digested or not requiring digestion, that is interchangeable among organisms; also, certain minerals used by plants.

**nutrient broth:** in the laboratory, a liquid solution of nutrients prepared to promote the growth and reproduction of microorganisms; on Earth long ago, water containing naturally-formed organic compounds.

**nutrition** (noo-TRIH-shun): the supply to a cell or organism of all its material and energy needs as nutrients or foods.

# O

**observation:** knowledge obtained from the environment by use of one or more of the senses, and with or without the aid of measuring devices and scientific instruments.

**Onychophora** (ah-nih-KAH-for-uh): the class of arthropods containing *Peripatus* and similar wormlike animals that appear closely related to both other arthropods and the annelids.

**open circulatory system:** a system in which the blood does not travel through the body completely enclosed in vessels; the return to the heart is usually through open body spaces called sinuses, as in the crayfish.

**optic nerve:** the nerve in vertebrates leading from the eye to the cerebrum of the brain.

**order:** the fourth-largest grouping, after kingdom, phylum or division, and class, in the biological classification system; a group of related families.

**organ:** an organized group of tissues that carries on a specialized function in a multicellular organism.

**organic compound:** a carbon compound in which carbon is combined chemically with hydrogen, usually oxygen, and often one or more of the elements nitrogen, phosphorus, and sulfur; many organic compounds in living things also contain an atom of a metal, or certain other atoms.

**organism** (OR-gan-iz-um): a living thing.

**organ system:** a group of related organs that work together in their specialized functions, as the organs of the digestive system.

**origin:** the fixed attachment of one end of a muscle to a part of the skeleton as an anchoring point.

**ornithologist** (or-nuh-THOL-uh-jist): a biologist who specializes in the study of birds.

**oscillograph** (AH-sil-uh-graf): an instrument that records or displays variations in electrical impulses in such structures as nerves.

**osmosis** (os-MOH-sis): the diffusion of water through a membrane.

**Osteichthyes** (os-tee-IK-thee-eez): a class of bony fishes.

**ovarian follicle** (oh-VAR-ee-un FOL-ih-kul): the structure within the mammalian ovary in which the egg develops.

**ovary** (OH-vuh-ree): an organ in sexually reproducing plants and animals in which eggs or egg nuclei are produced or develop.

**oviduct** (OH-vih-dukt): a tube in egg-laying animals that carries eggs from the ovary; in mammals, the oviduct leads to the uterus.

**ovulation** (ahv-yoo-LAY-shun): the release of an egg from an ovary, in egg-laying animals.

**ovule** (OH-vewl): a developing egg nucleus and its enclosing sac, in the ovary of a seed-producing plant.

**ovum** (OH-vum; plural, *ova*—OH-vuh): the egg, or female gamete.

**oxygen debt:** the condition of a muscle when lactic acid accumulates; as oxygen is again made available, the lactic acid is converted back to glycogen.

**oxyhemoglobin** (ok-see-HEE-muh-gloh-bin): hemoglobin with a high concentration of oxygen bound to the iron of its heme group.

**ozone** (OH-zohn): a form of oxygen, $O_3$, that provides a shielding layer in the atmosphere against ultraviolet radiation.

# P

**P** (parental cross): a cross between two organisms, usually purebred, selected to be the beginning organisms for a series of breeding experiments in genetics.

**pacemaker:** the neuromuscular tissue that generates the rhythmic impulses which spread to other heart muscles as the heartbeat.

**paleobotanist** (pay-lee-oh-BOT-un-ist): a botanist who specializes in the study of the fossil remains of plants that lived in the past.

**paleontology** (pay-li-un-TOL-uh-jee): the study of extinct organisms through their fossils.

**palisade** (pal-ih-SAYD) **layer:** the layer of cells in a green leaf inside the upper epidermis; one of the layers of leaf cells in which photosynthesis occurs.

**pancreas** (PAN-kree-us): a gland that secretes digestive enzymes into the small intestine. Other gland tissue, also in the pancreas, secretes the hormone insulin.

**pancreatic duct:** a tube from the pancreas to the small intestine.

**pancreatin** (pan-KREE-uh-tin): a mixture of enzymes in the pancreatic juices.

**Pangaea** (pan-JEE-uh): a supercontinent of Earth's major land masses, dating to hundreds of millions of years ago when the land masses were all joined.

**paper chromatography** (kro-muh-TOG-ruh-fee): a technique which results in the separation of the compounds making up a substance; filter paper is streaked with the substance and suspended in a liquid solvent; the compounds are separated as they migrate different distances up the filter paper from the solvent.

*Paramecium* (par-uh-MEE-see-um): a genus of one-celled or acellular protists with cilia, popular in laboratory studies.

**parasite** (PAR-uh-syte): an organism, often without a digestive system or digestive enzyme system, that lives in or on another organism from which it obtains digested foodstuffs.

**parasympathetic** (par-uh-sim-puh-THET-ik) **nervous system:** one of two divisions of the autonomic nervous system.

**parental cross:** the initial cross in a breeding experiment, abbreviated as P.

**pasteurization** (pas-tyoor-ih-ZAY-shun): a process named for its discoverer, Louis Pasteur, in which heat is used to kill bacteria in wine, milk, and other food products. *See also* sterilization; pasteurization stops short of complete sterilization in order not to destroy desirable taste qualities in wine or food.

**peck order:** a social hierarchy in chickens based upon pecking, or the threat of pecking.

**pedigree** (PED-ih-gree): a record of heredity over many generations, especially for animal breeds.

**penicillin** (pen-ih-SIL-in): an antibiotic originally extracted from the mold *Penicillium*.

**penis** (PEE-nis): the male organ through which nitrogenous wastes are discharged and sperm are ejaculated.

**pepsin** (PEP-sin): the active protein-digesting enzyme in the stomach.

**pepsinogen** (pep-SIN-uh-jen): the inactive form of pepsin, changed to the active form by hydrochloric acid.

**peptide** (PEP-tyde): a short chain of chemically bonded amino acids.

**peptide** (PEP-tyde) **bond:** the covalent chemical bond formed between amino acids in a peptide, polypeptide, or protein; it bonds the amino group of one amino acid to the acid group of the next, removing a hydrogen atom (H) from the former and a hydroxyl (OH) from the latter, forming water.

**peripheral** (peh-RIF-er-ul) **nervous system:** the cranial and spinal nerves.

**peristalsis** (pehr-ih-STAWL-sis): the rhythmic contractions of the muscles of the walls of the digestive tract which move food along.

**permeable** (PER-mee-uh-bul): a characteristic of many membranes, including a cell's plasma membrane, whereby molecules of many substances can pass through the membrane.

**petals:** leaflike parts of the flower, often brightly colored, that in varying numbers encircle the flower's reproductive organs. Often the petals form a cup, or two or three of the petals may completely enclose the reproductive organs, making the flower self-pollinating.

*p*H: the symbol for acid-base characteristics or the level of H$^+$ (hydrogen) ions in a solution as compared with the level of certain negatively charged ions (OH$^-$ and others).

**Phaeophyta** (fee-AHF-uh-tuh): a phylum of protists containing the brown algae.

**phage** (FAYJ): an abbreviation for bacteriophage, a virus that infects bacteria.

**phagocytosis** (fayg-oh-sy-TOH-sis): the process by which a cell engulfs other organisms or foreign particles; pseudopods are extended around the particle to be engulfed.

**pharynx** (FAR-inks): the part of the digestive tract between the mouth and the esophagus; in mammals it is shared by the respiratory system. Also, in flatworms, the tubelike muscular organ that takes in bits of solid food.

**phenotype** (FEEN-oh-type): the expression of a genotype in the appearance or function of an organism; the observed trait.

**pheromone** (FER-oh-mohn): a chemical messenger in animals such as insects. Some pheromones are sex attractants; others mark a trail to food; still others have other functions.

**phloem** (FLOH-em): sieve tubes and companion cells; the living tissue in higher plants that transports plant foods.

**phosphate** (FOS-fayt): an inorganic salt important as a mineral in the nutrition of organisms; as a particular grouping or bonding of a phosphorus atom to a hydrogen atom and to three oxygen atoms, it is important as a phosphate group in ATP, creatine phosphate, and some other cell compounds.

**phosphoglyceric** (FAHS-foh-glis-ER-ik) **acid:** an intermediate compound in the fermentation of glucose and in the synthesis of glucose in the carbon cycle of photosynthesis.

**photosynthesis** (foh-toh-SIN-theh-sis): the process by which living cells that contain chlorophyll use light energy to make organic compounds from inorganic materials.

**phylum** (FY-lum): the second-largest grouping, after kingdom, in the biological classification system for all organisms except plants.

**pigment:** a colored substance; a compound that absorbs some wavelengths of visible light and reflects others. An example is chlorophyll, which absorbs red and violet and reflects green.

**pinocytosis** (pin-oh-sy-TOH-sis): a process by which cells take in large molecules and liquids; infoldings or pockets in the plasma membrane fill with liquid and particles and move into the cell as vacuoles.

**pistil** (PIHS-til): the female reproductive organ of a flower; the stigma, style, ovary, and the ovules within the ovary make up the pistil.

**pith:** the tissue near the center of many plant stems.

**pituitary** (pit-TEW-ih-ter-ee) **gland:** an endocrine gland at the base of the brain that is acted on by the hypothalamus to produce a large number of regulatory hormones; the posterior pituitary also stores hypothalamic hormones.

**placenta** (pluh-SEN-tuh): the structure in the uterus of pregnant mammals that functions to exchange nutrients and waste products between the mother and the fetus.

**Plantae** (PLAN-tee): the plant kingdom.

**plant hormone** (HOR-mohn): any of the substances that promote or regulate growth and development in plants.

**plant inhibitor** (in-HIB-it-er): a hormone that slows down or prevents growth in plants. Inhibitors are active in seeds, preventing their premature germination.

**plasma** (PLAZ-muh): the liquid portion of blood, in which the blood cells and other formed elements are suspended.

**plasma membrane:** the lipid-protein-carbohydrate membrane that encloses a cell; the lipid material makes up the principal part of the structure.

**plasmid** (PLAZ-mid): a circular strand of DNA separated from a prokaryotic chromosome.

**plastid** (PLAS-tid): any of various specialized structures in the cytoplasm of cells of eukaryotic autotrophs. A chloroplast is one type of plastid.

**plate tectonics** (PLAYT tek-TON-iks): the theory and study of the great plates in Earth's crust and their movement, which produces continental drift and mountain-building activity, earthquakes, volcanic eruptions, and other major changes affecting life.

**Platyhelminthes** (plat-ih-hel-MIN-theez): a phylum of animals, the flatworms.

**pneumococcus** (new-moh-KOK-us): a bacterium of the group that includes an encapsulated strain causing pneumonia.

**poikilothermic** (poy-KIL-uh-THERM-ik): characterizing the body temperature of many animals in which regulatory mechanisms, if they exist, are insufficient to keep the body temperature regulated within narrow limits, especially in extreme heat or cold.

**polar bodies:** cells with little cytoplasm as a result of the unequal distribution of cytoplasm in meiosis.

**pollen grain:** any of the monoploid cells, produced by the anther of the stamen, that give rise to sperm nuclei.

**pollination:** the implanting of pollen grains on the stigma of a flower.

**pollution:** the contamination of the environment by both human and natural causes.

**polydactyly** (pol-ih-DAK-tih-lee): a genetic characteristic in which an individual has more than ten fingers or toes.

**polypeptide** (pol-ih-PEP-tyde): a long chain of chemically bonded amino acids.

**polyploidy** (POL-ih-ploy-dee): a multiple number of chromosomes in an individual—often two, three, or four times the diploid number. Polyploid organisms are common among plants.

**polysaccharide** (pol-ih-SAK-uh-ryde): a carbohydrate made up of six-carbon sugars such as glucose or fructose.

**population:** all the organisms of a particular species that live in the same area at the same time.

**population genetics:** the study of the genetics of an interbreeding group of individuals in order to determine the overall frequencies of different genes in the gene pool, the frequency of particular genotypes (especially for genetic diseases), the frequency of mutations, and patterns of stability or change for particular gene frequencies.

**Porifera** (poh-RIF-uh-ruh): a phylum of animals, the sponges.

**positive feedback:** feedback from one body process to another that accelerates the latter's rate, or accelerates production or secretion of its product.

**posterior** (pos-TIR-ih-er) **lobe:** the rear lobe of the pituitary gland; it stores and releases hypothalamic hormones, including antidiuretic hormone (ADH).

**prediction:** a probable explanation of a past event, or probable future consequence of present events, offered to suggest a test of a hypothesis.

**preformation** (pree-for-MAY-shun): the belief that a new individual, fully formed, exists in miniature in the egg or sperm.

**primary root:** the root that develops from the embryonic root of a seedling.

**principle of independent assortment:** a principle Mendel discovered in early genetics experiments with garden peas—that the genes for one trait were inherited independently of those for another. Later experiments showed that this principle holds true only when the genes are on different chromosomes or, if on the same chromosome, are separated by crossing-over.

**principle of segregation:** a principle Mendel discovered in early genetics experiments with garden peas—that the members of a gene pair separate into different gametes. Meiosis is the responsible process.

**producer:** in biology, an autotroph.

**progesterone** (proh-JES-tuh-rohn): a hormone active in the reproductive cycle of female mammals; along with estrogen it promotes build-up of the soft tissues of the uterus and an increase in the blood supply in these tissues.

**prokaryote** (pro-KARE-ee-oht): a cell or microorganism without a clearly distinguished cell nucleus and with no organized chloroplasts, mitochondria, or certain other structures found in eukaryotic cells. Only monerans have prokaryotic cells.

**prolactin** (pro-LAK-tun): a pituitary hormone in mammals that induces production of milk by the mammary glands.

**prophase** (PRO-fayz): an early stage in mitosis in which the replicated chromosomes become visible, the nuclear membrane disappears, and spindle fibers form.

**prostaglandin** (prah-stuh-GLAND-in): any of many hormone-like substances derived from fatty acids and synthesized by a variety of cells and tissues. Certain prostaglandins act to lower blood pressure and cause smooth muscle to contract; others are associated with male reproductive functions.

**prostate** (PROS-tayt) **gland:** a semen-producing gland in mammalian males; seminal vesicles also contribute to the semen.

**protein** (PRO-teen): an organic compound composed of one or more polypeptide chains of amino acids; most structural materials and enzymes in a cell are proteins.

**proteinase** (PRO-teen-ays): any of a group of protein-digesting enzymes.

**protist** (PROH-tist): *see* Protista.

**Protista** (pro-TIST-uh): a kingdom of mostly aquatic organisms whose cells are eukaryotic (with nuclei and other structures characteristic of higher organisms), but which are mostly microscopic. Exceptions in size include the larger seaweeds such as kelp.

**proton** (PROH-tahn): a particle bearing a positive electrical charge, found in the nuclei of all atoms.

**protozoa** (proh-tuh-ZOH-uh): heterotrophic protists.

**pseudopod** (SOO-doh-pod): literally, a false (pseudo) foot (pod), a term used to describe an amoebalike extension of a cell or one-celled organism. Pseudopods are used in locomotion and obtaining food, or, as in white blood cells of the human body, in engulfing bacteria and foreign particles.

**pulmonary** (PUL-muh-nar-ee) **artery:** the blood vessel that carries oxygen-depleted blood from the heart to the lungs.

**pulmonary** (PUL-muh-nar-ee) **vein:** any of the blood vessels that carry oxygenated blood from the lungs to the heart.

**pulmonary** (PUL-muh-nar-ee) **ventilation:** an indication of the efficiency of the lungs in gas exchange, measured during exercise.

**punctuated equilibrium:** a hypothesis that new species evolve from old in a series of major steps over a relatively brief period of geologic time; the new species thereafter tend to persist for long periods.

**pupa** (PYOO-puh; plural, *pupae* — PYOO-pee): a stage in the life cycle of many animals, notably insects, following an earlier stage as a larva; in the pupa stage, the organism confines itself in the pupal case or cocoon while it undergoes metamorphosis into the adult form.

**purebred:** homozygous for the alleles determining selected traits, as a result of many generations of selective breeding.

**purine** (PURE-een): a double-ring nitrogen base such as adenine or guanine.

**pyrimidine** (pih-RIH-meh-deen): a single-ring nitrogen base such as cytosine, thymine, or uracil.

**pyruvic** (pye-ROO-vik) **acid:** an intermediate compound in the respiratory breakdown of glucose in a cell; also, a breakdown product of the fermentation of glucose.

## Q

**qualitative** (KWAL-ih-tay-tiv): relating to, or involving, identification of materials or their ingredients, or identification of the biological or biochemical nature of a process.

**quantitative** (KWANT-ih-tay-tiv): relating to, or involving, precise measurements, such as mass, volume, temperature, *p*H, and many other physical and chemical characteristics.

**queen:** the fertile, fully-developed female of social bees, ants, and termites whose function is to lay eggs.

## R

**race:** a naturally-occurring strain or phenotypic variation in a species, perpetuated by geographic isolation or by other barriers to interbreeding.

**radiation:** transmission of energy in waves; the sun, life's principal source of radiation, releases energy at different wave-lengths as light, radio waves, X rays, and others.

**radioactive:** releasing short-wavelength energy that activates radiation detectors and that can ionize or otherwise damage substances in the bodies of organisms; mutations can be produced by such radiations.

**radioactive isotope:** an isotope with an unstable nucleus, from which energy is given off as high-energy (short-wavelength) radiations.

***Ramapithecus*** (rom-eh-PITH-eh-kus): a possible ancestor of australopithecines and humans, dating to 15 million years ago.

**random** (RAN-dum): occurring by chance, as opposed to any design or choice.

**ray cell:** any of the cells in the stems of woody plants that form a channel allowing the passage of materials laterally back and forth between the xylem and the phloem.

**reactant** (ree-ACK-tunt): a substance that takes part in a chemical reaction.

**receptor:** a specialized sensory structure or organ that receives stimuli.

**receptor organ:** an organ made up largely of specialized sensory receptors; an example is the eye.

**recessive** (re-SES-iv): denoting a hereditary trait that is not expressed in the presence of a related dominant trait.

**recombinant** (ree-COM-bin-ant) **DNA:** DNA to which added genes are spliced to modify an organism's genetic makeup. The added genes may be artificially synthesized or taken from a different species of organism.

**recycling:** reuse of materials in place of accumulating wastes. Such materials as nitrogen, carbon dioxide, and water can be used over and over again in an ecosystem.

**red blood cell:** a blood cell in vertebrates that carries hemoglobin and certain other blood proteins with highly specialized functions.

**red-green colorblindness:** an X-linked recessive trait in humans. The responsible allele is on the X chromosome. A male will have the trait when only one such allele is present, because the Y chromosome carries no allele at all for the gene.

**reflex activity** or **reflex behavior:** involuntary responses to stimuli.

**reflex arc:** a cell pathway in the nervous system that produces the simplest behavioral responses. At least two neurons (sensory and motor) and usually three (sensory, connector in spinal cord, and motor) are involved.

**regeneration:** regrowth of lost or damaged tissues or organs.

**relative humidity:** the amount of moisture in the air expressed as a percentage of the amount that the air can hold at a given temperature.

**replication** (rep-lih-KAY-shun): the process by which DNA forms new DNA; each of two DNA strands is used as a template for a new complementary strand. New DNA molecules have one new and one old strand.

**reptile** (REP-til): *see* Reptilia.

**Reptilia** (rep-TIL-ee-uh): a class of chordates containing turtles, snakes, lizards, crocodiles, and alligators.

**respiration:** usually, *cell respiration,* in which organic molecules of foodstuffs are broken down until only carbon dioxide and water remain, along with nitrogenous wastes from some of these molecules. More generally, respiration or *general respiration* means breathing and other processes by which an organism takes in oxygen for cell respiration and gives off carbon dioxide as a by-product of the cell respiration.

**respiratory chain:** a chain of electron-transfer enzymes and coenzymes in cell respiration. As electrons pass along the chain, energy is released and used in making ATP.

**response:** an organism's reaction to a stimulus, or the reaction of a tissue or organ within the organism to a stimulus.

**retina** (RET-in-uh): the inner lining of the eye in vertebrates, containing light-sensitive receptors, the rods and cones.

**RF:** the abbreviation for *releasing factors,* a group of hypothalamic hormones that stimulate the pituitary gland to secrete its hormones.

**Rh factor:** a blood protein for which some but not all persons (Rh-positive) carry the gene. An Rh-negative woman with an Rh-positive husband may become pregnant with an Rh-positive embryo and produce antibodies against the Rh factor. Usually a first child is unharmed, but in a later Rh-positive pregnancy the embryo could be endangered by increasing numbers of antibodies.

**Rhodophyta** (roh-DOF-uh-tuh): a phylum of protists containing the red algae.

**riboflavin** (rye-boh-FLAY-vin): a vitamin of the B complex, vitamin $B_2$.

**ribonucleic** (ry-boh-new-KLEE-ik) **acid:** *see* RNA.

**ribose** (RY-bohs): the five-carbon sugar in RNA and ATP.

**ribosomal RNA:** any of the RNA that forms a functioning part of a ribosome.

**ribosome** (RY-buh-sohm): any of many similar structural particles in the cytoplasm of both prokaryotic and eukaryotic cells where polypeptide chains of enzymes and other proteins are synthesized.

**RNA:** the abbreviation for *ribonucleic* (ry-boh-new-KLEE-ik) *acid,* the hereditary material of certain viruses, and the material coded by DNA of other cells to carry out specific genetic functions (for example, messenger-RNA and transfer-RNA).

**rod** (of eye): a sensory receptor in the retina of the eye that is sensitive to faint light and responsive in night vision.

**root hair:** a fine extension of an epidermal cell of a plant root; the hairlike extension absorbs water and minerals.

**root pressure:** the force of water absorbed and rising upward from the roots of a plant.

**Rotifera** (roh-TIF-er-uh): a phylum of microscopic, multicellular animals with a wheellike motion of cilia at their head ends.

## S

**saliva** (suh-LY-vuh): a secretion into the oral cavity that lubricates food and begins carbohydrate digestion.

**salivary** (SAL-uh-vehr-ee) **gland:** any of the glands that secrete saliva into the oral cavity.

**scanning electron microscope:** an electron microscope that scans a whole object or specimen with electrons and produces a three-dimensional image of it.

**Schwann cell:** a highly specialized cell whose coiled membrane surrounds an axon of a neuron.

**sclerotic** (skluh-ROT-ik) **coat:** the white outer coat of the mammalian eye, transparent only in the frontal area called the cornea.

**scrotum** (SCROH-tum): an outpocketing of the body wall in mammalian males, forming a sac in which the testes are located.

**second:** the basic unit of time in the metric system.

**secondary root:** any of the roots of a plant that develop by branching from the primary root.

**secondary sex differences:** male and female characteristics of appearance caused by, or partly by, effects of sex hormones on parts of the body other than the reproductive organs. Examples in humans are greater development of the larynx in males, leading to a deeper voice, and facial hair in males.

**second-order consumer:** an animal that eats herbivores; for example, humans are second-order consumers when eating beef, lamb, turkey, and chicken.

**secretin** (sih-KREET-in): a hormone, secreted by cells in the small intestine, that stimulates the pancreas to secrete pancreatic juice.

**secretion** (sih-KREE-shun): any substance other than waste produced and released by a cell or gland.

**sediment** (SED-ih-ment): particles that settle out of a liquid mixture, as in a streambed; sediment in streams, lakes, and the oceans often covers the remains of dead organisms and in time may become sedimentary rock with fossils.

**seed:** an embryonic plant enclosed within a coat with its initial food supply and with certain plant hormones that affect the time of germination.

**seed coat:** the tough, protective outer covering of a seed.

**selective breeding:** development of a purebreeding line with desirable hereditary characteristics, by repeated crossings of different organisms, each having some of those characteristics.

**selective permeability** (per-mee-uh-BIL-ih-tee): a characteristic of a membrane whereby passage of some particles but not others is permitted through it.

**self-pollination:** pollination of the stigma of a flower with pollen from the same flower's anthers.

**semen** (SEE-men): the thick fluid in which sperm are transported, in mammalian males.

**seminal vesicles** (SEM-ih-nul VES-ih-kuls): in mammalian males, structures in the reproductive system that together with the prostate gland produce semen; also, structures of varying function in male reproductive systems of other groups of organisms.

**seminiferous tubules** (sem-ih-NIF-er-us TOO-byools): the coiled, threadlike glands in which sperm are produced in the testes.

**sensory neuron** (NYOO-ron): a nerve cell that carries impulses from a receptor toward the central nervous system.

**sensory receptor:** *see* receptor.

**sepal** (SEE-pul): one of the green, leaflike growths from the plant stem that enclose and protect a flower bud and later provide support for the flower at its base.

**sex chromosomes:** chromosomes that include genes for the determination of the sex of the individual.

**sexual reproduction:** reproduction involving the contribution of genetic material from two parents.

**sickle cell anemia** (uh-NEE-mee-uh): a condition in which red blood cells become sickle-shaped, blocking small blood vessels and leaving part of the body without sufficient oxygen. Sickle hemoglobin is gene-determined; it differs from normal hemoglobin in one amino acid.

**sieve tube:** a column of phloem cells in a plant.

**sinus** (SY-nus): a body space through which blood passes in an open circulatory system.

**skeletal muscle:** muscle attached to the skeleton, as in arthropods and vertebrates.

**skeleton:** the supporting and protective framework of many animals, and the shell secreted around many microorganisms.

**smooth muscle:** in higher animals, a tissue usually in sheets lining the digestive tract, arteries, and other internal structures; the cells have single nuclei and no cross striations.

**society:** an organized population showing cooperative behavior.

**species:** a group of interbreeding organisms that is genetically isolated from all or most other such groups; usually, attempts to breed individuals of different species produce only sterile offspring, or no offspring at all.

**sperm,** or **spermatozoa** (spur-mat-uh-ZOH-uh): male gametes, each haploid in chromosome number.

**sperm duct:** a duct leading from a testis to the outside of the body, or to the urethra.

**sperm nucleus:** either of two like nuclei produced by the division of one of the nuclei of a pollen grain of a flowering plant. One of the two sperm nuclei fertilizes an egg nucleus.

**Sphenophyta** (sfen-OFF-ih-tuh): a plant division of horsetails.

**spicule** (SPIK-yool): a skeletal element in invertebrates such as sponges and echinoderms.

**spinal cord:** the dorsal nerve cord in adult higher vertebrates; it gives rise to spinal nerves.

**spindle:** a fibrous structure that forms during mitosis and meiosis, and along which the dividing chromosomes are arranged until they have moved to opposite ends of the cell.

**spiracle** (SPY-rih-kuhl): an opening into a trachea in insects.

**spirillum** (spy-RIL-lum; plural, *spirilla*—spy-RIL-luh): a spiral-shaped bacterium.

**spongy layer:** the layer of cells in a green leaf inside the lower epidermis; one of the layers of leaf cells in which photosynthesis occurs.

**spontaneous generation:** the erroneous belief that complex organisms could spring fully formed from mud, decaying animal or vegetable matter, and similar substances given the presence of some vital ''active principle.''

**spores:** one-celled reproductive bodies that are usually resistant to harsh environmental conditions and may remain inactive or dormant, in a dry covering or case, for long periods; in some organisms, spores are asexual and may initiate the growth of a new organism under favorable conditions; in other organisms, spores are sexual and must unite with those of the other sex before producing a new organism.

**Sporozoa** (spoh-ruh-ZOH-uh): a phylum of parasitic protists that have no means of locomotion and that reproduce by forming spores.

**stamen** (STAY-men): the male reproductive organ of a flower, consisting of the pollen-producing anther and its filament.

**starch:** a kind of carbohydrate made principally by plants; many common starches contain only repeating glucose units, which require only one type of digestive enzyme to digest, making these starches an almost universal plant and animal food.

**sterilization:** the process of killing all microorganisms on laboratory glassware and instruments or in a nutrient broth. Also, a procedure by which an organism is made unable to reproduce by sexual reproduction.

**stigma** (STIG-muh): the eyespot in some microorganisms; also, the pollen-receptive structure at the top of a pistil in a flower.

**stimulus** (STIM-yoo-lus): any change that induces a response in an organism.

**stoma** (STOH-muh; plural, *stomata*—STOH-muh-tuh): an opening in the epidermis of a plant leaf through which gases are exchanged.

**stomach:** an enlarged portion of the digestive tract in which mechanical breakdown of food and enzymatic digestion in an acid medium take place.

**stretch receptor:** a sensory receptor in striated muscle fibers that is activated by the contracting fibers; it carries impulses to the central nervous system that result in more impulses to other muscle fibers to contract.

**striated** (STRY-ayt-ed) **muscle:** in vertebrates, the skeletal muscle and related muscles in which the fibers have multiple nuclei and are banded by cross striations.

**style:** the narrow, necklike portion of a pistil connecting the stigma with the ovary in a flower.

**substrate** (SUB-strayt): a molecule on which an enzyme acts.

**sucrose** (SOO-krohs): the cane or beet sugar used as table sugar; a twelve-carbon sugar composed of two simpler, or six-carbon, sugars—glucose and fructose.

**symbiosis** (sim-bih-OH-sis): a metabolic relationship between two unlike organisms that live together in close association.

**sympathetic** (sim-puh-THET-ik) **nervous system:** one of two divisions of the autonomic nervous system.

**synapse** (SIH-naps): an open junction between neurons, across which an impulse is transmitted by a chemical neurotransmitter.

**synapsis** (sin-AP-sis): the coming together of the chromosomes of a pair before they attach to the spindle, during meiosis.

**syndrome** (SIN-drohm): a group of symptoms that almost always occur together, reflecting the same or a related cause.

**synthesis** (SIN-thuh-sis): putting together, as in organizing and constructing larger molecules from smaller ones, or organizing thoughts for their relationships.

**synthesize** (SIN-thuh-syz): to put together; to construct from parts.

**systematics:** the study of species and their classification by genus, family, order, and so on.

## T

**taphonomy** (ta-FON-uh-mee): excavation of sites at which animals have died both recently and in the ancient past, in efforts to understand geological and environmental conditions that affect preservation and scattering of the remains.

**taxis** (TAK-sus; plural, *taxes*—TAK-seez): a response of a protist or other lower animal in changing direction toward or away from an environment stimulus.

**taxonomy** (tak-SON-uh-mee): the study of species and their classification by genus, family, order, and so on.

**Tay-Sachs** (TAY-SAKS) **disease:** a human genetic disorder in which the "A" form of an enzyme—hexosaminidase A, or Hex A for short—is not produced, causing lipid accumulation and death in early childhood. A pair of alleles determines this recessive condition.

**technology** (tek-NOL-uh-jee): applied science; the discoveries of science put to work in new inventions and new ideas for industry, the home, and other applications.

**telophase** (TEL-oh-fayz): a stage in mitosis following anaphase; a set of chromosomes is at either end of the cell, and new nuclear membranes have begun to form around them.

**tendon:** a dense, white, fibrous connective tissue that fastens a muscle to a bone or to another muscle.

**territoriality:** the behavior of an animal in defense of its living area.

**territory:** the living space that an animal may defend.

**test cross:** a genetic cross that is made between an organism of unknown genotype for a trait and one with the recessive trait, in order to determine what the unknown genotype is. If no offspring show the recessive trait, the unknown genotype is assumed to be homozygous dominant.

**testis** (TES-tis; plural, *testes*—TES-teez): a male reproductive organ of many animals; it produces sperm, the male gametes.

**testosterone** (tes-TOS-ter-ohn): a principal male hormone, secreted by the testes.

**thalidomide** (tha-LID-oh-myd): a drug once widely used to relieve nausea during pregnancy, but which caused deformation of many offspring.

**theory:** a hypothesis that relates and organizes much of the knowledge in a science and has been tested with success many times, until it has been accepted.

**thiamine** (THY-uh-min): a vitamin of the B complex, vitamin $B_1$.

**third-order consumer:** a carnivore that preys upon second-order consumers.

**threshold stimulus:** a strength of stimulus below which no nerve impulse will be initiated.

**thrombin** (THROM-bin): an enzyme involved in blood-clotting reactions in mammals.

**thylakoid** (THY-luh-koyd): in a chloroplast, a flattened sac containing chlorophyll; a stack of thylakoids makes up a granum in the chloroplast.

**thymine** (THY-meen): one of the four nitrogen bases in DNA; it is present in equal amounts with adenine, with which it pairs.

**thyroid** (THY-royd) **gland:** an endocrine gland in the neck region of most vertebrates that controls the rate of cell metabolism in the body through one of its hormones, thyroxine.

**thyroxine** (thy-ROK-sin): a principal hormone of the thyroid gland; it regulates the rate of many cellular processes.

**tissue:** an organized group of like cells that accomplishes a specific needed function in an organism; skin tissue and gland tissues are examples.

**tissue culture:** the growth and reproduction of cells in a special nutrient medium in the laboratory. Many plant and animal experiments can be performed on cells and tissues grown in culture, instead of on the plants and animals directly.

**tobacco mosaic** (moh-ZAY-ik) **virus:** a virus that attacks and destroys leaves of tobacco; the first virus successfully isolated and purified in crystalline form, in early virus research.

**tongue:** a muscular organ in the oral cavity of many animals that serves to manipulate food. In vertebrates such as frogs and salamanders, the tongue can be flipped out to capture flies as food. In mammals the tongue also aids in forming sounds.

**toxicological** (tok-sih-kuh-LOJ-ih-kuhl): relating to poisons and their study.

**toxin** (TOK-sin): a poisonous substance produced by a living organism; an example is the toxin that causes botulism (a type of food poisoning) in humans.

**trachea** (TRAY-kee-uh): the windpipe of air-breathing vertebrates, connecting the pharynx with the lungs; in insects, one of the tubes in the tracheal system, also used in obtaining air.

**tracheid** (TRAY-kee-ud): one of two principal types of xylem cells, with pointed ends and thick walls with pits that connect the cell to nearby cells.

**trait:** a characteristic of an organism, genetically determined or environmentally determined, or partly both.

**transfer RNA:** RNA molecules coded for individual amino acids; they bind to amino acids in the cytoplasm of a cell and transfer them to ribosomes where polypeptides are being synthesized.

**transmission electron microscope:** an electron microscope that produces images from beams of electrons passed through a specimen.

**trial and error:** a learning behavior employing a variety of different responses until one is satisfactory.

**trisomy** (TRY-sohm-ee): the presence of three homologous

chromosomes instead of a pair, usually caused by nondisjunction in the egg or sperm.

**trivial name:** the second word in the binomial name of a species.

**tropism** (TROH-piz-um): a plant response either toward or away from a stimulus. Growth downward, as in roots, is positive geotropism; growth upward, as in stems, is negative geotropism.

**tropomyosin** (troh-poh-MY-oh-sin): a protein that covers active sites on striated muscle fibers.

**troponin** (tro-POH-nin): a protein associated with tropomyosin on striated muscle fibers.

**trypsin** (TRIP-sin): the active form of a pancreatic enzyme that digests proteins and peptides in the small intestine.

**trypsinogen** (trip-SIN-uh-jen): the inactive form of trypsin when secreted by the pancreas.

**TSH:** the abbreviation for *thyroid-stimulating hormone,* a hormone secreted by the pituitary and carried in the blood to the thyroid gland, where it stimulates production and secretion of thyroxine.

**TSH-RF:** the abbreviation for *thyroid-stimulating-hormone releasing factor,* a hormone that is produced in the hypothalamus and that acts on the pituitary, causing it to secrete TSH into the bloodstream.

**tube nucleus:** one of the two nuclei in a pollen grain; it is associated with directing the development of the pollen tube as the latter grows toward a plant ovary. The other pollen nucleus divides to form two sperm nuclei.

**Turner syndrome** (SIN-drohm): in humans, a congenital condition characterized by an XO sex chromosome pattern—that is, an X chromosome without a second X chromosome, or without a Y chromosome.

**2,4–D:** a synthetic auxin that destroys weeds by disrupting the regulation of their growth.

# U

**ultrasound:** high-frequency sound waves.

**ultraviolet radiation:** light outside the violet end of the visible light spectrum, of shorter wavelength than the range of light visible to humans. Ultraviolet light in the sun's spectrum was a source of energy long ago on Earth, but most of this radiation today is screened out by an ozone layer in the atmosphere.

**umbilical** (um-BIL-ih-kul) **cord:** in placental mammals, a tube formed by development of the amnion, connecting the embryo with the placenta.

**unicellular** (yoo-nih-SEL-yuh-lar): one-celled, as with many microorganisms.

**uracil** (YUR-uh-sil): one of the four nitrogen bases in RNA; it is present in equal amounts with adenine, with which it pairs.

**urea** (yoo-REE-uh): a nitrogenous waste of many animals, and the principal nitrogenous waste of humans.

**ureter** (YOOR-et-er): a tube that carries urine from a kidney to the bladder in vertebrates.

**urethra** (yoo-REE-thruh): the tube through which urine is carried from the bladder to the outside of the body in vertebrates.

**uric** (YOOR-ik) **acid:** a solid nitrogenous waste of many animals, especially insects, birds, and desert-adapted mammals; a small amount of uric acid is also excreted by humans.

**urine:** the form in which urea is excreted from the kidney in vertebrates; the urea is diluted in water.

**uterus** (YEW-ter-us): the organ in which the fetus develops and is nourished in female mammals; also, an organ in which eggs or young develop in certain other animals, such as in fishes that give birth to live young.

# V

**vacuole** (VAK-yuh-wohl): a membrane-enclosed structure in the cytoplasm of a cell or one-celled organism. Different kinds of vacuoles serve different functions.

**vagina** (vuh-JY-nuh): in female mammals, an organ that serves as the entrance for sperm into the reproductive system, and through which the fetus passes from the uterus during birth.

**vagus** (VAY-gus) **nerves:** nerves connecting the autonomic nervous system with the heart, and carrying impulses that slow the heartbeat.

**valve:** a flaplike structure in the heart and veins that prevents the backflow of blood.

**variable:** a condition subject to change, such as temperature, light intensity, rate of growth, availability of moisture, etc.; variables that are identified in biological experiments are controlled by exposing both experimental and control groups to the same variables in the same manner, except for a variable purposely changed for the experimental group.

**variations:** in genetics, differences in phenotype caused by different genotypes.

**vascular** (VAS-kyoo-lar) **bundles:** clusters of xylem and phloem forming tubes in many plant stems.

**vein:** in a plant leaf, a fluid-transmitting bundle of xylem and phloem cells; in animals, a blood vessel in which blood is carried toward the heart.

**ventricle** (VEN-trih-kul): in vertebrates, a large muscular chamber of the heart that pumps blood to the respiratory structures and to the body.

**verification:** repetition of an investigation or experiment by different investigators than the original ones, to confirm the original findings.

**vertebra** (VERT-uh-bruh; plural, *vertebrae*—VERT-uh-bree): one of the bones of the spinal column of a vertebrate.

**vessel:** one of two principal types of xylem cells, made up of a short tube with no end walls, continuous with other such cells end-to-end, forming a channel; in other organisms, any of a variety of tubelike structures including blood vessels.

**vestigial** (ves-TIJ-ee-ul) **organ:** an organ that has endured in the evolution of a species but is no longer useful. Two examples in humans are the appendix and, in embryos, the yolk sac.

**villus** (VIL-us; plural, *villi*—VIL-y): a tiny fingerlike projection of the intestinal wall into the cavity of the intestine; digested foods are absorbed through the villi into blood and lymph vessels. An embryonic membrane, the chorion, also has villi.

**virus** (VY-rus): an almost lifelike particle that carries on no activity outside a living cell but reproduces inside a living cell; viruses are composed of DNA and protein, or RNA and protein, and can be seen only with an electron microscope.

**visible light:** that portion of the spectrum from violet through blue, green, yellow, orange, and red that is visible to the human eye.

**vitamin** (VY-tuh-min): any of many different types of organic compounds that are essential in very small quantities in an organism's nutrition, often serving as coenzymes or acting in some other regulatory way. Frequently a vitamin is part of a coenzyme that acts as an electron acceptor, as in $NAD^+$ and flavoprotein in the respiratory chain, and $NADP^+$ in photosynthesis.

**white blood cell:** any of the nucleated cells in the plasma of the blood that are the first line of defense against invading organisms, which they surround and engulf; examples are macrophages, lymphocytes, and monocytes.

**worker:** in bee, ant, and termite societies, an individual that carries out all the activities of the society not related to reproduction or, often, to defense against invaders.

## X

**X chromosome:** the chromosome in many animals that is associated with the female sex or, paired with a Y chromosome, with the male sex.

**X-linked trait:** a trait determined by a gene carried on the X chromosome.

**X-ray diffraction:** the deflection or bending of X rays as they pass through a material. The diffraction pattern can be photographed and examined for clues to the molecular structure of the material.

**xylem** (ZYE-lem): the water- and mineral-conducting tissues of higher plants. The two principal types of xylem tissues are tracheids and vessels.

## W

**warm-blooded:** homeothermic; able to regulate internal body temperature within a narrow range independent of variations in the temperature of the external environment. Birds and mammals are warm-blooded.

**waste:** any excess or nonusable metabolic product that must be eliminated from a cell or organism.

**wavelength:** the measurement from the crest of one wave to the crest of the next, for any form of energy that shows wave behavior.

**wet mount:** a slide prepared for microscopic observation by placing a specimen in a drop of water on a slide.

## Y

**Y chromosome:** the chromosome in many animals that is associated with the male sex. It is usually shorter than the X chromosome and carries no alleles for many of the genes on the X chromosome.

**yolk sac:** one of four embryonic membranes in vertebrates, the one enclosing a food supply for the developing embryo. In placental mammals the yolk sac is vestigial.

## Z

**zoologist** (zoh-OL-uh-jist): a biologist who studies animals.

**zygote:** a fertilized egg.

# Index

# Index

Underlined page numbers indicate pages in the Investigations section of the textbook.

# Photo Credits

Part One introduction: John Hart

**Chapter 1** introduction: C. Allan Morgan. Figure 1–1 *a, e:* Jean K. Marsh; *b*, William V. Mayer; *c*, K. L. Tompkins/TOM STACK & ASSOCIATES; *d*, Betty R. Seacrest; *f, g, h,* C. Allan Morgan. Figure 1–3: Trustees of the British Museum (Natural History). Figure 1–4: Betty R. Seacrest. Figure 1–5 left: J. R. Waaland, University of Washington/ BPS; middle and right, Algamarine Ltd. Figures 1–6 and 1–7: Algamarine Ltd. Figure 1–8: John A. Moore. Figure 1–11: C. Allan Morgan.

**Chapter 2** introduction (page 16): D. P. Wilson/ERIC & DAVID HOSKING. Figure 2–4: BSCS. Figure 2–5: W. G. Whaley, University of Texas. Figure 2–6: BSCS. Figure 2–11: ANIMALS ANIMALS/E. R. Degginger. Biology Brief (pages 30–31): Manfred Kage—Peter Arnold, Inc.

**Chapter 3** introduction (page 34): C. Allan Morgan. Figure 3–1, upper left: Diane Pitochelli; upper right, Brownie Borden, Borden Productions, Inc.; center left, Walter Chandoha; center right, W. Perry Conway; bottom, Grant Heilman. Biology Brief (pages 46–47): left, Joyce G. Greene; center, Joyce G. Greene; right, BSCS.

**Chapter 4** introduction (page 64): C. Allan Morgan. Figure 4–1, left: Josef Muench; right, M. Woodbridge Williams. Figure 4–6: Courtesy of the American Museum of Natural History. Biology Brief (pages 72–73): center, Tanya Atwater/C. A. Hopson; right, Tanya Atwater/K. C. Macdonald.

Part Two introduction (pages 84–85): NOAA (National Oceanic and Atmospheric Administration).

**Chapter 5** introduction (page 86): Elso S. Barghoorn. Figure 5–3: Elso S. Barghoorn and J. W. Schopf. Biology Brief (page 106): Cyril Ponnamperuma and NASA (National Aeronautics and Space Administration). Figure 5–16, left: Harry Wessenberg; right, H. G. Bungenberg de Jong. Figure 5–17: University of California at Berkeley, Virus Laboratory.

**Chapter 6** introduction (page 112): C. Allan Morgan. Figure 6–1, left: Manfred Kage—Peter Arnold, Inc.; right, Gene Cox. Biology Brief (pages 116–117): BSCS. Figure 6–9: Courtesy of Adolph Coors Company. Figure 6–11: Dr. J. David Robertson.

**Chapter 7** introduction (page 132): C. Allan Morgan. Figure 7–2: BSCS/J. G. Zeikus, Department of Bacteriology, University of Wisconsin. Figure 7–3: Historical Picture Service, Inc. Biology Brief (page 137): Carlye Calvin. Figure 7–4: BSCS. Figure 7–6: BSCS. Figure 7–11: L. K. Shumway. Biology Brief (pages 150–151): BSCS.

**Chapter 8** introduction (page 154): William Ervin. Figure 8–7: Keith R. Porter. Biology Brief (pages 166–167): Lynn Margulis, Boston University.

Part Three introduction (pages 170–171): William Ervin.

**Chapter 9** introduction (page 172): Bert Kempers, West Wind Productions. Figure 9–8: Robley C. Williams. Figure 9–10: Courtesy of Biophysics Department, King's College, London. Figure 9–11, left and middle: United Press International; right, M. H. F. Wilkins. Figure 9–12: A. K. Kleinschmidt. Biology Brief (page 188), left: Walter Chandoha; right, Centers for Disease Control, Atlanta, Georgia.

**Chapter 10** introduction (page 190): C. Allan Morgan. Figure 10–1: BSCS/John Urban. Figure 10–8, left: Edward L. Tatum; right, George W. Beadle. Figure 10–9: Berwind P. Kaufman, University of Michigan. Figure 10–10: T. F. Anderson, E. L. Wollman, and F. Jacob. Figure 10–11: Stanley N. Cohen, Stanford University. Biology Brief (pages 210–211): left, BSCS; right, Culver Pictures, Inc.

**Chapter 11** introduction (page 214): John Hart. Figure 11–1: Courtesy of Dr. Mercedes R. Edwards, New York State Department of Health. Figure 11–3: W. G. Whaley, University of Texas. Figure 11–4: Courtesy of Carolina Biological Supply Company. Figure 11–5 right: BSCS/Slide courtesy of Connecticut Valley Biological Supply Company. Figure 11–6: BSCS. Figure 11–8: ANIMALS ANIMALS/ Oxford Scientific Films. Figure 11–13: Stephen G. Maka. Figure 11–14, left: Werner W. Schulz; upper right, BSCS; lower right, Joyce G. Greene. Figure 11–15: J. C. Allen and Son. Figure 11–16: Lynwood M. Chace. Figure 11–17: THE BIOLOGY OF THE LABORATORY MOUSE, by Jackson Laboratories, 1975, Dover Publications, Inc., NY. Figure 11–19, left and upper right: Courtesy of Carolina Biological Supply Company; lower right, ANIMALS ANIMALS/© Lloyd Beesley. Figure 11–22: Dr. Landrum B. Shettles. Figure 11–25: Gesell Institute, New Haven, Conn. Figure 11–26: Alan G. Fantel, University of Washington. Figure 11–28: Bert Kempers, West Wind Productions. Biology Brief (page 245): top, S. Arthur Reed; bottom, Holly Arrow.

**Chapter 12** introduction (page 244): C. Allan Morgan. Figure 12–7: BSCS. Figure 12–8: Courtesy of Carolina Biological Supply Company. Figure 12–9: Dr. Landrum B. Shettles. Biology Brief (page 265): Rick Stafford. Figure 12–16: Dr. Mark J. Brauer.

Part Four introduction (pages 270–271): William Ervin.

**Chapter 13** introduction (page 272): W. Perry Conway. Figure 13–1, upper left, lower left, and lower right: BSCS; upper right, C. Allan Morgan. Figure 13–4: Dr. C. Nash Herndon. Figure 13–5: BSCS. Figure 13–6: M. Hofer. Figure 13–8: Dr. Harold Edgerton, MIT, Cambridge, Mass. Figure 13–10: Herbert Gehr, LIFE Magazine © 1947, Time, Inc. Biology Brief (pages 292–293): BSCS.

**Chapter 14** introduction (page 296): W. Perry Conway. Figure 14–8: Courtesy C. Trunca, Ph.D. Figure 14–10: David Peakman, Reproductive Genetics Center, Denver. Figure 14–12: Ram S. Verma. Biology Brief (pages 310–311): left, Walter Chandoha; right, Media Services, State University of New York, Stony Brook. Figure 14–13: David Peakman, Reproductive Genetics Center, Denver. Figure 14–16: COLOR ATLAS OF LIFE BEFORE BIRTH, by Marjorie England, Year Book Medical Publishers, Chicago, and Wolfe Medical Publications Limited, London.

**Chapter 15** introduction (page 320): Betty R. Seacrest. Figure 15–1: Betty R. Seacrest. Biology Brief (pages 326–327): National Center for Toxicological Research, Jefferson, Arkansas. Figure 15–4: John A. Moore. Figure 15–5, top: American Brahman Breeders Association; middle, American Shorthorn Association; bottom, Santa Gertrudis Breeders International.

**Chapter 16** introduction (page 340): Taurus Photos/L. Weber. Figure 16–1: G. Woodruff, D. Premack, and K. Kennel, ''Conservation of Liquid and Solid Quantity by the Chimpanzee,'' *Science,* Vol. 202, pp. 991–994, Figure 1C, 1 December 1978; © 1978 by the American Association for the Advancement of Science. Figure 16–2: Society for French-American Cultural Services and Educational Aid. Figure 16–3: Courtesy of the American Museum of Natural History. Figure 16–4, top and middle: Anthro-Photo File/Kristina Cannon-Bonventre; bottom, R. I. M. Campbell. Figure 16–5: Institute of Human Origins. Figure 16–6: Robert Jurmain. Figure 16–7: R. I. M. Campbell. Figure 16–10: Anthro-Photo File/Erik Trinkaus. Figure 16–11, left: Collection Musee de l'Homme, Paris; right, Courtesy of the American Museum of Natural History. Biology Brief (pages 352–353): Anthro-Photo File/ Kristina Cannon-Bonventre. Figure 16–14, all photos except extreme upper right: BSCS; upper right, Nick Marble.

Part Five introduction (pages 360–361): Colorado Nature Photographic Studio/© Charles G. Summers, Jr.

**Chapter 17** introduction (page 362): BSCS. Figure 17–2, left: Courtesy of the Field Museum of Natural History, Chicago; right, Trustees of the British Museum (Natural History). Figure 17–3: J. H. Troughton and K. A. Card, Physics and Engineering Laboratory, Department of Scientific and Industrial Research, Lower Hutt, New Zealand. Figure 17–8: Martin H. Zimmerman. Figure 17–14: Dr. Mark J. Brauer.

**Chapter 18** introduction (page 386): C. Allan Morgan. Biology Brief (pages 392–393): DOCUMERICA/Environmental Protection Agency. Figure 18–5: Dr. Robert H. Fennell, University of Colorado Medical Center.

**Chapter 19** introduction (page 400): David C. Fritts. Figure 19–1: George Sheng. Figure 19–3: Werner W. Schulz. Figure 19–4: Oscar L. Miller and David M. Prescott. Biology Brief (pages 414–415): Courtesy of Pam S. Ford, Rocky Mountain Poison Center, Denver. Figure 19–11: Carl Struwe, Monkmeyer Press Photo.

**Chapter 20** introduction (page 418): Parco Scientific Company and Philip Harris Biological Ltd. Figure 20–1, left: © 1984 by Prentice-Hall, Inc., Englewood Cliffs, NJ, from *Discover the Invisible* by Eric V. Gravé. Figure 20–2: Jean K. Marsh. Biology Brief (pages 430–431): BSCS.

Part Six introduction (pages 434–435): David C. Fritts.

**Chapter 21** introduction (page 436): David C. Fritts. Biology Brief (pages 440–441): center, BSCS; right, Courtesy of Eli Lilly and Company. Figure 21–4: Courtesy of Carolina Biological Supply Company. Figure 21–5: Dr. Jacob Lerman.

**Chapter 22** introduction (page 452): David C. Fritts. Figure 22–1: Don Wong/Design Photographers International. Figure 22–4, left: Dr. Andrew Dixon; right, Dr. J. David Robertson. Figure 22–6: Edwin R. Lewis, Thomas E. Everhart, and Yehoshua Y. Zeevi. Biology Brief (page 461): Maggi Castelloe.

**Chapter 23** introduction (page 470): C. Allan Morgan. Figure 23–9: F. W. Schmidt. Figure 23–10: Manfred Kage—Peter Arnold, Inc. Figure 23–12: Gene Cox. Figure 23–13: H. E. Huxley. Figure 23–16: Wide World Photos. Biology Brief (pages 490–491): BSCS.

Part Seven introduction (pages 494–495): David C. Fritts.

**Chapter 24** introduction (page 496): C. Allan Morgan. Figure 24–2, top: John A. Moore; left, BSCS; middle and lower right, C. Allan Morgan. Figure 24–4: William Vandivert. Figure 24–6: Three Lions. Figure 24–7: Nina Leen, LIFE Magazine © 1964, Time, Inc. Biology Brief (pages 512–513): BSCS.

**Chapter 25** introduction (page 516): David C. Fritts. Figure 25–1: C. Allan Morgan. Figure 25–5: David C. Fritts. Figure 25–9: Bert Kempers, West Wind Productions. Figure 25–13: © 1965 National Geographic Society. Figure 25–14: BSCS.

**Chapter 26** introduction (page 536): James R. Eckert. Biology Brief (pages 542–543): Grant Heilman. Figure 26–7 (page 548) top: C. Allan Morgan; bottom, Union Pacific Railroad Photo; (page 549) upper left, BSCS; lower left, C. Allan Morgan; upper and lower right, Marathon Oil Company. Figure 26–9: U.S. Consumer Product Safety Commission. Figure 26–12 (page 556) upper left and lower right: BSCS; lower left, Peter Schweitzer; upper right and middle right, U.S. Department of Agriculture; (page 557) upper left, BSCS; upper middle, C. Allan Morgan; upper right, Sheryan P. Epperly; left center, American Airlines; right center, International Rice Research Institute; lower left and lower right, U.S. Department of Agriculture. Figure 26–14: C. Allan Morgan.

**Investigations** introduction (page 563): Andy Brilliant/Carol Palmer. Figure 4–B–1: H. B. D. Kettlewell/David Kettlewell. Figure 6–B–2: Andy Brilliant/Carol Palmer. Figure 11–A–1: BSCS. Figure 11–C–1: Lynwood M. Chace. Figure 15–A–1: BSCS. Figure 16–A–1: Dr. C. Lockard Conley. Figure 16–B–1: BSCS. Figure 17–B–1: BSCS.

**Appendixes** introduction (page 685): Andy Brilliant/Carol Palmer. Figure 11–A–1, left: Josef Muench; right, Hugh Spencer. Figure 17–F–2: Linda Hall Library. Figure 18–B–1: BSCS/William V. Mayer. Figure 19–B–1: Brown Brothers. Figure 21–C–1: Dr. Jacob Lerman. Figure 24–A–2: Courtesy of Ward's Natural Science Establishment. Figure 24–B–1: Shostal Associates.